A History
of Christendom
Vol. I

Warren H. Carroll

The Founding of Christendom

Warren H. Carroll

Christendom Press
Front Royal, VA 22630

ACKNOWLEDGMENTS

This first volume of my history of Christendom was written and published at Christendom College and owes much to the vibrant Catholic community established there. I am particularly indebted to Jeffrey Mirus, Director of Christendom Publications, for his critical reading of the manuscript and for making all the arrangements for its publication; to William Marshner, Chairman of the Theology Department at Christendom College, for his assistance with questions of the interpretation of Latin and Hebrew passages; and to Robert Hickson, Chairman of the English and Literature Department at Christendom College, for his critical reading of the manuscript. I would also like to express my particular appreciation for diligent assistance in the final preparation of this book for publication to Walter Janaro, Assistant Director of Christendom Publications; Mrs. Irene Furtado, who produced the type-set copy; Mrs. Kathleen Satterwhite, who did the layout; and to Katherine O'Brien, Darlene Summers, and Diana Weyrich who helped proofread it.

WARREN H. CARROLL

DEDICATED
to my beloved wife,
ANNE
whose bright example and unceasing prayer
brought to me the grace of faith
and membership in the Church of Christ

Contents

INTRODUCTION

What is Christendom? What kind of history can be written of it?

Christendom is the reign of Christ—that is to say, for the Christian, the reign of God recognized by men. Much of that reign is invisible, since His kingdom is not of this world. Much of it is personal, since the primary concern of this divine Person is with us as human and eternal persons. But some of it is public and historical. Where men of courage and missionary spirit recognize Christ as their Lord and proclaim Him, Christendom appears as a social, cultural and political presence in the world. It grows with that courage and profession, and above all by the silent impetus of prayer and example. It fades with timidity, indifference, apostasy, and lack of holiness.

Christendom has faded today, to the edge of invisibility. Here in the United States, when we founded a college to bear its name, we soon learned that most people could no longer define, or even pronounce it.

For fifteen centuries Christendom shaped the development of Western civilization. But it was not always so. In the spring days and nights of the year 30 A.D. in Jerusalem, between the feasts of Passover and Pentecost, all of Christendom met in one upper room of a nondescript house in an out-of-the-way street: a small group of men headed by a fisherman, and a few women from Galilee. Out of that one room streamed a historical force greater than any other ever known; no more than God Himself is it dead today. These years of Christendom's apparent eclipse are perhaps the best time to attempt the telling of its full historical story, from preparation through birth and growth, climax, division, and retreat—so as to be more ready for its coming resurrection. The six volumes projected for this history will cover each of those phases in the history of Christendom: founding (this volume, to 324 A.D.); building (324-1100); glory (1100-1517); cleaving (1517-1774); revolution against

(1774-1914); martyrdom (the twentieth century since 1914).

The history of Christendom differs from conventional histories of Christianity in that the latter concentrate very largely, if not almost exclusively on the institutional church or churches, and on clergymen. But clerics are far from being the only Christians; and the church is not, or at least need not be, the only Christian institution, though it will always be the most important, and unique. The history of Christendom includes as a major element the lay or temporal order insofar as it is penetrated and influenced by Christianity. The greater the degree of this penetration or influence, the more signficant is the temporal history so affected, for the historian of Christendom. He will therefore blend ecclesiastical and political history.

One of the greatest tragedies in the history of Christendom has been its division into competing churches. One of the relatively few immediately hopeful signs for the orthodox Christian in today's secularized world is the decline, at long last, of the internal bitterness and dissension among believing Christians as they discover the magnitude of their common ground and common interest in the face of an apostate civilization. True ecumenism does not mean the abandonment of conviction and truth for the sake of a superficial, meaningless agreement. It means building solidly on real convictions and truths which are found to be shared. Full reunion is still far away. But hostility and contention are receding.

This history is written by a Catholic, from the Catholic perspective, with the conviction that Jesus Christ founded a church and that the visible church He founded is the Roman Catholic Church which, through its succession of Popes in particular, has remained, is, and always will be His Church, and through which He acts in particular ways not available to members of most of the separated churches, notably in the Holy Eucharist by which He becomes really present on the altar at Mass, and reserved in the tabernacle. But He has other sheep who are not of the visible Catholic fold, members of His church through baptism by water or by desire. Many non-Catholic Christians have served Christ well—indeed, better than a great many Catholics have served Him. Their services are included in this history. Christendom—the idea and reality of a Christian public order—has been, historically, much more a Catholic than a Protestant concept and undertaking, but has echoes and reflections among many of the separated brethren (most notably in the Eastern Orthodox churches).

No history of Christendom as here defined has been published in English in the twentieth century. Of histories of Christianity and of the Catholic Church there have, of course, been many. Probably the best is that of Henri Daniel-Rops, translated from the French and published in many volumes (by Dutton and, in paperback, by Doubleday Image Books) in the United States from 1946 to 1966. But even Daniel-Rops' great and firmly orthodox work is not a history of Christendom, of the Christian public order and of devout Christian laymen working in and building that order, nearly so much as it is a history of the Church *per se*. It is marred by an anti-Hispanic bias which undervalues and misconceives the heritage of the more than half of the Catholic Church that speaks Spanish or Portuguese. Despite the profound and encyclopedic knowledge of the author, it is not properly speaking a work of scholarship, since it neither addresses scholarly controversies involved in the history recounted, nor cites sources.

The attempt is made in this history to combine vivid narrative in the text with thorough scholarship in the extensive notes at the end of each chapter. The majority of the citations in these notes refer to secondary sources—that is, to the work of modern historians on which the author has drawn. Primary sources—documents contemporary with the period under review—are used from time to time, particularly where there is a strongly controverted point, but comprise only a minority of the citations. This is simply because of the scope of this work, which renders it impossible for any one man in a reasonable period of time to master all or most of the applicable primary sources adequately; even if this were possible, it would not be a reasonable expenditure of time and effort, since so many painstaking and conscientious scholars have already investigated the primary sources with the utmost care and reported thoroughly on them. The overriding need is not for more monographs on original sources, but for synthesis from the Christian point of view, in a time when this kind of history has virtually ceased being written.

However, great care has been taken to cite every source used, even for statements which might reasonably be deemed "common knowledge," because of the passions and prejudices which have so often touched the telling of the history covered in these volumes, causing many to doubt or question even well-established facts. Each source cited is fully identified when it first appears in the notes to a particular chapter, and thereafter by the author's last name and an abbreviated version of the title (*op. cit.* is used only within a single note). The bibliography at the end of each volume will serve as a guide to works of history pertaining to Christendom, many of which have been almost completely forgotten, or never were adequately known.

Two points of possible objection call for further comment here: (1) the issue of historical objectivity; (2) the slight use made of social, economic, intellectual, and institutional (except ecclesiastical) history.

Regarding objectivity, every professional historian knows that the most difficult single task in historical research is pruning down and weeding out the original indigestible mass of raw material into the basis for a coherent presentation of the subject being researched and written about. Every historian must use principles of selection of what material is important and relevant to his general and particular task. Every historian (though not all are fully aware of this) has a world-view which has much to do with his choice of what is significant and relevant. For the historian to suppress evidence bearing directly on his own subject and conclusions is a grave dereliction; but for him to screen out irrelevant information is a duty, an essential part of his craft. In all honesty, every historian owes to his reader an identification and a statement of his own world-view.

Above all it is necessary to see the fundamental error in the widely held idea that the history of religion is "objective" when written by those who do not believe in the religion they are writing about (or, often, in any religion), but biased when written by a religious man. The rejection of some or all religious truth is every bit as much an intellectual position as is the acceptance of religious truth. Both the believer and the non-believer have a point of view. Both are equally tempted to bias; either may be objective by overcoming that temptation. Objectivity does not derive from having no point of view. History cannot be written without one. Objectivity does require honesty and respect for truth always.

This writer's own beliefs will be made very clear throughout these volumes. Facts and positions contrary to the conclusions stated herein will be noted to the fullest extent that a reasonable utilization of space permits. Again, due to the scope of the work and of the historical controversies concerning its subject matter, nothing like a definitive presentation of the contrary views can be attempted—after all, the primary purpose of these volumes is to present a Christian view, not today's much more common non-Christian view, of five thousand years of history. But the contrary arguments and especially the awkward facts, not appearing to fit the conclusions here stated, deserve to be, and will be, presented and dealt with explicitly.

Regarding social, political, and non-ecclesiastical institutional history, the writer would emphasize that as a Christian his interest is in *persons*. Persons in their earthly lives are indubitably very much affected by social and institutional structures and by economic conditions. But the person is ultimately, metaphysically independent of them. He is *not* their creature, but God's creature. It is surely no mere coincidence that the decline in political and ecclesiastical history and good biography in scholarly historical writing and the rise of social, economic, and temporal institutional history has paralleled so closely in time the erosion of Christianity in our civilization. Christians do not see men as primarily shaped or dominated by extrinsic and nameless forces, structures, and trends. They see the drama of human life as primarily composed of personal thought and action, above all by the working of the *will*. This is highlighted in political history but plays little part in social, economic, and institutional history.

Regarding intellectual history, the achievements of the mind are clearly a product of free will and therefore relevant to the concerns of this history, and where possible they will be introduced in these volumes. However, since the primary emphasis is on Christendom as a manifestation of the Faith in the public order, the more subtle and long-lasting effects of great intellectual achievements are difficult to fit into the organizational structure of this history, which covers relatively short chronological periods in sequence, and therefore only a very limited coverage of intellectual history is attempted. An intellectual history of Christendom, conceived on a different plan from these volumes, would be a most worthy and needed task for a properly equipped scholar to undertake.

The writer firmly holds the perhaps unfashionable belief that any good history should be a good *story*. Man's past is full of events more dramatic than any ever put on stage. The most dramatic of these events pertain directly to the supreme drama which is the action of Christ in the world, in preparing for His coming, in coming, and in living in His Church. There is no law of nature or of scholarship which says that a scholarly and reliable history must be dull, and no reason at all why it should be.

Since Christians today have almost ceased to write their own history as Christians, there is an immense void in historical scholarship. These volumes offer a synthesis of all history from the Christian viewpoint, and should often suggest promising avenues for further research and writing from that viewpoint. There is a crying need for rising young historical scholars possessing the gift of faith in Christ to answer the call for the reconstruction of Christian historiography. There are a hundred lifetimes' work to do. God willing, that work shall soon begin, and these volumes play some part in launching it.

Warren H. Carroll, Ph.D.
Christendom College
Front Royal, Virginia
United States of America

PROLOGUE
"IN THE BEGINNING"

In the beginning God created the heavens and the earth. The earth was without form and void, and darkness was upon the face of the deep; and the Spirit of God was moving over the face of the waters. And God said, "Let there be light"; and there was light.—Genesis 1:1-4[1]

God is; and God is love.[2] Only God, of all beings, must necessarily be. It is only God Whose Name can be, and must be, I AM.[3]

Because God is, He can create—give being to matter and energy in all their configurations throughout the length and breadth and height and depth and past and present and future of the Cosmos, to the last galaxy, and above all to the souls of men. Because God is love, He did create the material universe and its spiritual inhabitants. None of the tangible objects in the universe and none of its spiritual inhabitants necessarily is. None can explain or permanently preserve their being by their own efforts. All are contingent. The hardest mountain, the brightest star, the best man or woman unaided by Divinity must inevitably lose being in the visible universe as it moves down the corridors of time.

Time began with creation; history, in its broadest sense, began with man's appearance in the universe God had created. For the Christian, history has a center-point, a focus of ineffable radiance which alone gives it meaning, direction, and purpose. That focus is the person of One who was with God, is God, has acted in the universe and most especially in our world from the beginning, will act until the end, and will bring that end when He comes to judge the world.

In the beginning was the Word, and the Word was with God, and the Word was God. He was in the beginning with God; all things were made through him, and without him was not anything made that was made. In him was life, and the life was the light of men. The light shines in the darkness, and the darkness has not overcome it.[4]

That was He Who one day was to be born a human babe in Bethlehem—He Who lit the spark of all the galaxies, Who shot time's arrow upon its course, the master of all the light-years who was nailed to a cross in Jerusalem, at the Place of the Skull.

This happened upon the earth; and therefore in the order of ultimates, the order of Heaven, it makes our earth the center of the universe.

The earth came out of the starry heavens, and out of the earth came man. On both points the Book of Genesis and today's scientific theories agree. On the time span and the mechanism involved they seem to disagree, though they may be harmonized much more than is generally believed. But in the last analysis, questions of geologic time and organic evolution, though fascinating, are not of primary importance to the Christian. He needs to keep in mind that debate on these questions should not be foreclosed on either side, that it is possible for an orthodox Christian to accept the theory of man's bodily evolution—as a theory—so long as he unwaveringly affirms the direct creation of man's immortal soul by God and the descent of all men from an original pair whose sin of pride and disobedience, and its consequences, has indelibly stained the whole history of the human race. These two *de fide* doctrines no science can disprove. No fossil or rock stratum can ever tell us that the Garden of Eden and its inhabitants did *not* exist. Since all men are members of the same biological species which interbreeds with no other species,[5] no scientist can ever prove that we did *not* all descend from an original pair.

On the vexed question of the evolution of life and of man, the sure guide for the Roman Catholic must be the only magisterial pronouncement ever made on the subject, the encyclical *Humani Generis* by Pope Pius XII in 1950, which states:

The teaching authority of the Church does not forbid that, in conformity with the present state of human sciences and sacred theology, research and discussions on the part of men experienced in both fields take place with regard to the doctrine of evolution insofar as it inquires into the origin of the human body as coming from pre-existent and living matter—for Catholic faith obliges us to hold that souls are immediately created by God. . . . Some, however, highly transgress this liberty of discussion when they act as if the origin of the human body from pre-existing and living matter were already completely certain and proved by facts which have been discovered up to now, and by reasoning on those facts, and as if there were nothing in the sources of Divine revelation which demands the greatest moderation and caution in this question. When, however, there is a question of another conjectural opinion, namely polygenism, children of the Church by no means enjoy such liberty. For the faithful cannot embrace that opinion which maintains either that after Adam there existed on this earth true men who did not take their origin through natural generation from him as the first parent of all, or that Adam represents a certain number of first parents.[6]

On the other side of the evolution debate, no Christian can doubt that God had the power to create all men new, both body and soul, regardless of what had gone before; and once again, no scientist can disprove that or prove the contrary. There is considerable evidence of creatures living on earth from several hundred thousand to several million years ago whose bodies were intermediate in form between ape and man; but none of their remains show clear indications of spiritual awareness or imagination, the sure signs of humanity. They did not bury their dead; no religious objects or art have been found associated with them. A creature may be bodily intermediate between animal and man, but he cannot be spiritually intermediate. You either are a spiritual being or you are not.[7]

Thomas Aquinas teaches that body and soul cannot be permanently sundered or conceived as essentially separate, whatever the nature of the miracle involved in the soul's preservation during the period between bodily death and the resurrection of the body;[8] consequently, the idea of the soul of a man inserted into the body of an animal is a philosophical monstrosity. The being man was a whole new creation, whatever might have been his physical resemblances and antecedents in the preceding animal world—a new creation with a mind able to comprehend the Cosmos and to worship and glory in his Maker, as at the dawn of time "when all the morning stars sang together, and all the sons of God shouted for joy."[9]

These unique gifts we still possess, though we may not appreciate or use them; but the first man and the first woman had more. Their bodies were glorified by their uncorrupted souls. Souls are immortal by nature. Since soul and body were joined, their bodies would naturally have taken on the immortality of their souls, and in the beginning they did so. Any other condition would have been a contradiction, a clashing discord in the symphony of the Cosmos.

Yet that contradiction, that disharmony is the reality with which we live—a reality whose stark horror has been dulled by familiarity and made bearable by countless habitual evasions: the horror of an immortal soul bound in a mortal and corruptible body. The first tangible proof of the existence of true man on earth is to be found in the fact that the earliest true men buried their dead. To all animals death is a part of nature—sometimes to be mourned, as a mother beast will mourn her dead young, but never frightening or uncanny, because for an animal death is the end. But to all men—except those of our modern age most insulated from reality by sophisticated rationalizations—death is a ghastly mystery, a sign of fear. And so prehistoric man tied up his dead with thongs so that they could not walk about to haunt him, and surrounded them with goat horns to keep them in their graves by magic, yet left food to nourish and propitiate them in case neither bonds nor spells should work.[10] We think it natural that most men, especially primitive men, should be afraid of ghosts. But what in the world is natural about it? Nothing could be more helpless and harmless than a dead man, as any animal could tell us if it could think or speak; but it would be unlikely to convince us.

We fear the dead because in the depths of our being we feel that they ought not to be dead and might not stay dead; because they remind us of what we would much rather forget: That some day we will be as they; and because we cannot understand why this should be, and how it will be. Yet strange and ugly as it is, death no less than life is of the essence of humanity as we have known humanity. Death wars with the life in our bodies, and in time death always conquers. The victory of our "last enemy" is assured. No merely humanistic and materialistic philosophy can truly come to grips with the fact of death, because that fact makes dust and ashes out of the heart of their value systems, as it will make dust and ashes out of the body of every humanist and every materialist. Modern agnostic existentialists have at least faced the fact of death, but find in it only a blank wall of negation; the best they can tell us is to march into oblivion with courage. But what good is courage to a corpse?

There is just one adequate explanation in all the history of human thought for the terrifying and unnatural presence of inevitable death and bodily dissolution in human life. Materialism ignores the problem; agnostic existentialism is defeated by it; the doctrine of reincarnation merely multiplies it. Only one real answer has ever been given, in only one place:[11] in the third chapter of the Book of Genesis, which tells us that the first man and the first woman wished to sample the knowledge of evil,[12] believing this would make them like God, and that they did sample it in violation of God's express commandment and in disregard of His explicit warning that death would result from its violation.[13]

In that act and in that moment they lost their innocence and frustrated the purpose for which they had been given being: to know, to love, and to serve God. For nothing evil may behold Him Who is all good in His full glory, nor can one stained by sin worship Him with a pure heart. So the first man and the first woman learned when God moved through the Garden on that most terrible afternoon in the history of the world, and they tried to hide themselves from Him in their shame, only to find that there is no place to hide from God. He called them forth, listened to their sordid attempts to shift and evade personal responsibility for what they had done,[14] and passed the sentence which justice demands even from the Author of Justice:[15]

Cursed is the ground because of you;
in toil you shall eat of it all the days of your life;
thorns and thistles it shall bring forth to you;

and you shall eat of the plants of the field.
In the sweat of your face
you shall eat bread
till you return to the ground,
for out of it you were taken;
you are dust,
and to dust you shall return.[16]

From that day man was an exile upon the face of the earth; but in time, while still an exile, he was to become a pilgrim.

NOTES

[1] All quotations from the Old Testament are taken from the Revised Standard Version of the Bible (1952), as printed, with the additional books in the Catholic and Eastern Orthodox Bibles, in *The New Oxford Annotated Bible*, 2d ed. (New York, 1977).

[2] John 4:16.

[3] Exodus 3:14. See Chapter Three, below, for further discussion of the background and significance of God's self-revelation to Moses reported in this passage.

[4] John 1:1-5. All quotations from the New Testament are taken from the second edition of the Revised Standard Version of the Bible, New Testament translation (1971), as printed in *The New Oxford Annotated Bible*. (There is not yet a second edition of the Old Testament translation in the Revised Standard Version.) There is no difference between the Protestant and Catholic canons of the New Testament.

[5] Everett C. Olson, *The Evolution of Life* (New York, 1965), pp. 83-84. The distinction between our own species, *Homo sapiens*, and the species regarded by evolutionists as our immediate predecessor, *Homo erectus*, is clearly marked—especially in the shape of the head and the size of the brain—and there is no evidence of any interbreeding. On this point see W. E. Le Gros Clark, *The Fossil Evidence for Human Evolution*, 3rd ed. (Chicago, 1978), pp. 83-89, 118-123; Marcellin Boule and Henri Vallois, *Fossil Men*, rev. ed.136-138, 146; and William Howells, *Mankind in the Making*, 2nd ed. (New York, 1967), pp. 209-211, 215.

[6] Pope Pius XII, *Humani Generis* (1950). Philip G. Fothergill, *Evolution and Christians* (London, 1961), investigates the biological evidence and presents the case for evolution as a Catholic, strictly and explicitly under the guidance of the passages in *Humani Generis* pertaining to this question, indicating how closely the Genesis account and the scientific evidence in favor of evolution can be harmonized. For a vigorous and intelligent presentation of the opposing, anti-evolutionary viewpoint from an equally orthodox Christian, not a Catholic, see Duane T. Gish, *Evolution—the Fossils Say No!* (San Diego, CA., 1973). Those interested in pursuing the intricacies of this debate would do well to compare Fothergill and Gish point by point. The numerous standard scientific works on organic evolution are of limited value to the Christian concerned about this issue because almost all of them either ignore or ridicule the kind of questions which orthodox Christians naturally and necessarily ask about the theory of evolution.

[7] Most anthropologists define man as a tool-using animal. The crass materialism of this definition bears witness to an enormous philosophical poverty; nor does it even fit the evidence of the fossils any longer, since there is now good reason to believe that the primitive *Australopithecus*, with a brain hardly larger than a gorilla's, used chipped

stone tools (P. V. Tobias, *Olduvai Gorge 1951-1961*, ed. L. S. B. Leakey, Volume II [Cambridge, England, 1967], pp. 86-87; W. E. Le Gros Clark, *Man-Apes or Ape-Men?*, 2d ed. [New York, 1967], pp. 111-120). Man is more than an animal in any case; certainly he is more than a tool-using animal. The practice of chipping hard stones so as to use them in cutting up game to eat, and in striking down prey and enemies, grew naturally out of animal habits, for a number of animals will use stones to get at food such as shellfish, and chimpanzees will use them to drive off an attacker (Clark, *ibid.*; Adolph H. Schultz, "Some Factors Influencing the Social Life of Primates in General and of Early Man in Particular," in *Social Life of Early Man*, ed. Sherwood L. Washburn [New York, 1961], pp. 188-190). The deliberate shaping of stone tools was new, but hardly a unique adaptation in a world where creatures as diverse as ants, birds, and beavers use natural materials to build elaborate dwellings and other structures. The true mental distinction between man and animal was most pithily stated by G. K. Chesterton: "It is the simple truth that man does differ from the brutes in kind and not in degree; and the proof of it is here: that it sounds like a truism to say that the most primitive man drew a picture of a monkey and that it sounds like a joke to say that the most intelligent monkey drew a picture of a man" (*The Everlasting Man* [New York, 1955], p. 34). An excellent, philosophically sound modern investigation of the question of the essential mental difference between man and animal is Mortimer J. Adler, *The Difference of Man and the Difference It Makes* (Cleveland, 1968).

[8] Thomas Aquinas, *Summa Theologica*, I, Q 75, a. 4; Q 76, a. 1.

[9] Job 38:7.

[10] Grahame Clark and Stuart Piggott, *Prehistoric Societies* (New York, 1965), pp. 61-63; Henri Breuil and Raymond Lantier, *The Men of the Old Stone Age* (New York, 1965), pp. 236-237.

[11] Giuseppe Ricciotti, *History of Israel* (Milwaukee, 1955), I, 155-156, and Bruce Vawter, *A Path Through Genesis* (New York, 1956), p. 53, discuss the uniqueness of the account of the fall of man in the Book of Genesis. Vawter's more recent work has been increasingly marked by Modernism, but *A Path Through Genesis* is essentially sound and orthodox.

[12] Vawter, *A Path Through Genesis*, p. 58, points out several essential truths that many casual readers of the Genesis account of the fall of man miss: that the "knowledge" of evil spoken of is experiential knowledge, not mere intellectual knowledge, as in the familiar Hebrew idiom to "know" one's wife, so that to know evil in this sense is also to do it; and that the reference to knowledge of good as well as of evil does not mean "good *or* evil, but good-and-evil as a single unity," in keeping with the Hebrew language usage whereby binding-and-loosing meant judicial sentences, and going-and-coming meant walking about. The context establishes whether good or evil, binding or loosing, going or coming is meant. In the case of the Genesis account of the fall of man, it is evident that evil alone was meant.

[13] Genesis 2:17. Vawter, *Path Through Genesis*, pp. 65-66, points out that we have no way of knowing exactly what the sin of Adam and Eve was, since the eating of the fruit described in Genesis is almost certainly a symbolic rather than a literal description of what happened, but that we can be sure that "their sin was certainly at bottom one of pride."

[14] Genesis 3:8-13. See the excellent summary in Vawter, *Path Through Genesis*, pp. 66-67.

[15] We have grown so accustomed—having enjoyed, until recently, a culture primarily influenced by Christianity—to awareness of God's mercy that all too many have come to think they have a right to that mercy. No one has a right to mercy; if he did, it would not be mercy but justice. God is first of all just, and cannot violate the principles of

justice any more than He can fail to be good, or make both sides of a contradiction true.
   [16] Genesis 3:17-19.

1.
A DARKLING PLAIN

I saw a dream this night.
The heavens [roared], the earth resounded . . .
    . . . He transformed me,
Mine arms [were covered with feathers] like a bird.
He looks at me, leads me to the house of darkness,
  to the dwelling of Irkalla;
To the house from which he who enters never goes forth;
On the road whose path does not lead back;
To the house whose occupants are bereft of light;
Where dust is their food and clay their sustenance;
They are clad like birds, with garments of wings;
They see no light and dwell in darkness.
In the h[ouse of dus]t, which I entered.
I loo[ked at the kings], and (behold!)
    the crowns had been deposited.
        —Epic of Gilgamesh, Tablet VII[1]

The supernatural gifts were gone, the Garden vanished, and the first men on their own in a world full of enemies and haunted by death. Clothed in animal skins, taking up the crude stone tools by which alone they could now live, killing and being killed even by their own kind, they moved out upon the earth.[2]

The body which had been the receptacle for man's God-given soul was no longer fit to receive the graces which had come to man in his original innocence—graces not only of immortality, but of perfect harmony within his composite nature, and of effortless dominion over earthly creation. Without those graces, man's now corruptible body and fallen soul were inevitably at war with er even as they were estranged from God. That was the condition resulting from original sin. Man could neither merit salvation from God nor attain it on his own. The wonder is that such an offense against God and His creation was permitted to live at all; but God Who had made man and loved him would not destroy him.

To any human mind the problem posed by this situation was insoluble. God's solution finally came in a form that no man using only natural reason could ever have foreseen; and that solution had to wait until man, by halting efforts through many dark millennia, had at last reached the point where the solution could be understood and remembered and the news of it and the truth about it spread across the world despite all the evil which man carried with him wherever he went. That required writing, and civilization, and the beginnings of a disciplined rationality, all far beyond the ken of The Stone Age.

So man roamed the earth with shadowed spirit, dreaming strange dreams of magic and totem, of rituals that would command the invisible world[3] and bring back in some form what had come naturally to his ancestors, in the Garden. But behind and above the magic and the totems, the frenzies and the idols, all the perversions of worship into which sinful and desperate men prompted by the dark angels can fall, there remained an awareness and an acknowledgment—however faint and far—of the Divine King. In virtually every primitive mythology He is represented as the sky-god. Insofar as it can be disentangled from the later and usually degraded accretions of myth and rite, the concept of the sky-god originally included His creation of the world, His universal dominion and His absolute purity.[4] But the sky-god dwelt only in the sky; He did not come down to earth. Earth was where the dark gods and the wild gods roamed, the personifications of nature and of the passions of men. From the true God's Heaven there was no bridge to earth. Eden had been that bridge, and Eden was forever lost.

Yet still God called man to worship Him, because for this all men are made. The scattered voiceless remains which are all we have or can ever have from Stone Age men cannot tell us how God dealt with them or reached them. Was there a continuous or nearly continuous revelation—lost and renewed again and again —from the beginning, to those who were to be His Chosen People? The Book of Genesis indicates that it was so. Our modern archeological and anthropological studies cannot disprove it, and seem increasingly to support that thesis where its possibility is not ruled out *a priori* by anti-religious bias.[5]

Man increased and multiplied, and from his point of origin spread himself— though still very thinly—over almost the whole of the habitable earth.[6] But no new Eden lay at the end of any of the long, long trails of the Stone Age hunter. Everywhere his condition and way of life was fundamentally the same. It has been preserved into modern times by the Australian aborigines and the Bushmen of South Africa.[7]

Then came the Flood. However it may be explained by Christian or non-Christian scholars, the report of an immense deluge is much too widespread and deeply imbedded in the traditions of ancient and primitive peoples to be rationally attributed to mere cultural borrowing or diffusion, or to deny that it reflects the memory of an event that really happened. The great Oriental scholar and archeologist William F. Albright offers the following explanation:

> I see no reason any longer for refusing to connect the traditions of the Great Flood in most regions of Eurasia and America, including particularly Mesopotamia and Israel, with the tremendous floods accompanying and following the critical melting of the glaciers about 9000 B.C. It may not be accidental that there are no clear traditions of the Deluge in ancient Egypt, which must have escaped the worst of these floods.[8]

The low-lying plain of Mesopotamia could well have been completely inundated for a relatively brief period of time by a combination of heavy rains and rising seas. The Book of Genesis tells us that the distant ancestors of Abraham dwelling there were saved from the Deluge by God's special warning to Noah, with instructions to build the ark. For Noah and his family the Mesopotamian plain *was* the world, all of it they had ever known; from the ark upon that waste of waters, with no land in sight for tens or even hundreds of miles—for the Mesopotamian plain, flat as a board, extends for such distances —the Deluge could hardly seem other than world-wide. That catastrophic geological changes, sufficient to produce a world-wide inundation, took place at this time is not inconceivable and is suggested by some bits of otherwise unexplained evidence; real scientists are never quite so sure about such matters as their popularizers. But the weight of present evidence seems to tell against the explanation of the Deluge involving massive planetary catastrophe,[9] while pointing to heavy rainfall and rising seas at the end of the Ice Age as the more likely explanation, though for a more limited inundation. Neither alternative can be ruled out. Just as God could have made man literally and physically from the dust of the earth, so He could have covered all the surface of the earth with waters and soon afterward removed them together with most traces of their presence, and restored the earth's inhabitants.

The Middle East seems to have become increasingly arid after the Flood. Great deserts appeared in Egypt and Arabia; along their edges the forests shrank and the big game migrated away. Searching for new sources of food, men began to gather the wild grain which grew in the hill country and to domesticate the sheep and the goats they found there, in addition to the dogs which their hunting ancestors had tamed. The transition from hunting and food-gathering to farming and stock-raising occurred in the Middle East long before it happened anywhere else in the world. The earliest evidence for it comes from a valley in the Zagros Mountains separating northern Mesopotamia from Persia, and from several sites in Palestine, most recently dated to the ninth millennium (9000-8000) before Christ.[10]

This was the Neolithic or agricultural revolution.[11] It and the Industrial Revolution have been the only really fundamental economic changes in all history. Each made possible a great increase in population. The Neolithic Revolution also laid the foundation for civilization, which is distinguished from barbarism by two elements above all: the presence of cities and the use of writing.

The ancient city, seed of civilization, was three things: a shrine, a market, and a wall. It began with barbarian wanderers who settled upon the land and cultivated it. The shrine drew them together and made them more conscious of their community. Trade sprang up, as will always happen when men gather together with a reasonable degree of peace, and this was the market. Then the wall was built to protect the shrine and the market from those who would despoil them.

So it was that about 8000 B.C. a group of men gathered by a wondrous, ever-flowing spring near a river which ran through a deep straight valley, and built there a walled city which, so far as we now know, was the very first in all the world.[12] The river would one day be called Jordan, the city Jericho; and the land between the Jordan and the sea would be the substance of a promise and the seal of a covenant.

Take a map or a globe of the world and suppose yourself confronted with this problem: An event must occur, and truths must be taught, of supreme importance to every human being upon earth. That event and those truths must be made known to as many men as possible, as rapidly as possible, and as soon as possible in man's history, while technology is still primitive. For it is of the fundamental nature of this event that it can happen only at one time and in one place. The established culture of a civilized society is necessary to preserve the knowledge of it undistorted, and to provide a basis for the beginning of its worldwide propagation; but any delay not absolutely necessary is not to be considered. Thus it cannot wait until the progress of science has annihilated distance.

Where would you choose to have it happen?

Rarely are the reasons for a Divine decision so clear, in a material sense, to our finite minds. Studying map or globe with these criteria in mind, we can see at once why God chose Palestine for His Incarnation. For Palestine is "the center of the earth."[13]

It is not, of course, the center of the physical or geological world, which is a mass of nickel-iron four thousand miles beneath our feet. But it is the center of the human world, the point nearest to all the great concentrations of population before the European colonization of the Americas centuries after the Incarnation. Palestine stands near the junction of the three great continents of the Old World. Africa and Asia meet on its southwestern frontier. Europe is just a few days' sail away across the Mediterranean Sea to Crete. A circle drawn with Jerusalem at its center and a radius of three thousand miles includes modern cities as far apart geographically and culturally as Lisbon, London, Leningrad, Delhi, Kashgar in the Chinese province of Sinkiang, and Kinshasa on the Congo. Such a circle touches all the great races and civilized cultures of man, save only the strange civilizations developed in the Americas before Columbus. From this focal point, this cockpit of geography and history, the Word could most easily and quickly reach all the ends of the earth.

So Palestine was chosen as the place where mankind would be redeemed from the consequences of the Fall. But the very characteristics of Palestine which made it so eminently logical a choice for the site of the Incarnation also made it, from a temporal and human standpoint, a most unsuitable place for the long period of preparation which was the necessary prelude to the Incarnation, without which its true significance could never be understood or appreciated. For the necessary preparation required a long continuity in culture, and as every historian knows, that is precisely what is *not* normally found in the world's crossroads, where outside influences from all sides tend to produce rapid, kaleidoscopic change. Continuity in culture is naturally characteristic only of geographically isolated areas like the Nile valley of Egypt, surrounded by desert except for one short sea frontier to the north, or like China guarded by the immense mountains and deserts of Central Asia.

In fact, throughout recorded history Palestine has been repeatedly fought over, changing hands again and again, shifting from the Eastern to the Western cultural orbit and back again, ever the victim of force and violence. From the time four thousand years ago when "Amraphel king of Shinar, Arioch king of Ellasar, Chedorlaomer king of Elam, and Tidal king of Goiim . . . made war with Bera king of Sodom, Birsha king of Gomorrah"[14] and their allies, to the latest outbreaks of war between Arab and Israeli reported in yesterday's newspaper, this has been Palestine's fate. Yet through those same four thousand years something has been in that small land which not all the pomp and power and ferocity of men could expel, which has lasted through every storm, marking it out so unmistakably from all the rest of the world that even the unbeliever admits the uniqueness of its story.

For this was the Promised Land.

Jericho began with a shrine. Upon bedrock, at the very bottom of the huge mound built up by the accumulation of debris over thousands of years, the Kenyon expedition found its remains, a rectangular wall of stones with wooden posts set among them. Holes were bored through two of the stones apparently in order to hold totem poles or flagpoles.[15] It is believed that this structure marked a "place of pilgrimage, probably a sanctuary, visited by Mesolithic huntsmen who, like their quarry, came to the spring"[16]—the great life-giving spring of Jericho which made its site unique in the hot dry valley of the Jordan.

Here, ten thousand years ago, grew up a city of more than two thousand inhabitants. Its people, though still so primitive that they did not even know how to make pottery, to say nothing of writing, obtained valuable trade goods from distant places—obsidian from Anatolia (modern Turkey), turquoise from Sinai, cowrie shells from the Mediterranean shore. It has been suggested that they traded salt and tar from the Dead Sea for these valuables, as well as the food which they must have produced in quantity with irrigation from the great spring, under the unfailing sun.[17]

Having established a flourishing market, the people of Jericho soon learned their need of a wall. Built of immense stones some of which weigh several tons, standing more than twenty feet high and six feet wide, with thirty-foot watchtowers overlooking a moat 27 feet wide and nine feet deep, their wall was an amazing achievement, coming as it did five thousand years before the pyramids of Egypt.[18] The fact that it had to be built on such a scale, requiring an enormous effort at the very dawn of man's settled existence, tells us as clearly as any written record of the terrible new consequences of the rapacity of fallen man which the wealth created by the Neolithic revolution had unleashed.

By 6000 B.C. an even larger city had arisen in the north, on the Anatolian plateau, and there is reason to believe that men influenced by its culture spread south from the Taurus Mountains through Mesopotamia, Syria and Palestine during the ensuing millennium.[19] Not even its mighty walls could protect Jericho indefinitely; during this period it was conquered, devastated and abandoned, and the site was not reoccupied for nearly two thousand years.[20] By then there was a new walled city, on the flat low plain of southern Mesopotamia: Eridu of the Sumerians, apparently located on the shore of what was then a vast tidal lake. "All the lands were sea," runs an ancient Sumerian legend, "then Eridu was made." It was 25 acres in size and had a population of about four thousand, twice that of Jericho before it.[21]

Eridu lay just twelve miles from what was to be the site of the city of Ur, where Abraham was born.[22]

> As men migrated in the east, they found a plain in the land of Shinar and settled there. And they said to one another, "Come, let us make bricks, and burn them thoroughly." And they had brick for stone, and bitumen for mortar. Then they said, "Come, let us build ourselves a city, and a tower with its top in the heavens, and let us make a name for ourselves, lest we be scattered abroad upon the face of the whole earth."[23]

It is here, at the beginning of the eleventh chapter of the Book of Genesis, that the Bible moves into history as the world knows it—history which is elsewhere recorded. Henceforth the factual information found in Scripture can often be checked from independent sources; and we shall see that the overwhelming verdict of recent archeological and historical research is that the history recorded in the Bible is highly reliable. One by one the arguments and supposed evidence against Biblical historical veracity, so widely publicized in the past, have been discredited, so that the renowned Palestinian archeologist Nelson Glueck could state categorically that "no archeological discovery has ever controverted a Biblical reference."[24]

The reference in the Book of Genesis to the settlement of the plain of Sumer (Shinar) is the first example of this kind. The building of cities in the plain of southern Mesopotamia antedated the writing of the Book of Genesis by nearly three thousand years.[25] Yet the passage quoted preserves almost perfectly the memory of how it was done. Burnt brick and mud-brick, with bitumen (tar) as mortar, were the raw materials of almost all Sumerian architecture, because while there was plenty of clay in the alluvial plain of southern Mesopotamia, there was almost no stone. And very early in their history, when they had just begun to develop picture-writing into a medium which could represent the spoken word, the Sumerians at Uruk and Uqair built prototypes of the Tower of Babel: the first examples of the great stepped temples called ziggurats erected upon mounds rising high above the plain,[26] appearing even higher because of the absolute flatness of the plain, so that to the wondering eyes of tribesmen from the edges of the surrounding desert they might well seem to "reach to heaven."

In those days ten cities stood on the Sumerian plain between Eridu and the point where the Tigris and the Euphrates Rivers approach each other near the site of modern Baghdad and ancient Babylon. The greatest were Kish, Uruk and Ur; the others were Adab, Larak, Sippar, Shuruppak, Nippur, Lagash and Eshnunna. Far to the north two outlying cities, Ashur and Mari, were destined to transmit the culture of the Sumerians to Assyria in northeastern Mesopotamia and to the city of Harran in northwestern Mesopotamia together with adjoining regions of Syria.[27]

At the moment in history (about 2700 B.C.) when the kings of these cities begin to emerge from the mists of myth and to stand forth in Sumer's records as personalities in their own right, one titanic figure casts the longest shadow across the dun clay plain: Gilgamesh, king of Uruk, who defended his city against the aggression of Agga, king of Kish, and in consequence built Uruk's first city wall.[28] Sober history tells us this much of him; but for reasons we do not know, this king, like Achilles and Arthur, left behind him a mighty legend, woven into an epic tale of heroism against the dark background of an inexorable fate.

The epic of Gilgamesh is by far the most ancient composition of its kind. Inscribed upon imperishable clay tablets in the wedge-shaped characters of the cuneiform writing developed in Sumer, copies of portions of this tale nearly four thousand years old have come down to us; and the original sources undoubtedly went back several centuries earlier.[29] No other major work of literature—as distinct from royal or funerary inscriptions on monuments—

anywhere on earth dates from before 2000 B.C. and the age of Abraham.[30] In its final form the epic of Gilgamesh was preserved as carefully by the Mesopotamian scribes as the epics of Homer were later preserved by Greek intellectuals. Most of it came to light when the great clay tablet library of Ashurbanipal, one of the last kings of Assyria, was unearthed in the nineteenth century.

As befits its very early origin, many passages in the cuneiform epic are naive and childish, and it often lacks the kind of romance we expect in the telling of such a tale; yet its hero, in true epic fashion, sets forth with one brave companion to slay a dragon in a dark cedar forest, and succeeds in his mission. But the most striking characteristic of the epic of Gilgamesh is its absolute honesty in facing the riddle of death. Gilgamesh of Uruk, triumphant king, perfect knight, wall-builder, dragonslayer, goes forth in the end to meet the last enemy—for his dear friend and comrade-in-arms, the heroic Enkidu, is dead.

> Enkidu, whom I loved dearly,
> Who went with me through all hardships,
> He has gone to the lot of mankind,
> Day and night I have wept over him.
> For burial I did not want to give him up, thinking:
> "My friend will rise after all at my lamentations!"
> Seven days and seven nights,
> Until the worm fell upon his face.
> Since he is gone, I find no life.
> I have roamed about like a hunter in the midst of the
>   steppe.[31]

Before Enkidu died the nature of the after-life had been revealed to him in a dream, the appalling vision described at the head of this chapter: the "house of darkness" from which no man comes forth, the abode of dust for which king and commoner alike are destined.

One man had cheated death: Utnapishtim "the distant," the only survivor of the Deluge, to whom the gods—the quarrelling, capricious gods who were all Gilgamesh knew or dreamed of—were said to have given eternal life. Gilgamesh would find Utnapishtim, though Hell should bar his way:

> "Barmaid, which is the way to Utnapishtim?
> "The directions? Give me, oh give me the
>   directions!
> "If it is possible, the seas I will cross!
> "If it is not possible, I will roam over the
>   steppe."
> The barmaid said to him, to Gilgamesh:
> "Gilgamesh, there never has been a crossing;
> "And whoever from the days of old has come thus
>   far has not been able to cross the sea.
> "Valiant Shamash [the sun-god] does cross the
>   sea, who besides Shamash crosses?

"Difficult is the place of crossing, very
    difficult its passage;
"And deep are the waters of death, which bar
    its approaches.
"Where, Gilgamesh, wilt thou cross the sea?"[32]

Surpassing every barrier and danger by sheer power of will, Gilgamesh at last reaches Utnapishtim, only to be told:

Do we build a house [to stand] forever? Do we
    seal [a document to be in force] forever?
Do brothers divide [their inheritance to last]
    forever?
Does hatred remain in [the land] forever?
Does the river raise [and carry] the flood
    forever?
(line lost)
Does its face see the face of the sun [forever]?
From the days of old there is no
    [permanence]."[33]

Utnapishtim's eternal life was a privilege reserved to him alone. He could not share it, even if he would. The king and hero had gone upon his greatest quest where no man had ever been before, only to find that even at trail's end there was no hope:

Gilgamesh said to him, to Utnapishtim the distant:
"[What] shall I do, Utnapishtim, where shall I go
"As the robber has taken hold of my [member]s?
"Death is dwelling [in] my bedchamber,
"And wherever [I] set [my feet] there is
    death."[34]

In the five millennia since man first learned to write, no more terrible passage can be found than this cry of absolute despair stamped in strange wedges on broken tablets of clay by the industrious and talented people who built man's first civilization, but are now vanished utterly from the face of the earth—no more eloquent proof of the reality and consequences of original sin from a source which never knew the story of the Garden of Eden.[35] Beside that one pitiless fact that Gilgamesh at long last had to face, what mattered the pageant of cities and kings and conquerors with which early Mesopotamian history, like all temporal human history, was filled? Where was Sargon of Agade, who came out of the southern Mesopotamian plain to master the lands all the way to the Mediterranean Sea about 2350 B.C., the first great conqueror known to history? Where was his far-famed descendant who took the epithet of a god, Naram-Sin, "King of the Universe"?[36]

"They see no light and dwell in darkness.

"In the h[ouse of dus]t, which I entered,
"I loo[ked at the kings], and (behold!) the
    crowns had been deposited."[37]

The honesty with which they faced the truth about the human condition is
the measure of the real stature of the people of early Mesopotamia. It was no
mere chance that it was from their homeland, however stifled and corrupted,
that Abraham emerged, for there can be neither hope nor promise for man unless
there be first the willingness to face truth.

The two other centers of civilization which came into existence before 2000
B.C. showed no such willingness. In Egypt, as never to a comparable extent
in Mesopotamia, the king himself was a god—no mere demigod, but a full-
fledged member of the pantheon—whose status was determined by the size of
the tomb which was to guarantee him a happy eternity.[38] So the most gigantic
rock-piles in the history of mankind, not excluding the largest stone structures
of modern times, were erected early in the recorded history of Egypt to house
the mortal remains of Pharaohs. One can imagine what Utnapishtim would have
told Gilgamesh about the value of a pyramid.

In contrast to Mesopotamia, which during most of its history was a more
or less loose aggregation of city-states, Egypt and the third civilization, in the
Indus valley far to the east, were monoliths. The whole life of the nation and
the culture centered upon one or two capital cities, and was locked in a pattern
which remained essentially unchanged century after century. The building of
Egypt's political, economic and cultural monolith began with King Menes or
Narmer, who about 3100 B.C. unified the whole of the long narrow valley of
the Nile south of the cataracts, and its lush delta, into one state with its capital
at the city of the White Wall, later known as Memphis.[39] Egyptian writing was
probably derived from that of Mesopotamia in its earliest stages—though the
forms and appearance of hieroglyphic and cuneiform later became very
different—and such originality and inventiveness as Egyptian civilization possessed was exhausted after the first few centuries, by the beginning of the Pyramid
Age about 2600 B.C.[40] Though the unparalleled natural blessing of the fertility
created by the annual Nile flood gave rise to the greatest material abundance
in the ancient world—there is no better agricultural environment on earth than
the Nile valley—this only strengthened the monolithic character of the Egyptian system.[41] The Pharaoh himself could not change it; the one true genius of
Egyptian history, King Akhenaten, tried and failed.[42] From the beginning Egypt
was a land of bondage, from which the only escape was to leave. Yet this was
never easy, since the fertile valley of the Nile was surrounded on all sides by
desert and sea.

The other monolith was the still stranger civilization known as the Harappa, from one of its two chief cities in the Indus River valley in northwestern

India. Though probably also stimulated by Mesopotamia's example, since the Sumerians were periodically in contact with the Indus valley by sea, the form of its writing developed so differently from any other that there appears to be little hope of ever translating the few written records of the Harappa civilization which have survived. Aside from archeological remains, the only clues to its nature come from its ultimate conquerors, the Aryans whose triumph was recorded in the Vedas. The Vedas tell how invaders from the north overwhelmed a dark-skinned people huddled behind walls, the Dasyus. An Indian historian writes:

> In the Aryan view the Dasyus practised black magic. Such a belief is especially found in the *Atharva Veda*, in which the Dasyus appear as evil spirits to be scared away from the sacrifice. It is said that an all-powerful amulet enabled the sage Angiras to break through the Dasyus' fortresses. . . . It is believed that the Dasyus are treacherous, not practising the Aryan observances, and hardly human.[43]

And the British archeologist whose name has been associated with the Harappa civilization for more than a quarter of a century describes as follows a discovery in the excavation of the second city of that civilization, Mohenjo-daro:

> Particularly in the East, where decay is rapid, bodies are not left lying about amongst inhabited houses. The general inference from the thirty or more derelict corpses at Mohenjo-daro is that from the moment of death the place was uninhabited. The absence of skeletons (so far) from the citadel may imply that the raiders occupied and cleared this commanding position for their own momentary use. For the rest, it may be suspected that sporadic fires in the sacked city kept predatory animals away.[44]

Sacks are as old as cities themselves. Barbarian incursions and devastation mark the fall of every civilization. But in none was the physical destruction so complete and the initial rejection of existing culture so total as that of the Harappa civilization by the Aryans,[45] and it is hard to resist the impression that they felt they were crushing something abominable.

The Harappa civilization is distinguished from all others known by its extraordinary lack of change. For a thousand years (roughly 2500 to 1500 B.C.) it remained almost exactly the same, except for a very gradual decline towards the end. Its two great cities sprang up precisely planned, evidently by some supreme, unquestioned authority; and every smaller city and town of this civilization so far excavated has shown the identically, rigidly regular street pattern.[46] The cities contained neither monuments, nor inscriptions, nor decorations. Blank walls of mud-brick faced the long straight streets and the right-angle corners, hiding the small dark dwelling-places of the people behind them. In Harappa and Mohenjo-daro, gigantic granaries collectively stored the produce of the fields. No panoply of royalty nor clash of arms overawed potentially rebellious thousands. From all appearances Harappa had no kings, and its weapons were curiously weak. There were no swords, and the spearheads would have crumpled at the first hard thrust.[47]

In an evocative essay in his book *Lost Cities*, Leonard Cottrell asks: "Was this, perhaps '1984'—B.C.?"[48]

Merchants from Harappa sailed to Mesopotamia—whether in their own boats or in those of Sumer we do not know—and left relics of their presence in that foreign land, but we know of almost nothing they brought home. In Mesopotamia in 2300 B.C. they encountered a civilization technically advanced in many ways beyond their own. Yet after this contact just as before, the Melukhkhans (to give them the name of their country, the one word of their language that we know) continued to make tools of stone as well as of copper and cast bronze, and to grow grain without canal irrigation or deep plowing, though both these aids to agriculture—along with better metal tools—were used throughout Mesopotamia.[49]

In each city rose one great temple mound, and only one. In this the Indian historian D. D. Kosambi believes he has found the key to the cause of the utter stagnation of the Harappa civilization: domination by a single all-powerful priesthood which would allow no innovation.[50] The numerous seals used by individual Harappans which have been preserved depict a horned god who is a recognizable prototype of Shiva, the Hindu god of destruction, whose dark-skinned consort Kali was the goddess of the cult of the Thug stranglers who preyed for centuries on Indian travellers until finally exposed in the nineteenth century by a heroic British official. The pose of meditation shown on the Harappan seals is clearly that of yoga.[51]

A very substantial body of evidence from the history of Indian philosophy may be adduced to confirm the hypothesis that the Aryan destruction of the Harappa civilization, while physically complete, did not exorcise its ghosts, who returned to haunt the conquerors as wandering *gurus*.[52] In the Vedas there is none of the convoluted mysticism we now associate with Hindu India, but rather what Heinrich Zimmer calls a "roaring, world-affirmative" classical paganism.[53] But with the passage of the centuries the strange doctrines of the unreality of the objective universe,[54] the metaphysical nonentity of the individual,[55] and the endless cycle of reincarnation[56]—doctrines wholly unknown, or confined to a small esoteric minority, elsewhere in the world[57]—gained an ever-tightening grip on the Indian mind, along with their social expression which was caste.[58] Civilized society in India slowly petrified into an ultimate rigidity which neither time nor change could break.[59]

Though in the present (and likely future) state of our knowledge of the Indus civilization we cannot establish that these doctrines originated in it, and to postulate such a complex philosophy in so technically primitive a civilization appears at first sight very dubious to us of the modern West, so much influenced by the materialistic view of history, the hypothesis is strengthened by the complete absence of anything in Aryan Vedic culture which could account for the later development of Indian thought. Indo-European peoples closely related to the Vedic Aryans settled in Iran,[60] and others indubitably of the same stock and language family filled Europe, yet no religious and intellectual development remotely resembling the Indian occurred either in Europe or in Iran. Since the Indus valley civilization is materially and historically unique and later Indian philosophy, religion and culture is also unique, it is reasonable to look for the source of this uniqueness in the religion of the Harappans, which Kosambi suggests was so completely dominant in their culture.

When we learn that the uniform tradition of the Jaina religion of India[61] dates its origin not to its best-known historic teacher, Vardhamana the Mahavira (a contemporary of Gautama the Buddha) but to a remote pre-Aryan antiquity; that both the Mahavira and Parshva, his immediate predecessor in the traditional list of 24 supreme Jaina teachers or "Crossing-Makers" are described as very dark-skinned (as the Harappans, by contrast to the Aryans, were); and that the Jaina view of the world is and has always been, since the emergence of Jainism into recorded history, one of irremediable decline from earlier ages when their teachings were more widely accepted and practiced, the case for the origin of Jainism in the Harappa civilization becomes very strong.[62] Belief in reincarnation was a cardinal principle and starting point of Jaina doctrine.[63] But even Jainism is not the whole story, for there are no Jaina priests, though there is a clear link between Jainism and yoga;[64] who then were the Harappa priests? Were they, perhaps, the devotees of Shiva, the god of destruction? Shiva and Kali seem clearly to be Harappa deities assimilated into the Hindu pantheon;[65] in all probability they brought with them much more than mere names.

The building of civilizations in the great river valleys of the Nile, the Tigris-Euphrates and the Indus was an immense achievement. Yet this was how it ended: in the despair of Gilgamesh, in the loom of the pyramids, or broken on the ever-circling wheel of reincarnating fate which India calls *karma*. The answer which had eluded Old Stone Age man even at the ends of the earth was not to be found in the works of man's own hands in stone and clay and copper and bronze. To any human eye there was no answer; man stood

> . . . as on a darkling plain
> Swept by confused alarms of struggle and flight,
> Where ignorant armies clash by night.[66]

NOTES

[1] Alexander Heidel, *The Gilgamesh Epic and Old Testament Parallels* (Chicago, 1946),

p. 60. The quotation is from column iv of the Hittite recension of Tablet VII, lines 13-15 and 31-41.

[2] Genesis 3:21 and 4; Grahame Clark and Stuart Piggott, *Prehistoric Societies* (New York, 1965), pp. 59-61.

[3] Henri Breuil and Raymond Lantier, *The Men of the Old Stone Age* (New York, 1965), pp. 251-264.

[4] Wilhelm Schmidt, *The Origin and Growth of Religion* (New York, 1931, 1971), pp. 167-290.

[5] See Wilhelm Schmidt, *Primitive Revelation* (St. Louis, 1939).

[6] Clark and Piggott, *Prehistoric Societies*, pp. 112-113. The only habitable land Old Stone Age man did not reach was most islands separated from the mainland by several hundred miles of open water, the largest of these being New Zealand and Madagascar.

[7] Clark and Piggott, *Prehistoric Societies*, pp. 114-120.

[8] William F. Albright, *From the Stone Age to Christianity*, 2d ed. (New York, 1957), p. 9. See also *ibid.*, pp. 174-175, where Albright points out that the close similarity of the Flood tradition of the American Indians, even in southern South America, to the Flood tradition of Mesopotamia and Israel suggests that it goes all the way back to the original settlement of the Americas by Stone Age man at the end of the last glacial period.

[9] See Paul Heinisch, *History of the Old Testament* (Collegeville MN, 1952), pp. 28-30, for a particularly good discussion of this question by a clearly orthodox writer. The discovery by Sir Leonard Woolley in 1929 of a layer of sand laid down by a great flood at the lowest levels of the site of Ur in Mesopotamia, and his attribution of that layer to the flood described in the Book of Genesis, has been cited again and again by well-meaning Christians seeking scientific corroboration for a universal deluge. However, Woolley's find provides no such corroboration. There was very likely a great flood at Ur, probably about 3500 B.C., which left the deposit Woolley found, but the sites of the cities of Eridu and Lagash, just a few miles from Ur, have been excavated to the same level for the same period and show no trace of a flood. Traces have been found at a comparable level in the remains of two other early cities in southern Mesopotamia, Kish and Shuruppak, indicating that this particular flood was more extensive than most,but it certainly did not submerge all parts even of that flat and low-lying region. See *The Cambridge Ancient History*, Volume I, Part 1, 3rd ed. (Cambridge, England, 1971), pp. 353-354, and Heinisch, *History of the Old Testament*, . As G. Ernest Wright says, it is much more likely that the Genesis account of the Flood represents "an old tradition, going back to the end of the Stone Age before the present bounds of the oceans were fixed" (*Biblical Archaeology*, rev. ed. [Philadelphia, 1962], p. 120).

[10] *Cambridge Ancient History*, I (1) (3rd ed.), 249-258, 501-510.

[11] The term "Neolithic" refers to the polished stone implements which came into use in most areas at about the same time as the first controlled agriculture and domestication of animals (other than the dog), but the change in implements was considerably less significant than the development of agriculture and stock-raising.

[12] *Cambridge Ancient History*, I (1) (3rd ed.), 500-502. De Vaux, writing in this section of *The Cambridge Ancient History*, doubts the propriety of calling Jericho at this time a city, preferring to speak of a large village, but this seems an excess of scholarly caution. Anyone can go to Jericho today and see the ancient wall and gate for himself and make his own judgment as to whether it marked something impressive enough to be properly called a city—as the writer has done.

[13] Ezra 5:5, 38:10.

[14] Genesis 14:1-2.

[15] Kathleen M. Kenyon, *Archaeology in the Holy Land*, 3rd ed. (New York, 1969), p. 41.

[16] *Cambridge Ancient History*, I (1) (3rd ed.), 500.

[17] *Ibid.*, p. 502; Kenyon, *Archaeology in the Holy Land*, pp. 45-46; Emmanuel Anati, *Palestine Before the Hebrews* (New York, 1963), pp. 241-250.

[18] Kenyon, *Archaeology in the Holy Land*, p. 44; Anati, *Palestine Before the Hebrews*, pp. 243-246.

[19] James Mellaart, *Çatal Hüyük, a Neolithic Town in Anatolia* (New York, 1967), pp. 51-53; *Cambridge Ancient History*, I (1) (3rd ed.), 276-284.

[20] Kenyon, *Archaeology in the Holy Land*, pp. 55-56; *Cambridge Ancient History*, I (1) (3rd ed.), 519-520.

[21] *Cambridge Ancient History*, I (1) (3rd ed.), 330-332.

[22] *Ibid.*, p. 330. For a discussion of the argument over whether Ur was actually the birthplace of Abraham, see Chapter Two, Note 7, below.

[23] Genesis 11:2-4.

[24] Nelson M. Glueck, *Rivers in the Desert, a History of the Negev* (New York, 1959), p. 31.

[25] This presumes a date prior to 4000 B.C. for the founding of Eridu (Samuel N. Kramer, *The Sumerians, Their History, Culture and Character* [Chicago, 1963], p. 31) and a date somewhat later than 1000 B.C. (during the reigns of David and Solomon) for the commitment to writing of the Book of Genesis.

[26] *The Cambridge Ancient History*, Volume I, Part 2, 3rd ed. (Cambridge, England, 1971), pp. 81-84; Kramer, *Sumerians*, pp. 135-136, 302-306.

[27] *Cambridge Ancient History*, I (2) (3rd ed.), 96-98.

[28] *Ibid.*, pp. 110-112.

[29] Heidel, *Gilgamesh Epic*, p. 15.

[30] The Oriental civilizations have acquired a vastly exaggerated reputation for antiquity in the popular mind. In fact they possess no written texts (except for a few rock inscriptions) dating from before the birth of Christ, and the oldest compositions handed down by word of mouth and by written copies now lost go back no farther than 1500 B.C. in the case of the Vedas of India. Only in Egypt and in the Indus valley of India did writing exist in all the world outside Mesopotamia in 2000 B.C. So far as we can tell, it was not used for any literary purpose in the Indus valley. As for Egypt, the inscriptions and few papyri older than 2000 B.C. include no examples of a connected narrative of any length (*Cambridge Ancient History*, I [2] [3rd ed.], 201).

[31] Epic of Gilgamesh, Tablet X (Old Babylonian version), lines 2-11, in Heidel, *Gilgamesh Epic*, pp. 69-70. The Old Babylonian version of the Epic dates from the second millennium B.C. Heidel's excellent translation is reproduced except for the omission of many of his gratuitous insertions intended, by no means always necessarily, to clarify the existing text. Bracketed material represents the translator's most probable reconstruction of words missing in broken clay tablet copies.

[32] Epic of Gilgamesh, Tablet X (Assyrian version), column ii, lines 16-26, in Heidel, *Gilgamesh Epic*, p. 74. This version of the Epic was found in the cuneiform library of King Ashurbanipal of Assyria dating to about 650 B.C.

[33] Epic of Gilgamesh, Tablet X (Assyrian version), column vi, lines 26-32, in *ibid.*, p. 79. The tablet is unfortunately considerably broken and fragmented at this important point.

[34] Epic of Gilgamesh, Tablet XI (Assyrian version), lines 229-233, in *ibid.*, p. 90.

[35] It is often stated or implied that the early chapters of the Book of Genesis are little more than an adaptation of Sumerian and Babylonian myths. In fact, both the content and the style of these chapters are strikingly different from Mesopotamian or any other mythology. The universal tendency of mythic literature is to add ever more fantastic

accretions to the basic story, but the account of the creation and fall of man in Genesis is one of magnificent simplicity, whose scope and profundity go far beyond what could have been expected of any writer of that time without the help of Divine inspiration. While there are echoes in the Mesopotamian myths of the hopeless quest for immortality which is the great theme of the Epic of Gilgamesh, there is nothing in the Epic of Gilgamesh remotely resembling the Genesis account of man originally given immortality by God, but losing it through disobedience to Him. K. A. Kitchen, an authority on the ancient Orient, clearly demonstrates in *Ancient Orient and Old Testament* (Chicago, 1966), pp. 88-90, the fundamental differences between the Book of Genesis and Mesopotamian creation myths and the impossibility of the former deriving from the latter. Though Kitchen's book has no Catholic orientation, his conclusions are in complete agreement with this statement by Pope Pius XII in his encyclical *Humani Generis* (1950): "Whatever of popular narrations have been inserted into the Sacred Scriptures must in no way be considered on a par with myths or other such things, which are more the product of an extravagant imagination than of that striving for truth and simplicity which in the sacred books, also of the Old Testament, is so apparent." On the absence of anything like the Genesis account of original sin in Mesopotamian literature and the fundamental differences between the religious orientation of that literature and the Book of Genesis, see Giuseppe Ricciotti, *History of Israel* (Milwaukee, 1955), I, 155-156.

[36] Georges Roux, *Ancient Iraq* (New York, 1964), pp. 128-133; H. W. F. Saggs, *The Greatness That Was Babylon, a Sketch of the Ancient Civilizations of the Tigris-Euphrates Valley* (New York, 1962), pp. 404-405.

[37] Epic of Gilgamesh, Tablet VII (Hittite recension), lines 39-41, in Heidel, *Gilgamesh Epic*, p. 60.

[38] John A. Wilson, *The Burden of Egypt, an Interpretation of Ancient Egyptian Culture* (Chicago, 1951), pp. 49-52, 69-73; Saggs, *Babylon*, pp. 360-362.

[39] Wilson, *Burden of Egypt*, p. vii; *Cambridge Ancient History*, I (2) (3rd ed.), 6-7, 10-11, 14.

[40] Wilson, *Burden of Egypt*, pp. 36-40, 51-55; *Cambridge Ancient History*, I (2) (3rd ed.), 43-44.

[41] *Cambridge Ancient History*, I (2) (3rd ed.), 169-170.

[42] See Chapter Two, below, for a discussion of the character, thought, and significance of the Pharaoh Akhenaten.

[43] Ram Sharam Sharma, *Sudras in Ancient India, a Survey of the Position of the Lower Orders down to circa A.D. 500* (Delhi, 1958), p. 11.

[44] Mortimer Wheeler, *Civilizations of the Indus Valley and Beyond* (New York, 1966), pp. 82-83.

[45] Sharma, *Sudras in Ancient India*, p. 14; A. L. Basham, *The Wonder That Was India* (London, 1954), pp. 32-33.

[46] D. D. Kosambi, *The Culture and Civilization of Ancient India in Historical Outline* (London, 1965), p. 63; Stuart Piggott, *Prehistoric India to 1000 B.C.* (London, 1950), pp. 135-136, 140, 152-153, 229; B. B. Lal, "A New Indus Valley Provincial Capital Discovered: Excavations at Kalibangan in Northern Rajasthan," *Illustrated London News*, Vol. 240 (March 24, 1962), p. 454.

[47] Kosambi, *Ancient India*, pp. 63-64; Piggott, *Prehistoric India*, p. 189; Mortimer Wheeler, *The Indus Civilization*, supplementary volume to *The Cambridge History of India* (Cambridge, England, 1953), pp. 23-24.

[48] Leonard Cottrell, *Lost Cities* (New York, 1957), p. 125.

[49] Kosambi, *Ancient India*, pp. 69-70; Basham, *India*, p. 21; Wheeler, *Indus Civilization*, p. 94.

[50] Kosambi, *Ancient India*, pp. 69-70.

[51] Basham, *India*, pp. 22-23; Wheeler, *Indus Civilization*, p. 95. For the Thugs, see Francis Tuker, *The Yellow Scarf* (London, 1961).

[52] Heinrich Zimmer, *Philosophies of India*, ed. Joseph Campbell (Cleveland, 1956), pp. 219, 233, 281; Sharma, *Sudras in Ancient India*, pp. 20-21; Basham, *India*, p. 241.

[53] Zimmer, *Philosophies of India*, p. 220.

[54] *Ibid.*, pp. 8, 53, 306.

[55] *Ibid.*, pp. 153, 361, 442-444, 456.

[56] *Ibid.*, pp. 254, 299-300. This weird doctrine, taken for granted by all schools of Indian thought since at least 600 B.C. (Basham, *India*, pp. 242-243) is called *samsara* in Sanskrit.

[57] The concept of reincarnation is unknown until a late date in China, and the first and only expression of it in the West as a major part of a philosophical system is in the teaching of Pythagoras about 550 B.C. or a little later. The Greeks later ascribed this teaching of Pythagoras to Indian influence. (A. R. Burn, *The Lyric Age of Greece* [New York, 1964], pp. 373-383). Other Greek philosophers occasionally mention or even accept reincarnation, but make little of it.

[58] Zimmer, *Philosophies of India*, pp. 152-153.

[59] See Chapter Seven, below.

[60] For the character and religion of early Iran, see Chapter Seven, below.

[61] For a more extended discussion of Jainism, see Chapter Seven, below.

[62] Zimmer, *Philosophies of India*, pp. 182-183, 196n, 220, 226-227.

[63] *Ibid.*, pp. 226-227.

[64] *Ibid.*, pp. 281-283.

[65] *Ibid.*, pp. 568-569, for Kali. Zimmer regards Shiva as primarily if not solely in the Aryan-Brahmana tradition (ibid., pp. 597-598) but this would seem to be contradicted by the evidence of the horned god of the Harappa seals (see Note 51, above).

[66] Matthew Arnold, "Dover Beach."

2.
FATHER IN FAITH

Now the LORD said to Abram, "Go forth from your country and your kindred and your father's house to the land that
I will show you. And I will make of you a great nation and
I will bless you, and make your name great, so that you will
be a blessing. I will bless those who bless you, and him who
curses you I will curse; and by you all the families of the
earth will bless themselves."—Genesis 12:1-3

For just over a century Ur on the Euphrates River was the most splendid
city in the world. Egypt was temporarily in eclipse, a new dynasty taking over
at Thebes far up the Nile while Menes' capital of Memphis slipped into a long
decline; Harappa in India had stagnated utterly; but the old Sumerian stock of
lower Mesopotamia rose against the barbarian invaders and, expelling them from
the land, knit together a new empire with its capital at Ur. In those days tidewater
from the Persian Gulf reached Ur, making it a seaport as well as an overland
trade mart and capital of empire.[1] Like all such great cities before or since,
it was busy, teeming, cosmopolitan, bringing together the best and the worst
of the culture which had created it.

The city of Ur was dedicated to the moon-god, called Sin in Mesopotamia
and Laban in Syria.[2] The greatest of the ziggurats of Mesopotamia stood in Ur;
much of it remains to this day, looming up out of what is now wasteland.[3] Unlike
the pyramids of Egypt, the Mesopotamian ziggurats were not tombs but temples,

though their exact purpose and use is not yet clearly understood. Most probably they were intended to symbolize ascent to the sky, the abode of the gods, as is suggested by the story of the Tower of Babel and Jacob's dream of a ladder or stairway to heaven, full of ascending and descending angels.[4] But that kind of ascent was not yet open to man, as Gilgamesh had learned to his sorrow.

In the closing years of the third millennium before Christ, King Ibbi-Sin of Ur (2029-2006 B.C.) struggled in vain against the age-old nemesis of wealth gained by power: that it attracts those who will despoil it by power. His father had tried building a great wall all the way across Mesopotamia from the Tigris to the Euphrates to fend off Semitic Amorite invaders from the northwest; so far had civilized men come from the wall which was the mightiest work of the first city of Jericho. Like all such defenses it proved inadequate: the Amorites circled round it, the king's most trusted lieutenant betrayed him, and finally the Elamites took him in the rear and sacked his brilliant capital with a savagery remembered for centuries in this cuneiform lament:

> The city into ruins was made . . .
> Its people, not potsherds, filled its sides;
> Its walls were breached; the people groan,
> In its lofty gates, where they were wont to promenade,
>   dead bodies were lying about;
> In its boulevards, where the feasts were celebrated,
>   scattered they lay.
> In all its streets, where they were wont to promenade,
>   dead bodies were lying about;
> In its places, where the festivities of the land took
>   place, the people lay in heaps . . .
> Ur—its weak and its strong perished through hunger;
> Mothers and fathers who did not leave their houses were
>   overcome by fire;
> The young lying in their mothers' laps, like fish were
>   carried off by the waters;
> In the city, the wife was abandoned, the son was
>   abandoned, the possessions were scattered about.
> O Nanna! Ur has been destroyed; its people have been
>   dispersed.[5]

Some of the invaders, and some of the more peaceful wanderers along the edges of the desert who followed in their wake, resettled Ur along with a returning trickle of its former inhabitants; but it never again became more than a shadow of what it had been. Passed back and forth between Isin and Larsa, feeble heirs to its once-mighty empire, Ur retained from its days of greatness only the cult of the moon-god at the magnificent ziggurat. In 1830 B.C. it is recorded that Warad-Sin, the son of an Elamite princess who had usurped the throne of Larsa, appointed his sister priestess of the moon-god at Ur.[6] After that, in the course of time, the city became a town, the town a village, and the village one of the silent heaps of long-ago inhabited earth which the Arabs call a *tell*.

During these latter days of Ur, probably about the time that Warad-Sin set his sister over its temple to the moon, a band descended from the Amorites who had come to live there after the Elamite sack set out for the city of Haran several hundred miles away in northern Mesopotamia, in sight of the mile-high mountains of Armenia which mark the northern rim of the Middle East's "Fertile Crescent." They and their fathers and grandfathers had lived long enough in Ur to learn of its vanished glories and to make what remained of its culture their own.[7] They worshipped the moon-god.[8] Haran, their destination, was another center of the same cult, which was distinguished from others in Mesopotamia by not being tied to any one particular locality—since the moon, like the sun, rises and shines impartially upon all men everywhere.[9]

One of the migrants was named Thare, or Terah. He took with him his son Abram and Abram's wife Sarai, or Sarah. The couple had no children. They settled at Haran, where many tribes like theirs wandered freely in the absence of any strong centralized political authority in that region. Thare died there.[10] Further on, in Syria, lay the site of the city of Ebla, great and famous in the times of Sargon and Naram-Sin, whose recently discovered royal archives are written in a language showing many affinities to Hebrew, with names resembling some in the Book of Genesis—notably that of Ebrum, king of Ebla, which is very similar in form to the name of Abraham's ancestor Eber mentioned in Genesis 10 and 11.[11]

Ebla had carried on a far-flung commerce. Among the cities mentioned in its tablets are the five "cities of the plain"—Sodom, Gomorrah, Admah, Zeboim, and Zoar—listed in exactly the same order in which they later appear in the fourteenth chapter of Genesis in connection with the aid given them by Abraham, clear evidence that such cities existed in his time and were regarded as a group, as the Bible presents them.[12] Beyond this, despite some sensational and misleading reports, Ebla does not speak to our subject. There is no solid evidence that the true God, Whose Name was much later to be revealed to Moses as Yahweh, was worshipped there under any form of that Name. On the contrary, Ebla had the usual pantheon of false gods—over 500 of them, including several later worshipped by the Canaanites and previously by the Sumerians.[13]

Abraham still stands alone. And when he settled in Haran, there was nothing whatever to indicate that this "wandering Aramaean"[14] was to become the father in faith of billions of human beings—of every believing Christian, Jew and Muslim who lives, has ever lived or will ever live.

But this man God chose; this man God called. God made him a promise, and asked of him faith. Coming into a world of hideously distorted images of counterfeit divinity, of lewd ecstasies, of metaphysical terrors, of hopeless resignation, God sought a man who would listen and believe—simply, totally, without doubt or question, though what had happened to him ran counter to all the religious traditions and customs of men since the first shrine was built on the site which was to be Jericho. For in all that experience of men, the supreme sky-god never spoke at all, and the lesser gods did not send personal messages to individuals, or make promises to them, without temple or priest or ritual, without consultations and quarrels among the legion of themselves. They had no missions for men; rather, men came to them and sacrificed and prayed to them to avert their wrath or gain a transient favor.[15]

God promised Abram, if he would believe, a posterity to match the stars in the sky and the grains of sand in the desert.[16] Through Abraham's fatherhood in faith, that promise was kept.

There was a further promise: "In you shall all families on earth be blessed."[17] Through the direct descent of Jesus Christ from Abraham and His universal redemptive mission, that promise above all was kept.

From the day of the Call onward into eternity, Abram served no god but God.[18] His faith endured every test. And so it had to be, for faith was all he had. We know, as he could never know, the glory of the fulfillment of the promises made to him. Abram could only trust; and trusting, take the long road down from Haran across Syria and past the snow-capped peaks of Lebanon and the deep-laid Sea of Galilee to the hill country of Palestine where, first at Shechem and then at Bethel, the land at the center of the world was given, through him, to his posterity.[19]

Abram had not been long in the Promised Land when famine drew him to the rich fields of Egypt's Nile delta, very possibly during the reign of Amenemhet IV (1798-1789 B.C.), the last king of the Twelfth Dynasty which had restored the monolithic state there some two hundred years before, at about the time of the great sack of Ur. During the reign of Amenemhet IV Asiatics began to enter Egypt in large numbers[20] and were often called *'Apiru*—probably equivalent to "Hebrew," which in the language of that age was a generic name conveying something of the meaning of our words "freebooter," "nomad" or "tramp." Consequently most *'Apiru* (called *Habiru* in cuneiform documents) had nothing to do with Abram and his descendants, nor did they call themselves by this name; but others so called them, as the Book of Genesis records.[21] We have extensive archeological and historical evidence of a way of life very similar to that of the patriarchs as described in Genesis, in Palestine during the first two centuries of the second millennium B.C. (2000-1800).[22] An Egyptian text of the eighteenth century B.C. (1800-1700) actually contains a form of the name Abraham.[23]

The existence of the patriarchs of Genesis as real, historical individuals— once widely denied, and still sometimes denied today[24] —is attested "confidently" by modern historian of Israel John Bright.[25] Palestinian archeologist Roland de Vaux has estimated that the date of the wanderings of Abraham falls within the period 1900-1700 B.C., while the Biblical archeologist and Orientalist William F. Albright places it during the period 1900-1750 B.C.[26] A more recent review of the evidence by Kenneth A. Kitchen of the School of Archeology and Oriental Studies at the University of Liverpool, taking full account of recent criticisms, pronounces strongly in favor of the historical reliability of the Genesis narrative of the patriarchs. Kitchen points out that the newly discovered Ebla archives and other ancient Middle Eastern evidence prove the accurate retention of historical knowledge about early kings and founders over many centuries—over more than a thousand years in the case of the first name on the Assyrian king list, whose real existence the Ebla tablets have now established, and who predated Abraham by several centuries. There is no reason to suppose the Israelite tradition to have been less historically accurate than the Assyrian.[27]

Unlike many of the other wanderers from Asia who came to the Nile delta, Abram did not stay in Egypt. Remembering God's promise, he returned to Bethel as soon as he could, settling "by the oaks of Mamre, which are at Hebron, and there he built an altar to the LORD."[28] He gathered a clan about him; how many he may have brought with him from Haran, and how many may have joined him in Palestine, we do not know. But by the time of the invasion of the army of four kings—"Amraphel king of Shinar, Arioch king of Ellasar, Chedor-laomer king of Elam, and Tidal king of Goiim"—he mustered no less than 318 fighting men, with whom he harried the retreat of the invaders and recovered some of the prisoners and booty they had taken.[29]

On his return from this rescue and salvage expedition Abram was met by Melchisedek, priest-king of Jerusalem (Jerusalem's existence before this time is recorded in the archives at Ebla, and the city is mentioned again in Egyptian documents of the eighteenth century [1800-1700] B.C.).[30] Melchisedek blessed Abram in the name of "God Most High," to Whom he offered bread and wine; and Abram gave Melchisedek a tenth of all that he had recovered from the invaders.[31]

Who was "God Most High"? Elaborate attempts to explain this as the name of a local Canaanite deity remain unconvincing in the face of the name itself, which does not suggest one of many gods, nor a local god, nor even a chief god. It suggests nothing more nor less than what it actually says, and what most Christian and Jewish commentators before the nineteenth century A.D. naturally assumed it meant: that Melchisedek really was a priest of God Most High— namely, of God. That modern commentators should find this astonishing and incredible is more a judgment on them than on Melchisedek. Where one man had been given the beginning of an understanding of what God is, surely a neighbor of his might have learned it too! Talk of the unlikelihood of more special revelations so early is beside the point. Abram was living less than twenty miles from Jerusalem. Jerusalem's king—who, in view of the small size of the city at that time, would have been approximately the equal in status and authority to the leader of a clan mustering 318 fighting men—might well have been brought to the worship of God by the intercession and personal example of Abram. It would be far from the last time this has happened—though it may, indeed, have been the first.[32]

As for Melchisedek's offering of bread and wine, many modern commentators are quick to dismiss as coincidence the association that immediately leaps to the mind of every Christian reader of this passage. If it is a coincidence, it is the first of many of its kind in the Old Testament—which we will mention in due course as they appear. But with God there is no mere coincidence; nor is there anachronism.[33]

Now it was time for the promise to Abram to be sealed by a covenant. God renewed His promise of the land and of an innumerable posterity; in return Abram covenanted, for himself and his posterity, to serve God and to worship Him alone, and to mark themselves as His chosen people by circumcision. Thenceforth he was called Abraham, the Canaanite form of his Mesopotamian name Abram, as a sign that the Promised Land had become his home.[34]

Then Abraham had a vision of God appearing before his tent at noon, and discussed with Him the fate of Sodom and Gomorrah, the "cities of the plain" just south of the Dead Sea, upon which a cataclysm was about to break. The tale of the patriarchs is a tale of faith; there is little in their story specifying standards of conduct. Yet in this unique scene in the eighteenth chapter of the Book of Genesis, we find Abraham pleading with God for the people of the sinful cities, calling upon Him in the name of justice—and obtaining His promise—to spare those cities even if only ten good men could be found within them.[35] But not even ten could be found and the cities were consumed by fire, so that Abraham, standing in the place where he had spoken with God, "looked towards Sodom and Gomorrah, and the whole land of that country: and he saw the ashes rise up from the earth as the smoke of a furnace."[36]

Here we encounter the first of what have been called the "nature miracles" of the Old Testament. In considering what appears to be a nature miracle, the first question to be asked is this: Assuming the basic truth of the account, could there have been a natural explanation for what happened, not far-fetched or contrived? It is the same question the Catholic Church asks when beginning a formal investigation of miracles attributed to the Blessed Virgin Mary at Lourdes, or to persons proposed for beatification and canonization. To take a New Testament example of a nature miracle, Christ's walking upon the water, clearly no reasonable natural explanation is possible; the account must be either true or false, and if true —as the Christian must believe—then the event was supernatural. But many of the Old Testament miracles are susceptible of natural explanations, which does not make them any less the will and work of God, the Author of nature Who intended these events to occur when and where and as they did. In ancient times it was natural to speak of God having "rained upon Sodom and Gomorrah brimstone and fire . . . out of heaven," visualizing Him as personally hurling the fire; now it is more natural for us to speak of the fire and brimstone falling upon the cities because of an earthquake which released inflammable tar and gases ignited by lightning, with God allowing the seismic upheaval and the oxidation to take their natural course. But to a theist the difference is only a matter of conventions in thought and expression; in either case God is the direct cause of the event, when it occurs to accomplish His purpose.

However it was done, the "cities of the plain" were wiped from the face of the earth, never again to appear in history; since then a slow steady rise in the level of what Bruce Vawter refers to as "the malignant smear of water called the Dead Sea, deep in the cleft of the Jordan valley"[37] has covered their sites with fifteen feet of the saltiest water on earth. This has prevented archeological confirmation of the disaster, but the reports of Greek and Roman writers tell us that cities once stood there and that tar and sulfur (brimstone) were common in the area.[38]

Thus Abraham became a personal witness to the wrath of the God Who had deigned to make a covenant with him. Yet still more was needed. So there came a day, foreshadowing Gethsemane, when God told Abraham to take his son Isaac, his long-awaited God-given heir by Sarah who had been thought barren,[39] to Mount Moriah and there to sacrifice him to God as a burnt offering. Despite its other evils, Mesopotamia in Abraham's time had not known human sacrifice, but this was practiced in Palestine; for all Abraham knew, the God Who had revealed Himself to him, the God Who had destroyed Sodom and Gomorrah, might demand even this.[40] Familiar as it is, the passage describing what E. A. Speiser has called "the profoundest personal experience in all the recorded history of the patriarchs"[41]—a masterpiece of literature as well as of faith in action—deserves to be quoted in full.

> God tested Abraham, and said to him, "Abraham!" And he said, "Here am I." He said, "Take your son, your only son Isaac, whom you love, and go to the land of Moriah, and offer him there as a burnt offering upon one of the mountains of which I shall tell you." So Abraham rose early in the morning, saddled his ass, and took two of his young men with him, and his son Isaac; and he cut the wood for the burnt offering, and rose and went to the place of which God had told him. On the third day Abraham lifted up his eyes and saw the place afar off. Then Abraham said to his young men, "Stay here with the ass; I and the lad will go yonder and worship, and come again to you." And Abraham took the wood of the burnt offering, and laid it on Isaac his son; and he took in his hand the fire and the knife. So they went both of them together. And Isaac said to his father Abraham, "My father!" And he said, "Here am I, my son." He said, "Behold, here are the fire and the wood, but where is the lamb for a burnt offering?" Abraham said, "God will provide himself the lamb for a burnt offering, my son." So they went both of them together.

When they came to the place of which God had told him, Abraham built
an altar there, and laid the wood in order, and bound Isaac his son, and
laid him on the altar, upon the wood. Then Abraham put forth his hand,
and took the knife to slay his son. But the angel of the LORD called to
him from heaven, and said, "Abraham, Abraham!" And he said, "Here
am I." He said, "Do not lay your hand on the lad or do anything to him;
for now I know that you fear God, seeing you have not withheld your son,
your only son, from me."[42]

Such was the faith of Abraham, and the mercy of God.

Yet great trials were still to come. Abraham was forewarned in a dream,
soon after the blessing from Melchisedek: "Your descendants will be sojourners
in a land that is not theirs, and will be slaves there, and they will be oppressed
for four hundred years; but I will bring judgment on the nation which they serve,
and afterward they shall come out with great possessions."[43] But Abraham
himself died in peace. He was buried in the cave of Machpelah at the end of
the field which he had bought from Ephron the Hittite,[44] and there is good reason
to believe that his bones rest there still, in the great shrine (now Muslim) at
Hebron.[45]

Abraham's son Isaac went to his father's homeland in northern Mesopotamia
to find a wife; she bore him two sons, and they were sinners. Esau was a slave
of passion and appetite, Jacob a schemer and deceiver. Securing a blessing from
his dying father by an ugly trick, the younger Jacob displaced the elder Esau
as Isaac's heir[46] and, like Isaac, went to northern Mesopotamia to find a wife.
He found Rachel, who loved him deeply and truly, and became wealthy tending the flocks of his uncle Laban. At length, having made his fortune, he set
out for the Promised Land. But as he drew nearer his conscience began to gnaw
at him, for in that land he would meet the brother whom he had disinherited.
He feared Esau's vengeance; it seems he feared Another's. Perhaps he had heard
his grandfather describe the fate of Sodom and Gomorrah.

On the night before he was to meet Esau again:

He arose and took his two wives, his two maids, and his eleven children,
and crossed the ford of the Jabbok. He took them and sent them across
the stream, and likewise everything that he had. And Jacob was left alone;
and a man wrestled with him until the breaking of the day. When the man
saw that he did not prevail against Jacob, he touched the hollow of his thigh;
and Jacob's thigh was put out of joint as he wrestled with him. Then he
said, "Let me go, for the day is breaking." But Jacob said, "I will not
let you go, unless you bless me." And he said to him, "What is your name?"
And he said, "Jacob." Then he said, "Your name shall no more be called
Jacob, but Israel, for you have striven with God and with men, and have
prevailed." Then Jacob asked him, "Tell me, I pray, your name." But
he said, "Why is it that you ask my name?" And there he blessed him.
So Jacob called the name of the place Peniel, saying, "For I have seen
God face to face, and yet my life is preserved."[47]

So Israel came into being wrestling with God, as Israel was to wrestle with Him again and again down through the sixteen fierce centuries separating that night at the ford of the Jabbok from Christmas Day in Bethlehem. The magnificent serenity of Abraham's faith—which, so far as we know, was shared by Isaac—did not descend to the third generation. It had to be rekindled in the heart of a proud and obstinate man, called to account for his treachery and guile. Hence they grappled all through the night, Jacob and his Adversary; but in the end Jacob would not let Him go until he had been blessed.

It is the prototype of all conversion stories. The ford of the Jabbok prefigured the road to Damascus. For when God chooses a man and a man chooses God with his whole heart and soul, there is always a wrestling with the Almighty. He Whose touch made the galaxies swarm will never coerce a human will. But He can open any soul to Himself, even though it require a hand-to-hand combat of the spirit.[48]

Thenceforth there was a new life and a new spirit in Jacob become Israel. He humbled himself before his brother, asking and receiving his forgiveness.[49] When two of his sons took the city of Shechem by treachery and sacked it he reproved them, despite the fact that they had acted to avenge the rape of their sister Dinah by a son of Shechem's king;[50] in his last testament Jacob condemned their wanton destruction on strictly moral grounds and foretold that as a consequence their posterity would be scattered powerless among the other tribes of Israel.[51] Moving on from Shechem to Bethel, where he built an altar, Jacob ordered his family and all his companions to destroy every image of a god which they had with them. Here again a recurrent note in the history of Abraham's seed sounds for the first time: the purging of the idols from the midst of the people of the One Almighty God, among whom for many centuries idols never ceased to penetrate under the constant pressure of the polytheistic world around them.[52]

From the sons of Jacob sprang the tribes of Israel. The genealogies of the Old Testament, though very comprehensive, are not always complete; the number of tribes may not always have been precisely twelve, though this number had become fixed at least as early as the first Israelite invasion of Palestine after the Exodus.[53] But that Jacob was their common ancestor there is no reason to doubt. Ancient tribes were blood kin, often actually descended from a single family. And from the tribe of Judah, as Jacob prophesied at the end of his life, was to come "he . . . to whom it [the scepter] belongs, and to him shall be the obedience of the peoples"—He whom later generations of Israel were to learn to call the Messiah.[54]

All through the varying fortunes of his long life after the night he wrestled with God at the ford of the Jabbok, Jacob clung firmly to the Promised Land. But the wandering slave traders who brought his youngest son Joseph into Egypt after his jealous half-brothers had seized and sold him to them, set in motion a train of events by which the children of Israel came to dwell for generations in the land of the Nile.[55]

If Abraham lived during the greater part of the period 1850-1700 B.C. and we allow enough time for his grandson to have fathered many sons and for the youngest of them to have grown to manhood, we may very roughly estimate the date of Joseph's arrival in Egypt as falling within the period 1675-1625 B.C. This reckoning is based on the evidence we have reviewed for the existence of an historical Abraham and does not depend on the specific mention of Israel's four hundred years in Egypt, found in the Books of Genesis and Exodus,[56] which might be no more than a conventional way of expressing a very long time. But in fact independent evidence indicates that four hundred years was an accurate memory of the actual duration of this period, since there is good reason for dating the Exodus to the half century 1300-1250 B.C., during the long reign of the Pharaoh Ramses II.[57]

Egyptian history during the period 1675-1625 B.C. and immediately following—the Hyksos period—is wholly consonant with the Joseph story, which fits there much better than in any other period between the foundation of the Middle Kingdom of Egypt in Thebes before 2000 B.C. and the establishment of Israel in Palestine by about 1230 B.C.[58] There is no specific mention of the patriarch Joseph in any contemporary Egyptian record; but records from the Hyksos times are relatively scarce, and the picture of Egyptian society and government sketched in Genesis 39-50 is thoroughly authentic for this period, including literal translations of terms of Egyptian court etiquette and the correct price for a slave in Egypt in the eighteenth century B.C.—twenty shekels.[59] From about 1720 to 1670 B.C. the Hyksos, "rulers of foreign countries" from Asia, were in the process of taking over Egypt by a combination of infiltration and outright conquest.[60] Once in power they rapidly became Egyptianized; nevertheless the Hyksos kings of the Nile delta region, closest to Asia, were much more likely than any native Egyptian Pharaoh to appoint an Asiatic as chief minister.

In fact, the closest approach to a direct Egyptian confirmation of the Joseph story which the scanty records of the time provide is found in the records of the Hyksos king Mayebre Sheshi who ruled during the period 1650-1600 B.C. (when Joseph would have been in his prime) and appointed a Semite from Asia called Har as "Treasurer of the King of Lower Egypt," "Sole Companion [of the King]" and "Overseer of the Treasury"[61]—a position almost identical to that of Joseph as described in the Book of Genesis. During the same period, either as a direct contemporary of Mayebre Sheshi or just before or after his reign, another Hyksos king ruled in the delta whose name was written in Egyptian as Yakubher.[62] The first two syllables of his name are identical with Jacob. It is impossible to imagine the patriarch Jacob as a Pharaoh of Egypt, but the identity of name shows how closely the Hyksos were related to the children of Israel.

The Hyksos period in Egyptian history, then, was one during which a man like Joseph could readily have done what the Book of Genesis tells us Joseph did; and with this much support from independent historical evidence, there is no reason to doubt the historicity of the Genesis account of Joseph.

For just over a hundred years (1674-1567 B.C.) the Hyksos ruled all or most of Egypt below the First Cataract of the Nile, though they retained a native king in Upper Egypt as their vassal. We may assume that for a substantial part of that century Joseph stood high in the kingdom and was able to give protection and special benefits to his brethren of Israel. After a long and prosperous life he died in peace, probably during the more than forty-year reign of the last great Hyksos king, Apophis. While Jacob had insisted on being buried with Abraham and Isaac in the cave of Machpelah in the Promised Land, Joseph was content to be embalmed in the Egyptian manner and laid to rest in an Egyptian sarcophagus in the land of his adoption.[63]

Thus was the lot of the people of Israel cast with the monolithic state of the Pharaohs. For the first but by no means the last time, God's chosen were now to learn that their true kingdom is not of this world.

> Now there arose a new king over Egypt, who did not know Joseph. And he said to his people, "Behold, the people of Israel are too many and too mighty for us. Come, let us deal shrewdly with them, lest they multiply, and, if war befall us, they join our enemies and fight against us and escape from the land." Therefore they set taskmasters over them to afflict them with heavy burdens.[64]

This sudden reversal of fortune can best be explained by a shift from Asiatics to native Egyptians as rulers of Egypt. Such a shift occurred in 1567 B.C. and the years immediately following, when the Pharaohs Kamose and Ahmose of Thebes in Upper Egypt defeated the Hyksos and took their capital city of Avaris in the Nile delta, establishing the rule of the Eighteenth Dynasty throughout Egypt.[65]

Smarting from the century-long national humiliation of being subject to foreigners, whom the Egyptians during the first two thousand years of their tightly knit, isolated civilization despised with a fervor matched in more recent times only by the Chinese, the new Pharaohs sought to wipe out the bitter memory by a policy of militant imperialism. This was new to Egypt, which in the past had been content to confine almost all its attention to its own uniquely well-favored land. Pharaohs in war chariots carried fire and sword all through Palestine, Syria and Lebanon, while Asiatics in Egypt were ruthlessly enslaved just as the Book of Exodus describes. During this time Mesopotamian civilization was in temporary eclipse and the Hittite empire was only just beginning to develop in Asia Minor. Egypt was the greatest power in the world, all but irresistible within the reach of her arms. The pyramid-building god who was the Pharaoh of Egypt in the Fourth Dynasty (c. 2600 B.C.) had become a war-god in the Eighteenth Dynasty (1567-1350 B.C.).[66]

To live by power was to court and ultimately to meet the nemesis of power, as Ur and Harappa had met it. Their fate now awaited Egypt. "I will bring judgment on the nation which they serve," God had said to Abram. Since the establishment of the kingdom of Israel in Palestine, Egypt has been the footstool of a longer procession of conquerors than any other nation.[67] One man seems to have foreseen something of that fate and sought to avert it: the transcendent, tortured genius Akhenaten, who was King of Egypt in the second quarter of the fourteenth century (1375-1350) B.C.[68] If the essential course of Egyptian history were ever to be changed, only the god-king could change it. But to make a lasting change in that course the god-king must cease to be a god, to himself and to his people, so that a higher Power might be acknowledged and worshipped. Not even genius could surmount that fatal contradiction.

Akhenaten tried; no man, not more than human, could have done more. He broke with the royal past at Memphis and Thebes by moving his capital to a wholly new city which he named Akhetaten, the Horizon of the Disk of the Sun. He broke with militarism and imperialism, refusing to attack his neighbors or even to defend the territory in Asia which his predecessors had conquered. He broke with the long-fixed canons of artistic expression, inaugurating a flowering of beautifully naturalistic art as brief as it was exquisite. Most significant of all, he broke with the whole religious past of Egypt and flung his mind and spirit heavenward to reach for the reality of a single god reigning unchallenged and unequalled over the whole earth.[69]

But Akhenaten's reach exceeded his grasp, for his one god belonged primarily to him alone. His magnificent hymn to the Aten, the disk of the sun which he saw as the visible manifestation of his sole god—much of which appears to have been preserved in the 104th Psalm[70]—was the expression of a personal creed, not the living faith of a people. His new capital was filled far more with sycophants than with fellow-worshippers. For Akhenaten could not break away from the cornerstone of Egyptian civilization laid down by the first Pharaoh more than seventeen hundred years before him: the king as god. Even if he himself did not believe in his own divinity—and it seems that at least in a way he did believe in it—his subjects accepted it without question, and he did nothing to discourage them from accepting it.[71] But a god-king is a god only so long as he reigns, and earthly kings are mortal. Gradually abandoned by all whom he had trusted most, including his own family whom he dearly loved, Akhenaten died a mysterious death and underwent a secret burial.[72] After a few years of turmoil the old system was re-established virtually unchanged, and Egypt's fate was sealed.

As we approach the Exodus and the towering figure of Moses, two questions remain: Whence came Akhenaten's vision, and did it leave a legacy? They are natural questions in view of what Akhenaten did and tried to do, at a time when we have every reason to believe that the Isrᵃelites dwelt in his land worshipping the God of Abraham, of Isaac and of Jacob.[73] To guess at a connection is tempting, but it must be stressed that there is not a shred of specific evidence to support it except the parallel between the Aten hymn and the 104th Psalm, and no good explanation for how a king of Egypt and a group of despised foreign slaves could have come together in any circumstances allowing for a true exchange of ideas, even assuming—which many careful students of Egyptian history deny —that Atenism and the faith of the patriarchs were essentially comparable.[74] The two faiths existed in such very different spheres that any bridge between them must have been close to supernatural.

If there was a link, Akhenaten himself was the sole beneficiary, or one of a very few; for his faith died with him, never again to appear in the Egypt of the Pharaohs, while the faith of Israel was handed down from Abraham who lived long before Akhenaten. Nothing in all that we know of the creed and teaching of Moses suggests Atenism; rather, it is a certain element in Atenism that seems to approach the religion of Israel. If inspiration there was, it came from Israel and the God of Israel to Akhenaten far more than from Akhenaten to Israel. Something of what the children of Israel knew and loved came to him; their presence in his land when he had his unique vision can hardly be wholly coincidental. Beyond that we can only say with C. S. Lewis, in requiem for Akhenaten of Egypt:

> Meanwhile, what gentle heart can leave the topic without a prayer that this lonely ancient king, crank and doctrinaire though perhaps he was, has long seen and now enjoys the truth which so far transcends his own glimpse of it?[75]

NOTES

[1] *The Cambridge Ancient History*, Volume I, Part 2, 3rd ed. (Cambridge, England, 1971), pp. 599-600; Georges Roux, *Ancient Iraq* (New York, 1964), pp. 143-146.

[2] *Cambridge Ancient History*, I (2) (3rd ed.), 736. The name of the modern nation of Lebanon derives from Laban, which was the name of Abraham's nephew whom Jacob served (Genesis 29:5).

[3] *Cambridge Ancient History*, I (2) (3rd ed.), 599; Roux, *Ancient Iraq*, Plate 13 facing p. 176.

[4] Roux, *Ancient Iraq*, pp. 138-139; Genesis 11:4-9, 28:12. For the reasons for preferring the translation "stairway" for the very rare Hebrew word in Genesis 28:12 usually rendered into English as "ladder," see E. A. Speiser, *The Anchor Bible: Genesis* (New York, 1964), p. 218.

[5] Roux, *Ancient Iraq*, pp. 148-149.

[6] *Cambridge Ancient History*, I (2) (3rd ed.), 625-626, 631-634, 640-641.

[7] Alexander Heidel, *The Gilgamesh Epic and Old Testament Parallels* (Chicago, 1949), pp. 224-289. Speiser, *Genesis*, pp. 80-81, argues against accepting the statement in Genesis that Abraham once lived in Ur, making much of the anachronistic reference to "Ur of

the Chaldees," since the Chaldaeans did not arrive in Mesopotamia until after 1000 B.C. John Van Seters, *Abraham in History and Tradition* (New Haven, CT, 1975), p. 121, also argues against the historicity of Abraham on the grounds of anachronistic names for people and places in the Genesis account. Bruce Vawter in *A Path through Genesis* (New York, 1956), pp. 173-174, explodes this argument, though in a different context, by pointing out how common such anachronisms are in all but the most pedantic historical references, as "when we say that Caesar invaded England, or Clovis was the King of France, or that La Salle explored Texas" though in each case the name now used for the country had not in fact yet been given to it at the time of the historical figure mentioned, but is the name by which readers can most readily identify it now. "Palestine" is used in the same manner and for the same reason in this book. Speiser's and Van Seters' is a classic example of an argument "smelling of the lamp," divorced from practical reality. John Bright in *A History of Israel*, 3rd ed. (Philadelphia, 1981), p. 90, concludes that "there is nothing intrinsically improbable about" the statement that Abraham once dwelt in Ur. Probably the strongest case in support of the statements in Genesis (11:28, 11:31 and 15:7) that Abraham once dwelt in Ur, based on recent data, is set forth by the renowned and by no means always traditional archeologist and authority on the ancient history of the Middle East Roland de Vaux in *The Early History of Israel* (Philadelphia, 1978), pp. 190-192. De Vaux stresses the importance of the known Amorite migrations about 2000 B.C., the regular travel route from Ur to Haran, and the fact that some names in the story of the patriarchs appear on tablets from Lower Mesopotamia (the region including Ur) before they appear on tablets from Upper Mesopotamia (the region including Haran) —for example, Abraham's great-grandfather was named Serug and the cognate form Sa-ru-gi is found in a document of the Third Dynasty of Ur; Abraham's grandfather was named Nahor and the cognate form Na-ha-rum is found at Nippur near Ur at this period, while Ya-ah-qu-ub-el, a cognate of Jacob, appears in four documents from Uruk, also in the old Sumerian region (Lower Mesopotamia), about 1850 B.C.

[8] This is clear from the names of Abraham's relatives and wife (Terah corresponding to *yerah*, lunar month; Laban meaning white; Sarah corresponding to *sharratu*, an Akkadian translation of the Sumerian name of the consort of the moon-god Sin). It is confirmed, so far as their idolatry is concerned, by Joshua 24:2. See de Vaux, *Early History of Israel*, p. 192.

[9] *Cambridge Ancient History*, I (2) (3rd ed.), 736.

[10] Genesis 11:31-32; *The Cambridge Ancient History*, Volume II, Part 1, 3rd ed. (Cambridge, England, 1973), pp. 24-28. The tribe of the Benjaminites recorded in cuneiform tablets of this period at Mari in northern Mesopotamia may well have migrated from the Ur region as Terah and Abraham did, since their name means "sons of the south." The fact that there was a later Hebrew tribe of Benjamin suggests that Terah and Abraham might have been a part of this Benjaminite migration (André Parrot, *Abraham and His Time* [Philadelphia, 1968], pp. 49-51).

[11] Kenneth A. Kitchen, *The Bible in Its World* (Downers Grove IL, 1977), pp. 50-52; Chaim Bermant and Michael Weitzman, *Ebla, a Revelation in Archaeology* (New York, 1979), pp. 182-186.

[12] Bermant and Weitzman, *Ebla*, p. 187. The theory of David Noel Freedman that the mention of Damascus in the same tablet which mentions the five "cities of the plain" shows that they were located near it seems an unwarranted inference, especially in view of the explicit reference in Genesis 14 to the mustering of the troops of the five cities near the Dead Sea, which has usually been held to be their actual location (see Note 38, below).

[13] Bermant and Weitzman, *Ebla*, pp. 162-167, 178-182.

[14] Deuteronomy 26:5.

[15] See the comprehensive review of Mesopotamian religion in H. W. F. Saggs, *The Greatness That Was Babylon* (New York, 1962), pp. 299-358. Saggs is relatively sympathetic to Mesopotamian religion only because he quite obviously regards all religions, including Christianity, as intriguing but faintly amusing folly, and thus has great difficulty imagining the personal and psychological consequences of a genuine belief in the Mesopotamian pantheon and mythology. The striking contrast between Mesopotamian religion and the religion of the patriarchs is well brought out by Speiser, *Genesis*, pp. xliv-lii.

[16] Genesis 22:17.

[17] Genesis 12:3 as translated and explained by Paul Heinisch, *Christ in Prophecy* (Collegeville MN, 1956), pp. 12-13. The "Septuagint" Greek translation of the Old Testament, dating back before the Christian era, renders the promise to Abraham in Genesis 12:3 as "in you all the tribes of the earth shall be blessed" (ενευλογηθησονται εν σοι πασαι αι φυλαι της γης); parallel formulations of the same blessing in Genesis 18:18, 22:18, 26:14 and 28:14 have been held to mean "shall bless themselves by you" though in three of these four verses (all except 26:4) the Septuagint uses exactly the same form of the Greek verb as in 12:3, ενευλογηθησονται. The verb from in the Hebrew text used for this blessing in Genesis 12:3 can be either reflexive or passive (Speiser, *Genesis*, pp. 85-86). The traditional translation, in the passive, is found in the Catholic Douay Bible and in the original Protestant King James version, and has been widely regarded as a direct prophecy of Christ. The Revised Standard Version and most recent translations opt for the reflexive form, which can still be regarded as a prophecy, although somewhat less explicit, since in the normal course of events why would all the peoples of the earth bless themselves *by* an alien chief, however fortunate? Manuel Miguens, S.T.D., commented as follows on this matter in a letter to the author in 1975: "Gen 12:3, 18:18, 26:14 have the same form (*niphal*). Gen 22:18, 26:4 have the same form also (i.e. *hitpael*). It is true that the form *hitpael* usually has a reflexive meaning; it is also true that the form *niphal* can have a reflexive or passive meaning and, therefore, is ambiguous. But it is also true that even *hitpael* can occasionally have a passive meaning. In fact, the Jewish translation of the Soncino Books of the Bible renders 22:18 by "shall be blessed" (whereas 26:4 is rendered by "shall bless themselves"; in all other cases the passive is offered). However, the translation to the LXX [Septuagint] offers a passive rendering in each of the five cases (ενευλογηθησονται). Likewise, St. Paul understands the blessing in the passive sense, not only when he quotes from the Old Testament (Galatians 3:8) but in his entire reasoning in Galatians 3 (v. 9, 14); the passive form is kept in Acts 3:25 too. This should not be dismissed lightly."

[18] Volumes have been written in labored efforts to deny this simple fact, which not only the Genesis narrative but the whole subsequent history of monotheism stemming from Abraham should make so clear. Speiser (*Genesis*, p. xlvii) and Vawter (*Path through Genesis*, pp. 120-121), both profound and by no means always traditional exegetes of Genesis, do not hesitate to describe Abraham as a monotheist, although Bright (*History of Israel*, p. 102), despite his forthright assertion that "we may confidently believe that they [Abraham, Isaac and Jacob] were actual historical individuals" (*ibid.*, p. 92), feels constrained to deny it even while carefully pointing out many of the facts and arguments that show his conclusion to be wrong. Vast erudition has been expended to little purpose in finding supposed hidden evidence of polytheism in the different ways the patriarchs spoke of God (e.g., John Marshall Holt, *The Patriarchs of Israel* [Nashville TN, 1964], pp. 131-135); by the same logic one would conclude that Christians believe in a pantheon including (1) God, (2) the Lord, (3) the Almighty, (4) the Eternal, and (5) Our

Father, to name only a few. In our own language, nearly two thousand years after Christ, the God of monotheism is distinguished from a god of polytheism only by a capital letter (and ancient scripts were written entirely in capitals). Eventually the Hebrew language developed a convention, which at first sight seems strange to us, of referring to the true God only in the plural, *Elohim*, while the singular *el* stood for pagan gods. But in the time of the patriarchs *el* meant almost exactly what our English word "god" means, with or without the capital letter. As de Vaux points out, the patriarchs used the name El as Christians use God, to signify Him Who had revealed Himself to them (*Ancient Israel; its Life and Institutions* [London, 1961], pp. 293-294). On this point see especially the excellent discussion by Giuseppe Ricciotti, *The History of Israel* (Milwaukee, 1955), I, 154.

[19] Genesis 12:5-8, 13:3-17.

[20] John Van Seters, *The Hyksos, a New Investigation* (New Haven CT, 1966), p. 78.

[21] One of the clearest, best-balanced discussions of the much-debated Habiru problem is found in Holt, *Patriarchs of Israel*, pp. 40-59 and 89-90. See also Bright, *History of Israel*, pp. 93-95. All appearances of the term "Hebrew" in the Book of Genesis, except one, are in the story of Joseph, where they probably reflect Egyptian rather than Israelite usage. The one exception is in Genesis 14, which probably also reflects a non-Israelite source (Speiser, *Genesis*, pp. 101, 105-108).

[22] Kathleen M. Kenyon, *Amorites and Canaanites* (London, 1966), pp. 7-8, 15-18; Emmanuel Anati, *Palestine Before the Hebrews* (New York, 1963), pp. 365-366, 376-377, 379-380, 385-387; *Cambridge Ancient History*, I (2) (3rd ed.), 553-556; Nelson M. Glueck, *Rivers in the Desert, a History of the Negev* (New York, 1959), pp. 66-84. Archeological evidence from Palestine and information on conditions in Palestine contained in the famous Egyptian story of Sinuhe confirm each other and the Palestinian background established by the patriarchal narratives in Genesis. The semi-nomadic life of the patriarchs was characteristic of the hill country and the desert fringes of Palestine, and was carried on with surprisingly little contact with the cities along the coast and in the fertile plain of Jezreel. Two hill towns frequently mentioned in Genesis, Beersheba and Gerar, are known to have been in existence from about 2000 B.C. (Anati, *op. cit.*, p. 381). The mention of Abraham's use of camels, long regarded as an anachronism, has now been proved to be nothing of the kind by Babylonian cuneiform tablets dating from 2000-1700 B.C. which mention domesticated camels (K. A. Kitchen, *Ancient Orient and Old Testament* [Chicago, 1966], pp. 79-80). Though Glueck overstates his case when he describes the Negev settlements of this period as "another civilization of high achievement" (*op. cit.*, p. 11), as Kenyon properly points out (*op. cit.*, p. 64), Glueck's basic analysis is confirmed by the much more cautious Van Seters (*Hyksos*, pp. 11-14).

[23] Kitchen, *Ancient Orient and Old Testament*, p. 48.

[24] Notably by Van Seters, *Abraham*, pp. 121-122 (summary). Van Seters' conclusions not only go against the almost unanimous verdict of modern scholarship in ancient Middle Eastern history and Biblical archeology, but are very weakly supported, since he places the milieu of the Abraham traditions in the time of the neo-Babylonian empire of Nebuchadnezzar, when no one in Palestine was living as Abraham lived, by nomadic cattle-raising. Paul Heinisch, *History of the Old Testament* (Collegeville MN, 1952), pp. 61-62, points out that if the story of Abraham is a projection of later events into pre-Mosaic times, as Van Seters and the Wellhausen school have maintained, Abraham would surely have been glorified as a wonder-worker and master of the land, and presented as practicing the full later Jewish Law (according to which Abraham's marriage to his stepsister Sarah would have been incest, and his various altars to God schismatic). There

would assuredly have been some mention of conflict with the great later historic foes of the Israelites, the Canaanites and the Philistines; while the Book of Genesis as it actually stands presents relations with the Canaanites as uniformly peaceful and friendly and does not mention the Philistines at all (correctly enough, since they did not arrive in Palestine until after 1200 B.C.). The list of native peoples in Palestine given in the Book of Genesis includes the Rephaim, Zuzim or Zamzummim, Emim, and Horim (probably the Hurrians), who had all disappeared by the time of the Israelite conquest of Canaan. See the specific, detailed refutations of Van Seters' arguments by Kitchen, *Bible in Its World*, pp. 58-59.

[25] Bright, *History of Israel*, p. 92. He adds that "the stories of the patriarchs fit authentically in the milieu of the second millennium, specifically in that of the centuries sketched in the preceding chapter [2000-1500 B.C.], far better than in that of any later period. The evidence is so massive and many-sided that we cannot begin to review it all." (*ibid.*, p. 77)

[26] De Vaux, *Early History of Israel*, p. 265; William F. Albright, *From the Stone Age to Christianity*, 2nd ed. (New York, 1957), p. 200.

[27] Kitchen, *Bible in Its World*, pp. 59-73.

[28] Genesis 13:18.

[29] Genesis 14:1-16. Not one of these four rulers can be securely identified and dated, though such coalitions of kings are well known from all over Mesopotamia for the period 1900-1700 B.C. (*Cambridge Ancient History*, II [2] [3rd ed.], 178-182 and Kitchen, *Bible in Its World*, p. 72, Van Seters, *Abraham*, pp. 121-122 to the contrary notwithstanding. Van Seters even implies that invasions of Syria-Palestine from Mesopotamia did not occur before the first millennium B.C., although the campaigns of Sargon of Agade and Tiglath-pileser I to the Syrian shores of the Mediterranean, in the third and second millennium B.C. respectively, are solidly established.) Arioch, or Arriwuk, is probably a Hurrian name and Ellasar was probably a Hurrian realm in northern Mesopotamia or southeastern Asia Minor, but it is not surely attested in contemporary documents. We do know of an Arriwuk who was a vassal of King Zimrilim of Mari on the Euphrates about 1780 B.C. (Speiser, *Genesis*, p. 107; *Cambridge Ancient History*, II [1] [3rd ed.], 8-14). An alternative analysis identifies Ellasar with the city of Larsa, one of the two principal Mesopotamian cities between the fall of Ur and the rise of Babylon, and Arioch as an adaptation of a second reading of the cuneiform rendering of the name of Rim-Sin, king of Larsa (a contemporary of Hammurabi), Rim-Aku (Heinisch, *History of the Old Testament*, p. 52). Elam was a powerful kingdom at this time and the name Chedorlaomer, or Kudur-lagamar, is perfectly good Elamite—but we know of no king of Elam who bore it. There was a King Kudur-nahhunte of Elam about 1730 B.C. (Holt, *Patriarchs of Israel*, p. 86; *Cambridge Ancient History*, II [1] [3rd ed.], 266-267). Tidal, or Tudhaliyash, was the name of several kings of the Hittites of Asia Minor, who ruled over an assortment of peoples who might well have been collectively called "Goiim," the Hebrew word for "nations"; and the first Tudhaliyash was probably king of the Hittites about 1740 B.C., but nothing whatever is known of the events of his reign (Speiser, *Genesis*, pp. 107-108; O. R. Gurney, *The Hittites* [London, 3rd ed., 1961], p. 216). The most significant of all the four names could be "Amraphel, king of Shinar." Shinar is the Hebrew form of the name Sumer, over all of which Babylon had extended its rule late in the reign of the famous King Hammurabi (1792-1750 B.C. according to the most recent Mesopotamian chronology, accepted in the third edition of *The Cambridge Ancient History*). Was Amraphel Hammurabi? The names appear similar, but leading authorities on the Semitic languages have expressed doubt that the "h" sound would have been dropped and the "l" added to transform Hammurabi into Amraphel (Speiser,

Genesis, pp. 106-107; Holt, *Patriarchs of Israel*, pp. 85-86). Bright (History of Israel, pp. 83-84) states flatly that "the effort to equate Amraphel, king of Shinar, with Hammurabi . . . must be given up," yet cites a 1960 study which still maintains the identification (*ibid.*, p. 84n). Nevertheless it seems significant that Hammurabi's dates and his seat of power tie in so closely with the dates and realms of the other three kings mentioned in Genesis 14, insofar as they may be tentatively identified and located. Heinisch, *History of the Old Testament*, p. 52, points out that Genesis 14 by no means requires us to assume that any or all of the named kings personally commanded this foray; had they done so, larger forces would in all probability have been committed.

[30] *Cambridge Ancient History*, I (2) (3rd ed.), 555; Heinisch, *History of the Old Testament*, p. 52; Kitchen, *Bible in Its World*, p. 44.

[31] Genesis 14:18-20.

[32] Vawter, *Path Through Genesis*, pp. 132-134, at least gives a reasonably fair presentation of the arguments on both sides of this question, though in the end he concludes that Melchisedek was just another Canaanite pagan. Speiser is more peremptory in his flat assertion that El Elyon, "God Most High," was "an authentic Canaanite deity" (*Genesis*, p. 109). This is categorically denied by de Vaux (although he also disagrees with the interpretation given in the text, regarding the Melchisedek narrative as a later interpolation), who says: "Used alone without *el*, the word *elyon*, most high, is common in the rest of the Bible as a title or substitute for Yahweh. There is no evidence anywhere of El Elyon outside the Bible. In fact, El and Elyon are two different deities in the Canaanite-Phoenician pantheon." (*Early History of Israel*, p. 275).

[33] The association, of course, is with the Eucharist. Melchisedek is specifically mentioned in this connection in the Roman canon of the Mass in the Catholic Church. The facile judgment which sees nothing but anachronism in such associations must be firmly rejected in writing sacred history. These volumes will show that the consequences flowing from God's call to Abraham form a continuous skein of historical development, largely independent of the rise and fall of civilizations and the habits of thought of particular cultures —as one would expect if indeed they did have their origin in eternity. Anachronism is a warning sign of error in secular history; but it can be one of the best evidences of truth in sacred history.

[34] Genesis 17:1-14. Circumcision was a widespread but by no means universal practice in Abraham's world. The Egyptians definitely did circumcise; the Mesopotamian peoples apparently did not, and the Canaanites definitely did not (Genesis 34:14 ff.; Ricciotti, *History of Israel*, I, 122-123).

[35] Genesis 18:16-33. As Vawter (*Path through Genesis*, pp. 148-149) points out, Abraham did not actually see God, Whom no man has ever seen or can ever see face to face in this life upon earth; but the vision he saw may have been much more like God than most of our learned speculations about Him.

[36] Genesis 19:28.

[37] Vawter, *Path through Genesis*, p. 152.

[38] J. Penrose Harland, "Sodom and Gomorrah," in *The Biblical Archaeologist Reader*, ed. G. Ernest Wright and David N. Freedman (Chicago, 1961), pp. 45-67. Strabo and Josephus are the principal ancient authorities.

[39] The narrative of the birth of Ishmael in Genesis 16, in which Sarah urges Abraham to have a child by a slave-girl when she has failed to bear him a child herself and to all human appearance and knowledge is too old ever to do so, but later abuses the slave-girl after she bears Ishmael, is further confirmation of the historical accuracy of the patriarchal material in Genesis since the Hurrian laws of Nuzi, widely followed in Mesopotamia in the second millennium B.C., required a barren wife to provide her husband with another

wife to give him an heir (Speiser, *Genesis*, pp. 119-121; Bright, *History of Israel*, pp. 78-80; Kitchen, *Bible in Its World*, pp. 68-70).

[40] With a single possible exception, there is no record of human sacrifice in civilized Mesopotamia. The one possible instance, in the royal tombs of Ur at the very beginning of Sumerian history, about 2700 B.C., is still open to doubt, and in any case pre-dated Abraham by at least 900 years; and it did not recur (Saggs, *Babylon*, pp. 372-383). For human sacrifice in Palestine at this time see Glueck, *Rivers in the Desert*, pp. 61-62, and Vawter, *Path through Genesis*, p. 169.

[41] Speiser, *Genesis*, p. 164.

[42] Genesis 22:1-12.

[43] Genesis 15:13-14.

[44] Genesis 15:15; Genesis 23. Hittite law codes of the second millennium B.C. provide an answer to the otherwise very difficult question of why Ephron, the Hittite owner of the field facing Mamre and the cave which Abraham wished to purchase for a burial place, would not sell the cave without the field; for under Hittite law, any owner of specified property owed duties to the Hittite overlord as the owner, whether or not he was a Hittite himself, and Ephron evidently wanted to transfer to Abraham his obligations for this piece of property. This provides further independent confirmation of the historical validity of the Genesis account of Abraham (Holt, *Patriarchs of Israel*, pp. 121-123).

[45] The shrine of Abraham at Hebron is inside a great wall erected by King Herod the Great at the time that he built the third and last temple in Jerusalem. The Crusaders in 1119 announced the discovery of the bones of the patriarchs Abraham, Isaac and Jacob within this walled enclosure and built a church there, which was converted into a mosque after the Muslim reconquest by Saladin (Christopher Hollis and Ronald Brownrigg, *Holy Places* [New York, 1969], pp. 13-16; Hans E. Meyer, *The Crusades* [London, 1972], p. 166). The shrine came under the administrative control of the modern Jewish state of Israel only after the Six Days' War in 1967 and has still not been fully explored by the Israelis. It is known that the cenotaphs on the ground floor commemorating the patriarchs are empty; their actual burial place, the site of the original cave of Machpelah, is said to be underground. This shrine being one of the most obvious "flash points" where the three different and often conflicting religions which trace descent in faith from Abraham—Christianity, Judaism, and Islam—meet (the entire Jewish population of Hebron was massacred by the Arabs in 1925), the Israeli authorities have apparently decided not to undertake any exploration there that anyone might consider sacrilegious (information obtained by the writer on a visit to Hebron and the shrine of Abraham in 1971).

[46] Genesis 27:1-39. Once again at this point independent evidence helps confirm the historical validity of the patriarchal narratives. The Hurrian laws preserved on the cuneiform tablets at Nuzi expressly allowed an elder son to sell his birthright, and for it to be transferred to a younger son by a deathbed declaration (Speiser, *Genesis*, pp. 211-213).

[47] Genesis 32:23-31.

[48] The interpretation of Jacob's experience at Peniel here given generally follows that of Speiser, *Genesis*, pp. 256-257 (see also *The Jerusalem Bible*, ed. Alexander ones [New York, 1966] [Old Testament], p. 53, Note d, and Ricciotti, *History of Israel*, II, 132-134). There is every reason to suppose that Jacob had some such experience, as so many since him have had; and it was recounted in terms understandable to his age, when noctural struggles with divine beings, especially at river crossings, were a common theme of folklore (*The Jerome Biblical Commentary*, ed. Raymond E. Brown et al [Englewood Cliffs NJ, 1968], I, 34).

[49] Genesis 33:1-11.

[50] Genesis 34. The city of Schechem was established only during the Middle Bronze Age in Palestine—the period of the patriarchs—and its first city wall was constructed in the eighteenth century B.C., during the latter part of which (according to the chronology accepted in this book) Jacob lived. A palace was also built at Shechem during this period. See *Cambridge Ancient History*, II (1) (3rd ed.), 111-113, and Van Seters *Hykos*, pp. 38-39.

[51] Genesis 49:5-7; Speiser, *Genesis*, p. 257.

[52] Genesis 35:1-3; *Jerusalem Bible* (Old Testament), p. 57, Note b.

[53] See Heinisch, *History of the Old Testament*, pp. 87-89, for an excellent presentation of the case for the reality and antiquity of the traditional division of Israel among twelve tribes.

[54] Genesis 49:10. Heinisch, *Christ in Prophecy*, pp. 36-40, gives a thorough explanation and defense of the Messianic interpretation of this famous prophecy.

[55] Genesis 37. There has been much discussion as to whether in fact "all Israel" or only a part of the Israelites went to live in Egypt and were enslaved there. Genesis 46:8-27 and Exodus 1:1-7 clearly state that the ancestors of all of the twelve tribes migrated to Egypt and settled there when Joseph was chief minister to the Pharaoh, and that their descendants were later enslaved. If a substantial part of the people had been free and flourishing elsewhere, their exploits would surely not have been forgotten (see Vawter, *Path through Genesis*, pp. 241-242, on this point); yet nothing of the kind is mentioned in the Bible, and the evidence sometimes thought to point to Israelites in Palestine between the patriarchal period and the Exodus is tenuous and hypothetical. Such validity as it may have can easily be accounted for by assuming that some small groups of Israelites trickled back into Palestine before the bondage, or later as runaways, while much the greater part of the people remained in Egypt.

[56] Genesis 15:13; Exodus 12:40-41.

[57] See Chapter Three, below, Note 20.

[58] An inscription of the Pharaoh Merneptah about 1220 B.C. specifically refers to Israel established as a nation in Palestine, thereby furnishing "a *terminus ante quem* for the Exodus of the Children of Israel from Egypt" (John A. Wilson, *The Burden of Egypt* [Chicago, 1951], p. 255). Other dates for Joseph have been proposed, most often the "Amarna period" of the Pharaoh Akhenaten (c. 1375-1350 B.C.), discussed later in the text (e.g., H. H. Rowley, *From Joseph to Joshua* [Oxford, 1948], pp. 25ff., and Jack Finegan, *Let My People Go* [New York, 1963], pp. 2-3), but these brief and tumultuous years seem much too few into which to fit the whole story of Joseph, nor does Joseph's Pharaoh as described in Genesis at all resemble the unique Akhenaten, nor does that Pharaoh's capital city at all resemble the equally unique capital from which Akhenaten ruled, Akhetaten. Van Seters (*Hyksos*, p. 146) states that Rowley's "scepticism . . . in equating the period of Joseph to that of the Hyksos is quite unjustified," and many scholars now agree that Joseph's entry into Egypt most probably occurred during the Hyksos period (G. Ernest Wright, *Biblical Archaeology* [Philadelphia, 2nd ed., 1962], p. 57). Regrettably, however, Van Seters now seems to have changed his opinion, judging by his denial of the historicity of the patriarchs in *Abraham*.

[59] Wright, *Biblical Archaeology*, pp. 53-54; J. A. Thompson, *The Bible and Archaeology* (Grand Rapids MI, 1962), pp. 44-45; *Jerome Biblical Commentary*, I, 41; Ricciotti, *History of Israel*, I, 141-144; Kitchen, *Bible in Its World*, p. 74.

[60] *Cambridge Ancient History*, II (1) (3rd ed.), 52-53. For the meaning and derivation of the term "Hyksos," much misunderstood in the past, see Alan Gardiner, *Egypt of the Pharaohs* (Oxford, 1961), p. 156.

[61] *Cambridge Ancient History*, II (1) (3rd ed.), 60.

[62] *Ibid.*, pp. 59-60.

[63] *Ibid.*, pp. 58, 61-62; Genesis 49:26. A late tradition places the elevation of Joseph as prime minister in the seventeenth year of Pharaoh Apopi (Apophis), a name taken by three of the Hyksos Pharaohs.

[64] Exodus 1:8-11.

[65] Gardiner, *Egypt of the Pharaohs*, pp. 164-169.

[66] Wilson, *Burden of Egypt*, pp. 167-169, 199-201.

[67] This procession has included, over the past 3000 years, the Libyans, the Nubians, the Assyrians, the Persians, the Greeks, the Romans, the Arabs, the Turks, the French, and the English. During that entire period the native Egyptians were masters of their own destiny only during two brief epochs of a century or less (the Twenty-Sixth and Thirtieth Dynasties). Only since World War II has Egypt re-emerged as a significant world power governed by its own people.

[68] Akhenaten's exact chronology is still disputed, but the possible dates are all encompassed within this 25-year period.

[69] For an excellent summary of Akhenaten's revolution, with especially good treatment of the amazing change in art and the human drama of the situation, see Eleonore Bille-De Mot, *The Age of Akhenaten* (New York, 1966), though the author tends to overstate her hypothesis of an Indo-Aryan influence on Akhenaten through the nation of Mitanni in northern Mesopotamia, whence Akhenaten's beautiful wife Nefertiti may have come.

[70] Gardiner, *Egypt of the Pharaohs*, pp. 225-227.

[71] Wilson, *Burden of Egypt*, pp. 223-224.

[72] Gardiner, *Egypt of the Pharaohs*, pp. 232-235.

[73] See Note 18, above.

[74] Wilson, *Burden of Egypt*, pp. 224-229.

[75] C. S. Lewis, *Reflections on the Psalms* (New York, 1958), p. 89.

3.
FIRE ON SINAI

Then Moses said to God, "If I come to the people of Israel and say to them, "The God of your fathers has sent me to you," and they ask me, "What is his name?" "What shall I say to them?" God said to Moses, "I AM WHO AM." And he said, "Say this to the people of Israel," "I AM has sent me to you."—Exodus 3:13-14

Sinai is a stark land, sharp-edged against the sky. Rock peaks rear more than a mile and a half above the level of the sea, yet still gather only the rarest falls of rain. It lies hot and parched and silent under a relentless sun, no man's land, the very opposite of Eden.

It was to a shepherd in Sinai that He came, to a fugitive from the god-king of Egypt, one of Abraham's progeny who bore an Egyptian name but had been cut off from both his native and his adopted people for many years.[1] From out of the bush that burned but was not consumed, to the shepherd called Moses, came those words from eternity revealing the very core-truth of the Cosmos, Absolute Self-Existent Being, the Source and Sustainer of all else that is: God is He Who Is; His very name is I AM.[2] God's own proper name, here revealed for the first time,[3] in Hebrew "Yahweh" (YHWH, the sacred Tetragrammaton, in later years regarded as too holy even to be pronounced), almost certainly represents an early form of the Hebrew verb "to be," meaning "He Who Is" or "The Existing One."[4]

There is nothing like this direct personal avowal of Godhead, at a specific time and place to a specific man, in the history of any other religion on earth, just as the history which sprang from that moment in Sinai was to be utterly unlike any other history. The man to whom those supernal words were spoken went on to become the law-giver for a unique faith, one of the handful of truly towering personalities in the story of man.

The epic of Moses—together with the religious laws proclaimed by or attributed to him—is told in the Old Testament Books of Exodus, Leviticus, Numbers and Deuteronomy. Once thought to have been written in their entirety by Moses, these four extraordinary books have borne the brunt of the hurricane of critical assault on the authenticity of Scripture throughout the past two centuries. There are still "higher critics" and "historians of Israel" today who have so thoroughly explained away these books, at least to their own satisfaction, that they doubt the very existence of Moses and claim that, if he did live, almost nothing can be known about him.[5]

Such a conclusion is simply fantastic. Without Moses it is impossible, even in human terms, to account for the unique character of the religion of Israel—a uniqueness evident even to the unbeliever.[6] As John Bright says:

> There can be no doubt that he [Moses] was, as the Bible portrays him, the great founder of Israel's faith. Attempts to reduce him are extremely unconvincing. The events of exodus and Sinai require a great personality behind them. And a faith as unique as Israel's demands a founder as surely as does Chrisianity—or Islam, for that matter. To deny that role to Moses would force us to posit another person of the same name![7]

No more than three hundred years at most separated the Exodus from the earliest written compilation of the story of Moses—less time than separates us in America today from the first settlements at Jamestown and Plymouth. The preservation of historically accurate oral tradition over such lengths of time has been proved on many occasions.[8] But it is far from necessarily true that all or even most of the transmission of the material in the books of Moses was oral. There is no real basis for assuming that no writing was done in Israel before the kingdom of David and Solomon, often as this assumption is thoughtlessly made, for every other settled people in the Middle East was using writing by the time of Moses, and the earliest form of what was to become the Hebrew alphabet (and the ancestor of our own alphabet) actually appears in the Sinai peninsula *before* the Exodus.[9]

In light of this, there can be no good reason for doubting the explicit statement in the Book of Exodus that the holiest object in early Israel, the Ark of the Covenant, did in fact contain two tablets on which the Ten Commandments were inscribed,[10] nor any good reason for denying that at least substantial parts of the Mosaic books could have been written by order of Moses himself while Israel encamped on the plains of Moab just before he died, or at least within a few decades of the events they describe, preserving many of his actual words, just as we know that the Koran was written down by the only partly literate Arabs under quite similar circumstances within fifteen years of Muhammad's death, and preserves his actual words.[11] Indeed, such a conclusion is not only possible, but highly probable.

The fact is that we have in the Books of Exodus, Numbers and Deuteronomy a history of the times of Moses more complete than anything else available to us for any comparable period in the second millennium (2000-1000) B.C. The character of Moses emerges in this narrative with such vividness that he lives for us as no other man of that time ever has or ever will. Beside Moses even Akhenaten of Egypt is little more than a shadow. Any theory which could lead to denial or doubt of the historical reality of the Moses of the Old Testament must contain an error far more fundamental than mere misjudgment of a single historical figure or period.

The primary source for the history of Israel is the Old Testament. It ought to be read, without prejudice, as an historical document, checked as other historical documents are checked by reference to the records of other peoples and to the findings of archeology, rather than its interpretation being governed by theories developed and held in abstraction from this contemporary evidence as well as in denigration at almost every point of what that source says about itself. Neither orthodox Christian or Jewish belief, or the lack of it, should incapacitate the scholar from studying the Old Testament as history; though insofar as the evidence sustains the historical accuracy of the Old Testament it may rightly and reasonably be used for apologetic purposes as well as for more conventional history. Let Kenneth A. Kitchen of the University of Liverpool, an authority on ancient Middle Eastern literatures and history, writing as he says from no particular theological standpoint, state the case:

> The theories current in Old Testament studies, however brilliantly conceived and elaborated, were mainly established in a vacuum with little or no reference to the Ancient Near East, and initially too often in accordance with *a priori* philosophical and literary principles. It is solely because the data from the Ancient Near East coincide so much better with the existing observable structure of Old Testament history, literature and religion than with the theoretical reconstructions, that we are compelled—as happens in Ancient Oriental studies—to question or even to abandon such theories regardless of their popularity. Facts not votes determine the truth. We do not here merely advocate a return to "pre-critical" views and traditions (e.g., of authorship) merely for their own sake or for the sake of theological orthodoxy. Let it be clearly noted that *no appeal whatsoever* has been made to any theological starting-point in the body of this work . . . If some of the results reached here approximate to a traditional view or seem to agree with theological orthodoxy, then this is simply because the tradition in question or that orthodoxy are that much closer to the real facts than is commonly realized. While one must indeed never prefer mere orthodoxy to truth, it is also perverse to deny that orthodox views can be true.[12]

Undoubtedly there were varying recollections and accounts of past events in Biblical history as in other history strictly secular; undoubtedly there are occasional contradictions and a number of repetitions in the texts we have; probably some of the material ascribed to Moses in the Books of Exodus, Leviticus, Numbers and Deuteronomy—most likely some of the minute details of Jewish law—was not said or written by him in the words we have, but composed later as a commentary on the meaning of what Moses did say or write. But all this does not add up to "J," "E," "P," "D" and all the other hypothetical source-documents for these books which are supposed to explain every discrepancy and resolve every problem, but in fact create more discrepancies and problems than they solve. As Kitchen trenchantly states:

> Nowhere else in the whole of Ancient Near Eastern history has the literary, religious and historical development of a nation been subjected to such drastic and wholesale reconstruction at such variance with the existing documentary evidence. The fact that Old Testament scholars are habituated to these widely known reconstructions, even mentally conditioned by them, does not alter the basic gravity of this situation which should not be taken for granted. . . . Even the most ardent advocates of the documentary theory must admit that we have as yet *no single scrap* of extant, objective (i.e., *tangible*) evidence for either the existence or the history of "J," "E," or any other alleged source-document.[13]

We should, then, let Moses speak for himself—not through the medium of very possibly imaginary "redactors." We take up the story as he goes back out of the desert into lush, corrupt Egypt, armed only with his divine commission, "one man against an empire"[14] that had stood for eighteen hundred years.

> Moses and Aaron went to Pharaoh and said, "Thus says the LORD, the God of Israel, "Let my people go, that they may hold a feast to me in the wilderness." But Pharaoh said, "Who is the LORD, that I should heed his voice and let Israel go? I do not know the LORD, and moreover I will not let Israel go."[15]

Who was this Pharaoh? After Akhenaten had died his mysterious death and undergone his secret burial, and the reigns of the three successors of his own household had run their brief course, General Horemheb had taken over the dissension-torn land and restored, to all outward appearance, the majestic structure of the god-king's empire. The old pantheon was revived and every effort made to blot out the very memory of Akhenaten. After Horemheb's reign of some thirty years a new dynasty had begun, the nineteenth in Egypt's long history, which—for the first time since the Hyksos kings three centuries earlier—had moved the capital to the delta of the Nile in northern Egypt, near to Palestine. In the Wadi Tumilat leading east from the delta, the Pharaohs Seti I and Ramses II built the cities of Pithom and Ramses upon which we are told that the Israelite

slaves labored. The Wadi Tumilat region, the only fertile lateral valley extending out of the Nile valley at right angles to the great river, was somewhat isolated
from the main body of Egypt and included both good pasture and good farmland.
It was in all probability the land of Goshen in which the Bible tells us the Israelites
dwelt during their entire sojourn in Egypt.[16]

There is now general agreement among scholars that the Exodus took place
during the thirteenth century (1300-1200) B.C.; former support for an earlier
date, around the time of Akhenaten or even before, has dwindled away. The
evidence of the building of Pithom and Ramses in the first quarter of the century (1300-1275), together with the stele of the Pharaoh Merneptah (c. 1220
B.C.) locating Israel outside Egypt—but as a wandering nation, not yet settled—
and the remarkable accumulation of archeological evidence indicating a destructive conquest of central Palestine shortly before 1200 B.C., unite to provide
a convincing case.[17] Unless we do drastic violence to the text of the Book of
Exodus, a very substantial time must be allotted to the Exodus events—time
for a whole generation to grow old and die in the wilderness.[18] The relatively
brief reign of Merneptah (only about ten years) and the evidence that the Israelite
conquest of Palestine probably took place at about the same time as his reign—
very likely within it[19]—would not allow sufficient time for Israel's wandering
in the wilderness, while separating the Exodus by approximately half a century
from the building of Pithom and Ramses. Therefore the most probable hypothesis
is that the Exodus occurred during the first half of the long reign of Ramses
II, about 1275 B.C.[20]

Ramses II reigned for sixty-seven years. Few rulers in all history have approached him in splendor, prosperity, power, and length of reign. His colossal
statues of himself still loom over the ever-flowing Nile. Hieroglyphic inscriptions recounting his military prowess cover acres of stone. Yet most of his reign
was peaceful; though his slaves groaned under their burdens, by the world's
standards he was in every way a successful king. He died at the age of nearly
ninety, still an imposing figure as we can tell from his mummy which has been
well preserved.[21]

Yet this grand monarch was in all probability the Pharaoh of the Exodus.
It was he whom Moses and Aaron confronted and humbled; it was he who lived
through the ten plagues of Egypt before he would let God's people go.

Critical scholarship once blithely dismissed the plagues of Egypt as sheer
myth, or rearranged their number and sequence in accordance with the prevailing documentary hypothesis. But a brilliant analysis by Greta Hort, carefully
verified by references to geology, meteorology, biology, and bacteriology, has
shown that all but the last of the ten plagues are afflictions from which Egypt
suffered periodically in ancient times, that they are recorded in the text of the
book of Exodus in the proper sequence both as to time of the year and as to
mutual causality, and that the plagues which are said to have spared the Israelites

in Goshen (the Wadi Tumilat area) are precisely those which, for good scientific reasons, would not have reached, or not have affected so severely, that particular region. Her analysis not only shows that the plagues almost certainly did happen as the Book of Exodus recounts them, but also provides a striking confirmation of the general reliability and authentic Egyptian origins of the Mosaic account.[22]

According to Hort, the sequence of plagues began with a very high Nile flood in September, which carried great quantities of red earth and poisonous microorganisms down into Egypt from Ethiopia, turning the Nile blood-red at some points, killing fish and frogs, providing breeding grounds for unusual numbers of gnats, mosquitoes and flies, and infecting cattle and men with the dread disease anthrax, contracted from the dead frogs. These afflictions would have run their course from September to December; the later plagues of locusts and "thick darkness" (presumably one of Egypt's great sandstorms) are dateable by insect ecology and wind conditions to early spring, probably March. The fact that the Wadi Tumilat is a lateral offshoot of the Nile valley, rather than geographically a part of it, fully explains its having been spared the plagues of flies, pestilence, hail and sandstorm.[23]

Yet still Ramses II would not part with his valuable slaves. These afflictions had come upon his land before, and would come again. Unusually severe and close-packed though they had been for the six months from September to March following his first confrontation with Moses, he saw in them no necessary proof of the special power of this new deity of slaves called Yahweh. The world's most powerful monarch was not easily terrified. Once more he refused to let Israel go.

It was full moon in the first month of spring, late March or early April by our calendar, the time of an ancient rite of nomads who then sacrificed one of the first-born of their flocks and placed the animal's blood upon their dwelling places.[24] Whether the Israelites had observed this rite all through their generations as settled dwellers in Egypt or—as the Exodus narrative seems to suggest—it was revived by order of Moses at this critical juncture, we do not know for sure; but the houses of all the Israelites were marked with the blood of lambs on that early spring night in Egypt which the Jews have commemorated ever since as the Passover, and which for Christians fixes the date each year of the commemoration of the Passion and Resurrection of Jesus Christ, the Lamb of God.[25]

We may conclude from Hort's explanation of the other plagues that Egypt was rife with disease carriers that year, but that conditions were not nearly so bad in the area where the Israelites were living. Pestilence in ancient times could strike with appalling swiftness and mortality. An epidemic disease that spring could have swept over an Egypt, carrying off the Pharaoh's own eldest son and many others, and in the natural course of events the Israelites, partially protected by the Wadi Tumilat, might have been spared the worst of the epidemic.

But we are explicitly told that *all* Israel was spared and that *all* the first-born in Egypt died. For this no natural explanation will suffice. The believer, Christian or Jewish, will hardly dare deny the totality of the preservation—that God's chosen, their doors marked with the blood of the lamb, were indeed "passed over" by the angel of death—and must encounter the gravest difficulties in any attempt to get away from the totality of the destruction, however much our modern sensibilities may incline us to sympathize with the grief-stricken Egyptians. All men must die. For all our sensibilities, we of the twentieth century have inflicted death on a scale unimagined in the previous history of the world.[26] The Egyptians of the age of Moses had taken the sword and were ultimately to perish by the sword. If God brought the inevitable end to many in Egypt before what would normally have been their time, in order to demonstrate the enduring and unique significance of His preservation of His chosen people in a way they could never forget, and to fulfill His promise to Abraham that He would bring judgment on the enslavers of His people, it is not for us to question Him. By any standard of reason or faith, we cannot put "God in the dock."[27] If what happened on the first Passover makes us fear Him a little, we might recall the forgotten admonition that the fear of God is the beginning of wisdom.

So the children of Israel marched out under the Hand of God, perhaps six thousand men with their women and children,[28] and Ramses II, mourning his son and heir, made at first no move to stop them.

In those times only two ways out of Egypt toward Palestine were open to men on foot. One was the coastal route, along the shore of the Mediterranean, the main highway from Africa to Asia, the age-old thoroughfare of armies and conquerors, every mile of it under Pharaoh's constant watch and tight control. We are explicitly told that for this reason Israel did not take the coastal route.[29]

The other way was the way of the wilderness, the route through Sinai. It passed between a fresh-water lake called Timsah, or Crocodile Lake, at the end of the Wadi Tumilat, and two salt-water lagoons called the Bitter Lakes. These three bodies of water are now linked, and greatly changed in appearance, by the Suez Canal. In the time of Ramses II the dry land between Lake Timsah and the Bitter Lakes was about six miles wide. It was controlled by a powerful fortress whose commander apparently refused to allow the Israelites to pass. During this period the Bitter Lakes were probably connected with the Gulf of Suez and the Red Sea to the south by tidal channels and reedy marshland, the "Sea of Reeds" of the Hebrew text of the Book of Exodus.[30]

Having rejected the coastal route and been cut off from the starting point of the wilderness route, Israel was penned between sea and desert when the chariots and cavalry of the Pharaoh set out in pursuit, to recapture them and return them to slavery. But the water link between the Red Sea and the Bitter Lakes was shallow. The Book of Exodus tells us that "a strong easterly wind" blew all night and drove the waters back. A northeast wind combined with a strong ebb tide at this point could have opened up a passage, at least for men on foot and for animals, across what had been an especially shallow part of the channel, with water remaining in deeper basins on either side of the crossing place.[31] But such a ford, normally underwater, would still have been wet enough to mire chariots; and while the Egyptians were struggling to free them, a simultaneous shift of the wind and the tide could have overwhelmed them by the returning waters just as we are told happened.[32]

Such natural explanations may disappoint both enthusiasts for miracle and those who regard the Exodus narrative as largely or entirely myth, but they seem the most probable reconstruction of the actual event. After all, the Bible itself attributes the parting of the sea to a natural cause, the "strong easterly wind," rather than to any suspension of natural laws at that point. Once again we need to remember that God works first of all through nature, His creation, rather than against it. But that He *was* acting, that He was guiding and guarding the Israelites, cannot be reasonably denied in the face of the evidence. To attribute to pure chance the shift of wind and tide at precisely the right moment to let the Israelites through the Sea of Reeds and then to drown the pursuing Egyptians—especially in view of all the events of the preceding six months—is to pass beyond all measurable bounds of natural probability. The means used to effect the Israelites' escape, like the first nine plagues, seem to have been natural means; their timing, their obedience to the command of Moses in God's name, was clearly supernatural. In liberating His people God worked both supernaturally and naturally, in a way that will live in human memory until the end of time.

> Then Moses and the people of Israel sang this song to the LORD, saying,
> "I will sing to the LORD, for he has triumphed gloriously;
> the horse and his rider he has thrown into the sea.
> The LORD is my strength and my song,
> and he has become my salvation;
> this is my God, and I will praise him,
> my father's God, and I will exalt him.
> The LORD is a man of war;
> the LORD is his name.
>
> "Pharaoh's chariots and his host he cast into the sea;
> and his picked officers are sunk in the Red Sea.
> The floods cover them;
> they went down into the depths like a stone.
> Thy right hand, O LORD, glorious in power,
> thy right hand, O LORD, shatters the enemy."[33]

Israel's crossing of the sea closed a door forever on the past and opened a door forever into the future. Behind the surging tide which had overwhelmed the horsemen and the chariots of the absolute monarch who claimed godhead, oppression and misery lay heavy upon the land of Egypt for which henceforth all roads led downward, through all subsequent history to be "a broken reed."[34] Ahead in the stark loneliness of Sinai an experience awaited Israel such as no other people before or since has ever had, and which they were never to have again—an experience shared only with God. For eleven months it was as though the children of Israel dwelt outside time.

From one oasis and well to another they made their way. Moses, familiar with the country—he had lived there through the many years of his earlier exile[35]—knew how to obtain drinking water for them by treating brackish water with secretions from the branches of certain trees, and by sharp blows upon water-soluble limestone; very likely he also knew that at this season of the year (June) birds could often be easily caught for meat and the sap emerging from holes made by boring insects in the tree *Tamarix mannifera*, which congeals and drops to the ground during the night, gathered each morning as "manna." But since 6000 families could hardly have lived for long on these secretions alone, or primarily, as the Biblical account tells us they did, we may presume that God multiplied and fortified them to nourish the full host, as His Son was later to multiply the loaves and fishes in Galilee.[36]

Crossing the thornbush wilderness of Sin, Moses led his people to camp before the mountain where he had seen the bush that burned but was not consumed. Here, in the shadow of peaks rising to 8500 feet, was a plain providing space and water for a long encampment. Israel remained there for nearly a year, from July to May.[37]

> Moses went up to God, and the LORD called to him out of the mountain, saying, "Thus you shall say to the house of Jacob, and tell the people of Israel: You have seen what I did to the Egyptians, and how I bore you on eagles' wings and brought you to myself. Now therefore, if you will obey my voice and keep my covenant, you shall be my own possession among all peoples; for all the earth is mine, and you shall be to me a kingdom of priests and a holy nation. These are the words which you shall speak to the children of Israel."
>
> So Moses came and called the elders of the people, and set before them all these words which the LORD had commanded him. And all the people answered together and said, "All that the LORD has spoken we will do." And Moses reported the words of the people to the LORD.[38]

The people were told to prepare for two days. On the third day, there was fire on the mountain of Sinai.[39]

Not now did God come condescendingly, as to a little child, as He had come to Abraham. Not now did He come in self-revelation and with a special commission, as He had first come to Moses. Not now did He come open in love, vulnerable in peace, glorious in hope, as He would one day come to Palestine incarnate as a man. This time He came in smoke and thunder, staking out His mountain with a volley of skybolts, allowing only Moses and Aaron to approach Him, and then only to convey His words to their people:

"You shall have no other gods before me.

"You shall not make yourself a graven image, or any likeness of anything that is in heaven above, or that is in the earth beneath, or that is in the water under the earth; you shall not bow down to them or serve them; for I the LORD your God am a jealous God, visiting the iniquity of the fathers upon the children to the third and the fourth generation of those who hate me, but showing steadfast love to thousands of those who love me and keep my commandments.

"You shall not take the name of the LORD your God in vain; for the LORD will not hold him guiltless who takes his name in vain.

"Remember the sabbath day, to keep it holy. Six days you shall labor, and do all your work; but the seventh day is a sabbath to the LORD your God; in it you shall not do any work, you, or your son, or your daughter, your manservant, or your maidservant, or your cattle, or the sojourner who is within your gates; for in six days the LORD made heaven and earth, the sea, and all that is in them, and rested the seventh day; therefore the LORD blessed the sabbath day and hallowed it.

"Honor your father and your mother, that your days may be long in the land which the LORD your God gives you.

"You shall not kill.

"You shall not commit adultery.

"You shall not steal.

"You shall not bear false witness against your neighbor.

"You shall not covet your neighbor's house; you shall not covet your neighbor's wife, or his manservant, or his maidservant, or his ox, or his ass, or anything that is your neighbor's."[40]

When Moses told the people gathered below the mountain what God had said, "all the people answered with one voice, and said, 'All the words which the LORD has spoken we will do.'"[41]

The Ten Commandments were the heart of the covenant of Sinai and of the faith which sprang from that covenant, then and since.[42] In the text which has come down to us—though *not* in any of the scholarly reconstructions based on the documentary hypothesis—the Decalogue and the Book of the Covenant immediately following it, together with corresponding chapters in the Book of Deuteronomy, show a very close resemblance in form and structure to treaties between kings dating from the late second millennium (1500-1000) B.C., but not to such treaties of later date. This is one of the clearest proofs that the account of the Sinai covenant in the Book of Exodus does in fact go back to this period and not to a "redactor" at the time of the Babylonian exile in the sixth century (600-500) B.C., as many "higher critics" have held.[43] The Creator and Sustainer of the universe really did make this pact with the people of Israel soon after He brought them out of bondage in Egypt. To Abraham He had given the promise; from Moses and his people He demanded obedience to a specific and rigorous code of righteousness.

Israel pledged to obey. The witnesses of their pledge were Moses and Aaron, Aaron's two sons, and seventy elders of the people. They ascended Mount Sinai with Moses and saw the reflection of the glory of God upon the ground His presence had sanctified, which thereby had become "as it were a pavement of sapphire stone, like the very heaven for clearness."[44] But experience was to show that obedience to these commandments would not and could not be consistently given by fallen men, even God's chosen.

The first proof came very soon. While the divine fire still crowned Mount Sinai, and Moses was gone from the camp for many days and nights to stand in its Presence, the people to whom God had just given His Law proceeded to break it in the most spectacular and complete manner imaginable, by casting a golden bull or "calf" to worship, as had been done in Egypt. When at length Moses came down again from the mountain, he found all his people—including Aaron himself, who had actually cast the idol —far gone in apostasy. In anger and desperation Moses broke the Tablets of the Law which had just been inscribed on the mountain, and ground the golden "calf" to powder.[45] For this man, who had stood so close for so long to the fire on Sinai, knew far better than anyone else among his people what a fearful thing it is to offend God.

By prayer Moses turned away God's wrath, and after a struggle Israel returned to its divine allegiance under his leadership. But it was the first bitter lesson of a long series spanning the ensuing thirteen hundred years, as the Chosen People learned in the most painful ways that they could not keep the covenant of Sinai. Time and again they would rebel and fall away; time and again they would be brought back, in agony and with loss, to dedicate themselves anew to their obligation, only to begin sliding immediately toward another apostasy. For the Law alone was not enough for salvation.

Yet law man must have; so the Tablets of God's Law were inscribed a second time by the Divine Fire on the mountaintop, and the covenant was renewed. Yahweh granted Moses a glimpse of His glory—though not of His face.[46] He forgave His people, promising them both mercy and justice, and pledging Himself to be with them as they marched to the Promised Land.[47] When Moses descended from Mount Sinai for the last time he was so radiant from the glory he had beheld that the skin of his face shone, and Aaron and the people feared to approach him, until he called them; afterwards he veiled his face.[48]

The two stone tablets bearing the Ten Commandments, the tablets of the Covenant, were placed in a chest probably patterned after similar holy chests used in Egypt, 45 inches long and 27 inches wide, carried on poles overlaid with gold and bearing the figures of two angels with extended wings: the cherubim. This conformed to a well-attested practice of that age whereby the texts of covenants sealed by divine promises were placed at the feet of images of the ratifying gods. But this shrine, the visible heart of Israel's faith, differed essentially and fundamentally from every other in the world because of the absence of any image of a god (no one ever thought of the cherubim as gods). The text of the covenant of Sinai was laid before an invisible Spirit "enthroned upon the cherubim." Other peoples had worshipped some gods without images (though none had prohibited images altogether); but these gods did not guarantee covenants, nor speak to men and give them laws; vague and distant, they were increasingly eclipsed by those members of the pantheon who did have images. The invisible Lord, He Who Is and Who Causes To Be, had "pitched His tent" among this wandering people, and they pitched their tent for Him—the tent shrine, the tabernacle, which housed the Ark when it was not being carried with them on their wanderings.[49]

And so, chastened by their first fall, heartened by their first recovery, sustained by the new promise and the ineradicable memory of their special deliverance from Egypt, Israel set out, carrying the Ark of the Covenant, through the wilderness on a journey that shall not end until the world ends.

Israel emerged from Sinai into a world of enemies. Within the confines of Pharaoh's monolithic state there had at least been peace, though at the price of slavery; beyond lay anarchy. All the lands of the Eastern Mediterranean during the last half of the thirteenth century (1250-1200) B.C. were swept and scarred by merciless war, in which the consequence of defeat was total destruction.

The terror of those times thunders through the pages of the *Iliad*, for this was the age of the Trojan War, of the sacking and burning of splendid ancient cities all the way from Greece through Asia Minor, Syria, Lebanon and Palestine to Askelon near the border of Egypt. The Hittite empire in Asia Minor was eliminated from history at one stroke after five centuries of power; the great and fabulously rich port city of Ugarit on the north Syrian coast soon followed it into oblivion, in 1234 B.C. The palaces and strongholds of the Mycenaean Greeks and the people of the Aegean Sea were overwhelmed, wiping out the civilization they had been building for four hundred years and more. So complete was the destruction in Greece that, except for the *Iliad* and various half-mythologized legends, the civilization of Crete and Mycenae was lost without a trace or a memory until the archeological work of Schliemann in the nineteenth century; the art of writing itself—the Linear A and Linear B syllabaries—was lost in Greece, and therefore had to be developed all over again in a new way half a millennium later. The Philistines, tall men with feathered helmets armed with the first iron weapons, occupied the coast of southern Lebanon and Palestine, ravaging the cities of the Canaanites. Among the nomads upon the fringes of the desert and the petty kings of the surviving native cities of Syria and Palestine, strife was endemic. With Egypt having retreated into itself after the death of Ramses II, and with the Hittite empire gone, no great power remained to govern or pacify any significant part of this region.[50]

It is essential to keep these grim conditions clearly in mind in order to understand and appreciate the course which Israel followed from the time Moses led his people to the great oasis of Kadesh-barnea in the Negév desert south of Palestine, to their final settlement of the Promised Land. In that land, at that time, neither the thoughts nor the acts of peace could have any meaning. Palestine had filled up with a variety of peoples[51] in the four centuries since Abraham, Isaac, and Jacob had wandered there, relatively unmolested; more were on the way. The land at the center of the world had become, as it was so often to be in the future, everyone's target.

But it was the land of the promise, and it had to be taken.

Here at the dawn of the Iron Age, in a world scourged by marauding barbarians, a few thousand homeless tribesmen coming out of the Sinai desert with every man's hand against them could not possibly have accepted or practiced anything resembling the Sermon on the Mount. That lay more than twelve hundred years in the future. Every one of those years was needed to prepare the people of Israel for it.

Meawhile Israel must survive, and know its God.

Those parts of the law and teaching of Moses which bear on war were an iron creed for an iron age. "You must love your neighbor as yourself," Moses declared, in his most inspired moment, as recorded in the Book of Leviticus;[52] but the Israelites could not yet understand how their enemy could be their neighbor. The graces necessary for large-scale conversions among the Gentiles were not yet available. So conquered cities and their people could be, and on several occasions were, wiped out by the Israelites to the last man and even to the last living thing.[53]

For Israel had first of all to learn and to live the Great Commandment:

> Hear, O Israel: The LORD our God is one LORD; and you shall love the LORD your God with all your heart, and with all your soul, and with all your might. And these words which I command you this day shall be upon your heart; and you shall teach them diligently to your children, and shall talk of them when you sit in your house, and when you walk by the way, and when you lie down, and when you rise. And you shall bind them as a sign upon your hand, and they shall be as frontlets between your eyes. And you shall write them on the doorposts of your house and on your gates.[54]

All this the Israelites could never have done if their God had not become for them, during that critical and desperate time when every man's hand was against them and they had only Him to help, a God of battles.

Even with God's own assurance that He was with them and would give them victories, the Israelites repeatedly rebelled and despaired. They recoiled in fear from the reports the first scouts brought back of the might of the dwellers in Canaan, threatening to stone Moses and demanding another leader who would take them back to safety in slavery in Egypt. Once more Moses turned away by prayer God's wrath at this cowardice and lack of faith, but He decreed that because of their rebellion none of the Israelites over twenty years of age should set foot in the Promised Land, except Joshua and Caleb who alone, with Moses, had remained faithful and confident. Disregarding the punishment as they had disregarded God's promise, the people—unwilling to wait, now that their confidence was restored—set out again to the attack, without Moses and without the Ark, and were repulsed from Canaan's Sinai frontier. Humbled, once again believing and obedient, they returned to Kadesh-barnea where Moses and the Ark had remained during their mad adventure on their own.[55]

The Kadesh-barnea oasis became the center of their wanderings for the next 38 years, still entirely confined to the Sinai peninsula. During this long and often discouraging period other rebellions occurred. The Levites rose under Core, rejecting the rule of Moses and the priestly prerogatives of Aaron, and the popular support for the rebels was again punished, this time by a plague, which the prayers of Moses and Aaron finally checked. But evidently a far more serious apostasy took place—one so serious that Scripture draws a veil over its details and extent which the passage of time has thickened to near impenetrability. Whatever it was, it happened "by the waters of Meribah, on the day of Massa in the desert, when your fathers tested me though they had seen my works."[56]

The waters of Meribah were near Kadesh-barnea, probably one of the three separate springs which make this oasis. At Meribah the people complained of lack of water, once again regretting that they had ever left Egypt. (Presumably the springs had temporarily gone dry, or nearly so.) Moses rebuked them for their lack of faith and struck rock to bring out water, as he had done before; and as before, the water came. But he and Aaron were thereupon condemned by God for rebelliousness, for putting Him to the test, and for a lack of faith; consequently He ordained that they too, like all the other adult Israelites except Joshua and Caleb, should never set foot in the Promised Land.[57]

How had Moses rebelled? How had he lacked faith? How had he "put God to the test"? The account of his once again bringing forth water from the rock to meet the needs of the people when they complained—exactly as he had done in the past without Divine reproof—does not answer these questions. But weakening, even sin there must have been, to have called down upon his head such grievous punishment; and massive apostasy there evidently was, so complete that the fundamental covenanted rite of circumcision instituted by Abraham was abandoned, so that later Joshua had to circumcise his whole army just before beginning his invasion of the Promised Land.[58] At any other time in Israel's history the men of that army would have been circumcised in earliest infancy.

Israel's years in the desert were no idyll, despite the tendency of faithful Israelites in the age of the great prophets to see them as such. An apostasy so great as to touch even the magnificent Moses, enslaving for a time this giant among men to the sin that is our common heritage from Adam, may well have been the worst in Israel's history. We do not know. All we know is that, like all apostasies and rebellions against God, in the end it was surmounted by constancy in the essence of faith, together with repentance and expiation—that Moses, whatever his temporary lapse, eventually drew the strength to persevere and grow in faith from the Source of all true strength, accepting not only the truth of Him Who Is and the mission He had given to His people, but also the rightness of his own punishment. What must the road back have been like for the man who had stood before God on Sinai, yet had failed Him? We can hardly begin to imagine. Yet in the end, his greatness was the fuller and his strength the more splendid than before his fall, because he did come back.

With Moses their leader once again, and the forty years of wandering and waiting nearly over, Israel marched south of Edom to the head of the Gulf of Aqaba bordering Sinai on the east, then past the southern end of the Dead Sea to the land east of the Jordan River, which they conquered from its inhabitants after victories at Jahas against the Amorites under Sihon of Heshbon, at Edrei against Og king of Bashan, and against the Midianites. Controlling now almost the whole of the fertile area and good pasture of the present kingdom of Jordan, with a new generation grown up and ready for war, the long-delayed full-scale invasion of the Promised Land could at last begin.[59]

On the plains of Moab Moses took leave of his people. Here he gave them his final form of the law which ever afterward was to bear his name, written down and deposited near the Ark containing the tablets of the Ten Commandments which were its foundation. He renewed the covenant of Sinai with the people and ordered for the future a periodic reading of the whole law and renewal of the covenant. That during the 38 years in the desert, working back up from the sin and apostasy at Meribah, culminating in the preparation for the long-delayed invasion, Moses could have written everything in the books traditionally attributed to him is not only possible, but an entirely reasonable thing for him to have done. A people so "stiff-necked" and "hard-hearted," so relentlessly realistic yet so inconstant, clearly needed fixed, explicit, detailed laws as they faced a world full of danger and temptation. Whatever the actual history of their writing, whatever essentially peripheral additions may have been made later, it seems evident that Moses did in fact give his people such a code of laws.[60]

Finally, Moses set before Israel "a blessing and a curse: the blessing, if you obey the commandments of the LORD your God, which I command you this day, and the curse, if you do not obey the commandments of the LORD your God, but turn aside from the way which I command you."[61] And he told them for the first and only time of his Successor, one single future Prophet from their race, Whose words would be God's own and must be heeded and obeyed. He warned them that whoever did not heed the words of this Prophet would be answerable to Moses for his incredulity.[62]

Twelve hundred and fifty years later, speaking in the Temple at Jerusalem,

Jesus of Nazareth would recall that charge by the man who received the covenant and the commandments of God in fire upon the mountain of Sinai:

> Do not think that I shall accuse you to the Father; it is Moses who accuses you, on whom you set your hope. If you believed Moses, you would believe me, for he wrote of me.[63]

NOTES

[1] Exodus 2:15-24. The tradition recorded in Josephus, *Antiquities of the Jews* II:10-11, that Moses commanded an Egyptian army in a victorious campaign in Nubia or Ethiopia,and that intrigues by those he had defeated lost him Pharaoh's favor and led to his exile, is certainly possible if Moses was in fact brought up in the Egyptian court as Exodus 2:10 indicates, though it must be kept in mind that Josephus was writing nearly 1400 years after the events he purports to describe. If Moses was educated at Pharaoh's court and commanded an Egyptian army in Nubia, he very likely could read and write himself and certainly was familiar with the procedure of recording events in written documents and the value of doing so, and thus could have written or ordered written substantial parts of the Pentateuch, as all later Jewish tradition held that he did.

[2] St. Thomas Aquinas made God's declaration in Exodus 3:14 the basis and proof of the doctrine of self-existent being which is the cornerstone of the whole immense structure of his Christian metaphysics. See his *Summa Theologica*, Question 13, Article 11, and Etienne Gilson, *The Christian Philosophy of St. Thomas Aquinas* (New York, 1956), pp. 84-95.

[3] Roland de Vaux, *The Early History of Israel* (Philadelphia, 1978), p. 282.

[4] *Ibid.*, pp. 347-357. De Vaux criticizes the recent translation "I Am Who I Am" for God's self-identification to Moses in Exodus 3:14 (as in the Revised Standard Version quoted at the beginning of this chapter), stating that the older form "I Am Who Am" or "I am the Existing One" is preferable.

[5] For example, Martin Noth, *The History of Israel*, 2d ed. (London, 1960), pp. 134-136. John Bright, *Early Israel in Recent History Writing* (London, 1956), pp. 85-87, presents a devastating critique of Noth's view of Moses.

[6] Frank M. Cross Jr., "The Priestly Tabernacle," *The Biblical Archaeologist Reader*, ed. G. Ernest Wright and David N. Freedman (Chicago, 1961), pp. 207-209; William F. Albright, *From the Stone Age to Christianity*, 2d ed. (New York, 1957), pp. 258, 268.

[7] John Bright, *A History of Israel*, 3d ed. (Philadelphia, 1981), p. 127.

[8] For a discussion of the reliability of oral tradition, with specific reference to the traditions of Israel, see Albright, *Stone Age to Christianity*, pp. 64-65, 72-76. Several instructive examples are given by Giuseppe Ricciotti, *The History of Israel* (Milwaukee, 1955), I, 164-166. The writer has personally verified the preservation of accurate oral tradition over a 300-year period (1650-1950) in a rural community in Maine, by comparing twentieth century memory with seventeenth century documents.

[9] Bright states: "It must be stressed, and stressed again, that the age of Israel's origins was one of widespread literacy" (*History of Israel*, p. 118). K. A. Kitchen, *Ancient Orient and Old Testament* (Chicago, 1966), pp. 135-138, points out that written transmission of important material was much preferred to oral transmission during this period in the Middle East. For the Sinai alphabet, dating from the 15th century B.C., see John A. Wilson, *The Burden of Egypt* (Chicago, 1951), p. 191.

[10] Roland de Vaux, *Ancient Israel, Its Life and Institutions* (New York, 1961), p. 301; Ricciotti, *History of Israel*, I, 210-214.

[11] H. A. R. Gibb, *Mohammedanism, an Historical Survey*, 2d ed. (New York, 1962), pp. 49-50.

[12] Kitchen, *Ancient Orient and Old Testament*, pp. 172-173.

[13] Ibid., pp. 20, 23. The flimsiness and artificiality of many of the scholarly reconstructions of the Pentateuch is well demonstrated in the careful textual analysis of the Book of Deuteronomy in G. T. Manley, *The Book of the Law, Studies in the Date of Deuteronomy* (Grand Rapids MI, 1957). Good general presentations of the traditional view of the primarily and explicitly Mosaic authorship and largely unitary character of the books of the Old Testament, advancing many impressive arguments against the "documentary hypothesis" are (Protestant) Edward J. Young, *An Introduction to the Old Testament*, 2d ed. (Grand Rapids MI, 1960); (Catholic) John E. Steinmueller, *A Companion to Scripture Studies* (Houston, 1969), Volume II; (Jewish) Umberto Cassuto, *The Documentary Hypothesis and the Composition of the Pentateuch* (Jerusalem, 1961), especially pp. 98-105. See also Yehezkel Kaufmann, *The Religion of Israel from Its Beginnings to the Babylonian Exile* (Chicago, 1960), especially pp. 200-208 and 245-255, and Claus Schedl, *History of the Old Testament* (New York, 1972), II, 236-243. Kaufmann and Schedl accept the existence of "J," "E" and "P" but ascribe to them considerably greater antiquity and the use of much more contemporary and near-contemporary source material than most Old Testament scholars today will admit. Schedl also cites the very interesting though now almost forgotten theory of the great French Biblical scholar J.-M. Lagrange, accepting "J," "E" and "P" but making Moses himself their redactor and in large part their author. It is entirely unscholarly to regard the question of the Mosaic authorship of the Pentateuch as closed or the documentary hypothesis as finally proved. That this position has become in many quarters almost a badge of academic respectability is a sad commentary on the present condition of the Western academic world.

[14] A phrase powerfully used of Moses in the excellent motion picture "The Ten Commandments," based in large part on sound historical scholarship and many of the works cited in these Notes.

[15] Exodus 5:1-2.

[16] Alan Gardiner, *Egypt of the Pharaohs* (Oxford, 1961), pp. 242-250, 257-258; Kitchen, *Ancient Orient and Old Testament*, pp. 57-60; Jack Finegan, *Let My People Go* (New York, 1963), pp. 3-14, 25-39; Ricciotti, *History of Israel*, I, 167-171; G. Ernest Wright, *Biblical Archaeology*, 2d ed. (Philadelphia, 1962), pp. 58-60, 84.

[17] For the archeological evidence of the date of the Israelite conquest of central Palestine, see Chapter Four, Note 5, below; for the inscription of Merneptah, see Wright, *Biblical Archaeology*, pp. 70-71, which quotes it in full, and Ricciotti, *History of Israel*, I, 191-192. Kitchen, *Ancient Orient and Old Testament*, pp. 59-60, demolishes the arguments which Martin Noth and Otto Eissfeldt of the German school of higher Biblical criticism have advanced in an attempt to cast doubt on the Merneptah inscription as a specific reference to Biblical Israel.

[18] Even if the mention of forty years in the Book of Exodus is simply a conventional expression for "a long time" or a generation rather than a precise figure, the fact remains that at least this much time would have been required for most of those who were over twenty years old in the second year of the Exodus to die in the natural course.

[19] A fragment of a bowl marked with the Year 4 of an unnamed Pharaoh, found in the ruins of Lachish, is thought to refer to Merneptah (Wright, *Biblical Archaeology*, pp. 82-83), which would thereby date the destruction of Lachish by the invading Israelites to his reign.

[20] De Vaux, *Early History of Israel*, pp. 388-392. The reference in Exodus 2:23 to the death "after a long time" of the king under whom Moses was originally driven out of Egypt has sometimes been interpreted as referring to the very long reign of Ramses II (67 years) which would place the Exodus in the following reign, that of Merneptah. But the "long time" could also refer to the total length of the persecution of the Israelites in Egypt, or to the reign of the Pharaoh Horemheb in the late fourteenth century B.C. which lasted 30 years or more, when Moses could have been born and grown to manhood while still being in full vigor in 1275 B.C. The date of 1275 is suggested by the following negative indications, admittedly tenuous, but interesting: An exhaustive study of all the dated material from Ramses II's long reign (John D. Schmidt, *Ramses II, a Chronological Structure for His Reign* [Baltimore, 1973]), reveals that the second decade of that reign (1280-1270 B.C., according to the accession date of 1290 B.C. for Ramses II favored by Schmidt) is almost completely devoid of any indication of Egyptian military activity abroad or major enterprises at home, as might be expected in a nation heavily damaged during that decade by the first nine plagues of the Exodus and psychologically shocked as well as decimated by the tenth. It is hardly surprising that there is no Egyptian record of the Exodus. God-kings were not accustomed to commemorating their defeats, and they wrote or ordered written virtually all the political and military history for Egypt in the second and third millennia B.C. which we possess.

[21] See Pierre Montet, *Everyday Life in Egypt in the Days of Ramesses the Great* (New York, 1958), for a comprehensive account of Egypt under Ramses II.

[22] Greta Hort, "The Plagues of Egypt," *Zeitschrift für die alttestamentliche Wissenschaft*, LXIX (1957), 84-103, and LXX (1958), 48-59. This very important article is summarized by Finegan, *Let My People Go*, pp. 50-55, and by Wright, *Biblical Archaeology*, p. 54.

[23] Finegan, *Let My People Go*, pp. 50-55.

[24] *Ibid.*, pp. 68-69; de Vaux, *Ancient Israel*, pp. 489-490.

[25] The writer had the great good fortune to be in Jerusalem in April 1971, one of the rare years when Passover and Easter were both celebrated on the same weekend. The fact that both the Divine events they commemorate took place in early spring—the time of renewal of life also celebrated in ancient pagan rites such as that of the nomads sacrificing the first-born of their flocks (see Note 24, above)—is hardly accidental, nor should it arouse any qualms in the orthodox reader. Spring is the time of rebirth in nature, God's creation. It should not be surprising, to say nothing of disquieting, that He chose that symbolically appropriate time for the rebirth of His chosen people through their liberation from Egypt, and of all men through their liberation by Redemption from the bondage of sin. Insofar as the pagans responded to nature as it is, and not as human imagination distorted by sin and Satan often conceived it to be, they too were responding in their own way to God. As for the Passover feast prescribed in the law of Moses, it had no parallel elsewhere (Ricciotti, *History of Israel*, I, 182).

[26] See the appalling catalogue of the mass slaughters and exterminations of our age by Erik von Kuehnelt-Leddihn, *Leftism* (New Rochelle NY, 1974), pp. 417-419, including the effect of nuclear and incendiary bombing of cities by the United States as well as Nazi and Communist atrocities.

[27] Title of a famous essay by C. S. Lewis, written in 1948.

[28] The number of 603,500 for the Israelite host of the Exodus, given in the usual translations of Numbers 1:20-46, is clearly in error. No such multitude could have crossed the sea as the Exodus narrative describes, nor have maintained itself in the Sinai wilderness, nor ever have been in real danger from the Egyptian army. The best explanation for this passage would appear to be that *'elef*, the Hebrew word usually translated "thou-

sand," here refers to a family or clan within a tribe, as it does for example in Judges 6:15. On this interpretation, the list in Numbers indicates 598 families or clans, which may be estimated as containing ten men each (not counting women and children). See George E. Mendenhall, "The Census Lists of Numbers 1 and 26," *Journal of Biblical Literature*, LXXVII (1958), 52-66; Finegan, *Let My People Go*, pp. 90-93; Ricciotti, *History of Israel*, I, 192-193.

[29] Exodus 13:17-18. The "road to the land of the Philistines" mentioned here is clearly the coastal route, regularly used by the Egyptians (*The Jerusalem Bible*, ed. Alexander Jones [New York, 1966] [Old Testament], p. 95, Note 13e). In view of this clear statement and the excellent practical reasons for the Israelites to have avoided this route, it is surprising that many modern scholars (e.g. Wright, *Biblical Archaeology*, pp. 61-62) still regard the Exodus as having occurred somewhere near the Mediterranean coast. For an excellent summary of the reasons for *not* looking for it there, see Finegan, *Let My People Go*, pp. 78-81.

[30] Finegan, *Let My People Go*, pp. 81-87; Ricciotti, *History of Israel*, I, 168, 183-185.

[31] Finegan, *Let My People Go*, p. 88; Exodus 14:21. The reference to "walls of water" on either side of them (Exodus 14:23 and 14:29) would, on this theory of the manner of the Israelite crossing of the sea, be an understandable later poetic exaggeration.

[32] Exodus 14:24-28, which tells us that the chariot wheels were first mired, and then the sea returned. Ricciotti, *History of Israel*, I, 185, estimates that about a thousand Egyptian chariots and charioteers were engulfed.

[33] Exodus 15:1-6.

[34] So John A. Wilson entitles the final chapter of his *Burden of Egypt* (pp. 289-318). (See Isaiah 19:1-15.) Ramses II was the last really great Pharaoh, the last to be the most powerful monarch in the world. Within half a century of his death, the Pharaoh Ramses III barely succeeded in beating off a massive attack on Egypt by the Libyans and the "People of the Sea," and from then onward the judgment on Egypt foretold to Abraham took effect (see Chapter Two, Note 67, above).

[35] Since Moses had lived in Sinai before the Exodus and had encountered Yahweh there, some scholars (e.g. Murray Lee Newman Jr., *The People of the Covenant* [Nashville TN, 1962], pp. 83-90) have built up an elaborate hypothesis of the supposed "Kenite" origin of the worship of Yahweh, based on a tortured construction of Exodus 18 in which it is told how Moses met his father-in-law Jethro on the way to Sinai with Israel after the Exodus and Jethro praised Yahweh after hearing all that He had done for Israel. But the fact that Jethro said "*now* I know that Yahweh is greater than all the gods" (Exodus 18:11, emphasis added) certainly suggests that he had not known this before. See the detailed refutation of the "Kenite" theory by Kaufmann, *Religion of Israel*, pp. 242-244.

[36] Wright, *Biblical Archaeology*, p. 65; F. S. Bodenheimer, "The Manna of Sinai," *Biblical Archaeologist Reader*, pp. 77-79; Finegan, *Let My People Go*, pp. 98-99; Ricciotti, *History of Israel*, I, 198-202. British travellers in Sinai have reported that the Arabs treat brackish water with leaves and branches to make it more potable, much as Moses did, and a British officer actually observed an instance of water being "struck" from limestone in this region by a sharp blow, as Exodus tells us Moses did. The actual "manna" produced by *Tamarix mannifera* and the scale insect upon it (though there seems to be some disagreement as to whether the insect or the tree produces the secretion) closely resembles in appearance the manna described in the Book of Exodus, and like it must be gathered in the morning, since it soon melts in the sun's heat. Forests of *Tamarix mannifera* are still found on the west coast of the Sinai peninsula, nearest to Egypt, and about 600 pounds of the secretions are still produced annually. In view

of the widespread deforestation of the Middle East in historic times, the number of *tamarix* trees and the amount of this substance produced in Sinai was probably much greater in Moses' time. The similarity between this substance and the manna of Exodus was noted by Josephus, St. Ambrose and the early Arabs as well as by modern commentators. However, the *tamarix* secretions do not resemble bread and have a low nutritive value. That they were eaten by the Israelites of the Exodus seems almost certain, since the food was there where they were at exactly the season they arrived, but that the secretions as we know them could have fed so many people so well as the Exodus narrative describes, is impossible in purely natural terms. Since we are specifically told that a Divine action was involved, it seems most likely that it was a multiplication and enrichment of the existing manna rather than a special creation of manna—just as Christ multiplied existing loaves and fishes and changed existing water into wine rather than producing bread, fish and wine from nothing.

[37] Finegan *Let My People Go,* pp. 96-98. The traditional location of the Mount Sinai of Exodus is the 7519-foot peak of Jebel Musa (which means "mountain of Moses" in Arabic). The balance of evidence favors this as the correct location (Bright, *History of Israel,* pp. 124-125; Wright, *Biblical Archaeology,* pp. 63-64).

[38] Exodus 19:3-8.

[39] There has been much discussion as to whether the fire on Sinai was a volcanic eruption or lightning from a mountain thunderstorm. Attempts have even been made to relocate Mount Sinai in an area of Arabia where there are active volcanoes (Bright, *History of Israel,* p. 124). This is carrying the naturalistic explanation of these events rather far. By contrast to the passage accounting for the parting of the sea by a strong east wind, there is nothing in the Book of Exodus to suggest any explanation on this order for the phenomena on Mount Sinai. Mountain thunderstorms do not continue for days on end, and Israel would hardly have encamped for ten months under an erupting volcano.

[40] Exodus 20:3-17.

[41] Exodus 24:3.

[42] See, for example, the combination of deep faith and sound scholarship in Rabbi Solomon Goldman's *The Ten Commandments* (Chicago, 1956).

[43] K. A. Kitchen, *The Bible in Its World* (Downers Grove IL, 1977), pp. 79-85; G. A. Mendenhall, "Law and Covenant in Israel and the Ancient Near East," *The Biblical Archaeologist* XVII (1954), 26-46, 50-76; Wright, *Biblical Archaeology,* pp. 100-101. Kitchen summarizes the second millennium B.C. covenant form as including: (1) preamble or title; (2) historical prologue; (3) stipulations, basic and detailed; (4) deposition of a copy of the covenant in a sanctuary and periodic public reading of the covenant terms; (5) witnesses; (6) curses and blessings. In first millennium B.C. covenants, on the other hand, Kitchen points out that there is no historical prologue, there are no blessings, and witnesses and curses precede stipulations. The Mosaic equivalents to the above-listed six elements of the second millennium B.C. covenant form are: (1) Exodus 20:1 and Deuteronomy 1:1-5; (2) Exodus 20:2 and Deuteronomy 1:6-3:29; (3) Exodus 20:3-17 and 22-26 and Deuteronomy 4-11 (basic) and Exodus 21 and 25-31, Leviticus 1-25, and Deuteronomy 12-26 (detailed); (4) Exodus 25:16, 34:1 and 28-29 and Deuteronomy 10:1-5, 31:9 and 24-26; (5) Exodus 24:4 (memorial stones used in place of other gods ruled out by the First Commandment); (6) Leviticus 26:3-20 and Deuteronomy 28.

[44] Exodus 24:9-11. Though the text states that Aaron and his sons and the elders "saw the God of Israel," it is clear from the context that what they saw was not God Himself, but the sapphire pavement. Man on earth may not see God face to face and live (Exodus 33:20, John 1:18).

[45] Exodus 32; on the "calf" as a bull, see *Jerusalem Bible* (Old Testament), p. 119,

Note 32b.

[46] Exodus 33:18-23 and 34:1; see Note 44, above.

[47] Exodus 33:15-17, 34:6-10.

[48] Exodus 34:29-33.

[49] Ricciotti, *History of Israel*, I, 211-214; Frank M. Cross Jr., "The Priestly Tabernacle," *Biblical Archaeologist Reader*, pp. 208-215. The word "cherubim" creates many problems, despite the fact that throughout both Jewish and Christian history it has been clearly understood as referring to angels (later one of the nine choirs of angels). But the term is also sometimes applied to the huge Assyrian figures of winged beasts (which could hardly have been carried on poles through the desert!) and, much more recently, Renaissance art represented "cherubs" as winged babies, creating an entirely different image in no way suggesting the majesty and awe which real angels always inspire. The cherubim of the original Ark of the Covenant were most likely winged human figures, like our own best representations of angels, since this was the style for depicting such beings in Egypt from which the decorators of the Ark had come—a style which they would naturally use since it was the only kind of art most Israelites had ever seen.

[50] *The Cambridge Ancient History* Volume II, Part 2 (3rd ed.), (Cambridge, England, 1975), pp. 507-516; for an excellent and balanced account of the unveiling of the Cretan-Mycenaean civilization and the many intractable problems and fierce scholarly controversies that still becloud our understanding of it, see William A. McDonald, *Progress into the Past, the Rediscovery of Mycenaean Civilization* (New York, 1967). The situation in this field of study has become still more complicated and confusing since the publication of McDonald's book (see, for example, Hans G. Wunderlich, *The Secret of Crete* [New York, 1974]).

[51] Bright, *History of Israel*, pp. 115-120. The new peoples arriving since the time of the patriarchs included Hittites from the north and Hurrians and probably Indo-Aryans from the northeast, as well as other ethnic stocks whose origin is unknown or doubtful, such as the Jebusites, Girgashites and Perizzites.

[52] Leviticus 19:18.

[53] Numbers 24:4-8, 31:13-18; Deuteronomy 7:1-6, 20:15-18; Joshua 6:17-21, 7:25. See the excellent discussion of the meaning and background of the concept of "holy war" and the practice of the *herem*, or "ban" (which, in the rare instances when it was applied with full rigor, as by Joshua at Jericho, meant the annihilation of a vanquished enemy and of all his livestock and possessions) in de Vaux, *Ancient Israel*, pp. 258-263. Primitive and repellent as it is to us, the *herem* must not be regarded as an aspect of a war to impose one people's religion upon another. As de Vaux points out, since Israel knew itself to be God's chosen people, "all the institutions of Israel were invested with a sacred character, war just as much as kingship or legislation. This does not mean that every war was a religious war—a concept whch does not appear until very late, under the Maccabees: Israel did not fight for its faith, but for its existence. This means that war is a sacred action, with its own particular ideology and rites." (*ibid.*, p. 258) Or, more succinctly, Israel believed that "it was Yahweh who fought for Israel, not Israel which fought for its God" (*ibid.*, p. 262).

[54] Deuteronomy 6:4-9.

[55] Ricciotti, *History of Israel*, I, 215-217.

[56] Deuteronomy 33:8; Ricciotti, *History of Israel*, I, 217-218.

[57] Numbers 20:1-13; Ricciotti, *History of Israel*, I, 218-220.

[58] Joshua 5:4-9.

[59] Ricciotti, *History of Israel*, I, 222, 225-226.

[60] *Ibid.*, I, 226-227; Paul Heinisch, *History of the Old Testament* (Collegeville MN,

1952), pp. 94-101, 106-108.

[61] Deuteronomy 11:26-28.

[62] Deuteronomy 18:15-19. The fact that the Mosaic statement refers specifically to one prophet rather than many is sufficient to dispose of the frequent modern interpretation (e.g., *The Jerome Biblical Commentary*, ed. Raymond E. Brown et al [Englewood Cliffs NJ, 1968], I, 113 and *Jerusalem Bible* [Old Testament], p. 241, Note 18c) that the entire line of prophets in later Israel, or the "prophetic office" in general, was meant. This passage was given a Messianic interpretation not only by Christ Himself and by the Apostles, but by the Jews before Christ (*Jerome Biblical Commentary*, II, 771), and it is very hard to see on what grounds modern scholars prove that interpretation wrong—all aside from what surely ought to be an insuperable difficulty for a Christian scholar in disagreeing with the Son of God on a point of exegesis (see Note 63, below).

[63] John 5:45-46. Since there is no other comparable passage in the Pentateuch, Jesus' reference must be to Deuteronomy 18:15-19. This is confirmed explicitly by the Apostles Philip (John 1:45) and Peter in the first recorded Christian sermon after the Resurrection (Acts 3:22-23), as well as by St. Stephen, the first Christian martyr, before the Sanhedrin (Acts 7:37).

4.
THE PROMISED LAND

Why do the nations conspire,
and the peoples plot in vain?
The kings of the earth set themselves,
and the rulers take counsel together,
against the LORD and his anointed, saying
"Let us burst their bonds asunder,
 and cast their cords from us."

He who sits in the heavens laughs;
the LORD has them in derision.
Then he will speak to them in his wrath,
and terrify them in his fury, saying,
"I have set my king
 on Zion, my holy hill."

I will tell of the decree of the LORD
He said to me, "You are my son,
today I have begotten you,
Ask of me, and I will make the nations your heritage,
and the ends of the earth your possession."
  —Psalms 2:1-8

Moses was dead, and the Book of Deuteronomy tells us that God Himself buried him somewhere on the lower slopes of Mount Nebo, from which he had been granted a distant view of the Promised Land across the Jordan, and "no man knows the place of his burial."[1] The first place in Israel now passed to

Joshua son of Nun, a great leader and brilliant commander in the full human and military sense of those terms,[2] chosen to win the victories that Israel required lest she be swallowed up in the maelstrom of those dark and bloody years.

Just as the real existence of Abraham and even of Moses has been doubted by scholars drawn further and further from proved and probable fact by the siren songs of their own favorite theories, so has the historicity of Joshua and his conquests been challenged. The documentary critics have as usual carved up his book according to their preconceptions, claiming to find in it inconsistencies showing that the conquest of Canaan resulted from unplanned irruptions of separate Israelite tribes at different times and from different places, rather than from a coordinated attack by all Israel under the command of Joshua.[3]

This conclusion does obvious violence to the Biblical text, especially the first chapter of the Book of Judges, where a very specific plan of conquest is laid out which, as Yehezkel Kaufmann has demonstrated, could not have reflected the actual later ambitions of the various tribes as they became situated in Canaan, but only a preconceived plan drawn up by men not yet in possession of the territory they were to invade.[4] It is also contradicted by hard evidence from archeology. Of the nine cities of Canaan listed in the Book of Joshua as destroyed by the Israelites under Joshua's command, four (Lachish, Eglon, Debir, and Hazor) were in fact destroyed during this very period (1250-1200 B.C.); a fifth (Ai) is probably to be identified with nearby Bethel which was consumed by a "tremendous conflagration" at the same period, and three of the others (Makkedah, Libnah, and Hebron) have not yet been excavated so as to yield results applicable to this period.[5] Furthermore, the city of Gibeon, which plays an important part in the Book of Joshua as an ally of the Israelites, did exist as a prosperous settlement during this period and was *not* destroyed like its counterparts elsewhere, just as the Book of Joshua indicates.[6]

This leaves only Jericho as a possible archeological witness against the historical accuracy of the Book of Joshua. Once thought to confirm that Book, then thought to conflict with it, the results of excavations at Jericho now seem to show only that no reliable conclusions can be reached about the condition of the town from 1250 to 1200 B.C., because almost all of the soil which would have contained remains of that period has eroded away. It does appear that whatever sort of town may have been standing on the site when the Israelites arrived could not have been large, certainly not comparable to the great walled city built there six thousand years before, and therefore unlikely to have been a formidable military obstacle. Its walls may have been already half-ruined, requiring comparatively little effort to sap or breach, thereby bringing about the collapse recorded in the Book of Joshua —which includes the specific statement that a dweller in Jericho who befriended the Israelites, Rahab the harlot, was still alive at the time the Book was written.[7]

Finally, all the arguments previously advanced in favor of the historicity of Moses and the reliability of memories and records of the Exodus and the Sinai experience apply with even greater force to Joshua's campaigns which came after Moses, probably little more than two hundred years before the tenth century (1000-900) B.C. when it is generally agreed that written versions at least of parts of the Old Testament were in existence. The retention of substantially accurate and often very detailed memories of major historical events over a 200-year period has often been demonstrated. Such memories are likely to be preserved with special care and accuracy where they concern the origins of a people and how they came to occupy the land on which they dwell.[8]

Under Joshua, then, the twelve tribes of Israel thrust across the Jordan deep into Palestine. Palestine is a small country with a great range of elevation. Inland it is bounded by the great depression containing the Sea of Galilee, the Jordan River, and the Dead Sea, all of which lie below sea level. Immediately west of this depression is the hill country, rising to an altitude of nearly 3000 feet above sea level and sending a spur down to the Mediterranean at Mount Carmel. Along the coast is a plain, and in the north, between Mount Carmel and the Sea of Galilee, lies the thickly settled inland plain of Jezreel.[9]

Most of the land was occupied by the people known as Canaanites, of Semitic stock and language like the Israelites, dwelling in small cities and towns with a flourishing agriculture, worshipping primarily fertility deities—often with temple prostitution, homosexuality and various orgiastic rites —and with a fearsome cult of child sacrifice. Jezreel and the coastal plain were the main foci of Canaanite settlement, but the Canaanites had occupied many portions of the hill country also.[10]

Joshua struck first at the center of the hill country, establishing a foothold by taking Ai or Bethel; then, allied with the city of Gibeon, he defeated a coalition of five kings in the battle during which Joshua called upon the sun and the moon to stand still so that Israel might complete its victory by a total rout of the foe, already put to flight by a furious hailstorm. Joshua's call, we are told, was heard and answered. The sun did stop, the day was lengthened, and the victory completed.[11]

This famous passage has occasioned controversy ever since Galileo. Modern commentators tend to assume that its only possible explanation, taken literally, is that the earth stopped rotating for a time. Critics of the Faith point derisively to the massive suspension of scientific laws any such event would require; defenders reply (correctly, as a general proposition) that God can suspend any natural laws He chooses to suspend, since He made them. But as we have seen in discussing other nature miracles of the Old Testament, even His Providential and miraculous actions in nature usually display an economy of means, whereby existing natural conditions are adapted and improved for His special purposes, rather than massively set aside or catastrophically interfered with.

Suggestions have been made of a special meteorological phenomenon connected with the hailstorm, by which the sun seemed to set and then reappear,[12] though this involves either a substantial reinterpretation of the text or a quite extraordinary meteorology. More to the point is the example of the miracle of the sun at Fàtima in Portugal on October 13, 1917,[13] which seems never to have been applied to what happened on that distant day in Palestine, in the valley of Ajalon. Yet precisely the same sort of phenomenon was involved in both cases: an apparent change in the normal motion of the sun. No intelligent person who accepts the reality of the Fàtima miracle believes that the earth actually stopped rotating on October 13, 1917. But tens of thousands of people in Portugal saw the sun dance and fall in the sky on that day at Fàtima. A sun that can dance and fall can also stop. God Who made the light can change the light or keep it; leaving the sun in its actual astronomical place and the earth still rotating normally about it, He can nevertheless alter its appearance and behavior in a particular sky at a particular time. This He seems to have done at Fàtima, though the Church does not require of all the faithful belief in that particular miracle. This He also seems to have done at the valley of Ajalon, and something like this seems to have been what the Church did require Galileo to believe.

The victory at Ajalon won, Joshua then swept over the hill country south of Jerusalem (he did not conquer Jerusalem itself), taking the cities of Lachish, Eglon, and Debir which archeology shows to have been destroyed about this time, after which he marched north and won his most impressive military triumph of all against the powerful and flourishing city of Hazor in Galilee.[14] The conquest was not complete, the coastal plain and the Plain of Jezreel not having been attacked because the Canaanites there were still too numerous and strong; and several major cities of the hill country remaining unconquered, including Jerusalem. But by now Israel had taken the measure of the Promised Land. Their faith and their victories had given the Israelites absolute confidence that eventually all of it would be theirs. God had promised it.

So the Israelites settled into the land, becoming farmers instead of herdsmen, probably incorporating some of the native peoples yet firmly retaining their special identity. For the most part they shunned the corrupt life and debased religions of the Canaanite cities, preferring to build and dwell in smaller villages of their own.[15] The fortunes of war ebbed and flowed; some cities evidently had to be taken more than once,[16] while invaders from the fringes of the desert—coming as the Israelites themselves had come— had to be repelled. Not all the tribes rallied to the national cause even when these invaders struck, but in each crisis Israel found a leader able to hurl back the foe. There was not yet a monarchy, nor any sort of central government. Israel did not come to bring peace to the Promised Land. Except for a few brief periods, no longer than the span of one man's life, that land has never known peace since the first walls rose around the city of Jericho. For ten thousand years Palestine has been a mirror of the worst and the best in man.

Othniel delivered Israel from the Edomites from the south;[17] Ehud held the fords of the Jordan against the Moabires from the southeast;[18] and when the Midianites from the Arabian desert came on racing camels to lay waste the Promised Land, Gideon chose just three hundred men, marched to the Midianite camp, and routed them with the mighty cry: "A sword for the LORD and for Gideon!"[19] These leaders and others like them, whose title is traditionally translated "judges," were actually charismatic military commanders and adventurers, whose prowess God used to save His people from their thronging enemies, but whose own morality often left much to be desired. Gideon's son Abimelech sought to become king and in pursuance of his ambition killed all his brothers, so that his death by being struck in the head by a millstone thrown by a woman during a siege was seen as God's punishment for his crime.[20] Jephthah won a glorious victory over the hostile Ammonites from the east, but stained it horribly by sacrificing his own daughter afterwards as a "burnt offering" in imitation of the Canaanite rites, ignoring what God had told Abraham on Mount Moriah.[21]

Soon after 1150 B.C. the Israelites were solidly established in the hill country and ready to challenge the Canaanites for control of the Plain of Jezreel. Led by Barak as general and inspired by the prophetess Deborah, whose fierce battle song preserved in the Book of Judges so well reflects both the vigor and the savagery of this age, Israel inflicted a decisive defeat on a coalition of the Canaanite cities of that plain under Sisera.[22]

With the field now cleared of all lesser contenders, Israel about 1100 B.C. had to meet the greatest threat of all: the Philistines from beyond the sea, the mightiest warriors of their time, who had come from the world of Achilles and Hector to seize the coast of Palestine while Joshua was conquering the hill country, had challenged Pharaoh Ramses III at the delta of the Nile itself, and were now pressing inland to impose their barbaric mastery over the whole domain of the Promise. Israel met the Philistine army at Aphek on the edge of the coastal plain, and was defeated in its first engagement. The Ark of the Covenant—Moses' own Ark, enshrining the Ten Commandments—was then brought from its sanctuary at Shiloh to be carried into the decisive battle.[23]

The battle was lost. The Ark was taken. The Philistines carried it off as booty to their city of Ashdod, and all Palestine came under their rule and took their name. The shrine at Shiloh was destroyed.[24] To any outside observer, untouched by revelation, it would certainly have appeared that the curious episode of the twelve half-civilized wandering tribes who thought that the Creator of the Universe was with them had now come to its inevitable, inglorious end.

But the Philistines were uncomfortable with the Ark of the Covenant. The First Book of Samuel tells of an idol flung off its pedestal in Ashdod, and of a plague that struck Ashdod and every Philistine city to which the Ark was subsequently taken. Eventually the conquerors meekly returned the greatest prize of their victorious campaign to their beaten enemy, an act virtually impossible to explain except by the kind of events described in the Biblical narrative.[25] Still the Philistines kept the Ark and the Israelites under close surveillance and tight control; and Israel, stunned by the disaster at Aphek, appears to have found little consolation even in the remarkable providence of the Ark's return[26]—a fact which goes far to explain how necessary it was, at that early stage in their history as the Chosen People, for their God to be associated with military success.

Years passed—some dark and silent, some lit briefly and harshly by flares of open resistance that flickered for a time, only to die away into frustration and smoldering resentment. In this grim hour emerged Samuel, Israel's first primarily spiritual leader since Moses. He kept alive Israel's consciousness of a special destiny and unity as a people, even under alien domination. But Samuel, more priest than general, had to wait for real hope of liberation until his old age, when from beyond the Jordan where some Israelites still lived free, where Moses had passed the torch to Joshua for the conquest of Canaan, there came forth a proud and passionate man, battle-proven, ready and eager to be the champion of his oppressed people. His name was Saul. Upon popular acclamation, Samuel anointed him the first King of Israel.[27]

Other nations and settled peoples of the Middle East by then had kings as a matter of course. But in Israel the step to monarchy was taken reluctantly and with grave foreboding,[28] only under the compulsion of military necessity. To regain their freedom, the people must be united under firmly established, legitimate political and military authority. But it was hard to grasp the proper role of a king over a people committed for all time, by the most solemn of covenants, to the King of Kings. In truth, that royal role meant far more than anyone in Israel could then have dreamed.

The king and liberator of so unique a nation needed to combine the qualities of Saul and of Samuel, to be both militant and devout, both commander and intercessor. In all the four and a half centuries during which there was a crowned king in Israel, only one man attained and maintained this high and difficult standard. He was the king who established that standard, setting an example which none of his many successors wielding temporal power was ever able to match.

This was David, soldier, general, king . . . and psalmist and prophet, epic hero and humble worshipper of Yahweh.[29] David brought Israel from the depths of disaster to the heights of triumph and prosperity. That spectacular ascent left his people with a dream which centuries of disappointment, pettiness and corruption in high places, internal strife and foreign invasions, could neither dim nor extinguish, but only brighten by contrast. That the dream was conceived primarily in material terms was inevitable, for the Israelites were never a philosophic people—they would probably have soon argued themselves out of their covenant with God, through intellectual pride, if they had been. Yet as time passed their dream of an ideal king, the Messiah—the "Anointed One," in Greek "Christ"—was shot through with flashes and gleams of a kingdom transcending this world, whose origins lay outside time.

So it was David who did what Saul had hoped, but failed to do. Saul was a brave man, an able general and a sincere believer in Yahweh, capable of commanding great respect and personal devotion; but he was too emotional, headstrong and self-willed to be an effective ruler. Some have suggested that in his later years he was a victim of mental illness.[30] He harried the Philistines and won some significant victories, but he quarrelled with Samuel, flouting his priestly and prophetic authority, himself offering sacrifices to Yahweh after Samuel had told him to wait and first purify himself of sin.[31] So Samuel went, at God's command, to the house of Jesse in Bethlehem of Judah, where he secretly anointed David, the youngest of Jesse's eight sons, as king and Saul's successor. Thus the scepter of Israel passed to the tribe of Judah, as the patriarch Jacob's prophecy had long ago foretold.[32]

The Biblical narrative clearly implies that Samuel's anointing of David remained unknown to Saul, even later when he became consumed with jealousy of the young, handsome, talented and successful David. Yet since we are told that it was done in the presence of Jesse's entire family, including at least his seven other sons and very likely their wives and children as well, there is good reason to suspect that some hint of a secret so great which was known to so many would have come to Saul, inflaming his jealousy all the more. Be that as it may, we are told how David soothed Saul by his music, killed the Philistine champion Goliath and at least a hundred other Philistines single-handed, became the closest friend of Saul's dashing son Jonathan, and married Saul's daughter Michal. Saul's jealousy grew until even the entreaties of Jonathan and Michal could no longer control it. Saul hurled a spear at David, pursued him into his sanctuary with Samuel at Ramah, and dogged his trail all over the Promised Land.[33] David's personal quality in this extraordinarily trying and dangerous situation is best shown by the account of his penetration by night into Saul's camp on the hill of Hachilah by the Jeshimon road:

> So David and Abishai went to the army by night; and there lay Saul sleeping within the encampment, with his spear stuck in the ground at his head; and Abner and the army lay around him. Then said Abishai to David, "God has given your enemy into your hand this day; now therefore let me pin him to the earth with one stroke of the spear, and I will not strike him twice." But David said to Abishai, "Do not destroy him, for who can put forth his hand against the LORD's anointed, and be guiltless?" And David said, "As the LORD lives, the LORD will smite him; or his day shall come to die, or he shall go down into battle and perish. The LORD forbid that I should put forth my hand against the LORD's anointed; but take now the spear that is at his head, and the jar of water, and let us go." So David

took the spear and the jar of water from Saul's head; and they went away.[34]

We know of no other king of that far-distant, cruel age, with the possible exception of Akhenaten of Egypt, who would have been morally capable of such forbearance.

David was a true leader of men, of the kind who inspires intense personal devotion; even in his darkest hour he had with him no less than six hundred men who would risk everything for him, even unto death.[35] But most of the Israelites feared Saul even more than they loved David, and at length he was driven into the arms of the Philistines. They received him gladly, his prowess having become famous throughout the land. Achish of Gath gave him the town of Ziklag to rule, and David campaigned in the Negev desert, pretending to Achish that he was raiding Judah periodically, though in fact he never bore arms against his brother Israelites, campaigning exclusively against desert nomads.[36]

Taking advantage of the division and troubles in Israel and the weakening of Saul, the Philistines mounted a major assault against Israel on a familiar battleground, the plain of Jezreel, where Barak and Deborah had vanquished Sisera the Canaanite. The armies met at Mount Gilboa on the edge of the plain. Achish had ordered David to accompany the Philistine army, but the other Philistine princes, fearing that David would turn on them once battle was joined, demanded that he return to Ziklag. Spared a terrible and perhaps fatal choice, David agreed with alacrity. Samuel had died, but the desperate Saul, just before the battle, attempted to recall him to life through a "medium," the witch of Endor. The Book of Samuel tells us that Samuel appeared at the witch's call to give Saul a last warning from God that David was now His anointed king; but there being no other instance in all the history of the Faith of God's use of such means to speak to men, it seems most probable that the vision of Samuel was a product of Saul's own now deeply disordered imagination. Saul's conscience must for long have been suggesting to him that David was the new anointed king, even if he had not by this time heard a reliable report of the anointing ceremony at Jesse's house. Terrified by the apparition of Samuel, faint from a self-imposed fast, still Saul would not yield to David. He joined battle with the Philistines; his dispirited men were cut to pieces, Jonathan and two of his other sons were killed, and the first king of Israel, badly wounded, took his own life.[37]

Once again the Philistines were masters of the Promised Land. Beyond the Jordan, whence Saul had come, his son Ishbaal maintained a tenuous authority. But Israel did not yet generally recognize the principle of hereditary royal succession (David was to establish it) and in any case Ishbaal proved wholly ineffectual. The tribe of Judah anointed David king at Hebron, while presumably the Philistines continued to regard him as their vassal. After an indecisive trial of arms with David, Ishbaal and his (formerly Saul's) general Abner opened negotiations with him, during the course of which both Ishbaal and Abner were assassinated, apparently without David's prior knowledge or complicity. David was then anointed king of Israel by the elders of the whole people, with universal acclaim.[38]

Too late the Philistines realized that for them the game was up. History, so full of sudden unexpected reversals of fortune, shows none more startling and complete than that which now overtook these iron men from the western seas. In two short years they plunged from total victory over Israel under King Saul at Mount Gilboa to total defeat by Israel under King David at the Valley of the Rephaim near Jerusalem. Their kings became David's vassals, as he had so recently been their vassal. Never again did the Philistines play a significant part in the history of that land to which, by an ironic chance, they nevertheless left their name, as Palestine.[39]

It was through David that the promise of the Holy Land was finally fulfilled. During his reign Israel occupied and ruled the whole land from the mountains of Lebanon, Galilee and the Jordan to the desert and the sea. For his capital David chose Jerusalem, the city of Melchisedek, located in the central highlands not far from where Joshua had crossed the Jordan, long occupied by the Jebusites and protected by strong natural defenses as well as by formidable walls. Israel had never taken Jerusalem at any time during the conquest of Canaan. But David's soldiers penetrated its walls through an underground water conduit, and Jerusalem fell to him seven and a half years after the death of Saul, very close to the year 1000 B.C.[40]

To Jerusalem David brought the Ark of the Covenant, which had lain neglected at the town of Kiriath-jearim ever since the triumphant Philistines had so strangely sent it back to defeated Israel. Now the Ark was welcomed with joy and ceremony and sacrifice; David himself danced and sang before it in the streets.[41] And when the prophet Nathan, speaking in God's name, promised David and his heirs a throne forever, this victorious monarch, now one of the most powerful rulers in the world, replied in these extraordinary words:

> Who am I, O Lord GOD, and what is my house, that thou hast brought me thus far? And yet this was a small thing in thy eyes, O Lord GOD; thou hast spoken also of thy servant's house for a great while to come, and hast shown me future generations [and this is the determination of human fate],[42] O Lord GOD! And what more can David say to thee? For thou knowest thy servant, O Lord GOD! Because of thy promise, and according to thy own heart, thou hast wrought all this greatness, to make thy servant know it. Therefore thou art great, O LORD God, for there is none like thee, and there is no God besides thee, according to all that we have heard with our ears. What other nation on earth is like thy people Israel, whom God went to redeem to be his people, making himself a name, and doing for them great and terrible things, by driving out before his people a nation and its gods? And thou didst establish for thyself thy people Israel to be thy people for ever; and thou, O LORD, didst become their God. And now, O LORD God, confirm for ever the word which thou hast spoken concern-

ing thy servant and concerning his house, and do as thou hast spoken; and thy name will be magnified for ever, saying "The Lord of hosts is God over Israel," and the house of thy servant David will be established before thee. For thou, O LORD of hosts, the God of Israel, hast made this revelation to thy servant, saying, "I will build you a house"; therefore thy servant has found courage to pray this prayer to thee.[43]

Despite the efforts of modern Scriptural commentators to make of this magnificent prayer—and of the "royal" psalms which carry its themes even further—no more than a testament to the earthly pretensions of a reigning dynasty,[44] it is filled with the echoes of a message far greater, though still very imperfectly understood. Over the years it became clear, as the earthly fortunes of David's dynasty waned to the vanishing point, that something more than that must have been meant. In this Divine promise conveyed by Nathan is the foundation of the growing messianic hope of the people of Israel during the millennium separating David from Christ.[45]

Still more revealing is the 110th Psalm. In it we sense once again a sublime truth struggling for expression through human minds and in human words which can never be even remotely adequate to convey its sublimity. It is no accident that many of the most important passages of the Old Testament, foreshadowing the coming of the Son of God, are desperately difficult to understand and translate, because what they sought to say was so far beyond the reach of human imagination before the Incarnation. We must never forget that, despite all the pretensions reflected in most modern study of "comparative religions," the Incarnation is unique in the religious history of the world. Our present and historic familiarity with the idea, stupendous as it is, tends to blind us to how utterly strange it would have seemed when suggested in advance, especially in the context of the absolute monotheism of believing Jews.[46] When to the inherent difficulties of contemporary understanding and later translation are added the open hostility of rationalist exegetes in our own day and the timid evasions of scholars wishing to avoid theological controversy, the result is likely to be intellectual chaos such as the extraordinary variety in the translations of the 110th Psalm reveals.[47]

Like many of the other psalms, this one is specifically attributed to David himself. In conformity with the tendency so widespread among scholars, at least until recently, to reject out of hand the authorship and date assigned to older Old Testament books in their own text—the attitude which gave rise to the documentary hypothesis for the books of Moses—the Davidic psalms had been generally assumed to be much later compositions. But the current trend of scholarship runs counter to this assumption,[48] which has been shaken to its foundations by the rapidly accumulating literary and linguistic evidence from the tablets of Ugarit, a Canaanite city on the Syrian coast, showing that the language, style and many of the expressions in the psalms date back at least to the time of David, and in a number of cases even earlier. It is the conclusion of Mitchell Dahood, one of the world's foremost authorities on the Ugaritic texts, that from their evidence the 110th Psalm should be dated to the tenth century (1000-900) B.C.—which is the century of David.[49]

Here, then, are David's own words, as best we can reconstruct them from an extremely difficult text, in which the Greek of the Septuagint needs to be used to clarify the almost incomprehensible Hebrew:

> The LORD says to my lord:
> "Sit at my right hand,
> till I make your enemies your footstool."
> The LORD sends forth from Zion your mighty scepter.
> Rule in the midst of your foes!
> [With thee is the principality in the day of thy strength:
> in the brightness of the saints:
> from the womb before the day star I begot thee.][50]
> The LORD has sworn
> and will not change his mind,
> "You are a priest for ever
> after the order of Melchisedek."[51]

In interpreting the first line of this psalm we have the extraordinary benefit of an explicit statement by Jesus Himself, as reported in the Gospel of Matthew:

> Now while the Pharisees were gathered together, Jesus asked them a question, saying, "What do you think of the Christ? Whose son is he?" They said to him, "The son of David." He said to them, "How is it then that David, inspired by the Spirit, calls him Lord, saying,
>
>   'The Lord said to my Lord,
>   Sit at my right hand,
>   till I put thy enemies under thy feet'?
> If David thus calls him Lord, how is he his son?" And no one was able to answer him with a word, nor from that day did any one dare to ask him any more questions.[52]

Thus was the divinity of David's descendant—the Messiah—foreshadowed, and His eternal priesthood explicitly proclaimed. As evocative as it is mysterious, the phrase St. Jerome particularly loved, describing the Messiah's begetting— "from the womb before the day star I begot thee" in the Greek text, "from the womb of the dawn to you the dew of your youth" in the Hebrew[53]—despite all obscurities is like being brought back again to the first chapter of Genesis, but this time in the person of a human Savior-King Who was to transform the throne of David into the throne of God.

Yet David, greatest of all the crowned kings of Israel, was still very much a son of Adam. The almost irresistible temptations growing out of wealth and power began to work on him, and he succumbed. Not satisfied by completing

the conquest of the Promised Land, he struck outward in quest of empire, subjugating Ammon to the east, Moab and Edom to the south, and Aram to the
northeast including Damascus and reaching all the way to the Euphrates River.
David thus made Israel fully the equal of any power in the world of his time
(for Egypt and Mesopotamia persisted in their weakness). It was in the course
of these campaigns that he coveted Bathsheba, the wife of a loyal soldier in
his army, committed adultery with her, and ordered that her husband Uriah be
abandoned to the enemy in battle so that he would be killed. Thereby the anointed
King of Israel violated, in quick succession, three of the ten commandments
enshrined within the Ark of the Covenant that he had brought to Jerusalem with
such rejoicing.[54]

So once again, as on that last day in Eden, there came a judgment, this time
pronounced through the prophet Nathan who had conveyed God's towering promise to David's dynasty—a judgment fearfully executed in the years ahead:

> "Thus says the LORD, the God of Israel, 'I anointed you king over Israel,
> and I delivered you out of the hand of Saul; and I gave you your master's
> house, and your master's wives into your bosom, and gave you the house
> of Israel and of Judah; and if this were too little, I would add to you as
> much more. Why have you despised the word of the LORD, to do what
> is evil in his sight? You have smitten Uriah the Hittite with the sword, and
> have taken his wife to be your wife, and have slain him with the sword
> of the Ammonites. Now therefore the sword shall never depart from your
> house, because you have despised me, and have taken the wife of Uriah
> the Hittite to be your wife.' . . . David said to Nathan, "I have sinned against
> the LORD." And Nathan said to David, "The LORD also has put away
> your sin; you shall not die. Nevertheless, because by this deed you have
> utterly scorned the LORD, the child that is born to you shall die." Then
> Nathan went to his house.[55]

Bathsheba's first son by David did indeed die soon afterward; but later she
became the mother of Solomon. David's son Absalom murdered his brother
Amnon; Absalom in turn rose in rebellion against his father and was slain by
Joab, David's general. The king, who had given strict orders against this, cried
out in frantic grief. "Now therefore the sword shall never depart from your
house" . . . and it followed him to the edge of the grave when, fast failing
in mind and body, he abdicated in favor of Solomon in order to prevent another
son, Adonijah, from seizing the throne to which he had brought such power,
but was now powerless to defend. Thereupon Solomon had Adonijah murdered
and General Joab struck dead as he clung to the horns of the altar of God in
the tabernacle housing the Ark of the Covenant.[56]

Having thus summarily disposed of all major rivals and inherited a large
and flourishing realm, Solomon—still a young man and apparently without his
father's ambition for military victories—settled down, along with his people,
to enjoy its fruits. His long reign was a period of prosperity unequalled in the

history of Israel. Though shadows of God's judgment clouded the beginning
and end of this great and famous reign, the blessings of peace and unity marked
its middle years indelibly upon popular memory, as the age of "Solomon in
all his glory." Solomon's international fame, his reputation for wisdom, and
the rich embassies coming from distant lands to his court at Jerusalem became
themes of Hebrew song and story for centuries.[57] Israelite trade extended through
Arabia all the way to tropical Africa, and through the great Phoenician city of
Tyre on the Mediterranean (in what is now Lebanon) it reached across that sea
perhaps as far as Spain.[58] But Solomon's supreme accomplishment in the eyes
of posterity—and doubtless in his own eyes as well—was the building of the
temple of the Lord in Jerusalem, fulfilling a significant element in the prophecy
of Nathan, and in a sense prefiguring the Incarnation since God condescended
to take a material dwelling place among His people.[59]

Solomon's temple—the first of three, and only three, that were to stand in
that place—was under construction for seven years and was dedicated in the
eleventh year of his reign, about 950 B.C.[60] Its stone and wood were brought
from Phoenicia by Israelite labor, under the terms of an agreement with King
Hiram of Tyre. Much of the design and craftsmanship of the temple was Phoenician, for the Israelites had little or no architectural knowledge or tradition;[61]
but the temple was looked upon as the direct successor of the little tabernacle
of the wilderness wandering under Moses. Like the desert tabernacle, the temple was built to house in a fitting manner the Ark of the Covenant;[62] we are
explicitly told once again that "there was nothing in the ark except the two tablets
of stone which Moses put there at Horeb, where the LORD made a covenant
with the people of Israel, when they came out of the land of Egypt."[63] It was
the Ark that made Solomon's temple unique in the world.[64]

So important was Solomon's temple in the history and faith of Israel that
it is well to make a special effort to visualize it. Within its precincts the faithful
gathered from all over the Promised Land for the great annual feasts. There
the prophets spoke; in the third and last temple on the site where Solomon had
built, Jesus preached.

Occupying the rocky eminence atop Jerusalem's eastern hill, now crowned
by the Muslim Dome of the Rock—that rock having very likely been the actual
base of the Holy of Holies in Solomon's temple[65]—the temple stood in a great
courtyard which included Solomon's royal palace. It was probably approached
by a series of steps ascending to a broad platform. Flanking the steps at the
bottom were an altar 15 feet high for animal sacrifices on a grand scale, and
the famous bronze "sea," 15 feet across and weighing over 25 tons, supported
by twelve sculptured oxen—a huge basin filled with water for the ritual purification of the priests. Flanking the steps at the top were two free-standing bronze
pillars, more than 35 feet high and 18 feet around, cast (like all the temple
bronzework) by a Tyrian artist and named by him Jachin and Boaz. Between

the two bronze pillars and the actual entrance to the temple was an open porch. The main chamber of the temple, the Holy Place or sanctuary, was 60 feet long, 30 feet wide and 40 feet high; it held ten of the *menorah*—the famous seven-branched candlestick of Israel—an altar for incense, and a table for the "loaves of offering," which were twelve cakes made from pure wheat flour, representing the twelve tribes of Israel. The altar and table were of gold-plated cedar wood.[66]

Finally the Holy of Holies, a perfect windowless 30-foot cube, stood at the far end of the temple, opposite the entrance and probably raised above floor level, separated from the main chamber by a curtain through which the carrying poles of the Ark were thrust. In this lightless room the Ark of the Covenant reposed beneath the outstretched nine-foot wings of two cherubim of gold-plated wood—angels, probably still represented as in the desert by winged human figures, but invisible to the worshippers in the Temple. There, "enthroned upon the cherubim," Yahweh Himself was thought in a special sense to dwell, the darkness of the Holy of Holies corresponding to the divine cloud which had descended upon Mount Sinai before the fire burst forth from it.[67]

Thus was the covenant of Sinai enshrined, and its Author honored; and thus was the promise of the land fulfilled. All Palestine, and more, belonged to the house of David. But now, as in Egypt after the death of Joseph, Israel was once more to be taught her hardest lesson—that "My kingship is not of this world";[68] that the promises to Abraham and to Moses and to David had a meaning and a purpose far transcending material blessings and temporal dominion; that the triumphant monarchy of David and Solomon was only a stage—and an early stage, never to be repeated—in the fulfillment of the ultimate promise foreshadowed in God's first words to Abraham. Material blessings and temporal dominion were more likely to be an obstacle than a highroad to the attainment of that ultimate promise. Since the Fall man cannot stand prosperity for long. Not so would his rescue come.

Thus for all its glory the reign of Solomon ultimately degenerated into a tyranny, in which free-born Israelites were burdened with crushing taxation and conscripted in large numbers for forced labor on the king's mighty building projects, after the manner of the Pharaohs of Egypt whom they had escaped. Wealth was concentrated in the capital and at the port city of Ezion-geber built at the head of the Gulf of Aqaba connecting with the Red Sea. For the first time Israel had a class of the rich and powerful, whom the farmers and herdsmen increasingly resented. In his old age Solomon was to a large extent dominated by the women of his harem; he allowed them to build shrines to their favorite idols and even came himself to worship with them, in defiance of the First Commandment. Nevertheless Solomon's personal prestige remained so high that the gathering storm of revolt did not break while he lived. He retained the whole empire of David, with the significant exception of Damascus—which rebelled and became an independent state—and some cities along the Bay of Acre which he had to sell to the king of Tyre to help pay off his mounting debts. But immediately after Solomon's death in 922 B.C. the kingdom of the Promised Land split in two, not to be reunited as an independent state until the time of the Maccabees more than 750 years later.[69]

Solomon's son and successor Rehoboam, harsh and overbearing, sought to continue his father's oppression without the benefit of his father's prestige. The ten tribes of the north promptly rose in revolt under Jeroboam, an official whom Solomon had banished, and established their independence under the name of the Kingdom of Israel. Rehoboam retained for the dynasty of David only the southern half of Palestine, including Jerusalem but otherwise consisting mostly of uninhabitable desert, as the Kingdom of Judah.[70]

Prospects for prompt forcible reunion of the two kingdoms by either of their kings were virtually eliminated by the effects of a devastating attack by Sheshonk I, the Libyan general who had seized power from the faltering, obscure Pharaohs of Egypt's Twenty-First Dynasty during Solomon's reign. In the fifth year of King Rehoboam (917 B.C.) Sheshonk ravaged Palestine from end to end. He only spared Jerusalem upon receiving from Rehoboam a tribute so large that the Israelite king had to strip the gold from his palace and even from parts of the Temple to pay it. Though immediately afterward Egypt fell back again into weakness and internal instability, this single campaign and the heavy blows struck by Sheshonk played an important part in perpetuating the division of the people Israel.[71]

Thus, well within living memory of David, the Promised Land lay sundered and dangerously weakened, the Chosen People spilling their brothers' blood upon its soil, the two paltry successor states tempting prey for any new aggressive power arising in the Middle East. What now of the Promise and the Covenant?

NOTES

[1] Deuteronomy 34:1-6. The view of Palestine from Mount Nebo is graphically described by Rogers MacVeagh and Thomas B. Costain, *Joshua* (New York, 1948), pp. 59-62.

[2] This assessment of Joshua is based on MacVeagh and Costain's striking re-creation of his personality and career, summed up in pp. 159-162 and 211-214 of their *Joshua*.

[3] e.g., Otto Eissfeldt in *The Cambridge Ancient History*, Volume II, Part 2 (3rd ed.), (Cambridge, England, 1975), pp. 329-330; *The Jerome Biblical Commentary*, ed. Raymond E. Brown et al (Englewood Cliffs NJ, 1968), I, 123-124; John L. McKenzie, *The World of the Judges* (Englewood Cliffs NJ, 1966), *passim*.

[4] Yehezkel Kaufmann, *The Religion of Israel from Its Beginnings to the Babylonian Exile* (Chicago, 1960), pp. 245-247.

[5] G. Ernest Wright, *Biblical Archaeology*, 2nd ed. (Philadelphia, 1962), pp. 80-84; John Bright, *A History of Israel*, 3d ed. (Philadelphia, 1981), pp. 130-133; *Cambridge Ancient History* II (2) (3rd ed.), 334-337; *Jerome Biblical Commentary*, I, 136. These

conclusions are based on the generally, though not universally accepted identifications of the ruins of Eglon with the modern Tell el-Hesi and of Debir with Tell Beit Mirsim; also upon the identifications of Lachish with the modern Tell ed-Duweir and of Hazor with Tell el-Qadah, which appear to be accepted by all. (See Note 14, below, for Hazor.) That the conquest of the hill country of Palestine by the Israelites did take place at approximately this time (c. 1225-1175 B.C.) is accepted by most historians and archeologists of Palestine today, even those who have made considerable efforts to cast doubt on the archeological evidence of the destruction of the Canaanite towns by Joshua (e.g. Robert G. Boling, *The Anchor Bible: Joshua* [Garden City NY, 1982], particularly pp. 128-129).

[6] K. A. Kitchen, *Ancient Orient and Old Testament* (Chicago, 1966), p. 65.

[7] Joshua 6:25; Kitchen, *Ancient Orient and Old Testament*, pp. 62-63; Kathleen M. Kenyon, *Archaeology in the Holy Land*, 3rd ed. (New York, 1970), pp. 210-211; J. A. Thompson, *The Bible and Archaeology* (Grand Rapids MI, 1962), pp. 59-62. MacVeagh and Costain, *Joshua*, pp. 105-120, present an imaginative and plausible reconstruction of how the walls of Jericho might have fallen before Joshua. Though the archeological evidence they cite for a collapse of the walls at the time of Joshua's invasion is no longer held to be valid in light of Miss Kenyon's subsequent excavations, their point about the actual nature of Jericho's walls, as compared with the mental picture we customarily have of them, is very well taken. As they remind us, while we are inclined to imagine the walls of Jericho as imposing structures of solid masonry such as surrounded European cities in the Middle Ages, in fact, like most city walls in the Middle East at that time, they were built on rubble and held together only by crumbling mud-brick, and at that low point in Jericho's long history were probably in a very bad state of repair.

[8] Two examples, among many which might be mentioned, are the preservation of highly specific and accurate accounts of the settlement of Iceland by the Norsemen (the *Landnamabòk*) and of New Zealand by the Maoris.

[9] For a thorough survey of the geography of Palestine see *Jerome Biblical Commentary*, II, 633-652.

[10] Bright, *History of Israel*, pp. 114-118; Roland de Vaux, *Ancient Israel, Its Life and Institutions* (New York, 1960), pp. 444-446.

[11] Joshua 10:9-14; MacVeagh and Costain, *Joshua*, pp. 145-162; Giuseppe Ricciotti, *The History of Israel* (Milwaukee, 1955), I, 234-235.

[12] Ricciotti, *History of Israel*, I, 235.

[13] See William Thomas Walsh, *Our Lady of Fatima* (New York, 1947) for the best, most historically sound account of the great Marian apparitions at Fatima in the critical year 1917, discussed at length in Volume VI of this history.

[14] Joshua 10:29-43, 11:1-14; MacVeagh and Costain, *Joshua*, pp. 163-197. Hazor's population at the time is estimated to have been 40,000 and its area 175 acres, making it "one of the great cities of Syria and Palestine" (Wright, *Biblical Archaeology*, p. 83). Hazor's excavator states: "The striking similarity between the size of Hazor as revealed by the excavations and its description in the Bible . . . leave little doubt, it seems, that we actually found the Canaanite city of Jabin that was destroyed by Joshua" (Yigael Yadin, *Hazor, the Rediscovery of a Great Citadel of the Bible* [London, 1975], p. 145).

[15] Wright, *Biblical Archaeology*, p. 90; Kenyon, *Archaeology in the Holy Land*, pp. 235-237; Bright, *History of Israel*, pp. 118-119, 137-138, 142-143, 170-171.

[16] Such is the obvious explanation for the references in the Book of Judges to a conquest of Hebron and Debir by the tribe of Judah acting separately, and of Bethel (presuming it to be identical with Ai) by the Joseph tribes, even though Joshua had already taken these cities. The assumption that the opening words of the Book of Judges, which specifically place these campaigns after the death of Joshua, are merely a later editorial

harmonization is entirely gratuitous. See Kitchen, *Ancient Orient and Old Testament*, p. 69n, for a refreshingly common-sense comment on the evanescence of supposed contradictions between Judges 1 and the account of the conquest in the Book of Joshua, of which so much is made by Old Testament "higher criticism," e.g. McKenzie, *World of the Judges*, pp. 71-75.

[17] Judges 3:9-10. The Revised Standard Version uses the traditional "Mesopotamia" for the homeland of Othniel's foes, but more recent translations hold that Edom in the Negev is meant, which seems much more reasonable in light of the contemporary historical situation (*The Jerusalem Bible*, ed. Alexander Jones [New York, 1966] [Old Testament], p. 309, Note 3d; *Jerome Biblical Commentary*, I, 152).

[18] Judges 3:26-30.

[19] Judges 7:20, 6:1-6, 7:7-25.

[20] Judges 9:1-6, 50-56.

[21] Judges 11:29-40. De Vaux, *Ancient Israel*, p. 442, says that Jephthah's sacrifice of his daughter was regarded by his fellow Israelites "as a quite extraordinary and shocking incident."

[22] Judges 4-5; McKenzie, *World of the Judges*, pp. 126-130; Bright, *History of Israel*, pp. 179-180. The near-contemporaneity of the Song of Deborah with the battle it commemorates is generally agreed upon, as is the probable date of the battle (c. 1125 B.C.). Thus it is here, at long last, that we leave the period for which the reality of major historical events recounted in the Old Testament is widely challenged. The nature and scope of the challenges to the historicity of the Pentateuch, Joshua and Judges 1-2, and the obstinacy with which those challenges have been maintained in the face of the most imposing body of continuous historical documentation for so early a period existing anywhere in the world, which in recent years has been increasingly confirmed by independent evidence both from archeology and from the records of other contemporary nations, makes a very interesting study in bias.

[23] Bright, *History of Israel*, pp. 185-186. For the origin of the Philistines see *Cambridge Ancient History* II (2) (3rd ed.), 512-513; for their attack on Egypt during the reign of Ramses III see *ibid.*, pp. 242-243.

[24] 1 Samuel 4 and 5:1; Bright, *History of Israel*, p. 186; Yohanan Aharoni, *The Land of the Bible, a Historical Geography* (Philadelphia, 1967), pp. 252-253.

[25] 1 Samuel 5-6; *Jerome Biblical Commentary*, I, 167. Recent archeological evidence from Ashdod casts some doubt on the Biblical account of the fall of the idol of the male god Dagon, since only a mother-goddess seems to have been worshipped in the city at this period (Moshe Dothan, "Ashdod of the Philistines," *New Directions in Biblical Archaeology*, ed. David N. Freedman and Jonas C. Greenfield [New York, 1969], pp. 19-20). But the idol which fell could easily have been hers.

[26] Bright, *History of Israel*, p. 186.

[27] *Ibid.*, pp. 186-188. Saul had led a victorious campaign against the Ammonites shortly before or after he was proclaimed king. There appear to be three separate traditions of the actual circumstances of his anointing and acclamation, which are presented but not fully harmonized in 1 Samuel 9-11.

[28] Bright, *History of Israel*, pp. 188-190. As Bright rightly points out, the doubts and warnings about the monarchy voiced by Samuel in 1 Samuel 8 and 12 ought not to be regarded as simply "a reflection of subsequent bitter experience with the monarchy, as so many have done" since "it can hardly be doubted that a step as drastic as this, and involving such a break with tradition, evoked opposition from the beginning" (p. 188).

[29] The nature of David's personal faith emerges with particular clarity in the account of his meetings with the prophet Nathan (2 Samuel 7 and 12) and is emphasized by Yves

Congar, *The Mystery of the Temple* (Westminster MD, 1962), pp. 23, 61. For David's authorship of the psalms attributed to him, see *Jerusalem Bible* (Old Testament), pp. 783-784.

[30] Paul Heinisch, *History of the Old Testament* (Collegeville MN, 1952), pp. 173-175.

[31] *Ibid.*, pp. 165-167. During the early history of the Israelite monarchy it seems to have been regarded as permissible on special occasions for the king, even though not a priest, to offer sacrifice (Paul Heinisch, *Christ in Prophecy* [Collegeville MN, 1956], pp. 59-61).

[32] 1 Samuel 16:1-13; Heinisch, *History of the Old Testament*, p. 167.

[33] Heinisch, *History of the Old Testament*, pp. 167-170; Bright, *History of Israel*, pp. 192-193. Bright explains why the story of David and Goliath is probably historically reliable despite the brief conflicting reference in 2 Samuel 21:19 attributing the slaying of Goliath to an otherwise unknown Elhanan.

[34] 1 Samuel 26:7-12; Bright, *History of Israel*, p. 179.

[35] Heinisch, *History of the Old Testament*, pp. 170-171.

[36] *Ibid.*, pp. 171-172.

[37] *Ibid.*, pp. 172-173.

[38] 2 Samuel 2-5:5; Bright, *History of Israel*, pp. 195-197.

[39] 2 Samuel 5:17-25, 8:1; Bright, *History of Israel*, pp. 198-199. Despite its position in the narrative, it seems that David's defeat of the Philistines at the Valley of the Rephaim came before, not after he took Jerusalem (Bright, *op. cit.*, p. 198n).

[40] Bright, *History of Israel*, pp. 201-202; Kenyon, *Archaeology in the Holy Land*, pp. 240-243; 2 Samuel 5:5. The first precise date in the history of Israel that can be fixed with a high degree of probability is that of the death of Solomon, in 922 B.C. 2 Samuel 5:4 and 1 Kings 11:42 ascribe to David and Solomon reigns of 40 years each. While this is well known as a conventional figure in the Old Testament, both of these monarchs did have long reigns and therefore in their case it is probably close to the truth. Therefore David's anointing as king and taking of Jerusalem would have occurred just about 1000 B.C. (Bright, *History of Israel*, pp. 195n and 211n).

[41] 2 Samuel 6.

[42] Claus Schedl, *History of the Old Testament* (New York, 1972), III, 204, presents a brilliant exposition, drawing also on the analyses of other recent scholars, on the meaning of the mysterious phrase which defeated the translators of the Jerusalem Bible and was rendered "and hast shown me future generations" by the Revised Standard Version. The Hebrew is *torat ha'adam*, literally "the law for man." Schedl rightly calls these words "the whole leit-motiv of the statement." See also Schedl's important discussion of the meaning of the Hebrew word *'olam*, traditionally (and rightly, it would appear) translated "forever" (*ibid.*, p. 203), though now often translated "for years to come."

[43] 2 Samuel 7:18-24.

[44] e.g., de Vaux, *Ancient Israel*, pp. 108-110, and Bright, *History of Israel*, pp. 224-228. The most important of the "royal psalms" are 2, 72, and 110. Others are 18, 20, 21, 45, 89, 101, and 132.

[45] On this see particularly Congar, *Mystery of the Temple*, pp. 30-34, 44-45.

[46] No one has put this truth better than G. K. Chesterton, speaking of Jesus of Nazareth and Who He was: "It were better to rend our robes with a great cry against blasphemy, like Caiaphas in the judgment, or to lay hold of the man as a maniac possessed of devils like the kinsmen and the crowd, rather than to stand stupidly debating fine shades of pantheism in the presence of so catastrophic a claim. There is more in the wisdom that is one with surprise in any simple person, full of the sensitiveness of simplicity, who should expect the grass to wither and the birds to drop dead out of the air, when a strolling carpenter's apprentice said calmly and almost carelessly, like one looking over his

shoulder: "Before Abraham was, I am.'" (*The Everlasting Man* [New York, 1955], p. 201).

⁴⁷ See Note 50, below.

⁴⁸ K. A. Kitchen, *The Bible in Its World* (Downers Grove IL, 1977), pp. 94-100; Eugene H. Maly, *The World of David and Solomon* (Englewood Cliffs NJ, 1966), p. 91.

⁴⁹ Mitchell Dahood, *The Anchor Bible: Psalms I (1-50)* (New York, 1966), pp. xviii-xxx; William F. Albright, "The Impact of Archaeology on Biblical Research—1966," *New Directions in Biblical Archaeology*, pp. 9-10.

⁵⁰ The reader may judge for himself the chaos produced by recent attempts to re-translate or rewrite this third verse of the 110th Psalm, given in the text as it appears in the Catholic Douay version, by comparing the same verse as it appears in three distinguished recent translations: "Your people will offer themselves freely on the day you lead your host upon the holy mountains. From the womb of the morning like dew your youth will come to you" (Revised Standard Version); "Royal dignity was yours from the day you were born, on the holy mountains, royal from the womb, from the dawn of your earliest days" (Jerusalem Bible); "In the battle with your foes he was your Strong One, your Valiant as on the day of your conquest. When the Holy One appeared he was your Comforter, the dawn of life for you, the dew of your youth" (Anchor Bible). The Hebrew text is clearly corrupt, but ancient versions emphasize the element of mystery in the begetting (*Jerome Biblical Commentary*, I, 596). In contrast to the Hebrew text, the Greek of the Septuagint is quite clear, and is the basis for the Douay translation: Μετα σου η αρχη εν ημερα της δυναμεως σου, εν ταις λαμπροτησι των αγιων σου εκ γαστρος προ Εω-σφορου εγεννησα σε. Evidence from the Dead Sea scrolls has tended to support the high reliability of the Greek text of the Septuagint even against the original Hebrew as handed down in the Masoretic text, when the two differ (*Jerome Biblical Commentary*, II, 561-589; Patrick W. Skehan, "The Scrolls and the Old Testament Text," *New Directions in Biblical Archaeology*, pp. 89-100).

⁵¹ Psalms 110:1-4.

⁵² Matthew 22:41-46.

⁵³ For the Greek text, see Footnote 50, above; the literal Hebrew reading is given in *Jerusalem Bible* (Old Testament), p. 897, Note 100e, but is left in a footnote while the translators present quite a different rendering in their version of the psalm.

⁵⁴ 2 Samuel 8-11; Bright, *History of Israel*, pp. 197-201; Aharoni, *Land of the Bible*, pp. 261-264. The weakness of Mesopotamia at this period is indicated by the fact that at the same time David was defeating and subjugating the Aramaeans of Damascus and northeastern Syria, they in turn were defeating the Assyrians east of the great bend of the Euphrates (*Cambridge Ancient History*, II [2] [3rd ed.], 533-535).

⁵⁵ 2 Samuel 12:7-10, 13-15.

⁵⁶ 2 Samuel 13-15, 18; 1 Kings 1-2.

⁵⁷ 1 Kings 3, 5:1-14, 10. The literature collected in the Book of Proverbs—Chapters 10-22 and 25-29 of which are specifically attributed to Solomon in the text—probably did in fact begin to develop during Solomon's reign (Bright, *History of Israel*, pp. 215-216).

⁵⁸ Bright, *History of Israel*, pp. 214-217; Heinisch, *History of the Old Testament*, pp. 196-197; *Cambridge Ancient History*, II (2) (3rd ed.), 525-526.

⁵⁹ Congar, *Mystery of the Temple*, pp. 30-39, 49-53.

⁶⁰ 1 Kings 6:37-38; Bright, *History of Israel*, p. 195n.

⁶¹ 1 Kings 5:15-32, 7:13-14; de Vaux, *Ancient Israel*, pp. 317-318.

⁶² De Vaux, *Ancient Israel*, pp. 294-302. As de Vaux points out, the chapters in the Book of Exodus describing the desert tabernacle (25-27 and 35-38) are probably idealiz-

ed since they depict it as an exact half-size replica of the later temple; nevertheless he says these chapters "do preserve an authentic tradition" (p. 302) of the Ark enshrined with all available ornamentation in a tent sanctuary in the wilderness.

[63] 1 Kings 8:9.

[64] Other sanctuaries existed, notably at Gibeon near Kiriath-jearim where the Ark had been before David moved it to Jerusalem—it had a tabernacle with a mosaic altar where the Zadokite priesthood had presided since the days of Samuel (Heinisch, *History of the Old Testament*, pp. 179, 208)—and at Arad, where a recent dig has revealed it (Yohanan Aharoni, "The Israelite Sanctuary at Arad," *New Directions in Biblical Archaeology*, pp. 25-39); but from the time of Solomon the temple at Jerusalem was unquestionably the center of the worship of Yahweh (de Vaux, *Ancient Israel*, pp. 320-321, 331-339).

[65] For a good statement of the arguments for and against accepting the present location of the Dome of the Rock as the base of the Holy of Holies, inclining toward the conclusion that this hypothesis is correct, see Congar, *Mystery of the Temple*, pp. 101-103.

[66] 1 Kings 6-7; de Vaux, *Ancient Israel*, pp. 312-320, 422; Ricciotti, *History of Israel*, I, 297-302; Wright, *Biblical Archaeology*, pp. 138-141; *Jerome Biblical Commentary*, II, 714-716 (including an excellent diagram). The porch of the Temple was called the Ulam and the main chamber or sanctuary was called the Hekal.

[67] 1 Kings 6:19-32, 8:6-13; de Vaux, *Ancient Israel*, pp. 313-314, 319, 325-327; Ricciotti, *History of Israel*, I, 302. The Holy of Holies was called the Debir. See Chapter Three, above, for the cherubim.

[68] John 18:36.

[69] Bright, *History of Israel*, pp. 220-224, 229; Ricciotti, *History of Israel*, I, 307-309; Kenyon, *Archaeology in the Holy Land*, pp. 254-259, 346. For the Maccabees see Chapter Eleven, below.

[70] Bright, *History of Israel*, pp. 230-232.

[71] *Ibid.*, pp. 229-230; Aharoni, *Land of the Bible*, pp. 283-290; K. A. Kitchen, *The Third Intermediate Period in Egypt* (Warminster, England, 1973), pp. 294-302, 432-447. Kitchen adopts a somewhat earlier date for the death of Solomon and the succession of Rehoboam, and therefore of the invasion of Shoshenk (or Sheshonk) I, than that used by Bright and other authorities whose chronology is followed in this history.

5.

THE DIVIDED KINGDOM (922-721 B.C.)

Do horses run upon rocks?
Does one plow the sea with oxen?
But you have turned justice into poison
and the fruit of righteousness into wormwood—
you who rejoice in Lo-debar,
who say, "Have we not by our own strength
taken Karmain for ourselves?"
"For behold, I will raise up against you a nation,
O house of Israel," says the LORD, the God of hosts,
"and they shall oppress you from the entrance of Hamath
to the Brook of the Arabah."—Amos 6:12-14

    Much the greater part of the fertile land and available wealth of Solomon's kingdom lay to the north of the line of the division, in the successor state which took the name of Israel and included all the historic tribes except Judah and a part of Benjamin. The northern kingdom ran from Dan above Galilee down to Jericho and the northern end of the Dead Sea, and from the Mediterranean to the eastern desert; it included the fertile plain of Jezreel still thickly settled with the original Canaanite population. Since Jerusalem and the Temple remained with Judah and the dynasty of David, the rebel Jeroboam who founded the northern kingdom felt it necessary to build substitute temples, one at the old patriarchal shrine at Bethel, the other at Dan in the far north. The temple at Bethel was built hurriedly and poorly; the temple at Dan was erected primarily as a favor to the far northern tribes who in the wake of Jeroboam's rebellion were developing separatist tendencies of their own. In both the Bethel and the Dan temples Jeroboam placed a golden bull as a sign of the strength and power of Yahweh.[1]

Modern commentators have been very free with excuses for this extraordinary act of Jeroboam's, perhaps in a sort of reaction against the blistering denunciation of it in the Book of Kings; but the Christian historian should be very cautious about reactions against Scripture. When every possible allowance has been made for Jeroboam's political problems and the justified resentment created by Solomon's and Rehoboam's heavy taxation, forced labor and abuses of royal authority, the fact remains that what Jeroboam did repeated *precisely* the sin of Aaron at Sinai which caused Moses in fury to break the tablets of the Ten Commandments which God Himself had inscribed. Jeroboam must have known he was doing this; every Israelite must have known it. They had hardly forgotten Moses. In fact many in the north, particularly priests and Levites, were well aware that Jeroboam's action amounted to apostasy and therefore left the northern kingdom in protest, to dwell in Judah—so many that Jeroboam soon had to appoint laymen as priests, contrary to the law of Moses. That the bull was a generalized symbol of godlike strength and power is true; but it was also the visual symbol of Baal, the child-eating god of the Phoenicians and the Canaanites, whose evil rites the Israelites had been commanded to cast out forever when they conquered the Promised Land, and who still dwelt in large numbers within and around the northern kingdom.[2]

The prophet Ahijah of Shiloh in the northern kingdom had foretold to Jeroboam the division of the kingdom and his royal future when he was fleeing from Solomon's wrath, urging him to rule uprightly in the sight of God. Jeroboam sent his wife to Ahijah when his son fell ill; she found the prophet aged and blind but still vigorous,[3] and received from him the first of the terrible prophetic curses which were to fall upon a disobedient Israel in the centuries to come:

> Thus says the LORD, the God of Israel: "Because I exalted you from among the people, and made you leader over my people Israel, and tore the kingdom away from the house of David and gave it to you, and yet you have not been like my servant David, who kept my commandments and followed me with all his heart, doing only that which was right in my eyes, but you have done evil above all that were before you and have gone and made for yourself other gods and molten images, provoking me to anger, and have cast me behind your back, therefore behold, I will bring evil upon the house of Jeroboam, and will cut off from Jeroboam every male, both bond and free, in Israel, and will utterly consume the house of Jeroboam as a man burns up dung until it is all gone. Any one belonging to Jeroboam who dies in the city the dogs shall eat, and any one who dies in the open country the birds of the air shall eat, for the LORD has spoken it." Arise therefore, go to your house. When your feet enter the city, the child shall

die. And all Israel shall mourn for him, and bury him; for he only of
Jeroboam shall come to the grave, because in him there is found something
pleasing to the LORD, the God of Israel, in the house of Jeroboam. Moreover
the LORD will raise up for himself a king over Israel, who shall cut off
the house of Jeroboam today. And henceforth the LORD will smite Israel,
as a reed is shaken in the water, and root up Israel out of this good land
which he gave to their fathers, and scatter them beyond the Euphrates.[4]

Jeroboam's sick son died as the prophet had said. In 901 B.C. Jeroboam
was succeeded by another son, Nadab, who had reigned but a single year when
he was assassinated by Baasha, a military officer, who slew all members of
the short-lived royal family of Jeroboam. Baasha's own fate was identical. After
his reign of 23 years his son too was murdered after a one-year reign, along
with all members of his family. Zimri, the assassin, reigned just one week,
perishing in the flames of the royal palace when Omri, a capable general and
administrator who was probably not even an Israelite, moved in to restore order
and impose a firm military dictatorship on the Kingdom of Israel.[5] (For these
reigns and others of this age, see the Chronological Table of Middle Eastern
Kings, 922-721 B.C., facing page 104.)

The Kingdom of Judah, more homogeneous in population (the great majority of its people were directly descended from the Israelites of the conquest),
more compact in its territory, and above all unwaveringly faithful to the dynasty of David, was inherently much more stable than the northern Kingdom of
Israel.[6] After Rehoboam and his short-lived son and successor Abijah, two
kings—Asa and Jehoshaphat—reigned unchallenged in Judah for no less than
sixty-four years. Orthodox and faithful worshippers of Yahweh, they acted firmly
to expel idolatry from Jerusalem and from public shrines throughout Judah,
though they permitted private shrines to remain even when contaminated by
false gods. Asa's mother had set up a phallic image in the Temple itself; Asa,
when he became king, had it thrown into the Kedron canyon far below the Temple
mount. Jehoshaphat set up an organized apostolate, sending officials and Levites
throughout the country to teach the Mosaic Law to the people; we are specifically
told that his teachers carried written books of the Law.[7]

In the north, Omri built a capital for his kingdom upon virgin soil at Samaria,
dominated by a splendid "royal quarter" at the highest point in the city. He
intended it to be a rival to Jerusalem, and so it became, not only during the
period of the two kingdoms but long afterward when it gave its name to the
half-alien people who settled around it after the fall of the northern kingdom
and became known as the Samaritans, much hated by the Jews.[8]

Omri took steps to restore the alliance with the Phoenician cities of the coast,
especially Tyre, that had been a feature of Solomon's reign. However, in the
intervening half-century Phoenician wealth and power had grown through their
great development of overseas trade while Israelite wealth and power had

decreased, so that Tyre now had an opportunity to become the dominant partner. The King of Tyre in Omri's time was Ittobaal, a former high priest of the fertility goddess Astarte. Like Omri, Ittobaal had murdered his way to the throne. Omri sealed his alliance with Tyre by marrying his son, the crown prince Ahab, to Ittobaal's daughter Jezebel, who shared her father's dedication to the hideous worship of Baal and Astarte.[9] When in 869 B.C. Ahab became king and Jezebel queen, the stage was set for the northern kingdom, already including a large Canaanite population devoted to Yahweh in name only (if that),[10] to experience an open attempt—the first in a long history—to use the powers of government to eliminate the worship of the God Who Is by outright persecution.

King Ahab broke the First Commandment, setting up an altar to Baal and a "sacred pole" in Samaria, protesting that he and his people could worship both He Who Is, and these others, without impiety. Jezebel had those who publicly denounced this killed. An official of Bethel named Hiel undertook the rebuilding of Jericho and sacrificed two of his sons as foundation offerings in the Phoenician/Canaanite manner; one was buried under the new town and the other under its gates. Those loyal to the old faith hid in caves, living on bread and water; they grew fewer every day.[11]

Then the rains failed for an entire season,[12] and Ahab called the priests of Baal—who was first and foremost a rain-god[13]—together on the great high promontory of Mount Carmel, facing the western sea from which any rain there was to be must come, to pray for rain. And there came also to Carmel, like a meteor, a strange wild figure clad only in a hair cloak and a leather loincloth: Elijah.[14]

> And Elijah came near to all the people, and said, "How long will you go limping with two different opinions? If the LORD is God, follow him; but if Baal, then follow him." And the people did not answer him a word. Then Elijah said to the people, "I, even I only, am left a prophet of the LORD; but Baal's prophets are four hundred and fifty men. Let two bulls be given to us; and let them choose one bull for themselves, and cut it in pieces and lay it on the wood, but put no fire to it; and I will prepare the other bull and lay it on the wood, and put no fire to it. And you call on the name of your god and I will call on the name of the LORD; and the God who answers by fire, he is God." And all the people answered, "It is well spoken." . . .

> And at the time of the offering of the oblation, Elijah the prophet came near and said, "O LORD, God of Abraham, Isaac, and Israel, let it be known this day that thou art God in Israel, and that I am thy servant, and that I have done all these things at thy word. Answer me, O LORD, answer me, that this people may know that thou, O LORD, art God, and that thou hast turned their hearts back." Then the fire of the LORD fell, and consumed the burnt offering, and the wood, and the stones, and the dust, and licked up the water that was in the trench. And when all the people saw it, they fell on their faces; and they said, "The LORD, he is God; the LORD, he is God."[15]

Then the first rain cloud appeared far out over the sea, sweeping toward the Carmel lookout; and the rains came and fell in torrents upon thirsty Israel.[16]

As the distinguished Old Testament scholar H. H. Rowley has pointed out,[17] no naturalistic explanation of the miracle on Carmel will suffice. The priests of Baal were no ignorant multitude readily deceived by sleight-of-hand tricks such as substituting inflammable oil for water; moreover, lightning cannot strike from a cloudless sky. And if, as Rowley says, we then attempt to dismiss the whole account as unhistorical legend, we are left without any explanation for the source of the successful resistance to the introduction of the Phoenician pantheon into Israel—or, we might add, for the later fame of Elijah which endured so vividly down to the time of Christ 850 years later, and still lives today, especially among orthodox Jews.

Elijah lived long before the days of martyrs being led meekly to the executioner; it was still much too early in the history of salvation for that. He had all the priests of Baal who had been with him on Carmel slaughtered on the spot, and consequently—despite the miracle of the fire and the ending of the drought—he had to flee the country when Jezebel sought to kill him in turn. He betook himself straight to Mount Sinai, to the very cleft in the rock from which Moses had seen the glory of God pass by.[18] Only at this point, in all of the Old Testament after the books of Moses, do we hear of a return to Sinai. Stark and empty as ever, that hallowed wilderness enfolded Elijah in its loneliness. Through wind and fire and earthquake he waited, until at last the voice of his Lord came to him in a gentle breeze, "still and small," asking him why he was there.[19] Elijah replied:

> "I have been very jealous for the LORD, the God of hosts; for the people of Israel have forsaken thy covenant, thrown down thy altars, and slain thy prophets with the sword; and I, even I only, am left; and they seek my life, to take it away." And the LORD said to him, "Go, return on your way to the wilderness of Damascus; and when you arrive, you shall anoint Hazael to be king over Syria; and Jehu the son of Nimshi you shall anoint to be king over Israel; and Elisha the son of Shaphat of Abelmeholah you shall anoint to be prophet in your place. And him who escapes from the sword of Hazael shall Jehu slay; and him who escapes from the sword of Jehu shall Elisha slay. Yet I will leave seven thousand in Israel, all the knees that have not bowed to Baal, and every mouth that has not kissed him."[20]

This passage strikes the great recurring theme of the Remnant, the counterpoint to the repeated apostasies of Israel which had begun with the casting of the golden "calf" at the foot of Mount Sinai. And it carries also a message and a warning all too easily misunderstood as the word of a cruel and vengeful God. For Elijah did call Elisha as prophet to succeed him, and Elisha did anoint Jehu King of Israel, and Jehu and Elisha, in the bloodiest purge of Israel's history, did massacre the Baalists and the whole court at Samaria, including not only

Jezebel—who was thrown from a window and trampled—and King Jehoram of Israel, but also King Ahaziah of Judah together with forty-two of his family. This happened eight years after Ahab had died in battle with the army of Damascus in 850 B.C.[21]

Yet the prophet Hosea in the next century, also speaking for God, condemned Jehu's massacre unequivocally, proclaiming that it brought a curse upon his house.[22] Our problem here is that we are so much more inclined to philosophical and theological argument than were the ancient Israelites. It needs to be stressed again and again that there probably has never been a people less philosophical and more concrete and earthy in their thinking than Israel's People of the Covenant. Very likely this is one of the principal reasons God chose them, since the unique experiences they were to have made it imperative that they trust first of all in their own God-given perceptions of a reality above and beyond themselves, and not dismiss Divine revelation as fantasy in the manner of so many skeptics both ancient and modern. The Israelites were honestly not concerned "to justify the ways of God to man." God was to them far too great, immediate and concrete a reality to need justifying to anybody, as is clearly demonstrated in the climactic passages of the Book of Job.[23] The doubts and philosophical questions of a later age simply did not occur to the Israelites of Elijah's time. As best we can reconstruct it, their thinking went something like this: The price of sin is death. Ahab and Jezebel and their families and retainers and all who had apostatized from Yahweh to Baal sinned grievously. The price of their sin was a particularly grievous death. But those who massacred them sinned also through cruelty and excess. They too paid the penalty. God had commanded the anointing; He had simply prophesied the massacre. He brought good out of evil, and He was not mocked.[24]

Massacres will not cease so long as men are men, in the grip of original sin and all its consequences. But though such deeds are not God's will, they cannot ultimately frustrate His will. Adam knew death because he broke God's law. Jehoram and the apostates of Israel met violent death when they broke His first commandment. The house of Jehu, which had taken the sword, died by the sword. But God's purpose endured until "in the fullness of time" the Chosen People and the Promised Land brought forth a Prince of Peace.

Elijah left Israel as he had come, mysteriously and meteorically. Soon after Ahab's death in battle, before Jehu's purge, he departed from his land and his people, taken—according to the Second Book of Kings—by Yahweh in a fiery sky-chariot, giving rise to the belief that some day he would return.[25] Exactly what happened we cannot tell. But we might remember that Moses and Elijah, the two men of the Old Testament who were to appear with Christ at the Transfiguration, in the presence of the apostles Peter and James and John,[26] had both encountered God on Sinai and seen His glory as no other Israelite had been privileged to see it —and that, despite their lasting fame among their peo-

ple, no memory was preserved of a tomb or a grave or any sort of burial place
for either one.

With the single exception of the campaign of the Egyptian Pharaoh Sheshonk
I shortly after Solomon's death, which was never followed up, Palestine had
not experienced or even been threatened by a major foreign invasion since the
Philistines and the Israelites themselves arrived in the land about 1200 B.C.
The only outside menace had come from the half-civilized tribes of the desert
fringes, who were readily repulsed even before the period of the united
monarchy.

By the time of Ahab and Jezebel this long immunity, unique in the history
of the land at the center of the world, was drawing to its inevitable end. Out
of the welter of barbaric strife which filled all the Middle East during the years
of the conquest of Canaan a resolute, disciplined and brutal nation had emerged
in northern Mesopotamia, led by iron-hearted kings claiming the right to rule
every land and people under the sun, in the name of their god Ashur.[27] This
nation was Assyria, whose ravaging warriors ranged from the highlands of Iran
to the shores of the Mediterranean. We should not exaggerate their particular
cruelty, for as we have seen, theirs was a merciless age; but their insatiable
lust for plunder and dominion in distant lands set them apart from most other
civilized peoples of their time—such as the Egyptians, the Babylonians and the
Israelites—who were generally content with their own land and sought additional territory, if at all, primarily for defensive purposes.[28]

In the great days of Ur before Abraham was, Assyria had been just another
province in that city's imperial domain. After Ur's fall Assyria had emerged
briefly as a major power during the first half of the reign of King Hammurabi
of Babylon. As Hammurabi's kingdom grew in size and strength, Assyria had
declined and been all but lost to sight during the invasions of the Hurrian and
other barbarians of Mesopotamia's "Dark Age"[29] while the Israelites were dwelling in Egypt.

As the centuries unrolled in strife, the first indication appears in Assyrian
annals of the terrible policy which was to make their name feared and hated
throughout the Middle Eastern civilized world—the policy responsible for removing ten of the tribes of Israel forever from the Promised Land, the policy which
ultimately led to the exile and captivity of the remainder of the Chosen People
"by the waters of Babylon." An inscription of King Ashur-dan I of Assyria,
dating from about 1160 B.C., reports that he marched against the peoples of
Zaban, Irria and Ugarsallu in central Mesopotamia, defeated them, and deported
them to Assyria. These "displaced persons" were presumably replaced, as was
the later policy, by other deportees from distant regions who, as aliens in a strange
land owing all they had to the King of Assyria and having nothing in common
with the remaining inhabitants of the area, could be expected to remain loyal
to Assyria or at least not to rebel. Half a century later the conqueror Tiglath-

pileser I followed Ashur-dan's example.[30]

Since the Hittite empire of Asia Minor and Syria had collapsed at the time of the massive barbarian irruption that brought the Philistines to Palestine, there was no great power to bar Assyria's way to the Mediterranean Sea through northern Syria. About 1110 B.C. Tiglath-pileser I marched by this route to the Mediterranean, where he took ship for a short distance along the north Phoenician coast, killed a dolphin and a narwhal to symbolize his new power upon the seas, and received the tribute of the Phoenician cities of Byblos and Sidon.[31] But the mountains of Lebanon still interposed their snow-capped bulk between the victorious Assyrian army and the Promised Land, where the Israelites were then establishing themselves in the time of the "judges," and Tiglath-pileser I never came into contact with them.

Tiglath-pileser I had overextended himself and his kingdom. Though so far as we know he died in peace, his reign was immediately followed by civil strife among rival claimants to the throne and increased pressure on both Assyria and Babylonia from the half-civilized Aramaean peoples who had occupied Syria and northwestern Mesopotamia in large numbers following the disintegration of the Hittite empire.[32] Silence now falls on the history of the whole of Mesopotamia, continuing throughout the century of David and Solomon. When it begins to lift, after the division of Solomon's kingdom, we find Babylonia reduced to virtual impotence and the Assyrian kings thrown back upon their original homeland on the upper Tigris River. But the Assyrian royal succession had been maintained, and a veteran soldiery, tried and tempered in the struggle for survival during those two hundred years of obscurity and conflict, was now ready to serve as an instrument for the greatest conquests the world had yet seen.[33]

The year before Omri became King of Israel, Ashurnasirpal II of Assyria, following the course of Tiglath-pileser I, swept across northern Syria to the Mediterranean Sea and took tribute from the rich cities of Phoenicia, including Tyre where Jezebel was then a young princess. Ashurnasirpal's son likewise marched to the Mediterranean and proceeded to consolidate control of the land within the westward bend of the Euphrates, incorporating it fully into the Assyrian realm. Confronted by this unmistakable proof that Assyria aimed at permanent conquest rather than merely occasional plunder, the kings of Syria and Phoenicia formed a defensive alliance under Ben-Hadad II of Damascus. Ahab of Israel joined them, contributing 2,000 chariots and 10,000 infantry to the 70,000-man army of the alliance which met 120,000 Assyrians under Shalmaneser III at the drawn battle of Qarqar in Syria in 853 B.C.[34]

Thus was the Kingdom of Israel finally brought into direct armed conflict with the far more powerful Kingdom of Assyria. The historic paths of the peoples of Mesopotamia and the children of Abraham crossed again on the battlefield of Qarqar, almost exactly a thousand years after Abraham left Ur.

The alliance between Israel and Damascus scarcely outlasted the Qarqar campaign. As we have seen, Ahab died in battle against his erstwhile allies in 850 B.C., just three years after the Battle of Qarqar. Shalmaneser III of Assyria returned to the attack in 841, besieging the city of Damascus and devastating the lands around it, carving his portrait next to that of Ramses II in the curious gallery of conquerors cut into a cliff above the mouth of the Dog River in Phoenicia near Beirut. One wonders if anyone in Israel marked the juxtaposition and the warning, as their old oppressor's face in stone looked down upon the marching armies of the new oppressor who had by this act proclaimed his intention to seek and exercise the same kind of power. On Mount Carmel where Elijah had challenged the false god, Shalmaneser received tribute from Tyre and Sidon—and from Jehu, who had just become King of Israel after his great massacre the year before. Shalmaneser's "Black Obelisk" shows Jehu making obeisance to him and identifies the Israelite king and his country by name—the first explicit mention of an Israelite historical figure in the contemporary records of another people.[35]

An outbreak of civil strife in Assyria then gave a respite to Syria, Phoenicia and Palestine, but the only result was to encourage their kings to turn on one another again. King Hazael of Damascus struck so hard at Jehu's son Jehoahaz that he and the Kingdom of Israel were virtually reduced to vassalage; the rich city of Megiddo on the Plain of Jezreel was destroyed. But in 801 B.C., in yet another turn of the kaleidoscopic fortunes of war, the power of Damascus was broken forever by the Assyrian king Adad-nirari III.[36] No effective buffer of any kind—political or geographic—now remained to separate the northern half of the divided kingdom of God's Chosen People from the rapacious empire which was advancing from Abraham's ancient homeland.

Judah was hardly in a better or safer position. Despite a better start, the southern kingdom had fallen heir to most of the evils of the northern, even to having its own wicked queen of Jezebel's line: Athaliah, daughter of Ahab and Jezebel. Her husband Jehoram of Judah had massacred his brothers and many of the elders of the kingdom when he succeeded the good King Jehoshaphat after his long reign finally ended in 849 B.C. After Jehoram's death from a loathsome disease and the slaying of his son and successor Ahaziah in Jehu's purge, Athaliah put to death all her sons and grandsons whom she could find, so as to establish herself on the throne of David. This monstrous crime—worse than any recorded even of Jezebel—was frustrated in the completion of its purpose by a sister of Ahaziah, the wife of the high priest Joaida, who saved one of her nephews from the massacre, a year-old baby named Joash, hiding him in the Temple area for five years. The boy was then brought forth on a Sabbath day, presented to the Temple guard as the true successor of David, and acclaimed king; Athaliah was deposed and killed, and the line of David preserved.[37]

Athaliah had damaged the Temple; Joash restored it, ruling wisely once he reached his majority so long as his mentor, the high priest Joaida, lived. But after Joaida's death Joash turned to idolatry, killing Joaida's son Zachary when reproached by him for it. Then came the heavy stroke of King Hazael of Damascus against the northern kingdom. Joash was forced to make a humiliating peace, sending the treasures of Jerusalem and the Temple to Damascus. Angered by this and by the murder of the high priest's son, the leaders and people of the southern kingdom killed Joash in turn, at just about the time the Assyrians destroyed the power of Damascus. Joash's son and successor Amaziah began his reign well, restoring stability, exercising clemency and regaining much of Edom. But then he attacked the northern kingdom unprovoked, seeking to restore Solomon's realm by force of arms, and was defeated and captured at Beth-shemesh. The army of the northern kingdom marched to Jerusalem, occupied it, and levelled a long section of its wall. But they left Amaziah on David's throne.[38]

A peaceful reunion of the divided kingdom seemed impossible and the paltry ambitions of the kings—both Davidic and non-Davidic—insatiable, even in the face of the looming Assyrian thundercloud in the northeast, on the verge of engulfing them both.

Now, upon the brink of disaster for all the people of Israel, came a pause in the march of threatening events. For more than a generation, during the reigns of three successive sons of Adad-nirari III, royal weakness stayed the Assyrian sword. This 36-year period coincided very closely with the reigns of King Jeroboam II of Israel and King Uzziah in Judah. Both rulers took advantage of the power vacuum resulting from the earlier Assyrian campaigns in Syria to extend their spheres of commercial and political influence into the now disorganized and leaderless north. A degree of prosperity and power was attained by both halves of the divided kingdom approaching that of the great days of Solomon.[39]

But the situation was now fundamentally different. In Solomon's time there had been no monarch in all the world stronger than he. No significant danger of external aggression and foreign conquest had existed. In the time of Jeroboam II and Uzziah it was only necessary for Assyria to find a king to match her all-conquering army and the imperial potential her earlier rulers had built up, to become irresistible. In 745 B.C. such a king was crowned: Tiglath-pileser III, the ablest leader Assyria ever had, a great general and excellent administrator, who during an 18-year reign decisively defeated every nation bordering his empire,[40] leaving Israel and Judah with no source of succor except hopelessly decadent Egypt, when the final blow fell, first upon one and then upon the other. Once again, as when the Philistines had captured the Ark of the Covenant, it seemed there could be no hope—that God must have abandoned His people.

It was then that the great prophets appeared in Israel. There is nothing like them in the history or the religion of any other land and people. They are unique.[41]

"Higher critics" of the Old Testament once thought that the "classical" prophets, beginning with Amos and reaching a towering summit in Isaiah, invented in all essential respects the monotheism of the Israelites. All responsible scholars know better now; they know that these prophets built on a foundation already sturdy and deep-laid.[42] Nevertheless it is true that the prophetic books stand in such striking contrast to the rest of the world of their time as to cry aloud for an explanation.

To Abraham had come the promise; to Moses, the covenant. Both concerned only the people Israel. Even the great drama of the Exodus was understood primarily if not solely as proof that the Lord of the universe was with Israel and had chosen her for His own. Now convinced at last of their divine election, the Israelites had actually begun to take this supernal favor for granted. Confident that God would live up to His obligations, they were making less and less effort to fulfill their own. The prophets came to tell them that because of this they would be chastised by foreign nations, also guilty of the gravest sins in the sight of God, which nevertheless He would use as rod and flail to strike down the pride, injustice, and sordid materialism which were staining His Chosen People. For Yahweh was the Lord of history. All the nations—even the greatest, even the worst, even Assyria—did His bidding.[43]

That teaching pierces the tidal ebb and flow of history like a sharp black rock amid foaming surf. It is familiar and not particularly startling to us only because our civilization grew up with it, as our heritage from the prophets through Christ. No other people or civilization, not influenced by the faith of Israel or by Christianity, ever imagined it.[44] Elsewhere, if gods were angry, it was because they had not been sufficiently propitiated with sacrificial rites; and the Israelites, whatever their sins, were nothing if not punctual in carrying out the ritual or worship and sacrifice prescribed by the Law of Moses. The prophets repeatedly condemned them for relying on this alone, without a clean heart. There was no easy or merely formal way to please and to serve the One True God, Who demanded justice and would punish them if they did not manifest it. Yet for a people to worship a God Who raised up foreign monarchs and armies to lay waste their land as punishment for their immorality, entirely unconnected with ritual and sacrifice, was a thing unheard of, undreamed of in the world of imperial Assyria and its victims.

But the prophets spoke before kings, and were not ashamed. They suffered abuse and martyrdom. Still many Israelites could and did believe in a God Who sent Assyria upon them "like a wolf on the fold" to punish them for their sins. And in that they displayed a difference from all their contemporaries so great as to bear convincing witness that the Old Testament prophets really were what they claimed to be—direct spokesmen for the God Who Is—and that their people knew this and were helped by God to believe it even while, through the mouths of the prophets, He was denouncing their sins.

The first of them was Amos, a shepherd. He came from Tekoa south of Jerusalem in a rocky, desolate region of the Kingdom of Judah,[45] but he preached in the more corrupted and more immediately threatened Kingdom of Israel. His short book is like a clap of thunder.

> Thus says the LORD:
> "For three transgressions of Israel,
> and for four, I will not revoke the punishment;
> because they sell the righteous for silver,
> and the needy for a pair of shoes—
> they that trample the head of the poor into the dust of the earth,
> and turn aside the way of the afflicted;
> a man and his father go into the same maiden,
> so that my holy name is profaned;
> they lay themselves down beside every altar
> upon garments taken in pledge;
> and in the house of their God they drink
> the wine of those who have been fined.[46] . . .
>
> 'Woe to those who are at ease in Zion,
> and to those who feel secure on the mountain of Samaria,
> the notable men of the first of the nations,
> to whom the house of Israel come! . . .
>
> The Lord GOD has sworn by himself
> (says the LORD, the God of hosts):
> "I abhor the pride of Jacob,
> and hate his strongholds;
> and I will deliver up the city and all that is in it."[47]

All the world was stained then as now by sins like these; but in all the world of 750 B.C. only one man and his hearers knew a God who hated those sins and would judge their perpetrators—and that man a simple shepherd, whom the mighty Tiglath-pileser III would never have condescended to notice. Yet men still honor Amos' words today, twenty-seven centuries later; and where are the armies of Assyria?

Amos preached late in the reign of King Jeroboam II of Israel,[48] who died in the year before Tiglath-pileser III came to the throne. In the next ten years there were four kings of Israel; three of them died by assassination. Jeroboam's son Zechariah was murdered after a reign of just one year (746-745) by Shallum ben Jabesh, who became king but was murdered one month later by Menahem ben Gadi, whose son Pekahiah was murdered in 737 by Pekah.[49] Tiglath-pileser III was then consolidating his direct rule in Syria and Lebanon, and Pekah sought to take advantage of the disaffection over his new taxes and tribute by forming a new Syro-Palestinian coalition against Assyria in 734. When Judah refused to join the coalition, Pekah and King Rezon II of Damascus attacked it, causing

Judah's King Ahaz to appeal to Assyria for aid, after spurning the warning of the prophet Isaiah which included his glorious prediction of the virgin birth of Immanuel.[50]

Tiglath-pileser III responded promptly and decisively to the challenge. In two crushing campaigns he overwhelmed the allies and conquered the greater part of the kingdom of Israel, annexing the Plain of Jezreel which Barak and Deborah had won from the Canaanites four hundred years before, all of Galilee which Joshua had claimed by virtue of his great victory over the powerful city of Hazor, and the land east of the Jordan whence Moses had gazed upon the Promised Land. All three regions were incorporated into the Assyrian empire. The kingdom of Israel was reduced to a mere hill country principality around Samaria. In 732 Pekah, a discredited failure, was assassinated by Hoshea, who promptly paid his tribute to Assyria.[51]

Meanwhile Babylonia, which had been ruled by a king friendly to Assyria, fell into strife and rebellion when he died. Tiglath-pileser III marched down the Tigris, crossed it and took Babylon, where in 729 he had himself crowned king of Babylonia under the throne name of Pul, thereby uniting the whole of Mesopotamia under the direct rule of the Assyrian king. Tiglath-pileser III's empire now extended from the Persian Gulf to the borders of Egypt, and included substantial portions of Asia Minor.[52]

Tiglath-pileser III died in 727. Seizing upon a forlorn hope, King Hoshea of Israel refused tribute to his son and successor, Shalmaneser V. In 724 Shalmaneser appeared before Samaria with the invincible Assyrian army and took Hoshea prisoner when he came to ask for terms. This time there would be no forgiveness, no restitutions; the kingdom of Israel was to be utterly destroyed. After a three-year siege Samaria fell to Shalmaneser's successor Sargon II, who wrote its epitaph in Assyrian clay: "I besieged and captured Samaria, and led away as booty 27,290 inhabitants of it." They never returned.[53]

In just thirty years, the terrible prophecy of Amos had been fulfilled.

Another and greater prophet followed immediately after Amos in the northern kingdom, in the darkest days just before its fall: Hosea, the prophet of God's love. Hosea was the first to develop the sublime image of God's chosen people as His bride, His beloved, whom He would forgive and rescue even though she had been unfaithful to him.[54] The fervor of Hosea's commitment to such a God, even in the midst of final disaster for his country, shines like a diamond star through the gloom of the tempest. God would never forget His people; some of His people would always remember God. Hosea could denounce the sins of Israel inwords even more searing than the words of Amos; yet he also spoke of hope—a hope whose full measure was not to be realized and understood for more than seven hundred years:

> Come, let us return to the LORD;
> for he has torn, that he may heal us;

he has stricken, that he will bind us up.
After two days he will revive us;
on the third day he will raise us up,
that we may live before him.
Let us know, let us press on to know the LORD;
his going forth is sure as the dawn;
he will come to us as the showers;
as the spring rains that water the earth.[55]

NOTES

[1] John Bright, *A History of Israel*, 3d ed. (Philadelphia, 1981), pp. 237-238 and Plate vi (map); Paul Heinisch, *History of the Old Testament* (Collegeville MN, 1952), pp. 224-225.

[2] Heinisch, *History of the Old Testament*, pp. 224-225.

[3] 1 Kings 14:1-6.

[4] 1 Kings 14:7-15. While the Book of Kings was probably completed about 600 B.C. when the complete fulfillment of Ahijah's prophecy had become only too clear (*New Oxford Annotated Bible*, ed. Herbert G. May and Bruce M. Metzger [New York, 1977], p. 438), this by no means proves that Ahijah's prophecy was not made in Jeroboam's lifetime. Implicit denial of the possibility of accurate predictive prophecy is the false and heretical proposition which stalks almost all modern Biblical scholarship, even the best. See the discussion of the prophecies of Isaiah in Chapter Six, below.

[5] Bright, *History of Israel*, pp. 238-239; Heinisch, *History of the Old Testament*, pp. 225-226. For the non-Hebraic character of the name Omri, see *The Jerome Biblical Commentary*, ed. Raymond E. Brown et al (Englewood Cliffs NJ, 1968), I, 193.

[6] Bright, *History of Israel*, pp. 230, 239.

[7] Giuseppe Ricciotti, *History of Israel* (Milwaukee, 1955), I, 358-361.

[8] Kathleen Kenyon, *Archaeology in the Holy Land*, 3rd ed. (New York, 1970), pp. 261-269.

[9] Bright, *History of Israel*, pp. 241-242; Sabatino Moscati, *The World of the Phoenicians* (London, 1968), pp. 14-15. Astarte was the principal female deity of both Tyre and Sidon, the leading cities of Phoenicia at this period (Moscati, *op. cit.*, pp. 33-35). Since Jezebel was a princess of Tyre, it is highly likely that Astarte was the goddess who, along with the god Baal, was the chief object of her worship (*Jerome Biblical Commentary*, I, 194). However, a gloss on the text of the Book of Kings identifies Jezebel's goddess as ''Asherah'' (*The Jerusalem Bible*, ed. Alexander Jones [New York, 1966] [Old Testament], p.445, Note 18d), who was the consort of El, the chief god in the Canaanite and Phoenician pantheon. G. Ernest Wright accepts this identification and guesses that Jezebel thought Asherah was Baal's consort instead of El's (*Biblical Archaeology* [2d ed., Philadelphia, 1962], pp. 107-110). For details about the Earth-Mother goddess and the fertility cult, see Bright, *op. cit.*, pp. 116-117; Wright, *op. cit.*, pp. 110-113; and William F. Albright, *From the Stone Age to Christianity*, 2d ed. (New York, 1957), pp. 230-235. For child sacrifice in Phoenicia, see Roland de Vaux, *Ancient Israel, its Life and Institutions* (New York, 1961), pp. 441-446. De Vaux shows that child sacrifice was never approved in Israel even in times of crisis and great danger, but there are Biblical references to its practice there nevertheless—one of the earliest coming, significantly, from the reign of Ahab and Jezebel (see Note 11, below).

[10] The persistence of Canaanite cults is indicated by the substantial number of religious

objects associated with fertility rites which have been recovered by archeologists from sites in Palestine dating from the century of David and Solomon (Kenyon, *Archaeology in the Holy Land*, pp. 251-256). However, it is very significant that, with only a single exception, no image of a *male* god has ever been found in any Israelite town of this period—and no images purporting to be of Yahweh are known from any period (Wright, *Biblical Archaeology*, pp. 117-118). No Israelite ever broke the First Commandment with regard to Yahweh Himself—an example of doctrinal fidelity unique in the history of the pre-Christian world.

¹¹ 1 Kings 16:32-34, 18:13. The probable nature and extent of the persecution is outlined in Bright, *History of Israel*, pp. 245-247. Hiel's child sacrifice is attributed to Phoenician influence by de Vaux, *Ancient Israel*, p. 442.

¹² Bright, *History of Israel*, pp. 244-245. This drought is also attested, probably independently of the Old Testament, by the classical writer Menander of Ephesus, who says it lasted one full year. This may be harmonized with the three years recorded in 1 Kings 18:1 by presuming that it ran from the spring rains of one year to the fall rains of the year following, thus including one full year and part of two others (*ibid.*, p. 245n).

¹³ Wright, *Biblical Archaeology*, p. 108.

¹⁴ 2 Kings 1:8. While the story of Elijah probably derived originally from oral tradition, the nature of the Hebrew in which it is written in the books of Kings indicates that it was written down little more than a century after the events which it describes took place (Albright, *Stone Age to Christianity*, pp. 306-307).

¹⁵ 1 Kings 18:21-24, 36-39.

¹⁶ 1 Kings 18:41-45.

¹⁷ H. H. Rowley, "Elijah on Mount Carmel," *Bulletin of the John Rylands Library*, XLIII (1960), 190-219.

¹⁸ 1 Kings 19:1-9; *Jerusalem Bible* (Old Testament), p. 447, Note 19c.

¹⁹ 1 Kings 19:11-13.

²⁰ 1 Kings 19:14-18.

²¹ 1 Kings 19:19-21, 22:29-38; 2 Kings 9 and 10:1-27; Bright, *History of Israel*, pp. 250-251.

²² Hosea 1:4-5.

²³ Especially Job 42:1-6.

²⁴ The commentary on Hosea 1:4 in *Jerome Biblical Commentary*, I, 256, supports this interpretation.

²⁵ 2 Kings 2:1-12; Malachi 3:23-24; *Jerome Biblical Commentary*, I, 198.

²⁶ Matthew 17:1-5.

²⁷ Georges Roux, *Ancient Iraq* (New York, 1964), pp. 235-236; Jörgen Laesse, *People of Ancient Assyria* (New York, 1963), pp. 95-97.

²⁸ H. W. F. Saggs, *The Greatness That Was Babylon* (New York, 1962), pp. 235-240; Roux, *Ancient Iraq*, pp. 237-238; de Vaux, *Ancient Israel*, pp. 262-265. As discussed in Chapter Four, above, the Israelites displayed their full share of ferocity in the original conquest of the Promised Land under Joshua; but after that, their wars were essentially defensive. Even David's extension of his realm into Syria was primarily for the purpose of securing peace on the frontiers, and his successors never went beyond, or even maintained his boundaries.

²⁹ A. Leo Oppenheim, *Ancient Mesopotamia, Portrait of a Dead Civilization* (Chicago, 1964), pp. 153-154, 163-175; *The Cambridge Ancient History*, Volume II, Part 2 (3rd ed.), (Cambridge, England, 1975), pp. 21-27.

³⁰ *Cambridge Ancient History*, II (2) (3rd ed.), 451, 462.

³¹ *Ibid.*, pp. 461, 463.

³² *Ibid.*, pp. 467-470; Oppenheim, *Ancient Mesopotamia*, pp. 59-60.

³³ Roux, *Ancient Iraq*, pp. 231-232, 234.

³⁴ Saggs, *Babylon*, pp. 109-110; Roux, *Ancient Iraq*, pp. 239-246, 289; Moscati, *World of the Phoenicians*, pp. 14-16; Wright, *Biblical Archaeology*, pp. 158-160.

³⁵ Roux, *Ancient Iraq*, p. 246; Wright, *Biblical Archaeology*, pp. 158-160.

³⁶ Bright, *History of Israel*, pp. 253-255; Wright, *Biblical Archaeology*, p. 159. Although Damascus was allowed to retain its own kings until its formal incorporation into the Assyrian realm by Tiglath-pileser III in 732, it never exercised significant military power in the ancient Middle East after its great defeat in 801 B.C.

³⁷ Ricciotti, *History of Israel*, I, 361-365.

³⁸ *Ibid.*, I, 347-348, 365-366.

³⁹ Roux, *Ancient Iraq*, p. 251; Bright, *History of Israel*, pp. 256-259, 270-271. In 743 and 742 B.C. King Tiglath-pileser III of Assyria campaigned in Syria against a coalition led by a monarch identified in the Assyrian inscriptions as "Azriyau, King of Ya'diya" (Roux, *op. cit.*, p. 255). Despite the virtual phonetic and linguistic equivalence of this ruler's name and nation to Uzziah (also known as Azariah), King of Judah, many scholars have refused to accept Uzziah as a leader in Syria at this time, due to its distance from Judah and the earlier weakness of the southern kingdom. But in view of the power vacuum left in Syria by the earlier Assyrian campaigns and the subsequent Assyrian withdrawal due to internal troubles, there would seem to be insufficient basis for this skepticism. After all, since Ben-Hadad II of Damascus in Syria led an allied army against the Assyrians at Qarqar in 853 which included an Israelite contingent, there is no good reason why an Israelite king could not have led an army against the Assyrians in Syria with Syrian contingents, a century later.

⁴⁰ Roux, *Ancient Iraq*, pp. 255-257.

⁴¹ Bruce Vawter states: "There is no non-Israelite parallel for classical prophecy, either in form or in content. There seems to be no valid reason to alter the judgment made over 50 years ago by a man who was never reluctant to minimize what was unique in Israel, that 'the results of a search for genuine Babylonian prophecies are disappointing' and who then ventured 'to doubt [that Babylonia and Assyria] had any prophecies at all' (T. K. Cheyne, *The Two Religions of Israel* [London, 1911], 7-8). Neither has such a search proved to be productive elsewhere." (*Jerome Biblical Commentary*, I, 229). See also K. A. Kitchen, *The Bible in its World* (Downers Grove IL, 1977), pp. 116-118, on this point.

⁴² Bright, *History of Israel*, pp. 264-266.

⁴³ Abraham J. Heschel, *The Prophets* (New York, 1962), pp. 159-186; Yves Congar, *The Mystery of the Temple* (Westminster MD, 1962), pp. 62-63.

⁴⁴ A possible exception to this generalization is found in the Moabite stone of Mesha, king of Moab, dating from the reign of Jehoram in Israel (849-842 B.C.), which tells of the wars between Moab and the dynasty of Omri and attributes the initial success of Israel in these wars to the anger of the Moabite god Chemosh against his people (Ricciotti, *History of Israel*, I, 339-340). But there is not the slightest hint in this Moabite document of any moral or ethical concern by Chemosh as a cause of his anger, which may therefore be presumed to have been thought either as mere caprice, or due to some inadequacy in sacrifices and rites, in conformity with the general character of polytheistic imagery in that time. Such echoes of the Israelite view of God's anger as a cause for the ill fortune of a people as this inscription nevertheless displays may be fully accounted for by the proximity of the Moabites to the Israelites during nearly four centuries (1250-850 B.C.) during which this concept was an essential element of the Israelite faith, discussed since the time of Moses (who had issued his last tremendous warning to Israel on the consequences of disobeying God, on the plains of Moab).

[45] *Jerome Biblical Commentary*, I, 246.

[46] Amos 2:6-8.

[47] Amos 6:1, 6:8.

[48] *Jerome Biblical Commentary*, I, 245-246.

[49] 2 Kings 15:8-25.

[50] Bright, *History of Israel*, pp. 273-274; Saggs, *Babylon*, pp. 118-119. See Chapter Six, below.

[51] Bright, *History of Israel*, pp. 274-275.

[52] Saggs, *Babylon*, pp. 119-121.

[53] Wright, *Biblical Archaeology*, p. 166; Bright, *History of Israel*, pp. 275-276; P. R. Ackroyd, "Samaria," *Archaeology and Old Testament Study*, ed. D. Winton Thomas (Oxford, 1967), p. 347. Since obviously many more people had been living in the northern kingdom than the 27,290 Sargon II deported plus any reasonable estimate of casualties in the wars with Assyria, the genocide was not complete; but if the Assyrians followed their usual practice of taking particular care to deport all the leaders of the defeated people and their families, the result would have inevitably been exactly what in fact we find: the remainder of the ten tribes in Palestine merging with the remaining Canaanites and Philistines and the new peoples brought in by the Assyrians to replace the deportees, to form a mixture holding only an attenuated version of the Judaic faith—the Samaritans (Ricciotti, *History of Israel*, I, 354-356). See also Chapter Seven, below.

[54] Heschel, *The Prophets*, pp. 50-60. This is a particularly thoughtful and well-balanced treatment of the often vexed question of the relationship of Hosea's account of the troubles of his own marriage and his symbolism of the Chosen People as God's bride.

[55] Hosea 6:1-3.

6.
THE HOLY CITY
(721-582 B.C.)

How the faithful city
has become a harlot
she that was full of justice!
Righteousness lodged in her
but now murderers.
Your silver has become dross,
your wine mixed with water.
Your princes are rebels
and companions of thieves.
Every one loves a bribe
and runs after gifts.
They do not defend the fatherless,
and the widow's cause does not come to them.

Therefore the Lord says,
the LORD of hosts,
the Mighty One of Israel:
"Ah, I will vent my wrath on my enemies,
and avenge myself on my foes
I will turn my hand against you
and will smelt away your dross as with lye
and remove all your alloy.
And I will restore your judges as at the first,
and your counselors as at the beginning.
Afterward you shall be called the city of righteousness,
the faithful city."

Zion shall be redeemed by justice,
and those in her who repent, by righteousness.

But rebels and sinners shall be destroyed together,
and those who forsake the LORD shall be consumed.
   —Isaiah 1:21-28

   Jerusalem remained—with the Temple, and the dynasty of David. One tribe
of Israel still dwelt in the Promised Land. The little kingdom of Judah,[1] where
David had risen to power, where the royal succession had been in one unbroken
line of direct descent from David for more than two centuries, lodged precariously on the edge of Assyria's bloated domain. It seemed that all now depended
upon its fate.
   In the year that King Uzziah died, Isaiah the son of Amoz stood in the temple at Jerusalem. He saw a vision of God within the sanctuary, and prepared
to die because he knew that sinful man may not look upon God and live. But
an angel cleansed his sin with a burning coal upon his lips.[2]

   And I heard the voice of the Lord saying, "Whom shall I send, and who
   will go for us?" Then I said, "Here I am! Send me."[3]

   Unlike Moses before him and Jeremiah afterward, Isaiah accepted his mission immediately and totally, without doubt or reservation, with the whole of
his being. The only parallel is with Abraham. Isaiah was a genius, the greatest
Hebrew stylist who ever lived,[4] a man who knew the whole world of his time
on the level of a statesman[5]—yet he had a shepherd's faith, the faith of the man
to whom God spoke when first He chose His people. And Isaiah needed all
that faith, especially when he heard the appalling words which came next:

   "Go, and say to this people:
   'Hear and hear, but do not understand;
    see and see, but do not perceive.'
   Make the heart of this people fat,
   and their ears heavy,
   and shut their eyes
   lest they see with their eyes,
   and hear with their ears,
   and understand with their hearts,
   and turn and be healed."[6]

   Given that commission, seemingly so contrary to the goodness of God, Isaiah
asked only: "How long, O Lord?" And the answer came:

   "Until cities lie waste
    without inhabitant,

and houses without men,
and the land is utterly desolate,
and the LORD removes men far away,
and the forsaken places are many in the midst of the land.
And though a tenth remain in it,
it will be burned again,
like a terebinth or an oak
whose stump remains standing
when it is felled.''[7]

How could God have told Isaiah to help shut the eyes and ears of His own people to the message of repentance? Because the day of the nation of Judah, and of the First Temple—the Temple of Solomon—which was its heart, was nearly done. Its people must pay for their sins with the life of their nation; but that would not be the end. Far more was intended for the dynasty of David than that it produce an endless line of petty Middle Eastern kings; far more was intended for the people Israel than that they should have a contented life with worldly blessings in Palestine. Their degradation would become exaltation; but before the exaltation could come, the degradation must be almost complete. Their rejection of Isaiah's message was a necessary part of that necessary process, and therefore incorporated into the purpose for which he was sent.[8]

So Isaiah went forth on perhaps the most extraordinary mission ever given to a man in the history of the world. He must have been quite young at the time, because his awesome presence loomed in Judah for more than 55 years after that supernal moment in the Temple.[9] During all that time he played a leading part in affairs of state, while repeatedly denouncing the sins of his people as Amos and Hosea had done in the northern kingdom, and predicting the eventual defeat and destruction of his country. That would have been mission enough, and more than enough, for any other man. But Isaiah's mission included a whole additional dimension—one our modern age finds almost impossible to accept, but which is absolutely essential to understanding what he accomplished, and what he was.

For Isaiah really was a prophet. He foretold the virgin birth, the Galilean origin, the divine and human nature, and the passion and ultimate glory of Jesus Christ, and the spread of faith in the one true God far beyond Israel. He prophesied the downfall of Assyria and then of Babylon, followed ultimately by Babylon's depopulation. He predicted the destruction of Jerusalem and of the First Temple, the exile of his people, and their return to rebuild the Temple. He even predicted the name of the conquering Persian king who was to be their liberator two hundred years later: Cyrus. And all these things that he predicted, came to pass.

To us, strait-jacketed in our twentieth-century mind-set and the intellectual arrogance which is its hallmark, this is so startling and unpalatable a conclusion that a personal note may be in order at this point. The writer did not come to the preparation of this history and to the study of the prophet Isaiah holding the view that a single prophet named Isaiah, living in the late eighth century B.C., actually prophesied all these things—a position which has been almost completely abandoned in recent Biblical scholarship of all religious affiliations.[10] It was forced upon him by the solid evidence of the Scriptural text and the historical facts, and by some hard logical arguments.

Specific references to the fall of Assyria, the fall of Jerusalem, the exile in Babylon, the fall of Babylon to Cyrus and his Median troops, and the return of the exiles to Jerusalem all appear unmistakably in the text of the Book of Isaiah. Modern Biblical criticism regards them as later additions, interpolations and redactions. The theory of a "second Isaiah" is advanced to account for them. This nameless hypothetical writer, whose style by some marvel of imitation closely resembles that of the real Isaiah,[11] is assigned to just the right historical period to have known Cyrus in the natural order and then to have written chapters 40 through 55 of the Book of Isaiah in which this Persian king is mentioned. Chapters 56-66 are sometimes attributed to a "third Isaiah."

Now we have the testimony of Jesus ben Sirach, author of the Book of Ecclesiasticus written in the second century (200-100) B.C., and the evidence of the Dead Sea scroll of Isaiah dating to 100 B.C. or earlier, to support the unanimous verdict of tradition that there was never more than one Book of Isaiah;[12] while Josephus, the historian of the Jews for the Romans, tells us that Cyrus himself was impelled to authorize the rebuilding of the temple in Jerusalem because he knew that Isaiah had named him and predicted his victories two hundred years before his time.[13] An anonymous prophet would be unique in Israelite prophecy, since the prophets invariably announced themselves as personally selected spokesmen for God, not composers of literary continuations of the manuscripts of their predecessors.[14] Modern scholars may question the date of Isaiah; even second century B.C. scholars, so much closer to his own time, may have been wrong about him; but the people to whom the hypothetical "second Isaiah" supposedly preached most certainly knew that the real Isaiah was dead by then and that the books he had ordered written down in his lifetime[15] contained none of these new revelations.

But suppose answers can be found, however tortuously,[16] to all these objections. The "second Isaiah" hypothesis still leaves the critic scarcely better off than when he started. He has disposed of Cyrus, but not of his army. The Medes still march in their stern, upright, and pitiless array[17] against Babylon in Chapters 13 and 21, and the great city falls, while Assyria lies prostrate, in Chapters 14 and 31—all in the first part of the book which is still acknowledged to be the work of the "first Isaiah," living a century before the fall of Assyria and the rise of the Medes, and two centuries before the Medo-Persian conquest of Babylon. Still more interpolations and redactions must be conjured up to deal with these awkward facts. A plethora of Isaiahs is in the making. Analysis has ended in chaos.

As Edward J. Young, one of the very few modern Old Testament scholars who did not succumb to this extraordinary set of rationalizations, well states:

> If one begins to separate or divide Isaiah, it is impossible to rest with two or even three large divisions. One is compelled to continue analyzing and dividing until only a conglomeration of fragments remains.[18]

With regard to the prophecies of Christ, the theory of continuators, interpolators and redactors will not do, since the Septuagint Greek text of Isaiah and the Dead Sea scroll Hebrew text, both substantially identical with the text found in our Bibles today, pre-date Christ by a century or more. The Greek text of Isaiah 7 explicitly predicts the virgin birth of "Immanuel," meaning "God-with-us"—and the degree of ambiguity in the Hebrew word which the Septuagint translators here rendered as "virgin" does not justify our concluding that twenty-two centuries later we can translate it better into our languages than they did into theirs, at a time when both Hebrew and ancient Greek were living tongues.[19] Isaiah 9 predicts the appearance *in Galilee* of "a child . . . a son" given to us, who will be named "Wonderful Counsellor, Mighty God, Everlasting Father, Prince of Peace." The child to be born is explicitly identified as God, *el*; yet heavy stress is laid on the word "child," which no aspect of the Old Testament God even suggests. And He is called a wonder or miracle, *pele*—the same word used for the miracles of the Exodus.[20] Isaiah 53 predicts the Passion of Christ with such accuracy and detail—the Flagellation, the Crucifixion, the burial in a rich man's tomb, the Resurrection, and the redemptive effect of His sufferings and death—that it has been called a "fifth gospel."[21]

Nevertheless, most modern commentators shy away like frightened horses from the obvious meaning of these passages, intimidated where not convinced by "the modern mind." The main thrust of the usual argument against the integrity of the Book of Isaiah ultimately resolves itself into a perfect circle: Actual prophecy of the future cannot occur; therefore anything appearing to be actual prophecy was written later than it claims to be; therefore there are no accurate prophecies, because all passages appearing to be such were written later. We are even told that prediction was not characteristic of Israelite prophecy, despite the explicit statement in the Book of Deuteronomy that accurate prediction of future events is the *only* proof of a genuine prophetic mission.[22]

We may not be so far from Isaiah's own generation as we think. Perhaps it was not only to ancient Israel that his mission, through his book, is to "make the heart of this people fat, and their ears heavy, and shut their eyes; lest they see with their eyes, and hear with their ears, and understand with their hearts, and turn and be healed."[23]

Seven years after King Uzziah died and the prophet Isaiah received his mission, the kingdom of Judah was attacked on all sides by a coalition led by her brethren of the northern kingdom of Israel. King Ahaz, who had just come to the throne in Jerusalem, appealed for help—to Assyria. Isaiah strove mightily to dissuade him from an alliance with the great imperial aggressor, calling on him to trust in God rather than in the warlords of the east, giving him God's own promise that "these two smoldering stumps of firebrands" (Pekah of Israel and Rezon II of Damascus, the leaders of the coalition) would not prevail, but warning that "if you will not believe, surely you shall not be established" in God's favor.[24] Seeing that Ahaz was nevertheless resolved on carrying out his plan for an alliance with Assyria, Isaiah offered a miracle—"ask for a sign of the Lord your God"—to prove that his words and counsel truly came from Him. Ahaz refused, on the hypocritical plea of not putting God to the test.[25]

An understanding of this historical and personal background is essential to show why this was the occasion for the great prophecy of the Virgin Birth of Christ. The occasion was no mere petty war or political dispute, nor even just the crisis produced by the advance of imperial Assyria. It was a deliberate act of the will by the direct descendant of David—and ancestor of Christ—then reigning in Jerusalem, rejecting God's promise, scorning His power, choosing instead the worldly power of Assyria. It was treason and apostasy rolled into one; and this was what caused Isaiah to say: "Hear then, O house of David? Is it too little for you to weary men, that you weary my God also?"[26] No longer does he speak of the Lord Yahweh as Ahaz's god, as he had done earlier; now he speaks only of "my God," for Yahweh has abandoned Ahaz. But He will never abandon His people, and will Himself send them the supreme sign: Immanuel, born of a virgin, brought up in poverty.[27] And this is the wonder-child, Mighty God, Everlasting Father, Prince of Peace, the great light that is to appear in Galilee, as Isaiah prophesied soon afterward, when the Assyrians had swept over the north—the "shoot from the stump of Jesse," appearing when to human eyes the house of David had been cut off forever from power and glory, who would bring justice, peace and holiness to the whole earth, including the Gentiles, in the Messianic kingdom.[28]

Tiglath-pileser III of Assyria probably did not need Ahaz's request as a pretext for launching his devastating assault of 734 B.C.[29] on northern Palestine. But it meant that he could now legitimately extend his overlordship to Judah as well as her northern neighbors, since Judah's king had asked for his protection. Ahaz became an Assyrian vassal, and so he remained throughout the whole period of the death struggle and the fall of the northern kingdom.

In the Assyrian and later Babylonian empires the condition of vassalage was not only political and economic but also religious; the vassal king had to pay homage to the gods of his overlord. This Ahaz did, the Law of Moses to the contrary notwithstanding. He erected a new bronze altar in the temple at

Jerusalem, patterned after one favored by his Assyrian masters, and dismantled the "bronze sea" which had stood just outside the Temple—probably to obtain the highest quality metal for the new altar, possibly to help pay his tribute to Assyria. This opened the floodgates to popular acceptance of alien cults of all kinds, including the worship of trees and posts and the veneration of "high places," in massive violation of the First Commandment. Ahaz himself seems to have sacrificed one of his sons according to the hideous Canaanite practice.[30]

Isaiah and his contemporary, the prophet Micah who predicted the Messiah's birth in Bethlehem,[31] denounced in the classic prophetic manner the widespread apostasy, along with the personal and social immorality inevitably accompanying it. Under Ahaz conditions were hardly better in the southern kingdom than they had been in the northern, in contrast to the generally higher level of fidelity and morality that had earlier prevailed in Judah. The fact that Isaiah and Micah, along with Amos and Hosea, had accurately predicted the fate of the northern kingdom of Israel lent weight— after their predictions were so grimly fulfilled in 721 B.C.—to their repeated warnings that a similar fate impended for Judah.[32]

When Hezekiah succeeded Ahaz as King of Judah in 715 B.C., he made an attempt at reform, very likely in response to the messages of these four prophets. Pagan sanctuaries and cult objects were destroyed. Local shrines, once dedicated to Yahweh but now given over to alien gods, were closed. There may even have been some attempt to curb the dishonest practices in trade and the exploitation of the poor that the prophets had so magnificently condemned.[33]

But the relatively abundant historical material which has come down to us from the first half of the reign of Hezekiah indicates that his primary emphasis was not so much on either religious or secular reform, as on regaining national independence—which was necessary to complete any real religious reform, since only then could the gods favored by imperial Assyria be purged from the temple in Jerusalem. Egypt had just emerged again, very briefly, as a major power, following her conquest by the vigorous Nubian or "Ethiopian" dynasty of Piankhi from the region of the Fourth Cataract of the Nile in what is now Sudan, near Khartoum (see the Table of Middle Eastern Kings, 721-582 B.C., facing p. 105). It seemed that Egypt might be played off against Assyria so that Palestine could be preserved as a free buffer between the two great powers. Ashdod and several other Philistine cities in the coastal region of Palestine were enticed by this prospect into rebellions against Sargon II of Assyria, the destroyer of the northern kingdom of Israel. They urged Hezekiah to join them. He was very much inclined to do so, but Isaiah would have none of it. Egypt, he said —was he remembering Abraham's dream, a thousand years before? —can succceed in nothing; God has confused Egypt so that she staggers like a drunken man.[34] The history of Egypt during the next two centuries fully confirms that judgment.

This time Isaiah's counsel prevailed. Hezekiah did not join the revolt against Sargon II, so Judah was spared when in 711 B.C. Ashdod and its allies were humbled by the might of Assyria. Egypt did nothing whatsoever to help them.[35]

In 705 B.C. the great Sargon died on a campaign against barbarians in the far north, and his less able son Sennacherib became king of Assyria. A chain reaction of revolts crackled around the Assyrian empire. The city of Babylon and the whole of southern Mesopotamia erupted into full-scale rebellion under the able leadership of Merodach-baladan the Chaldean. He sent emissaries to every king and nation subject to Assyria whom he thought might join him; Hezekiah of Judah was one of them. Egypt offered its aid, for whatever that was worth. There appeared to be a genuine prospect of success; in fact, it was just such a concerted uprising that totally destroyed the Assyrian empire less than a century later.[36]

Despite Isaiah's renewed warnings, Hezekiah felt he could not let pass what seemed to be his and Judah's greatest temporal opportunity. He formally renounced allegiance to Assyria and made a treaty with Egypt. In vain Isaiah told him that his ambassadors were carrying gifts to a nation that would be of no use to them, "that brings neither help nor profit, but shame and disgrace."[37] Through all the year 702 B.C. Hezekiah prepared for a desperate struggle. It was at this time that the famous Siloam tunnel, a remarkable feat of ancient engineering, was dug to bring the water of the only spring near Jerusalem within the city walls underground, for use during a prolonged siege.[38]

These preparations were only too necessary. Merodach-baladan proved a better diplomat and advocate than warrior. Sennacherib defeated him, took Babylon, and marched west in 701 B.C. to capture Tyre, the great Phoenician port. Tyre had prospered mightily since the days of Jezebel, founding Carthage far across the Mediterranean Sea in North Africa, opposite Italy. But as Isaiah had foretold, Tyre's days of greatness were now at an end. She was never more to be her own master. As Ezekiel was later to prophesy, her island would eventually become a bare, uninhabited rock used only by fishermen as a place to spread their nets.[39]

Most of Palestine and Phoenicia submitted to Sennacherib after the fall of Tyre, but Hezekiah held out, counting on his Egyptian allies. This time they actually did send a relieving force, which the veteran Assyrian infantry easily repulsed at Eltekeh. Sennacherib proceeded to take 46 of the towns of Judah, deporting many of their inhabitants, and shutting up Hezekiah and his army in Jerusalem "like a bird in a cage."[40]

Hezekiah sued for peace. He offered a large tribute and indemnity, which Sennacherib seems to have accepted; but then, according to our two Biblical accounts of these events, he nevertheless demanded the unconditional surrender of the holy city.[41] Hezekiah defied him, this time with Isaiah's blessing. The prophet proclaimed:

Thus says the LORD concerning the king of Assyria: He shall not come into this city, or shoot an arrow there, or come before it with a shield, or cast up a siege-mound against it. By the way that he came, by the same he shall return, and he shall not come into this city, says the LORD. For I will defend this city to save it, for my own sake and for the sake of my servant David.[42]

The Egyptians probably brought another army to Pelusium on their northeastern border. Their tradition as well as the Biblical narrative preserved the vivid memory of a sudden, overwhelming disaster to the Assyrian army. The terrible invaders were laid low by no human hand; tens of thousands died. The Egyptians told a strange tale of mice gnawing the Assyrian soldiers' bowstrings; the Israelites saw in what happened the work of an "angel of the Lord." A pestilence is the most likely natural explanation for both traditions. The imperial tyrant retreated headlong, leaving Jerusalem unscathed, and laying the foundation for the later conviction of the people of Judah that God would never permit His holy city to be taken by an enemy under any circumstances.[43]

But Isaiah made no such promise. He never ceased to predict Jerusalem's eventual conquest and the exile of its people,[44] while at the same time also predicting that the yoke of Assyria would ultimately be broken[45] and that Babylon, her imperial successor, would end also in utter desolation:

> Babylon, the glory of kingdoms,
> the splendor and pride of the Chaldeans,
> will be like Sodom and Gomorrah
> when God overthrew them.
> It will never be inhabited
> or dwelt in for all generations;
> no Arab will pitch his tent there,
> no shepherd will make their flocks lie down there.
> But wild beasts will lie down there,
> and its houses will be full of howling creatures.[46]

This spectacular prophecy, so astonishing to those who first heard it applied to the queen city of the Middle East for the past thousand years, came true *to the letter* across the next thousand years.[47] After the Persian, Macedonian, and Roman conquests and a long decline, when the Roman emperor Septimius Severus reached its site in 199 A.D. he found it completely deserted— and 150 years later, the space within its crumbling walls was actually used as a Persian royal game park. Said an Elamite Christian who passed by Babylon on his way to Jerusalem, quoted by St. Jerome: "The whole area within the walls is a wilderness inhabited by all manner of wild animals."[48] Never since inhabited by men, it has remained to this day a haunt of foxes and jackals.[49]

Hezekiah died in 687 or 686 B.C. and was succeeded by his son Manasseh, a young boy. The regents who ruled for him made peace with Assyria, and throughout his reign of over forty years he remained Assyria's loyal vassal. At Manasseh's accession, Isaiah must have been well over seventy years old.[50] Most probably it was then that, like the Apostle John in his old age, Isaiah brought forth—in the clear, serene detachment from worldly concerns that comes to great spirits at the end of a long, full life—his supreme revelation, set forth in the last twenty-seven chapters of his book.[51]

He was given the grace to see, far down the corridors of time, a liberator named Cyrus marching out of the mountains of the east with Median troops, and the return at last from exile of the remnant of his people, which he had first foreseen at the beginning of his mission when he named his elder son Shear-jashub, meaning "a remnant shall return."[52] And God enabled him to see further still—this man who in the fullness of his faith and the strength of his youth had said to the Holy Spirit: "Here I am! Send me!" and had spoken at His bidding through more than half a century—to the end of the long, long trail of rise and fall, exile and return, disaster and glory, humbling and hope for his people, where waited One in agony, "despised and rejected by men, a man of sorrows . . . [But it was for our sins that he was pierced][53] . . . wounded for our transgressions . . . bruised for our iniquities," given "a grave with the wicked," placed in a rich man's tomb "although he had done no violence, and there was no deceit in his mouth." Yet "upon him was the chastisement that made us whole, and with his stripes we were healed."[54] After sacrificing his life he would live again;[55] "he will see the light and be filled."[56] Flagellation, Crucifixion, redemptive suffering and death, burial, and Resurrection—all are here in vivid foreshadowing, though with many of the usual difficulties of Messianic textual interpretation compounded by rationalistic, anti-supernatural exegesis.

Yet when all is said and done, who else but Jesus Christ could the prophet possibly be referring to? As Paul Heinisch rightly reminds us, "in all religious history we find but One who suffered and died to redeem mankind, and One who rose to new life from a grave—Jesus."[57] The Suffering Servant in Isaiah 53 is unquestionably innocent, his suffering unquestionably redemptive, his death and burial and return to life clearly attested. Was the Servant a personification of Israel, as has often been suggested? Evidently not, for this sufferer is sinless, and where does Isaiah or any other prophet depict Israel as sinless? The whole thrust of the prophetic message is that Israel is being justly punished for her many and grievous sins. Even the rationalist exegete John McKenzie is forced to reject this popular interpretation, and opt for an otherwise unknown individual as the Servant.[58] But the point is that the individual Whom these words signify is obvious, if only the critics would drop their fixed preconception that predictive prophecy cannot occur, and realize that all time is present to the eternal God, Who can and does reveal truth to us.

Who has performed and done this,
calling the generations from the beginning?
I, the LORD, the first,
and with the last; I am He.[59]

Late tradition held that the aged Isaiah was killed during the reign of Manasseh, and it could well be true, for so long as he lived he would be a standing reproach to those who brought back idolatry and apostasy to Judah during that reign, on a larger scale than ever before, and presecuted all who remained faithful to Yahweh and His commandments. (This was probably the occasion of the scornful denunciations of idolatry in the later chapters of the Book of Isaiah, rather than their reflecting the later experience of the exiles in Babylonia, as is assumed by those who hold to the hypothesis of a "second Isaiah.") At any rate, we know that by the time of Christ Jerusalem was called the "killer of prophets."[60]

In Manasseh's reign Jerusalem became a killer not only of prophets, but of children. The Satanic Canaanite rites of child sacrifice had returned with idolatry. Manasseh's own son was burned upon an altar as an offering to the dark spirit Jezebel had served, two hundred years before.[61] Such altars now stood in the Temple itself, along with an image of Asherah. Pavilions were built within or close by the Temple for the "sacred" prostitution of both men and women. The king consulted mediums, soothsayers and wizards.[62]

Meanwhile, Assyria was lord of the world. Sennacherib had died at the hands of two of his sons in 681 B.C., but the murderers did not succeed him; another son, Esarhaddon, became king and conquered Egypt, taking Memphis in 671. Egypt revolted as soon as he had left it; he died on the way back to regain it, but his son and successor Ashurbanipal accomplished the reconquest. When yet another revolt sprang up there—for the Pharaohs of this period came from Nubia far up the Nile where they could retreat and regroup unmolested each time they were defeated—Ashurbanipal devastatingly sacked the enormously wealthy 1500-year-old capital of Thebes in Upper Egypt, in 663 B.C.[63] The whole of the Middle East now lay at Assyria's feet —virtually the whole civilized world of that time, west of India.

But Assyria had no tradition of, nor real capability for lasting incorporation and rule of foreign lands, only a splendid army;[64] so she could never go beyond the incessant military campaigning that comprises practically all we know of her bloody history. Eleven years after the great sack of Thebes, Babylonia and Elam were in revolt and Egypt had regained independence. In this general revolt, spearheaded and probably planned by Ashurbanipal's own brother Shamash-shum-ukin who was viceroy of Babylonia, there is reason to believe that Manasseh of Judah joined; for the Book of Chronicles tells us that late in his reign he was dragged with hook and chain to Babylon by order of the Assyrian king. Ashurbanipal's siege of Babylon took three years; we know of no other occasion during his reign when he would have brought a captive vassal king there rather than to his own capital of Nineveh, and all we know of Manasseh's character indicates that he would never have risked revolt without very good reason to expect victory. The revolt of Shamash-shum-ukin was the most formidable Assyria had ever faced up to that time, led as it was by a member of Assyria's own royal family. But it failed; Ashurbanipal took Babylon in 649 B.C. Manasseh, in his humiliating captivity, underwent a conversion. Praying to God for forgiveness, he was restored to his kingdom, and in the few years remaining to him (he died in 642) he did all he could to undo the effects of the massive apostasy he had earlier permitted, if not inspired. His son Amon reigned just two years before he was assassinated by his own servants, and an eight-year-old boy, Josiah, became king of Judah.[65]

Meanwhile Assyria turned on rebellious Elam and ravaged it with such ferocity and thoroughness—even disinterring and desecrating the bones of the dead—that this once populous and prosperous country in what is now southwestern Iran, which had existed for well over a thousand years, was virtually eliminated from history in 639 B.C.[66]

So was Assyria itself, just thirty years later.

For Ashurbanipal, growing old, doted upon his son Sin-shar-ishkun, though it seems probable that another son, Asur-etillu-ili,[67] was the Crown Prince; he made Sin-shar-ishkun his coregent, and in 627 B.C. the old king died. The two sons went to war with each other for their imperial inheritance, and the whole outwardly imposing structure of the Assyrian empire collapsed like the house built upon sand.[68]

In Jerusalem King Josiah was twenty-one now, ruling on his own; and in that very year, the year of old Ashurbanipal's death, God's call came to a young man, probably about Josiah's age, named Jeremiah, who dwelt in the village of Anathoth three miles northeast of Jerusalem. Jeremiah was probably a direct descendant of the priestly family of Eli who had been custodians of the Ark of the Covenant at Shiloh in the days before the Philistine conquest;[69] he was to live to see the Ark, now enshrined in the Holy of Holies in the Temple at Jerusalem, destroyed forever as he had prophesied.[70] The words of God's call to Jeremiah echo down the centuries; they would be quoted at critical moments in the history of Christendom by the great Popes of the High Middle Ages:[71]

> "Before I formed you in the womb I knew you,
>   and before you were born I consecrated you;
>   I appointed you a prophet to the nations."
> Then I said, "Ah, Lord God! Behold, I do not know how to speak, for
> I am only a youth." But the LORD said to me,
> "Do not say, 'I am only a youth';
>   for to all to whom I send you you shall go,

and whatever I command you you shall speak.
for I am with you to deliver you, says the LORD.''
Then the LORD put forth his hand and touched my mouth; and the LORD
said to me,
    "Behold, I have put my words into your mouth.
    See, I have set you this day over nations and over kingdoms,
    to pluck up and to break down,
    to destroy and to overthrow,
    to build and to plant.''[72]

It was indeed a time of uprooting and of rebuilding. In October of the year
after God called Jeremiah, Nabopolassar of Babylon defeated the Assyrians just
outside the walls of his great city; in November he assumed the title of King
of Babylon, marking the beginning of the end for the Assyrian empire. In Judah
King Josiah, freed at last from Assyrian vassalage, set out to restore the realm
of his ancestor David by taking control of the former northern kingdom of Israel,
whose people were now a mixture of the surviving Israelites with the new tribes
the Assyrians had brought in to settle there, and thoroughly permeated with
paganism. As an essential part of this restoration, Solomon's temple in Jerusalem
was repaired. During the repairs, in 622 B.C., the high priest Hilkiah found
in some forgotten niche of the holy structure a "book of the law" as given to
Moses, and took it to the king.[73]

It was St. Jerome who first suggested that the book Hilkiah found was
Deuteronomy, the fifth book of the Pentateuch; modern scholars generally agree
with his conclusion.[74] No book of the Old Testament contains more vehement
denunciations of idolatry and apostasy than Deuteronomy; the glory of its blessings and the fire of its curses still strike sparks even today, across thirty-two
centuries. Whatever King Josiah had begun to do in his land so deeply corrupted
by the evils given free rein under Manasseh, it was clear to him upon reading
the Book of Deuteronomy that he had not done nearly enough. He rent his clothes,
crying: "Great is the wrath of the LORD, that is kindled against us, because
our fathers have not obeyed the words of this book."[75]

Josiah assembled all the people who could be gathered together at the Temple, almost certainly including the young prophet Jeremiah. All solemnly
covenanted to live by the Law they had almost forgotten, which had been so
dramatically revealed to them again. The Temple was purged of every object
connected with the false gods; they were burned on the slopes above the Kedron
canyon and their ashes taken away to Bethel. The priests who had used them,
the mediums and the soothsayers and the wizards and the cult prostitutes, were
all driven away. The alien shrines around and beyond Jerusalem were ceremonial-
ly defiled, particularly Tophet where the children had been sacrificed, in the
deep valley of Ben-Hinnom which, most appropriately, was to give its hellleniz-
ed name of Gehenna to be one of the names of Hell.[76]

Josiah and his men then proceeded to the north, where they tore down the shrines of the old northern kingdom, originally dedicated to Yahweh, but long since perverted by the rituals of other gods; the Book of Deuteronomy called for public worship of the One True God at the Temple alone, and so it now must be. The next spring (621 B.C.) the Passover was celebrated for the first time in centuries. Its commemoration had actually lapsed ever since the time of the ''judges''—this alone clear proof of how far the Israelites had fallen away from the teachings of Moses, and therefore of how well founded the prophets' denunciations had been; now it was renewed according to the prescriptions of the Law of Moses.[77]

It was the greatest reform in the history of the children of Israel since their occupation of the Promised Land; yet still it was not sufficient. It proved far too much a reform ''from the top,'' by official edict, rather than a repentance of the heart, a genuine turning back to God by the people as a whole. As Jeremiah was to declare later, public and private morals had been little changed; only the liturgy and the suppression of idolatry were involved.[78] And now presumption was joined with continuing sin: the Temple had been purified according to God's Law; very well, now everyone could go about his business as before, except for the new restrictions on ritual. Surely God would never permit their holy city with His holy Temple to be destroyed!

Meanwhile the wolves were gathering about the lair of their brethren in Nineveh. Nabopolassar of Babylon made an alliance with Cyaxares, King of the Medes, in 620 B.C.; the Medes were an Iranian people, with no historical connection with Mesopotamia, vigorous, now expansion-minded, and outstanding soldiers. The Babylonians attacked Assyria from the south, the Medes attacked it from the east, and the wild barbarians known to the Babylonian chronicles as Umman-manda and to the Greeks as Cimmerians and Scythians attacked it from the north. The desperate Sin-shar-ishkun made an alliance with Egypt. A combined Egyptian-Assyrian army fought the Babylonians to a standstill in 615, but the next year the Medes broke through and took and destroyed Ashur, the most ancient city in Assyria, which bore the name of their god of battles.[79]

Few people have left so grim a memory as the Assyrians; but one must admire their courage in the last fatal hour. They fought to the end. In 613 they drove back the Medes and counter-attacked Babylonia; but in 612 the allies—Babylonians, Medes, Umman-manda—came together in a final smashing invasion, dammed the Tigris River, flooded the walls of Nineveh, and stormed and looted the imperial capital of the treasures accumulated by centuries of raiding. Sin-shar-ishkun died in the flaming city—we may presume, sword in hand.[80]

The Assyrian remnant retreated to Haran, the ancient city of Abraham. They had a new king, their last, Ashur-uballit II. The Umman-manda and the Babylonians followed close; Haran too was taken and sacked. Ashur-uballit escaped, fleeing southward, seeking sanctuary and help in Egypt. What was left of his army and that of Egypt counter-attacked, to no avail; and Ashur-uballit II and his nation pass out of history.[81]

Egypt had a new Pharaoh in the year Haran fell (610 B.C.), the vigorous and enterprising Necho,[82] who decided to lead the main Egyptian army into Syria, presumably to pick up as many as he could of the pieces of the shattered Assyrian empire. He marched in the spring of 609, taking the old familiar route of the conquerors up the coast of the Mediterranean in Palestine almost to Mount Carmel, then across the plain of Jezreel to Megiddo, site of so many battles. At Megiddo King Josiah met him with the comparatively tiny army of Judah, fought a battle against great odds, and died on the field; his body was brought back to Jerusalem in his royal chariot, with great lamentation. Necho marched on to the Euphrates River, which temporarily became the border between the Egyptian and Babylonian empires; the Medes had returned to their distant Iranian plateau and the Umman-manda, with no more cities to loot, had vanished into the northern wilderness. As for Palestine, for the moment it belonged, though very briefly, to Egypt.[83]

In the summer of 609 B.C. Pharaoh Necho asserted his new authority over defeated Judah by deposing and imprisoning Josiah's son Jehoahaz and appointing in his place Josiah's eldest son Eliakim, whom the people had previously rejected, evidently knowing well the base character which his later history reveals. Necho ordered his creature to change his name to Jehoiakim, meaning "Yahweh establishes." This change of the king's name to incorporate the Divine *Ya* is significant, showing that despite what must have been the appalling shock of the disaster at Megiddo to loyal worshippers of Yahweh, faith in Him remained strong enough in Judah so that even the alien victor felt he must recognize it in this way. But perhaps the faith had been weakened to the point where this gesture alone sufficed for the people, for under Jehoiakim Josiah's reform lapsed almost completely.[84]

Now the prophet Jeremiah's hour had come—the hour foretold in his second call from God, when he was to be made like "a fortified city, an iron pillar, and bronze walls, against the whole land, against the kings of Judah, its princes, its priests, and the people of the land"[85] with a message of destruction and disaster and death. The sin of the long years of the reign of Manasseh had not been purged by the largely external and ritualistic reform of Josiah, and was now returning under Jehoiakim. Foreign domination was no excuse. God expected loyalty from His people even without temporal reward, even in the face of temporal punishment; He had given no automatic perpetual guarantee of physical protection to a faithless people. So Jeremiah stood at the gate of the Temple in the winter of 609-608 B.C. to proclaim to that people his crushing Temple Sermon:

Thus says the LORD of hosts, the God of Israel, Amend your ways and your doings, and I will let you dwell in this place. Do not trust in these deceptive words: "This is the temple of the LORD, the temple of the LORD, the temple of the LORD!"

For if you truly amend your ways and your doings, if you truly execute justice one with another, if you do not oppress the alien, the fatherless or the widow, or shed innocent blood in this place, and if you do not go after other gods to your own hurt, then I will let you dwell in this place, in the land that I gave of old to your fathers for ever.

Behold, you trust in deceptive words to no avail. Will you steal, murder, commit adultery, swear falsely, burn incense to Baal, and go after other gods that you have not known, and then come and stand before me in this house, which is called by my name, and say, "We are delivered!"—only to go on doing all these abominations? Has this house, which is called by my name, become a den of robbers in your eyes? Behold, I myself have seen it, says the LORD. Go now to my place that was in Shiloh, where I made my name dwell at first, and see what I did to it for the wickedness of my people Israel. And now, because you have done all these things, says the LORD, and when I spoke to you persistently you did not listen, and when I called you, you did not answer, therefore I will do to the house which is called by my name, and in which you trust, and to the place which I gave to you and to your fathers, as I did to Shiloh.[86]

And there had been the children —the children who had died screaming in the valley of Ben-Hinnom, Gehenna, the Valley of Hell, blood offerings to the powers of evil. One ritual defilement of Tophet had not atoned, could not come near atoning, for such a crime. Only acts of charity and love, of whole-hearted service and total obedience to God, could wash that stain away; without them in sufficiency, it remained. "Vengeance is Mine." So the words of judgment came to Jeremiah—words which speak also to us, the worst child-murdering generation in the history of the people of God:[87]

"For the sons of Judah have done evil in my sight, says the LORD; they have set their abominations in the house which is called by my name, to defile it. And they have built the high place of Topheth, which is in the valley of the son of Hinnom, to burn their sons and their daughters in the fire; which I did not command, nor did it come into my mind. Therefore, behold, the days are coming, says the LORD, when it will no more be called Topheth, or the valley of the son of Hinnom, but the valley of Slaughter: for they will bury in Topheth, because there is no room elsewhere. And the dead bodies of this people will be food for the birds of the air, and for the beasts of the earth; and none will frighten them away. And I will make to cease from the cities of Judah and from the streets of Jerusalem the voice of mirth and the voice of gladness, the voice of the bridegroom and the voice of the bride; for the land shall become a waste.[88]

When he was done, those who had been listening in mingled horror and fury rushed upon him and seized him, crying: "You shall die!" They brought him to trial; the priests—forerunners of Annas and Caiaphas—presented the indictment: "This man deserves the sentence of death, because he has prophesied against the city, as you have heard with your own ears."[89]

Jeremiah said:

> Behold, I am in your hands. Do with me as seems good and right to you. Only know for certain that if you put me to death, you will bring innocent blood upon yourselves and upon this city and its inhabitants, for in truth the LORD sent me to you to speak all these words into your ears.[90]

Then the princes and the people began to have second thoughts. Had not, after all, the earlier prophets prophesied very similarly, if not quite so scathingly? Suppose Jeremiah was speaking God's word; what would then be the consequences of putting him to death? In the end it was Ahikam, son of Shaphan, one of Josiah's original group of reformers, who saved the prophet's life; but still Jeremiah's words were not heeded.[91]

Egypt remained, as ever since the Exodus, a "broken reed." In the spring of 605 B.C. the brilliant young crown prince Nebuchadnezzar[92] led the Babylonian army in an attack on the Egyptian army at Carchemish on the Euphrates, and routed it. Pursuing swiftly into Syria, he defeated the Egyptians again near Hamath, but then (in August) received an urgent message from Babylon that his father, King Nabopolassar, had just died. Nebuchadnezzar had to hurry back for his coronation, which took place in September. The next year the new king was in the field again, besieging the old Philistine city of Ashkelon in Palestine, which fell in December 604. In that very month, Jeremiah collected all of God's words to him about the impending fate of Judah, and had his secretary Baruch write them on a scroll which was taken to King Jehoiakim, in a last effort to gain his repentance and that of the people. The scroll contained the warning that Judah and all the surrounding nations would serve the king of Babylon for seventy years.[93]

King Jehoiakim listened attentively to the reading of the whole scroll. As each three or four columns were read and finished, he took out a knife, cut them off, and threw them on the fire that was keeping the winter chill at bay. Three of his aides protested; he ignored them. When the systematic destruction of the scroll was complete, he sent orders for the arrest of Jeremiah and Baruch. But they could not be found. God, we are told, had hidden them.[94]

By the next year (603) Nebuchadnezzar had established his rule over Judah—Jehoiakim became his vassal instead of Pharaoh Necho's—and over all of Syria-Palestine, just as Jeremiah's scroll had said; and that Babylonian dominion lasted sixty-five years. It is the most precise historically verified time prophecy in the Bible.[95]

Determined to gain for himself and his Babylonian dynasty the full extent of the former Assyrian empire, Nebuchadnezzar invaded Egypt in 601 B.C., but was repulsed from the frontier with heavy losses. This convinced Jehoiakim that the time had come to change sides again, and he repudiated his allegiance to Babylon. It took Nebuchadnezzar a year to reorganize his army after the defeat, and in 599 he was occupied elsewhere, but in December 598 he was back in Palestine and Jehoiakim was dead—very possibly killed by his own people. Nebuchadnezzar besieged Jerusalem; no Egyptian help came; in three months the holy city surrendered. Its new young king Jehoiachin, his mother, high officials, leading soldiers and citizens, and skilled artisans, to the number of about 10,000 men (at least 30,000 including their wives and children who accompanied them) were deported to Babylonia along with all the gold in the Temple. The long-predicted exile of the people of Judah from the Promised Land had begun.[96]

Jehoiakim's brother Zedekiah was now made king, or regent, by Nebuchadnezzar's order, though many in Judah continued to regard the exiled young Jehoiachin as their only rightful king; and the great tragedy continued to unfold. For the Israelites were not yet ready to submit. The greater part of them could not believe that God had indeed delivered His people into the hands of the Babylonians as punishment for their sins, as Jeremiah had been telling them. Did not the holy city of Jerusalem, with the fountainhead of holiness that was its Temple, still stand, even though now shorn of its gold? Had not many of the prophets foretold a triumphant return of God's people from exile? Probably that return was imminent, and all would be well again. It is hardly surprising that they thought thus; no people in any age, however much aided by Divine grace, would have found such a message as Jeremiah's easy to accept. The amazing fact is not that so many angrily refused to follow his advice, but that they listened to him at all, and remembered and in the end honored him for all that he had said; for no man in all history has quite so relentlessly condemned the people he loved, whose fate, combined with God's orders that he foretell it, brought him agonies of spirit that plumb the profoundest depths of human suffering.[97]

In the year 594 B.C., when a new rebellion was being plotted at a conference in Jerusalem of representatives of Edom, Moab, Ammon, Tyre, Sidon, and Judah, Jeremiah came to the plotters with an ox yoke on his shoulders, and this message:

> Thus says the LORD of hosts, the God of Israel. This is what you shall say to your masters: "It is I who by my great power and my outstretched arm have made the earth, with the men and animals that are on the earth, and I give it to whomever it seems right to me. Now I have given all these lands into the hand of Nebuchadnezzar the king of Babylon, my servant."[98]

To King Zedekiah personally Jeremiah was equally blunt: "Bring your necks under the yoke of the king of Babylon, and serve him and his people, and live."[99]

In the same year Jeremiah wrote to the exiles in Babylonia, warning them not to heed the false prophets who spoke of an imminent return, but rather to settle down, build homes, plant gardens, marry and have children, ''for thus says the LORD: When seventy years are completed for Babylon, I will visit you, and I will fulfill to you my promise and bring you back''—but not before.[100] And when Zedekiah himself went to Babylon that same year, Jeremiah sent a message by his quartermaster to be read aloud in Babylon, foretelling the end of the new imperial city:

> Though you rejoice, though you exult,
> O plunderers of my heritage,
> though you are wanton as a heifer at grass,
> and neigh like stallions,
> your mother shall be utterly shamed,
> and she who bore you shall be disgraced.
> Lo, she shall be the last of the nations,
> a wilderness dry and desert.
> Because of the wrath of the LORD she shall not be
>   inhabited,
> but shall be an utter desolation.[101]

In 589 B.C. a new Pharaoh, Hophra, came to the ancient throne of Egypt and it seems that his promises of aid were the decisive factors in persuading Judah to rise in one last, suicidal rebellion. Only Ammon and Tyre joined them this time; Zedekiah was very dubious, but was overborne by his bellicose advisors. So, in an act of matchless folly, the invincible Nebuchadnezzar was challenged again; and he was in Palestine before the year was out. In January 588 he was already besieging Jerusalem, and the other strong points in Judah were taken one by one, their defenders massacred and the towns destroyed.[102] Zedekiah asked Jeremiah if God would help Judah in this extremity. No, answered Jeremiah inexorably, it is too late; now God Himself is fighting against Israel. He will neither pity nor spare Zedekiah and his people. The holy city ''shall be given into the hand of the king of Babylon, and he shall burn it.''[103]

The all too familiar story of the ''broken reed'' was now acted out again for the last time. Pharaoh Hophra marched with his army into Palestine and the Babylonians had to raise the siege of Jerusalem to meet him, giving Judah a temporary respite until the Egyptians suffered their usual defeat and were driven back to their homeland. During the period when the siege was raised Jeremiah, leaving Jerusalem to return temporarily to his ancestral lands in Anathoth, was arrested on suspicion of desertion to the Babylonians, since he was suspected (not unreasonably, from the standpoint of the strictly worldly-minded) of collaboration with them. Thrown into a mud-filled cistern to die, he was rescued by a black eunuch after a plea to Zedekiah, who promised to protect his life.[104]

But Zedekiah could protect no one's life much longer. The siege of Jerusalem was resumed, now with no hope of rescue for the defenders. By July 587 all food in the city was gone, and the veteran Babylonian troops were driving in through a great breach in the walls. Zedekiah, his sons, and his remaining soldiers tried to flee at nightfall. They were caught in the desert near Jericho. Zedekiah and his sons were brought before Nebuchadnezzar. This time he showed no mercy. He killed the sons before their father's eyes, then blinded him and sent him in chains to Babylon to die. All the bronze was stripped from Solomon's temple, including the great bronze pillars Jachin and Boaz, and on July 30 the holy city was put to the torch. What remained of the Temple after the fire was torn down, along with the walls of the city. The Ark of the Covenant, with the tablets of the Law—the Ten Commandments inscribed on Sinai—disappeared, never to be seen again.[105] Among the exiles in Babylon, the prophet Ezekiel wrote that he had seen God departing from the Temple in a vision.[106]

Much of the remaining population of Judah—at least 30,000, possibly as many as 60,000 more—was deported to Babylon to join the 30,000 exiles of 597.[107] Many went in chains. Jeremiah was fettered with them, but at the last moment Nebuzaradan, the commander of the Babylonian royal guard, found and released him, for he had orders to treat him well—Nebuchadnezzar believed Jeremiah had helped him attain his victory. Jeremiah was told that he was free to go wherever he wished. He chose to stay in his shattered country.[108]

Gedaliah, son of that Ahikam son of Shaphan who had been one of King Josiah's ardent reformers and had saved Jeremiah's life after his Temple Sermon in 608, was made governor of what was left of Judah, but he was soon assassinated. Most of the Israelites who had remained in the neighborhood of ruined Jerusalem, fearful of being blamed by Nebuchadnezzar for the crime, fled to Egypt, despite a last warning by Jeremiah that if they went they would die there, abandoned by God. They took the old prophet with them—presumably by force, since he would hardly have voluntarily subjected himself to the fate of the emigrants to Egypt which he so graphically described—and so this man, called to as hard a mission as ever God gave one of His own, passes out of history and out of time, awaiting the coming of his Savior Whom, in a single passage, he foresaw as the just and triumphant king of the future, descendant of David and Vindicator of His people.[109]

The Holy Land and the Holy City lay waste. There was yet another deportation of about 2,300 of the remnant still dwelling in Judah, in 582 B.C.; then the very name of Judah seems to have been abolished, and most of its territory merged with the province of Samaria.[110] The glory of the Chosen People of God was a fading memory:

> By the waters of Babylon,
> there we sat down and wept,
> when we remembered Zion.
> On the willows there
> we hung up our lyres.[111]

Yet there remained the voice of Jeremiah the doomsayer, Jeremiah the prophet of destruction and desolation—but Jeremiah who yet spoke for the Lord of history, Who is love:

> Behold, the days are coming, says the LORD, when I will make a new covenant with the house of Israel and the house of Judah, not like the covenant which I made with their fathers when I took them by the hand to bring them out of the land of Egypt, my covenant which they broke, though I was their husband, says the LORD. But this is the covenant which I will make with the house of Israel after those days, says the LORD: I will put my law within them, and I will write it upon their hearts; and I will be their God, and they shall be my people. And no longer shall each man teach his neighbor and each his brother, saying "Know the LORD," for they shall all know me, from the least of them to the greatest, says the LORD; for I will forgive their iniquity, and I will remember their sin no more.[112]

NOTES

[1] How small it really was is graphically demonstrated by Hilaire Belloc's statement "that a man walking out from Jerusalem eastward or northward or westward would have reached its boundaries in a morning" (*The Battleground: Syria and Palestine* [Philadelphia, 1936], p. 115).

[2] Isaiah 6:1-7. That this event, so supremely important in Isaiah's life, took place in the Temple is alone sufficient to dispose of the oft-heard argument that the great prophets were fundamentally opposed to the Temple worship (Yves Congar, *The Mystery of the Temple* [Westminster MD, 1962], pp. 54-57).

[3] Isaiah 6:8-9.

[4] Henri Daniel-Rops, *Israel and the Ancient World* (New York, 1964), pp. 257-258.

[5] See Norman K. Gottwald, *All the Kingdoms of the Earth* (New York, 1964), for a thorough exploration of this aspect of Isaiah's mind and career—but only for this aspect, since Gottwald writes with the evident presupposition that the supernatural never touches history.

[6] Isaiah 6:9-10.

[7] Isaiah 6:11-13.

[8] *The Jerusalem Bible*, ed. Alexander Jones (New York, 1966) (Old Testament), p. 1153, Note 61; Edward J. Young, *The Book of Isaiah* (Grand Rapids MI, 1965-1972), I, 258-259.

[9] According to the chronology adopted in John Bright's *A History of Israel*, 3d ed. (Philadelphia, 1981), and in this book, the year of King Uzziah's death and of Isaiah's inaugural vision in the Temple was 742 B.C., and Isaiah was still active at least until 688 near the end of Hezekiah's reign (Bright, *op. cit.*, pp. 290, 293).

[10] *e.g.*, *The Jerome Biblical Commentary*, ed. Raymond E. Brown et al (Englewood Cliffs NJ, 1968), I, 266, 366 (Catholic) and *The Interpreter's Bible*, ed. George A. Buttrick et al, Volume V (New York, 1965), pp. 382-383 (Protestant). Most Jewish scholars take the same view. A typical justification for this position appears in the Jerusalem Bible's "Introduction to the Prophets": "Almighty God could, of course, have conveyed the prophet into the distant future, severing him from his own time, transforming his imagery and cast of thought. This would mean, however, a duplication of the author's

personality and a disregard for his contemporaries—to whom, after all, he was sent—for which the Bible provides no parallel" (*The Jerusalem Bible* [Old Testament], p. 1125). This astonishing statement not only disregards the continuity of history (especially sacred history) and the utility, which should be self-evident, of prophecy which comes true, but is clearly wrong in asserting that this kind of prophecy is found only in Isaiah ("the Bible provides no parallel"). Jeremiah predicted the fall of Babylon; the Book of Daniel contains many long-range prophecies; Jesus Himself predicted the Roman destruction of Jerusalem in 70 A.D., forty years after His death and Resurrection. Roman Catholic readers will take note that the Pontifical Biblical Commission stated in 1908 that the theory of the multiple authorship of Isaiah had not been proved, and that this position has never since been changed by the Vatican. This remains true despite the fact that this decree is now mostly honored in the breach; as *The Jerome Biblical Commentary* states (II, 629), "in those instances where there is a real dispute few modern Catholic scholars adhere today to the position on the authorship, the dating, and the unity of the biblical books proposed" by the Commission in 1908, and by other authoritative decrees of the Roman Catholic Church. For a summary of the 1908 statement—a very moderate and reasonable position indeed—see Edward J. Kissane, *The Book of Isaiah* (Dublin, 1943), II, lviii.

[11] *Jerome Biblical Commentary*, I, 367; *Interpreter's Bible*, V, 383; Kissane, *Book of Isaiah*, II, lx; and see especially Rachel Margalioth, *The Indivisible Isaiah* (New York, 1946), for an exhaustive linguistic analysis of the similarities of word usage in the earlier and later chapters of the Book of Isaiah. As she points out, the magnificent classical Hebrew in which the entire book is written contrasts sharply with the changing language of the exilic period. She concludes: "If, therefore, both parts of Isaiah have in common an unusual number of the same unique attributes of God, specific designations for the Jewish people, the same special formulas of prophecy, similar words of consolation and rebuke, similar expressions on the future of Zion and Jerusalem, and the ingathering of the exiles, the same forms for emotions of joy and gladness, failure and destruction—all this points to a common and single mentality. This indicates not only a uniformity of style, but also a uniform trend of thought. This reveals the innermost recesses of human thinking, wherein idea and language are woven into one web, and there can be no room for a stranger. This is the style of a man which is the man himself." (pp. 41-42) John E. Steinmueller, *A Companion to Scripture Studies*, 2nd ed. (New York, 1942), II, 241-242 also points out similarities in style between the earlier and later chapters of Isaiah, for example the use of the term "Holy One of Israel" for God 12 times in the first part of Isaiah and 14 times in the second part, but only five times elsewhere in the whole Old Testament, and the use of the imperfect tense for "thus says the Lord" instead of the usual prophetic perfect in the first chapter and in the 40th and 41st; Steinmueller adds that Isaiah clearly knew Palestine rather than having grown up in Babylonia during the exilic period, since he "designates by name various trees which are indigenous in Palestine and not in Babylonia, for instance, the cedar (44:14), the myrtle, the olive, the fir, the elm and the box (41:19)." It is only fair to add that many scholars have found significant differences between the style of the earlier and that of the later chapters of the Book of Isaiah, and that some differences are apparent even in translation. The writer, not being a student of Hebrew, cannot express an informed opinion on the details of the controversy, but is certainly entitled to point out that the carefully reasoned and researched conclusions of Mrs. Margalioth and Father Steinmueller deserve, at a minimum, respectful attention and a detailed, categorical response, which they do not appear to have received from modern Biblical scholarship.

[12] Edward J. Young, *Introduction to the Old Testament*, 2d ed. (Grand Rapids MI, 1960), pp. 204, 207. For the Dead Sea scroll of Isaiah, see *Jerome Biblical Commen-*

tary, II, 565. On that scroll, "chapter 40 begins on the very last line of the column which contains 38:9-39:8. The last words on the one column are "'cry unto her'; and the first words in the next column are "that her warfare is accomplished'" (Oswald T. Allis, *The Unity of Isaiah* [Philadelphia, 1950], p. 40). Although the generally accepted date for the scroll is c. 100 B.C., the great Oriental scholar William F. Albright has dated it to 150 B.C. (Allis, *op. cit.*, p. 40).

[13] Josephus, *Antiquities of the Jews*, XI.1.2.

[14] Young, *Introduction to the Old Testament*, p. 209; C. F. Whitley, *The Prophetic Achievement* (London, 1963), pp. 37-38.

[15] See Isaiah's specific commands to write down his words, in 8:16 and 30:8.

[16] *Interpreter's Bible*, V, 383, says that to treat the later chapters of Isaiah as true prophecy has "led to the most tortuous kind of reasoning." A bit of projection is apparent here. It is the efforts to explain away the prophecies which are an integral part of the Book of Isaiah as we have it—as it was written down over 2,000 years ago in the scrolls preserved at Qumran—which are truly tortuous reasoning; their acceptance, however simple-minded some may think it, is the straightforward response.

[17] The Medes had a great reputation in the ancient world for rigid morality and stern discipline, conveyed by Herodotus' well-known phrase "the law of the Medes and the Persians, which altereth not" (see Richard N. Frye, *The Heritage of Persia* [Cleveland, 1963], p. 100). The Medes were ethnically and historically very close to the Persians; Cyrus of Persia was to rule them early and recruit many of them into his army (see Chapter Seven, below).

[18] Young, *Introduction to the Old Testament*, pp. 209-210.

[19] For contrasting views of this long-drawn-out controversy, see *Interpreter's Bible*, V, 218-219 and Young, *Book of Isaiah*, I, 281-289. The chief difficulty with all the non-Messianic interpretations of this passage is their inability to account reasonably for who else but the Messiah Isaiah might be talking about. The Hebrew word *'almah*, best translated "maiden," does not normally refer to a married woman and certainly does not mean a married woman of distinction, which disposes of the two most frequently heard modern interpretations, that either Isaiah's own wife or the Queen of Judah was meant (see John Mauchline, *Isaiah 1-39, Introduction and Commentary* [New York, 1962], pp. 98-99, on this point). Since the mother herself will name the child, evidently it has no father at hand to do so (normal procedure in the strongly patriarchal Middle East); therefore, if on the merely natural level, the child is illegitimate. Why Ahaz, Hezekiah, Isaiah or anyone else should regard the birth of an illegitimate boy in Judah in 735 B.C. as a sign of anything significant—to say nothing of being proof that "God is with us"— no one has explained. At any rate, all agree that *'almah* can mean "virgin" as the Greek Septuagint version of the Old Testament translates it, by the Greek word *parthenos*; the only difficulty is in explaining why Isaiah used *'almah* rather than *bethulah* which is the more specific Hebrew word for "virgin." Young (*op. cit.*, I, 288, citing Joel and later Aramaic incantation texts) thinks that *bethulah* might mean a married woman, but this would leave Hebrew without a word for "virgin"; Young's argument seems rather thin at this point. On balance it seems most reasonable to trust the Septuagint translation, which is at least as old as the Qumran scroll of Isaiah, since nothing in the Hebrew contradicts it at this point, and otherwise it is almost impossible to imagine how this prophecy could have had the importance Isaiah obviously intended to give it.

[20] Young, *Book of Isaiah*, I, 333-338; Paul Heinisch, *Christ in Prophecy* (Collegeville MN, 1956), pp. 89-94. Young's brilliant linguistic and literary analysis solidly establishes the divine meaning of these names for the Messiah. See also Young's refutation of the theory of a royal enthronement ceremony in Judah in which such terms were allegedly

used (*op. cit.*, I, 496-499). The explicit prophecy in Isaiah 9:1 of the Galilean origin of the Messiah has been curiously overlooked or downplayed even by many orthodox exegetes. It is one of the most significant and clear-cut prophecies in the entire Old Testament, since virtually every scholar who accepts the existence of an historical Jesus will at least admit that He was a Galilean, yet at the time the prophecy was made, Galilee had just fallen to the Assyrians, who introduced an alien population which was to predominate in that area for centuries. Galilee had never been part of the southern kingdom of Judah where Isaiah lived and preached. There was hardly a less likely place in all the traditional territory of the Twelve Tribes for the Messiah to come from. Matthew 4:15-16 specifically cites this prophecy in reference to the Galilean ministry of Jesus.

21 See Notes 53-58, below, for further commentary and sources on Isaiah 53.

22 Deuteronomy 18:21-22.

23 Isaiah 6:10.

24 Isaiah 7:1-9; Bright, *History of Israel*, pp. 271-272; Heinisch, *Christ in Prophecy*, pp. 82-83.

25 Isaiah 7:10-12; Heinisch, *Christ in Prophecy*, p. 83.

26 Isaiah 7:13.

27 Isaiah 7:14-15; Heinisch, *Christ in Prophecy*, pp. 83-85.

28 Isaiah 9:1-7, 11:1-9; Heinisch, *Christ in Prophecy*, pp. 89, 93-105. Toward the end of the Book of Isaiah appears a very significant reference to the choosing of priests from among the Gentiles in the Messianic kingdom (66:21).

29 Bright, *History of Israel*, p. 274; see Chapter Five, above.

30 Bright, *History of Israel*, pp. 276-277; 2 Kings 16:3, 10-18.

31 Micah 5:1-3; Heinisch, *Christ in Prophecy*, pp. 109-112.

32 Bright, *History of Israel*, pp. 277-280; Paul Heinisch, *History of the Old Testament* (Collegeville MN, 1952), pp. 278-281.

33 Bright, *History of Israel*, pp. 282-284.

34 Isaiah 19:11-15; Genesis 15:12-14; Heinisch, *History of the Old Testament*, p. 25.

35 Bright, *History of Israel*, pp. 281-282.

36 *Ibid.*, pp. 284-285; H. W. F. Saggs, *The Greatness That Was Babylon* (New York, 1962), pp. 127-128.

37 Isaiah 30:5.

38 G. Ernest Wright, *Biblical Archaeology* (Philadelphia, 1957), pp. 169-171; Bright, *History of Israel*, p. 285.

39 Isaiah 23; Bright, *History of Israel*, pp. 285-286; Ezekiel 26:4-5. The complete and literal fulfillment of Ezekiel's prophecy occurred after the Muslims devastated the last remains of ancient Tyre during the wars of the Crusades. The ancient site of the island city is today a bare rock where fishermen spread nets (Nina Jidejian, *Tyre through the Ages* [Beirut, 1969], p. 139).

40 Bright, *History of Israel*, p. 286.

41 Even though we have a record of these events from Sennacherib (the Taylor prism) as well as in both 2 Kings and Isaiah, the sequence of events is sufficiently unclear to have given rise to a widely accepted theory that Sennacherib conducted two campaigns in Palestine: the first in 701 B.C. ending with the Assyrians victorious, Isaiah's warnings against rebellion proved correct, and Hezekiah paying a large tribute and indemnity; and another in some later year of Sennacherib's reign, in which the Assyrian king demanded the unconditional surrender of Jerusalem and planned the deportation of its people, Isaiah counselled firm resistance and promised that God would save Jerusalem, and Jerusalem was saved by a disaster (probably a pestilence) that struck the Assyrian army (see Note 43, below). For an extended presentation of the case for this "two-

campaign theory" of these events, see Bright, *History of Israel*, pp. 298-309; for an account assuming that only one campaign was involved, see Giuseppe Ricciotti, *The History of Israel* (Milwaukee, 1955), I, 380-387. K. A. Kitchen, *The Third Intermediate Period in Egypt* (Warminster, England, 1973), pp. 154-161 and 383-387, argues strongly against the two-campaign theory, with specific reference to Bright's arguments. Bright's claim that the Biblical mention of Taharka as Pharaoh of Egypt in connection with the 701 campaign proves that a later campaign was involved since Taharka did not become Pharaoh until 690, is answered effectively by Kitchen with the argument that Taharka was a prince commanding the Egyptian army in 701 and Pharaoh when the account of this period was written in the Book of Kings, so would naturally then be identified by the royal title he bore at the time of writing. Bright's other arguments are somewhat more persuasive, particularly that which highlights the difficulty of accounting for what seems to be first an acceptance by Sennacherib of tribute, indemnity, and loss of territory as sufficient punishment for rebellious Judah, and then a demand for unconditional surrender. But Assyrian kings were hardly noted for honor in diplomacy. Bright's argument based on attribution of particular passages in Isaiah not explicitly referring to Sennacherib's invasion or invasions, to one or the other of his supposed two campaigns in Palestine, reads far too much into the text; many of these references are not so precisely attributable to known historical events. Bright himself admits that postulating only a single campaign "might be held to satisfy the evidence as well as any reconstruction were it not for the mention of "Tirhakah"" (*op. cit.*, p. 303) which Kitchen has fully explained.

[42] Isaiah 37:33-35.

[43] The Egyptian tradition is recounted in Herodotus II, 141—a source clearly not dependent in any way on the Bible and therefore giving very strong support to the historical reality of a great disaster having befallen the Assyrian army at this time. Mice would naturally be associated with a pestilence, which would be seen by the Israelites as the sign of a destroying angel. It is hardly surprising that this episode is nowhere mentioned in Assyrian annals. For an account combining particularly well the Egyptian and Israelite memories of this event, see Ricciotti, *History of Israel*, II, 384-386; for a discussion of the regrouping of the Egyptian army see Kitchen, *Third Intermediate Period in Egypt*, p. 385n (*pace* Bright, *History of Israel*, p. 304).

[44] One of many such predictions was made when Hezekiah was receiving the ambassador of Merodach-baladan (Isaiah 39:6-7). Another appears in the immediate context of Isaiah's reassurance that Assyria would not triumph after Sennacherib had demanded the surrender of Jerusalem (Isaiah 37:30-32).

[45] Isaiah 14:24-25. The language could hardly be more explicit: Yahweh has sworn "to break the Assyrian in my land, and upon my mountains trample him under foot; and his yoke shall depart from them, and his burden from their shoulder."

[46] Isaiah 13:19-21.

[47] With two notable exceptions (Jeremiah 25:11 and Daniel 9:24-26) the prophets do not give precise dates for the events they foretell; their time perspective is God's own eternal present. Events of the near and of the distant future stand side by side. As Paul Heinisch well states: "Just as the eye discerns no depth dimension in the stars of the heavens and regards the rays from the various stars as equidistant while the actual light distance may vary by millennia, so in spirit the prophet beheld as contemporaneous events that would take place at various times. Accordingly, the prophets before and during the exile do not distinguish sharply between preparations for the Messianic kingdom (e.g. the return from exile) and the Messianic kingdom itself." (*Christ in Prophecy*, p. 206) Therefore a long historical perspective is often necessary to see just how the prophecies were fulfilled.

48 James Wellard, *Babylon* (New York, 1972), pp. 198-199; Georges Roux, *Ancient Iraq* (Cleveland, 1964), p. 353. The extant Qumran scroll of the Book of Isaiah antedates the final fulfillment of his prophecy about Babylon, with the specific detail of the wild animals in the ruined houses, by some 400 years; therefore no theory of interpolators and redactors can cope with the precise fulfillment of that prophecy. But that precise fulfillment is little known. Even Edward J. Young in his monumental three-volume commentary on Isaiah, who rarely misses an opportunity to help establish the Divine inspiration of the prophet and his prophecies, is apparently unaware of it. The quotation from St. Jerome was discovered only by fortunate chance in the course of research for this history.

49 An archeologist's eyewitness testimony graphically demonstrates the fulfillment of the prophecy, on the site of ancient Babylon: "Here only is real death. Not a column or an arch still stands to demonstrate the permanency of human work. Everything has crumbled into dust. . . . Under my feet are some holes which have been burrowed by foxes and jackals. At night they descend stealthily from their haunts in their difficult search for food, and appear silhouetted against the sky. This evening they appear to sense my presence and stay in hiding, perhaps wondering at the stranger who has come to disturb their peace. The mount is covered with white bones which represent the accumulated evidence of their hunts. . . . A jackal is now sending forth his howl, half-cry and half-threat. . . . I should like to find a reason for all this desolation. Why should a flourishing city, the seat of an empire, have completely disappeared? Is it the fulfillment of a prophetic curse that changed a superb temple into a den of jackals? Did the actions of the people who lived here have anything to do with this, or is it the fatal destiny of mankind that all its civilizations must crumble when they reach their peak?" (Edward Chiera, *They Wrote on Clay* [Chicago, 1938], pp. xiii-xiv)

50 Isaiah was called in 742 B.C. (see Note 9, above). The nature of his response does not suggest a young boy. If he were 20 at the time, he would have been 75 in the probable year of Manasseh's accession, 687 B.C.

51 Young, *Book of Isaiah*, I, 411.

52 Isaiah 7:3, 10:20-21; *Jerusalem Bible* (Old Testament), p. 1153, Note 7b.

53 Translation of Isaiah 53:5 by Heinisch, *Christ in Prophecy*, p. 145. The Revised Standard Version, the Douay (old Catholic) translation, and the Knox translation use "wounded" rather than "pierced," as does the Greek of the Septuagint. Two of the most recent complete Bible translations, however—the Jerusalem Bible and the New English Bible—use "pierced" as Heinisch does.

54 Isaiah 53:3, 5, 9. Heinisch, *Christ in Prophecy*, p. 147, rejects the Revised Standard Version (and more usual) translation "with a rich man in his death," claiming it to be a textual corruption. On this point, significant in view of Jesus' actual burial in the tomb of the rich man Joseph of Arimathea, the Jerusalem Bible supports the Revised Standard Version, and defends this translation in a footnote (*Jerusalem Bible*, Old Testament, p. 1229) while the New English Bible rejects it, and the Douay and Knox translations are equivocal.

55 He had been "cut off out of the land of the living" (Isaiah 53:8) and put in his grave (53:9) yet "he shall see his offspring, he shall prolong his days" (53:10)—conventional expressions for a long life.

56 The Revised Standard Version has "he shall see the fruit of the travail of his soul and be satisfied" (Isaiah 53:11). But Heinisch (*Christ in Prophecy*, pp. 145, 148n) gives the translation quoted in the text, pointing out that "the Septuagint reading, light, is confirmed by a Hebrew manuscript found in 1947 north of the Dead Sea from pre-Christian times which has *'or*, light."

[57] Heinisch, *Christ in Prophecy*, p. 148.

[58] John L. McKenzie, *The Anchor Bible: Second Isaiah* (Garden City NY, 1968), pp. xliii-liv.

[59] Isaiah 41:4.

[60] Matthew 23:35-37. See Ricciotti, *History of Israel*, I, 389, on the persecution by Manasseh.

[61] 2 Kings 21:5-6; see Chapter Five, above.

[62] Ricciotti, *History of Israel*, I, 102, 388.

[63] Saggs, *Babylon*, pp. 131-137; Kitchen, *Third Intermediate Period in Egypt*, pp. 391-395. The Assyrian destruction of Thebes is graphically described by the prophet Nahum (3:8-10).

[64] The technological superiority of the Assyrian army is explained by A. R. Burn, *Persia and the Greeks* (New York, 1962), pp. 24-25.

[65] Ricciotti, *History of Israel*, I, 389-391; Saggs, *Babylon*, pp. 138-140.

[66] Saggs, *Babylon*, pp. 140-141.

[67] This name is sometimes rendered Ashur-etil-ilani.

[68] This reconstruction of the course of events in Assyria after Ashurbanipal's death follows John Bright in *The Anchor Bible: Jeremiah* (New York, 1965), pp. xxxvi-xxxviii; that of Saggs, *Babylon*, pp. 141-142 differs slightly.

[69] Bright, *Jeremiah*, pp. lxxvii-lxxxviii.

[70] Jeremiah 3:16.

[71] Notably by Pope St. Gregory VII (pontificate 1073-1085); see Volume Two, Chapter Nineteen of this history.

[72] Jeremiah 1:5-10.

[73] Bright, *Jeremiah*, pp. xxxvii-xxxviii; 2 Kings 22:8-10.

[74] Bright, *History of Israel*, p. 319n.

[75] 2 Kings 22:13.

[76] 2 Kings 23:1-10. For Gehenna, see *Jerome Biblical Commentary*, II, 648 (with reference to Matthew 5:22).

[77] 2 Kings 23:15-23; Bright, *Jeremiah*, p. xl. For the development of the Passover feast, see Roland de Vaux, *Ancient Israel, its Life and Institutions* (New York, 1961), pp. 484-493.

[78] Heinisch, *History of the Old Testament*, p. 261.

[79] Saggs, *Babylon*, pp. 142-144; Burn, *Persia and the Greeks*, pp. 27-28.

[80] Saggs, *Babylon*, p. 145.

[81] *Ibid.*, pp. 145-146; Alan Gardiner, *Egypt of the Pharaohs* (Oxford, 1961), p.358.

[82] These characteristics of Necho are evident from two separate accounts in Herodotus, of his commencement of an 80-mile canal from the Nile to the Red Sea and of his sending a naval expedition manned by Phoenicians on no less a mission than the circumnavigation of Africa, which he states that they accomplished in three years (*Persian Wars*, II:158, IV:42). On the expedition circumnavigating Africa, see Walter W. Hyde, *Ancient Greek Mariners* (New York, 1947), pp. 234-240, who states that "the weight of recent opinion" supports the conclusion that the circumnavigation was actually accomplished.

[83] Bright, *Jeremiah*, p. xlvi; A. T. Olmstead, *History of the Persian Empire* (Chicago, 1948), p. 33.

[84] Bright, *Jeremiah*, pp. xlvi-xlviii; Ricciotti, *History of Israel*, I, 403-405.

[85] Jeremiah 1:18.

[86] Jeremiah 7:3-14.

[87] Legal abortions in the United States of America alone approached a million a year

within three years of the U. S. Supreme Court's decision January 22, 1973 legalizing abortion on demand at any time during the first six months of pregnancy and in most cases thereafter, right up to the moment of birth. By 1982 virtually unlimited abortion had also been legalized in most other Western and nominally or once Christian countries, with the notable exceptions of Ireland, Poland, and most of those speaking Spanish or Portuguese, so that the overall annual total of unborn babies killed—though reliable statistics for that total were unavailable—may have run as high as three million or even more.

[88] Jeremiah 7:30-34.

[89] Jeremiah 26:11.

[90] Jeremiah 26:14-15.

[91] Jeremiah 26:16-19, 24.

[92] This is the form of his name long familiar from the most used translations of the Bible. It is retained in the Revised Standard Version used in this history, and therefore is employed uniformly in the text. The more technically correct but rather pedantic "Nebuchadrezzar" (the actual transliteration of the name in Babylonian cuneiform is Nabu-kudurri-usur) is not used. Nebuchadnezzar was the real builder and only strong figure of the short-lived Babylonian or Chaldean empire, appearing after the fall of Assyria.

[93] Bright, *Jeremiah*, pp. xlviii, ci, 181-182. The prophecy of the seventy years' subjection to Babylon appears in Jeremiah 25:11 in a discourse specifically dated to the year 604 B.C., the first official year of Nebuchadnezzar's reign, which was also the year the scroll was prepared (Jeremiah 36:1).

[94] Jeremiah 36:21-26.

[95] The 65 years run from the fall of Ashkelon to Nebuchadnezzar in December 604 B.C. (for verification of the date see Bright, *Jeremiah*, p. xlviii with citations) to the fall of Babylon to Cyrus of Persia in October 539 B.C. (Olmstead, *Persian Empire*, p. 50).

[96] Bright, *History of Israel*, p. 327; Heinisch, *History of the Old Testament*, pp. 268-269; 2 Kings 24:12-16.

[97] See particularly Jeremiah 8:18-23 ("Is there no balm in Gilead? Is there no physician there?"), 15:10-21 ("Why is my pain unceasing, my wound incurable, refusing to be healed?"), and 20:14-18 ("Cursed be the day on which I was born!").

[98] Jeremiah 27:4-6.

[99] Jeremiah 27:12.

[100] Jeremiah 29:4-10.

[101] Jeremiah 50:11-13. The accuracy of this and other prophecies of Jeremiah on the destruction of Babylon has been impugned because of the fact that the Persian conqueror Cyrus entered the city without a battle and treated its inhabitants with the utmost consideration (Wellard, *Babylon*, pp. 183-184). But it was hardly the purpose of the prophets to write a complete future history; the issue is not what details they left out, but the accuracy of the predictions they actually made. Jeremiah nowhere explicitly linked the time of the destruction of Babylon with the end of its 70 years of imperial rule. Just 17 years after Cyrus' conquest Babylon had to be retaken by King Darius, this time with plenty of destruction and bloodshed; Darius tore down its walls and gates, plundered its royal tombs, and impaled 3,000 of its leading citizens on stakes. Later, after Babylon rebelled again, Darius' son Xerxes as King of Persia dismantled the city's great shrine to its god Marduk and degraded it to the level of a provincial town, putting it on the road to the eventual, final desolation (Olmstead, *Persian Empire*, p. 115; Wellard, *Babylon*, p. 186; and see Note 48, above).

[102] Bright, *Jeremiah*, pp. li-lii; Kathleen Kenyon, *Archaeology in the Holy Land*, 3rd ed. (London, 1970), pp. 290-296. Lachish is specifically mentioned in a collection of letters on ostraca found in its ruins as having been the last fortress outside Jerusalem

holding out in 588; one of the letters comments starkly that only from Lachish are signals still to be seen. Two thousand skeletons were found dumped in a single tomb in the ruins of Lachish; they are believed to have been victims of the massacre that occurred when the besiegers finally broke in. After the siege of 588 the town of Lachish was never again occupied.

[103] Jeremiah 34:2.

[104] Bright, *Jeremiah*, pp. lii, cviii-cx; Jeremiah 38:16.

[105] Bright, *Jeremiah*, p. liii; Heinisch, *History of the Old Testament*, pp. 272-273; 2 Kings 25:3-17; Kenyon, *Archaeology in the Holy Land*, pp. 291, 351; Kathleen Kenyon, *Royal Cities of the Old Testament* (New York, 1971), pp. 148-150. No specific mention is made in the Bible of what happened to the Ark itself. Perhaps the subject was simply too painful to discuss. We are told that the gold and sacred vessels of the First Temple were preserved in Babylon, ordered returned to Jerusalem by Cyrus, and actually brought back for installation in the Second Temple by Sheshbazzar (Ezra 5:13-16, 6:5); but nothing is said of any preservation or return of the Ark. Perhaps the Babylonian conquerors, unable to conceive of any sacredness or value in a rude structure of wood and two old stone tablets (as compared to objects of precious metal used in regular public ritual) simply cast them aside into the general destruction. The Holy of Holies of the Second Temple and later of Herod's Third Temple was entirely empty, as the Roman conqueror Pompey discovered to his astonishment (see Chapter Twelve, below).

[106] Ezekiel 10:4, 18-19, 11:22; see commentary by Congar, *Mystery of the Temple*, p. 67.

[107] Heinisch, *History of the Old Testament*, p. 312n.

[108] Jeremiah 40:1-6.

[109] Jeremiah 23:5-6; Bright, *Jeremiah*, pp. liii-liv, cxi, 144 (see p. 144 for the translation of *Yahweh-sidqenu* [Jeremiah 23:6] as "Vindicator" rather than simply "our righteousness" as in the Revised Standard Version). Jeremiah 43:8-44:30 preserves the last recorded words of the prophet, uttered in Egypt apparently shortly after his arrival there; being then in his late sixties (presuming he was born about 645 B.C.) and worn out with spiritual anguish and by the rejection of his people, it is probable that he died soon afterward. In these last prophecies and warnings in Egypt, Jeremiah foretold that Pharaoh Hophra would be delivered into the hands of his enemies who sought his life, as indeed happened in a revolt led by Ahmose (Amasis) in 570 B.C. (Herodotus, *Persian Wars*, II:169; Gardiner, *Egypt of the Pharaohs*, pp. 361-362) and that Nebuchadnezzar would smite Egypt, as he did in 568 (Gardiner, *ibid.*; Saggs, *Babylon*, p. 149). Since no details of Nebuchadnezzar's invasion are known (our principal source, the Babylonian Chronicle, is not extant for the years 594-556 B.C.—D. Winton Thomas, ed., *Documents from Old Testament Times* [New York, 1958], p. 75), we are hardly in a position to arrive at any conclusions, as Gardiner (*op. cit.*, p. 362) rashly does, about what Nebuchadnezzar did or did not accomplish in Egypt or how much destruction he wreaked. He could perfectly well have done there in 568 all that Jeremiah said he was going to do, including setting up his throne at Tahpanes (Daphnae) where the group of exiles with Jeremiah settled—this would have been a logical place for this to have been done, being very close to the eastern frontier of Egypt (Jeremiah 43:8-10; Bright, *History of Israel*, p. 346). All we know from extra-Biblical sources is that Nebuchadnezzar led a military expedition to Egypt in 568 B.C. and then departed, and that Pharaoh Ahmose retained his throne. It is notable that Jeremiah's prediction specifically states that "he [Nebuchadnezzar] shall go away from there in peace" (Jeremiah 43:12).

[110] Bright, *History of Israel*, p. 344; Heinisch, *History of the Old Testament*, p. 313. The southern part of what had been Judah, later to be Idumaea, was gradually occupied by Edomites from further south. The population of Judah, estimated at 125,000 even

after the deportation of 597 B.C., was reduced by the two later deportations and by war, famine, pestilence, and flight to so low a figure that when the first group of exiles returned half a century later, there were only about 20,000 Jews in Palestine (Bright, *ibid.*).

[111] Psalms 137:1-2.

[112] Jeremiah 31:31-34.

7.
THE QUEST AND THE CHOSEN (582-499 B.C.)

Thus says the LORD to his anointed, to Cyrus,
whose right hand I have grasped,
to subdue nations before him
and ungird the loins of kings,
to open doors before him
that gates may not be closed:
"I will go before you
and level the mountains,
I will break in pieces the doors of bronze
and cut asunder the bars of iron,
I will give you the treasures of darkness
and the hoards in secret places,
that you may know that it is I, the LORD,
the God of Israel, who calls you by your name.
For the sake of my servant Jacob
and Israel my chosen,
I call you by your name,
I surname you, though you do not know me."
    —Isaiah 45:1-4

"By the waters of Babylon" the survivors gathered. They wept for Zion lost; they built for Zion to come. The prophet Ezekiel outlined for the exiles their ideal city of the return; their teachers and scribes preserved the Law and the Prophets, collecting the sacred books brought from Judah and writing down those carried in memory, assembling the greater part of what we now know as the Old Testament.[1] The prophets had been proved right in their warnings; they would also be proved right in their promises. Under the iron rod of Nebuchadnezzar the exiles cemented a deathless loyalty and devotion which has lasted ever since, and shows every indication of enduring—redeemed or unredeemed—to the end of time. God had punished them justly, even allowed the destruction of His own temple, but they were still His Chosen and would cling to Him, despite all sin, error and weakness, world without end. It was a titanic, heaven-storming resolve, utterly unique in history, affecting Jews who never returned to the Holy Land almost as much as the Jews who did return. This division, so familiar in our own day, was already clearly apparent before the sixth century B.C. ended. Some went back to the Promised Land; others remained, prosperous and successful, in alien lands; but the Chosen People held together. The promised restoration would soon occur; but the great *diaspora*, the scattering of the children of Israel all over the world, had begun as well, and continues to this day.[2]

A Messiah would come, descendant of David, to bring the ultimate fulfillment of the Divine promise; somehow, with the glory of his triumph an immense, cosmic suffering would be associated. So the Prophet Isaiah had told them. But first must come the restoration, so often foretold by so many of the prophets. For this, and for a new ordering of the world, the Lord of history called Cyrus of Persia by name, as His anointed for this task, though Cyrus did not know Him. From the clay plains of Babylon the exiles were to raise their eyes to the hills toward the sunrise, whence would come their help. And there is good reason to believe that God's Word had already been brought to that high eastern land by others of His Chosen People.

Thirty-eight years after the destruction of the Temple, three years after the death of the mighty Nebuchadnezzar, an insignificant prince named Cyrus was ruling the small province of Anshan (called Parsa by its inhabitants) in southwestern Iran, just east of old, shattered Elam. Cyrus held this land as a vassal of his maternal grandfather Astyages, king of the Medes, ruler of the western portion of the Iranian plateau, son of that Cyaxares who had helped bring down Assyria. Cyrus' people were as close as any known to history to the ancestral Indo-European or Aryan stock of central Asia, men straightforward like spears, trained to "ride and shoot and speak the truth," worshipping the sky-god who was always the closest to the true God in the ancient pantheons, and the fire as a beneficent warrior against darkness and cold. They had their ancient priesthood, the Magi, who sacrificed, but not to idols. Air, earth, water, fire—the primal elements—were to be kept pure and undefiled by human corruption.[3]

Late in the reign of Ashurbanipal of Assyria the first Cyrus of Parsa, paternal grandfather of Isaiah's Cyrus, had sent tribute after the Assyrian devastation of Elam, borne to Nineveh by his eldest son. Assyria then ruled over a substantial portion of what was soon to become the Median kingdom in northwestern Iran.[4] It was to these distant provinces on the Iranian plateau that Sargon II of Assyria had sent his 27,290 captives, the flower of the northern kingdom of Israel, the "lost ten tribes," in 721 B.C. Fantastic were the speculations about their fate through the Christian centuries; total has been the abandonment of the question in our time. When mentioned now in any standard work on the history of Israel or of the ancient Middle East, these captives (very unlike those from Jerusalem in Babylon later) are simply said to have merged with the local population, disappearing from history without a trace.[5]

Yet vital evidence to the contrary appears in every Catholic Bible. The Book of Tobit tells of God-fearing Israelites of the northern tribe of Naphtali living in Nineveh in its last years, with friends and kinsmen in the cities of the Medes in Iran—in Ecbatana (modern Hamadan), the Median capital, and in Rhages near the site of present-day Tehran. The story of Tobit concludes with the old man, his son and his new wife setting out from Nineveh, warned of its imminent fall by Nahum's prophecy, to take refuge in Media, to dwell there permanently and show forth the holiness of the lives an angel had touched.[6]

The combination of its special literary merit, its giving the most extensive presentation of an angel in the entire Bible, and the fact that through pure happenstance it was preserved only in a Greek text and therefore excluded from the Hebrew and later Protestant Bibles—though the existence of a Hebrew or Aramaic original is generally acknowledged[7]—has made the Book of Tobit an historical orphan. With one forgotten exception,[8] every commentator seems to have missed the enormous significance of Tobit's and Tobias' life and character and journeyings with reference to the history of Iran during the childhood of the great Cyrus, the rescuer and restorer of Israel. For as soon as Nineveh fell in 612 B.C., the Median kingdom succeeded to the rule of all the old Assyrian provinces in Iran, including those where the Israelite captives from the northern kingdom had been settled; and probably in 588 B.C., just 24 years later, Zarathustra (Zoroaster), the prophet of the Persians, the first great religious founder-leader known to history outside Israel, converted King Vishtaspa of Bactria to his new faith after (according to Zoroastrian tradition) having been driven out of his original home further west in Iran. One tradition places that home in that very city of Rhages to which Tobias was originally sent, at the very time when young Zarathustra would have been living there, if this tradition is correct.[9]

This is not to say, of course, that either Tobit or Tobias ever actually met Zarathustra—after all, we are told that Tobias never reached Rhages. Nor does the point being made even depend on the actual historicity of Tobit and Tobias—though to this writer, as to most earlier Catholic commentators, there seems no good reason for denying it.[10] The point is that the Book of Tobit clearly reflects the existence and persistence of Jewish colonies, descended from the ten tribes of the northern kingdom of Israel rather than from the later exiles from Judah, in the region of Iran from which Zarathustra came, at the time when he was there. The "lost ten tribes" did *not* disappear in a generation or two, becoming indistinguishable from the local population; they endured at least for the century and more from the fall of Samaria to the fall of Nineveh (721-612 B.C.) and almost certainly longer, to merge not with the local population but with the general Jewish *diaspora* after the fall of Jerusalem; and some of the lost ten tribes kept the faith. Considering all the later history of the Jews, it would surely have been much more astonishing if all of them had lost it.

We have solid historical proof of how deeply the Jews of the *diaspora* influenced Muhammad in Arabia twelve centuries later. There is every reason to suppose that their colony in his home city of Rhages, and in neighboring cities like Ecbatana, had a similar influence on the Persian prophet, so utterly unlike any other Gentile up to this point in history in his character and teaching and mission: a humble man, called by God to preach His justice, His love of right, His abhorrence of evil, His ultimate reward of the good and punishment of the wicked, the great battle which would be His triumph at the end of the world—an all-powerful Creator-God Who nevertheless could be addressed, as Zarathustra like the psalmists addressed Him, as an intimate friend." Zarathustra felt that he knew God. His doctrine strongly suggests that some of God's revealed truth had come to him, giving his religion, with its glorious prayers, its heroic image of a cosmic-historic battle against evil which was far from the later perversion of Manichaeanism, a quality much more akin to the Biblical faith of God's Chosen People than any other religion in the world before the Incarnation.

When this fact is noted at all, it is usually attributed to Zoroastrian influence on Judaism, though how this could have been exerted on men with the ironclad, exclusive, penitential mentality of Ezekiel and Ezra—Giuseppe Ricciotti calls theirs the mentality of the *gadher*, of the walled city[12]—is almost impossible to imagine. How much more reasonable to see Zoroastrianism as a mingling of the partly understood teaching of exiled Jews like Tobit with the native virtues and world-view of the Iranians—an offshoot of revelation, the product of a questing mind and heart working on Divine truth only partly heard, destined ultimately to wither and die as all branches cut off from the one true vine must wither and die, but drawing its initial nourishment from the same root.

There is only one religion in the world. Beyond it, as G. K. Chesterton so memorably expresses it in *The Everlasting Man*, there are only the story-tellers and the philosophers —and never, till Bethlehem, could the twain meet.[13]

When the Magi came to Bethlehem from the east to worship the Child, did they bring the faith of Zarathustra home at last?

Was Cyrus of Persia a Zoroastrian? Though we do not have positive proof, as we have for the third Persian emperor, Darius, everything in Cyrus' career and character and policies that we know supports this hypothesis. The Zoroastrian religion was well established in the Persian empire as it moves into history; Cyrus was universally recognized in his time as one of the noblest of all ancient rulers, ethically far advanced over any of his predecessors. When in 550 B.C. he revolted against the Median king Astyages, who had become a cruel oppressor, and took over his whole kingdom, the change seems to have met no significant resistance after the initial clash; yet Cyrus employed no terror tactics, no massacres and deportations. By 547 B.C. Cyrus ruled most of Iran, when an ambitious and wealthy king of the far west, Croesus of Lydia in Asia Minor near the Aegean Sea, made the mistake of invading Cyrus' new territories in eastern Asia Minor.[14]

Cyrus may have been one of history's greatest commanders; we cannot say for sure, because his three opponents—Astyages, Croesus, and Nabonidus of Babylon—all seem like men of straw before him, falling at the first push. Was it because they were all so weak, or Cyrus so overwhelming? Or was indeed, as Isaiah said, the hand of the Lord directly at work in smoothing his way? Be the cause what it may, each of Cyrus' three great wars, overthrowing three mighty kingdoms, lasted less than a year. In November 547 B.C. Persian spearmen stood on the "impregnable" citadel of Lydia's capital of Sardis; Cyrus was giving his law to the Greeks of the Ionian shore; what had been the world of Nebuchadnezzar was transformed.[15] The days of Babylon's power were numbered; the prophecies were being fulfilled. We can only begin to imagine— but it is worthwhile to try—the emotion with which the Jewish exiles heard the supernal words of Isaiah and Jeremiah, one and two centuries old, echoing back down the corridors of time in justifying thunder.

What was more, now they had a new prophet: Daniel. Taken from Jerusalem as a boy and raised at the court of Nebuchadnezzar,[16] yet he kept the faith of his people while rising high in the king's favor, as we know that at least one Jewish interpreter of signs and dreams rose in the later reign of Nabonidus of Babylon.[17]

The Book of Daniel bristles with difficulties—textual, historical, and theological. Many of these were apparent even before the modernism and rationalism of those "higher critics" who explicitly or implicitly deny the possibility of real predictive prophecy, was applied to it. The book as we have it has portions in three different languages: Hebrew, Aramaic, and Greek. Full texts in different languages, or one which could be regarded as a translation from an original written by Daniel, would be another matter, but here we have the unique case of a book containing long sections (not simply brief passages or quotations) in three languages as far back as we can trace it. In such a situation, it seems that we must assume that what we have in the extant Book of Daniel are oral accounts of Daniel's prophecies and adventures, circulated among the Israelites particularly of the *diaspora* (since Daniel never returned to Jerusalem), and written down long after his death in separate fragments in the language each writer preferred to use, the most authoritative of which were later collected into our present book. The attempts to link these fragments by chronological tags and name references which do not match Persian history as we know it, need not therefore be attributed to Daniel himself, who would have known these facts more precisely.[18]

Except for these chronological tags, nothing in the Book of Daniel contradicts the known history of the sixth and seventh centuries B.C. It is often claimed that the account of Nebuchadnezzar's temporary insanity, which Daniel predicted, is a projection back in time of the insanity suggested by the contemporary accounts we have of the withdrawal of Nabonidus, the last Babylonian king, for ten years, virtually incommunicado, to the isolated Arabian oasis of Tema.[19] But the fact is that our Babylonian sources tell us almost nothing about the last decade of Nebuchadnezzar's reign[20]—indeed, the silence is so complete as to be almost suspicious—and accumulating evidence about Nabonidus' stay in Tema indicates not insanity but a forceful and innovative imperial policy which, but for the advent of Cyrus, might have greatly extended and strengthened the Babylonian empire.[21] As for Belshazzar, called "king" and son of Nebuchadnezzar in the Book of Daniel, he had been regent during Nabonidus' long absence and may well have been Nebuchadnezzar's grandson if Nabonidus married one of the old king's daughters, as it would have been very reasonable and politic for him to do.[22] Though Nabonidus returned to Babylon before Cyrus' final blow fell, it is obvious from contemporary accounts that, being then very aged, he was totally incapable of conducting its defense; furthermore, Herodotus—a completely independent authority—says that there was indeed a great feast in Babylon the very night of Cyrus' final approach, just as the Book of Daniel tells us, and Belshazzar disappears from history with Babylon's fall (the Book of Daniel tells us that he was killed the night of the feast). The Persians "weighed, measured and divided" the land and wealth of the conquerors of the Chosen People, as the handwriting on the wall which Daniel had read, had said that they would.[23]

That Daniel lived and prophesied in the time of Nebuchadnezzar, Nabonidus and his son Belshazzar, and early in the reign of Cyrus, may therefore be taken as historical fact. The historical confusion, if such it be, in the chronological tags no more disproves the historical existence of Daniel than comparable chronological confusion in secular historical sources (a far from uncommon occurrence) vitiates the historical reality of the persons and events they describe. Daniel is located by the sources in a well-known, highly civilized age among well-known historical personages, not in a time of shadowy figures on the borderland of history and myth. The spectacular rise of the Persians provided the occasion and the need for great prophecy. Those who attribute the prophecies regarding Cyrus to a "second Isaiah" contemporary with the Persian empire-

MIDDLE EASTERN KINGS
582-499 B.C.

BABYLONIA	IRAN	EGYPT	JERUSALEM
	Media		
Nebuchadnezzar 605-562	Astyages 585-550	Hophra 589-570	
Amel-marduk 562-560		Amasis 570-526	
Neriglissar 560-556			
Labashi-marduk 556			
	Persia		
Nabonidus 556-539 (Belshazzar regent in Babylon)	Cyrus 550-530		the Return 537
	Cambyses 530-522	Psamtik III 526-525	
	Bardiya 522		
	Darius I 522-486		Haggai 520
			Zachariah 519
			Temple rebuilt 515

builder naturally give this role to him; but if in truth there was only one Isaiah, as we have contended, then Daniel stands alone as the world-prophet of this age, distinct from the much more local emphasis of the prophets primarily concerned with the repeopling of Jerusalem and the rebuilding of the Temple. If there were any doubt as to Daniel's importance as a prophet, surely Christ Himself laid it forever to rest, not only by so often quoting Daniel with approval, but above all by adopting for Himself Daniel's mysterious appellation "Son of Man" for the glorious King to come, and by applying to Himself, as He stood on trial before the Sanhedrin, Daniel's prophecy of the coming of the Son of Man to judge the world.[24]

Babylon fell in 539 B.C. Cyrus had diverted the Tigris River so as to skirt the "Median wall" which Nebuchadnezzar had built between the two rivers of Mesopotamia to protect Babylon. After a battle at the wall, Cyrus marched in and took the city unopposed.[25] Turning over its administration first to an official named Gobryas, who died soon afterward,[26] and then to his son Cambyses, he proceeded at once to redeem his pledge to the peoples Babylon had ruled: to restore their gods to their homes, and the people themselves where they had been deported and still wished to return. It was a remarkable promise; still more remarkably, it was faithfully kept.

For the exiled children of Israel Cyrus promptly issued his immortal decree, the first fulfillment of all the prophecies of the Return:

> Thus says Cyrus king of Persia: the LORD, the God of heaven, has given me all the kingdoms of the earth, and he has charged me to build him a house at Jerusalem, which is in Judah. Whoever is among you of all his people, may his God be with him, and let him go up to Jerusalem, which is in Judah, and rebuild the house of the LORD, the God of Israel— he is the God who is in Jerusalem; and let each survivor, in whatever place he sojourns, be assisted by the men of his place with silver and gold, with goods and with beasts, besides free-will offerings for the house of God which is in Jerusalem.[27]

The decree is dated to Cyrus' first year as king of Babylon, into which he had made ceremonial entry October 29, 539 B.C. The joyful eagerness of the response is shown by the fact that in the spring of 537 B.C., less than eighteen months after the fall of Babylon and probably little more than a year after Cyrus issued this decree, the repatriation caravan departed from Mesopotamia with no less than 42,360 Jews returning to the Promised Land. The caravan bore the implements of precious metal from the destroyed Temple that had been preserved as spoils of war at the Babylonian court, freely given back to the rightful owners by Cyrus; it was jointly led by Zerubbabel, a scion of the Davidic dynasty (the last known to history before Christ) appointed governor by the Persians, and by Joshua, grandson of the last high priest who had served in Jerusalem.[28]

The returning exiles brought with them the titles to the former property of their families, from records which had been kept in Babylonia. They found some of the land occupied by squatters, with whom special arrangements for property exchanges had to be made and to whom substantial sums of money often had to be paid. Seven months after their arrival the men of the Return rebuilt the altar amidst the ruins of Solomon's Temple, on the exact spot where it had formerly stood. Then they laid the foundations of a new Temple, considerably smaller than Solomon's; but due to the exhaustion of their funds and opposition from the local inhabitants, mainly Samaritans, they were unable at that time to complete the project. For nearly twenty years the worship of the One True God was conducted once again in its designated place, but in the open air, on a lonely bare altar set in rubble. All work on the Second Temple had ceased by the end of the year 536 B.C.[29]

Glorious as the Return was, it was not going to usher in the Messianic Age right away, however easy it had been so to read the prophecies of Isaiah; for prophecy often telescopes time, as the prophecies of the fall, desertion and desolation of Babylon had done.[30] The Return was a type, no more, of the founding of Christendom. The material circumstances of the repatriates were poor and would remain poor for centuries. Their political liberation was not in sight. The world would ignore them; only their fellow Jews in other lands would help sustain them.

Many Jews remained in Mesopotamia, supporting their brethren in Palestine both economically and politically. Among them was Daniel, now of great and venerable age, who continued to be a highly respected and influential figure in the land to which he had been brought captive long ago as a boy. His last revelations range down the centuries, past all the Persian kings and past Alexander the Great to the great oppressor Antiochus Epiphanes nearly 400 years later, and from him to the Antichrist of whom, as St. Jerome points out, Antiochus Epiphanes was clearly a type. Needless to say, those who reject the possibility of genuine prophecy are quick to date Daniel—or at least these parts of his book—to the time of Antiochus Epiphanes, about 165 B.C. There is not a fully developed "second Daniel" hypothesis; the modern scholarly consensus seems to be that the whole book was written at the time of Antiochus Epiphanes, but made use of some older traditions.[31]

Since most modern scholars assume that the prophetic parts of the Book of Daniel were written after, or contemporary with the events prophesied, by an odd twist it becomes in this case acceptable by modernist academic standards to try to identify the specific nations and kings referred to. Alexander the Great and Antiochus Epiphanes are unmistakable, and the Greeks are mentioned by name; but the figures of the other rulers and kingdoms, as even a cursory examination of the extensive and involved Danielic literature will show, are far from self-evident. Daniel is only somewhat more circumstantial than the earlier prophets. It was not the business of any of them to write a detailed, specific future history that could be dealt with like a conventional historical document. Here we approach the fringes of the profound—and, to time-bound mortals, essentially insoluble—mystery of Divine foreknowledge and free will. A prophecy too detailed would amount to a denial of free will; one too vague would amount to a denial of Divine foreknowledge. What the true prophets give us is therefore something intermediate—outlines, suggestions, parts of a pattern, even some specific names and events, but not the whole story, not even all the high points and prime movers.

Nor do the prophets give us exact dates. The Book of Daniel has many numbers, but even the conservative and literal Protestant exegete Edward Young is firm in his conclusion that all of Daniel's numbers indicating historic time are symbolic.[32] We are not told just when the prophesied events are going to happen nor just how long they are going to last. At most, the suggested time intervals are approximations of the coming truth. Jeremiah's prophecy of a 70 years' captivity in Babylon was five years too long; Daniel's prophecy of 69 weeks of years (483 years) from the Return to the time when "an anointed one shall be cut off, and shall have nothing'' is a little less than a hundred years too short if it refers to the Crucifixion and a little more than a hundred years too long if it refers to the murder of the high priest Onias during the early stages of Antiochus Epiphanes' persecution.[33]

The great Cyrus died in the far east, in battle against the wild Massagetai of central Asia, in 530 B.C. It was left to his son Cambyses to complete the unification of all the ancient Middle Eastern realms by conquering Egypt. At first he had his father's fortune; the hoary kingdom of the Pharaohs fell in a single year, 525 B.C.—as Media and Lydia and Babylon had each fallen in a single year—after one great battle at Pelusium and a relatively short siege of Memphis. Cambyses occupied the Egyptian oases as well as the Nile valley, and marched far up the Nile into Nubia where he suffered a reverse, the truth about which has been obscured by later propaganda.[34] But we know for certain that he, like his father, favored the Jews; he found a Jewish garrison which had been stationed on the island of Elephantine at the First Cataract of the Nile, the southern border of Egypt, by the last Pharaohs, presumably drawn from the refugees from the destruction of Jerusalem who had come to Egypt with or after the group including the prophet Jeremiah. Cambyses confirmed the favored position of the Jewish garrison with its schismatic temple (only at Elephantine did Jews of the pre-Christian *diaspora* build a temple of their own, if the Samaritans are excluded as non-Jews; no evidence or speculation so far has suggested why the Elephantine temple was built).[35]

Cambyses' troubles mounted. Rebellions threatened in Egypt, particularly after his reverse in Nubia; he destroyed some Egyptian temples and put to death the last Pharaoh, Psamtik III, whom he had defeated at Pelusium and Memphis. Despite many marriages, Cambyses had no sons. Then in 522 B.C. word came to him in Palestine, near Mount Carmel, that his brother Bardiya had risen in revolt and been proclaimed king. Scarcely had Cambyses received this news than he was dead—one of the many mysterious deaths of the mighty in history, that neither contemporary sources nor later hypotheses have been able to explain convincingly.[36]

Bardiya, supported by the Magi, proclaimed peace throughout the empire and relief from the war-tax for three years. Certain temples were damaged or destroyed, perhaps indicating a Zoroastrian urge for purification from idolatrous worship, since it is believed—though not known for certain—that the Persian Magi at this period were predominantly Zoroastrian. Then a thirty-year old prince named Darius, of another Achaemenid line parallel to that of Cyrus, whose father Hystaspis was satrap of Parthia and who had served as Cambyses' spear-bearer in Egypt, suddenly came forth proclaiming Bardiya to be not Bardiya at all, but a Magian impostor named Gaumata who looked almost exactly like him. The real Bardiya, Darius claimed, had been secretly killed by order of Cambyses—who, being conveniently dead, could not deny it. This dubious charge seems to have commanded little if any belief at the time, until Darius with six hard-bitten henchmen fell upon the reigning king and his court in Media and killed them, seven months later.[37]

Circumstantial evidence tells heavily against Darius as a regicide and usurper, and so sensitive was he to the accusation that he carved the enormous rock inscription of Behistun in three languages—Old Persian, Babylonian cuneiform and Elamite—to deny it to all the world and present his "cloak and dagger" version of the events of the hectic year 522 B.C. The Behistun inscription stands to this day, but Darius' credibility does not; for all his thunderings in good Zoroastrian language about how his opponents personified "the Lie," it appears more likely that Darius himself was the liar, that there was no impostor Gaumata, and that Bardiya was really Bardiya and the rightful king when Darius assassinated him.[38]

For when Bardiya—real or impostor—had fallen under Darius' sword, the empire flared in revolt from end to end. Only three Iranian provinces stood with Darius. But Cambyses' battle-proved army from Egypt with which he had served, orphaned by the mysterious death of Cyrus' son and the peace policy of Bardiya, followed Darius. He gained Media in the spring of 521, but it seemed very doubtful that he could take and hold Cyrus' western conquests. A young man from Armenia claiming to be a Babylonian prince, son of Nabonidus, calling himself Nebuchadnezzar, sought to re-establish the Babylonian empire. A brilliant historical reconstruction, comparing the Book of Judith with Darius' Behistun inscription, shows the strong probability that they are describing some of the same events. According to this reconstruction, Nebuchadnezzar's strategy was to take over Babylon himself while his general Holofernes occupied Syria and Palestine. (Syria is regularly called "Assyria" in the Behistun inscription, which could help explain the use of that designation in the Book of Judith for an army in the service of the King of Babylon.) The Jews, naturally pro-Persian and anti-Babylonian after their recent experiences, determined to resist Nebuchadnezzar and Holofernes. When Judith killed Holofernes, probably in the late summer of 521, his army broke up. Darius then took Babylon from Nebuchadnezzar and restored the Persian empire at its full extent.[39]

Seeing God's hand at work in their dramatic rescue from Holofernes, the Israelites were ready to resume the task of rebuilding the Temple. Summoned by the prophet Haggai in a ringing sermon probably delivered at the restored altar in the ruins of Solomon's Temple on August 29, 520 B.C., the people began the work again with renewed enthusiasm. Nothing like the magnificence of Solomon's Temple was possible at this time; a modest building would have to suffice. But a Temple there must be. Haggai promised that eventually God would fill it with splendor, while the contemporary prophet Zechariah added to the accumulating treasury of foreknowledge of the Messiah that He would enter Jerusalem riding upon a donkey, symbolizing His peaceful rule, and that the day of mourning for the Messiah's "piercing" would also be a fountain of cleansing from sin. The Hebrew text of Zechariah's prophecy of the Pierced One contains the explicit statement that God Himself will be pierced.[40]

Hostile reports of the rebuilding project were sent to Tattenai, the Persian satrap of Aber-Naharim,[41] by the enemies of the Jews—probably the Samaritans—and Tattenai sent an investigating committee in 519 B.C. to ascertain by what right the work was being done. The Jews appealed to the decree of Cyrus. Tattenai, who evidently had never heard of this decree, reported their claim to Darius, suggesting that a search be made in the royal archives to see if it existed. It says much for the basic moral quality of the early Persian imperial regime, the heritage of Cyrus and of Zarathustra, that this appeal was not only accepted but the decree actually found in the royal archives, and that Darius did not hesitate to abide by it through apparently he had not known of it before, any more than Tattenai. Darius gave his official approval to the rebuilding of the Temple, asking in return only prayers for his life and for his children. Plotter, murderer, ruthless conqueror, man of iron—Darius was all these, and he was to live to see his pride humbled by a tiny Greek city at the battlefield of Marathon—yet here is a human touch of his, at the place and in the context where it mattered most. The Samaritans made their peace (temporarily) with the Jews of the Return, and the Second Temple was completed in the short period of four and a half years and dedicated in March of 515 B.C.[42]

Amid the crashing and upraising of empires, amid all the tumults of history, God had brought His people home as He had promised, and once more "pitched His tent" among them. Beyond them, and those whom they had touched, man's highest aspirations only left him stumbling through the dark. Let us see how it was in the world which revelation had not yet reached, in this amazing sixth century B.C.—the *Achsenzeit*, as it has been called, the Axis Age, when great minds in several very different, widely separated civilizations almost simultaneously began to seek ultimate truth with a burning passion.

At about the time the Second Temple was completed in Jerusalem, Darius sent an expedition down from the highlands of Kabul to the Indus River, and thence around Arabia to Egypt. This expedition, which included Skylax of Karyanda, a countryman of Herodotus the historian, brought India into direct contact with the West for the first time since the days of the Sumerian empire of Ur in 2000 B.C.; while Darius' Persian empire now included most of the Indus valley, once the heartland of the Harappa civilization.[43] Thus Persia and her essentially familiar Western-type culture met the fantastically alien civilization that had been growing up in the Indian subcontinent and at this very moment, 515 B.C., had reached a kind of climax in the lives of two extraordinary men: Siddhartha of the Sakyas, called the Buddha—the "Enlightened One"; and Vardhamana of Vaisali, called the Mahavira—the "Great Victor"—by the Jains. Near contemporaries, the Buddha and the Mahavira were already launched and about to launch, respectively, upon their India-wide teaching missions.[44]

The sinister mien of early Indian civilization has already been sketched;[45] and the Harappa theme intensifies as we move through the almost unknown centuries of the Vedic age in India to the age of the Buddha and the Mahavira. The earliest Vedic poems, prayers, and pantheon are almost identical with what we know or surmise of the literature and religion of the earliest Persians,[46] yet no two cultures could be more different than the Persia of Darius and the India of the Buddha. It is evident that in India the largely healthy naturalism of the Vedas was swallowed up by something so extraordinary as to be historically unique, a cast of mind which no other culture has developed or resembled except where itself influenced by the Indian. Mention has already been made of a central component of that cast of mind: the unquestioning belief in reincarnation, which there is good reason to hold to have been derived solely from the Harappa civilization, since it is not found in the Vedas or in the earliest Upanishads.[47]

To begin to grasp what had happened in India, we should try to visualize, as clearly and sympathetically as we can, one of history's most gifted men, Prince Siddhartha of the Sakyas, in the full bloom of his powers at the age of 35, at just about the time Cambyses was conquering Egypt and the repatriates in Jerusalem were husbanding their resources for the rebuilding of the Temple, sitting down under a large pipal tree outside the town of Gaya with a mighty resolve to remain sitting there "though his bones wasted away and his blood dried up"[48] until he had thought of a way to escape the innumerable rebirths and the illimitable suffering which reincarnation entails. And then we should consider what Cyrus, Cambyses, Zerubbabel or the High Priest Joshua would have thought of his problem, or what *any* other leader or thinker in *any* other culture, not greatly influenced by the Indian, would have thought of it.

Any such man, confronted with the spectacle of Prince Siddhartha's heroic but fantastic challenge to imagined cosmic horror, would surely have asked in astonishment why he did not first demand some real evidence that reincarnation is true before committing his bones and his blood to working out a way to escape from it.

There are few more mystifying—indeed, more frightening—facts in history than that not only did the Buddha never ask that question, but neither did any other respected thinker or leader or teacher in India before the time of Christ.[49]

Is it any wonder that of all the apostles, that one was sent to India who had refused even to believe in the Resurrection of Christ until he could put his fingers into the holes made by the nails in the hands of the Risen Lord, and his hand into the wound in His side made by the Roman lance-thrust while He hung upon the Cross?[50] Is it any wonder that when the great Jesuit Roberto de Nobili followed in the footsteps of the Apostle Thomas some fifteen centuries later, his Indian converts hailed him as "Teacher of Reality"?[51]

To descend into the universe of Indian thought before Christ is like a diver's descent into the depths of some gaudy South Seas coral reef, studded with designs of astonishing beauty, but full of dark caverns whre hideous, many-tentacled creatures lurk. Unless the diver holds firmly to his life-line he is lost, for in that world there is no choosing, no either-or, no law of non-contradiction;[52] everything and anything can be true, nothing is false. And because of reincarnation there is no way out—unless one followed the Buddha, the Mahavira, or the Brahmanic philosophers of the Upanishads and the Vedanta, and what they offered was no exit, but the end.

Historians, hobbled by a prejudice against "value judgments" (except for those, like the modern Western economic interpretation of history, of which they are largely or entirely unconscious because of familiarity) are not supposed to deal with this kind of question. Yet any attempt at serious consideration of Indian history which fails to do so becomes rank absurdity. For the primary characteristic of Indian history, before and outside the impact of the West, is that it hardly exists; and the reason it hardly exists is that almost no one bothered to write it, because in view of the endless cycle of rebirth and the illusory nature and/or positive evil of all temporal activity of existence, which Indian philosophy taught, there was no point in writing it. No Indian writing of any kind, earlier than about 250 B.C., survives; nor is there good evidence of any great lost written works before then.[53] Alexander the Great first gave India the idea of large-scale political organization.[54] But the shocks from him and from later Greek penetrators were like stones falling into a still pond, producing long slow ripples which eventually died away into stillness again. Not until Islam hammers into India with fire and scimitar does she at last begin to open her eyes; not until the British *raj* is the nightmarish sleep at last cast off. As the great—and generally admiring—Indologist Heinrich Zimmer put it:

> One cannot but feel that such a sublime flight as India's into the transcendental realm would never have been attempted had the conditions of life been the least bit less hopeless. Release (*moksa*) can become the main preoccupation of thought only when what binds human beings to their secular normal existence affords absolutely no hope—represents only duties, burdens, and obligations, proposing no promising tasks or aims that stimulate and justify mature ambition on the plane of earth.[55]

The early Brahman philosophers who wrote the Upanishads, while still desperately trying to cling to the dissolving remnants of the truth of the sky-god their forefathers had known[56] despite the encroachments of the atheism or "transtheism" of the Jains, were turning inward in their quest for "release." They had developed a concept of the Self as a devouring pantheism summed up in the phrase that was the heart of their teaching: *tat tvam asi*, "you are that."[57] So the sage Aruni taught in the Chandogya Upanishad, perhaps as early as 700

B.C.:[58]

> "Put this salt in water, and come to me in the morning."
> The son did as he was told. The father said: "Fetch the salt." The son
> looked for it, but could not find it, because it had dissolved.
> "Taste the water from the top," said the father. "How does it taste?"
> "Of salt," the son replied.
> "Taste from the middle. How does it taste?"
> "Of salt," the son replied.
> Then the father said: "You do not perceive that the one Reality exists
> in your own body, my son, but it is truly there. Everything which is has
> its being in that subtle essence. That is Reality! That is the Soul! And you
> are that, Svetaketu!"[59]

The point is the last sentence, the *tat tvam asi* ("you are that") formula.
Up to that point it could be taken (as a Western philosopher would naturally
take it) as simply a statement that only God gives being to matter. But when
Aruni tells Svetaketu that he is himself identical with the source and essence
of existence, he declares in effect that the only way to reach the real is to become
like the dissolved salt. Otherwise life, suffering and death go on forever, world
without end—and without purpose or meaning. An old Indian proverb speaks
of the joys in endless lives being as small as a mustard seed, and the sorrows
as big as Mount Meru.[60] Elsewhere in the world before Christ the soul's prospect was to die, and then to wait. In India it was to die . . . and to die . .
and to die . . . and to die . . . or to vanish.

Such soul-shattering horror is not natural; it is of Hell. Why early India
became Hell's special victim we cannot know. But the immense distorting effect of that Satanic spiritual climate is unmistakable in the Buddha and the
Mahavira—noble spirits, full of generosity and love as many of their ethical
teachings bear witness, and the Buddha personally lovable, unfailingly kind and
considerate, to a degree and in a manner vividly reminding a Roman Catholic
of the personal qualities of some of the saints he knows so well. It is no wonder
that the mainspring of Buddhism so soon became devotion to the personal
memory of its founder, developing long afterward into a full deification. But
the early Buddhist scriptures make it very clear that the Buddha himself claimed neither a divine nature nor divine powers, that he saw himself simply as a
man like other men, who had attained "enlightenment" by his own unaided
efforts under the pipal tree at Gaya. He had nothing to teach about God. He
taught a Way, good and pure in itself, but its goal was to escape personality,
to escape reality, not as in the manly dualism of Zarathustra to defeat evil, but
to transcend good and evil so as to desire neither any more, no more the good
than the evil; to be blown out as a lamp is blown out, not annihilation, but only
because *nirvana* is not really anything at all, including itself.[61] Incredible as
it must seem to any reasoning mind, the ultimate teaching of Buddhism is that

nothing really exists—not even *nirvana*, not even the Buddha himself.[62]

And the Mahavira's Jainism was worse.

While the Buddha claimed to introduce an entirely new doctrine, the Jains said they were harking back to ancient truths steadily being lost, which had been far more strongly and widely held in the distant past—evidently, in the Harappa civilization.[63] While Buddhism has its sacred scriptures, including many which evidently include actual words and teachings of the Buddha, recognized and accepted by all Buddhist sects, the rigorous Digambara sect of the Jains[64] insists that their sacred scriptures have all disappeared in this declining age,that no direct word of the Mahavira survives In the year 497 B.C. the Mahavira had his supreme illumination, the *kevala*, and collected about him—as the Buddha was doing at exactly the same time—large communities of monks. He discarded all his clothing; finally, at the age of 72, he starved himself to death. Only by such means, the Jains taught, could the soul be purged of the *karma* necessitating rebirth. Once purged, the soul entered *kevalatva*, "the state of self-subsistence." It became an omniscient, self-existent being; the fully developed Jain was the victor soul, rising through the lesser entities of the universe—including all the gods—until it reached the top where it dwelt in unapproachable splendor, as much "He Who Is" as the One Who had spoken to Moses from the burning bush in Sinai.[65]

The blasphemy takes a Christian's breath away; he smells the very smoke of the Antichrist. Was this doctrine—which Heinrich Zimmer (writing from no detectable Christian perspective) calls "as inhuman as an icicle . . . like a pillar of some supraterrestrial, unearthly substance"[66]—the dark heart and demonic presumption of what dwelt in the huddled ancient houses and streets of Harappa and Mohenjo-daro? May India's native civilization have been overtly Satanic?

Yet the Mahavira himself was not an evil man. He was the greatest teacher of *ahimsa*—respect for life—in Indian history; he taught truthfulness, honesty, and mercy.[67] But, as with the Buddha, all this was simply part of the Way out of the world and into a false godhead whose very imagining turns man inside out and violates the most fundamental fact of his nature: the contingency of his being, his dependence for existence itself on a Power outside of himself.

And this Jain teaching was later to find echoes beyond the relatively small number of its declared adherents—in yoga, in Mahayana Buddhism, eventually in Brahmanism whose declared goal came to be to make men, by their own efforts, sharers in all the attributes of the Supreme Being: not simply seeing God, as in the Christian Beatific Vision, but *being* God.[68]

Such was the India upon which Skylax of Karyanda looked down from the heights of Kabul as he prepared to set sail upon the Indus River in great King Darius' name, some five hundred and fifteen years before the Word was made flesh.

Beyond the sky-piercing Himalayas, in this questing sixth century B.C., a totally independent civilization was growing up to face the great questions of human life. China is, has always been, and remains as different from India as it is different from the West. Any concept of "the Orient" as more than a geographical expression must be dropped as soon as one begins to deal seriously with the two great non-Western Asiatic civilizations. In religion and philosophy the difference between them is enormous, and may be summed up as follows: While India found truth only in rejection of the world, China from the beginning of its known history saw little or nothing beyond the world; it is the closest to a genuinely agnostic civilization of which we have record.

A kind of after-life was believed in, so that it made sense to venerate and sacrifice to ancestral spirits, though they were thought to continue to dwell very close to the old hearth. There remained the vague concept of a ruling sky-god, Heaven, under whose decree China's emperors were believed in a special way to operate, so that whatever of good or ill befell China under a particular emperor's rule was seen as reflecting Heaven's attitude toward that emperor. But there was no pantheon as in both India and the West, and—outside of the rather static concept of the "decree of Heaven"—no idea of gods acting among men. Religion was significant only in a practical sense, as a means of keeping good social order through its public rites, of strengthening family ties through ancestor worship, and in an unspecified manner helping to keep man in tune with the harmonies of nature. Confucius best summed up the Chinese view of religion when he included, in a definition of wisdom given to his disciple Fan Ch'ih, the following counsel: "Respect the spirits and maintain the proper distance from them."[69]

Unlike both Greece and India, China had little speculative philosophy, and no metaphysics; the Chinese aim was a static good society and individual contentment. Especially during the five centuries of strife between the rise of a feudal nobility with great estates in the eighth century (800-700) B.C. and the final unification of the Chinese empire under strong centralized authority in the third century (300-200) B.C.—all well chronicled historically, for unlike the Indians the Chinese had a strong sense of the importance of history and kept excellent historical records—China confronted all the evils which accompany the pursuit of power, wealth, and fame. Some Chinese responded by withdrawing from public life, in a manner somewhat reminiscent of the Indian withdrawal but far more genial, without the hideous Indian metaphysics; these came to be known as Taoists, followers of "the Way" of Lao Tzu (probably no more than a pseudonym for an unknown, disillusioned writer living near the end of this period, long after Confucius) and Chuang Tzu.[70] But the principal and most characteristically Chinese response was that of Confucius and his followers.

Confucius was born in 551 B.C., the year before Cyrus rose up against Astyages the Mede to become ruler of Iran.[71] At almost exactly the same time that the Buddha and the Mahavira were wandering teachers in India—the last

two decades of the sixth century and the first two of the fifth century, roughly
520-480—Confucius became known as the premier teacher in China. Long a
loosely organized agricultural realm under an emperor reigning and revered from
the very beginning of its recorded history about 1400 B.C. and apparently even
before then,[72] China by Confucius' time had seen the emperor become a
powerless figurehead while once feudal territories of the aristocracy were coalesc-
ing into the nation-states whose incessant warring scarred the two and a half
centuries from Confucius' death to the iron-handed unification of China by the
Emperor Shih Huang Ti in 221 B.C.[73] The natural law morality which every
man carries in his heart was revolted by the immense abuses of this scramble
for power. Confucius made it his life's work to establish a firm set of moral
and ethical standards for society and statecraft in China.

Like all such undertakings, it was essentially an exercise in distilling common sense. Every sane man knows that he is not supposed to lie, cheat, steal,
defraud, and murder, and that if most men do these things regularly with im-
punity, society will break down and all will suffer. Confucius, who seems to
have been the first full-time educator or schoolmaster, almost in the modern
sense, in world history, had an extraordinary gift for presenting these common-
sense ethical truths in a comprehensive, reasonable and convincing system whose
principles became the foundation of Chinese social order, and which he regarded as much more important than any transcendental religious questions.[74]

The void at the center remained. Again there was only a Way—a different
and better Way than that of India, whether that of the cheerful though self-
centered Taoists who rejected all public action and ambition, or the dedicated,
altruistic public service of the Confucians trying to keep society wholesome and
curb abuses by moral teaching illustrated by historical examples; but yet no more
than a Way, with nothing at the end but those spirits from whom it was part
of wisdom to keep a safe distance. Beyond the Chosen People there were still
only quests without ending, searches without finding, from the Mediterranean
all across broad Asia to the Yellow Sea.

But what of the land to which Skylax of Karyanda finally came home?

Second only to the Jews, the Greeks are the most extraordinary people in
history. They were the wonder-people of the ancient world; even when their
temporal power and wealth had faded, their prestige remained so high that one
Roman emperor after another loved Greece more than his native land, and finally
the first Christian emperor moved the imperial capital to Greece, where as great
Constantinople it held the pass for Christendom against the assaults of Islam
all through the Middle Ages. When at last Constantinople fell the Renaissance
had begun, making Greek learning an essential part of European higher education. Only our own century, which has lost so much else, has lost or is losing
its respect for the Greek mind and achievements.

Following the Renaissance, the division and subsequent decline of Christendom, the Greeks have sometimes been idolized, their pre-Christian thought set

up as a sort of human substitute for revelation, seen as more refined and therefore more valuable and significant than the thought of the less intellectually oriented Jews. But perhaps the finest testimony to the greatness of the Greeks is that, with a few relatively unimportant contemporary exceptions, they themselves have not fallen into this error. There has been no massive rejection of Christianity in Greece so as to idolize Plato or Demosthenes or Myron of the Discus-thrower, no move to tear down their churches and build new Parthenons. The Greeks were thoroughly converted to the Christian faith and by and large have remained so, despite the tragic schism perpetuated by the Fourth Crusade which has set them apart from the Roman Catholic Church, despite nearly four centuries of Turkish rule followed by modern Westernization.[75] The Greeks ultimately found Christianity intellectually convincing as well as the gift of faith. As many of the early Christian writers pointed out, their own earlier triumphs of the mind had led them toward the fullness of truth in the fullness of time, preparing them for its reception, its teaching, and its exploration by the mind as well as by the heart and the soul.

When Crete and Mycenae fell—however they fell—the knowledge of writing itself was lost to the Greeks, to be brought back about 750 B.C. in the new alphabetic form by the Phoenicians.[76] At that time Hellas was already set in the social and political pattern which was to be retained for more than a thousand years: a collection of city-states, unable or unwilling to unite themselves, capable of being united only by a strong outside authority. This inability or unwillingness of the Greek city-states to unite, or to remain united, has been the subject of long continued and often vehement criticism, from the great Greek historian Thucydides right down to the present, and it certainly was unique; nowhere else did cities of such wealth and culture in so small a geographical area, speaking the same language, remain independent and in conflict with each other for so long. Yet out of their freedom came a glorious flowering of philosophy, poetry, art and culture which permanently transformed the world. The Greeks truly seemed to feel they might find something at the end of their minds' quest, while for Buddha and for Confucius there had been, at the end, only the void.

Greek poets—especially the diadems of the Lyric Age, buoyant Archilochos and joyous Sappho[77]—sought and made beauty; their philosophers sought truth. From Thales of Miletus early in the great sixth century (600-500) B.C. all down through the years covered in this chapter, they were seeking truth with a determination and realism unmatched elsewhere. Thales and his successors tried to see if various familiar substances or processes—water, air, earth, fire—could be taken as the ultimate reality, but could find no convincing explanation. Then came Parmenides of Elea, startlingly enough *an exact contemporary* of the generation of the Return, of King Darius, of the Buddha, the Mahavira, and Confucius.[78] He tells us that it seemed a chariot bore him into the presence of the white goddess of truth, and from her he learned:

For this shall never prevail, that the things which are not
are; but from this way of search hold back thy thought
nor let thyself be forced upon this way
by oft-tried habit here along to aim
a heedless eye, resounding ear and tongue
but judge by Reason this disputed proof
spoken by me. The only tale which yet
remains to tell of the Way is that *it is*;
and many signs there are upon this path
that it *is* Unborn and is without destruction,
for Whole is it of limb and still unquaking
and without fatal End, nor *was* it ever
nor *will* it be, since now it *is* Together
All and One, Containing; for what birth
wilt thou seek for it? How and whence
could it increase? I shall not let thee say
nor think it came from *what is not*,
for it is unuttered and unthought, that *it is not*;
and what need could have stirred it up to grow
rather now than then, if it began
from Nothing? Therefore must it altogether
Be, or not at all.[79]

Here was the beginning of the concept and understanding of absolute self-existent being in Western philosophy. Yet it remained only a vision, with which even the best Greek minds could not really work, since without an understanding of the Creation even Being remains a static and actually imprisoning idea, divorced from the world of change and contingency in which men live. "Old Parmenides," Plato called him, "a man much to be respected, and much to be feared."[80] Not for the Greeks the Indian perversions. Their quest would go on, but Parmenides' vision of being would be remembered, until Christ came to reconcile the Creator and the world.

NOTES

[1] Giuseppe Ricciotti, *The History of Israel* (Milwaukee, 1955), II, 64-72.

[2] *Ibid.*, II, 61-63, 169-190.

[3] Richard N. Frye, *The Heritage of Persia* (New York, 1966), pp. 45-47, 70-71, 102-103; A. T. Olmstead, *History of the Persian Empire* (Chicago, 1948), pp. 24-28; A. R. Burn, *Persia and the Greeks; the Defence of the West* (New York, 1968), pp. 37-38, 63-66, 78-79; H. C. E. Zacharias, *Protohistory* (St. Louis, 1947), pp. 350-351; Herodotus, *Persian Wars* I, 136.

[4] Frye, *Heritage of Persia*, pp. 93-94; Burn, *Persia and the Greeks*, pp. 25-26; H. W. F. Saggs, *The Greatness That Was Babylon* (New York, 1968), pp. 123-125, 134. The extent of the Assyrian rule in Iran is not known precisely at any period in Assyrian history, largely due to our ignorance of the location of many of the places named in the Assyrian records describing this region, but it is clear that the Assyrian domain in-

cluded at one time or another most of Azerbaijan, all of Khuzistan (Elam) and at least the western part of Media proper.

⁵ e.g., Saggs, *Babylon*, p. 121; John Bright, *A History of Israel*, 3rd ed. (Philadelphia, 1981), p. 275.

⁶ Tobit 1:1-6, 10-14; 7:1-5, 14:1-15. For Rhages (Raga in Medo-Persian) see Olmstead, *Persian Empire*, p. 30.

⁷ Bernard Orchard et al, *A Catholic Commentary on Holy Scripture* (London, 1952), p. 393.

⁸ Zacharias, *Protohistory*, pp. 354-355.

⁹ Frye, *Heritage of Persia*, pp. 50-53; Burn, *Persia and the Greeks*, pp. 70-73. The date of Zarathustra is still disputed, but we have a specific reference in medieval Muslim sources, declaring that they draw on earlier Zoroastrian tradition, that the central event in the life of Zarathustra occurred 258 years before the death of Darius III, the last Achaemenid king of Persia, and the triumph of Alexander the Great. Darius III died in 330 B.C., which would put this event—very likely the conversion of the king of Bactria by Zarathustra—in 588 B.C. A confirming tradition tells us that a cypress tree, planted by Zarathustra to commemorate the conversion of Vishtaspa of Bactria, was 1,450 years old when cut down by order of the Caliph Mutawakkil in 846 A.D.; correcting for the Muslim lunar year, this gives a date of 597 B.C. for the conversion, very close to the date computed from the death of Darius III. These two independent but convergent chronological traditions would appear to establish a solid probability of the correctness of the date for Zarathustra given in the text, despite the late date of the written sources. Some writers (e.g. Olmstead, *Persian Empire*, pp. 102-104) have held that the Vishtaspa whom Zarathustra converted was not a king of Bactria in the time of the Median empire but the Persian satrap Hystaspes of Parthia, father of Darius I. Burn provides a convincing refutation of this proposed identification (*Persia and the Greeks*, pp. 70-71). With regard to Zarathustra's original homeland, Frye (*Heritage of Persia*, p. 52), while admitting that Zoroastrian tradition places Zarathustra originally in western Iran, emphasizes that most of the events of his life seem to have taken place in eastern Iran and expresses doubt that he would have moved so far east as Bactria if he had been born in western Iran. In view of the explicit account in the Zoroastrian *Yasna* of the prophet's flight from his original homeland, and similar *hegiras* in the lives of other great religious leaders (*e.g.*, Moses, Muhammad, and the Buddha), there seems no good reason for Frye's skepticism here. Zoroastrian tradition holds that Zarathustra was 42 years old when he converted King Vishtaspa; if the date of 588 B.C. is correct for that event, Zarathustra would then have been born in 630 B.C., 18 years before the fall of Nineveh, shortly before which Tobias was sent to Media.

¹⁰ Orchard et al, *Catholic Commentary on Holy Scripture*, pp. 394-395.

¹¹ Olmstead, *Persian Empire*, pp. 98-100; Burn, *Persia and the Greeks*, pp. 73-77; Zacharias, *Protohistory*, pp. 352-356. For the influence of the Psalms on Zarathustra, see Yves Congar, *The Mystery of the Temple* (Westminster MD, 1962), p. 89.

¹² Ricciotti, *History of Israel*, II, 105.

¹³ G. K. Chesterton, *The Everlasting Man* (New York, 1925), pp. 208-223.

¹⁴ Burn, *Persia and the Greeks*, pp. 37-39, 63-64, 80; Frye, *Heritage of Persia*, p. 105; Ricciotti, *History of Israel*, II, 82.

¹⁵ Burn, *Persia and the Greeks*, pp. 39-44.

¹⁶ Daniel 1. Daniel could have been brought to Babylon to serve Nebuchadnezzar at any time after King Jehoiakim became his vassal, in 604 or 603 B.C. (see Chapter Six, above). Sending the youths to Babylon, as described in Daniel 1, could have been a condition of the state of vassalage imposed by Nebuchadnezzar, rather than part of the first great deportation from Judah by the Babylonians in 597. This still does not push the

date of Daniel's departure from Palestine quite back to "the third year of Jehoiakim" (606 B.C.), where Daniel 1:1-3 seems to place it, but on closer examination it is evident that the sending of the youths to Babylon (Daniel 1:3) came *after* that year. Nebuchadnezzar, even as Crown Prince and field commander in Syria and Palestine (as he definitely was during the year before his accession to the throne—see Chapter Six, above) apparently could not have besieged Jerusalem before 605 B.C., the year of the Battle of Carchemish in which he defeated Pharaoh Necho of Egypt, and probably not during that year; but he could well have besieged it, at least briefly, in the following year (604) when he campaigned against the Philistine cities. This would make the chronological reference in Daniel 1:1, of whose apparent error so much is made by Louis F. Hartman and Alexander DiLella, *The Anchor Bible: Daniel* (Garden City NY, 1978), pp. 33-34, 47-48, in totally denying historical reality to Daniel, only two years off. Such small chronological divergences are not uncommon in even the most reliable historical sources.

[17] Burn, *Persia and the Greeks*, p. 49.

[18] Orchard et al, *Catholic Commentary on Holy Scripture*, pp. 622-623. The "chronological tags" are references to the reigns of Persian kings, in Daniel 5:31, 6:28, 9:1, 10:1, and 11:1. It is difficult to avoid the impression that the writer or editor who inserted these references believed that King Darius of Persia reigned before Cyrus, especially since he explicitly states that "Darius the Mede received the kingdom" of Babylonia immediately after Belshazzar's feast (Daniel 5:31). Several of the other references imply the same belief. It is possible that the naming of Darius in Daniel 5:31 may be a corruption of Gobryas or Gubaru (Ugbaru), who was first put in charge of captured Babylon by Cyrus for a short period (see Note 26, below), but Gobryas was not a Mede but a Babylonian. The references to a "Median kingdom" pose no real problem (*pace* Hartman and DiLella, *Daniel*, pp. 35-36) for there indubitably was a Median kingdom exercising broad imperial rule before the Persian empire was created; Cyrus the Great combined the Median regime with his own Persian realm rather than simply obliterating Media, so that the wholly independent authority Herodotus always refers to it as the kingdom "of the Medes and the Persians." Whenever the text of Daniel was first written down, it is very unlikely to have been as late as the Maccabean period, as the "higher critics" would have it. Virtually complete manuscripts of the Book of Daniel found in the Qumran caves are dated to about 120 B.C., and it is most improbable that they would have been kept and accepted there if only composed in that same century (K. A. Kitchen, *The Bible and Its World* [Downers Grove IL, 1977], p. 152; Edwin M. Yamauchi, *The Stones and the Scriptures* [Philadelphia, 1972], p. 183).

[19] e.g., Saggs, *Babylon*, p. 154, and Burn, *Persia and the Greeks*, p. 45.

[20] Almost no deeds of Nebuchadnezzar are recorded between his conquest of the Phoenician city of Tyre in 571 B.C., after a siege lasting many years, and his death in 562 B.C.

[21] Saggs, *Babylon*, pp. 148-155; Burn, *Persia and the Greeks*, pp. 33-35. Saggs describes Nabonidus' move to Tema as "a remarkable attempt to move the center of gravity of the empire westwards and secure the trade routes from south Arabia" (p. 153) and notes the very significant fact that five of the six Arabian oases where Nabonidus says he established garrisons and planted colonies were, a thousand years later at the time of Muhammad, occupied by Jews (whose religion strongly influenced Muhammad). From this, and from the known presence of so much of the exiled population of Judah in Babylon at the time of Nabonidus, Saggs' conclusion that Nabonidus' Arabian garrisons and colonies included substantial numbers of Jews, whose descendants remained there, seems almost unavoidable.

[22] Edward J. Young, *The Prophecy of Daniel* (Grand Rapids MI, 1949), pp. 115-119; Saggs, *Babylon*, p. 153; Orchard et al, *Catholic Commentary on Holy Scripture*, p. 630.

[23] Burn, *Persia and the Greeks*, pp. 54-55; Young, *Prophecy of Daniel*, p. 128; Orchard et al, *Catholic Commentary on Holy Scripture*, p. 631. The text adopts the interpretation of St. Jerome of the handwriting on the wall, *mene teqel uparsin*, as "weighed, measured, divided," referring to the kingdom of Babylonia, rather than the modern and widely accepted, but surely less reasonable "numbered a mina, a shekel and two half minas," which can only be applied to the fall of Babylon to Cyrus by the most extraordinary numerological contortions (cf. Orchard et al, *ibid.*).

[24] Matthew 26:44; Mark 15:62; Luke 22:69. Any theory regarding the literary genre of Daniel (*e.g.* Hartman and DiLella, *Daniel*, pp. 46-54) which is intended to be more than a simple literary exercise must come to grips with this central question: even presuming that Daniel is a work of a genre comparable in some respects to our "historical fiction" (a presumption far from being proved, and certainly not self-evident), was the central character and spokesman, Daniel himself, invented? If so, how was he expected to stand on a par with the other prophets, whom almost all scholars admit to have been real people? If Daniel was a real person about whom later traditions and writings of a "midrashic" genre gathered, then such literary analysis has its place. But if there were never such a person as Daniel—if he were as fictitious as David Copperfield or Ben Hur—then the millions of Christians and Jews who for two thousand years fervently believed otherwise have been misled, and at least at the beginning must have been deliberately misled. This is a serious issue, which cannot be brushed off with arrogant talk of modern scholarly consensus and of "so-called conservatives" who do "the Word of God a huge disservice by insisting that the book [of Daniel] does in fact deal with real persons and events in the seventh and sixth centuries B.C.," or by what must be called the hypocritical pretense that total rejection of the historicity of Daniel does not undermine the authority of Scripture (Hartman and DiLella, *op. cit.*, pp. 53-54). Furthermore, the use that Christ makes of Daniel cannot be ignored in examining this question, as in Hartman and DiLella's extraordinary feat of devoting seventeen erudite pages to the exegesis of Daniel's term "Son of Man" without once mentioning that Christ repeatedly applied it to Himself (Hartman and DiLella, *op. cit.*, pp. 85-102).

[25] Burn, *Persia and the Greeks*, pp. 54-55.

[26] *Ibid.*; see Note 18, above.

[27] Ezra 1:2-4.

[28] Burn, *Persia and the Greeks*, p. 56; Ricciotti, *History of Israel*, II, 83-85. Ricciotti's argument that Zerubbabel and Sheshbazzar, who are mentioned in almost identical contexts in several passages in the Book of Ezra, are identical is here accepted over the views of Bright (*History of Israel*, pp. 362-363) and of Paul Heinisch (*History of the Old Testament* [Collegeville MN, 1952], p. 325) that they were distinct.

[29] Ricciotti, *History of Israel*, II, 85-91.

[30] See Chapter Six and its Notes 47-49, above.

[31] Orchard et al, *Catholic Commentary on Holy Scripture*, pp. 623-624; *The Jerusalem Bible* (Garden City NY, 1966) (Old Testament), pp. 1131-1133. On Antiochus Epiphanes as a type of the Antichrist, see St. Jerome's commentary on Daniel 11:21-45 reprinted in Young, *Prophecy of Daniel*, pp. 306-317. On Daniel's age, if he were thirteen years old—*bar mitzvah* age—when he was sent to Babylon, and if he were sent in 604 B.C. (as is suggested by the reference to his reading of Nebuchadnezzar's dream in Nebuchadnezzar's second year [Daniel 2:1], which would have been 603), he would have been 78 years old at the time of Cyrus' conquest of Babylon. The infirmities often accompanying such age would easily explain why he himself did not return to Palestine.

[32] Young, *Prophecy of Daniel*, pp. 220-221, 261-264.

[33] Not even an attempt can be made here to sample the enormous literature on this

question deriving from Daniel 9:24-27. For an orthodox Protestant review of it, see Young, *Prophecy of Daniel*, pp. 191-221; for an orthodox Catholic review of it, see Paul Heinisch, *Christ in Prophecy* (Collegeville MN, 1956), pp. 183-190. The point is that none of the hundred or more proposed chronological reconciliations of this prophecy with subsequent history can be made to fit exactly. Every scheme has an error factor on the order of decades.

[34] Burn, *Persia and the Greeks*, pp. 81-88.

[35] Ricciotti, *History of Israel*, II, 155-168.

[36] Burn, *Persia and the Greeks*, pp. 81, 88-93; Frye, *Heritage of Persia*, p. 296, n. 56 on the disputed question of whether the Persian word *huvamarshiyush* used in Darius' inscription to describe Cambyses' death indicates suicide or a natural death. Frye favors the interpretation of natural death. Clearly Darius' account is intended to exclude all thought of murder. Since by his own admission Darius personally slew the claimant to the Persian throne who followed Cambyses, one would at least like to know where Darius, who had been Cambyses' spear-bearer in Egypt (Herodotus, *Persian Wars* III, 39) was at the time of Cambyses' death in Palestine. Was he still the king's spear-bearer? If so, he could have had an opportunity to kill Cambyses himself.

[37] Burn, *Persia and the Greeks*, pp. 90-95.

[38] *Ibid.*; Olmstead, *Persian Empire*, pp. 107-113. Frye (*Heritage of Persia*, pp. 114-118) covers the same ground and, while admitting that the case against Darius is strong, rightly points out that it is not, and in the nature of the available evidence from so long ago cannot be, proved; and that the burden of proof rests with the accusers of Darius. While this is true in a strictly legal sense, the entire proceedings give grounds for deep suspicion. Insufficient emphasis seems to have been given to the fact that Darius killed his rival himself, with only six companions, in an operation that was far more a carefully planned assassination than a military or judicial action against an impostor and usurper believed to be such by a substantial portion of the empire.

[39] Claus Schedl, *History of the Old Testament* (New York, 1972), V, 92-111. One of the most impressive arguments Schedl advances in support of this reconstruction is the dating of Nebuchadnezzar's reign in the Book of Judith to precisely the number of years (17 and 18) separating the two years of revolts against Darius from Cyrus' conquest of Babylon ending Nabonidus' reign (*ibid.*, p. 98).

[40] Ricciotti, *History of Israel*, II, 91-93; Haggai 2:7; Zechariah 9:9-10 and Heinisch, *Christ in Prophecy*, pp. 167-168; Zechariah 12:10-13:1 and Heinisch, *Christ in Prophecy*, pp. 168-171. The reference to the piercing of Yahweh Himself is in the Hebrew text of Zechariah 12:10. Heinisch's doubts about the correctness of the text—"It can hardly be said that Yahweh would be pierced through. And although the Messiah was truly God, we are still in Old Testament times, the age of preparation; it is certain that no pre-Christian reader would have understood the text in this manner" (*op. cit.*, p. 169)—are a rare lapse into rationalistic skepticism by this generally sound exegete. As we have seen, the Old Testament contains a number of other passages, notably Isaiah 9:5-6, clearly indicating the Messiah's divinity, while Isaiah 53 clearly predicts the Messiah's shameful death. It is true that until the Crucifixion few if any could have understood Zechariah's full meaning, but this is the obvious sense of the text we have.

[41] Persian records mention a satrap Tattanu in the twentieth year of Darius, 502/501 B.C., who is probably identical with the Tattenai of the Book of Ezra (Heinisch, *History of the Old Testament*, p. 330n).

[42] Ricciotti, *History of Israel*, II, 93-97.

[43] Burn, *Persia and the Greeks*, pp. 115-117; Olmstead, *Persian Empire*, pp. 144-145.

[44] India's immemorial indifference to history creates chronological problems unmat-

ched in the reconstruction of the past of any other civilized people. Solidly established dates for major reigns and events of Indian history are not reached (with a few exceptions such as the rock edicts of the Mauryan emperor Ashoka in the third century B.C.) until about 600 *A.D.*, some 1200 years after writing came into use in Hindu India. However, because many Indians did regard the Buddha and the Mahavira as very important—unlike secular historical figures—and chronicled the events of their lives with some care, it is possible to determine their dates within a few years. The Buddha lived roughly from 560 to 480 B.C., these figures being subject to an error factor of about five years (A. L. Basham, *The Wonder That Was India* [New York, 1954], p. 257; Edward Conze, *Buddhism, Its Essence and Development* [New York, 1959], p. 34). The Mahavira may have been about twenty years younger than the Buddha, living from about 540 to 468 B.C. (Basham, *India*, pp. 287-288).

[45] See Chapter One.

[46] Frye, *Heritage of Persia*, pp. 44-47.

[47] Heinrich Zimmer, *Philosophies of India* (Cleveland, 1956), pp. 252-254.

[48] Basham, *India*, p. 258.

[49] There were some skeptical and materialist thinkers in India during this period, but their thought was decisively rejected and soon disappeared (Basham, *India*, pp. 296-297).

[50] John 20:24-27. The evidence that the Apostle Thomas did in fact go to India, preach and win converts there, and die there—probably a martyr—is well presented in George Moraes, *A History of Christianity in India A.D. 52-1542* (Bombay, 1964), pp. 13-45. See Chapter Seventeen, below, for an extended discussion of this subject.

[51] Vincent Cronin, *A Pearl to India* (New York, 1959), pp. 127-128.

[52] Basham, *India*, pp. 271-278, 279, 328, 501-503; Zimmer, *Philosophies of India*, pp. 25-27, 463. Zimmer, who seems to be no friend of Christianity and admires much in Indian thought, describes the classic formulation of this anti-logic in the paradoxes of Sankara, architect of Vedanta, as "mind-destroying" (*op. cit.*, p. 463).

[53] Basham, *India*, pp. 394-398; Zimmer, *Philosophies of India*, p. 68n.

[54] Basham, *India*, pp. 50, 79, 83. See Chapter Nine, below.

[55] Zimmer, *Philosophies of India*, pp. 82-83.

[56] Originally Dyaus, Father Heaven, the counterpart and cognate of the Greek Zeus, then Varuna, then Indra (Zimmer, *Philosophies of India*, p. 344).

[57] Zimmer, *Philosophies of India*, pp. 3, 354, 357, 360-361.

[58] Basham, *India*, pp. 24-25.

[59] Chandogya Upanishad VI, 13. Translation in Basham, *India*, p. 251. Cf. Brhadaranyaka Upanishad II, 412.

[60] H. C. E. Zacharias, *Human Personality, Its Historical Emergence* (St. Louis, 1950), p. 79. Basham (*India*, p. 9) argues that the "life-negating" (to use the term first applied to Indian thought by Albert Schweitzer) philosophy of the Upanishads, Buddhism and Jainism is not really typical of Indian character and life, that it received only "lip-service" from the masses, who enjoyed life and were remarkably kind and gentle. Such popular sayings as that quoted in the text should at least give pause to a ready acceptance of Basham's conclusion. Evidently the majority of the Indian people did not accept the Brahmana, Buddhist or Jain metaphysics fully, or they would all—like the Mahavira— have killed themselves. It is a universal observation that simple people everywhere retain more "common sense"—more awareness of cosmic reality and joy in it—than the learned. But in India the pressure against this natural, God-given "common sense" was stronger than in any other culture, and remained so at least up to a century ago, as we will have occasion to show in the course of this history; and reincarnation, a doctrine whose clear tendency is toward discouragement and despair, is still generally believed even by ordinary people in India, as it has been ever since the time of the first Upanishads.

See also Zimmer, *Philosophies of India*, pp. 220, 413-414, in which he calls "world-renouncing" and "life-chilling" the synthesis of Jain, Buddhist, yoga and Upanishadic ideas which became Vedanta.

[61] Basham, *India*, pp. 256-261, 270-271. Once, in answer to a question, the Buddha specifically denied that Nirvana is annihilation, but only on the grounds that it is undefinable by any human term, including that one.

[62] Zimmer, *Philosophies of India*, pp. 479-483.

[63] See Chapter One, above.

[64] These went naked until forced by the Muslims to put on clothes. The Greeks who came with Alexander the Great called them "gymnosophists" (naked philosophers). Many of their texts still have not been published in any language. See Zimmer, *Philosophies of India*, pp. 210-211, and Basham, *India*, p. 289.

[65] Basham, *India*, pp. 287-289; Zimmer, *Philosophies of India*, pp. 182, 203-204, 233, 260-261.

[66] Zimmer, *Philosophies of India*, p. 212.

[67] Basham, *India*, pp. 292-293.

[68] Zimmer, *Philosophies of India*, p. 602. The conclusion of Zimmer's great work here provides this summary of the goal of Indian philosophy: "In contrast to the attitude of Job who cried out to Yahweh: "What is man, that thou shouldest magnify him?' the Indian, by shattering his ego, equates himself with God, transcends God, and is at peace in the knowledge of himself as Brahman."

[69] H. G. Creel, *Confucius and the Chinese Way* (New York, 1960), pp. 113-117; H. G. Creel, *The Birth of China* (New York, 1937), pp. 336-343, 367-375.

[70] Creel, *Confucius*, pp. 194-198; Thomas Merton, *The Way of Chuang Tzu* (New York, 1965), pp. 15-32.

[71] Creel, *Confucius*, pp. 25, 296-297.

[72] Creel, *Birth of China*, pp. 57, 132-137; Dun J. Li, *The Ageless Chinese* (New York, 1965), pp. 36-37. Writing in China may go back as early as 2000 B.C.; the traditional dates of the Hsia dynasty, which preceded the Shang, are 2205-1766 B.C. (Li, *op. cit.*, pp. 36-37, 41). Of actual writing during the time of the Shang dynasty (traditional dates 1766-1122 B.C.) we have only inscriptions on oracle bones, which were used to ask the spirits of the dead questions about future events (Creel, *Birth of China*, pp. 185-196). It seems very likely that books were written, even as early as Shang times, on strips of wood or bamboo tied together by cords, like some which have been preserved from about the time of Christ; but we have no extant Chinese manuscripts older than that, nor copies of any book written before the advent of the Chou dynasty in 1122 B.C. The disappearance of the Shang books is probably explained by a combination of the destructive effects of the Chou conquest, the great book-burning by Emperor Shih Huang Ti in 213 B.C., and the ravages of time on the perishable materials of the books in China's relatively damp climate (Creel, *Birth of China*, pp. 171-173). (Throughout this history, the Wade-Giles system of transliteration of Chinese names will be used rather than the Pinyin system which the present Chinese mainland government has tried to impose on the entire world, despite the facts that it is unmanageable and unpronounceable to English speakers without constant reference to a key, and that it renders obsolete all bibliographical entries concerning China by scholars writing in English for the last 150 years and more.)

[73] Li, *Ageless Chinese*, pp. 49-50. Chinese historiography conventionally divides this period into two parts, the "Spring and Autumn" period (771-479 B.C.) and the period of the "Warring States" (479-221 B.C.). The "Spring and Autumn" period takes its name from the brief annals of Confucius' native state of Lu from 722 to 479 B.C., the latter date being the year of Confucius' death (Creel, *Confucius*, pp. 55, 103-104). In

the year 771 B.C. occurred a long-remembered barbarian sack of the imperial capital of Hao, followed by the removal of the capital to Loyang and a rapid and long-continued weakening of imperial authority; hence, this year was chosen as the beginning of the long period of civil war in China.

[74] Creel, *Confucius*, pp. 75-99, 122-125, 142-172.

[75] The deep-rooted Christianity of the Greek people, the profusion of shrines and small churches along with the many larger ones, and the widespread evidence of living popular devotions, greatly impressed the writer while travelling in Greece at the time of the Greek Orthodox Easter in 1971.

[76] A. R. Burn, *The Lyric Age of Greece* (New York, 1967), p. 54.

[77] *Ibid.*, pp. 161-174, 226-237.

[78] *Ibid.*, p. 391 for the date of Parmenides (*floruit* 504 B.C.).

[79] Parmenides 28, translated by Charles H. Kahn, in Moses Hadas, ed., *The Greek Poets* (New York, 1953), p. 157.

[80] Plato, *Theaetitus* 183E. That the great Plato could both respect and fear this tremendous, intractable teaching of Parmenides shows that the Greeks were aware of the possibility of distortion of this truth in the way that the Indian philosophers had distorted the unicity and self-existence of Being, and would not accept such distortions even in the absence of a full capability of using Parmenides' insight.

8.
TWO HOPES
(499-404 B.C.)

Behold, I send my messenger to prepare the way before me, and the Lord whom you seek will suddenly come to his temple; the messenger of the covenant in whom you delight, behold, he is coming, says the LORD of hosts. But who can endure the day of his coming, and who can stand when he appears?

For he is like a refiner's fire and like fullers' soap; he will sit as a refiner and purifier of silver, and he will purify the sons of Levi and refine them like gold and silver, till they present right offerings to the LORD.—Malachi 3:1-3

The Temple had been rebuilt, God's worship there resumed as He had commanded, the Return was complete—and what had come of it all? God's people were still wholly subject to an alien king and his governors. They were hard pressed by hostile neighbors. They were very poor, some almost destitute. They had no influence upon the world. Never in all their history, at least since Joshua conquered the Promised Land, had they been so utterly insignificant in worldly terms. A cloud of cynical despair spread over many of them. Was this all that the glorious prophecies of the Return had meant? Was it of no more than this that Isaiah and Daniel had so magnificently sung?

From the beginning, from Abraham, faith and hope were the keynotes of life and thought for the children of Israel. By faith and hope they had survived the devastating blow of the exile; taught by the prophets, they had confidently awaited the Return. The prophets had seemed to say that the Return would usher in the era of glory for God's Chosen People. It had not. Very well, those prophecies must have applied to a future age (had not Daniel warned of that, however obscurely, with his "seventy weeks of years"?). They knew as well (or better) than we do, that prophecy telescopes time. So the faith and hope that were the heart of Israel led them now to an increasing emphasis on the Messiah, God's anointed one, the savior of his people who would bring the fulfillment of all God's promises. Malachi, the last of the prophets until John the Baptist, preaching about 450 B.C., voiced this growing Messianic hope while solemnly warning that the Savior's coming would be no cause of rejoicing for sinners—and predicting the offering, in times to come, of a pure sacrifice to God all over the world.[1]

Disillusionment and degradation combined with undying faith brought the Messianic hope to the people of Israel with new strength and clarity. Steadily it grew during the almost silent years that followed, the three long centuries from Ezra to the Maccabees when the People of God hardly speak to us at all,[2] until it had become the central element in Judaism. The Messiah would be "the judge and ruler of the world."[3] He would rule from Jerusalem, with the Chosen People as his legates. Creation itself would be transformed and glorified under his scepter. Pious and just Israelites who had died before his coming would be resurrected, and judged according to their deeds. The Messiah would be a man, endowed with unique God-given powers, chosen by God before the creation of the world, born in Bethlehem, hidden by God until the foreordained time of his appearing. Despite the revealing words of the prophets previously discussed, there is no sign that the Israelites of these centuries had the slightest awareness that the Messiah would be God Incarnate. There was always a strong political and even militaristic element in the Messianic hope, intensified in later times when the Jews had regained and then again lost their political freedom by military means. But in these early days the development of the Messianic hope went on quietly, non-violently, with so little record that it is exceedingly difficult to trace or follow. The small amount of evidence we have has been twisted into veritable contortions to fit various writers' theories of religious evolution.[4] But far more was involved than the development of an idea. God was still calling His people.

There was another hope in the world of the prophet Malachi— a strictly human hope, and therefore bound in the end to fail, but unforgettably brilliant while it lasted. This was the hope of the Greeks, to master the world through knowledge and create beauty in word and painting and statue and building such as no men had ever seen before. Aeschylus voiced it best, in the *Agamemnon*:

> A shining wind out of this dark shall blow,
> Piercing the dawn, growing as great waves grow,
> To burst in the heart of sunrise.[5]

There was nothing metaphysical or spiritual about the Hellenic hope, for nothing in their religion or philosophy offered that, as their sadly resigned sepulchral decorations and inscriptions testify. The Greeks' "shining wind" was not sent by God or dependent on His will; it was to be their own creation. The Jews might mourn the loss of their freedom, but they could live and grow without it. The Greeks of their golden age *required* freedom; without it they had nothing. Yet as the fifth century B.C. opened, they stood precariously on the leading edge of the vast domain of imperial Persia, within which the little Jewish community dwelt totally unknown to the Greeks.[6] In 513 B.C. King Darius had personally led a major military expedition which secured the Straits—the Hellespont (now the Dardanelles) and the Bosporus—separating Asia from Europe, and established Persian rule in eastern Thrace and along the coast of the Black Sea as far as the mouth of the Danube. He already ruled the numerous Greeks on the eastern shore of the Aegean.[7]

Centuries before the rise of Persia, the Ionian Greeks had crossed the Aegean Sea to settle upon the shores and the close-in islands of the western coast of Asia Minor.[8] They had been—at least nominally—subjects of the Lydian kingdom when Cyrus came and conquered them. Rightly fearing that Persian rule would be much more restrictive, they asked for help from old Greece. A herald from Sparta came to Sardis, the Lydian capital, where Cyrus was holding court, to warn him not to tamper with any Greek cities, since "the Spartans would not tolerate it." The man who had overwhelmed the mightiest kingdoms of the ancient world in one year for each, who reigned from India to Europe, looked in astonishment at this spokesman for one paltry little city on a rocky peninsula westward, and asked:

"Who *are* the Spartans?"[9]

The epic war between the Greeks and the Persians for the freedom of the West has stirred men's hearts from that day to this. The Greek victory in the Persian wars created and defined the West as a self-conscious historical entity—the West where, alone so far in history, Christendom has been built. Persia has never been converted, despite a splendid effort and many martyrs during the century of Constantine the Great; every land and people under Greek rule for long, or significantly penetrated by Greek culture (except far-distant Bactria in central Asia) eventually was converted (even though many of these lands and peoples were subsequently lost to Islam). So here, prospectively, lies the Christian significance of the Persian wars. That the Greeks misused the freedom they so gloriously won has been a commonplace of both ancient and modern historical commentary; that the Greeks were not crushed, but were able to develop the genius of their thought and their individualism limited only by their own sins rather than by an alien rule from distant Iran, should be of greater significance both to Christian and to non-Christian historians.

Persian rule had begun, under Cyrus, at the highest natural level of probity and clemency; already, under Darius, it had descended (probably) to fratricidal assassination by the King of Kings himself. There is no reason to suppose that the long decay of the Persian empire which followed the repulse of Xerxes from Greece would have been any different if Greece had been conquered; but in that case, the world would have had no alternative to it. Even the noble elements in Zoroastrianism availed little in checking the Persian decay. The future of God's action in the world lay, in 500 B.C., primarily with the Jews and the Greeks. And over all the Greeks, from the eastern shores of the Aegean to western Sicily, the Persian shadow loomed in the year 499 B.C. when King Darius' Ionian Greek subjects on the coasts of Asia Minor rose in revolt against the lord of the world.

The queen city of the Ionian shore was Miletos, home of Thales the first Greek philosopher and of the explorers of the Euxine (Black) Sea. Located on the mainland, Miletos could only have been helped to withstand the onslaught of the Persian army by a full mobilization of old Greece—particularly of the full forces of its two leading cities, Athens and Sparta. That mobilization did not then come. The Athenians and Spartans gave just enough encouragement and assistance to the Ionians to throw down the gauntlet to the Persian king, but not enough to be effective in sustaining the rebellion.[10]

The striking differences between Athens and Sparta, so often remarked, have obscured essential elements in common of which citizens of both states during the Persian Wars were well aware. Sparta, with its own Laconian lands and those of Messenia which it had conquered, was ruled by a tight military oligarchy under two kings reigning simultaneously;[11] Athens with its peninsula of Attica had been governed, since the reform of Cleisthenes in 508 B.C., by its much admired democracy.[12] But the adulation of democracy as a political system is a strictly modernistic and historically conditioned phenomenon of the last century and a quarter. As we shall have many occasions to see in the course of this history, the *form* of government is never so important as its *substance* or *manner*. Almost any reasonable system of government will work if conducted by men of generally good moral character in a society valuing such character. Both Sparta and Athens in 500 B.C. lived by a rule of generally respected law. In Athens there was excessive materialistic greed and personal political ambition, and in Sparta a cruel system of educating boys which violated the natural moral laws of family life. Our sympathies tend to lie with the Athenians. Yet in the great war against Persia it was the Spartan leaders who were trusted above all others to put the interests of the whole of Hellas first, rather than their own personal interests or the interests of their own city. The lives and acts of the Spartan kings Cleomenes (until he became insane late in life), Leonidas and Archidamos, spanning most of the fifth century B.C., provide one of history's noblest examples of public virtue, worthy of the best of the Romans. Beside them, so far as sheer rectitude goes, even Themistocles and Pericles—much more brilliant men—leave something to be desired.

The Spartans were the Greek soldiers *par excellence*; the Athenians—a vigorous trading people—were famed for their skill in shipbuilding and naval warfare. The Persian Wars are the classic example of the triumph of quality over quantity, of free men at arms over conscript masses; and these essential elements of the Greek victory apply equally to Sparta and to Athens. The poison of their later rivalry and strife should not be brought back unhistorically and injected into their earlier, heroic alliance against the mammoth invader.

The Ionian revolt ended with the fall of Miletos in 494 B.C. Mardonios, a capable young Persian officer married to Darius' daughter, whose father was one of the six assassins whom Darius had taken with him to kill Bardiya whom he calls Gaumata, came up to command an expedition to punish Athens for its aid to the rebels. Mardonios' fleet was wrecked rounding Mount Athos in 492 and he was badly wounded in Thrace; but the Persians, with all the resources of their enormous empire behind them and the iron will of Darius the Great pushing them on, soon returned to the attack under Datis the Mede. In the summer of 490 a Persian expeditionary force disembarked on the plain of Marathon on the coast of Attica, within easy striking distance of Athens.[13]

The Persians were far superior to the Greeks in cavalry and archers; the shielded, helmeted and corseleted Greek hoplites (heavily armed infantrymen) were superior in hand-to-hand combat. Consequently the Athenians under Miltiades refused to advance into the Marathon plain, holding a defensive position until word came to the Persians that a Spartan army was on the march to the aid of the Athenians, after having been delayed by the sacred Spartan festival of the Karneian moon. Realizing that he must strike, if at all, before the arrival of the Spartans, Datis sent the bulk of his cavalry by ship to land on the beaches before Athens itself, while making a feint to contain the Athenians before him. Throwing caution to the winds, Miltiades led an immediate attack with his whole line, omitting the usual advance missile barrage to gain time and surprise; the Persians were barely able to form line before the charging Athenian hoplites were upon them.[14]

Fighting under the best possible conditions for them, the hoplites won a smashing victory, killing 6,400 Persian soldiers at the cost of only 192 of their own. At once they turned and marched back to Athens, arriving in time to forestall the planned landing on the beaches there.[15] It was a splendid, storied victory for Athens; but it should be remembered that the march of the Spartans out of the protection of their isthmus to the south was an essential element in it—and also that the main forces of neither side had yet been engaged. The one-sidedness of the victory greatly encouraged the Greeks, but there is no indication that it significantly discouraged the Persians. Mardonios was recovering from his wound and planning an assault on Greece that would dwarf all previous military operations in Persian history, and Darius gave him full support.

The launching of Mardonios' grand assault was delayed by the outbreak of revolt in Egypt (not apparently connected with the Greeks) and the death of Darius in the same year, 486 B.C. But Xerxes, son of Darius and grandson of Cyrus, now in his mid-thirties and looking every inch a king, seemed a worthy successor. The revolt of Egypt was put down savagely in the single year that always seemed to suffice for the Persians except when they were fighting Greeks. All the energies of the empire were then turned to the great campaign against Greece.[16]

The center of the Athenian line at Marathon had been commanded (under the overall generalship of Miltiades, who died the year after the battle) by the two principal leaders of Athens during the ensuing critical decade: Themistocles and Aristeides, called the Just. The two were rivals, notably on a vital question brought forward in the year 483 B.C., when an extremely rich vein was struck in the Attic silver mines at Laureion. Themistocles carried in the assembly the resolution to use this silver windfall to double the size of the Athenian fleet, rather than distributing it among the citizens as Aristeides proposed. Shortly afterward Themistocles procured the banishment of Aristeides from Athens through the curious device of ostracism, whereby any man named in a majority of more than 6,000 potsherd ballots cast for this special purpose was exiled from the city for ten years. These two events, occurring almost simultaneously, dramatize both the strength and weakness of Athens: Themistocles, a political and military genius, foreseeing that only a navy greater than any Greek city had ever imagined before could save Greece from the Persians, seizing this opportunity to finance the building of that navy, which was to win the decisive Battle of Salamis over the Persians; yet at the same time the display of petty rancor both of the great man and of other Athenians against Aristeides of whom, as one of those who voted to banish him spitefully declared, he was tired of hearing called the Just.[17]

It is a saga that never grows old, how mighty Xerxes, king of kings, marched out of the east with his innumerable host, changing the very face of earth and sea as he came—cutting a canal through the isthmus behind Mount Athos, off whose stormy peak the Persian fleet had once been wrecked; bridging the Hellespont with boats; overwhelming northern Greece by the sheer magnitude of his forces, so that one after another its people and cities surrendered to him without a fight; marching past Olympus, over the mountains, along the coast road opposite the island of Euboea to the narrow place called Thermopylae where King Leonidas of Sparta awaited him with 7,000 men, three hundred of them Spartans, along with Themistocles and 380 trireme warships at the Straits of Artemision between Euboea and the mainland. The Persian fleet was so large that even after severe storm damage it was still approximately equal to the Greek. The naval battle of Artemision was a Persian victory, though at heavy cost. When Xerxes' army lapped round Thermopylae after being stopped there for six days, Leonidas and his three hundred Spartans stood *alone* as the rear guard against a host which, when all of Herodotus' famous numerical exaggerations (five million men!) are pruned down to reasonable size, still probably consisted of some 200,000—odds of more than six hundred to one. Every single Spartan died at his post, fighting in the end with fists and teeth when all weapons were gone; they held the whole horde of Asia from dawn to mid-afternoon, so that the rest of the army lived to fight again and help win later at Plataea; Leonidas and his three hundred became a byword for valor all down the ages; and the would-be conquerors of the world had learned who were the Spartans.[18]

Tell them in Lakedaimon, passer-by,
Carrying out their orders, here we lie.[19]

The Persians pressed on, carrying fire and sword through Attica. They burned Athens, driving its people for refuge to the island of Salamis just offshore, where the fleet of all Greece—half of it Athenian—stood at bay. The Peloponnesians had built a wall across their isthmus, but it would avail nothing without control of the sea. The survival of a free Hellas, the whole future of the fledgling West, depended on the outcome of the clash between the fleets at Salamis. Themistocles tricked the Persians by a false message and a pretended retreat into advancing into a difficult position in narrow waters, then counterattacked with his whole force under the very eyes of Xerxes, who had set up a throne on the shore to watch the battle. The Greeks sank 200 Persian warships while losing only 40 of their own; the Phoenician contingents of the Persian fleet were so decimated and dispirited that they did not fight again for ten years. Xerxes returned to Asia Minor, leaving Mardonios with some 70,000 men to go down to defeat the next year before about half that number of Greek hoplites led by the Spartan Pausanias at the Battle of Plataea, in which Mardonios was slain. The Greeks sailed at once to liberate their brethren in Ionia whose revolt had begun the whole struggle; their victory was complete.[20]

But the Greeks of their golden age were still fallen men, who cannot stand prosperity for long. Pride, ambition, and envy trailed their cold fire across the laurels of the victors. Within ten years Themistocles of Athens who had won the Battle of Salamis and Pausanias of Sparta who had won the Battle of Plataea were both gone in disgrace—Themistocles ostracized, accused of treasonable dealings with the Persians, eventually to settle in one of the very few Greek cities (Magnesia in inland Asia Minor) still under Persian rule, and to die there; Pausanias condemned by his own people on the same charge, left in a temple sanctuary until starving, then dragged out and slain. Of Pausanias' guilt there seems little doubt, of Themistocles' much more; yet one has to wonder how Themistocles of all men could have ended his days under the sway of the power he had fought so magnificently, if he had not in fact been corrupted by it, for surely he could have escaped westward, if escape he must, to the Greek colonies in southern Italy and Sicily long before established, which had also won a great victory against enemies of Asiatic origin, the Carthaginians, in the very year of Salamis.[21]

Still the fruits of the glorious Greek victory were not lost. Even in the darkest hours of the Peloponnesian War at the end of the fifth century when the Greeks shed one another's blood for twenty-seven years, no Persian ever crossed the Hellespont in arms again. The erstwhile aggressors hoped for nothing more than to regain control of the Greek cities on the eastern shore of the Aegean, which they eventually did for a time after their successful defense of Egypt culminating in a military disaster for the Greeks on the Nile in 454 B.C. By then Athens had laid the foundations for a maritime empire of her own. It originated as a free alliance, the Delian League, but its true character was made evident by the removal of the League treasury from the island of Delos to Athens in the year of the disaster in Egypt, and was sealed by the forcible prevention of secession and collection of tribute. Annual payments originally intended for prosecuting the war with Persia were collected by Athens even after she had made the Peace of Kallias with Persia. These revenues were applied to the great building programs of Pericles, crowned by the Parthenon and the Propylaea on the Athenian Acropolis. Meanwhile in 464 B.C. had come the terrible revolt of the subjected Messenian "helots" against Sparta, when a great earthquake seemed to have laid their masters low. Though by the courage of young King Archidamos the Spartans prevailed, a legacy of bitterness remained which virtually eliminated the memory that Spartan helots had fought at Thermopylae.[22]

For all the immorality of Greek politics, there were Greeks who knew a God Who loves right and will not suffer evil to go unpunished—knew Him even without the help of revelation, through natural law and reason—and none of them greater than Aeschylus, veteran of Marathon, the supreme dramatist of his age and perhaps of any age, who once wrote:

> But one there is who heareth on high
> Some Pan or Zeus, some lost Apollo—
> That keen bird-throated suffering cry
> Of the stranger wronged in God's own sky;
> And sendeth down, for the law transgressed,
> The Wrath of the Feet that follow.[23]

But who was that "One"? Greek culture and tradition could give no answer. Even Pericles' Funeral Oration, the lofty summit of all that the golden age of Athens dreamed of and hoped for itself and in its most exalted moments imagined itself already to be, could tell the Hellenes for whom Athens proclaimed hserself above all the teacher, only this:

> Knowing the secret of happiness to be freedom and the secret of freedom
> a brave heart, do not idly stand aside from the enemy's onset.[24]

Fine words, with a special appeal to our time—or rather, perhaps, to a generation ago in our time. But in what lies man's happiness? How shall he rightly use his freedom? To what kind of cause shall he commit his courage? Man is *not* "the measure of all things," as the early Sophists falsely taught; Socrates of Athens devastatingly demonstrated their errors and duplicity, but he too had no more than the questions which made his teaching method famous, the personal goodness (resembling in many ways that of the Buddha) which bound his students to him, and the humility to admit how little he really knew.

While Pericles was building the Parthenon, Nehemiah was building a wall around Jerusalem. Though our information about events in Jerusalem between the completion of the Second Temple in 515 B.C. and the arrival of Nehemiah in 445 B.C. is sparse, spotty, and chronologically confused,[25] it is clear that at some time before 445 the Jews attempted to build a wall around their city but were checked by the opposition of the Samaritans and local Persian officials. These obtained an order from King Artaxerxes I—successor of the Xerxes whom the Greeks defeated at Salamis, who was assassinated in 465 B.C.—halting all work on the wall and commanding the destruction of what had already been built. A wall was an essential protection for any ancient city of significant size and prosperity, whether or not politically independent, for there was always a possibility of barbarian raids and even more of civil strife. Yet the Jews' neighbors resented and opposed the re-walling of Jerusalem because it would tend to establish the repatriated Jewish settlement more permanently and strengthen their claim to a God-given position in Palestine.[26]

Nehemiah was a Jewish layman who had risen to the trusted post of cupbearer to the Persian king. On hearing what had happened in Jerusalem, Nehemiah assumed a mournful countenance before the king. When asked the reason, he explained that the walls of his native city had been destroyed and its gates burned, and asked permission to go with a royal order to rebuild both. By the intervention of the queen his request was granted, even though some years before Artaxerxes himself had ordered a halt to the building of the walls of Jerusalem.[27] Perhaps in the intervening time, in the manner of many government officials both ancient and modern, he had simply forgotten his earlier order; more likely his mind was changed by his queen and his favorite. The story of Esther, attributed to the prior reign of Xerxes, shows how the Jews would go quite spectacularly into and out of favor at the Persian court, as they were to go into and out of favor similarly with later Greek and Roman rulers.[28]

Nehemiah's announcement of his authorization from the King of Persia to rebuild the walls was greeted with a wave of enthusiasm, though some, especially among the wealthy who had established profitable ties with the Samaritans and local Persian officials opposed to the rebuilding, held back. Nevertheless the rebuilding was completed in just 52 days. The workmen went armed for protection against barbarian raids stirred up by the enemies of the Jews, while

Nehemiah avoided every trap and plot laid by the local officials and their allies. The rapid completion of the work was evidently made possible by the fact that the previous destruction of the walls had been done simply by breaching (with the probable exception of the most strategic part, in the north) so that the cast-down stones were still ready at hand for the reconstruction.[29]

When the work was finished a great dedication festival was held, presided over by the high priest Eliashib who had taken charge of rebuilding the especially important north wall. Since after Zerubbabel who helped lead the first caravan of the Return the royal line of David had fallen into obscurity—for reasons not altogether clear, though Persian suspicion of an attempt to regain Judah's independence under the old dynasty may have been responsible—the high priest was now the effective leader of the Jewish people, and remained so for the next three hundred years. Eliashib was the second in succession from the high priest Joshua who had also been in the original caravan of the Return. Eliashib was succeeded by his son Joiada, he by his son Johanan who is known to have been high priest in 410 B.C., and he by his son Jaddua who lived to a great age, since he was still high priest when Alexander the Great arrived in 332 B.C.[30]

Nehemiah remained in Jerusalem twelve years. He encouraged more of the people to move into the now-protected holy city from the surrounding countryside, and required the money-lenders who had become rich from the sufferings and poverty of their fellow Jews to cancel all outstanding debts and interest. Probably at the beginning of the year 443 B.C. the people assembled at the Temple to hear the Law read from the Books of Moses and to renew their covenant with God to obey it. The reader of the Law may well have been the scribe Ezra, who according to the chronology here accepted would then have been a young man of about thirty, recently come from Babylon where the exiles had assembled with loving care all the Scriptures written up to that time, most especially the Pentateuch or Torah, the five books of Moses containing God's law. The reading of the Law continued all through the week-long Feast of Tabernacles in the autumn, which the Law commanded.[31]

> The law, which was then read, was the Pentateuch in essentially the same form as we now have it. Isolated passages may have been subsequently interpolated, but with respect to the main substance, these need not be taken account of. Henceforward then *the law given by God through Moses was acknowledged by the people as the binding rule of life, i.e. as canonical.* For it is in the very nature of the law that its acceptance *eo ipso* involves the acknowledgment of its binding and normative dignity. Hence this acknowledgment was from that time onwards a self-evident assumption to every Israelite. It was the condition without which no one was a member of the chosen people, or could have a share in the promises given to them. "He who asserts that the Torah is not from heaven, has no part in the future world."[32]

The whole community confessed and lamented their past failure to observe the commandments of God and solemnly renewed their covenant with Him in writing. Nehemiah's name heads the list of signers, followed by the principal priests and Levites and other eminent laymen. Later Nehemiah founded a library where the Books of the Law, together with other books and documents concerning the kings of the Israelites from the time of David, and the books of the prophets, could be properly preserved so that no future generation need lose sight of any of them again.[33]

In 433 B.C. Nehemiah returned to Persia and to his place at the court of King Artaxerxes. But shortly before the king's death in 424 Nehemiah had to come again to Jerusalem in response to reports of widespread profanation of the Sabbath and the establishment of a bank in the Temple precincts by Tobias the Ammonite, an old foe and one of those responsible for the razing of the walls of Jerusalem which had originally brought Nehemiah there. The presence of Tobias' men and money in the Temple, permitted by the high priest Eliashib shortly after Nehemiah's departure, had so antagonized many Jews that they had stopped paying their tithes. Upon his return Nehemiah expelled Tobias and his bank from the Temple, reimposed tithes, and insisted that the gates of Jerusalem remain closed during the Sabbath, with no foreign merchant permitted even to approach its walls on the holy day. Nehemiah also took action against Jews who had married foreign women, including a son of Joiada son of Eliashib, though Joiada was now the high priest. With this last reform and renewal of his people's obedience to the Law of God, Nehemiah—his mission accomplished—disappears from history. He left a Jerusalem walled both materially and spiritually against the Gentiles, firmly preserving its God-given heritage, in which the foundations of what the world would later come to know as Judaism were solidly and enduringly laid.[34]

Meanwhile in Greece, Athens and Sparta, partners in victory in the great war against the Persian empire, had entered into mortal combat—a combat which the ambition of Athens and the pride of Sparta would not allow to end until one or the other had conquered. This conflict, the Peloponnesian War, immortalized by Thucydides' classic history, has always been regarded as the second decisive turning point in Hellenic history, the first being the repulse of the Persian invasion. For Athens alone among the Greek city-states of the fifth century B.C. had wealth, population, and sea power sufficient to unify all or most of the far-flung Greek peoples under her leadership. Despite the heroism of her soldiers, Sparta was too small, too poor, and, in maritime Greece, too exclusively a land power to do so. The failure of Athens meant that ultimately unification must be imposed from without; that Greece, while still the teacher, would never be the political leader of the ancient world. Athens failed because of her own greed and lack of imagination: the cities under her were treated as subjects instead of allies. The idea of a common citizenship, such as Rome later developed

.in Italy, never seems to have occurred to any Athenian.

This was due in no small part to Athens' vaunted democracy. The Athenian assembly had no intention whatever of sharing its powers and privileges with anyone, and all too often acted out of temporary emotion without thought of long-term consequences. A memorable example occurred in 428 B.C., the third year of the Peloponnesian War, when after the city of Mytilene on the island of Lesbos had revolted against Athens, the democratic assembly of Athens voted death to the entire male population of Mytilene (including Athens' friends there, who had helped put down the revolt) and slavery for all its women and children. A ship was sent immediately to carry the grim orders to Lesbos. The next day the better men in the assembly had second thoughts. After sharp debate and by a very narrow majority, the death decree was reversed. Another ship was sent in hot pursuit of the first, which had 24 hours' head start. Rowing frantically, the messenger of reprieve caught up with the messenger of death just as the latter was entering Mytilene harbor.[35]

Later in the war, when hearts had become more hardened, the Athenians visited the fate Mytilene had barely avoided upon the blameless inhabitants of the island of Melos, though they had never been part of the Athenian empire, had never fought against Athens, and their only crime was refusal to surrender on demand that they accept Athens as overlord.[36]

Sparta's oligarchy was little better; exactly the fate the Athenians almost inflicted on Mytilene and did inflict on Melos was inflicted on Plataea by Sparta early in the war—though only after Plataea had held out in arms against Sparta for two years, and all military history shows how passions rise during a long siege. (Athens had no such excuse in either the case of Mytilene or that of Melos.) Sparta's capacity for political leadership never matched her capacity for military heroism; her morally admirable King Archidamos could think of no way of preventing Sparta from going to war against Athens, though he personally opposed it.[37]

Athens alone, with a wiser policy and more far-seeing leadership, could have led the way to ordered liberty for all Hellas; but she did not. After Pericles died in 429 B.C. her democracy produced no leader both competent and trustworthy, so that Athens herself became more and more anarchical even while imposing ever tighter control on her subjects in the name of preserving democracy. When the Sicilian expedition of 415 B.C. was mounted, Athens' only competent leader was young Alcibiades, notorious for his loose morals, whom nobody trusted, while the good and pious Nicias was disastrously inept as a military commander. Alcibiades was exiled and betook himself to Sparta; Nicias threw away the whole Athenian army and fleet in Sicily in a series of colossal blunders, and Athens was fatally weakened.[38]

Alcibiades recommended to Sparta the strategy—immediately adopted—of establishing a permanent military base in Attica; its steady pressure on Athens was one of the principal military causes of her downfall. But Alcibiades made enemies in Sparta as he had in Athens, notably King Agis; in 412, after less than three years in Sparta, he had to flee from it under sentence of death. He persuaded the Athenians to take him back, carrying on political intrigues and military enterprises with ingenuity and skill, but a residue of natural distrust remained, and in 406 he withdrew to a private fortress on the Hellespont.[39]

The demagogue Cleophon the lyre-maker now dominated the Athenian assembly. In 406 B.C. came the last Athenian naval victory, at the Battle of the Arginusae Islands. But a storm arose suddenly the evening after the battle, the survivors of the wrecked Athenian ships were not picked up, and 5,000 Athenian sailors perished. The volatile assembly demanded payment in blood for these losses. Six of the victorious commanders of the Athenian fleet were condemned to death as a group by majority vote. Even in the Athenian "pure democracy" such a proceeding was illegal; and it happened that the lot on the day of the fatal vote fell on none other than Socrates the philosopher to be a member of the presiding council. He objected to putting the illegal question. His objection was overridden and the commanders were executed. Among them was the younger Pericles, only son of the great Pericles and his beloved Aspasia.[40]

Sparta, her fleet shattered, offered to withdraw from her military base in Attica and make peace on the basis of the status quo elsewhere. Cleophon, coming to the assembly drunk, nevertheless persuaded the Athenians to refuse this fair and honorable offer.[41]

Such a state, once so glorious, did not deserve to survive. The irony of membership in the presiding council on this critical occasion falling by lot on the greatest Athenian of the age, and his counsel and ruling then being summarily rejected, bites like acid through the pages of history. A viable political order does not choose its presiding officers by the luck of the draw; one that does, will not benefit even when chance turns up the best.

What remained of the Athenian fleet now held the Hellespont to ensure the continued flow of Ukrainian wheat which Athens, which had long lived by trade, must import or starve. Its incompetent commander, presumably a friend of Cleophon's, drew up his ships on a beach at a place called Aegospotamoi. Irony piled upon irony; Alcibiades' refuge was only a short distance away, and he saw the last fleet of his native city helpless and exposed, inviting total destruction. Rogue and renegade though he was, it may be that there stirred in his heart some flicker of real patriotism at the eleventh hour—or he may only have been hoping to curry favor for another return. At any rate, he knew war, and he rode down to tell the commander to get his ships off that beach before it was too late. Told to mind his own business, Alcibiades rode sadly back to his fort. Athens would listen neither to Socrates' voice for reason and justice nor to Alcibiades' voice of military experience. So Lysander the Spartan came to Aegospotamoi with a fleet paid for by Persian gold, captured no less than 170 Athenian warships on the beach, and slaughtered almost all the Athenians captured with the ships, to the number of about 3,000. The erstwhile queen of the Hellenic seas had only ten war vessels remaining; the Peloponnesian War ended the next year, 404 B.C., with Athens' unconditional surrender.[42]

Sparta was victorious, but the victory had been won only with the help of Persia. The city of the immortal Leonidas of Thermopylae had sold its honor.

Out of Athens during the Peloponnesian War had come great drama—all the plays of Euripides, most of those of Aristophanes, and some of those of Sophocles were written then; great art—the Erechtheion with its exquisite Porch of the Maidens was built then;[43] and the teaching of Socrates, which inspired his student Plato to become the greatest philosopher in history up to that time. But Plato's thought and writings on politics and society were distorted for the whole of his life by what he saw during the Peloponnesian War, climaxed for him by the subsequent execution of Socrates at the order of the Athenian democracy. Seeing the Greeks apparently unable to govern themselves, Plato proposed in his *Republic* an inhuman totalitarianism which, if ever put into practice, would have destroyed the civilization that produced him and his mentor. The confidence in their capacity to achieve in freedom, which had brought about the superb creative flowering of the Hellenes of the golden age, was passing; the cosmic despair which lies at the end of every pagan road, even the most brilliant, drew closer.

In Jerusalem the faithful moved quietly through their daily rounds of work, watching, waiting. The world took no notice of them. They had suffered in many respects far more, and certainly far longer, than Greece in the Peloponnesian War. But their hope only burned the brighter; and they knew why.

NOTES

[1] Giuseppe Ricciotti, *The History of Israel* (Milwaukee, 1955), II, 108-110; Paul Heinisch, *Christ in Prophecy* (Collegeville MN, 1956), pp. 171-176; Malachi 1:11. As Heinisch points out, despite the opinion of some modern exegetes, it is almost impossible to imagine a Jewish prophet with Malachi's special interest in pure sacrifices approving those of the Gentiles. His use of the present tense in describing pure sacrifices outside Israel must be taken in a prophetic sense. The Roman Catholic Church has historically seen in this verse a clear reference to the Mass, which Christ was to institute at the Last Supper and which for centuries has been offered throughout almost all the known world.

[2] Ricciotti, *History of Israel*, II, 140.

[3] Emil Schürer, *A History of the Jewish People in the Time of Jesus Christ* (New York, 1891), II(2), 130.

[4] *Ibid.*, II(2), 130-135, 160-162. Schürer, though still rightly regarded as the best authority on Judaism from Ezra to Bar-Kochba, is by no means immune from this tendency himself. He presents the whole Messianic idea as post-exilic. While it is certainly true

that the great flowering of popular Jewish Messianism took place after the Return, for the reasons explained in the text, there are far too many references to a personal Messiah in the prophets and in the earlier history of the Israelites to fit the mechanical kind of religious evolution that Schürer outlines, in which first only the nation as a whole is seen as the recipient of God's special favors, and the concept of a personal Messiah is not developed until later.

[5] Aeschylus, *Agamemnon* (Gilbert Murray translation).

[6] Despite some modern theories to the contrary, there is no hard evidence of *any* contact between Greeks and Jews before the time of Alexander the Great. On this point see Arnaldo Momigliano, *Alien Wisdom, the Limits of Hellenism* (Cambridge, England, 1975), pp. 74-84.

[7] A. R. Burn, *Persia and the Greeks, the Defence of the West, 546-478 B.C.* (New York, 1962), pp. 127-169; A. T. Olmstead, *History of the Persian Empire* (Chicago, 1948), pp. 141-150.

[8] See particularly G. L. Huxley, *The Early Ionians* (New York, 1966).

[9] Burn, *Persia and the Greeks*, p. 44.

[10] *Ibid.*, pp. 193-217; A. R. Burn, *The Lyric Age of Greece* (New York, 1960), pp. 114-120, 330-336.

[11] The unique Spartan political and social system was ascribed in antiquity to a single great lawgiver, Lykourgos (Lycurgus), whose laws were dated by the predominant ancient tradition to the early eighth century B.C. The evidence now at our disposal indicates that this, like many other traditional dates in early Greek history, is too early. The Spartan system attributed to Lykourgos in all probability arose after, and as a result of the conquest of neighboring Messenia and the reduction of its people to serfdom (helotry) by the Spartans about the end of the eighth century; the most probable date for the Lykourgan reforms is therefore about 650 B.C. But this change of date is no reason to dismiss Lykourgos as an entirely mythical figure, often as this has been done. For a thorough and balanced discussion of this vexed question, see W. G. Forrest, *A History of Sparta, 950-192 B.C.* (London, 1968), pp. 35-60.

[12] Burn, *Persia and the Greeks*, pp. 176-187, gives a very sympathetic view of the Cleisthenic reform. However, it certainly was not "democracy" as we think of it. Though all adult male citizens acted as the legislature in Athens, only a minority even of its male inhabitants were citizens; many were slaves, and many others were resident aliens.

[13] Burn, *Persia and the Greeks*, pp. 221-223, 236-242.

[14] *Ibid.*, pp. 242-249.

[15] *Ibid.*, pp. 249-252.

[16] *Ibid.*, pp. 276-278, 313-317.

[17] *Ibid.*, pp. 291-293. For ostracism, see Raphael Sealey, *A History of the Greek City-States* (Berkeley, CA, 1976), pp. 164-166.

[18] Burn, *Persia and the Greeks*, pp. 313-420.

[19] Epitaph at Thermopylae, attributed to Simonides of Ceos.

[20] Burn, *Persia and the Greeks*, pp. 423-554.

[21] *Ibid.*, pp. 564-565, 476-480; J. B. Bury, *A History of Greece* (New York: Modern Library, n. d.), pp. 319-321. Ancient historians state that the Carthaginian invasion of Sicily in 480 B.C.—by far the largest military expedition Carthage had undertaken up to that point in her history—was urged by Xerxes and carried forward at least to some extent in concert with him; and this seems probable (Gilbert C. and Colette Picard, *The Life and Death of Carthage* [New York, 1968], pp. 78-79). Even if there were no direct cooperation between the two foes of the Greeks, it seems at least very likely that the occurrence of these two invasions in the same year was no coincidence—that the Car-

thaginians were attempting to take advantage of the troubles of old Greece by attacking the Sicilian colonies at a time when their mother cities could send them no aid.

[22] Bury, *History of Greece*, pp. 321-327, 344-345, 348-356; Burn, *Persia and the Greeks*, pp. 378-379, 421; A. R. Burn, *The Pelican History of Greece* (New York, 1974), pp. 209-210.

[23] Aeschylus, *Agamemnon* (Gilbert Murray translation).

[24] Pericles' Funeral Oration as translated by Alfred Zimmern, *The Greek Commonwealth*, 5th ed. (Oxford, 1931), p. 207.

[25] Ricciotti, *History of Israel*, II, 98-107; John Bright, *A History of Israel*, 3rd ed. (Philadelphia, 1981), pp. 391-402; W. Stewart McCullough, *The History and Literature of the Palestinian Jews from Cyrus to Herod* (Toronto, 1975), pp. 44-49. All three authorities agree that Nehemiah must have preceded Ezra in Jerusalem, despite the initial impression created by the Old Testament text that Ezra came first. Ezra 7:7 identifies the date of Ezra's principal mission to Jerusalem as the seventh year of an unnumbered Artaxerxes All three authorities reject the seventh year of Artaxerxes I (458 B.C.) as the correct date; Ricciotti and McCullough favor the seventh year of Artaxerxes II (398 B.C.). Ricciotti belives that Ezra also visited Jerusalem earlier, during the time of Nehemiah, to read the Law; Bright favors 428 B.C., assuming that a letter was dropped in the text which should have read the *thirty*-seventh year of Artaxerxes I. As Bright himself admits, such a convenient emendation is hard to justify; and Bright's arguments against the 398 B.C. date depend on such long chains of inference that they can hardly prevail over the actual wording of the extant text which, if not meaning 458 B.C., must mean 398 B.C. For a contrary view, accepting 458 B.C. as the date for Ezra and his priority in time over Nehemiah, see Paul Heinisch, *History of the Old Testament* (Collegeville MN, 1952), pp. 330-338.

[26] Ricciotti, *History of Israel*, II, 100-101.

[27] *Ibid.*, II, 99, 110-111.

[28] See R. K. Harrison, *Introduction to the Old Testament* (London, 1970), pp. 1090-1098, for an excellent argument supporting the historicity of the Book of Esther. Particularly noteworthy is the discovery of a cuneiform tablet referring to a high official named Marduka (cognate with the "Mordecai" of Esther) at the Persian royal court at Susa during the reign of Xerxes I, exactly when and where the Book of Esther places him (*ibid.*, p. 1097).

[29] Ricciotti, *History of Israel*, II, 114-120; Heinisch, *History of the Old Testament*, p. 339.

[30] Ricciotti, *History of Israel*, II, 121-124, 107-108, 142-143; Bright, *History of Israel*, pp. 371-373, 377, 401n-402n.

[31] Ricciotti, *History of Israel*, II, 127-129.

[32] Schürer, *History of the Jewish People*, II(1), 306-307.

[33] Ricciotti, *History of Israel*, II, 129-132.

[34] *Ibid.*, II, 132-135.

[35] John V. A. Fine, *The Ancient Greeks, a Critical History* (Cambridge MA, 1983), pp. 470-474; Bury, *History of Greece*, pp. 395-400.

[36] Thucydides, *The History of the Peloponnesian War*, tr. Richard Crawley (New York, 1950), pp. 400-410. The famous "Melian Dialogue" contained in these pages should be read in its entirety to grasp the full extent of Athenian moral degradation revealed by this act of unprovoked aggression and massacre.

[37] Bury, *History of Greece*, pp. 392-395; A. H. M. Jones, *Sparta* (Cambridge MA, 1967), pp. 70-71.

[38] Sealey, *Greek City-States*, pp. 351-355. An entire book, and an excellent one, devoted

to the Sicilian expedition is Peter Green, *Armada from Athens* (Garden City NY, 1970).

[39] Sealey, *Greek City-States*, pp. 355-375.

[40] Bury, *History of Greece*, pp. 485-486.

[41] *Ibid.*, p. 486.

[42] *Ibid.*, pp. 486-489; Fine, *Ancient Greeks*, pp. 516-518.

[43] Burn, *Pelican History of Greece*, pp. 297-298.

9.
THE MARCH
ACROSS THE WORLD
(404-301 B.C.)

Behold, a he-goat came from the west across the face of the whole earth, without touching the ground; and the goat had a conspicuous horn between his eyes. He came to the ram with the two horns, which I had seen standing on the bank of the river, and he ran at him in his mighty wrath. I saw him come close to the ram, and he was enraged against him and struck the ram and broke his two horns; and the ram had no power to stand before him, but he cast him down to the ground and trampled upon him; and there was no one who could rescue the ram from his power. Then the he-goat magnified himself exceedingly; but when he was strong, the great horn was broken, and instead of it there came up four conspicuous horns toward the four winds of heaven. —Daniel 8:5-8[1]

The great historical themes of the fourth century (400-300) B.C., seen in Christian perspective, were manifested in three striking events occurring in widely separated parts of the civilized world—in Jerusalem, in Athens, and in the hinterlands of the Persian empire—in the three years from 401 to 398 B.C.

In Jerusalem in 398 the venerable scribe Ezra, now 75 years old, famous for his knowledge of the Law of God since his reading of the Books of Moses in the Temple in 443 B.C., returned at the head of a caravan from Babylon consisting of 1,800 men and including 250 "servants of the Temple." The caravan brought rich offerings for the Temple from the Jews of Babylon together with a special offering from King Artaxerxes II of Persia (404-358 B.C.), who commissioned Ezra in a decree very likely drafted for him by a Jew (perhaps even by Ezra himself) "to make inquiries about Judah and Jerusalem according to the law of your God, which is in your land."[2]

For it would seem that reports had again reached the Jewish community in Babylon of a decline of fervor, a lessening of resolve by the Jews in Jerusalem to maintain the Law and their closed society in full purity. To the Jewish colony at Elephantine in Egypt the Lord of the universe had already become no more than "first among equals." The way of cultural amalgamation was the way of the Samaritans, who had consistently opposed the resettlement of Jerusalem, the rebuilding of the Temple, and the re-walling of the holy city. Rigorous adherence to the Law was essential to the preservation of all that was unique in the faith of Israel.[3]

Ezra was the supreme authority on the Law and had been Nehemiah's partner in his first restorative mission. He was the logical choice as the next reformer. This mission he carried out with a success so decisive and lasting as quickly to make him a figure of legend as well as of history. To Ezra were uncritically attributed many of the later Pharisaic reinterpretations and supplements to the Law, greatly burdening the people, which Christ condemned. Apocryphal books borrowed Ezra's name. (It should be noted, however, that none were represented as *continuations* of his canonical books, as the theory of a second or third Isaiah posits regarding the Book of Isaiah, but as later books of Ezra, separately numbered.)[4] Of what Ezra actually taught and did in 398 we are told only that he insisted that Jews should marry only among themselves, and send away all the foreign wives they had acquired along with the children born to them.[5] Harsh as this requirement seems to us, it was indispensable in the circumstances of the time, when only the faith of the Jews could preserve their identity, and history and psychology unite to show us that in the normal course of life the religion of children follows that of the mother.

As reformed by Ezra, what remained of the Jewish homeland and the people of God dwelling in it was a small quadrilateral in the hill country of Palestine, centered in every sense of the word on Jerusalem and the Temple, fully accepting the Persian authority and devoid—then and for more than two centuries to come—of secular political and military ambition. The attitude of the people of Jerusalem and its environs toward the world of the fourth century B.C. is best reflected in the Books of Chronicles which were in all probability composed shortly after Ezra's final visit to Jerusalem—a new version of the history of Israel in which the Temple and the priesthood play a more dominant role than in earlier books.[6]

In Athens in 399, the year before Ezra's final mission to Jerusalem, the great

Socrates had been executed by the Athenian democracy, restored after Sparta imposed a brief period of rule by tyrants. The most brilliant of his students, Plato, dedicated his life to enhancing man's awareness of incorporeal and conceptual realities and to raising the level of moral and ethical understanding, and the best of Plato's teaching was conveyed through dialogues in which Socrates was presented as the ideal teacher of morality and truth. The "Socratic problem"—the question of how much of the actual Socrates there is in Plato's Socrates, and how much of Plato himself—will in all probability never be solved, since there is no indication that Socrates ever wrote down any of his own teachings, but it does a grave injustice to Plato's obvious devotion to the memory of his master to suppose that he would have fundamentally altered or transformed his teaching. Undoubtedly Plato clarified, supplemented and systematized in his writing what Socrates had explained orally; but the essential sources of Plato's philosophy surely must have been in Socrates' own thought.[7]

Socrates was philosophy's first martyr, and has remained its greatest. Through Plato's genius, his thought shaped that of all the philosophical schools of the Greek world for the next eight hundred years. Aristotle was a student of Plato at Athens, and Aristotle refined reason itself into a system, providing for the first time in history explicit standards for intellectual judgment universally valid at any time and in any culture. Through Aristotle's teaching the mind could know itself, know that it knew external, objective reality, and know *how* it knew that reality—an achievement of enormous magnitude for one man so early in the history of thought.[8]

In 401 B.C.—three years before Ezra's mission to Jerusalem, two years before Socrates drank the hemlock—ten thousand Greek mercenary hoplites had been recruited by the Spartan Clearchus for an expedition organized by the Persian prince Cyrus the Younger against his elder brother Artaxerxes II, King of Persia and friend of the Jews, who had succeeded to the throne of Persepolis in 404 B.C. One of the officers of the Greek ten thousand was Xenophon, an Athenian who had studied under Socrates. The army of Cyrus the Younger reached Babylonia and won the Battle of Cunaxa there, but Cyrus died on the battlefield and his Asiatic support immediately dissolved. The ten thousand Greeks, abandoned and cut off, refused to surrender. After Clearchus and his fellow generals were treacherously seized and slain, the army elected Xenophon general and commenced its famous winter march through the uplands, mountains and rivers of eastern Asia Minor until at last they reached the sea at Trapezus. No force at the disposal of the King of Persia or any of his governors could destroy or even halt them. In one year Xenophon's ten thousand had marched 2500 miles through the Persian empire and returned virtually unscathed. The Persian colossus had feet of clay.[9]

A greater than Xenophon would follow in his footsteps, and march far beyond them.

Meanwhile in Greece it had become apparent that the Peloponnesian War had settled nothing except that Athens should not be supreme. Spartan predominance lasted less than ten years; in 395 B.C. a coalition, supported like Sparta herself earlier by Persian gold, drove Sparta back into the Peloponnesus. Athens regained a navy and rebuilt the Long Walls to the port of Piraeus; at the same time neighboring Thebes began to grow in power, absorbing the smaller cities in surrounding Boeotia. For the next 35 years there was a three-cornered struggle among Sparta, Athens, and Thebes. The Persian satraps skillfully played them off against one another, thereby preventing the weakness so spectacularly revealed by Xenophon's march from being exploited. Persia's need for this policy was all the more emphatically demonstrated by the successful revolt of Egypt from its control and the regular repulse of periodic Persian efforts to regain it, primarily due to the fighting qualities of the Greek mercenaries whom the last native Egyptian kings hired to defend them.[10]

In 358 B.C. Artaxerxes III came to the throne of Persia. Cruel but able, he was resolved to restore the strength and power of the Persian empire. Murdering all his close relatives to prevent future conspiracies against him, he set himself the task of reconquering Egypt. Repulsed in 351, he was faced with a revolt of Phoenicia, Cyprus, and part of Syria, apparently including some Palestinian Jews since a number of them were deported to Iran when the revolt was put down. Some persecution of Jews may have ensued;[11] but this is the period, out of all their history since Moses, when we know least about the Jews, when they seem lost and forgotten, hidden from the whole world. In 345 the Persians finally reconquered Egypt, but seven years later Artaxerxes III was poisoned by his chief eunuch, who also killed the crown prince, Artaxerxes' successor Arses (338-336 B.C.) and his sons two years later, and was preparing to kill Arses' successor Darius III when discovered and executed in 335.[12] So far down had Persia come from the days of Zarathustra and the great Cyrus.

Meanwhile the unity which the city-states of Hellas had been unable to attain by themselves was being imposed on them by the semi-Greek state of Macedon to the north. Insignificant up to this point in history, by the end of the Peloponnesian War Macedon was emphasizing its Hellenic character, bringing Euripides among many other famous writers, musicians and artists to its court. But in one essential respect Macedon remained wholly different from all other Greek states: it was a full monarchy, the king's authority being limited only by the requirement that he gain the approval of an assembly before putting any free-born Macedonian to death. Macedon therefore had no politics, as the rest of the Greek world knew politics.[13]

In 359 B.C. King Perdiccas II of Macedon was killed in battle with the Illyrians. His son and heir was a child; Perdiccas' brother Philip, who had lived several years at Thebes as a hostage and learned war from its able generals schooled by the brilliant tactician Epaminondas, became regent and effective ruler of the kingdom at the age of twenty-four. He took the city of Amphipolis to protect the development of the gold mines around Mount Pangaeus near the Macedonian border. Athens, which had claimed Amphipolis ever since the Peloponnesian War when it had been much fought over, protested vehemently when Philip(after pretending to have conquered it for them, refused to hand it over)) but not even the most wily and experienced Greeks of the older cities were a match for Philip in Machiavellian diplomacy.[14]

Now solidly established in the north, with growing wealth and power, Philip reorganized the Macedonian army to take advantage of the military lessons learned in the almost unending Greek wars of the past seventy years. He established the famous phalanx of pikemen (bearers of the 18-foot *sarissa*), nearly impenetrable yet reasonably mobile on the battlefield, along with an elite corps of 3,000 lighter-armed shock troops known as the Royal Shield-Bearers. Balancing these were the superb Companion cavalry, the principal assault force in pitched battles. In 357 B.C., cresting the wave of his early successes, Philip married a brilliant, passionate and beautiful princess, Olympias of Epirus, and in October 356 their first child, a son, was born. He was named Alexander, one of the traditional names of the Macedonian royal line.[15]

During the next ten years Philip took over first Thessaly, then Thrace, then the peninsula of Chalcidice. With unerring strategic vision, he next concentrated all his efforts on securing the pass of Thermopylae, the gateway to the heart of Hellas. In the so-called "Sacred War" he stirred up the priests of the oracle of Delphi, the principal shrine of Greece, and the other members of the Amphictyonic League around Delphi against Phocis, the small state in that area which had grown rich from the revenues of Delphi—and which held Thermopylae. The troops defending the pass were suborned and Philip took it without a battle. He obliterated Phocis, breaking up its cities into villages, eliminating it from history. It was now obvious that Philip was moving deliberately toward mastery of the whole of Hellas.[16]

The peerless Athenian orator Demosthenes, determined to preserve the traditional independence of the city-states, sought to rally opposition to Philip. With his famous "philippics" he roused Athens, which gained the alliance of Thebes, directly in Philip's path. The Athenian and Theban armies, with their allies, met the Macedonians under Philip at Chaeronea in Boeotia in 338 B.C. Alexander, now eighteen, commanded the cavalry and broke the Thebans, while Philip outgeneralled the Athenian hoplites and won a decisive victory. Greece lay at his feet. He marched unopposed across the Isthmus into the Peloponnesus, announced a panhellenic congress at Corinth, and called upon every Greek state to send delegates. Every one did, but Sparta. The congress established a Hellenic Confederacy to support an invasion of Persia, to begin in 336.[17]

But Philip now gave way to his lusts. Tiring of his queen Olympias, he divorced her to marry the niece of his general Attalus. He even publicly questioned his own paternity of Alexander to throw shame upon his first wife, whereupon Alexander flung a drinking-cup in his father's face. Philip would have killed his son, and thereby changed the whole course of history, had he not been too sodden with wine to hold a sword. Alexander took Olympias back to her home in Epirus and withdrew to the northern mountains. Soon afterward Philip was struck down at his daughter's wedding by the dagger of an assassin Olympias probably encouraged.[18]

It was the summer of 336 B.C. Alexander was twenty years old. The kings of Persia were falling by poison even as the king of Macedon and overlord of Greece fell by a dagger. The bonds of legitimacy and order were dissolving; the hope of Hellas was being drowned in endless internecine bloodshed; the great Plato was dead in near despair of the world, and the Chosen People in their closed society in Jerusalem were cut off from their fellow-men by the invisible walls that Ezra's teaching of the Law had raised once the material walls of Nehemiah were in place. The world seemed without direction or purpose. God's law benefitted only the few who knew it; the glory of God's gift of reason was understood and celebrated only by a handful of little-noticed teachers and their students in the declining, no longer free cities of Greece.

In just thirteen years that world was to be transformed as no single mortal man before or since has transformed it, united and ordered all the way from Greece to the shrouded heart of India, with Greek language and culture and learning and reason spreading all through that vast expanse, a whole new amalgamated civilization of West and Middle East created by a march across the world led by the greatest commander of this or any other age—a march of more than eleven thousand miles across some of the most forbidding terrain on earth, on which he won every one of the many battles he had to fight.[19]

In Alexander the Great were joined the firm resolution and extraordinary political sagacity of his father Philip, the blazing passion of his mother Olympias, and the discipline and expansion of mind resulting from his tutoring for at least three years (343-340 B.C.) by the incomparable Aristotle.[20] Alexander's goal was not simply the conquest of all the immense empire of Persia; it was to reach the very end of the earth, the shore of the River Oceanus which Aristotle had taught him ringed the inhabited world.[21] There is good reason to doubt that any other conqueror in history, with the probable exception of Napoleon Bonaparte, actually and deliberately aspired to rule the whole civilized world. Alexander not only aspired to it; he very nearly achieved it. Had he lived a normal life span he was entirely capable of having achieved it, for before his premature death he was concretely planning the conquest of Arabia and all the shores of the Mediterranean,[22] which would have left, of civilized lands, only eastern India and China outside his domain. He would have had thirty years and more to conquer them. "You, Zeus, hold Olympus," he had inscribed on his official statues, "I set the earth beneath me."[23]

What drove this man? There is no convincing evidence that he loved and sought power and wealth for their own sake, like so may lesser leaders. Though marred by occasional gusts of uncontrollable passion—the heritage of his mother—his rule was generally just and remarkably far-sighted. The cultural unification of East and West was his explicit, announced objective; its attainment was well begun even in his own short lifetime, and despite his early death was achieved and preserved in large part for nearly a thousand years.[24] Yet for all Aristotle's teaching there is no clear indication that Alexander sought the good for its own sake, or would ever have become anything like a philosopher-king. Of contemplation, of intellectual detachment, of an altruistic sense of duty there is no sign in Alexander, who was above all a man of action, a romantic, Homeric hero[25] who led his men into battle, fought hand-to-hand in the front ranks, and on one unforgettable occasion leaped down *alone* into a besieged citadel on the Ravi River in the Punjab of India. Was it simply the romance, the desire to rival Achilles, the thrill of opening up new lands and seas that drove him? But the romantic mentality is notoriously foreign to fixity of purpose, and Alexander was nothing if not overpowering in his perseverance.

So the central motivation of Alexander remains locked in mystery. He himself seems to have felt the thrust of some supernatural impulse, which he attributed to his special patron, the god Zeus Ammon whose oracle spoke to him at the Egyptian oasis of Siwah.[26] Dare we speculate that in truth One Whom neither Alexander nor any of his people could yet truly know, was urging him on? For upon his titanic achievement was built the world of East and West united into which the Incarnate Lord of Heaven and earth was to be born a little over three hundred years later, into which His apostles were to go far and wide with His message, writing the New Testament in the language that Alexander and his army spoke.

Yet when Alexander came to the throne of his murdered father all this was undreamed of; the Greeks and nearby barbarians saw only an inexperienced youth whose immaturity they could at once take advantage of. First to rise against him was Thessaly. Marching on its vale of Tempe, Alexander found the pass leading to it—five miles long and so narrow that it could only accommodate horsemen single file—strongly defended. His father would have bought off or tricked the defenders, or come again another year. Alexander had steps cut in the cliff face of Mount Ossa facing the sea (afterwards men called them "Alexander's ladder"), marched his whole army where no man had ever walked before, outflanked the pass,and appeared in the plain of the Peneus without losing a man. The Thessalians, first to behold the Alexandrian thunderbolt in action, submitted at once. (Their cavalrymen were later to ride with him all the way to India.) The next spring, campaigning against barbarians in the north, Alexander flung all the men of his phalanx across the broad Danube in a single night on fishing boats and hay-filled tent-skins, marking his frontiers where later were to be drawn the *limes* of the Roman empire.[27]

Now his presence cast an aura of fear and mastery, and his enemies had to hope for his death. Deceived by a report that he had been slain in Thrace, Thebes rose. Alexander was there in two weeks, marching faster than the messengers reporting his advent. He carried the city by assault and razed it to the ground, sparing only the house of Pindar, considered the greatest poet of the Hellenes. There was no more trouble from old Greece.[28]

In the spring of 334 B.C., with an army of some 32,000 men—less than half Macedonian, 9,000 in the phalanx, 3,000 Shield-Bearers and 1,800 Companion cavalry, and the rest from old Greece—Alexander crossed to Asia to offer sacrifice on the hill of storied Troy, to garland the tomb of Achilles, and to take from its temple the holy shield, said to date back to the Trojan War, to guard him on his mission. After thus symbolically identifying himself with Homer's heroes, he struck the first Persian army to challenge him at the river Granicus, meeting its commanders and their guards head-on in person in a clash at the center of the battle line. Barely escaping death (his life was saved by his bodyguard Cleitus), he broke the Persians, captured thousands of their Greek mercenaries whom he killed or sold into slavery for fighting against the panhellenic cause, and was master of Asia Minor.[29]

Behind Alexander was the Phoenician fleet of the Persian empire, some 400 warships, outnumbering his navy more than two to one; it forced Miletos to retract its surrender to Alexander and return to allegiance to the King of Persia. Disdaining to challenge this powerful enemy naval force in its own element—Macedon had never had a navy—Alexander adopted a typically Alexandrian counter-strategy, as breathtakingly audacious as it was eventually effective: capture all the Mediterranean ports of the Persian empire, all the way from Miletos round to Egypt, leaving the hostile fleet no base. Exactly this he proceeded to do during the next two years, beginning with Miletos itself, which he besieged and took; then, after defeating King Darius III in person at the Battle of Issus where the Mediterranean shore turns south to become the coast of Syria, capturing the island city of Tyre, queen of Phoenicia, by no less a tactic than extending the land out to reach it. For six hundred years, since the days of Kings Hiram and Solomon, Tyre on its island had been mistress of the eastern seas. To take it, Alexander built a mole from the mainland to within 100 yards of the island, easy artillery range; so well did he build the mole that it remained permanently, a new addition to the map, joining the island unbreakably to the mainland, and Tyre began its long decline to the poor fishing village it is today—as the prophets of Israel had predicted long before.[30]

Having secured the coastlands, Alexander was hailed as Pharaoh by the ancient priesthood of Egypt and founded Alexandria at the western edge of the Nile delta.[31] Passing within a few miles of Jerusalem without making any contact with it, though punishing Samaria for killing his governor by colonizing it with Macedonians,[32] Alexander turned east for the march across the world. At Gaugamela in Mesopotamia, where civilization began, he met the last great Persian army.

Darius III, who had fled for his life from the battlefield of Issus, may have been personally a coward, though this would be very surprising in a Persian king. It is more likely that he was simply unnerved by the experience of twice facing, head to head, the premier battle captain of all time. We know more of Alexander's tactics at Gaugamela than at Issus—how he opened the lines of the phalanx to receive harmlessly the deadly scythe-bearing chariots, then closed them again to meet the Persian center; how he sent the Companion cavalry oblique to the right, broke the Persian line in an irresistible charge, then halted it, faced about, and shattered the Persian center. Never hesitating, never wavering, never making a mistake, Alexander conducted the decisive battle for the Persian empire like a skilled surgeon in his operating room, cutting the Persian host to pieces with methodical incisions, until the Great King lost heart and fled again. At Arbela Alexander found his chariot, shield, and bow; Darius, an almost defenseless fugitive, was riding frantically into the mountains of Media.[33]

The battle of Gaugamela was fought October 1, 331 B.C. The triumphant Alexander looked in at Babylon, staying there about a month; he looked in at Susa, staying there about a month; by then winter gripped the high harsh plateau of Iran. No matter, the march across the world must go on. In January Alexander's army was at the Persian Gates, the pass through which ran the only road to Persepolis from the west. It was guarded by thousands of troops who repulsed the first attack.[34]

Alexander the Great on the march was more like an elemental force than a mortal man; he simply could not be stopped by a physical obstacle. On this occasion he took half his army eleven miles by night along a snowy track over the back of the mountains overlooking the pass, struck the Persians in the rear, and routed them. Proceeding by forced marches to the Persian capital, he took it and burned the palace of Xerxes. No building ever rose again upon its site. The ashes of the palace of Xerxes symbolized the total collapse of the power that had unified all the civilized lands from India to Greece, and at the height of its long-departed glory and magnanimity had restored the Chosen People to the Promised Land.[35]

Alexander intended a wholly new order to take the place of the ruined empire—an order that would put Greek and Persian on an equal footing as citizens, to be a fusion of peoples and cultures rather than a simple domination of Hellene over Asiatic. At Ecbatana, capital of Media, the troops from old Greece, who had marched under the banner of the panhellenic war of revenge against the ancient Persian foe, were paid off and allowed either to return home or to enlist in what was now unequivocally Alexander's own army, to be led wherever he willed for whatever purposes he chose. Many did re-enlist, and almost all the Macedonians remained (though with numerous complaints about the new favors given the Persians and the adoption by Alexander of some forms of Persian court etiquette).[36]

Still fleeing from his relentless adversary, Darius III was now beyond the Caspian Gates, in the land bordering the Caspian Sea on the southeast, known as Hyrcania (later Parthia). As ever, Alexander followed. Darius wished to turn at bay and fight, but Bessus, satrap of Bactria further to the east, decided to fall back on Bactria and claim there whatever might be left of the power and authority of the Great King. As Alexander with five hundred picked horsemen bore down on them, Bessus and his co-conspirators stabbed Darius and rode away. By a spring some 45 miles east of Thara a Macedonian soldier found the King of Kings, abandoned by all, breathing his last. So ignominiously ended the line and achievement of the dynasty of the great Cyrus, after 220 years. The conqueror was just twenty-six years old.[37]

The march went on. After zigzagging through central Iran imposing peace on restive satraps, the army crossed the two-mile-high Hindu Kush Mountains (called by the Greeks Paropamisadae, the "peaks over which the eagle cannot fly") in March 329, finding shelter only in huts submerged beneath enormous snowdrifts, eating nothing but herbs and the meat of their own baggage animals—meat which was raw because there was no wood to cook it. Alexander was approaching "the roof of the world," but still no natural barrier could stop him.[38]

Bessus, like his murdered king, fled. Was he too a coward, as Darius III is alleged to have been? Surely he knew that Alexander would come; he had gone to Bactria, his homeland, specifically to hold it against him, had even "scorched the earth" on the slopes Alexander must descend to penetrate it. Cowardice in both men is too easy an explanation. Rather we must try to imagine the state of mind of the proud former governor in the fertile valley of the province he had ruled, now wearing the upright headdress of the Great King whose successor he claimed to be, having last heard of Alexander far to the south trying to establish his rule in other provinces, the great heights and the passes all buried deep in snow, suddenly confronted with the news that this inescapable thunderbolt of a man was coming like a ghost out of the white silences of a high mountain winter to strike again, *now,* with his invincible army.

In Sogdiana beyond the Oxus River, the last province of the Persian empire on the edge of the endless, uncivilized central Asian steppe, Bessus was seized and delivered up to Alexander, who had him scourged and executed for the murder of Darius. Alexander took Samarkand (Maracanda) and marched all the way to the Jaxartes River in the heart of Asia where he set his ultimate frontier, founded a city he called Alexandria-the-Farthest, and routed a Scythian force which had assembled on the far bank to challenge him. Alexandria-the-Farthest stood at the point where the Jaxartes River flows out of the vale of

Ferghana. The vale of Ferghana leads to the pass over the Tien-Shan Mountains into the orbit of China, then still more than a century from its unification by the Emperor Shih Huang Ti, in its "period of the warring states."[39] Divided, it too could have been conquered.

China does not know Alexander. But it was more than a thousand years before another army from the west reached this point.[40]

Hearing that Sogdiana had risen in revolt behind him under its former satrap Spitamenes, Alexander marched an almost incredible 180 miles in three days in the broiling heat of a central Asian summer to relieve Maracanda and drive off Spitamenes' army. A whole year was required to subdue this distant province. At last Spitamenes was slain and the "impregnable" crag fortress called the Sogdian Rock scaled by Macedonian volunteers, one in ten of whom fell to their deaths on the way up. Alexander then married Roxana, daughter of the commander of this stronghold, thereby gaining enough support in Sogdiana to establish peace.[41]

Recrossing the Hindu Kush, Alexander set his face toward India. The core of his army was still the peerless Macedonian cavalry and infantry. Periodic drafts of reinforcements had been dispatched; but among the Royal Shield-Bearers and the Foot Companins of the phalanx who marched through the Khyber Pass and down into the Indus valley in the fall of 327 B.C. were still many who had crossed the Hellespont with Alexander seven years before. There were numerous Asiatics in the army now, enlisted primarily from Bactria and Sogdiana, but they were only auxiliaries. Whatever might be Alexander's dreams and plans of *homonoia*—concord—among all men of his empire, and of a common Graeco-Persian citizenship, it was only upon the farm boys from Macedon that he could ultimately depend in the mysterious, shadowed land of Harappa and the Vedas and the Upanishads and the Buddha and the Jains that he was now entering, the first Greek since Skylax of Karyanda (so far as we know) even to see it, yet daring to come as its conqueror. It seems clear that he intended to conquer it all, not just the Indus province once (but not for well over a century) part of the Persian empire. No less an authority than Chandragupta Maurya, the first king of all India, who as a young man witnessed Alexander's invasion, testified that Alexander could have taken the whole of India, and almost did.[42]

Across the Indus Alexander came; then across, one by one, the five mighty rivers of the Punjab. At the second, the Jhelum, (called by the Greeks Hydaspes), King Porus awaited him with a great army, defending all of the few fords, and 200 war elephants. No Greek soldier had ever faced elephants in sufficient numbers to be decisive in battle; they had seen only the few used largely for show by the Persian kings. Alexander depended on his heavy cavalry as his primary assault force, and no cavalry untrained in elephant warfare would face the enormous trumpeting beasts for a moment.

What followed was a battle unique in the annals of war. Somehow Alexander found enough boats to embark 5,000 cavalry and 10,000 infantry, the pick of his army; he sent them 16 miles to the south and ferried them by night to an island in the river where they disembarked, re-formed, crossed the remainder of the river by a ford through water up to their chests, re-formed again, and marched the 16 miles back for a dawn attack on Porus. Alexander drew the Indian cavalry to one flank, away from the protection of the elephants, then surrounded them with his cavalry which promptly attacked. The Indian survivors fell back on the elephants, whereupon the Macedonian *foot* soldiers came up to challenge them, spear to tusk.[43]

Fifty years later a much smaller force of elephants was to defeat two Roman consular armies in their native Italy before the legions learned how to fight them; and no soldiers in the ancient world matched Rome's. But the Macedonians under Alexander the Great, four thousand miles from home in the heart of India, surpassed the legions in this battle. They actually surrounded the whole elephant force, penning it in an iron ring of spears, maddening the elephants with wounds until they ran wild and began to kill the Indian troops encircled with them. Elephants and infantry broke, Porus was taken captive on the battlefield, and Alexander's great horse Bucephalas died of exhaustion. Another victory, the most astonishing of all, had been won.[44]

Here it is necessary to step back for a moment from the rush of events to gain a clear perspective. Consider a Macedonian infantryman, raised on a farm in the gentle green valley of the Axios River near Pella, in the heart of Macedon. His horizon is bounded by his native hills. At the call of the golden youth who is his king, he forsakes his home and marches east, into the great empire which has overshadowed all Hellas for generations. An incredible eleven thousand miles he marches through seven years, conquering that empire on the way—across rivers and deserts, twice across mountains two miles high in winter, into the steppe, to the gates of China, and finally into the Indian jungle among the weird philosophers, where armies rely on the power and the terror of unknown colossal beasts—apparitions such as the monsters of science-fiction would be to men of today—until he stands on the bank of the second of the five rivers of the Punjab, charging an elephant with his spear. No commander ever led men as Alexander the Great led men.

One more river . . . one more . . . one more. Across the Chenab, swollen by monsoon rains to a mile and a half of rolling brown flood, into the land of Porus' nephew, who submitted at once (Porus presumably having told him what manner of man he faced). Across the Ravi, to a battle with the warlike Cathaeans, taking their capital, Sangala. To the Beas, the monsoon rains never stopping, the hooves of their horses worn away, their weapons battered, their clothes rotted to rags, cobras slithering away from the rising waters a perpetual menace of instant death. An immense weariness overtook the army, and a creeping terror as they realized at last how incredibly far they had come from home and how strange was this new world they had entered. Ahead lay a great desert; beyond it, upon the Ganges River, was the mighty kingdom of Magadha which had existed since the Buddha's time, ruled by Dhana Nanda from his palace at Palimbothra, master of 200,000 infantry and 4,000 elephants. We may imagine wild tales of this hitherto totally unknown empire flying through the ranks. But Porus, now Alexander's firm ally, was giving him solid information about Magadha: however externally imposing, its king was the son of a barber and universally detested; his facade of power would crumble under one hard blow. The Bay of Bengal, the end of India, was only three months' march away.[45]

Alexander would go.

His army would not.

World's end was too far. The Macedonians halted at the Beas River. No one dreamed of overthrowing Alexander. They would follow him still—anywhere but further east.[46]

Alexander waited three days, hoping for a change of heart. It did not come. So he set up twelve altars to the twelve great gods of Olympus and turned away at last from the rising sun.[47]

No trace of the twelve altars has ever been found. Like some vast quicksand, India has swallowed them up. But she remembered the Yavanas (a corruption of "Ionians"), the men from the west; some knowledge of their culture and learning and poetry spread gradually all through India, so that more than five hundred years later in Ceylon a native writer could quote Homer; and the contact begun by Alexander's invasion remained unbroken until the Apostle Thomas followed the monsoon trade route to the Malabar coast in the far south of India, in the first century after God became man.[48]

Alexander built a fleet and sailed southward down the rivers of the Punjab toward the sea. At the confluence of the Chenab and the Ravi the fierce tribe of the Malloi defied him from the fortress of Multan. He prepared to storm its citadel with ladders, but the ladders broke under the weight of his men. Standing alone on the rampart, Alexander leaped down inside the fortress. Just three men followed him. Alexander slew the Mallian chieftain and beat off all attackers, his back to the wall, until he fainted for loss of blood from a severe wound in his chest. The heroic Peucestas, one of the three who had come after him, held over him the sacred shield of Troy, taken so long ago from the temple at Ilion, saving his life until the Macedonians finally broke in the gates and put every defender to the sword. Alexander lived, but there is reason to believe that he never fully recovered from the wound, inflicted by a yard-long arrow that apparently pierced his lungs.[49]

South along the Indus the Brahmins stirred up the people to oppose Alexander, but he put them down, and by the summer of 325 B.C. had reached the Arabian Sea. He sent part of his army under Craterus to suppress rebellions in central Iran and took the rest across the frightful desert of Makran (Gedrosia) while a fleet under Nearchus sailed along the parched coast from the mouth of the Indus to the Persian Gulf. The risks were enormous and Alexander's losses substantial, but as always his irresistible drive carried him and his men through.[50]

Returning to the center of his empire, Alexander found that many of his provincial governors had been unfaithful to their charge during his long absence, embezzling tax funds and royal treasure or planning rebellion, and that some of his troops had looted and plundered. Even the tomb of Cyrus the Great had been despoiled. The guilty were punished with ruthless, efficient severity.[51]

Alexander proceeded immediately to develop further and begin to carry out his plans for a united Graeco-Persian realm. Ten thousand Macedonians were persuaded to take Asiatic wives; Greek military schools were established in every province and Asiatics were enlisted even in the heretofore exclusively Macedonian Companion cavalry. Macedonian resentment flared up in a brief mutiny, followed by a passionate reconciliation. Ancient Babylon was selected as the capital of the new Alexandrian empire. So to Babylon, in the winter of 323 B.C., came ambassadors from Greek Italy, from Carthage and the Phoenician colonies in Spain, from Ethiopia far up the Nile, and from the Libyans, Celts and Scythians. (Did any come from the young Rome? We cannot be sure; the sources disagree.) Everyone was wondering and waiting to see where the invincible world conqueror would strike next.[52]

His choice was for Arabia, on whose southern coasts valuable spices were to be found, and which looked out upon the sea route from Egypt to India. An expedition was planned for the circumnavigation and conquest of Arabia; a fleet of a thousand ships was ordered built for it. Regular commerce was to be opened up with India; the Caspian Sea was to be explored, and possibly a voyage undertaken to circumnavigate Africa. Following that, another fleet of a thousand ships was to be built in Phoenicia and Syria and sent with a great army against Carthage and thence all the way around the shores of the Mediterranean to include all its coastlands in the empire, as Rome was later to establish her rule on every Mediterranean coast—but only after centuries of struggle, while Alexander proposed to do it in one campaign. Peucestas, who had held the shield of Troy over Alexander in the citadel of the Malloi in India, had recruited 20,000 Persians whom Alexander integrated into the phalanx to make a new, more mobile formation, with the heavy-armed Macedonians in the outer ranks while the lighter-armed Persians remained in the center from which they would sally to strike the enemy. The world conqueror never relaxed, hardly slept. Along with his stupendous plans and preparations went a daily round of gargantuan festivity and gorgeous ceremonials, many in honor of his closest friend Hephaistion who had died a few months before. Alexander's superhuman energy was unabated, but his body could stand the constant strain no longer; suddenly he was seized by a raging fever, which worsened through ten days, and on June

13, 323 B.C. Alexander the Great died. He was thirty-three years old.[53]

He left an illegitimate, imbecile half-brother and a posthumous son born of Roxana. No arrangements had been made for a successor; it was as though no one, including himself, could imagine this enormously vital young man dying. A triple regency was decided upon after prolonged, acrimonious negotiations: the elderly but steady, loyal and competent Antipater to continue as viceroy of Macedon and Greece, a position he had held all through Alexander's mighty march, and Generals Perdiccas and Craterus to divide the regency in Asia, with Perdiccas holding chief power. But no such makeshift arrangement could work in the face of the enormous temptations inherent in the disposition of the greatest empire the world had ever seen. The meddling and jealousy of Alexander's mother Olympias heightened tensions, and a lesser general named Ptolemy, who had had the foresight to claim rich, easily defensible Egypt as his province, lit the fires of civil war in 321 by seizing the body of Alexander as it was being sent home to Macedon, and conveying it to Egypt for burial at Alexandria. Antipater and Craterus joined Ptolemy against Perdiccas, Craterus died in battle, while Perdiccas was murdered by his own officers after a defeat. The one remaining regent, Antipater, then died of old age in 319, leaving all in confusion. Every general's hand was against every other. Antipater's chosen successor and his second-in-command went to war with each other; Perdiccas' military commander in Asia Minor was still fighting; and a rebellious commander, Antigonus the One-Eyed, was making his own way to power, allying himself with first one and then another of the contenders as his needs and plans of the moment dictated, aiming to become the full successor of Alexander.[54]

Olympias herself now led an army from Epirus into Macedon. Alexander's veterans would not fight her. She seized poor Philip Arrhidaeus, Alexander's imbecile half-brother, and had him killed. The next year she herself met the same fate at the hands of Cassander, Antipater's cruel and faithless son, who finally prevailed in Macedon and by 310 had Alexander's young son and only legitimate heir quietly put to death along with Alexander's queen, Roxana.[55]

While Ptolemy held Egypt, Seleucus—who had been a highly placed officer under Alexander—established himself in Babylon, from which he could draw on the resources of the vast eastern reaches of the empire. Alexander's victory had been so complete that there were no native rebellions all through the territory of the former Persian empire, despite the turmoil of civil war among the Greek successors; all Iran was at Seleucus' disposal. But India was different; there the young prince Chandragupta, learning from the example of Alexander and enlisting mercenaries from among the Greek troops who had stayed there as garrisons, overthrew Dhana Nanda ''the son of a barber'' and made himself master of the kingdom of Magadha on the Ganges, founding the Mauryan empire in India. Marching westward, Chandragupta invaded the Punjab. Seleucus, too preoccupied with the struggle for the empire in the west to make a major effort to hold India, gave the Punjab up to Chandragupta in return for five hundred war elephants.[56]

By this time (305 B.C.) Seleucus in Babylon, Ptolemy in Egypt, Cassander in Macedon, and Lysimachus in Thrace had proclaimed themselves kings of their respective portions of Alexander's realm. Forming a coalition against the ambitious Antigonus and his son Demetrius the Besieger, they met the father and son in battle at Ipsus in Asia Minor. The contending forces were approximately equal in numbers; Seleucus' elephants, for which he had sold Alexander's Indian conquests, decided the issue. Antigonus died on the field.[57] As the prophet Daniel had foretold, the heritage of Alexander was divided into four parts. It was never again to be fully united politically, only in part even at the apogee of Rome; but Hellenization provided a cultural unity, and the bridge between East and West that Alexander had built would endure for a thousand years, until the coming of Islam.

NOTES

[1] For arguments on the date of Daniel, see Chapter Seven, above. The reference in the quoted passage is evidently to Alexander. Most modern commentators refuse to call it prophecy, claiming that the Book of Daniel was written after the events described; Robin Lane-Fox (*Alexander the Great* [New York, 1974], p. 200), for example, notes that the symbol of the god Amon, whom Alexander adopted as a special patron after hearing his oracle in the Siwah oasis in the Egyptian desert, was a ram's horn, later shown on his coins and those of his successors, and in this context states that "in the Book of Daniel, he [Alexander] appears in the guise of the ram-horned conqueror." Unhappily for this neat rationalistic theory, Lane-Fox has confused goats with sheep. A ram is a male sheep, not a male goat; the sequence in Daniel as well as the description of the actions of the he-goat makes it clear that the ram in Daniel symbolizes the *Persian* empire which came from the east, not the new empire brought from the west by Alexander. Scripture knows nothing of Alexander's pagan symbolism; it has its own.

[2] Giuseppe Ricciotti, *The History of Israel* (Milwaukee, 1955), II, 136-137. For the controversy over the date of Ezra and a summary of opinions differing from the conclusions presented in the text, see Chapter Eight, Note 25, above.

[3] Ricciotti, *History of Israel*, II, 136-137, 147-148, 166-167.

[4] The so-called later Books of Ezra were never regarded as canonical either by official Judaism or by the Roman Catholic Church, or by any of the Church Fathers.

[5] Ricciotti, *History of Israel*, II, 138-139.

[6] Elias Bickerman, *From Ezra to the Last of the Maccabees* (New York, 1949), pp. 20-31; William F. Albright, *Recent Discoveries in Bible Lands* (New York, 1955), p. 105; Paul Heinisch, *History of the Old Testament* (Collegeville MN, 1952), pp. 156, 355. The Books of Chronicles, long dated by "higher critics," for no particularly good reason, to the third or even the second century B.C., are now assigned by most scholars to the fourth century. Heinisch presents a solidly convincing case for dating them at the beginning of the fourth century, almost contemporaneous with the final visit of Ezra to Jerusalem according to the chronology adopted in the text. He points out that the last high priest mentioned in Chronicles is Johanan, who is known from the Elephantine papyri

to have been ruling in the late fifth century (up to at least 408 B.C.), and that with its dominant interest in the Temple and the high priesthood the Books of Chronicles would almost certainly have given a complete account of high priests right down to the time of its writing. Consequently it would appear that Johanan was still high priest when the Books of Chronicles was completed. The exact date of the end of Johanan's pontificate is not known, but his successor Jaddua was high priest for a very long time, up to the coming of Alexander the Great, and a rough approximation of the dates would extend Johanan's pontificate to about 370 B.C. (Ricciotti, *History of Israel*, II, 142-143). John Bright, *A History of Israel*, 3rd ed. (Philadelphia, 1981), pp. 396-397, agrees on this date for the writing of the Books of Chronicles.

[7] Joseph Owens, *A History of Ancient Western Philosophy* (New York, 1959), pp. 165-175.

[8] *Ibid.*, pp. 294-306.

[9] J. B. Bury, *A History of Greece* (New York, Modern Library edition, n.d.), pp. 501-515; John V. A. Fine, *The Ancient Greeks, a Critical History* (Cambridge MA, 1983), pp. 538-541.

[10] Bury, *History of Greece*, pp. 525-612.

[11] A. T. Olmstead, *History of the Persian Empire* (Chicago, 1948), pp. 424-425, 432-440; Ricciotti, *History of Israel*, II, 141; Heinisch, *History of the Old Testament*, pp. 341-342.

[12] Olmstead, *Persian Empire*, pp. 489-490.

[13] Fine, *Ancient Greeks*, pp. 605-614.

[14] *Ibid.*, pp. 615-618; Bury, *History of Greece*, pp. 671-674.

[15] Bury, *History of Greece*, pp. 674-675; Lane-Fox, *Alexander the Great*, pp. 72-79.

[16] Bury, *History of Greece*, pp. 690-698.

[17] *Ibid.*, pp. 698-719.

[18] *Ibid.*, pp. 720-721; Lane-Fox, *Alexander the Great*, pp. 17-25.

[19] For the total distance marched (11,250 miles) see Lane-Fox, *Alexander the Great*, p. 369. The distance "as the crow flies" from the Hellespont to the Beas River in India is about 3,500 miles.

[20] Ulrich Wilcken, *Alexander the Great* (New York, 1967), pp. 53-58.

[21] *Ibid.*, pp. 173-175; Lane-Fox, *Alexander the Great*, pp. 210, 275-278, 331-333, 367-376. N. G. L. Hammond, *Alexander the Great, King, Commander and Statesman* (Park Ridge NJ, 1980), in an appendix calls the idea that Alexander aspired to rule the whole inhabited earth a "misconception" (p. 306), but earlier quotes Plutarch against himself: "Alexander considered that he had come from the gods to be a general governor and reconciler of the world" (p. 269).

[22] Wilcken, *Alexander the Great*, pp. 223-230. Hammond, *Alexander the Great*, decisively disposes of doubts about the genuineness of these "last plans" of Alexander (pp. 300-304).

[23] Lane-Fox, *Alexander the Great*, p. 331.

[24] *Ibid.*, pp. 417-429, 478-495; Hammond, *Alexander the Great*, p. 264.

[25] Lane-Fox, *Alexander the Great*, pp. 496-498.

[26] *Ibid.*, pp. 210-217.

[27] *Ibid.*, pp. 68, 116; Bury, *History of Greece*, pp. 724-727; Hammond, *Alexander the Great*, pp. 44-48.

[28] Bury, *History of Greece*, pp. 730-732; Hammond, *Alexander the Great*, pp. 57-63.

[29] Hammond, *Alexander the Great*, pp. 68-76; Lane-Fox, *Alexander the Great*, pp. 109-116. Lane-Fox's otherwise excellent biography of Alexander—in the opinion of this writer the most penetrating book in English about this meteoric man, though disfigured for the Christian reader by its anti-Christian bias—is marred by an attempt to rewrite

the history of the Battle of the Granicus in a manner contrary to all other modern, and all but one ancient presentation of the battle, wich requires major surgery on all but the one ancient account. Lane-Fox's explanations for what his theory requires him to regard as massive historical falsification of the facts of this battle are far from convincing. Hammond's account of the battle, written after that of Lane-Fox, specifically rejects it (*op. cit.*, p. 310).

30 Bury, *History of Greece*, pp. 740, 751-756. See Figure 108, p. 752 (*ibid.*) for a map showing the ancient coastline of Phoenicia opposite island Tyre and the present coastline which joins the former island to the mainland on either side of the mole of Alexander. For the prophecies of the decline and depopulation of Tyre see Chapter Six, Note 39, above.

31 Lane-Fox, *Alexander the Great*, pp. 196-198, 222.

32 Bickerman, *Ezra to the Maccabees*, pp. 41-46; Victor Tcherikover, *Hellenistic Civilization and the Jews* (Philadelphia, 1959), pp. 42-48.

33 J. F. C. Fuller, *The Generalship of Alexander the Great* (New Brunswick NJ, 1960), pp. 176-180; Hammond, *Alexander the Great*, pp. 137-148.

34 Bury, *History of Greece*, pp. 764-766.

35 Lane-Fox, *Alexander the Great*, pp. 255-261; Hammond, *Alexander the Great*, pp. 166-167.

36 Lane-Fox, *Alexander the Great*, pp. 267-272.

37 Bury, *History of Greece*, pp. 768-770.

38 Lane-Fox, *Alexander the Great*, pp. 293-294; Hammond, *Alexander the Great*, p. 188.

39 Lane-Fox, *Alexander the Great*, pp. 299-301. China was unified more than a hundred years later; its divisions at the time of Alexander were profound (Dun J. Li, *The Ageless Chinese, a History* [New York, 1965], pp. 54-59).

40 At the peak of the explosive initial expansion of Islam, a Muslim army under Qutaiba marched through the vale of Ferghana to Kashgar in 713 A.D. (John B. Glubb, *The Empire of the Arabs* [Englewood Cliffs NJ, 1965], pp. 153-154).

41 Lane-Fox, *Alexander the Great*, pp. 302-306, 314-317.

42 *Ibid.*, pp. 372, 331; A. K. Narain, *From Alexander to Kanishka* (Varanasi [Benares], India, 1967), pp. 1-3.

43 Fuller, *Generalship of Alexander the Great*, pp. 186-197.

44 *Ibid.*, pp. 197-198.

45 Lane-Fox, *Alexander the Great*, pp. 363-368.

46 *Ibid.*, p. 369; Hammond, *Alexander the Great*, pp. 214-215. As Hammond points out, under Macedonian law the army had to approve a new war against a new enemy— the king's authority over Macedon and particularly over its army was not absolute. Alexander never issued a positive order to advance beyond the Beas River. Technically, therefore, the army did not actually mutiny.

47 Lane-Fox, *Alexander the Great*, p. 370.

48 *Ibid.*, pp. 470, 492. See Chapter Seventeen, below, for the Apostle Thomas.

49 Bury, *History of Greece*, pp. 795-796.

50 Hammond, *Alexander the Great*, pp. 229-235; Lane-Fox, *Alexander the Great*, pp. 387-399.

51 Lane-Fox, *Alexander the Great*, pp. 403-410.

52 *Ibid.*, pp. 417-429, 448; Howard H. Scullard, *A History of the Roman World from 753 to 146 B.C.*, 3rd ed. (London, 1961), p. 114n. Also see Note 22, above.

53 Lane-Fox, *Alexander the Great*, pp. 448-472.

54 M. Cary, *A History of the Greek World from 323 to 146 B.C.*, 2nd ed. (London,

1963), pp. 1-3, 10-26.
    [55] *Ibid.*, pp. 20, 29.
    [56] *Ibid.*, pp. 28, 65-68.
    [57] *Ibid.*, pp. 35-41.

10.
THE FORTITUDE OF ROME
(301-201 B.C.)

Nobody understands the romance of Rome, and why she rose afterwards to a representative leadership that seemed almost fated and fundamentally natural, who does not keep in mind the agony of horror and humiliation through which she had continued to testify to the sanity that is the soul of Europe. She came to stand alone in the midst of an empire because she had once stood alone in the midst of a ruin and a waste. After that all men knew in their hearts that she had been representative of mankind, even when she was rejected of men. And there fell on her the shadow from a shining and as yet invisible light and the burden of things to be. It is not for us to guess in what manner or moment the mercy of God might in any case have rescued the world; but it is certain that the struggle which established Christendom would have been very different if there had been an empire of Carthage instead of an empire of Rome. We have to thank the patience of the Punic wars if, in after ages, divine things descended at least upon human things and not inhuman. . . . If, after all these ages, we are in some sense at peace with paganism, and can think more kindly of our fathers, it is well to remember the things that were and the things that might have been. For this reason alone we can take lightly the load of antiquity and need not shudder at a nymph on a fountain or a cupid on a valentine. Laughter and sadness link us with things long passed away and remembered without dishonour; and we can see not altogether without tenderness the twilight sinking around the Sabine farm and hear the household gods rejoice when Catullus comes home to Sirmio. *Deleta est Carthago.* — G. K. Chesterton, *The Everlasting Man*, pp. 154-155

The proof was in; Alexander the Great was one of a kind, no man could fill the empty place which he had left. Not Antigonus the One-Eyed, dead on the battlefield of Ipsus in 301 B.C. Not his son Demetrius the Besieger, who on his attempt to duplicate Alexander's march got no farther than the Taurus Mountains of Cilicia in Asia Minor, where he was captured and drank himself to death in 285. Not cautious Ptolemy, content with Egypt, Palestine, Phoenicia and a fringing of Mediterranean islands until his death in 283. Not Lysimachus, whom Seleucus slew at the Battle of Corupedion in 281; and not even Seleucus, heir to the greater part of the Alexandrian domain, who fell ignominiously by the dagger of Ptolemy's disinherited son Ceraunus as he stepped out of a boat after crossing the Hellespont in 280.[1]

Yet there was one who still dreamed of Alexandrian conquests. Since they were clearly not possible among his contending successors in the east, who invariably joined to pull down the strongest, then in the west, in Italy and Sicily where the old Greek settlements were in decline and non-Greek invaders moving against them. Young, brilliant, dashing and red-haired, vaultingly ambitious, King Pyrrhus of Epirus next to Macedon, looking for a western world to conquer, gladly seized on a request for help from the Greek city of Tarentum on the instep of the Italian boot, close to Greece, against a confederation of northern barbarians that was beginning to press them hard. In 280 B.C., the year of the assassination of Seleucus, Pyrrhus landed in Italy with an excellent professional army of 25,000 men, very similar in composition and character to the army Alexander had taken across Asia to India—and with 20 elephants, creatures never before seen in Italy.[2]

Certain of victory, Pyrrhus and his army marched to meet the barbarian challengers at Heraclea—a mere militia who assuredly could never stand against the phalanx, let alone the elephants. The kind of infantry Alexander had led so far and so triumphantly toward world's end, the great beasts he had brought back from world's end, were hurled against a formation of Italian farmers who had never in all their history faced a professional army in battle.

But those farmers' formation was a legion, and it bore the eagles of Rome—a city which, step by step over two centuries, had grown from an insignificant riverside town to the mistress of most of peninsular Italy, welding its people into a public order in which every city had its recognized and rightful place and its own local self-government, a state like none the world had yet seen, a city which for an almost incredible 797 years (387 B.C. to 410 A.D.) never knew the tramp of a foreign enemy in arms upon its streets.

Few moments in all of military history match the drama of this unexpected, unheralded clash of Alexandrian phalanx and Roman legion, each utterly confident of victory, neither with any initial conception of the quality of the other.

The result was a bloody draw; neither side would break, and at last the elephants—and they alone—won the battle for Pyrrhus by stampeding the Roman cavalry horses. The Romans held their fortified camp and retreated in good order at their leisure. They left 7,000 dead, but Pyrrhus lost 4,000, 16 per cent of his whole army—and he was much farther away from home.[3]

Nothing if not bold, Pyrrhus immediately marched on Rome, calling on the other Italians to rise and join him, counting on discouragement in Rome after the defeat and disaffection among her subordinates and allies. There was neither discouragement nor disaffection. The southern cities of the Roman confederacy shut their gates against their self-proclaimed liberator; the country people harassed his advance; the consul he had defeated at Heraclea hung undaunted on his heels. The Romans brought up fresh legions. Pyrrhus halted forty miles from Rome and sent his personal ambassador, the urbane Cineas, to offer peace and alliance.[4]

Cineas came before a body of stern dignity and rectitude, the Senate, composed of all who had ever held high office in the Roman state. He offered the senators lavish gifts for themselves and their wives, which they firmly rejected as bribes. He presented Pyrrhus' terms: an end to the war and a restoration of prisoners in return for autonomy for the Greek cities and the relinquishing of some Roman-conquered territory to the Lucanians and Samnites. A few senators spoke for accepting these proposals.[5]

Then former censor Appius Claudius, for whom the Appian Way is named, was led into the Senate. Perhaps eighty years old, now blind, he could remember the final defeat of the Gauls—the last enemy to sack Rome—by the son of the great Marcus Furius Camillus; he, a patrician, had made himself a champion of the plebs, the common people, to build a stronger society; through the many years of his public service he had done much to hammer a stable and prosperous state out of the tough metal of turbulent, still half-barbaric Italy through his people whose iron resolution to endure and to prevail never weakened. Would that he had become deaf as well as blind, Appius Claudius cried, that he might not have to hear Romans discussing even the possibility of accepting peace terms from an invader. Rome should never negotiate with an enemy in arms upon her soil.[6]

He spoke for the very heart of early Rome. The record of his speech—the oldest such record in Roman archives—was preserved for at least 250 years. His doctrine was to remain a cardinal principle of Roman policy.[7]

So there would be no peace, and Pyrrhus marched up along the Apennines to Asculum, where in 279 B.C. he met another Roman army and fought another drawn battle, technically a victory for him because the Romans had to fall back on their camp and then retire, but the occasion which has made his name a byword ever since for a victory too costly to bear—"one more such victory and I am ruined." At Asculum Pyrrhus lost 3,500 men and most of his officers, and was himself wounded. He made a truce with Rome, planning to recoup his fortunes in anarchic Sicily.[8]

Before Pyrrhus left Italy an Epirote traitor wrote to Fabius, one of the two Roman consuls for 278, offering to poison Pyrrhus for a sizeable sum of blood money. As Ptolemy Ceraunus had shown at the Hellespont, the successors of Alexander had no compunction about using assassination to further their ends. But although Rome had already lost 13,000 men to Pyrrhus, when Fabius received the traitor's offer he promptly sent the letter on to the Red King. Rome would not win her wars that way.[9]

But she would win them. When Pyrrhus came back to Italy three years later he was decisively defeated at Beneventum by the army of consul Manius Curius. Returning to Greece, Pyrrhus was soon killed during street fighting in Argos by a tile thrown by an old woman on a roof. At the news of his death Tarentum surrendered, and all Italy south of the plain of the Po was in Roman hands. Ptolemy II of Egypt sent an embassy to seek Roman friendship. A new power had come into the world.[10]

Why this one particular little town, of all the thousands of little towns apparently just like it all over the Mediterranean region, rose to become the ruler of the civilized Western world, remains a mystery. The distinctive characteristics of Rome at the time of Pyrrhus are clear enough: an altogether extraordinary degree of resolution, perseverance and moral probity; a unique governmental structure which presented a veritable thicket of obstacles to the concentration of unlimited authority in the hands of any individual or special interest group for any substantial period of time; and a policy of allowing many former enemies to retain local autonomy and even to gain some of the benefits of Roman citizenship once they came firmly under Roman rule. But whence came all this, and why? Why in Rome—and nowhere else but in Rome?

As an historical problem, the early history of Rome bears more than a passing resemblance to the early history of Israel. Here once again we find "higher critics" going expansively to work, sweeping away large parts of the extant written accounts because of their late date (nearly five centuries after the traditional date of the founding of the Roman Republic, 509 B.C.) and dismissing one long-standing Roman tradition after another as legendary and mythical.[11] Legend and myth there evidently are, in what we are given as early Roman history as in the early traditions of all ancient peoples; bold would be the historian who would take a stand for the full historicity of Romulus and Remus as founders of Rome being suckled by a wolf, or for the Trojan ancestry of the Romans celebrated in Vergil's *Aeneid*. Yet even here a moderating touch on the destructive enthusiasm of the critics is in order: there are on record cases of human children raised by animals, and a fairly strong body of historical, linguistic, and archeological evidence indicates that the Romans' near neighbors, the mysterious Etruscans, did in fact migrate to Italy from eastern Asia Minor—the region of Troy—not long after the Trojan War.[12] At least a scrap of historical truth usually lies at the root of even the most efflorescent legends which are tied to a particular time, place and people; and the closer we come to the first written historical accounts (in Rome they first appeared in the third century B.C., the period covered by this chapter) the more historically reliable the traditions become.

Be that as it may, the state of our knowledge of Roman history during the century following the end of Etruscan royal domination (immediately replaced, according to tradition, by the Roman Republic) is not such as to give a clear answer to the abiding and fascinating question of the cause of Rome's historical uniqueness. A good case can be made, even by those who more reasonably accept a genuinely historical core in the early Roman traditions, that few if any signs of that uniqueness developed during the fifth century (500-400) B.C., the age of Themistocles and Pericles in Athens, except perhaps an unusual concern for clearly stated law as revealed in the demand for legal codification which took the form of the famous Twelve Tables of the Law about 450 B.C.[13] The extreme slowness of Rome's growth during its first republican century is best shown by the fact that not until 396 B.C. did Rome finally subdue the strong rival Etruscan city of Veii—just fifteen miles away![14]

In 387 B.C. a thunderbolt struck in the form of ferocious Gallic barbarians from the north. They came surging down the Tiber, defeated the Roman army at the Allia River, and sacked and burned the entire city except for the Capitoline hill, which withstood a seven months' siege. Here, as best we can determine from our incomplete knowledge, was the historical watershed. For Rome's reaction to the Gallic catastrophe was like nothing that might have been expected, or that was characteristic of other cities superficially like her. Other ancient cities in like case were either permanently damaged or destroyed, or recovered and went on much as before. Rome, on the contrary, learned from her defeat that fundamentally different and better concepts were needed in both the state and the army. Probably Rome could not have learned this lesson so well without a man of genius to show the way. That man, by all indications, was Marcus Furius Camillus, said to have been five times dictator and the architect of the recovery after the Gallic catastrophe.[15]

Though we know much less of him personally, it is highly probable from what we may reasonably conclude to have been his work that Camillus was an even greater statesman than the much admired Pericles, who after all got Athens into the war that ended her primacy in Greece, while Camillus seems to have built much of the public order and policy that gave Rome primacy in Italy. But we may reasonably doubt that any leader could have persuaded the Athenian people as they were during the Peloponnesian War (or later, right down to the time of Alexander the Great) to extend their citizenship, to bring other peoples into an Athenian domain in which those peoples had clearly understood, guaranteed and respected rights.[16] Nor was this only an Athenian problem. It was the curse of all the ancient city-states, and the more successful they were and the greater their achievements—intellectual as well as political—the more they seemed to fall under it, refusing until the very last extremity, and usually then as well, to consider the possibility of any sort of genuine federation. They seemed unable to imagine any condition for a city other than full sovereignty or total subjection.

Rome was different, at least from the time of the Gallic sack and Camillus. A limited but clearly defined and much prized Roman citizenship was extended to other Latin cities, creating a Latin rather than merely a Roman state, beginning with Tusculum in 381 B.C. and completed after the dissolution of the Latin League in the time of Lucius Furius Camillus, Marcus' son (338-332 B.C.). And so it came about that when Pyrrhus was marching on Rome after his costly victory at Heraclea, he found almost none to join him; the cities of Campania and Latium, which according to all his Greek experience should have risen joyfully against their oppressive ruler once he gave them the opportunity, regarded themselves too as Romans and closed their gates against him.[17] And along with Rome's supremely important and far-seeing political reconstruction after the Gallic sack went a military reconstruction, very likely also the work of the elder Camillus, which established the legion as a formation of small, highly maneuverable, tightly disciplined groups of fighting men—the maniples, arranged on the battlefield like a checkerboard, which were the heart of the defense against Pyrrhus and his phalanx.[18]

Meanwhile Rome had developed a remarkably well constructed system of checks and balances to prevent the domination of their government either by the patrician class that had apparently been largely in control during the first century of the Republic or by the kind of popular assembly whose inconstancy had doomed Athens.[19] As we shall have more than ample opportunity to see in the course of this history, even the best political structure is of very little value without public and private moral virtue and respect for the natural law; but all this the people of the early Roman republic had, in an impressively high degree. These early Roman moral qualities and the system of government of the early Roman republic, complementing each other, laid the foundation for their eventual dominion over the Western civilized world, though not until Rome had been tested and annealed in the crucible of the Punic Wars with sinister Carthage could this potential be realized.

The major executive powers in Rome were divided among no less than five *classes* of magistrates independently elected: the consuls, the censors, the praetors, the quaestors, and the tribunes. There were two consuls, elected together annually; two censors, elected for five-year terms; and varying numbers of praetors, quaestors and tribunes, but always more than one, with the total tending to increase as the years passed. The most powerful officials, the two consuls, could each nullify the action of the other (except, interestingly enough, in the convocation of the senate or an assembly). Practical problems of constant interference which this dual authority might have caused were largely avoided by assigning most routine administrative duties to each consul in alternating months, though the second consul could step forward at any time to check his colleague. The consuls represented the state in dealings with foreign powers, commanded the army, kept internal peace and order, and scheduled meetings of the senate and assemblies. One or the other presided over meetings of the senate, and either could introduce legislation.

Though the dual consular military command succeeded surprisingly well—it was used in all three of the battles against Pyrrhus—the Roman constitution from the beginning provided for a single commander, the dictator, to serve for no more than six months in a crisis. Not until Sulla and Caesar in the first century B.C. did any dictator exceed this sharply limited term of office.

The consuls were elected annually by the *comitia centuriata*, an assembly open to all Roman citizens who could meet a standard property qualification. The constitution forbade the re-election of a consul within ten years, and rigid custom decreed that candidates for consul must have passed through a prescribed succession of lesser executive offices, the *cursus honorum*, before becoming eligible for the highest office.

The *comitia centuriata* also elected the censors and praetors. The censors assessed property for taxes, prepared lists of eligible voters, and interpreted and enforced laws regarding membership in Rome's governing bodies. It was a censor, for instance, who at some time between 339 and 312 B.C. interpreted the recently passed Ovinian Law to confine senate membership exclusively to ex-magistrates, which did so much to make and keep the senate a unique reservoir of talent in statesmanship. The praetors carried out judicial duties similar in some, though not all respects to those of trial court judges.

The fourth class of magistrates, the quaestors who administered the treasury, were elected by the two popular assemblies—the *comitia tributa* and the *concilium plebis*—which, unlike the *comitia centuriata*, had no property qualification for voting. Each Roman citizen had one vote within one of 35 tribal units, each of which in turn cast its vote according to that of the majority of its members present and voting. Only four of these 35 voting tribes resided in the city of Rome; the others drew their members from the Italian countryside. Citizens of nearby cities were enrolled in some of these tribes during the fourth century (400-300) B.C. as part of the system of Latin unity set up by Rome after the Gallic catastrophe; others more distant received citizenship rights but without the vote, which they were too far away to cast in significant numbers.

The *concilium plebis* elected the unique fifth class of Roman officials, the tribunes. Their powers grew out of the class dispute between patricians and plebeians in early Rome. After 457 B.C. there were ten tribunes, later still more.

Their duty was to protect the individual citizen, especially the plebeian, from arbitrary action by any magistrate. To carry out this duty, each tribune independently was authorized to prosecute any magistrate for illegal and unjust acts, to convoke the senate and assembly and present matters for its consideration (including proposed legislation), and to veto any bill so as to prevent it from becoming law. To protect the tribune in the exercise of his duties and the casting of his veto, the Roman constitution provided one stark penalty: instant death. Any man laying violent hands upon a tribune could be executed without trial by any Roman citizen.

Statutory laws could be passed by any one of the three assemblies—the *comitia centuriata* of the propertied citizens and the *concilium plebis* and *comitia tributa* of the common people. Since either consul could prevent assembly consideration of any bill and every tribune had an absolute veto, the Republic of Rome had few laws—only those clearly perceived as necessary by almost all citizens who concerned themselves with public affairs. There was a correspondingly great respect for those laws which did exist.

The primary policy-making body in the Roman Republic was not any of the popular assemblies nor any of the colleges of magistrates, but the senate. The fact that it was composed entirely of ex-magistrates gave the Roman senate a combination of experience and disinterestedness unmatched among large governing bodies known to history. Senators served for life. Approximately twenty new members entered the senate each year after completing their term in one of the major offices; the running total membership was about six hundred. Not the senate itself, but the two censors were the judges of the qualifications of its members.

The senate had no formal powers; under the Roman constitution it was simply an advisory body. But until the last century of the Republic its advice was almost always taken, especially on matters of foreign policy and domestic taxation which were its chief concern.[20] The senate of Rome had no committees, no agenda, and for a long time it had no organized parties and never took a vote by division of the house. Decisions were made by consensus. Where there was no consensus, the *status quo* was left unchanged.

Such was the system of government in republican Rome. It worked, and Rome advanced and prevailed, because the Roman people at least from the time of the Gallic catastrophe were marked to an extraordinary degree by two of the cardinal virtues: prudence and fortitude. Most very brave men tend to be rash; most very prudent men tend to shrink from a confrontation. The early Romans for the most part avoided both these weaknesses. They rarely courted trouble; but when it came, they faced it down with a wall of iron. With these great virtues were associated a relentless perseverance unparalleled in the ancient world and rarely equalled in all history, and an unusually strong sense of justice and personal moral accountability. It is beside the point to show, as many historians have rather caustically done, that the Romans could be exceedingly devious in negotiation, that they were often very vain, and that as their power and wealth grew, more and more of them became corruptible. Of course all this is true, of them as of every other people in history. As with the children of Israel, what is significant in the history of early Rome is not the Romans' share of the sins that are our common heritage from Adam, the ways in which they were like everybody else then and since, but rather the ways in which they were different. Those differences made Rome literally unconquerable.

Rome was defeated more than once in the two hundred years following the Gallic sack—by the Samnites in 321 B.C., by Pyrrhus in 280 and 279, by the storms of the Mediterranean in the First Punic War against Carthage (255, 253, and 249), by Hannibal (218-216)—but each disaster was only the signal for a renewed and greater effort. Like the giant Antaeus in Greek mythology, when thrown to earth Rome grew in strength. No people has ever been so dangerous when beaten. The fortitude of Rome has no peer in history before the Incarnation.

We may well see in Roman valor a type of Christian valor, in Rome's ability to rise again stronger after each defeat a Gentile prefiguring of the pattern of fall, repentance and Divine rescue that is the history of Israel and the spiritual life of the individual Christian. The Roman empire, pagan and mortal, vanished long ago. But Rome lives still, and until the end of time the Bishop of Rome will be Vicar of Christ. In what Rome was from her early days lay the germ, however much later transfigured, of what she was to be both to the world and to the Church.

Thus it was all the more appropriate that, as G. K. Chesterton explains in his brilliant chapter "The War of the Gods and Demons" in *The Everlasting Man*, early Rome with its natural virtues and perhaps supernaturally reinforced perseverance and fortitude should be brought face to face, just eleven years after the defeat of Pyrrhus, with none other than the successor of Jezebel's Tyre: Carthage. Surely it is no coincidence that the only regular, long continued and widely practiced cult of child sacrifice known in the history of civilized man appears among the original inhabitants of the Promised Land whom God's Chosen were commanded to conquer or destroy. Canaanites in Phoenicia founded Tyre; Tyrians went to Tunisia and founded Carthage, bringing baby sacrifice with them. Carthaginian babies were still being thrown to the fires of Baal during the climactic struggle of Carthage with Rome.[21]

In this third century (300-200) B.C. the translation of the Hebrew scriptures into Greek was begun in Alexandria, very likely with help from the scribes of Jerusalem; Aristotle's pupils Theophrastus and Clearchus provided the first reasonably perceptive account of the Jews and their faith for a Gentile audience; Hecataeus of Abdera notes with amazement that these people raise *all* their children[22] (in contrast to the Greeks, who often put their newborn girl babies out on mountainsides to die). But there is no Elijah in this age, thundering on Carmel against the priesthood of Satan. Rather it is the Roman legions going into battle against the hosts of Baal, against the commander who bore Baal's name, as the Greeks began to soften and decline, with the whole future of Europe hanging in the balance. Rome against Carthage . . . farmer against trader, mistress of Italy against mistress of Africa, elephants over the Alps and "Hannibal at the gates," the wooden dolls which were the household gods of Italy[23] against the dark angel who ate babies. But there was more with Rome than wooden dolls. The nature, history, and future of the combatants all indicate that the battle of Rome with Carthage resounded in Heaven as well as on earth. And Rome lives, atop countless strata of glorious history human and divine, while Carthage lies a bleak, sandswept ruin, even as Babylon.

So far as we can tell, in all the third century B.C. the one event really important to the history of salvation and the future of Christendom was the struggle to the death between Rome and Carthage. It began in 264 and was decided by 201, though Carthage was to linger in the shadow of destruction for another half century before the final Punic War ended with Roman salt sown in her soil. It is an epic which, like the last stand of the Spartans at Thermopylae and Alexander's march to world's end, still has power to stir the blood after more than twenty centuries. Rome went on from that supreme effort to triumph after triumph; Carthage fell, in Chesterton's words, "as nothing has fallen since Satan."[24] The world since has known many evils vast and hideous; it has not known the deliberate, ritual sacrifice of young children as a social and religious norm. Even today's mass abortion is not quite this; it is "murder in the dark," while Carthage's was murder in the very light of Hell's furnace.

Not until the Second Punic War did the full dimensions of the conflict become apparent to the combatants. The First Punic War, though one of the longest and hardest fought in ancient history, was more a testing ground for Roman and Carthaginian military capacity than a fight to the finish. The main theater of war was Sicily, so often fought over, though Carthaginian fleets harried the coast of Latium and a Roman expeditionary force landed in Africa, where it was defeated and its commander captured. The war began with a relatively trivial dispute over control of the Sicilian city of Messina on the narrow strait that separates Sicily from Italy; it ended with Carthage renouncing by treaty all claim to Sicily. It was a Roman victory, but not finally decisive, and the Barcid family of Carthage, whose scion Hannibal was made to swear eternal hatred for Rome at the age of nine, led a rally in which Carthage gained more in Spain than she had lost in Sicily.[25]

The great story of the First Punic War was the rise of the Roman navy. When the war began Rome owned not a single warship; her consul had to be ferried across the Straits of Messina in a borrowed trireme.[26] Carthage, by contrast, had been a great naval power in the central and western Mediterranean for at least three hundred years.[27] Yet in a single year (261 B.C.) Rome built a fleet of 160 warships, larger than Carthage's, and in 260 won the naval Battle of Mylae, boarding and capturing 50 Carthaginian warships. In the next five years Rome won four major naval victories; only once during the entire war did Carthage defeat Rome on the sea, where Carthage had formerly ruled unchallenged. Yet on three separate occasions the still landlubberly Roman sailors lost almost their entire fleet in a storm. More than 150 ships were destroyed in each one of these maritime disasters. Each time the indefatigable Romans proceeded to build another fleet and try again. It was the last of these new fleets that won the final victory in the First Punic War, at the Battle of the Aegates Islands in 241 B.C.[28]

But the peace of 241 was no real peace. Once Rome had come out of Italy she stood squarely facing Carthage; neither city could place any real trust in the other. The question was not so much whether to renew the struggle, as when. The Hellenistic star was setting; the Mediterranean was now the road to empire, and either Carthage or Rome would take it—they could not both do so. No genuine alliance, still less amalgamation of two such different societies, was possible. The only choice was victory or death.

At this critical moment Carthage produced, in Hannibal Barca, a battlefield genius whose name appears on every list of history's greatest generals. His Battle of Cannae displays probably the nearest to tactical perfection of any battle ever fought. Hannibal was not Alexander; he did not think in planetary terms like the Macedonian titan, but only of conquering Rome. But for him to have achieved that would have changed the course of history at least as much as Alexander's epochal march changed it.

Hannibal's strategy for conquering Rome was to strike directly at her Italian homeland. Since Rome, thanks to her great feats of shipbuilding in the First Punic War, was in such complete command of the seas that Carthage—the erstwhile leading naval power—could no longer even challenge her in that element, Hannibal's attack must be made overland from Spain, where he had trained his army. This meant crossing the Alps, for there is no other way to get into Italy by land.

It was done, by a lightning march from Spain where the Second Punic War had begun in 218, bypassing the Roman armies. Most of Hannibal's famous elephants left their hulking gray bodies and long curved tusks in the Alpine snows, and all the rest but one died within a few months of reaching Italy; many of his soldiers were lost as well; but the army of Carthage came through still strong and splendidly disciplined, and the consuls of Rome marched against it to disaster. Tiberius Sempronius and Publius Cornelius Scipio the elder attacked across the Trebia River on a bitter cold December day; Hannibal almost encircled them, destroying two thirds of their force. The next year Hannibal crossed the Apennines, ambushed two legions in a heavy fog rising from Lake Trasimene, and cut them to pieces, killing the new people's consul, Flaminius. Reviving its ancient tradition, Rome appointed a dictator in the crisis: Quintus Fabius Maximus, known to history as Fabius Cunctator, the Delayer.[29]

During his brief six months' tenure of office—the dictator's traditional term—Fabius avoided battle, keeping pressure on Hannibal with a minimum of risk to Rome's depleted forces, though when he finally did seek battle Hannibal avoided it by creating a spectacular diversion, driving two thousand oxen with torches tied to their horns through the Roman position at night. Meanwhile Hannibal was meeting the same response in Italy that had been given to Pyrrhus more than half a century before. Virtually every town shut its gates against him, refusing to rise against Rome. The invader was seen as alien, menacing; Rome was friend and protector.[30]

But loyalty is a virtue whose genuine depth must be tried by adversity. The crisis came in the year 216 B.C. Hannibal seized a Roman grain storage depot at Cannae on the Aufidus River. The two consuls for 216, L. Aemilius Paullus and C. Terentius Varro—the latter a popular leader, like Flaminius whom Hannibal had killed at Lake Trasimene—marched out to give him battle with four reinforced legions on ground of his own choosing, directly contrary to the strategy of Fabius. They were the victims of Hannibal's tactical masterpiece. Using his superiority in cavalry to counterbalance his inferiority in infantry, Hannibal defeated crushingly—it seemed, fatally—the best soldiers in the world. Out of 50,000 legionaries who marched to Cannae, fully one-half were slain and 10,000 captured. Less than a third escaped. Hannibal's loss was only 5,700, one-sixth that of Rome.[31]

Consul Paullus was dead on the battlefield of Cannae, Consul Varro in flight. Now the Italian cities began to join Hannibal in substantial numbers—not because they preferred Carthage to Rome (their rejection of Hannibal's overtures after his previous victories shows that) but because they had now become convinced that Rome must lose the war. Most of southern Italy shifted allegiance from Rome to Carthage: many of the old Greek cities including Capua, the second largest city in Italy; Samnite hill towns; many of the towns of the rich Campanian plain. Hannibal's Gallic allies overwhelmed the two Roman legions in northern Italy; the skull of their commander was set up in a Gallic temple. By all normal human standards of judgment, the end of Rome was at hand, and the dark power of Carthage was about to become the ruler of the greater part of the Mediterranean world. Roman patricians made ready to flee—where, they did not know, but somewhere very far away.[32]

Casualties at Cannae had been 70 per cent. It is a military axiom that armies which have suffered losses of this magnitude are broken, useless for months. The survivors of Cannae were not even assembled together as a single organized body, but scattered in groups of varying sizes, confused, leaderless, apparently helpless. Four thousand were at Canusium. When the Senate learned that two young tribunes of distinguished lineage who had given proof of special valor were among these survivors—Publius Cornelius Scipio the younger, whose father as consul had shared command at the Battle of the Trebia and was now in northern Spain with a small army, and Appius Claudius Pulcher, descendant of the great Appius Claudius who had inspired Rome's defiance of Pyrrhus—it gave them temporary command over the four thousand. Young Scipio was just twenty years old. There was a meeting of self-appointed leaders of the men, taking counsel of despair, talking of places of refuge. Scipio came to the meeting with drawn sword and demanded an oath on its naked blade. Every man was to swear never to desert Rome. Every man swore.[33] The four thousand marched to Venusia where Consul Varro, who had survived Cannae, had gathered another nucleus of fugitives. The two young tribunes reported to Varro. Varro reported to the Senate that he had an army ready to fight again; he was at their orders, for disgrace or a second chance. The assembly of Periclean Athens would have had Varro's head. The Senate of Rome publicly thanked him for not despairing of the Republic, and the war went on.[34]

Every able-bodied man, free or slave, stood to arms. (Later Rome would know and fear slave insurrections; but the Rome of 216 B.C. did not fear to arm her slaves against Carthage.) The property tax was doubled. Rome's navy of 200 ships and 50,000 men was kept up to full strength. Six legions had been lost in 216; within four years, no less than 25 were in the field. Marcus Junius Pera was appointed dictator, with the full support of every political and social faction in Rome. Disdaining to retire behind the city's walls, Pera took his stand on the Latin Way near Teanum, covering the road to Rome, daring Hannibal to attack.[35]

Hannibal did not come. Instead, he consolidated his position in Campania. He needed reinforcements to deal the final blow Rome's heroic fortitude had rendered necessary. As Rome still commanded the sea, only a trickle of help could reach Hannibal directly from Africa. The bulk of the aid he required would have to come the long way round, as Hannibal himself had come, through Numidia (Algeria), Mauritania (Morocco), Spain, southern Gaul, and across the Alps. Blocking the way was the Roman army commanded by young Scipio's father and uncle on the Ebro River in northern Spain. Through five critical years (216-211) the brothers—Publius Cornelius Scipio the elder and Gnaeus Scipio—held fast. Finally they counterattacked and were destroyed by superior Carthaginian forces when their Spanish allies deserted them. But they had prevented any significant reinforcement from reaching Hannibal during all that time; when at last they perished, the tide was turning in Italy. Syracuse in Sicily, which had risen against Rome in 215, was retaken in 211; that same year the Romans retook Capua after Hannibal had tried to raise their siege of it by a brief demonstration before the walls of Rome—the only time he ever actually saw them. The great commander was isolated in southeastern Italy. His only hope was his brother Hasdrubal in Spain, where Publius Cornelius Scipio the younger—he who had rallied the survivors of Cannae with sword-blade and oath—had now been sent to take command, in place of his slain father.[36]

Scipio Africanus, to give him the name which posterity awarded him for his eventual victory over Hannibal, in 209 captured the principal Carthaginian base in Spain—New Carthage, now Cartagena—by taking advantage of a remarkable phenomenon: the driving back of the waters of the shallow lagoon on the landward side of the city by a strong wind at the height of the assault. (The similarity of this event to the Biblical account of the Israelites' departure from Egypt has been noted by Scipio's most recent biographer. Scipio's men regarded it as proof that the gods favored their cause and their commander. In view of their exceedingly limited and erroneous conceptions of divinity, the effects of this event even so understood could in no way correspond for them to the effects of the Exodus sea crossing for the Israelites, who knew the fullness of God's power and sovereignty. But the possibility that even in the case of Scipio's victory there was more than coincidence in the fortunate timing of this wind should not be totally dismissed, for if Chesterton is right that this was a war against demons, in such a conflict God is not necessarily restricted to confirming the fortitude of the demons' opponents.)[37]

The next year Hasdrubal Barca led his army—the largest of the three Carthaginian armies in Spain—off to reinforce Hannibal in Italy, for it was now obvious that Hannibal must be heavily reinforced if Carthage were to have any hope of final victory in the war. Adopting new tactics similar to those of Hannnibal, Scipio defeated Hasdrubal at Baecula, but was unable to keep him from marching out of Spain on his mission to Italy. Across the Alps, in the footsteps of his brother, came Hasdrubal—once again, with elephants—making Carthage's last bid for imperial dominion.[38]

Rome now had 23 legions in arms. C. Claudius Nero, consul for 207, held Hannibal with six; his colleague M. Livius Salinator held Hasdrubal with four. Leaving the bulk of his force facing Hannibal, Claudius Nero—another of the famous family of Appius Claudius—took 7,000 picked men in an amazing forced march along the Adriatic coast road. Cheered on by the women and children of the villages through which they passed, covering forty miles a day for six consecutive days, they thundered into Livius' camp on the Metaurus River in the dead of night and took the field at dawn. Hasdrubal retreated; Claudius Nero pursued. Battle was joined the following day. Claudius Nero outflanked the elephants that had crossed the Alps, outflanked Hasdrubal's fierce Gauls, marched clear round the Carthaginian army, attacked from the rear, and won a total victory. Hasdrubal died fighting; Claudius Nero cut off his head, carried it south with him, and flung it into Hannibal's camp.[39]

Not so had the Romans treated Pyrrhus; not so should just wars be fought. But the stakes were ultimate and the darkness pressed close; it was still a pagan world outside the closed society of the Chosen People, and Rome had been at bay—and Italy systematically devastated—for eleven terrible years.

Later, lesser Carthaginian efforts to reinforce Hannibal were futile. Scipio

Africanus took all of Spain; in 204 he landed in Africa. The next year he won a major battle in the plain of the Bagradas River and then took Tunis, within sight of Carthage itself. A truce was agreed on; Carthage sued for peace. Scipio offered terms quite generous in view of the passions aroused by the long and terrible war; Carthage was to give up all her overseas possessions and pay an indemnity of 5,000 talents, but to retain her independence. Carthage accepted. The proposed terms were sent on to Rome.[40]

From the Senate came back the relentless reply of Appius Claudius: We do not negotiate with an enemy in arms upon our soil. While Hannibal remains in Italy, the war must go on.[41]

So Hannibal sailed back to Carthage, after nearly sixteen years in Italy. In his favor had been his military genius and the perpetual military advantage of the offensive. Never once had he been beaten in the field—his record was still Alexandrian in this respect—and his victories had been military classics. He had defeated the elder Scipio, Flaminius, Paullus and Varro; he had outwitted cautious Fabius and held bold Claudius Nero. He had maintained himself in enemy territory for the better part of a generation. Yet he had lost. It must have been very hard for him to understand how, or why. It is only just to the memory of a great captain to say that, for all the horror that was Carthage, Hannibal himself never participated in or promoted the rites of child sacrifice; by no means all Carthaginians did.[42] But he lived with them, like all his countrymen; he had made his choice for the devil he knew, against the good he did not know.

It is no disparagement of the military capacity of Scipio Africanus, which was also of a high order, to stress that Hannibal and Carthage were already beaten when Hannibal came home to Africa and met Scipio at the Battle of Zama. Carthage, in bitter fury, had broken the truce just before news arrived of Rome's acceptance of the terms previously proposed by Scipio—accepted as soon as Hannibal had left Italy. Encouraged by the return of their peerless general, the leaders of Carthage took the mad decision to renew the war against the triumphant Romans; to seal it, the ship carrying the Roman ambassadors back from their final negotiation was treacherously attacked and nearly all on board were slain, though the ambassadors themselves were rescued by a Roman patrol.[43]

The armies that met at the Battle of Zama in 202 B.C. were approximately equal in numbers, but very different in morale. The army of Rome consisted of tried and confident veterans of a 16-year struggle under a brilliant and beloved young commander. The once victorious army of Hannibal had been largely dissipated in Italy. The force he commanded at Zama was primarily composed of emergency levies from Carthage itself and of barbarian mercenaries. Only a relatively small proportion were Hannibal's veterans. At the crisis of the battle an event occurred which may have been unique in military history. The Carthaginian army seems to have gone to war against itself. In the front line stout Spanish and Berber troops, hard pressed by the Roman veterans, suddenly turned in startling fury on the second line, composed of Carthaginian city-dwellers, and began to cut them down. The historian Polybius ascribes this to their anger at the failure of the Carthaginian levies to support them, because of what seemed cowardice to the mercenaries. Perhaps. But it is very rare indeed for soldiers in the middle of a battle to turn away from their antagonists and begin fighting men on their own side. Individual or mass desertion or flight would normally be expected in such a situation, not a pitched battle between two formations of the same army. Had something happened suddenly to open the eyes of the Spaniards and the Berbers to the real nature of the society and the cause for which they were fighting? This too would be strange, for mercenaries are notoriously resistant to moral scruples. The mystery remains, but it was the cause of Hannibal's only defeat. His mercenaries and levies departed to the wings, fighting each other; his veterans held the center for a time against hopeless odds, but at length were overwhelmed. Rome had won the Second Punic War.[44]

Rome could now dictate new peace terms, and did so—doubling the indemnity previously agreed upon and setting up King Masinissa of Numidia as a Roman client on Carthage's borders, an established and protected rival to whatever would remain of Carthaginian power in Africa. Hannibal told his people they had no choice but to accept the new terms. Still reluctantly, they did so; in 201 B.C. the treaty of peace was finally concluded. Scipio Africanus returned to Rome for the greatest ceremonial triumph ever seen in the city.[45] Rarely has a celebration been so well earned.

The road was open for Rome to become ruler of the Western world. Now that the western Mediterranean was secured, the road to empire led east, to the lands of the Greeks, the conquests of Alexander the Great, and the Promised Land of the children of Israel.

NOTES

[1] M. Cary, *A History of the Greek World from 323 to 146 B.C.*, 2nd ed. (London, 1951), pp. 37-57.

[2] *The Cambridge Ancient History*, Volume VII (Cambridge, England, 1954), pp. 642-643.

[3] *Ibid.*, p. 645.

[4] *Ibid.*, p. 646; Plutarch, "Life of Pyrrhus."

[5] *Cambridge Ancient History*, VII, 646.

[6] *Ibid.*, pp. 531-535; Howard H. Scullard, *A History of the Roman World from 753 to 146 B.C.*, 3rd ed. (London, 1961), p. 121.

[7] *Cambridge Ancient History*, VII, 647. See Note 41, below, for Rome's rejection of peace terms with Carthage in 202 B.C. so long as Hannibal remained on Italian soil, and Chapter Twelve, below, for the use of the same principle of policy by Quintus Cicero in response to rebellious Gauls.

[8] *Cambridge Ancient History*, VII, 647-648; Plutarch, "Life of Pyrrhus."

⁹ Plutarch, "Life of Pyrrhus."

¹⁰ *Cambridge Ancient History*, VII, 214-215, 652-653.

¹¹ e.g., *ibid.*, pp. 312-332.

¹² *The Cambridge Ancient History*, Volume IV (Cambridge, England, 1930), pp. 387-392. The outpouring of literature on the Etruscans and their mysteries continues unabated. Unless and until their writings can be read, there is little hope of extracting solid history out of these discussions; yet, as the pages cited in *The Cambridge Ancient History* demonstrate, there is sufficient evidence of the origin of the Etruscans in Asia Minor to make a good case for it.

¹³ Scullard, *Roman World 753-146 B.C.*, pp. 58-61.

¹⁴ *Cambridge Ancient History*, VII, 511-516.

¹⁵ *Ibid.*, pp. 561-567.

¹⁶ John L. Myres, *The Political Ideas of the Greeks* (New York, 1927), pp. 350-351.

¹⁷ *Cambridge Ancient History*, VII, 569; Scullard, *Roman World 753-146 B.C.*, pp. 87-89.

¹⁸ *Cambridge Ancient History*, VII, 568.

¹⁹ An excellent, clear brief survey of the Roman constitution is found in George Lee Haskins' introduction to John Dickinson's posthumously published *Death of a Republic* (New York, 1963), pp. 4-13. The summary in the text is based on Haskins and Dickinson.

²⁰ Scullard, *Roman World 753-146 B.C.*, pp. 104-105.

²¹ Gilbert C. Picard and Colette Picard, *The Life and Death of Carthage* (New York, 1968), pp. 177-178, 224-225.

²² Paul Heinisch, *History of the Old Testament* (Collegeville MN, 1952), p. 412; Elias Bickerman, *From Ezra to the Last of the Maccabees* (New York, 1949), pp. 46-51, 74-76; Simon Dubnov, *The History of the Jews from the Beginning to Early Christianity* (New York, 1967), I, 532. Bickerman states that modern critical rejection of the tradition of the sponsorship of the translation of the Hebrew Pentateuch into Greek by King Ptolemy II Philadelphos of Egypt is "without the slightest reason" (*op. cit.*, p. 74) and points out that "this venture of translating [sacred books] was unique in antiquity" (*op. cit.*, p. 75).

²³ G. K. Chesterton, *The Everlasting Man* (New York, 1955), pp. 146-147.

²⁴ *Ibid.*, p. 153.

²⁵ Scullard, *Roman World 753-146 B.C.*, pp. 142-145, 150-152, 157-158; Picard, *Carthage*, p. 217. The Barcids were virtual kings in Spain; in fact, Hasdrubal the elder, who succeeded his brother-in-law Hamilcar Barca (Hannibal's father) in command there in 229 B.C., actually wore a crown, despite the fact that Carthaginian law proclaimed Carthage a republic (Picard, *op. cit.*, pp. 219-220).

²⁶ *Cambridge Ancient History*, VII, 670, 673; Scullard, *Roman World 753-146 B.C.*, p. 148.

²⁷ *Cambridge Ancient History*, IV, 350-351.

²⁸ Scullard, *Roman World 753-146 B.C.*, pp. 149-150, 152-157; *Cambridge Ancient History*, VII, 678-694.

²⁹ *The Cambridge Ancient History*, Volume VIII (London, 1954), pp. 36-48.

³⁰ Scullard, *Roman World 753-164 B.C.*, pp. 192-193.

³¹ *Ibid.*, pp. 194-195.

³² *Ibid.*, pp. 195-196, 206; Howard H. Scullard, *Scipio Africanus, Soldier and Politician* (Ithaca NY, 1970), p. 30.

³³ Scullard, *Scipio Africanus*, pp. 29-30.

³⁴ *Ibid.*, p. 30; *Cambridge Ancient History*, VIII, 72.

³⁵ Scullard, *Roman World 753-146 B.C.*, pp. 205-206.

[36] *Ibid.*, pp. 196-199, 202-205, 208-211.

[37] Scullard, *Scipio Africanus*, pp. 39-67.

[38] *Ibid.*, pp. 68-85.

[39] Scullard, *Roman World 753-146 B.C.*, pp. 217-219; T. A. Dorey and D. R. Dudley, *Rome Against Carthage, a History of the Punic Wars* (New York, 1972), p. 84.

[40] Scullard, *Roman World 753-146 B.C.*, pp. 220-224.

[41] Scullard, *Scipio Africanus*, pp. 136-137; Dorey and Dudley, *Rome Against Carthage*, pp. 141-142.

[42] Picard, *Carthage*, pp. 224-225. See *Cambridge Ancient History* VIII, 107, for an excellent summary of Hannibal's generalship.

[43] Scullard, *Scipio Africanus*, pp. 138-139.

[44] *Ibid.*, pp. 143-154.

[45] *Ibid.*, pp. 155-160.

11.
ROME ASCENDANT, THE TEMPLE REGAINED (201-133 B.C.)

> But Mattathias answered and said in a loud voice: "Even if all the nations that live under the rule of the king obey him, and have chosen to do his commandments, departing each one from the religion of his fathers, yet I and my sons and my brothers will live by the covenant of our fathers. Far be it from us to desert the law and the ordinances. We will not obey the king's words by turning aside from our religion to the right hand or to the left."—1 Maccabees 2:19-22

After the great victory over Carthage, Rome did not rest on her laurels for so much as a single year, but at once turned east.

There is no evidence of specifically imperial ambition on Rome's part—neither at this time, nor for decades to come—and much evidence against it. But Rome, so nearly conquered in so great a war, was determined with all the iron resolve that had beaten Hannibal and the dark gods of Carthage, never again to be threatened in her very existence by a great power.[1]

With Carthage humbled past all prospect of significant recovery, no threat remained in the west, still barbarian except for the handful of former Carthaginian and Greek colonies. Danger could come only from the Hellenistic east. There the long dreary strife of the successors of Alexander the Great, and their successors, had "shaken down" into two empires—the Seleucid, based on Syria, and the Ptolemaic, based on Egypt—ruled absolutely by kings claiming (at least officially) descent from the gods;² the kingdom of Macedon, much smaller than the two empires but still formidable, whose ruling dynasty descended from the redoubtable Antigonus the One-Eyed; some smaller kingdoms in Asia Minor, of which the most important was newly established Pergamum on the Aegean coast;³ and the conglomerate cities, islands and leagues of old Greece, factious and disunited as ever, but now for the most part lacking in resources to match their ambitions. The best supplied of them was the island of Rhodes, a major sea power and banking and commercial center.⁴

In 223 B.C. a vigorous and capable young king, Antiochus III later called the Great, took the Seleucid crown. It was his fixed purpose to regain *all* the lands which had been possessed by his ancestor, the founding Seleucus who had been Alexander's general—including Palestine, Bactria, Parthia, most of Asia Minor, and even Thrace in nothern Greece which Seleucus had been in the process of claiming when he was assassinated in 280. In a six-year campaign Antiochus III defeated Parthia, made favorable terms with Bactria, negotiated near Kabul with an otherwise unknown Indian prince, and came back in 205 B.C. with an Alexandrian halo. His achievements, though considerable, did not justify this reputation since the eastern kingdoms all resumed full independence almost as soon as he had left. Yet for the moment Antiochus III stood forth as a prospective world conqueror, in the reflected glory of the memory of Alexander.⁵

Just two years after Antiochus' return Ptolemy IV of Egypt died suddenly and mysteriously. His new, corrupt and highly unpopular prime minister Agathocles then killed the Ptolemaic queen, forged a will appointing him guardian of Ptolemy IV's six-year-old son and heir, and announced himself ruler of Egypt. Few there or elsewhere had any confidence in Agathocles' government. There were both Greek and native Egyptian revolts. Antiochus III and Philip V of Macedon concluded (probably in 202 B.C.) an agreement to divide all the Ptolemaic possessions outside Egypt between them. Philip promptly attacked the eastern coast of the Aegean, regarding as fair game any city that had ever been controlled by the Ptolemies no matter how long ago—along with attacking some which had never been subject to the Ptolemies—and sold into slavery the entire population of the first two cities that resisted him.⁶

Pergamum, the kingdom on the threatened coast, and Rhodes—just off it—appealed to Rome for help. (Meanwhile Antiochus was moving on Syria and Palestine.) It was late in the summer of 201 B.C. Rome's formal treaty of peace with Carthage had been concluded that spring; the cheers for Scipio Africanus' great triumph had scarcely died away in her streets. Italy had been exhausted by the titanic struggle. Yet the Senate appears to have decided almost immediately on a favorable response to the appeal of Pergamum and Rhodes. In the spring of 200 three senatorial legates were sent to demand from Philip reparation for Pergamum and a pledge never again to make war on any Greek state. This demand having no legal or treaty basis—Pergamum was merely a past ally of Rome, and Rhodes not even that—Philip refused to respond to it, and proceeded to attack both Athens and Thrace. With this further provocation the Senate was able to persuade the naturally reluctant spokesmen of the war-weary Roman people in the centuriate assembly to declare war on Macedon in July of 200 B.C.[7]

Why did the Senate take this bellicose action—of immense significance to the history of the world and of Christendom, since it made Rome ultimately the real heir of Alexander the Great and the bridge between Europe and the Promised Land—so soon after the great war with Carthage? The most likely motive would seem to have been fear of the growing power and supposed world-conquering ambition of Antiochus III, brought to a head by his agreement with Philip V to divide the Ptolemaic empire between them. It was the obvious argument, and the only really good one, that the skillful Pergamene and Rhodian envoys could make to the Senate for Roman intervention in their favor.[8]

In 200 B.C.—the year Rome declared war on Macedon—the army of Antiochus III shattered the incompetently led army of the Ptolemies at Panion near the sources of the Jordan and all Palestine, including Jerusalem, fell to him and was lost forever to the Ptolemies who had held it for over a century. This change of masters was to have major consequences for the Chosen People, who gave substantial assistance to Antiochus, and it constituted a considerable access of power to the rising young warrior-emperor.[9] But Philip and his small Macedonian army proved no match for the Roman veterans who had beaten the greatest general since Alexander. In three years Philip met utter defeat at their hands at Cynoscephalae in Thessaly.[10]

Titus Quinctius Flamininus, the victor of Cynoscephalae, had served among the Greeks of southern Italy during the war with Hannibal. An ardent philhellene, speaking fluent Greek, he gloried in a dramatic announcement at the Isthmian Games in 196 B.C. of Rome's pledge to restore complete freedom to every Greek city and state. Within two years no Roman soldier remained east of the Adriatic, an example of honor and selflessness all too rare in the history of war and international politics. But Greek unity remained an impossible dream, and Greek particularism meant virtually unceasing war and the constant cynical playing off of one ally against another. The Greeks could no longer use freedom well. Only a master from outside Hellas could keep the peace—could keep them, in the end, from destroying themselves.[11]

Meanwhile there remained "the shadow of Antiochus,"[12] darkened now by a still more ominous shadow: Hannibal. The peerless Carthaginian general was still very much alive. Elected chief magistrate of his city in 196 B.C., he had instituted reforms limiting the power of the ruling oligarchy and making possible full payment in just five more years of the huge indemnity demanded by the peace treaty with Rome. Reports came to Rome that Hannibal was intriguing with Antiochus. They are usually dismissed today as falsifications by his political enemies at Carthage, and so they may have been; but it is at least curious that as soon as Hannibal learned that the reports had been made, he did not wait even to try to exculpate himself with the Romans, but fled by night to Antiochus. We do not know enough about Hannibal's real character, and of how his hatred for Rome balanced against his loyalty to his native city, to be able to form a good estimate of his motivation in this situation. But this much can be said: It must have been very clear at this time to a commander of Hannibal's consummate ability that no force remained in the ancient world capable of withstanding the full strength of Rome and even defeating her, unless it were the potential might of the vast Seleucid empire. If he did wish to continue the fight against Rome, only this ally offered him any real hope.[13]

Antiochus had now attained his announced objective of restoring Seleucid power in all lands any Seleucid had ever ruled or inherited (with the exception of Pergamum, whose territorial integrity he had personally guaranteed). He had occupied the whole western portion and coast of Asia Minor, outside of Pergamum, and crossed the Hellespont into Europe, where he began building a city in Thrace as a residence for his son. Here, he said, his ambitions ended. But he had come too far—and Hannibal was at his court.[14]

Rome presented Antiochus with an ultimatum: either withdraw from Thrace or restore freedom to the Greek cities on the Aegean coast of Asia Minor. Antiochus tried to temporize; delays in the negotiations made the situation more explosive. The igniting spark was supplied by the unprincipled robber-state in west central Greece, the Aetolian League. The Aetolians invited Antiochus to come to "free the Greeks" from Rome; when asked by Flamininus for a copy of the invitation, the Aetolian general Damocritus replied with incredible arrogance that he would deliver it on the banks of the Tiber. The Aetolians then seized by surprise attack the great fortress of Demetrias in Thessaly, formerly a Macedonian stronghold, whose freedom had been guaranteed by the Roman peace settlement.[15]

It was an act of madness for the Aetolians, who were eliminated from history three years later; consul Glabrio chained their envoys together with iron collars when they protested his demand for unconditional surrender.[16] Antiochus' decision to let the Aetolians commit him to war with Rome was scarcely more rational. Though he may have rightly regarded the conflict as eventually inevitable, he was not ready for it in 192 B.C., the year of the Aetolian capture of Demetrias; he had only 10,000 men under arms. The Greek cities hesitated; many rejected Antiochus' bid for their support. As he laid siege to Chalcis in Euboea, one of his generals massacred 500 Roman troops at Delium. The war that perhaps nobody but Hannibal and the Aetolians really wanted, had begun.[17]

Rome called once more upon the great Scipio Africanus. Petty jealousies of him were forgotten; the constitutional requirement that he could not serve again as consul in less than ten years (he had been consul in 205 and in 193) was ingeniously evaded by electing his brother Lucius one of the consuls for 190 with the understanding by all concerned that Scipio Africanus would exercise his authority. By then the energetic and merciless Glabrio had shattered Antiochus' expeditionary force at storied Thermopylae and driven the emperor out of Greece. Scipio pushed on into Asia; he and the Senate had decided that Antiochus must be expelled from Asia Minor forever. Since Seleucid emperors were accustomed to commanding their own armies in the field, it was probably too much to expect him to hand over the field command to Hannibal. Instead he gave Hannibal the novel employment of raising a fleet in Phoenicia and bringing it into action. Even the greatest of generals is unlikely to be successful as an admiral; Hannibal was defeated at sea by a Rhodian named Eudamus. Then Scipio fell ill and had to be left behind, so by curious chance neither of the two great antagonists was present on the decisive battlefield of Magnesia, just inland from Smyrna. The Roman army was outnumbered 75,000 to 30,000 and was commanded in Scipio's absence by an otherwise little-known Domitius Ahenobarbus; but Scipio's veterans were steady as ever, Antiochus threw away his best opportunities, his phalanx was broken by his own stampeding elephants—and Hannibal was not there. Two-thirds of the Seleucid army was slain.[18]

Antiochus had no choice but to make peace—the Treaty of Apamea, which established the supremacy of Rome in the whole of the ancient Mediterranean world. He had to pay an indemnity of 15,000 talents, the largest known in ancient history, and to withdraw all the way to Syria, behind the Taurus Mountains. And he had to expel Hannibal, who fled to the king of Bithynia; a few years later he took his own life when the implacable Romans pursued him even there. Meanwhile Antiochus, once the Great, died ignominiously in Iran at the hands of a mob when he tried to rob their temple to help pay his huge indemnity to Rome.[19]

Eighteen years of peace followed, during which there was constant debate in Rome between the spokesmen of the old order, led by Marcus Porcius Cato—Cato the Censor, the upright, unbending champion of the old Roman virtues—and those who wished to bring Rome more quickly and fully into the Greek world, which now lay for all practical purposes at Rome's feet. Cato greatly feared corruption of the pristine Roman character by excessive wealth and power—the future was to show how well founded were his fears—and strove to check this tendency by law, notably through the prosecution of corrupt officials. Cato held that Rome should not involve herself more deeply in Greek affairs, now that there was obviously no more serious military danger from the east; but he never forgot the war with Hannibal (in which he had fought as a young soldier), and at the great age of 85, it was Cato who brought about the final destruction of Carthage in the third and last Punic War (149-146 B.C.).[20]

But the troublesome Greeks continued to appeal their every petty quarrel to Rome, and there seemed to be no end to them. The Third Macedonian War grew out of a combination of exhausted patience and cupidity on Rome's part. The charges that Macedon's new young king Perseus was plotting against Rome seem to have been baseless, but the Romans struck and destroyed him and his kingdom at the Battle of Pydna in 168 B.C.[21] The vigorous new Seleucid emperor Antiochus IV Epiphanes took advantage of Rome's temporary preoccupation by this last war with Macedon and of strife between partisans of two Ptolemaic boy kings (Ptolemy VI Philomater and VII Physcon) to invade Egypt and besiege Alexandria. The Ptolemaic factions, unable to defend Egypt effectively, promptly united and appealed to Rome. The Senate sent the ex-consul Gaius Popillius Laenas to deal with the problem. If the remnants of the Seleucid empire were united with wealthy Ptolemaic Egypt under vigorous leadership such as Antiochus IV might provide, there was just a chance that a new power could be built up to rival Rome. Popillius waited until the consul Aemilius Paullus had won the final victory over the Macedonians at Pydna (he did not have to wait very long) and then promptly set sail for Egypt. He met Antiochus IV just outside Alexandria. It was now a truly imperial Rome giving orders: Antiochus was to quit Egypt immediately with all his army. The king asked time to deliberate, to consult advisors. With his walking stick Popillius drew a circle in the sand around Antiochus. "Deliberate here!" he said, demanding an answer before the monarch stepped out of the circle.[22]

It was a successor of Alexander the Great that Popillius addressed—a mature and capable ruler bent on building up his great heritage, the commander of a successful army, humiliated as few proud rulers in all history have been humiliated while still retaining their crown, by one old man with a walking stick. Antiochus was intelligent enough to know that he had no choice but to submit to Popillius' demand or be destroyed in another Zama, Cynoscephalae, Magnesia or Pydna. He swallowed what must have been an almost berserk fury, and meekly retreated from Egypt.[23] The confrontation between Antiochus and Popillius has an importance much greater than an especially picturesque episode in Rome's rise to world empire. For there is good reason to believe that this experience permanently unbalanced the mind of Antiochus IV, leading him to persuade himself in compensation that he really was the god the official cult proclaimed him to be,[24] and thereby shaping him into the architect of the first religious persecution in the history of the Graeco-Roman world, directed against God's Chosen People.

Since Nehemiah built his wall around it, Jerusalem had virtually dropped out of history. Alexander the Great had marched past it without even a second look; the Jews play no part whatever in the historical events of the third century (300-200) B.C.; but when Antiochus III arrived at Jerusalem after defeating the Ptolemaic army in the Battle of Panion in 200 B.C., we hear of Jewish militia helping him expel the Egyptian garrison from the citadel in Jerusalem, and of a charter Antiochus gave the city which included recognition of the "scribes of the sanctuary" as a specially privileged group. These scribes were scholars devoted to the study, development, exposition, and administration of the Mosaic law and its accompanying and derived traditions. Through many of the silent years in Jerusalem they had worked in relative obscurity, with little reward for their labors, their motivation and satisfaction being love for the study of God's word and strict observance of His law. The priests had been, by and large, only slightly interested in their work, sometimes actively hostile. But at the time of the transfer of Palestine from Ptolemaic to Seleucid control, two extraordinary, holy men had taken steps to unite scribes and priests as leaders of the Jewish people. The great High Priest Simon the Just, remembered and revered for long afterward, had given scribal interpretations of the Law and the tradition the force of law. He had personally encouraged the scribes most devoted to the Law to identify themselves and their followers as moral guides for the people—the Hasidim or "pure," later the Pharisees. Under Simon, Jesus ben Sirach became the great spokesman for the scribes. About 190 B.C. he wrote the Book of Ecclesiasticus, in which both priests and scribes are highly praised. Though, like Simon the Just, a supporter of the Seleucids, Ben Sirach saw danger in Greek intellectual pride. He noted that the most devout and faithful Jews tended to be the poor, while the rich often turned to Hellenistic customs and heretical ideas.[25]

Early in the reign of Antiochus IV we hear for the first time of plans to hellenize Jerusalem. The heterogeneous Seleucid empire was knit together by the Hellenistic culture of its overlords and its Greek colonists—and by nothing else. Rome's defeat of Antiochus III had shown the fundamental weakness of this empire despite its imposing size. A program of accentuated hellenization seemed necessary and Palestine, as ever the land of contention, an especially good place to begin it. Precisely this was proposed to Antiochus IV, not so far as we know originally by any of his own ministers or advisors, but by the brother of the High Priest Onias III, named Jesus, who had taken the Greek name of Jason and was associated with a faction of the wealthy Tobiad family based in Ammon across the Jordan—the same Tobiad family which had set up the bank in the Temple precincts which Nehemiah expelled about 425 B.C.[26] Antiochus IV welcomed Jason and his plans. He decreed the deportation of Onias III and named Jason High Priest in his stead.[27]

Jason's hellenization was limited in scope, consisting mainly of building a gymnasium and promoting its use by the young men of the city as both a cultural and an athletic center. Money was also sent from Jerusalem for the offering of sacrifices to pagan gods elsewhere. Antiochus IV perhaps felt that Jason was not moving fast enough, and in any case was promised much money by Jason's associate Menelaus if he would remove Jason as high priest and put Menelaus in his place, even though Menelaus was not of priestly lineage. Antiochus was quick to agree, and Jason like Onias III was forced into exile; but Menelaus could not after all supply the promised money. He sent his brother Lysimachus to take enough treasure from the Temple in Jerusalem to make up what was lacking, and the people of Jerusalem rose up and killed Lysimachus.[28]

Thus matters stood when Antiochus IV stepped out of Popillius Laenas' circle in the sands of Egypt. The report of his humiliation sped before him, growing in the telling; when it reached Palestine, it had him actually dead of shame. Jason, believing the report of the emperor's death, promptly seized Jerusalem from Menelaus and his supporters, so that on returning to his own domain Antiochus found "moderate" and "radical" hellenizers in Jerusalem at each other's throats.[29]

Here was a target upon which he could safely vent his fury. He brought his army into Jerusalem, drove Jason out, massacred many of the population and sold many others into slavery, and completed Menelaus' plundering of the Temple, stripping it of every object of monetary value. He broke down Nehemiah's walls and built a fortress, the Akra, on a commanding height within the city itself, manning it with a strong garrison. But Antiochus IV wanted more than money and military security; he wanted a hellenized Jerusalem. His Jewish collaborators seemed incapable of establishing it. Therefore he brought in "an old Athenian" to be the architect of the destruction of the religion of the Jews and its replacement by Hellenistic cults. An idol—probably a statue of Jupiter Olympus—was erected in the Temple itself; it may have had Antiochus IV's own features. On December 25, 167 B.C., the Temple was dedicated to the pagan god with the sacrifice of a pig, in deliberate mockery of the Law of Moses. The Temple courts began to be used for ritual sexual prostitution.[30]

This deliberate maximum profanation was accompanied by a thorough and carefully planned religious persecution. Idols were set up in the streets and squares in Jerusalem and in even the smallest towns and villages, with pigs frequently sacrificed on their altars. The local residents were required to join in the sacrifices and eat the sacrificed meat, usually pork. All copies of the Books of the Law were ordered destroyed. Circumcision of the new-born, observance of the Sabbath, or possession of the Sacred Books of the Law were all punishable by death, and the death penalty was frequently imposed for these "offenses." Martyrs were made under circumstances very similar to those of the later Christian martyrdoms. Those who kept the faith and lived had to flee to the countryside, into caves or into the desert.[31]

At first there was no active resistance. Against the might of the Seleucid empire—which, however roughly that empire had been handled by Rome, was still overwhelming from the standpoint of a Jewish farmer in Palestine—it seemed utterly futile. The ordinary Jews of the countryside, as distinct from political factions in the city of Jerusalem, had not, so far as we know, borne arms in any cause since the days of Nebuchadnezzar four hundred years before. It seemed that, for the faithful, only martyrdom remained.

Later, against the power of Rome, there was indeed to be no hope in armed resistance. But the Seleucid empire of Antiochus IV was not the Rome of Scipio Africanus. It was rotten with moral and material corruption. The later, degenerate Seleucids and their henchmen would not know how to deal with men ultimately resolved either to die for their faith or to live and fight for it, as God should give them the opportunity.

In the little village of Modein about twenty miles from Jerusalem dwelt—unknown, unheralded—one of the most remarkable families in all history. The father, well advanced in years, was Mattathias, a priest, known as the Hasmonean (either because his ancestors came from the district of Heshmon in Judah, or because his great-grandfather was named Hasmoneus).[32] Mattathias had five strong sons who shared his total dedication to the service, the law and the love of the God Who Is. Their names (in order of birth) were John, Simon, Judas, Eleazar, and Jonathan. Every one of them was to die, separately, at the hands of the enemies of God's people. Not one ever wavered, ever changed fundamentally, ever broke faith. By the time the last of them had died, they had freed God's people and re-established His law. From Judas, called Maccabeeus—the hammer—the five came to be known as the Maccabees.

It was probably in the spring of the year 166 B.C., shadowed by the December 25 profanation of the Temple and the apparent helplessness of God's people, that an officer of Antiochus IV came to Modein to enforce the new laws upon its inhabitants, to build an altar to Zeus and to compel the Jewish people to join in sacrificing a pig upon it and in the eating of its flesh. He called upon Mattathias to be the first to sacrifice, and was met by the reply quoted at the beginning of this chapter. Though the whole world should submit to this royal command, Mattathias and his family would never abandon God's law.[33]

But one of their fellow townsmen was weaker; he agreed to join in the desecrating ritual. As he advanced to the altar, Mattathias rushed upon him and killed him, then turned upon Antiochus' representative and struck him down as well. The remaining villagers set upon the rest of the patrol which had been sent to Modein, and killed them all.[34]

They were rebels now and could expect no mercy—one old man, his five sons and probably most of the inhabitants of one small village, without allies or any kind of military support. Like Moses before him, Mattathias the Hasmonean in this hour stood as "one man against an empire." But as news of his defiance spread among the Jews of the countryside, the refugees and the bravest among those under the Seleucid yoke came to join him. Some of those who were Hasidim were caught and killed because they refused to fight on the Sabbath, even to save their lives. Mattathias then ruled, on his own authority, that in this crisis self-defense on the Sabbath was lawful. In less than one year he had become the recognized spiritual and temporal leader of the Jewish faithful.[35]

For about a year the Seleucid authorities paid little attention to the rebels. The Maccabees and their men carried on guerrilla warfare, destroying the pagan altars in the Jewish villages, circumcising the boy babies found in them, and from time to time ambushing Seleucid patrols. The forces at their command, and their support in the countryside, steadily grew. Then old Mattathias felt death approaching, and called his sons together to give them this stern final counsel:

> Arrogance and reproach have now become strong; it is a time of ruin and furious anger. Now, my children, show zeal for the law, and give your lives for the covenant of our fathers. . . . Observe, from generation to generation, that none who put their trust in him [in God] will lack strength. Do not fear the words of a sinner, for his splendor will turn into dung and worms. Today he will be exalted, but tomorrow he will not be found, because he has returned to the dust, and his plans will perish.[36]

He named his second son Simon as counsellor and father to his other sons, and his third son Judas as commander of their army. He chose well.[37]

By 165 B.C. it had finally become clear to the Seleucid authorities that the rebellion of the Maccabees had to be taken seriously. Apollonius, commander of the Seleucid forces in Palestine, assembled an army he thought large enough to overcome the rebels easily. Marching south from Samaria, he was ambushed by Judas, probably in a defile on the Samaria-Jerusalem road near the Gophna hills which are believed to have been the original place of refuge of the Maccabees after their flight from Modein. Apollonius' force, amounting to perhaps 2,000 men, was surprised and routed. Apollonius himself was killed and Judas Maccabeus took his sword, which he carried in all his subsequent battles.[38]

As soon as possible after receiving news of this startling defeat, the Seleucids sent a force perhaps double the size of that of Apollonius toward Jerusalem by a different route, along the coast and then inland. General Seron commanded it. Judas ambushed him at the pass of Beth-Horon ten miles northwest of Jerusalem and disposed of him exactly as he had disposed of Apollonius: Seron's army was routed and the Seleucid general was slain.[39]

No longer was the situation in Palestine merely a matter for provincial governors. The rebellion had now become a major problem for the whole empire, of grave concern to Antiochus IV himself. (So far had their zeal and resolution brought the Maccabees in just a year and a half from their hour of decision at Modein.) Antiochus IV was hard beset, for at the same time he faced an even more serious challenge from the Parthians in the east, who were making major inroads on his Iranian provinces which were much larger and richer than Palestine. Antiochus had prepared a large-scale military expedition for Iran in 165 B.C. and refused to let the Jewish rebellion turn him aside from that campaign. But on his departure he left strict orders with Lysias, his regent who was to stay behind and rule from Antioch during his absence, to send a substantial army to Palestine to put down the Jewish rebellion once and for all, and to punish the Jewish people by selling many of them into slavery.[40]

At least 20,000 Seleucid soldiers were thereupon put under the command of the generals Nicanor and Gorgias. Encamping at Emmaus near Beth-horon, these generals—now fully respecting the military prowess of the Maccabees—neither attacked frontally nor exposed themselves to another ambush while on the march. Instead Gorgias took 6,000 of his men for a surprise night attack on the Jewish camp. Probably apprised of this by his excellent intelligence service developed with the enthusiastic cooperation of the country people, Judas at once abandoned his camp and sent his men against the Seleucid camp, whose defenders were seriously weakened by the absence of Gorgias. By this masterly generalship Judas defeated in detail an enemy outnumbering him at least three to one, and perhaps as much as six to one: first Nicanor's portion was routed, then Gorgias' was forced into retreat. The slave dealers brought with the expedition to take charge of the prisoners expected to be acquired, went home disappointed.[41]

Now the time of the Seleucid generals was over. Lysias the regent took the field in person in 164 B.C. His army circled far to the south, along the fringes of the Negev desert, where the Maccabees still lacked a strong following. In this way his army was able to advance unopposed to within a day's march of Jerusalem. But there, at Beth Zur, the Maccabees joined battle once more, and once more gained the victory. Lysias survived, and it appears that the greater part of his army was not engaged, but a portion suffered heavy losses. He returned immediately to Antioch, not only because of the defeat, but probably also because of news coming from the east about Antiochus' troubles there, including a false report of his death.[42]

Only the garrison of the Akra in Jerusalem remained to uphold the fading Seleucid claim to the Promised Land. The Maccabees did not yet possess the means to reduce a strongly fortified citadel. But Judas nevertheless brought his army right into Jerusalem. Under cover of its archers, the Temple (within easy bow-shot of the Akra) was reoccupied by the people of God. It was a grim sight—the altar profaned, the doors burned, the buildings run down, the courts overgrown with weeds. The priests promptly set about its purification. They tore down the profaned altar and built a replacement. The Temple was repaired, restored, re-consecrated. On December 25, 164 B.C.—three years to the day after the first pagan sacrifice had profaned the Temple—the sacrifices commanded by the Law of Moses were resumed. The day was designated as a great annual festival, the first Jewish festival not mentioned in the Mosaic law, now called Hanukkah. The Temple was regained. The band of brothers from Modein had attained, against all odds, the primary goal for which they had taken up arms, in just three years.[43]

Antiochus IV died in Iran, probably early in the next year.[44] Both the First Book of Maccabees and the history of Josephus record that he died repentant, recognizing that his plundering of the Temple in Jerusalem and his persecution of the Jews had been evil acts and the cause of his subsequent misfortunes and early death.[45] It is not reasonable to dismiss this report from two separate sources whose authors lived not very long after the Maccabees' century—two of our three primary sources for the history of this struggle—as mere self-serving legend. Would it not have been obvious to any clear-sighted man by the time of Antiochus IV's death that his Jewish policy had been a disastrous failure? It had fatally weakened him by diverting badly needed troops and money from his eastern campaigns. He could well have triumphed in them if only he had kept his hands off the practice of the Jewish religion, which none of his predecessors, Ptolemaic or Seleucid, had ever interfered with. Had his Jewish policy not been perhaps more a product of his burning anger against the Rome of Popillius Laenas than of rational calculation for the good of his realm, or even for his own good? Yet how could he have known the hidden power of the apparently helpless people he had challenged? Was there more to this strange invisible God of theirs than any Greek had ever imagined? Had Antiochus heard the story their sacred writings told, of the long-ago humbling of great Pharaoh when he had stood in the way of that God's command?

Meanwhile there was politics as usual in the land of the living. Antiochus, before his death, had become disenchanted with Lysias—perhaps reports had reached him of plans and intrigues by the regent to gain control of the empire through his young son—and appointed his favorite officer Philip as his successor. Lysias and Philip began maneuvering for position before the inevitable collision. While they were doing so, Judas Maccabeus assaulted the Akra.[46]

It was too soon. The victorious Maccabeean army was still not trained or equipped for siege warfare, while the Akra garrison most definitely was. They held out firmly and appealed to Lysias for help. If the Maccabees took the Akra, Palestine was irretrievably lost to the Seleucids. Since Philip now controlled what was left of the eastern provinces, without Palestine Lysias would have only Syria remaining to him out of the whole once-vast empire.[47]

So Lysias marched on Judea a second time, taking with him the boy king Antiochus V in whose name he was ruling, and 32 war elephants. Employment of the elephants was a direct breach of Antiochus III's Treaty of Apamea with Rome, which bound the Seleucids to refrain from ever again using elephants in war. But Lysias and his commanders had met the Maccabees too often unsuccessfully in battle to have any real confidence in their ability to defeat them without special help. It seemed that war elephants—usually irresistible against troops who had never seen them in action—would provide that necessary help. Lysias' willingness to risk a breach with Rome to conquer the Jews shows just how much he now respected and feared the Maccabees.[48]

The Maccabees met Lysias' army and elephants at Beth Zachariah just south of Jerusalem. The elephants had their usual effect on an army unfamiliar with them; even Roman legionaries had faltered when Pyrrhus first confronted them with war elephants. When the Maccabee brothers saw the battle going against them for the first time, Eleazar, the fourth, rushed into the midst of the enemy host, actually *under* the largest elephant, and killed it single-handed with an upward thrust of his sword. The huge beast fell dead upon him, crushing out his life—and now there were four Maccabees instead of five.[49]

What was left of the Jewish army retreated either to Jerusalem or back into the hills where the struggle had begun. Judas was besieged on the Temple mount. Since they lacked food supplies for a long siege, the condition of the Temple defenders soon became desperate. But as they approached their extremity, Lysias learned that his rival Philip was marching on Antioch with the late king's army from Iran. Lysias must settle with him or defeat him; there was not a moment to lose. So in February 162 B.C. he offered peace to the Maccabees, pledging not to interfere any longer with their religion, and executing the renegade high priest Menelaus. He strengthened the Akra garrison and hurried back to Antioch, where he defeated and probably killed Philip. Scarcely had this happened when Gnaeus Octavius, head of a Roman commission sent to investigate Seleucid breaches of the Treaty of Apamea including the use of war elephants against the Jews (the commissioners had the elephants hamstrung or killed), had been assassinated in Lysias' own Syria.[50]

There was never any evidence that the assassination was more than the work of a lone fanatic, and Lysias was profuse in his apologies to the Senate. But the Senate was unhappy with his breach of the treaty and had already sent a letter to the Jews indicating interest in their affairs and sympathy with their cause. The rightful heir to the Seleucid throne was actually not Antiochus V but Demetrius, the 23-year-old son of Seleucus IV—Antiochus IV's predecessor and elder brother—who had lived in Rome as a hostage since boyhood. While officially denying Demetrius permission to leave Rome, the Senate appears to have deliberately allowed him to escape. He landed in Syria toward the end of 162 and was promptly acclaimed king by the people, with their traditional loyalty to the legitimate Seleucid heir. Lysias and young Antiochus V were executed.[51]

Demetrius appointed a new hellenizing high priest, Alcimus (born Eliakim) to replace the dead Menelaus. Since Alcimus had been of the hellenizing party, Judas refused to allow him to approach the altar, regarding him as polluted by his past collaboration with the persecutors. Others in the Jewish community accepted the legitimacy of Alcimus' high priestly office, so civil war broke out again. Alcimus twice requested help from Antioch; Nicanor, one of the generals Judas had beaten at Emmaus, was sent in response in 161 B.C. with orders to capture the Maccabees. Judas and his men routed Nicanor's army by an ambush followed by a vigorous pursuit. Judas then sent ambassadors to Rome where they obtained a treaty of alliance which, however, Rome at that point apparently did not intend to honor.[52]

Demetrius now applied himself to the Jewish problem and worked out what seemed at last to be a feasible solution. He would grant full religious freedom to the Jews while sending another large army to Palestine to subdue the rebels. He replaced the incompetent Nicanor with the very competent Bacchides and put 22,000 of his best soldiers under his command. Judas' army, 10,000 strong at its peak, had now dwindled to 3,000 in what seemed to many Jews to be the absence of any genuinely religious motive for continuing the struggle. At the sight of the imposing enemy force Judas' 3,000 melted away to only 800. Battle was joined ten miles south of Jerusalem in April of 160 B.C. against odds of thirty to one, prohibitive even for Judas the Hammer. He was overwhelmed and died fighting, and the Maccabees were now three.[53]

The surviving brothers and their few remaining adherents fled to the forbidding desert around the Dead Sea, where the eldest Maccabee, John called Gaddis, the Forager—the supply master—was killed by hostile tribesmen; and now the Maccabees were two.[54] Simon continued in his role as father-counsellor; Jonathan, the youngest of the brothers, took command of what was left of the army. But the cause now seemed more hopeless that at any point since the original day of decision at Modein.

For a time the victors kept their promise of allowing uninterrupted traditional worship at the Temple, while conducting a methodical political purge of all the leading supporters of the Maccabees they could catch. But then Alcimus' hellenizing proclivities came to the fore. He ordered the wall of the inner courtyard of the Temple, which was reserved for Jews only, to be broken down so as to allow pagans to mingle with the Jews right up to the sanctuary itself. The predictable storm of protest arose, and Alcimus had a stroke and died just before demolition of the wall of the inner courtyard was to begin. General Bacchides, now acting governor in Judea, decided not to replace the high priest, who seemed to bring nothing but trouble, whoever he was. There followed two years of peace, during which Jonathan gradually rebuilt the Maccabeean movement, strengthened by disunion among the hellenizers and a growing hope for the full independence of the Jews. Eventually Bacchides, who had returned to Antioch, had to come back to campaign in Judea again, besieging Simon in the desert fortress of Beth-basi. Jonathan struck his rear, Simon sallied from the fortress, and once again a Seleucid force went down to defeat at the hands of the Maccabees.[55]

By this time Bacchides was understandably weary of the apparently endless struggle—it had gone on for ten years—and utterly exasperated with the hellenizing Jews, who always underestimated the strength of the Maccabees and by bad judgment and quarrels among themselves kept driving the Jewish people into their arms. Bacchides executed several of the leading Jewish hellenizers, and like Lysias made a truce with the Maccabees. But his truce, unlike that of Lysias, was not made due to the pressure of events elsewhere, but solely because the Maccabees had proved unconquerable. They received amnesty, permission to return and live in Judea, the release of their prisoners, and a renewed guarantee of religious freedom.[56]

Like every Seleucid king of whose reign we have substantial records, Demetrius was in time abandoned by fortune. His own people disliked him and he antagonized his fellow Hellenistic kings. They promoted an apparent impostor, one Balas, named Alexander for the occasion, who resembled the dead Antiochus IV and claimed to be his son. Bidding against Demetrius for the support of Jonathan Maccabeus, Balas topped Demetrius' concession of release of hostages and authorization to raise an army and in effect govern Judea in the emperor's name, by offering to name Jonathan high priest, the office having remained vacant since the days of Alcimus. Jonathan accepted Balas' offer with alacrity—apparently seeing no incongruity in obtaining from a Gentile the highest position then open to one of God's people—and as high priest presided over the Feast of Tabernacles in October 152 B.C. Jonathan gave aid to Balas, who thereby was helped to vanquish and kill Demetrius in 150.[57]

With a pretender on the Seleucid throne, however stoutly supported by the Maccabees, the scramble for the spoils of the disintegrating empire reached fever pitch. A young son of Demetrius appeared under the wing of a Cretan adventurer to claim his inheritance; Ptolemy VI of Egypt, though he had married his daughter to Balas, turned against him in an effort to regain Palestine for his dynasty. Jonathan took control of the coastal plain of Palestine. A battle between Balas and Ptolemy VI resulted in the death of both. Riots swept Antioch; the young king Demetrius II appealed to Jonathan for help, promising to evacuate the Akra in return. Maccabeean troops saved the king's life, whereupon he broke his promise by holding on to the Akra. A former supporter of Balas now made his bid for power in the style of Lysias, putting forward a baby son of Balas with himself as regent, taking the name Tryphon. A man utterly without honor or principle, Tryphon inveigled Jonathan into supporting him by playing on his well-justified anger at Demetrius' breach of faith over the Akra. But Tryphon was to prove much more accomplished at betrayal than Demetrius. He invited Jonathan to visit him at Ptolemais on the coast, and the Maccabee came unsuspecting, with a thousand men. The gates of the walled city clanged shut behind them; the thousand men were massacred and Jonathan held in close confinement.[58]

Tryphon and the other enemies of the Jews might now have thought that at last they had worked their way down through the Maccabee brothers to the one who was not a man of war: Simon. But Simon too had learned the deadly trade in the twenty-three years of strife since it all began at Modein. He took command of the Maccabeean army and challenged Tryphon, who promised to release Jonathan for 100 talents in silver and two of Jonathan's sons as hostages. Simon sent the money and the boys. Tryphon took them—and killed Jonathan. Of the five Maccabee brothers only one now remained, he whom old Mattathias had appointed a father to all the others in his stead.[59]

Simon's feelings toward Tryphon may readily be imagined; he turned to young Demetrius, whose treachery in the matter of the Akra now paled into insignificance by comparison with the treachery of Tryphon. He offered Demetrius military support in return for recognition of the full independence of Judea. Demetrius agreed. In 141 B.C. the Akra at long last was surrendered to the Jews, after a quarter of a century of constant menace in the heart of the holy city. At a great assembly in Jerusalem the following year, the priests and people proclaimed Simon their leader and high priest—but not king—"until there should arise a faithful prophet." His secular title was "Prince of the People of God," or Ethnarch.[60] The liberated children of Israel were at last able to enjoy the fruits of their long struggle in full peace and security, "each man under his vine and his fig tree."[61]

But the thirty years' war of the Jews for freedom had one last victim to claim. In 134 B.C. Simon's own son-in-law, plotting to seize Judea and probably to deliver it to the new Seleucid king Antiochus VII, killed Simon and two of his sons at a banquet which he had prepared for them. Of the five sons of the priest Mattathias—five heroes to whom, as a family, history shows few equals—now there were none.[62]

Simon had a third son, John called Hyrcanus, the Tiger. He was not with his father on the fatal night, but in the city of Gezer. A friendly messenger outran the assassins sent to kill him. The Tiger struck; the assassins were slain and the gates of Jerusalem closed against the party of the murderer. John Hyrcanus took his father's place as high priest and leader of the nation, and set himself to the task of restoring the ancient kingdom of David, now that the Seleucid empire was no longer strong enough to prevent it.[63]

What had it all meant, the saga of the Maccabees? A genuine epic, to lighten the hearts and raise the spirits of the Chosen People then and afterward, the regaining, restoration and rededication of the Temple gave the Jews their Christmas: Hanukkah, the Festival of Lights. No one thought of any of the Maccabees as the long-awaited Messiah, who was universally expected to be far more than even they had been; but it is reasonable to suppose that their spectacular success caused many Jews, now of a more martial turn of mind, to see the Messiah as a glorified military commander who would lead them to victory and dominion over the Gentiles. The nobility of the Maccabee brothers blinded them and their people to the dangers of power abused; could any Jew in 134 B.C. have imagined that in little more than a century his people would be ruled by a king of their own whose morals matched Tryphon's? But it is given to no man but a prophet to see the future, and there had been no faithful prophet in Israel for three hundred years.[64]

The Maccabees lived and fought, suffered and died for the love and in the service of God and of His people. Inspired by Him, they had become His people's champions. In a world where it seemed no man could be trusted, where brother cut down brother in all the great royal families, they never failed to trust one another and to earn and keep the trust of their people. No just man can hold the Maccabees responsible for the errors and evils into which their achievement ultimately led. Rather we should note the vivid contrast of the moral commitment and perseverance of the Maccabees with the character of every one of the Gentile leaders—even the Roman senators—with whom they had to deal. Because of that, the Maccabees were unconquerable. Their invincibility was type and foreshadowing of the indestructibility of the Church of Christ that was to come, when the Son of God at last entered His Father's house which the Maccabees had saved and restored.

NOTES

[1] Howard H. Scullard, *A History of the Roman World from 753 to 146 B.C.*, 3rd ed. (London, 1961), pp. 235-236.

[2] In Egypt the Ptolemaic dynasty appropriated the immemorial Egyptian tradition of the divine Pharaoh. But there was no such tradition in Asia, and in both regions the Greek settlers themselves actively promoted the cult of living rulers as a substitute for the old gods of the city-states which no longer seemed significant in the new countries they had colonized. It also seemed to make the absolute rule of the Ptolemaic and Seleucid kings more acceptable to the once freedom-loving Greeks. But when these explanations have all been given and duly weighed, it remains clear that the practice of paying divine honors to living men marked a sharp decline in genuine religious feeling even in the pagan sense, whether or not the practitioners of the king-cult or the kings themselves actually believed in their alleged divinity. See M. Cary, *A History of the Greek World from 323 to 146 B.C.*, 2nd ed. (London, 1951), pp. 367-370, and *The Cambridge Ancient History*, Volume VII (Cambridge, England, 1928, 1954), pp. 113-115, 161-164.

[3] For the history of Pergamum (Pergamon in Greek) see Esther V. Hanson, *The Attalids of Pergamum* (Ithaca NY, 1947).

[4] *Cambridge Ancient History*, VII, 207-208.

[5] *The Cambridge Ancient History*, Volume VIII (Cambridge, England, 1930), pp. 139, 142, 184; Cary, *Greek World 323-146 B.C.*, pp. 56-57.

[6] *Cambridge Ancient History*, VIII, 148-152.

[7] *Ibid.*, pp. 152-166; Cary, *Greek World 323-146 B.C.*, pp. 186-189; Scullard, *Roman World 753-146 B.C.*, pp. 230-234, 441-442. The Athenian ambassador Cephisodorus seems to have arrived in Rome to add his city's plea for help to that of Pergamum and Rhodes, just before the Roman declaration of war on Macedon. It is certain that Philip's aggression in the Aegean began hostilities, but it is by no means established that Pergamum struck first against Macedon following the Macedonian attack on the Aegean cities. A recent proposed rearrangement of the uncertain but very important chronology of the

years 202-200 B.C. would place the Pergamene declaration of war only after Philip's actual invasion of Pergamene territory. Since Attalus of Pergamum was known as a friend of Rome, this would somewhat strengthen the legal and moral basis for Rome's intervention in the east at this time. See Scullard, *op. cit.*, pp. 441-442 on this point.

[8] On the long-vexed question of the origin of Rome's Second Macedonian War the text follows the persuasive argument of Maurice Holleaux in *Cambridge Ancient History*, VIII, 156-159, which is supported by Scullard, *Roman World 753-146 B.C.*, p. 441, and by F. W. Walbank, *Philip V of Macedon* (Cambridge, England, 1940), pp. 127-128. For an argument against this interpretation see R. M. Errington, *The Dawn of Empire, Rome's Rise to World Power* (Ithaca NY, 1972), p. 283.

[9] *Cambridge Ancient History*, VIII, 165-166; Victor Tcherikover, *Hellenistic Civilization and the Jews* (Philadelphia, 1959), pp. 76-77; Sean Freyne, *Galilee from Alexander the Great to Hadrian* (Wilmington DE, 1980), pp. 28-33. Freyne dates the Battle of Panion to 201. He makes the excellent point that the Jews almost certainly favored the Seleucids over the Ptolemies because the latter had a much more centralized and restrictive bureaucratic administration of government, thereby posing a greater threat to Jewish control over their own internal affairs as a people. The Seleucid practice, deriving from the vast extent and great cultural diversity of the lands they ruled, had been to grant much more local autonomy. There was nothing in the time of Antiochus III to suggest the dramatic reversal of this policy, so far as the Jews were concerned, which was to be made by Antiochus IV in 167 B.C. (see below).

[10] Scullard, *Roman World 753-146 B.C.*, p. 242. Scipio did not have a command in this war because of political jealousies in Rome (H. H. Scullard, *Scipio Africanus, Soldier and Politician* [Ithaca NY, 1970], p. 185).

[11] Scullard, *Roman World 753-146 B.C.*, pp. 242-246; Cary, *Greek World 323-146 B.C.*, pp. 193-194.

[12] Scullard, *Scipio Africanus*, p. 190.

[13] Scullard, *Roman World 753-146 B.C.*, pp. 298-299.

[14] *Ibid.*, pp. 247-249; Errington, *Dawn of Empire*, pp. 158-160.

[15] Scullard, *Roman World 753-146 B.C.*, pp. 249-252; Errington, *Dawn of Empire*, pp. 164-166; Cary, *Greek World 323-146 B.C.*, p. 194.

[16] Errington, *Dawn of Empire*, pp. 171-175; Cary, *Greek World 323-146 B.C.*, p. 196.

[17] Scullard, *Roman World 753-146 B.C.*, pp. 252-254; Cary, *Greek World 323-146 B.C.*, p. 195.

[18] Scullard, *Roman World 753-146 B.C.*, pp. 254-259; Scullard, *Scipio Africanus*, pp. 202-206; Errington, *Dawn of Empire*, p. 178.

[19] Cary, *Greek World 323-146 B.C.*, pp. 212-213; Edwyn R. Bevan, *The House of Seleucus* (New York, 1902), II, 120.

[20] Scullard, *Roman World 753-146 B.C.*, pp. 272, 293, 328-329, 356-361; Errington, *Dawn of Empire*, pp. 263-268.

[21] Errington, *Dawn of Empire*, pp. 206-241. The resulting conquest of Macedon brought so much booty to Rome that all taxes on Roman citizens were lifted, while 150,000 largely unoffending Epirotes were sold into slavery, Macedon was made a Roman province in 147 B.C., and many of the cities of old Greece were placed under the authority of the governor of that province the next year, after they rose in one last rebellion.

[22] Errington, *Dawn of Empire*, pp. 253-255; Bevan, *House of Seleucus*, II, 144-145.

[23] Errington, *Dawn of Empire*, p. 255.

[24] Glanville Downey, *A History of Antioch in Syria, from Seleucus to the Arab Conquest* (Princeton NJ, 1961), pp. 95-96.

[25] Elias Bickerman, *From Ezra to the Last of the Maccabees* (New York, 1949), pp.

54-56, 63-71; Tcherikover, *Hellenistic Civilization and the Jews*, pp. 80-81, 125-126, 144-145, 150-151; Emil Schürer, *A History of the Jewish People in the Time of Jesus Christ* (New York, 1891), II (1), 320-321, 335-338, 355-356.

[26] For the Tobiads, see Giuseppe Ricciotti, *The History of Israel* (Milwaukee, 1955), II, 207-213, and Chapter Eight, Note 34, above.

[27] Ricciotti, *History of Israel*, II, 217.

[28] *Ibid.*, II, 218-220, 222.

[29] *Ibid.*, II, 222-223.

[30] *Ibid.*, II, 223-225; Abraham Schalt, ed., *The World History of the Jewish People*, First Series, Volume VI - "The Hellenistic Age" (New Brunswick NJ, 1972), pp. 138-140.

[31] Ricciotti, *History of Israel*, II, 225-228.

[32] *Ibid.*, II, 237n.

[33] Solomon Zeitlin, *The Rise and Fall of the Judaean State* (Philadelphia, 1962), I, 94-95; Bickerman, *Ezra to the Maccabees*, p. 93. For an excellent popular retelling of the whole heroic story of the Maccabees, based on the best historical sources and opinion, see Moshe Pearlman, *The Maccabees* (New York, 1963).

[34] Schalt, ed., *World History of the Jewish People*, VI, 148.

[35] Ricciotti, *History of Israel*, II, 238; Bickerman, *Ezra to the Maccabees*, pp. 98-100.

[36] 1 Maccabees 3:49-50, 61-63.

[37] Ricciotti, *History of Israel*, II, 238.

[38] Schalt, ed., *World History of the Jewish People*, VI, 149-155.

[39] *Ibid.*, VI, 155-157.

[40] Ricciotti, *History of Israel*, II, 45, 240-241.

[41] *Ibid.*, II, 241-242.

[42] The date of the death of Antiochus IV, the number and date of the military expeditions into Palestine which Lysias personally commanded, and the authenticity of the letters from Antiochus IV, Antiochus V, and Lysias contained in the Second Book of Maccabees together constitute a long-standing historical problem which we lack sufficient first-hand evidence to solve completely. The sequence of these events as reported in the two Books of Maccabees appears to be different. Consequently many earlier scholars jumped to the conclusion that 2 Maccabees is historically unreliable and that the above-mentioned letters appearing in it are forgeries (e.g. *Cambridge Ancient History*, VIII, 707-710). But as we have pointed out repeatedly in discussing problems of this kind, it is always preferable to seek a reasonable reconciliation of such a conflict than to reject out of hand a major historical document when there is nothing but the one apparent conflict to justify doing so. The best reconciliation in this case appears to be that of Ricciotti (*History of Israel*, II, 242-244 and notes), attributing the documents in 2 Maccabees referring to Antiochus IV as dead when according to 1 Maccabees he was still alive, to a widely believed false report of his death, possibly deriving from his having been driven out of the very same temple in Iran where his father Antiochus III had in fact been killed. Solomon Zeitlin, *The Second Book of Maccabees with Introduction and Commentary* (New York, 1954), pp. 56-68, makes a strong defense of the authenticity of the documents in 2 Maccabees (*pace Cambridge Ancient History*, VIII, 707-710); reconciles the apparently conflicting chronology by an argument that the Seleucid era as used in Judea began a year earlier than the Seleucid era used in Antioch; and points out the high probability, based on the military and political situation, that Lysias would have immediately invaded Judea after the defeat of Nicanor, while Antiochus IV still lived, and again in the year after his death when Lysias saw an opportunity for a decisive victory through the use of elephants (see Note 62, below). But Zeitlin's conclusion that

Antiochus IV died in 165 B.C. runs counter to that of the great majority of authorities on Hellenistic history who date his actual death to 163 (e.g. *Cambridge Ancient History,* VIII, 514; Cary, *Greek World 323-146 B.C.,* p. 220; Downey, *Antioch,* p. 99). The text follows Ricciotti's reconstruction—a false report of Antiochus IV's death in 165 and the actual death in 163—except in the matter of the first attack of Lysias in 164, which Ricciotti dismisses as a mere "show of force" rather than another major effort to put down the entire Maccabeean rebellion, as Zeitlin—correctly, in this writer's view— interprets it.

[43] Zeitlin, *Judaean State,* pp. 102-104; Bickerman, *Ezra to the Maccabees,* pp. 120-121.

[44] Bickerman, *Ezra to the Maccabees,* p. 122; see Note 42, above.

[45] 1 Maccabees 6:8-13; Josephus, *Antiquities of the Jews,* XII, 9.

[46] W. Stewart McCullough, *The History and Literature of the Palestinian Jews from Cyrus to Herod* (Toronto, 1975), p. 120; *Cambridge Ancient History,* VIII, 516-517; Bickerman, *Ezra to the Maccabees,* pp. 122-123.

[47] Ricciotti, *History of Israel,* II, 248.

[48] Israel Abrahams, *Campaigns in Palestine from Alexander the Great* (London, 1927), pp. 30-31.

[49] Zeitlin, *Judaean State,* pp. 109-110.

[50] *Ibid.,* pp. 111-113; Bickerman, *Ezra to the Maccabees,* pp. 124-126; McCullough, *Palestinian Jews,* pp. 120-121; Downey, *Antioch,* p. 119n.

[51] *Cambridge Ancient History,* VIII, 518; Zeitlin, *2 Maccabees with Commentary,* pp. 67-68.

[52] Ricciotti, *History of Israel,* II, 250-255; Bickerman, *Ezra to the Maccabees,* pp. 128-130.

[53] Zeitlin, *Judaean State,* pp. 114-117.

[54] Ricciotti, *History of Israel,* II, 257-258.

[55] Zeitlin, *Judaean State,* pp. 118-120; Schalt, ed., *World History of the Jewish People,* VI, 186.

[56] Schalt, ed., *World History of the Jewish People,* VI, 186-187.

[57] *Cambridge Ancient History,* VIII, 521-523.

[58] Ricciotti, *History of Israel,* II, 47, 265-269; Downey, *Antioch,* pp. 122-124.

[59] Ricciotti, *History of Israel,* II, 269-270.

[60] *Ibid.,* II, 271-274; 1 Maccabees 14:41.

[61] 1 Maccabees 14:12.

[62] Ricciotti, *History of Israel,* II, 276-278.

[63] *Ibid.,* II, 280-283.

[64] Malachi (see Chapter Eight, above) was generally recognized as the last of the faithful prophets, through the time of the Maccabees.

12.
ROME AND CAESAR
(133-44 B.C.)

The Roman Empire was recognized as the highest achievement of the human race, and also as the broadest. A dreadful secret seemed to be written as in obscure hieroglyphics across those mighty works of marble and stone, those colossal amphitheatres and aqueducts. Man could do no more.

For it was not the message blazed on the Babylonian wall, that one king was found wanting or his one kingdom given to a stranger. It was no such good news as the news of invasion and conquest. There was nothing left that could conquer Rome; but there was also nothing left that could improve it. It was the strongest thing that was growing weak. It was the best thing that was going to the bad. . . . Many civilizations had met in one civilization of the Mediterranean sea . . . The peoples had pooled their resources and still there was not enough. The empires had gone into partnership and they were still bankrupt. No philosopher who was really philosophical could think of anything except that in that central sea, the wave of the world had risen to its highest, seeming to touch the stars. But the wave was already stooping; for it was only the wave of the world.—G. K. Chesterton, *The Everlasting Man*, p. 167 (Image Books edition)

By the time of the death of the last of the heroic Maccabee brothers, Rome had reached—primarily by her special qualities of moral greatness and logical hardihood—a unique position of unchallengeable dominance in the ancient civilized world. Certain inexperienced barbarian tribes of Europe's northern and central forests had yet to learn that truth; Gaius Marius and Julius Caesar would be their teachers. The Oriental kings of lands never fully hellenized by the successors of Alexander—Pontus and Armenia in Asia Minor, in particular—had yet to learn it; Lucius Cornelius Sulla and Gnaeus Pompey would be their teachers. By 133 B.C. everyone else in what was to be the Roman empire at the time of the birth of Christ, coterminous with the Western civilized world, already knew it. The great Greek historian Polybius had seen this truth so clearly that, in selecting Rome's rise to world power as the subject of his history, he declared that no comparably significant historical theme could be found.[1]

Rome was genuinely reluctant to rule the whole ancient civilized world directly. Only gradually did necessity bring her, step by step, to this position.[2] But so overwhelming was her power that, given the absence of any other recognized supreme authority in the ancient world (outside the still almost unknown revelations of the God of the Jews), it was impossible *not* to exercise it; the disordered condition of human affairs demanded it. The first objective of every contender for power or seeker after justice on any large scale in the first century B.C. European and Mediterranean world had to be the support, or at least the benevolent neutrality, of Rome. For nothing in that world, from Britain to Iran, could stand against the might of Roman arms and the resolution of spirit that made them invincible.

It is essential to keep this overriding political and human reality clearly in mind in approaching the bloody history of Caesar's century. The perpetual counterpoint to the rapacity of the senatorial oligarchy, the tax-farming bankers and publicans, and the generals and their armies coming off campaign, was the invincibility of the Roman soldier. When badly led he might lose a battle; he never lost a war. In virtually every conflict with non-Romans during this century he was outnumbered, often vastly. Yet in every conflict his ultimate victory was certain, and the only real danger came from an opposing army of his own kind—that is, composed of other Roman legions.

It is of the nature of such power, however nobly built and originally won, that it must corrupt; after no external enemy remains capable of seriously threatening or long resisting it, then it turns upon itself. In the lifetime of Julius Caesar Rome had nothing fundamentally to fear from any alien, everything to fear from itself. Yet even this internal threat was for a time surmounted. It was a near thing, but Rome survived, despite an explosion of prolonged civil conflict dwarfing the Peloponnesian War which had ruined the prospects of old Greece for political leadership of the ancient world and the quarrels among the Hellenistic kings which had so depleted the heritage of Alexander the Great.

That Rome survived, continued to grow, and at length established full peace in the Mediterranean world in the very last generation before the Incarnation was due almost entirely to the work of two men: Caius Julius Caesar and his nephew and adopted son and heir Octavian, later called Caesar Augustus. So enormous was their impact on history that the very name Caesar was still used as a royal title twenty centuries later in a very different successor civilization, not disappearing until Kaiser Wilhelm, the German emperor, and Czar Nicholas II, the last monarch of Russia, were deposed in the twentieth century.

Neither of the two original Caesars needs an apologetic, though both have often—especially in the past—received one. No one can reasonably advance a full moral justification for all or even most of their acts. They were not Christians, nor Jews. They did not have access to the treasury of spiritual resources and revealed moral teachings available to the Maccabees. They knew the natural law, though imperfectly, as all men know it. But they had no vision of what was to be—nor, so far as we can tell, anything like the strange intuition of Alexander the Great that some divine power was urging him on. Their official deifications after death and quasi-deifications while ruling were strictly political, not religious acts. They were heirs of old Rome, valuing highly the best in Rome's great tradition, but also and most emphatically practical men of affairs living in a century when even the most brilliant man who kept his integrity—Cicero comes immediately to mind—had virtually no chance of prevailing. But both Caesars were geniuses; by and large they did display more moral sense than their opponents; and both triumphed against all odds. In the end Caesar Augustus brought peace to the world—the peace glorified by St. Luke in his gospel account of the Nativity, the peace which emerging Christianity required to spread, to be heard, to sink roots in the Gentile world that in time would bear the rich fruit of a Christian civilization. To what extent this achievement was a case of God bringing good out of evil, and to what extent it reflected real personal good in the two Caesars themselves, only their ultimate Judge knows.

The corruption of Roman politics came, as political corruption always comes, from wealth and power and too many opportunities to get more of both. Wealth and power are inseparable in public affairs. Money begets power; power begets money. The now imperial Roman republic had the authority and the opportunity to dispose of a very substantial proportion of all the wealth of the ancient world. Members of the senate, which had once rejected Pyrrhus' bribes with scorn, now eagerly accepted bribes from a petty African client prince-claimant of illegitimate birth named Jugurtha.[3] Magistrates and ex-magistrates were among the wealthiest men in Rome, matched only by the tax-farmers and their banker associates. The senators used their wealth to buy more and more land, until huge estates sprawled over the Italian countryside, swallowing up the small farmers which had nurtured the yeoman soldiery that defeated child-murdering Carthage.

Two idealistic young men, the brothers Tiberius and Gaius Gracchus, elected tribune in 133 and 123 B.C. respectively, sought to remedy this unjust and dangerous concentration of economic power by land reform legislation, and succeeded in having such legislation passed despite the angry opposition of most of the senate. Each brother was slain while seeking re-election as tribune despite the prohibition, by long-standing Roman tradition, on re-election to successive terms in the same office. Yet at the same time a cardinal principle of that tradition was the sacrosanctity of the person of a tribune. In the name of the tradition against re-election the tradition of the security of the tribune's person was disregarded. Tiberius Gracchus was clubbed to death in the Forum at the instigation of Senator Scipio Nasica; Gaius, besieged on the Aventine hill by the consul Opimius, asked his slave to kill him when all was lost. Three hundred died with Tiberius Gracchus in the Forum, three thousand with Gaius Gracchus on the Aventine. The consul Opimius, later prosecuted for putting Roman citizens to death without trial, was acquitted on the grounds that the state had been in danger from the ambitions of the Gracchi.[4]

Thus were born in blood the two parties which contended for Rome through almost a hundred years, the *optimates*—the senatorial aristocrats—and the *populares*, who challenged the senate in the name of the people and their assemblies and tribunes. The Gracchi and their partisans were *populares*; Scipio Nasica and Opimius and their partisans were *optimates*. Like all political labels these were more flattering than accurate. The *optimates* (literally, "better men") were not noticeably more good than their opponents, nor were the *populares* more genuinely popular, being led by rival aristocrats and financed by the tax-farming and merchant class. But the *optimates* did for the most part seek to uphold the old constitution with a minimum of change, while the *populares* were ready to carry out any number of changes to check the concentration of wealth and power which the old constitution no longer seemed able to prevent.[5]

It was soon apparent that no permanent solution to the quarrel could be attained by peaceful means. To the *optimates* every popular leader and every successful general was a potential tyrant, whom it was morally permissible and even positively virtuous to kill. To the *populares* every defender of the old constitution was a man for sale to the highest bidder, interested only in retaining his class privileges so as to go on milking Rome, Italy and the world of hard-earned goods. There was enough truth in both accusations to be believable even when clear injustices were done to the more honorable men on either side. Compromises failed; mutual trust faded; hostilities escalated. The popular general Gaius Marius restored Rome's military honor against Jugurtha in Africa and defeated a massive barbarian invasion of northern Italy after corrupt senatorial commanders had failed against the invaders, but while doing so he held the office of consul for five successive years (104-100 B.C.), an even more flagrant violation of the constitution than the re-election of a tribune, since the consuls were the chief magistrates. He established the precedent of enlisting a professional volunteer army rather than the old citizen soldiers—an army which owed its primary loyalty to its own generals, with whom the soldiers had taken service.[6]

It was during this five-year unconstitutional rule of Marius in Rome that the long life of John Hyrcanus, son and successor of Simon the last of the Maccabees, drew to a close in Judea (see Table Six, "Rome and the Jews, 133-4 B.C.").

CHRONOLOGICAL TABLE OF ROME AND THE JEWS
133-4 B.C.

ROME	THE JEWS
tribunate of Tiberius Gracchus 134-133	John Hyrcanus 134-104
tribunate of Gaius Gracchus 124-121	
Jugurthine War 112-106	
consulships of Marius 105-100	Aristobulus I 104-103
	Alexander Jannaeus 103-76
Social War (Rome v. Italy) 91-88	Jewish civil war 96-87
First Mithridatic War 88-85	
Sullan civil war 85-82	
dictatorship of Sulla 81-79	
Third Mithridatic War 74-70	Queen Alexandra Salome 76-67
Fourth Mithridatic War 69-66	Aristobulus II 67-64
Pompey's conquest of the east 66-63	Hyrcanus 64-40 (Antipater)
consulship of Cicero 63	
First Triumvirate 60	
Caesar's Gallic Wars 59-51	
Roman civil war (Caesar v. Pompey) 50-48	
dictatorship of Caesar 47-44	
Antony and Octavian 44-31	Antigonus 40-37
Octavian as Caesar Augustus from 27	Herod the Great 37-4

John Hyrcanus had extended the Maccabean frontiers substantially while maintaining his position against the weakening Seleucid rulers and occasionally defeating them. In the south he had conquered Edom, obliging its people to accept Judaism and its men to be circumcised—the first forcible conversion on a large scale in the history of the Chosen People (it was because of this that

Herod, an Edomite or Idumaean, was born a Jew). In the north he conquered the Samaritans and destroyed the separatist temple they had built on Mount Gerizim, probably soon after the death of Alexander the Great. He was regarded as a friend of Rome and there may have been one or more direct Roman interventions on his behalf, and even on behalf of Jews living outside Palestine.[7]

But despite John Hyrcanus' successes, there was growing concern among the faithful about the union of the office of high priest with that of ruler of the people Israel. No such union had ever existed before. Even Moses had separated the temporal and spiritual offices by making his brother Aaron the high priest. This separation had been central to the history of Samuel, Saul, and David. During the monarchy, from Solomon to Nebuchadnezzar's destruction of the Temple, we hear little of the high priests; but their line continued, separate from the royal line of David. The family of the Maccabees—the Hasmoneans—though of priestly lineage, had no Scriptural or traditional title to the high priesthood. The Hasidim—the "pure"—who had arisen in the time of the High Priest Simon the Just and revered his memory, urged John Hyrcanus to give up his high priestly office. Angrily he refused, and from that time his earlier piety noticeably cooled.[8]

The more radically strict among the Hasidim found this situation intolerable. They fled to the desert, following a priest of the old line whom they called the "Teacher of Righteousness" in contrast to the "Wicked Priest"—probably Simon Maccabeeus—and the "False Oracle," perhaps John Hyrcanus. They formed a community at Qumran near the Dead Sea, which they saw as a "counter-Israel," the sole remaining repository of God's mission for His people. They lived a monastic and ascetic life, the first of its kind in community to emerge in the history of Israel, in which a substantial proportion of the members seem to have practiced celibacy (often held by scholars, before the discovery of the "Dead Sea scrolls" which this community left at Qumran, to be unknown as a vocational choice among Jews). The community grew and flourished during the ensuing century as the corruption of the regime founded by the Maccabees became more and more evident and ugly. Its members laid great stress on full obedience to the law of Moses, rigorous separation from the "impure" who accepted Hasmonean authority in any form, and apocalyptic visions and hopes connected with the future coming of the Messiah, which—quite naturally, in their circumstances—they emphasized even more than other Jews. It was in the Qumran community that the advent of the Messiah was most explicitly and closely linked with catastrophic phenomena which were to mark the end of the world as men have known it. The majority of Jews did not assume this linkage, but expected the Messiah to establish his kingdom first in this world.[9]

In 104 B.C. John Hyrcanus died and was succeeded by his eldest son Aristobulus I (his use of a Greek name is very significant). Josephus tells us that Aristobulus immediately imprisoned his mother, who was starved to death, and his three brothers, one of whom he soon killed.[10] So had the Seleucids treated their own, not so the glorious Maccabees. Aristobulus reigned only a single year; but during that year he took Galilee from the Seleucids, reuniting it with the domain of Jerusalem for the first time since the fall of the northern kingdom of Israel to Sargon of Assyria 617 years before, and forcibly converting its non-Jewish inhabitants, the Itureans, as John Hyrcanus had forcibly converted the Idumaeans.[11]

Aristobulus was succeeded by his brother Alexander Jannaeus, who promptly had himself crowned king along with being proclaimed high priest. No longer was the ruler of the Chosen People, liberated by the Maccabees, to be a special kind of prince, awaiting the coming of a faithful prophet and respecting God's anointing of the dynasty of David despite its fall into complete obscurity.[12] (We should note the element of mystery in that obscurity. With the rising opposition to the Hasmoneans it would have been natural—almost inevitable in normal secular circumstances—for a scion of the old dynasty of David to step forward as a popular champion against the oppressor. But none ever did. After the exile, Jesus was to have no worldly precursors in His royal line.) Now the ruler of the Jews was to be a king just like his Hellenistic rivals. Thus, in striking parallel, the corruption and decline of the rulers of God's People went hand in hand, historically speaking, with the corruption and decline of the city, once so strongly marked by natural virtue, which was to become the seat of Christ's Vicar on earth.

The ascetics at Qumran (almost certainly the group later known as the Essenes)[13] had removed themselves totally from the political struggle in Judea, but many remaining in Jerusalem followed the teaching and tradition of the scribes and Pharisees from the days of Simon the Just and Jesus ben Sirach, author of the Book of Ecclesiasticus. They formed an unyielding opposition to the greedy, tyrannical rule of Alexander Jannaeus. The newly self-proclaimed king of the Jews was, however, able to find some support among the priestly class and the wealthy aristocrats, from those willing to put personal and worldly advantage above doctrinal purity. His priestly supporters were the origin of the later Sadducees. The civil wars and massacres in Rome during the terrible decade of the 80's were matched, on a smaller scale, by those of Alexander Jannaeus during the same period in Jerusalem. Fifty thousand Jews are estimated to have died in the civil war between Alexander Jannaeus and his priestly and military supporters on the one hand and the people led by the scribes and Pharisees on the other. The war lasted from 96 to 87 B.C. When at last it ended with Alexander Jannaeus victorious, he crucified hundreds of the leaders of the revolt. Those he hated most had to watch their wives and children killed before their eyes as they hung upon their crosses.[14]

Thus did the method of execution, which a hundred years later was to be inflicted upon the Son of God, become familiar in Judea.

In Italy the long-continued gradual extension of Roman citizenship and voting rights to other Italians had stopped. Those in control at Rome, whether *optimates* or *populares*, had generally no wish to share their increasingly lucrative powers and privileges with anyone else. Gaius Gracchus as tribune in 122 B.C. and Livius Drusus as tribune in 91 B.C. each introduced bills for Italian enfranchisement; both men were killed as a result. It seemed a fundamental reversal of the policy that had made Rome great. Immediately following the murder of Drusus, many of Rome's Italian allies rose in revolt, proclaiming the new nation of Italia. From the bitterly fought contest emerged as Roman victors old Marius; the younger, adroit Lucius Cornelius Sulla, who excelled both as diplomat and as warrior; and the brutal Pompeius Strabo, father of Pompey the Great. But this "Social War" was won only after Rome enfranchised all loyal Italians, by cities or individually.[15]

Then in 88 B.C. a heavy blow suddenly struck Rome in the east. King Mithridates of Pontus, a slightly hellenized region in eastern Asia Minor, had established a Black sea empire.[16] He coveted Rome's province of Asia, which had been the Hellenistic kingdom of Pergamum in western Asia Minor, willed to Rome by its last king who died without issue in 133 B.C.[17] Rome's richest province, it had been systematically fleeced by the tax-farmers for a generation. Mithridates' men and local rebels, working together, killed every Italian in the province they could catch. Mithridates then crossed the Aegean, occupying the island of Delos and massacring the Italian traders there, and took over much of old Greece. In Rome Sulla was consul, but Marius wanted the eastern command. Marius was of the *populares*, Sulla of the *optimates*. Marius expelled Sulla from Rome; Sulla rallied troops, returned, took Rome (the first time a Roman army had captured Rome) and exiled Marius. The Roman state and empire seemed on the verge of breaking up.[18]

What followed was an astonishing demonstration of the tenacious constancy of the Roman soldier despite all turmoil behind and around him, and his invincibility when even reasonably well led. Sulla, taking only two or three months to make a paper-fragile settlement in Rome that collapsed as soon as he left the city, led five legions to Greece to fight the Pontic invaders. Consul Cinna of the *populares* declared Sulla an outlaw; old Marius plunged into an insane orgy of revenge in Rome until he died. Before Sulla was the victorious army of Mithridates; behind him were his irreconcilable foes in power at Rome. Sulla had no support anywhere in the world, except for his five steadfast legions. With them alone, he triumphed. Despite his total lack of strategic support, he smashed Mithridates' army in two battles in Greece in 86 B.C. and forced the Pontic king to sue for peace, imposing terms very favorable to Rome. When another Roman army, raised by Cinna, arrived in Asia to arrest Sulla, he won its soldiers over to his side; their commander killed himself.[19]

With his victorious legions and the new recruits from his enemies, Sulla landed in Italy at the beginning of 83. His immense achievements for Rome should, in any rational judgment, have led to immediate peace and reconciliation between him and his opponents, especially since both Marius and Cinna were now dead. Young Gnaeus Pompey, son of the deceased Pompeius Strabo of the Social War and formerly a supporter of Marius as his father had been, saw this clearly; he raised a legion and brought it to Sulla. But most of the *populares* would hear of no reconciliation; they must fight Sulla to the end. Roman armies ravaged Italy; overborne by Sulla's military skill, the *populares* called on the Samnites, Rome's fierce opponents from the old days of the unification of Italy before Pyrrhus, to join them against him. A reign of terror by the *populares* took many lives in Rome. The final battle of this civil war took place late in 82 B.C. at Rome's Colline Gate, between a huge Samnite army and Sulla's veterans of the Mithridatic War. It raged from late one afternoon all through the night into a grisly dawn. Fifty thousand men were slain. Sulla barely escaped with his life when the part of the army he commanded was routed; but due to the steadiness of the rest of his men, he finally prevailed by the narrowest of margins. He had himself proclaimed dictator for an indefinite term, contrary to the constitution, butchered six thousand prisoners, and ordered some three thousand leaders and supporters of the *populares* "proscribed," which meant that their names were published on a death list; they were killed and their property confiscated to pay off his troops.[20]

After all this, it is hardly surprising that Sulla's attempt to re-establish the peaceful regime of the old senate ended in failure, though his personal prestige was so great that his settlement was not challenged until after his death in 78. A constitution which can be restored only by its own violation is moribund. The memory of Sulla's proscriptions remained vivid with burning hatred so long as their victims' children lived, and those who had witnessed these horrors in their youth. Cicero, 25 years old at the time, never forgot them. Nevertheless, Sulla's serious attempt, however ill-fated, to restore the senate and his abdication from the dictatorship a year before he died show that he was still seeking a solution to Rome's problems at a higher level than mere personal despotism.[21]

Mithridates of Pontus was still making war against Rome whenever he could, and had obtained as an ally his neighbor king Tigranes of Armenia, who had recently conquered nearly all that remained of the once-vast domain of the Seleucids. Some years after Sulla's death Gnaeus Pompey, now Rome's leading general, was sent east. He led the irresistible legions on a triumphal march through Pontus and Armenia to the Caucasus Mountains, then down to Syria— which he made a Roman province—and on into Palestine. There, three years before, Alexander Jannaeus' widow and successor, Alexandra Salome, had died. Her reign had been most remarkable. As her husband approached death in 76 B.C. he repented of the evils he had brought upon God's people, and instructed Alexandra Salome to obey the Pharisees in everything, as he had never done. She carefully followed his dying counsel. The effective ruler in Jerusalem during Alexandra's reign was the rabbi Simeon ben Shetah, leader of the Pharisees, who made the Jewish council of elders, the Sanhedrin (resembling in some ways the Roman senate) a far more influential body than ever before, filled with his supporters. True to the special emphasis on research, academic disputation and learning characteristic of the scribes and Pharisees, Simeon ben Shetah made basic education compulsory for all Jewish children. But when "good Queen Alexandra" died in 67 B.C. she left two sons, Hyrcanus II and Aristobulus II, as rivals for the throne. Hyrcanus, the elder, was unambitious but much influenced by his very ambitious counsellor Antipater; Aristobulus, the younger, was much more enterprising. Hyrcanus surrendered the high priesthood and the kingship to Aristobulus after only three months in office, but was then induced by Antipater to try to take them back. War broke out, and the two brothers were still at odds when Pompey arrived.[22]

At Damascus, in the spring of 63 B.C., Pompey heard the case between the brothers. Both came to plead, along with an independent Jewish delegation asking that neither be recognized and the people of God go back to rule by the high priest alone within the structure of the dominant empire, now to be Roman. Pompey and his advisors knew very little of this strange people, with whom Rome had had only distant and occasional previous dealings; they did not really understand the character and significance of the high priestly office. Pompey at first put off a decision between Aristobulus and Hyrcanus. Aristobulus knew just enough about the Romans to be afraid of them without knowing enough to realize the utter futility of any sort of military challenge to them. Vacillating, he shut himself up in Jerusalem to defend it against Pompey, then changed his mind and decided to surrender it to him, but the troops in Jerusalem refused to obey his command to surrender. A majority of the people of the holy city were for Hyrcanus and therefore promptly capitulated to Pompey, but some Jewish soldiers held out in the Temple itself. The Akra having been finally demolished by the Maccabees, the Temple was now not only the religious focus but the prime military strong point of Jerusalem. It stood a three months' siege from Pompey's veterans. They finally broke in on a Sabbath, killing 12,000 of the defenders, who fought right up to the altar of sacrifice itself. When at last the carnage ended, Pompey stood facing the mysterious black-curtained cube, the Holy of Holies, containing he knew not what. Rumor said it held an ass's head. It might hold something worse. Could it hold anything better?[23]

Pompey walked up to the Holy of Holies and drew aside the curtain—the first Gentile to approach or touch it since the rededication of the Temple after the profanations of Antiochus IV Epiphanes 101 years before. Within he saw—nothing. The stone tablets of the Ten Commandments inscribed on Sinai which had once been there, enshrined in the Ark of the Covenant, had long since disappeared, lost in the Babylonian sack over half a millennium before. In all probability Pompey knew nothing of them. Did this strange people worship only a void?

We do not know what Pompey thought about what he saw, and did not see, in the Temple; but he ordered the sacrifices resumed, confirmed Hyrcanus as high priest and "ethnarch," but not king, and prepared for his return to Rome where in that same year, 63 B.C., Cicero had been consul and had put down the conspiracy of Catiline.[24] Contrary to the fears of many senators, Pompey—a rather phlegmatic, good-natured man with little political ambition though a strong desire for popularity—made no attempt to set himself up as a dictator as Sulla had done. He held a magnificent triumph in 61 B.C., parading the wealth of the east which he had conquered for Rome. With this he seemed, at least for the moment, content.[25]

In the next year after Pompey's triumph a forty-year-old pro-praetor just returned from a campaign in the barbaric hinterland of Spain asked for a triumph and permission to run for consul. His name was Caius Julius Caesar. He was of the *populares*; his aunt had been Marius' wife; Sulla had wished to include him, even as a very young man, in the list of the proscribed, but had been dissuaded by some of Caesar's relatives—and by the Vestal Virgins, who found some indefinable but impressive charisma in him. Yielding to these entreaties, Sulla—an excellent judge of men—nevertheless remarked: "In that boy I see many Mariuses."[26]

Caesar, having kept his head and moved slowly but steadily forward through the deadly welter of Roman politics for the twenty years since Sulla (for example, adroitly avoiding the conspiracy of Catiline when it became wild and fantastic, though he had played some still obscure part in an earlier version of it),[27] was now ready to aim for the top. He joined with Pompey and Crassus the financier, the two most powerful men in Rome outside the *optimates*, to form the "First Triumvirate," had himself elected consul, married his daughter to Pompey, and put through a package of reform legislation. It was the usual program of the *populares*: land reform, land for demobilized soldiers, and more effective checks on the rapacity of provincial governors. With Pompey's troops, Crassus' money and Caesar as the cutting edge, the laws were passed by riding roughshod over constitutional obstacles validly raised by Caesar's consular colleague, the *optimate* Bibulus. Desperate to get Caesar out of Rome, the senate voted him a five years' command in Gaul.[28]

Away from the cauldron of Roman politics, sanity and constancy could surface once more. Caesar, one of the sanest men who ever lived—whatever one may say of his political morality—found himself confronting masses of well-armed, bellicose Celtic barbarians whose ancestors had sacked Rome in 390 B.C. and whose near neighbors had tried to do it again, and almost succeeded, in the time of Marius. So far, all Rome's expansion had been into the old civilized lands of the Mediterranean shore. Even in Spain, Carthage had first showed the way for Rome. But Caesar had campaigned in interior Spain which was almost as barbaric as Gaul, and had prevailed. He knew these wild men could be tamed. He dared imagine a Romanized Gaul, a whole new land and people brought into the orbit of Western civilization, strengthening it instead of threatening it. This was a momentous departure from all previous Roman policy, for until then all Western civilization had revolved around the Mediterranean. Now Julius Caesar was to make Europe as we know it, the Europe of which France (Gaul) has always been the keystone.

He came first not as aggressor but as protector. The entire tribe of the Helvetians from western Switzerland—368,000 men, women and children—left their old homes in a mass migration in the spring of 58 B.C., just as Caesar took over his Gallic command. They intended to settle somewhere in Gaul, displacing whoever might already be living in the region they chose, and crossing Roman territory where necessary for their movement. Obligated to defend the Roman province in southern Gaul against any such locust-like incursion, and asked for help by the independent Aedui of central Gaul who were directly in the path of the invaders, Caesar checked the Helvetians at Geneva, followed them across the Jura Mountains, and shattered their army near Bibracte. The remnant meekly returned to Switzerland. Then, again, at the request of the Aedui, Caesar marched to the Rhine to defeat the treacherous Germans under King Ariovistus, who revealed to Caesar in a conference where Ariovistus tried to kill him that the Roman senate had offered him great favors in return for Caesar's head.[29]

It was still only the fall of 58, less than a year into the five-year term of Caesar's command, and already he had become the arbiter and protector of all of Gaul. The tribes of the Gallic north—notably the Belgae and the Nervii—correctly saw in this the harbinger of full Roman rule. The next year they mounted a major assault on Rome's allies in Gaul, now including the tribe of the Remi near what was to become Paris. Caesar besieged and captured the town of Noviodunum where the Belgic king had sought refuge, and despite a massive surprise attack by the Nervii, rallied his troops and won a decisive victory.[30]

In the year 56 the triumvirs met at Lucca to renew their alliance. Pompey and Crassus were to be consuls for 55, Caesar was to continue in his Gallic command for five more years, Pompey was to get a five-year command in Spain, and Crassus a command in Syria. These arrangements were to be imposed on the senate and assemblies, if necessary by Pompey's troops. Cicero created a sensation by supporting the decisions made at Lucca, declaring that Caesar ought to be continued in his command in Gaul because of the magnitude and significance of his victories there, despite the fact that Cicero was devoted to the old constitution, had previously taken the side of the *optimates* against the triumvirs, and had been exiled from Rome for a year and a half (58-57 B.C.) with the triumvirs' tacit consent. So for a moment there was substantial concord among the leaders of Rome. Cicero's brother Quintus took service as a legate with

Caesar's army in Gaul.[31]

With this greatly extended span of time at his disposal in the Gallic command, Caesar set about completing his conquests. The lands on the Gallic coast of the English Channel were subdued. He led two expeditions across the Channel to Britain in 55 and 54, winning battles with the inhabitants there though not yet extending Roman rule to the great island. But northern Gaul, so far from Rome and the Mediterranean world and so new to civilized order, was restive. Ambiorix, chief of the Belgic tribe of the Eburones, tricked the Roman legate Sabinus, commanding a legion and a half in winter quarters in Belgium, into leaving the protection of his fortified camp and annihilated the entire Roman force; hardly a man survived. A horde of Gauls, wild with victory, descended totally without warning on the camp at the river Sabis held by Quintus Cicero with a single legion.[32]

For four days hand-to-hand fighting raged along the palisades and ditches of the camp, the attackers outnumbering the defenders twelve to one. On the fifth day Ambiorix sent a herald. All Gaul had risen, he announced; the Germans were across the Rhine; the Fourteenth Legion of Sabinus was wiped out. If the Roman commander surrendered, he would get safe conduct out of the country.[33]

There was no word from Caesar; the messengers sent to summon help from him had been caught and killed. Quintus Cicero was totally isolated and his position seemed hopeless. He had none of his brother's mercurial genius, but all of the old Roman courage. He gave Ambiorix's herald the reply of Appius Claudius: Rome never negotiates with an enemy in arms on her territory. If Ambiorix and his army would surrender to him, he would ask Caesar to pardon them.[34]

Once more Roman courage and constancy won the day. When at last Caesar heard what had happened and rushed to Quintus' relief, he found the camp still holding out—but barely one-tenth of the defending legion unwounded, a casualty rate of ninety per cent![35]

The stand of Quintus Cicero and the victory of Caesar that followed should have ended the war in Gaul, and probably would have ended it had not the Romans once more displayed what appeared to be clear indications of a general collapse at home and in the east. At Carrhae in Mesopotamia Crassus met the Parthian horse-archers on a waterless plain and proved that even Roman legions could be defeated when commanded by a banker. Crassus was killed along with two-thirds of his army.[36] In Rome, later in the year 53, disorder and corruption reached such a fever pitch that no magistrates for the next year could be elected. Rival gangs led by Clodius of the *populares* and Milo of the *optimates* fought actual battles in and around Rome, culminating in a clash on the Appian Way in which Clodius was killed. Pompey took over as emergency sole consul and restored order, but not before a young, high-born Gallic chieftain named Vercingetorix had planned, organized, and proclaimed a general rebellion of central Gaul against Caesar, trusting that a Rome shocked by the defeat of Crassus and paralyzed by civil strife would not give Caesar the support he needed to put down so great an uprising.[37]

But Julius Caesar was incapable of shock or paralysis. He struck at the heart of Vercingetorix's coalition at Gergovia, but lost the battle there due to the impetuosity of his troops, who attacked at a critical moment without orders. Retreating, apparently beaten, through the territory of the once-friendly Aedui who had now joined Vercingetorix, Caesar responded to the attack intended to destroy him by a sweeping counterattack that drove Vercingetorix and the whole leadership and best troops of Gaul back into the fortress city of Alesia. Caesar ringed it with a double line of trenches and ramparts, stood off sallies from within by Vercingetorix and attacks from without by a relieving force (at one point his men were fighting two battles at once, one facing their front and the other facing their rear), and by the middle of the year 52 he had forced Vercingetorix to surrender.[38]

Gaul never rebelled again on its own behalf. It became thoroughly Latinized in language and culture,[39] and as France has remained a central part of the Latin world ever since. Few conquests have endured so well.

Caesar's work in Gaul was done, his prolonged command there drawing toward its legal close. The senatorial *optimates* had not forgotten or forgiven their grievances against this man whom they saw clearly as the ablest of their enemies, whom some of them had tried to bribe Ariovistus to kill. There was no longer a triumvirate, for Crassus was dead; Pompey and Caesar remained. The *optimates* had now concluded that Pompey, unlike Caesar, was not ambitious enough to be a real threat to them, and that he could be manipulated in their interests. Playing upon his growing jealousy of Caesar, they sought to make him their champion. After months of intrigue, they succeeded.[40]

Caesar had wished to return to Rome as consul, and until taking office to remain in Gaul with his command and his legions. He knew that to return to Rome as a private citizen, with neither army nor office, would be to invite imprisonment and execution by his many enemies. Pompey offered some concessions; he was willing to let Caesar stand for consul *in absentia*. But he insisted on Caesar's giving up his command by a fixed date, *before* taking office if elected. He promised Caesar, his long-time friend and ally, protection. But Caesar now trusted nobody but his own peerless soldiers. He demanded that Pompey lay down his own military powers if Caesar were required to do so. Partly for the same reasons as Caesar, partly from injured pride, Pompey would not. By the end of the year 50 Pompey had made up his mind that war with Caesar was inevitable. On January 7, 49 B.C., he pressured a reluctant Senate into passing its "ultimate decree," the herald of war, calling for all necessary measures for the safety of the state.[41]

Caesar's choice was exile or conquest. The cisalpine portion of Gaul where he still legally commanded extended as far as the little Rubicon River in northern Italy. To cross that river in arms was to make himself formally a rebel and an outlaw, to plunge Rome into a new civil war. Caesar made his decision—"the die is cast!"—and crossed the Rubicon with his legions, later in January of 49.[42]

The *optimates*—moderates and extremists alike—rallied as one to Pompey against Caesar as a destroyer of the constitution. Very reluctantly, against his better judgment, Cicero went with them, though he had very little confidence in their ability to prevail over Caesar. The people of Rome and Italy generally supported Caesar, so much so that Pompey had to flee almost immediately to Greece. In sixty days, with that lightning quickness of movement which was the chief of his military gifts, Caesar was master of Italy. Pompey and the optimates held Greece, Africa, and Spain, together much outnumbered Caesar, but their geographical separation allowed Caesar to defeat them in detail. First overcoming the Pompeian legions in Spain and obtaining their capitulation, Caesar then crossed the Adriatic in the teeth of a winter gale to challenge Pompey in Greece. After a brilliant campaign he won a total victory at Pharsalus in the summer of 48. Pompey fled to Egypt, where a general in the Ptolemaic army, presumably in collaboration with the prime minister Pothinus who ruled in the name of the boy-king Ptolemy XII, had him beheaded.[43]

Caesar followed, landing in Alexandria in the full panoply of a Roman consul to collect a debt owed by Egypt to Rome and to settle the dispute between the young Ptolemy XII (age 13) and his older sister Cleopatra (age 22), who had been expelled from Egypt earlier in the year. Since Ptolemy XI "the Piper," the preceding ruler who died in 51, had made Rome the guarantor of his will specifying that Ptolemy XII and Cleopatra were to rule Egypt jointly, Caesar had strong legal grounds for his intervention. But it was fiercely resented by the largely anti-Roman populace of Alexandria. Pothinus took the lead in organizing resistance, stirring up street riots against the Romans and assembling a large military force.[44]

Cleopatra smuggled herself into the royal palace in Alexandria where Caesar was beleaguered (tradition has it, very possibly correctly, that she arrived rolled up in a carpet) and the two of them at once formed that personal and political liaison which has been the theme of so much great drama. Cleopatra, the last and perhaps the greatest of the descendants of Alexander, was aiming at a universalist world empire ruled by a dynasty uniting Roman leadership with the Ptolemaic Hellenistic royalty which she represented; but she could not dominate Julius Caesar as she later dominated Mark Antony. Yet Caesar listened to her, was captivated by her, and later brought her to Rome and installed her in his villa across the Tiber. She had a son whom she named Caesarion and identified as his. If this was true (as it probably was), this was the only son Caesar ever had.[45]

From early December of 48 B.C. to late February of 47—three full months—there was almost constant fighting in Alexandria. At one point Caesar, engaged in battle beside his men on the mole joining the island of Pharos with the mainland and forming the double harbor of Alexandria, was forced into the water and had to swim for his life. But in March the army of relief he had summoned finally arrived and smashed the Ptolemaic army. The boy-king Ptolemy XII was drowned in the Nile, and the siege of Caesar in the royal palace was at last lifted.[46]

One of the largest contingents in the army that saved Caesar on this occasion was commanded by Antipater of Judea, the chief counsellor of Hyrcanus II; it consisted of 3,000 Jews. Not only did they play a very significant part in Caesar's Egyptian victory, but also they did much to persuade the large Jewish communities in Egypt (it has been estimated that as much as two-fifths of the population of Alexandria at this time was Jewish) to support Caesar rather than Ptolemy.[47] Consequently Caesar showered favors on Antipater and the Jews. In the spring of 47 he confirmed Hyrcanus, Antipater's puppet, as high priest and ethnarch (offices originally granted him by Pompey); made Antipater a Roman citizen and Roman procurator of Judea; granted permission to rebuild the walls of Jerusalem, which Pompey had torn down; and while levying some tribute, decreed that Judea should not be occupied by Roman troops or subjected to Roman military requisitions, and that it should be exempt even from ordinary tribute every seventh year in view of the Mosaic law requiring the land to be left fallow then. Going still further, Caesar recognized the common bond among Jews throughout the world and extended to all of them, wherever resident, the special protection of Roman law so that they would not be forced to act contrary to their Law and their faith, and could worship freely in their synagogues. Julius Caesar thus became in a real sense the protector and emancipator of the Chosen People.[48]

By now the great Diaspora, or dispersion of Jews throughout the ancient world, was reaching its climax. It is one of the most remarkable phenomena in all history. Since Alexander the Great, Jewish emigrants—already strongly established in Babylonia and Egypt—had spread through the whole Mediterranean region. They went to Rome with other Greek-speaking traders and exiles; the influx of slaves captured during Pompey's wars in Palestine substantially enlarged Rome's Jewish community. It is estimated that in the time of Julius Caesar there were about eight million Jews in the Roman empire. Most of them were outside Palestine; there were a million in Egypt alone. In the eastern provinces of the empire they comprised about twenty per cent of the total population. Wherever they went they stood out, by their rigorous exclusiveness based on their following of the Law of Moses and its increasingly restrictive interpretations by the scribes and Pharisees; by their internal coherence—every Jewish community had its own college of directors and its synagogues, so different in every way from pagan temples; by their insistence on a special Divine destiny for their whole people, wherever located, which was so closely linked with their continuing veneration and unfailing support for the Temple in Jerusalem and its priesthood; and above all, by their unwavering faith in the invisible world-ruling Spirit they worshipped, Whom Pompey had found so strangely honored in the empty room which was the Holy of Holies. Jews refused absolutely to be absorbed by the Hellenistic or Roman culture surrounding them. Not all were as total in their rejection of foreign ways as the Maccabees; but a Jew never forgot who he was, no matter how far from Jerusalem he might be, nor did anyone who knew him. They were a people within a people, almost a state within a state. Julius Caesar fixed their place in the Roman empire which he did so much to establish and extend. The legal privileges he gave the Jews long outlasted him; they were still in effect when the building of the Church of Christ began, and its missionaries always preached first to the Jews in their clearly visible communities, in every city to which they came.[49]

After a luxurious cruise up the Nile with Cleopatra and a lightning campaign against a last outbreak of rebellion in Pontus (the occasion for Caesar's famous despatch: *"Veni, vidi, vici"*—"I came, I saw, I conquered"), Caesar finally returned to Rome in September of 47 B.C.[50] More than a year had passed since the Battle of Pharsalus. Caesar's long stay in Egypt and consequent detachment from affairs at Rome had given his senatorial enemies time and opportunity to regroup. Under the leadership of Marcus Porcius Cato, a direct descendant of Cato the censor of "Carthage must be destroyed" fame, they had established themselves in Africa with a considerable army. Caesar had to win back his veteran legions from a threatened mutiny; they were understandably weary of endless civil wars, but still responsive to his personal charisma. Leading them to Africa, he crushed the senatorial forces at Thapsus in March of 46; Cato committed suicide. Returning to Rome in triumph, Caesar was proclaimed dictator for ten years, then for life. Even Sulla had not gone this far; it meant the end of the old constitution.[51]

No longer dependent on the *populares*, Caesar could finally call a halt to their long-lasting and ever-growing vote-buying scheme of "free" grain for most of the people of Rome. He cut the number of recipients of this grain by more than 50 per cent.[52] He enfranchised all of Cisalpine Gaul and Sicily, and extended the privileges of Roman citizenship to selected non-Italians for the first time, individually and by whole cities (including several cities in southern Gaul and Spain)[53]—a step of the greatest importance in maintaining the unity of the Mediterranean world by means more constructive and lasting than sheer military force. With the aid of the Alexandrian astronomer Sosigenes, Caesar reformed the calendar, adding 80 days to the year 46 B.C. to bring the calendar back in line with the seasons, and setting January 1 as the first day of the new year of 45 B.C.[54] This Julian calendar remained in use throughout the Western world until the Gregorian improvement in 1582 (not accepted by the English-speaking peoples until 1752 and not accepted by Russia until 1918).

Yet the struggle for the future of Rome was not yet entirely decided. Enmity toward Caesar persisted. In March of 45 he had to fight a last battle, at Munda in Spain, against a new army his foes had recruited there; he almost lost it, having at one point to rush into the front lines with sword and shield like a private (at the age of 55) to rally the best of all his legions, the famous Tenth, with the cry: "Are you not ashamed to deliver your old general into the hands of boys?"[55] Back in Rome the surviving *optimates* denounced Caesar as a tyrant only waiting for the best moment to assume a royal crown, the ultimate anathema in Roman political tradition. He set up a statue of Cleopatra in the temple of Venus in Rome, augmenting the already widespread hatred of his foreign consort.[56]

As the year 44 opened, Caesar himself seems to have grown weary of the struggle, slipping into a kind of fatalism which often overtakes men who achieve mightily while lacking a clear sense of higher purpose. He refused a bodyguard, despite repeated warnings of threats and plots against his life, saying that none could be so mad as to plunge Rome once again into the horrors of civil war by killing him. It is hard to imagine that a man so realistic as Julius Caesar truly believed that; for it was precisely the lack of such common sense in political matters that had almost destroyed Rome—and had been demonstrated again just the year before by the rebels at Munda. He was planning a great campaign against Parthia, the last unconquered civilized people in the world Rome knew and that her empire touched, which would take him away from Rome perhaps for years; Cleopatra would probably accompany him. But even this prospect of a last road to glory did not arouse his old vigor; his health was failing, and he was heard to say that he had lived long enough. On March 15, 44 B.C., the Ides of March, two days before he was to leave for the east, Julius Caesar was struck down by the daggers of Brutus and Cassius of the old aristocracy and their friends, in history's most famous assassination, on the floor of the senate chamber while it was in session.[57]

Caesar's work remained unfinished. There was still more blood to be shed, still more reconstruction to be done. When he was slain no man could have foreseen that he would have an heir worthy of him and more than worthy, who would at last bring peace with a large measure of justice to the war-weary Roman world.

NOTES

[1] Michael Grant, *The Ancient Historians* (New York, 1970), pp. 148-151.

[2] See the thorough review of this question, supporting the conclusion stated in the text, by E. Badian, *Roman Imperialism in the Late Republic*, 2nd ed. (Ithaca NY, 1968).

[3] *The Cambridge Ancient History*, Volume IX (Cambridge, England, 1932, 1957), pp. 117-120; James A. Froude, *Caesar* (New York, 1908), pp. 35-41. Since our only authority for the history of the Jugurthine wars is a pamphlet by Sallust, a partisan of Caesar in the later civil wars, writing more than half a century after the events he describes, modern historians have often been reluctant to credit fully the appalling picture of senatorial venality and corruption which Sallust's account conveys. (Froude, *op. cit.*, is an exception.) But when Sallust wrote the Jugurthine war was still well within the 90-year span of living memory. He may have distorted or exaggerated the facts about Jugurtha's bribery of senators, but could hardly have invented his charges out of whole cloth. There must have been some substantial basis for them—some significant bribes offered by Jugurtha and accepted by influential senators.

[4] *Cambridge Ancient History*, IX, 1-93.

[5] Lily Ross Taylor, *Party Politics in the Age of Caesar* (Berkeley CA, 1949, 1964), pp. 1-24; Ronald Syme, *The Roman Revolution* (Oxford, 1939, 1960), pp. 65-77.

[6] M. Cary, *A History of Rome*, 2nd ed. (London, 1954), pp. 303-313. For the Roman professional soldier of the first century B.C. see Michael Grant, *The Army of the Caesars* (New York, 1974), pp. xvii-xxxiv.

[7] Giuseppe Ricciotti, *The History of Israel* (Milwaukee, 1955), II, 281-284; James D. Purvis, *The Samaritan Pentateuch and the Origin of the Samaritan Sect* (Cambridge MA, 1968), pp. 98-109, 113; Michael Grant, *The Jews in the Roman World* (New York, 1973), pp. 32-33.

[8] Ricciotti, *History of Israel*, II, 284-286; Emil Schürer, *A History of the Jewish People in the Time of Jesus Christ* (New York, 1891), II (2), 26-27.

[9] Frank Moore Cross Jr., *The Ancient Library of Qumran and Modern Biblical Studies*, 2nd ed. (Garden City NY, 1961), pp. 58-60, 76-99, 127-160; Schürer, *History of the Jewish People*, II (2), 142-143, 158-159; see also Chapter Sixteen, Note 79, below.

[10] Ricciotti, *History of Israel*, II, 287-288. It is possible that the mistreatment of his mother and brother which Josephus ascribes to Aristobulus I may have actually been the work of his brother and successor Alexander Jannaeus, who was fully capable of such crimes and had a much longer period in power to carry them out.

[11] Stewart Perowne, *The Life and Times of Herod the Great* (New York, 1957), p. 18. For the significance of the prophecy of Isaiah 9:1 that the Messiah would come from Galilee, then in the hands of the Assyrians and resettled with non-Jews, see Chapter Six, above. While the non-Jewish Ituraeans who lived in Galilee were forcibly circumcised and brought into Judaism as the Idumaeans had been (Ricciotti, *History of Israel*, II, 288), Perowne (*loc. cit.*) is incorrect in implying that it was only because of these forced conversions that Jesus of Nazareth was born a Jew. As His genealogies show, Jesus was of the line of David; some of His neighbors in Nazareth may have been descended from forced Ituraean converts, but not He. Sean Freyne, *Galilee from Alexander the Great to Hadrian* (Wilmington DE, 1980), pp. 37-45, argues strongly—with supporting citations from several other distinguished scholars, in opposition to the conclusion of Schürer, *Jewish People in the Time of Christ*—that Galilee was predominantly Jewish throughout the Hellenistic period. But that there was a sharp break in its Jewishness at some point between the Assyrian conquest in the eighth century B.C. and Hellenistic times (*pace* Freyne, *op. cit.*, pp. 23-26), is evident from the strong and enduring tradition of the "lost ten tribes," several of which had originally had Galilee for their home. Once Galilee was included in the Jewish domain through the efforts of John Hyrcanus and Aristobulus, there was considerable Jewish immigration and settlement there, due

to the fertility of the land, the good fishing in the Sea of Galilee, and the fact that Galilee had been part of the Land of the Promise, of Joshua's original conquest and of the territory of the twelve tribes. By Jesus' time the area was known for its fervent faith.

[12] Ricciotti, *History of Israel*, II, 273-274, 288-289.

[13] Cross, *Ancient Library of Qumran*, pp. 76-99.

[14] Ricciotti, *History of Israel*, II, 289-292.

[15] Cary, *History of Rome*, pp. 316-324.

[16] *Cambridge Ancient History*, IX, 211-233.

[17] The bequest of Pergamum was only accepted because it happened to fall in the year Tiberius Gracchus was tribune (133 B.C.). Tiberius, who had family connections with the Pergamene royal house, learned of the bequest before the senate did, and had the assembly, which he then controlled, pass a law accepting the bequest so as to provide additional revenue for carrying out his land reform program. See Badian, *Roman Imperialism*, pp. 21-23.

[18] Cary, *History of Rome*, pp. 324-326, 333.

[19] G. P. Baker, *Sulla the Fortunate* (New York, 1927, 1967), pp. 189-232.

[20] *Ibid.*, pp. 237-267; Cary, *History of Rome*, pp. 338-339; Peter Greenhalgh, *Pompey, the Roman Alexander* (London, 1980), pp. 12-22, 33.

[21] Baker, *Sulla*, pp. 267-291.

[22] Cary, *History of Rome*, pp. 348-356, 369; Ricciotti, *History of Israel*, II, 293-299; *The World History of the Jewish People*, ed. Alexander Schalt, Volume VI ("The Hellenistic Age, 332-67 B.C.") (New Brunswick NJ, 1972), pp. 248-254.

[23] Ricciotti, *History of Israel*, II, 299-303.

[24] *Ibid.*, II, 303; Torsten Petersson, *Cicero* (New York, 1963), pp. 240-285. There is an enormous literature on the conspiracy of Catiline, because of our thorough knowledge of it due to the preservation of Cicero's classic orations against Catiline and other documents of his consulate. But historically this conspiracy is relatively insignificant, there having been during this period in Rome a conspiracy of generally similar character to Catiline's every two or three years.

[25] *Cambridge Ancient History*, IX, 509-511.

[26] Froude, *Caesar*, pp. 92-94, 175-176, 182-183; Matthias Gelzer, *Caesar, Politician and Statesman* (Cambridge MA, 1968), pp. 19-21.

[27] *Cambridge Ancient History*, IX, 488.

[28] Cary, *History of Rome*, pp. 375-376; Greenhalgh, *Pompey, the Roman Alexander*, pp. 197-227 (a very full, modern, excellent and well-written account of the First Triumvirate).

[29] *Cambridge Ancient History*, IX, 547-553; Froude, *Caesar*, pp. 235-237. For an excellent popular account of Caesar's conquest of Gaul and of his role in the civil war that followed, see Fletcher Pratt, *Hail, Caesar!* (London, 1938).

[30] *Cambridge Ancient History*, IX, 553-555.

[31] *Ibid.*, IX, 614-619; Petersson, *Cicero*, pp. 333, 339-340.

[32] *Cambridge Ancient History*, IX, 555-563.

[33] Froude, *Caesar*, pp. 307-308, 311.

[34] *Ibid.*, pp. 308-309.

[35] *Ibid.*, pp. 310-311.

[36] *Cambridge Ancient History*, IX, 606-612.

[37] *Ibid.*, IX, 620-626, 565-566.

[38] *Ibid.*, IX, 566-570.

[39] *The Cambridge Ancient History*, Volume XI (Cambridge, England, 1936, 1965), pp. 506-507.

[40] Cary, *History of Rome*, pp. 393-397.

[41] *Cambridge Ancient History*, IX, 629-637; Frank B. Marsh, *A History of the Roman World from 146 to 30 B.C.*, 3rd ed. (London, 1963), pp. 222-228, 395-399; Peter Greenhalgh, *Pompey, the Republican Prince* (London, 1981), pp. 89-132.

[42] *Cambridge Ancient History*, IX, 636-637; Plutarch, "Caesar."

[43] Cary, *History of Rome*, pp. 399-403; Petersson, *Cicero*, pp. 483-493; Michael Grant, *Cleopatra* (New York, 1974), pp. 57-58.

[44] Grant, *Cleopatra*, pp. 61-64, 69-70.

[45] *Ibid.*, pp. 63-67, 83-85; Gelzer, *Caesar*, p. 257n; *The Cambridge Ancient History*, Volume X (Cambridge, England, 1934, 1952), pp. 35, 38, 76-77. The paternity of Caesarion is a long-vexed question; but there is good evidence to show that he was born in September 47, nine months after Caesar and Cleopatra were besieged together in the palace at Alexandria (Grant, *Cleopatra*, pp. 83-84); Antony said that Caesar had acknowledged the boy as his son; and though Antony and Cleopatra had an obvious interest in having an heir to Julius Caesar in their house, it is very difficult to imagine Cleopatra finding another father for Caesarion at that particular moment in her life.

[46] Grant, *Cleopatra*, pp. 70-78.

[47] *Ibid.*; Ricciotti, *History of Israel*, II, 309; E. Mary Smallwood, *The Jews under Roman Rule, from Pompey to Diocletian* (Leiden, 1981), pp. 37-38.

[48] Ricciotti, *History of Israel*, II, 309-311; Smallwood, *Jews under Roman Rule*, pp. 38-43.

[49] Ricciotti, *History of Israel* II, 169-190; Grant, *Jews in the Roman World*, pp. 59-63; Smallwood, *Jews under Roman Rule*, pp. 120-136.

[50] Grant, *Cleopatra*, pp. 80-82, 85. Grant makes a strong case for the full historicity of Caesar's and Cleopatra's Nile cruise, famous in romance -- and historically significant because it diverted Caesar for a considerable time (probably the greater part of April and May of 47) from the organization and settlement of his rule in the Roman empire. Gelzer (Caesar, p. 255) also accepts the historicity of the Nile cruise.

[51] Cary, *History of Rome*, pp. 405-406.

[52] The practice was begun by Gaius Gracchus, though it appears that he did not simply give away the grain, but stored and sold it, under the authority of the government, at a low fixed price, below market value. His successors as leaders of the *populares* took advantage of the demagogic potentialities of this system by steadily lowering the price and enlarging the quantity distributed, until by the time of Caesar's rise to power, 320,000 Roman citizens were receiving grain at state expense, as handouts for which they paid nothing. See F. R. Cowell, *Cicero and the Roman Republic* (London, 1948), pp. 84-86.

[53] Cary, *History of Rome*, pp. 409-411.

[54] Grant, *Cleopatra*, p. 89.

[55] *Cambridge Ancient History*, IX, 703-704; Plutarch, "Caesar."

[56] Grant, *Cleopatra*, pp. 87-88.

[57] Cary, *History of Rome*, pp. 415-417; Froude, *Caesar*, pp. 490-493, 512-514.

13.
THE WINNING OF THE
ROMAN PEACE
(44-8 B.C.)

With vows and prayers your country calls for you . . . for
with you here the ox plods the fields in safety, Ceres and
bounteous happiness enrich our farms; our sailors sail waters
unvexed by pirates; public honor stands inviolate; chaste
homes are stained by no adulteries, and punishment follows
swift on crime. . . . Who fears Parthian, Scythian, German
or Spaniard if Augustus be safe? Each man sees day close
in peace on his native hills.—Horace, *Odes*, IV, 5

Just eighteen and a half years old on the Ides of March in 44 B.C., Julius
Caesar's great-nephew Octavian was a boy of delicate health and no worldly
experience, though manifesting a grave and deliberate reserve in striking contrast to his youth, with a steady piercing gaze which few could meet for long.[1]
In the ferocious world of Roman politics in the first century B.C. it seemed
that this young man, whatever high potential he might have had in better times,
stood hardly any chance.

Yet Julius Caesar, a superb judge of men, had seen in his young relative
the seeds of genius. When his will was opened in the house of Mark Antony,
his most honored military subordinate who had fully expected to be his heir,
it designated Octavian instead. To Octavian was to go Caesar's own name and

three-quarters of his vast fortune. As Octavian, who had looked up to his great-uncle as to no other man, told doubters: he could not think himself unworthy of the role for which Julius Caesar had by his will pronounced him worthy.[2]

This was the man who was to win at last the Roman peace.

The killers of Caesar had no plan for action other than the assassination itself. They appear to have expected the old republican constitution to begin working again smoothly, almost automatically, as soon as the dictator was dead. Even Cicero, prey to illusion though he had now become, knew better than that. He still dreamed of restoring the old constitution, but was well aware of how difficult it would be.[3]

Antony had a plan, simple and straightforward as befitted his soldierly character and experience: Stir up the people against Caesar's murderers, get them out of Rome, build on all available Caesarian sentiment and support, and take over the empire himself.[4] If Caesar had designated Antony his heir instead of Octavian, Antony would almost certainly have succeeded in this initial aim, but it is most unlikely that he would ever have brought peace to the Roman world. Did Caesar know this, or guess it? Very possibly he did. By naming Octavian his heir he made him a counterweight to Antony, able to rally much of the old, deep Caesarian loyalty of the Roman legionaries that would otherwise have gone to Antony.[5]

Yet Antony was a veteran commander, probably the best Roman general alive, while young Octavian had never even seen a battle.[6]

Standing alone except for a few close friends and advisors not much older than himself and the emotional but unorganized sympathy of many of Caesar's old soldiers, Octavian found himself caught between Antony with his dream of military empire and Cicero with his dream of a restored civilian constitutional republic. Octavian could not concede supreme power to Antony, over whom Caesar had chosen himself; he could not forget that Brutus had called out Cicero's name as he daggered Caesar and that Cicero had openly approved the assassination.[7] But with a sagacity astonishing in one so young, Octavian played off the two men and their parties against each other, preventing either from prevailing while he built up his forces until he had eight legions with him.

It was July, 43 B.C. More than a year had passed since Caesar's assassination. The two consuls for 43—both republicans—had died fighting Antony, and Octavian marched on Rome to demand for himself and his uncle Pedius the consulships for the rest of the year. The senate gave in to him, and made the appointments. In November he met Antony and Marcus Lepidus at Bononia (Bologna) and the three of them formed another triumvirate.[8]

Brutus and Cassius, the leaders among Caesar's murderers, had raised an army in Greece, like Pompey before them. To maintain and strengthen their forces so as to defeat this republican army, the triumvirs required much money. Consequently they ordered a proscription, following the example of Sulla. Three hundred senators and two hundred of the commercial class were on the death list, their property and their lives forfeit to the triumvirs. It is said that Octavian was unhappy with the decision for the proscription and tried to mitigate its rigor for some individuals; but for the most part, once the decision was made, he was as ruthless as his colleagues. One of the first victims of this proscription was Cicero. He died by the sword of a Roman soldier, face to face in the old Roman way.[9]

Meanwhile Brutus and Cassius had been building up their army by means no less atrocious. The whole population of Xanthus was forced into suicide by their merciless exactions; Tarsus—whence St. Paul was to come—was fined the colossal sum of 1,500 talents; 700 talents were demanded from Judea, some Jews were sold into slavery to help raise it, and Antipater was poisoned by an intriguer hoping to curry favor with the angry people. Antipater's son Herod took over, ruling for a time through the weak Hyrcanus as his father had done. In the next year, 42 B.C., Antony and Octavian triumphed at Philippi in Greece; Brutus and Cassius committed suicide.[10]

But peace did not come with the elimination of the republican assassins. The scramble for Caesar's mantle began to take on much of the appearance of the melee that had followed the premature death of Alexander the Great. Conditions at the beginning of the year 40 B.C. approached chaos. Antony was in Egypt, absorbed in revelry with Cleopatra, who was now resolved to fulfill her dreams of power through him;[11] his legitimate wife Fulvia, almost equally ambitious, joined with his brother Lucius to raise a major rebellion against Octavian;[12] Pompey's son Sextus held Sicily against all Caesarians, still in the name of the old republic which his father had purported to defend.[13] Under the circumstances it was hardly surprising that the Parthians, whose victory over Rome at Carrhae had remained unavenged, concluded that the time had come for them to conquer the Roman empire in Asia. They launched a two-pronged invasion, the right prong under a renegade Roman general striking deep into Asia Minor while the left prong under Crown Prince Pacorus took Syria and then Jerusalem.[14] Antony tore himself from Cleopatra's arms, rushed back to Italy, and was caught immediately in a fantastic vortex of confusion and misunderstanding at Brundisium which found him propelled into alliance with Domitius Ahenobarbus, a proscribed surviving assassin of Caesar, against Octavian, after having denounced his own wife Fulvia for rising against Octavian and sending her away to die.[15]

Not for the only time in these later stages of Rome's long and bloody civil wars, the soldiers now intervened on their own, clamoring for their commanders to make peace with one another. Negotiations were opened, Antony and Octavian embraced, and in October of 40 B.C. they renewed their alliance by the Pact of Brundisium, sealed by the marriage of Octavian's own sister Octavia to the just-widowed Antony.[16]

Within a month of the Pact of Brundisium, Herod of Judea came to Rome to meet with the two new rulers of the Roman world. Antigonus, nephew and rival of the high priest and ethnarch Hyrcanus in whose name first Antipater and then Herod had ruled, had welcomed the Parthian invaders. He offered them 1,000 talents and 500 women to make him king of the Jews. (Such was the price set on David's throne by the great-grandson of heroic Simon the Maccabee.) With his own teeth Antigonus bit off Hyrcanus' ear so that he could never again serve as high priest, since, according to the Mosaic law, the high priest had to be without physical blemish. Herod's brother Phasael, despairing, killed himself by the horrible method of dashing his head against a stone. Herod escaped into the desert, but found every door closed against him. Rome, where he and his father had always found favor, was his last hope. Only with the aid of Cleopatra, whom he detested and who detested him, was he able to make his way there.[17]

He arrived at a moment opportune beyond his highest expectations. Antony and Octavian were in full agreement that the Parthians must promptly be expelled from the Roman east and then, as soon as possible, conquered in their homeland. Who better to aid them in a Parthian war than this man who had suffered so much at Parthian hands? Antony had met Herod in Syria after the Battle of Philippi and had been impressed by his ability; Octavian remembered the great service Herod's father Antipater had rendered to Julius Caesar when he was gravely imperilled in Alexandria. Since Rome's arrival in Palestine the Hasmonean dynasty in Judea had shown itself again and again to be hostile or incompetent or both. For all these reasons, Antony and Octavian decided, contrary to the usual Roman policy with client kingdoms, to reject the established dynasty in Judea altogether, and sent Herod the penniless suppliant back to Jerusalem as King of the Jews. Even with the help of two of the invincible Roman legions, it required Herod three years to establish his bitterly resisted royal dominion in the Land of the Promise, climaxed by a five months' siege of Jerusalem ending in a massacre and a sack which spared only the Temple itself.[18]

Most Romans, longing for peace, welcomed the Pact of Brundisium with enthusiasm, the more so because Antony's marriage to Octavia seemed to presage a full dynastic union of the two potential rivals since Octavian had as yet no children of his own.[19] But for such a union a male heir was needed, and the first-born of Antony and Octavia was a girl. Still Octavia's very presence was almost a guarantee of peace. She was a woman whose virtue came as close to holiness as any pagan's can—W. W. Tarn calls hers "perhaps the loveliest nature which the ancient world can show."[20] She mediated between her brother and her husband whenever misunderstanding or jealousy arose. For three years she tamed the wild Antony, guiding and inspiring him, working at his side as he reorganized Asia while sending his capable general Ventidius to drive out the Parthians in two successful campaigns in 39 and 38 B.C.[21]

Antony would not let matters rest there. He was determined to carry out Caesar's plan, aborted by his assassination, for a massive invasion and conquest of Parthia. For this he needed either Octavian's support, or Cleopatra's. Octavian was involved in a protracted naval conflict with Sextus Pompey, who still held Sicily; Antony had sent ships to help Octavian there. Had Antony waited for Octavian's victory over Sextus Pompey he probably could have had his support, with the intercession of Octavia, for his Parthian campaign. The view that Antony was motivated solely or primarily by his military, political or economic ambition at this point, in choosing Cleopatra over Octavian and Octavia, does not fit the realities of the situation. Antony was a Roman and in a campaign against Parthia he needed above all Roman help, not Egyptian. Egypt could provide ships and money, but only Rome could give him the essential: the world's best fighting men. The alliance with Octavian was now solid, and welcomed in Rome. As victor over Parthia, with Octavia at his side, Antony's position would be unchallengeable—not total power, but at least an equal and probably a dominant role in a Rome which still greatly admired military success. The arguments from self-interest and military realism dovetailed with the arguments from morality and duty. Octavia was pregnant with their second child, who could be the longed-for male heir cementing in his person the alliance of the Antonian and Caesarian houses. Antony sent Octavia back from Greece to Italy for the birth and sailed for the east in the fall of 37 B.C. with no hint of what he was about to do on the way.[22]

Then at Antioch he summoned Cleopatra to meet him, gave her most of the coast of the Mediterranean from Egypt round to Cilicia in Asia Minor along with substantial areas of the hinterland, acknowledged her three-year-old twins as his, and settled down to live with her exactly as though they were married.[23] Unwilling though stodgy or prudish historians may be to admit it, there is no plausible explanation for these actions other than sexual infatuation with Cleopatra.

The shock to Roman opinion was great, for a substantial regard for moral virtue had survived even the degradation of the last years of the republic. Octavia was beloved, Octavian respected, and Cleopatra hated.[24] But for the moment, military issues held center stage. In July of 36 B.C. Octavian was locked in a final struggle with Sextus Pompey, having constructed a large fleet for an attack on Sextus' main Sicilian base, while Antony was coming down out of the mountains of Armenia to the plateau of Media in Iran with one of the finest Roman armies ever put into the field.[25] Then, in August, both men suffered totally unexpected defeats.

Octavian had crossed the Strait of Messina with three legions and a squadron of ships; Sextus Pompey outmaneuvered him (Octavian never became a really competent battle commander), cut him off, and destroyed his ships in a twilight engagement. As night fell, Caesar's heir had to struggle across the turbulent waters of the Strait in a small boat, with just one man remaining with him. Dragging himself ashore exhausted on the Italian side, for once in his life overcome by despair, he who was to be Caesar Augustus asked his lone companion to kill him. With the future of Rome hanging in the balance, the man refused.[26]

In Iran, Antony had divided his army, leaving only two legions to guard the long baggage train with the huge siege engines required for the capture of the fortified Parthian cities. Fifty thousand Parthian horse-archers descended upon this inadequate force, annihilated the two legions, and destroyed the baggage train, cutting Antony off in the heart of Asia with no means of victory and no way to get help.[27]

Yet in both men, whatever military errors they had made, an old Roman flame burned—and in Octavian something more, a growing consciousness of a higher destiny that had preserved him again and again from death, from his recurrent severe illnesses and his many enemies, to return always reinvigorated to the fray.[28] The day after his brush with ultimate despair and suicide on the shore of the Strait of Messina, Octavian learned that his boyhood friend and skilled admiral Agrippa had won a victory over Sextus Pompey's fleet while he was being defeated. The three legions, which Octavian had landed in Sicily and then had to abandon, were rescued. Within a few days Sextus Pompey was brought to battle again at Mylae and this time decisively defeated. He fled east, where he met his death.[29]

As for Antony, at first his Roman pride would not let him turn back. He laid siege to the Median capital, but without siege engines it was a futile exercise. As autumn cold began to set in on the high Iranian plateau he had to retreat—a retreat which has been compared to Napoleon's from Moscow. One day mutiny threatened among his troops and Antony, like Octavian, thought of suicide. But like Octavian he recovered his nerve the next day, carried on, won the admiration of his men and even a tribute to his courage from the Parthians. But he left 22,000 of Rome's best soldiers dead in the harsh highlands of Iran and came back with nothing whatever to show for the whole mighty expedition. Caesar's best general, attempting to carry out Caesar's own plan of eastern conquest, had come, had seen—and had lost.[30]

On November 13, 36 B.C., Octavian entered Rome in an impressive ceremony of public thanksgiving for the end of the civil wars; later that same month Antony was waiting by the sea at an obscure fishing village in Syria where he had called Cleopatra to come to rescue him, rushing daily from his dinner to look for her sails on the horizon.[31] The turning point in the careers and relations of the two men had come. Antony, a beaten general, was now fully in Cleopatra's power. Octavian, Caesar's heir, was in control at Rome, the seat of empire.

Not all Cleopatra's ruthless, resilient genius, not all the fabled Treasure of the Ptolemies which she actually carried with her everywhere, could now overcome the power that had prevailed over the whole Mediterranean world, marshalled by one who knew how to bring forth all that remained of old Roman pride and patriotism against the wicked foreign queen who had enslaved through lust the once popular, but now increasingly discredited Antony. Against a still divided Rome, Antony and Cleopatra might have succeeded. Against a Rome united and at peace under Gaius Julius Caesar Octavianus—for such was his full legal name—they were entirely outclassed.[32]

In the autumn of 34 B.C. Antony and Cleopatra threw down the gauntlet to Octavian and old Rome. In a glittering ceremony in Alexandria Antony, dressed as the god Dionysius-Osiris, with Cleopatra beside him garbed as the Egyptian goddess Isis, proclaimed Caesarion, now thirteen years old, the *legitimate* son of Julius Caesar and Cleopatra (although they had not, according to Roman law, been married to each other at the time of his birth) with the title King of Kings, co-ruler of Egypt with Cleopatra. She was given the title Queen of Kings and confirmed in her rule of Cyprus, Lebanon, and the coast of Palestine. Alexander Helios, the six-year-old son of Antony and Cleopatra, was proclaimed king of recently conquered Armenia, currently allied with Antony against Parthia; his twin sister Cleopatra Selene was given Cyrenaica and Crete, despite the fact that the two territories had been a Roman province for decades. Ptolemy Philadelphus, Cleopatra's two-year-old son by Antony, was made overlord of all the Roman client kings of Asia Minor.[33]

The remaining territory in the Roman east—the provinces of Macedonia (including Greece), Asia, Bithynia, and Syria—remained theoretically Roman under Antony's authority; but thousands of Roman denarii were minted with Cleopatra's head and full royal titulary in Latin along with Antony's head and title, clearly indicating that she now shared his authority as joint ruler over the Roman provinces as well. The two were aiming at rule of all of the Roman empire— evidently Cleopatra's design for herself from the beginning of her involvement with the great men of Rome.[34] Antony had accepted her design and made it his own. Though he was not yet totally dominated by her,[35] everything about the Donations of Alexandria and Antony's policy after his return from Parthia shows that she had become the stronger of the two, the guiding intellect and planner. The east saw her as its champion against Western rule; Rome saw her as bent on supplanting its regime with an alien oriental despotism. Anonymous eastern prophets linked her with dreams of a golden age. But there is no good evidence that Cleopatra ever sought anything beyond power and pleasure for herself.[36]

In the spring of 33 B.C. Octavian sent a letter of remonstrance to Antony, objecting particularly to his liaison with Cleopatra, his recognition of Caesarion as Julius Caesar's legitimate son, and his harsh treatment of Octavia, whom Antony had forbidden in 35 B.C. to come east. Antony made an insulting reply, accusing Octavian of grand-scale adultery. During the year 33 a propaganda polemic on behalf of the two rulers of the Roman world developed with steadily increasing vituperation.[37]

Antony had an enormous navy of 500 ships manned by 150,000 men—mostly paid for by Cleopatra—and 19 legions, but Octavian had or could raise even stronger forces. He had less money than Antony, but made up for that by an income tax of 25 per cent on all citizens and a capital levy of one-eighth on all freedmen. At first there was considerable resistance to the collection of these high taxes, but as the nature of the conflict became more apparent to the people of Italy, support for Octavian grew and opposition to the tax diminished. Cleopatra insisted on remaining with Antony's army and navy. Those of Antony's followers who were most conversant with public opinion in Italy pleaded with him to send her away. Once he did order her to go, but she refused to obey, and he gave in to her. Late in the spring of 32 Antony sent Octavia a formal notice of divorce. She had remained faithful to him during all the years of his infidelity flaunted before the whole world, continuing to raise his children. Now she was driven weeping from his house by those enforcing the divorce proclamation, to the sympathy of virtually all Rome and the cold anger of her brother Octavian. The timing of this action could hardly have been worse from Antony's standpoint; it is hard to see any explanation for it other than Cleopatra's jealousy and fear that, as Antony drew closer to Italy, somehow he and Octavia would meet again and she would draw him away from her. If this was the reason, it clearly shows that her ascendancy over him was now complete.[38]

All Italy rallied to Octavian. Town after town swore a special allegiance to him for the coming campaign. Antony was formally stripped of all his powers. Stories of depraved luxury, sorcery, and every kind of unnatural vice were told of the court of Alexandria and of Cleopatra personally. Octavian revived an ancient ritual by declaring war as a priest before the temple of Bellona. The war was declared against Cleopatra alone.[39]

Early in the year 31 B.C., during which Octavian held his third consulship, he crossed with his army to Greece where Antony was encamped near the Gulf of Ambracia. The Actium campaign that followed has been debated among historians at often tedious length because of the inadequacy and confusion of our sources regarding its strategy and tactics. But the determining element, obvious in every account, is the rising tide of desertions from Antony by his commanders, soldiers and sailors, Roman and non-Roman. Every engagement brought major new desertions. Whether the Battle of Actium on September 2, 31 B.C. was intended by Antony and Cleopatra as a genuine effort to defeat Octavian's navy and win command of the sea or was simply a bungled attempt to escape through his naval blockade, it was a shattering disaster for them. The greater part of their fleet simply surrendered without fighting at all. Though both Antony and Cleopatra got away, Antony was left in numb despair on the deck of his flagship, tagging after Cleopatra back to Egypt, knowing that very few Romans would ever fight for him again.[40]

Cautious and deliberate in victory as in adversity, Octavian made his way eastward during the year 30 B.C. At Rhodes he met Herod, who had killed both old Hyrcanus, the former high priest, and young Aristobulus while he was high priest, and had been very close to Antony despite the mutual hatred between Herod and Cleopatra. Herod simply told Octavian that he would serve him well, as he had always served Antony well. Octavian decided to overlook the fate of Hyrcanus and Aristobulus, and confirmed Herod as King of the Jews.[41]

Herod had feared a different outcome. Before departing for Rhodes he had left orders with his minister Sohaemus to kill his wife Mariamne, granddaughter of Hyrcanus whom he had killed and brother of Aristobulus whom he had killed, if he did not return. Herod was passionately in love with Mariamne and apparently could not bear the thought of her ever being married to another man, even if he was dead. Mariamne, who had never cared much for Herod especially in view of his crimes against her family, learned of this order after his safe return, and began to reject him. Believing a lying story of his sister Salome, that Mariamne's rejection was due to a sexual liaison between her and Sohaemus, Herod ordered both Sohaemus and Mariamne killed—and then went almost mad with grief for her.[42]

Rarely has sexual passion played so major a role in history as in these years of Antony and Herod, Cleopatra and Mariamne. The contrast with the calm balance of Octavian and his fifty-two years of serenely happy married life with Livia[43] is most striking. In the perspective of time and eternity, there is a far more profound contrast. For there is good reason to believe that it was during these years that St. Joseph, the ever-chaste head of the Holy Family, was born in Bethlehem of Judea.[44]

On the first of August—the month later named for him—in 30 B.C. Octavian finally arrived in Alexandria. Antony had remained almost despairing ever since Actium. Cleopatra had considered fleeing to India, but was foiled by the destruction of the ships she had brought to the Red Sea to take her and Antony there.[45] On Octavian's arrival Antony killed himself. Cleopatra locked herself in a tower with her famous, long-hoarded treasure of the Ptolemies, thinking to bargain with Octavian by threatening to burn it. It was a childish stratagem to try on the master of the world. The tower was seized with Cleopatra and the treasure intact.[46] She and Octavian met. Ancient historians tell us she tried to seduce him. Most modern historians deny it, regarding our accounts of their meeting as legendary or "rhetorical." But Cleopatra's whole history and character strongly suggest that this is exactly what she would have done in that situation. In her experience, these methods had never failed to work. But in Octavian she found at last a Roman leader who would not yield to her. So Cleopatra too committed suicide, allegedly by the bite of a "sacred" snake, to avoid being displayed in Octavian's triumph like some common barbarian princess.[47]

Rarely if ever in history has one man possessed unchallenged power of the magnitude that now belonged to Octavian. The whole Mediterranean world was united and encompassed in the empire he ruled. To the east the ramshackle Parthian regime[48] might have given the appearance of a threat, but it was only the Roman divisions and civil wars that had made possible the Parthian invasions and occasional battle victories over the Romans. In the year of Actium there were 60 Roman legions in arms. Even after extensive demobilization, 28 remained—some 200,000 peerless fighting men.[49] Octavian commanded them all, to the last javelin. Alexander the Great had almost conquered the whole civilized world with a force one-sixth that size. He was an unparalleled genius, and cautious Octavian was the last man to have sought to emulate him by marching to the end of the world, though almost certainly he could have done so had he wished—he was only three years older than Alexander had been when he died, and nothing between the Euphrates River and the Sea of Japan could have stood against those 28 legions, well led.

However, Octavian's purpose was not more conquests, but a lasting peace. In the year 29 B.C. he made that unmistakably and publicly clear by closing the temple of Janus, an ancient ceremony marking a period of peace that had occurred only twice before in all of Rome's war-filled history.[50] In keeping his peace he then had absolutely nothing to fear externally and, for the moment at least, nothing to fear from internal dissension, of which the Romans had had more than enough during the past hundred years.

To sit upon such a pinnacle of power would have overwhelmed or terrified a weaker man, driven mad a less well-balanced man, rotted with corruption any man even normally subject to temptations of the flesh. Exactly these things— separately or together—were to happen to each of the four immediate successors of Caesar Augustus.[51] None of them happened to him. Was it entirely because of his old Roman virtues, his cultivation of the personal qualities which his clear vision told him he must have to be the architect of an enduring peace? Human nature is too weak for that to be a sufficient explanation. For his work was not only Rome's, but God's. The central event of history was drawing very close. The Prince of Peace needed to begin His work in a time of peace.

On August 13, 29 B.C., Octavian celebrated his splendid triumph, despite a strong personal distaste (very unusual in a Roman) for public displays of this kind. During the following autumn and winter he was ill, but seems to have taken the opportunity to plan in meticulous detail with his two principal advisors—the ever-faithful, hard-headed military commander Agrippa and the brilliant civilian Maecenas—the permanent reconstruction of the Roman and imperial government. As *princeps* (first citizen) with the title ''Augustus'' (one specially favored by the gods) he would be consul every year, with a hand-picked colleague; he would simultaneously hold the proconsular imperium for all the frontier provinces where virtually all of the army was stationed, thereby maintaining his full command over it; he would exercise the powers of both censor and tribune under the old constitution even though not formally designated as the holder of these offices (as a patrician he was technically ineligible to be a tribune, a plebeian office), so that he might control membership in the senate and introduce legislation; he would associate the senate with himself in the government, so as to gain the benefit of all that remained of its ancient prestige and political experience; and he would obtain all this authority, at least in theory and appearance, from the senate and people of Rome—he would not be a king. He called the entire arrangement a "restoration of the republic."[52]

There was hardly a whisper of opposition, for Octavian was both obviously irresistible and honestly seeking peace and harmony for Rome and the empire. The old republican case had faded to mere nostalgic sentiment, and Octavian had no surviving political or military rival. Indeed, by virtue of past senatorial grants he already possessed most of the powers required for his permanent rule. But he saw a need for the formal ratification of his status including all of the powers together, sealed by the grant of his new title. On January 13, 27 B.C., he went before the senate and solemnly relinquished to it all of his powers; three days later the senate gave all of them and more back to him, along with the title "Augustus." The Roman world would never be the same again.[53]

Regarding the Jews, Augustus confirmed all the privileges Julius Caesar had granted them, and assigned to the Jewish population of Rome (now numbering as much as 40,000) the region just across the Tiber adjoining the Vatican hill, where St. Peter's now stands.[54]

Augustus used his unmatched military power to advance the Roman empire (including the now totally subservient client kingdoms) to readily defensible frontiers which could be held firmly and indefinitely against external assault. This involved some substantial extensions of the territory directly ruled by Rome, together with the renunciation of some tempting prospects for conquest which would not really be worthwhile to defend. The Atlantic Ocean to the west and the Sahara Desert to the south were obvious natural frontiers. East of the Euphrates River was the Parthian domain, which Antony had sought in vain to conquer. Augustus saw that Rome's interests did not require a conquest of the very large and distant Iranian plateau so long as the Euphrates frontier was securely held, and Parthian pride in their past victories over Rome memorably humbled. In 20 B.C. Augustus, assembling large Roman forces in Syria and Armenia, put such pressure on the Parthian king Phraates that he had to agree to restore the Roman battle standards taken a generation earlier at Carrhae. This symbolic gesture had the desired effect. Except for continued conflict over the mountainous border region of Armenia, Parthia did not trouble Rome significantly again for 200 years.[55]

Augustus held the north shore of the Black Sea through the client Bosporan kingdom, centered in what is now called the Crimea.[56] From the Black Sea, his plan was to extend the frontier to the broad Danube River. This involved substantial new conquests in eastern Europe, notably in Hungary (Pannonia) and Serbia (Illyricum), valuable not only in bringing the empire up to the easily defensible river line but also in greatly improving east-west land communications in Europe via the valley of the Save River in Illyricum where the important Latin city of Sirmium grew up.[57] This area was to become a stronghold of Latin civilization in its declining years.

From the Danube Augustus' plan was to complete the northern frontier by conquering Germany east to the Elbe River, but not following Julius Caesar's lead across the English Channel into Britain. Here his policy was to prove mistaken and to be changed by his successors, for Britain proved conquerable but central Germany not. Augustus' stepson Drusus conducted a brilliant campaign in Germany between the Rhine and the Elbe from 12 to 9 B.C. but died at the end of it, and this bellicose, uncivilized region could not be held. The Rhine was to remain the Roman frontier in Germany up to the end of the empire in the west.[58]

In 9 B.C. a beautiful altar in honor of Augustus' Roman peace was dedicated in the Field of Mars near Rome. Much of it still survives. Its friezes depict Augustus taking his place with others in his city's celebrations and rites, not glorified or set apart in the manner of oriental royalty, but sharing his honors with the senate and the people. To this extent it was true that he had restored the republic, for he always respected and honored its sound traditions, however much he subtly changed the character of its government which had failed. A particularly significant feature of the Ara Pacis is its lovingly realistic depiction of children, quite different from Greek art, reminding us what Europe had escaped—for all the corruption and civil strife that darkened the late Roman republic—by being saved by Rome from rule by Carthage.[59]

While Augustus was settling the empire as he had settled Rome, Herod was building a new temple in Jerusalem. Herod never really understood the Jewish faith he professed, into which his recent ancestors had been brought by compulsion; but he was anxious to demonstrate how splendidly he honored all its outward symbols, and he was a great builder. He replaced the smaller structure built by the returned exiles from Babylon in the time of King Darius I with what he claimed to be an exact replica of Solomon's temple, but which actually seems to have been much larger and taller than the original. Surrounded by much enlarged outer courts and resting upon an immense stone platform, it towered over Jerusalem to a height of no less than 450 feet from the top of its highest pinnacle to the bottom of the Kedron canyon directly below the city. Herod's version of Solomon's famous temple porch was five times the width of the original and dropped sheer for a great distance on three sides.[60] As A. H. M. Jones describes it:

The whole structure was a fantastic *tour de force* and must have presented a most startling appearance, more like a modern skyscraper than any known building of antiquity.

No expense was spared in the materials of the structure or in its decoration. It was built after the manner of many Syrian temples—Baalbek is a striking example which still survives—of huge blocks of stone; Josephus gives as typical dimensions of a single block 45 by 6 by 5 cubits. The stone employed was a brilliant white marble; Josephus compares the general aspects of the building seen at a distance to a mountain covered with snow. The east front of the Holy Place was plated with gold which reflected the rays of the rising sun with dazzling splendour. The great folding doors of the Holy Place were likewise plated with gold, and across them was drawn a magnificent embroidered veil whose four colours typified the four elements. Over the doorway hung a giant golden vine—replacing that which Aristobulus had given to Pompey—whose clusters were as large as a man.[61]

Construction of Herod's Temple began in January of 19 B.C. The temple proper was completed in just eighteen months, whereupon it was immediately consecrated; the outer courts were completed eight years after that, in 10 B.C. However, some construction work on the Temple continued up to as late as 64 A.D. Within, the regular routine of the animal sacrifices prescribed by the law of Moses continued on every day of every year; and on every day of every year Jewish men and women, rich and poor, came to pray in the vast new courtyards added by Herod, their faces turned toward the curtained darkness of the Holy of Holies in unwavering faith that the Creator-God, the Lord of Hosts Whom no man could see and live, dwelt in a special way in that one place.[62]

Probably only a year or two before the beginning of Herod's rebuilding of the Temple, the Blessed Virgin Mary was born in the little back-country village of Nazareth in Galilee, north of Judea. As the new temple of stone and wood and costly ornaments was rising, she whose womb was to be the first home of God incarnate was simultaneously growing up.[63]

The Messiah the Blessed Virgin Mary was to bear was eagerly, passionately awaited by God's people of Israel. But by now most of them had come to see his advent and his purpose primarily in political and even military terms. The Messiah would free them from the galling Roman yoke and give them the dominion of the world. But this was not what the prophets had actually said; and by no means all of their message had been lost or totally distorted. There remained a vivid though unspecific awareness that the Messiah would be far more than an ordinary man, far more even than an inspired worldly leader. He was not seen as God Himself, but as much more closely associated with God than any other man, indeed as existing with God and cooperating with Him from and in the creation of the world, higher and greater than the angels. The post-Christian rabbinic commentaries on the prophecies of Isaiah as well as the pre-Christian "similitudes" of the Book of Enoch both show a definite belief in the premundane existence, godlike character, and special supernatural origin of the Messiah. There are even two references in rabbinic commentaries which seem distinctly to suggest the virgin birth and direct Divine paternity of the Messiah, by speaking of His "Seed which is to come from another place."[64]

The fullness of the Jews' vision of the Messiah in the days of King Herod was clouded above all by their hatreds. Those who closely followed the teachings of the rabbis, the scribes and the Pharisees had an actual abhorrence of all Gentiles, except for the few who made a serious attempt to live at least in large part by the Mosaic law.[65] There was no sense of a Messianic mission to convert the Gentiles, only a fierce anticipation of savoring a God-given triumph over them which would utterly humiliate them. The Jews alone would be righteous, and their righteousness would win the admiration of all; but there was to be no conversion of the world. Israel ruled by the Messiah would be God's perfect servant, but not the servant of suffering mankind. In their pride and hatred, the harshest of the Jewish leaders were not nearly so far from Herod as they liked to think. This was the climate of opinion that made the Crucifixion possible.

In 9 B.C. Herod was sixty-five years old and had nine sons by seven wives. As each son grew up Herod began to fear him; his fear grew to the verges of paranoia, and blossomed evilly in insane delusions. Herod had a great deal on his conscience. His eldest son Antipater (by his first, Idumaean wife Doris) made every effort to feed his guilt-laden suspicions of his second and third sons, Alexander and Aristobulus, whose mother Mariamne the beautiful Hasmonean he had so passionately loved, killed in a jealous rage, and bitterly grieved for, and whose grandfather, the high priest Hyrcanus, he had also killed. Alexander and Aristobulus had been educated at Rome and were well regarded there. In 12 B.C. Herod accused them to Augustus of plotting his death. Augustus' calm good sense was unruffled by Herod's twisted fantasies and the boys' youthful imprudence (they had from time to time made public reference to the fate of their mother and grandfather) and he arranged a reconciliation. But intrigues—real or imagined—involving his sons continued, Herod made war on the Nabataean Arabs without first consulting Augustus and obtaining his permission as client kings were required to do, and in 9 B.C. Augustus wrote Herod curtly that he would no longer treat him as a friend, but as a servant.[66]

Though the misunderstanding between Augustus and Herod regarding the Nabataean campaign was soon cleared up (even in his most deranged moments Herod never intended to offend all-powerful Rome), Herod's demented suspicion of his sons kept on growing, with the inevitable result that it began to make real a danger which at first had been mostly, if not wholly imaginary. By 9 B.C. there probably were plots against Herod, purely in self-defense, for he was now striking out at any friend or associate of his sons who caught his attention, including their tutors who had long been among his most trusted adherents. A reign of terror began at his court.[67]

NOTES

[1] John Buchan, *Augustus* (London, 1937), pp. 19-20.

[2] *The Cambridge Ancient History*, Volume X (Cambridge, England, 1934, 1952), pp. 2-7.

[3] *Ibid.*, pp. 1-2; Torsten Petersson, *Cicero* (New York, 1963), pp. 594-604.

[4] *Cambridge Ancient History*, X, 3-4.

[5] *Ibid.*, pp. 9-12.

[6] Octavian had the opportunity to accompany Julius Caesar on both his African campaigns culminating in the Battle of Thapsus (46 B.C.) and on his last Spanish campaign culminating in the Battle of Munda (45 B.C.), but on both occasions he was prevented by ill health from arriving in time for the battle, though joining his uncle very shortly afterward (Buchan, *Augustus*, pp. 24-25).

[7] Petersson, *Cicero*, pp. 592-594.

[8] *Cambridge Ancient History*, X, 15-20.

[9] *Ibid.*, pp. 20-22; Buchan, *Augustus*, pp. 67-74.

[10] *Cambridge Ancient History*, X, 22-25; Giuseppe Ricciotti, *The History of Israel* (Milwaukee, 1955), II, 313.

[11] Michael Grant, *Cleopatra* (New York, 1972), pp. 111-123; *Cambridge Ancient History*, X, 39-40.

[12] *Cambridge Ancient History*, X, 28-29.

[13] *Ibid.*, pp. 23, 27.

[14] *Ibid.*, pp. 47-48.

[15] *Ibid.*, pp. 41-43.

[16] *Ibid.*, pp. 43-44.

[17] Ricciotti, *History of Israel*, II, 316-317; Grant, *Cleopatra*, pp. 127-128.

[18] Ricciotti, *History of Israel*, II, 317-318, 314-315; E. Mary Smallwood, *The Jews under Roman Rule, from Pompey to Diocletian* (Leiden, 1981), pp. 53-59.

[19] Antony and Octavia were married in November of 40 B.C.; Octavian, by his unhappy and soon terminated marriage to Scribonia, was childless until January 14, 38 B.C., when Julia, his only child, was born. Three days later Octavian divorced Scribonia and married Livia, to whom he remained devoted for the remaining 52 years of his life (see Note 43, below).

[20] *Cambridge Ancient History*, X, 51.

[21] *Ibid.*, pp. 49-54.

[22] *Ibid.*, pp. 54-55, 66; Grant, *Cleopatra*, pp. 133-134. Grant takes the position, criticized in the text, that Antony's liaison with Cleopatra was of great practical advantage to him at this point.

[23] *Cambridge Ancient History*, X, 67-68.

[24] *Ibid.*, pp. 76-77; Buchan, *Augustus*, pp. 110-113.

[25] *Cambridge Ancient History*, X, 58-60; Grant, *Cleopatra*, pp. 146-147.

[26] *Cambridge Ancient History*, X, 60-61.

[27] *Ibid.*, pp. 73-74.

[28] Buchan, *Augustus*, pp. 102-103.

[29] *Cambridge Ancient History*, X, 61-62.

[30] *Ibid.*, pp. 74-75; Grant, *Cleopatra*, p. 148.

[31] *Cambridge Ancient History*, X, 64, 74.

[32] *Ibid.*, pp. 76-83. For the "treasure of the Ptolemies" see Grant, *Cleopatra*, pp. 211, 216, 218, 223-224.

[33] Grant, *Cleopatra*, pp. 161-167.

[34] *Ibid.*, pp. 168-170.

[35] *Ibid.*, p. 171.

[36] *Ibid.*, pp. 171-180; *Cambridge Ancient History*, X, 80, 83. It is the view of this writer that both W. W. Tarn in *The Cambridge Ancient History* and Michael Grant in his outstanding biography of Cleopatra glorify the statesmanship of their glamorous subject too much. That some imaginative eastern writers associated visions of a golden age with Cleopatra certainly does not prove that she was aiming to create one for anyone but herself. Nothing in her actions and career clearly indicates anything more than personal ambition combined with great personal ability.

[37] Grant, *Cleopatra*, pp. 185-190.

[38] *Ibid.*, pp. 199, 200; *Cambridge Ancient History*, X, 96-97, 100.

[39] *Cambridge Ancient History*, X, 98-99; Grant, *Cleopatra*, pp. 194-195.

[40] *Cambridge Ancient History*, X, 101-105.

[41] Stewart Perowne, *The Life and Times of Herod the Great* (New York, 1957), pp. 70-80.

[42] *Ibid.*, pp. 84-86; Ricciotti, *History of Israel*, II, 329-332.

[43] Buchan, *Augustus*, pp. 250-253.

[44] While Christian scholars generally agree that St. Joseph is most unlikely to have been an old man at the time of his betrothal to the Blessed Virgin Mary, opinion is still divided as to whether he is more likely to have been of the usual marrying age for a Jewish man of that time—18 to 20—or of somewhat more mature years (*e.g.*, Henri Daniel-Rops, *The Book of Mary* [Garden City NY, 1963], pp. 30-31; Francis L. Filas, *Joseph: the Man Closest to Jesus* [Boston, 1962], pp. 65-73; Denis O'Shea, *Mary and Joseph, Their Lives and Times* [Milwaukee, 1949], pp. 81-89). Dating the betrothal of Mary and Joseph to 7 B.C. (see Chapter Fourteen, below), St. Joseph would therefore probably have been born no earlier than 50 B.C. (age 43 at betrothal) and no later than 25 B.C. (age 18 at betrothal) with a greater probability that his birth fell in the latter part of this 25-year period, the decade 35-25 B.C. which saw the climax of the association of Antony and Cleopatra and the domestic tragedy of Herod.

[45] Grant, *Cleopatra*, pp. 217-222.

[46] *Ibid.*, pp. 223-224.

[47] *Ibid.*, p. 225; *Cambridge Ancient History*, X, 109-110; Perowne, *Herod the Great*, p. 81. Grant, with his usual skepticism of anything romantic, doubts that the meeting between Cleopatra and Octavian even took place; Tarn in *The Cambridge Ancient History* accepts the fact of the meeting but not Dio Cassius' account of the attempted seduction, which is quoted by Perowne.

[48] The Parthian kingdom never advanced beyond a primitive feudalism. It remained at a considerably lower economic and political level than both its predecessor, the Achaemenian Persian empire founded by Cyrus which Alexander conquered, and its successor, the Sassanid Persian empire which dealt such blows to the later Roman and Byzantine empires, and upon eastern Christendom. See *Cambridge Ancient History*, X, 257-258.

[49] *Cambridge Ancient History*, X, 120, 222-223, 228.

[50] Buchan, *Augustus*, p. 13.

[51] Tiberius, Gaius "Caligula," Claudius, and Nero. See Chapters Fifteen and Seventeen, below.

[52] Buchan, *Augustus*, pp. 138-146.

[53] *Ibid.*, pp. 147-157.

[54] Alfred Edersheim, *Life and Times of Jesus the Messiah* (New York, 1896), I, 68; H. J. Leon, *The Jews of Ancient Rome* (Philadelphia, 1960), p. 135.

[55] *Cambridge Ancient History*, X, 254-257, 260-264.

[56] *Ibid.*, pp. 265-270.

[57] *Ibid.*, pp. 355-358.

[58] *Ibid.*, pp. 358-363, 376.

[59] *Ibid.*, pp. 546-548.

[60] A. H. M. Jones, *The Herods of Judaea* (Oxford, 1938), pp. 106-107; Perowne, *Herod the Great*, p. 133.

[61] Jones, *Herods of Judaea*, pp. 107-108.

[62] *Ibid.*, pp. 105-106; Perowne, *Herod the Great*, pp. 132, 140-141.

[63] The average age of betrothal for Jewish girls at this period was 14 or 15. Dating the betrothal of the Blessed Virgin Mary and St. Joseph to 7 B.C. (see Chapter Fourteen, below), that would make the year of the Blessed Virgin's birth 21 or 22 B.C. See Daniel-Rops, *Book of Mary*, pp. 29-30.

[64] Edersheim, *Jesus the Messiah*, I, 171-179; F. E. Bruce, *New Testament History* (New York, 1971), pp. 131-133. The "Similitudes of Enoch" is the title often given to 1 Enoch 37-71, whose pre-Christian authorship has been generally accepted by both nineteenth and twentieth century scholars, though its composition was very close in time to Christ. The Son of Man is identified in this portion of Enoch as the "Elect One of righteousness and faith" dwelling "under the wings of the Lord of Spirits" (1 Enoch 39) and as the "Anointed One" of the Lord (1 Enoch 48:10 and 52:4) and is said to have been "named before the Lord of Spirits . . . before the sun and the signs were created, before the stars of heaven were made" (1 Enoch 48).

[65] Edersheim, *Jesus the Messiah*, I, 84-92.

[66] Perowne, *Herod the Great*, pp. 152-162.

[67] *Ibid.*, pp. 162-163.

14.
THE INCARNATION
OF THE LORD
(8-4 B. C.)

And the Word became flesh and dwelt among us, full of
grace and truth; we have beheld his glory, glory as of the
only Son from the Father.—John 1:14

For the believing Christian, the dividing line between history and apologetics
is always rather shadowy and artificial, since all truth is fundamentally one,
and Christianity is pre-eminently an historical religion. The distinction, both
in reason and in faith, vanishes when one comes to deal with the Incarnation
itself. Unlike other historical events, even those specifically Christian, the Incarnation cannot logically be discussed at all apart from its apologetic dimension. To make any serious study of the life of Christ is to meet at every turn
the question: "Who do men say that I am?" And the reader has every right
to ask, first and always, of the historian of Christ: "Who do *you* say that He is?"

In answering this question the historian necessarily passes beyond the bounds
of his intellectual discipline into an area intimately concerned both with the salvation of his own soul, and the souls of his readers. For history cannot in itself
prove any spiritual truth beyond the shadow of a doubt. Christ is proved and
accepted in far higher realms than the historian's. Yet history has a vital part
to play in approaching Him, for it was through history that He came to us; it

is in the context of the historical evidence about Christ that we must make our decision about Him.

Consequently, a forthright avowal of belief or disbelief is the only honest starting point for writing the history of His time that includes or even mentions Him. Yet most modern historians, both Christian and non-Christian, in a sorry spectacle of timidity or confusion of diffidence with charity, pretend that the great question can be evaded or put aside, that one can talk about the life of Christ without drawing any conclusions about His divinity, or by reserving such conclusions to some hypothetical realm of "faith alone," outside of history— as though Christians had not been proclaiming every Sunday at church for twenty centuries, and to non-Christians all over the world for most of that time, their belief in a God Who took on flesh and blood, walked among us, and died on a cross under Pontius Pilate. Hence the fashionable references to the "kerygma" and "catechesis" of the early Christians, as though they were teaching merely an abstract set of doctrinal propositions, rather than the living truth about a living man, a member of the most totally monotheistic people in the world, Who had said in living memory that He was the Son and equal of the Almighty and Ineffable God.

Let there be no mistake about the fact that He did say this—and not only in the Gospel according to St. John. He was condemned to death for blasphemy for saying it. On this all four Gospels are agreed and explicit.

> And the high priest said to him, "I adjure you by the living God, tell us if you are the Christ, the Son of God." Jesus said to him, "You have said so. But I tell you, hereafter you will see the Son of man seated at the right hand of Power, and coming on the clouds of heaven." Then the high priest tore his robes, and said, "He has uttered blasphemy. Why do we still need witnesses? You have now heard his blasphemy. What is your judgment?" They answered, "He deserves death."—Matthew 26:63-66

> Again the high priest asked him, "Are you the Christ, the Son of the Blessed?" And Jesus said, "I am; and you will see the Son of man sitting at the right hand of Power, and coming with the clouds of heaven." And the high priest tore his mantle, and said, "Why do we still need witnesses? You have heard his blasphemy. What is your decision?" And they all condemned him as deserving death.—Mark 14:61-64

> When day came, the assembly of the elders of the people gathered together, both chief priests and scribes; and they led him away to their council, and they said, "If you are the Christ, tell us." But he said to them, "If I tell you, you will not believe; and if I ask you, you will not answer. But from now on the Son of man shall be seated at the right hand of the power of God." And they all said, "Are you the Son of God, then?" And he said to them, "You say that I am." And they said, "What further testimony do we need? We have heard it ourselves from his own lips."
>
> Then the whole company of them arose, and brought him before Pilate.

And they began to accuse him.—Luke 22:66-23:2

> So Jesus came out, wearing the crown of thorns and the purple robe. Pilate said to them, "Here is the man!" When the chief priests and the officers saw him, they cried out, "Crucify him, crucify him!" Pilate said to them, "Take him yourselves and crucify him, for I find no crime in him." The Jews answered him, "We have a law, and by that law he ought to die, because he has made himself the Son of God."—John 19:5-7

Furthermore, St. Matthew's Gospel tells us that He said: "All things have been delivered to me by my Father; and no one knows the Son except the Father, and no one knows the Father except the Son and any one to whom the Son chooses to reveal him." (11:27) If Jesus' claim to divinity is given somewhat less stress in the Gospels of Mark and Luke, it is because—and on this point all Scriptural interpreters, orthodox and modernist, agree—those Gospels were written primarily for a Gentile audience (Roman and Greek) whose understanding of divinity was debased by centuries of polytheism with its gross and absurd myths of divine and semi-divine generation. They needed not so much to hear the claim of divinity as the proof, through the miracles, that Jesus Christ was Lord of nature rather than simply a part of it like their imagined gods.

In the end, questions and disputes about Jesus Christ as an historical figure always come back to the reliability and credibility of the gospels as historical sources. If all four gospels are accepted as historically reliable, no honest reader can escape the question: Who was this man? nor, in answering, avoid the salvational choice between worshipping Him and rejecting Him. In view of the profound dislike of modern man for being pressed into making that choice, it is not surprising that the gospels—and the New Testament in general—have been subjected during the last two centuries to a critical assault far more intense than that ever directed against any other historical documents.[1] It is even denied that the gospels are, or were intended to be, or should be regarded as historical documents, since (as their authors state) their primary purpose is to instil faith. But a document does not cease to be historical because written for some higher purpose than insertion in an archive!

So before approaching the events described in the gospel narratives, we must first survey the bizarre obstacle course set up by this critical barrage. There is scarcely a verse or a line in any gospel that some critic, somewhere, usually equipped with good scholarly credentials, has not contradicted or distorted. One could spend a lifetime simply learning and cataloguing all these contradictions and distortions, often flying straight in the face of the common-sense meaning of the passage in context. How this super-critical mind-set really works was best summed up by Ferdinand Prat, author of one of the great orthodox lives of Christ:

> Let us cease treating the Evangelists as men on trial whose every word

is suspect. When one of them is alone in stating something, certain modern critics who pride themselves on their independence reject his testimony as isolated; when several say the same thing, it seems, we are told, that they must have copied from one another, and their testimony is equally worthless. Were such radical norms applied to profane writers, history could not be written.[2]

Are the gospels reliable accounts of historical events that actually happened as they are described? Sound historical scholarship responds to that question as it would respond to any problem regarding later and widely controverted reports of great events, asking essentially the following questions: (1) Do they present direct eyewitness testimony? (2) Were they written within living memory of the events they describe, and therefore subject to verification or contradiction by others who remembered or witnessed these events? (3) Do they contain obviously fabulous, legendary or mythical material? (4) Are they corroborated at significant points by external, independent testimony from persons not directly involved with the writers or their particular beliefs and goals?

(1) *Eyewitness testimony.* The gospels declare themselves to be the work of four men known to Christians as the Evangelists. Two of these men, Matthew and John, were among the Twelve Apostles selected by Christ early in His public ministry. The Evangelist Mark may also have been an eyewitness of some of the events he narrates, but his principal source was Peter, chief of the apostles. The Evangelist Luke says specifically that he was not an eyewitness, but carefully gathered the testimony of eyewitnesses before writing his Gospel. This evidence about the Evangelists, where not explicitly set forth in their own narratives, is derived from Papias, bishop of Hierapolis in Asia Minor, writing about 125 A.D.—an old man at that time, who could clearly remember the latter part of the Apostolic Age.[3]

It is interesting to note that the authorship of the Gospels of Mark and Luke, who do not claim to have been eyewitnesses of the events they describe, is rarely challenged even by the most radical Biblical critics, while the authorship of the Gospels of Matthew and John by the Apostles bearing their names has been challenged and denied again and again. All human experience testifies to the greater probative value, as a general rule, of personal eyewitness testimony over second-hand information, however diligently researched. It is hard to escape the suspicion that this is the real reason for the persistent attempts of so many critics to prove that the Gospels of Matthew and John were not written by St. Matthew and St. John, while having no difficulty in accepting the almost identically based tradition that the Gospels of Mark and Luke were written by St. Mark and St. Luke.

Actually there is no more reason to deny that St. Matthew and St. John were the authors of the gospels bearing their names than to deny that St. Mark and St. Luke wrote their gospels. It would have been natural and obvious for the apostle most practiced in writing among the Twelve to be the first asked to write an account of the life, death, and resurrection of Christ, primarily for the Jews to whom Christ said He was sent first of all. Matthew, the former tax collector, was according to all we know of the Apostles the most accustomed to writing, because of the profession in which he was engaged when Christ called him. This argues strongly both for the authenticity of his authorship and for his having been the first gospel written (in Aramaic, later rendered into our present Greek version very likely by Matthew himself, who like many Jews at this time, especially those with official connections, was in all probability bilingual.) This is the uniform tradition of the Church. While many Biblical critics have denied the correctness of this tradition, a re-evaluation in favor of the priority of Matthew is now developing, and has recently been championed by none other than the Anglican Bishop John Robinson, long known as a leading exponent of Modernism in Christianity. Nor did the old tradition ever lack able scholarly defenders, though their work was often curiously ignored. In 1951 B. C. Butler, Abbot of Downside, published a brilliant study entitled *The Originality of St. Matthew* in which he carefully and thoroughly explored and exploded the theory of a mysterious ''Q'' source from which the Gospel of Matthew was allegedly drawn, presented the evidence for an Aramaic original and for the priority of the Gospel of Matthew over the Gospel of Mark, and concluded:

> Once it is admitted that Matthew is not based on Mark or on Q, there is a great deal to be said for, and virtually nothing against, the view that it emanated in its Aramaic form from the body of our Lord's own companions before they dispersed beyond the borders of Palestine.[4]

St. Mark's Gospel has long been considered by many Biblical critics to have been the first gospel written, because it is more simply constructed, and because most of the material included in it also appears in St. Matthew's Gospel along with much additional material not found in Mark. But surely these facts are equally well or better explained by concluding that Mark wrote more simply because he was a more simple, less educated man, not because no other gospel existed at the time he wrote; and that he was trying to reach Gentiles, very different in background and habits of thought from the Jews to whom Matthew's Gospel was primarily addressed, and so selected the material which he and St. Peter thought most likely to open Gentile minds and hearts to the truth about Christ. That there are no substantial contradictions between Mark's and Matthew's gospels proves that they were true to the facts of Christ's life and teaching; the differences in style and scope of treatment simply reflect the individuality of the writers and the differing emphases of their later apostolates.

We do not know just what sources St. Luke consulted in researching for his Gospel, but his intimately detailed narrative of the Annuncianon, birth and infancy of Christ contains much that could only have been known originally to the Blessed Virgin Mary. It is a very ancient tradition that Luke did in fact obtain this information directly from her, and he could easily have done so.[5]

The Gospel of John is generally recognized as the last written; but St. John, alone among the Twelve Apostles, is known to have lived to a very great age. A young man at the time of the Crucifixion, perhaps twenty years old, he died at the end of the first century A.D., when he would have been about ninety years old.[6] The definite differences in thought and style between John's Gospel and the other three gospels (often called the "synoptics" because their narratives fit closely together, with fewer points of contact with John's) are most reasonably explained as the fruit of a lifetime's reflection and mystical contemplation on the Incarnation. Christian mystics from the death of St. John to this day have meditated on the redemptive Passion of Christ; St. John alone among them all who left us words in writing, alone even among the Twelve Apostles, personally beheld the Passion in the flesh. Along with the Blessed Virgin Mary and Mary Magdalene and another Mary of whom we know too little, he stood at the foot of the True Cross all during the three hours of God's agony. Is it any wonder, with that experience burned forever into his mind and soul, that St. John writes differently—and more gloriously—than the other Apostles and Evangelists?

Yet many modern critics persist in denying that the words in the Gospel of John are the words of St. John the Apostle, the son of Zebedee the fisherman, or that the words of Christ which he gives us accurately reflect what Christ said and meant, particularly about His divinity. They deny that this Gospel is eyewitness testimony. But rarely if ever do they come to grips with two extraordinary passages in this Gospel which, if human communication means anything, are directed *straight at these critics themselves*:

> So the soldiers came and broke the legs of the first, and of the other who had been crucified with him; but when they came to Jesus and saw that he was already dead, they did not break his legs. But one of the soldiers pierced his side with a spear, and at once there came out blood and water. *He who saw it has borne witness—his testimony is true, and he knows that he tells the truth—that you also may believe.* For these things took place that the scripture might be fulfilled, "Not a bone of him shall be broken." And again another scripture says, "They shall look on him whom they have pierced."—John 19:32-37 (emphasis added)

> Peter turned and saw following them the disciple whom Jesus loved, who had lain close to his breast at the supper and had said, "Lord, who is it that is going to betray you?" When Peter saw him, he said to Jesus, "Lord, what about this man?" Jesus said to him, "If it is my will that he remain until I come, what is that to you? Follow me!" The saying spread abroad among the brethren that this disciple was not to die; yet Jesus did not say to him that he was not to die, but, "If it is my will that he remain until I come, what is that to you?"

> *This is the disciple who is bearing witness to these things, and who has*

written these things; and we know that his testimony is true. —John 21:20-24
(emphasis added)

Who is speaking in the italicized passages? First of all St. John himself;
then, confirming him and testifying for him, his first hearers, who presumably
aided him in the physical task of committing his words to paper. The very truths
about the composition and witness of his Gospel which modern critics reject
are here most solemnly and explicitly avowed, in a context where surely any
man who believed that Christ would come to judge the world and everyone in
it (can anyone doubt that whoever wrote John's Gospel must have believed that?)
would tremble to tell a lie. Rarely if ever does the critic who denies that St.
John's Gospel presents eyewitness testimony, that it accurately reports the words
of Christ, that it was in fact written by the Apostle John, the son of Zebedee
the fisherman, dare to assert openly that these two statements are sheer per-
jury. Yet that is precisely what the position he holds requires him to believe.
The battle is joined. Either the Gospel speaks falsely or the critic does. There
can be no third position; there can be no compromise.

(2) *Date of Writing Within Living Memory.* The original modernist critical
assault relegated all the gospels to the second century A.D. or even later. As
evidence mounted that at least the first three could not possibly be that late,
the critics continued to insist that St. John's Gospel, at least, was written well
beyond the bounds of living memory[7] of the events it described.

(Here again we find St. John's Gospel at the eye of the hurricane. Why?
Is it, can it really be, for any other reason than that this gospel poses most starkly,
most inescapably, the sundering question: *Who was this Man?*—this Man Who
declared, as only St. John tells us, "Before Abraham was, I AM"?[8] Was this
the principal reason that St. John wrote his Gospel as he did, to make the question and the choice inescapable for any honest man who read and believed him?)

Then came the enormously important discovery of the Rylands papyrus fragment of St. John's Gospel in a remote area of Upper Egypt, in 1935. The fragment, word for word in accord with our standard text, was dated by paleographic
analysis (analysis of the manner in which the letters were formed) to the first
decades of the second century, probably about 130, very possibly earlier.[9] This
fits perfectly with the traditional dates of 95-100 A.D. for St. John's death and
the commitment of his Gospel to writing, especially since the place where the
Rylands papyrus fragment was found, at the very edge of the ancient civilized
world far down into Africa, nearly two thousand miles from Ephesus where
St. John died, indicates a very wide dissemination of his Gospel by 130 and
consequently a considerably earlier date of original writing.

As for the date of the first three gospels, virtually all critics would now put
them before 90, and the majority before 70, well within living memory of the
events of Christ's life, death, and resurrection. Even critics proceeding from

assumptions about the composition and character of Scripture very different from those maintained here are now beginning to discover strong arguments from their own premises for pushing the dates of composition of the Gospels of Matthew and Mark back to the 40's and 50's A.D. (the period when tradition always held they were written) and to accept the clear evidence from the point at which the Book of Acts ends and the manner of its conclusion, that it was written in 62 or 63 A.D., with Luke's Gospel a little earlier.[10] No one had ever really refuted the traditional dating; it had simply been abandoned by academic fashion and out of theological prejudice, so often the fate of old and sound positions in our change-obsessed age.

The full significance of this steady retreat by the critics and move toward the restoration of traditionally early dates for the composition of the gospels has not yet been sufficiently appreciated by Christian historians and apologists. Since by almost everyone's reckoning the gospels are now seen to have been written well within living memory of Christ, the capability of the authors to distort the truth about Him—even if not deliberately, even presuming that this is what they were doing—is sharply curtailed. If Christ did not claim to be God, perform miracles, rise from the dead and appear resurrected in the flesh, then there were many still alive when the gospels were first written and circulated who knew what He had really taught and done, and in faithfulness to His memory would have resisted and denounced the innovations of writers attributing to Him claims of divinity He never made. All religions and ideologies produce strong and active opposition to attempted major innovations and reinterpretations. But there is absolutely no evidence of any group in the first century which claimed to follow Christ, but did not accept His divinity.[11] Surely in all the controversial letters of St. Paul, at least, there would have been some reference, however derogatory, to such a group and its beliefs, if it existed. There is none. Only in the second century A.D., after the close of the Apostolic Age and beyond the limits of living memory of Christ, does the Ebionite sect of Christian Jews appear, denying that Jesus of Nazareth was the Son of God though honoring Him as one through whom God spoke and acted in a special way.[12] What the critics who deny the Incarnation must regard as the original and correct interpretation of the life of Jesus therefore turns out to have almost exactly the same late date they originally attempted, without lasting success even on their own academic terms, to impute to the gospels.

(3) *Use of Fabulous, Legendary or Mythical Material.* The first problem is to define such material accurately and without prejudice. The non-Christian historian characteristically assumes *a priori*, without proof, argument or justification, explicitly or implicitly, that *all* reports of the miraculous fall into this category. An increasing number of historians and other writers who still claim some Christian affiliation now make the same assumption, usually on the grounds that this has become the academic standard. Such writers should be asked to

explain on what basis they assume that no miracle can ever happen and that therefore, automatically, any document reporting a miracle is fabulous, legendary, or mythical. An atheist writer at least has a logically consistent position up to a point, though in the end it must founder upon the rock of human contingency. But if, as is usually the case, the writer still acknowledges God, his argument comes down to a mere assertion of his personal opinion that God would never work a miracle—an opinion which by any fair standard of judgment is insufficient to reject solemnly avowed testimony out of hand.

On the other hand, clearly there are such things as fables, legends, and myths. They tell, not of miracles, but of magic. Whatever our modern habits of thought may incline us to assume, the two are fundamentally different. God works miracles to help save souls, heal bodies, open the way to faith, or give special aid in desperate situations. Magic has no purpose but to astonish; magical events are trivial where not unnatural or diabolical. Such magical events constitute the fabulous element in literature, a marked characteristic of the apocryphal gospels and purported accounts of the works of the Apostles which the Church refused to include in the canon of the New Testament. It is immediately obvious in comparing these apocrypha, or other contemporary mythological literature even when involving Christian themes, with the canonical gospels, that the canonical gospels are fundamentally different in form, style, emphasis, and purpose. They have none of the fabulous and magical material at all.

(4) *Independent Verification*. Most men tend to make the strongest possible case for that in which they believe, and are often tempted to distort facts to strengthen the case in support of their beliefs. Even in the absence of internal evidence of distortion, when a set of reported facts is highly unusual or widely controverted, its credibility is always enhanced by corroboration from sources holding a different belief, or uncommitted. Rarely can every challenged point be independently corroborated in this way; but whatever of such corroboration there may be strengthens the argument in favor of the historical reliability of the narrative in question.

A major independent source, the Romanized Jewish historian Flavius Josephus, who wrote—like the Evangelists—in the first century A.D., provides direct corroboration of the gospels' report on the life of Christ at several vital points. Josephus' principal works are his immense history of his own people, *The Antiquities of the Jews*, and his account of the origins and events of their great war with the Romans which ended with the destruction of the Temple in 70 A.D., *The Jewish War*. All extant manuscripts of the *Antiquities* contain a passage referring explicitly to the life, miracles, crucifixion, and resurrection of Jesus, along with the suggestion that these reports and their evident factual basis prove Him to have been something more than a man. The passage, as translated by the noted Josephan scholar H. St. John Thackeray, runs as follows:

Now about this time arises Jesus, a wise man, if indeed he should be called a man. For he was a doer of marvellous deeds, a teacher of men who receive the truth with pleasure; and he won over to himself many Jews and many also of the Greek (nation). He was the Christ. And when, on the indictment of the principal men among us, Pilate had sentenced him to the cross, those who had loved (or perhaps rather ''been content with'') him at the first did not cease; for he appeared to them on the third day alive again, the divine prophets having (fore)told these and ten thousand other wonderful things concerning him. And even now the tribe of Christians, named after him, is not extinct.[13]

The Jewish War contains several passages referring to Jesus, but only in a Slavonic (Old Russian) translation, first edited and published in 1906. The Jewish scholar Robert Eisler, in a work unfortunately marred by anti-Christian animus and by exaggerated and fanciful theorizing, despite these flaws presents a powerful case for the Slavonic manuscript having been translated from an early edition of The Jewish War which is nowhere else preserved.[14] The most important of the passages referring to Jesus in the Slavonic translation of The Jewish War are as follows:

It was at that time that a man appeared—if ''man'' is the right word—who had all the attributes of a man but seemed to be something greater. His actions, certainly, were superhuman, for he worked such wonderful and amazing miracles that I for one cannot regard him as a man; yet in view of his likeness to ourselves I cannot regard him as an angel either. Everything that some hidden power enabled him to do he did by an authoritative word. Some people said that their first Lawgiver had risen from the dead and had effected many marvellous cures; others thought he was a messenger from heaven. However, in many ways he broke the Law—for instance, he did not observe the Sabbath in the traditional manner. At the same time his conduct was above reproach. He did not need to use his hands: a word sufficed to fulfill his every purpose.

Many of the common people flocked after him and followed his teaching. There was a wave of excited expectation that he would enable the Jewish tribes to throw off the Roman yoke. As a rule he was to be found opposite the City on the Mount of Olives, where also he healed the sick. He gathered round him 150 assistants and masses of followers. When they saw his ability to do whatever he wished by a word, they told him that they wanted him to enter the City, destroy the Roman troops, and make himself king; but he took no notice. . . . When the crowds grew bigger than ever, he earned by his actions an incomparable reputation. The exponents of the Law were mad with jealousy, and gave Pilate 30 talents to have him executed. Accepting the bribe, he gave them permission to carry out their wishes themselves. So they seized him and crucified him in defiance of all Jewish tradition. . . .

In the days of our pious fathers this curtain [of the Temple] was intact, but in our own generation it was a sorry sight, for it had been suddenly rent from top to bottom at the time when by bribery they had secured the execution of the benefactor of men—the one who by his actions proved that he was no mere man. Many other awe-inspiring "signs" happened at the same moment. It is also stated that after his execution and entombment he disappeared entirely. Some people actually assert that he had risen; others retort that his friends stole him away. I for one cannot decide where the truth lies. A dead man cannot rise by his own power; but he might rise if aided by the prayer of another righteous man. Again, if an angel or other heavenly being, or God Himself, takes human form to fulfill his purpose, and after living among men dies and is buried, he can rise again at will. Moreover it is stated that he could not have been stolen away, as guards were posted round his tomb, 30 Romans and 1,000 Jews.[15]

In a normal historians' controversy this contemporary testimony from an obviously disinterested party, independently verifying the gospel accounts of Jesus' miracles, death, and reported resurrection, would be decisive. But in this dispute far more is at stake than in any other, so the critics return to the attack with a challenge to the authenticity of all these passages in Josephus, fortified by some real difficulties they present—notably, the phrase "he was the Christ" in the passage from the *Antiquities*,[16] and the clear implication in the passage from the Slavonic translation of *The Jewish War* that the Jews allowed the Temple curtain to remain in place for many years while torn from top to bottom[17]. Some Christian editing or interpolation is possible. But, as Thackeray emphasizes for the passage on Christ in *The Antiquities of the Jews* and as the historian S. G. F. Brandon emphasizes for the passages on Christ in the Slavonic version of *The Jewish War*, not only do they show clear characteristics of Josephus' style, but overall they are simply not the kind of writing that a Christian forger or commentator of patristic or medieval times would have done.[18] The puzzled, sophisticated doubt which Josephus expresses as he reviews what he knows of the life of Jesus is very characteristic of his pagan world (illustrated by Pilate's famous question to Christ: "What is truth?") as it is of our own time, but emphatically not of the Christian centuries.

In light of all these considerations, the Christian need not hesitate to proclaim the Incarnation a fact of history, as well attested as any other historic fact in ancient times, indeed better documented than most. (There are long spans of time in ancient history when the greater part of our knowledge of major historical events depends on a single book, in some cases originally available to scholars of the modern age only in a single manuscript. The history of Tacitus is a well-known example.) Some may doubt or deny the historical reality of the Incarnation, just as all human testimony, no matter how truthful or well substantiated, may be doubted or denied by some members of a fallen race. But by all normal standards of historical judgment on sources and evidence the Incarnation is a fact, and would unquestionably be almost universally recognized as such if the existing testimony and evidence referred to any morally and spiritually neutral event reported for this period. Therefore we may proclaim it so, proceeding to the life of Christ which the gospels relate, and leaving a point-by-point answer to the fine-spun theories of the "demythologizers" to some other series of volumes which, to be complete, would have to be at least as long as this one.

As we of the twentieth century return to these timeless and surpassingly beautiful documents, the Good News of the Incarnation, we should have one constant care: never for an instant to forget that when we are reading about Jesus, we are reading about God. Other ages have been captivated by the opposite danger, of forgetting that He is man, of seeing His humanity swallowed up in His divinity, going even to the point of the Docetist heresy that His humanity was no more than an appearance, like a projection on a screen. But Docetism is far from being today's popular or intellectually fashionable heresy. The whole thrust of our age and culture and mind-set, stemming from a hundred different sources, is to dwell on the humanity of Jesus at the *expense* of His divinity, thinking only of how He was a man like us and as little as possible—or not at all—of how He was and is and ever shall be the Eternal, Transcendent, Immutable, Uncreated God.

We are told that this modern approach to Jesus will make Him more lovable, more understandable, more real. These great goods do indeed flow from a vivid awareness of the humanity of God the Son. But if we do not also always keep clearly in mind that He *is* God, we shall never grasp the essential significance of His humanity. He will become just another prophet or teacher, even if called the greatest of these; all that He tells us about Himself will be omitted or distorted. Whenever the gospel narratives show us Jesus speaking or acting, we of the twentieth century need forcibly to remind ourselves that this is God speaking and acting, as well as man. It is not for us to plumb the depths of the mystery of two natures in one person, the stupendous miracle of the Incarnation. That is the province of theology, ultimately of faith alone. But believing Christians know that Jesus is God Incarnate, fully God and fully man, divine and human, His every word and action consequently touched both by His divinity and by His humanity.

Nowhere is this more evident than in the circumstances of His advent.

The year was 747 of the Roman era—*ab urbe condita*, reckoned from the legendary founding of the imperial city by Romulus and Remus the wolf-children—according to our calendar (distorted at this point by a relatively minor historical error on the part of its original designer, the monk Dionysius the Little), 7 B.C.[19] Half-demented King Herod, grown monstrous with bitter age (67) and raging hate, had just executed his two sons by Mariamne, his one-time great love whom he had also murdered many years before; Caesar Augustus commented that it was better to be Herod's pig than his son. The boys had died by the strangler's noose, along with 300 officials at Jericho suspected of collusion with them. The king had dyed his white hair black, the better to pretend that he was young again. The world and the Chosen People looked upon this spectacle of evil with the mixture of fear and unhealthy fascination such spectacles always evoke.[20]

Yet in the Promised Land, blessed long ago by God Himself when He led His Chosen People there and gave it to them, were two temples for Him: one the mighty structure of stone on the site where (except for the fifty years of the exile in Babylonia and the three years of Antiochus IV's profanation at the time of the Maccabees) He had been honored with sacrifice and incense and prayer and vows[21] for just short of a thousand years; the other of flesh and blood, a girl about fourteen years old, "a virgin betrothed to a man whose name was Joseph, of the house of David, and the virgin's name was Mary."[22] Mary and Joseph lived in Nazareth, a little village tucked away in the Galilean hills in the northern part of Palestine. There is good reason to believe that before her betrothal Mary had pledged her virginity to God, so that her marriage to Joseph was only to give her a protector and legal status in a society which—except for the Essene communities at Qumran and elsewhere—had no place for the consecrated celibate life.[23] In the temple at Jerusalem the sacrifice of lambs and the burning of incense went on, morning and afternoon, every day of every year. Some twenty thousand priests, descendants of Aaron and Levi, were eligible to offer the incense on the golden altar of the sanctuary, alone before the curtain which screened the Holy of Holies. Each one, chosen by lot, did so just once in all his life.[24]

It was probably in this year 747 a.u.c./7 B.C. that the priest Zachary was chosen for this highest honor that life could bring to an ordinary Israelite of the priestly tribe.[25] Zachary and his wife Elizabeth had lived holy lives, striving always to please God and to keep His commandments; but they were old, and Elizabeth had borne no children. As Zachary offered the incense, wholly alone before God, he prayed—probably then, as certainly earlier, for a son; and certainly, as pious Jewish men prayed regularly and especially on this most holy occasion of offering their once-in-a-lifetime priestly sacrifice to God, for the long-awaited coming of the Messiah.[26] Amidst all the attention rightly given to the Annunciation to Mary and the birth of Christ in Bethlehem, it has not often been remembered that the whole stupendous drama of the Incarnation, as it happened to our human sight, began with this prayer of Zachary. Prayer has a power of which even two millennia of Christianity have not always made us sufficiently aware.

The Angel Gabriel, "who stands in the presence of God," came to Zachary in the sanctuary, to tell him first of all that he came in answer to his prayer. Zachary would have a son, who should be called John, whose mission would be "to make ready for the Lord a people prepared."[27] John the Baptist was to be the last and the greatest of the prophets of the old covenant, and the herald and immediate precursor of the new.[28] Zachary emerged from the sanctuary dumb; he told only his wife, by writing, about the revelation he had received, and they went into seclusion for six months.[29]

Since she was not yet living with Joseph,[30] Mary must still have been at the home of her parents, according to tradition named Joachim and Anne.[31] Presumably, like most dwellers in Nazareth then and for long afterward, they lived in a natural cave in the soft rock built up at the entrance so as to serve as a humble home.[32] Luke's language clearly indicates that the Angel Gabriel actually entered the dwelling and spoke with Mary alone inside,[33] using the words whose millions upon millions of repetitions have been counted in Heaven through all the centuries the Rosary has been prayed: "Hail Mary, full of grace, the Lord is with you."[34] Then the angel told her that she had been chosen to be the Mother of the Eternal God, Whose kingdom has no end—if she agreed. She asked how this could be, in view of her vow of virginity, and the answer came in those glowing, perfect words: "The Holy Spirit will come upon you, and the power of the Most High will overshadow you."[35] Her Divine Son was to have no human father, only His Father in Heaven.[36]

Gabriel went on to tell Mary of the miraculous conception of John the Baptist in the previously barren womb of Elizabeth, who was related to Mary, reminding her that "with God nothing will be impossible."[37] Then came Mary's humble acceptance—on which, as a free act of her own will, depended the fate of billions of souls, the whole destiny of the human race. There in the room of the cave-house in little, forgotten Nazareth, alone except for the angel, utterly unknown to the mighty of the world then hanging in the balance, she paused, while the King of the Universe waited upon her answer.

"Behold, I am the handmaid of the Lord, let it be done to me according to your word."[38]

In that moment, according to most orthodox theologians, the Incarnation was accomplished.[39] For the next nine months Mary Immaculate carried God in her womb.

As soon as she could arrange it, Mary left Nazareth to visit Elizabeth, her relative whose special blessing of a son the Angel Gabriel had reported to her. It is most unlikely that Joseph accompanied her.[40] She may have travelled alone or with a caravan, riding a donkey or on foot—but probably in company for safety and on foot because of her poverty. If she wore the usual women's costume of that time and country, she was clad in a blue dress with a red cloak, or a red dress with a blue cloak, with a large white veil. The journey to Ain Karem near Jerusalem, the probable site of Zachary's and Elizabeth's home, would have taken at least four days; the roads were often steep and rocky.[41] Even if with a caravan, Mary was in a human sense utterly alone during that journey, for no one in all the world knew or could possibly have begun to imagine her secret, that she carried in her body the salvation of mankind. Her attention must have been focussed constantly on the glory within her. Mary's lonely journey from Nazareth to Ain Karem on the occasion of the Visitation would seem to merit more attention than it has generally received in theological and devotional works.

When she arrived at Elizabeth's home and Elizabeth came to greet her, Mary at last found another whom God had enlightened about her Son. Elizabeth welcomed her as "the mother of my Lord" and John the Baptist in Elizabeth's womb "leaped for joy" as, according to orthodox Catholic theology, he was baptized and sanctified by Christ from Mary's womb.[42] Mary responded with her sublime Magnificat:

> My soul magnifies the Lord,
> and my spirit rejoices in God my Savior,
> for he has regarded the low estate of his handmaiden.
> For behold, henceforth all generations will call me blessed;
> for he who is mighty has done great things for me,
> and holy is his name.
> And his mercy is on those who fear him
> from generation to generation.[43]

It seems overwhelmingly probable that Mary remained with Elizabeth until John was born, only then returning to Nazareth.[44] It had now been nearly four months since the Incarnation, and Mary's pregnancy had become visible; yet still, not having been directed to reveal it, she kept her cosmic secret even from Joseph. Knowing her to be spotlessly pure, and knowing at the same time that the child she was carrying could not possibly be his because of the total continence of their relationship, he struggled to decide what he should do. Public denunciation and repudiation of Mary—the usual action of a Jewish man under such circumstances—was unthinkable; but to proceed with the marriage without knowing the truth about this child seemed wrong for a just man, a descendant of David who lived by the Law and honored all the traditions of his people. So Joseph, debating with himself, inclined toward a private separation. When the child was born it would be assumed to be his, for Jewish betrothal customs of that time apparently often involved intercourse between betrothal and marriage, which was not regarded as a serious sin. Whatever public blame there might be would fall upon him rather than upon her, since people would assume that had Mary been guilty of infidelity Joseph would have denounced her.[45]

But the choice was extraordinarily difficult. Joseph's own profound love for Mary must have impelled him, despite the tyranny of custom, to the course that naturally suggests itself to us: stand by her, marry her regardless of the unexplained pregnancy, and wait for God to reveal the truth. The language of the terse Greek text of St. Matthew's Gospel which is our only source for Joseph's ordeal on this occasion—in the original, though not in most translations—indicates a firm decision on his part not to defame Mary in any way, and only a tentative leaning toward the separation.[46] In his doubt and great distress he would have prayed much for God's help and enlightenment, and Mary would have been praying constantly for him; and so another angelic message came, to reassure Joseph that it was right for him to take Mary as his wife, and informing him of the virginal conception and salvific mission of Jesus.[47]

Thus Joseph became, to all outward appearance at the time, the father of Jesus; and through his adoptive or foster fatherhood he transmitted to Jesus juridically the lineage of David, which was sufficient in Jewish law and custom to establish the descent of Jesus from David which the prophets had foretold of the Messiah.[48]

While Joseph and Mary dwelt together in Nazareth and the time neared for the birth of their Divine Son, a command in the name of the far-distant ruler of their world, Caesar Augustus of the Roman peace, crashed into their quiet, hidden life. Augustus' orderly mind, which made him so great an administrator, sought accurate, detailed records of the available human and material resources of the Roman empire. Consequently he ordered a series of censuses. In 28 B.C. there had been a census of Roman citizens throughout the empire, and of all the inhabitants of Gaul. In 8 B.C. there had been another general census of Roman citizens. Now there was to be a census in Palestine, conducted in the Jewish manner, with every man registering in his ancestral home, but with the returns to go to the Roman authorities in Syria who had ultimate responsibility for affairs in Palestine, even though juridically Palestine was a separate client kingdom under Herod. That this census was probably ordered for a larger area than Palestine is strongly indicated by the evidence of a Roman census in Egypt at this very time, 6-5 B.C.[49]

Whether Herod played any part in the taking of this census in Palestine we do not know, but traditionally the Jews had always resented and resisted any enumeration of their people, even by a government of their own. (King David himself had once ordered a census, then repented it and confessed it to God as a sin, choosing a pestilence upon the land as a punishment.)[50] Resentment and resistance to a census ordered by a Gentile ruler could be expected to be still greater. The later Roman census of 6 A.D., under Coponius as procurator of Judea, was the immediate cause of a major revolt by Judas the Galilean, supported by many of the Pharisees, which originated the long-lasting revolutionary movement of the Zealot party, active in Palestine until their short-lived triumph in the great revolt of the Jewish War.[51] Though we have no explicit evidence of a connection, there is a strong possibility that Herod's known demand early in the year 6 B.C. that all his people swear a special oath of loyalty to Caesar Augustus, followed by his harsh punishment of leading Pharisees for inducing 6,000 people to refuse this oath, grew out of popular opposition to a Roman census in progress or imminent at that time. In any case, the imposition of this oath by Herod clearly shows the lack of real significance in the juridical distinction between client kingdom and province, sometimes used as an argument against the historicity of the report in Luke's Gospel of the census being taken in Palestine at the time of Christ's birth.[52]

There remains the historical problem arising from Luke's statement that this census was ordered when "Quirinius was governor of Syria" and the fact that Quirinius, though he was later governor of Syria, definitely held a position of military authority in the region of Syria earlier, and was probably also governor at an earlier date, was not the regular governor at any time between 8 and 4 B.C., when that office was held by C. Sentius Saturninus (8-6) and P. Quinctilius Varus (6-4). There is no doubt, however, that Quirinius was very active in the Roman East during the last decade of the first century B.C. as well as the first decade of the first century A.D. We have independent verification from the later Christian writer Tertullian that the census at the time of the birth of Christ was in progress when Saturninus was governor (8-6 B.C.). No anachronism has been proven, merely a lack of knowledge on our part of the detailed arrangements for Roman administration in the Syrian region at this period and of the exact length of time required for a general census. Probably the two best solutions to the long-standing, much-discussed historical problem of Quirinius and the census at the time of Christ's birth are: (1) that the principal governor was assisted from time to time by a second high official for specific purposes such as census taking, and that Quirinius was that second official in this case; (2) that Quirinius was governor of Syria before 8 or after 4 B.C., and either began in 9 the census which Saturninus completed by 6, or completed by 3 the census which Saturninus began in 6. That there was a census under Saturninus, whose term of office ran to 6 B.C., is surely established by Tertullian's evidence as well as many generally accepted historical facts for that ancient period can be authenticated. Both Justin Martyr, writing in the middle of the second century within living memory of the Apostolic Age, and Tertullian writing at the end of that century, explicitly state that the records of this census were preserved down to their time in the archives of Rome.[53]

The requirement of registration at each man's ancestral home meant that Joseph would have to travel almost a hundred miles to Bethlehem, whence the family of David had so spectacularly sprung a thousand years before. He could not leave Mary behind, for her Son's birth was imminent; not only would Joseph's love for Mary never have permitted separation at such a time, but for the foster father of the Incarnate Lord to be absent on His day of birth was unthinkable. So Mary made the journey with him, over mostly the same roads she had travelled on her visit to Elizabeth in the spring.

Thus Mary and Joseph came to Bethlehem, in the "silent night" which Christians ever since have taken to their hearts, and in a cave-stable with none but those two at first to adore Him, the Maker of the Cosmos invaded the world He had crafted and was constantly sustaining in being, coming secretly, underground, speechless and helpless in His infant humanity, yet still and always the Lord of the galaxies and the light-years, the Savior Who was to conquer death and open the gates of Heaven. The angels sang of His coming above the pastures around Bethlehem, and shepherds heard them—men despised as unclean by doctors of the Law, scribes and Pharisees,[54] yet true Israelites who yearned for the Messiah and, now that He had come, were humble enough to accept Him on His own terms rather than demanding that He conform to their preconceived ideas about Him. After Mary and Joseph, the shepherds of Bethlehem were the first of all men privileged to know and to worship their Lord and Redeemer in the flesh. They enter history on Christmas night; they drop out of history the next morning. But they left a mark—and not only in Nativity sets.

It was of the fundamental nature of the Incarnation that it could happen only once. There could be only one Divine-human life, as there was only one God the Son; once only could God be a baby. And so it is natural and proper that the place where the Divine infant lay, the home of the shepherds who were the first after Mary and Joseph to adore Him, should be uniquely blessed.

Bethlehem . . . There was no room at its inn for the Mother of God, but there was room in its shepherds' hearts, and God does not forget. Bethlehem . . . Two hundred years passed, the Jews were driven out, pagans entered in, Christianity was proscribed and persecuted, the little town had few visitors yet, but Origen could write: "In Bethlehem you are shown the cave where he was born, and within the cave, the manger where he was wrapped in swaddling clothes. These things which they show you are recognized in the district."[55] Bethlehem . . . Eleven hundred years passed; the Muslims—the Scourge of God, Christendom's deadliest enemies of all time—had ruled Palestine for nearly half a millennium and converted most of its population from Christianity to Islam; even in Nazareth there was hardly a Christian to be found; yet when the First Crusade arrived, Bethlehem welcomed the Crusaders as deliverers, for it had remained almost entirely a Christian town.[56] Bethlehem . . . in 1266 the fanatically anti-Christian Sultan Baybars of Egypt drove all Christians out of the town and demolished its walls; but within a very few years, they came back.[57] Bethlehem . . . shortly after 1517 the terrible Sultan Selim the Grim of Turkey demolished the entire town and filled up its moats; but an Italian traveller of 1586 reported still finding Christians there.[58] Bethlehem . . . Almost two thousand years have now passed since the first Christmas, and through all this twentieth century after Our Lord, Bethlehem has been a plaything of war and power politics, passed from Turk to Briton to Arab to Jew, now on the debatable ground of Israeli-occupied Arab Palestine, the "West Bank"—yet still, a quiet light shining through storm and turmoil and strife, *almost entirely a Christian town.*[59]

The shepherds of the first Christmas—they and theirs, for eighty generations—with the unfailing help of God who was born there a man and blessed them from His manger, have kept the Faith. Dare we predict that Bethlehem, at least, will still be Christian when the world ends? Will there be one at least from Bethlehem to answer "yes" to that terrible question: "When the Son of Man comes, will he find faith on earth"?[60]

Some hint of this deathless loyalty in Bethlehem may have come to Mary and Joseph despite its initially inhospitable reception of them, for it appears that they now decided to remain in Bethlehem rather than return to Nazareth, and took up their abode in a house there.[61] Jerusalem and the Temple were only seven miles away. Forty days after Jesus' birth they went to present Him in the Temple as the Law of Moses prescribed, and to make the offering for a first-born son which the Law commanded.[62] In the Temple the infant God was recognized and adored by two old and holy people who had waited in prayer for many years for the opportunity to see the Messiah in the flesh: Simeon and Anna. Simeon may have been the man of that name honored by the Jews as one of the holiest and most learned teachers in all their history, the son of the great Rabbi Hillel and the father of the Rabbi Gamaliel, who was later to defend the Christians before the Sanhedrin.[63]

Returning to Bethlehem with the Child, Mary and Joseph were about to have a new visitation, of a kind they could hardly have imagined, since all those so far who had recognized Jesus had been deeply believing Israelites. But Jesus had come to bring salvation to the Gentiles as well, and they too were to send representatives to welcome and worship Him in Bethlehem.

By now it was probably 5 B.C. The seven miles separating Bethlehem from Jerusalem were like a bridge from Heaven to Hell. In a poor little house in Bethlehem Joseph worked at his carpenter's bench; Mary's radiant face bent over the Christ-Child, to bring forth His first smile; angels hovered. In his splendid palace at Jerusalem Herod felt the hatred of his people like a licking flame; with impotent fury he knew how they would rejoice when he was dead. A cancer was seeding in his bowels. He had more sons to kill: Antipater, his eldest, was next. (Herod would slay him just five days before his own hideous death.) Pretenders and false Messiahs were awaiting their opportunity. Herod knew that his patron Augustus despised him now, for the emperor was in most respects a decent and honorable man; he preferred not to deal with monsters. The world held nothing more for Herod. Abysses yawned beneath his stumbling feet.[64]

His spies brought word that sages from the east were in Jerusalem inquiring about a king of the Jews, most certainly not he. They seemed to be talking about a newborn baby. Herod questioned them himself. They spoke of an extraordinary astronomical sign, probably the recent conjunction of three planets in the constellation Pisces (the Fishes) during the preceding winter,[65] and of a king so holy He was to be worshipped, whose reign meant splendid new hope for the whole world. Apparently their Divine King was the Israelite Messiah. How had they known of Him? If they came from Iran, as the references to them as "magi" clearly suggest (Magi were found only in Iran), they were in the Zoroastrian tradition, whose ancient links with the revelation to Israel we have examined;[66] there is an echo of the Messianic hope in the Zoroastrian *Avesta*.[67] By study of the Hebrew Scriptures they could have come to understand these links themselves, thereby being prepared to hear and answer the call of the sign in the sky. Or they might have come from Arabia, where also many Jews had penetrated from the days of the Babylonian exile and the desert colonies established there by the last Babylonian king, Nabonidus.[68] By the first century B.C. the time of Jewish exclusiveness had ended; wherever Jews went, their neighbors learned a great deal about their faith and their hope.

On the advice of the Sanhedrin, the Jewish high priestly court, Herod told the sages from the east to go to Bethlehem, where the prophet Micah had said that the Messiah would be born, and to let him know if they found their new-born king there. They went to Bethlehem, found the Holy Family, and presented their offerings of gold, incense and myrrh to the Christ-Child; but immediately on their departure an angel warned them not to return to Herod, while St. Joseph was told to flee to Egypt because Herod would try to kill the Child.[69]

So the Holy Family crossed the grim desert running down from Mount Sinai, reversing the route of the Exodus, until they arrived in the Nile delta region. Falling into one of his fearsome rages, Herod ordered every male child two years old or under in Bethlehem to be slaughtered. There were probably only about 25 of these children, for Bethlehem was then a very small town; but the grief of a mother for her baby slain cannot be measured by numbers. The Holy Innocents died. The Church of Christ has honored them through almost all her history as the first martyrs who, like soldiers in a rear-guard though all unknowing, gave their lives that the King might escape and live.[70]

There were many Jews in Egypt; Mary and Joseph could feel as much at home there as anywhere outside the Promised Land, while they waited for a better day. In April of 4 B.C. Herod died at last, leaving orders that hundreds of prominent citizens whom he had imprisoned be killed so that mourning would accompany his funeral, since he knew there would be no mourning for him. Even his vicious sister Salome, who for many years had come close to matching Herod in evil, would not carry out these orders. Herod's eldest surviving son Archelaus succeeded him; Augustus hesitated some time before confirming his succession, and then allowed him only the title "ethnarch," not king, and only for Judea (the area around Jerusalem), not for Galilee. Augustus knew that Archelaus was essentially the same sort of man as his father, but less competent.[71]

Joseph knew this too. He abandoned his plan of settling permanently in Bethlehem, which was in the region now to be ruled by Archelaus, and returned to Nazareth in Galilee where a less evil son of Herod—Herod Antipas—now reigned as client king.[72] Here the boy Jesus grew up.

NOTES

[1] In all essentials the attack on the gospels for the purpose of denying the divinity of Christ began in modern times with the 4000-page *Apologia for the Rational Worshippers of God* by H. S. Reimarus, professor of Oriental languages in Hamburg, Germany, completed in 1768 just before his death and first published in part in 1774. The history of modernist and rationalist criticism of the gospels and of the life of Christ is summarized and its main lines of development up to 1940 outlined from the orthodox viewpoint by Giuseppe Ricciotti, *The Life of Christ* (Milwaukee, 1947), pp. 179-216. Its assumptions and characteristics as there outlined have remained essentially unchanged, though some of its more sweeping conclusions are now expressed with greater caution; however, there has been a corresponding lessening in the strength and numbers of the scholarly opposition, so that the significance of certain recent concessions and retreats by the rationalists has not always been clearly seen and commented on. Unfortunately there are few Ricciottis writing today.

[2] Ferdinand Prat, *Jesus Christ, His Life, His Teaching, and His Work* (Milwaukee, 1950), I, 29.

[3] St. Irenaeus later in the second century described Papias as "a hearer of John and a companion of Polycarp, a man of primitive times" (Against Heresies V, 33, 4).

[4] R. C. Butler, *The Originality of St. Matthew, a Critique of the Two-Document Hypothesis* (Cambridge, England, 1951), p. 165. His entire book deserves careful study. It is significant to note the convergence of arguments in favor of the traditional dating in two earlier, staunchly orthodox works -- Ricciotti, *Life of Christ*, pp. 98-101, and Constant Fouard, *St. Peter and the First Years of Christianity* (New York, 1915), pp. 206-226, and a much more recent work proceeding from many modernist premises in Scripture study, John A. T. Robinson, *Redating the New Testament* (Philadelphia, 1976), pp. 3-9, 103-107.

[5] Ricciotti, *Life of Christ*, p. 122; Manuel Miguens, *The Virgin Birth, an Evaluation of Scriptural Evidence* (Westminster, MD, 1975), pp. 128-132; Henri Daniel-Rops, *The Book of Mary* (Garden City NY, 1960), pp. 23-24.

[6] Ricciotti, *Life of Christ*, pp. 135-136.

[7] As Hilaire Belloc often pointed out, "living memory" is a very important though somewhat elastic concept in the study of history. Events remain within living memory when some men still live who can clearly remember their occurrence. Since very few men live more than a hundred years with mental faculties unimpaired, and very few children under ten remember details about historical events, the span of living memory is about 90 years.

[8] John 8:58.

[9] Ricciotti, *Life of Christ*, pp. 141-142.

[10] Robinson, *Redating the New Testament*, pp. 86-117.

[11] The writer is indebted for this excellent argument to his colleague William H. Marshner, Professor of Theology at Christendom College, who presents a detailed exposition of it in the College's apologetics textbook, *Reasons for Hope*, ed. Jeffrey A. Mirus, 2nd ed. (Front Royal VA, 1982), pp. 65-84.

[12] Karl Baus, *From the Apostolic Community to Constantine* (Volume I, *Handbook of Church History*, ed. Hubert Jedin and John Dolan) (New York, 1965), pp. 154-156; Sean Freyne, *Galilee from Alexander the Great to Hadrian* (Wilmington DE, 1980), pp. 351-356. Freyne, a Jewish writer, states: "Clearly, however the relationship between the Ebionites and the Nazoraioi is to be worked out, it is important to recognize that a number of external influences have been operative on their different development

in the Transjordan region during the second century. One cannot therefore take their beliefs and practices *in toto* and use them for determining trends and attitudes in early Christianity, and more specifically in Galilean Christianity'' (pp. 351-352).

¹³ Josephus, *Antiquities of the Jews*, XVIII, 63f., translated by H. St. John Thackeray, *Josephus, the Man and the Historian* (New York, 1929), pp. 136-137. As Thackeray points out, the authenticity of this passage—formerly almost universally denied—has been accepted in the twentieth century by such renowned scholars as von Harnack and Burkitt.

¹⁴ Robert Eisler, *The Messiah Jesus and John the Baptist* (London, 1931), pp. 128-140; S. G. F. Brandon, *The Fall of Jerusalem and the Christian Church* (London, 1970), pp. 114-117, including a considerable discussion in footnotes of the scholarly controversy over Eisler's book. See Chapters Sixteen and Seventeen, below, for a critique of the Eisler-Brandon theory that the references in these passages to the people's hopes for a politico-military Messiah being projected upon Jesus mean that he *was in fact* a leader of this kind.

¹⁵ Josephus, *The Jewish War*, tr. and ed. G. A. Williamson, rev. ed. (London, 1970), pp. 398-400. Williamson vigorously defends the authenticity of the ''Slavonic additions'' to *The Jewish War*.

¹⁶ At first sight it would appear that this phrase must be an interpolation, particularly since Origen, writing in the third century in our earliest Christian reference to this famous passage, says that Josephus ''did not admit our Jesus to be Christ'' (*hemon ou katadexamenos einai Christou, Comm. in Matt.* X, 17), and ''disbelieved in Jesus as Christ'' (*kaitoi ge apiston to Iesou hos Christo, Contra Celsum* I, 47). On the apparent contradiction between these quoted statements of Origen and Josephus' words ''He was the Christ'' which appear in our text of the *Antiquities*, entire theories at total variance with Christian texts and tradition have been erected, such as that of Eisler and Brandon that the original passage on Christ in the *Antiquities* presented Jesus as a political revolutionary and consequently was later expurgated by Christian editors or copyists. But Thackeray— even though, following Eisler, he regards the passage as having been altered by a Christian hand to eliminate an original unfavorable reference to Christ—also points out that a Christian interpolator would have written ''He *is* the Christ,'' not ''He was the Christ,'' and that the phrase may simply mean ''this was the Christ of whom you have heard tell'' (as Josephus later referred to James as ''the brother of Jesus who was called Christ,'' *Antiquities* XX, 197-203, a passage generally accepted as authentic), or ''He was believed to be the Christ'' (as Jerome later suggested) with the verb ''believed to be'' later dropped by Christian copyists (Thackeray, *Josephus*, pp. 138-139, 146-147). The hypothesis of an original passage strongly hostile to Christ or depicting him as a revolutionary appears to this writer entirely gratuitous. Origen's statement is clearly explicable as a comment on the striking fact that Josephus, knowing as much as he does about Christ, shows no inclination to make up his own mind about Who He is. It does not necessarily need to refer to the specific terms he used in naming Him.

¹⁷ Eisler, *Messiah Jesus*, pp. 146-147, is convincing on this point, though characteristically he tries to carry it much too far, attributing the whole story of the rending of the Temple curtain in this passage to tourists in Rome seeing among Roman war trophies the curtain torn down at the time of the sack of Jerusalem in 70 (for the independent evidence of a rending of the Temple curtain forty years before the destruction of the Temple, see Chapter Sixteen, below) and by going on to challenge the paragraph on the Resurrection in the Slavonic text of *The Jewish War* as an interpolation by a Judaizing Russian heretic (Eisler, *op. cit.*, pp. 149-164). Despite the immense learning and ingenuity lavished by Eisler on this elaborate and extraordinary hypothesis, it must founder on the rock of the *Antiquities* passage on Christ, which says much the same thing in

much the same tone; and whoever wrote that passage, it was most certainly not a Judaizing Russian heretic.

[18] Thackeray, *Josephus*, pp. 129-131, 141-142, 144-146; Brandon, *Fall of Jerusalem*, pp. 116-117.

[19] The one certain date on which all chronologies of the birth of John the Baptist and of Christ, and of the events of Jesus' infancy, must be built is the death of Herod, which occurred at the end of March or the beginning of April in 4 B.C. (Prat, *Jesus Christ*, I, 454-455; Giuseppe Ricciotti, *The History of Israel* [Milwaukee, 1955], II, 353). The conclusive evidence for this dating, based on a precisely dateable lunar eclipse, proves Dionysius Exiguus' calculation of the Christian era to have been in error by at least four years, since Christ was born before Herod died. Sufficient time must be allowed between Christ's birth and Herod's death for the forty days of purification required by the Mosaic Law before Mary could have presented Jesus in the Temple, and for the subsequent visit of the sages from the east (since it is inconceivable that Mary and Joseph would have taken Jesus to the Temple in Jerusalem after Herod had ordered Him killed) and for Herod's residence at Jericho during the last weeks of his life seeking relief from the pains of his fatal illness at its hot springs, since we are told that the sages found Herod at Jerusalem and not at Jericho (see Ricciotti, *Life of Christ*, pp. 155-156, and Jules Lebreton, *The Life and Teaching of Jesus Christ* [New York, 1957], I, xxii, on these points). These time intervals are sufficient to push the date of Christ's birth back to at least 5 B.C., while to put it before 6 B.C. seems to make Him improbably older than the ''about thirty'' mentioned by Luke (3:23) as His age at the beginning of His public ministry, probably early in 28 A.D. (see Chapter Fifteen, below, for this dating). Christ's birth in 5 B.C. would fit here better than birth in 6, making him 32 at the outset of His public ministry. On the other hand, the best conclusions that can be drawn from the references in Luke and later writers to the census at the time of Christ's birth (see the text and Notes 49-53, below) tend to point to 6 B.C., as does the astronomical evidence regarding the Star of Bethlehem (see Note 63, below). Consequently the date 6 B.C. is here adopted, in harmony with the conclusions of Prat, *Jesus Christ*, I, 114 and Henri Daniel-Rops, *Jesus and His Times* (New York, 1954), pp. 98-99. There is no evidence of the celebration of December 25 as the date of Christ's Nativity before the fourth century; both that day and January 6 (Epiphany) were pagan feasts which the Church most likely appropriated soon after the conversion of Constantine. But one of the reasons for this appropriation clearly seems to have been ''a rather widespread opinion at least as early as in the second century that the conception was in the spring and the birth of Jesus near the midwinter'' (Jack Finegan, *Handbook of Biblical Chronology* [Princeton NJ, 1964], p. 254).

[20] Ricciotti, *History of Israel*, II, 346-349.

[21] See the accounts of the ceremony particularly in Prat, *Jesus Christ*, I, 58-62, and L. C. Fillion, *The Life of Christ*, 2nd ed. (St. Louis, 1928), I, 243-246).

[22] Luke 1:27.

[23] Andres Fernandez, *The Life of Christ* (Westminster MD, 1958), pp. 83-86; Ricciotti, *Life of Christ*, pp. 225-228; Miguens, *Virgin Birth*, pp. 77-82. The two principal objections to the traditional interpretation that Mary had made a vow of perpetual virginity before the Annunciation—excluding the views of those who reject the historicity of the Infancy narratives altogether or in large part—are philological and historical. It is objected that Mary's question to the angel refers only to her immediate present condition of being unmarried, and that she takes the angel's statement as indicating an already accomplished conception (e.g. Reginald Fuller et al, eds., *A New Catholic Commentary on Holy Scripture* [London, 1969], p. 996). This objection is most thoroughly and con-

vincingly refuted by Miguens' learned review of the philological questions pertaining to this point, in his pages cited. His main point is that the Greek present tense used for Mary's words in Luke 1:34 corresponds not to the Hebrew and Aramaic perfect, indicating a condition limited to the past or the present, but to the Hebrew and Aramaic active participle indicating a permanent condition. He concludes that Mary's words in Aramaic were *ki enneni yodaat ish*, the *yodaat* indicating a permanent condition of virginity (Miguens, *op. cit.*, p. 81). The historical objection, that consecrated virginity was unknown among Jews of Mary's time and mentioned in the entire Old Testament only in the case of the prophet Jeremiah, has lost most of whatever force it had by the discovery of the remains and records of the largely celibate community at Qumran during this period (Frank M. Cross Jr., *The Ancient Library at Qumran and Modern Biblical Studies* [London, 1958], pp. 71-74), referred to by Fernandez, *loc. cit.* In any case, to have rejected the *possibility* of a vow of virginity by Mary before the Annunciation, because it was uncommon or even unknown at the time, is akin to rejecting the Incarnation itself on the grounds that the Jews were not generally expecting the Messiah to *be* God. Mary's early vow of virginity is not *de fide*, but the historical and logical case for it is very strong—much stronger than most modern scholars and students appear to realize.

[24] Prat, *Jesus Christ*, I, 58-59.

[25] See Note 19, above.

[26] Fillion, *Life of Christ*, I, 248-250; M.-J. Lagrange, *The Gospel of Jesus Christ* (Westminster MD, 1951), I, 13; Bernard Orchard et al, *A Catholic Commentary on Holy Scripture* (London, 1951), p. 940.

[27] Luke 1:13-19.

[28] *Cf.* Jean Danielou, *The Work of John the Baptist* (Baltimore, 1966).

[29] Prat, *Jesus Christ*, I, 60-61. The dumbness of Zachary is described as a punishment for his hesitancy to believe the angel's message (Luke 1:20).

[30] Matthew 1:18. According to contemporary Jewish custom, betrothal was in most respects as binding as marriage. It was usually entered into about a year before the wedding, which took place when the bride actually moved into her husband's house. Between betrothal and wedding the couple were regarded as married in virtually every way except cohabitation, and the same legal proceedings were required for divorcing a betrothed as a married couple. See Prat, *Jesus Christ*, I, 43-44 and Ricciotti, *Life of Christ*, p. 226.

[31] The names of the Blessed Virgin Mary's parents do not appear in the New Testament, but do appear in the earliest portion of the most doctrinally orthodox and historically reliable of the New Testament Apocrypha, the Protevangelium of James (whose early attribution to the Apostle James cannot be correct in view of the ignorance of Jewish life and custom which it displays, inconceivable in one who became Bishop of Jerusalem). The probable date of the portions of the Protevangelium of James referring to Joachim and Anne is about 130 or 140 A.D., not long after the probable date of composition of St. John's Gospel and the close of the canonical New Testament. In view of the tenacious genealogical memory of ancient and rural peoples, and especially of the Jews, it is most unlikely that the names of Mary's parents were forgotten or confused by this early date. See Daniel-Rops, *Book of Mary*, pp. 63-64 and Prat, *Jesus Christ*, I, 12, 42.

[32] Ricciotti, *Life of Christ*, pp. 222-223.

[33] *Ibid.*, p. 225; Franz M. Willam, *The Life of Jesus Christ in the Land of Israel and Among its People*, ed. Newton Thompson (St. Louis, 1938), p. 9.

[34] Luke 1:28 (traditional Catholic translation, in the Douay-Rheims and other Catholic versions of Scripture). The translation "full of grace" is based on the Latin *gratia plena* in Jerome's Vulgate. The translation in the Revised Standard Version usually used for Scriptural quotations in this book is "Hail, favored one, the Lord is with you." The

phrase in question in the Greek text of Luke's Gospel is κεχαριτωμενη, which has been explained as "meaning one endowed with favor or grace, χαπις, *in permanent fashion*. It is God's favor which is indicated" (emphasis added) (Orchard et al, *Catholic Commentary on Holy Scripture*, p. 941). It should be noted that Paul had done most of his work in developing the Christian theology of grace and explaining it in his epistles before the probable date of the composition of Luke's Gospel (62 A.D. or a little earlier—see Robinson, *Redating the New Testament*, pp. 88-92) and that Luke was Paul's intimate friend and disciple. In selecting the proper word to render into Greek what the angel had said to Mary in her language, Aramaic (which Mary herself had most likely repeated to him), Luke would in all probability have been guided by this understanding, indicating that a far more than ordinary favor was involved. According to Roman Catholic belief, Mary alone of all mankind except her Divine Son was conceived without stain of original sin. For an explanation and defense of the dogma of the Immaculate Conception, infallibly proclaimed by Pope Pius IX in 1854, see J. B. Carol, ed., *Mariology*, Volume I (Milwaukee, 1955), pp. 328-394, "Mary's Immaculate Conception," by Aidan Carr and German Williams.

[35] Luke 1:35.

[36] On the historicity of the Virgin Birth and the total absence of any belief in the early Christian community that Joseph was the natural father of Jesus, see Manuel Miguens' brilliant and conclusive *The Virgin Birth, an Evaluation of the Scriptural Evidence*. He points out that even the Gospels of Mark and John, which make no explicit reference to Christ's virgin birth, clearly imply a knowledge and acceptance of this fact in their references to Mary as Jesus' only human parent. On the general historicity of the narratives of Christ's infancy in Matthew and Luke, often challenged by modernist intepreters of the New Testament, see Jean Danielou, *The Infancy Narratives* (New York, 1968).

[37] Luke 1:36-37.

[38] Luke 1:38.

[39] Lagrange, *Gospel of Jesus Christ*, I, 21.

[40] Fernandez, *Life of Christ*, p. 98.

[41] *Ibid.*, pp. 98-100; Fillion, *Life of Christ*, I, 267; Prat, *Jesus Christ*, I, 62-63.

[42] Prat, *Jesus Christ*, I, 64.

[43] Luke 1:46-50.

[44] Prat, *Jesus Christ*, I, 66; Fernandez, *Life of Christ*, pp. 104, 107-108. Though the text of Luke's Gospel seems to imply that Mary had left Elizabeth just before the birth of John the Baptist, if she did leave it would have been very close to the time of his birth, since we are told in Luke 1:36 that Elizabeth was in her sixth month of pregnancy at the time of the Annunciation and in 1:56 that Mary remained with her "about three months." Adding the unspecified length of time between the Annunciation and the Visitation, at least a week and probably two to three weeks, Mary must have left either immediately before the birth or very soon after it. Surely the latter is much more likely. As Prat says in the page cited, we would hardly expect any other woman spending the last three months of a relative's pregnancy with her to leave just before the birth; still less would we expect such an action by the Mother of God on the occasion of the birth of the angelically heralded precursor of the Incarnate God she carried in her womb.

[45] Daniel-Rops, *Book of Mary*, pp. 42-43; Fernandez, *Life of Christ*, pp. 108-111.

[46] Prat, *Jesus Christ*, I, 68-73; Fillion, *Life of Christ*, I, 283n. The point is of sufficient importance, and this analysis of it sufficiently rare, to justify quoting Prat's linguistic analysis of this passage at length. First he translates Matthew 1:19 as follows: "Because he was a just man (δικαιος ων), he did not wish (μη θελων) to discredit her (δειγματισαι); he purposed (εβουληθη) to send her away secretly (απολυσαι λαθρα)." Prat then

continues: "The very rare word, δειγματιζειν, has the same meaning as παραδειγματι-ζειν, "to make an example of,' "to disgrace.' . . . For Mary, disgrace would be exposure to feminine raillery and gossip. This is what Joseph wishes to avoid (μηθελων) at any price. He deliberates (εβουληθη) what to do. Βουλεσθαι is not a synonym for θελειν. It means "desire,' "plan'; and Plato in the *Protagoras* gently chides a Sophist who finds a shade of difference between βουλεσθαι and επιθυμειν. Besides, the meaning is explained further on: 'While he was reflecting on these things (ταυτα αυτου επιθυμηθεντος).' [Matthew 1:20] He had not yet come to a definite decision." (Prat, *op. cit.*, I, 70n).

⁴⁷ Matthew 1:20-21; Prat, *Jesus Christ*, I, 70-71.

⁴⁸ Most modern authorities—orthodox included—reject the opinion, not advanced until the sixteenth century, which resolves the ancient question raised by the divergence between the genealogies of Jesus in Matthew and in Luke by attributing the former to Joseph and the latter to Mary. Both genealogies are now generally held to be Joseph's, one by natural and one by levirate succession, according to the ancient Jewish law wich obliged a man whose brother had died without male issue to marry his brother's widow to perpetuate his brother's line, and/or by other forms of adoption. The fact that Joseph was not related to Jesus according to the flesh was not, oddly to modern eyes, seen as an objection to the use of his genealogy to prove the Davidic descent of Jesus, until the sixteenth century. See Prat, *Jesus Christ*, I, 478-482; Ricciotti, *Life of Christ*, p. 236n; Fillion, *Life of Christ*, I, 310-325. Danielou (*Infancy Narratives*, p. 18) states that "the genealogy was certainly not something contributed by the apostles, but was found in the archives of Jesus' family"—presumably, both versions of it.

⁴⁹ *The Cambridge Ancient History*, Volume X (Cambridge, England, 1934, 1971), pp. 192-193, 304; Prat, *Jesus Christ*, I, 78-79; Ricciotti, *Life of Christ*, p. 168. The date of the Egyptian census mentioned in the text is probable but not certain (*Cambridge Ancient History*, X, 304n). Though we have no specific evidence linking it with a census in Palestine at the same time, the coincidence of dates suggests a connection, especially in light of Tertullian's evidence that the census took place under Saturninus, whose tenure as governor ended in 6 B.C. (see Note 53, below) and the chronological arguments advanced in Note 19, above.

⁵⁰ 2 Samuel 24:1-17.

⁵¹ Ricciotti, *History of Israel*, II, 369-372.

⁵² *Ibid.*, II, 349-350; Prat, *Jesus Christ*, I, 79. With regard to the issue of whether the Romans would ever have imposed a census on a client kingdom or other self-governing tributary state, conclusive evidence is provided by the city-state of Apamea in Syria, with a population of 117,000, which minted its own coins, and yet had a census taken within it by none other than Quirinius himself, who was involved as governor of Syria in the census taken at the time of Christ's birth (Finegan, *Handbook of Biblical Chronology*, p. 237).

⁵³ Finegan, *Handbook of Biblical Chronology*, pp. 234-238; Prat, *Jesus Christ*, I, 483-485; Ricciotti, *Life of Christ*, pp. 168-173; Fillion, *Life of Christ*, I, 579-590. The attempt in *Cambridge Ancient History* X, 877-878 to remove Quirinius from Syria altogether until the first decade of the first century A.D. runs counter (as its author admits) to an "almost universally accepted" view that Quirinius had an earlier term as governor of Syria during which he led a campaign against the Homanadenses in Asia Minor near Syria (in the Taurus Mountains) at some time between 11 B.C. and 1 A.D. (*ibid.*, pp. 271-272). This evidence, together with that of Tertullian that the census at the time of Christ's birth took place during Saturninus' tenure as governor (of such importance as to deserve verbatim quotation in the original: "Sed et census constant actos sub Augusto tunc in Judaea per Sentium Saturninum apud quos genus eius inquirer potuis-

sent"—*Adv. Marcionem* IV, 1) and the legitimate inferences from the census in Egypt in 6-5 B.C. and the oath of loyalty to Augustus demanded of the Jews by Herod in 6 B.C., provides a very impressive counterweight to the common presumption among modernist historians and Scriptural commentators that Luke's statement must be an erroneous reference to the known census of Palestine in 6 A.D. when Augustus deposed Herod's son and successor Archelaus and established direct Roman rule in Judea, at which time Quirinius is known for certain to have been governor of Syria, and the revolt of Judas the Galilean grew out of Jewish resistance to the census.

[54] Ricciotti, *Life of Christ*, p. 243.

[55] *Contra Celsum* I, 51. On the cave of the Nativity in Bethlehem as the best authenticated of all the holy places in Palestine, see Clemens Kopp, *The Holy Places of the Gospels* (New York, 1963), pp. 6-47.

[56] Henri Daniel-Rops, *Cathedral and Crusade* (New York, 1957), pp. 445-446.

[57] Maria Petrozzi, *Bethlehem* (Jerusalem, 1971), p. 25.

[58] *Ibid.*, pp. 25-26.

[59] Prat, *Jesus Christ*, I, 85; personal verification by the author on a visit to Bethlehem in 1971. The population is almost all Christian, a slight majority being Catholic and most of the remainder Greek Orthodox.

[60] Luke 18:8.

[61] Ricciotti, *Life of Christ*, pp. 238, 245-246; Prat, *Jesus Christ*, I, 113.

[62] Prat, *Jesus Christ*, I, 90-92.

[63] Fillion, *Life of Christ*, I, 330-338. The Simeon who was son of Hillel and father of Gamaliel, at one time president of the Sanhedrin, was so highly regarded for his learning that he was called "Rabban," master above all others, rather than simply "Rabbi." The identity of Rabban Simeon with the Simeon of Luke's Gospel is vigorously defended by Constant Fouard, *The Christ the Son of God* (New York, 1890, 1924), I, 56-57, and much more recently by A. Cutler, "Does the Simeon of Luke 2 Refer to Simeon the Son of Hillel?", *Journal of the Bible and Religion* XXXIV (1966), 29-35, supported by Danielou, *Infancy Narratives*, pp. 103-104. It is denied without circumstantial explanation by Prat, *Jesus Christ*, I, 92-93 and by Ricciotti, *Life of Christ*, p. 247.

[64] Ricciotti, *History of Israel*, II, 349-353, 356; *Cambridge Ancient History* X, 336; Prat, *Jesus Christ*, I, 90.

[65] Good discussions of the Star of Bethlehem are found in Prat, *Jesus Christ*, I, 97-100, 492; Fillion, *Life of Christ*, I, 344-348; Alfred Edersheim, *The Life and Times of Jesus the Messiah* (New York, 1886), I, 204-213; and especially David Hughes' recent *The Star of Bethlehem, an Astronomer's Confirmation* (New York, 1979). Twentieth-century orthodox commentators and historians have abandoned too quickly the once widely held theory of the great astronomer Kepler that the Star of Bethlehem was the remarkable conjunction of three planets—Jupiter, Saturn, and Mars—in February of 6 B.C. The three planets very close together would have made a most striking appearance; this happens only once in 800 years. The coincidence in time, if such it be, is so extraordinary that it is exceedingly hard to dismiss it even in the face of assurances that the word used in Matthew's Gospel to describe the Star of Bethlehem, *aster*, never refers to a stellar grouping (as its cognate *astron* may) but only to a single luminary. Gerhard Kittel's *Theological Dictionary of the New Testament* (Grand Rapids, MI, 1964), I, 503, qualifies this assertion somewhat by stating that "*aster almost* always denotes a single star" (emphasis added), and this distinction—more significant to our scientific mind-set than to the story itself—might not have been made by Matthew with the astronomical precision now being attributed to him. Hughes (*op. cit.*, pp. 245-250) dates the Star and the birth of Christ to 7 B.C. when a closer conjunction of Jupiter and Saturn took place than the later, but not quite so close conjunction of Jupiter, Saturn, and Mars

in 6; but birth in 7 B.C. seems improbably early to match the other chronological data regarding Christ's life (see Note 19, above). Geographical difficulties raised by the usual translation "we have seen his star in the East"—since the sages came from the East and were travelling west—are obviated by the equally defensible translation "we have seen his star at its rising" (Edersheim, *op. cit.*, I, 204n). The only other tenable interpretation of the Star of Bethlehem, for those accepting the fundamental reliability of the gospel narrative, is that it was wholly miraculous and supernatural, unrelated to any known or pre-existing celestial object—as the report of its moving to stand over the house where Jesus was, does tend to suggest.

[66] See Chapter Seven, above.

[67] Ricciotti, *Life of Christ*, pp. 250-252, citing the studies of G. Messina. There is substantial evidence that Jewish messianic prophecies were quite widely known in Iran by the first century B.C. and were linked with expectations of a Zoroastrian "helper" (*saushyant*) to come, and possibly also with expectations of a great temporal leader to command a victorious counteroffensive against the Graeco-Roman culture and political order then prevailing east of the Euphrates. On this last expectation, see the remarkable and penetrating study by Samuel K. Eddy, *The King Is Dead, Studies in Near Eastern Resistance to Hellenism* (Lincoln NE, 1961), especially pp. 16-23.

[68] See Chapter Seven, above. The case for an Arabian origin of the sages is well stated by Lagrange, *Gospel of Jesus Christ*, I, 42-43, and has been quite widely held (partly because frankincense and myrrh, two of the three gifts brought by the sages to the Christ-Child, are Arabian products) but it seems very difficult to explain the specific reference to "Magi," who were solely associated with Iran, on any basis other than an Iranian origin of the sages.

[69] Matthew 2:1-12; Ricciotti, *Life of Christ*, p. 253.

[70] Ricciotti, *Life of Christ*, pp. 256-259.

[71] Ricciotti, *History of Israel*, II, 354-358, 382; *Cambridge Ancient History*, X, 337-339.

[72] Prat, *Jesus Christ*, I, 113-114; Lagrange, *Gospel of Jesus Christ*, I, 48; Ricciotti, *History of Israel*, II, 359-361.

15.
GOD IN GALILEE
(4 B.C.-29 A.D.)

And when they had performed everything according to the law of the Lord, they returned to Galilee, to their own city, Nazareth. And the child grew and became strong, filled with wisdom, and the favor of God was upon him. . . He went down with them and came to Nazareth, and was obedient to them; and his mother kept all these things in her heart. And Jesus increased in wisdom and in stature, and in favor with God and man.—Luke 2:39-40, 51-52

As he walked by the Sea of Galilee, he saw two brothers, Simon who is called Peter and Andrew his brother, casting a net into the sea; for they were fishermen. And he said to them, "Follow me, and I will make you fishers of men." Immediately they left their nets and followed him.—Matthew 4:18-20

Jesus said to them: "I am the bread of life; he who comes to me shall not hunger, and he who believes in me shall never thirst. . . . For I have come down from heaven, not to do my own will, but the will of him who sent me; and this is the will of him who sent me, that I should lose nothing of all that he has given me, but raise it up at the last day. For this is the will of my Father, that every one who sees the Son and believes in him should have eternal life; and I will raise him up at the last day."—John 6:35, 38-40

The town of Nazareth in Galilee, where God dwelt unrecognized and unheralded for thirty years, occupied the lower slopes of a small valley in the hill country between the Sea of Galilee and the plain of Esdraelon. Lovely but isolated, away from all major trade and travel routes, Nazareth had no history. It is nowhere mentioned in the Old Testament, nor in any contemporary historical source before the gospels.[1] Being in that part of Palestine assigned to Herod Antipas, it remained in peace and security, in contrast to tormented, turbulent Judea.[2] No one imagined that anything or anyone of importance would ever emerge from Nazareth.[3] Even so had the prophet Micah told God's people that the Messiah would be born in Bethlehem, but no one had guessed the cave; and the prophet Isaiah had said that the Messiah's light would shine forth in "Galilee of the nations,"[4] but no one had guessed Nazareth. As Isaiah had reminded the Chosen People, God's ways are not our ways.[5]

In Nazareth the Holy Family lived in that silent sanctity which has been an inexhaustible fountain of contemplation for Christians through all the centuries since. Into their sanctuary only prayerful meditation can lead us; like Heaven, it lies outside and beyond history. Yet Nazareth was in history even though not recorded there. Its people were as real as any of us, living ordinary human lives filled with everyday human concerns. Nazareth's children of the 750's of the Roman era knew and played with God as a little boy; growing up with Him, in time they did business with God as a carpenter. All those years He lived with them solely as a man, with no hint of more, the Lord of the universe dwelling incognito among His creatures. The truth about Jesus was never really understood at Nazareth, except by a few of those closest to Him. Yet He never condemned the Nazarenes for their unbelief as He was to condemn the unbelieving people of Capernaum, Bethsaida, and Chorazin, though (so far as we know) He had been worse treated by the Nazarenes than by them. He must have loved the people of Nazareth in a special way, for they had been companions and brothers in God's unique *personal* experience as a man, unrecognized in His divinity.[6]

From the hills just above Nazareth the shore of the Mediterranean Sea is visible, the blue expanse of its waters, and the snow-capped peak of Mount Hermon.[7] As a boy, Jesus must surely have gone up to the top of those hills, to look out with His human senses into the wider world He had come to save. No more than the unfathomable mystery of the Incarnation itself will we ever in this life conceive the coexistence of divine and human knowledge in the growing Jesus;[8] but, some aberrant modern theology to the contrary notwithstanding, divine knowledge there must have been—God Incarnate cannot fail to know Who He is. This knowledge must have included full awareness of His mission. Anything less is incompatible with the full divinity of the God-Man. And this is clearly implied by Jesus' solitary visit to the Temple when He was twelve years old, and by His response to Mary's reproach when at last she found Him: "Did you not know that I must be about my Father's business?"[9]

What passed before the gaze of the Child God looking out from the hills of Nazareth upon the Mediterranean Sea no man, short of the Beatific Vision, will ever know. But the historian can tell us something of what was out there, humanly speaking, to be seen—of the impending tragedies of the mighty beyond the blue waters, which were to shape the Roman political background of God's life on earth. Jesus never came directly into contact with Roman politics, approaching it only at brief moments—notably when He stood before Pontius Pilate. But since the world He came to save was first of all, in point of time, that Roman world, its condition during His lifetime helps to show in an especially striking manner how great was its need of Him.

For Caesar Augustus' purpose in the divine preparation for the coming of Christianity had been fulfilled with the winning of the Roman peace. He could do no more. The dark side of paganism—and of the general condition of fallen humanity—was now to reassert itself. To win the peace Augustus had concentrated in his steady and capable hands a power greater than the world had ever seen, except for the brief coruscant hour of Alexander the Great. Caesar Augustus was incorruptible and almost indestructible. But he was not immortal. He could use the power he had won, in general, wisely and well; all the world knew it. But to whom would he—to whom *could* he—pass it on?

As the Christian era opened, in the year 1 A.D. (Jesus of Nazareth was five years old), Caesar Augustus celebrated his sixty-fourth birthday. His thirty-nine years of marriage to the high-born, beautiful and virtuous Livia had been childless. His only child was his daughter Julia by his first wife Scribonia, whom he had divorced to marry Livia. Julia had been the wife of Augustus' truest, most loyal friend, stout-hearted Agrippa. She had borne him three sons and a daughter. When Agrippa died, Augustus had forced a marriage between Julia and his stepson Tiberius—a marriage which required Tiberius to divorce his wife Vipsania, the only woman he ever loved. Tiberius and Julia had one child, who died in infancy. After that they drew steadily apart. They had strong, almost diametrically opposite personalities. Tiberius was an old Roman. His father, an ardent republican, was of the famous family of Claudius Nero, which included the general who had beaten Hannibal's brother at the Metaurus after the long heroic march at the final crisis of the Second Punic War in Italy. Only after his father died, when Tiberius was nine years old (33 B.C.), did he come to live with his mother Livia and her new husband Octavian, not yet Caesar Augustus. Tiberius was a man of immense mental and physical strength, for long impeturbable in a crisis, who could crush an apple in his hand; but he lacked imagination, dash and daring. His virtue was solid but cold. And he was only the emperor's stepson. Julia was warm, witty, beautiful, vivacious, increasingly immoral—and the emperor's own daughter, the only heir of his body. Between these two dislike turned to revulsion, then to a hatred so deep and terrible that it sears across centuries of history. Julia wrote to Augustus accusing Tiberius—of what we do not know, but probably of some kind of disgusting immorality, the charge that would hurt a man of Tiberius' type most. Two years later, wholly unexpectedly and without explanation, Tiberius demanded that Augustus permit him to retire from all public life, to the island of Rhodes. He was only thirty-six. When Augustus demurred, Tiberius went on a hunger strike. Then he was allowed to go.[10]

It was 7 B.C., the year of Zachary's vision in the Temple.

Five years later the truth about Julia's flagrant immorality, long the subject of salacious gossip in Rome, was finally brought home to Augustus. So evil was her conduct as reported to him that he actually considered having her—his only child—executed. Finally he sentenced her to close confinement on the island of Pandataria.[11] Upon these two islands, Rhodes and Pandataria, across the sea which could be seen from the hills above Nazareth, Tiberius and Julia nurtured the hatred of each other that was consuming them.

For a time Augustus hoped to bypass them both by training Julia's oldest son Gaius as his successor. But Gaius died in 4 A.D. of a wound received in the wild mountains of Armenia; his brother Lucius was already dead; his other brother, Agrippa Postumus, was going insane. Tiberius was brought back from Rhodes and made heir to the empire—on one condition, that he adopt his nephew Germanicus as his heir in preference to his own son by Vipsania, Drusus. Then Augustus had Germanicus marry Julia's only daughter, Agrippina.[12]

It was the worst mistake Caesar Augustus ever made. He had been too long master of the world. Always a rather cold man, he had forgotten that there is a point beyond which natural human feelings cannot be violated for the supposed good of the state and have any actual good for the state result. First he had forced Tiberius to give up his beloved wife Vipsania to marry Julia; now he was forcing him to give up his son by Vipsania, Drusus, in favor of Julia's son-in-law—despite the fact that Julia had proved herself utterly unworthy of all that Augustus stood for, that she hated Tiberius with an undying passion, and that Tiberius would succeed Augustus as head of the empire.

From this point on the story unfolds like that of King Lear. Indeed, there is much of Lear in Tiberius, except that Tiberius was a stronger man than Shakespeare's king, and so in his own way suffered even more. No thought of abdication seems to have entered his mind; it was his duty as a Roman to serve—and in any case the heir to the mastery of the civilized world could not simply lay down his inheritance; as Tiberius himself said, the emperor of Rome was like a man "holding a wolf by the ears."[13] Tiberius took command of the army in Germany, marched through its dark forests to the Elbe River, and sent his fleet to the shores of Denmark—the only imperial Roman vessels ever to touch there. He had to bring most of his forces rushing back to put down a great revolt in Illyria, whereupon the Germans rose and annihilated three legions at the Battle of the Teutoberg Forest. Their beaten commander, Quinctilius Varus (who had been Rome's legate in Syria when the Holy Family dwelt in Bethlehem) killed himself. Tiberius returned to Germany, restored order and morale, and held the frontiers.[14] In 14 A.D. Caesar Augustus died at the age of seventy-six; Tiberius duly succeeded him. Julia died that same year. Men said she starved herself to death rather than live in a world where Tiberius was Emperor.[15]

In Nazareth the next year, 15 A.D., Jesus was twenty years old. An ancient tradition holds that it was in this year that St. Joseph died, in the arms of the Blessed Virgin Mary and of his foster son Who was God.[16] But Mary and Jesus were not left entirely alone. They had the company of Jesus' "brethren," James and Joseph and Simon and Jude, who seem to have been the children of St. Joseph's brother Cleopas and of Cleopas' wife Mary by previous marriages;[17] James later became one of the Twelve Apostles; Simon and Jude probably became disciples.[18] Jesus Himself now took charge of Joseph's carpentry shop, making plows and yokes and other wooden implements for the people of Nazareth. For more than a decade the King of Kings worked as a simple artisan, earning His living and His mother's by His hands.[19]

Far away in Rome, the kind of hatred that Jesus had come to cast out with love, or to bear upon the Cross, continued its devouring course. Julia was dead, but her hatred for Tiberius lived on and grew in her daughter Agrippina, married to the rather shallow and vainglorious but popular Germanicus, who imagined himself the conqueror of Germany, though he had been extricated from a defeat there which would have been as disastrous as that of Varus only by the magnificent old Roman courage and military skill of his general Caecina.[20] Tiberius recalled Germanicus; he accepted the recall with little protest and undertook a triumphal tour in the east, in the midst of which he suddenly sickened and died at Antioch, at the early age of thirty-three.[21]

Agrippina cried poison. She accompanied Germanicus' ashes in a theatrical journey back to Italy, with her partisans demanding judical action against the alleged poisoner, Calpurnius Piso, said to have been acting for Tiberius. Nothing about poisoning could be proved. Piso was tried on other charges and driven to suicide, but the whispering against Tiberius continued. Behind it, like a reincarnation of her mother Julia, was Agrippina, who had now apparently lost everything because for obvious reasons Tiberius preferred his own son Drusus as heir, to her sons by Germanicus. One Libo Drusus was executed on a charge of attempting to procure the emperor's death by sorcery. Tiberius re-fashioned an old law against crimes injuring the state—the law of *maiestas*—to apply to all forms of speech or action, derogatory or insulting words or gestures, directed against the government or its head. He organized a system of paid informers, the delators; today we would call it a secret police. The classic techniques of totalitarianism were being established.[22]

Worse was to come for Tiberius. Drusus, his son and only child, was married to Livilla, Tiberius' niece and the sister of the dead Germanicus. Twin sons had been born to them. Drusus was very much in love with Livilla, she less so with him. Tiberius, increasingly isolated and surrounded by enemies, pursued by Julia's hatred from beyond the grave through her unyielding daughter Agrippina, placed more and more trust and power in the hands of Lucius Sejanus, a wily Etruscan. Sejanus was made head of the Praetorian Guard, the military garrison which held Rome and kept the emperor in power. He was in charge of the enforcement of the law of *maiestas* and the secret police. His ambitions kindling, he ingratiated himself with Livilla; she became his mistress. Drusus protested to Tiberius, who ignored the matter. Once Drusus actually struck Sejanus. In 23 A.D. Drusus suddenly died at the age of about forty.[23]

Tiberius, a man of iron, took the terrible blow without public flinching. When, after waiting for what he thought was a decent interval, Sejanus requested permission to marry Livilla and become the guardian of her children, Tiberius refused. Duty to the state demanded that all possible steps be taken to avoid the succession of a child to the rule of the empire. He would pass over his own grandson, and return for the succession to the family of Germanicus and Agrippina—to the grandsons of Julia.[24]

But Agrippina and her partisans could not believe in his sincerity—and Sejanus worked to stir up their suspicions still more, so that he might destroy her and her children. For Sejanus wanted the empire for himself. Though only a very few people yet knew it and Tiberius was not to find it out until the tragic climax of his life the year after the Passion and Resurrection of Christ, Sejanus and Livilla had poisoned Drusus. Tiberius' only son had been killed by his son's wife, acting with his own chief minister who had ravished her.[25]

Did Tiberius, emperor of the Western world, have a single friend or loved one left? There was his mother, Livia, the widow of Augustus, now 83 years old and still vigorous. Did he go to her for help in his agony, to seek her reassurance and support? We do not know; but we are told of a fearful quarrel between mother and son in 26 A.D. over some petty question of official patronage, culminating in her showing him derogatory letters which Augustus had long ago written to her about him. This final rebuff brought Tiberius to the breaking point. Suddenly, without explanation, he left Rome, where he had dwelt uninterruptedly since his reign began, to settle permanently on the island of Capri off the south Italian coast, governing the empire through Sejanus. He never returned to Rome.[26]

So matters stood in the world of men, the great world of public affairs and human achievement, as the hidden life of God in Galilee drew toward its close.

For the fall of 27 A.D. began the fifteenth year of Tiberius as emperor, as it was counted in Antioch, the capital of Syria, the province which included Judea;[27] and that was the year when "the word of God came to John the son of Zechariah in the wilderness, and he went into all the region about the Jordan, preaching a baptism of repentance for the forgiveness of sins."[28] Long ago now, in 6 A.D., Herod's cruel, incompetent son Archelaus had been deposed by Augustus and sent away to die in Gaul; Roman procurators ruled Judea in his stead. The year Tiberius went to Capri, a bad-tempered middle-echelon bureaucrat named Pontius Pilate had been assigned this unrewarding and unpleasant post, governing the troublesome, ever-restless Jews.[29] The following table presents the rulers of Rome, Galilee and Judea during these years.

RULERS OF ROME, JUDEA AND GALILEE
4 B.C.-37 A.D.

ROME	JUDEA	GALILEE
Augustus 27 B.C.-14 A.D.	Archelaus, King A.D. 4 B.C.-6 A.D.	Herod Antipas, King 4 B.C.-39 A.D.
	ROMAN PROCURATORS	
	Coponius 6-9 A.D.	
	Marcus Ambivius 9-12 A.D.	
	Annius Rufus 12-15 A.D.	
Tiberius 14-37 A.D.	Valerius Gratus 15-26 A.D.	
	Pontius Pilate 26-36 A.D.	
	Marcellus 36-37 A.D.	

Who was John the Baptist? Where had he been since that glorious, joyous day in the home of Zachary and Elizabeth at Ain Karem where, already sanctified through the Mother of God carrying God in her womb, he had been born?

He said that he was not Elijah; yet he was the fulfillment of the prophecies of the return of Elijah.[30] He said that he was not the one supreme prophet foretold by Moses, for Christ was that prophet; yet he was the culmination of the line of prophets that had begun with Moses.[31] And he said that he was not the Messiah, for he came as the Messiah's herald.[32] Yet Christ Himself tells us: "Truly, I say to you, among those born of women there has risen no one greater than John the Baptist."[33] Alone he had lived, at least since his aged parents died; so he had not seen Jesus at least since he was old enough to remember Him, despite the unique bond that joined their two families.[34] There is little basis for the oft-heard theory that he was a member of an Essene or Qumran-type community. Nothing in the descriptions of John the Baptist suggests anything but a wholly solitary ascetic, a man clad in the garments of Elijah who appears as if from nowhere, like Elijah. Nor does his teaching resemble in any significant way that of the Essenes or of Qumran.[35] Strange and fierce, full of fire and yet of love, he stands unique, the living link between the old covenant and the new. His moral teaching was simple, straightforward, the common sense of the natural law; he warned of chastisement, but offered repentance; his horizons extended far beyond his Judean desert, to encompass all those distant sons and daughters whom God was about to raise up, as from stones, to be children to Abraham, their father in faith.[36] Through and above all shines John's love for the Master Whom he has never seen: "After me comes he who is mightier than I, the thong of whose sandals I am not worthy to stoop down and untie. I have baptized you with water, but he will baptize you with the Holy Spirit."[37]

At length He came—quietly, unnoticed, the young carpenter of Nazareth mingling with the crowd of penitents from all over the Holy Land on the banks of the Jordan in the great deep cleft leading to the Dead Sea, just a few miles from where the world's first city was built at Jericho. There was nothing visible to distinguish Him from all the others. Yet John knew Him at once, even before the sign of the Dove which came at His baptism. It was the first time Jesus had been recognized for Who He was since the coming of the Magi.[38]

Over the Jordan valley, a thousand feet below sea level, tower the rocky outlines and waterless chalk slopes of Jebel Qarantal, the Mount of the Forty Days. Tradition identifies it as the place where Jesus went shortly after His encounter with John the Baptist, to fast and to pray. It is close to the site of His baptism. It was the winter of 28 A.D.[39] In such places John the Baptist had spent much of his life. Great missions for God often begin with fasting and purgation. This was the greatest mission of all, in time and for eternity. Jesus had no sin to be purged. But the forty days of fasting and prayer were to mark the transition from the happy life in Nazareth, shared as an apparently ordinary man with ordinary men, to the colossal demands of His mission of salvation. He had a fully human body and a fully human will. Both must be girded in a special way for what was to come.

By the bone-dry chalk peak He stayed, day after day, eating nothing, praying, preparing Himself. Presumably He brought some water with Him, because we hear nothing at this point of the torments of thirst; they were to come to Him on the Cross. But the fast was total, and Jesus' human body suffered from it just as our bodies would suffer. When the forty days were over He was weakened, and longed for food. Some of the rocks strewn over the mountainside were shaped like loaves of bread. Perhaps He looked on them, and wished that they were bread. Then Satan appeared, to urge Him to turn them into bread and eat them.[40]

It is the general view of orthodox exegetes that Satan cannot then have known fully and for certain Who Christ was, or he would not have dared to try to tempt Him. If so—and it seems most probable—then the secret of Who had been dwelling in Nazareth for the past thirty years had been kept from Hell as well as from earth. The little town in the vale off the beaten track in Galilee, and the house of the Holy Family, had been protected even better than we know. Satan presumed that Jesus was the Messiah; it seems he did not know, or was not sure, that He was God and therefore incapable of sin.[41]

Said Our Lord to His adversary: "It is written, 'Man shall not live by bread alone, but by every word that proceeds from the mouth of God.'"[42]

Then Christ actually surrendered Himself to being transported by Satan—was it for this, among other fearful indignities, that He had steeled His body and will during the long fast?—to the top of the Temple, from which Satan urged Him to throw Himself down so that angels might spectacularly save Him in the sight of all the people. Christ answered: "It is written, 'You shall not tempt the Lord your God.'"[43] Then Satan "showed him all the kingdoms of the world and the glory of them"—mighty Rome, with Emperor Tiberius broken-hearted in Capri; far-flung Parthia, where kings, when they took the throne, often murdered all their brothers as a necessary safeguard against rebellion; glittering India, where Satan's gods still reigned supreme; busy, wealthy China, far beyond the ken of the world Christ knew as man, honoring human wisdom, still unable to understand that human wisdom alone is never enough—and said: "All these I will give you, if you will fall down and worship me."[44] The leader of the revolt of the angels was trying to claim for himself the Savior Whom God had sent to mankind by pandering to the false idea of the Messiah as a political and military leader. So long as Satan did not know, or was not sure, that Jesus the Messiah was God, he had some reason to hope for success.[45]

"Begone, Satan! for it is written, ''You shall worship the Lord your God and him only shall you serve.'"[46]

Down from the Mount of the Forty Days came Christ, Victor—and back to the Jordan where John, still baptizing, hailed Him as "the lamb of God."[47] The reference can hardly be other than to the 53rd chapter of Isaiah, the great prophecy of the Suffering Servant and the Passion—little as this prophecy was then cited among Jews.[48] Soon afterward, this time accompanied by just two of his disciples, John the Baptist saw Jesus again, repeating to them: "Behold the lamb of God!" At once they set off to follow Jesus.[49]

These two were the first of the Twelve, symbolizing the Twelve Tribes of Israel in the new dispensation, who were to be called "apostles," meaning men sent on a special mission.[50] One of them was named Andrew; he and his brother

Simon, sons of John, were fishermen on the Sea of Galilee. The other was (in all probability) a young man of about twenty named John, the son of Zebedee, a fishing boat owner.[51] Jesus took them with Him to His temporary dwelling in a hut or cave near the Jordan, and talked with them there for hours. As soon afterward as he could, Andrew went to his brother Simon to bring him to meet Jesus, crying out joyfully: "We have found the Messiah!" When Simon came, Jesus told him: "You shall be called Rock."[52] Only much later was the meaning of this new name—Cephas in Aramaic, Petros or Peter in Greek, never before used as a proper name among Jews[53]—to be explained. For this was not yet the final call of the Twelve Apostles; Jesus' "hour had not yet come."[54]

Travelling northward toward Galilee in March of 28 A.D.,[55] Jesus met Philip, who like Andrew and Simon came from the town of Bethsaida on the Sea of Galilee. It seems likely that Philip was introduced to Him by the two brothers who were accompanying Jesus. To Philip, Jesus said simply, "Follow me"— and Philip followed.[56] Very possibly near Bethel, where Jacob sixteen centuries before had seen his unforgettable vision of the ladder or stairway with angels ascending to and descending from Heaven,[57] Philip found a friend named Nathanael from the Galilean village of Cana near Nazareth, and told him that the Messiah had come and was actually with them: "Jesus of Nazareth, the son of Joseph." Nathanael demurred: "Can anything good come out of Nazareth?" But he came to Christ, Who read his heart. Nathanael confessed Him to be "the Son of God . . . the King of Israel." Jesus replied with the assurance that "you shall see heaven opened and the angels of God ascending and descending upon the Son of Man"—probably a reference to His Ascension to come, in the context of Jacob's vision.[58] Nathanael became, in all probability, the Apostle Bartholomew, which means *bar-tolmai*, son of Tolmai, and is therefore the equivalent of a surname rather than a given name such as Nathanael.[59]

In Cana, Nathanael Bar-Tolmai's home town, Jesus rejoined His mother at a wedding feast. It is one of the most beloved of all the incomparable stories from His life, how the wine ran out and at Mary's pleading, despite His initial hesitation ("my hour has not yet come") He changed some 150 gallons of water in six great stone jars into the finest of wines.[60] (Puritanical types then and now would have been much better satisfied if He had turned wine into water; but He had come to bring joy to the world, and this was a sign of it, as well as a foreshadowing of His special blessing upon marriage as an indissoluble, sacramental bond.) Then He turned about and set His steps toward Jerusalem to begin His public life at the Passover, the greatest annual celebration of the Chosen People, just two years before the Passover at which He was to die.[61] The following table shows the chronological reconstruction of Jesus' life during these two years which is the basis of the narrative here set forth.

THE PUBLIC LIFE OF CHRIST, 28-30 A.D.

(*Note*: The chronology of Jesus' public life is not known with certainty and is disputed even among orthodox exegetes. What follows is the reconstruction on which the narrative in Chapters Fifteen and Sixteen is based, justified at major points of controversy in the chapter notes.)

March, 28	Jesus goes to Jerusalem for the Passover and drives the money-changers from the temple
April, 28	Jesus' conversation with Nicodemus in Jerusalem further testimony of John the Baptist to Jesus; arrest of John
May, 28	Jesus, returning to Galilee, encounters the Samaritan woman at the well Jesus' first preaching and cures in Galilee second calling of Andrew and Peter; calling of James and John
June, 28	cure of the paralytic in Capernaum calling of Matthew and the others of the Twelve
July, 28	Sermon on the Mount
Aug.-Sept., 28	Jesus raises the son of the widow of Naim the message from John the Baptist and Jesus' reply Mary Magdalene, cleansed and forgiven, anoints the feet of Jesus
October, 28	Jesus calms the storm Jesus cures Jairus' daughter, the woman with the hemorrhage, and the Gerasene demoniac the "Day of Parables"
Nov.-Dec., 28	Jesus sends the Twelve on their first missionary journey Jesus visits Nazareth and is driven out
Jan.-Feb., 29	execution of John the Baptist
Mar.-Apr., 29	the second Passover in Jesus' public life first multiplication of the loaves and fishes Jesus' discourse on the Bread of Life, at the synagogue in Capernaum
May-June, 29	Jesus goes to Phoenicia
July, 29	Jesus among the Gentiles of the Decapolis; second multiplication of the loaves and fishes

THE PUBLIC LIFE OF CHRIST, 28-30 A.D.

	Peter's confession of faith on the road to Caesarea Philippi; Jesus' commission to Peter as head of His Church
August, 29	the Transfiguration; final teachings in Galilee
September, 29	condemnation of the sinful cities; Jesus departs from Galilee
October, 29	Jesus in Jerusalem for the Feast of Tabernacles; cure of the man born blind
November, 29	Jesus in Judea; the mission of the Seventy-Two
December, 29	Jesus at Bethany, then in Jerusalem for the Feast of Dedication
Jan.-Feb., 30	Jesus' teachings in Peraea
March, 30	Jesus' teaching on the indissolubility of marriage the raising of Lazarus; the Sanhedrin orders the arrest of Jesus Jesus sets out for Jerusalem for the Passover; his arrival in Jericho, welcome by Zacchaeus, cure of Bartimaeus
April, 30	(2) Palm Sunday
	(3) second cleansing of the Temple
	(4) Jesus teaching in the Temple—denunciation of the Pharisees
	(4) Jesus' teaching to the Apostles on Mount Olivet regarding the end of the world
	(5) Judas offers to betray Jesus to the Sanhedrin
	(6) Holy Thursday—the Last Supper; the agony in the Garden of Gethsemane
	(7) Good Friday—the arrest and condemnation of Jesus; the Passion
	(8) Holy Saturday—Jesus in the tomb; the Passover
	(9) Easter—the Resurrection of Jesus

The immense annual pilgrimage to Jerusalem for the Passover brought Jews by the hundreds of thousands—possibly by the millions—from all over the Mediterranean world.[62] It was the religious climax of every year, the Chosen People assembling in all the strength of their faith and hope, drawing still more strength and faith and hope from their numbers and their fervor. Yet they had no real leader any longer. Pontius Pilate, a despised Gentile, governed Judea for Rome; the effective head of Israel was Annas the former high priest, now ruling through his sons, but he and they were venal, corrupt and hated.[63] John the Baptist, still in the desert at this Passover, would soon be arrested and imprisoned until he was slain. There could have been no time and place nearly so appropriate for Jesus Christ to begin His public life as the Passover in Jerusalem, in the presence of so large a proportion of His people. This He did, in unexpected and highly dramatic fashion, by using a whip He made Himself to drive from the courtyards of the Temple the animal sellers and the money-changers who swarmed there with the permission and encouragement of the priestly authorities, to extort, in noisy bargaining, large profits from the pilgrims whom the Law required to present animals for the sacrifices, and shekel coins for offering rather than Roman currency.[64]

As all Christians know, love is the heart of Christ's ministry and mission. Yet His public life begins with an act of holy anger against lack of reverence for God the Father, Who sanctified the Temple by His special presence within it, and against economic injustice to the poor. Some may wish to emphasize His striking against the irreverence, others His striking against the economic injustice. He did not separate the two. Nor did He hesitate to use physical force, thereby establishing once and for all, contrary to modern pacifists, that the use of physical force is not always evil in itself. The teaching of love would come when men were prepared to listen. But first they must know that One had come among them with a power which was God's.

Questioned as to the authority by which He had driven the money-changers and the animal sellers from the Temple, Jesus replied only: "Destroy this temple, and in three days I will raise it up."[65] Scoffing, His hearers nevertheless remembered what He had said, though only in garbled form; later they were to testify at His trial that He had threatened to destroy the Temple.[66] It was a prophecy of His Resurrection, a warning of the consequences of continued profanation of the Temple and all it represented,[67] and a foreshadowing of the Church, His Mystical Body, which would replace it.

Jesus withdrew from Jerusalem, but spent a few spring weeks in Judea. Some of His disciples began to give a baptism like John's (almost certainly not sacramental baptism, since the Trinity had not yet been revealed);[68] some of John's disciples protested, since John was still baptizing not far away. But John replied with a new and beautiful testimony to Jesus, reiterating his role as precursor, calling himself "the friend of the Bridegroom," and concluding: "He must increase, but I must decrease."[69]

It was the end of John's public ministry; for very soon afterward he denounced the bigamous and incestuous "marriage" of Herod Antipas of Galilee to Herodias, his brother's wife and his niece, and was betrayed—presumably by the Pharisees, whom he had denounced in his earlier preaching by the Jordan—into Herod Antipas' hands. John was imprisoned in the fortress of

Machaerus in the wild scored desert southeast of the Dead Sea, where Herod Antipas often came because of the threat to his frontiers in this region from Aretas, king of the Nabataeans, whose daughter he had put away in order to marry Herodias.[70]

The Pharisees' betrayal of John was a clear warning that Jesus, Who had already incurred their enmity at the time of His cleansing of the Temple,[71] might soon face similar treatment if He remained near Jerusalem, the center of their power.[72] It was not time for this. First He must preach in Galilee. Those among whom Jesus had lived unknown during the silent years must now hear His voice and His message.

The shortest road from Judea to Galilee ran through Samaria, though so great was the hostility between Jews and Samaritans that Jewish pilgrims tried to avoid travelling that road if at all possible.[73] But Jesus had no fear. His worst enemies were among His own people; no pagan or non-Jew ever really threatened Him. His Word was to break down the 2000-year-old barrier between Jew and Gentile, though He was sent first of all "to the lost sheep of the house of Israel."[74] Among the Jews, for a long time, He could not openly proclaim Himself the Messiah without immediately being cast in the role of political and military leader, which it was His fixed purpose to avoid at all costs.[75] But there was one other people—just one—who, like the Jews, knew that the Messiah would come and eagerly awaited his advent. They were the Samaritans. It was to one of them, an uneducated and sinful woman drawing water from Jacob's Well, that Jesus, in a scene of matchless tenderness and condescension, revealed Himself for the first time explicitly as the Messiah.[76]

Blooming, proverbially fruitful, Galilee lay before her Savior as He came down from the hill country around Nazareth on the way from Jerusalem and Samaria to the deep basin where lay the beautiful harp-shaped lake called Gennesareth, the Sea of Galilee. The great fertility of the volcanic soil, the abundance of fish in the cool waters of the lake which drained the high mountains of Lebanon, and the working of a long-established and well-designed irrigation system supported a large population along its then well-wooded shores, in striking contrast to its denuded loneliness today outside the one city surviving from Christ's time, Tiberias. One of the largest of the flourishing now-vanished cities of the shore of the Sea of Galilee was Capernaum. Unlike Tiberias, it was inhabited almost entirely by Jews. In Capernaum Jesus established what was, in effect, the headquarters for his Galilean mission, which probably lasted about 500 days, from May of 28 A.D. through September of 29 A.D., including one intercalary lunar month in the spring of 29.[77]

Jesus had worked His first miracle at the wedding feast at Cana, by changing the water into wine; again at Cana, on his way back from Jerusalem and the encounter with the Samaritan woman, He healed the son of an official of Herod Antipas' court who resided in Capernaum.[78] His reputation as a miracle worker preceded Him to Capernaum, ensuring a large and eager audience as He preached in the synagogue there and in the synagogues of surrounding towns, upon the necessity of repentance and the imminent coming of the kingdom of God.[79] In the synagogue at Capernaum, one Sabbath day, He performed a public exorcism, followed later that same day by a miraculous healing of Simon Peter's mother-in-law. Reports of these extraordinary events spread quickly, and by the evening of that Sabbath Jesus was veritably besieged by sick people and victims of diabolical possession, many of whom He healed.[80]

The miracles of Jesus fall into two broad categories: miracles of healing, physical and spiritual; and miracles of special aid and provision, such as the changing of water into wine, the multiplication of bread and fish, and the calming of the storm on the Sea of Galilee. All these miracles were the outpouring of a merciful love, to overcome various consequences of sin and the fall of man; hence they manifested in a special way Christ's role as Savior. Most were widely publicized. Although in many cases Jesus asked the beneficiary of the miracle to tell no one what had happened, His request was usually not heeded; and in many other cases—such as the exorcism in the synagogue at Capernaum—He performed the miracle in public, before a large crowd. Clearly the miracles had a twofold purpose: the direct and immediate purpose of curing or providing and the broader long-range purpose of proving His Divine power, thereby authenticating His authority and gradually opening the minds of the people so that some at least could begin to understand the Incarnation. This was exceedingly difficult, because the Messiah was not expected to *be* God, nor was His sacrificial role in expiation of sin anticipated, despite the 53rd chapter of Isaiah. Without the evidence of the miracles to support His credibility, few would have found themselves able to believe.

The miracles, often worked before groups including Jesus' deadly enemies, were beyond the possibility of natural explanation then, and remain beyond it now. In most instances the lack of modern scientific knowledge by the people of Jesus' time has no bearing on the matter whatsoever, because we of the late twentieth century can explain the event as reported no better than could Jesus' contemporaries. For example, the son of Herod Antipas' official at Capernaum was cured at the instant Jesus announced that He would cure him, in Cana, at one o'clock in the afternoon, twenty miles away.[81] No theory of faith healing by suggestion can account for this instantaneous cure at a distance, without any reason for anticipation by the person cured that the healing would occur at that particular time—nor for the restoration of sight to a man born blind or the raising of a man four days dead and in the tomb, to mention only two of the most spectacular later miracles.

The one class of Jesus' miracles we may think we can explain naturally while His contemporaries could not, is the exorcisms. To many moderns it seems obvious that these were all cases of mental illness cured by psychological means.

But this begs the question of what mental illness really is, and how many of its causes we really know. Physical illness may be defined by the presence of a disease-causing organism, a bacillus or virus. Mental illness may, and usually does exist without detectable differences in the organism between the sick and the healthy. There are known ways of treating mental illness—ways which by no means always succeed—but its cure is not a science. Demonic possession can exist as well as "normal" mental illness, and few psychiatrists today, given their world-view, could or would attempt to tell them apart. Yet exorcisms continue today, in Christ's Name—and succeed.

The north shore of the Sea of Galilee, where Capernaum lay, was home to Andrew and John, whom John the Baptist had first directed to Jesus by the Jordan, saying "Behold the Lamb of God!"—home also to their brothers, Simon Peter and James, respectively.[82] It is likely that these four, or at least some of them, had remained with Jesus since first meeting Him in March.[83] In Capernaum, Jesus was probably living in Simon Peter's house.[84] But, having returned home, it seemed reasonable to the two pairs of brothers that they should resume their usual work of fishing. They were not very poor men, but neither were they rich;[85] the necessities of life still had to be provided, and they did not yet know exactly what their Master expected of them. So once again, as in the past before they had beheld the Lamb of God, they took their boats out into the deep waters of the lake by night, letting down their nets and hauling in their catch.[86] Neither they, nor any man who knew them, excepting only Him Who knows all, could have imagined the life and work and death that lay ahead of them: the cross and crown of martyrdom in far-distant lands, the rulership of the Church of Christ, the authorship of the sublime Fourth Gospel. Only the Maker of the stars which glinted down through the clear night sky upon the dark lake and its toiling fishermen knew; and not yet did those fishermen fully realize that it was He Who had come to them as their countryman and their brother.

All one night they labored without catching anything. Their nets were empty. When morning came they drew them ashore and began to wash them. Jesus came by, surrounded by the crowd that now seemed to follow Him everywhere He went. He wished to speak to them and they to hear Him, but there was no elevated or isolated place—no natural pulpit—from which He might address them. So He asked Simon Peter for his boat, to speak from it, just offshore on the still waters. When Jesus had finished speaking, He turned to Peter and said: "Put out into the deep and let down your nets for a catch."[87]

Peter was astonished, knowing that very few fish could be netted there in the morning, but he obeyed; and the happy miracle that followed is almost the only one of Christ's that we can actually visualize in the making without presumption or fantasy. For it is most unlikely that the Lord of life suddenly created from nothing the great shoal of fish which appeared in Peter's net on that unforgettable occasion; the lake was already full of them, though not normally swimming at levels where they could be caught in quantity in the morning, and what He most probably did was to call them. From their haunts in the deep waters the fish, His creatures, came at their Maker's bidding, swimming into Peter's net. So, at the call of grace, were millions to come into Christ's Church. The fish was for long a well-known, semi-secret symbol for a Christian in the ancient world.[88]

Simon Peter fell to his knees, the first overwhelming presentiment of an infinite and eternal destiny surging over him, engulfing the hard-headed practicality that was so much a part of his forthright character, bringing an immense awe and a penetrating sense of his own unworthiness: "Depart from me," he cried, "for I am a sinful man, O Lord."[89] But Jesus raised him up, with his brother Andrew, saying: "Follow me, and I will make you fishers of men."[90] Close by on shore were James and John, mending their nets with their father Zebedee. They too were called; they too followed, with Peter and Andrew, then and forever. From that hour began their total commitment to the apostolic life.[91]

Jesus then moved out from Capernaum to smaller towns and villages in Galilee, preaching and healing.[92] Reports of His activity, of the unique authority with which He taught and the unparalleled miracles He was working, came to the Pharisees of Galilee,[93] local representatives of that sect which from the time of the decline of the Maccabees had arrogated the role of moral judges of Israel. To accept a higher authority than their own, whatever the evidence, was more than most of them, in their pride, were then spiritually capable of doing. But they were intelligent men; they knew they faced a phenomenon unprecedented in their individual or collective experience. The easy rationalizations of many modern commentators were not sufficient to satisfy these enemies at the time and on the scene. Jesus was in a class by Himself.

When He returned to Capernaum from His first missionary journey the Pharisees were waiting for Him, mingling with the crowd that gathered about the house—probably still Peter's—where He was staying.[94] So great was the crush of the throng at the door that the bearers of a paralyzed man, brought on a litter, hoping for a cure, could find no way to get him through. Consequently they took advantage of the loose construction of Palestinian houses of that time by making a hole in the roof big enough to let him down on his litter into the room beside Jesus, Who said to him simply: "My son, your sins are forgiven."[95]

The significance of these words of Jesus seems to have been largely lost on Modernist commentators, but the Pharisees understood it perfectly: "Why does this man speak thus? It is blasphemy! Who can forgive sins but God alone?"[96] Who, indeed? Any man may forgive a sin or offense against himself, but he is hardly entitled to forgive sins committed against others by a total stranger. Only God is offended by all sin; therefore only He may forgive any sin, no matter by whom or against whom committed. Here was a clear assumption by Jesus of an exclusively Divine prerogative. The Pharisees knew it; and Jesus knew what they were thinking, even though they had not spoken it aloud:

> "Why do you question this in your hearts? Which is easier, to say to the paralytic, 'Your sins are forgiven,' or to say, 'Rise, take up your pallet and walk'? But that you may know that the Son of man has authority on earth to forgive sins"—he said to the paralytic—"I say to you, rise, take up your pallet and go home." And he rose, and immediately took up the pallet and went out before them all.[97]

In choosing His next apostle, Jesus deliberately and dramatically flouted Pharisaic prejudice. His choice fell upon Levi, a tax collector or publican, hence despised by most Jews and especially by the Pharisees. Levi must have heard of Jesus, for his tax collection booth was located very near Capernaum; we are not told whether he had ever talked or worked with Jesus before being called by Him, but in view of the instant response of Levi's whole being to that call when it came, it would seem likely that he had already loved Him from afar. For Jesus said to him simply: "Follow me," and Levi rose from his booth and followed. He became the Apostle Matthew the Evangelist.[98]

Levi/Matthew gave a great banquet to celebrate his conversion and his vocation. Jesus attended the banquet, despite the fact that other publicans and sinners were invited. The Pharisees had a particular horror of eating with people outside the Law (for this reason it was absolutely forbidden for any Jew to eat with a Gentile); they demanded of Jesus' disciples—not daring to ask Jesus directly—why He ate with publicans and sinners. Jesus answered that it was sinners He had come to help and to heal.[99]

It was now early summer in Galilee.[100] Jesus had made Himself known, proclaiming and proving His authority, though not yet stating clearly Who He was. He had called in a special way five men to be His apostles: Simon Peter and Andrew, James and John the son of Zebedee, and Levi/Matthew. His mission must now take on more definite shape. There was need for a clear exposition of the radical difference between the Truth and the Way and the Life He brought and was, and what fallen man in his flawed nature tends to believe and how fallen man usually lives. And since no doctrine stands in a vacuum, there must be a college of men—imperfect, fallen, wayward men, yet devoted to Jesus and sanctified by that devotion—to teach and live that Truth and Way and Life with and for Him: the Apostolic College, the Twelve.

So He went up on a mountain to pray all night in preparation for their final selection. At dawn He called all His followers together and formally announced His choices: Peter first; then the three other "fishers of men," Andrew, James, and John; then Philip, whom he had first called in the country of John the Baptist; Nathanael/Bartholomew who was Philip's friend; Levi/Matthew the new convert; and Thomas, a twin, of whom we have not heard before—a man hard-headed as Peter himself, cautious, steady, unimaginative, yet as time and grace were to show, utterly relentless in pursuit of a missionary goal, of starkly indestructible courage.[101]

That made eight. Of the last four, the first in all the lists is James the son of Alpheus, in all probability Jesus' cousin, son of the wife of St. Joseph's brother Cleopas, by her first marriage.[102] With him was Jude Thaddeus[103] and Simon the Zealous.[104] Finally there was Judas Iscariot from Judea, the traitor-to-be, who seems to have been the only non-Galilean apostle.[105]

That Judas Iscariot was wholeheartedly devoted to Jesus at this time there is no good reason to doubt. Jesus often showed His love for Judas, trying to draw him back from his fatal course when he began to change. The presence of Judas Iscariot in the Apostolic College is perpetual proof that the Church of Christ, from its beginning to the end of the world, will contain men willing to betray their Lord, or able to be drawn into doing so.[106]

The Apostles chosen, Jesus proceeded to instruct them, and the other disciples from among whom He had chosen the Twelve, and others who had come to Him in search of truth and healing. His instruction was the Sermon on the Mount—that sublime address embodying the greatest revolution of moral principles in all history, the veritable title-deed for the Christian conquest of the world, a spiritual conquest whose like no man had imagined before. These were the words, as William Thomas Walsh says, ''that would send lusty men into deserts and monasteries, draw lovely girls into grilled cells, bring sinners to their knees with tears, and give martyrs the strength to die . . . A reverie like an ineffable music weaving a world of dreams; a trance like that high prayer in which truth and beauty and goodness are seen, heard, and felt.''[107]

There was a sinful woman who had been living in the town of Magdala in Galilee, in whose body seven devils raged; might she have been one of the hearers of the Sermon on the Mount? Did it speak to the depths of her soul? We do not know, but it is possible; for the gospels present us with four scenes of a woman at the feet of Christ, meek and mournful and poor in spirit yet overflowing with love: once, soon after the Sermon on the Mount, to anoint His feet at a banquet given by a leading Galilean Pharisee; once to anoint His feet again at a banquet in Bethany near Jerusalem, given just a week before the Passion by a man whom Jesus had cured; then, at the foot of the Cross; finally, on Resurrection morning. At the house of Simon the Galilean Pharisee, this woman poured out the tribute of her lovez—first in the most costly perfume, then in her tears, then in an ecstasy of homage and adoration as she wiped Christ's feet with her hair. Forgiving her sins, He made her whole by love, while Simon glared and argued uncomprehendingly. In the humility, pardon, and exaltation of this once sinful woman, side by side with the Pharisee's self-centered pride, stands in living tableau much of the lesson of the Sermon on the Mount. It is here maintained, contrary to most modern Biblical scholarship including orthodox, that the woman in all these four scenes was the same: Mary of Magdala ("Tower of Fishes") on the Sea of Galilee. The glory of her redeemed soul stamps each scene with an indelible, inimitable character: John's Gospel (11:1-2) makes it quite clear that the two anointings were both performed by Mary of Bethany, who had evidently been living in Galilee when she first came to follow Jesus, just as we are told of Mary Magdalene.[108]

Jesus continued to travel through Galilee. He taught—more and more often now in His famous parables—and continued to heal, most dramatically in restoring to life the son of the widow of Naim (a little town about eight miles from Nazareth)[109] and the young daughter of Jairus of Capernaum,[110] both of whom had just died. He sent the Twelve in pairs on missionary journeys of their own to "the lost sheep of the house of Israel," commanding them to travel in poverty, proclaim the kingdom of God, cast out devils, and heal the sick, giving them instructions and guidance that are a charter for Christian apostolates through all time.[111] At length He returned to Nazareth, to announce Himself to His fellow townsmen as the Messiah. But they would not believe . . . "Is not this the carpenter's son?" They tried to kill Him when because of their lack of faith He worked too few miracles among them to suit them; but He escaped, because this was not the time or the place for Him to die. His mother must have suffered especially on this occasion, for these would-be murderers of her Son were her people, and this was her ancestral home.[112]

In the bleak fortress of Machaerus in the desert, Herod Antipas put on a grand party to celebrate his birthday. As the drunken revelry reached its climax, his daughter Salome danced the brilliant, lascivious dance she had learned when living in Rome with Herodias and her first husband. Herod Antipas promised Salome anything she might ask as a reward, up to half his kingdom. At her vengeful mother's bidding, Salome asked for the head of John the Baptist, who had long been imprisoned there in Machaerus. Very reluctantly, afraid to break his oath before the many guests, Herod Antipas agreed, committing murder for the sake of worldly respect. The Forerunner, the "voice crying in the wilderness" prophesied so long ago by Isaiah, acclaimed by the Son of God as great a man as was ever born of woman, was slain.[113]

Far away in Italy the Emperor Tiberius from Capri vented his hatred on Julia's daughter Agrippina, charging her (it seems rightly) with insolence and immorality, condemning her, and sending her to the same little island where her mother had been imprisoned by Augustus. Agrippina refused to eat; Tiberius had her force-fed. She raged and fought so savagely that in one struggle she lost an eye.[114]

The grass was green as spring came again to Palestine in 29 A.D.,[115] and the multitudes following Jesus were now enormous. More than five thousand men, with many women and children, accompanied Him to the eastern side of the Sea of Galilee, where He had gone to seek a little privacy with the Apostles.

Taking pity on the people, who seemed to Him "like sheep without a shepherd," He spoke to them about the kingdom of God and healed some of the sick among them. The place where they had all come was sparsely settled, almost a wilderness; there was nothing available there to eat. A boy had brought five barley loaves and two little salted fish. Jesus told the worried Apostles to seat the people in groups of fifties and hundreds. Arranged thus in their multi-colored garments on the blooming grassy plain, they looked, the evangelists tell us, like beds in a beautiful flower garden. Jesus blessed the bread, broke it, and gave it to the Apostles for distribution to the multitude. The food flowed in an unending stream until all those present—probably ten thousand, possibly even more—had eaten their fill.[116]

At some point during the distribution of the food the truth about what was happening began to dawn on the crowd. Perhaps those closest to Jesus noted that all this largesse was coming from a single small basket; perhaps some had overheard the Apostle Andrew tell Jesus that there were only five loaves and two little fish.[117] Here was a public miracle for all, in contrast to the individual miracles of healing and the secret transformation of water into wine at Cana; here was a very material miracle, which set everyone thinking of the manna in the desert at the time of the Exodus.[118] As the people finished their meal and excitement began to build as they discussed where it had come from—we must visualize tidings of the miracle passing from one group of fifty or a hundred to another, all across the plain—Jesus abruptly dismissed all the Apostles, ordering them to take their boat (the only one immediately available) and return to the vicinity of Capernaum.[119] Reluctantly they obeyed. Hardly had they left when the crowd, convinced by the miracle that Jesus was *the* prophet foretold by Moses and in all probability the Messiah, prepared to proclaim Him king— but a king according to their own standards and expectations, a political and military champion to give them empire. Jesus escaped them, and as night fell He went alone to a mountain to pray.[120]

Out in the lake the wind was rising, soon becoming of such intensity that the Apostles in their boat could make almost no headway against it.[121] About three o'clock in the morning Jesus came walking toward them over the water. The scene is memorably described by Alfred Edersheim, on the very probable supposition that the Passover moon was shining in a sky laced with clouds broken by the wind:

> All at once, in the track that lay behind them, a Figure appeared. As It passed onwards over the water, seemingly upborne by the waves as they rose, not disappearing as they fell, but carried on as they rolled, the silvery moon laid upon the trembling waters the shadows of that Form as It moved, long and dark, on their track. St. John uses an expression [*theorein,* John 6:19], which shows us, in the pale light, those in the boat, intently, fixedly, fearfully, gazing at the Apparition as It neared still closer and closer.[122]

They thought Him a ghost; He reassured them, and St. Peter, greatly daring, asked if he might come to Jesus over the tossing waves. Jesus said: "Come." Peter came, by faith, a few steps; then fear overwhelmed him and he began to sink. Jesus rescued him, brought him into the boat, and as He had done before, calmed the storm, while the Apostles fell at His feet in awe. When the crowd that had been fed by the multiplication of the loaves and fishes returned to Capernaum, they found Jesus already there, though they knew the Apostles had left without Him in the only boat. They asked Him in amazement how and when He had arrived in Capernaum, but He would not gratify their curiosity, reproaching them for being impressed only by the material benefit of His miracle on the previous day.[123]

At some time later in this immensely important day, Jesus spoke at the great synagogue in Capernaum.[124] His purpose was to explain the real significance of what He had done the day before on the meadow across the lake. It was far more than to minister to the immediate needs of their bodies. It was to prepare them for both the material and the spiritual reality of the means He had chosen, beginning just one year in the future at the Last Supper, to forge the mystical bond between Him and those who believed in Him and heeded His words: the reception of His body and blood in the great sacramental mystery of the Holy Eucharist.[125]

> "I am the bread of life; he who comes to me shall not hunger, and he who believes in me shall never thirst. . . . I am the living bread which came down from heaven; if any one eats of this bread he will live for ever; and the bread which I shall give for the life of the world is my flesh."
> The Jews then disputed among themselves, saying "How can this man give us his flesh to eat?" So Jesus said to them, "Truly, truly, I say to you, unless you eat the flesh of the Son of man and drink his blood, you have no life in you; he who eats my flesh and drinks my blood has eternal life, and I will raise him up at the last day. For my flesh is food indeed, and my blood is drink indeed. He who eats my flesh and drinks my blood abides in me, and I in him. As the living Father sent me and I live because of the Father, so he who eats me will live because of me."[126]

It was the supreme challenge to faith, before the Crucifixion itself; for this teaching, clear as it is to Catholics who have known the Mass and the Eucharist for twenty centuries, was far from clear to anyone then. Jesus' hearers, in their still all too materialistic imaginations, had horrible visions of cannibalism, possibly even of madness. But this was the Man Who only the day before had fed ten thousand people with five loaves and two fishes, Who only the night before had crossed the Sea of Galilee by walking upon its stormy waters (and even those who had not seen Him doing that knew that He could not have reached Capernaum ahead of them by any natural means). They had followed Him because of His miracles and because of His goodness. Their experience of both gave them more than ample reason to accept even a "hard saying" of His, simply because it was He who said it.

But many, even of His disciples, would not accept; they "drew back and no longer went about with him."[127] The Twelve remained. Jesus looked at them. He saw the struggle within them. Every one of them, like Mary at the Annunciation, had the fullness of free will, and so could have denied or left Jesus at any time; furthermore, none of them were free from sin as Mary always was. What Jesus would have done had all twelve deserted Him, no man can say or guess; the thought is terrible to contemplate. We may be sure, given His great love for the Apostles, that it was a still more terrible thought for Him.

"Do you also wish to go away?"[128] Jesus asked the little wavering line of men whom He had chosen to build His Church.

"Simon Peter answered him, 'Lord, to whom shall we go? You have the words of eternal life; and we have believed, and have come to know, that you are the Holy One of God.'"[129]

St. Peter had stood fast; but perhaps some of the others, at least for a moment, had doubted; and St. John tells us that in this moment Jesus knew that Judas Iscariot had abandoned all faith in Him. All He said to them was this:

"Did I not choose you, the twelve, and one of you is a devil?"[130]

Yet, whether temporarily doubting or not, the other Apostles had held on; the teaching mission of Jesus could continue, but not at this point primarily in Galilee or Judea, for He had temporarily lost the popular support that had been sustaining Him against the intrigues of the Pharisees and the Sadducees. So Jesus and the Twelve departed for the pagan lands north and east of Galilee—Phoenicia on the Mediterranean coast, the Greek cities of the Decapolis beyond the Jordan, and the slopes of Mount Hermon where the Jordan rose. Through those lands they journeyed until midsummer of 29 A.D., probably with one brief visit to Galilee, where Jesus was immediately challenged by the Pharisees and responded with His first direct attack upon their empty formalism. This was Jesus' first and only visit to the Gentile world (except for His sojourn in Egypt as a baby) and here too He found hearers and even faith, presaging His universal mission through His Church. Here He fed four thousand Gentiles in the Decapolis region with seven loaves of bread and a few fish miraculously multiplied, as at the beginning of that spring He had fed some ten thousand of his Jewish followers by the Sea of Galilee.[131]

It was during this journey in the north, on the road to Caesarea Philippi at the foot of snow-capped Mount Hermon, at the principal source of the Jordan River,[132] that Jesus held His decisive dialogue with Peter, which will ring down to the end of the world:

> "Who do men say that the Son of man is?" And they said, "Some say John the Baptist, others say Elijah, and others Jeremiah or one of the prophets." He said to them, "But who do you say that I am?" Simon Peter

replied, "You are the Christ, the Son of the living God." And Jesus answered him, "Blessed are you, Simon Bar-Jona! For flesh and blood has not revealed this to you, but my Father who is in heaven. And I tell you, you are Peter, and on this rock I will build my church, and the powers of death shall not prevail against it. I will give you the keys of the kingdom of heaven, and whatever you bind on earth shall be bound in heaven, and whatever you loose on earth shall be loosed in heaven."[133]

The plain meaning of these words is inescapable. Simon had explicitly recognized and confessed Jesus not only as the Messiah, but as divine, "the Son of the Living God."[134] In return, Jesus had declared his name to be Rock,[135] and that He would found His Church upon the rock that Peter was, a Church to endure forever, teaching God's truth, indestructible by man or devil. That Church of Christ, founded by Him upon Peter, continued under the authority of Peter's legitimate successors,[136] would hold the keys and the powers of the kingdom of Heaven, or the kingdom of God, of which Jesus had so often spoken during His public preaching.

As with Jesus' sermon on the Bread of Life, the meaning of His response to the confession of Peter, the famous *Tu es Petrus*, is so clear that many Modernist critics join orthodox Catholic exegetes—in contrast to Protestants—in affirming that the words do mean what they evidently say. But the Modernists then insist that, precisely because of this clear meaning, Jesus could not have said these words, because in their view He had no intention of founding a church. Yet as scholar after scholar has pointed out, the Aramaic character of the language in this passage is unmistakable.[137] Any falsification of Jesus' words must therefore have preceded the catastrophe of 70 A.D. which destroyed Jewish, Aramaic-speaking Christianity; thus it would have fallen well within living memory of Jesus. Yet there is no hint that the authenticity of the promise to Peter was ever challenged in early Christian times, and it was cited by Christian authors as early as the second century.[138]

Why are Christ's words to Peter found only in Matthew, and not in the other gospels? Because Matthew was there, with Peter and the Twelve, on the road to Caesarea Philippi in the summer of 29 A.D.; he heard the dialogue himself, in his own Aramaic language. Mark the Evangelist was not there; his information came from Peter, and we have very early testimony that out of humility Peter did not include Christ's praise of him in his catechesis.[139] John had the other gospels before him as he wrote, and rarely repeated what they had already reported. Only Luke's silence is difficult to explain; but he did not hear the dialogue either, and writing when Peter was still alive and the Papal succession had therefore not yet begun, and while Paul was doing such great work for the Church, he perhaps did not fully realize the significance of this declaration by Christ. That the passage stands in Matthew, the First Gospel, is enough for the Christian believer.

Jesus now began to instruct the Apostles explicitly regarding the suffering, shameful death, and glorious resurrection that awaited Him. Knowing Him to be the Messiah and Divine, they must be brought to understand as quickly and as fully as possible how different was God's plan for the Messiah His Son than self-glorifying Jewish Messianic expectations had led them to believe. But at that time they found the truth too much to bear; they did not want to understand it. The gospels tell us again and again how they did not really grasp it until the Resurrection had occurred.[140]

Out of the Twelve, the closest now to Jesus, the most developed spiritually, were Peter and the sons of Zebedee, James and John. It was these three who were singled out for the extraordinary privilege of beholding what only John the Baptist had seen before them: direct visible and audible testimony of God the Father to the glory of His Son. Upon a mountain—probably Mount Tabor not far from Nazareth[141]—which Jesus had climbed with these three, He was transfigured before their eyes, radiant with Divine light; and they saw conversing with Him Moses the Lawgiver and Elijah the great early prophet, the two men of the Old Testament who, tradition held, had never really died.[142] The prophet Malachi had predicted Elijah's return before "the great and terrible day of the Lord"—and here he was. Jesus was discussing with Moses and Elijah His coming Passion and death which would achieve the salvation of mankind.[143]

As the three Apostles watched in awe, a shining cloud came and enveloped the two men of the old covenant; from it a voice testified to the Divine Sonship of Jesus. Afterward, Jesus told Peter and James and John to tell no man—not even the other Apostles—what they had seen, until He should have risen from the dead.[144] Thus once more, in a stupendous, ineffable way, was the hard lesson taught to the builders of Christ's Church that He was God—and that He must die.

From Mount Tabor Jesus and the Twelve made their way back to Capernaum. He continued with the instruction and spiritual formation of the Apostles. But the people of Galilee, once so enthusiastic for Him, now seem to have paid little attention to Him—except for a peremptory demand by local officials that He pay His taxes. In human terms, the Galilean mission had been a failure. Only eleven men and a handful of women truly followed Jesus. Others had watched Him, benefitted from His miracles, talked about Him, felt the impulse to seek out and find what He offered—but in the end, did little or nothing to follow through, to understand deeply and truly, to make a lasting commitment.[145] There had been so much promise—the simple, unspoiled people, good-hearted, straightforward, in their blooming land by their beautiful lake, the very own countrymen of Jesus of Nazareth, the Messiah, God Incarnate. But they had not been nearly so good or responsive as they had seemed. The promise was not to be fulfilled there.

The Galilean mission of Jesus ends on a note so grim that few would wish to dwell on it. But rejection is an essential part of the history of Jesus and His Church. Rejection of God began with Adam and will end only with the Antichrist. "He came to his own home," says John the Evangelist, who saw it happen, "and his own people received him not."[146] He looked back on Galilee for the last time before He would return in His Risen Body, and it was probably then[147] that he said:

> Woe to you, Chorazin! woe to you, Bethsaida! for if the mighty works done in you had been done in Tyre and Sidon, they would have repented long ago in sackcloth and ashes. But I tell you, it shall be more tolerable on the day of judgment for Tyre and Sidon than for you. And you, Capernaum, will you be exalted to heaven? You shall be brought down to Hades. For if the mighty works done in you had been done in Sodom, it would have remained until this day. But I tell you that it shall be more tolerable on the day of judgment for the land of Sodom than for you.[148]

Today, nearly two thousand years later, the once lovely land on the shores of the Sea of Galilee lies mostly waste and silent. There is one city, Tiberias—where Jesus never went. There are Christian pilgrims and Christian churches built with money sent from distant lands, but few native believers. Of Capernaum only the ruins of the synagogue remain; for more than a millennium and a half no man knew where the city had been. Scholars dispute whether Bethsaida in Galilee ever existed. Of Chorazin, "nothing is known of it but its doom."[149]

So God came out of Galilee in September of 29 A.D. with only twelve men with Him, one of them a traitor; and the Galilee where God had been, slipped into the everlasting night.

Jesus of Nazareth was on His way to Jerusalem—and to victory over death.

NOTES

[1] Ferdinand Prat, *Jesus Christ, His Life, His Teaching and His Work* (Milwaukee, 1950), I, 41; Giuseppe Ricciotti, *The Life of Christ* (Milwaukee, 1947), pp. 222-223.

[2] L. C. Fillion, *The Life of Christ, a Historical, Critical and Apologetic Exposition*, 2d ed. (St. Louis, 1928), I, 373-374.

[3] *e.g.*, Nathanael's remark quoted in John 1:46.

[4] Isaiah 9:1; M.-J. Lagrange, *The Gospel of Jesus Christ* (Westminster MD, 1938), I, 126. See the discussion of this prophecy in Chapter Six, above.

[5] Isaiah 56:8-9.

[6] See the extended discussion of the development of Christ's human personality in Fillion, *Life of Christ*, I, 388-476.

[7] Henri Daniel-Rops, *Jesus and His Times* (New York, 1956), p. 113.

[8] See the commentary of Prat, *Jesus Christ*, I, 127-132, on this point.

[9] For a well documented statement of the case for the translation "about my Father's business" rather than "in my Father's house" (the Revised Standard Version translation now favored by the majority of exegetes) see Andres Fernandez, *The Life of Christ* (Westminster MD, 1958), p. 156n; for a good review and discussion of the finding of

the Child Jesus in the Temple, see Ricciotti, *Life of Christ*, pp. 262-264. For a scholarly, thoroughgoing defense of the proposition that Jesus always knew that He was God, see William G. Most, *The Consciousness of Christ* (Front Royal VA, 1980).

[10] *The Cambridge Ancient History*, Volume X (Cambridge, England, 1934), pp. 144, 151-155; G. P. Baker, *Tiberius Caesar* (London, 1929), pp. 5-25, 44-51, 62-75.

[11] Baker, *Tiberius*, pp. 78-81.

[12] *Ibid.*, pp. 83-90.

[13] *Cambridge Ancient History*, X, 612.

[14] *Ibid.*, pp. 368-376.

[15] Baker, *Tiberius*, pp. 130-131.

[16] Daniel-Rops, *Jesus and His Times*, pp. 111-112.

[17] An excellent discussion and resolution of this old and difficult problem appears in Prat, *Jesus Christ*, I, 132-137 and 500-506, especially the summary on p. 506. The otherwise clear and brilliant exposition is marred only by the use of the term "sister" in several places to refer to the Blessed Virgin Mary's sister-in-law, Mary the wife of Cleopas, who was later to stand with the Blessed Virgin and Mary Magdalene and St. John at the foot of the Cross. Although there is some evidence of a blood relationship between the Blessed Virgin Mary and her sister-in-law, it is exceedingly unlikely that they were full sisters since they bore the same name, and not much more likely that they were half-sisters, for the same reason. On the proposition, still advocated by many who reject Mary's perpetual virginity, that James and Joseph and Simon and Jude, or some of them, were Jesus' full blood brothers, see the decisive refutation in Lagrange, *Gospel of Jesus Christ*, I, 204-205, who points out that Mary the mother of James and Joseph is several times mentioned in the gospels and clearly distinguished from Mary the mother of Jesus.

[18] Prat, *Jesus Christ*, I, 138-139, 504-509. Prat accepts the Apostle James the Less, later Bishop of Jerusalem, as that James who according to his reconstruction was a son of the Blessed Virgin Mary's sister-in-law Mary by a previous husband (before Cleopas) named Alpheus. Galatians 1:18-19—"I went up to Jerusalem to visit Cephas [Peter], and remained with him fifteen days. But I saw none of the other apostles except James the Lord's brother"—would seem to furnish clear proof that James was one of the Twelve. Prat (*loc. cit.*) further identifies Simon, son of the Blessed Virgin Mary's sister-in-law Mary by Cleopas, as the Simeon who succeeded James as Bishop of Jerusalem, and Simon's full brother Jude as the author of the canonical epistle in the New Testament bearing his name. See Notes 102 and 103, below.

[19] Franz M. Willam, *The Life of Jesus Christ in the Land of Israel and Among Its People*, ed. Newton Thompson (St. Louis, 1938), pp. 51-52.

[20] Baker, *Tiberius*, pp. 172-179.

[21] *Ibid.*, pp. 185-194.

[22] *Ibid.*, pp. 194-220.

[23] *Ibid.*, pp. 221-228; *Cambridge Ancient History*, X, 623-631.

[24] Baker, *Tiberius*, pp. 229-232.

[25] *Cambridge Ancient History*, X, 631-632, 638. The truth of this intensely dramatic report from our ancient sources is sometimes questioned, *e.g.* by Barbara Levick, *Tiberius the Politician* (London, 1976), pp. 161-162. But it is affirmed by the *Cambridge Ancient History* and by Frank B. Marsh, *The Reign of Tiberius* (London, 1931), pp. 163-165, 198-199, and regarded as probable by Robin Seager, *Tiberius* (London, 1972), pp. 181-187. The event as described to us is neither very improbable nor by any means unprecedented in the lives of the mighty.

[26] Baker, *Tiberius*, pp. 241-245.

[27] This is based on the usual practice of the time, of reckoning as the first year of

a reign the interval, regardless of its actual chronological length, between the ruler's accession and the next civil new year, which began in Syria on the first day of the month Hyperberetaios or Tishri, roughly our October. Since Augustus died and Tiberius succeeded on August 19, 14 A.D., counting Tiberius' first year from then to October of 14 A.D., his fifteenth year would begin in October of 27 A.D. See Ricciotti, *Life of Christ*, pp. 157-159; Jack Finegan, *Handbook of Biblical Chronology* (Princeton NJ, 1964), pp. 88-92, 260, and Table 128 on p. 268; Eugen Ruckstuhl, *Chronology of the Last Days of Jesus* (New York, 1965), p. 6; Harold W. Hoehner, *Herod Antipas, a Contemporary of Jesus Christ* (Grand Rapids MI, 1972), pp. 308-312. If one grants the very likely premise that Luke, the only New Testament writer to mention this date (3:1), who was a citizen of Antioch, was using the Syrian system for dating the beginning of the year which in any case would probably have been the official standard since Syria was the nearest Roman province, it is unnecessary to resort to the much more dubious hypothesis of Finegan, *op. cit.*, pp. 259-260, and others, that the dating was from Tiberius' assumption of joint rule of the Roman provinces with Augustus in 12 A.D. rather than from his becoming Emperor on Augustus' death in 14. Or, if Luke was using the Julian year of Rome but counting Tiberius' first year from August to December only, the fifteenth year of Tiberius would begin January 1, 28 A.D.—only three months later than the Syrian reckoning.

[28] Luke 3:2-3.

[29] Giuseppe Ricciotti, *The History of Israel* (Milwaukee, 1955), II, 358-373.

[30] John 1:21; Malachi 4:5; Matthew 11:14.

[31] John 1:21; Deuteronomy 18:15; Matthew 11:13; John 5:45-46. See Chapter Three, above, Notes 62 and 63.

[32] John 1:20, 25-27.

[33] Matthew 11:11.

[34] Ricciotti, *Life of Christ*, p. 271.

[35] *Ibid.*, p. 267; Fernandez, *Life of Christ*, pp. 173-174; Prat, *Jesus Christ*, I, 146-148; Alfred Edersheim, *The Life and Times of Jesus the Messiah*, 3d ed. (New York, 1896), I, 324-335. There is no trace in all that we are told of John the Baptist of the extraordinary concern with ritual purity and the exaggerated sabbatarianism—going far beyond even that of the Pharisees—which characterized the Essenes and the Qumran community, nor of their Gnostic contempt for the body and for all material creation. Even John the Baptist's ascetic diet of locusts, being animal food, was directly contrary to Essene law (Edersheim, *op. cit.*, I, 264).

[36] Fernandez, *Life of Christ*, pp. 183-188.

[37] Mark 1:7-8.

[38] Fernandez, *Life of Christ*, pp. 190-197.

[39] Ricciotti, *Life of Christ*, pp. 272-274. If, following clear indications in the Gospel of John, we accept with all the major authorities on the life of Christ cited herein that there were three Passovers during Christ's public life—that of 28 A.D. at the beginning, that of 29 in the middle, and that of 30 at the end—and if John the Baptist's public ministry could have begun no earlier than October of 27 (see Note 27, above), then, allowing a reasonable time for John's preaching as forerunner to be carried on before Christ came to him for baptism, only the winter of 28 A.D. remains available for Christ's fast and temptation before entering on His public life with the Passover of 28.

[40] Daniel-Rops, *Jesus and His Times*, pp. 140-143.

[41] Prat, *Jesus Christ*, I, 157; Fernandez, *Life of Christ*, pp. 198-201.

[42] Matthew 4:4.

[43] Matthew 4:5-7.

[44] Matthew 4:9. For the Parthian royal practice of eliminating brothers, see *Cambridge*

Ancient History, X, 257, and Neilson C. Debevoise, *A Political History of Parthia* (Chicago, 1938), pp. 120-121.

⁴⁵ Fillion, *Life of Christ*, II, 63-64.

⁴⁶ Matthew 4:10.

⁴⁷ Prat, *Jesus Christ*, I, 165-166. For the rabbinic understanding of the daily sacrifices of lambs as a means for the forgiveness of sin, see Edersheim, *Jesus the Messiah*, I, 342-344.

⁴⁸ Paul Heinisch, *Christ in Prophecy* (Collegeville MN, 1956), p. 156; Daniel-Rops, *Jesus and His Times*, p. 73. Edersheim (*Jesus the Messiah*, I, 337) describes the mind of John the Baptist as "saturated" with the prophecies of Isaiah.

⁴⁹ John 1:35-37.

⁵⁰ Manuel Miguens, *Church Ministries in New Testament Times* (Westminster MD, 1976), pp. 4-21.

⁵¹ Ricciotti, *Life of Christ*, p. 308.

⁵² Fernandez, *Life of Christ*, pp. 214-215.

⁵³ Ricciotti, *Life of Christ*, p. 279.

⁵⁴ John 2:4.

⁵⁵ The month is defined by the estimated date of Jesus' baptism by John in late 27 A.D., and the Passover of the year 28, which was either March 30th or April 28th (Ricciotti, *Life of Christ*, p. 162). See Note 39, above, and Note 61, below. The intervening period included the forty days' fast followed by the first call to the Apostles.

⁵⁶ Ricciotti, *Life of Christ*, p. 280.

⁵⁷ See Chapter Two, above, for commentary.

⁵⁸ Ricciotti, *Life of Christ*, pp. 280-281; Ronald Knox, *A Commentary on the Gospels* (New York, 1952), pp. 206-207.

⁵⁹ Prat, *Jesus Christ*, I, 233-234.

⁶⁰ John 2:1-11. The problem of Jesus' apparently harsh response to Mary's intercession (John 2:4, translated "O woman, what have you to do with me?" in the Revised Standard Version; "What wouldst thou have me do, woman?" in the Catholic Douay-Confraternity version; "Nay, woman, why dost thou trouble me with that?" in Ronald Knox's translation; and "Woman, why turn to me?" in the Jerusalem Bible, is fully and well discussed by Fernandez, *Life of Christ*, pp. 226-232; see also Ricciotti, *Life of Christ*, p. 284, on the use of "Woman" as an especially honorable title of address, like *Madonna* in Renaissance Italy or "Milady" in nineteenth-century English, totally without the connotation it carries in English today. The basic difficulty, as the variant translations indicate, is that we are dealing with an essentially untranslatable Semitic idiom. Its meaning in the context is given by Fernandez, *loc. cit.*, as "Don't ask me to do this."

⁶¹ Ricciotti, *Life of Christ*, pp. 159-161. The year of the first Passover of Jesus' public life may be dated with remarkable precision by the reference in the Gospel of John describing it (2:20) to the Temple having been in the process of building for 46 years up to that Passover. Since we know that construction of the Temple began during the eighteenth year of King Herod, including parts of the years 20 and 19 B.C. by our reckoning, 46 years after that would be 28 A.D. (keeping in mind that there is no "year zero"). See Lagrange, *Gospel of Jesus Christ*, I, 97-98.

⁶² Fernandez, *Life of Christ*, pp. 244-249.

⁶³ *Ibid.*, pp. 679-680. There is abundant rabbinic testimony to the vast ill-gotten wealth and massive corruption of the High Priests of this period in general and of Annas and his family in particular; see Edersheim, *Jesus the Messiah*, I, 367-372. Edersheim's old but still very useful life of Christ is particularly valuable for the wealth of information drawn from rabbinic sources.

[64] Prat, *Jesus Christ*, I, 180-182; II, 327-328. The Talmud reports that one time during the control of the high priesthood by the family of Annas, the price of pigeons for the Temple sacrifices was driven up by their monopoly to the unheard-of level of one gold denarius per bird.

[65] John 2:19.

[66] Matthew 26:61; Mark 14:58.

[67] Constant Fouard, *The Christ the Son of God* (New York, 1924), I, 168.

[68] Lagrange, *Gospel of Jesus Christ*, I, 105-106; Prat, *Jesus Christ*, I, 188.

[69] John 3:25-30.

[70] Ricciotti, *Life of Christ*, pp. 19-20; Willam, *Life of Jesus Christ*, pp. 100-102. On the Pharisees' probable role in the betrayal of John the Baptist, see Prat, *Jesus Christ*, I, 193n.

[71] This is evident in the fact that Nicodemus, a member of the Sanhedrin—the highest authority in Judaism—and a Pharisee, had to visit Jesus in Jerusalem secretly at night, shortly after His cleansing of the Temple. See Fernandez, *Life of Christ*, pp. 257-258.

[72] Fernandez, *Life of Christ*, pp. 277-278.

[73] Prat, *Jesus Christ*, I, 193-196.

[74] Matthew 15:24.

[75] This fixed purpose of avoiding any political or military role is so obvious in passage after passage of the gospels, even before His unequivocal statement to Pilate that "My kingdom is not of this world" (*e.g.* Matthew 22:21, 26:52; John 6:15; and all the "Messianic secret" passages, *e.g.* Mark 5:43, 7:26 and 8:30; Matthew 16:20; Luke 9:21) that one marvels at the bias of the many who still describe Jesus as coming largely or entirely as a temporal "liberator." This position can only be maintained by a wholesale rejection of the historicity of the gospels and a substitution for them of hypotheses crafted mostly from sheer imagination. To quote a recent outstanding history of Galilee in these times by a Jewish author: "It is clear that Jesus, with his explicit rejection of the Zealot ideology, could never have functioned as the charismatic prophet that a revolutionary Galilee would have required." (Sean Freyne, *Galilee from Alexander the Great to Hadrian* [Wilmington DE, 1980], p. 229)

[76] Ricciotti, *Life of Christ*, pp. 296-301. See Prat, *Jesus Christ*, I, 201-203, for a refutation of the view, once widely accepted, that the reference in this story to a farmers' proverb "yet four months and the harvest comes" is meant literally and so dates this episode, and hence Jesus' return to Galilee to begin His ministry there, in December or January, being four months before the harvest, rather than in May when it actually took place, according to the chronology herein adopted.

[77] Prat, *Jesus Christ*, I, 209-213; Freyne, *Galilee*, pp. 129-134; Willam, *Life of Jesus Christ*, pp. 111-113; Daniel-Rops, *Jesus and His Times*, pp. 166-167, 173-175. Tiberias was founded by Herod Antipas about the beginning of the rule of the Emperor for whom it was named. Its mixed population was formerly thought to have been mostly pagan; Freyne, *loc. cit.*, gives evidence that Jews had settled there, probably a majority of the inhabitants, but many under coercion since the city was ritually impure, having been built partly on a cemetery. Other Galilean Jews tended to avoid it throughout Herod Antipas' reign; Jesus never went there.

[78] Ricciotti, *Life of Christ*, pp. 301-302.

[79] See Prat, *Jesus Christ*, I, 216-220, for an excellent brief discussion of the often obscure meaning of the phrase "kingdom of God." The word formerly always translated into English as "kingdom," now sometimes as "reign," is *malkuth* in Hebrew, *basileia* in Greek, and *regnum* in Latin. As Prat points out, all these words have "three meanings which modern languages distinguish . . . the sovereign power of God . . . the exer-

cise of this power, and . . . the domain in which it is exercised'' (*op. cit.*, I, 216).

[80] Ricciotti, *Life of Christ*, pp. 303-304.

[81] See Note 78, above.

[82] Ricciotti, *Life of Christ*, pp. 279-280, 308. It is likely that the four formed a fishing partnership in the legal sense of the time, a business association rather similar to our present-day legal partnerships (Ricciotti, *op. cit.*, p. 308n; Willam, *Life of Jesus Christ*, pp. 134-138).

[83] Prat, *Jesus Christ*, I, 224-225; Ricciotti, *Life of Christ*, p. 306.

[84] He is known to have stayed there at least at the time of the cure of Peter's mother-in-law (Mark 1:29-31).

[85] Willam, *Life of Jesus Christ*, pp. 133-134.

[86] *Ibid.*, pp. 137-139, for a description of fishing on the Sea of Galilee.

[87] Luke 5:4; Ricciotti, *Life of Christ*, pp. 306-307. Willam, *Life of Jesus Christ*, p. 140, notes that Jesus' phrase "put out into the deep," used by fishermen when they are going out to let down their nets for a catch, is still used in Palestine as *bitna nitla al bahr*.

[88] Prat, *Jesus Christ*, I, 225-226.

[89] Luke 5:8.

[90] Matthew 4:19.

[91] Ricciotti, *Life of Christ*, p. 308. The text follows the general (though not unanimous) opinion of recent orthodox exegetes that the calling of Andrew, Peter, James, and John described in Matthew 4, Mark 1, and Luke 5 refers to the same event, despite some differences of detail.

[92] Fernandez, *Life of Christ*, pp. 310-312.

[93] Lagrange, *Gospel of Jesus Christ*, I, 134-135.

[94] Fernandez, *Life of Christ*, pp. 316-318.

[95] *Ibid.*; Mark 2:5.

[96] Mark 2:7.

[97] Mark 2:8-12.

[98] Fernandez, *Life of Christ*, p. 320; Edersheim, *Jesus the Messiah*, I, 517-519. It is only Matthew himself, in his own Gospel, who identifies himself as the former publican. Mark and Luke describe the call to Levi, list Matthew among the Twelve, but do not mention that they were one and the same.

[99] Fernandez, *Life of Christ*, p. 321.

[100] The final calling of the Twelve Apostles and the Sermon on the Mount are both dated to June of 28 A.D. by Daniel-Rops (*Jesus and His Times*, p. 456). Since Jesus' Galilean apostolate began in May (deducible from the fact that it was already quite warm when He was passing through Samaria on His way back to Galilee after attending the March or April Passover celebration in Jerusalem in that year and preaching for a time in Judea, when He talked with the Samaritan woman at the well), and everything about the call of the Twelve and the Sermon on the Mount indicates that they came early in His Galilean mission, Daniel-Rops' dating is most plausible.

[101] For a thorough review of this final calling of the Twelve Apostles and a discussion of the way their names are listed in Matthew, Mark, Luke, and Acts and the significance of the manner of the listing, see Prat, *Jesus Christ*, I, 226-235. The personality of the Apostle Thomas emerges much more clearly when we understand the extraordinary character of the work he seems to have done in India (see Chapter Seventeen, below).

[102] See Note 18, above.

[103] Jude is identified in Luke 6:16 and Acts 1:13 ambiguously as "Jude of James," Ιοξδαν Ιαχωβοξ. This is now usually translated "son of James," as in the Revised Stan-

dard Version. While the Greek is ambiguous, Aramaic usage and the Old Syriac version of the New Testament both support the translation "son" rather than "brother" which many older authorities had favored because the Scriptural references to Jesus' "brethren" included a Jude whose descendants were leaders in the Church in Jerusalem (Eusebius, *Ecclesiastical History*, III, 19). On the distinction between Jude the relative of Jesus and Jude the Apostle, see Emil G. Kraeling, *The Disciples* (New York, 1966), pp. 203-204, and the editorial comment by Roy J. Deferrari in the edition of Eusebius in *The Fathers of the Church* series of Catholic University of America, Volume 19 (New York, 1953), p. 166n. It is difficult to see either James the son of Zebedee, John's brother, or James the cousin of Jesus as old enough at the time of Christ's public ministry to have had a son of mature age, in view of the known ages of the Apostle John and of Christ. Therefore the Apostle Jude was probably not the son of either of these (the name James was relatively common among Jews at this time). The author of the Epistle of Jude in the New Testament identifies himself, this time explicitly, as the brother of James, αδελφηος δε Ιακωβοξ (Jude 1), but not as one of the Twelve. Since this epistle was certainly written after James the first bishop of Jerusalem had become especially famous among Christians, the Jude of the Epistle is probably his brother, and this has tended to influence the translations of Luke 6:16 and Acts 1:13 and to support the identification of the Apostle Jude with the Jude who was Jesus' cousin and James' brother (or, more properly, half-brother—see Prat, *Jesus Christ*, I, 506). Jerome (*De Viris Illustribus* 4) identifies the Jude of the New Testament Epistle as the brother of James, but not as one of the Twelve. An additional argument against the identification of the author of the canonical Epistle and/or cousin of Jesus with the Apostle is found in John 7:5, "even his brothers did not believe in him." If the second James was an Apostle, as we have contended (see Note 18, above), then this statement in John could still be accurate if at the time of Jesus' Galilean ministry three of His cousins disbelieved while only one believed (keeping in mind that the Twelve had already been chosen before this remark was made). It becomes much harder to explain John's reference if two of the four cousins—half the total number—were among His Apostles. The fact that two more of his cousins—Simon and Jude—probably later became disciples (see Chapter Seventeen, below) does not even weaken this argument if at this point in Jesus' life they had not yet come to believe in Him.

[104] Great confusion has grown up around the word added to distinguish the name of the second Simon in the Apostolic College—*qanana* in Aramaic (sometimes translated "the Cananean" or mistranslated "the Canaanite") and Ζηλωτην in Greek, meaning in the Aramaic "zealous one"—reaching what is surely one of the lowest points of recent Biblical translation in the New American Catholic Bible's rendering of this word as "Zealot party member." It is as though some future historian of the United States were to find a literary or other intellectual figure of our time described as "democratic" and for that reason alone identified him as part of the late Mayor Daley's political machine in Chicago. There is not a shred of proof that the Apostle Simon the Zealous was ever a member of the murderous revolutionary gang known as the "Zealots" or that everyone called "zealous" was in that gang. Lagrange refers to "Simon surnamed *qanana*, Aramaic for zealous but not necessarily 'the zealot,' though there is only one word for both meanings in Greek." He adds: "We use the term Zealots to denote a Jewish sect inspired with a fierce zeal for the independence of Israel . . . But as Simon's surname is retained in the list of the Apostles we ought to understand it in its more general sense of fervent zeal for God." (*Gospel of Jesus Christ*, I, 148). More recent studies make the same point. See F. F. Bruce, *New Testament History* (New York, 1971), p. 94, and especially Freyne, *Galilee*, who says (p. 223) that "Simon was one of that class of Jews known from rabbinic sources as the *qannaim*, those specially zealous for the

law and its observance who later formed a party of zealous defenders of the temple." By "later" Freyne refers to the period of the Jewish war, 66-70 A.D., long after Simon became an Apostle.

[105] Fernandez, *Life of Christ*, p. 326.

[106] Fillion, *Life of Christ*, II, 264-266.

[107] William Thomas Walsh, *Saint Peter the Apostle* (New York, 1948), pp. 92-93. No further commentary on the Sermon on the Mount will be attempted here. It soars far beyond the bounds of history.

[108] Raymond-Leopold Bruckberger, *Mary Magdalene* (New York, 1953), *passim*, especially pp. 204-216, 245-250, and 258-259; J. E. Belser, *History of the Passion* (St. Louis, 1929), pp. 30-33. Bruckberger's analysis of the significance of the use of the Greek aorist (historical past) tense in John 11:2, as showing that John meant in that passage to refer to Luke's account of the anointing in Galilee, is masterful and, to this writer, conclusive on this much-debated point (*op. cit.*, pp. 204-209). Bruckberger grants that the case for the identity of Mary Magdalene with the Mary of the anointings is not provable beyond a doubt, but it is exceedingly strong. We are told specifically that it was Mary Magdalene who stood at the foot of the Cross and went to the Holy Sepulcher on Easter morning, where she met the Risen Christ. As both Bruckberger and Belser emphasize, it is hardly conceivable that Mary of Bethany, who had twice anointed Christ's feet and to whom Christ had paid His glorious tribute: "Truly I say to you, wherever this gospel is preached in the whole world, what she has done will be told in memory of her" (Matthew 26:13), would not even have put in an appearance at either the Passion or the Resurrection, especially since other women adoring Christ were present at both. But if Mary Magdalene and the Mary of the anointings were the same, the difficulty vanishes. For a contrary view, see Prat, *Jesus Christ*, I, 292-293; for Magdala, see Ricciotti, *Life of Christ*, p. 307.

[109] Ricciotti, *Life of Christ*, pp. 339-340.

[110] *Ibid.*, pp. 356-357.

[111] On the special character and significance of this first Christian mission, see especially Jules Lebreton, *The Life and Teaching of Jesus Christ Our Lord* (New York, 1957), I, 286-291, and Fouard, *The Christ*, I, 325-335.

[112] Ricciotti, *Life of Christ*, pp. 365-369. A number of orthodox exegetes—though a minority of those whose works are primarily relied upon here—hypothesize two separate episodes of public preaching by Jesus in Nazareth, the earlier described in Luke 4:15-32 and the latter in Matthew 13:54-58 and Mark 6:1-6. For this position see Lagrange, *Gospel of Jesus Christ*, I, 123-124; Fillion, *Life of Christ*, II, 195-204; and Edersheim, *Jesus the Messiah*, I, 452-457. Generally speaking, it seems a better principle of exegesis in historical perspective not to multiply closely similar events reported in the life of Christ by different evangelists when a harmonization of the essential facts is possible.

[113] Ricciotti, *Life of Christ*, pp. 361-365. The account of the martyrdom of John the Baptist in the gospels is confirmed to a remarkable degree by Josephus, except that he says nothing of Salome's dance and the banquet, attributing Herod's execution of John to his fear of him as a revolutionary. But the one story and motive certainly does not exclude the other (nor, incidentally, does Josephus' account do anything whatever to establish, in the face of overpowering gospel evidence to the contrary, that John was in fact a revolutionary; tyrants are notorious for seeing revolutions and revolutionaries where they do not really exist). See Lagrange, *Gospel of Jesus Christ*, I, 209-218; for the thesis that John the Baptist was a political revolutionary (in its most extreme form) see Robert Eisler, *The Messiah Jesus and John the Baptist* (London, 1931), pp. 257-270; for a moderate and well-balanced harmonization of the two accounts, see Harold W. Hoehner, *Herod Antipas*, pp. 136-146.

[114] Baker, *Tiberius*, pp. 251-254.

[115] John 6:4 specifies that the Passover "was at hand."

[116] This miracle is the only one narrated in detail in all four gospels. See Prat, *Jesus Christ*, I, 359-363 and Fillion, *Life of Christ*, II, 474-479. Edersheim (*Jesus the Messiah*, I, 682-683) points out very significantly that the Gospel of John (6:9) alone specifies that the fish involved was not the larger fish eaten for a main meal, but a small dried or pickled fish (*opsarion*) eaten with bread, like sardine or herring. This is clear evidence of John's intimate knowledge of Galilean life—and fisheries. Edersheim further points out that exactly the same kind of fish, designated in John 21:9-13 by the same word *opsarion*, is used when the Risen Lord offers breakfast to the Apostles who had been fishing all night on the Sea of Galilee—thereby linking the two events and recalling the great miracle.

[117] John 6:8-9.

[118] John 6:31. See Walsh, *Peter the Apostle*, pp. 108-109.

[119] Prat, *Jesus Christ*, I, 363-367; Fillion, *Life of Christ*, II, 480-481. Mark 7:45 states that Jesus "made his disciples get into the boat and go before him to the other side, to Bethsaida, where he dismissed the crowd." This reference to Bethsaida on "the other side" of the lake from the eastern, non-Galilean shore where they were at the time, together with the reference in John 12:21 to the Apostle Philip's home town as "Bethsaida in Galilee" and the fact that Jesus was with the Apostles in Capernaum the next day, would seem to provide more than enough evidence to support solidly the contention of Prat and Fillion (as against Fernandez, *Life of Christ*, pp. 409-412 and Ricciotti, *Life of Christ*, pp. 385n-386n) that there were *two* Bethsaidas on the Sea of Galilee, one the known Bethsaida Julias in Gaulanitis near which Jesus had performed his first multiplication of the loaves and fishes (Prat, *op. cit.*, I, 359) and the other near Capernaum. The point is of some importance because Peter, Andrew, James, John, and Philip among the Twelve all came from Bethsaida—evidently the Bethsaida in Galilee—and Bethsaida was later one of the cities solemnly cursed by Christ.

[120] Ricciotti, *Life of Christ*, pp. 384-385.

[121] For a description of these sudden severe storms on the Sea of Galilee and their frequency, see Fillion, *Life of Christ*, II, 432, 482-483.

[122] Edersheim, *Jesus the Messiah*, I, 692-693.

[123] Fillion, *Life of Christ*, II, 483-485; John 6:22-27.

[124] Edersheim, *Jesus the Messiah*, II, 25-33; John 6:59. Only the ruins of a synagogue remain from all of ancient Capernaum. Although these ruins, recently excavated, are apparently from a building constructed after Jesus' time, it probably stood on the same site and perhaps incorporated parts of the very building in which Jesus preached on the Bread of Life. The great synagogue was Capernaum's particular pride. See Ricciotti, *Life of Christ*, pp. 286-287 and Daniel-Rops, *Jesus and His Times*, pp. 164-167.

[125] On the clear Eucharistic meaning of Christ's teaching on the Bread of Life reported in John 6, see especially Prat, *Jesus Christ*, I, 369-379 and Fillion, *Life of Christ*, I, 488-502 and 698-700. The Eucharistic meaning of John 6 is now accepted by all except "fundamentalist" Protestants—who on this point are anything but "fundamentalist" since they reject the literal meaning of Scripture. Modernist interpreters, while accepting that the Eucharist is meant by John 6, deny by their arbitrary chronology of the development of the Church that Jesus could have actually said these words. See Ricciotti, *Life of Christ*, p. 392n.

[126] John 6:35, 51-57.

[127] John 6:66.

[128] John 6:67.

[129] John 6:68-69.

[130] John 6:70.

[131] Fernandez, *Life of Christ*, pp. 417-429; Prat, *Jesus Christ*, I, 393-402; Edersheim, *Jesus the Messiah*, II, 37-67. Edersheim (*op. cit.*, II, 65) presents the most thorough justification, among the sources for the life of Christ used here, for the two multiplications of loaves and fishes as separate events despite certain mostly inevitable similarities in the gospel accounts of them. He notes particularly Jesus' blessing of the bread alone (not the fish) for the Jews "in strict accordance with Jewish custom," but blessing both the bread and the fish for the Gentiles, and the contrast of the reference to the people seated, for the first multiplication, "on the grass"—that having happened in early spring, at Passover time, when the grass is green in Palestine; and, for the second, "on the ground"—that having happened in late spring or summer, when the grass in Palestine has mostly been burned dead by the hot sun.

[132] For a vivid description of the area of Caesarea Philippi and Mount Hermon, see Edersheim, *Jesus the Messiah*, II, 72-74.

[133] Matthew 16:13-19.

[134] For the significance of the formulation "Son of the living God" as testimony to Christ's full divinity as God the Son, see Lagrange, *Gospel of Jesus Christ*, I, 259-260, and Fillion, *Life of Christ*, II, 536-538.

[135] The play of words involved in naming Simon "Rock" is as clear in Aramaic as in English, if we use the literal translation "Rock" for the Aramaic *Kepha* rather than "Peter" which is derived from the Greek *Petros*. In Greek the noun for rock is feminine. Therefore it is unsuitable for a man's name, and Peter is named *Petros* while the precise word for "rock" is *petra*, making the meaning a little less clear. But Christ's words to Peter were spoken in Aramaic and first recorded in Aramaic in Matthew's Gospel; furthermore, we know that Peter was later often called *Kepha* or *Cephas* as well as *Petros*. See Prat, *Jesus Christ*, I, 413n.

[136] Michael M. Winter, *Saint Peter and the Popes* (Baltimore, 1960), pp. 18-19. The doctrine of apostolic succession is explicitly stated by Clement I, third in succession to Peter as Bishop of Rome, who had known Peter personally, in his Epistle to the Corinthians 42 and 44. See Chapter Eighteen, below.

[137] Prat, *Jesus Christ*, I, 411; Winter, *St. Peter and the Popes*, pp. 6-18.

[138] Fillion, *Life of Christ*, II, 704-705.

[139] *Ibid.*, II, 705-706. That Peter's humility did thus influence the composition of Mark's Gospel—far from being merely a modern pious speculation—is testified by Victor of Antioch, the first commentator on Mark, and by Eusebius of Caesarea, both in the early centuries of Christian history.

[140] Fernandez, *Life of Christ*, pp. 436-441.

[141] The case for Mount Tabor rather than Mount Hermon as the site of the Transfiguration is best stated by Prat, *Jesus Christ*, I, 422-423. A fairly strong alternative case can be made for Mount Hermon (with the proposed site of the Transfiguration there on its higher slopes rather than on its peak, which can be reached easily only by experienced mountain climbers) but is wholly unsupported in Christian tradition; see Edersheim, *Jesus the Messiah*, II, 92-97.

[142] See Chapters Three and Five, above.

[143] Fillion, *Life of Christ*, II, 560-566.

[144] Prat, *Jesus Christ*, I, 425-426; Edersheim, *Jesus the Messiah*, II, 97-98, 102-103.

[145] Ricciotti, *Life of Christ*, pp. 413-418. For the holy women who accompanied Christ, see Fernandez, *Life of Christ*, pp. 313-316, and Bruckberger, *Mary Magdalene*, pp. 76-80.

[146] John 1:11.

[147] For the time of the curse on the unbelieving cities of Galilee, see Prat, *Jesus Christ*, I, 443n.

[148] Matthew 11:21-24.

[149] Walsh, *Peter the Apostle*, p. 130; Prat, *Jesus Christ*, I, 442-444; Lagrange, *Gospel of Jesus Christ*, I, 290-291; observations by the author on a visit to Galilee in 1971. See Note 119, above, on the question of the existence of Bethsaida in Galilee.

16.
"I AM THE RESURRECTION AND THE LIFE" (29-30 A.D.)

Jesus said to her, "I am the resurrection and the life; he who believes in me, though he die, yet shall he live, and whoever lives and believes in me shall never die."—John 11:25-26

"Let not your hearts be troubled; believe in God, believe also in me. In my Father's house are many rooms; if it were not so, would I have told you that I go to prepare a place for you? And when I go and prepare a place for you, I will come again and will take you to myself, that where I am you may be also. And you know the way where I am going." Thomas said to him, "Lord, we do not know where you are going; how can we know the way?" Jesus said to him, "I am the way, and the truth, and the life; no man comes to the Father, but by me. If you had known me, you would have known my Father also; henceforth you know him and have seen him."—John 14:1-7

"When the days drew near for him to be received up, he set his face to go to Jerusalem."[1] Thus does St. Luke introduce the transcendent, eternal story of the last six months in the mortal life of Jesus Christ. From early October of 29 A.D. to early April of 30 A.D. by our calendar,[2] these days, weeks and few months tower in Christian history like a mountain touching the sun. In that infinitely precious, timeless historical moment, so brief that no secular historian can chronicle it from his sources, the world was transformed, made over new, all changed—everywhere, fundamentally, imperishably, unalterably. What had been lost was found. The way to Heaven was opened. The ancient quest of Gilgamesh was attained in the fulfillment of the hope of Abraham. And all of the world that did not know it then or soon afterward, would hear of it through the forthcoming two thousand years of the history of Christendom.

To Jerusalem! The Holy City, where God dwelt in the Temple and where vows must be fulfilled. The killer city, where the prophets died victims to a stiff-necked people. The city of David, who took Jerusalem for God's Chosen, whose heir was Jesus. The city of Melchisedek, who offered bread and wine to God in the days of Abraham. The city of the Scribes and Pharisees, who feared and hated Jesus, knowing that whatever the final result of His mission to Galilee, He had displayed power there which they could neither match nor understand. The city of the *anawim*, the Poor of Yahweh, like the well-known beggar upon its streets who had been blind from birth.

> O Jerusalem, Jerusalem, killing the prophets and stoning those who are sent
> to you! How often would I have gathered your children together as a hen
> gathers her brood under her wings, and you would not![3]

It was the Feast of Tabernacles, one of the three greatest feasts of the Jewish religious year (the others were Passover, greatest of all, and Pentecost), held in early fall, at grape harvest time. The Law of Moses directed each family to dwell for eight days in a makeshift house or "booth" of boughs, in commemoration of Israel's wandering in the wilderness when God had led them by day and by night, and fed them with manna, thirteen centuries before. Each day during the Feast of Tabernacles there was a procession to the famous Pool of Siloam, whose waters came from a spring flowing through a tunnel that King Hezekiah had dug in the days of the Prophet Isaiah, to bring some of Siloam's water to the Temple in a golden vessel, with the singing of psalms, and to sprinkle the water on the altar. Each night during the Feast of Tabernacles the light from great branching candelabra, 150 feet high, illuminated the city almost as though it were day. There was music, dancing, festivity of all kinds.[4]

At this Feast of Tabernacles, many in Jerusalem—some enemies, some friends, others merely curious—had heard startling stories about Jesus of Nazareth and His extraordinary works in Galilee.[5] They gathered to hear what He had to say—and saw before them a man of noble, commanding presence, with large eyes set wide in a long, splendidly proportioned face with firm mouth and a short, slightly forked beard. He was about five feet eleven inches tall and weighed about 170 pounds. His body, like his face, was beautifully proportioned.

For centuries most Christian scholars believed that we would never know in this world how Jesus Christ truly looked in the flesh. Even the saints and mystics who saw Him could not describe His appearance in such a way that others could clearly visualize it. The once widely circulated description on which the familiar reproduction of His appearance is based has long been known to be a forgery. But—like His mother as Our Lady of Guadalupe—He has in fact left us His picture. It is imprinted on the cloth of the shroud in which He was wrapped when He was laid in the tomb after the Crucifixion. This shroud—the Holy Shroud of Turin—has been preserved through two thousand years and a series of extraordinary historical changes, concealments, removals, and catastrophes which are only just now being fully traced; but the accumulated scientific evidence for its authenticity, attested by recognized authorities in many different fields of knowledge, has become powerfully convincing. Evidence from the Holy Shroud of Turin will therefore be used in this book as equally valid with other solid historical evidence available, and the later history of the Shroud will be carefully followed as it appears, disappears, and reappears down the Christian centuries.[6] The latest dramatic development in our unfolding knowledge of this most precious and most historically important of all Christian relics is the discovery of an imprint on the cloth, over one of the eyes of the dead Jesus, of six clearly identifiable Greek letters from a Roman coin minted by Pontius Pilate—minted only by him, only in Palestine, and *only in the sixteenth, seventeenth, and eighteenth years of the Emperor Tiberius* (October 28-October 31 A.D.). This is immensely important evidence confirming the authenticity of the Holy Shroud of Turin, and also powerful support for the chronology of the public life of Christ set forth in this book (see the table in Chapter Fifteen, above).[7]

Speaking far more clearly about Himself to the crowds assembled for the Feast of Tabernacles in Jerusalem than He had ever publicly spoken in Galilee, Jesus proclaimed Himself the fulfillment of the prophecies and of the very symbolism of this feast: the Source of "living water"—"If any one thirst, let him come to me and drink" (which may have been said very soon after the solemn ceremony of bringing the water of Siloam to the altar of the Temple); "the light of the world" (which may have had specific reference to the great blazing candelabra of this feast).[8] The Pharisees challenged Him openly, with increasing bitterness. They tried to have Him seized and imprisoned; "but no one arrested him, because his hour had not yet come."[9] He called upon the people to believe in Him; some among them cried out that because Abraham was their father, they had no need of Him. "Truly, truly, I say to you," Jesus replied, "if any one keeps my word, he will never see death."[10] But Abraham was dead; did Jesus claim to be greater than Abraham?

"Your father Abraham rejoiced that he was to see my day; he saw it and

> was glad." The Jews said to him, "You are not yet fifty years old, and
> have you seen Abraham?" Jesus said to them, "Truly, truly, I say to you,
> before Abraham was, I AM."[11]

The Name announced to Moses out of the burning bush of Sinai, the true
personal name of the Ineffable, Eternal, All-Sustaining God, Self-Existent Being, He Who Is—Jesus had assumed it for Himself. It was His Name. "I AM."
The carpenter of Nazareth, Who had taught on a mountain in Galilee that the
meek shall inherit the earth, here proclaimed in Jerusalem, in God's house, in
God's presence, that He is God. "I AM."

The Jews cried blasphemy, and prepared to stone Him. He "hid himself,
and went out of the temple."[12]

Soon afterward Jesus passed the beggar blind from birth, on his street corner in Jerusalem. He told the apostles who were with Him that the blind man
had been afflicted precisely so that "the works of God might be manifest in
him." Jesus put spittle and clay upon the blind man's eyes and sent him to wash
in the Pool of Siloam; and as the beggar later said, "I went, I washed, and
I saw."[13]

The Pharisees called the man, furiously questioning him, trying with increasing desperation to find some way to discredit him and the truth about what
had happened to him. He held firm in his overwhelming gratitude to his Healer,
and a dawning faith. The Pharisees, closing their minds and hearts to the
evidence, cursed the man and excommunicated him. Hearing of this, Jesus went
in search of him:

> Having found him he said, "Do you believe in the Son of man?" He
> answered, "And who is he, sir, that I may believe in him?" Jesus said
> to him, "You have seen him, and it is he who speaks to you." He said,
> "Lord, I believe," and he worshipped him.[14]

It was a confession worthy of St. Peter himself. We hear no more of the
once blind beggar of Jerusalem, so strikingly cured; but a faith so well tested
and so forthrightly avowed is not likely to have failed. In all probability we
should place him in the ranks of the first disciples. It was of such material as
this man, not of the proud and the rich and the learned, that Jesus was to fashion
His kingdom on earth and in Heaven, His Mystical Body.

It was not yet Jesus' "hour," but that hour was drawing near; and the gospel
had not yet been preached to the greater part of the "lost sheep of the house
of Israel."[15] Even excluding the Jews of the Dispersion (to whom St. Paul, in
city after city across the eastern Roman world, was subsequently to go, always
before preaching to the Gentiles) there were many in Palestine who had not
yet been touched by His truth. Since the time was growing short, Jesus would
send out a larger mission than that of the Twelve in Galilee[16]—indeed, six times

that number.

The mission of the seventy-two in all probability began very soon after the Feast of Tabernacles in early October of 29 A.D. and ended no later than mid-December, as the Feast of Dedication drew near.[17] The disciples again went out two by two, with instructions very similar to those Jesus had given to the Twelve for their mission in Galilee.[18] The seventy-two were sent to the towns and villages, presumably both those in Judea itself outside Jerusalem, and in Perea, the Jewish territory just across the Jordan where John the Baptist had preached, which was included in Herod Antipas' kingdom.[19] No record of their names has come down to us.[20] But we may see Jesus in the process of selecting them, as He meets the prospective but doubtful disciples who hesitate in their decision about following Him, in the scenes recorded in the Gospels of Luke and Matthew as they describe His journey to Jerusalem.[21] And we may see Him instructing them as He repeats for them His perfect prayer, the "Our Father"— which, it would seem from its inclusion in Matthew's Gospel in connection with the Sermon on the Mount, He had taught His first followers long before in Galilee.[22] When the new missionaries returned rejoicing over their success, particularly in having cast out devils by simply invoking Christ's Name, He rejoiced with them and for them in the glorious words of thanksgiving and promise recorded by Luke and by Matthew:

> In that same hour he rejoiced in the Holy Spirit and said, "I thank thee, Father, Lord of heaven and earth, that thou hast hidden these things from the wise and understanding and revealed them to babes; yea, Father, for such was thy gracious will. All things have been delivered to me by my Father; and no one knows who the Son is except the Father, or who the Father is except the Son and any one to whom the Son chooses to reveal him."[23]

> "Come to me, all who labor and are heavy laden, and I will give you rest. Take my yoke upon you, and learn from me, for I am gentle and lowly in heart, and you will find rest for your souls. For my yoke is easy, and my burden is light."[24]

When He went up to Jerusalem again for December's Feast of Dedication, commemorating the cleansing and rededication of the Temple by the Maccabees in 164 B.C., He once again proclaimed His Godhead publicly, in the most explicit language, on the great portico called Solomon's Porch, later to be hallowed ground for Christian assemblies.[25] Urged to declare openly if He were the Messiah—which He could not yet do because of the false and grossly materialistic expectations most Jews entertained for the Messiah—He replied by pointing to His miracles and then transcending the question to state Who He ultimately is: "I and the Father are one."[26] His enemies again cried blasphemy; first they tried to stone Him and a little later to arrest Him, but once more He escaped them.[27]

It was in all probability either just before or just after this new expulsion of God the Son from His own holy city, that He dwelt for a time at a house in Bethany three miles to the east, where a man named Lazarus lived with his two sisters, Martha and Mary—this Mary being, according to the traditional view here upheld and defended, Mary Magdalen.[28] It is from this visit that St. Luke draws his unforgettable story of the busy Martha and the contemplative Mary, whom Jesus said "has chosen the good portion, which shall not be taken away from her."[29]

Leaving behind these dear friends and devoted disciples in Bethany and His enemies in Jerusalem, during the winter months of 30 A.D. Jesus journeyed and preached in Perea across the Jordan, where it would seem that He gained for Himself a considerable number of those who had heard and loved John the Baptist—and had remembered what John had told them about Jesus.[30] These journeyings were filled with teaching to the crowds, to the apostles and disciples, and to the Scribes and Pharisees who now dogged His footsteps. There were miracles, as always—the cure of a man with dropsy, of a woman stooped over with arthritis for eighteen years, of ten lepers[31]—but above all there was now a growing note of urgency, of demand that a choice be made for Jesus immediately, whatever the consequences:

> I come to cast fire upon the earth, and would that it were already kindled! I have a baptism to be baptized with, and how I am constrained until it is accomplished! Do you think that I have come to give peace on earth? No, I tell you, but rather division; for henceforth in one house there will be five divided, three against two and two against three; they will be divided father against son and son against father, mother against daughter and daughter against her mother.[32]

The Pharisees, in their incessant questioning, at last found an issue on which Jesus would lay down a law directly opposite to the law of Moses. For the law of Moses permitted divorce, and the Jews had availed themselves wholesale of that permission; the school of Rabbi Hillel actually went so far as to declare that a husband might divorce his wife for any fault that displeased him, even if it were no more than burning his dinner. This teaching by the People of God would have shamed an old Roman, or any other virtuous pagan. The human suffering it must have caused is appalling. Surely the thought of His mother was in Jesus' mind and heart as He proclaimed, once and for all, in the fullness of His Divine authority:

> From the beginning of creation, "God made them male and female." "For this reason a man shall leave his father and mother and be joined to his wife, and the two shall become one flesh." So they are no longer two but one flesh. What therefore God has joined together, let not man put asunder. . . . Whoever divorces his wife and marries another, commits adultery.[33]

Whatever the meaning of the celebrated apparent exception to this universal command in the parallel text of the Gospel of Matthew,[34] it is a fact that Christ's followers then, and all Christians for at least three centuries afterward, accepted His words as ordaining the indissolubility of marriage for all who acknowledged Him as Lòrd and God.[35] This became, and has remained, the enduring, indefectible teaching of the Roman Catholic Church. It has shaken empires and toppled kings. It has been a sword against the arrogant and a shield for the defenseless, a stumbling block for the ambitious and a rock of refuge for the virtuous, a guarantor of hearth and home and a scandal to the worldly, for two thousand years. Terrifying in its purity as an angelic lance, it frightened the disciples when they first heard it, as Matthew's account shows, almost as much as it frightened Henry VIII. It is virtually impossible to exaggerate the historical importance of this unprecedented doctrine which Jesus Christ laid down in the last climactic weeks of His preaching as the cornerstone of the new Christian law of the family. So powerful and lasting was its effect that even among Christians separated from the Catholic Church and rejecting the doctrine of the total indissolubility of marriage, divorce never became really widespread until our present age of secularism and apostasy.

While Jesus was teaching in Perea, a message came to him from Martha and Mary in Bethany: "Lord, he whom you love is ill." Lazarus, their brother, had in fact already died when the message reached Jesus, nearly a day's journey away. Knowing this, and what was to come, Jesus continued His work in Perea, regardless of the message, for two full days. Only then did He set out for Bethany to "awaken" Lazarus. The Apostles were now very fearful of any approach to Jerusalem, the stronghold of Christ's enemies; but Thomas spoke up: "Let us also go, that we may die with him."[36]

As Jesus approached Bethany He was first met by Martha, from whom He drew an almost Petrine confession of faith, and then by Mary Magdalen, who fell at His feet weeping for her brother.[37] Jesus wept with her, and with all the bereaved and the victims of death, the wages of sin.[38] They went to the tomb, followed by a large group of mourners, including both friends and enemies of Jesus.[39] The tomb—like the one in which Jesus Himself was to lie just a few weeks later—was cut out of Palestine's soft limestone and closed by a large stone.[40] Jesus ordered the stone removed, despite practical Martha's warning that Lazarus' body, four days dead, would already have begun to decay.[41] Jesus prayed, and then:

> He cried with a loud voice: "Lazarus, come out." The dead man came out, his hands and feet bound with bandages, and his face wrapped with a cloth. Jesus said to them, "Unbind him, and let him go."[42]

It was the greatest of all the miracles of Jesus' public life; and one of the most striking testimonies to the perversity of human nature which history records is that a significant number of those present, after having seen with their own eyes a man four days dead, who should have been a decaying corpse, climb up the stairs of his own tomb bound in his burial cloths at the command of Jesus Christ, should still have refused to believe in Him, and run off to plot with the Pharisees against Him. But many who saw the miracle did believe, and the news of it spread rapidly and greatly augmented the number of Jesus' supporters among the people.[43]

The raising of Lazarus plays such a central, causative part in the whole account of the Passion in the Gospel of John that it is logically impossible to dismiss it as a later Christian myth, subsequently interpolated, and retain any historical value for John's narrative, or any honesty for him. As Lagrange puts it, bluntly and decisively:

> If he [St. John the Evangelist] invented the miracle [the raising of Lazarus] then it is not lawful to call it a symbol; it is a lie. We shall be told that it is a poetical fiction, invented by one who is the divinely inspired poet of friendship, grief and tears, of the irrepressible hopes of mankind. This is all very beautiful, but it is not what St. John wanted to show. It was his desire to render testimony to the truth: to the truth of religion, certainly, but first of all to the truth of actual facts.[44]

The one real difficulty for the orthodox exegete is to explain the complete absence of any reference to this great miracle in the other three gospels. The usual explanation, that their structure confines them to describing the public life of Jesus in Galilee, where many great miracles were performed, and His Passion in Jerusalem, leaving out all else that He did in Judea, falls short of being altogether convincing in view of the magnitude of this particular miracle. A more probable explanation is suggested by Lagrange and buttressed by the evidence we have given for an early date for the first three gospels, that when they were written the family at Bethany—Martha, Mary, and Lazarus—was still living there, just two miles from Jerusalem, subject to the persecution of the Jews; so, to protect them, they were not clearly identified in these gospels.[45]

The reaction of Jesus' enemies to the raising of Lazarus brings to the forefront, for the first time, the High Priest and his circle. At least since 6 A.D., when the rule of the Roman procurators began in Judea after Augustus dismissed Herod's son Archelaus, the high priesthood had been controlled by Annas and his family. His son-in-law Caiaphas was High Priest at this time. Annas and his circle were Sadducees. Theologically they differed with the Pharisees about the resurrection of the dead, which the Sadducees denied; the raising of Lazarus was therefore a direct challenge to Sadduceean belief. Politically, the Sadducees were collaborators with the Romans, while the Pharisees tended to be rebellious—the same position both groups had taken toward constituted authority in the days of Alexander Jannaeus.[46] But concerning Jesus, both groups were as one. The Sadducees saw in Him a threat to their dominant position in Judaism; the Pharisees saw in Him a threat to the Law (or to their interpretation of it). For both groups, the miracles were only further evidence of the danger from Jesus. Most of them could not or would not face the question of the reality and significance of the miracles themselves.

Both Pharisees and Sadducees were members of the Sanhedrin, the great aristocratic council of seventy-one that ruled Judaism, presided over by the High Priest.[47] The Sanhedrin met to discuss what to do about Jesus very soon after receiving the report of the raising of Lazarus from some of those who had witnessed it. Concern was expressed that Jesus was about to gain so large a following and cause so much disturbance that the Roman legions would march in and destroy Jerusalem. Never in all His public life had Jesus said or done anything that could lead any just and reasonable man to believe that He would create a political uprising or provoke such a reprisal—which the Romans of the early imperial period were not in the habit of making for trivial reasons.[48] Yet the decision was made to kill Him; the High Priest Caiaphas declared: "It is expedient for you that one man should die for the people." In so speaking, as St. John points out, Caiaphas unwittingly prophesied the redemptive character of Christ's death.[49]

Knowing that His death had now been definitely decided upon, Jesus withdrew from Bethany to Ephrem, a Judean town about twenty miles north of Jerusalem at the edge of the desert. The Sanhedrin ordered that anyone who knew where He was should report it to them, so that He might be arrested.[50]

The Passover of 30 A.D. was near. Many in Jerusalem and at the Temple were asking with growing curiosity and excitement if Jesus, under the Sanhedrin's threat, would come to the great feast. He did not stay long in Ephrem, but soon set out for Jerusalem by the Jericho road, with the Apostles and disciples following fearfully. Jesus called the Twelve to Him and told them what would happen, giving a detailed and specific account of His coming betrayal, trial, and death; but still they could not believe or really grasp what He was saying to them.[51]

In Jericho Jesus dined with Zacchaeus, chief of the publicans of the city, whom He called down from the tree he had climbed in order to see Him; Jesus forgave his sins, and Zacchaeus pledged half his wealth to the poor and four-fold restitution to those he had wronged in his financial dealings. There also Jesus taught the parable of the talents, a vivid warning against the still strong expectation among His followers that He was about to establish an immediate, material and worldly Messianic kingdom; for in this parable the king went away to a far country where he remained for a very long time, leaving some of his wealth with trusted servants, who were judged according to how much they had increased what had been left with them. Jesus too was soon to go away for a long time, and the future of His work on earth would depend on how well

His servants used and multiplied the spiritual wealth He had entrusted to them.[52]

It was, in all probability, on Friday, March 31, 30 A.D.—exactly one week before His Passion and death—that Jesus and His followers left Jericho for Jerusalem, some twenty miles to the west. Their immediate destination was the house of Martha and Mary at Bethany, where they stayed for the next two nights and the intervening Sabbath. On the second of these nights a banquet was held in Bethany for Jesus by Simon, formerly a leper, who had very possibly been cured by Jesus.[53] It was at this banquet that Mary Magdalen came to anoint her Lord and Beloved once again, with a full pound of the precious perfume called nard, made from a plant which grew only on the high far slopes of India's mighty Himalayas.[54] Judas Iscariot angrily protested against this as waste, and some of the other apostles also objected. But Jesus said that she had done "a beautiful thing," that "wherever the gospel is preached in the whole world, what she has done will be told in memory of her."[55] And so it has been. It seems likely it was then that Judas made his final decision to betray Christ. The devil had been in him ever since the sermon on the Bread of Life at Capernaum; now, the intimate proximity with Mary Magdalen's holy love may have proved too much for his shadowed, resentful soul to bear. Judas—who had free will always—turned his will against Christ, and there it remained fixed.[56]

Now it was time for Jesus to enter Jerusalem. Long ago the prophet Zechariah had foretold that the Messiah would enter His city riding upon a humble donkey. The rabbinic commentators had wrestled with the contrast between this prophecy and Daniel's, that the Son of Man would come on the clouds of Heaven. But both were true; the first coming would be on the donkey, the second on the clouds. So Jesus sent some of the Apostles to procure His predestined mount. Thousands of pilgrims coming to the Passover, led by the considerable number who seem to have joined Jesus during His travels of the past few months in Judea and Perea, or had come to Him because of the raising of Lazarus, formed a grand procession. Hailing Him the Messiah, crying out "Hosanna to the Son of David!" and waving palms and other branches, they escorted Him toward the city.[57]

The procession probably began at Bethany, and followed the road to Jerusalem over the brow of the Mount of Olives. There, Jerusalem suddenly appears before the traveller in a magnificent panorama, still one of the most impressive sights in the world.[58] In Jesus' day the Holy City was far more splendid even than it is today; the Temple was one of the most magnificent structures in existence, surrounded by hundreds of forty-foot columns of pure white marble topped with cedar, a golden grapevine over the door with each grape the size of a man, the stones of the foundations enormous—fifteen feet long or more.[59] Jesus looked upon it all, wept, and prophesied:

> Would that even today you knew the things that make for peace! But now

they are hid from your eyes. For the days shall come upon you, when your enemies will cast up a bank about you and surround you, and hem you in on every side, and dash you to the ground, you and your children within you, and they will not leave one stone upon another in you; because you did not know the time of your visitation.[60]

This famous prophecy was fulfilled, word for word, exactly forty years later.[61] As William Thomas Walsh says:

It was not the white glory of the Temple and the palaces on the western hill that He saw now, but the Tenth Legion camping on the very spot where He paused; on the right and left of Him the battering rams and mounds; the four trenches around the Castle Antonia; the dead bodies falling from the walls, the unburied corpses in the streets, the children eating dung, the silence of death falling, the despairing priests leaping into the flames.[62]

The Temple, the center of the history of God's Chosen People for almost exactly a thousand years, was indeed to be left with not one stone standing upon another: only a part of the vast stone platform on which it was built was to survive, where to this day orthodox Jews go to bewail its destruction.[63]

Thus was the Messiah's triumphal entry into the Holy City, so long awaited, so ardently desired, accomplished at last—to the accompaniment of the tears of God.

After a brief visit to the Temple, Jesus returned to Bethany,[64] in all probability to stay for the night at the house of Martha and Mary and Lazarus, where He always found simple, total devotion. It is likely that He stayed there on each of the next three nights as well; for His following was surely now very substantial in the town where Lazarus had been raised from the dead, and would protect Him from any attempt by His enemies in Jerusalem to come and arrest Him. The Son of God, Who during His journeying in Judea near the time of the Feast of Tabernacles had said, "Foxes have holes, and the birds of the air have nests, but the Son of man has nowhere to lay his head,"[65] had at last found a place of love and refuge during the cosmic struggle that filled the last week of His mortal life.

The next two days He went to the Temple. On Monday, April 3, 30 A.D., the preponderance of evidence suggests that for a second time He drove the money-changers and the animal sellers out of the Temple, the circumstances and His words being very similar to those of His first "cleansing of the Temple" at the beginning of His public ministry two Passovers before.[66] It was this that probably prompted the first challenge flung at Him on that day of ultimate verbal battle, Tuesday, April 4, 30 A.D.: "By what authority are you doing these things, or who gave you this authority to do them?"[67] Jesus' answer was a counter-question: "Was the baptism of John from heaven or from men? Answer me."[68] His enemies dared not answer, because the people venerated the memory of John the Baptist and would have been furious if their leaders had publicly denied that God had sent John; yet if they admitted that, they could have no reason for continuing to resist Him Whose coming and glory John had proclaimed. Jesus' response was far from a mere debating trick; it was both an answer in essence to the question He had been asked—for John *was* sent by God, and John had called upon all to follow Jesus—and at the same time an effective exposure of the hypocrisy and malice of the Pharisees.[69]

After that, it was all-out war between Jesus and His foes. They could not seize Him in the Temple, much as they wished to do so, because the crowds that had hailed Him on Palm Sunday were still strongly with Him. Therefore they had to find a way to turn the people against Him. They were proud, highly intelligent men, accustomed to having their way, equally adept at intrigue and public disputation; and whatever may have been the case with Annas and Caiaphas and their inner circle, it is obvious from the dialogues of that day that— despite all Jesus had done—most of them still had no idea that they were dealing with anyone more than a clever impostor. Again and again they tried to trap Jesus with trick questions that would force Him upon the horns of a dilemma, either horn of which would help discredit Him with the people. This contention of human with divine wisdom had, each time, its inevitable result. Most memorable and significant was His transcending of the dialectic involved in the question as to whether it were lawful to pay taxes and tribute to Caesar. Humanly speaking, there seemed no escape from the dilemma it posed to one hailed two days before as the Messiah. Since the Messiah was supposed to make Israel the ruler of the world, anyone claiming that role could not retain the belief and support of the people if he accepted the rule of Rome; but if he refused to accept it, he could immediately be denounced to the Roman authorities. Jesus' reply, after calling for and showing a Roman coin of the tribute with the head of the Emperor Tiberius on it, is one of the most familiar of all his statements. The working out of its meaning has comprised a substantial part of the history of Christendom.

"Render to Caesar the things that are Caesar's, and to God the things that are God's."[70]

Some, even among the questioners, listened to what Jesus was really saying, and were impressed; to one of them Jesus eventually said: "You are not far from the kingdom of God."[71] But most of them were only overborne in helpless anger at their debating failures; they were not really listening, not open to be convinced of Jesus' truth. And most of the people who had acclaimed Jesus on Palm Sunday were so fixed in their belief that the Messiah would bring immediate political power and great wealth to Israel that, no matter what Jesus said or did, their support for Him was sure to fade when they realized He was not going to do anything of that kind.[72] This spiritual blindness was not the result of any special evil in the Chosen People as a whole, who had received so many graces through nearly two thousand years; in truth, all mankind was involved in the rejection of the Savior. But to a very considerable extent that blindness was the result of the pride and hypocrisy of the spiritual leaders and intellectual guides the Chosen People then had, to whom God had given the talents which could have been used to correct the popular errors, but who instead had vastly magnified them.[73] Those spiritual leaders and intellectual guides, the Scribes and Pharisees, had long since closed their minds and hearts to God's truth, because it threatened their position and practices. Pride, power, privilege—to these great perennial temptations they had succumbed, yet they "sat on Moses' seat" and pretended to be God's most holy worshippers. They recognized no spiritual authority above their own. There was no way to reach them; they were walled off from grace as from truth. And this, for the sake of their own salvation, the people who admired them so much and followed them so faithfully must know.

> Woe to you, scribes and Pharisees, hypocrites! for you are like whitewashed tombs, which outwardly appear beautiful, but within they are full of dead men's bones and all uncleanness. So you also outwardly appear righteous to men, but within you are full of hypocrisy and iniquity. . . . You serpents, you brood of vipers, how are you to escape being sentenced to hell? Therefore I send you prophets and wise men and scribes, some of whom you will kill and crucify, and some you will scourge in your synagogues and persecute from town to town, that upon you may come all the righteous blood shed on earth . . . Truly I say to you, all this will come upon this generation.[74]

As He departed from Jerusalem, Jesus once more looked back upon the Temple, as He had looked out upon it during the triumphal Palm Sunday procession, and said again: "Truly, I say to you, there will not be left here one stone upon another."[75]

For the disciples, Jesus' prophecy of the destruction of Jerusalem and the Temple in "this generation" could only mean that the end of the world was near. Faithful Jews could not imagine a world without Jerusalem and the Temple at the center. So, as the Apostles walked back with Him toward Bethany that Tuesday evening and He sat down with them on the Mount of Olives, they pressed Him to tell them more about this coming catastrophe, to explain its signs and forewarnings.

Jesus' answer was much the most detailed, comprehensive and significant of all His prophecies, and has been the source of endless discussion and argument almost from the day He spoke it. It contains, in close juxtaposition, a passage in which He appears to place the end of the world and the Last Judgment in a specific chronological framework which has long since passed ("Truly, I say to you, this generation will not pass away till all these things take place")[76] and another in which He declares that only the Father knows when it will happen ("But of that day or that hour no one knows, not even the angels in heaven, nor the Son, but only the Father").[77] Taking the former passage in total isolation not only from the rest of Jesus' life and teaching, death and resurrection, but even from the latter passage which follows so closely upon it, the "eschatological school" of Biblical critics claims that it alone proves Jesus could not have been God.[78] Granting that the passage presents serious difficulties, to explain the rest of the gospels on the assumption that Jesus is *not* God is, to say the least, a great deal more difficult.

It would be presumptuous indeed for an historian to pretend to offer a full solution to an exegetical problem which has taxed the best minds of the Church for two thousand years. But some very significant clarifications of the issue can be made. First of all, contrary to many assertions made on the basis of the apocryphal apocalyptic books of the time which were later rejected from both the Christian and the Jewish canons of divinely inspired Scripture, the great majority of Jews of Christ's time were *not* expecting an imminent end of the world.[79] The hypothesis that Christ was expecting it is incompatible not only with His Divine knowledge and the manifold evidence of His Divinity, but with His actions to found a Church reported by the same Matthew whose account of the great prophecy presents the most serious difficulties, and with His many parables stressing the importance of faithfulness during a long wait for the Master's return, including three given at exactly this time.[80] Finally, the early portions of the prophecy contain a remarkably accurate prediction of the events of the Roman siege and destruction of Jerusalem in the years 68-70 A.D., which were also years of turmoil and convulsion for the whole Roman empire (69 was always remembered as "the year of the four emperors"; even in the last stages of the collapse of the Western Roman Empire, never again were that many generally recognized emperors elevated to power in a single year).[81] Jesus made it very clear that this catastrophe could be escaped by flight: He expressly directed His followers in Judea at that time to "flee to the mountains."[82] Obviously flight to the mountains will avail nothing on the eve of the end of the world. Therefore at least a very substantial time interval between the two events is logically indicated by Jesus' discourse, even though the manner in which Matthew and Mark reproduce it does not always convey a sense of that interval.[83]

At any rate, the catastrophic destruction of Jerusalem in 70 A.D., fulfilling to the letter Christ's prophecies about it, occurred in exactly the traditional span of a Biblical generation from the time of the prophecy: forty years. As for the date of the end of the world, the whole of Christ's teaching in any way pertaining to this subject shows that He had no intention of giving any hints of when it was to happen. The *parousia*, His second coming, must always be an event that could occur at any moment, suddenly and unexpectedly, though it would be preceded by warnings signs that some would see as heralds of the Last Day.

> Know this, that if the householder had known at what hour the thief was coming, he would not have left his house to be broken into. You also must

be ready; for the Son of Man is coming at an unexpected hour.[84]

Except for the astronomical phenomena—which *may* have been intended simply as literary devices, familiar at the time, to underscore the shattering character of this final event in the world's history[85]—almost all the events and tendencies Christ gives as signs of the end have appeared again and again in history, as they appeared before the destruction of Jerusalem in 70. So evident is this that many orthodox authors have seen most of the description of the "great tribulation" as referring only to the circumstances surrounding that destruction.[86] The visitation of evil in the world's last hours will not necessarily be visible to most men as an unmistakably new and uniquely hideous assault of Hell. More probably it will simply be an intensification of conditions every Christian historian knows and chronicles. That is how the Last Day could come unexpectedly, yet with the signs.

Jesus concluded His discourse on the Last Day with a description of the Judgment itself, in which all men will come before Him and be judged primarily on the love they have borne, and showed by works of charity, to their fellow men. This was another clear assertion of His Godhead, since all Jewish teaching proclaimed God alone the ultimate Judge of the souls of men, never the Messiah— presuming as they did that he would be no more than human.[87]

The gospels tell us nothing about where Jesus was or what He said or did on Wednesday, April 5, 30 A.D. The most probable assumption is that, as so often before during His public life when great moments impended, He spent most of the day and night in prayer.[88] All we know of that Wednesday is the darkest deed in recorded history, when the Apostle Judas Iscariot went to a secret meeting of the members of the Sanhedrin most hostile to Jesus, in Caiaphas' house, and agreed with them to betray the Son of God for thirty shekels—the price of a slave.[89] The betrayal was to enable Caiaphas' men to seize Jesus in a secluded place where there would be no friendly multitude to defend Him.

Much has been written and conjectured about the psychology of Judas, to little avail since we have far from enough information to begin to penetrate his mind and heart. That he longed for wealth and power is evident; St. John emphasizes that he was a thief; that he shared the common expectation of an opulent earthly Messianic kingdom and was disgusted when Jesus refused to use His power to establish such a kingdom (in which Judas surely expected a high position), is virtually certain. But Judas' failure to drive a hard bargain with Caiaphas and his adherents, his evident overmastering desire to help them dispose of Jesus quickly without much regard to the personal advantage he might gain by it, reveal a much greater and deeper evil than avarice. First there was consuming hatred of Jesus; then—after the betrayal was accomplished—that total despair of the possibility of forgiveness which is the ultimate rejection of Christ's love. Indeed, as St. Luke says, Satan had "entered into" him. It is very difficult to read Christ's words about Judas at the Last Supper—"it would have been better for that man if he had not been born"—in any other way than as a statement of Judas' eternal damnation.[90]

On the evening of Thursday, April 6, 30 A.D., Jesus celebrated the paschal meal with the Twelve. A celebrated controversy, extending through almost the entire history of the Church, arises because the first three gospels, clearly describing the Last Supper as a Passover meal, seem to contradict St. John who states in his Gospel that Jesus died on the day *before* the Passover, the "preparation day," in which case the paschal meal would normally have been eaten on Friday evening rather than on Thursday evening.

Now the Passover was always celebrated on the 15th day of the Jewish month Nisan; and all four gospels are unanimous, as is the entire tradition of the Church, that Christ died on a Friday. If He died on the Passover, therefore, it must have been in a year when the 15th Nisan fell on a Friday. Two separate, detailed, and highly accurate calculations have been made of the days of the week on which the 14th and 15th Nisan fell during these years. Both agree that *the 15th Nisan did not fall on a Friday in any year from 28 through 33 A.D.*[91] Since almost all commentators have concluded that the Crucifixion must have occurred in one of those six years, this means that John must be right.

Why then did Jesus eat the paschal meal with the Twelve a day early?[92] Obviously, since He knew He was to die the next day, this was the only time He could have eaten it; and we probably need look no further than this for the explanation. While it is true that the gospels do not report any surprise on the part of the Apostles that they were eating the paschal meal with their Lord that particular night, by this point they were obeying His commands instantly and unquestioningly;[93] and His words at the beginning of the Supper quoted by Luke clearly indicate that this Passover is not to be completed on earth, and carry a suggestion of a special modification of the normal conduct of the great feast so that He may share it with the Apostles before He dies:

> I have earnestly desired to eat this passover with you before I suffer; for
> I tell you I shall not eat it until it is fulfilled in the kingdom of God.[94]

The Last Supper was held at a U-shaped table in the upper room of a house in Jerusalem which may have belonged to the parents of Mark the Evangelist. Peter and John had the places next to Jesus; this had given rise to a petty argument among the Twelve about precedence, which Jesus had terminated in unforgettable fashion by washing the feet of all of them beginning with Peter—and including Judas—as a sign both of the humility to which Christians are so urgently called, and of purification for the forthcoming Eucharist. The prescribed ritual of the paschal meal was in all probability followed without change; but during it, Jesus announced that one of those present would betray Him.[95]

"Is it I, Lord?" each of the Twelve asked fearfully, their then still characteristic presumption for once in abeyance as they contemplated the magnitude of the crime and the certainty with which the Lord had predicted it. Judas joined in the question; to him alone Jesus replied, inaudibly to the others: "You have said it." Then John, leaning against Jesus with his head on His breast—as Prat well says, "the memory of that privilege was to sweeten his whole life"[96]—at the prompting of Peter, asked Jesus who the traitor was, and to him alone Jesus identified Judas Iscariot. "What you are going to do, do quickly," Jesus then told Judas, who went out at once; John's Gospel adds starkly, "and it was night."[97]

Only the faithful remained. More than a year ago, at the synagogue in Capernaum, Jesus had scandalized many of His hearers and puzzled His Apostles by declaring His flesh to be real food, the Bread of Life, which men must eat to have divine life in them; it seems to have been then that Judas abandoned Him in spirit.[98] Now that promise was to be fulfilled in the Christian feast of love, the Eucharist, in which Jesus Christ gives His own Body and Blood to His disciples to unite them more closely with Him. He took some of the remaining unleavened Passover bread, blessed and broke it, and said: "This is my body which is given for you. Do this in remembrance of me." Then He took the cup of wine and said: "This cup which is poured out for you is the new covenant in my blood." "Do this, as often as you drink it, in remembrance of me." The meaning of the verb is not "signifies," but *is*.[99]

Thus the central rite of Christianity was inaugurated. The words of institution, repeated in St. Paul's first letter to the Corinthians less than twenty-five years later, in the context of participation by all the faithful make it very clear that Jesus intended not that the Apostles partake of His Body and Blood only on this unique occasion, but that they and their successors should continue to partake of It until the end of time. The repetition of the words of institution as the heart and center of an ongoing rite (later to be called the Mass) show also that Christ had given the Apostles the power to transform bread and wine into His real, actual Body and Blood by saying those words in union with the Church and for the purposes for which the Lord had first spoken them at the Last Supper, thereby re-enacting (in an unbloody manner) His sacrifice on Calvary. That is to say, Jesus at the Last Supper instituted and administered what came to be called the sacrament of holy orders, empowering the Apostles as priests to make and celebrate the Eucharist as He had done. The sacrificial character of the rite is vividly evident in St. Paul's words to the Corinthians: "As often as you eat this bread and drink this cup, you proclaim the Lord's death until he comes."[100]

In His discourses that followed, Jesus spoke over and over again of love. Though declaring that in the coming hour of apparent disaster to Him they would scatter and flee, that Peter would deny Him three times, that all would seem totally lost and hopeless, yet still He proclaimed that He loved them "to the end" and would keep them safe; that He had prayed to His Father that Peter's faith would not fail under Satan's temptation, and that after his fall Peter would recover and confirm his brethren; and that "in a little while" the Apostles would see Jesus again.[101]

> This is my commandment, that you love one another as I have loved you. Greater love has no man than this, that a man lay down his life for his friends. You are my friends if you do what I command you. No longer do I call you servants, for the servant does not know what his master is doing; but I have called you friends, for all that I have heard from my Father I have made known to you. You did not choose me, but I chose you and appointed you that you should go and bear fruit and that your fruit should abide; so that whatever you ask the Father in my name, he may give it to you. This I command you, to love one another.[102]

The discourse of the Lord recorded by St. John, reaching if possible even greater heights than this was climaxed by His last sublime prayer to the Father for the Apostles and their mission.[103] Then He set out with them, through the night into which Judas had gone, for the Garden of Gethsemane.

Gnarled, ancient olive trees—some of which may have grown from the stumps of those there that night, later cut down by the Roman soldiers who destroyed Jerusalem—still cast their crooked shadows on Gethsemane's stony soil. There is a formal garden around them now; it is most unlikely that there was anything of the sort then. Now as then, beyond the immediate vicinity of the trees, the soil is hard, gritty, rock-studded, almost lifeless where not artificially watered. The site lies in the deep gully of the Kedron wadi, which is a "brook" or "torrent" only for a few weeks in the rainy season. The word Kedron comes from the Hebrew *qadar*, meaning dark or muddy. Though the paschal moon was full, down at the bottom of the canyon there were many areas of almost total darkness; the air was cold. Far above towered the walls and buildings of Jerusalem. They loomed even higher that night than they do today—the Holy City, become the domain of the killers of the Son of God.[104]

Taking Peter and James and John with Him—the witnesses of His Transfiguration and, with Andrew, the recipients of His final teaching about the end of the world—Jesus went off a little way from the others to pray. In a few minutes He had flung Himself face down on the harsh ground. The cruel rocks must have cut into His flesh like rasps.[105]

Foreseeing in every detail what would be inflicted upon Him the next day, His human will recoiled, and He prayed to the Father to let this cup pass from Him—but only if it were the Father's will. It was not the Father's will. The Apostles, worn out with grief and apprehension, fell deeply asleep; they "could not watch for one hour" with their Lord. In some way it seemed that the Father Himself withdrew from the Son.[106] All was abandonment; all was pain. Upon

Jesus Christ face down upon the rock-laced grit of Gethsemane fell the appalling weight of innumerable human sins, the vivid awareness of the despair of lost souls, the future sufferings of the good, the endless war that would be waged against Him and His with undying ferocity through all the centuries of the Christian era. The historian can imagine the array of great malefactors and human monsters who gibbered at Him that night out of the years to come, after His blood had been poured out for the salvation of mankind: the Emperor Nero; the terrible Romula, harpy of the Great Persecution of the Christians which bears the name of the Emperor Diocletian; Attila the Hun; al-Hakim the mad Caliph, destroyer of the Holy Sepulcher; the Old Man of the Mountain, founder of the Assassins; Genghis Khan; Tlacaellel, architect of the Aztec system of mass human sacrifice; Caesar Borgia, the son of a Pope; the Anabaptists of Münster; the Marquis de Sade; Marat and Robespierre and Saint-Just of the French Revolution and the guillotine; Rasputin and Lenin and Stalin; Hitler and Heydrich and Adolf Eichmann. But no man can begin to imagine the additional weight of those secret and personal sins which history cannot chronicle. All of it fell on Him. The bloody sweat burst from His pores, and God sent the Angel of the Agony to strengthen Him.

From the black wadi came the scrape of many feet on the rocks, the clank and clash of arms, the gleam of lanterns. Against eleven exhausted, bewildered men armed with exactly two swords—and the Son of God—came marching a force of several hundred including temple guards armed with swords and clubs and led by members of the Sanhedrin, and more than 100 fully armed Roman soldiers commanded by no less a personage than the officer in charge of the Jerusalem garrison.[107] Just ahead of them was Judas Iscariot. He went up to Jesus and kissed Him. It was the identifying signal to the captors.

Jesus defied the Sanhedrin's men momentarily, as He had done before when physically threatened, by a look which caused them to fall to the ground,[108] but only long enough to identify Himself to them. Then he submitted: "This is your hour, and the power of darkness."[109] Peter swung a sword wildly, striking off the ear of the high priest's servant Malchus; Jesus healed Malchus by a touch.[110] (History tells us no more of Malchus, but one wonders about him. Was he so blinded by hate that even the totally unmerited blessing of Jesus' last healing miracle failed to impress him? Did he remember in the future, as he touched his restored ear, the Person who had healed it? Did he become, at length, a Christian? It is possible, perhaps even likely.)

The Apostles fled. Jesus was hustled out of the deep dark valley and up into the looming city to confront the High Priest who ruled in His Father's name.

Annas and Caiaphas and their adherents in the Sanhedrin had long since resolved on Jesus' death. But for them to put a man to death required confirmation of the sentence by the Roman governor, the Procurator Pontius Pilate, a man who detested them—and, indeed, all Jews and their religion.[111] He was quite likely to refuse to endorse their death sentence on a purely religious charge. But Pilate was very much on his guard against agitators claiming to be the Messiah the Jews were expecting to bring them world-wide political power. To accuse Jesus to Pilate as such an agitator was a most promising course of action for the Sanhedrin. At the same time they must find at least some appearance of legal justification for what they were doing; as the world knows, the Pharisees set great store by appearances.

Consequently, in the trial before the Sanhedrin—probably held in the last hours of the night, around three or four o'clock in the morning[112]—it was at first attempted to convict Jesus by perjured testimony. When this failed becase the perjurers did not agree, Caiaphas himself took charge. Face to face with Jesus, he hurled the decisive question, intended to condemn the accused simultaneously in Jewish and Roman eyes, so put that Jesus, Who had been almost completely silent up to that point, could not fail to answer in loyalty to His Father:[113]

"I adjure you by the living God, tell us if you are the Christ, the Son of God."[114]

Jesus answered: "I am; and you will see the Son of man seated at the right hand of Power, and coming with the clouds of heaven."[115]

As previously explained,[116] despite some minor differences of detail each of the four gospels makes it unmistakably clear that Jesus was condemned to death by the supreme council of Judaism for claiming Divinity for Himself. He had said the same publicly, and been threatened with death for it, at the Feast of Tabernacles six months before and at the Feast of Dedication three months before. Now the Sanhedrin condemned Him with a unanimous shout, and the Temple guards and servants who had been holding Him in custody began to beat Him.

Meanwhile Peter and another apostle, probably John, had managed to make their way into the courtyard of Caiaphas' palatial residence where the Sanhedrin was meeting. They must have heard the shouts of condemnation and abuse, perhaps the sickening crack and thud of the blows falling on Jesus' body. Suspicious looks and questions had already been directed at Peter, a big man with a marked Galilean accent who found it hard to hide. Up to this point Peter may well have been expecting some new exertion of Christ's miraculous powers. But as the curses and blows began falling unrestrained, he must have realized that no such powers would now be used. As at the time of Christ's arrest when he had fled with the other Apostles, fear overwhelmed Peter; but from the enclosed courtyard it was not easy to flee. Then one of the men who had been with the arresting party in the Garden of Gethsemane, a relative of Malchus, suddenly realized that the burly man near the fire was the man who had swung the sword in defense of Jesus. "Did I not see you in the garden with him?" he cried; and Peter was challenged on all sides as a follower of the condemned man. He was literally in the enemy's camp, and it seemed that his Lord had surrendered. So he began to curse and swear that he did not even know Christ.[117]

At that moment, in the half-light of earliest dawn, the long crow of a rooster rang out; and Christ appeared in the clutches of His captors and looked across the courtyard at Peter, who broke down in bitter weeping. As William Thomas Walsh memorably comments:

> Years later, when men saw deep furrows on his cheeks, they said they had been worn by the tears he had never ceased to shed for that moment. Those tears themselves were evidence that he had not lost the faith which Jesus Himself had promised at the supper to pray for. When divine grace had been withdrawn to let him be humbled for his rash presumption and to teach him many lessons for the future, he had yielded, under a sudden and irresistible temptation, to a fear that he might have to share the suffering accepted by his Lord. Cowardice made him lie and curse. And with those falsehoods and imprecations already smothered by sobs of remorse, he stumbled out of the court into the street and was swallowed up by the vast obscurity of that hellish night.

> Where he went or what he did no one has ever known. For some forty-eight hours or more he disappears from the history of the Passion. . . . He did not go to the Mount of Golgotha with John, because he was ashamed to face the beautiful and stricken innocence of the Blessed Mother whose Son he had denied. But he loved Jesus, now in his remorse more than ever; and it is inconceivable that he could have torn himself away from the knowledge of what was happening to Him. The chances are that when the cold wind failed, and a brazen dawn brought back the parched breath of the Dead Sea and the desert to Jerusalem, Peter was somewhere at the edge of the crowd that saw the trial before Pilate in front of the Citadel Antonia.[118]

As for Judas Iscariot, he felt remorse as terrible, but in the unfathomable mystery of iniquity, no genuine repentance and no hope for forgiveness. He hanged himself. His shattered body was buried close by Tophet, in the valley of Gehenna, where Satan's own had made Israelite children into burnt offerings in the Prophet Jeremiah's time.[119]

In his hall of judgment, the Praetorium, Pontius Pilate commenced the day's business, as was customary among Romans and Greeks, at sunrise.[120] It was, in all probability, April 7, 30 A.D.[121] There was nothing in the least distinguished about Pontius Pilate. He was a very ordinary Roman official—arrogant, narrow-minded, unimaginative, affecting a rough "practical" skepticism, yet still possessing both in himself and as a living tradition of government some of that sense of natural justice and law that had brought the Roman peace to the Western world. There is no doubt that, left to himself, Pilate would have acquitted Jesus immediately and unreservedly. He recognized His innocence and the malice of His accusers. The Sanhedrin could put various kinds of pressures on him, and in the course of that murderous morning they tried them all; but none succeeded until the last one, because all that was good in Pontius Pilate revolted against what they wanted him to do. In one dialogue Jesus explicitly told His executioner that his was far from the greatest sin in this matter.[122]

Hoping to appeal to the pity of the crowd that was clamoring for Jesus' death by giving Him a lesser though severe punishment, Pilate at length ordered Him scourged with some sixty lashes of a bone-studded whip, after which his soldiers "crowned" Jesus with a crude cap of thorns pressed against His head by a circlet of rushes, inflicting approximately 20 bloody lacerations on His scalp. Pilate then showed Him to the crowd, saying: "Behold the man!" But there was no pity in the crowd that morning, at least in any who dared to speak. The spectacle of Jesus' whip and thorn wounds may well have further convinced some who had acclaimed Him just five days before on Palm Sunday that He could not be the Messiah—because He was obviously not the kind of Messiah they were expecting—and so must be an impostor deserving death.[123]

Still Pilate held out against the Sanhedrin and the mob. He only gave way when their spokesmen finally invoked the prospect of the wrath of Tiberius—Tiberius the world's ruler and victim, so terribly alone on Capri with his accumulated hatreds and desires for vengeance, Tiberius whom all the world feared because so much of the world had wronged him, Tiberius who so desperately needed the love of Christ Whom he was never to know on this earth, Who was killed in his name:

> Pilate sought to release him, but the Jews cried out, "If you release this man, you are not Caesar's friend; every one who makes himself a king sets himself against Caesar." When Pilate heard these words, he brought Jesus out and sat down on the judgment seat at a place called The Pavement, and in Hebrew, Gabbatha. Now it was the day of Preparation of the Passover; it was about the sixth hour [close to noon]. He said to the Jews, "Behold your king!" They cried out, "Away with him, away with him, crucify him!" Pilate said to them, "Shall I crucify your king?" The chief priests answered, "We have no king but Caesar." Then he handed him over to them to be crucified.[124]

Crucifixion was the most terrible death inflicted in the ancient world—the most painful and the most degrading. It was a "development" of impalement; there is reason to believe that it was originally invented by those masters of satanic cruelty, the Phoenicians and their descendants the Carthaginians.[125] Posts were set up at the place of execution and the victim, stripped naked,[126] was forced to carry a hundred-pound beam to that place, where he was put on his back and his wrists were nailed to the beam. There was a small space where a nail could easily be driven through a hollow just back of the heel of the hand, so that it would support much of the weight of a hanging body—but on its way through this space the nail pierced a major nerve, causing very intense pain.[127] The victim was then "lifted up" and the beam attached as a crossbar to the post, into which his feet were nailed by a single nail driven either through the middle of both feet or through the heels.[128] The weight of the lower body rested either on a wooden projection called a *sedile* or simply upon the ankle-bones above the nail in the feet. If there was a *sedile* the victim lived considerably longer, for the immediate cause of death in crucifixion was asphyxiation; after a time breathing was only possible by raising the body to take some of the weight off the arms, and this could be done for a longer time on an external support than on the ankle-bones of nailed feet. In either case, each raising of the body produced great pain in the extremities, and each sagging of the body great pain in the chest. The torture was constant. Most crucified men took a full day to die. Death could be hastened by breaking their legs, causing almost immediate asphyxiation.[129]

The Holy Shroud of Turin gives clear proof that all these tortures were endured by Jesus Christ—and He had no *sedile*. In 1968, for the first time, the skeleton of a man who had been crucified, with the nails still in his feet, was found just outside Jerusalem, confirming in many respects the data from the Shroud on the manner of crucifixion and the place of the wounds inflicted.[130]

Upon "The Pavement" outside the Antonia fortress Jesus, bloody from the scourging, His face ravaged by blows from a two-inch cudgel which had broken His nose and battered His eyebrows and cheeks,[131] staggered under the weight of the beam of His Cross as He set out surrounded by a troop of Roman soldiers under a centurion, and followed by the bloodthirsty crowd.[132] The destination was Golgotha, the Place of the Skull, just outside the city walls perhaps a thousand yards from the Antonia.[133] The Via Dolorosa led downward into the Tyropoeon valley, then upward out of it; toward the end, therefore, Jesus had to climb uphill under the weight of the beam bearing down upon shoulders that had been scourged after having first sweated blood. He could not do it; He fell. We know from the Shroud as well as from the gospels that He fell, adding wounds on His knees to all His other wounds.[134]

The procession would now have been approaching a gate in the walls; the centurion in charge saw a man named Simon, originally from the African city of Cyrene, coming in from work in the fields. The centurion requisitioned Simon to carry Jesus' cross. "Take up your cross and follow me!" Jesus had told His disciples; and here was a man to do exactly that, though under duress. We are not told that a single word was exchanged between Jesus and Simon of Cyrene; but later Scriptural references make it almost certain that Simon of Cyrene and his sons, most fittingly, became Christians.[135]

At Golgotha the nails were driven through flesh into the wood of the crosses, and the condemned men were raised up in agony for their long dying. Jesus said: "Father, forgive them, for they know not what they do."[136] On each side of Him hung a robber. One reviled Him; the other adored Him. Jesus canonized the penitent thief from the Cross: "Today you will be with me in Paradise."[137] But there were others, dearest of all to Him, who yet adored, whom He could see even with His dimming human vision at the foot of the Cross: His mother, who now reappears in the gospels for the first time since Cana and Nazareth; her sister-in-law Mary;[138] Mary Magdalen; and St. John, the only one of the Twelve to stand by him at the end. "Woman, behold thy son," said Jesus to Mary of John and all the faithful to the end of time; and "Behold thy mother" to John and all the faithful to the end of time, of the Blessed Virgin Mary.[139] Then there burst from Him the terrible cry: *Eloi, Eloi, lama sabachthani—* "My God, my God, why hast thou forsaken me?"[140] G. K. Chesterton says of this moment:

> There were solitudes beyond where none shall follow. There were secrets in the inmost and invisible part of that drama that have no symbol in speech; or in any severance of a man from men. Nor is it easy for any words less stark and single-minded than those of the naked narrative even to hint at the horror of exaltation that lifted itself above the hill. Endless expositions have not come to the end of it, or even to the beginning. And if there be any sound that can produce a silence, we may surely be silent about the end and the extremity; when a cry was driven out of that darkness in words dreadfully distinct and dreadfully unintelligible, which man shall never understand in all the eternity they have purchased for him; and for one annihilating instant an abyss that is not for our thoughts had opened even in the unity of the absolute; and God had been forsaken of God.[141]

He thirsted, and was given vinegar to drink.[142] The sky had grown strangely dark.[143] Jesus' work was done. He, God and man, had suffered the utmost agony possible to man, both mental and physical; from the beginning of His prayer in Gethsemane to the consummation on Golgotha, He had borne and expiated the sins of men and reconciled the human race with its Creator. Theologians may debate how and why; but the fact is that this is what He did. Isaiah had predicted it in his fifty-third chapter, and David in the Twenty-Second Psalm; He Himself, in the course of His teaching and ministry, had predicted and explained it. The gospels and the Shroud tell us how much He suffered; the gospels and the Shroud then provide the final confirmation of His Godhead through their evidence for His Resurrection.

"It is finished. . . . Father, into thy hands I commend my spirit."[144]

The ground shivered. Across the valley and beyond the wall from Golgotha, the lintel of the great double-winged entrance to the sanctuary or "Holy Place" of the Temple, where stood the altar for incense, the table for the Showbread, and the seven-branched gold candelabrum (the *menorah*) facing the Holy of Holies, cracked down the middle. The huge ornate curtain hanging from it—a Babylonian carpet in white, purple, blue, and red, 82 feet by 24—tore in two. A brass gate of the inner Temple building that normally required twenty men to move it, swung open by itself. The central light of the great candelabrum went out. Much of this information comes to us from Jewish, not Christian sources (Josephus and the Talmud), substantially and very significantly supplementing the brief reference to the rending of the Temple curtain in the gospels. The Talmud even dates the strange opening of the brass gate specifically to the year 30 A.D.[145]

Jesus was dead. The mocking crowd had fallen silent at the frightening phenomena in the sky and earth. They began to fear that a great sin had been committed, and "returned home beating their breasts."[146] And the Roman centurion who had ordered the nails driven into the flesh of Jesus and had commanded His raising up on the Cross, exclaimed: "Truly this was the Son of God!"[147]

Perhaps emboldened by the natural prodigies and this reaction among the people, the two members of the Sanhedrin who are known to have been supporters of Jesus—Joseph of Arimathea and Nicodemus—now stepped forward to see that at least He received an honorable burial. Joseph had a new tomb, never yet used, just 22 yards from Golgotha. He obtained Pilate's permission to bury Christ there. Pilate was surprised that Jesus had died so soon; but His death was soon confirmed. One of the troop of Roman soldiers assigned the grisly duty of carrying out crucifixions, ordered to break the legs of the men crucified that day so that they would die more quickly and therefore might be taken down from their crosses before sunset when Passover began, found Jesus apparently already dead. Consequently the soldier did not break His legs; but he made sure of His death by a lance thrust straight into His heart. It left a gaping wound the size of a man's hand.[148]

We may be sure that the Blessed Virgin Mary and the other women who had been at the foot of the Cross never left His Body for a moment until It was laid in the tomb. It was carried the short distance from Golgotha to the tomb probably by five bearers, two at the ends of the terrible crossbeam to which His hands were still nailed, two supporting the middle of His body with a sheet, and the fifth supporting His right heel. In the tomb His hands were at last withdrawn from the beam, the blood-soaked carrying sheet was discarded, and His body was laid on a linen shroud that Joseph of Arimathea had just bought. His hands and feet were bound (a necessity because the tetanic contraction of muscles in those who died by crucifixion would otherwise have caused them to return to the position of the torture) and His chin was supported by small linen bands.[149]

The Sabbath was very close now. There was not time to wash or properly to anoint the Body. The hundred pounds of spices that Nicodemus had bought were quickly packed tight around It to help preserve and freshen It despite the five great wounds and the many open lacerations from which some of His Precious Blood still seeped. The sun had set; in a moment the appearance of the first three stars would signal the beginning of the Passover Sabbath. The massive blocking stone was rolled in front of the entrance to the tomb. Under the Law, nothing more could be done until Sunday.[150]

Wherever Jesus went that night, it was beyond the bounds of history and of the world. The early Christians firmly believed that as one dead He had joined all the other dead, from Adam to Gilgamesh to the Good Thief, in the place of waiting, the Limbo of Hell, and that night brought forth the just to be with Him. His recorded words from the Cross to the Good Thief provide strong evidence that something of this kind did happen.[151]

Meanwhile His murderers were uneasy. Whatever their public demeanor, they had hardly gone unaffected by what had happened in their precious Temple that afternoon. Very likely they began to remember, and at last to understand more truly, His words: "Destroy this Temple, and in three days I will raise it up."[152] They dared not risk any possibility that the people might come to believe that such a thing had occurred. How easy it would be for His disciples to steal His body and proclaim a resurrection, especially since, in the tomb owned by Joseph of Arimathea, It was now directly under their control! So on the Sabbath day the spokesman of the Sanhedrin went to Pilate and obtained a guard of Roman soldiers for the tomb. They went with this guard to the tomb and sealed it, in such a way that any opening would leave clear marks.[153]

Did they look inside before the sealing? Almost certainly they did, though we have no specific testimony to the fact, because they would have felt it necessary to determine that no body-stealing had yet taken place. But there lay Jesus, silent, motionless, untouched, in His Shroud. It seemed death ruled Him, as it had ruled every man since Adam.

The Sabbath ended, the initial Passover celebration completed, and the second night fell upon the Holy Sepulcher. It was Sunday, April 9, 30 A.D., the 16th day of the month Nisan.[154]

Guard detachments of Roman soldiers, such as the one on duty at Jesus' tomb, usually consisted of sixteen men, with four on watch at all times.[155] Sleeping on watch was punishable by death. These were still the same kind of soldiers who had conquered most of the known world for Rome. To imagine all sixteen of them asleep, on duty only six hundred yards from Pilate's praetorium,[156] simply beggars the imagination—however dull and unimportant their curious duty that night may have initially seemed to them.

At the Transfiguration on Mount Tabor, Peter and James and John had seen Jesus radiating light from His body and clothes, in a manner outside all earthly experience. The evidence of the Holy Shroud of Turin, analyzed scientifically by micro-densitometer, VP-8 image analyzer, spectroscope, and other modern scientific instruments and methods, suggests that the extraordinary impressions upon its cloth could only have been formed by a brief scorching flash at a level of energy approaching the thermonuclear.[157]

"Let there be light . . ."

Christ had slain death, the last enemy. He had come back from the fathomless abyss from which no man had ever emerged.

The Roman guard lay huddled, prostrate. An angel wreathed in lightnings rolled back the stone at the entrance of the tomb. Before such power, the shields and swords that had won the Western world were toys. When at last the soldiers could struggle to their feet, they fled.[158]

Earliest dawn glimmered in the eastern sky beyond the pinnacle of the Temple. The women who had been at the foot of the Cross were hastening to complete the work upon the Body of their Lord that the coming of the Sabbath Friday evening had interrupted—the washing and anointing. Some went to buy spices and perfumes. One ran on ahead, to come back just as quickly as she could to all that remained of her beloved Master. It was Mary Magdalen.[159]

But one was not there at all: the Blessed Virgin Mary, the Mother of God. As His mother, Mary loved Jesus as no other human being has ever loved or could ever love Him. Is it conceivable that she would have left others to attend Him in the tomb, if like them she believed Him to be still there? Here is the best evidence for the truth of the ancient Christian tradition that it was to His mother that Christ first appeared after His Resurrection. The Blessed Virgin Mary did not go to the tomb on Easter morning because she knew that her Son had already left it.[160]

Reaching the tomb first, Mary Magdalen found it empty. She ran back to tell Peter and John. They ran at top speed to the tomb, John outrunning Peter because he was much younger and lighter; but at the tomb John waited for Peter, so that they went inside together. They saw, lying on the rock within, the linen bands which had been round Jesus' wrists, ankles and chin, and one burial cloth, which may well have been the Shroud itself, "rolled up in a place by itself." No grave robbers or body stealers would have done this; they would have taken the Body as it was, in the shroud. John tells us that after beholding the burial linens he "saw and believed." In light of all that we now know about the Holy Shroud, it seems very likely that John saw immediately the unique picture of Jesus on the cloth which, along with its position, convinced him that a supernatural event had taken place, that Jesus Christ had risen from the dead as He had predicted, though the Apostles—even John—had not until then understood just what His prediction really meant.[161]

Jesus had risen in His glorified body, which could pass through walls, move from place to place without traversing space as we know it, and was not always immediately recognizable even to those who had known Him best. During that Easter day He appeared to the ineffably loving Mary Magdalen, to the other women who came a little later to the empty tomb, to Peter alone, to two disciples on the road to Emmaus, and to all the eleven Apostles except Thomas, gathered in the Cenacle. He took care to impress upon them that He was really, physically present—that it was in His own body, flesh and blood, that He stood before them, while also emphasizing that He would soon ascend to His Father after a last brief sojourn with them in Galilee.[162]

Also that morning, Annas and Caiaphas took the testimony of the bewildered guards, and the Sanhedrin (or its leaders) met to consider what to do. Reason gave them only two choices: to believe the story of the guards, or to disbelieve it. If they believed the guards, they had no rational alternative to admitting that Jesus had risen from the dead by Divine power, thereby giving final proof of the truth of His claim to be God, for making which they had killed Him. If they disbelieved the guards, then their obvious course was to denounce them to Pilate and arrest the Apostles for stealing Jesus' body either with the complicity of the guards or because of their negligence. Otherwise the very claim of a resurrection which the leaders of the Sanhedrin had posted the guard to prevent, could be very convincingly made. But instead of doing this, Annas and Caiaphas and their immediate associates bribed the guards to say that Jesus' disciples had stolen His body while they slept—and promised to protect them from Pilate. The absurdity of such an explanation for what had happened is so patent—St. Augustine put it best: "How is this? Do you call upon witnesses who were asleep?"—that it speaks volumes that this was the best story these highly intelligent men could devise. Evidently it was the only story that offered any hope of convincing at least some of the people of a natural explanation for what had happened to the body of Jesus, while preventing any close questioning of the guards that could cause them to tell more people what they had actually seen—a telling that the leaders of the Sanhedrin had evidently concluded was, and would be very persuasive. The whole proceeding casts grave doubt on the sincerity of Annas and Caiaphas, at least. It strongly suggests that they knew the guards were telling the truth and that Jesus had risen from the dead by His own power, yet still maintained their adamant refusal to believe in Him.[163]

Among the Apostles, only Thomas had not yet seen the Risen Jesus. Thomas was another Peter, or even more so, in his stubbornly literal mind and outlook. He insisted that he would never believe what the others were telling him about the Resurrection unless and until he not only saw but touched the flesh of the Risen Lord and the marks of His wounds. Such truculent skepticism would have seriously endangered many souls; therefore Christ said to him, after offering the proof he demanded: "Blessed are those who have not seen and yet believe!"[164] But Thomas had been made for a mission, and for that mission the very qualities he here displayed in an unlovely manner would, when perfected by grace, be indispensable.

The forty days from Resurrection to Ascension were, above all, the preparation for the Church and its universal mission. Before the followers of Christ could understand the Church and its mission, they must know its Founder in His fullness, understand the Redemption He had wrought, humble themselves before the Victor over death. All this they achieved, as their preaching on and soon after Pentecost, reported in the Book of Acts, makes very clear. Every one of the eleven had fallen in the hour of trial, except John, and even he had fled from Gethsemane; but now they were restored, Peter above all as he made his humble threefold confession of love at the Mensa Christi rock on the beautiful, quiet little bay of Tabgha of the Sea of Galilee, atoning for his threefold denial of Christ in the courtyard of the high priest. Peter's primacy was restored, his commission as head of the Church given by Christ, to continue with God's guarantee of unfailing constancy until the hour of his martyrdom: "Feed my lambs. . . . Feed my sheep. . . . Follow me."[165]

Somewhere, during this period, the Risen Jesus appeared to no less than five hundred of His followers gathered together.[166] It could have been in Galilee, where His mission had begun, or in Jerusalem where it ended. Wherever it was, the five hundred were made sharers in the cosmic mission which Jesus most explicitly proclaimed to the Eleven on a mountain in Galilee:

> All authority in heaven and on earth has been given to me. Go therefore and make disciples of all nations, baptizing them in the name of the Father and of the Son and of the Holy Spirit, teaching them to observe all that I have commanded you; and lo, I am with you always, to the close of the age.[167]

For two thousand years the Word had been confined to the Chosen People. Now it was to go out to all the world.

In His last hour on earth with the Apostles, in response to a thoughtless and backsliding question about when He was going to "restore the kingdom to Israel," Jesus repeated the same universal theme:

> You shall receive power when the Holy Spirit has come upon you, and you shall be my witnesses in Jerusalem and in all Judea and Samaria and to the ends of the earth.[168]

Then He took them out from Jerusalem and up the Mount of Olives, looking from its highest point across on the one hand to the Holy City where He had died and conquered death forever, and on the other hand to Bethany where He had loved and been loved so much. He raised His arms in blessing, was lifted up into a cloud, and returned to his Father.[169]

NOTES

[1] Luke 9:51.

[2] For very good summaries of the evidence for dating the Passion of Christ in April of 30 A.D. see Eugen Ruckstuhl, *Chronology of the Last Days of Jesus* (New York, 1965), pp. 1-9; Giuseppe Ricciotti, *The Life of Christ* (Milwaukee, 1947), pp. 161-167, and Jules Lebreton, *The Life and Teaching of Jesus Christ Our Lord* (New York, 1957), I, xxx-xxxii. See also Notes 7 and 121, below. For the date of the Feast of Tabernacles

at Jerusalem to which Jesus went in October of 29 A.D., see Andres Fernandez, *The Life of Christ* (Westminster MD, 1958), p. 464.

[3] Luke 13:34.

[4] Ferdinand Prat, *Jesus Christ, His Life, His Teaching, and His Work* (Milwaukee, 1950), II, 39-40, 47-48, 51-52; L. C. Fillion, *The Life of Christ, a Historical, Critical, and Apologetic Exposition* (St. Louis, 1943), III, 6-7.

[5] Prat, *Jesus Christ*, II, 42-44.

[6] By far the best recent presentation of the extraordinary detective work—scientific and historical—that has been done on the Holy Shroud of Turin is Ian Wilson, *The Shroud of Turin* (New York, 1978). Wilson discusses the physical appearance of Jesus Christ as revealed by the Shroud on pp. 13-22. Much of the book reports the results of Wilson's own researches which give strong support to the identity of the Shroud with the Byzantine "Mandylion"—a picture of Christ "not made by hands," found in Edessa in Syria in the sixth century. Wilson's brilliantly developed theory and evidence of this identity has by no means received the attention among historical scholars which it deserves; this writer views it as a landmark advance in Christian history. However, Wilson's study does stand in need of supplementary argument and data insofar as it relates to the early history of Edessa (before 300 A.D.). This volume attempts to meet that need in the text and especially in the notes of Chapter Seventeen, below. For further evidence authenticating the Holy Shroud of Turin in connection with the Crucifixion of Christ, see Notes 123, 125-131, 148-150, and 161, below.

[7] Francis L. Filas, "The Dating of the Shroud of Turin from Coins of Pontius Pilate" (privately published, Youngtown AZ, 1980), together with materials supplied by Filas to the writer on June 3, 1980, and a report in the Washington *Post*, December 14, 1983, on the further progress of Filas' researches ("results of the first complete computer analysis show shroud imprints fitting six Greek letters of a Pontius Pilate coin from 29 A.D., shortly before Christ's crucifixion, said the Rev. Francis Filas"). Filas, a Jesuit, is Professor of Theology at Loyola University of Chicago and has been studying questions pertaining to the Holy Shroud of Turin for nearly thirty years. For the dating of the coins, Filas relies on Frederic W. Madden, *History of Jewish Coinage* (London, 1864), p. 149—a still authoritative treatment of the subject. The dating of the coin which made the impression on the Shroud to the 16th, 17th, or 18th year of Tiberius— and to no other years of his reign—is obviously of the greatest importance, especially in light of the specific reference in Luke 3:1 to the beginning of the preaching of John the Baptist in the *15th* year of Tiberius.

[8] John 7:37-38, 8:12; Alfred Edersheim, *The Life and Times of Jesus the Messiah*, 3rd ed. (New York, 1886), II, 157-161, 164-166.

[9] John 8:20. An earlier attempt to arrest Jesus, which also failed for the same reason, was explained by the arresting officers very simply: "No man ever spoke like this man!" (John 7:46).

[10] John 8:51.

[11] John 8:58.

[12] John 8:59.

[13] John 9:3, 11, 15,

[14] John 9:35-38.

[15] Matthew 15:24.

[16] See Fillion, *Life of Christ*, III, 626-627, for a summary of the very strong case for clearly distinguishing this mission from that of the Twelve in Galilee.

[17] Ricciotti, *Life of Christ*, pp. 439-441.

[18] Prat, *Jesus Christ*, II, 13-14.

[19] M.-J. Lagrange, *The Gospel of Jesus Christ* (Westminster MD, 1938), II, 4-6, 51-52.

[20] As Prat says (*Jesus Christ*, II, 18): "Eusebius informs us that in the fourth century there existed no authentic list of their names. The lists fabricated later, linking them with famous names, are devoid of all historical value. Still it is natural to number among them St. Matthias who was destined to fill out the number of the Twelve, and also his competitor Joseph Barsabas surnamed Justus, for both of them had followed the Savior from the beginning. And, considering the role that he played in the history of the primitive Church, the name of Barnabas may be added to these. All else is empty conjecture."

[21] Though the encounters with these half-hearted disciples are usually placed before the Feast of Tabernacles, Lagrange (*Gospel of Jesus Christ*, II, 2-4) points out that they fit in equally well just afterward, as part of the careful selection process preceding the sending out of the seventy-two. Indeed, we may reasonably suppose that some or all of these men attended the Feast, heard Jesus there, and were drawn to Him while still holding back from a total commitment.

[22] Ricciotti, *Life of Christ*, pp. 446-447; Edersheim, *Jesus the Messiah*, II, 195-196. As Ricciotti points out, it is very hard to imagine Jesus waiting to give His followers the only prayer He ever spelled out for them, until almost the end of His public ministry. Even though Matthew's Gospel by no means always adheres to chronological order, its placement of the first teaching of the Our Father—in a fuller version than Luke's—at the time of the Sermon on the Mount is probably chronlogically accurate, since this was the great occasion for Jesus' fundamental instruction on the Christian faith to His first followers. But the circumstantial details given by Luke, which clearly place his account of the teaching of the Our Father at the period of the Judean and Perean ministry toward the end of 29 A.D., suggest a request for guidance in prayer from one of the new disciples (see Note 21, above) who had not been in Galilee at all. This would readily account for the reports of Jesus' teaching the Our Father at two widely separated times and places in His public life.

[23] Luke 10:21-22.

[24] Matthew 11:28-30. As Fillion remarks (*Life of Christ*, III, 26-27) this is the one gospel passage specifically mentioning the Sacred Heart of Jesus, the object of a strong and widespread Roman Catholic devotion since the time of St. Margaret Mary Alacoque, in the seventeenth century.

[25] Prat, *Jesus Christ*, II, 73-74, 77.

[26] John 10:30.

[27] Prat, *Jesus Christ*, II, 75-77.

[28] See Chapter Fifteen, Note 108, above.

[29] Luke 10:38-42.

[30] Fernandez, *Life of Christ*, pp. 494-495.

[31] *Ibid.*, pp. 513, 519-520, 539-540.

[32] Luke 12:49-53.

[33] Mark 10:6-9, 11.

[34] Matthew 19:9. For an explanation to the effect that Jesus was teaching that even under the Mosaic law (which He had just abrogated with regard to divorce) adultery should have been the only grounds for divorce, see Fernandez, *Life of Christ*, pp. 543-547. For the more usual explanation that the exception refers only to an invalid marriage, see Prat, *Jesus Christ*, II, 79-83. A particularly good discussion of this ancient and much disputed question is that of Lagrange, *Gospel of Jesus Christ*, II, 85-92; he inclines to the view that only separation is here meant by "putting away." It is a very significant point, emphasized by Lagrange, that it is Matthew's Gospel—the only one containing the apparent exception to the doctrine of the indissolubility of marriage—which stresses

more than any other the astonishment and shock of the disciples at the novelty and difficulty of Jesus' doctrine of marriage.

[35] Prat, *Jesus Christ*, II, 82n-83n.

[36] John 11:16; Fillion, *Life of Christ*, III, 188-191.

[37] R.-L. Bruckberger, *Mary Magdalene* (New York, 1953), pp. 103-106.

[38] Fillion, *Life of Christ*, III, 196; Lebreton, *Jesus Christ*, II, 128-130.

[39] Prat, *Jesus Christ*, II, 140-141. Jewish custom involved visits to bereaved relatives and friends by all who knew them well, for a full week after the death, with particular emphasis on the fourth day after death, when decomposition of the body began and it was thought that the soul finally departed from the neighborhood of the body. As Prat (*loc. cit.*) says, "since the family of Lazarus was very well known in the environs of Jerusalem and in the city itelf, there was a considerable gathering of people present when the approach of Jesus was announced." Their comments at the time and their subsequent behavior shows the group of mourners that day to have included both friends and enemies of Jesus, along with others previously uncommitted who were convinced by the miracle.

[40] Prat, *Jesus Christ*, II, 143-144.

[41] John 11:38-40. The characterization of Martha is superb. In many ways she is a feminine counterpart of Peter.

[42] John 11:43-44.

[43] Lebreton, *Jesus Christ*, II, 132-133; J. E. Belser, *History of the Passion, Death and Glorification of Our Savior Jesus Christ* (St. Louis, 1929), pp. 34-36.

[44] Lagrange, *Gospel of Jesus Christ*, II, 103.

[45] *Ibid.*, II, 103-104.

[46] Ricciotti, *Life of Christ*, pp. 29-41, 47-49; Belser, *History of the Passion*, pp. 3-4; see Chapter Twelve, above.

[47] Ricciotti, *Life of Christ*, pp. 53-57.

[48] This is the thesis developed at length and with full scholarly apparatus by Robert Eisler, *The Messiah Jesus and John the Baptist* (London, 1931) and more recently supported, in large part, by S. G. F. Brandon, *The Fall of Jerusalem and the Christian Church* (London, 1970). These works—Eisler's in particular—are extreme examples of the kind of massive rewriting of history in which scholars who reject the authenticity, contemporaneity and historical reliability of the gospels feel free to engage. Their reconstructions are a tissue of scattered bits of "evidence" from writers who lived four, six, or eight centuries after the life of Christ on earth, yet purport to know aspects of His life wholly unreported by the Evangelists; of strained deductions from the relatively little that is known from non-Christian sources of Jewish and Roman provincial history in Jesus' time; of highly tenuous hypotheses of what Josephus supposedly said before supposed Christian forgers and revisers cut up his manuscript; and of sheer flights of imagination about what Romans and Jews of Jesus' time "must have thought" and "must have done," even when there is no contemporary or near-contemporary evidence or indication whatever that they thought and did anything of the kind, or would logically have done so. Two illustrations, common to both Eisler and Brandon, will suffice to show the quality of their analysis: both seriously argue that Jesus' driving the money-changers out of the Temple the day after Palm Sunday (see Note 66, below) indicates an actual military insurrection posing a dangerous threat to Roman rule (Eisler, *op. cit.*, pp. 480-493; Brandon, *op. cit.*, pp. 103-104) and that the two swords Peter and another brought to Gethsemane betoken an actual attempt, contemplated or already undertaken, to seize political power in Palestine (Eisler, *op. cit.*, pp. 510-513; Brandon, *op. cit.*, pp. 102-103). The only appropriate rejoinder would seem to be that a power which felt,

or could be seriously threatened by the overturning of a few bankers' tables and two very unskilled swordsmen could hardly have governed a village, much less an empire.

[49] John 11:50-52.

[50] Ricciotti, *Life of Christ*, p. 506.

[51] *Ibid.*, pp. 506-507.

[52] Lebreton, *Jesus Christ*, II, 140-149.

[53] Fillion, *Life of Christ*, III, 222.

[54] Prat, *Jesus Christ*, II, 189.

[55] Mark 14:6, 9.

[56] Lebreton, *Jesus Christ*, II, 152-154.

[57] Ricciotti, *Life of Christ*, pp. 518-522; Prat, *Jesus Christ*, II, 190-194; Edersheim, *Jesus the Messiah*, II, 365-373. See especially Edersheim, *op. cit.*, II, 371-372, for a very thorough explanation of how the popular acclamations for Jesus on Palm Sunday were drawn from liturgies used at all the great Jewish feasts, of what kind of branches were actually waved, and of where they were obtained—points on which challenges to the accuracy of the gospel narratives have often been mounted, *e.g.* by Eisler, *Messiah Jesus*, pp. 476-480. The frequently heard statement that palm branches could not actually have been among those used to hail Jesus, because the palm tree does not grow at the altitude of Jerusalem, overlooks the fact that many of the pilgrims—including Jesus Himself—had come to this Passover from across the Jordan and from Jericho, where palms grew in abundance. It was customary to bring branches to the feast, and palm branches were regarded as a sign of special honor (Edersheim, *op. cit.*, II, 372). It would have been natural for Jesus' new followers from Perea and Jericho to have brought palm branches with them to help give Him a royal reception in Jerusalem.

[58] It is etched unforgettably on the memory of the writer, who first beheld it on Palm Sunday 1971—as is the memory of the Palm Sunday procession of our day, which to a remarkable degree recaptures the spirit of the original one.

[59] Ricciotti, *Life of Christ*, p. 545; Fillion, *Life of Christ*, III, 323.

[60] Luke 19:42-44.

[61] Jerusalem was besieged, the Temple destroyed, and most of its people killed by the Romans at the climax of the Jewish war in 70 A.D. See the conclusion of Chapter Seventeen, below.

[62] William Thomas Walsh, *Saint Peter the Apostle* (New York, 1948), p. 156.

[63] The "Wailing Wall." For a discussion of its physical relation to the former Temple, see Fillion, *Life of Christ*, III, 323-324, and Kathleen M. Kenyon, *Jerusalem* (New York, 1967), pp. 139-141.

[64] Mark 11:11.

[65] Luke 9:58.

[66] For excellent statements of the case for *two* Temple cleansings by Jesus, one at the beginning of His public ministry as recounted in John's Gospel and the other in the last week of His mortal life as recounted in the other gospels, see Prat, *Jesus Christ*, II, 202-204 and Belser, *History of the Passion*, pp. 56-58. Certainly the recurrence of the abuse is not difficult to understand; as Prat says, "inveterate abuses are almost ineradicable" (*op. cit.*, II, 203n). A very significant difference between the two accounts, indicating that they refer to two different events, concerns the challenge to Jesus' authority to take such action in the Temple and His response. In the Temple cleansing described in the Gospel of John, He replies: "Destroy this temple, and in three days I will raise it up" (John 2:19). After the Temple cleansing described in the Synoptic Gospels He replied with a counter-question about the origin of John's baptism. Since the response regarding John the Baptist was an important part of His great debate of Tuesday in Holy

Week, while the response regarding a destruction of the Temple was used as evidence against Him in His trial before the Sanhedrin, it seems clear that both responses were actually made; and John's Gospel, so much more chronologically oriented than the other gospels, clearly places the "Destroy this temple" response at the outset of Jesus' public ministry.

[67] Mark 11:28.

[68] Mark 11:30.

[69] Lebreton, *Jesus Christ*, I, 162-164.

[70] Mark 12:17. There is a particularly good discussion of the significance and perfect truth of Jesus' answer regarding tribute to Caesar (sometimes called evasive, *e.g.* by Brandon, *Fall of Jerusalem*, p. 104) in Belser, *History of the Passion*, pp. 67-68, 78-80.

[71] Mark 12:34.

[72] Even the Apostles were still asking Him after His Resurrection when He was going to "restore the kingdom to Israel" (Acts 1:6). If after all His teaching and His Crucifixion they still cherished some of the old illusion, we can imagine how it controlled the minds of the crowds in Jerusalem on this Passover of 30 A.D.

[73] This point has been firmly clarified at the highest level of authority in the Roman Catholic Church by the Declaration on the Relationship of the Church to Non-Christian Religions, proclaimed by the Second Vatican Council with the approval of Pope Paul VI, which states: "Even though the Jewish authorities and those who followed their lead pressed for the death of Christ (cf. John 19:6), neither all Jews indiscriminately at that time, nor Jews today, can be charged with the crimes committed during his passion. It is true that the Church is the new people of God, yet the Jews should not be spoken of as rejected or accursed as if this followed from Holy Scripture" (Austin Flannery, ed, *Vatican Council II; the Conciliar and Post-Conciliar Documents* [Collegeville MN, 1975], p. 741). See the excellent discussion of the Pharisees' special influence having been the principal reason for the manner in which Jesus addressed them, and the general review of Jesus' attitude toward the Pharisees, in Lagrange, *Gospel of Jesus Christ*, II, 152-170.

[74] Matthew 23:27-28, 33-36. Belser (*History of the Passion*, pp. 85-87) soundly surmises that the reason Matthew gives so much more full a report on Jesus' mighty condemnation of the Pharisees in the Temple debates during Holy Week than Mark or Luke, is that Matthew was writing for Jewish readers at a time when the Pharisees were still very powerful in Judea. Therefore, the same factors that had impelled Jesus to make this shattering public denunciation of them in 30 A.D. were still operative in the 40's when, according to Belser's view (also the view here accepted) the original Aramaic version of Matthew's Gospel was written.

[75] Mark 13:2.

[76] Matthew 24:34; Mark 13:30 is virtually identical.

[77] Matthew 24:36; Mark 13:32 is identical.

[78] Lagrange, *Gospel of Jesus Christ*, II, 172. Reimarus, the founder of modern rationalistic anti-supernatural criticism of the Bible (see Chapter Fourteen, Note 1, above) declared that "this one text was enough to prove for him that the Founder of Christianity was convicted of error and Christianity of being false" (Lagrange, *loc. cit.*).

[79] Ricciotti, *Life of Christ*, pp. 201-203; Edersheim, *Jesus the Messiah*, II, 434-445. Edersheim's very thorough review of the evidence solidly establishes this often forgotten or ignored point. Furthermore, as Edersheim makes clear (*op. cit.*, II, 441-442) the visions of the Last Judgment held and taught by the rabbis are at an immense moral distance from the teaching of Christ on the Last Judgment, showing almost nothing in common with it.

[80] The parables of the wicked servant (Matthew 24:45-51), of the ten virgins (Matthew 25:1-13), and of the talents (Matthew 24:14-30). See Lebreton, *Jesus Christ*, II, 197-201.

[81] See Chapter Seventeen, below. Ricciotti (*Life of Christ*, p. 548) quotes Tacitus' memorable description of that year when "four princes were cut down by the sword" as "filled with calamities, black with battles, torn by sedition, cruel even in its very peace."

[82] Matthew 24:16; Mark 13:14.

[83] Lagrange strongly and very rightly emphasizes this point (*Gospel of Jesus Christ*, II, 181-184).

[84] Luke 12:39-40.

[85] Note on this point the comments and citations of Fernandez, *Life of Christ*, p. 613, whose total orthodoxy is unquestionable.

[86] *e.g.*, Ricciotti, *Life of Christ*, pp. 546-549, and Belser, *History of the Passion*, pp. 111-115.

[87] Lebreton, *Jesus Christ*, II, 202.

[88] Fillion, *Life of Christ*, III, 360.

[89] Ricciotti, *Life of Christ*, p. 558; Prat, *Jesus Christ*, II, 254. By worldly standards the amount of money paid Judas for his betrayal was absurdly inadequate in a matter of this importance. If Judas had been motivated primarily by avarice, as many orthodox writers have rather unreflectively held, he would certainly have exacted a much higher price for his treason. The high priest and his circle had plenty of money, and could and surely would have paid far more than 30 shekels for the safe and easy delivery of Jesus into their hands. Judas' primary motive must have lain in far deeper and darker realms than Mammon's.

[90] Luke 22:3; Mark 14:21. See especially the excellent analysis and reconstruction of Judas' betrayal by Edersheim, *Jesus the Messiah*, II, 472-477.

[91] Jack Finegan, *Handbook of Biblical Chronology* (Princeton NJ, 1964), Table 140 and pp. 292-296. Furthermore, the Passover was observed like a Sabbath, with most if not all of the sabbatarian restrictions on servile work and business activity in effect. The descriptions of the events of Friday in all four gospels show unmistakably that no such restrictions were being enforced that day by the Jewish leaders in Jerusalem. As Lagrange conclusively states: "All the busy comings and goings of the chief priests and the leaders of the Pharisees, the appearance of Jesus before the Sanhedrin, His prosecution before Pilate, everything in fact that all the four evangelists by common consent assign to the Friday, could not possibly have taken place on the most solemn feast of the year. In particular, the Synoptists state that the Jews wished to have the matter finished before the feast began. It must therefore be regarded as certain that the feast of the Pasch did not fall on Friday that year, but on Saturday." (*Gospel of Jesus Christ*, II, 192) Finally, the 14th Nisan, the day before the Passover, was specifically remembered and commemorated as the day of Jesus' death on the Cross in the tradition of the eastern churches for two centuries (Jules Lebreton and Jacques Zeiller, *The History of the Primitive Church* [New York, 1946], II, 717-718).

[92] Numerous other theories have been advanced to explain why Jesus and the Apostles might have eaten the Passover a day early; for a summary and review of many of them, see Prat, *Jesus Christ*, II, 488-499. It is proposed (a) that different groups of Jews may have used different lunar observations to date the Passover (for the difficulty and variation of the lunar observations setting the beginning of Nisan, see Ricciotti, *Life of Christ*, pp. 164-165); (b) that some Jews ate the Passover supper a day early when the Passover fell on a Sabbath so as to avoid breaking the Sabbath rest by slaughtering the lambs at dusk (Lagrange, *Gospel of Jesus Christ*, II, 192-195); (c) that the high priest's circle

and the Sadducees might have celebrated the Passover a day later than other Jews because of their insistence that Pentecost always fall on a Sunday, 50 days after the Passover (Fernandez, *Life of Christ*, pp. 632-634); (d) that Galileans still counted days as beginning at sunrise instead of at sunset as the high priests now counted them, so that for them the day of the Crucifixion, the day before the official Passover, was the Passover and the 15th Nisan (Finegan, *Handbook of Biblical Chronology*, pp. 290-291). Arguments against the first three theories are presented by Ruckstuhl, *Last Days of Jesus*, pp. 28-32; all four of them suffer from the near-fatal defect of assuming that any large group of Jews in Jerusalem at Passover time could safely defy the high priest and all the recognized religious authorities, slaughter their own Passover lambs at the time they preferred even though they had to do so in the Temple which was the priests' own domain, and observe the holy occasion on a different day while conducting business as usual on the official day of its commemoration. Given the temper of the high priest, the Sadducees and the Pharisees so clearly revealed in the Gospels, such assumptions are, to say the least, unlikely. Ruckstuhl's explanation, that Jesus and the Apostles were celebrating the Passover according to the curious rigid calendar of Jubilees believed to have been used by the Qumran or Essene community, in which Passover always fell on a Wednesday (*op. cit.*, pp. 72-134), encounters all the force of the above objection plus the strong internal evidence of the gospel narratives that Jesus' arrest, trial and crucifixion took only twelve hours or less. Many events were indeed crowded into this short period, but despite Ruckstuhl's arguments it seems clear that they could have happened this quickly, and early Christian tradition is almost unanimous that they did. For a detailed argument specifically supporting the feasibility of the events described in the Gospels from Jesus' arrest to his crucifixion occurring in the stated twelve-hour period, see George Ogg, review of Mlle. Jaubert's *La date de la Cène, Novum Testamentum* III (1959), 156-160.

[93] For example, the manner in which He commanded and they obeyed in obtaining His unexpectedly humble mount for His triumphal Palm Sunday entry into Jerusalem (Matthew 21:1-9; Mark 11:1-10; Luke 19:28-38; John 12:12-18).

[94] Luke 22:15-16.

[95] The dining arrangements were those of the Roman *triclinium*; despite the commandment in the Law of Moses that the Passover meal be eaten standing, to commemorate the abrupt departure of the Israelites from Egypt, the Jewish religious authorities at the time of Christ permitted it to be eaten reclining, a practice derived originally from Iran, which had become universal in the ancient Mediterranean world (with the odd exception of Crete). Jesus reclined in the place of honor at the middle of the crossbar of the U in the table, with Peter at His left, John at His right, and Judas at John's right. See Prat, *Jesus Christ*, II, 260, 268-270, on these points. Edersheim (*Jesus the Messiah*, II, 493-495) proposes a different arrangement, with Judas at Jesus' left and Peter lower, hypothesizing that it was Judas' taking of this place of honor that provoked the strife over precedence the gospels report at the beginning of the Last Supper. But there is no solid evidence to support this; the conversations with or about Judas on this occasion, reported in the gospels, can equally well be explained by his having been seated at John's right, easily accessible to Jesus across the bend of the table. Peter also needed to be near Jesus to converse privately with him as he did, and by this time his precedence among the Twelve was clearly established by Christ's own words. For the evidence that the house where the Last Supper was held belonged to the family of Mark the Evangelist, see Fernandez, *Life of Christ*, pp. 625-628. It has also been conjectured on fairly sound grounds that the Garden of Gethsemane also belonged to Mark's family and that Mark, then little more than a boy, was sleeping there that night and that he was the young man who ran

away naked after Jesus' arrest, as Mark's Gospel alone reports, without naming the young man; see Ricciotti, *Life of Christ*, pp. 586-587, 593-594. For the significance of the washing of the feet, see Lebreton, *Jesus Christ*, II, 226-228; for the ritual of the paschal meal that Jesus in all probability followed throughout, see Fillion, *Life of Christ*, III, 384-387.

⁹⁶ Prat, *Jesus Christ*, II, 270.

⁹⁷ John 13:23-30; Lebreton, *Jesus Christ*, II, 229. It has been the opinion of most orthodox exegetes in the twentieth century that Judas left before the Eucharist began and so did not receive Holy Communion, which would have been an appalling sacrilege.

⁹⁸ See Chapter Fifteen, above.

⁹⁹ Luke 22:19-20; 1 Corinthians 11:23-25. Unleavened bread must have been used, because the Law of Moses allowed no leavened bread in the house on the night the Passover was celebrated, and this law was still rigorously observed (Prat, *Jesus Christ*, II, 272-273). The controversial literature on the institution of the Eucharist is of course enormous. But the words of institution are so vividly clear, repeated in essentially the same form in all three Synoptic Gospels (except that Matthew and Mark do not include "do this in remembrance of me") and in Paul's first letter to the Corinthians, that it is very difficult to escape their plain meaning without resorting to the usual Modernist practice of denying authenticity to Scriptural passages disagreed with. For learned linguistic analyses of the words of institution and their evidently Semitic origin, see Joachim Jeremias, *The Eucharistic Words of Jesus* (New York, 1966), pp. 189-203, and Belser, *History of the Passion*, pp. 237-245; Belser stresses the point that although Aramaic does not use a copulative verb in a phrase like "this is my body," the copulative sense is clearly understood, while the Greek *estin* used to translate it can only mean "is." Lebreton notes Jesus' special care to tell his very literal-minded Apostles when He is using figures of speech and when He is not; as he says: "Surely it is impossible to pretend . . . that in His last farewell meal He had no other intention than to put before His Apostles an insoluble enigma, which from the morrow of His death onward was to be interpreted by the whole Church in the wrong way?" (*Jesus Christ*, II, 241). Fillion quotes most appropriately none other than Martin Luther on this subject: " 'I would like to find a man able to prove that there is only bread and wine in the Eucharist; he would render me a great service. I have sweat a great deal over the study of this question, but I feel bound, the Gospel text is very clear. . . . Doctor Carlstadt tortures the pronoun "this"; Zwingli is captivated by the verb "is"; Oecolampadius twists the word "body"; others inflict martyrdom on the whole text. . . . I challenge them to bring me a Bible where we find the words: This is the sign of my body.' " (*Life of Christ*, III, 653). The Protestant Edersheim also admits that the meaning is clearly "is," not "signifies" (*Jesus the Messiah*, II, 511-512). For an excellent, while rather satirical survey of the prolonged step-by-step process whereby Modernist scholars have chipped away at the texts on the institution of the Eucharist until finally eliminating the historical reality of them all, at least to their satisfaction, see Ricciotti, *Life of Christ*, pp. 576-579.

¹⁰⁰ 1 Corinthians 11:26; Manuel Miguens, *Church Ministries in New Testament Times* (Arlington VA, 1976), pp. 122-127. Although Miguens finds no specific reference in the New Testament to persons called priests in celebrating the Eucharist (the word "priest" is applied only to Christ Himself during this period) (*ibid.*, pp. 127-129), the repetition of the rite was unquestionably commanded by Christ when He said "do this in remembrance of me," and it was unquestionably carried out regularly and faithfully by the early Christian community. Since only the eleven faithful Apostles were present at the institution of the Eucharist, only they could have been empowered directly by Christ to continue it. No such power could have been given to anyone earlier since the rite

had not yet been inaugurated, so no follower of Jesus would have known exactly what it was to be or exactly how he should conduct it; nor could it have been done afterward (except possibly after the Resurrection, when we have no hint of anything of the kind) since there was no time. Therefore the Apostles alone must have received from Christ on the night of the Last Supper the power to transform bread and wine into His Body and Blood—a power they could and did pass on to others ("apostolic succession") through the sacrament of holy orders. See Belser, *History of the Passion*, pp. 256-258, 283-287, and Fillion, *Life of Christ*, III, 402-404.

[101] Fernandez, *Life of Christ*, pp. 646-650; Lebreton, *Jesus Christ*, II, 257-258. For the significance of Christ's words to Peter as they pertain to his leadership in the Church, see Michael M. Winter, *Saint Peter and the Popes* (Baltimore, 1960), pp. 19-20.

[102] John 15:12-17.

[103] John 17.

[104] Prat, *Jesus Christ*, II, 309, 311-313; Fernandez, *Life of Christ*, p. 663n; personal observations by the writer on a visit to Jerusalem in 1971, when the paschal moon was full. The coldness of the night is evident from the fires burning later in the courtyard of the high priest.

[105] During an hour's meditation on Holy Thursday evening in 1971 conducted by the Franciscan Fathers on a slope adjacent to the Garden of Gethsemane, the writer was particularly impressed by this harshness of the soil and rocks. His earlier visualization of Jesus throwing Himself down on grass to pray could hardly have been further from the truth.

[106] Lebreton, *Jesus Christ*, II, 292-296, 314-316; Prat, *Jesus Christ*, II, 317-320. These authors compare Jesus' experience of a feeling of the Father's withdrawal with the "dark night of the soul" experienced by the great mystics of the Church, notably St. John of the Cross and St. Teresa of Avila, while recognizing that much deeper mysteries regarding the essential nature and operation of the Holy Trinity—impenetrable to human wisdom—are involved in Jesus' agony in Gethsemane. See also the text and Note 141, below, on Jesus' cry from the Cross: "My God, my God, why hast thou forsaken me?"

[107] Belser, *History of the Passion*, pp. 336-337, 343-347. For the number of Roman soldiers probably involved, see Fernandez, *Life of Christ*, p. 668.

[108] There is considerable disagreement as to whether this falling down was natural—a confusion and entangling caused by reaction to Jesus' overawing presence (*e.g.*, Lagrange, *Gospel of Jesus Christ*, II, 234)—or an actual miracle (*e.g.*, Belser, *History of the Passion*, pp. 339-340). In either case the purpose and effect of Jesus' action is the same: to show that He is not being taken captive against His will, but submits voluntarily, in conformity with the Father's will, to all that is to happen that day.

[109] Luke 22:53.

[110] John 18:10; Luke 22:50-51.

[111] Prat, *Jesus Christ*, II, 332-333, 365-366; Fillion, *Life of Christ*, III, 481-482; Lagrange, *Gospel of Jesus Christ*, II, 248-250.

[112] The Sanhedrin apparently met twice on this occasion, once at the time indicated in the text and again at dawn. Reliable authorities are almost evenly divided on whether the actual trial and condemnation of Jesus took place at the night session, with the morning meeting simply for the purpose of concerting the best approach to Pilate, as the Gospels of Matthew and Mark suggest (the view of Fernandez, *Life of Christ*, pp. 699-700; Prat, *Jesus Christ*, II, 346; and Fillion, *Life of Christ*, III, 462-471, 477-478) or at the morning session, with the night meeting devoted solely to preliminary questioning, as Luke's Gospel suggests (the view of Ricciotti, *Life of Christ*, pp. 597-598; Lagrange, *Gospel of Jesus Christ*, II, 243; and Lebreton, *Jesus Christ*, II, 345). But since speedy action

characterized the whole plan and proceedings of Jesus' foes that night and day; since all three Synoptic Gospels agree that the beating of Jesus took place before the morning session of the Sanhedrin and it is more likely to have come after the condemnation than before it; and since the indications of condemnation at the night meeting of the Sanhedrin seem to the writer much clearer in Matthew and Mark than do the indications in Luke that it was delayed until the morning meeting (Luke's account of the morning meeting, 22:66-71, sounds very much like a repetition and confirmation of an earlier action) the view of Fernandez, Prat and Fillion that the condemnation took place at the night session is here adopted. It has been strenuously argued that this meeting, or at least the night session, was not a regularly constituted meeting of the Sanhedrin and was contrary to Jewish law (*e.g.* by Edersheim, *Jesus the Messiah*, II, 553-557; Ruckstuhl, *Last Days of Jesus*, pp. 35-48; and by various Jewish scholars). This may be true—though our rabbinic data on the procedures of the Sanhedrin probably represent more a later idealization than first-century reality (Prat, *Jesus Christ*, II, 332-334)—but it is clear that the Sanhedrin was acting collectively under the cover of its recognized authority; and, being the highest court in Judaism, there was no appeal from its decisions on procedural grounds.

[113] Prat, *Jesus Christ*, II, 336-337; Lebreton, *Jesus Christ*, II, 349-350.

[114] Matthew 26:63. In light of his immediate response to Jesus' affirmative answer to this question, and Jesus' previous public declaration of His Divinity at the Feast of Tabernacles, there can be no reasonable doubt that Caiaphas had in mind the correct and full meaning of the term "Son of God" as Jesus had used it, rather than some loose popular sense of one specially favored by God. On this point see especially Lebreton, *Jesus Christ*, II, 350-353.

[115] Mark 14:62. Matthew and Luke give Jesus' response in the rather odd elliptical form sometimes used for affirmation at that period: "You say that I am." For the strictly affirmative sense of this, see Fillion, *Life of Christ*, III, 494n.

[116] See Chapter Fourteen, above.

[117] Fernandez, *Life of Christ*, pp. 692-695; Walsh, *St. Peter*, pp. 188-189. So much ink has been spilled over the essentially insignificant questions of whether Annas and Caiaphas had separate palaces or shared a palace, and exactly how many denials Peter made, that commentators have almost lost sight of the point—of capital importance in fully understanding Peter's denial—of what was happening to Jesus when Peter denied Him most forcefully. Fernandez and Walsh rightly emphasize the effects on Peter of the cruel and humiliating abuse that Jesus was permitting His enemies to inflict upon Him at that moment. The sequence of events set forth in the text, following Fernandez and Walsh, seems much the most probable reconstruction, given that the formal condemnation of Jesus took place at the night session of the Sanhedrin (see Note 112, above).

[118] Walsh, *St. Peter*, pp. 189-190.

[119] Lagrange, *Gospel of Jesus Christ*, II, 246-248; Edersheim, *Jesus the Messiah*, II, 575-576. Edersheim presents an excellent resolution to the old problem of why Matthew (27:3-10) appears to attribute to Jeremiah a quotation known to be from Zechariah, based precisely on Jeremiah's prophecies against Israel because of the child sacrifices at Tophet in the Valley of Gehenna.

[120] Prat, *Jesus Christ*, II, 348-349.

[121] Given that Jesus was crucified on Friday, 14 Nisan (see Note 91, above), the year must have been either 30 or 33, these being the only years when the 14th of Nisan fell on Friday during the range of possible dates for the Crucifixion (27-34 A.D.). Although 33 seems to have been gaining support recently, compared to twenty years ago when scholars accepting the historicity of the Gospels were virtually unanimous in favor of

30, the arguments against 33 remain very strong and have not been refuted. As Ruckstuhl says, "there are no serious objections against 30 A.D. as the year of the Crucifixion" (*Last Days of Jesus*, p. 6), while dating it in 33 requires a span of at least four years from Jesus' baptism by John to His Crucifixion, although even the longest estimates of His public life do not exceed three years. Furthermore, Friday the 14th of Nisan in 33 A.D. was April 3; but a strong consensus of tradition in the early Church points specifically to April 7 (Friday, 14th Nisan, 30 A.D.) as the day of the Crucifixion. See Ruckstuhl, *op. cit.*, pp. 5-9.

[122] John 19:11. Firstly, political charges were brought against Jesus: that He had proclaimed Himself Messiah and king and was stirring up sedition, telling people not to pay their taxes to Rome. Pilate quickly disposed of these charges by his questioning of Jesus; in any case he probably knew them to be false, for it was his duty as governor to keep very careful watch on alleged Messiahs who might lead revolts. See Lebreton, *Jesus Christ*, II, 359-363. Lebreton emphasizes the importance of Pilate's complete refusal to believe the political charges against Jesus as "the most decisive confirmation of everything we know already of Christ's ministry and its purely religious character. If in such turbulent times so suspicious a Roman governor found in our Lord's activities nothing to justify His prosecution, it was indeed because there was nothing that could have given rise to the slightest suspicion" (*ibid.*, II, 361n-362n). Once again the modern theory of Jesus as a political agitator or "liberator" is conclusively disproved. After the political charge had failed, the Jewish leaders brought before Pilate their own charge of blasphemy, demanding that he confirm their sentence of death upon Jesus as a gesture of respect for their local law; but this only aroused in Pilate a new interest in and respect for the Prisoner, and a feeling (most eminently justified!) that he was becoming involved in matters far beyond his ken, from which it would be wise to remove himself (*ibid.*, II, 381-382).

[123] Lebreton, *Jesus Christ*, II, 373-374. Clear evidence for the number of strokes in the scourging of Jesus and the shape and construction of the crown of thorns appears in the Holy Shroud of Turin as explained by two physicians who have studied it closely: Dr. Pierre Barbet (*A Doctor at Calvary* [New York, 1953], pp. 83-87) and Dr. David Willis, whose unpublished notes are cited in Wilson, *Shroud of Turin*, pp. 23-24.

[124] John 19:12-16. Mark 15:25 gives the time of the condemnation as "the third hour," which if used precisely of a 12-hour day—as John's Gospel fixes time—would have meant about 9:00 a.m. But in view of the absence of anything resembling clocks in general use in Judea, the common people usually divided the day into only four parts, which were called the first, third, sixth, and ninth hours. Presumably Mark was following this practice. Hence his "third hour" could mean any time from 9:00 a.m. to noon. See Ricciotti, *Life of Christ*, pp. 635-636, and Prat, *Jesus Christ*, II, 508-510, *pace* Ruckstuhl, *Last Days of Jesus*, pp. 46-48. Ruckstuhl claims the reconciliation of Mark and John explained above "is contradicted by Mark 15:33," in which Mark says the preternatural darkness of the Crucifixion fell "when the sixth hour came." There is surely no "contradiction" unless we impose a veritable stopwatch accuracy on the Evangelists. There is no need to suppose that more than an hour elapsed between condemnation and crucifixion; some of that hour may have been before noon and the rest of it afterward. Furthermore, it must never be forgotten that John was there, an eyewitness of all that happened; Mark may not have been there, and if he were, it was as a very young man. "The Pavement," or Lithostratos, which was just outside the Antonia fortress, has recently been excavated. It is quite unmistakable, consisting of 2700 square yards of large stone slabs, some six feet long and 18 inches thick, some with marks cut for games played by the Roman soldiers. See Ricciotti, *Life of Christ*, p. 612; L. H. Vincent, "Le Lithostrotos Èvangelique," *Revue Biblique* 59 (1932), 513-530; Pierre Benoit, "Prètoire,

Lithostrotos et Gabbatha," *ibid.*, pp. 531-550. The Lithostratos may be examined by any tourist in Jerusalem today.

¹²⁵ Ricciotti, *Life of Christ*, p. 626; Barbet, *Doctor at Calvary*, pp. 41-42.

¹²⁶ Ricciotti, *Life of Christ*, p. 629; Barbet, *Doctor at Calvary*, pp. 62-65. The usual practice, as all authorities admit, was to crucify men naked, though this may not have been universal. But the evidence of the Shroud indicates that Jesus was crucified naked.

¹²⁷ Barbet, *Doctor at Calvary*, pp. 48-50, 94-105. Barbet's research has been upheld and confirmed by later medical investigation and stands as a major contribution both to proving the authenticity of the Holy Shroud of Turin and to explaining what actually happened at the crucifixion of Christ (Wilson, *Shroud of Turin*, p. 27).

¹²⁸ Wilson, *Shroud of Turin*, pp. 27-28, 35.

¹²⁹ Barbet, *Doctor at Calvary*, pp. 45, 68-69, 74-80.

¹³⁰ Wilson, *Shroud of Turin*, pp. 35-36. The most striking confirmation was the clear indication in the skeleton of the crucified man discovered in 1968, that he had been nailed through the wrists close to the position indicated by the Shroud and by Dr. Barbet's researches.

¹³¹ Barbet, *Doctor at Calvary*, pp. 71, 82-83; Wilson, *Shroud of Turin*, p. 22 (notes of Dr. David Willis). Some of the facial wounds might have been inflicted by the beating after Jesus' condemnation by the Sanhedrin, but the detail of the cudgel—shown by the character of some of the wounds—and the use by St. John of a word meaning "to beat with a stick" to describe the abuse of Jesus by the Roman soldiers at the time of the scourging, strongly indicates that the worst of the facial wounds were inflicted then.

¹³² Lebreton, *Jesus Christ*, II, 386-387.

¹³³ See Fernandez, *Life of Christ*, pp. 716-725, for an excellent review of the much debated question of the authenticity of the location of Golgotha at the present Church of the Holy Sepulcher, now generally but still not universally admitted. It was just outside the wall surrounding Jerusalem at the time of the Passion, but was enclosed within a new wall built around Jerusalem by Herod Agrippa a few years later (Kenyon, *Jerusalem*, pp. 153-154).

¹³⁴ Prat, *Jesus Christ*, II, 375-376; Barbet, *Doctor at Calvary*, pp. 88-89.

¹³⁵ Fillion, *Life of Christ*, III, 524-525; Prat, *Jesus Christ*, II, 376.

¹³⁶ Luke 23:34.

¹³⁷ Luke 23:39-43.

¹³⁸ See Chapter Fifteen, Note 17, above.

¹³⁹ John 19:25-27.

¹⁴⁰ Mark 15:34.

¹⁴¹ G. K. Chesterton, *The Everlasting Man* (New York, 1925), pp. 260-261.

¹⁴² John 19:28-29.

¹⁴³ Ricciotti, *Life of Christ*, pp. 638-639. The darkness would appear to have been preternatural, but this is not entirely certain, nor is its nature and extent; we are not given enough information about it.

¹⁴⁴ John 19:30; Luke 23:46.

¹⁴⁵ Flavius Josephus, *The Jewish War*, translated with notes and commentary by G. A. Williamson (London, 1970), p. 399; Belser, *History of the Passion*, pp. 542-543, 546-548; Fillion, *Life of Christ*, III, 551-552; Prat, *Jesus Christ*, II, 397-398; Edersheim, *Jesus the Messiah*, II, 610-612. Jerome extensively reviewed this whole subject, aided by his access to Jewish sources but hampered by the lapse of time between the event and his researches. He alone reports the cracking of the lintel, citing the apocryphal Gospel to the Hebrews; but this is so related to the opening of the Temple gate on its own, which is reported in the Talmud, that it seems reasonable to accept this evidence and combine the two reports. Though many orthodox exegetes hold that it was the inner

curtain of the Holy of Holies that was torn (and it may indeed have been torn along with the outer curtain), Josephus' statement in *The Jewish War* seems to indicate the outer curtain, and Jerome states explicitly that the outer curtain was torn (Lagrange, *Gospel of Jesus Christ*, II, 273). However, Josephus' implication that the curtain remained torn but in place for years is surely in error; the Temple authorities would obviously have replaced it just as quickly as possible, which would have been very quickly since they had a considerable supply of curtains on hand (Edersheim, *op. cit.*, II, 611).

[146] Luke 23:48.

[147] Matthew 27:54; Mark 15:39.

[148] Ricciotti, *Life of Christ*, pp. 642-644; Belser, *History of the Passion*, p. 562; Barbet, *Doctor at Calvary*, pp. 52-53, 113. This one fact alone, fully congruent with Roman practice as well as attested by the gospels, is sufficient to dispose of all the "Passover plot" theories, ancient and modern (the first was proposed by the pagan Celsus in the third century) to the effect that Jesus was still alive when put in the tomb, and later somehow escaped in a natural way. Roman soldiers did, after all, know how to kill men; and St. John saw the lance penetrate Jesus' heart (John 19:34). No one survives such a wound.

[149] Barbet, *Doctor at Calvary*, pp. 129-132, 135-138; Wilson, *Shroud of Turin*, p. 39.

[150] Barbet, *Doctor at Calvary*, pp. 138-141; Wilson, *Shroud of Turin*, pp. 40-41; Fernandez, *Life of Christ*, pp. 743-744; Matthew 27:60. The Holy Shroud of Turin shows that Jesus' body cannot have been washed before being placed in the tomb on Friday, despite Christian traditions to the contrary; none of the gospels refer specifically to a washing of the Body. The final anointing with perfumes would be done by rubbing and the Body would have to be washed before this was done. The explanation is simple, and clearly suggested by the gospels: the women attending the Body simply ran out of time before the Sabbath began when the first stars came out after sunset on Friday.

[151] Prat, *Jesus Christ*, II, 404-405; Lagrange, *Gospel of Jesus Christ*, II, 282.

[152] John 2:19.

[153] Ricciotti, *Life of Christ*, pp. 646-647; Fernandez, *Life of Christ*, pp. 750-751.

[154] See Note 121, above.

[155] Fillion, *Life of Christ*, III, 563.

[156] Barbet, *Doctor at Calvary*, p. 134.

[157] Wilson, *Shroud of Turin*, pp. 198-211.

[158] Matthew 28:2-4; Fernandez, *Life of Christ*, pp. 752-753.

[159] Barbet, *Doctor at Calvary*, p. 141; Lagrange, *Gospel of Jesus Christ*, II, 283-284.

[160] Prat, *Jesus Christ*, II, 414-416.

[161] John 20:1-9; Wilson, *Shroud of Turin*, pp. 44-45; Barbet, *Doctor at Calvary*, pp. 142-149. Barbet gives a most interesting argument, based on Aramaic and later Latin usage, for translating the Greek word *soudarion* used in John 20:7 as "shroud" rather than the usual "napkin" or "handkerchief."

[162] Lebreton, *Jesus Christ*, II, 408-415; Prat, *Jesus Christ*, II, 421-423; Belser, *History of the Passion*, pp. 592-594.

[163] Walsh, *St. Peter*, pp. 198-199; Ricciotti, *Life of Christ*, pp. 653-654. Most recent Christian writers have been very reluctant to comment on the possibility that Annas and Caiaphas may have known that the Resurrection really happened, while still refusing to believe in Christ, perhaps because of concern that more widespread awareness of the likelihood of this would intensify anti-Jewish feeling among Christians. But the importance of examining every fact and reasonable inference pertaining to the Resurrection as an historical occurrence is so great, and the manner in which Annas and Caiaphas conducted themselves immediately after the Resurrection so very germane to its historicity,

that the issue ought not to be avoided, even for good motives.

[164] John 20:29.

[165] Prat, *Jesus Christ*, II, 441-445; Fernandez, *Life of Christ*, pp. 775-782; Winter, *St. Peter and the Popes*, pp. 21-23. The Mensa Christi rock still stands, now enclosed in a little church reconstructed by the Franciscans, on the very edge of the clear waters of the Sea of Galilee. Incredibly, this very holy and beautiful place is now almost never visited by pilgrims or tourists. Nowhere in Palestine is the atmosphere of a New Testament story easier to evoke, as the writer can testify from unforgettable personal experience.

[166] 1 Corinthians 15:6.

[167] Matthew 28:18-20.

[168] Acts 1:8.

[169] Lebreton, *Jesus Christ*, II, 427-430; Bruckberger, *Mary Magdalene*, pp. 187-189. For some curious reason, the Ascension is a particular stumbling block to belief for a certain type of mind, whose aversion to it apparently stems from a feeling that it localizes God "in the sky" in a manner that is astronomically absurd. But Luke's narrative in Acts does not speak of Christ rising indefinitely up into the sky, but of His being "lifted up" and then enfolded in cloud. Nothing astronomical is indicated by this. The cloud is an ancient Israelite symbol for God, Who led Moses and his people by a pillar of cloud by day and of fire by night (see Chapter Three, above), while an upward motion toward reigning Divinity is common to the imagery, liturgy, and religious language of most peoples, including the Jews, whatever their astronomical conceptions or lack thereof.

17.
HE CHOSE TWELVE—AND PAUL (30-70 A.D.)

Therefore take the whole armor of God, that you may be able to withstand in the evil day, and having done all, to stand. Stand therefore, having girded your loins with truth, and having put on the breastplate of righteousness, and having shod your feet with the equipment of the gospel of peace; besides all these, taking the shield of faith, with which you can quench all the flaming darts of the evil one. And take the helmet of salvation, and the sword of the Spirit, which is the word of God.—Ephesians 6:13-17

I have fought the good fight, I have finished the race, I have kept the faith. Henceforth there is laid up for me the crown of righteousness, which the Lord, the righteous judge, will award to me on that day, and not only to me but also to all who have loved his appearing.—2 Timothy 3:7-8

Jesus ascended into Heaven on May 19, 30 A.D.[1] Gathering daily in the "upper room," the Cenacle, where the Last Supper and the first Eucharist had been celebrated,[2] the Apostles watched and waited with the Blessed Virgin Mary, Mother of God and Mother of the Church; with Jesus' kinsmen from Nazareth, the sons of Cleopas and Alphaeus, now all believers at last;[3] and with a number of other disciples that grew to 120 during the ten days between the Ascension and the feast of Pentecost. During that time Peter called for the selection of a twelfth Apostle, to fill the place vacated by the treason of Judas, from among the disciples who had been with Jesus from the beginning, and were witnesses to His Resurrection. These were not many, other than the Eleven who had been with Jesus throughout His public life. Only two were there in the Cenacle: Joseph Barsabas, and Matthias. The choice between them was made by lot, which fell upon Matthias.[4]

The feast of Pentecost fell that year on a Sunday, May 29. It was the harvest festival for the Jews, since late spring is harvest time for wheat in Palestine. Two loaves, and other special sacrifices, were offered at sunrise.[5] Once again God was to act both in reality and as sign and symbol; for the Church of Christ was to be the harvester of souls, and it was born this day.

> When the day of Pentecost had come, they were all together in one place. And suddenly a sound came from heaven like the rush of a mighty wind, and it filled all the house where they were sitting. And there appeared to them tongues as of fire, distributed and resting on each one of them. And they were all filled with the Holy Spirit and began to speak in other tongues, as the Spirit gave them utterance.[6]

Many Jews from distant lands of the Dispersion came to Jerusalem for the feast of Pentecost as for Passover, or remained there from Passover to Pentecost. We are specifically told that in that year there were Jewish pilgrims in Jerusalem for Pentecost not only from all over the Roman empire, but from several areas of the Parthian realm as well, and from Arabia. The Apostles came out to address them, and each listener heard their words perfectly in his own native language. All timidity, confusion, doubt, and obstinate adherence to erroneous popular Jewish ideas of the Messiah were gone from the Apostles now, blown away forever by the breath of the Holy Spirit, the Third Person of the Blessed Trinity, Who had conferred His precious gifts upon them, most especially understanding and fortitude.[7]

Peter said:

> Men of Israel, hear these words: Jesus of Nazareth, a man attested to you by God with mighty works and wonders and signs which God did through him in your midst, as you yourselves know—this Jesus, delivered up according to the definite plan and foreknowledge of God, you crucified and killed by the hands of lawless men. But God raised him up, having loosed the pangs of death, because it was not possible for him to be held by it. . . . This Jesus God raised up, and of that we all are witnesses. Being therefore exalted at the right hand of God, and having received from the Father the promise of the Holy Spirit, he has poured out this which you see and hear. . . . Let all the house of Israel therefore know assuredly that

God has made him both Lord and Christ, this Jesus whom you crucified.[8]

This time there was no argument, no hostile questioning, no demand for new confirming signs; for the Sign of the Holy Spirit—the gift of tongues—rang in the ears of the audience, and none could withstand Him. By nightfall, no less than three thousand of the pilgrims had been baptized in the name of the Father, of the Son, and of the Holy Spirit. The Church had grown thirtyfold in a single day. With the convert pilgrims' return home, the world-wide expansion of the Church began.[9]

It was probably not long after this Pentecost that Peter, invoking the Holy Name of Christ, healed a crippled beggar at the gate of the Temple called the Beautiful. When the people heard of the miracle and flocked around Peter, he preached to them again as he had on Pentecost, so that two thousand more came into the Church. The Sanhedrin could no longer ignore what was happening. Those who had brought about the crucifixion of the Son of God now became the first of the enemies of Jesus Christ and His Church to confront in wrathful dismay that phenomenon, against all rational calculation, which has baffled and frustrated them for twenty centuries: the persistent refusal of that Church, the Mystical Body of its Founder Who had been killed and buried in a tomb but had risen from it, to stay dead. On Good Friday morning Peter had fled, denying Christ, when he heard the first blows fall upon his Master's body. Now he defied the whole Sanhedrin when it ordered him never again to speak or teach in the Name of Jesus, rejoicing when they scourged him for doing so, because this meant that he had been found worthy to suffer for his Lord.[10]

The infant Church in Jerusalem grew and flourished. Its members lived their lives in total dedication to their faith and their mission. They cherished one another, partook of the Body and Blood of Christ frequently together in private, held all their goods in common, and prayed together in the Temple[11]—for they were still all Jewish Christians, carefully observing the full Mosaic Law.[12] Even some of their enemies were impressed; voices were raised in their favor in the Sanhedrin itself. Two of the most respected rabbis, Gamaliel and Eliezer, were believed to be favorable to the Christians. Gamaliel firmly opposed their persecution in the very earliest days of the Church; a rather vague but suggestive dialogue with Eliezer preserved in rabbinic tradition strongly indicates that he was familiar with Christ's words describing Himself as the Good Shepherd and held so nearly Christian a view of those words that he did not dare to answer directly, without evasion, probing questions from the other rabbis on his view of Jesus.[13]

As the Church grew, it embraced more and more dwellers in Jerusalem of diverse origins, including those who had been of the Dispersion and spoke Greek as well as the natives of Palestine who spoke Aramaic—though still all Jews. Eventually it became necessary to select a special body of men—the first members of the Church hierarchy, other than the Apostles themselves, of whom we have record—to serve the Greek-speaking Jewish Christians in Jerusalem. The Apostles chose seven deacons, ordaining them by the laying on of hands, to preach and to minister to the needs of this body of the faithful. Outstanding among them was Stephen, young and ardent, whose forceful preaching particuarly scandalized the Pharisees.[14]

For nearly seven years after the Resurrection the Emperor Tiberius continued to live and rule. In the year after the Resurrection he learned at last of the long-time treachery and ambition of his prime minister Sejanus, who aimed to supplant him. Tiberius carefully and cleverly arranged for the overthrow and execution of Sejanus; but when this had been accomplished, he learned that his daughter-in-law Livilla had conspired with Sejanus some years before to poison his beloved son Drusus, her husband, who had loved and trusted her completely. Grimly desperate, disgusted with the human race, Tiberius withdrew still more deeply into his embittered isolation on the island of Capri. Yet, despite the almost unbearable intensity of his private anguish and some indications of consequent mental disorder, he still insisted on good government in the provinces. So well was this insistence of his known and heeded that when Pontius Pilate, in one of his characteristic fits of exasperation, ordered the massacre of a group of harmless Samaritan pilgrims gathered at the foot of their holy mountain Gerizim, Vitellius, legate of Syria, at once sent Pilate to Rome to answer personally to the emperor for the injustice.[15] It was fitting that Pilate should in the end have been called to judgment by the very emperor in whose name he had condemned Christ.

But Tiberius did not live to judge Pontius Pilate. The procurator of Judea was suspended from office probably in December, 36 A.D.; when he reached Rome he found that Tiberius had died on March 16, 37 A.D., and that Gaius "Caligula," the 25-year-old surviving son of Germanicus, was the new emperor.[16] At this point Pilate disappears from verifiable history into efflorescent Christian legend, too late and too varied to tell us anything substantial about his actual fate.

After dismissing Pilate and sending him to Rome, Vitellius had appointed one Marcellus as Pilate's provisional replacement in Judea. Like all high official appointments, it lapsed with the death of the emperor reigning when it was made. Gaius quickly appointed a procurator for Judea, whose name is given in the single reference we have to him in all our sources as Marullus—possibly a copyist's error for Marcellus. During the ensuing two years Gaius permitted a much greater degree of autonomy in the provinces than had Tiberius, which may explain why we hear nothing more about Marcellus or Marullus in Judea. Even though we are told that Gaius appointed him within a few days of becoming emperor, the vagaries of sea travel may have delayed the receipt of the report of his appointment in Judea; or the general uncertainty about the policy of the new emperor, together with the disgrace of Pilate and its cause, may have persuaded Marcellus or Marullus not to intervene with force to uphold the prohibition against the Sanhedrin carrying out executions without Roman approval. In any event, the prohibition was temporarily suspended; and the Sanhedrin promptly put Deacon Stephen on trial for his life for preaching against the Temple, the Law, and Jewish tradition in the Name of Jesus of Nazareth.[17]

It appears that Stephen had spoken somewhat more openly and explicitly than the Apostles were then speaking about the coming days, foretold by Jesus, when His Church would be no longer bound by the Law and Jewish tradition, and the Temple would lie destroyed. Stephen charged his judges with obstinate resistance to God, with the murder of Christ, and with breaking the Law themselves. As, in furious anger, they threatened him, he cried out: "I see the heavens opened, and the Son of man standing at the right hand of God."[18]

The Sanhedrin screamed that this was blasphemy. Abandoning all pretense of legal procedure, they dragged Stephen outside the city, flung him into a hollow, and immediately inflicted the ancient form of capital punishment for blasphemers: stoning. Watching it all with great approval was a young Jew from the city of Tarsus in Cilicia, a "Pharisee of the Pharisees," Saul—called in Greek, Paul. He held the garments for members of the Sanhedrin so that they might better hurl the stones at Stephen. With his last breath, St. Stephen the first martyr prayed that God would forgive his killers.[19]

A general persecution now began, aimed particularly at the Hellenistic Jews in Jerusalem like Stephen. Many of them fled to surrounding regions. But in the vacuum of authority left by the death of the grim old emperor and the coming of a feckless young one, the Sanhedrin could exert power even outside Judea, for it was recognized by the Jews of the Dispersion as holding supreme authority in Judaism throughout the world. So the avid persecutor Paul was sent to seek out Jewish Christians in the Syrian city of Damascus as he had sought them out in Jerusalem. In all probability he set forth in the late spring or early summer of the year 37.[20]

Damascus is the oldest continually inhabited city on earth, fundamentally little changed down the millennia. An aerial photograph taken in the twentieth century still shows the Street Called Straight crossing the city like a transfixing arrow. It was to be known as the military key to Syria and Palestine, as the home of the world's best sword-blade steel. But above all Damascus has been, is, and shall ever be best known and remembered for what happened on a bright hot summer day on the road entering the verdant oasis in which it lies, when the caravan led by the relentless Paul approached the city from the direction of Jerusalem. For Paul, sinner and persecutor, was that rarest of men: a man of total personal and intellectual honesty.[21] He had hunted down the Christians because he honestly believed them to be God's enemies. He sought no glory for himself, no personal reward, no satisfaction of private hatreds. He was capable of complete, lifelong, deathless dedication. This capacity, when harnessed by grace, can move mountains, transform history; and that was the kind of work for which God had chosen Paul before the foundation of the world.

Supernal light blazed, eclipsing the noonday sun of the Syrian desert in summer. Damascus disappeared before Paul's blinded eyes. His horse reared, and he fell. A voice came, like a mutter of thunder to his companions, but Paul could hear every word like deep-toned bells:[22]

> "Saul, Saul, why do you persecute me?"
> "Who are you, Lord?"
> "I am Jesus, whom you are persecuting." . . .
> "What shall I do, Lord?"
> "Rise, and go into Damascus, and there you will be told all that is appointed for you to do."[23]

Paul wrote to the Philippians, years later: "Christ Jesus laid hold of me." The Greek word he used may also be expressed as "took me by surprise" or "vanquished me" or "took me as prey."[24]

Still unable to see, Paul was led to a house on the Street Called Straight, and there Ananias of the Christian community of Damascus came to him at God's call, restored his sight, and baptized him. For a few weeks Paul preached Christ in the synagogues of Damascus, astonishing Jews and Christians alike. The Jews plotted to kill him, and he had to flee for a time into Arabia, where he prepared himself in prayer and contemplation for his coming mission.[25]

Meanwhile the scattering outside Judea of the Hellenistic Jews who had been associated with Stephen strengthened and extended the Church. One of the seven original deacons, Nicolaus, was a proselyte from the great Syrian Greek city of Antioch; it is reasonable to assume that he now returned to his native city and helped lay the foundations for the Christian community there which soon became very important.[26] Deacon Philip (not to be confused with the Apostle Philip)[27] went to Samaria and won many converts. Christ Himself had first brought the Good News to the Samaritans, the only people in the world not accepted in Jerusalem as Jews who nevertheless observed the Law of Moses; they were now ripe for His harvest. Unfortunately they were much influenced at this time by an extraordinary charlatan known as Simon the Magician, who claimed to be "the great Power of God." He accepted baptism from Philip, but when he found it did not bring the miraculous powers the Holy Spirit was giving to many who preached Christ, he came with a bag of gold to buy those powers from Peter when the chief of the Apostles visited Samaria to confirm the new converts. Appalled, Peter warned Simon that "your heart is not right before God" and that Hell awaited the man who would try to buy the gifts of the Holy Spirit. Only mildly abashed, Simon went on to become one of the founders of the weird far-flung heresy which came to be known in the next century as Gnosticism.[28]

Deacon Philip moved on to the Palestinian coastal plain, where on the road from Gaza to Jerusalem he met a eunuch from the royal court of Ethiopia (that is, the kingdom of Meroë in what is now the Sudan, where the Blue Nile and the White Nile converge), a distant land and people known to the Jews from the time of the prophet Isaiah when "Ethiopian" kings had ruled Egypt as Pharaohs.[29] Some Jews of the Dispersion had penetrated even to this far-off realm. The eunuch may have been one of them, for he knew the Book of Isaiah which mentioned his country and prophesied that some day its people would worship the One True God. Philip explained to him how Isaiah had prophesied Christ; the Ethiopian believed, and was baptized. So difficult was access to the Upper Nile that it was more than three hundred years before Christian missionaries of whom we have record reached it; when they arrived, they found people who knew the sign of the Cross, though they had forgotten its meaning.[30] The eunuch of the Ethiopian court, Deacon Philip's convert, may well have been the first evangelizer of his people, and have labored with some success; a few years later the Apostle Matthew may have followed him there. Their faith renewed by the fourth century mission, the Ethiopians have remained Christian ever since, even after being totally surrounded by Islam. Ethiopia's Christian kings were the source of the famous legend of Prester John, the hidden Christian monarch of the east, which so fired the imaginations of the first Portuguese and Spanish explorers.

As Peter had come to Samaria to confirm Deacon Philip's converts and to strengthen his foundations, so he came to the Palestinian coastal plain, probably in the year 39.[31] In the city of Joppa he raised the beloved widow Tabitha from the dead. The greatest city on the coast was pagan Caesarea, where Herod had built a breakwater to make the first port on the harborless shore of Palestine. In Caesarea was stationed Cornelius, a Roman centurion attracted—as many of the more virtuous Romans in this period were attracted—by the faith and high moral teachings of the Jewish people of the country in which he found himself. Cornelius had become their admirer and benefactor, but not a Jewish proselyte since he remained uncircumcised. Peter had never heard of him, nor he of Peter. But to Peter in Joppa came a vision of animals both clean and unclean according to the Law of Moses, mingled together so that all contracted ritual impurity, and a command that he kill and eat some of them. His protests about the Law were answered with: "What God has cleansed, you must not call common [unclean]." Meanwhile Cornelius was summoned by an angel to send men to Joppa to find and bring Peter to him, and Peter was commanded by the Holy Spirit to go with these men, despite the age-old prohibition on Jews visiting the homes of pagans. Peter went, accompanied by six probably very dubious Jewish Christian disciples. He stayed in Cornelius' pagan household, ate at his ritually unclean table, preached Christ, and saw the Holy Spirit descend upon these pagans as soon as they believed, just as He had descended upon the Jewish Christian Apostles and disciples at Pentecost in Jerusalem. Cornelius and his household were baptized, the first Gentiles to enter the Church of Christ.[32]

This startling news flew through the infant Church. It was well known in

Jerusalem before Peter returned there, so that he was immediately challenged about it and had to explain the reasons for what he had done and justify his action at some length. Once they had heard the whole story, centering on the vision Peter had received, most of the faithful in Jerusalem accepted what he had done and rejoiced in it, though some still doubted. The fundamental issue of whether all Christians must live as Jews under the Mosaic Law had been settled once and for all, in the first decade of the Church's history, by the head of the Church. The news must have come very soon to Antioch, for it was just at this time that the Greek-speaking Jewish Christians in that city first began to preach Christ to their Gentile neighbors, and to make converts among them. This evangelization of Gentiles in Antioch met with so much success that the next year (40 A.D.) Peter himself went to Antioch (shortly after his first meeting with Paul, in Jerusalem) to take personal charge of this new and vitally important work. It was in Antioch that the faithful were first called Christians— probably by the Roman authorities, since the name has a Latin derivation.[33]

In this same year 40, deadly danger threatened Judea from Rome. The young Emperor Gaius was in the process of establishing the dark axiom of Roman imperial history that almost always when a man assumed the purple and ruled in his own right under the age of thirty-five, it drove him insane.[34] From the death of his sister, the only good influence on him, in the second year of his rule, Gaius' megalomania grew. He took the official cult of the reigning emperor with utter seriousness and demanded ever more elaborate testimonials to his own divinity. The Jews, as a specially privileged group under Julius Caesar's laws, had always been exempt from the requirement to practice the imperial cult. Gaius refused to maintain this privilege. When the Jews still resisted, he ordered a colossal statue of himself to be erected in the Temple in Jerusalem, with two legions to beat down any resistance. The generous and heroic Petronius, successor of Vitellius as governor of Syria, delayed enforcement of this fatal order, at the risk of his life, until Herod Agrippa, a grandson of Herod the Great who had a long-standing friendship with Gaius, was able to prevail upon him not to insist on the destruction of the people Herod Agrippa hoped to rule as his grandfather had done (Gaius had already given him Herod Antipas' former authority over Galilee, in 39). The danger suddenly ended when Gaius' reign of terror in Rome provoked his assassination in January of 41. The Praetorian Guard replaced him with his uncle Claudius, a retiring scholar whom few thought capable of truly ruling; but in many respects Claudius governed well. He restored the privileges of the Jews, and awarded Herod Agrippa (who had taken care to cultivate him as well) with the coveted realm of his grandfather, including all of Judea and Samaria (see "Rulers of Rome and Judea, 37-70 A.D.," below).[35]

These arrangements probably took several months to complete; we have no explicit evidence of Herod Agrippa in Palestine until October of 41.[36] The Apostles had every reason to expect the worst from him. they well remembered

RULERS OF ROME AND JUDEA, 37-70 A.D.

Rome	Judea
Gaius "Caligula" 37-41	Procurator Marullus (or Marcellus) 37-41
Claudius 41-54	King Herod Agrippa I 41-44
	Procurator Cuspius Fadus 44-46
	Procurator Tiberius Alexander 46-48
	Procurator Ventidius Cumanus 48-52
	Procurator Antonius Felix 52-60
Nero 54-68	Procurator Porcius Festus 60-62
	Procurator Albinus 62-64
	Procurator Gessius Florus 64-66
	Jewish War (leadership: John of Gischala) 66-70
Galba 68-69	
Otho 69	
Vitellius 69	
Vespasian 69-79	

how his grandfather had sought to kill the Infant Jesus. They knew that the leading Jews hated them more than ever and that the support they had previously enjoyed among many of the Jewish people was dwindling as it became known that the Christians now sanctioned disregard of the Law of Moses in preaching to the Gentiles, and welcomed association with them. Herod Agrippa was no Pharisee; he was exclusively concerned with wealth and power and cared little or nothing for the Jewish religious doctrines which he professed. But he was almost sure to curry favor with the Pharisees by pandering to their prejudices and desires, so long as they did not conflict with his own. The virtually complete removal of the Roman power by the restoration of the kingdom of Herod left the Christian community naked to its enemies. Even Pilate had almost saved Jesus from crucifixion; Stephen had been martyred only after, and because of Pilate's departure and Tiberius' death; Petronius had saved the Temple from Gaius' madness. There was still some genuine respect for natural justice in Rome and among the better of the imperial officials, but far less among the enemies of the Christians in Jerusalem.

An early, well attested Christian tradition dates the dispersion of the Apostles very precisely to twelve years after the Resurrection—the Passover of 42 A.D.[37] There is good reason to believe the dispersion did take place then, having been carefully planned as soon as the Apostles had news of the Emperor's establishment of Herod Agrippa's full kingdom, to include Jerusalem. Christ's discourse on the destruction of Jerusalem and the end of the world had clearly indicated that a community of the faithful was to remain in Jerusalem until its destruction was imminent; though this might have seemed to be impending during Gaius' last year, it was the last thing Herod Agrippa wanted. So a Christian community must remain the city where Christ had died and risen, with one of the Apostles left to lead it. The one chosen was James the Lord's cousin, known throughout Jerusalem—to Jews as well as Christians—as James the Just. He was constantly in the Temple praying, the skin of his knees hardened like a camel's from his hours spent upon them in prayer. His devotion to the Law of Moses had won him the respect even of the Pharisees, though he always remained utterly dedicated to Christ above all.[38]

As for the others, the decision as to where they should go and when they should leave could not be quickly made; it was too important, and extensive preparations were necessary in view of the distances they expected to be travelling. In all probability the most important of these preliminaries was the preparation of the first written record of the life and teaching of Jesus as the Apostles had experienced it, set down (probably with regular consultation with the other Apostles) by Matthew, as a former publican being the Apostle most practiced in writing. He was asked to leave behind for the faithful in Judea an account in their own language—either Hebrew, the language of their Scriptures and liturgy, or the Aramaic they spoke—of what Christ had said and done during His public life and after His Resurrection. For the Jews of the Dispersion who spoke and wrote only Greek (a large number), a Greek Gospel was also needed. This too Matthew probably prepared at this time, or very soon after leaving Jerusalem. Almost all Matthew's official writing as a publican would have been in Greek. He was probably fully bilingual, as many Galileans of that time were, which would account perfectly for the fact—so long discussed by Scripture scholars and critics, on which so many elaborate and dubious theories have been built—that the Greek text of the Gospel of Matthew, the only text we have, does not always read like a translation despite the uniform testimony of the Fathers of the Church and substantial internal evidence that it was first written in Aramaic or Hebrew. Finally, for lands and peoples beyond the Roman empire where little or no Greek was understood, the Apostles sent to them would bring the original Gospel, very likely with a view to some day translating it into the native languages.[39]

The Church later celebrated on July 15 a feast day commemorating the dispersion of the Apostles; possibly this reflects a valid tradition of the day it was decided upon, for that date would fit almost perfectly the circumstances of the Christian community of Jerusalem in the year 41 as we know them, though there would hardly have been time for Matthew to have written his Gospel between the arrival of the news of Herod Agrippa's new royalty, and then. But there is good reason to believe that by the Passover of 42 Matthew's Gospel had been written, and that all of the Apostles had departed from Jerusalem except James the Just, James the son of Zebedee and brother of John the Evangelist, and Peter.

It was at that paschal season that the persecution of the Christians, which the Apostles had evidently foreseen, most probably began, launched by the new king to please the Jewish leaders. James the son of Zebedee was beheaded, the first of the Apostles to suffer martyrdom for Christ. Peter was thrown into prison, condemned to the same fate. Only James the Just remained untouched, because he was so much admired for his austere piety even by many who disliked or despised all other Christians.[40]

Miraculously liberated from prison, Peter—after a last brief reunion with the disciples at the house of Mark and his family where the Cenacle probably was—departed from Jerusalem. It was natural that the head of the Church should go to Rome, the capital of the empire which the Church was to evangelize as its primary mission now that Christ's truth had been well and thoroughly preached to the Jews; and Rome was his ultimate destination. But there is good reason to believe that he went first to Antioch, to make sure that the very important church there was in good hands. The Jewish Christian disciple Barnabas, the friend of Paul, had for some time been the effective leader of the church in Antioch; but he was a man of so much talent and zeal that Peter doubtless expected him soon to be called for evangelization elsewhere (as he was, with Paul). So Peter chose for bishop of Antioch a Greek convert (very likely a former pagan) named Evodius, who governed the church in that city until succeeded by the great St. Ignatius.[41]

From Antioch, probably by way of Asia Minor, Peter then made his way to Rome, where a convergence of later tradition from many sources indicates that he arrived before the end of the year 42—the year in which he had been forced to leave Jerusalem at Passover time.[42] To the fisherman from Galilee, the enormous, teeming city must have seemed overwhelming at first sight and sound. Its population at this time probably exceeded one million, enormous for the ancient world. Contemporary writers often refer to the nerve-shattering noise rising constantly from its narrow, winding streets overhung by precariously erected apartment houses up to six stories or even more in height. All day the streets swarmed with people; all night they resounded to the wheeled thunder of the carts which were rigidly excluded during the day.[43] Through the great roaring capital, unnoticed, unknown, strode the bluff and burly, rustic and humble fisherman who was the Vicar of Christ, the earthly head of the Church of God, the trustee of the King of Kings. Of every thousand men who saw him upon the streets of Rome in the forty-second year of the Christian Era, hardly one would have known who he was.

It seems almost sure that he would have gone to live in the large community of poor Jews in the Fourteenth District of Rome, extending along the right bank of the Tiber and up the slopes of the Vatican hill—an undesirable area, full of the stench of tanneries. At least among his own people he could find an oasis of familiar customs; some rumors of Christianity had probably already reached them, and there may have been a few actual Christians among them.[44] But in all probability Peter was soon treated as the Apostle Paul was to be treated by the Jewish communities in the cities he evangelized, where he always made it a point to go to them first: acceptance by a few, rejection by the majority, and soon, expulsion and hatred.

In such circumstances, Paul always turned at once to the Gentiles. Peter would surely have done the same in Rome. He could have had some useful introductions from friends and relatives of his first Gentile convert, the centurion Cornelius who had been stationed in Joppa on the coast of Palestine, and served in a cohort of Italian volunteers. By the next year after his arrival Peter seems to have made his first notable Roman convert: Pomponia Graecina, wife of Aulus Plautius, the general commanding the Roman armies then engaged in the conquest of Britain, who had sought consolation for the execution of a beloved friend and found it in an unnamed "foreign superstition," to which she held with unflagging perseverance throughout the remaining forty years of her long life, though it isolated her from the normal social life of Roman matrons and led to much gossip and criticism. Her "foreign superstition" was not Judaism and does not seem to have been any Greek or Asiatic mystery cult; in all probability it was Christianity, preached to her by Peter.[45]

Where had the other Apostles gone? Here the historian encounters the greatest gap in the written record in the whole history of the Church. For Jesus Christ had chosen the Twelve, as we have seen, with the utmost care, as founders of the Church He was establishing to last until the end of time. Therefore each one of these twelve men must have been of special, unique importance for the building of that Church. Up to this point they had acted together in all things, always under Peter's direct leadership; it is only of Peter, among the Twelve, that significant individual actions are recorded during the first twelve years of the history of the Church. Now James the son of Zebedee is martyred; James the Just becomes bishop of Jerusalem; Peter becomes bishop of Rome. John, the beloved disciple, is not mentioned again at this point, but we know from his later writings that he dwelt for much of the rest of a very long life in Asia Minor. But the other eight Apostles vanish at this point from well-documented and generally accepted history and fade into legend.

Nevertheless, much more can be done to fill this gap than is usually believed. Later tradition, even when containing many obviously legendary elements, is by no means always to be despised if it can be linked with historically reliable corroborative material. It may, and often does, reflect a considerable memory of real events even when much overlaid with myth. It is not reasonable to attribute less persistence to Christian memory of the men Christ chose to found His Church, and of the work they did, than to Israel's memory of the work of its founders, the patriarchs, whose remarkable accuracy over the centuries we have demonstrated.[46] Even the silences may be made to speak, if we ask ourselves how it could be that in the case of several of the Apostles tradition and legend preserved so little. An important part of the answer emerges when we list the regions where, according to the traditions we have, the other eight Apostles carried out their mission after leaving Jerusalem:[47]

Andrew - Scythia (barbarian Ukraine) and perhaps Greece

Bartholomew - south Arabia (and perhaps India)

Jude Thaddaeus - Mesopotamia (and perhaps Armenia and Iran)

Matthew - Media or Ethiopia

Matthias - entirely unknown

Philip - Asia Minor (Phrygia)

Simon the Zealous - Iran

Thomas - Parthia and India

The most striking fact about this list is that, with the single exception of Philip, every one of these Apostles about whose missionary work even the scantiest memory was preserved, went *beyond the boundaries of the Roman empire*. With the exception of the Ukraine and Ethiopia (if Matthew did go there rather than to Media) none of the lands and peoples to which they went became and remained predominantly Christian—and those two countries were then quite barbarous, with very few written records and almost none preserved. This made conditions much less favorable for the preservation of extensive and accurate traditions of the work of these Apostles.[48] The exception, Philip, proves the rule, for we have the testimony of Bishop Papias of Hierapolis, who wrote about 125 A.D. and had known Philip and his four daughters well, to the essential work he had done in the evangelization of central Asia Minor. We do not have Papias' own writings, only quotations from him given by later Christian writers.[49] In lands never fully Christianized, those who had known the Apostles or collected information from those who had known them, like Papias, were much less likely to have their words recorded and preserved for posterity.

The truth therefore seems to be (as we should have expected, though in our narrow vision may find hard to believe) that Christ really meant exactly what He said when He spoke to the disciples after His Resurrection of carrying His message to the ends of the earth, and had no intention of waiting for the development of aircraft and television so that it might be done more easily. Peter, His Vicar, with matchless boldness and confidence took the whole world as the Church's mission field in 42 A.D., just as the Popes have always done ever since. To James the Just went the children of Israel; to himself in Rome and to John and to Philip and later to Paul went *all the rest of the Roman empire*.

That left seven Apostles, more than half the Apostolic College, for the shadowy, distant lands where no Roman legion had ever marched and no writ of Caesar ever run.

Of two of those seven, and only of two—Thomas and Jude Thaddaeus—do we have enough evidence to hazard a reasonably probable historical reconstruction of what they did. In the case of Thomas the evidence has long been available and given substantial credence by most of the small number of historians who are really familiar with it. In the case of Jude Thaddaeus the evidence is very new and challenges almost all existing scholarly opinion. But that evidence and those reconstructions deserve to be presented; and the unique drama of the stories which our limited data can only hint at, convey most memorably the power and glory and romance of the apostolate of Christ.

First, then, let us follow, according to the best reconstruction we can make from the available evidence, the Apostle Thomas—once doubting, now forever sure; Thomas the Twin, a good, solid, rather unimaginative and hard-headed young Israelite who almost certainly had never been out of Palestine in his life. The hour of the dispersion of the Apostles came. Some traditions say the choice of countries was made by lot; we might guess at an assignment by Peter as head of the Church, or an individual choice by each Apostle; we do not know. However the decision was made, Thomas' assignment was . . . India—India the ancient, the shadowed, her teeming millions yearning for the hope they had not known since the Harappan heart of darkness engulfed the thought and spirit of its Vedic conquerors, a thousand years ago. To the land of the unreal, of negation, of double truth and untruth, of yearning for non-existence, of beatitude through death by starvation, he, Thomas, was to bring and to teach the utter reality, the shining glory, the triumphant and eternal and *human* existence of the Risen Christ, the Way, the Truth, the Life . . . " 'Put your finger here, and see my hands; and put out your hand, and place it in my side; do not be faithless, but believing.' Thomas answered him, 'My Lord and my God!' "[50]

He found a Jewish merchant (possibly a Christian) named Habban, who had come from India—there was regular trade now between the Roman empire and India—and told him that King Gundofarr (Gondophernes in Greek), a prince of the royal house of Parthia ruling the Indus valley region from his capital at Taxila whence Alexander's army had descended into India, had need of a carpenter. Evidently Thomas, like his Lord, had once practiced this trade. Aramaic was spoken in Taxila, due to its past connections with the Persian empire which had used Aramaic as its official language, so it was possible for Thomas to make himself understood in Taxila, while having every opportunity to learn one or more of the Indian languages while residing there. A Jewish colony probably existed in Taxila, as in virtually all major cities in both the Roman and the Parthian empires. If so, Thomas could have gone to it first to preach Christ, as Paul did in city after city in the Roman world before moving on to the Gentiles, and as Peter probably did in Rome. On his way to or from Taxila, Thomas may have gone overland, establishing churches on the way, for there is a very old and strong tradition in all the Syriac-Aramaic churches of Mesopotamia and Iran that the Apostle Thomas was their founder, even though his ultimate destination and mission was India.[51]

King Gundofarr was a Parthian and therefore a Westerner by blood and speech, but it would not have been long after arriving that Thomas would have learned that he had become a devotee of the god Shiva, the deity of destruction, the consort of devouring Kali, whose image appears on the Harappa seals.[52] The evidence suggests that Thomas remained for several years at Taxila—long enough to learn a great deal about Shiva and Kali and the magnitude of the evil he faced. Of his work in Taxila and the Punjab, we know only that he won some converts, and that when he departed, never to return, he gave this new Christian communty into the care of one of them, who appears to have been a native Indian named Gaurasva, "auburn horse." Not long afterward Kushan barbarians invaded the Punjab and extinguished the kingdom of Gundofarr. The community Thomas had built disappeared in the storm.[53]

But his apostolate in India had not ended; it had only begun.

Some years earlier, in the city of Edessa in northwestern Mesopotamia, about 350 miles north of Galilee (roughly the same distance as from Galilee to the Nile delta in Egypt, which the Holy Family had travelled on their return to Nazareth after Herod's death), King Abgar the Black had been stricken by a dread disease, probably leprosy. As a relatively near neighbor of the Jews and speaking a language almost identical to theirs, he had heard of Jesus, and especially of His healing miracles. He sent a message to Jesus, begging for a cure. A very ancient tradition in Edessa, widely known throughout the Middle East and already set down in writing as early as the third century, tells us that Jesus received Abgar's message and replied to it. While His reply was later said to have been in the form of an autograph letter and it is very unlikely that any such document ever existed (Jesus is not known to have left any written documents of His own), the contact itself and an oral message from Jesus are reasonable enough. Neither the scorn of modern critics nor the later, unhistorical accretions to the story and the documents should cause historians to dismiss it out of hand as most of them have done. The message was clear, and characteristic of Jesus: Abgar is praised for his faith; Jesus cannot come to him, because His mission is in Palestine and after completing it He must return to "Him that sent me"; but after that return, He will send one of His disciples to Abgar.[54] But it seems most unlikely that this promise to Abgar would have been fulfilled until Peter's baptism of the centurion Cornelius in the year 39 had opened the way for the reception of Gentiles into the Church.

Since the day of the Resurrection the Apostles had reverently, and in all probability secretly, retained the shroud that had wrapped Jesus' body, which Peter and John had found neatly rolled up in the empty tomb on Easter morning. It bore a miraculous imprint not only of Jesus' ravaged body, but most clearly of His Holy Face. Assuredly this holy object had been given to them to spread faith in Him Who was depicted upon it; but so far they had been unable to think of an appropriate way to use it. The Law of Moses prohibited any visual representation of the human face and figure, and held any object which had touched a dead body to be ritually unclean. The Shroud and its image were therefore doubly unacceptable to any Jew. But not only would the pagan King Abgar have no objection to a picture of Jesus; he would welcome it, especially since he had expressed a strong desire to see Jesus in person. Why not bring the Shroud to him? But it should not be brought and shown as a shroud, for all people and cultures have a natural revulsion toward objects which have been in close contact with the dead. Therefore, before being brought to King Abgar, the cloth seems to have been folded—"doubled in four"—and decorated so that it showed only the portrait-like image of the Holy Face of Jesus.[55]

The oldest Edessan tradition, which appears in the ancient Syriac document called "The Doctrine [Teaching] of Addai" whose original form probably existed in the third century and certainly by the fourth century, reports a picture of Christ brought to Abgar and the arrival of a man named Addai, sent by Jesus, who cured and baptized Abgar and established Christianity in Edessa. Eusebius, the first Christian historian, calls this man Thaddaeus. Both sources describe him as one of the seventy-two disciples sent out by Christ toward the end of His public life; but St. Jerome, writing later in the third century, identifies Addai/Thaddaeus as the Apostle Jude Thaddaeus.[56] For a mission of this importance it would seem more reasonable to have chosen one of the Twelve, particularly if it took place at about the time of their dispersion, as the regnal dates of King Abgar the Black (4 B.C.-7 A.D., 13-50 A.D.)[57] combined with the date of Peter's baptism of Cornelius, indicate that it did. A later tradition places the martyrdom of the Apostle Jude in Iran, but also tells of prior missionary work by him in Mesopotamia, which includes Edessa;[58] and Edessan tradition preserves no clear memory of a burial place there of their own evangelizer,[59] indicating that he may have moved on and died elsewhere, as the tradition of Jude holds. Finally, later Christian iconography often represents the Apostle Jude carrying a picture of Christ.[60]

The Doctrine of Addai and Eusebius both refer to a "vision" seen by Abgar on the face of Thaddaeus, with his cure following shortly afterward. Although this "vision" is not directly linked to the picture of Jesus in the Doctrine of Addai, it is so linked by later accounts, and the link seems reasonable, especially in view of the solid body of evidence now available which indicates that it was the Holy Shroud which was brought to Edessa at this time. That evidence primarily relates to its rediscovery after a long period of concealment, and its later history.[61]

According to the Doctrine of Addai, Christianity flourished in Edessa during the remainder of Abgar the Black's reign and the ensuing reign of his eldest son Manu V (50-57).[62] But in 57 a second son, Manu VI, came to the throne and rejected the new faith. By this time, the head of the Christian community in Edessa was Aggai, the maker of the king's silks and headdresses—very possibly the man who "doubled in four" and decorated the Shroud to make it into a portrait. Refusing to make a pagan headdress for the apostate Manu VI, Aggai was martyred by him. The portrait-like Shroud was hidden away for safekeeping in a hollow place in one of the city gates—so well hidden that the very knowledge of its whereabouts was soon lost, accounting for the fact that there is no further mention of the miraculous picture of Christ at Edessa in Christian literature until the sixth century.[63] It appears that the Christian community in Edessa was almost totally destroyed by the persecution of Manu VI. Not until about a hundred years later did a revival of the faith take place under Palut, who was consecrated Edessa's first bishop by Serapion, Bishop of Antioch, at the very beginning of the third century.[64]

This reconstruction of the apostolate of Jude Thaddaeus, based primarily on recent research on the Holy Shroud of Turin, stands at variance with almost all previous scholarly (including orthodox) opinion of the last hundred years, which did not make a connection between the picture of Christ at Edessa and the Shroud and its later history. But an unbroken trail of evidence now connects that picture with the Shroud—evidence ranging from pollen grains found on the cloth of the Shroud from a plant which grows only on the Anatolian plateau near Edessa, to the fifteen separate points of similarity to the physiognomy of the Shroud face shown by pictorial and iconic representations of the face of Christ which began to appear immediately after the sixth-century discovery and growing fame of a picture of Christ at Edessa said to be "not made by hands," to the subsequent emergence of the relic as we know it in Constantinople, where the picture from Edessa had been taken in the tenth century after Edessa fell under Muslim control.[65] And while the very existence of a Christian community in Edessa in the first century has been roundly denied, the city's proximity to Palestine and its even closer proximity to the first Gentile Christian community at Antioch, as well as its status as a major trade center, makes it naturally likely that it would have been evangelized very early; and the considerable evidence of Edessa's close contact with the Apostle Thomas, before and during his mission to India, requires an existing community with which he could have communicated during his lifetime.[66]

After the departure of most of the Apostles, the martyrdom of James the son of Zebedee, and the miraculous escape of Peter, Herod Agrippa rose rapidly to a dizzying height of popularity and glorification, hailed as a god by his pagan subjects and as a brother by his Jewish subjects. Then suddenly, at a great feast in honor of the Emperor Claudius early in the year 44, he was struck down by a searing pain in his bowels and died after five days of agony. He was the last King of the Jews. By 45 a Roman procurator, Cuspius Fadus, was once again governing in Jerusalem.[67]

Paul was in Jerusalem when Herod Agrippa died, bringing gifts from Antioch where he had been evangelizing, to the persecuted Christian community of James the Just.[68] Seven years had passed since Christ appeared to him on the Damascus road. In solitude in Arabia and in Tarsus, in the active apostolate at Damascus and Antioch, Paul had prepared himself to work as a full Apostle, though "one born out of time," to achieve as mightily as any of the Twelve. Christ had specially chosen them during His mortal life; but He had specially chosen Paul directly from Heaven. In this small, rather ugly, unprepossessing man burned the flame of total dedication that had been his God-given strength all his life, now directed unwaveringly toward its true and ultimate Object, the Lord Incarnate, the Word Made Flesh. Paul went forth to win an empire for Christ. Much as Peter, John, and Philip undoubtedly accomplished (and we can reconstruct some, though by no means all of their achievements) Paul's contribution to the evangelization of the Roman empire was unquestionably the greatest, as well as much the most amply documented, of all the Apostles' missions.

Paul had waited a long time for the decisive call. It came, not from any private revelation (though he received many such) but from the Holy Spirit through the Church. The faithful of Antioch gathered for the Eucharist, having been fasting and praying for guidance about the direction of their missionary work. So important was this Mass and the gathering that it is likely that almost every member of the Christian community of Antioch came. It was, in all probability, the year 45. Five men presided—a remarkably cosmopolitan group, already clearly representing the universal Church. There was Joseph called Barnabas, Son of Consolation, from Cyprus—an early friend and advocate of Paul, the brightest light of the church of Antioch; there was Simon called Niger, the black, from Cyrene, who may well have been that Simon of Cyrene who, at first unwillingly, carried the Cross of Christ up that last punishing slope of Calvary; there was Lucius of Cyrene; there was Manahen, foster brother of the old "fox" Herod Antipas, now converted to the faith Herod Antipas had scorned on the day of the Crucifixion; and there was Paul. During the prayers, one of the faithful who had the charism of prophecy suddenly announced: "Set apart for me Barnabas and Saul for the work to which I have called them." The words were accepted as coming from the Holy Spirit; Paul and Barnabas had their commission.[69]

Accompanied by young Mark, Barnabas' cousin, at whose house in Jerusalem Peter had sought refuge after his miraculous escape from prison during Herod Agrippa's persecution, Paul and Barnabas went first to Cyprus, Barnabas' homeland. They crossed the sixty-mile-long island, preaching mostly to the large Jewish communities there. When they reached Paphos, at the western end of

Cyprus, they were invited to explain their doctrine to the Roman proconsul, Sergius Paulus. They were opposed by Bar-Jesus, a Jewish magician who had attached himself to the proconsul. Condemning Bar-Jesus as "full of all guile and of all deceit, son of the devil," Paul struck him temporarily blind. Sergius Paulus was deeply impressed; we are told that he then "believed," though we do not know whether he was baptized and became a practicing Christian.[70]

From Cyprus Paul sailed to Pamphylia in Asia Minor at the foot of the towering Taurus Mountains, their peaks rising nearly two miles high and their passes nearly a mile. Only a few Jews had penetrated the harsh interior uplands beyond the Taurus; this was the real beginning of the mission to the Gentiles. Robbers lurked along the rough trails; for long distances there was neither food nor man-made shelter. Mark could not at that time see any point in venturing into such country, and returned home. Paul and Barnabas—two men alone, with Christ—pressed on through the gorges of the Cayster River and up the rocky slopes until they reached Antioch in Pisidia, a Roman military colony where Caesar's famous Legion of the Lark (Alaudae), recruited in Gaul, had been stationed. It was now the largest town of the region, with a cosmopolitan population including some born Jews and a considerable number of proselytes and "God-fearers," who admired the Jewish faith but would not accept circumcision and the full rigor of the Law.[71]

In the synagogue at Antioch in Pisidia, on the first Sabbath after his arrival, Paul proclaimed Jesus as Messiah and Redeemer, the Savior of all men both under and outside the Law. When on the following Sabbath an enormous crowd, consisting mostly of Gentiles, appeared to hear more of the new teaching, many of the Jews debated with Paul and cursed him.[72] Quoting the prophet Isaiah, Paul and Barnabas responded:

> It was necessary that the word of God should be spoken first to you. Since
> you thrust it from you, and judge yourselves unworthy of eternal life, behold,
> we turn to the Gentiles. For so the Lord has commanded us, saying
> > "I have set you to be a light for the Gentiles,
> > that you may bring salvation to the uttermost
> > parts of the earth."[73]

Expelled from the synagogue, Paul and Barnabas continued to work among the Gentiles of Antioch in Pisidia until a flourishing Christian community had been formed. Eventually driven out by the intrigues of their enemies among the Jews, they went on to the city of Iconium, about a hundred miles to the southeast, where their experiences in Antioch were repeated: preaching first in the synagogues; rejection by the majority of the Jews; preaching to the Gentiles with many of them accepting Christianity; expulsion from the city by Jewish intrigue.[74]

It now seemed best to go to an area where there were hardly any Jews. The isolated, backward region of Lycaonia, tucked away in the southward bend of the Taurus range, was not far away, and Paul and Barnabas went there next. Even in Lycaonia, where most of the people still spoke their ancient and barbarous tongue, Greek was widely understood, so that Paul could preach to the crowds in it.[75] The heritage of Alexander the Great was serving the Apostle to the Gentiles well.

In Lystra in Lycaonia Paul healed a lame man in Christ's name, as Peter had done years before at the Beautiful Gate in Jerusalem. The townspeople immediately set about to honor Barnabas and Paul as Zeus and Hermes; the missionaries repelled the attempt in horror. Unsettled by this, the people of Lystra were open to be convinced by Jews from Antioch in Pisidia and from Iconium who came to warn them that Paul and Barnabas were deceivers and sorcerers. Paul was seized, stoned as Stephen had been, and left for dead. He survived, but ever afterward bore the scars of that stoning—"on my body the marks of the Lord Jesus."[76] It was in Lystra, probably at this visit, that he first met the half-Jew Timothy, later to be one of his dearest disciples. After the stoning Paul went on to recover and preach in the Lycaonian town of Derbe, about forty miles southeast of Lystra. Then he retraced his steps to each of the four cities he had evangelized, confirming and strengthening the new brethren, until he and Barnabas had returned to the Pamphylian coast opposite Cyprus where they had originally landed. From there they took ship back to Antioch in Syria, probably in the year 49, four years after their departure on this, Paul's first great missionary journey.[77]

Seven years had now passed since the dispersion of the Apostles. So successfully had Peter evangelized in Rome that the resulting controversies among Christian converts, followers of Simon Magus who had now come to Rome, and those holding to traditional Judaism rose to the threshold of public consciousness, probably causing the Emperor Claudius, in this very year 49, to banish all Jews from Rome because (a pagan historian tells us) of "tumults" raised by "Chrestus."[78] We know that Peter was in Jerusalem by late 49 or in 50. He may have come, with other Jewish Christians expelled from Rome by this edict, by way of the rich and decadent Greek city of Corinth, planting the seeds of Christianity there.[79]

Or he may have come for another reason. Tradition indicates that about the year 49 the Blessed Virgin Mary, under the care of the Apostle John for the nineteen years since the Crucifixion and Resurrection, "fell asleep" in Jerusalem and was assumed body and soul into Heaven, and that all the Apostles were recalled from their far-flung missions to be present for her last hours on earth in her mortal body. We know for certain that Peter and John, as well as James the Just, were in Jerusalem when Paul came there soon after the completion of his first missionary journey. Though no others of the Twelve are mentioned by name in our sources as being present at that time, the account in the Book of Acts of the ensuing Council of Jerusalem repeatedly mentions "apostles" in a way that suggests a considerable number. It is by no means impossible that the whole Apostolic College, excepting only the martyred James the son of Zebedee, was present for the Council. The best reconstruction of Thomas' apostolic labors in India shows a gap at precisely this point between his preaching at Taxila in far northwestern India and his concluding mission to south India, which would have permitted a return to Jerusalem. John's presence clearly implies Mary's, if she was then still living. To picture Mary, the Mother of God, tenderly taking leave of her first and dearest spiritual children, the Apostles, on the eve of the Apostolic Council, is an entrancing vision; to date her Assumption then is magnificently appropriate. The dating and the occasion cannot be said to be historically provable in the fragmentary condition of our evidence, though it is both reasonable and likely; the Assumption itself—defined as infallible dogma by the Roman Catholic Church—is strongly indicated historically by the absence of any tradition of a burial place of the Blessed Virgin Mary or any veneration of relics thought to be hers, combined with the tradition of her "falling asleep" (Dormition) in Jerusalem.[80]

The presence of the full living Apostolic College at the Council of Jerusalem, meeting to consider the persistent problem of how much if any of the Mosaic Law to impose upon Gentile converts to Christianity, would help explain its outcome, which has surprised so many historians.[81] For all of the Apostles except James the Just had been sent out in the dispersion; all had worked among largely Gentile populations and had made at least some Gentile converts (such as Peter's Cornelius and Pomponia Graecina, Thomas' Gaurasva, and Jude's King Abgar); all, therefore, except James—and not Paul alone—could see from their own experience the correctness, both theological and practical, of not attempting to bring the Gentile converts under the Law nor segregating them from the rest of the Church and its Jewish Christian leaders. Their united witness, along with his own charity and good sense, would have helped to persuade James who had virtually no personal experience of Gentile Christians. In the end, Peter as head of the Church made the basic decision, the charter of the Church's universality:

> Brethren, you know that in the early days God made choice among you, that by my mouth the Gentiles should hear the word of the gospel and believe. And God who knows the heart bore witness to them, giving them the Holy Spirit just as he did to us; and he made no distinction between us and them, but cleansed their hearts by faith. Now therefore why do you make trial of God by putting a yoke upon the neck of the disciples which neither our fathers nor we have been able to bear? But we believe that we shall be saved through the grace of the Lord Jesus, just as they will.[82]

Then followed the Council decree, specially praising Barnabas and Paul as "men who have risked their lives for the sake of Our Lord Jesus Christ,"[83] asserting the fullness of his own, and the Apostles' God-given authority:

> It has seemed good to the Holy Spirit and to us to lay upon you no greater burden than these necessary things: that you abstain from what has been sacrificed to idols and from blood and from what is strangled and from unchastity.[84]

Paul returned to Antioch for a few months, soon followed by Peter; this was probably the famous occasion when Peter, under pressure from some of the Jewish Christians still not reconciled to a universal Church of equals in which observance of the Law of Moses was no longer required of all, ceased eating with the Gentile converts until Paul vigorously objected ''to his face.'' Peter was certainly not going back on his own decree, so recently issued; he had simply fallen again, briefly, into his old weakness of subservience to human respect. He humbly accepted Paul's correction.[85] From this point on, though ''Judaizers'' continued to appear from time to time to disturb the Church, they never again obtained the slightest support from the Church's recognized leaders.

Peter may have remained some time at Antioch, giving rise to the tradition of a seven-year Petrine episcopate there. Then he probably went into northern Asia Minor—Bithynia, Pontus, Cappadocia—and evangelized these provinces during the remainder of the reign of Claudius. It seems likely that Silas, Paul's former missionary companion, accompanied him. These regions, especially populous and prosperous Bithynia, had numerous Christians by the end of the first century. Later traditions strongly connected them with Peter, but with no other Apostle. His first Epistle is directed specifically to them.[86]

Mark now wished to join Paul and Barnabas again; but Paul, remembering his earlier faintheartedness at the foot of the Taurus passes, would not have him. So Barnabas took Mark and went to Cyprus, where Barnabas stayed to become the apostle of his native land, while eventually Mark joined Peter in Rome.[87] Paul set off again into Asia Minor with Silas, who had come from Jerusalem to Antioch; they were joined in Lystra by Timothy, who became Paul's most beloved friend and companion.[88] Passing through wild Galatia in north central Asia Minor, Paul was taken seriously ill, but was well cared for by the people with whom he stayed; even during his illness he preached to them, and when he departed he left behind another Christian community to which he was always particularly devoted.[89] He reached the Aegean near Troy, where his disciple and historian Luke joined him, and crossed to Europe to begin the most fruitful of all his missions, that to Macedon and to Greece.[90]

It was probably early in the year 51 that Paul arrived in Philippi in Macedon. There were too few Jews in Philippi even to have built a synagogue; Paul found only a handful of women gathered by a stream for the Jewish ablutions, on the Sabbath. One of them was called Lydia, a seller of purple dye, a wealthy woman and a Gentile who, like many other Gentiles, had been attracted to the holiness and moral purity of the Jewish religion. Soon Paul had baptized her and her whole family. Later, after he had exorcised a slave girl whose "prophecies" while possessed had brought a substantial income to her owners, they stirred up a crowd in the city against Paul. He was beaten with rods and imprisoned. Released from his bonds and with the doors of his cell opened by a miraculous earthquake, Paul did not escape, but used the occasion to convert his jailer. Then, revealing his Roman citizenship, he forced the city authorities into a virtual apology for their treatment of him and was able to leave his first European church safe under the guidance of Luke and Timothy, who remained for some time in Philippi. Paul's later Epistle to the Philippians shows the fullness of the Christian comradeship and brotherhood he always felt for his converts there.[91]

At the larger city of Thessalonica, the principal port of Macedon, there was a considerable Jewish community and consequently the familiar hostility when Paul, after proclaiming Christ in the synagogue, went among the Gentiles to build a new church. Before he was driven out, he had won so many converts that the church in Thessalonica flourished despite years of continuing hatred by the Jews so virulent that the Christians there dared not let Paul return because of the danger to his life. To this forcible separation we owe Paul's first two canonical epistles, those to the Thessalonians, in which he cautions them against expecting the Second Coming of Christ in the near future, since Christ specifically stated that no man can know its time. Thus, in the very earliest New Testament writing (except, according to the dating here accepted, the Gospel of Matthew) the "eschatological interpretation" of Christ, so popular among rationalists and Modernists, is explicitly rejected and refuted.[92]

From Thessalonica Paul went to the smaller inland Macedonian city of Beroea. At first well received, he was soon driven out through the efforts of a delegation of his Jewish enemies sent from Thessalonica for that purpose. Silas remained in Beroea. All of Paul's companions now had assignments in the new churches of Macedon; but he, virtually a hunted fugitive, had to leave Macedon altogether. He took ship for storied Athens.[93]

Up the colonnaded, statue-lined avenues of Athens came Paul. For five hundred and fifty years the greatest intellectual luminaries of the ancient world had paraded their learning on its marble-crowned heights: the Acropolis of Phidias and Pericles, the Areopagus where Themistocles had rallied the West against the Persians. Now the brilliance was fading in a twilight of sophistry and cynicism, idle curiosity and apathy; the mind's quest for truth had become a mirage; hope deferred had become hope forgotten. Paul saw Athens' whole tragedy summed up in an inscription on one of the multitudinous altars: "To an unknown god." In one of the most dramatic moments of all history, the little ugly Jew of Tarsus, whom God had "taken as prey" on the road to Damascus, marched *alone* up the Areopagus by the coldly exquisite beauty of the Parthenon to proclaim to the intellectual capital of the world: "What therefore you worship as unknown, this I proclaim to you."[94]

Subsequent commentators, like Paul himself, have dwelt on the failure of his sermon on the Areopagus, scorned by most of his audience, accepted only by a man named Dionysius, a woman named Damaris, and a handful of others.[95] Paul said that after that experience he resolved to preach only Jesus Christ and Him crucified, "a stumbling block to Jews and folly to Gentiles, but to those who are called, both Jews and Greeks, Christ the power of God and the wisdom of God."[96] But little else could have been expected. Intellectual pride is always the greatest single obstacle to the growth of the Church, to evangelization, to conversions. Rather, what is significant is the magnificent audacity of Paul's challenge, ringing down the centuries.

From Athens Paul made his way to infamous Corinth, where he found rampant sins of the flesh far less an obstacle to his missionary work than the intellectual pride of Athens. Christ Crucified did not always seem so foolish to the prostitute, the dissolute, the drunkard and the thief as He did to the philosophical word-twister who had lost all vision of truth. More often than their intellectual betters, the sinners of Corinth could *feel* the evil into which they had fallen, and welcomed the news of salvation. Aquila and Priscilla, refugees from Claudius' edict banishing all Jews from Rome and very likely converts of Peter's, were now living in Corinth, and Paul lodged with them. Crispus, the president of the synagogue of Corinth, became a Christian, though as usual the majority of the Jewish community held back and tried to influence the Roman governor against Paul—unsuccessfully, since the governor was the noble and upright Gallio, brother of a great philosopher who still respected truth: Seneca.[97]

In the very years when Paul was challenging the pride of Greek paganism, Thomas renewed the Christian challenge in India. Some time previously, the Greek seaman Hippalos had discovered the monsoon sailing route directly across the Arabian Sea to south India, which shortened the time of a sea voyage to India from about a year to only forty days. This faster route was being increasingly used, particularly by the 50's A.D.[98] If Thomas did come back to Jerusalem for the Dormition of Mary and the Apostolic Council, he could therefore have reached southern India readily, after the Council, by this means; and there is a strong tradition, both Christian and Hindu, that he arrived at Cranganore on the Malabar (southwestern) coast of India in the year 52 (while Paul was in Corinth).[99] The chronological dovetailing at this point of our very different sources, so widely separated in time and space and culture, carries solid conviction of historical truth. It is rendered even more impressive by the good evidence that Thomas stopped at the large island of Socotra off the south coast of Arabia, lying directly on the new sea route to India, and spent considerable time there evangelizing the people of the island. "A multitude of Christians" remained on Socotra in 530; there was still a substantial Christian community in its wild hills, honoring the Apostle Thomas as its founder, when St. Francis Xavier visited the island in 1542, on *his* way to India, and after that up to 1800 when it was destroyed by the fanatically Muslim Wahhabis of Arabia.[100] We may therefore visualize Thomas, after his return to Jerusalem and attendance at the Apostolic Council in 50, departing for the east in the monsoon sailing season of 51, spending a year on Socotra, and then completing his journey in the monsoon sailing season of 52 when we are told that he arrived at Cranganore.

Cranganore was the capital of the Chera kingdom, one of the three ancient realms comprising the southern tip of India, where the Tamil language was spoken. It was roughly equivalent to the present Indian state of Kerala. The development of Graeco-Roman commerce with south India via the monsoon sea route had not yet had time to modify significantly the utter strangeness of the place. There was no Jewish colony in south India until 68.[101] Thomas had no interest in preaching to Greek and Roman traders; they would soon be leaving India as they had come, and his fellow Apostles and their disciples could reach them at their homes in the Mediterranean world. Native India was Thomas' objective, the India untouched by the West, the India that by sheer immensity and alien shadow had at last turned back even the invincible Alexander the Great. As far as we know, Thomas was *alone*. The thought of that is staggering, even more so than Paul's penetration of Athens alone; but none of the Indian traditions of St. Thomas mentions companions on his arrival.

"Lo, I am with you always"[102] . . .

He landed at the mouth of the Periyar River. Ahead of him was the royal palace, to the left (north) the quarter of Trkanamatilakam with a great shrine of Shiva, the terrible god of Harappa.[103] In the face of universal spiritual tyranny, speaking in the Prakrit he had probably learned in the north on his previous mission and increasingly in the Tamil he doubtless soon began to acquire, Thomas proclaimed Jesus Christ King, Lord and Savior, and denounced the evil he found for what it was.

The tenacious memory of the Brahmins follows him. Their Keralolpattis tell how "Thoman, an opponent of all vedas" came to the Malabar coast and converted "many prominent people in the land."[104] The Nagargarandhravaryola of the family Kalathu Mana notes: "Kali year 3153 [A.D. 52] the foreigner Thomas Sanyasi came to our village, preached there causing pollution. We therefore came away from that village." This was in Palayur, where a Christian church stands to this day on the ruins of a Hindu temple. The tradition of the Jews who came to Cranganore in 68 is that a Christian community already existed there when they arrived.[105] Christian tradition tells of the cures of hundreds and the baptism of thousands by the Apostle Thomas.[106] No reliable written record survives;[107] the apocryphal "Acts of Thomas," which provides some solid information about his northern Indian apostolate, is almost valueless for the southern. It may be the greatest lost epic in the history of the Church. The proof of its essential nature, despite the paucity of evidence, lies in the flourishing Christian community of Kerala which the Apostle Thomas founded and which, loving and honoring him still, endures to this day with a membership of hundreds of thousands and a native priesthood which at least in one family is traced back through no less than sixty generations.[108]

For seventeen years Thomas continued his mighty work on the Malabar coast, until he saw the Church's foundations deeply and firmly laid in the Chera kingdom, Christ's beachhead in the teeming mass of India, and decided that the time had come for him to move on across the peninsula, to preach the faith in the Chola kingdom on the opposite, Coromandel coast. He came eventually to Mylapore on a barren part of the shore near the great city of Madras. Nearby was a temple of Kali, the Satanic goddess of death and dismemberment, patroness of the Stranglers. One day in 72 A.D. Thomas was praying in a cave on a hill called the Little Mount. Brahmins from the temple of Kali attacked him. One pierced his heart with a lance—just as Christ's heart had been pierced, one of the wounds Thomas had demanded to touch before he would believe in the Resurrection. He was buried at Mylapore, where ever since Indian Christians have venerated his tomb.[109]

"Let us go up to Jerusalem," Thomas had said, in that long-ago winter of 30 A.D. in Judea when Redemption was at hand, "and die with Him."[110] Now he had done so—"on the stone at Mylapore,"[111] overlooking the Bay of Bengal, in the kingdom of the Cholas three thousand miles from home, having brought into the domain of the dark gods of Harappa the inextinguishable light and love of Christ.

The Roman empire had been reasonably well governed during the reign of Claudius. The old picture of this emperor as a degenerate weakling has been substantially modified by accumulating evidence of his high sense of public responsibility particularly in the administration of the provinces. After the completion of the conquest of southern Britain and the suppression of a minor Jewish revolt in 47, there was uninterrupted peace (except for the usual endemic skirmishes along the frontiers). The last seven years of Claudius' reign were therefore ideal for the initial apostolic work of the Church of Christ among the Gentiles.[112]

In the year 48 Claudius had married the younger Agrippina, a daughter of the ill-fated Germanicus and his own niece. A fearsomely ambitious harridan, Agrippina bent all her energies toward securing the imperial succession for her son by her previous marriage to L. Domitius Ahenobarbus, scion of a Roman family which had long had a sinister reputation. The boy, originally named for his natural father and later renamed Tiberius Claudius Nero, was five years older than Claudius' own son by his previous marriage, Britannicus. When it seemed that the prize might slip from her grasp as Claudius was warned against her, Agrippina poisoned him in a dish of mushrooms; in October 54 Nero was proclaimed emperor at the age of only sixteen, and the next year Britannicus too was poisoned.[113]

For five years the consequences of these crimes remained in abeyance; the philosopher Seneca and the incorruptible praetorian prefect Burrus governed the empire in young Nero's name, so well that the period from 54 to 59 became known as "the golden quinquennium"—a further extension of the seven years of peace at the end of the reign of Claudius which had been so beneficial to the Church. But the megalomania of young emperors was growing in Nero, complicated and intensified by a classic psychopathic love-hate relationship with his murderous mother. In the spring of 59 he had her killed after a bungled attempt to sink the ship on which she was travelling (she survived by swimming, long enough to learn before she died that her own son was her murderer); Seneca and Burrus consented to the matricide.[114]

These years from 54 to 59 included Paul's long residence in Ephesus, during which he founded a large Christian community there, and saw the Faith begin to spread rapidly among the 500 cities of the province of Asia, in which Ephesus was located. Paul kept closely in touch with the church he had founded in Corinth, sending at least four letters there, of which only the two canonical epistles to the Corinthians are extant. Their primary theme was unity, for factionalism had already begun to trouble the young church. Driven out of Ephesus after a residence of three years by a riot of the silversmiths, whose idol-making business he had damaged by drawing many of the city's people away from idolatry to Christianity, Paul returned to Greece, revisiting Macedon and Corinth, and writing from Corinth his theological masterpiece, the Epistle to the Romans.[115]

Paul does not mention Peter in that epistle, though including greetings to many others in Rome. It is very hard to imagine any reason for him not to have greeted Peter as well, if in fact Peter was in Rome at the time Paul wrote. But it seems that Peter had probably taken advantage of the lapsing of the decree banishing all Jews from Rome when Claudius, its author, was murdered, returning to Rome by 55 where he then ordained his two future successors as Bishop of Rome and head of the Church: Linus and Cletus. If Peter stayed in Rome through 57, leaving shortly before the dispatch of Paul's epistle to the Romans, these three years would have been the most likely time for the writing of Mark's Gospel, since it is known to have been written in Rome and is generally believed to have preceded Luke's Gospel, which was written during Paul's imprisonment in Rome in 61 and 62. During those years Paul's several letters from Rome make no mention of Peter, entitling us to conclude that Peter did not return to Rome for some five years following his departure before Paul's epistle to the Romans was written.[116]

Mark may well have accompanied Peter on his departure from Rome in 57. A mature, dedicated missionary now stood in the shoes of the timorous young

man who had flinched when Paul first prepared to plunge into the wilds of the
Taurus Mountains. While Peter probably resumed his work in the region of
Bithynia, Pontus, and Cappadocia—for we have no record or hint of his presence
elsewhere during this period, and this was a large area—Mark made his way
to Alexandria. The large Jewish community of this most populous city of the
ancient world had not yet received any complete instruction in Christianity. Even
those who had heard of, and admired Christ knew only of the baptism of His
precursor John. This was clearly evident from the deficient theology of the Alexandrian semi-Christian Jew Apollos when he went to Corinth and Ephesus in
the early 50's, as reported in the Book of Acts.[117]

Mark would then have founded the church in Alexandria, probably in 58,
presenting his new Gospel to its members. According to the much later Christian historian Eusebius, he remained there until 62, when he was succeeded by
Anianus. But Mark certainly did not die then, since Peter's later First Epistle
includes greetings from "my son Mark" in Rome. This provides good reason
for concluding that Mark left Alexandria in 62 because Peter asked him to return
with him to Rome that year—which fits the evidence that Peter was not in Rome
from 57 to 62 as well as the other evidence convincingly establishing that he
returned soon after 62. A strong and ancient tradition among Egyptian Christians holds that Mark was martyred in Alexandria in the year 68, when Easter
fell on the same day as the festival of Serapis, one of the most popular of the
old Egyptian gods; and a mob of hostile Serapis-worshippers dragged Mark,
bound with cords, along the rough stones of Alexandria's streets until he died.
The date fits; for after Peter was martyred in Rome in 67, there would have
been no reason for Mark to stay longer in Rome, and every reason for him to
return to the church he had founded.[118]

On the basis of the evidence so far presented, together with that to be
presented concerning Peter's first Epistle and his martyrdom in Rome, we may
now construct a probable timetable for Peter's entire reign as head of the
Church—the first pontificate.

After writing his epistle to the Romans, Paul, like his Lord, steadfastly "set
his face to go to Jerusalem."[119] The Holy Spirit had "bound" him to go, he
explained to his colleagues who were alarmed (with good reason) for his safety, and he was pledged to bring money from his Gentile converts for the upkeep
of the church in Jerusalem. Avoiding ambushes and plots against him by taking
a roundabout route, he was unable to reach Jerusalem in time for the Passover
of 58, but was there for Pentecost that year.[120] James the Just welcomed him,
and defended him against his Jewish Christian critics. (Not the least of the glories
of sanctity of James the Just is that, though always expected by the divisive
and factionally minded among the Christians of his time to oppose Paul—whose
apostolate, doctrinal emphases and missionary methods he had every reason,
humanly speaking, to reject—he never did reject Paul, but instead constantly

defended and supported him. It is one of the delicious ironies of Christian history that rationalists, Modernists, and "higher critics" of our time are still perpetually casting James in the same role his shortsighted contemporaries were always expecting him to play, though in fact he always nobly refused to play it.)[121]

THE PONTIFICATE OF ST. PETER, 30-67

30-37	head of the Church in Jerusalem
38-39	missionary journeys in Samaria and on the coast of Palestine
40-41	in Antioch
42	imprisonment in Jerusalem, escape, and departure thence
42-49	first sojourn in Rome
49	expulsion from Rome by the edict of Claudius against its Jews
49-50	in Jerusalem for the Apostolic Council
50-54	in Antioch, Bithynia, Pontus, and Cappadocia (or some of them)
54-57	second sojourn in Rome; Gospel of Mark written under Peter's direction
57-62	in Bithynia, Pontus, and Cappadocia (or some of them); Mark in Alexandria
62-67	third sojourn in Rome; canonical Epistles of Peter; Mark with Peter in Rome
67	martyrdom in Rome and burial at the Vatican

Paul's Jewish enemies were tracking him, and eventually set upon him in the Temple court. They would have beaten him to death if the Roman guards there had not intervened to save his life. For two years Paul was confined at Caesarea on the coast while two successive procurators—Antonius Felix and Porcius Festus—and the last of Herod's line to exercise any authority in Palestine, Herod Agrippa II, tried to decide what to do with him. Finally Paul appealed to Caesar, as was his right as a Roman citizen. He was promptly dispatched to Rome, which eventually he reached after his famous stormy autumn voyage and shipwreck on the island of Malta.[122]

The Caesar to whom Paul had appealed was Nero the matricide; but Seneca and Burrus, though declining in influence, were still in office when he arrived in Rome early in 61. Justice could still be had in Roman courts if the pressures and the price did not rise too high. The Jews did not press their accusations against Paul, nor even communicate their charges against him to the synagogues in Rome. Paul was held approximately two years, then released for lack of evidence. During the two years of his imprisonment in Caesarea and the additional two years of his imprisonment at Rome, Luke was never far from him.

There is almost conclusive evidence that both his Gospel and the Book of Acts were written then (the Gospel in Caesarea and the Book of Acts in Rome), despite the tyranny of academic fashion among Biblical scholars which caused most of them to deny it for the better part of a century, until very recently—although one of the greatest of them, Adolf von Harnack, while rejecting many orthodox premises, gave as his final conclusion on this question that the abrupt ending of Acts can only be explained by its having been written before the Neronian persecution began in 64.[123]

Released in 63, with Peter probably back in Rome, Paul appears to have departed immediately on his longest missionary journey, to Spain at the western edge of the Roman world. Most unfortunately, no record or tradition has survived giving any hint of his activities in Spain.[124] In Rome, Nero was being devoured by moral degeneracy and megalomania. He divorced his wife to marry his mistress, forced Seneca into retirement after Burrus died, made the vicious Tigellinus praetorian prefect in Burrus' place, began executing anyone who criticized him in any way, and insisted more and more on public glorification of his imagined artistic talent.[125] But the Christians had no reason to expect an immediate crisis. Most of their converts had been from the lower classes, attracting little notice from the imperial authorities.[126] When noted at all, they were dismissed as an aberrant sect of Judaism. Almost all their troubles and persecutions so far had resulted from the animosity of the Jews, from which Roman officials had often protected Christians. Luke could work on the composition of the Book of Acts with the relistic hope that its impressive and convincing story, written in good literary Greek, would justify Christians against future Jewish calumny and even win more highly place converts.[127]

Then came the lurid red night of July 18, 64 A.D., and everything was changed. Two hundred and fifty years of persecution by the unchallenged rulers of the Western civilized world began when it occurred to the increasingly psychotic Nero to blame the Christians for the uncontrollable fires which started that night, and in nine infernal days destroyed the greater part of the city of Rome.[128] From then until Constantine's Edict of Milan in 313, it was a capital offense simply to confess oneself, or to be proved to be, a believer in Jesus Christ.

The lengthy scholarly discussions of the juridical basis of the prohibition of Christianity and the varying manner of the enforcement of that prohibition[129] have tended to obscure its extraordinary, indeed unique character. Nor do the usual explanations of secular-minded historians nearly suffice to explain it. After Nero was overthrown in 68 and his memory unanimously execrated in Roman tradition, why was his outlawing of the Christians—alone of all his acts—kept in effect? Tertullian asked this question at the end of the second century, and few modern scholars have answered it.[130] The Romans did not treat Christianity like other "Oriental superstitions" because they sensed in it far more than just another Oriental superstition. The only adequate explanation is that memorably given by G. K. Chesterton:

> New tortures have been invented for the madmen who have brought good news. That sad and weary society seems almost to find a new energy in establishing its first religious persecution. Nobody yet knows very clearly why that level world has thus lost its balance about the people in its midst, but they stand unnaturally still while the arena and the world seem to revolve around them. And there shone on them in that dark hour a light that has never been darkened; a white fire clinging to that group like an unearthly phosphoresence, blazing its track through the twilights of history and confounding every effort to confound it with the mists of mythology and theory; that shaft of light or lightning by which the world itself has struck and isolated and crowned it; by which its own enemies have made it more illustrious and its own critics have made it more inexplicable; the halo of hatred around the Church of God.[131]

In his gardens across the Tiber by the Vatican hill, near where Peter had probably lived when he first came to Rome 22 years before, Nero held the circus games which could no longer be held in the two great amphitheaters, damaged in the fire. During those games in the fall of 64, many of the Christians whom Nero's police had arrested were thrown to the wild beasts in the arena. Others were dressed in clothing soaked in pitch and sulfur and lit as human torches along the Appian Way, as Nero raced by in his chariot. Even the bloodthirsty mob murmured at this; and the glorious constancy of these first Christian victims of mass martyrdom seems to have made a deep impression on at least two leading Romans: the philosopher Seneca (formerly chief minister, now in retirement) and the city prefect, Flavius Sabinus, brother of the future emperor Vespasian and father of Flavius Clemens, later probably a Christian martyr himself during the persecution of the Emperor Domitian.[132]

If it was illegal for a man to be a Christian in Rome, it was equally illegal in the provinces. The persecution soon spread to Asia Minor where, following Paul's missionary journeys and Peter's extended apostolic work there, many flourishing Christian communities were to be found.[133] Peter wrote from Rome to the churches of Asia Minor which he had evangelized, to strengthen and inspire them as he had been strengthening and inspiring the martyrs in Rome:[134]

> Beloved, do not be surprised at the fiery ordeal which comes upon you to prove you, as though something strange were happening to you. But rejoice in so far as you share Christ's sufferings, that you may also rejoice and be glad when his glory is revealed.[135]

In Rome, when the Neronian persecution broke out, Luke abruptly broke off the Book of Acts at the point he had then reached in his composition—during Paul's first imprisonment in Rome, but before his acquittal in 63—and accompanied Paul, after his return from Spain, on a new journey to Greece. In 66 Paul seems to have crossed the Aegean to Asia, been arrested at Troy, and taken to Rome a prisoner again—now abandoned, due to the fear engendered among Christians by the persecution, by many he had counted friends and disciples, and this time kept in close confinement.[136]

It was a dark hour for the Church everywhere. In Jerusalem, James the Just had been martyred in 62 by Ananas, son of the High Priest Annas, one of the murderers of Christ, after the good procurator Porcius Festus had suddenly died that year.[137] There is good reason to believe that the Epistle to the Hebrews, written probably by a disciple of Paul with an excellent command of literary Greek, was sent to guide and strengthen the now leaderless and greatly endangered Jewish Christian community in Jerusalem shortly after the Neronian persecution broke out.[138] Festus' two successors as procurators of Judea— Albinus and Florus—were typical officers of the later years of Nero's reign, greedy, brutal, and stupid. The Zealots or Sicarii—"daggermen"—grew ever stronger among the Jews under these conditions, until the High Priest was prevailed upon to end public prayers for the Emperor in the Temple. The Roman garrison in Jerusalem was induced to surrender under promise of safe conduct out of Judea; once they had laid down their arms, they were massacred. The legate of Syria brought down the Twelfth Legion to suppress the rebellion. Repulsed from Jerusalem, the legion was set upon by the Zealot army at the pass of Bethhoron, famous in the history of Israel, where Joshua had commanded the sun to stand still and Judas Maccabeus had defeated the Seleucid general Seron. The Twelfth Legion was routed, with 5,000 casualties and the loss of its eagle. It meant war to the death between Rome and the Jews.[139]

When the news reached him at the end of 66, Nero was in Greece, beginning the year of incredible orgies and buffooneries which were to make his name as infamous among pagan Romans as it already was among the Christians. Yet somewhere in his disintegrating mind, a gleam of sanity and common sense still flickered. Nero was a coward who had never seen a battle and could not face one. But to meet the crisis of the Jewish rebellion he chose the best man who could have been found: Titus Flavius Vespasianus, a 57-year-old general of Sabine farming stock, a man who preserved in his character much of the best of old Rome, of enormous patience and perseverance, indomitable, inexorable, invincible. Nero sent Vespasian to Palestine with three legions.[140]

During the year 67 Vespasian mastered all Palestine outside Judea itself; during that same year in Rome, the continuing persecution of the Christians begun by Nero reached its culmination with the martyrdom of both Peter and Paul. Of the details we eagerly seek there are almost none, though the cumulative historical evidence that both men were martyred in Rome—sometimes questioned in the past—is now generally admitted to be convincing, even by secularly oriented historians.[141] Paul, arrested in the east and brought back to Rome, defended himself with his usual skill, once again taking advantage of his Roman citizenship; it required two court sessions before he was finally condemned to death by beheading. The sentence was executed three miles outside Rome on the Ostian Way, near where the world-famed Church of St. Paul's Outside the Walls stands today, after he had endured the last in the long series of scourgings for Christ that had marked his missionary years.[142] For Peter, who had neither Paul's Roman citizenship nor his forensic abilities, the legal process was undoubtedly much more summary. He was condemned to be crucified as his Lord had been, and had foretold for him. Tradition tells us that out of humility Peter asked to be crucified head downward, and that this was done.[143] It is most unlikely that the Roman authorities had any real idea whom they were killing.

Peter's cross stood on the Vatican hill, in the gardens of Nero where the persecution had begun. He was buried at the foot of the hill, in a poor grave scratched out of the earth. Above that poor grave of the crucified fisherman of Galilee rise today, going straight up, level upon level, the following: (1) a simple red wall to mark the grave site, with an underground shrine, probably built in the time of Pope Anicetus (155-166), with an adjoining wall built later and covered with graffiti (including numerous representations of the key-symbol deriving from the letter P and indicating Peter), under which the bones now confirmed as most likely to be Peter's were found in 1942, misplaced through an extraordinary accident, rediscovered in 1953, and identified by strong circumstantial evidence in 1965;[144] (2) a church erected by Constantine the Great, the first Christian emperor, between 315 and 330, with Peter's grave and bones enclosed in a marble housing never disturbed until the twentieth-century excavations; (3) an altar built by Pope St. Gregory the Great (590-604); (4) a church built by Pope Calixtus II (1119-1124); (5) the present immense church of St. Peter's and the altar of Pope Clement VIII (1592-1605), under the canopy supported by Bernini's famous twisted columns; (6) the soaring dome planned by Michelangelo.[145]

The leadership of the Church passed to Linus, whom Peter had ordained, who had attended Paul in his lonely last hours. Linus had been, and perhaps still was, a slave.[146] Of Linus the man, the first successor to Peter as Vicar of Christ, we know only this: that Paul had loved him, and that Peter had trusted him. It is enough.

In Jerusalem it was the time of the abomination of desolation. On the Via Dolorosa Jesus had said:

> Daughters of Jerusalem, do not weep for me, but weep for yourselves and for your children. For behold, the days are coming when they will say, "Blessed are the barren, and the wombs that never bore, and the breasts that never gave suck!" Then they will begin to say to the mountains, "Fall on us," and to the hills, "Cover us." For if they do this when the wood is green, what will happen when it is dry?[147]

In the winter of 68 a Zealot army under the ferocious John of Gischala and an Idumaean army under the priest Eleazar entered the city and slaughtered by the Temple every man suspected of Roman or aristocratic sympathies, to the number of 8,500. Josephus tells us that "a lake of blood" lay outside the Temple after this prodigious massacre. Remembering Jesus' warnings to them, the Christian community of Jerusalem fled to Pella beyond the Jordan, probably at this time.[148]

Meanwhile Vespasian was tightening his net. He took Perea beyond the Jordan, then the coast around Lydda and Jamnia, then Jericho. In June of 68 Nero, terrified by uprisings all over the western part of the empire, died whimpering. The whole structure Augustus had built seemed on the verge of disintegration. Emperor Galba was slain in January of 69; Emperor Otho committed suicide after a defeat in March; Emperor Vitellius entered Rome in May, but quickly proved to be a hopelessly self-indulgent wastrel. In Jerusalem the Zealots went from murder to rape and perversion, making the Temple more than ever a place of sacrilege and horror. The few good men left, in desperation, invited the brigand chieftain Simon bar Giora into Jerusalem to expel John of Gischala. Simon took most of the city, but John held the Temple mount. Then there was a schism among the Zealots, and a faction headed by the priest Eleazar the Idumaean took control of the highest part of the Temple, including the sanctuary. Three mutually hostile parties of Jews were ensconced in Jerusalem as the Roman legions approached. It seemed that madness reigned everywhere.[149]

But though the sky be falling, nothing could shake the solid peasant practicality and the relentless determination of Vespasian. In July of 69 his legions proclaimed him Emperor; in August the legions on the Danube hailed him likewise. His generals Antonius and Mucianus led them in a march on Rome, which they took in December; Vespasian turned the war in Judea over to his able son Titus.[150] The *pax romana* was to be restored—at the price of Jerusalem. Jesus, weeping over Jerusalem, had prophesied:

> For the days shall come upon you, when your enemies will cast up a bank about you and surround you, and hem you in on every side, and dash you to the ground, you and your children within you, and they will not leave one stone upon another in you, because you did not know the time of your visitation.[151]

A great number of pilgrims came to Jerusalem for the Passover of 70, despite the war. Titus let them all go into the city. Then he brought up his legions. After their first assaults had failed, he surrounded the whole city with a wall of circumvallation, as Caesar had done at Alesia in Gaul, and as Jesus had foretold. The wall ran along the lower slopes of the Mount of Olives, where the Tenth Legion was encamped; the olive trees in the Garden of Gethsemane were cut down to furnish wood for the towers. Starvation soon gripped the city, with the population vastly swollen by the paschal pilgrims, now unable to get out.[152] (On the Mount of Olives three days before He died, Jesus had said: "So when you see the desolating sacrilege . . . then let those who are in Judea flee to the mountains; let him who is on the housetop not go down to take what is in his house; and let him who is in the field not turn back to take his mantle."[153]) Men ate leather and hay; every day those dead of starvation were flung out in rotting heaps into the surrounding ravines. A mother ate her own child. At last even the Temple sacrifices stopped, because not enough men were left able to conduct them. Still the Zealots refused to consider surrender, though Titus repeatedly offered them generous terms.[154]

The deed that followed reverberates down the centuries, echoing loud and clear in the Holy Land to this day. Titus led the final assault in person. The crazed defenders fought his men step by step into the Temple precincts. For a whole day, the 9th of August 70, they fought hand-to-hand through the outer court, the Court of the Gentiles, which Jesus had twice cleansed. The Romans set fire to the gate and portico of the inner court, which burned and smoldered throughout the night. Next morning the struggle was resumed in the inner Court of the Israelites. Ahead was the Golden Window opening into the "holy place," the sanctuary itself. A legionary flung a firebrand through it. The old wood of the sanctuary blazed up. Titus ordered the fire put out. His raging men would not listen or obey. Titus plunged into the burning room. He turned to push away his men. More firebrands were flung behind his back. The Holy of Holies, that had been God's thousand-year sign of His special presence with Israel, exploded in flame.[155]

The Temple burned down to its bare stones; every combustible object in it was consumed. Titus now had no mercy left for anything in Jerusalem. He ordered the Temple and the city razed. Not one Jew was to be allowed to live there—only the Tenth Legion, Caesar's own, which set up a permanent encampment upon the ruins. In 71 Titus celebrated a long-remembered triumph in Rome. The great seven-branched candlestick—the *menorah*, symbol of Judaism—which he had extorted from the High Priest as the price of his life, was carried in his procession through the streets of the imperial city, along with John of Gischala and Simon bar Giora, in chains. In the deepest dungeon of the Mamertine prison Simon met his death. History tells us nothing of the fate of John.[156]

The Temple was gone forever. In all the years since that apocalyptic 10th of August, 70 A.D., only one attempt has ever been made to rebuild it, by the Emperor Julian the Apostate in 363, as a deliberate defiance of the prophecy of Christ. A sober classical historian, Ammianus Marcellinus—a pagan, not a Christian—tells of the earthquakes, the landslides, and the balls of fire coming out of the ground, that prevented the completion of the work.[157]

The Church of Christ looked out upon a new world: a world without the Temple, a world without Jerusalem; a world in which only one Apostle, John the Evangelist, remained; a world in which Linus the slave stood in the shoes of the fisherman, the little-known head of a small, poor, largely hidden and widely scattered band of Christian faithful in an empire where it was illegal for them to exist.

NOTES

[1] The Ascension occurred forty days after the Resurrection (Acts 1:3). For the dates of the Crucifixion and the Resurrection, see Chapter Sixteen, above.

[2] Acts 1:13-14; Constant Fouard, *St. Peter and the First Years of Christianity* (London, 1892), pp. 1-2. While it is true that, as Jules Lebreton and Jacques Zeiller (*The History of the Primitive Church* [New York, 1949], I, 166n) point out, that we do not know for certain that the Apostles were still using the same "upper room" that had been used for the Last Supper seven weeks before, it seems from every standpoint most unlikely that they would have ceased to assemble in what must have been for them, even more than for all the generations of Christian pilgrims ever since, a most holy place—in every sense of the word, the first Christian church building.

[3] Fouard, *St. Peter*, p. 2. For Jesus' cousins, see Chapter Fifteen, Notes 17, 18, and 103.

[4] Acts 1:15-26; Fouard, *St. Peter*, pp. 2-5; Manuel Miguens, *Church Ministries in New Testament Times* (Arlington VA, 1976), pp. 19-26. Miguens explains why this replacement of an Apostle and filling up of the Twelve to their full number was necessary just this once, but never again: because only Judas among the Twelve betrayed Christ. The others all died as Apostles, most of them as martyrs, thereby continuing to be in Heaven as they had been on Earth, pillars of the Faith. But the place left empty by Judas' desertion had to be filled so that the Church, the new Israel, would continue to have its Twelve Apostles, corresponding to the twelve tribes of old.

[5] Fouard, *St. Peter*, pp. 6-7.

[6] Acts 2:1-4.

[7] Fouard, *St. Peter*, pp. 8-11; William T. Walsh, *St. Peter the Apostle* (New York, 1948), pp. 207-210.

[8] Acts 2:22-24, 32-33, 36.

[9] Acts 2:41; Fouard, *St. Peter*, pp. 9-11. The importance of this conversion of substantial numbers of pilgrims who would soon be returning to their own homes in distant lands and could spread the Faith there has often been missed because we have no specific information about what any of them did. But this fact probably explains why, for instance, there are indications of Christianity in the Parthian realm as far back as we can trace Western contacts with it, after Christ.

[10] Acts 5:28-32, 40-41; Fouard, *St. Peter*, pp. 32-37; Walsh, *St. Peter*, pp. 216-221.

[11] Acts 2:44-47; Fouard, *St. Peter*, pp. 14-18.

[12] Fouard, *St. Peter*, p. 13. The question of whether Gentile converts to Christianity must be required to observe the whole of the Mosaic Law, which troubled the Church during its second and third decades, had not yet been faced. Presumably it was taken for granted at this time that all Christians would observe the Law, as all the first members of the Church did. But as the circumstances of the conversion of Cornelius the centurion were soon to make clear, there was no basis for this assumption, since the salvation Jesus brought was available to all men, and did not depend on the Law.

[13] Acts 5:33-40; Alfred Edersheim, *The Life and Times of Jesus the Messiah*, 3rd ed. (New York, 1896), II, 193-194.

[14] Lebreton and Zeiller, *Primitive Church*, I, 176-179; Miguens, *Church Ministries*, pp. 40-45.

[15] *The Cambridge Ancient History*, Volume X (Cambridge, England, 1934), pp. 636-638; G. P. Baker, *Tiberius Caesar* (London, 1929), pp. 255-277; Giuseppe Ricciotti, *The History of Israel* (Milwaukee, 1955), II, 376.

[16] Ricciotti, *History of Israel*, II, 376; E. Mary Smallwood, "The Date of the Dismissal of Pontius Pilate from Judaea," *Journal of Jewish Studies* V (1954), 12-21. "Caligula" was a soldiers' nickname for Gaius as a boy. He did not like or use it, for obvious reasons, since it is best translated "Booties."

[17] Ricciotti, *History of Israel*, II, 363, 376; Fouard, *St. Peter*, pp. 66-67, 391-392. The martyrdom of Stephen is often dated in 36, assuming that it occurred after Pilate had left Jerusalem for Rome, but while Tiberius was still reigning (e.g., Lebreton and Zeiller, *Primitive Church*, I, 182, and W. L. Knox, *St. Paul and the Church of Jerusalem* [Cambridge, England, 1928], p. 53). More recent writers (e.g. George Ogg, *The Chronology of the Life of Paul* [London, 1968], pp. 24-30) date it to 31 or 34, depending on their date for the Crucifixion, on highly speculative grounds (an imagined correspondence of an apocryphal tradition of an 18-month stay on Earth by Christ after His Resurrection, with the span of time between that event and Paul's conversion). But the very careful reconstruction of the evidence by E. Mary Smallwood in the penetrating article cited in Note 16, above, indicates that Pilate did not leave Jerusalem until almost the very end of the year 36 and that Vitellius arrived in Jerusalem within a few days of Pilate's departure, bringing Marcellus with him. Since Vitellius had taken the responsibility of removing Pilate from his post and sending him to Rome, he would have taken special care to ensure that no preventable civil disturbances broke out as a consequence of Pilate's absence. According to Smallwood's reconstruction, Vitellius was personally in Jerusalem in early January of 37 and again at Passover time in April, when he received the news of Tiberius' death just as he was preparing to march, at Tiberius' command, against the Nabataean Arabs in support of Herod Antipas. Vitellius immediately withdrew from Syria and took no further part in Judean affairs. From this it would seem likely that the martyrdom of Stephen took place in the month following Vitellius' departure—May of 37—when either the news of Marullus' appointment (or Marcellus' reappointment, if the name Marullus be a copyist's error for Marcellus) had not arrived, or the new or acting procurator was unsure of his authority. This dovetails very well with the evidence from the account of his conversion that Paul's meeting with Christ on the Damascus road took place on a bright, hot day, therefore in late spring or summer—according to this reconstruction, in June, July, or August of 37. A somewhat different reconstruction, that of Harold W. Hoehner, *Herod Antipas, a Contemporary of Jesus Christ* (Grand Rapids MI, 1972), pp. 255-257, 313-316, agrees with Smallwood that Pilate did not leave Judea until the very end of 36, puts Marcellus in his place at once, and has Vitellius withdrawing from Palestine in May 37 upon a somewhat later receipt of the news of Tiberius' death. This still makes May or early June 37 the most likely date for the martyrdom of Stephen (though Hoehner, like Smallwood, does not discuss Stephen in this connection).

[18] Acts 7:56. The speech of Stephen fills the whole seventh chapter of Acts. Fouard (*St. Peter*, pp. 67-74) argues that it is taken from an actual stenographic report in the archives of the Sanhedrin, and makes a good case. The argument of Knox (*St. Paul and the Church of Jerusalem*, pp. 40-44, 54-56), that Stephen's speech was a *condemnation* of the Law and all Temple worship as evil and corrupt from the beginning, is a truly fantastic exaggeration entirely without warrant in the text of Stephen's words which we have in Acts (and only there). Equally unwarranted is Knox's attempt to read into the speech an argument or even hint of the terms on which Gentiles were to be brought into the Christian Church. That subject is simply not mentioned by Stephen. His speech, like Peter's at Solomon's Portico (Acts 4:11-26) though considerably harsher, was a denun-

ciation of the sins of the Chosen People in the classic prophetic manner, and a call for their repentance with particular reference to the crucifixion of Christ.

[19] Giuseppe Ricciotti, *Paul the Apostle* (Milwaukee, 1953), pp. 183-186, 201-203.

[20] *Ibid.*, pp. 203-205. For the nature, background, and attitudes of the Jewish Christian community in Damascus at this time, see Jean Danielou and Henri Marrou, *The Christian Centuries*, Volume I: "The First Six Hundred Years" (New York, 1966), pp. 22-24.

[21] Ricciotti, *Paul the Apostle*, pp. 220-222; Fouard, *St. Peter*, pp. 117-118; Walsh, *St. Peter*, p. 237; Hilaire Belloc, *The Crusades* (Milwaukee, 1937), pp. 95-109.

[22] Ricciotti, *Paul the Apostle*, pp. 207-210; Fouard, *St. Peter*, pp. 118-119.

[23] Acts 9:4-5, 22:10.

[24] Philippians 3:12; Ricciotti, *Paul the Apostle*, p. 219. The Greek verb Paul used is $\kappa\alpha\tau\epsilon\lambda\eta\phi\theta\eta\nu$. See Ricciotti, *op. cit.*, pp. 211-219, for a comprehensive refutation of the various psychological and naturalistic theories which have been advanced in modern times as attempts to account for Paul's conversion without reference to the supernatural. It simply cannot be done. As Ricciotti points out, many even among rationalist and Modernist scholars dismiss his experience on the road to Damascus as an insoluble problem. A very profound and penetrating discussion of the event from the orthodox Christian viewpoint is founded in Joseph Holzner, *Paul of Tarsus* (St. Louis, 1944), pp. 35-44.

[25] Ricciotti, *Paul the Apostle*, pp. 127-128, 221-227. It is Ricciotti's conclusion, which seems well founded, that Paul remained less than a year in Arabia and then returned to Damascus where he stayed for almost two years until finally driven out, in the famous incident in which he was let down the city wall in a large basket (Acts 9:25). According to the chronology herein adopted (see Note 17, above), this would bring his sojourn in Arabia probably into 38 and his return and later stay in Damascus from 38 to 40.

[26] Glanville Downey, *A History of Antioch in Syria* (Princeton NJ, 1961), p. 273; Lebreton and Zeiller, *Primitive Church*, I, 177-178.

[27] Danielou and Marrou, *Christian Centuries*, I, 40; John Chapman, *John the Presbyter and the Fourth Gospel* (Oxford, 1911), pp. 64-71. The circumstantial account in Acts 6 of the seven Hellenist deacons, including Philip, clearly indicates that this was an office subordinate to the Apostles and that the Apostles themselves did not serve in this capacity (Miguens, *Church Ministries*, pp. 40-45). Hence Apostle Philip and Deacon Philip must have been two separate persons, as most later Christian writers held.

[28] Fouard, *St. Peter*, pp. 78-90. The sin of simony—the sale and purchase of Church offices, benefits, charisms, or sacraments—takes its name from Simon Magus.

[29] Fouard, *St. Peter*, pp. 90-94. See also Chapter Six, above, and P. L. Shinnie, *Meroe, a Civilization in the Sudan* (New York, 1967). The reigning queen at the time (up to 41 A.D.) was Aminatare, who left many inscriptions in Nubia and a memory of fame and power (Shinnie, *op. cit.*, p. 61). The "Candace" of Acts 8:27 undoubtedly represents one of her royal titles (Roy J. Deferrari, ed., Eusebius' *Ecclesiastical History*, The Fathers of the Church, Volume 19 [New York, 1953], p. 87n).

[30] Fouard, *St. Peter*, pp. 92, 97n; Isaiah 28. See Volume II, Chapter One, of this history.

[31] This date is strongly indicated by several converging lines of evidence. If the martyrdom of Stephen and the conversion of Paul are to be dated to 37, as we have argued (see Note 17, above), a reasonable time must be allotted for the work of Deacon Philip and St. Peter in Samaria and then for Philip's work on the Palestinian coastal plain, before the coming of Peter to the coast. At least a year, perhaps somewhat more, would seem to be called for. Eusebius, the first Church historian, placed the date of Peter's first visit to Antioch in the third year of the Emperor Gaius, from March 39 to March 40

(Downey, *Antioch*, p. 584). That visit was most probably occasioned by the rapid growth of the church in Antioch due to the opening of the Church to uncircumcised pagans signalized by the baptism of Cornelius (see Note 33, below). Consequently the baptism of Cornelius would fall in 39.

[32] Acts 9:36-10:48; Fouard, *St. Peter*, pp. 144-154.

[33] Acts 11:1-18; Fouard, *St. Peter*, pp. 154-156, 164-166; Downey, *Antioch*, pp. 274-276, 282; Danielou and Marrou, *Christian Centuries*, I, 24; Ricciotti, *Paul the Apostle*, pp. 122-128, 227-243; see Note 31, above. Paul dates his first visit to Jerusalem at three years after his conversion (Galatians 1:18)—therefore in 40, according to the chronology here adopted. Fouard (*op. cit.*, pp. 164-166) dates Peter's first visit to Antioch in 40 but places the baptism of Cornelius after it. It seems much more likely that Peter would have gone to Antioch after its church began to grow rapidly due to the admission of Gentiles, with the consequent problems regarding the extent to which the Mosaic Law was to be imposed on Gentile converts. It is commonly assumed (*e.g.*, Downey, *op. cit.*, p. 274) that the Hellenistic Jewish Christians in Antioch had proceeded on their own to baptize Gentiles, and only gradually became aware of the problems this created. This seems most unlikely. So momentous a step (see Ricciotti, *Paul the Apostle*, pp. 272-273, for an excellent explanation of how momentous and extraordinary it really was, in light of the ironclad exclusiveness that had characterized the people of Israel through nearly 2000 years since Abraham) would hardly have been taken on any significant scale without Apostolic authority. Peter himself—no innovator by nature—would have been most unlikely to take that step without some such direct and explicit guidance from the Holy Spirit as he received on the occasion of the baptism of Cornelius. Modern historians of early Christianity have tended to lose sight of these hard facts and clear circumstances amidst the multitude of scholarly theories that have proliferated, like the apocryphal legends of old, from the simple and sober accounts we actually have of the controversy over whether and to what extent Christians were still obliged to follow the law of Moses. Though certainly important, this controversy has been exaggerated out of all reasonable proportions. The fact is that the basic issue was *settled at the beginning* by the baptism of Cornelius, an uncircumcised pagan, by Peter personally, without any requirement that Cornelius henceforth observe the Mosaic law. Later criticism and opposition to this procedure by some Jewish Christians never had Apostolic support (not even from James the Just) and never changed the policy. (On this point see especially Gregory Dix, *Jew and Greek, a Study in the Primitive Church* [London, 1953], pp. 35-37). Therefore this controversy cannot be, as so many have presented it, the key to understanding the whole history of the Church from Pentecost to the destruction of Jerusalem. Rather, as this chapter will show, that key was the concept of the universal apostolate of Christ taught by Jesus Himself and firmly held by all of the Twelve, who were thereby in essential harmony with Paul.

[34] Other examples: Nero (age 17 at his accession in 54), Domitian (age 30 at his accession in 81), Commodus (age 19 at his accession in 180), Caracalla (age 25 at his accession in 211), and Elagabalus (age 14 at his accession in 218).

[35] *Cambridge Ancient History*, X, 656-668; J. P. V. D. Balsdon, *The Emperor Gaius* (Oxford, 1934), pp. 124-125, 135-139; Ricciotti, *History of Israel*, II, 377-382; Arnaldo Momigliano, *Claudius, the Emperor and His Achievement* (Oxford, 1934), pp. 30-31.

[36] *Cambridge Ancient History*, X, 680.

[37] Lebreton and Zeiller, *Primitive Church*, I, 323-324. For the dating of the Crucifixion and Resurrection see Chapter Sixteen, above (Note 2).

[38] Eusebius, *Ecclesiastical History*, II, 23, quoting Book Five of the Memoirs of Hegesippus, who assiduously gathered information about the early Church and worked

within living memory of the Apostolic Age, from about 130 to 190 (Deferrari, ed., *Fathers of the Church*, XIX, 253n); Fouard, *St. Peter*, pp. 190-196.

[39] Fouard, *St. Peter*, pp. 216-226. After a long period during which the very cogent arguments set forth by Fouard and other writers of his time were, for no particularly good reason, almost totally rejected by New Testament critics (even those thoroughly orthodox), the proposition that the Gospel of Matthew was after all written first, before any of the other gospels—as Church tradition had always maintained—is now being revived even by critics whose premises and methods are very different from those accepted herein, *e.g.*, John Robinson, *Redating the New Testament* (Philadelphia, 1976), pp. 92-99. See also a foreshadowing of this change of view in Danielou and Marrou, *Christian Centuries*, I, 25. For a brilliant summation of the linguistic arguments for an Aramaic original of St. Matthew's Gospel, see John Chapman's almost forgotten *Matthew, Mark and Luke, a Study in the Order and Interpretation of the Synoptic Gospels* (London, 1937), pp. 182-214; for a similar summation of the arguments for the Apostle Matthew's authorship of the Gospel which bears his name, see *ibid.*, pp. 253-260. St. Jerome (*De Viris Illustribus* 3) says that the original version of Matthew's Gospel, in "Hebrew," was extant in his time, a copy being preserved in the library of the famous early Christian scholar Pamphilus (c. 300) at Caesarea in Palestine; and Eusebius (*Ecclesiastical History*, V, 10) says a copy of the "Hebrew" Gospel of Matthew was taken to India by the Apostle Bartholomew and found there at the end of the second century by the Christian scholar and traveller Pantaenus. In his commentary on Eusebius' Chronicle (*Patrologia Latina* XXVII, 577-578). Jerome dates the composition of the Gospel of Matthew to the last year of Gaius (40 A.D.), just one year before the date here proposed.

[40] Fouard, *St. Peter*, pp. 171-181, 191, 393-395; George Edmundson, *The Church in Rome in the First Century* (London, 1913), pp. 42-43. The account of Herod Agrippa's persecution in Acts 12 makes no mention of the presence of any other Apostle in Jerusalem at the time except the martyred James the son of Zebedee (12:2); James, the head of the Christian community in Jerusalem (12:17); and Peter. Presumably, therefore, the others had already departed before the persecution began and were safely beyond its reach. The persecution is often dated to 44, because the account of Herod Agrippa's sudden and dramatic death, known to have occurred in that year during some great festival, appears at the end of Acts 12 which mentions the Passover at its beginning. But Acts 12:19 ("then he [Herod Agrippa] went down from Judea to Caesarea, and remained there") seems clearly to indicate a considerable lapse of time. And Fouard (*op. cit.*, pp. 394-395) demonstrates that the festival at which Herod Agrippa died in 44 was most probably that celebrating the accession of Claudius as emperor on January 24th. Fouard also gives very persuasive reasons for supposing that Herod Agrippa would have begun his persecution of the Christians by the first Passover of his reign as King of the Jews, rather than waiting until his third year. This dating makes still more difficult the already almost impossible task of developing a plausible reconstruction of the apostolic career of James, son of Zebedee, that would bring him all the way to Spain and back before his martyrdom in Jerusalem. But his relics may well have been brought to Spain later, and found their way to the famous site at Compostela which became Spain's greatest shrine. For the best case that can now be made for St. James' purported visit to Spain— which its author repeatedly admits is very difficult to defend—see Zacarías Garcia Villada, *Historia Ecclesiástica de España* (Madrid, 1929), I, 41-66.

[41] Downey, *Antioch*, pp. 282-286, 584-585. Oscar Cullmann, *Peter: Disciple, Apostle, Martyr*, 2d ed. (Philadelphia, 1962), makes the astonishing argument that Peter resigned as head of the Church when he left Jerusalem, giving way to James! Since Cullmann

admits the authenticity of Matthew 16:18, he asks us to believe that the man whom the Incarnate God named Rock removed himself as the Church's cornerstone within a few years. Cullmann's principal authority for this hypothesis is the pseudo-Clementine romances of the third century. For further refutation of this thesis of Cullmann, see Jean Dauvilliers, *Les temps apostoliques* (Paris, 1968), pp. 273-275.

[42] Arthur S. Barnes, *Christianity at Rome in the Apostolic Age* (London, 1938), pp. 2-10; Fouard, *St. Peter*, pp. 246-249. Jerome (*De Viris Illustribus* 1) gives 42 as the date of Peter's first arrival in Rome. This fits in very well with the evidence that Herod Agrippa's persecution, which forced Peter to leave Jerusalem, occurred in the spring of that year (see Note 40, above). The utter scorn of W. L. Knox (*St. Paul and the Church of Jerusalem*, p. 176) for the very idea that Peter could have gone to Rome in 42 is attainable only by totally ignoring the evidence for a strong Christian community in Rome by the year 49 (see Note 78, below) and, even more clearly, in 58 (the most likely date for Paul's Epistle to the Romans [Ricciotti, *Paul the Apostle*, pp. 390-398]); see particularly Romans 16:7. As George Edmundson states, with reference to that Epistle: "There was in Rome a Christian community not of yesterday, but of many years' standing: an important community, whose faith and whose high repute were well known in all churches of the Empire with which the writer was acquainted. Further that St. Paul himself for some years past had been longing to visit this Roman community, but had been hindered from doing so by the restriction he had imposed upon himself of not building on another man's foundation. If again the question be repeated—Who was this man? with greater emphasis than before the same answer must be returned—It cannot be any other than St. Peter." (*Church in Rome*, pp. 55-56)

[43] Jerome Carcopino, *Daily Life in Ancient Rome*, ed. Henry T. Rowell (New Haven CT, 1940; New York, 1971), pp. 18-58.

[44] Fouard, *St. Peter*, pp. 249-271; Edersheim, *Jesus the Messiah*, I, 66-72; Edmundson, *Church in Rome*, pp. 56-57.

[45] Barnes, *Christianity at Rome*, pp. 131-137; Ludwig Hertling and Englebert Kirschbaum, *The Roman Catacombs and Their Martyrs*, 2d ed. (Milwaukee, 1956), pp. 27-28; Edmundson, *Church in Rome*, pp. 57, 85-86; E. Mary Smallwood, *The Jews under Roman Rule, from Pompey to Diocletian* (Leiden, 1981), p. 218n, affirming the likelihood that Pomponia Graecina was a Christian.

[46] See Chapter Two, above.

[47] Fouard, *St. Peter*, pp. 203-205. A. C. Perumalil, *The Apostles in India*, 2d ed. (Bangalore, India, 1971), pp. 105-140, presents a well-reasoned argument for the Apostle Bartholomew also having gone to India—specifically, to the Bombay region. But his own evidence shows considerable confusion over the precise extent and geographical position of India in many of the early sources mentioning an Indian apostolate for Bartholomew. The absence of any native tradition of an apostolic foundation for Christianity in the Bombay area, by contrast to the strong tradition in south India of the apostolate of Thomas there, and the countervailing indications of an apostolate of Bartholomew in south Arabia—where we know there were numerous Christians by the century before Muhammad—would seem to make it more probable that Bartholomew did not reach India proper, or if he did, that he did not stay there long. But *all* traditions about Bartholomew take him beyond the frontiers of the Roman empire. Regarding Matthew, confusion arises because in classical times there was an "Ethiopia" in Iran near the Caspian Sea as well as the larger and better known Ethiopia in Africa; the later traditions of Matthew are divided as to which Ethiopia he evangelized. On this see Emil G. Kraeling, *The Disciples* (New York, 1966), pp. 163-165, and E. Jacquier's article on the Apostle Matthew in *The Catholic Encyclopedia* (1913). For the Apostle Andrew, see the very valuable study by Francis Dvornik, *The Idea of Apostolicity in Byzantium and the Legend*

of the Apostle Andrew (Cambridge MA, 1958), one of the few extended scholarly studies of the traditions of the lesser known Apostles available in English. On pp. 198-201 and 211-214 of this work, Dvornik presents a strong argument in support of locating Andrew's apostolate entirely in Scythia and the Ukraine, outside the borders of the Roman empire, where Eusebius (*Ecclesiastical History*, III, 1, with note by its editor Roy Deferrari, *Fathers of the Church*, XIX, 137-138) places it, rather than in Greek Achaea within the empire, as some later traditions held. A Greek apostolate for Andrew would clearly have overlapped that of Paul and impinged closely upon areas whose evangelization was well known to Luke and described by him in some detail in Acts. Yet Luke nowhere mentions Andrew in Acts.

⁴⁸ The old, forgotten work of the great French Syriac scholar J. P. Paulin Martin, *Les Origines de l'Église d'Édesse et des Églises Syriennes* (Paris, 1889), pp. 6-7, is the only scholarly source known to the writer to make this exceedingly important point.

⁴⁹ Constant Fouard, *St. John and the Close of the Apostolic Age* (New York, 1905), pp. 73-74; Fouard, *St. Peter*, p. 204; Danielou and Marrou, *Christian Centuries*, I, 40. Polycrates, Bishop of Ephesus, wrote to Pope Victor I late in the second century specifically identifying the Philip who evangelized the region of Hierapolis and lived there with his daughters as one of the Twelve (Fouard, *St. John*, p. 73n).

⁵⁰ John 20:27-28. There is an old tradition, reported in the "Acts of Thomas," that he resisted for a long time before accepting this assignment, fearing its extraordinary difficulty, but finally submitted as a slave to the Will of Christ. See the striking reconstruction of the possible truth behind this tradition by J. N. Farquhar, "The Apostle Thomas in North India," *Bulletin of the John Rylands Library* X (1926), 93-94.

⁵¹ George M. Moraes, *A History of Christianity in India, A.D. 52-1542* (Bombay, 1964), pp. 25-30; Farquhar, "The Apostle Thomas in North India," *Bulletin of the John Rylands Library* X, 86-89, 102-103; *The Cambridge Ancient History*, Volume XI (Cambridge, England, 1936), pp. 111-112; Neilson C. Debevoise, *A Political History of Parthia* (Chicago, 1938), p. 66; George Woodcock, *The Greeks in India* (London, 1966), pp. 140-147; Martin, *Les Origines de l'Église d'Édesse*, pp. 17-30. Farquhar thinks Thomas went by sea from Egypt on all his journeys to India, and came back by sea to Egypt on any returns he made.

⁵² Moraes, *Christianity in India*, pp. 30-31; see Chapter One, above.

⁵³ Moraes, *Christianity in India*, pp. 32-34. Gaurasva's name appears in the Greek text of the "Acts of Thomas" as Xanthippus.

⁵⁴ Eusebius, *Ecclesiastical History*, I, 13. For a thorough summary of the usual modern view of the story of Abgar and Jesus, see J. B. Segal, *Edessa, the Blessed City* (Oxford, 1970), pp. 62-74; for the view upheld in the text, see Martin, *Les Origines de l'Église d'Édesse*, pp. 103-108, and Herbert Thurston, "The Letter of Our Saviour to Abgar," *The Month*, LXXVI (Sept.-Dec. 1892), pp. 39-61. The message of Christ is specifically declared to be oral in one of the two primary sources, the Doctrine of Addai. As Thurston points out (*art. cit.*, pp. 60-61), the written documents seen by Eusebius, including the short alleged letter of Christ, are almost certainly a later retelling of the original story rather than documents contemporary with King Abgar the Black and with Christ. The antecedent improbability of a letter from Christ, Who is not known to have made any written communication whatever during His life, is very high; but the oral message would be entirely consistent with His methods.

⁵⁵ Ian Wilson, *The Shroud of Turin* (New York, 1978), pp. 98-113; Pierre Barbet, *A Doctor at Calvary* (New York, 1953), pp. 145-159. The cloth "Mandylion" bearing the image of Christ, later found at Edessa, is described in the Acts of Thaddaeus as τετραδυπλον—"doubled in four"—a word that appears nowhere else in Greek literature. See Alexander Roberts and James Donaldson, eds. *The Ante-Nicene Fathers* (Grand Rapids

MI, 1957), VIII, 558, and Wilson, *op. cit.*, p. 260. The Mandylion is described as having the aspect of a horizontal rather than an upright rectangle (landscape rather than portrait shape), which together with the "doubling in four" suggests the preparation of the Shroud to serve as a picture (Wilson, *op. cit.*, pp. 98-99).

[56] Eusebius, *Ecclesiastical History*, I, 13; George Phillips, ed., *The Doctrine of Addai the Apostle* (London, 1876), p. 5; Jerome, Commentarium in Evangelium Matthae I, 10, 57, *Patriologia Latina* XXVI, 61; Aziz S. Atiya, *History of Eastern Christianity* (Notre Dame IN, 1968), pp. 315-316; Henri Leclercq, "La Légende d'Abgar," *Dictionnaire d'Archéologie chrétienne et de liturgie*, I (1), 89; Segal, *Edessa*, p. 80; Martin, *Les Origines de l'Église d'Édesse*, pp. 29-36. Roy Deferrari, in editing Eusebius, pronounces his statement that the apostle of Edessa was one of the Seventy-Two rather than one of the Twelve to be an error comparable with his statement elsewhere that Cephas was one of the Seventy-Two and a different person from Peter (*Fathers of the Church* XIX, 76n).

[57] Segal, *Edessa*, p. 15n.

[58] *Butler's Lives of the Saints*, edited, revised and supplemented by Herbert Thurston and Donald Attwater (New York, 1956), IV, 213-214. Thurston and Attwater, in common with many other authorities, regard the Apostle Jude as the author of the canonical Epistle of Jude in the New Testament. However, its author does not identify himself as an Apostle, but only as the "brother of James" and therefore probably the cousin of Jesus. There is good reason to doubt that the Jude who was the cousin of Jesus was the Apostle Jude Thaddaeus. See Chapter Fifteen, Note 103, above.

[59] Henri Leclercq states: "St. Addai or Thaddaeus nowhere had a distinct and conspicuous tomb. Reports are divergent enough on the circumstances of his death, wholly uncertain on his sepulcher. The tomb of his successor Aggai was known; it was in plain sight, inside the principal church. As for Addai, one report buries him in the cemetery of the kings of Edessa, another in Armenia, a third transports him to Rome." ("*Saint Addai ou Thaddée, n'y avait nulle part un tombeau distinct et apparent. Les récits sont assez divergents sur les circonstances de sa mort, absolument flottants sur sa sépulture. On connaissait la tombe de son successeur Aggai, elle se trouvait bien en vue, à l'intérieur de l'église principale. Quant a Addai lui-même, un récit l'enterre dans la sépulture des rois d'*Édesse, un autre en Armenie, un troisième le fait transporter jusqu'/a Rome.*" (*Dictionnaire d'Archéologie chrétienne et de liturgie*, "Édesse," IV [2], 2076). However, Leclercq goes on to hypothesize that the famous tomb of the Apostle Thomas in Edessa is actually Addai's, which seems most unlikely in view of the very strong, ancient, and general tradition of a translation of Thomas' body from India to Edessa at a comparatively early date (Martin, *Les Origines de l'Église d'Édesse*, pp. 42-50).

[60] The inclusion of the reference to Christ's face imprinted on a cloth "doubled in four" and brought to Edessa, in the Acts of Thaddaeus (see Note 55, above), may account for this. There is little mention in standard works and references on Christian iconography of the representation of the Apostle Jude with a picture of Christ; but the writer has seen him so represented on holy cards and in statuary, notably at St. Peter's Church in Munich.

[61] Wilson, *Shroud of Turin*, pp. 108-109.

[62] Segal, *Edessa*, pp. 64-69, presents a comprehensive and learned argument against the historicity of the conversion of Edessa in the reign of Abgar V Ukkama (the Black). Segal's principal arguments are: (1) "the conversion to Christianity of an important monarch at this early period would not have been ignored by Christian writers for close on 300 years"; (2) "Edessa was, from, at any rate, the third century, under the ecclesiastical jurisdiction of Antioch, but her Christian community is unlikely to have ac-

cepted this subordinate role had her ruler and the majority of her citizens adopted Christianity shortly after the crucifixion''; (3) the story as we have it shows marked parallelism with the story of the conversion to Judaism in 36 A.D. of King Ezad of Adiabene in Mesopotamia beyond the Tigris, and also to some of the accounts we have of Manichean missionary activity in this area in the late third or early fourth century, which also mention an Addai and a Thomas. In reply, (1) as Segal himself states, ''at the beginning of the Christian era Edessa lay in the Parthian, not the Roman, sphere of interest, and its people spoke Syriac not Greek'' (*op. cit.*, p. 65). Most of the records of early Christianity that have come down to us derive from the Graeco-Roman world; and their total volume is small. We have virtually nothing from the Parthian world before the beginning of the third century (200). Therefore we are unlikely to find among our extant Graeco-Roman documents historical reports on a city in an alien realm, its people speaking an alien tongue, who had the faith only briefly and then lost it. When records of Christianity east of the Roman empire begin to appear, the story of Addai and the conversion of Edessa very soon appears as well; and by the time of Eusebius in the early fourth century, the early conversion of Edessa is featured. (2) The fact that Antioch always kept a strong Christian community from its initial evangelization, while Edessa's first Christian community was virtually snuffed out, would alone suffice to account for Antioch's primacy over Edessa in the Church. Furthermore, according to the reconstruction presented in the text, Antioch was evangelized first in any case, immediately after the baptism of Cornelius, and claimed Peter himself, the head of the whole Church, as its founder. So its title to ecclesiastical primacy over Edessa was clear. (3) Parallels can be found between any two historical events with sufficient effort. In this case they have been compounded by the natural practice of Syriac Christians in naming their children, generation after generation, for Thaddaeus (Addai) and Thomas, of whose missionary career they were well informed (see text and Note 66, below). There have been many Thomases in the Church for two thousand years, but this does not entitle historians to assume any two of them to be identical without solid evidence. Danielou and Marrou, *Christian Centuries*, I, 46, present evidence that Edessa was in fact evangelized from Palestine in the first century, though Danielou accepts the view that the first Christian king was not Abgar V Ukkama but Abgar IX ''the Great'' (177-212).

[63] Wilson, *Shroud of Turin*, pp. 110-119, 235-251; Segal, *Edessa*, pp. 76-78, 214-216; Ernst von Dobschütz, *Christusbilder* (Leipzig, 1899), pp. 102-117. Wilson translates in full the Byzantine ''Story of the Image of Edessa'' prepared for the court of Constantine Porphyrogenitus in 945 when the Shroud had just been brought from Edessa to Constantinople. Under other circumstances so late an account, even though presented as— and giving internal indications of actually being—based on careful historical research, would be of only limited value. But in this case the Shroud itself provides remarkable confirmation of the accuracy of the Byzantine account, as Wilson demonstrates in detail. It seems to have occurred to no modern researcher before Wilson that the lack of any mention of the picture of Christ in Edessa by writers of the fourth, fifth, and early sixth centuries, so often advanced as conclusive evidence for rejecting altogether its connection with the first-century Abgar (*e.g.* by Dobschütz, *loc. cit.*), is clearly and satisfactorily explained by the report in the Byzantine account mentioned, of the concealment of the picture for 500 years following the first-century persecution (Wilson, *op. cit.*, pp. 243-244). There is nothing surprising about either its concealment or its preservation under such circumstances, for a span of time not so long as the Holy Shroud of Turin is known to have been preserved since its emergence in France in the fourteenth century.

[64] This is the most likely explanation for the most celebrated ''anachronism'' in the Doctrine of Addai, used by modern authorities as the principal argument for rejecting

it entirely as a source of reliable historical evidence: its reference to the ordination of Palut as bishop of Edessa by Bishop Serapion of Antioch (198-212), with the implication that Bishop Palut was the immediate successor of the martyred Aggai (Phillips, ed., *Doctrine of Addai*, p. 50; Segal, *Edessa*, p. 81; Leclercq, "¢Edesse,'' *Dictionnaire d'Archéologie chrétienne et de liturgie*, IV [2], 2073-2074). Martin, *Les Origines de l'Église d'Édesse*, pp. 51-56, 82-103, vigorously attacks the reliability of the Palut reference as a later interpolation, a position which to some extent begs the question of when the document as a whole was written. The evidence that Palut was regarded as a sort of second founder of the church in Edessa (Leclercq, *loc. cit.*, cols. 2082-2083) strongly suggests that it was he who reconstructed it after its long eclipse following the persecution of Manu VI. The one major difficulty with this hypothesis arises from the three references in the Doctrine of Addai to a Palut who was indubitably a companion of Aggai. But this could simply have been a different Palut. It is not intended here to claim full historical accuracy for the Doctrine of Addai—only the essential truth of its main points. Its author was no historical scholar; but he was dealing with a living tradition. That tradition was altogether too widely known and believed at too early a date to have been entirely an invention or a baseless legend. Martin rightly hammers on this theme: "If one wished to draw up a complete bibliography of books where allusion is made to Abgar, to Addai and to the evangelization of Edessa in apostolic times, it would make a small volume. I do not believe that there was a Syriac author of any length who does not speak, at one time or another, of these events or these persons." ("*Si on voulait dresser un bibliographie complète des livres ou il est fait allusion à Abgar, à Addai et à l'évangelization d'Édesse aux temps apostoliques, on ferait un petit volume. Je ne crois pas qu'il y ait un auteur syrien un peu étendu qui ne parle, une fois ou l'autre, de ces évenements ou de ces personnages.*") (*Les Origines de l'Église d'Édesse*, p. 49n).

[65] Wilson, *Shroud of Turin*, pp. 61-64, 82-85, 133-147. Several of the numerous Christian writers, beginning in the sixth century, who mention the picture "not made by hands" (*acheiropoietos*—a most apt designation of the Shroud image) are explicit that the image was on cloth (Leclercq, "La Légende d'Abgar," *Dictionnaire d'Archéologie chrétienne et de liturgie*, I [1], 94-95).

[66] Martin, *Les Origines de l'Église d'Édesse*, pp. 13-17; Farquhar, "The Apostle Thomas in North India," *Bulletin of the John Rylands Library*, X, 82-83, 106. Farquhar presents a good case for his hypothesis that the Apostle Thomas sent a letter to the church in Edessa describing his work in India.

[67] Ricciotti, *History of Israel*, II, 387-388, 393; Fouard, *St. Peter*, pp. 182-184.

[68] Ricciotti, *Paul the Apostle*, pp. 129, 245-246.

[69] Acts 13:1-3; Holzner, *Paul of Tarsus*, pp. 97-100; Ricciotti, *Paul the Apostle*, p. 242.

[70] Acts 13:4-12; Holzner, *Paul of Tarsus*, pp. 101-106; Ricciotti, *Paul the Apostle*, pp. 252-255.

[71] Ricciotti, *Paul the Apostle*, pp. 256-259; Holzner, *Paul of Tarsus*, pp. 112-113.

[72] Acts 13:44-45; Ricciotti, *Paul the Apostle*, pp. 259-261.

[73] Acts 13:46-47.

[74] Acts 13:48-14:5; Ricciotti, *Paul the Apostle*, pp. 261-265.

[75] Ricciotti, *Paul the Apostle*, pp. 265-266; Constant Fouard, *St. Paul and His Missions* (New York, 1899), p. 38.

[76] Acts 14:8-19; Ricciotti, *Paul the Apostle*, pp. 266-270; Galatians 6:17.

[77] Acts 14:20-26; Ricciotti, *Paul the Apostle*, pp. 266, 270-271.

[78] Acts 18:2; *Cambridge Ancient History*, X, 500-501; Hubert Jedin and John Dolan, eds., *History of the Church*, Volume I: "From the Apostolic Community to Constantine" (New York, 1965), pp. 128-129 (this volume was originally published under the title *Handbook of Church History* for the general series); Momigliano, *Claudius*, pp.

32-33, 36. The pagan authority is Suetonius in his life of the Emperor Claudius. The date is given by Orosius, *History Against the Pagans*, VII, 6. "Chrestus" was a natural Latin misspelling of the Greek *Christos* (Edmundson, *Church in Rome*, pp. 9-10). The plausibility of Orosius' date is pointed out by Vincent M. Scramuzza, *The Emperor Claudius* (Cambridge MA, 1940), p. 287: "For it was just in the period 47-52 A.D. that Claudius was engaged in his campaign to restore the old Roman rites and check the growth of foreign cults." It is also brilliantly defended by Smallwood, *Jews under Roman Rule*, pp. 210-216. For an excellent argument for the historical authenticity of Simon Magus' visit to Rome (often denied) see Edmundson, *Church in Rome*, pp. 60-65.

[79] Lebreton and Zeiller, *Primitive Church*, I, 286, 288; Fouard, *St. Paul and His Missions*, pp. 158-161; Barnes, *Christianity at Rome*, pp. 27-28. Corinth may also have been evangelized by Peter on his way from Asia back to Rome after the Apostolic Council. Peter's presence in Corinth is explicitly attested by Bishop Dionysius of Corinth, writing about 170 (Eusebius, *Ecclesiastical History*, II, 25; IV, 23) and clearly implied by 1 Corinthians 1:12.

[80] Walsh, *St. Peter*, p. 178; Fouard, *St. John*, pp. 71-72; Henri Daniel-Rops, *The Book of Mary* (New York, 1960), pp. 69-70, 192-214. St. John Damascene (c. 730), a great Marian theologian and sharp critic of the Apocrypha, specifically states that, despite the unreliability of much of the material in the Apocrypha, the tradition recorded in the apocryphal "The Passing of Mary" of the presence of all living members of the Apostolic College at the deathbed of the Blessed Virgin Mary in Jerusalem is worthy of belief. There is an allusion in the acts of the Ecumenical Council of Ephesus in 431 suggesting that Mary died in that city, and a like tradition there, but the tradition of her death and Assumption in Jerusalem seems better attested (Fouard, *op. cit.*, p. 72n). It seems most unlikely that the Apostle John, with Mary in his care, could have lived in Ephesus for any considerable period of time before the year 54 when Paul arrived there on his third missionary journey (Ricciotti, *Paul the Apostle*, p. 343), since Paul found in Ephesus only a small group of semi-Christians who had not even heard of the Holy Spirit and so had not been validly baptized (Acts 19:1-6). It is almost impossible to believe that the Apostle John, had he been there earlier, would have left them in such ignorance, and no other converts in Ephesus. Paul stayed in Ephesus until 57 (Ricciotti, *op. cit.*, p. 133) and still we hear nothing of John in that city. By that year the Blessed Virgin Mary, if still living on earth, would have been at least seventy-seven years old, presuming she was fourteen at the time of Christ's birth (see Chapter Fourteen, above). It seems most improbable that John would have taken her out of her homeland and far away to alien Ephesus for the first time at so advanced an age. The tradition of her "Dormition" in Jerusalem about 49, when she would have been sixty-nine years old (or just a year or two older), is evidently more probable. For references to the apostles in a manner suggesting a considerable group of them gathered for the Council of Jerusalem, see Acts 15:6 and 15:22.

[81] There is a vast, tendentious and over-subtle literature on the Apostolic Council, much of which sees forbidding problems in reconciling Galatians 2 and Acts 15 and immensely complicates the basically clear and straightforward account we have of it. See Note 33, above; Ricciotti, *Paul the Apostle*, pp. 129-131, 272-281; and Dix, *Jew and Greek*, pp. 37-51, for much-needed corrective analysis (though Dix, in his otherwise excellent rebuttal to the common scholarly misinterpretation of the Apostolic Council, accepts in this writer's view much too late a date for the writing of Acts and hypothesizes on insufficient evidence a very negative reaction by Paul to the quite minor concessions made to the Judaizers by the Council). For the opposing viewpoint magnifying the historical problems of the Apostolic Council, see Kirsopp Lake and Henry J. Cadbury,

eds., *The Beginnings of Christianity*, Volume V (London, 1933), pp. 195-212.

[82] Acts 15:7-11. Peter's first sentence seems clearly to refer to his baptism of Cornelius.

[83] Acts 15:26.

[84] Acts 15:28-29. The formulation "it has seemed good to the Holy Spirit and to us" is a remarkable testament to the extent of the Apostles' authority (Walsh, *St. Peter*, p. 271).

[85] Fouard, *St. Paul and His Missions*, pp. 75-79.

[86] 1 Peter 1:1; Lebreton and Zeiller, *Primitive Church*, I, 286, 293-294; Danielou and Marrou, *Christian Centuries*, I, 50; Fouard, *St. Paul and His Missions*, p. 215; Edmundson, *Church in Rome*, p. 77.

[87] Acts 15:37-39; Fouard, *St. Paul and His Missions*, pp. 80-86. Fouard here partially retracts his earlier position (*St. Peter*, pp. 367-381) that Mark's Gospel was written in Rome during the reign of Claudius. (Fouard attributes this view to Eusebius in his *Ecclesiastical History*, II, 15, but that chapter of Eusebius does not mention the reign of Claudius, which is referred to only in the preceding chapter in connection with Peter's arrival and early preaching in Rome.) In fact it is most unlikely that Mark was in Rome with Peter for any considerable length of time before the Council of Jerusalem, since we know that Mark was available in Palestine to join Paul and Barnabas on their first missionary journey in 45 and that he returned to Palestine after leaving them at the foot of the Taurus in 46, while Peter (according to the reconstruction here adopted) left Jerusalem in 42 and returned there from Rome in 49. Furthermore, Mark's timidity and uncertainty in apostolic work, as indicated by his unwillingness to penetrate upland Asia Minor with Paul in 46, strongly suggests that he was a novice in such work at that time. But Mark could have come to Rome with Peter immediately *after* the reign of Claudius, when the edict banishing Jews from Rome presumably lapsed with that emperor's death in 54, and there is good reason to believe that Peter did return to Rome at that time. See Note 116, below. In any case, Mark is specifically mentioned in Colossians 4:14 and Philemon 24 as in Rome during Paul's first imprisonment, in 61 and 62.

[88] Acts 15:40-16:3; Holzner, *Paul of Tarsus*, pp. 165-171.

[89] Ricciotti, *Paul the Apostle*, pp. 292-295. In these pages Ricciotti presents a convincing case against the theory, widely held even by orthodox writers, that the "Galatia" referred to at this point in Acts, and in Paul's Epistle to the Galatians, was not Galatia proper in north central Asia Minor (the region of Ancyra, modern Ankara) but Pisidia and Lycaonia which Paul had evangelized on his first missionary journey, and which were administratively included in the Roman province of Galatia (but, as Ricciotti shows, were still normally referred to by their older names).

[90] Ricciotti, *Paul the Apostle*, pp. 293-296.

[91] Acts 16:12-40; Ricciotti, *Paul the Apostle*, pp. 296-305, 474-477.

[92] Ricciotti, *Paul the Apostle*, pp. 305-313, 331-340.

[93] *Ibid.*, pp. 313-314.

[94] *Ibid.*, pp. 314-322; Acts 17:23; Fouard, *St. Paul and His Missions*, pp. 140-157.

[95] Acts 17:34; Ricciotti, *Paul the Apostle*, pp. 323-324.

[96] 1 Corinthians 1:23-24.

[97] Acts 18:1-17; Ricciotti, *Paul the Apostle*, pp. 324-331; Fouard, *St. Peter*, pp. 345-346; Edmundson, *Church in Rome*, p. 10. Gallio was proconsul in Achaia (Hellenic Greece) from May 51 to May 52 (Ogg, *Chronology of the Life of Paul*, pp. 104-111).

[98] *Cambridge Ancient History*, X, 416-417; Woodcock, *Greeks in India*, pp. 138-146. Hippalos' discovery of the monsoon route, formerly dated to 47 A.D., is now generally ascribed to the late first century B.C. But the maximum utilization of his discovery did not develop until the reign of Nero (54-68). The Kushan conquest of the north Indian realm of Gundofarr, to which Thomas had gone on his first Indian mission, came about

50 A.D. (Woodcock, *op. cit.*, p. 130) and Thomas may have had news of this and consequently changed his destination to the more peaceful south India. Peace and public order were very important prerequisities for the success of early Christian evangelization (which was one of the main reasons that it flourished more in the Roman empire under the *pax romana* than elsewhere).

[99] Moraes, *Christianity in India*, pp. 34, 40; George Woodcock, *Kerala, a Portrait of the Malabar Coast* (London, 1967), pp. 110-111. Cranganore was also known as Muziris.

[100] Moraes, *Christianity in India*, pp. 34-35, 37-38; James Brodrick, *St. Francis Xavier* (New York, 1952), pp. 110-112; Douglas Botting, *Island of the Dragon's Blood* [Socotra] (New York, 1958), pp. 214-223.

[101] L. W. Brown, *The Indian Christians of St. Thomas* (Cambridge, England, 1956), p. 62. Cf. H. S. Kehimkar, *The History of the Bene-Israel of India* (Tel Aviv, 1937).

[102] Matthew 28:20.

[103] Moraes, *Christianity in India*, p. 35.

[104] Woodcock, *Kerala*, pp. 110-111.

[105] Moraes, *Christianity in India*, p. 40; A. Mathias Mundadan, *Sixteenth Century Traditions of St. Thomas Christians* (Bangalore, India, 1970), pp. 64-65; A. Sreedhara Menon, *A Survey of Kerala History* (Kottayam, India, 1967), p. 99. The traditions mention seven churches as foundations by the Apostle Thomas himself in south India (J. N. Farquhar, "The Apostle Thomas in South India," *Bulletin of the John Rylands Library*, XI [1927], 22-23).

[106] Mundadan, *Traditions of St. Thomas Christians*, pp. 60-63.

[107] It is largely due to the absence of written records that Western historians have generally remained very skeptical of India's traditions of the Apostle Thomas (though one must note lamentable failures to investigate the question carefully, even on the part of some of the best and most orthodox). But the fact is that, except for a few inscriptions, all our knowledge of early Indian history comes from oral tradition which, where it pertains to major religious leaders and founders, is generally regarded by historians of India as reliable. The Vedas were transmitted orally for more than 1,500 years before being written down—approximately the length of time that the Thomas traditions were preserved orally until the coming of the Portuguese, if their dates are correct. See Chapter Seven, above. One striking example of the historical accuracy of the oral tradition of the St. Thomas Christians is the preservation in that tradition of the earliest of all designations for believers in Christ, Nazrani (Nazarenes or Nazoreans) as their name for themselves. The designation Christians, first given by the Romans to Greek converts in Antioch in the 40's, did not reach India for centuries. But the St. Thomas Christians knew and remembered the first century name of their brethren in far-off Palestine (Perumalil, *Apostles in India*, p. 97).

[108] Woodcock, *Kerala*, p. 113; Perumalil, *Apostles in India*, pp. 95-96; Henri Daniel-Rops, *The Church of Apostles and Martyrs* (New York, 1960), p. 106n. For an excellent description of the tenacious faith and high morality of the St. Thomas Christians and the great respect accorded them by other Indians of the Tamil region despite the difference in religion, at the time of the arrival of the Portuguese in 1498, see Moraes, *Christianity in India*, pp. 175-203. Doctrinal misunderstandings and aberrant practices deriving from the long centuries of separation were of remarkably little significance, and today most St. Thomas Christians are members of the Roman Catholic Church. A. Mingana trenchantly sums up the strength of the case for the historicity of the evangelization of India by the Apostle Thomas: "It is the constant tradition of the Eastern Church that the Apostle Thomas evangelized India, and there is no historian, no poet, no breviary, no liturgy, and no writer of any kind who, having the opportunity of speaking of Thomas, does not associate his name with India. Some writers also mention Parthia and Persia

among the lands evangelized by him, but all of them are unanimous on the matter of India. The name of Thomas can never be dissociated from that of India." ("The Early Spread of Christianity in India," *Bulletin of the John Rylands Library*, X [1926], 447-448).

[109] Perumalil, *Apostles in India*, pp. 71-89; Mundadan, *Traditions of St. Thomas Christians*, pp. 63, 72; Placid J. Podipara, *The Thomas Christians* (Bombay, 1970), pp. 22-25; Farquhar, "The Apostle Thomas in South India," *Bulletin of the John Rylands Library*, XI, 23, 34. The lance-head with which Thomas was killed was actually found when his tomb was opened by the Portuguese in 1523, and the bricks used to construct his original tomb have recently been shown to be of first century A.D. manufacture. Travellers' reports in extant writings dating from the sixth century attest to the uninterrupted veneration of Thomas' tomb at Mylapore.

[110] John 11:16.

[111] Henry Hosten, *Antiquities from San Thomé and Mylapore* (Mylapore, India, 1936), p. 307, reports that as late as the seventeenth century the Malabar Christians, when asked where St. Thomas died, would reply "at Maliapur Calurmina"—"on the stone at Mylapore."

[112] *Cambridge Ancient History*, X, 674-701. See Momigliano, *Claudius*, for a full statement of the case for a revised and more favorable view of Claudius as emperor.

[113] *Cambridge Ancient History*, X, 672-673, 696-697, 709-710. Fletcher Pratt in *Hail, Caesar!* calls the Ahenobarbus family Rome's "hereditary evil genius." The Domitius Ahenobarbus active during the last stages of Rome's civil wars certainly played a most devious and destructive role, exceeding almost all other participants in the frequency and perfidy of his betrayals.

[114] *Cambridge Ancient History*, X, 702-716; B. H. Warmington, *Nero, Reality and Legend* (New York, 1969), pp. 47-48. Warmington, who tries in many ways to tone down the traditional picture of Nero as a monster, nevertheless admits that the ancient sources which state categorically that Nero was involved in an incestuous relationship with his mother may well be correct.

[115] Ricciotti, *Paul the Apostle*, pp. 343-399.

[116] Edmundson, *Church in Rome*, pp. 80-85. Edmundson points out that the Liberian Catalogue of the Bishops of Rome erroneously states that Peter's Roman episcopate ended in 55, and attributes the error to a misunderstanding of the significance of the ordination of Peter's two successors at that time, which almost certainly would have been done by Peter himself while he was in Rome. That this occurred in the very year following the death of Claudius and the consequent lapsing of his edict banishing the Jews from Rome is strong presumptive evidence in support of Edmundson's thesis that Peter returned at this time to Rome, as soon as he was legally able to do so. On Peter in Rome during this sojourn, see also Walsh, *St. Peter*, pp. 279-282, 288-289, and F. F. Bruce, *Paul, Apostle of the Free Spirit* (Exeter, England, 1977), p. 392; on the writing of Mark's Gospel, see Fouard, *St. Peter*, pp. 367-380, and Chapman, *Matthew, Mark and Luke*, pp. 90-92. Chapman presents a very impressive argument that Peter actually used the Gospel of Matthew in giving Mark the catechesis for his Gospel. Holding that Peter was in Rome when Paul wrote his Epistle to the Romans, Barnes (*Christianity at Rome*, pp. 44-50) argues that Paul would not have "built on another man's foundation" by writing to the Christian community in Rome if Peter were *not* there. For a good explanation of why he might in fact have done exactly that, see Ricciotti, *Paul the Apostle*, pp. 390-391.

[117] Acts 18:24-28, 19:1-3; 1 Corinthians 1:12, 3:5-6.

[118] Eusebius, *Ecclesiastical History*, II, 15, 24; Fouard, *St. Peter*, pp. 379-380; Atiya, *History of Eastern Christianity*, pp. 27-28; see Note 141, below. Fouard's arguments for the historicity of the Marcan foundation of the church of Alexandria are at least strong enough to arouse astonishment at the cavalier dismissal of this long-established tradition even in orthodox histories (*e.g.*, Lebreton and Zeiller, *Primitive Church*, I, 365-366). Eusebius preserves a complete dated list of the early bishops of Alexandria, beginning with St. Mark. This is just the kind of list that the church in a city as literate and historically conscious as Alexandria would have been most careful to keep. We know that Eusebius regularly consulted original sources, including both church and public archives. The dovetailing of Eusebius' dating of Anianus' succession with Peter's probable return to Rome adds significantly to the probability that Eusebius' information on this matter was correct.

[119] Luke 9:51; Acts 20:16.

[120] Acts 20:16, 22; Ricciotti, *Paul the Apostle*, pp. 398-407.

[121] On this point see Lebreton and Zeiller, *Primitive Church*, I, 300-304, and Constant Fouard, *The Last Years of Saint Paul* (New York, 1900), pp. 28-46.

[122] Ricciotti, *Paul the Apostle*, pp. 413-452. The traditional chronology of the procuratorship of Festus (60-62), which has recently come under considerable attack, is well defended by Ogg, *Chronology of the Life of Paul*, pp. 146-170.

[123] *Ibid.*, pp. 452-458, 100-102, 111-112; Robinson, *Redating the New Testament*, pp. 89-91.

[124] Ricciotti, *Paul the Apostle*, p. 480; Fouard, *St. Peter*, pp. 407-408; Garcia Villada, *Historia Eclesiástica de España*, I, 147. John J. Gunther, *Paul: Messenger and Exile, a Study in the Chronology of His Life and Letters* (Valley Forge PA, 1972), pp. 144-148, makes the interesting and quite plausible suggestion that Paul was exiled to Spain by the Roman authorities when insufficient evidence was brought forward in his case for a capital conviction.

[125] *Cambridge Ancient History* X, 720-721; Warmington, *Nero*, pp. 49-50.

[126] Fouard, *St. Peter*, pp. 335-342; Ricciotti, *Paul the Apostle*, pp. 329-330.

[127] Ricciotti, *Paul the Apostle*, pp. 92-94, 101; Lebreton and Zeiller, *Primitive Church*, I, 375.

[128] *Cambridge Ancient History* X, 722-725; Walsh, *St. Peter*, pp. 299-303.

[129] On this much-debated issue see Lebreton and Zeiller, *Primitive Church*, I, 375-381; Fouard, *Last Years of St. Paul*, pp. 130-138; W. H. C. Frend, *Martyrdom and Persecution in the Early Church* (New York, 1967), pp. 126-130; A. N. Sherwin-White, "The Early Persecutions and Roman Law Again," *Journal of Theological Studies*, n.s. III (1952-53), 199-213. All sides in the debate agree that most Christians during the early persecutions were executed simply for being Christians—for bearing the Name. No other specific charge had to be made and proved against them to obtain a death sentence. Hence the martyrs' other designation: confessors. Fouard (*op. cit.*, pp. 137n-138n) quotes the very powerful—and much neglected—argument of the French jurist Guérin on the significance of this designation: "The avowal made thus before a magistrate was styled *confessio*, and the delinquent who had recourse to it was known as a *confessus*, against whom it was no longer necessary to bring any proof of the facts alleged. The *confessio* carried with it certain very serious consequences to the prisoner at the bar; once uttered, there was no more defence possible, and the assistance of an advocate became superfluous. The penalty inflicted by the law must be at once pronounced, and Roman lawyers were wont to say, in their terse and energetic style, that the accused passed sentence on himself. . . . It is worthy of note that the Christians adopted this name of *Confessi*, or Confessors of the Faith, as a glorious title indicating that they had affirmed their faith in the face

of a magistrate. Had they been prosecuted for sacrilege, *lese majeste*, or any other of-
fence, they certainly would never have done this. For the *confessio* was then applied
to this misdemeanor, and not to the Christian Faith.''

¹³⁰ Tertullian, *Ad Nationes* I, 7, 9 and *Apologeticus* 5; Jedin and Dolan, *History of
the Church*, I, 130. Tertullian was, after all, a highly intelligent practicing lawyer who
had personally observed the trials of Christian martyrs; it is rather absurd to behold preten-
tious scholars 1,700 years later lecturing him on his ignorance of the law against which
he was striving, by insisting that Christians were *not* condemned—as Tertullian said they
were condemned—under a general law which denied their right to exist, but rather under
other general legislation or police regulations not designed specifically for them (*e.g.*,
Sherwin-White in the article cited in Note 129, above). Timothy D. Barnes, *Tertullian,
a Historical and Literary Study* (Oxford, 1971), on p. 140 declares there was no general
law making Christianity a criminal offense, but on p. 146 admits that an individual's
mere affirmation that he was a Christian was equivalent to a plea of guilty! This is not
to presume that we know exactly what form the law banning Christians took, nor to
overlook the fact that the ban—like most prohibitive laws where no overtly dangerous
conduct is involved—was by no means uniformly or always rigorously enforced.

¹³¹ G. K. Chesterton, *The Everlasting Man* (New York, 1925), p. 197.

¹³² Fouard, *Last Years of St. Paul*, pp. 124-129; Fouard, *St. John*, p. 45; see Chapter
Eighteen, below.

¹³³ It is puzzling to discover how many otherwise sound histories of the Apostolic
Age doubt or even deny that the Neronian persecution extended to the provinces, when
we have the clear evidence of the first letter of Peter speaking of the ''fiery ordeal''
which the churches of Asia Minor were about to undergo. To doubt or deny the extension of the Neronian persecution to the provinces is therefore a logical position only
for the historian who explicitly denies the authenticity of 1 Peter. But its authenticity
is much more widely accepted among Biblical scholars today than is the authenticity
of 2 Peter, *e.g.*, C. E. B. Cranfield, *I and II Peter and Jude, Introduction and Commentary* (London, 1960), pp. 14-176. *Cambridge Ancient History* X, 725-726 at least
recognizes that we have no evidence *against* the extension, but fails to mention 1 Peter.
Lebreton and Zeiller, *Primitive Church*, I, 374-375, favor the extension but also do not
mention 1 Peter. Frend, *Martyrdom and Persecution*, p. 52, and Jedin and Dolan, *History
of the Church*, I, 130-131, flatly deny the extension, but also without mentioning 1 Peter.
In fact, the Neronian persecution was ever afterward recognized as the origin of the
outlawry of Christians throughout the empire.

¹³⁴ See Note 86, above; Fouard, *Last Years of St. Paul*, pp. 138-153; Barnes, *Christianity at Rome*, pp. 102-103; Walsh, *St. Peter*, pp. 303-305. 1 Peter states that it is
written from ''Babylon,'' a common symbolical name for Rome at this time among both
Jews and Christians (Lebreton and Zeiller, *Primitive Church*, I, 289-290). The fluent
Greek in which the letter is written is almost certainly not Peter's own, but can readily
be explained by the editing and polishing of Silvanus (Silas) ''by'' whom, Peter says,
''I have written'' (1 Peter 5:12).

¹³⁵ 1 Peter 4:12-13.

¹³⁶ Ricciotti, *Paul the Apostle*, pp. 480-485.

¹³⁷ Eusebius, *Ecclesiastical History*, II, 23; Fouard, *Last Years of St. Paul*, pp. 28-46;
Smallwood, *Jews under Roman Rule*, pp. 279-280.

¹³⁸ Ricciotti, *Paul the Apostle*, pp. 490-497. St. Simeon, the successor of James the
Just as bishop of Jerusalem, was not elected until after the Christian community in
Jerusalem had fled to Pella and Jerusalem had been destroyed (Lebreton and Zeiller,
Primitive Church, I, 307). Consequently the community was leaderless from 62 to 70.

¹³⁹ Ricciotti, *History of Israel*, II, 399-406, 240; Smallwood, *Jews under Roman Rule*,

pp. 292-298; Fouard, *Last Years of St. Paul*, p. 194.

[140] *Cambridge Ancient History*, X, 735-737, 828; Ricciotti, *History of Israel*, II, 409-411.

[141] For a good, though somewhat over-cautious recent review of the evidence establishing Peter's presence and martyrdom in Rome (there has never been much serious question regarding Paul's) see Jedin and Dolan, *History of the Church*, I, 112-118; for Vespasian's campaign of 67, see Ricciotti, *History of Israel*, II, 411-416. The traditional date of 67 for the martyrdom of Peter and Paul in Rome rests ultimately on the authority of Jerome (Edmundson, *Church in Rome*, pp. 147-151; see also Fouard, *St. Peter*, pp. 407-408). Sound chronological reconstructions of Paul's life, based on the premise that all his canonical epistles are authentic, require at least two years of continued ministry after 64 (Ricciotti, *Paul the Apostle*, pp. 480-485). There is no good reason to believe, as is commonly and unreflectively held, that Nero's persecution of the Christians was confined entirely to the year of the Great Fire in Rome, 64, and that Peter and Paul were necessarily martyred in that year, as leaders of the Church and consequently prime targets of the persecution. On the contrary, our evidence indicates that Paul was not even in Rome that year (see Note 124, above), though Peter very probably was. Nor is it likely that the Roman authorities in Nero's reign yet understood enough about the structure and history of the Christian Church to know how especially important Peter and Paul were. Bruce, *Paul*, says Paul was executed during Nero's persecution, without special emphasis on his personal significance, and that his martyrdom was in 65 or 66 rather than in 64 (p. 450).

[142] Eusebius, *Ecclesiastical History*, II, 22; Ricciotti, *Paul the Apostle*, pp. 499-502.

[143] Fouard, *Last Years of St. Paul*, pp. 250-253; Dauvilliers, *Les Temps apostoliques*, pp. 287-288; John E. Walsh, *The Bones of St. Peter* (Garden City NY, 1982), pp. 164-165. Walsh points out that the bones finally identified as Peter's, while containing at least fragments of most of the bones of the body including the fingers, include no foot bones at all, suggesting in explanation that Peter's feet might have been severed by the Roman soldiers when they took his body down from the cross after his crucifixion head downward.

[144] For the extraordinary history of the excavation under St. Peter's and the probable finding of the Apostle's bones, see especially Walsh, *Bones of St. Peter*, *passim*; the earlier account in Englebert Kirschbaum, *The Tombs of St. Peter and St. Paul* (New York, 1957) thoroughly reports the excavations but was written before the bones under the graffiti wall, most probably Peter's, were discovered. The bones found directly under the altar, originally thought and reported to be Peter's and still believed to be his by Kirschbaum when he wrote his cited book, were later proved to be the bones of an elderly woman. Walsh sets forth very well the strong circumstantial evidence supporting the authenticity of the bones found under the graffiti wall, on which Pope Paul VI relied in his announcement June 27, 1968 that the bones of St. Peter had been found. The bones seem to have been moved from the original grave during the worst periods of persecution of Christians by the emperors, in the 250's under Decius and Valerian and in the first decade of the fourth century (300-310) by Diocletian and Galerius. That Peter, in any case, was known by the early Christians to be buried on Vatican hill under the present St. Peter's is now firmly established, despite doubts and reservations expressed in Jedin and Dolan, *History of the Church*, I, 117-118 and the flat denials of Cullmann, *Peter*, pp. 138-157. The case for Peter's martyrdom and burial in Rome is well summed up by Dauvilliers, *Les Temps apostoliques*, pp. 288-292, though Dauvilliers does not accept the identification of the bones of St. Peter by Pope Paul VI and Margharita Guarducci, as set forth in Walsh, *op. cit.*

[145] Margherita Guarducci, *The Tomb of St. Peter* (New York, 1960), pp. 182-183.

[146] 2 Timothy 4:21; Fouard, *Last Years of St. Paul*, p. 236; Fouard, *St. John*, p. 49.

[147] Luke 23:28-31.

[148] Ricciotti, *History of Israel*, II, 417-418; Frend, *Martyrdom and Persecution*, pp. 131-132, 455. This withdrawal, attested by Eusebius (*Ecclesiastical History*, III, 2-3) and in two places by Epiphanius two centuries later, is alone sufficient to dispose of the hypothesis that Jesus and His followers were revolutionaries allied with the Zealots (see Chapter Sixteen, above). Therefore one of the advocates of this hypothesis, S. G. F. Brandon, in *The Fall of Jerusalem and the Christian Church* (London, 1957), pp. 168-173, presents an elaborate argument against the historicity of the flight on grounds of military improbability at any stage of Vespasian's campaign in Palestine. His arguments against the flight occurring or being feasible in the years 66 and 67 have merit, but his argument against a flight in the year 68 seems to be based entirely on the assumptions that (1) the Christians could not have got out of Jerusalem, even before it was besieged, because the nationalist leaders hated deserters and killed them whenever they could catch them; and (2) if they had got out, the Romans would have massacred them because they hated all Jews. Hatred was unquestionably virulent during these terrible years, but the experience of refugees in all wars tells decisively against both these assumptions as reflecting a general rule justifying the rejection of otherwise reliable and well attested historical evidence. Not all or even most refugees are killed by either side in a war, however bitterly contested.

[149] Ricciotti, *History of Israel*, II, 418-423; *Cambridge Ancient History*, X, 738-741, 811-829. A particularly good and thorough account of the "year of the four emperors" is that of Kenneth Wellesley, *The Long Year—A.D. 69* (London, 1976).

[150] *Cambridge Ancient History*, X, 829-839.

[151] Luke 19:43-44.

[152] Ricciotti, *History of Israel*, II, 423-433.

[153] Matthew 24:15-18.

[154] Ricciotti, *History of Israel*, II, 433-436.

[155] Josephus, *Jewish War*, VI, 255-277; Ricciotti, *History of Israel*, II, 437-439. Smallwood, *Jews under Roman Rule*, pp. 324-326, doubts Josephus' testimony that Titus wished to spare the Temple and that his soldiers refused to obey him in this regard, giving credence rather to an account by Sulpicius Severus three centuries later. Josephus' contemporary report is clearly to be preferred.

[156] Ricciotti, *History of Israel*, II, 440-442; Michael Grant, *The Jews in the Roman World* (New York, 1973), p. 201.

[157] See Giuseppe Ricciotti, *Julian the Apostate* (Milwaukee, 1960), pp. 223-226.

18.
THE SEED IN THE EARTH (70-249)

See what love the Father has given us, that we should be called children of God, and so we are. The reason why the world does not know us is that it did not know him. Beloved, we are God's children now; it does not yet appear what we shall be, but we know that when he appears we shall be like him, for we shall see him as he is. And every one who thus hopes in him purifies himself as he is pure.—1 John 3:1-3

As the great world had not known, and barely noticed Jesus Christ when He was physically dwelling within it, neither did it, for a very long time, know or more than barely notice His followers who came after Him, and the Church they were building. For no less than 179 years of Roman history after the fall of Jerusalem, Christianity remained almost invisible to contemporaries. During that period it also remains obscure to us, even after the most careful historical investigations. Lofty theories and many-chambered reconstructions must be built up from single sentences or paragraphs in the few Christian writings or notices about Christians which have come down to us from that long span of some seven generations. Toward the end of it the Church emerges a little more into public view. Yet in the reign of Alexander Severus (222-235) it was still possible for Cassius Dio to write an immense and authoritative history of the world in many volumes without once mentioning the Christians.[1]

The seed Christ had sown was in the earth, hidden from most human eyes.

But like the germinating seed in fertile soil, it was putting forth sprouts and roots in the sheltering dark, so that when at last it broke through into the open air, not all the storms and stress of the greater world could kill it.

Yet the Church had a false dawn, of which we know only the faintest outlines. In the year 90, less than a century after the Incarnation, the two young heirs to the empire seem to have been Christians.[2] If they had attained power and kept the Faith, the whole of subsequent history might have been different; for the Roman empire of the year 90 was a much more healthy, salvageable society than that of 313 which the first Christian emperor, Constantine, came to rule.

But it was not to be. Probably the Church was not yet ready for so great an apparent opportunity. It had come about in a way whose details must remain conjectural. Titus Flavius Sabinus, elder brother of the Emperor Vespasian, had been prefect of the city of Rome in 64, during Nero's persecution. In all probability he was converted to the martyrs' faith then, or soon afterward, by the power of their sacrifice, example, and prayers.[3] His wife may have been a daughter of the great lady Pomponia Graecina who was probably one of Peter's first Roman converts.[4] Their son Flavius Clemens, also a Christian, married Vespasian's granddaughter Flavia Domitilla, who became a Christian. Their two sons, at ages six and five, being raised as Christians, were proclaimed heirs to the childless Emperor Domitian, their great-uncle, in 90.[5]

Up to this point the policy of the Flavian emperors—Vespasian and his sons Titus and Domitian who succeeded him—had been uniformly and entirely tolerant toward Christianity, probably due to the presence of so many Christians or Christian sympathizers in their family. Not a single martyrdom or persecution under them is recorded from 70 to 90.[6] Popes[7] Linus and Cletus ruled the Church in peace. (See Chronological Table of Emperors and Popes 70-249.) Of Cletus we know only that, like Linus, he had been a slave, named derisively Anencletus or "blameless"; on becoming head of the Church he changed his name to Cletus, "the one called."[8] Christianity made considerable progress during these years, particularly in Asia Minor. But it was not yet really known or understood by more than a very few people in Rome. Christians were seen as misanthropic crypto-Jews, who renounced and despised human society. Even the Flavian emperors did not repeal Nero's laws against them, merely suspending their enforcement and consequently leaving the Christians totally dependent for their security upon the continuation of imperial good will.[9]

When Cletus died—in 92, according to Eusebius—his successor was Clement, whom Peter himself had ordained. Since the principal patron of Christianity at this time was probably the Emperor's cousin Flavius Clemens, father of the heirs to the empire, the similarity of the fourth Pope's name to his is unlikely to be coincidental. It has been speculated, with good reason, that Clement was a freedman, formerly a slave in the h;ousehold of Flavius Clemens, who had taken the name of his former master and the Christians' benefactor,

---

CHRONOLOGICAL TABLE OF ROMAN EMPERORS AND POPES
(70-249)

Roman Emperors	Popes (dates approx. before 189)
Vespasian 70-79	Linus 67-81
	Titus 79-81
Domitian 81-96	Cletus 81-92
Nerva 96-98	Clement I 92-101
Trajan 98-117	Evaristus 101-108
	Alexander I 108-115
Hadrian 117-138	Sixtus I 115-125
	Telesphorus 125-136
Antoninus Pius 138-161	Hyginus 136-140
	Pius I 140-155
	Anicetus 155-166
Marcus Aurelius 161-180	Soter 166-175
Commodus 180-192	Eleutherius 175-189
Pertinax 193	Victor I 189-199
Didius Julianus 193	
Septimius Severus 193-211	Zephyrinus 199-217
Caracalla 211-217	
Macrinus 217	
Elagabalus 217-222	Callistus I 217-222
Alexander Severus 222-235	Urban I 222-230
	Pontian 230-235
Maximus Thrax 235-238	Anteros 235-236
Gordian III 238-244	Fabian 236-250
Philip the Arab 244-249	

---

in gratitude after being freed.[10] In these circumstances there was a distinct possibility that the head of Christ's Church would soon become the close advisor of a future emperor.

But then an ugly change came over Domitian. He had ruled reasonably well for nine years. Now he appointed to the annual consulate, one after another, members of his family and others who probably were, or may possibly have been Christians, and then proceeded to eliminate them. He ordered Acilius Glabrio, consul for 91, to fight wild beasts in the arena. When Glabrio slew the lion set upon him, Domitian sent him into exile, accusing him of "novelties"—probably religious—and later executed him. Glabrio's family later became Christian, but it is not known definitely that he did. In 93 M. Arrecinus Clemens, a relative of the emperor and of Flavius Clemens, was made consul and then executed. Next came Titus Flavius Sabinus III, son of the Christian of the same name who had been prefect of the city of Rome during Nero's persecution, the husband of Domitian's niece and the brother of Flavius Clemens. He was made consul in 94 and then executed. The consul and victim for 95 was Flavius Clemens himself, charged with "atheism," "Jewish practices," and *maiestas* (lack of respect for Roman institutions)—a combination of charges almost certainly adding up to Christianity as Roman law then viewed it. He too was executed.[11]

Hating and fearing all the world to the point of insanity—a story is told of how he spent most of his time in a specially constructed hall of polished surfaces acting as mirrors so as to be able to see anyone who might be creeping up behind him—Domitian's last days were a horror for himself and for those he ruled resembling the last days of Herod. In the year 96 he was struck down by the dagger of Stephanos, a freedman of his victim Flavius Clemens, acting in concert with the praetorian prefects and other palace officials, who then had an elderly and virtuous senator named Nerva proclaimed emperor. Though a very good man, Nerva knew nothing of Christianity and showed no interest in learning about it. We do not know what happened to the two little Christian boys who had been Domitian's heirs.[12]

The persecution of Domitian was directed against Christians throughout the empire as well as against Christian members of the imperial family. Christians in the province of Bithynia in Asia Minor were forced to renounce their faith.[13] John, the last of the Apostles, now about eighty years old,[14] was sent to the bleak Aegean island of Patmos, where he received the cosmic vision recorded in his Apocalypse, sent with a letter warning seven of the churches of Asia Minor against the consequences of an evident decline in the original fervor of their faith.[15] First of all, John called on the church of Ephesus to repent for a lessening of love despite "your works, your toil and your patient endurance."[16] There is good reason to believe that Timothy—St. Paul's Timothy—was still bishop at Ephesus, and that, taking St. John's strictures very much to heart, he challenged the licentious public rituals for the goddess Diana (in whose name St. Paul had been driven out of that same Ephesus) and was martyred for it in the year 97.[17]

Elsewhere, peace and obscurity returned to the Church during the brief reign of Nerva (96-98). It was in all probability then that Pope Clement I wrote to the church in Corinth directing its members to end a revolt against their elders, and offering extensive guidance on living the Christian life through the imitation of Christ. His letter, commanding obedience, is the earliest Christian document we possess outside the New Testament. Its explicit assumption of authority over a distant church speaking another language (Greek), while the last of the Apostles still lived, stated in a manner clearly indicating that no challenge to the authority of its writer is anticipated or would be entertained, is the most striking of all the historical proofs of the general acceptance by Christians, from the beginning of the Church, of the Bishop of Rome as the successor of Peter and the head of the whole Church. The most authoritative language in the letter is Clement's warning: "If some shall disobey the words which have been spoken by Him [Christ] through us, let them know they will involve themselves in no small transgression and danger."[18]

Almost as significant in the letter of Clement as this clear-cut assertion of the Roman primacy in the Church is its statement about the apostolic succession of bishops. The letter of Clement falls within the period of the primitive church, by any reasonable definition of that term; likewise it clearly falls within the Apostolic Age. Together with the epistles of St. Ignatius, Bishop of Antioch, about twenty years later, it supplies proof of the existence in that primitive Christian church, in the Apostolic Age, of a well-developed episcopate in direct succession from the Apostles. (However, collegial government by a group of bishops and elders was apparently the practice in many churches—including that of Corinth itself—from the martyrdom of Peter and Paul to the time of Ignatius, when administration by a single bishop became almost universal.)[19] Clement stated:

> The apostles preached the gospel to us from the Lord Jesus Christ. Christ, therefore, is from God, and the apostles are from Christ. Both things, accordingly, came in proper order by the will of God . . . They [the apostles] went forth preaching the gospel. . . . As they preached, therefore, in the countryside and in the cities, they [regularly][20] appointed their first fruits— after having tested them through the Spirit—to be bishops and deacons of the future believers . . .[21]

> Our apostles also knew that there would be strife for the name of bishop. For this cause, therefore . . . they appointed those who have been already mentioned [bishops and deacons] and afterwards gave [it as a rule][22] that if they should fall asleep other approved men should succeed to their ministry.[23]

Though there is no solidly authentic evidence for his martyrdom, nor any significant contemporary or near-contemporary information about him except that he had personally known and been taught by the Apostles Peter and Paul, and wrote the letter to the Corinthians, Pope Clement I became a heroic and romantic figure in Christian lore from an early date. Wondrous legends and anonymous writings gathered about his revered name. His letter was never forgotten. It continued to be widely read and was accorded an authority second only to Scripture itself.[24]

When Pope Clement I died about the year 101, the Apostle John was approximately ninety years of age.[25] He had settled in Ephesus, probably immediately after Timothy's martyrdom there in 97, and remained in that city until his death, preparing his gospel with the help of assistants, and writing his canonical letters. He did not become bishop of Ephesus, for his authority as the last of the Apostles was unique in the whole Church; Onesimus, Philemon's

runaway slave whom Paul had so kindly received, and mentioned so affectionate-
ly in his letter to Philemon, was bishop of Ephesus somewhat later, and was
probably Timothy's immediate successor.[26]

Soon afterward there came to the province of Asia one Cerinthus, who had
been trained in the great intellectual melting-pot of Alexandria. He had been
a Jew; he was circumcised and still kept the Sabbath. Now he called himself
a Christian. But he taught a new, strange doctrine: that the creator of the world
was not God, but some inferior though supernatural being who did not even
know God; and that Jesus was not the Christ, not God Incarnate, when He was
born or when He died, but only for the period of His public life from His baptism to Gethsemane, where God did in fact abandon Him. It was only the poor
human Jesus of Nazareth Who had died on the Cross, and His body had never
risen at all. God had never really come to earth to "pitch His tent" among men,
except in some vague spiritual sense; He was "utterly other," alien to the world
as the world was alien to Him. This was the higher knowledge—*gnosis*. This
was Gnosticism.[27]

John, the son of Zebedee, had stood at the foot of the Cross. He had lived
through that hideous afternoon when, if ever in all time and history, God had
seemed withdrawn from creation—yet John knew that God had been there, body,
blood, soul and divinity, on Calvary. John had seen Mary's face as the nails
were hammered through the flesh of the Lord of Light, her Son. He was ninety
years old and it had been seventy years ago, but it was burned into his mind
and heart with the immediacy of eternity. No man could tell John the Evangelist
that Jesus Christ was not God; no man could tell John the Evangelist that Jesus
Christ was not human. John had seen Him live, seen Him die, seen Him risen.
Jesus Christ had reconciled God and the world. Through Him, by Him and
because of Him, God could never again be a stranger, never an "utterly other."

Cerinthus and most of his followers were not really Christians, but disappointed Jews who could not endure the shattering of their hopes by the catastrophe
that had struck Jerusalem in 70. In the shadow of that disaster, their hatred for
the created world grew. Among the Jewish rabbis there had remained many
noble souls, good and profoundly sane even in the face of cataclysm, who clung
to most of the truth God had given their people, in the old dispensation; within
Judaism they had largely prevailed. But the world-haters had left Judaism while
never embracing Christ. Outcasts from both faiths, they had made up their own
synthesis with elements drawn from the degeneracy of Hellenistic philosophy,
a pale mask of pride over the face of death. It is probable that Cerinthus condemned marriage and childbirth as coming from Satan, as did the Gnostics Sator-
nil in Antioch and Basilides in Alexandria who came soon after Cerinthus. It
was only a short step from the Gnostic doctrine of an evil world created by
a spirit alien to God, to making Satan the *creator*, not merely the dethroned
ruler, of the world of men.[28]

John abhorred this blasphemy to the depths of his being. His disciple Polycarp often recalled how, when he went to the baths of Ephesus one day and saw Cerinthus there, he rushed out—once again the "Son of Thunder"—exclaiming: "Let us fly, lest even the bath-house fall down, because Cerinthus, the enemy of the truth, is within."[29]

Living on into the reign of Trajan, Nerva's hand-picked successor, a hard but in many ways virtuous general from Spain, John probably died during the first decade of the second century (100-110), before the martyrdom of Ignatius of Antioch, which probably took place in 116.[30] Since copies of John's Gospel had spread as far as southern Egypt by 130, and St. Ignatius appears to have known it, his Gospel was probably first published about 105 or 110.[31] In his last years John was constantly repeating to his flock: "My little children, love one another."[32] In his second and third Epistles he calls himself simply "the elder."[33] This man, whom Jesus and Mary so dearly loved, who may have been the finest writer humanity has ever known, in the fullness of his authority as the last of the Apostles, through whom revelation still continued, with whose death it ceased, was the humblest of men, at the service of all. Stories were told and retold of how John would work and pray and fast and travel, despite his advanced age, to bring back even one who had fallen away from the Faith.[34] In view of the surpassing, gentle charity which radiates from every sentence of his letters and his Gospel, one is appalled to read in his third epistle of Diotrephes, a bishop or priest in charge of a church in Asia Minor, who "does not acknowledge my authority" and "is prating against me with evil words."[35] How grim a foreshadowing of the Church's millennial struggle against enemies within—almost always more dangerous than enemies without—to find here, as early as the end of the first century of the Christian era, a priest of Jesus Christ refusing to acknowledge the authority of the last survivor of the Twelve Apostles, who was actually living nearby, and "prating against [him] with evil words"!

About the time of the Apostle John's death, Emperor Trajan had completed his conquest of Dacia (now Rumania), triumphantly extending the Roman frontier in eastern Europe well to the north of the Danube River, where it had been fixed for more than a century.[36] It seemed that the victorious, popular, and militarily capable emperor might usher in a whole new age of conquests. Of mature years (45) when he became emperor, through his first decade he had ruled well. When his governor Pliny in Bithynia in Asia Minor reported the great growth of the sect called Christian, which led many of the neighbors and foes of these Christians to denounce them to the authorities, Trajan accepted as a matter of course and tradition the outlawry of Christianity, but ordered Pliny not to initiate prosecution of Christians nor entertain anonymous accusations against them.[37]

This combination of an apparently genuine desire to mitigate the suffering caused by an utterly unjust law, with a total lack of interest in even considering that law's origins, reasons for being, and prospective repeal, tells us a great deal about Trajan and the other "good emperors" who followed him during the second century of the Christian era. For them, the essential structure of the empire was never to be changed. They strongly felt an obligation to administer it well. But social, cultural, and intellectual growth was at an end for old Rome. Trajan was the last emperor to attempt even physical expansion, and Dacia was his only enduring success along that line. The Christian could not look upon the Roman empire and its preservation as the highest good. This made him automatically guilty of *maiestas* and liable, following public denunciation and proof of his affiliation, to death.

So had died, in the year 107, Simeon, bishop of Jerusalem in exile, at Pella beyond the Jordan where he and his Jewish Christian community had lived since the siege and destruction of Jerusalem in 70, from which Jesus' forewarning had rescued them. There is good reason to believe that this martyr bishop was one of the cousins of Jesus mentioned in the gospels, together with James and Joseph and Jude (Simeon being simply a variant way of writing or saying the name "Simon," which is linked with these other three in the gospels). He need not have been of improbably great age for this to be true; if he were of approximately the same age as the Apostle John or just a little younger (which the gospel references, mentioning him only briefly and in passing, by no means preclude) he would not yet have been a centenarian in 107.[38] The practice regarding Christians which Trajan outlined five years later to Pliny in Bithynia was followed by the Roman authorities in Palestine in the case of Simeon. No action was taken against him until others formally denounced him. His accusers were Christian heretics of the Judaizing sect later known as Ebionites. They seem to have formerly been members of a Qumran-type Essene community broken up in the upheavals that accompanied and followed the Roman destruction of Jerusalem. Isolated as Essene communities were, it would probably not have heard any clear and circumstantial account of the events of 30 A.D. in Jerusalem—of the Passion and the Resurrection. Persons coming out of this kind of community, impressed by the teaching of Christ but still devoted to the Jewish Law and their own Essene traditions, would look upon Jesus as a great teacher but not as God Incarnate Who rose from the dead—just as the later Ebionites regarded him. Simeon, who knew the truth first-hand, would have tried to demonstrate their error and lead them to a full understanding and appreciation of the divinity of Christ. The Qumran documents reveal a very aggressive, unbending mentality. Some among these Essene semi-Christians, very likely reacting to correction with hatred, apparently brought about Simeon's martyrdom. The informers too were executed, having been found to be—at least by the government's standards—Christians like the man they had accused and so, like him, under the ban.[39]

The year after Pliny expressed his worries about the Christians in Bithynia to the Emperor Trajan, war flared up in the east between Rome and Parthia over an old bone of contention: Armenia. Each power supported its own candidate for king of that ever-debatable territory, once more embroiled in civil strife. Trajan made his base for military operations at Antioch. Abgar VII of Edessa, caught in the middle, tried unavailingly to mediate. Full of confidence because of his victory in Dacia, Trajan moved forward massively, occupying Armenia and northern Mesopotamia and establishing a strong frontier line. Victorious again, to all appearances, he returned to Antioch late in 115.[40]

At dawn on December 13, 115 a devastating earthquake struck Antioch. Great buildings cracked and tumbled; thousands were killed, including one of Rome's consuls for that year. The emperor himself was injured. After-shocks continued for days. As in Rome after the Great Fire of 64, the people found a scapegoat in the Christians, and began denouncing them in large numbers. By his own rules as explained to Pliny, Trajan could not overlook such formal accusations; he had to condemn to death the accused who were found to be truly Christians.[41]

As with Simeon at Pella, the first Christian to be denounced in this sudden persecution at Antioch was the bishop of the city. His name was Ignatius—a Latin name in Semitic Syria, though he was a native Syrian. Apparently a convert, he speaks of himself as "one born out of time," like Paul.[42] His seven letters, which contain virtually all we know of him, blaze across the obscurity deriving from the scant Christian records of that early age like a shower of brilliant meteors. All of them were written from Smyrna and Troas on the east coast of Asia Minor during two or three weeks in the summer of 116, when he was already on his way from Antioch to Rome to be thrown to the wild beasts in the arena.[43] (Trajan had a particular fondness for the bloody gladiatorial games, presenting them on a scale never before seen in Rome; it is the darkest blot on his character. He conducted no less than 123 consecutive days of them in 107 to celebrate his conquest of Dacia.)[44] The circumstances are little known and somewhat puzzling. Transportation of Christian prisoners from other parts of the empire to Rome for martyrdom in the arena is known in few if any other cases. But no games could then be held in Antioch because of the earthquake damage, and for some reason this was the death Trajan decided Ignatius must die, perhaps because of his very prominence in the Church. He had been at least thirty years a bishop, probably trained by the Apostle John, and was apparently at this time the most venerated living member of the whole Church. (Nothing whatever is known—beyond their names, nationality and approximate dates—of the reigning Popes during these years: Evaristus, Alexander I, and Sixtus I.)[45]

In his letters to the churches in Asia, Ignatius explains and condemns the principal heresies of his time, already mentioned—that of the Gnostics, which he rejected in glowing words about the Incarnation almost worthy of John the Evangelist; and that of Judaizers like the Ebionites, who had betrayed Simeon.[46]

Ignatius repeatedly emphasized the central, predominant role of the bishop in the Christian community—the bishop who must above all be respected and obeyed in all matters concerning the Church, who alone may authorize the celebration of the Mass. There can be no doubt that Ignatius held a concept of the office of bishop virtually identical to that held by the Catholic Church ever since, and by the Greek Orthodox and Episcopalian (Anglican) churches throughout their histories. Of alleged primitive congregationalism there is no trace, though this was in all probability still within ten or a dozen years of the death of the last Apostle.[47]

Then Ignatius wrote "to that church which presides in the region of the Romans, worthy of honor, worthy of blessing, worthy of praise, worthy to be heard, worthy in purity, presiding in the love."[48] The unusual phrase "presiding in *the* love" suggests a view of the whole Church as a community representing "the love"—the love of Christ—over which the Roman Church presides.[49] But the letter of St. Ignatius of Antioch to the Romans soars far above questions of Church government, even the most important. One can only quote its climactic passages, and meditate upon them; comment would be superfluous, or worse.

> You can do me no greater kindness than to suffer me to be sacrificed to God while the place of sacrifice is still prepared. Thus forming yourselves into a chorus of love, you may sing to the Father in Jesus Christ that God gave the bishop of Syria the grace of being transferred from the rising to the setting sun. It is good to set, leaving the world for God, and so to rise in Him. . . . Beg only that I may have inward and outward strength, not only in mind but in will, that I may be a Christian not merely in name but in fact. For, if I am one in fact, then I may be called one and be faithful long after I have vanished from the world. . . . Christianity is not the work of persuasion, but, whenever it is hated by the world, it is a work of power.
>
> I am writing to all the churches to tell them that I am, with all my heart, to die for God . . . Let me be thrown to the wild beasts; through them I can reach God. I am God's wheat; I am ground by the teeth of the wild beasts that I may end as the pure bread of Christ. . . . Fire and cross and battling with wild beasts, the breaking of bones and mangling of members, the grinding of my whole body, the wicked torments of the devil—let them all assail me, so long as I get to Jesus Christ.
>
> Neither the kingdoms of this world, nor the bounds of the universe can have any use for me. I would rather die for Jesus Christ than rule the last reaches of the earth. My search is for Him who died for us, my love is for Him who rose for our salvation.[50]

With these imperishable words, St. Ignatius of Antioch dons his crown of glory. We have no historically reliable details of his martyrdom in Rome. After his letter to the Romans, we do not need them. We know how he gave the gift of his sacrifice to God.

There could be no more eloquent contrast than that between the heaven-storming spiritual heroism of the last letters of St. Ignatius of Antioch and the also famous last poem of the next "good emperor," Trajan's successor Hadrian (117-138), its haunting Latin melody a testament of despair for himself, his people who had not yet found the Christian faith, and all he stood for:

Animula vagula blandula	Little soul, little wanderer, charmer,
Hospes comesque corporis	Body's companion and guest,
Quae nunc abibis in loca,	What places will you leave for now,
Pallidula, rigida, nudula,	Little pale thing, stiff, little naked thing,
Nec ut soles dabis iocos?	And you won't make your usual jokes?[51]

Three years before his death Hadrian suppressed a last Jewish revolt in Palestine after he outlawed circumcision and ordered Jerusalem rebuilt as a pagan city, Aelia Capitolina. No Jew was any longer allowed even to approach it.[52] Nor was the new Israel spared. Hadrian had received pleas for Christianity; in what he must have thought the height of magnanimity, he offered Christ a place in his Pantheon![53] (In the end Christ was to have His rightful place there, when Hadrian's Pantheon was converted into a Christian church.) Gradually Hadrian learned—for he was a very intelligent man—that this was a fundamentally different kind of being. Something stirred behind his sophisticated mask and agitated his despairing soul; he ordered the Pope, St. Telesphorus, executed.[54]

The Church gathered in the darkness, remembering Ignatius. When the immediate danger was past, Hyginus was elected Pope.[55]

With Hadrian the expansion of the Roman empire ended forever. Mesopotamia, which Trajan had conquered in his last campaign, was given back to the Parthians. Hadrian built frontier forts and walls, like that wall in the north of England bearing his name, of which some portions still stand.[56] All the old thrust and drive was gone from Rome now; but during the reign of Hadrian's adopted son and successor Antoninus Pius (138-161) the new defenses held, and the old peace. An occasional pagan protest against Christianity was heard, and an occasional Christian apology.[57] But for the most part the growth of the Church was slow and silent, though steady. The seed was still in the earth. When heresy made its first systematic assaults on Rome, most of the world had no idea at all of what was happening.

The Gnostics came first. Two of the leading teachers in what was now—despite the denunciations of John the Evangelist and Ignatius of Antioch—a very widespread movement, arrived in Rome during the short pontificate of Hyginus: Cerdo and Valentine.[58] Gnosticism had flourished in the cultural milieu of

Hellenistic Judaism; the response to it in Rome, where the practical common sense which had always been characteristic of Romans was outraged by the fantastic mental castle-building of Gnostic speculation,[59] was at first thoroughly negative. Cerdo temporarily admitted errors and made an appearance of conforming to orthodoxy before his final, open break with the Church.[60] But Valentine, the founder of the principal Gnostic school of thought, appears to have aimed at nothing less than control of the whole Church of Christ. Tertullian tells us that he intrigued to become Pope, either at the death of Hyginus or more probably at the death of his successor Pope Pius I, in whom the heretics found an unexpectedly firm obstacle.[61]

Pius I (c.140-154)—three of whose namesakes were to guide the Church in the twentieth century after his Lord, amid perils of which he never could have dreamed—is the first Pope after Clement I to emerge from the shadowlands of history into at least a dim glow of awareness of his personality. Like Linus and Cletus, he had been a Greek slave;[62] he may even have still been a slave while Pope. He had a brother, probably named Hermas, also born into slavery, but freed by a generous mistress. The boys had been brought up in prosperity, probably as Christians, but Hermas at least had not really grasped the meaning of his faith until he had experienced the humiliation of being sold as a slave and sent far away.[63] Hermas was a simple man, largely uncultured though not unlettered, with a warm sincerity and a rich charity, as we know from his book, which he called simply "The Shepherd."[64] Not a word from Pius I survives; but we know several of his most important actions as Pope, and they bespeak the same kind of personality, devotion, and profound and practical Christianity that is conveyed by his brother's book.

So Hermas has the Angel of Repentance address him:

> "First of all believe that there is one God, that He created all things and set them in order, that He caused all things to pass from non-existence to existence, and that though He contains all things, He is Himself uncontained. Trust Him then, and fear Him, and in this fear be continent. Observe this mandate and throw far from you all wickedness. Clothe yourself with every excellence that goes with justice and you will live to God, provided you observe this command."
> He said to me: "Hold fast to simplicity of heart and innocence. Yes! Be as infants who do not know the wickedness that destroys the life of man."[65]

By contrast, hear the Gnostic Valentine in his "Gospel of Truth":[66]

> Since Oblivion [the lower world] came into existence because they [the Aeons] did not know the Father, Oblivion becomes of that very instant non-existent. That, then, is the Gospel of Him whom they seek and which [Jesus] revealed to the Perfect.[67]

Between two such different minds, such different conceptions of Christ and responses to Him, there was almost no common ground. For Valentine the hidden knowledge of God, given only to the Perfect (among whom he was naturally included), brought power and salvation. For Hermas and his brother Pope Pius I, God called all men to repentance and gave all men sufficient grace to repent; He made the world, loved it, maintained it in being. In Gnosticism breathed the same dark spirit which the Apostle Thomas had seen in full panoply of power in India; and Pope Pius I, from all we know or can guess of him, seems a man very much like Thomas. Valentine made little progress in Rome while Pius I was Pope, nor did he later have any success in persuading the clergy of Rome to elect him Pius' successor; they preferred the much less famous and less articulate Anicetus.[68]

Also to the Rome of Pius I, early in his pontificate, came Marcion—an enthusiast from Pontus in Asia Minor, a bishop's son,[69] wealthy, impressive, vehement. He gave the Roman Church a large sum of money. Then he asked its interpretation of two sayings of Christ in St. Luke's Gospel, his favorite among the sacred writings: "A good tree can bring forth only good fruit," and "No man puts new wine into old bottles." Marcion wanted the Gnostic answer to his question: that the God of Jesus is not the creator of the world we live in, nor the God of the Chosen People of the old Israel, and could not have been, because the world and Israel contain evil; the world must be the creation of the inferior and often evil Demiurge. But Marcion, more nearly Christian than the other Gnostics, felt compelled—as they, with their doctrine of a secret knowledge held only by the Perfect, did not—to justify his position by a simultaneous appeal to the Scriptures he liked and a rejection of those he did not like, including the whole Old Testament.[70]

We do not have the reply of Pius I to Marcion; but from the "Shepherd" of his brother Hermas we may almost reconstruct much of its probable content and tone:

> Behold the God of Hosts, who has created the world with His invisible power, strength and surpassing intelligence and who in His glorious good pleasure, has clothed His creation with beauty and His mighty Word has firmly fixed the heavens and set earth's foundations on the waters, Who in the wisdom and providence that is His alone has founded His holy Church and blessed it, behold! He is moving away the heavens, the mountains, the hills and seas, and all is becoming level for His elect, to fulfill the promise He made in fullness of glory and joy—provided they observe in great faith the commands received from God. . . . My children, listen to me. I brought you up in great simplicity and innocence and reverence, because of the Lord's mercy. He instilled justice into you, that you might be justified and sanctified from all wickedness and all perversity. But you did not wish to desist from your wickedness. Now, then, hear me: Be at peace among yourselves, look after one another, help one another. . . . All creatures fear the Lord,

but not all creation keeps His commandments. But, life with God is for
those who both fear Him and keep His commandments.[71]

So Marcion's arguments, his enthusiasm, his wealth and pride and power
fell like thistledown from the Vicar of Christ. As against the brilliant philosopher
Valentine, so against Marcion the proud and skillful organizer and the exegete
of a distorted Scripture, the slave's brother, his simple faith annealed by suffering, stood upon the Rock of St. Peter in defense of the fullness of Christian
truth and the goodness of God's creation. Marcion went away angry and
rebellious. In July 144 he established his own church, the first to be set up in
defiance of the Pope.[72] There would be many more.

Soon after Pius I died and was succeeded by Anicetus, there came to Rome,
probably in the summer of 154, the man who had become the Church's last
living link with the Apostles: Polycarp, Bishop of Smyrna. Chosen and trained
by the Apostle John, recipient of one of the famous letters from St. Ignatius
of Antioch, now eighty-five years old yet still sound in mind and body, Polycarp
vividly remembered John's eyewitness accounts of Christ's miracles and
teaching, how John looked and sounded, the way in which he would walk about
as he taught. Thus, near the outermost limits of doubled living memory, a witness
only one life removed from Christ's sojourn on earth was available to counter
the Gnostics and the Marcionites with the conclusive argument of continuous
tradition handed down by the Apostles: Christ's truth is one and public; it is
in the Scriptures and in the Church; there are no secret revelations of a ''higher
truth''; Valentinian and Marcionite doctrines were mere human invention, or
worse (Polycarp, normally the mildest of men, once called Marcion ''the first-
born of Satan''). Polycarp's vigorous preaching in Rome upon these themes
brought many Gnostics and Marcionites back into the Church.[73] We may even
reasonably speculate that it was Valentine's unsuccessful attempt to become Pope
in succession to Pius I who had so firmly held out against him, that helped im-
pel Polycarp, despite his advanced age, to go to Rome to strengthen Pope
Anicetus as he began his chapter of the struggle against heresy.

Another reason for Polycarp's journey—and of this reason we are explicitly
told—was to discuss the question of the proper date for celebrating Easter.
Polycarp's own church, like all those which had been closely associated with
the Apostle John, had always celebrated Easter on the 14th day of the old Jewish
month Nisan, the day of the Crucifixion, regardless of the day of the week on
which it fell; they fasted during the day and celebrated the Eucharist commemorating the Resurrection in the evening. Elsewhere the Church uniformly
celebrated Easter on the first Sunday following the 14th Nisan, with the Crucifixion commemorated the preceding Friday. Polycarp and Pope Anicetus could
not agree on this question. For Polycarp, the practice of the Apostle John was
sacrosanct, and the Pope did not at this time insist on his conforming, though

not persuaded by his arguments in favor of the "quartodeciman" practice. The memorable visit of Polycarp to Rome concluded with a special invitation to him from Pope Anicetus to say Mass for the faithful in Rome, probably at the first shrine over St. Peter's grave, which Anicetus had erected.[74]

It appears probable that Polycarp brought with him, on this visit to Rome, his pupil Irenaeus, later bishop of Lugdunum (Lyons) in Gaul and redoubtable adversary of the Gnostics, who was later to recall in his writings the apostolic tradition passed on to him from John the Evangelist through Polycarp, which above all pointed to the Bishop of Rome as the ultimate source of contemporary magisterial authority on doctrinal and theological issues. Irenaeus remained teaching in Rome when Polycarp returned to Smyrna.[75]

Within a few months Polycarp, the aged witness to the truth of Christ, became His witness by blood. At the League festival of the province of Asia celebrated in special honor of the emperor in Smyrna in February 155 or 156,[76] some anti-Christian outbursts induced a few unwisely ardent Christians from nearby Phrygia—soon to become the stronghold of the fanatical pentecostal Montanist heresy—to volunteer for arrest and martyrdom. When ten of them had been tortured and thrown to the wild beasts in the arena, the crowd began shouting for Polycarp, the bishop. His many disciples and friends had hidden him, but he was sought out. After two hours of prayer for all the persons he had known during his long life, and for the Church, he was brought to the stadium and condemned by the proconsul in deference to the howling mob, when he refused to obey a command to revile Christ: "Eighty-six years have I served Him and He has done me no wrong. How can I blaspheme my King Who has saved me?" Sentenced to burning at the stake, Polycarp stood untouched by a fire that arched over him instead of burning in the normal way; an executioner had to kill him with a dagger. The account of the passion of Polycarp in Smyrna is the first of a long, long succession of acts of Christian martyrs that has come down to us—a succession that continues to this day in Communist-controlled countries, and will in all probability continue until the end of the world.[77]

In 161 Emperor Antoninus Pius died after a reign of 23 years. He had been probably the best of all the heirs of Caesar Augustus. Unlike so many of his predecessors and successors who died by violence, in storm and stress, or in despair, his passing was tranquil; his last watchword to his guard was "Equanimity."[78] There is no indication that Antoninus Pius ever personally favored or encouraged punitive action against any Christian, in contrast to his predecessors Hadrian who had martyred Pope Telesphorus and Trajan who had martyred St. Ignatius. Gibbon to the contrary notwithstanding, the "Age of the Antonines" was no golden era of superabundant happiness, for by and large neither its people nor its leaders had a clear sense of purpose in life, of lasting goodness; metaphysical and spiritual despair were never far from them. But Antoninus Pius seems to have been spared it, and under him the Roman peace of Augustus returned almost in full. And Antoninus Pius' adopted son and successor Marcus Aurelius was Plato's dream come true at last: the philosopher-king. For Marcus Aurelius, a Stoic and author of the world-famous *Meditations*, is one of history's leading philosophers; and he was more than a king, he was the Emperor.

But Marcus Aurelius was to die in 180 at Vindobona (later Vienna) on the Danube frontier, facing barbarians with whom he had warred inconclusively for the greater part of a decade,[79] leaving to his incompetent son and heir Commodus a plague-stricken,[80] obviously declining empire in which only the Christians seemed to know how to live and how to die. Once only, in his *Meditations*, does Marcus Aurelius mention them. These Christians, he says, die *in formation*, as though marshalled in line of battle. They never fought; but the word that occurred to him to describe them was *parataxis*, the military term for drawing up troops in combat formation.[81]

G. K. Chesterton has memorably expressed Marcus Aurelius' insight for our time:

> It was not exactly what these provincials said; though of course it sounded queer enough. They seemed to be saying that God was dead and that they themselves had seen him die. This might be one of the many manias produced by the despair of the age; only they did not seem particularly despairing. They seemed quite unnaturally joyful about it, and gave the reason that the death of God had allowed them to eat him and drink his blood. According to other accounts God was not exactly dead after all; there trailed through the bewildered imagination some sort of fantastic procession of the funeral of God, at which the sun turned black, but which ended with the dead omnipotence breaking out of the tomb and rising again like the sun. But it was not the strange story to which anybody paid any particular attention; people in that world had seen queer religions enough to fill a madhouse. It was something in the tone of the madmen and their type of formation. They were a scratch company of barbarians and slaves and poor and unimportant people; but their formation was military; they moved together and were very absolute about who and what was really a part of their little system; and about what they said, however mildly, there was a ring like iron.[82]

So, as the contrast between the state of the Christians and the state of the empire grew more striking in the eyes of those—probably, by now, a majority—who had heard of them and knew at least something of them, persecutions became more common, occurring in many different parts of the empire. St. Justin the apologist and first Christian philosopher was martyred in the great plague year 167,[83] the year after Pope Anicetus died, having crowned his pontificate with the construction of the first shrine over the grave of Peter.[84] We hear of at least three bishop martyrs in Asia Minor and Greece directly contemporary with the martyrdom of Justin, and of numerous Christians condemned to hard labor in the mines and receiving aid from the Church of Rome during the pontificate of Soter, the successor of Anicetus.[85] In the summer of 177, at Lugdunum (now Lyons), where a Christian community—the only one in Gaul with a resident bishop—had been established by emigrants from the province of Asia who had known Polycarp at Smyrna and whose aged Bishop Pothinus had possibly known the Apostle John[86], the hatred for the Church of Christ blazed out more fiercely than at any time since the human torches in the gardens of Nero began 248 years of outlawry and agonizing death for Christians in the Roman empire.

The tortures inflicted on the martyrs of Lyons by the authorities in that city, without even waiting for an imperial command and under great popular pressure to be merciless, pass all rational understanding. Nothing that any Christian could have been imagined to have done could have justified in the mind of any sane man what was done to these Christians. It was not simply a matter of throwing grown men to wild beasts in the arena. A woman, Blandina, was tortured until "her whole body was broken and opened"; ninety-year-old Bishop Pothinus was beaten to death; several of the Christians were roasted in an iron chair; and when at last Blandina was offered to the beasts, she was hung on a stake for them like a haunch of meat—but not one of the savage half-starved animals would touch her. As often happened in these hellish scenes, the beasts felt the presence and power and goodness of their Maker in their victims, when men would not. All through days and weeks of almost inconceivable horror the martyrs of Lyons held fast to Christ: Vettius Epagathus the young aristocrat, Sanctus the deacon, Maturus the novice, Attalus the Pergamene, Ponticus the fifteen-year-old boy, Alexander the honest doctor who tried to save them, the aged Bishop Pothinus himself, above all Blandina, whose passion reached a height of sacrificial glory matching all that we can imagine of the passion of St. Ignatius of Antioch.[87] The last act of the cosmic drama in Lyons in 177 furnishes the final proof of the true nature of the malignant power that crafted their sufferings:

> The bodies of the martyrs, after being exhibited and exposed in every way for six days, and then burned and turned to ashes, were swept by the wicked into the Rhone River which flowed near by, in order that not even a trace of them might still appear upon the earth. And this they did as if able to conquer God and to deprive them of the rebirth, in order, as they said, "that they might not even have hope of resurrection, by trusting in which they introduced among us a strange and new religion."[88]

While in prison awaiting this fate, the martyrs of Lyons—even as their hour of supreme trial approached, never losing their care and concern for the whole Church—had sent Irenaeus, the pupil of Polycarp who was a member of their community, to Rome with letters for their brethren in Phrygia in Asia Minor where a new heresy, Montanism, was rising, and a letter of introduction for Irenaeus to the new Pope, Eleutherius.[89]

Montanism was a growing problem. It had originated in the wilds of the Phrygian-Mysian border in Asia Minor with a recent convert, probably a former priest of the ancient pagan goddess Cybele whose rites combined uncontrolled enthusiasm with a rigorous insistence on ritual purity. This man, Montanus, began to prophesy and to "speak in tongues." He was soon followed by two women, Priscilla and Maximilla, who left their husbands to devote themselves to his mission. Their theme was the imminent end of the world, to be heralded by wars and revolutions; the necessity for the strictest asceticism to prepare for it; and a call for the gathering of the faithful in the little Phrygian town of Pepuza as the new Jerusalem. In the voice of Montanus, they claimed, could be heard the Paraclete Himself Whose coming Jesus had foretold, but Who had never been fully manifested until now, even at the first Christian Pentecost in Jerusalem. Montanist preachers called upon their hearers to renounce marriage, to give up their worldly goods to their spiritual leaders (they would not be needed any longer, since the end of the world was at hand), to seek martyrdom wherever possible, and to repudiate all civil obligations. Though rejected by almost all the bishops, the Montanist call struck responsive chords all over Asia Minor; the whole church of Thyatira, for example, went over to them—Thyatira's church which the Apostle John had warned, in his letter to the seven churches of Asia in the Book of the Apocalypse, to beware of a prophetess whose teaching led to immorality.[90]

Though there is some evidence of a pronouncement by Pope Eleutherius against Montanism, after an initial favorable reaction on his part due to the Montanists' appearance of great zeal for the Faith and their general doctrinal orthodoxy,[91] it appears more probable in light of all the evidence that no great danger was apprehended from the Montanists and no general condemnation issued until a renewed growth of this sect was occasioned by the public catastrophes of the years 193-197 that shook the Roman empire to its foundations.

The firm clear understanding of Christian orthodoxy which remained, as ever, the mainstream of the Church—despite the Gnostic and Marcionite assault and the Montanist aberrations—was voiced most memorably about 182 by the Church's most publicly distinguished martyr of the second century, Apollonius the Apologist, who was in all probability a Roman Senator.[92] Denounced as a Christian, put on trial, and called upon to explain why he would not give up his illegal religion, Apollonius replied:

> The Word of God who brought into existence men's souls and bodies, became man in Judea—our Savior Jesus Christ. Perfectly righteous and filled with divine wisdom, He lovingly taught us what the God of all is like, and what is the end of virtue, befitting the souls of men with a view to social order and dignity. By His own suffering He put a stop to sins in their very beginning. He taught us to relieve sorrow, to be generous, to promote charity, to put away vainglory, to abstain from taking revenge, to despise death—

not when inflicted for wrongdoing, but in patient endurance of the wrong-doing of others. He taught us to obey the law laid down by Himself, to honor the king, to worship the immortal God, and Him only, to believe our souls to be immortal, to look forward to judgment after death, to expect the reward of the toils of virtue to be given by God after the resurrection of those who have lived good lives. All this He taught us plainly.[93]

The first great general defense of orthodoxy was written at this time by Irenaeus, who had become Bishop of Lyons—in all probability the sole bishop in Gaul at that time[94]—in succession to the martyred Pothinus. His lengthy, detailed work, entitled *Against Heresies*,[95] marshalled all available arguments against the prevalent errors, Gnosticism in particular. After carefully and patiently following the labyrinthine intricacies of Gnostic thought, for one precious moment he lets a flash of Christian laughter sparkle through:

> There is a certain Proarche, royal, surpassing all thought, a power existing before every other substance, and extended into space in every direction. But along with it there exists a power which I term a *Gourd*; and along with this Gourd there exists a power which again I term *Utter-Emptiness*. This Gourd and Emptiness, since they are one, produced (and yet did not simply produce, so as to be apart from themselves) a fruit, everywhere visible, eatable, and delicious, which fruit-language calls a *Cucumber*. Along with this Cucumber exists a power of the same essence, which again I call a *Melon*. These powers, the Gourd, Utter-Emptiness, the Cucumber, and the Melon, brought forth the remaining multitude of the delirious melons of Valentinus.[96]

But argument and satire were not enough. Ultimately there must be *authority*—decisive, unshakable authority in matters of doctrine, authority to which all Christians could look to obtain the answers they needed on the road to salvation, however well or ill versed in theological subtleties an individual believer and questioner might be. Irenaeus—the disciple of Polycarp, who was the disciple of the Apostle John—knew exactly where to look for that necessary authority; and it was not to Polycarp or to John, holy and glorious though they were. Irenaeus affirmed that ultimate Christian authority in this world in what is deservedly the most famous passage in all his writings:

> By pointing out the Apostolic tradition and creed which has been brought down to us by a succession of bishops in the greatest, most ancient and well-known church, founded by the two most glorious Apostles Peter and Paul at Rome, we can confute all those who in any other way, either for self-pleasing or for vainglory or blindness or badness, hold unauthorized meetings. For with this church [at Rome], because of its stronger [or higher] origin, all churches must agree, that is to say, the faithful of all places, because in it the Apostolic tradition has always been preserved.[97]

Then Irenaeus lists the full succession of Popes from Peter to Eleutherius then reigning, the oldest such list that has come down to us.[98]

Since supreme authority in the Church was vested in Rome, it was from Rome that the decision must come on which of the many Christian books in circulation were truly inspired Holy Scripture. The Muratorian fragment, dating from close to the end of the second century, gives an almost complete list of the canonical books of the New Testament. It was "made by the Roman congregation or one closely attached to it."[99]

On the last day of the year 192 the Emperor Commodus, unworthy son of Marcus Aurelius, who had become a megalomaniac like Nero, imagining himself to be Hercules, was strangled in his bath. Three months later his successor Pertinax was assassinated in Rome by the Praetorian Guard, which literally put the empire up for auction. Didius Julianus, the richest man in Rome, bought it for 25,000 sesterces per praetorian. Such a transaction was too much even for a decadent, profoundly materialistic Rome. The people of the city stoned Didius Julianus and rose to welcome the grim African Septimius Severus, as he marched his legions into the city and was acclaimed emperor by the senate. But Pescennius Niger had also proclaimed himself emperor at Antioch; soon afterward Albinus proclaimed himself emperor in Britain; then the Parthians attacked on the eastern frontier, as they were always ready to do when Rome was in trouble. For four years Septimius Severus marched and countermarched from one end of the empire to the other, and even beyond it, to punish the Parthians[100]—it was in 197 that he passed the ancient site of Babylon and found it totally deserted, the hunting ground of wild animals, just as the prophets of Israel had long ago foretold[101]—and the events of these angry years helped convince the self-appointed prophets of apocalypse and their hearers that the end of the world was indeed at hand. Heresy and schism gained new strength. Once again its leaders beat a path to Rome, where they found Pope Victor I, resolute and imperious, who had unmistakably exercised his authority as head of the whole Church by commanding uniformity everywhere on the date of celebrating Easter,[102] barring their way.

To Rome came Theodotus of Byzantium, who had denied Christ under persecution, and when reproached for it, compounded his sin by denying Christ's divinity, saying, "It is not God I have denied, but a man." Pope Victor excommunicated him, and he and his followers fell back on human reason as an alternative to the truth taught by the Church. Christ is not the truly begotten Son of God, but only His *adopted* son, Theodotus claimed, thereby rejecting the mystery of the Trinity and above all, the Incarnation itself. Known as Adoptionists, Theodotus' sect found itself a bishop in Rome and for a time maintained a schismatic church there; but the bishop, Natalis, repented and was reconciled with the Catholic Church, and the heresy faded until renewed half a century later in a new form by Paul of Samosata.[103]

To Rome at this time came Monarchianism or Modalism, the heresy of

Noetus of Smyrna, which abolished the distinction of Father and Son, denying the triad of persons in the one God, teaching instead that the Son and the Holy Spirit are "modes" of the divine being. By merging the Father and the Son, Noetus claimed to be glorifying Christ.[104] Unable to match his dazzling rhetoric and display of Scriptural learning, the elders of the church in Smyrna—Polycarp's church—nevertheless knew that something was profoundly wrong with it. They called on Noetus to abandon his novel opinion, setting against his fine-tuned arguments the simple Catholic sense of their hearts:

> We also confess truly one sole God; we confess the Christ; we confess the Son who suffered as He suffered, who died as He died, who rose again the third day, who is at the right hand of the Father, who will come to judge the living and the dead. And this we say as we have learnt.[105]

Noetus too founded a church. His disciple Praxeas brought his ideas to Rome, where initially he gained Papal favor by providing a full and accurate report on the dangers of the recent rapid growth of Montanism in his native Asia Minor. But when the essential elements of Praxeas' Monarchian teaching became known, Pope Victor promptly condemned him as well. Like Natalis, Praxeas repented and withdrew his errors.[106]

Monarchianism reappeared in Rome in the next pontificate, that of Zephyrinus. Epigonus, another disciple of Noetus, set up a Monarchian school there. One of its students, Sabellius, soon emerged as the leader of the Monarchian sect not only in Rome but throughout the empire. Zephyrinus held aloof from the controversy, refusing to condemn Sabellius, though he had finally issued the long-awaited general condemnation of Montanism.[107]

At this moment, probably in the second year of Zephyrinus' pontificate (201), Emperor Septimius Severus issued an edict prohibiting conversion either to Christianity or to Judaism, and demanded its full and immediate enforcement. The bad impression created by the Montanist preachers of apocalypse, whom pagan emperors and officials were unlikely to try to distinguish from the main body of sober and orthodox Christians, was probably one of the principal causes for this edict.[108]

At the new Roman city of Carthage in North Africa in 203, two young women catechumens, Vibia Perpetua and Felicity, both mothers of newborn babies, were given to the wild beasts in the arena for disobeying this imperial edict by seeking baptism. The narrative of their passion, universally accepted as contemporary and authentic, is one of the most beautiful of its kind. The girls entered the arena singing, "as if they were on their way to heaven, with gay and gracious looks; trembling, if at all, not with fear but joy. Perpetua followed with shining steps, true bride of Christ and darling of God, abashing with the high spirit in her eyes the gaze of all." Exposed to a savage cow, set upon her in mockery of her sex, Perpetua was tossed and Felicity knocked down; Perpetua rose, tidied her hair so that she should still be seen as joyful rather than in mourning, and helped Felicity to her feet; the cow, like the beasts to which St. Blandina had been exposed in the arena at Lyons, did not attack again. The martyrs gave each other the kiss of peace and awaited the triumph of death for Christ. The gladiator ordered to kill St. Perpetua could not do it; with his sword upon her throat he missed, dealing great pain but not death, so that she herself had to guide his hand in the mortal thrust which was her baptism of blood.[109]

In Alexandria this persecution went on for five years or more; the flourishing catechetical school founded in that city by the great Christian scholar and teacher Clement was temporarily broken up, and the young Origen who was to succeed Clement as its head saw his father and many of his friends martyred. But it was not only young Christians who treasured the memory of the martyrs and saw their lives changed fundamentally by the power of their example. The rough soldier Basilides was given the duty of leading the beautiful young Christian virgin Potamiaena to the most painful kind of death, by slow immersion in a vat of boiling pitch. He was kind to her, protecting her from the bloodthirsty mob as long as he could; she promised to pray for him, and that he would be rewarded for what he had done for her. ("Truly, I say to you, as you did it to one of the least of these my brethren, you did it to me.") A few days later Basilides astonished his comrades-in-arms by announcing himself a Christian. He was immediately beheaded. It is one of many well-attested instances in which the persecutors and executioners themselves were converted by the prayers and the example of loving and joyous constancy offered by their victims.[110]

Exhausted and cynical, Septimius Severus died far away from Rome, in the north of Britain at York; his last words to his two sons and successors (one of whom was soon to kill the other) were: "Do not disagree between yourselves; give money to the soldiers, and despise everyone else."[111] Caracalla, the survivor of this pair, was assassinated in 217 by Macrinus, who in turn was put to death that same year by Caracalla's aunt Julia Maesa, acting on behalf of her young, mad grandson Elagabalus, a priest of the Syrian Baal at Emesa.[112] In Rome Pope Zephyrinus died in that same bloody year; he was succeeded by the man he had trusted more than any other, whom he had put in charge of the catacomb cemeteries which had become the first substantial property owned by the Church: Callistus, a former slave and convict who had suffered for years in the prison mines of Sardinia, from which few emerged alive.[113] He assumed the leadership of a church which in that hour seemed in scarcely better condition than the Empire.

Her greatest writer, champion and apologist in the west, Tertullian of Africa, had left her to join the Montanists.[114] Her second greatest western writer and scholar, Hippolytus, incensed at Pope Zephyrinus' failure to condemn the Monarchian heresy of Sabellius, had fallen into the opposite heresy of ditheism—that Christ and the Father are two gods—and set himself up against Callistus as the first antipope.[115] Tertullian and Hippolytus and their followers took it upon themselves to deny absolution to all persons who had committed mortal sins of the flesh, however genuine and profound their contrition.[116] The category of "unforgivable sins," according to these proud and learned puritans, was large. Did anyone still remember what Christ had said to the woman taken in adultery, or that He had told Peter that a Christian should forgive "not seven times, but seventy times seven"?

The Pope who had been a slave and a convict laborer in the mines, having the mind of Christ, remembered. He confirmed the availability of confession and absolution even for those guilty of the most grievous sins, who sincerely repented.[117] He excommunicated Sabellius as an irreconcilable heretic—only to have Hippolytus respond that the Pope was a secret Monarchian who had acted against Sabellius only to throw his critics off the track![118] There seemed to be no pleasing this vain, irascible scholar. Yet Callistus saw good in him still, saw that despite all Hippolytus had said and done and his bitter hostility toward Callistus personally, he still loved Christ and the Church, was honestly misled; so he bore Hippolytus' slashing attacks in silence, refusing to condemn him publicly. In the end Callistus' judgment was vindicated. Hippolytus died a martyr for the Faith in those very mines of Sardinia where Callistus had once labored in chains, side by side with a later Pope, Pontian, his pride forgotten, reconciled at last to the Church, honored by her as a saint—the only antipope ever canonized.

Pope Callistus I reigned for five years, during which he had to endure the savage invective of Tertullian as well as of Hippolytus—Tertullian, a lawyer and a master of scorn and sarcasm, who said that the decree, which Callistus had issued or authorized, confirming that the sacrament of penance could be received by those confessing mortal sexual sins, should be posted on the doors of brothels.[119] Callistus' detractors gained new impetus from his ruling permitting Christian women to contract marriages valid before God with their social inferiors, although such marriages would not be recognized by Roman civil law. This was the Church's declaration of independence from the state regarding the sacrament of marriage, one of the most momentous steps in the history of her relations with temporal power. But Hippolytus could see in it only more immorality, high-born women having affairs with low-born men, claiming to be married in the sight of the Church while aborting their children to conceal the relationship from others for the sake of worldly respect. (For Christianity had brought into the Graeco-Roman world, where abortion and infanticide had long been common and tacitly approved, all the old Jewish horror of the killing of babies, and more.)[120] But to use the possibility of abortion as an argument against marriage made no sense to Pope Callistus. Availability of the sacraments should have nothing to do with social position. Other sins which might arise from the corruption of the society then encompassing Christ's people were separate problems.

Thus, hated by the rebel intellectuals and the puritanical moralists, scorned by the "better elements" in society, Pope St. Callistus I carried his cross with Christ, loving his enemies, pardoning sinners, serving his people. In the end he gained the martyr's crown—not dramatically and gloriously like the beautiful Perpetua walking "with shining steps" into the arena of death, but darkly, as on Calvary it fell dark. He was set upon by a mob and thrown to his death from a height. The circumstances are obscure; but it came to be honored as a martyrdom.[121]

We have not one word from Pope Callistus himself. The preservation of what is called his slave collar, and the oldest church in Rome (now Santa Maria in Trastevere), which he built—the first known Papal construction—attest "to the deep impression he made upon his contemporaries."[122] Otherwise, he lives for us in the impassioned attacks of his enemies, Tertullian and Hippolytus, which comprise almost all we know about him. Out of their mouths, unwittingly, comes his praise; history and the light of truth and charity turn their venom into honey. What they condemn him for having taught and done, we can clearly see now was his glory. Dimly through the shadows of the distant past, from those days of Popes before the tiara as we live in the days of Popes after the tiara, emerges the figure of a sane, solid, loving man in a disintegrating age, one of the greatest of all the Popes,[123] and one of the kindest.

The martyrdom of Pope Callistus occurred several months after the assassination of Elagabalus (March 222), who was replaced as emperor by his thirteen-year-old first cousin Alexander Severus, under the virtual regency of his mother Julia Mamaea, niece of Septimius Severus. Mother and son were (or became) relatively sympathetic to Chrisianity, but this did not suffice to save Pope Callistus. (Later, while residing in Antioch, Mamaea invited the great Origen to give her instruction in the Christian faith; but there is no evidence of her baptism, nor of her specifically calling herself a Christian or acting as a Christian would.)[124] Callistus' successor was Urban I, of whose pontificate virtually nothing is known up to its final year, 230.

The years from 222 to 230 were a time of peace, recovery, and some last intellectual flowering at Rome, and of upheaval beyond the eastern frontier, where a momentous change had taken place. The shaky, disorganized 450-year-old Parthian empire had fallen at last. From Cyrus the Great's homeland of Persia proper, a vigorous, autocratic and strongly Zoroastrian dynasty, the Sassanids, had taken power from the Parthians and re-established the Persian empire, as they formally proclaimed in 226.[125] This empire, like the Parthian, included most of Mesopotamia, in which Christianity—restored to Edessa after its first-century apostasy and spreading eastward from there[126]—was already firmly rooted, with twenty bishops in the region of the Tigris River by 224.[127] During this whole period there is no record of any persecution of Christians by the Parthian government. A Christian church was openly built and decorated at Dura-Europos on the Euphrates in 238,[128] and as early as 134 Rakbakt, prince of Adiabene on the Tigris, is recorded as a Christian convert.[129]

By the year 230, having mopped up the last remnants of Parthian resistance, the founder of the new Persian empire, Ardashir (Artaxerxes) I, prepared to march west for the avowed purpose of regaining the full extent of the ancient Persian empire which Alexander the Great had destroyed. He invaded western Mesopotamia, which Rome ruled. The thoroughly unwarlike 21-year-old Alexander Severus and his hovering mother had to come to grips with an unexpected, serious military crisis.[130]

Preoccupied with this suddenly emergent danger in the east, so close to their home city of Emesa on the Orontes in Syria south of Antioch,[131] it is unlikely that Alexander Severus and Julia Mamaea paid the slightest attention to a great drama of Christian martyrdom most probably enacted that same year in Rome. Indeed, there is no evidence that any of the Roman emperors of their time ever took concrete action to protect the Christians from the local persecutions and malicious denunciations which periodically fell upon them even in the reigns of the most tolerant emperors, because of the law—still in effect—which made the simple profession of Christianity a crime punishable by death.[132]

Cecilia, a girl small in stature and strikingly beautiful, a descendant of one of the noblest ancient Roman families and a secret Christian vowed to virginity, was married on the orders of her parents to Valerian, a young pagan. On their wedding night she revealed to him her Christian faith and her vow. He consented to go to Pope Urban for instruction in the faith, and was soon baptized, together with his brother Tiburtius. The two converts began to teach their new faith openly, and consequently were summoned before the prefect of the city of Rome to be questioned about it. They confessed Christ; converted Maximus, one of the prefect's subordinates; and were martyred by the sword on the prefect's order and taken by Cecilia for burial in the catacomb of Praetextatus on the Appian Way. Maximus was then likewise condemned, beaten to death by blows to the head with leaded whips, and buried near Valerian and Tiburtius. Cecilia's own faith was now well known and the prefect would soon proceed against her; before her arrest, she gave her large house to the Church. Confronting the prefect, clad in a robe of gold and silk, she refused to deny Christ and sacrifice to idols. Wishing to avoid the public execution of a member of so distinguished a family, the prefect unsuccessfully attempted to have her scalded to death in her bath. He then ordered her beheaded; but as with Perpetua in Africa, the abashed executioner could not fully carry out his task, though he left her deeply cut in the neck and bleeding copiously. Her admirers gathered about her, applying linen cloths to stanch the flow of blood. They remained with her three days, until she died in peace and joy, her witness to Christ fulfilled. Pope Urban buried her in the catacomb of Callistus, still clad in her robe of gold and silk, with the linen cloths which had absorbed the blood at her feet.[133]

Soon afterward, in May of 230, Pope Urban was himself martyred and buried in the catacomb of Praetextatus near his martyred converts Valerian, Tiburtius, and Maximus.[134]

This account of St. Cecilia's martyrdom is taken first of all from her *Acts*, written about the year 500 and therefore more than 250 years after the events they purport to describe, though very possibly based on more nearly contemporary documents.[135] So beautifully was the story told that it brought about a great increase in devotion to St. Cecilia, and her inclusion among the select few mentioned in the canon of the Mass. Historical criticism has looked with growing disfavor upon this story during the last 300 years, until today it is impossible to find a single authority writing in any language who upholds it as a reliable account of actual historical events. Its date, in particular, has been universally rejected. Even those who still see some historical truth in the Acts of St. Cecilia insist that she did not live and suffer martyrdom during the pontificate of Urban, in the reign of Alexander Severus, though her Acts (unlike the Acts of many martyrs which are only loosely or inaccurately tied, if at all, to other dateable historical events) state explicitly that this was when she lived and suffered. Prosper Guéranger himself, the great defender of the historicity of St. Cecilia in the nineteenth century, toward the end of his life abandoned the defense of the chronology given in her Acts.[136]

Like many of the other Acts and Passions of martyrs in the early Christian centuries, St. Cecilia's have been thrown out of court as largely or entirely mere romance. While it is admitted that a house belonging originally to someone of the family of the Caecilii was an important early property of the Church in Rome, it is argued that Alexander Severus was not a persecutor; that the name of the persecuting prefect of Rome in the Acts of St. Cecilia, Turcius Almachius, is not Roman; that no mere girl would have been allowed to defy the prefect of Rome with long speeches such as the Acts of St. Cecilia report; and that writers of the fourth century (300-400), such as Pope Damasus, St. Ambrose, and Prudentius, who have much to say of other martyrs including the virgins Agnes and Eulalia, never mention Cecilia.[137] Though the Acts of St. Cecilia contain relatively little of the miraculous and nothing of the magical or the absurd, the narrative as its stands—with its late date and indubitably romantic character, meeting this battery of objections—inevitably arouses doubts in the critical historian even of strong and orthodox faith.

But in the case of St. Cecilia we are not dependent on the much later, romantic narrative of her martyrdom alone for concrete evidence. Her small cypresswood coffin[138] has been twice opened: once by Pope Paschal I in 821 and a second time by Cardinal Sfondrato in 1599. On both occasions her body was found incorrupt, lying just as it had lain when she died, with the blood-soaked linens at her feet, dressed in a robe of gold and silk, all exactly as her Acts tell us. On the second occasion the sword wounds in her neck were seen and reported. On both occasions the sarcophagus containing the bodies of Valerian, Tiburtius, and Maximus were also opened, displaying two skeletons remarkably similar (Valerian and Tiburtius, be it remembered, were identified in the Acts of St. Cecilia as brothers) with the head removed from one of them, and a third skeleton whose skull had been severely damaged by blows from heavy objects, matching the account of Maximus being beaten to death by leaded whips applied to the head. The sculptor Stefano Maderna carved an unforgettably lovely replica of St. Cecilia's body exactly as he saw it lying in the coffin in 1599, as he testifies in an inscription on the statue itself, which remains today in full public view at the Basilica of St. Cecilia in Rome. The first opening of the coffin was witnessed by Pope Paschal I himself, as testified by the contemporary historian Anastasius "the librarian." The second opening was witnessed by the first great modern Catholic historian, Caesar Baronius; by Cardinal Sfondrato; by the Bishop of Iserna; by James Buzzi, canon of the congregation of the Lateran; by the Jesuit priests Peter Alabona and Peter Morra; and later by Pope Clement VIII in person.[139] To quote Baronius' eyewitness account of the viewing, though the "very light" silken coverings upon her body were not removed, "these, when pressed down, showed the position and posture of the body." When Pope Clement VIII viewed it, he "recognized each and every member through the covering cloths."[140]

The presence of the Church's most distinguished living historian at the opening of St. Cecilia's coffin in 1599 is an event unique in the history of hagiography. Critical twentieth century historians who have attempted to deal with Baronius' circumstantial report in any detail (these are few and far between, since most prefer to ignore it entirely or are honestly unaware of it) have had to allege or imply that he and the others were in such a state of "pious exaltation" that they could not distinguish an incorrupt body under the cloths from a skeleton, and even thought the body had a head when it didn't! (Anastasius' much earlier account indicates that St. Cecilia's head was detached in 821; at that point he must have been in error, since the eyewitness testimony of 1599 contradicts it.)[141]

As in the case of the Holy Shroud of Turin and the Gospel accounts of the Crucifixion, the physical remains discovered in the tomb of St. Cecilia confirm her Acts at every point where they could confirm them. Paul Allard, the great historian of the martyrs, sums it up: "Rarely has a document of this nature undergone a test more conclusive, and emerged from it better justified."[142] So complete is the confirmation that it establishes a powerful presumption in favor of the accuracy of the Acts of St. Cecilia on chronology as well. In light of the accuracy of the Acts as thus confirmed, the "argument from silence" by fourth century writers and deductions from our limited knowledge of the personal involvement of emperors of this period in the persecution of Christians (we know that persecutions and executions of Christians were periodically carried out whether encouraged by the reigning emperor or not)[143] should not be allowed to prevail. And this eyewitness evidence, so widely ignored—not to say suppressed—by today's historians of the early Church,[144] most emphatically calls for a re-evaluation, not only of the historicity of the passion of St. Cecilia, but also of the entire pattern of instant, automatic dismissal as historically worthless of all Acts and Passions of the martyrs which are not demonstrably contemporary, and a recognition that a romantic style of writing and the intrinsically romantic and heroic nature of the events these narratives report by no means preclude the possibility that solidly factual historical sources were used by their authors to obtain the essential information they give.

Alexander Severus brought his Persian campaign to an inconclusive end after a drawn battle in 232. Though the Persians did not then pursue their invasion, his military incapacity had been revealed. Increasingly his troops looked down on the bookish young man as a coward. As he prepared for war in Germany in 235, he was killed in a mutiny of the army in camp at Mainz at the instigation of a brutal soldier of huge stature, Maximin the Thracian. The army hailed Maximin as emperor. He promptly issued an edict against the Christians, aimed specifically at bishops—thereby demonstrating more shrewdness than is usually attributed to Maximin. The first and principal victims of Maximin's edict were Urban's successor, Pope Pontian, and Callistus' old foe Hippolytus. Both were condemned to the mines of Sardinia. Pontian resigned his office, the first Pope to do so, probably because he was sure he would not return from the mines, possibly to help persuade Hippolytus to give up his schism. As the two old men labored together, awaiting the release and triumph of death which in that place of punishment for their Faith would be martyrdom, Hippolytus was reconciled with the Church by the ex-Pope himself, and sent word to his remaining followers to rejoin the Church under the new Pope. When Pontian's successor Anteros died after a pontificate of only six weeks, the farmer Fabian was unexpectedly elected in his place. Fabian was later able to bring back Pontian's body from Sardinia for burial in the crypt of the Popes in the catacomb of Callistus, very near the original grave of St. Cecilia. He maintained vigilance against heresy, denouncing the Bishop of Lambesa in Africa, and receiving a letter from Origen defending himself against charges of unorthodoxy.[145]

As peace returned to the Church, Pope Fabian addressed the ever-pressing task of evangelization, sending several priests—probably close in number to, if not precisely, the traditional seven—to bring the Faith to the vast areas of Gaul, outside the region of Lyons, that were still hardly touched by Christianity. They became the founding bishops of the Christian communities they established. St. Saturninus went to Toulouse in the Gallic south, where he was later martyred by being tied to an enraged bull and dragged through the streets. St. Dionysius (Denis) went to Paris in the north, made many converts, and eventually was martyred by beheading. St. Gatian went to Tours in the center of Gaul, where he lived in a cave in a neighboring hillside as he struggled, with only limited success, to penetrate the deeply rooted paganism there; perhaps by his very choice of abode, withdrawn from the mob, he escaped the martyr-dom of his fellow missionaries.[146]

While Fabian led Christ's Church, a young man named Mani, born in Ctesiphon in Mesopotamia in the last days of the Parthian empire of which it had been the capital, had sailed for India to teach and to learn. Mani had pro-bably been brought up a Mandaean Gnostic (a sect which still exists in Mesopotamia, and was more numerous then) and aspired to found and lead a universal religion. Jesus, Buddha, and Zoroaster, he declared, were his forerun-ners; he was the seal of the prophets. In India he absorbed the world-denying doctrine of Buddhism and very likely some Hindu philosophy as well, which he combined with the sharp cosmic dualism into which Zoroastrianism had developed in Iran and some heretical Christian ideas, to form a syncretic religion which his genius as a church organizer could promote as no form of Gnosticism had ever been promoted before. The innate evil of the material world, the utter transcendence of the unreachable God, the impossibility of a real Incarnation, were the foundations of his creed. The human body, he taught, was of Satanic origin both in substance and in design. Mani came back from India to preach in the new Persian empire with the encouragement of its second king, Shapur I, beginning in 241.[147] His work would extend Gnosticism far down the cen-turies and bring to the West a breath of India's hidden hell. A full thousand years after Mani, Manichees would distort the faith in Europe and threaten Christendom at its very center, in France, the "eldest daughter of the Church," which Fabian's missionary bishops were at this time evangelizing. So does the battle for Christ leap across the millennia.

Of all men and women who have ever lived, one alone can claim the Incar-nation as, in a real sense, her own, since it actually occurred within her body—one glorified creature who knows as no other human being except her Divine Son can know, how good in essence material creation is. Her name is Mary. Two years after Mani came back from India to begin the worldwide preaching of his doctrine of the hatred of material creation, Mary appeared—the first of her many recorded apparitions in Christian history—to St. Gregory Thaumaturgus, about to begin his great work of evangelization in eastern Asia Minor (Cappadocia and Pontus), to explain to him the truth of the Trinity he was to expound.[148]

In 248 Rome celebrated the completion of its first millennium, from the tradi-tional date of its founding by Romulus and Remus in 753 B.C. Philip the Arab, a known Christian sympathizer, was emperor.[149] (Despite his Christian sym-pathies he permitted a large-scale massacre of Christians in Alexandria in 248 or 249, which helps to show how Pope Urban, St. Cecilia and her friends could have been martyred in Rome in 230 despite the sympathy toward Christianity which had been shown by the then reigning emperor Alexander Severus).[150] Origen published his great refutation of the pagan Celsus' comprehensive intellectual attack on Christianity, the first such attack which the pagan intelligentsia had thought it needful to make.[151] No longer could the Church of Christ be ignored or merely scoffed at. It was now clearly visible from Persia to Scotland, and had been planted even farther out, in India and possibly in Ethiopia. In its very weakness was a strength that even its enemies were beginning, with growing disquiet, to sense. The pagan world faced a peaceful rebellion from within, armored with a gentle invincibility that none of its weapons could touch. Seedtime was becoming harvest. Saint Cecilia—small, smiling, exquisite—best expressed and exemplified it, facing the prefect of Rome:

> Did you not say that your princes have conferred upon you the power of life and death? You well know that you have only the power of death. You can take away life from those who enjoy it, but you cannot return it to the dead. Say then, that the emperors have made you a minister of death, and nothing more. . . . Christ alone can save from death, and deliver the guilty from eternal fire.[152]

NOTES

[1] Hubert Jedin and John Dolan, eds. *History of the Church*, Volume I: "From the Apostolic Community to Constantine" (New York, 1965), p. 132 (this volume was originally published under the general title *Handbook of Church History*).

[2] *The Cambridge Ancient History*, Volume XI (Cambridge, England, 1936), pp. 31, 255.

[3] See Chapter Seventeen, above (Note 132).

[4] Arthur S. Barnes, *Christianity at Rome in the Apostolic Age* (London, 1938), pp. 129-133, 138-139, 147-150. The suggestion that Titus Flavius Sabinus, the elder brother of Vespasian, married a daughter of Pomponia Graecina and Aulus Plautius, was first made by the great nineteenth century Roman archeologist John Baptist de Rossi and was seconded by the Anglican Bishop Joseph B. Lightfoot, a well-known authority on the Apostolic Age. Barnes' attempt to identify this hypothetical lady with the otherwise unidentified St. Petronilla, described in the Roman Martyrology as "St. Peter's daughter," is ingenious and very possibly true, but in the state of the evidence it must remain only a possibility.

[5] Jules Lebreton and Jacques Zeiller, *The History of the Primitive Church* (New York, 1949), I, 384; Barnes, *Christianity at Rome*, p. 142; Ludwig Hertling and Engelbert Kirschbaum, *The Roman Catacombs and Their Martyrs*, 2nd ed. (Milwaukee, 1956), pp. 22-24.

[6] Barnes, *Christianity at Rome*, p. 126.

[7] Our English word "Pope" is simply an anglicization of *Papa*, Father. For many centuries in the West it has designated exclusively the Bishop of Rome, the successor of Peter as head of the Catholic Church, though in the early Christian centuries it could be applied to any major bishop or Church leader (E. G. Weltin, *The Ancient Popes* [Westminster MD, 1964], p. 20). Since the papal office was always essentially the same, as we shall take care to demonstrate, it seems sound and reasonable to follow the practice of most Catholic histories and use the term "Pope" for the Bishops of Rome throughout their entire history.

[8] Constant Fouard, *St. John and the Close of the Apostolic Age* (New York, 1905),

pp. 49-50.

[9] *Ibid.*, pp. 45-47; Lebreton and Zeiller, *Primitive Church*, I, 384-386.

[10] Eusebius, *Ecclesiastical History*, III, 13, 15; Fouard, *St. John*, p. 138; Lebreton and Zeiller, *Primitive Church*, I, 411n; Weltin, *Ancient Popes*, p. 60.

[11] Eusebius, *Ecclesiastical History*, III, 18; Barnes, *Christianity at Rome*, pp. 153-155; Fouard, *St. John*, pp. 59-61; Jedin and Dolan, *History of the Church*, I, 131-132; Hertling and Kirschbaum, *Roman Catacombs*, pp. 24-27. It is frequently argued today (*e.g.*, W. H. C. Frend, *Martyrdom and Persecution in the Early Church* [New York, 1967], pp. 157-162) that all Domitian's noble victims accused of religious irregularities were Jewish converts or Jewish sympathizers rather than Christians. While their Christianity cannot be proved beyond question since none of our sources explicitly identify any of them as such and they were not later honored by the Church as martyrs, the strong indications of their Christian faith in our sources find substantial confirmation in the evidence from the excavations of early Christian cemeteries in Rome that the descendants of both Acilius Glabrio and Flavia Domitilla were definitely Christian. The very vagueness and confusion in the charges against Domitian's victims suggests that nothing so well known and understood to most Romans as ordinary Judaism was involved. See Hertling and Kirschbaum, *op. cit.*, pp. 198-199.

[12] Fouard, *St. John*, pp. 54, 68-69; Barnes, *Christianity at Rome*, p. 156; Lebreton and Zeiller, *Primitive Church*, I, 388.

[13] Jedin and Dolan, *History of the Church*, I, 131. This is even clearer than in the case of Nero's persecution, in view of the strong tradition that St. John suffered in the persecution of Domitian and the specific reference to Christian apostasies in Bithynia in the contemporary letter of Pliny to the Emperor Trajan (see Note 14, below). Melito of Sardis, writing within living memory of Domitian's persecution, grouped him with Nero as an opponent of Christianity.

[14] The references to the Apostle John in the gospels all suggest a very young man, but not a boy. We may therefore reasonably estimate his age at the time of Jesus' Passion and Resurrection in 30 A.D. as 18 to 20, which would put his birth year at 10 to 12 A.D. (see Chapter Sixteen, above). The speculations of Barnes (*Christianity at Rome*, pp. 163-191) that John would have been too old to have survived the rigors of Domitian's persecution because he was "between ninety and a hundred years old" when Domitian began his policy of persecution in 96" (ibid., p. 166), involve both a mathematical and an historical error. If Acilius Glabrio, sent to the arena in 91, was a Christian and if Pliny the Younger in Bithynia was at all close to chronological accuracy when he wrote in 112 of Christians rejecting their faith under pressure in that province about twenty years earlier (see Note 13, above, and Frend, *Martyrdom and Persecution*, pp. 162-164), Domitian's persecution began in 91, not 96; if John was 18 in the year of the Passion, as is quite possible, he would still have been one year short of eighty in 91 rather than "between ninety and a hundred"—a very considerable difference, which vitiates most of Barnes' objections. Men of 79, even when not supernaturally aided (a possibility that certainly cannot be ruled out, especially in this case) have sometimes proved remarkably resistant and durable.

[15] Irenaeus, *Against Heresies*, V, 30.3; Fouard, *St. John*, pp. xxv-xxvii, 70-134; John Chapman, *John the Presbyter and the Fourth Gospel* (Oxford, 1911), pp. 50n-51n. No one in this life will ever have "the last word" on St. John's Apocalypse—either as to its content or its composition. That it is a very different sort of literary production from the Fourth Gospel is obvious. That one man filled with grace, guided by the Holy Spirit, and receiving by revelation the last of the deposit of faith entrusted by Christ to the Apostles could have written both books is a proposition no literary or historical critic can ever

disprove. Substantial similarities and common patterns in the use of words in the two books have been found. Many differences may be explained by the use of different assistants for transcribing and editing the two books. We know that St. John had such assistants in preparing the Fourth Gospel, since they occasionally insert their independent testimony to his verity (*e.g.*, John 19:35, 21:24). On this point see Chapman, *op. cit.*, pp. 88-94.

[16] Apocalypse 2:2.

[17] Fouard, *St. John*, pp. 93-94.

[18] Clement 59, 1; Manuel Miguens, *Church Ministries in New Testament Times* (Arlington VA, 1976), p. 156; Lebreton and Zeiller, *Primitive Church*, I, 412-413, 416-417; Michael M. Winter, *Saint Peter and the Popes* (Baltimore, 1960), pp. 119-121. The great St. Ignatius, Bishop of Antioch, writing to other churches in Asia on his way to martyrdom, explicitly says that he does not command them (Ephesians 3). Clement, on the other hand, *does* explicitly command the church in Corinth (Clement 57, 1-2; 63, 1). No attempt to challenge the strength of the evidence for Papal primacy from the Apostolic Age furnished by the letter of Clement has obtained significant support even in today's intellectual climate generally hostile to Papal authority. One counter-argument which appears from time to time, that Corinth was rebuilt in 44 B.C. as a Roman colony and therefore had unusually close secular ties with Rome which could explain the intervention of the Bishop of Rome in its religious affairs without implying his universal primacy, fails on the simple fact that the Corinthians spoke Greek, not Latin. Corinth was still a Greek city and Latin colonists who continued to speak Latin remained a minority, if indeed any significant number of them still existed by the end of the first century A.D., 150 years after the resettlement of the city.

[19] Miguens, *Church Ministries*, pp. 145-160; Lebreton and Zeiller, *Primitive Church*, I, 478-480.

[20] The verb καθιστανων, here translated "appointed," is in the imperfect tense which conveys the meaning of a common, customary, regular or repeated action. See Miguens, *Church Ministries*, pp. 150-151.

[21] Clement 42, 24 (as translated by Miguens, *Church Ministries*, p. 150).

[22] επινομην. For the proper translation of this difficult word see Miguens, *Church Ministries*, p. 206 (note 235).

[23] Clement 44, 1-2 (as translated by Miguens, *Church Ministries*, p. 150). The Greek verb Miguens translates "succeed" is διαδεχονται. He defines its meaning as "to receive (in turn) from a former owner or series of owners, to succeed; this is a technical term that indicates a succession in a series of kings or emperors, it indicates the receiving of the kingdom or empire ''through' the predecessors" (*Church Ministries*, p. 151).

[24] Weltin, *Ancient Popes*, pp. 60-61.

[25] See Note 14, above. Eusebius dates Clement's death to 101 (*Ecclesiastical History*, III, 34).

[26] Fouard, *St. John*, pp. 155-156; John Knox, *Philemon among the Letters of Paul* (Chicago, 1935), pp. 50-56. Knox makes a very convincing case for the identity of the Onesimus, Bishop of Ephesus, who is repeatedly mentioned in the letter of St. Ignatius of Antioch to the Ephesians, with the Onesimus of Paul's epistle to Philemon. F. F. Bruce, *Paul, Apostle of the Free Spirit* (Exeter, England, 1977), pp. 399-406, agrees with Knox.

[27] Irenaeus, *Against Heresies*, I, 26.1; Jean Danielou and Henri Marrou, *The Christian Centuries*, Volume I: "The First Six Hundred Years" (New York, 1964), pp. 59-60; R. M. Wilson, *The Gnostic Problem* (London, 1958), pp. 104-108. Most general studies of Gnosticism have been marked by an extraordinary sympathy for the Gnostics and an explicit or implicit downgrading of the orthodox Christian analysis and rejection of

Gnostic teachings. Despite much initial scholarly enthusiasm, the discovery of a complete Gnostic library at Nag Hammadi (the ancient Chenoboskion) in Egypt shortly after World War II has added relatively little to our knowledge of Gnosticism insofar as it bears on the general history of Christianity. The most thorough review of Gnosticism in English, incorporating these recent discoveries, is the second edition of Hans Jonas, *The Gnostic Religion; the Message of the Alien God and the Beginnings of Christianity* (Boston, 1963).

[28] Irenaeus, *Against Heresies*, I, 24.2; Danielou and Marrou, *Christian Centuries*, I, 62, 64-65.

[29] Irenaeus, *Against Heresies*, III, 3.4. Irenaeus explicitly attributes this memorable anecdote to Polycarp, a disciple of John and Irenaeus' own teacher. The authority could hardly be stronger unless the account had come from St. John himself. There is no basis whatever for any hesitation in accepting it as historical fact.

[30] See Note 43, below, for the probable date of Ignatius' martyrdom.

[31] Jedin and Dolan, *History of the Church*, I, 119.

[32] Fouard, *St. John*, p. 220.

[33] 2 John 1; 3 John 1. The precise term used is "presbyter." This bears on the continually renewed speculation arising from a confusing passage in Papias and first given wide currency by Eusebius (*Ecclesiastical History*, III, 39), that there were two different Johns of great reputation in Asia Minor in the late first century, the Apostle John and the Presbyter John, one of whom wrote the Apocalypse while the other wrote the Fourth Gospel (critics who accept this speculation "take their pick" as to who wrote which). But Papias' words can equally well be interpreted as referring to just one John, the Apostle, also known as the Presbyter (elder). Internal evidence is strong that 2 and 3 John were written by the author of the Fourth Gospel (Herbert G. May and Bruce M. Metzger, eds., *The New Oxford Annotated Bible* [New York, 1977], p. 1489); and as we have seen (Chapter Fourteen, above) the Fourth Gospel is clearly identified internally as the work of the Apostle John (note especially John 21:20-24). That the Apostle John also wrote the Apocalypse is not only the unanimous witness of tradition but is also explicitly confirmed at a very early date (150 or earlier) by St. Justin Martyr (*Dialogue with Trypho* 81; Thomas B. Falls, ed., *St. Justin Martyr*, Volume 6 in *The Fathers of the Church* series [New York, 1948], p. 12). On this entire question see especially Chapman, *John the Presbyter, passim*. In this writer's opinion Chapman stands in the very highest rank of scholars both for erudition and for sound judgment.

[34] Eusebius, *Ecclesiastical History*, III, 23; Fouard, *St. John*, pp. 215-216. Eusebius' source for this story is Clement of Alexandria, writing only about a hundred years after St. John's death.

[35] 3 John 9-10.

[36] *Cambridge Ancient History*, XI, 224-231.

[37] *Ibid.*, pp. 198-199; Frend, *Martyrdom and Persecution*, pp. 162-164; E. G. Hardy, *Christianity and the Roman Government* (New York, 1894, 1971), pp. 102-140.

[38] Matthew 13:55, Mark 6:3, Luke 4:22; Eusebius, *Ecclesiastical History*, II, 11, 32; Ferdinand Prat, *Jesus Christ, His Life, His Teaching, and His Work* (Milwaukee, 1950), I, 504-506; Lebreton and Zeiller, *Primitive Church*, I, 389-390.

[39] Lebreton and Zeiller, *Primitive Church*, I, 389-390; Danielou and Marrou, *Christian Centuries*, I, 56-57; Virginia Corwin, *St. Ignatius and Christianity in Antioch* (New Haven CT, 1960), pp. 58-63.

[40] *Cambridge Ancient History*, XI, 240-247; Glanville Downey, *A History of Antioch in Syria* (Princeton NJ, 1961), pp. 212-213; F. A. Lepper, *Trajan's Parthian War* (Oxford, 1948), pp. 120-125.

[41] Downey, *Antioch*, pp. 213-215.

[42] Maisie Ward, *Saints Who Made History* (New York, 1959), p. 5; Miguens, *Church Ministries*, p. 157.

[43] Corwin, *St. Ignatius*, pp. 17-20; Downey, *Antioch*, pp. 292-293. The usual date given for the arrest and martyrdom of St. Ignatius of Antioch is 108/109, the 11th year of Trajan, on the authority of Jerome. But Jerome's chronological reference is not linked to any other contemporary historical events, and may be based on an artificial chronological reconstruction from lists of bishops only. On the other hand, the chronicle of John Malalas, actually compiled at Antioch in the early sixth century and making use of local sources, specifically links Ignatius' condemnation with the earthquake which occurred in 115 when Emperor Trajan was in the city. Malalas' general reliability for major events in Antiochene history and the dating of Ignatius' arrest to 115—often challenged—are well defended by the greatest modern authority on Antioch, Glanville Downey (*op. cit.*, pp. 37-40, 292n, 293n) and by a careful study of Trajan's Parthian war (Lepper, *Trajan's Parthian War*, pp. 54-83). As Downey points out, many scholars have not accepted the 108/109 date of Jerome even though rejecting or ignoring Malalas' date of 115 as well.

[44] *Cambridge Ancient History*, XI, 215.

[45] Downey, *Antioch*, pp. 292n, 297; Weltin, *Ancient Popes*, pp. 65-67.

[46] Lebreton and Zeiller, *Primitive Church*, I, 426-428; Corwin, *St. Ignatius*, pp. 52-61.

[47] Miguens, *Church Ministries*, pp. 157-161; Lebreton and Zeiller, *Primitive Church*, I, 421-424.

[48] St. Ignatius of Antioch, Epistle to the Romans, introduction. The Greek phrase translated "presiding in the love" is προκαθημενη της αγαπης .

[49] Winter, *St. Peter and the Popes*, pp. 122-124.

[50] St. Ignatius of Antioch, Epistle to the Romans 2-6.

[51] Anthony Birley, *Marcus Aurelius* (Boston, 1966), pp. 58-59.

[52] *Cambridge Ancient History*, XI, 313-314; Stewart Perowne, *Hadrian* (London, 1960), pp. 148-149, 163-165; Giuseppe Ricciotti, *The History of Israel* (Milwaukee, 1955), II, 453-459. Recent excavations have brought to light a number of letters by, or concerning Bar-Kokhba, the leader of the Jewish rebellion against Hadrian, confirming his passionate dedication to Judaism but also the essential hopelessness of his uprising. The documents say nothing about his reputed Messianic pretensions. See Yigael Yadin, *Bar-Kokhba* (New York, 1971). Yadin's researches have established for the first time that Bar-Kokhba's rebellion broke out in 132 (*op. cit.*, p. 183). The edict prohibiting circumcision was revoked by the tolerant and peaceable Antoninus Pius, Hadrian's successor, shortly after becoming emperor (Perowne, *Hadrian*, p. 148).

[53] Bernard W. Henderson, *The Life and Principate of the Emperor Hadrian* (London, 1923), p. 223.

[54] Weltin, *Ancient Popes*, p. 67.

[55] *Ibid.*

[56] Henderson, *Hadrian*, pp. 57, 153-162.

[57] The principal Christian apology known from the reign of Antoninus Pius is that of St. Justin Martyr, probably presented to the emperor in 154 (Lebreton and Zeiller, *Primitive Church*, I, 547-555; Birley, *Marcus Aurelius*, pp. 146-148). There was an earlier Christian apology by Aristides, about ten years previous to Justin's (Lebreton and Zeiller, *op. cit.*, I, 536-538). The Cynic philosopher Crescens was spreading evil reports about Christians in Rome in 152-153, which helped induce Justin to prepare his apology (Danielou and Marrou, *Christian Centuries*, I, 88).

[58] Irenaeus, *Against Heresies* III, 4.3.

[59] That this aspect of Gnosticism, which is one of the first and most forcible negative

impressions its doctrines make on a modern reader, was felt also by the ancients is clear from Irenaeus' celebrated satirical passage on its theories of generation (*Against Heresies*, I, 11.4), quoted later in the text.

[60] Irenaeus, *Against Heresies* III, 4.3.

[61] Tertullian, *Against Valentinus* 4.

[62] Shepherd of Hermas, *Visions* I, 1.1 (written in Greek).

[63] *Ibid*. III, 6.7; Lebreton and Zeiller, *Primitive Church*, I, 444.

[64] See text in *The Fathers of the Church* series, Volume I: *The Apostolic Fathers* (New York, 1946), pp. 233-250, from which all quotations herein are taken, and commentary in Lebreton and Zeiller, *Primitive Church*, I, 443-456. It is not absolutely certain that "Hermas" was the writer's own given name.

[65] Shepherd of Hermas, *Mandates* I, 1; II, 1.

[66] For the attribution of the "Gospel of Truth"—a complete copy of which, in Coptic translation, was found in the ancient Gnostic library discovered at Nag Hammadi in 1945—to Valentinus, see Jonas, *Gnostic Religion*, pp. 178-179.

[67] *Ibid*., p. 195.

[68] Danielou and Marrou, *Christian Centuries*, I, 99; Weltin, *Ancient Popes*, p. 56.

[69] Clerical celibacy was not yet the rule in any part of the Church, although quite commonly practiced.

[70] Lebreton and Zeiller, *Primitive Church*, II, 641-653; Weltin, *Ancient Popes*, pp. 71-73; E. C. Blackman, *Marcion and His Influence* (London, 1948), pp. 42-60, 82-87, 113-124.

[71] Shepherd of Hermas, *Visions* I, 3.4; *Mandates* III, 9.1-2; VII, 5.

[72] Lebreton and Zeiller, *Primitive Church*, II, 643; Weltin, *Ancient Popes*, p. 71; Blackman, *Marcion*, pp. 1-14.

[73] Irenaeus, *Against Heresies* III, 3.4; Irenaeus to Florinus, in Eusebius, *Ecclesiastical History* V, 20. The gentleness of Polycarp's character is evident from his one extant writing, the Letter to the Philippians (about 135).

[74] Irenaeus to Pope Victor I, in Eusebius, *Ecclesiastical History* V, 24 (see note in the translation of this book of Eusebius' history in *The Fathers of the Church* series, Volume 19, p. 338); John E. Walsh, *The Bones of St. Peter* (Garden City NY, 1982), pp. 176-177.

[75] Jean Colson, *Lyon, Baptistère des Gaules* (Paris, 1975), pp. 117-118.

[76] The correct date for Polycarp's martyrdom has been much argued. The majority of authorities favor 155 or 156 over the alternative date of 167 derived from Eusebius. For a brief statement of the case for 155, see Cecil J. Cadoux, *Ancient Smyrna, a History of the City from the Earliest Times to 324 A.D.* (Oxford, 1938), p. 355n; for a statement of the case for 156, see Lebreton and Zeiller, *Primitive Church*, I, 396. More recently, support for the retention of the 155 or 156 date as against 167 is given in Jedin and Dolan, *History of the Church*, I, 136, while Frend, *Martyrdom and Persecution*, pp. 197, 471, citing several authorities, upholds the minority view for 167.

[77] *Martyrdom of Polycarp* 9, 3 for the quotation. The most detailed modern account of the martyrdom of Polycarp appears in Cadoux, *Ancient Smyrna*, pp. 355-364.

[78] Birley, *Marcus Aurelius*, pp. 149-150.

[79] Marcus Aurelius departed for the Danube frontier in the autumn of 169 (Birley, *Marcus Aurelius*, p. 222); he remained there almost continuously until the summer of 175 when he had to go east following a rebellion there (*ibid.*, p. 262); then, three years later, new barbarian incursions compelled him to return to the Danube frontier (*ibid.*, pp. 281-283) where he remained until his death in March of 180 (*ibid.*, pp. 286-288).

[80] A severe plague—perhaps the most severe in ancient history—was brought back

by Roman troops returning in 167 from a campaign in Mesopotamia. It ravaged the empire for several years, causing very high mortality (Birley, *Marcus Aurelius*, pp. 202-206, 214-219).

[81] Birley, *Marcus Aurelius*, p. 210.

[82] G. K. Chesterton, *The Everlasting Man* (New York, 1925), pp. 195-196.

[83] The Acts of Justin's martyrdom, whose authenticity is almost universally acknowledged, are printed in full with notes in E. C. E. Owen, *Some Authentic Acts of the Early Martyrs* (London, 1927), pp. 47-52.

[84] Engelbert Kirschbaum, *The Tombs of St. Peter and St. Paul* (New York, 1957), pp. 129-137; Frend, *Martyrdom and Persecution*, p. 179.

[85] Lebreton and Zeiller, *Primitive Church*, I, 398-399.

[86] Élie Griffe, *La Gaule Chrétienne à l'époque romaine* (Paris, 1964), pp. 25-28; Colson, *Lyon*, pp. 121-122. Pothinus, about 90 years old in 177, would therefore have been at least thirteen in the year 100, shortly before the Apostle John's death. Although too young to have been extensively instructed by St. John as Polycarp was, he certainly could have seen and heard him, and would have been old enough to understand the importance of this man and to remember him vividly, if he had met him as a boy in the province of Asia.

[87] A detailed account of these martyrdoms, whose authenticity is unquestioned, appears in Eusebius, *Ecclesiastical History* V, 1-2.

[88] *Ibid.* V, 1.

[89] *Ibid.* V, 3-4.

[90] Apocalypse 2:20; Frend, *Martyrdom and Persecution*, pp. 217-221; Jedin and Dolan, *History of the Church*, I, 199-201; Lebreton and Zeiller, *Primitive Church*, II, 656-659.

[91] Weltin, *Ancient Popes*, pp. 80-82, accepts the older tradition of a condemnation of Montanism by Pope Eleutherius which the other authorities cited in Note 90, above, now attribute to Pope Zephyrinus about 200. Danielou and Marrou, *Christian Centuries*, I, 103, emphasize (perhaps over-emphasize) Montanism's doctrinal orthodoxy.

[92] Hardy, *Christianity and the Roman Government*, pp. 198, 202-208. As Hardy explicitly states (p. 208), Apollonius was executed simply and solely for being a Christian. To be charged with bearing the Name, and not to retreat from it, were sufficient grounds for the death penalty, and had been as far back as we have record of persecution and martyrdom of Christians by Roman officials. This clear evidence, along with that of the certainly authentic Acts of the Scillitan martyrs in 181 (Hardy, *op. cit.*, pp. 198-200), makes it especially difficult to understand why so many modern scholars, including Hardy himself—one of the principal authorities on this subject—have been so resistant to the thesis of a general law in the Roman empire which made it illicit simply to be a Christian, opting instead for variations on Hardy's theme of "local police regulations" as the basis for the persecutions and executions of Christians from Nero to Decius. The wide geographical distribution of Christian martyrdoms in the Roman empire even before the well-organized universal persecution of Decius began in 250 (see Chapter Nineteen, below) and the remarkable uniformity of the legal proceedings, once instituted, as reported in all the early Acts of the martyrs, surely indicate not variant local regulations, but a uniform law—not always rigorously enforced, but enforced in the same way and on the same basis whenever charges were brought against Christians and their trials undertaken. See Chapter Seventeen, above, especially Notes 129-133.

[93] Butler's *Lives of the Saints*, edited, revised and supplemented by Herbert Thurston and Donald Attwater (Westminster, MD, 1956), II, 120.

[94] Griffe, *La Gaule Chretienne*, pp. 74-79.

[95] It is astonishing that no English translation of this exceedingly important book has

been published in the twentieth century. Neither of the principal Roman Catholic series of patristic volumes—Fathers of the Church and Ancient Christian Writers—includes it. The only English version in existence is in the complete edition of the Ante-Nicene Fathers, edited by Alexander Roberts and James Donaldson, originally published in Scotland in the nineteenth century and reprinted in Grand Rapids, Michigan in 1957—fiercely Protestant, but at a high level of scholarship.

[96] Irenaeus, *Against Heresies* I, 11.4

[97] *Ibid.* III, 3.2, translation of Winter, *St. Peter and the Popes*, p. 126, with commentary following, pp. 126-129. The famous crux in this passage is the phrase translated by Winter "because of its stronger origin," in our text *propter potentiorem principalitatem*. However, our text is an ancient Latin translation of the Greek original, which we do not have, and the translation at this point is not very good or clear Latin. Alternate renderings to "stronger origin" are "the greater authority of its origin" (Jedin and Dolan, *History of the Church*, I, 356n); "special priority" (Herbert Musurillo, *The Fathers of the Primitive Church* [New York, 1966], p. 139); and "outstanding pre-eminence" (Cyril Richardson, *Early Christian Fahters* [New York, 1970], p. 372). Winter thinks the original Greek for *principalitatem* was πρωτεια , "priority"; other authorities have suggested αρχη, "ancient origin." But Winter's "stronger origin" is definitely not good English; "special priority" and even "outstanding pre-eminence" beg the question by avoiding the concept of origin; and the word "authority," while seeming to clarify the matter, is simply not in the text we have. "Higher" would seem to convey the sense of *potentiorem* better, at least in English, than "stronger." The precise nuance of meaning, both in the original and in any translation, of the two words here represented by *potentiorem principalitatem* is obviously of the greatest importance. We may hope that some day the rainless sands of Egypt will yield up a papyrus containing the original Greek of this vital phrase. Whatever its exact meaning, it seems hardly possible to imagine that it does not refer to the Roman church described with such enthusiastic praise in the preceding sentence, despite some attempts to cast doubt even upon this (Jedin and Dolan, *History of the Church*, I, 357n).

[98] Irenaeus, *Against Heresies* III, 3.3.

[99] Jedin and Dolan, *History of the Church*, I, 196-197.

[100] Anthony Birley, *Septimius Severus, the African Emperor* (New York, 1972), pp. 136-202; *Cambridge Ancient History*, Volume XII (Cambridge, England, 1938), pp. 1-38.

[101] See Chapter Six, above.

[102] Lebreton and Zeiller, *Primitive Church*, II, 719-725; Jedin and Dolan, *History of the Church*, I, 268-271, 357-358.

[103] Leoreton and Zeiller, *Primitive Church*, II, 726-730.

[104] *Ibid.*, pp. 730-734; Cadoux, *Ancient Smyrna*, pp. 370-372.

[105] Hippolytus, *Against Noetus* 1.

[106] Lebreton and Zeiller, *Primitive Church*, II, 734-735.

[107] *Ibid.*, pp. 736-737; Jedin and Dolan, *History of the Church*, I, 257-258.

[108] Lebreton and Zeiller, *Primitive Church*, II, 753-754; Danielou and Marrou, *Christian Centuries*, I, 141-143. Lebreton and Zeiller present the arguments for dating the edict to 201 rather than the more commonly attributed date of 202; the 201 date is also supported by *Cambridge Ancient History*, XII, 18, 481.

[109] Owen, *Acts of the Early Martyrs*, pp. 78-92; the quotation is on p. 89. Much of the text of the Acts of Sts. Perpetua and Felicity represents the actual words of Perpetua, which she—a well-educated woman—either wrote or dictated herself; the remainder was edited and very possibly written by none other than Tertullian. For the date, background, and composition of the Acts of Perpetua and Felicity see Frend, *Martyrdom and Persecu-*

tion, pp. 268-271 and Lebreton and Zeiller, *Primitive Church*, II, 754-755.

[110] Matthew 25:40; Eusebius, *Ecclesiastical History* VI, 1-5; Jean Danielou, *Origen* (New York, 1955), pp. 3-12; Lebreton and Zeiller, *Primitive Church*, II, 897. The intellectual history of the "school of Alexandria" and the questions surrounding the theology, Scriptural exegesis and fusion of Christian and Hellenistic learning by Clement and Origen are outside the scope of this history. For a brief but excellent introduction by one of the greatest authorities on Origen, Cardinal Danielou, see Danielou and Marrou, *Christian Centuries*, I, 127-136, 181-186; for a fuller treatment see Lebreton and Zeiller, *Primitive Church*, II, 891-985. Because of his special interest in Origen, Eusebius the historian was very familiar with events in Alexandria at this period and so can be relied upon when conveying the tradition of the martyrdom of Potamiaena and Basilides.

[111] Birley, *Septimius Severus*, p. 268.

[112] *Cambridge Ancient History*, XII, 43-53.

[113] Lebreton and Zeiller, *Primitive Church*, II, 1124-1125; Danielou and Marrou, *Christian Centuries*, I, 167-168; Hertling and Kirschbaum, *Roman Catacombs*, p. 29.

[114] Lebreton and Zeiller, *Primitive Church*, II, 835-842, present an excellent analysis of the elements in Tertullian's mind and character that made him the only Church Father to leave the Church. His slide into Montanism began about 206 (Jedin and Dolan, *History of the Church*, I, 202) and was complete by 213 (Stuart A. Donaldson, *Church Life and Thought in North Africa, A.D. 200* [Cambridge, England, 1909], p. 37).

[115] Lebreton and Zeiller, *Primitive Church*, II, 736-741, 1124-1125; Weltin, *Ancient Popes*, pp. 100-101; Louis Duchesne, *The Early History of the Christian Church* (London, 1909), I, 232-233. Some writers, *e.g.*, Danielou and Marrou, *Christian Centuries*, I, 144-151 and Jedin and Dolan, *History of the Church*, I, 245, deny that Hippolytus ever proclaimed himself, or was formally proclaimed Pope. But that he was in schism, refusing to accept Callistus' Papal authority, is evident from his writings; and there seems little basis in the sources for assuming, as Danielou does (*op. cit.*, I, 146) that Hippolytus was not only reconciled with the Church under Callistus' successor Pope Urban I but also was asked by Urban to work out in more detail the chronology of Easter. It is more consistent with the known facts to assume, with Duchesne *loc. cit.*, that his work on the chronology of Easter was written because of his position as a rival to the regular Papal line. The reconciliation of Hippolytus in the Sardinian mines is too well attested, especially by the evidence of Pope Damasus, to justify any historical reconstruction which would put that reconciliation at any other time (see Note 145, below).

[116] Tertullian, *De pudicitia* 1-5; Hippolytus, *Philosophumena* IX, 12. Speaking of "adulterers and fornicators," Tertullian says at the end of the first chapter of *De pudicitia*: "They will shed tears barren of peace and receive from the Church nothing more than the publication of their shame." The editor of Tertullian's two works on penance does not exaggerate when he declares: "The heartless cruelty of this sentence is unparalleled, even in a work conspicuous for intolerance and severity." (William P. Le Saint, ed., *Tertullian: Treatises on Penance, Ancient Christian Writers* series, Volume 18 [Westminster MD, 1959], p. 197).

[117] Lebreton and Zeiller, *Primitive Church*, II, 709-713; Weltin, *Ancient Popes*, pp. 103-104. There is every reason to believe that Callistus took this position, even if the specific bishop's edict confirming the availability of penance to those guilty of adultery and fornication, which Tertullian so scathingly denounces in the first chapter of *De pudicitia*, is not the Pope's but that of a bishop of Carthage or elsewhere in North Africa, as many modern scholars hold (*e.g.*, Jedin and Dolan, *History of the Church*, I, 326). Hippolytus' criticisms of his principles on penance make it evident that the edict quoted

by Tertullian accurately reflects the Pope's policy, no matter who issued it. The much-debated phrase in *De pudicitia* 21, directed by Tertullian in hectoring courtroom style to the author of the edict: "You presume that the power of binding and.loosing has devolved upon you also, that is, upon every church which is akin to Peter [*ad omnem ecclesiam Petri propinquam*]. Who are you to prevent and to change completely the manifest will of Christ, who grants this to Peter personally?" is far from being conclusive (*pace History of the Church, loc. cit.*) or even strongly suggestive either that the edict was the Pope's or that of a local bishop. The same power is asserted on the same basis by the Catholic Church, and denied by Tertullian, in either case, so long as the local bishop is acting in harmony with the Pope. See the excellent commentary by Le Saint, ed., *Tertullian: Treatises on Penance*, pp. 284-286. See also Le Saint's introduction to *De pudicitia* (*ibid.*, pp. 46-51) for a discussion of the question of whether all sins were regarded as forgivable even before the pontificate of Callistus. The best evidence that they were is provided by Tertullian's own *De paenitentia* (4), written before he became a Montanist, in which he explicitly affirms that all sins may be forgiven. Confirming evidence is provided by the Shepherd of Hermas (written about 150) and by a letter from Bishop Dionysius of Corinth about 170, which specifically mentions that forgiveness for heresy may be obtained through penance (Jedn and Dolan, *History of the Church*, I, 321-324.). Tertullian's statements in *De pudicitia* that only adultery and not murder and apostasy, of the capital sins, are now to be forgiven by the Church in union with Rome need not be taken at face value in view of the intensely polemical character of *De pudicitia* and the weight of this other contemporary and earlier evidence to the contrary.

[118] Lebreton and Zeiller, *Primitive Church*, II, 736.

[119] Tertullian, *De pudicitia* 1. See Note 116, above.

[120] Lebreton and Zeiller, *Primitive Church*, II, 711-712; Weltin, *Ancient Popes*, pp. 105-106; Jedin and Dolan, *History of the Church*, I, 308.

[121] Duchesne, *Early History of the Christian Church*, I, 320; Weltin, *Ancient Popes*, p. 96; Frend, *Martyrdom and Persecution*, p. 247; Hertling and Kirschbaum, *Roman Catacombs*, p. 39.

[122] Weltin, *Ancient Popes*, pp. 96-97.

[123] This is the verdict of the great English Catholic scholar John Chapman in his outstanding article on Pope St. Callistus I in *The Catholic Encyclopedia* (1913).

[124] *Cambridge Ancient History* XII, 56-57; Lebreton and Zeiller, *Primitive Church*, II, 1128; Downey, *Antioch*, pp. 305-306; Danielou, *Origen*, pp. 20-22. The traditional date of Pope St. Callistus I's martyrdom is October 14, his feast day.

[125] *Cambridge Ancient History* XII, 109-111.

[126] See Chapter Seventeen, above; Jedin and Dolan, *History of the Church*, I, 372; Downey, *Antioch*, p. 304; Danielou and Marrou, *Christian Centuries*, I, 188-190; Paul Allard, *Ten Lectures on the Martyrs* (London, 1907), pp. 48-50.

[127] Danielou and Marrou, *Christian Centuries*, I, 192.

[128] Frend, *Martyrdom and Persecution*, pp. 228-229.

[129] *Cambridge Ancient History* XI, 111.

[130] *Ibid.*, XII, 69; Godfrey Turton, *The Syrian Princesses* (London, 1974), pp. 186-188.

[131] Turton, *Syrian Princesses*, pp. 3, 132-134.

[132] See Chapter Seventeen, above (text and Notes 129-134) and Note 92 for this chapter. The letter of Trajan to Pliny and the rescript of Hadrian to Minucius Fundanus are not exceptions, since they are directed only against malicious *false* accusations of Christianity. Actual Christians denounced must still be executed (Lebreton and Zeiller, *Primitive Church*, I, 393-394).

[133] Prosper Guéranger, *Life of Saint Cecilia, Virgin and Martyr* (Philadelphia, 1866),

pp. 28-31, 52-130; H. Quentin, "Sainte Cécile," *Dictionnaire d'Archéologie chrétienne et de liturgie* (DACL), II (2), 2713-2721; J. P. Kirsch, "Cecilia, Saint," *The Catholic Encyclopedia* (1913). Guéranger and Quentin both quote extensively from the Acts of St. Cecilia in the original Latin; the English translation of Guéranger's work provides much the largest body of quotations from this document available in English.

[134] There has been much historical and archeological confusion and prolonged controversy over the correct location and attribution of the graves of Cecilia, Valerian, Tiburtius, Maximus, and Pope Urban I. The principal relevance of the controversy to this history concerns the historical accuracy of the tradition of the burial of these martyrs as later recorded in the Acts of St. Cecilia and, still later, in the Acts of Pope St. Urban I. The body of St. Cecilia had been moved from the catacomb of Callistus by 821 when it was rediscovered by Pope Paschal I in the catacomb of Praetextatus. See H. Leclercq, "Cécile, Crypte et Basilique de Sainte," DACL, II (2), 2753-2756, and Louis Duchesne, *Le Liber Pontificalis, Texte, Introduction et Commentaire* (Paris, 1892), I, 64-65. Roman tradition, the later Acts of Pope St. Urban I, the Acts of St. Cecilia, and the Liber Pontificalis all agree in placing the grave of Pope Urban I in the catacomb of Praetextatus near the graves of his martyred converts (cf. Duchesne, *op. cit.*, p. xciv). Discovering an inscription reading "URBANUS E[piskopos]" (Bishop Urban) in the catacomb of Callistus in the same area where many of the subsequent third century Popes were buried (it has come to be known as the "papal crypt"), the great archeologist de Rossi developed a theory that Pope Urban I was buried in the catacomb of Callistus with his immediate successors and that the Urban buried in the catacomb of Praetextatus was a simple bishop, also honored as a martyr. De Rossi's theory has been widely accepted. But two strong arguments may be made against it: (1) none of Urban's *predecessors* were buried in the "papal crypt," the first certain burials there having been carried out by Pope Fabian of his predecessors Pontian (Urban's immediate successor) and Anteros (Hertling and Kirschbaum, *Roman Catacombs*, p. 41), so there is no real evidence that the practice was established at the time of Urban's death, leaving us only with the evidence of the inscription, which cuts both ways since the Urban buried in the catacomb of Callistus could have been the simple bishop, and the Pope could then have been buried in Praetextatus as tradition and our other sources state; (2) epigraphic evidence indicates that the lettering on the "URBANUS" inscription in the catacomb of Callistus is considerably later in date than the third century (J. P. Kirsch, "Urban I, Saint, Pope," *The Catholic Encyclopedia* [1913]). Kirsch concludes: "It seems necessary to accept the testimony that Pope Urban is buried in the Catacomb of Praetextatus while the Urban lying in St. Callistus was a bishop of later date from some other city." (*ibid.*) Though Kirsch dismisses the Acts of St. Cecilia as "purely legendary" (*ibid.*), his own data actually provide an impressive confirmation of the historical accuracy both of the Acts of St. Cecilia and of the Acts of Pope St. Urban I. The authenticity of the latter in particular, long almost universally denied, is well defended by Guéranger, *St. Cecilia*, pp. 131-137.

[135] Guéranger, *St. Cecilia*, pp. 139-158; Quentin, "Sainte Cécile," DACL, II (2), 2719-2720. The earliest date Quentin considers possible for the composition of the Acts of St. Cecilia is 486. As Guéranger points out, the careful preservation by the Church of contemporary written accounts of the martyrs is clearly attested by Pontius in his very early life of St. Cyprian, the great martyr bishop of Africa (*Early Christian Biographies*, ed. Roy J. Deferrari [New York, 1952], Volume 15 in *The Fathers of the Church* series, p. 5).

[136] Prosper Guéranger, *Sainte Cécile et la Sociéte Romaine aux deux premiers siècles*, 8th ed. (Paris, 1897), II, 84. Of the many alternative datings proposed, the most widely accepted has been that drawn from Adon of Vienne, writing more than three centuries after the probable date of composition of the Acts of St. Cecilia, who says she was mar-

tyred during the joint reign of Marcus Aurelius and Commodus toward the end of Marcus Aurelius' life—that is, about the time of the great martyrdom of Lyons (177). Adon is supposed to have used some ancient lost source giving this as the correct date of Cecilia's martyrdom. (See Paul Allard, *Histoire des Persécutions pendant les deux premiers siècles*, 2d ed. [Paris, 1892], pp. 427-429.) In a learned and brilliant analysis, the French scholar H. Quentin has shown that Adon's principal and probably only sources for the information he gives on St. Cecilia were her Acts and misunderstood and misapplied data from Bede's Chronicle, in which the old official names of the Roman emperors are used: Elagabalus, the immediate predecessor of Alexander Severus, is given as Marcus Aurelius Antoninus; while the emperor whom we call Marcus Aurelius is given as Marcus Antonius Verus. On the other hand, neither does Quentin accept the historical validity and chronological accuracy of the Acts of St. Cecilia; he suggests that she was martyred in Diocletian's persecution of 304-312 (Quentin, "Sainte Cécile," DACL, II [2], 2722-2725).

[137] Hippolyte Delehaye, *Étude sur le Legendier romain, les Saintes de Novembre et de Decembre* (Brussels, 1936), pp. 77-88; Quentin, "Sainte Cécile," DACL, II (2), 2729-2731; Allard, *Persécutions pendant les deux premiers siècles*, pp. 434-435. The name of the prefect, Turcius Almachius, is half Roman—Turcius is a known Roman name, though a rare one; Almachius is not. The surname may have been corrupted in the tradition or by an early copyist of the Acts (the only place it appears), or—following the edict of Caracalla extending citizenship to all free provincials—non-Romans may by this time have begun to hold high office even in the city of Rome itself.

[138] Cecilia's stature has been excessively reduced by those who have taken the length of her coffin—four feet three inches—to represent her full height. The body was found in a curved position, and some contraction had very likely taken place (though the usual physical and anatomical laws and probabilities obviously do not entirely govern in the case of a body which remained incorrupt for more than a thousand years). Still, her stature was probably slightly below five feet, not at all uncommon for a woman of that time, especially if (as is probable) she was in her middle teens at the time of her martyrdom.

[139] Guéranger, *St. Cecilia*, pp. 198-217, 221-228, 265-302; H. Leclercq, "Cécile, Crypte et Basilique de Sainte," DACL, II (2), 2749-2753. The principal accounts are those of Baronius, *Annales Ecclesiastici*, Tomus Quartusdecimus (820-863) (1868 ed.), Year 821, 1-20, pp. 12-16, and of Antonio Bosio, *Historia passionis sanctae Caeciliae* (Rome, 1600), a very old and rare book of which this writer has not been able to obtain a copy. However, Guéranger includes numerous lengthy quotations from Bosio, both in the original Latin and in English translation, in his pages cited. The differences between Baronius' and Bosio's accounts, of which much is made by critics, do not appear major, and may readily be explained by the simple fact that Baronius was an eyewitness to the opening of the coffin while Bosio, though a contemporary, was not present. For the statement of Maderna the sculptor, see Butler-Thurston-Attwater, *Lives of the Saints* IV, 404, though the editors cast doubt on the veracity of Maderna and Baronius in reporting what they actually saw, in a manner that, in the absence of concrete evidence of falsification or major internal evidence of contradictions, seems to this writer both unwarranted and reprehensible. Maderna's statue and inscription may be seen today in the Basilica of St. Cecilia by any visitor to Rome. Leclercq, *loc. cit.*, col. 2752, explains the devices in use in the early medieval period by which the lower portion of Cecilia's coffin could readily have been moved without disarranging the body.

[140] Baronius, *Annales Ecclesiastici*, Tomus Quartusdecimus, Year 821, 16 and 19, pp. 15-16. The writer is indebted to his colleague, Professor William Marshner, chair-

man of the Theology Department of Christendom College and a fine Latin scholar, for his careful translation of Baronius' Latin in these decisive phrases describing the examination of the body of St. Cecilia, which are fundamental in establishing the accuracy of the reported findings.

[141] Delehaye, *Légendier romain, Saints de Novembre*, pp. 94-95; H. Quentin, "Sainte Cécile," *DACL* II (2), 2735-2737. The diametrical opposition of the views of Quentin and Leclercq on the authenticity and reliability of the observations of St. Cecilia's incorrupt body in 1599, in successive articles in the DACL, is truly remarkable. The weight of expert and intelligent testimony by the distinguished witnesses of that opening of her coffin appears to this writer overwhelming. However, there is clearly a contradiction with Anastasius' ninth century history in the matter of St. Cecilia's head. Baronius' attempts to explain the contradiction away (*Annales Ecclesiastici*, Tomus Quartusdecimus, Year 821, 11, p. 15) are unconvincing. Guéranger suggests that the relics later venerated as Cecilia's, including the head, were mostly from Tiburtius, whose head was not found at the examination of 1599, pointing out that it was customary in the ninth century to remove parts of a saint's body as relics when it was found, and that Anastasius would therefore have expected this to have been done with St. Cecilia's body, leading him to assume that some of Tiburtius' relics were hers (*St. Cecilia*, pp. 224-226). The critic Quentin (*loc. cit.*) cites Guéranger's explanation and admits that it is possible, but clings to his conclusion that the eyewitnesses of 1599 did not notice that the head of the body at which they were gazing so intently, was missing. With all due respect to the great French scholar, such a conclusion seems simply incredible. Eight people do not view a body so carefully and reverently without noticing that the head is missing, if in fact it is missing; and Baronius testifies explicitly that Pope Clement VIII personally determined that every member of St. Cecilia's body was intact (see Note 140, above).

[142] Allard, *Persécutions pendant les deux premiers siècles*, p. 439: "Rarement un document de cette nature a subi une épreuve plus concluante, et en est sorti mieux justifié."

[143] Emperor Hadrian said nothing to encourage persecution of Christians, and in fact attempted to discourage it in his rescript to Minucius Fundanus, yet Pope Telesphorus was martyred in Rome during his reign; Marcus Aurelius certainly did not order and would never have approved the hellish tortures inflicted on the martyrs of Lyons in 177, yet they were inflicted on his authority. With specific reference to Alexander Severus, Timothy D. Barnes states: "Alexander [Severus] may still have been emperor when earthquakes and the subsequent outcry led Licinius Serenianus, the governor of Cappadocia, to lend his hand to attacks on the Christians of the province" (*Tertullian, a Historical and Literary Study* [Oxford, 1971], p. 157).

[144] *E.g.*, the astonishingly inadequate statement on this matter in the generally outstanding history of the early Church by Lebreton and Zeiller: "The *Passion* which represents Cecilia as the virgin spouse of Valerian, brother to Tiburtius, is only a late romance; but the account it gives of the death of Cecilia, condemned to be suffocated in the bath of her own house, and finally decapitated [this is erroneous; St. Cecilia's Acts clearly specify that she survived three days with deep wounds in her neck, but definitely not decapitated], has been at least partially confirmed by remarkable archeological discoveries" (*Primitive Church*, I, 402)—but the nature of these "remarkable archeological discoveries" is never specified! Information on this whole subject is extraordinarily difficult to come by, and almost totally unavailable in English. (One noteworthy exception is Horace K. Mann in his very comprehensive *The Lives of the Popes in the Early Middle Ages*, III, 150-153, with reference to the exhumation by Pope Paschal I, but also including a summary of the exhumation of 1599. See also Joan C. Cruz, *The Incorruptibles* [Rockford IL, 1977], pp.43-46.) It would seem that there has been a reluctance,

even on the part of orthodox Catholic historians, to "get involved" in the controversy, though the available evidence strikingly demonstrates the accuracy of a great martyr's Acts which the usual canons of critical scholarship would have dismissed (and, despite the evidence, have still dismissed) as unhistorical.

[145] *Cambridge Ancient History* XII, 70-71, 129; Turton, *Syrian Princesses*, pp. 192-197; Lebreton and Zeiller, *Primitive Church*, II, 759-760, 862, 1129-1130; Eusebius, *Ecclesiastical History* VI, 29; Hertling and Kirschbaum, *Roman Catacombs*, p. 41. Postulating a second Hippolytus as the martyr in the mines (*e.g.*, Jedin and Dolan, *History of the Church*, I, 245) should be avoided in the absence of clear proof. The hypothesis of doubling so readily resorted to by many historians needs sharp cuts of Occam's razor. See Note 115, above, for the martyrdom of Hippolytus, and Note 133, above, for the original placement of the grave of St. Cecilia in the catacomb of Callistus.

[146] T. Scott Holmes, *The Origin and Development of the Christian Church in Gaul during the First Six Centuries of the Christian Era* (London, 1911), pp. 60-73; Griffe, *La Gaule Chrétienne*, pp. 114-115, 148-152; Joseph Stiglmayr, "Denis, Saint," *The Catholic Encyclopedia* (1913); Henri Leclercq, "Denis," DACL, IV, 588-606. There is considerable reason to believe, as Gregory of Tours reports four centuries later, that Sts. Trophimus of Arles, Paul of Narbonne, and Martial of Limoges were also in this group, but the great accumulation of legend around their names has made it almost impossible to ascertain anything historically reliable about their apostolic work. If the group did go to Gaul at the same time, it is highly probable that they went at least several years before Saturninus' martyrdom, which is securely dated in 250.

[147] Jedin and Dolan, *History of the Church*, I, 261-268; Lebreton and Zeiller, *Primitive Church*, II, 1010-1016; Jonas, *Gnostic Religion*, pp. 206-236. See L. J. R. Ort, *Mani, a Religio-Historical Description of His Personality* (Leiden, 1967), *passim*.

[148] Lebreton and Zeiller, *Primitive Church*, II, 1035-1040.

[149] *Ibid.*, II, pp. 761-762; *Cambridge Ancient History* XII, 91-92; Frend, *Martyrdom and Persecution*, p. 299. On the alleged Christian belief of Emperor Philip the Arab, see Jedin and Dolan, *History of the Church*, I, 221-222, and Downey, *Antioch*, pp. 306-308, as well as Lebreton and Zeiller, *ibid.* Almost all modern authorities who have carefully investigated the question doubt very much, or simply deny, that Philip the Arab was actually the first Christian emperor, noting for example that he presided over the thoroughly pagan ceremonies commemorating the millennium of Rome with no indication of any of the conscientious scruples which any real Christian must have felt in doing so. The evidence indicates no more than a strong sympathy for Christianity on Philip's part; but this he clearly had. Its origin is unknown, but if it related to his Mesopotamian childhood home, it would be further evidence to add to the growing body of data indicating the extensive penetration of Christianity into that region, both within and outside the Roman frontiers (see Notes 127-129, above).

[150] Eusebius, *Ecclesiastical History* VI, 41; Lebreton and Zeiller, *Primitive Church*, II, 762-763; Frend, *Martyrdom and Persecution*, pp. 298-299. Opponents of the historicity of the Acts of St. Cecilia have long relied, as a principal argument, on the Christian sympathies of Alexander Severus to state or imply that he would not have permitted such martyrdoms in Rome while he was emperor. See Note 143, above.

[151] Lebreton and Zeiller, *Primitive Church*, II, pp. 971-983; Danielou, *Origen*, pp. 99-120.

[152] Guéranger, *St. Cecilia*, pp. 122-123.

19.
BLOOD OF THE MARTYRS
(249-311)

You have endured, even to the consummation of glory, the hardest questioning; you have not yielded to torments, but rather the torments have yielded to you. An end of sorrows which torments did not give, crowns have given. The butcher's stall has persisted for a time for this, not to cast down your abiding faith, but to send men of God more quickly to the Lord. The multitude of those present, admiring the celestial and spiritual combat of God, the battle of Christ, saw that His servants stood with a free voice, an incorruptible mind, a divinely inspired valor, stripped, indeed, of worldly weapons, but believing, armed with the arms of faith. The tortured stood braver than the torturers; and battered and wounded limbs conquered hammering and tearing nails. . . .

How joyful was Christ therein! How willingly in such servants of His has He both fought and conquered as Protector of the faith, giving to the believers as much as he who receives believes he can take! He was present at His own struggle; He lifted up, strengthened, animated the defenders and protectors of His Name. And He Who once conquered death for us always conquers it in us. . . . If the line of battle has called you, if the day of your struggle has come, fight bravely; struggle constantly, knowing that you are fighting under the eyes of God who is present, that you are coming to His glory by the confession of His name who is not such that He only looks upon His servants, but He Himself struggles in us; He Himself joins battle; He Himself in the contest of our struggle both crowns and is likewise crowned.—Bishop St. Cyprian of Carthage to the martyrs and confessors of Jesus Christ, 250 (Epistle 10)

Within and throughout the Roman empire now there was a Presence, becoming evident even to many of the pagans. For 220 years Christianity had been hidden from most of the world its Founder had conquered. It could be hidden no longer. Henceforth it would shape history as much through the deathless hatred of its foes as by the deathless love of its own.

"I have not come to bring peace, but a sword . . . ."[1]

Emperor Decius was a strong man, highly motivated, rigorous, inflexible. In another age he could have been the savior of Rome. He saw himself in that role. This was no flabby, deluded Nero; no haunted, paranoid Domitian; no cynical Septimius Severus. This was a Roman senator like the senators of old. But the day of his kind had passed; Christ had made all things new. Decius seems in a way to have sensed this, and he could not endure it. His Roman world must be one, hard, strong, bonded in unity under the old gods, the slow rot—now spreading for all to see—ruthlessly cut out. The Christians would conform or die.[2]

Four months after Decius became emperor, in January 250, he issued his edict of persecution: Every man, woman and child in the Roman empire must make a public sacrifice before the idols of the pagan gods. Anyone refusing to do so would be killed. He began by killing the Pope, the farmer Fabian, and let it be known that he would rather face a rival claimant of the imperium than hear of the election of another Bishop of Rome.[3]

The shock was truly universal, utterly unexpected. There had been no general persecution throughout the whole empire since Nero's, with the partial exception of Domitian's, both already far back beyond living memory. The sporadic persecutions of the second century and the first half of the third century (100-250) had grown out of local problems and tumults; though Christianity had remained illegal ever since Nero, there had not been during those 150 years a deliberate general imperial initiative to eliminate the new religion. In Nero's time there had been Peter himself to lead and inspire the Church until almost the end of the first great imperial persecution; during Domitian's persecution there remained throughout, at the head of the Church, Peter's own hand-picked Clement. Pope Fabian had been a deeply good, strong and simple man;[4] but Decius knew exactly who he was and why he was important (as Nero had never known with Peter, nor Domitian with Clement) and so had killed him first. There was no time to gird spiritual armor; the demand for the pagan sacrifices was immediate and universal; the Church was leaderless. With Decius in Rome, no successor to Pope Fabian could be elected; the bishops of Carthage and Alexandria disappeared;[5] the bishops of Antioch and Jerusalem died in prison.[6] The Bishop of Smyrna—Euktemon, of Polycarp's see—apostatized.[7] So did thousands of the formerly faithful.[8]

It was March of 250. Decius' persecuting edict was scarcely two months old, and its success was almost complete.

The elder Pionius of the church of Smyrna, a little man named Asclepiades, and an escaped slave-girl called Sabina stood against the tide. At that moment, so far as they knew, the whole Christian hope as the world might see it had departed. But it had not departed for them. To the warden of the pagan temple at Smyrna Pionius declared: "We do not worship your gods, and we do not bow down to the golden image."[9]

Pagan friends in the listening crowd urged Pionius to save his life. He replied: "It is good to live, but that life for which we yearn is better. And good it is to see the light [of day], but to see the true light is better. And all these things are good: but the reason we flee from them is not that we long for death, or hate God's words, but because of the surpassing greatness of other things."[10] The apostate bishop was brought in to urge the three to give way, fruitlessly. With joy on their faces they prepared for martyrdom. Pionius was nailed to a stake as his Lord had been nailed to a cross, and burned to death as Polycarp had been.[11]

And after all, they were not alone. Dionysius, the gentle and holy bishop of Alexandria, had been taken away against his will by a crowd of sympathetic peasants after waiting four days in his home for arrest and martyrdom; and while the rich and influential among his flock almost all apostatized, an old invalid, a mother of many children, a virgin, and a fifteen-year-old boy stood forth among others to bear witness to Christ before the judges and the mob of the turbulent Greek city. The aged Origen in Palestine once more confessed his faith heroically under torture.[12] At Rome young Celerinus, not yet twenty years old, a visitor from Africa, refused to make the pagan sacrifice even in the presence of Decius himself, and in consequence spent nineteen consecutive days in the torture of the stocks, unyielding and steadfast. At length released, a scarred cripple, he returned to Carthage to prepare for the priesthood of Christ Whom he had so magnificently confessed.[13]

In Asia Minor Nestor, the bishop of Magydus in Pamphylia, died proclaiming: "With my Christ I have ever been, with Him am I now, and with Him I shall be for evermore";[14] in Ephesus Maximus, a tradesman, was stoned to death for not sacrificing to Diana;[15] in Lampsacus young Peter was broken on the wheel for refusing to sacrifice to Venus; on Chios off the coast, Isidore, an official of Decius serving with the Roman fleet, was denounced as a Christian and died constant in the Faith.[16] In Cappadocia where St. Gregory Thaumaturgus labored, there were numerous martyrs and confessors.[17] The Christian community of Crete produced ten renowned martyrs, to whose intercession the Cretans later gave credit for their preservation from heresy during the Arian, Nestorian, and Monophysite controversies of the ensuing centuries.[18] In the province of Africa Mappalicus held firm through every torture unto death, even though his mother and sister lapsed;[19] in Sicily the virgin martyr Agatha left a radiant, enduring memory of sublime Christian heroism of which, most unfortunately, we lack historically precise details.[20]

By the fall of 250 the tide had turned. Decius was in the Balkans, fighting against Gothic barbarians who had invaded across the Danube. They defeated him in Thrace. In his absence, with his prestige waning, the persecution of the Christians was relaxed. The next spring Decius vanished into the marshes of the Dobrudja around the mouth of the Danube, never to emerge alive;[21] meanwhile in Rome it was possible to elect a new Pope. With near unanimity the bishops and clergy present chose the humble, unsophisticated Cornelius, passing over the distinguished rhetorician and theologian Novatian—as the Gnostic Valentinus had been passed over for Pope in favor of the unpretentious Anicetus a century before, and the theologian Hippolytus for Callistus a generation before. Novatian set himself up as antipope, condemning Cornelius for showing too much willingness to forgive the sin of those who had lapsed during the persecution—once again, men scandalized by the superabundant mercy of Christ and His Vicar. Novatian proceeded to try to take full control of the Church, appointing new bishops in sees all over the Roman empire. Here is the first clear historical proof of the general acceptance of the authority of the Bishop of Rome, as Pope, to appoint or approve bishops anywhere in the world.[22]

Bishops Cyprian of Carthage and Dionysius of Alexandria came at once to the support of the legitimate Pope. In the fall of 251 a synod of sixty bishops, convened at Rome under the direction of Pope Cornelius, excommunicated Novatian and his schismatic followers and specified the precise penitential requirements for readmitting various categories of the lapsed to full communion with the Church.[23]

Decius' successor Gallus did not move strongly to renew the persecution for more than a year. Then he challenged Pope Cornelius and the Christian community in Rome, possibly responding to popular demand for a scapegoat because of a severe plague. But now the Church had been tried by fire. In contrast to the numerous apostasies at the beginning of the Decian persecution, this time the Christians of Rome stood solidly with their bishop, whom Gallus apparently feared to kill as Decius had killed Fabian. Cornelius was sent into exile where he died, acclaimed a martyr because of his sufferings for the Faith, in June 253. By then Gallus too was dead, overthrown by yet another of the Roman army revolts that had now become endemic in the declining empire. Lucius, who had accompanied Pope Cornelius into exile, was elected his successor while still in exile, and restored to Rome when the new Emperor Valerian had established his authority there—for at first Valerian, later a great persecutor, was friendly to the Christians.[24] (See Chronological Table of Popes and Emperors, 249-324, below.)

CHRONOLOGIAL TABLE OF ROMAN EMPERORS AND POPES
249-324

Roman Emperors (Augusti)	Popes
Decius 249-251	Fabian martyred 250
Gallus 251-253	Cornelius 251-253
Valerian 253-259	Lucius I 253-254
	Stephen I 254-257
	Sixtus II 257-258
Gallienus 259-268	Dionysius 259-268
Claudius II Gothicus 268-270	Felix I 269-274
Aurelian 270-275	
Tacitus 275-276	Eutychian 275-283
Probus 276-281	
Carus 281-283	
Carinus (West), Numerian (East) 283-284	Caius 283-296
Diocletian (whole empire)284-293	
Diocletian (E.), Maximian (W.) 293-305	Marcellinus 296-304
Galerius (East) 305-311	(interregnum) 305-307
Constantius Chlorus (West) 305-306	
Constantine (West) 306-323	
Severus (West) 306-307	
Maxentius (West) 307-312	Marcellus I 308-309
Licinius (East) 311-323	Eusebius 310
Maximin Daia (East) 311-313	Miltiades 311-314
Constantine (whole empire) 323-337	Sylvester I 314-335

Lucius died after a pontificate of less than a year and was succeeded by Stephen I, whose strong and decisive character was displayed first by his firm adherence to the policy established by Pope Cornelius regarding the readmission of the lapsed to communion, and also by his defense of bishops who followed this policy despite often vehement criticism by Novatianist rigorists. He laid down principles for judging a bishop accused of excessive laxity or rigor, or of having lapsed himself, and made it clear that the final decision in such cases rested with him as head of the Church. In 256 Pope Stephen ordered Bishop Cyprian of Carthage and the African episcopate which followed his lead to discontinue the practice of re-baptizing persons who had originally received baptism from heretics. In this Stephen upheld the consistent position of the Roman Church, that it is the power and action of Christ that confers baptism and its remission from original sin, not the worthiness or unworthiness of the minister of the sacrament, and the traditional practice of most of the Church, to accept as valid any baptism which had invoked the Trinity. Pope Stephen specifically called for obedience on this matter by his authority as the successor of Peter.

Cyprian refused to obey, despite his earlier statements affirming and glorifying the Petrine primacy and the unity of the Church. But when Pope Stephen died the next year, his successor Sixtus II decided, probably in response to a conciliatory initiative by Bishop Dionysius of Alexandria, not to press the issue further and to tolerate for a time, without explicitly approving, the practice of rebaptism in those areas (Africa, Asia Minor, and Syria) where it was then commonly followed. Despite this important disagreement and Cyprian's actual disobedience, he was never excommunicated, and remained in close contact with Rome.[25]

The pontificate of Stephen was, for the Church's external relations, a brief lull between storms. The persecution which had ceased in 253 when Emperor Gallus was overthrown broke out again in 257 when there was a complete reversal in Emperor Valerian's policy toward the Christians. The change seems clearly to have been connected with the severe trials and dangers the empire was then confronting. Along with the continuation of the plague, there were barbarian assaults almost all along the northern or European frontier, both by land and by sea. The Goths struck Greece, the Sarmatian Borani from south Russia crossed the Black Sea to attack Asia Minor, the Marcomanni marched right through Pannonia (Hungary) all the way into northern Italy as far as Ravenna, and the Franks appear in history for the first time with a massive raid across the Rhine. In the east the newly invigorated Persians launched the greatest invasion of Roman territory from Iran in three hundred years, sweeping across the Euphrates and probably taking and burning Antioch in 256.[26]

Valerian and his son Gallienus fought back bravely in the east and west, respectively. Gallienus regained control of the Rhine frontier and crossed it to punish the barbarians—the last Roman emperor to do so.[27] Valerian marched to Syria, repelled the Persians, and regained and rebuilt Antioch.[28] But the cost was staggering. For many years the Roman empire had been in an economic and population decline. Taxation had become confiscatory for the upper middle class, upon whom the empire depended for effective local government; no considerable financial reserves remained anywhere in the empire. Consequently there was massive depreciation of the currency; the silver *antonianus* lost 98 per cent of its real value in a few years following 256; prices in Egypt rose by 14 to 20 times in 25 years; the population of the empire fell from about 70 million to 50 million.[29]

Under these severe pressures, Valerian and his advisors not only felt the increased concern for tighter social unification of the empire that had helped make Decius hostile to the Christians, but also began to listen to the whispers of highly placed enemies of the Christians that they were secret traitors concealing vast wealth which the empire required for its survival.[30] By all indications Valerian was originally a man of high moral character who saw much good in Christianity, and his first action against the Christians was mild except in one respect. Their leaders, the bishops of major cities in particular, were to be asked to sacrifice to the pagan gods; those who refused were to be exiled into the remote countryside. The death penalty for Christians was not to be invoked simply on account of their faith. But they were explicitly prohibited from assembling in cemeteries; the penalty for that would be death. Here we have the first specific contemporary historical reference to the catacombs. Obviously the Roman authorities were by now well aware of how the Christians had been using them.[31]

Valerian's first persecuting edict was issued in midsummer 257, and immediately enforced against Bishops Cyprian of Carthage and Dionysius of Alexandria, who were officially sent into exile, as they had gone into exile during the Decian persecution. Bishop Demetrianus of Antioch had already been carried off captive by the Persians. Pope Stephen died at exactly this juncture, and it is hard to dismiss this as coincidence even though there is no historically reliable account of his martyrdom. He may have been ordered to leave Rome instantly and, if he was in bad health, this could have brought about his death. But in general this new form of persecution proved ineffective. The exiled bishops continued to administer their sees from a distance, and the clergy of Rome proceeded at once to elect Sixtus II Pope in succession to Stephen.[32]

As reports flowed in to Emperor Valerian from the frontier provinces during 257 and 258, the magnitude of the crisis facing the empire became ever more clear. Gallienus had stabilized the Rhine frontier, but there were still invading barbarians in northern Italy. The Goths had been driven out of Greece, but had joined with the Borani of Russia for another and larger invasion of Asia Minor. The Persians were preparing another and greater invasion. The treasury was almost empty. Plague was decimating the Roman armies, which in any case were far from what they had been. No longer were Roman foot soldiers the best fighting men in all the world. Persians and even barbarians were defeating them with increasing ease. For the first time in Roman military history, heavy cavalry emerged as of equal importance with infantry.[33]

Valerian rallied all the strength he had. He held a great review of his armies and generals at Byzantium in the summer of 258, giving chief honor to the fierce, inflexible general Aurelian, nicknamed "Hand-to-Hilt," who seems to have been the real "strong man" of the empire during the ensuing twenty years of unremitting peril.[34] What part Aurelian may have played in counselling an even harsher policy toward the Christians we do not know, but such counsel would have fitted his character and motivation, which were much like that of Decius. Aurelian could have argued, with apparent plausibility, that in this ultimate crisis every Roman must give his highest loyalty to the empire, and every available denarius to its preservation. So had Rome survived earlier maximum crises, though there had been none like this since Hannibal. The Christians were an alien element, apparently rich. Their organization, the church, must be crushed and its treasure appropriated for the sake of a more united and effective imperial defense.

Valerian issued a second edict condemning all Christian bishops, priests, and deacons to death.[35]

But the Rome of Valerian and Aurelian was five hundred years from the Rome that had defeated Hannibal. Upon their Rome was the mark of death. Only among the Christians was there enduring life. Jesus Christ had said: "Unless you eat the flesh of the Son of man and drink his blood, you have no life in you."[36]

The Pope and the faithful had gathered in the catacombs in the evening of August 6, 258,[37] for just this purpose. Being Christians in a cemetery, theirs was an illegal assembly punishable by death even under Valerian's first persecuting edict; it was clear from the second that full enforcement was now demanded. Valerian was not in Rome, but the officials acting for him there knew how to proceed and where to begin—with the Pope, as Decius had begun with Pope Fabian.

The congregation must have known of the new edict. There is every reason to believe that the catacomb Mass that evening was to be offered specifically to strengthen the faithful to endure the new persecution, in surroundings which would most vividly call to mind the martyrs of the past—probably the papal crypt, one of the largest rooms in the catacomb of Callistus, where among others the martyred Popes Pontian and Fabian were buried.[38]

Pope Sixtus was preaching. With a trampling rush, soldiers burst into the crypt. The congregation drew together before them, baring their breasts and extending their necks to signify that they were ready to die to protect the Pope. But Sixtus, like his Lord in Gethsemane, would have none of that. He came forward and they took him, along with four of his deacons who presumably were to assist him in the celebration of the Mass.[39]

Another deacon, Lawrence, cried out: "Father, where are you going without your deacon?" Sixtus replied: "I do not leave you, my son. You shall follow me in three days."[40]

The Vicar of Christ was taken up the nearby stairs to the open air and beheaded on the spot, along with the four deacons.[41] For some 1,500 years his name was mentioned in the canon—the great central prayer of consecration—at every Mass said by every Catholic priest of the Latin rite, anywhere in the world.

Deacon Lawrence was temporarily spared in order to give the persecuting officials access to the treasure supposedly accumulated by the Roman church. (The acquisition of such imagined treasure was, as we have seen, probably a prime motive of this persecution.) He promised to show the Church's treasure in three days; but then, according to our accounts, what he actually brought forth before the prefect of Rome was not gold and silver, but a representative group of the poor and needy to whom had been given whatever surplus wealth the Roman church had. The angry prefect commanded that Lawrence be roasted to death on a gridiron, as eighty years before some of the martyrs of Lyons had been roasted to death in an iron chair, and as 1,628 years later some of the black martyrs of Uganda were to die. The prefect's sentence was executed upon Lawrence, while he prayed for the conversion of Rome, and even joked with his executioners about turning his body over because "one side is broiled enough."[42]

Despite major scholarly challenges to its authenticity in recent years, the basic facts about St. Lawrence's famous martyrdom stand up very well under criticism. While the full written account of his martyrdom is not always historical-ly reliable, the circumstances of his death as recounted here are attested by no less than four major authorities during the fourth century, only a little more than a century after his martyrdom. These authorities are St. Ambrose, St. Augustine, the historian-Pope Damasus, and the poet Prudentius. It is hard to believe that four minds of this caliber could be so uncritical as some modern writers allege, or that just a few years beyond the bounds of living memory of Lawrence's martyrdom it would have been possible for a largely baseless legend to have arisen about how it took place.[43]

It was probably at almost this same time—very likely August 12, 258, just two days after Lawrence's martyrdom—that another Christian congregation, meeting for Mass in a crypt near the tomb of Sts. Chrysanthus and Daria on the first anniversary of their martyrdom (about which we have little historically reliable information) was trapped by soldiers and buried alive under an avalan-che of stones and sand. Later, when it became possible to excavate the site in the Christian Roman empire during the pontificate of Damasus (366-384), the skeletons of the martyrs at this Mass—men, women, and chidren—were found in their buried crypt, with the priests and deacons still holding the sacred vessels for the Body and Blood of Christ. This scene was on view for pilgrims to the catacombs, through a window in a wall constructed there by Pope Damasus, for more than two hundred years.[44]

No account of the martyrdoms connected with the Eucharist in Roman times would be complete without mention of Tarsicius, the deacon or acolyte whose martyrdom Pope Damasus later described in glowing words. Tarsicius was car-rying the Body of Christ to the home of a Christian when he was accosted by soldiers who demanded to see what he was carrying so carefully (presumably, again, thinking it might be some of the fabled Christian silver and gold). When Tarsicius guarded it from them, they beat him to death. We do not know exact-ly when this happened, but the evidence strongly suggests the persecution of Valerian.[45]

After Pope Sixtus II came the turn of Bishop Cyprian of Carthage. He who had so long been encouraging and inspiring other martyrs and confessors—notably through his letters, many of which have been preserved—now obtained the crown for himself. His people, like the congregation at Pope Sixtus II's last Mass, asked to die with him. Kneeling in prayer, watched in silence and loving awe by thousands, Bishop Cyprian bore his witness to Christ, as a centurion struck off his head.[46] During the ensuing year his memory was constantly before the additional martyrs of the African church who followed where he had led the way, glorying in their brotherhood of sacrifice for Christ.[47] And in Spain, in January 259, Bishop Fructuosus of Tarragona became the first martyr of that land and its people, to leave a substantial account of himself. Fructuosus died by fire, giving testimony to the universality of the Church which the Christian people of Spain were later to do so much to show forth, when he declared: "I must have in mind the Catholic Church, which is dispersed from the East even unto the West."[48]

By the summer of 259, for reasons we do not know, the persecution had been relaxed in Rome to the point that it was possible for its clergy to elect a new Pope, Dionysius, who had been a leader in the Roman church since the pontificate of Stephen.[49]

Meanwhile the enemies of Rome, whose menace had been the excuse for all this horror and killing, were laying waste the Roman east. The aging Valerian wore out the plague-thinned ranks of his army marching to and fro against them. Finally, camped before Christian Edessa,[50] he entered into peace negotiations with the formidable and ruthless King Shapur I of Persia, who demanded a personal interview. Valerian came with only a small guard. He was seized and carried off a prisoner to Persia, never to return. It was the first time in history that a Roman emperor had been captured by the enemies of Rome. For five years or more Valerian lived in the utmost degradation, loaded with chains, dressed in his robes of imperial purple for constant mockery; Shapur mounted his horse by placing his feet on Valerian's neck, and when the former emperor finally died, disgraced and forgotten at Rome, his skin was stuffed with straw and hung up in a Persian temple.[51] Like the last years of Diocletian, the emperor whose decision launched the next great persecution, the last years of Valerian were a living death. The two men are curiously alike—personally virtuous and highly motivated, giving way in their sixties to fears and bad advice in ordering persecution of the Christians, evidently going against their own better judgment and, it would seem, their own consciences. Both paid a penalty which involved the extinguishing of every earthly hope.

For the next ten years the Roman empire was absorbed in a struggle for survival so desperate that the whole mighty structure came within a hairsbreadth of complete destruction. Centralized authority almost collapsed. Everywhere the barbarians were breaking through; in 268 no less than 320,000 of them descended upon Greece, and the next year an estimated quarter million were in Italy. Temporarily successful or merely ambitious generals fleetingly occupied one or two embattled provinces, proclaiming themselves emperors for the moment. Valerian's son Gallienus was the "legitimate" emperor from 260 to 268 and was able to maintain a force in being, but that was all. His decree of toleration for the Christians in 260 appears less a carefully considered change of policy than a token of unwillingness to become involved in any undertaking not immediately and obviously related to imperial survival.[52]

"Hand-to-Hilt" Aurelian was the man for this grim hour, and he more than the flippant and feckless Gallienus[53] seems to have prevented total disintegration. Aurelian was a leader in the conspiracy that eventually overthrew Gallienus; when Gallienus' successor Claudius II died of plague after a great victory over the horde of Goths and Heruli which had penetrated Italy itself, Aurelian took the purple in 270.[54] He restored a semblance of order in the west, then turned on the curious Arabian desert state of Palmyra whose sudden rise under one Odenath and his Jewish wife Zenobia[55] had provided Rome with a shield against predatory Persia when she needed it most. But Palmyra under Zenobia (Odenath was assassinated in 267) aimed to rule the Roman east, and for some years had in effect ruled the great Hellenistic city of Antioch, one of the jewels of the Roman empire. Aurelian prevailed, destroyed Palmyra forever, and came back to Rome to be hailed as restorer of the world and to hold an old-fashioned triumph in 274 with Zenobia and the latest Gallic pretender displayed in golden chains.[56] Meanwhile Aurelian had ordered the building of a wall twelve miles long, twenty feet high, and twelve feet wide all around the city of Rome,[57] which had needed no such defense since Hannibal was at its gates. With peace restored and the frontiers stabilized, Aurelian prepared, immediately after his triumph, decrees to launch a new persecution of the Christians. Before he could put them into effect, he was murdered by his own officers.[58]

During these years the Church of Christ was ruled by Popes Dionysius and Felix I. Of the latter we know almost nothing;[59] but the former holds an important place in the history of dogma. His namesake Bishop Dionysius of Alexandria, one of the heroes of the persecution of Valerian, had become deeply distressed and angered by the widespread Sabellian or Monarchian heresy in Libya— the heresy, originally launched by Noetus of Smyrna at the end of the third century (c. 200), in the pontificate of Victor, which suppressed the distinct personality of Christ. Like Hippolytus who had earlier engaged in the same controversy against the same heresy, Dionysius of Alexandria fell into the opposite error of tritheism, presenting Christ as a lesser divinity, created in time by the Father. His writings against the Libyan Monarchians nowhere defined the Son as of the same substance (*homoousios*, "consubstantial") with the Father. In a magisterial letter which had fortunately been preserved entire, Pope Dionysius clarified this difficult but essential issue with a brilliant exposition of orthodox Trinitarian theology. Bishop Dionysius humbly accepted the Pope's correction and affirmed the orthodox Trinitarian doctrine, including specifically the use of the term *homoousios*.[60]

Monarchianism was revived in a still more objectionable form by Paul of Samosata, the Syriac bishop imposed on Antioch by Odenath and Zenobia of

Palmyra during the period of their dominant influence in that city. Paul denied Christ's divinity altogether; he was both a Monarchian and an Adoptionist, and may well have been guided by, or responding to Zenobia's Jewish beliefs in formulating his theology. Two councils were held in Antioch during the pontificate of Dionysius to call Paul to account both for heresy and for abuse of his office by excessive arrogance and ostentation. The second council deposed him; for a time he held on in the city, but was finally driven out when Aurelian defeated Palmyra. But Paul of Samosata left a legacy of theological confusion which was to trouble the Church all through the next century. For while Bishop Dionysius of Alexandria had been criticized for *not* using the term *homoousios* (consubstantial) to describe the Son in relation to the Father, Paul of Samosata had used it as a way of denying the distinct divine personality of the Son. Therefore the council of Antioch in 268, which proclaimed Paul deposed and his doctrine heretical, acting hastily and without due consideration, condemned the use of the term *homoousios* as well. Probably the council meant to condemn it only in the heretical sense Paul had given it, since there is reason to believe that at least some of the bishops in the council had been among those who had criticized Dionysius of Alexandria for not using this term just eight years before, and surely most of them knew that after his correction by Pope Dionysius, he had apologized for not having used it. But if this was its intention, the council did not make itself clear. The Arians of the next century were to cite this action of the council of Antioch in 268 as one of the strongest official supports for their position against the use of *homoousios*. There is no indication whatever that this particular pronouncement of the council of Antioch ever received approval either from Pope Dionysius, who died the year it was held, or from his successor Felix I.[61]

After the brief reign of the aged emperor Tacitus, Probus—a former high officer of Aurelian's—became emperor. Successful for a time, his reign ended after six years like so many others in this century. When Probus was put to death by his own troops in 282, he became the eleventh out of the last fifteen Roman emperors to die at Roman hands (and of the other four, two—Decius and Valerian—were victims of the enemies of Rome.)[62] During the next three years the pace of emperor-killing accelerated. Probus' successor Carus reigned less than a year before dying under very suspicious circumstances in Mesopotamia (one story was that he was killed by a convenient bolt of lightning!); his son Numerian who succeeded him as emperor of the east was secretly slain in a litter covered and darkened because of an eye disease from which he was suffering; Carus' other son Carinus who succeeded him as emperor in the west was murdered by one of his officers whose wife he had violated. An Illyrian officer named Diocles killed the supposed murderer of Numerian and emerged as sole emperor in 285 after the murder of Carinus. As emperor, Diocles lengthened his name to Diocletian.[63]

Diocletian was at this time a clear-headed and reflective man, imbued with the profound loyalty to the Roman imperial tradition which had been particularly characteristic of Illyria at least since the time of Decius. He saw that the sequence of events which had brought him to the purple could not continue to be the pattern if the empire, so gravely menaced just a few years before, were to survive. He must break the pattern.[64]

He began by recognizing that the whole empire could no longer safely be governed by one man. The burdens and temptations of such vast power were too great; any single man in that position was too vulnerable. The emperor must have a colleague, as in the old Roman consular system. Diocletian picked as his colleague a rough but competent, honest and loyal Illyrian comrade-in-arms named Maximian. Then, he decided, each of the co-emperors must have a designated successor who actually exercised power, thus establishing an imperial college of four. The two senior emperors were called Augusti; one was to rule in the east (the Greek-speaking portion of the empire, and Illyria) and the other in the west (the Latin-speaking area, except Illyria). The two junior rulers and designated successors to the Augusti were called Caesars. Diocletian, ruling as Augustus in the east, chose for his Caesar a younger, even tougher Maximian, an Illyrian of gigantic physique named Galerius and nicknamed "the Drover." As Caesar in the west, under Maximian as Augustus there, Diocletian chose a very different sort of man, though also an Illyrian, who was intelligent and reflective like Diocletian, calm and kind, almost gentle—a very surprising quality to find in a Roman emperor of those days, even if only one of four. This was Constantius "Chlorus," father of Constantine the Great.[65]

So long as Diocletian held power to guide the development of the new imperial system—and so long as he had not yet molested the Christians—he knew success and prosperity. By no means all of the empire's economic problems could be solved—the failure of Diocletian's experiment in price controls is notorious—but he restored a sound currency in gold, ended disorder in the provinces, and constructively reorganized the entire administrative structure of the empire. It seemed that the period of greatest trouble and danger had passed—that the decline of the empire had been stopped and stability at last achieved.[66]

As for Christianity, Diocletian, a syncretist, felt drawn to it in some degree, and his wife and daughter were still more interested; they may actually have been catechumens.[67] Like Valerian during the first years of his reign, Diocletian as emperor long displayed no hostility toward Christianity, and doubtless would have been astonished, during those years, to know that his name was to go down in history indelibly linked with the greatest, most terrible persecution of Christians in two thousand years.

The Church of Christ had been exceedingly quiet during the whole last quarter of the third century. Pope Felix I died in 274, the year Aurelian drafted his persecuting decrees against the Christians which were never put into effect, because of his assassination. About that time Porphyry, a disciple of the neo-

Platonic philosopher Plotinus, was writing an attack on Christianity which was widely circulated, and answered by the Christians.[68] After that, during the years of Probus and Carus, of the establishment of Diocletian's power and his great reorganization of imperial government and the succession, we hear virtually nothing of the Church. Popes Eutychian (275-283) and Caius (283-296) are no more than names to us, though between them they ruled the Church for more than twenty years; not a single act of either is known as reliable history. Of Caius' successor Marcellinus (296-304), we also know nothing whatever until the great persecution broke out.[69]

About the opening of the year 303, Galerius came to Diocletian's palace at Nicomedia in Asia Minor near the Straits, to ask the senior emperor to marshal all the resources of the now peaceful, victorious and firmly governed empire to destroy Christianity once and for all. There had been a series of incidents involving Christians in the army, disturbing the generals: men had refused military service because they were, or had become Christians[70] (though no official Church teaching or major Christian writer had adopted the position of total pacifism which some of these men were upholding); officers and soldiers had been ordered to sacrifice to pagan gods, and some who were Christians had refused and been executed, probably including the famous martyr Sebastian.[71] This was the only development that could even be considered a Christian provocation to the empire at this time. The Church had never been quieter, less conspicuous or less aggressive than in the generation preceding the Diocletianic persecution.

Galerius the Drover is an improbable figure as a great persecutor. He was neither of the Neronian nor of the Decian type, and it is hard to see in him the imagination to understand Christianity and to care about it sufficiently to resolve so firmly on its utter destruction. Yet there is strong evidence that originally he was the only promoter of the Great Persecution among the four members of the imperial college. Diocletian resisted ordering even the most limited measures against the Christians, for about six weeks. During all that time Galerius kept up the pressure on him, until finally the much older emperor gave way. The best source on the Great Persecution tells us that it was Galerius' mother Romula, a priestess of the wild, orgiastic mountain gods, who most of all thirsted for the blood of the Christians, dominating on this issue her big, brutish though able son, who in turn was eventually able to dominate Diocletian. At all events, Diocletian finally decided to order the removal of all Christians from public office, to close the courts to them, to prohibit the emancipation of Christian slaves, and to destroy the Christian churches and sacred books. But Diocletian declared explicitly that no one was to be killed simply for being a Christian.[72]

The edict of persecution containing these provisions was issued in Nicomedia February 23, 303 and the Christian church of that city, then the eastern capital of the Roman empire, was destroyed that same day. The edict of persecution was posted. A Christian named Euetius tore it down, and was promptly burned to death for disrespect to the emperor. During the next month two fires broke out in Diocletian's palace in Nicomedia, for which he (no doubt still under Galerius' relentless prodding) blamed the Christians. In terror of assassination (the fate of so many of his predecessors) he extended the persecution. His wife and daughter, Christian sympathizers and possibly even catechumens, were forced to sacrifice to pagan gods. Bishop Anthimus of Nicomedia was beheaded, and many of his flock were slaughtered with him. All Christians who could be found among the emperor's palace staff were ordered to sacrifice. Those who refused were tortured and killed; one named Peter was roasted over a slow fire, according to Eusebius' almost contemporary testimony—exactly as St. Lawrence of Rome had been, according to later testimony often challenged.[73] From this point Diocletian, prematurely aged and caught up in a cosmic struggle whose infinite dimensions he seems in some way to have *felt* without ever approaching intellectual understanding, became increasingly confused, fearful, and irrational.

Though Diocletian still refrained from the general and indiscriminate imposition of the death penalty on all Christians, he soon issued two further persecuting edicts for the eastern part of the empire (where Galerius ruled with him), ordering the imprisonment of all Christian clergy and the torture of all among them refusing to sacrifice to the pagan gods. From Antioch in Syria, whose bishop Cyril was arrested and condemned to the marble quarries, to Córdoba in Spain, whose Bishop Ossius of later fame throughout the Christian world gained the title of confessor at this time, the original edicts of February 23, 303 against the Christians were rigorously enforced. There are reports that in Rome Pope Marcellinus himself so far weakened as to give up copies of Holy Scripture to the persecutors.[74] The lector Procopius was martyred at Caesarea in Palestine for refusing to sacrifice to the genius of the four emperors; later in the year the deacon Zachaeus and the lector Alphaeus were also martyred there. Bishop Felix of Thibiuca in Africa was martyred for refusing to deliver the Scriptures to the persecutors, helping to make up for the weakness of the Pope. As in past persecutions, substantial numbers of the clergy apostatized under duress. But in every region there were also martyrs—except, for the most part, in Gaul and Britain, which escaped the full persecution under the mild and humane rule of Constantius "Chlorus."[75]

In the fall of 303 Diocletian began the twentieth year of his imperial rule.[76] No Roman emperor had lasted for twenty years since the good and peaceful Antoninus Pius 150 years before. A traditional triumph followed by the traditional bloody "games" was held for Diocletian in Rome in honor of his "vicennalia." But he disliked Rome; he found the round of ceremonies grueling and the licentiousness of the people disgusting.[77] Was his conscience nagging him?

Had he begun to reflect on the fact that every one of the great persecutors of Christians before him—Nero, Domitian, Decius, Valerian—had died horribly, two of them mad, the third a scorned captive whose stuffed skin now hung in a Persian temple, the other swallowed up in a swamp?

Abruptly, Diocletian left Rome for Ravenna in northern Italy, just a week before the climax of debauchery which was the great pagan Roman festival of the Saturnalia following the winter solstice. An extraordinary episode during the games may have helped provoke his sudden departure. There is a tradition, later written in several versions of acts of the martyrs, that a comedian named Genesius was called upon to burlesque Christian baptism on the stage as part of the entertainment presented during this visit of Diocletian to Rome. (That this chronological reference is clear and accurate is one of the strongest arguments in favor of the authenticity of the essential facts in the story of the martyrdom of Genesius.) While in the very process of mocking the sacrament, Genesius was seized with a great desire to receive it in truth, and gave his testimony to Christ from the stage, in Diocletian's presence. He was then beaten, tortured by Diocletian's order, and eventually executed.[78] If Diocletian were beginning to doubt the wisdom and justice of his persecution of the Christians, such a startling face-to-face challenge from a mere actor would undoubtedly have disquieted him still more.

At all events, it appears that the next month, in Ravenna, Diocletian underwent a psychological collapse which rendered him incapable of transacting any business for months. For the whole year 304 he was out of touch with government and people, first travelling very slowly through his native Dalmatia, then shut away in his palace at Nicomedia. When at last he emerged in March of 305, his appearance was so changed that he was almost unrecognizable.[79]

Meanwhile Galerius for all practical purposes took over the empire in the east, and surely was responsible for the final persecuting edict issued in the spring of 304 which, like that of Decius, required all Christians regardless of age, sex or position to sacrifice to the pagan gods or die.[80]

This edict only confirmed what by then had become standard practice. Diocletian's collapse removed the last restraint on the persecution anywhere in the empire outside of Constantius' Gaul and Britain.[81] During the winter of 304 occurred the celebrated martyrdoms of Bishop Philip of Heraclea in Asia Minor, with two companions; of the priest Saturninus from Abitina in Africa near Carthage for saying a Mass, and of about fifty fellow Christians for having assisted at that Mass; and of the three sisters of Thessalonica in Greece given the names, in Christ, of Agape, Irene and Chione—Love, Peace, and Snow—for concealing copies of the Scriptures in order to preserve them from the persecutors. All these martyrdoms are thoroughly authenticated historically and are reported in considerable detail.[82] Here are some recorded words of the martyrs:

Bishop Philip of Heraclea: "Tear then with any torture you wish this weak body of mine. Over that you have power but over my soul you have none."[83]

Emeritus of Abitina, when asked why he allowed the priest Saturninus to say Mass in his house for a Christian congregation: "They are my brethren; they came to celebrate the *dominicum* [Eucharist] without which we cannot live."[84]

The dialogue of Chione of Thessalonica with Dulcitius, governor of Macedonia:
DULCITIUS: "Who put these ideas into your head?"
CHIONE: "Almighty God."
DULCITIUS: "Somebody must have persuaded you to this folly; who was it?"
CHIONE: "Almighty God and his only-begotten Son, our Lord Jesus Christ."[85]

The same spirit animated the host of martyrs all across the Roman empire during the fearful year 304, the most terrible in the whole history of Christianity after the Passion of Christ on Calvary, which was then recapitulated in many ways, in many places, by many who put all their hope and trust in Christ Who had suffered as they were suffering. The cruelty of the tortures is almost beyond imagining. Hear the Satanic words of Numerian Maximus, governor of Cilicia, to the martyrs Tarachus and Probus: "Strike him upon the mouth. . . . Break his jaws. . . . Strip him and lash him with ox's sinews. . . . Turn him, and strike him on the belly. . . . Look, fool, at your mangled body; the ground is covered with blood." (Later, in the arena, the bear and the lion which were supposed to tear them to pieces came to lick their wounds instead.)[86] In Upper Egypt the persecution reached a pitch of overwhelming horror, which no man even in this permissive age would dare visually depict, at which it remained for years, according to the testimony of Eusebius the historian, who himself witnessed some of the Egyptian martyrdoms:

> The outrages and sufferings which the martyrs in the Thebais endured surpass all description, their whole bodies being torn to pieces by shells instead of claws even until life was gone; and women were tied by one foot and were raised on high through the air, head downwards, by certain machines, with their bodies completely naked and without even a covering, and they furnished this most shameful and cruel and inhuman sight of all to all the onlookers; and others again died on being fastened to tree trunks and stumps; for having brought together the very strongest of the branches by certain machines, and stretching the legs of the martyrs one by one on each of these, they released the branches to be carried back to their natural position, planning a sudden separation of the limbs of those against whom they devised this. And all these things, indeed, were carried out not for a few days or a short time, but for a long interval of entire years,

sometimes of more than ten, sometimes more than twenty in number being destroyed, sometimes not less than thirty and then again nearly sixty; and again at other times one hundred men in a single day, together with very young children and women were slain.[87]

Christian children were often chosen victims. No martyrs left quite so bright a memory as these: Agnes of Rome, aged twelve;[88] Eulalia of Mérida in Spain, aged twelve;[89] Justus and Pastor of Complutum (Alcalá de Henares) in Spain, aged thirteen and nine, who ran from school to the place where the persecutor was interrogating and sentencing Christians, to give him their testimony to Christ; Maxima and Secunda of Thumbarbo in Africa, aged fourteen and twelve, who with their friend Domitilla were the only Christians of their town to remain faithful unto death.[90]

Amid this sea of Christian blood, a cult of martyrdom arose in some areas, notably in Africa among those rigorists who were soon to become the Donatist heretics. Leaders of the Church were expected to be martyrs; any who were not, were viewed with suspicion. In Egypt, some condemned Bishop Peter of Alexandria for going into hiding rather than offering himself for martyrdom; they refused to accept him any longer as their bishop, and went into schism (though their leader, Meletius, was not martyred either, and Peter later was).[91] It appears that the death of Pope Marcellinus in October 304 was natural, which surprised those who expected the Bishop of Rome and head of the Church to be martyred in this crisis as many of his predecessors had been. Much later reports circulated by the Donatists to the effect that Pope Marcellinus lapsed by sacrificing to pagan gods are almost certainly false; no such extraordinary fall from grace could have been kept secret by all other writers, and the Donatists had an obvious interest in encouraging belief in such calumnies. It has been suggested that Marcellinus may have purchased immunity for himself and for much of the Roman church from local officials, since we hear of few martyr-doms at Rome in 304, nor do we hear of any concealment of the Pope. This would fit with the evidence of his weakness provided by the better authenticated report of his surrender of the Scriptures to government officials, and would help account for the confused rumors from which the Donatists, after having rejected Papal authority, drew their story of the lapsing of the Pope. The best evidence that some act at least arguably dishonorable occurred is later Roman tradition, which was markedly ambivalent or embarrassed regarding this particular Pope (his name, for instance, is often left out of Papal lists.)[92]

Whatever the full explanation may be, the contrast between Pope Marcellinus in the persecution of Diocletian and Galerius, and Pope Fabian in the persecution of Decius and Pope Sixtus II in the persecution of Valerian, is striking. No Pope has ever apostatized; but by no means all have been equal in moral courage.

After Marcellinus' death, the Holy See of Rome remained vacant for more than two years, possibly for as much as four. The delay in electing his successor was due first to the persecution, then to internal divisions of the church in Rome over the question of the penances to be required of the lapsed before they could be readmitted to the Church—the same question which had been so troublesome after the Decian persecution.[93]

By the end of 304, therefore, the Church had no Pope, and no immediate prospect of regaining one. No end of the persecution was in sight. Clearly it was Galerius' objective to destroy the Church, and it seemed he had the power to do it. The glorious testimonies of the martyrs went on and on,[94] impressing many, converting some even though the price of a public avowal of conversion in the circumstances of the martyrdoms was almost instant death. But in the human and material sense the Church had no protection at all—except in the two provinces Constantius still ruled, and he was now a sick man.[95]

Diocletian, a mere shadow of his former self, appeared again in public in March 305. Galerius, who had evidently been expecting him to die, now virtually ordered him to abdicate, which would also involve the abdication of Maximian. Whether or not Diocletian then wanted to abdicate, he was much too weak to resist any pressure. Galerius could not think of a way to prevent Constantius from succeeding Maximian as Augustus in the west, in accordance with the plan of succession which was now to make Galerius Augustus in the east. But he probably suspected that Constantius would not live long, and carefully insisted on choosing both the new Caesars: for the west Severus, "a general who was much attached to him and even more to wine and debauchery," and for the east his own nephew "Daia or Daza, a great beast of a barbarian who had lately begun calling himself Maximin so as to have something Roman about him."[96]

These arrangements entirely left out a young man who had a very immediate interest in them, since he had himself expected, and had been widely expected, to be named Caesar of the west: Constantine, the only son of Constantius by his first wife Helena, an innkeeper's daughter[97]—about thirty years old, tall, vigorous, handsome, ambitious, a dominating personality, much admired by the soldiers. It must have been a great shock to him not to be appointed Caesar, as Diocletian himself had intended that he should be; and on the morrow of the surprise ceremony May 1, 305 when Severus and Daia were presented to the army as the new Caesars after Diocletian's abdication, Constantine must have come abruptly to the chilling realization that not only had he lost the position of heir to half the empire, but now he stood in the most deadly personal danger. For at Nicomedia, where he had long resided, he was in the power of Galerius; his father was sixteen hundred miles away. Galerius might not dare to let him live much longer, for his very existence as a deprived heir posed a standing threat.[98]

Constantius was ill, and the barbarian Picts were attacking his troops in Britain. He wrote Galerius asking that his son be allowed to join him. Galerius temporized. Finally one evening, for reasons which remain unclear, he gave Constantine permission to depart, evidently without really meaning it. He may have been playing a cat-and-mouse game; he may have planned to arrange for Constantine's death on the way; he may have been temporarily and uncharacteristically in a generous mood; or he may (as his long sleep that night and the following morning tends to suggest) simply have been drunk. In any case, he certainly did not expect Constantine to leave at once. But in this first great crisis of his life, he who was to become the first Christian emperor and the founder of political Christendom showed the capability for instant decision and daring action that marks all of history's great leaders of men. The moment Galerius had gone to bed after a hearty dinner, Constantine was on a horse. All through the quiet spring night he rode along the post road to the west in a thunder of galloping hooves. At each post-station he vaulted from his frothing horse, hamstrung it, selected the best fresh mount, hamstrung the others, swung back into the saddle, and rode on, leaving behind at the station sleepy men bewildered by the sudden whirlwind apparition, but never considering raising a hand against the son of the Augustus of the west.[99]

It is fifty miles from Nicomedia to the Bosporus. Any good horseman can cover that distance in a night of hard riding with an unlimited supply of fresh mounts. So we must picture Constantine at dawn on the ferry that plied, then as until just a few years ago when the first bridge was finally built upon the Bosporus, that turbulent, fast-running, historic waterway which separates Europe from Asia. Galerius was still asleep far back in his palace; he did not rise that day until noon. All morning Constantine was riding like the wind up the great highway from the Bosporus toward Hadrianople. When Galerius finally woke up and realized what had happened, Constantine had fifteen hours' head start—and there were no uninjured horses at any of the post-stations with which to pursue him. Galerius nearly wept with vexation.[100]

History is a cosmic battleground between Heaven and Hell, an almost unimaginably complex web of human actions and relationships in the matrix of time. But it has moments when the course of events for a thousand years can be decisively shaped by one man's strong arm and mind and heart. This was such a moment. With young Constantine that spring night in the Year of Our Lord 305 rode the future of Christendom. Christian generations yet unborn could give thanks that none of his succession of horses stumbled and fell.

Constantine's pace presumably slowed somewhat as he drew farther away from Nicomedia and Galerius, but he would not have slackened it more than absolutely necessary. Up the Egnatian Way to Sirmium in Illyria (Serbia); along the Danube through Noricum (Austria) and Rhaetia (Switzerland); across the young Rhine; past the battlefields of Caesar in north central Gaul, past Lutetia (Paris), upon the famous Roman roads built during half a millennium of empire, for all of those sixteen hundred miles, Constantine rode. At Bononia (Boulogne) on the English Channel he met his father, who welcomed him with astonishment and joy. Next year, in July 306, Constantius died at York in Britain, his son at his side. The Roman army in Britain at once proclaimed Constantine his successor as Augustus of the west.[101]

There was of course no legality in this action, but Diocletian's attempt to establish a generally recognized and respected legality in the process of imperial succession was already failing. Galerius was furious when he heard the news, but in view of the loyalty of Constantine's troops and the unpopularity of Severus and Daia among his own troops, Galerius did not dare to reject Constantine totally. He contented himself with recognizing him as Caesar in the west rather than Augustus, designating Severus as the western Augustus. Meanwhile the persecution of Christians continued in the east, since Daia was as enthusiastic a persecutor as Galerius. In the spring of 306 Daia issued an edict like that of Decius, providing that everyone should be called up from census lists to sacrifice in public to the pagan gods to prove that they were not Christians. Still more fiendish ingenuity was applied to the infliction of horrible deaths upon Christians; the young martyr Ulpian of Tyre was condemned in that year to be thrown into the sea inside an ox-skin with a live dog and a poisonous snake.[102]

In Egypt the persecution continued with the particular horror so graphically described by Eusebius. Probably in this same year Phileas, Bishop of Thmuis— young, nobly born, learned and rich, generally beloved—was called upon to sacrifice. His pagan wife and many pagan friends, and even officials of the court and lawyers, pleaded with him to do so to save his life, and for the sake of his family. Resolutely he refused; he would never deny Christ. Philoromus, an important Roman official present, at length cried out:[103]

> Why do you try uselessly the constancy of this man? Why do you wish to make unfaithful one who is faithful to God? Why do you want to force him to deny God just to satisfy men? Do you not realize that his eyes do not see your tears, that his ears do not hear your words? He who contemplates heavenly glory is not moved by earthly tears.[104]

No less constant unto death was Cyril, bishop of great Antioch, who had been condemned to the marble quarries at the very beginning of the persecution. A true pastor to the end, regardless of his position and his sufferings, he converted five sculptors who were doing their work there, before he died.[105]

Within a year of Constantius' death, Galerius and his henchmen had totally lost control of the Roman west. Maxentius, son of Diocletian's co-Emperor Maximian, had taken over Rome by promising to restore its one-time privileges as the imperial capital, including immunity from taxation, which Galerius had imposed upon it; Severus was captured and killed after a disastrous campaign against Maxentius; Galerius was expelled from Italy in 307. Maximian tried to fish in the troubled waters in order to regain the power he had been forced to give up when he and Diocletian abdicated in 305, but was driven from Rome by his own son, who established a corrupt and licentious tyranny.[106] Old, broken Diocletian was brought out of his cabbage-growing retirement at Salona in Dalmatia for a conference at Carnuntum arranged by Galerius in November 308, whose real purpose was to put together a coalition against Maxentius. This proved impracticable. The only significant result of the conference at Carnuntum was to bring in a new member of the "imperial college": Licinius, another Illyrian, an old friend and comrade-in-arms of Galerius, whose later career showed that he would persecute or befriend the Christians with equal readiness, insofar as either policy advanced his own position. Licinius was given the title of Augustus and presented as the successor of Severus in the west, but in fact he had no power there unless he could defeat Maxentius. Constantine did not participate in the conference.[107]

During these years of political maneuvering (307 and 308) there was a relaxation of the persecution in some parts of the eastern empire (though not at all in Egypt and only briefly in Palestine) and an almost complete remission of persecution in the west.[108] Maxentius, controlling Italy and perhaps Spain (an adventurer named Domitius Alexander had now been proclaimed emperor in Africa) appears to have been relatively neutral toward Christianity.[109] A new Pope, Marcellus, had at last been elected, but in 307 or 308 he was driven from Rome in riots stirred up by disaffected Christians who thought his penances for the lapsed too rigorous. Soon afterward he died.[110] His successor, Eusebius (not to be confused with Eusebius the historian) reigned even more briefly, being driven out within a year (probably in 308) by the opposite faction, rigorists who thought the lapsed should never be forgiven. Eusebius died in exile in Sicily shortly after his expulsion from Rome.[111] As the policies and fates of Marcellus and Eusebius show, the Popes in that ancient, critical hour were rejecting, as ever, both extremes, holding to the heart and center of Christian truth, maintaining the balance of justice and charity.

There were now no less than eight regularly constituted, irregularly constituted, or former emperors—Galerius, Licinius, Daia, Constantine, Maxentius, Domitius Alexander, Maximian, and Diocletian—with Galerius still the most powerful among them. He and Daia remained resolved to destroy Christianity. In 309 a new edict by Daia renewed full-scale persecution in the east.[112] There were notable martyrdoms in Palestine and in Edessa, now under Roman control and indubitably an almost entirely Christian city,[113] as few if any other cities in the Roman empire yet were. The Palestinian martyrs included the great Scripture scholar Pamphilus, already tortured for the Faith in 307, who had been the teacher of Eusebius the first Christian historian; five Egyptians who were on their way to comfort and assist Christians imprisoned in the Cilician mines; and two young men—Seleucus and John—and one very old man, Theodulus, who came up and kissed the martyrs, and for that expression of love alone were sentenced to die with them.[114]

In February 310 Maximian was done to death—by execution or by his own hand; our sources disagree—after attempting to overthrow Constantine either by military action or by assassination (again the sources disagree; it has been theorized that both attempts were made, and that Constantine pardoned Maximian after the revolt and only executed or forced suicide upon him after the assassination attempt)[115]. Whichever account of these confused events we follow, however, shows Constantine clearly master of the situation, more than a match for the former co-emperor. It was probably at this time that Constantine's full imperial ambitions awoke. Later in the year 310 he suddenly announced a claim to direct descent from the Emperor Claudius II the Goth-slayer (268-270) and his special patronage by Sol Invictus, the Unconquered Sun—a step toward the usual deification of Roman emperors. This clearly indicates that there was not yet any real Christian belief in Constantine—but, on the other hand, also no sign of any hostility toward Christianity.[116]

When the old ex-emperor Diocletian heard of Maximian's sorry death and of how the rising Constantine was effacing Maximian's name from public monuments, often along with Diocletian's name because the two were too closely joined in the inscriptions to be separated, he wept, raved, and begged for death. Gradually he starved himself. At some time during the next three years, abandoned, alone, the man who had so reluctantly approved the launching of the Great Persecution, which made his name a synonym for horrible death down through all the Christian centuries, ended his life in an ocean of misery that only a psychiatrist—or a priest—could penetrate.[117]

As Diocletian began to die, so did Galerius. Venereal disease produced a hideous ulcer. As with the dying Herod, the foul smell of his corruption filled every room he entered. The palace at Nicomedia, where he had advocated and brought about the Great Persecution seven years before, became an abode of horror. Galerius the Drover had never been an imaginative man. But now, recoiling from a ghastly death, he began to think seriously for the first time of what he had done, of the immense weight that bore down upon whatever conscience he possessed. We are told that this once strong man whimpered in his terror like a child.[118]

At this point the Christian historian can only wish to be able to report evidence of a conversion. Tragically, there is none, only evidence of a fear of the vengeance of the Christian God, without even a glimmer of awareness of His forgiving love. Galerius' last gesture bears all too close a resemblance to Judas flinging the thirty pieces of silver for which he had betrayed Christ at the feet of the high priest's men, and then going out to hang himself. On April 30, 311

Galerius issued a decree of toleration for the Christians—a document extorted from him by fear, and nothing else. Most of it insults the Christians; only at the end, briefly, grudgingly, does it ask them to pray that their angry God will turn away His wrath from him.[119]

Six days later Galerius was dead; two weeks later he was buried in Romulianum in Illyria, the city named for his mother the pagan priestess who may have set his feet on the fatal road. But his edict of toleration was honored for a time, even by Daia.[120] Let Eusebius, who personally experienced this glorious moment, describe it for us, the first fruits of the blood of the martyrs:

> It was possible to see, like a light shining suddenly forth out of a dark night, churches being put together in every city, and crowded assemblies, and rites being performed at these according to custom. And every one of the unbelieving heathen was struck not a little at these things, marveling at the wonder of so great a change, and proclaiming the God of the Christians as great and alone true. Those of our people who had faithfully and courageously endured the struggle of the persecutions again took on an air of confidence before all, and such as had become diseased of faith and storm-tossed in soul eagerly strove for their own cure, beseeching and begging the strong for a right hand of safety, and supplicating God to be merciful to them. Then, also, the noble athletes of piety, being freed of their evil plight in the mines, returned to their own homes, going through every city, exulting and beaming with joy and filled with unspeakable happiness and confidence that one cannot describe in words. Populous throngs in the midst of thoroughfares and market places went on their way praising God with songs and psalms, and you would have seen those who shortly before had been driven from their fatherlands in bonds under a very harsh punishment resuming their fireside with happy and joyous countenances, so that even those who before were stained with our blood, on seeing the marvel contrary to all expectation, rejoiced with us at what happened.[121]

NOTES

[1] Matthew 10:34.

[2] W. H. C. Frend, *Martyrdom and Persecution in the Early Church* (New York, 1967), pp. 300-302; Jules Lebreton and Jacques Zeiller, *The History of the Primitive Church* (New York, 1949), II, 791-792.

[3] Frend, *Martyrdom and Persecution*, pp. 300-302; John A. F. Gregg, *The Decian Persecution* (Edinburgh, 1897), pp. 70-81, 94-96.

[4] Cyprian, Epistle 9, 1; E. G. Weltin, *The Ancient Popes* (Westminster, MD, 1964), pp. 108-113.

[5] For Cyprian's withdrawal and his rather embarrassed response to the criticism it aroused, see his Epistles 8, 9, and 19, and Lebreton and Zeiller, *Primitive Church*, II, 848-849.

[6] Frend, *Martyrdom and Persecution*, p. 301; Glanville Downey, *A History of Antioch in Syria* (Princeton NJ, 1961), p. 308.

[7] Cecil J. Cadoux, *Ancient Smyrna, a History of the City from the Earliest Times to*

324 A.D. (Oxford, 1938), p. 293.

[8] Frend, *Martyrdom and Persecution*, pp. 302-306.

[9] Cadoux, *Ancient Smyrna*, pp. 380-384 (citing *Mart. Pion.* IV, 23). The authenticity of the account we have of the martyrdom of Pionius is generally admitted (unlike that of many other martyrs' Acts); see *Butler's Lives of the Saints*, edited, revised and supplemented by Herbert Thurston and Donald Attwater (Westminster MD, 1956), I, 224-225.

[10] Cadoux, *Ancient Smyrna*, pp. 384-385 (citing *Mart. Pion.* VII, 1).

[11] *Ibid.*, pp. 393-399.

[12] Eusebius, *Ecclesiastical History*, VI, 39-41. The old man, John, and the virgin, Ammoniaron, were martyred after terrible tortures; the mother, Dionysia, was slain by a sword-thrust; the boy, Dioscorus, though he held out magnificently, was spared because the governor particularly liked and admired him.

[13] Ludwig Hertling and Englebert Kirschbaum, *The Roman Catacombs and Their Martyrs*, 2d ed. (Milwaukee, 1956), pp. 111-112; Cyprian, Epistle 39; Celerinus to Lucius, Epistles of Cyprian 21. For a review of known and probable martyrs and confessors at Rome during the Decian persecution see Gregg, *Decian Persecution*, pp. 99-110. Only six Christians are known or believed to have died at Rome for their faith during this persecution; the best attested (after Pope Fabian) is the presbyter Moses, who died in prison after great sufferings.

[14] Butler-Thurston-Attwater, *Lives of the Saints*, I, 422. Several authorities cited therein uphold the substantial authenticity of the Acts of Nestor.

[15] *Ibid.*, II, 198. Maximus' brief Acts seem to be authentic, but add little to our knowledge of the Decian persecution.

[16] *Ibid.*, II, 319-320. The description of these martyrdoms is late and may be heavily romanticized, but their actual occurrence is hard to question.

[17] Gregg, *Decian Persecution*, pp. 227-230.

[18] Butler-Thurston-Attwater, *Lives of the Saints*, IV, 599.

[19] Cyprian, Epistles 10, 4 and 27, 1.

[20] J. P. Kirsch, "Agatha, Saint," *The Catholic Encyclopedia* (1913).

[21] *The Cambridge Ancient History*, Volume XII (Cambridge, England, 1939), pp. 143-145; Frend, *Martyrdom and Persecution*, p. 307.

[22] John Chapman, *Studies in the Early Papacy* (London, 1928), pp. 41-45, and his articles on St. Cyprian, Pope St. Cornelius, and Novatian and Novatianism in *The Catholic Encyclopedia* (1913); Lebreton and Zeiller, *Primitive Church*, II, 852-854. The conclave that elected Pope Cornelius included 16 bishops and the greater part if not all of the Roman clergy then existing: 46 priests, 7 deacons, and 7 sub-deacons. Whether the 42 acolytes and 52 doorkeepers were also electors we do not know for certain, but it seems unlikely. Pope Cornelius' lack of sophistication is presumed from the contrast of his colloquial Latin with the much more polished Latin of Novatian and Cyprian (cf. Chapman's article on Pope St. Cornelius in *The Catholic Encyclopedia*).

[23] Cyprian, Epistles 44, 45, 47, 48, 51, 52, 55; Eusebius, *Ecclesiastical History* VI, 45 (letter from Bishop Dionysius to Novatian); Gregg, *Decian Persecution*, pp. 192-206.

[24] Cyprian, Epistles 60 and 61; Eusebius, *Ecclesiastical History* VII, 10; Lebreton and Zeiller, *Primitive Church*, II, 798-799; Gregg, *Decian Persecution*, pp. 278-287; *Cambridge Ancient History*, XII, 168-169; Joseph Fichter, *St. Cecil Cyprian* (St. Louis, 1942), p. 157.

[25] Lebreton and Zeiller, *Primitive Church*, II, 860-873, 1135-1139; Charles J. Hefele, *A History of the Christian Councils* (Edinburgh, 1871, 1896), I, 103-116; Fichter, *Cyprian*, pp. 200-201; Chapman, *Early Papacy*, pp. 28-50, and the article "Cyprian, Saint" in

The Catholic Encyclopedia (1913); Firmilian to Cyprian, Epistles of Cyprian 75, 17.

[26] *Cambridge Ancient History*, XII, 139, 146-148, 157, 169-171; Downey, *Antioch*, pp. 256-258, 593-595.

[27] *Cambridge Ancient History*, XII, 158; Patrick J. Healy, *The Valerian Persecution* (Boston, 1905), pp. 252-253.

[28] Downey, *Antioch*, pp. 259-260.

[29] *Cambridge Ancient History*, XII, 262-268.

[30] Healy, *Valerian Persecution*, pp. 109-127.

[31] *Ibid.*, pp. 108-109, 136-139, 173-175. It is quite likely to have been at this time that the bones of St. Peter were moved from their original grave to the nearby concealed location under the graffiti wall adjoining the red-wall shrine or Tropaion, which was probably built at this period (John E. Walsh, *The Bones of St. Peter* [Garden City NY, 1982], pp. 48, 132-135). This would have helped protect them from desecration in a raid on the shrine, such as Roman soldiers made when Pope Sixtus II was arrested and martyred while saying Mass in the catacombs later in this decade (see Notes 37-41, below).

[32] Healy, *Valerian Persecution*, pp. 131-136, 142-152; Downey, *Antioch*, p. 309.

[33] *Cambridge Ancient History*, XII, 134-135, 148, 216-217.

[34] *Ibid.*, pp. 192-193; Healy, *Valerian Persecution*, pp. 156-161.

[35] Healy, *Valerian Persecution*, pp. 162-165, 168-173.

[36] John 6:53.

[37] The precise date is fixed by Cyprian in an immediately contemporary letter to his brother Successus, the next to last in the collection of his Epistles that has come down to us (Number 80).

[38] Hertling and Kirschbaum, *Roman Catacombs*, pp. 44-45.

[39] *Ibid.*, p. 45.

[40] Butler-Thurston-Attwater, *Lives of the Saints*, III, 297.

[41] Hertling and Kirschbaum, *Roman Catacombs*, p. 45.

[42] Butler-Thurston-Attwater, *Lives of the Saints*, III, 297-298; see Note 43, below.

[43] Butler-Thurston-Attwater, *Lives of the Saints.*, III, 298-299; Lebreton and Zeiller, *Primitive Church*, II, 830n; Healy, *Valerian Persecution*, pp. 179-185. All these sources reject the historicity of most of the account of the Lawrence's martyrdom which has come down to us. Its historicity is vigorously defended by the great French scholar Henri Leclercq in the articles "Gril" and "Laurent" in *Dictionnaire d'Archéologie chrétienne et de liturgie* (DACL), VI (2), 1827-1831 and VIII (2), 1912-1925. The earliest patristic source is Ambrose, *De officiis*, I, 41. Prudentius' poem *Peri Stephanon* was composed in honor of St. Lawrence and confirms many of the most famous details of the story of his martyrdom given in the text. The later Acts of Lawrence reveal their remoteness from the event they are describing most clearly by representing both Decius and Valerian as personally present at Lawrence's martyrdom, though in fact Decius was then seven years dead and Valerian far distant in the east, campaigning. But it seems to have been insufficiently appreciated by many critical writers that historical errors in Lawrence's *Acta* do not in any way affect the historical reliability of the far more nearly contemporary authorities mentioned. Even Healy (*op. cit.*, pp. 181-184), who tends to find more historical reliability in traditional accounts of saints' lives and martyrdoms than more recent writers, is very skeptical of the dramatic details of the martyrdom of Lawrence. Yet, to mention just two of his (and others') objections, the dialogue of Lawrence and Pope Sixtus as the Pope was being led away to martyrdom, reported by St. Ambrose and quoted in the text, is entirely natural and likely, being both brief and poignant, rather than "lengthy" and "savoring . . . of the tragic drama;" while the fact that torture of Christian martyrs was rare in the persecution of Valerian surely does not mean that it

never happened, and it would have been an understandable and indeed a likely response in an arrogant official angered by what he would almost certainly have seen as deliberate mockery in Lawrence's introducing the poor and needy as "the treasures of the Church" when the official was looking for, and expecting to get, literal treasure. Leclercq (DACL, VI [2], 1827-1831) emphasizes the importance of the parallel of the roasting in the iron chair of some of the martyrs of Lyons in 177 (see Chapter Eighteen, above); there is a similar close parallel in the martyrdom of Peter of Nicomedia in 303 (see text and Note 73, below).

⁴⁴ Healy, *Valerian Persecution*, pp. 128-129, 144-145; Butler-Thurston-Attwater, *Lives of the Saints*, IV, 196-197. Healy attributes the original martyrdom of Chrysanthus and Daria to the year 256 and the mass martyrdom of the worshippers in their crypt to the following year, on the first anniversary of their death. But since we know of no active persecution of Christians in 256, it seems more reasonable to date the martyrdom of Chrysanthus and Daria to 257, shortly after the promulgation of Valerian's first persecuting edict (which did specify the death penalty for Christians meeting in catacombs), and that of the worshippers to 258—especially since its probable date, according to the reconstruction of Delehaye (*Lives of the Saints*, IV, 197) was August 12, just six days after the "crackdown" on Christians worshipping underground began with the arrest and martyrdom of Pope Sixtus II. The preservation of the scene of martyrdom visible through the window was noted in 587 by Gregory of Tours in his *De Gloria Martyrum*, I, 38.

⁴⁵ Healy, *Valerian Persecution*, pp. 143-144; Hertling and Kirschbaum, *Roman Catacombs*, pp. 129-130; Butler-Thurston-Attwater, *Lives of the Saints*, IV, 335. The date of the feast commemorating the martyrdom of St. Tarsicius, August 15, fits very well with the facts and dates cited above regarding the sudden access of severity in Valerian's persecution in August of 258 following his second persecuting edict, with particular emphasis on thwarting or breaking up Christian assemblies. Tarsicius may have been carrying the Eucharist to his fellow Christians precisely because of the serious risks then involved for the faithful in assembling anywhere in significant numbers for Mass.

⁴⁶ Healy, *Valerian Persecution*, pp. 188-200. The Acts of Cyprian's martyrdom are among the most indubitably authentic of all such documents; see text and commentary in E. C. E. Owen, *Some Authentic Acts of the Early Martyrs* (London, 1927), pp. 93-99. A contemporary biography of Cyprian by his disciple Pontius is also clearly authentic (see text and introduction in *The Fathers of the Church* series, Volume 15: *Early Christian Biographies*, ed. Roy J. Deferrari [New York, 1952], pp. 3-24).

⁴⁷ Healy, *Valerian Persecution*, pp. 200-232. Notable among these martyrs were Montanus, Lucius, and companions, and James and Marian. See Butler-Thurston-Attwater, *Lives of the Saints*, I, 409-411, quoting the "Acts of Montanus and Lucius" which the often highly critical authors hold to be a "document . . . unhesitatingly commended as a reliable narrative of contemporary date." The text of the Passion of James and Marian appears in Owen, *Authentic Acts of the Early Martyrs*, pp. 105-118. The full authenticity and historical reliability of this *Passio* is generally accepted (Butler-Thurston-Attwater, *Lives of the Saints*, II, 199).

⁴⁸ Healy, *Valerian Persecution*, pp. 233-239; Owen, *Authentic Acts of the Early Martyrs*, pp. 100-104. Virtually all critics accept as historically reliable the account of Fructuosus' martyrdom which we possess (Butler-Thurston-Attwater, *Lives of the Saints*, I, 138).

⁴⁹ J. P. Kirsch, "Dionysius, Saint, Pope," *The Catholic Encyclopedia* (1913). In *Valerian Persecution, passim*, Healy mentions a number of other martyrs whom he sees some reason to date during this persecution: Eugenia; Rufina and Secunda; Protus and Hyacinth; Pancras (Pancratius); the martyrs of the "Massa Candida" at Utica in Africa;

Cyril of Caesarea in Cappadocia; Nicephorus of Antioch; Leo and Paregorius of Lycia. Evidence assembled or cited in Butler-Thurston-Attwater, *Lives of the Saints*, in the respective entries for these saints, gives reason for seriously doubting the historicity of most of the alleged information we have about them, though this evidence may not be quite so conclusive as the authors would have us believe. Only with Leo and Paregorius is there a firm and specific basis for defending their historicity, since their Acts mention a known Roman of Valerian's time, Lollianus, as proconsul of Lycia who ordered their execution (see Healy, *op. cit.*, pp. 246-248). But the story we have gives the cause of their execution as their attack on a pagan temple, the only report of this kind from the whole of this persecution; there is nothing to date or link it with other events of the Valerian persecution except the reference to Lollianus, who is not otherwise known as a persecutor.

⁵⁰ The Christianization of Edessa was completed during the third century, as even those scholars firmly rejecting the account in "The Doctrine of Addai" of the original conversion of the King Abgar who was contemporary with Christ, will admit. See J. B. Segal, *Edessa, the Blessed City* (Oxford, 1970), pp. 62, 69-71; Jean Danielou and Henri Marrou, *The Christian Centuries*, Volume I: "The First Six Hundred Years" (New York, 1964), pp. 188-191; Herbert Jedin and John Dolan, *History of the Church*, Volume I: "From the Apostolic Community to Constantine" (New York, 1965), pp. 372-373 (this volume was originally published under the general title *Handbook of Church History*).

⁵¹ Healy, *Valerian Persecution*, pp. 258-262; *Cambridge Ancient History*, XII, 135-136, 171-172.

⁵² *Cambridge Ancient History*, XII, 148-149, 158, 172-174, 184-189, 721-723; Frend, *Martyrdom and Persecution*, pp. 325-326.

⁵³ See Healy, *Valerian Persecution*, pp. 265-266, for this estimate of the character of Gallienus.

⁵⁴ *Cambridge Ancient History*, XII, 189-192.

⁵⁵ St. Athanasius, well within living memory of these events, states explicitly that Zenobia was Jewish (*Hist. arianorum ad monachos* 71) and she is mentioned in the Talmud as protecting Jewish rabbis (*Talm. Jer. Ter.* VIII, 46b). The great English scholar John Chapman accepts the attribution of Judaism to her without question, in his article "Paul of Samosata" in *The Catholic Encyclopedia* (1913), and there seem to be no real grounds for doubting it, though Downey (*Antioch*, p. 312) says it is "not certain."

⁵⁶ *Cambridge Ancient History*, XII, 173-180, 302-307; Downey, *Antioch*, pp. 310-318.

⁵⁷ *Cambridge Ancient History*, XII, 300.

⁵⁸ *Ibid.*, p. 310; Lebreton and Zeiller, *Primitive Church*, II, 807-808.

⁵⁹ J. P. Kirsch, "Felix I, Saint, Pope," *The Catholic Encyclopedia* (1913).

⁶⁰ Lebreton and Zeiller, *Primitive Church*, II, 1027-1035. For Monarchianism, see Chapter Eighteen, above.

⁶¹ Lebreton and Zeiller, *Primitive Church*, II, pp. 1050-1056; Downey, *Antioch*, pp. 310-315; John Chapman, "Paul of Samosata," *The Catholic Encyclopedia* (1913).

⁶² *Cambridge Ancient History*, XII, 313-318. Of the fifteen emperors following Septimius Severus—not counting those who "reigned" less than three months or only in a part of the empire—Caracalla, Macrinus, Elagabalus, Alexander Severus, Maximinus Thrax, Gordian III, Philip the Arab, Gallus, Gallienus, Aurelian, and Probus were all killed by Romans (by assassins or by the army). Decius died on campaign in a manner unknown, Valerian in enemy captivity, and Claudius II and Tacitus of diseases at least partly brought on by the strain of incessant military campaigning.

⁶³ *Cambridge Ancient History*, XII, 322-324.

⁶⁴ Giuseppe Ricciotti, *The Age of Martyrs* (Milwaukee, 1959), pp. 6-7.

⁶⁵ *Ibid.*, pp. 7-8, 13-15; John Holland Smith, *Constantine the Great* (London, 1971),

p. 22; G. P. Baker, *Constantine the Great and the Christian Revolution* (New York, 1967), pp. 57, 65. Henri Leclercq particularly notes Constantius' "kindness and gentleness" (*bienveillance et douceur*) which "drew the Christians toward him" (DACL, VIII [1], 935).

[66] Smith, *Constantine*, pp. 11-15.

[67] Ricciotti, *Age of Martyrs*, pp. 29-30.

[68] Lebreton and Zeiller, *Primitive Church*, II, 808, 877-890; Jedin and Dolan, *History of the Church*, I, 390-394; J. P. Kirsch, "Felix I, Saint, Pope," *The Catholic Encyclopedia* (1913).

[69] Weltin, *Ancient Popes*, pp. 144-145; J. P. Kirsch, "Marcellinus, Saint, Pope," *The Catholic Encyclopedia* (1913).

[70] Following the refusal in 295 of the 21-year-old conscript Maximilian to serve along with his father in the army in Numidia, for which he was martyred, Diocletian began with a purge of Christians and their sympathizers from the army, which involved the martyrdom of the centurion Marcellus and the court secretary Cassian in Mauretania Tingitana probably in 298 or 299, and of Julius and companions at Durostorum in Lower Moesia, probably in 302. See Ricciotti, *Age of Martyrs*, pp. 36-41; Butler-Thurston-Attwater, *Lives of the Saints*, II, 405; *Cambridge Ancient History*, XII, 338-339; Timothy D. Barnes, *Constantine and Eusebius* (Cambridge MA, 1981), pp. 18-19.

[71] Sebastian is said by his Acts to have been commander of the "first cohort" of an unnamed legion (Ricciotti, *Age of Martyrs*, pp. 145-146). His martyrdom could well have come when Diocletian and Galerius ordered military commanders to require their officers and men to sacrifice to the pagan gods, about 299 (Barnes, *Constantine and Eusebius*, pp. 18-19, though he does not mention Sebastian specifically). No modern scholar known to the writer has attempted a defense of the historicity of any part of the Acts of Sebastian, except for the historical reality of his martyrdom and the probability that he was an army officer purged for Christianity before the Great Persecution; his Acts are unhesitatingly rejected in *The Catholic Encyclopedia* of 1913 and in Butler-Thurston-Attwater, *Lives of the Saints*, I, 128-130. Yet his story is for the most part logical and straightforward, without notable excess of marvels and miracles; it is generally attributed to the fifth century in the final form of its composition, which we have (Butler-Thurston-Attwater, *op. cit.*, I, 130) and "shows an intimate knowledge of the topography of Rome" (Ricciotti, *op. cit.*, p. 146); the memory of this martyr's burial place seems to have been accurately preserved from the beginning of the fifth century in the crypt now crowned by the Basilica of St. Sebastian (*ibid.*) The authentication of the burial site and the admitted date of the writing of the Acts are both somewhat earlier than the corresponding dates for burial site authentication and the writing of the Acts of St. Cecilia, whose historicity has been defended at length herein (see Chapter Eighteen, above). His Acts present St. Sebastian as assisting martyrs and confessors in a time of severe persecution, bringing about conversions of pagans and persecutors, defying Diocletian to his face after the emperor had initially befriended him before learning that he was a Christian and then demanded that he renounce his faith, and finally martyred by being shot to death with arrows (Butler-Thurston-Attwater, *op. cit.*, I, 129). There seems no *a priori* reason why the greater part of this narrative should not be substantially true. However, indications of the date of these events are confused since some of the features of the earlier, solely military persecution are mingled with other features characteristic of the later general persecution, thus preventing us from locating them precisely in history even if we accept their basic validity. Does the scholar live today who is bold enough to take up the cause of the substantial historic reality of the narrative in the Acts of St. Sebastian as Prosper Guéranger took up the cause of St. Cecilia?

⁷² Ricciotti, *Age of Martyrs*, pp. 14, 41-42; Frend, *Martyrdom and Persecution*, pp. 362-363; Baker, *Constantine*, pp. 70-74; Smith, *Constantine*, pp. 45-46. Lactantius is the source of our information about the role of Romula. Karl Baus in Jedin and Dolan,*History of the Church*, I, 396-397, rejects Lactantius' testimony, arguing, against long-held scholarly opinion as well as the best (and contemporary) source, that Diocletian himself was the prime mover of the persecution. Insufficient evidence is adduced to justify so drastic a rewriting of the history that has come down to us.

⁷³ Ricciotti, *Age of Martyrs*, pp. 42-45; Frend, *Martyrdom and Persecution*, p. 365; Barnes, *Constantine and Eusebius*, pp. 22-24; Eusebius, *Ecclesiastical History*, VIII, 5-6. Eusebius was of mature years at the time of the Great Persecution, which he describes as occurring in "our own times" (*ibid.*, VII, 26).

⁷⁴ Ricciotti, *Age of Martyrs*, pp. 45-47; Barnes, *Constantine and Eusebius*, pp. 23-24, 38, 303; Downey, *Antioch*, p. 329; Victor C. De Clercq, *Ossius of Cordova* (Washington, 1954), pp. 118-133; Zacarías Garcia Villada, *Historia Ecclesiastica de España* (Madrid, 1929), I, 279-281. Ossius is more often, but less correctly, spelled "Hosius." De Clercq presents convincing evidence that Spain was under the authority of Maximian rather than Constantius up to the abdication of Diocletian and Maximian in 305. There was extensive persecution but relatively few executions of Christians in Spain during 303. The famous martyrdom of St. Vincent, deacon of Zaragoza, probably falls in that year. His extant Acts may have been embellished by later unreliable additions, but a large element of historical truth remains in them, for we have St. Augustine's word that he had seen and read Acts of the martyrdom of St. Vincent of Zaragoza within little more than a century of its occurrence. The governor of Zaragoza, Datianus, appears to have become so personally involved in the struggle to break down Vincent's Christian constancy through torture that he disregarded the imperial instructions against inflicting death on Christians (as they were also disregarded on several occasions in Palestine that year—see Note 75, below). See de Clercq, *op. cit.*, pp. 131-133, and Butler-Thurston-Attwater, *Lives of the Saints*, I, 142-144.

⁷⁵ Ricciotti, *Age of Martyrs*, pp. 45-47, 114; Butler-Thurston-Attwater, *Lives of the Saints*, IV, 188, 366; Frend, *Martyrdom and Persecution*, pp. 372-374.

⁷⁶ Baker, *Constantine*, p. 80. Diocletian reckoned his regnal years from the death of Carus in 283. Historians unaware of this have done arithmetical contortions trying to account for Diocletian's twentieth regnal year being celebrated in what was actually his nineteenth.

⁷⁷ Ricciotti, *Age of Martyrs*, pp. 49-50; Smith, *Constantine*, pp. 53-54; *Cambridge Ancient History*, XII, 340.

⁷⁸ Smith, *Constantine*, p. 54. Paul Allard, *La persécution de Dioclétien et le Triomphe de l'Église* (Paris, 1908), I, 7-12, presents the case for the historicity of Genesius; Butler-Thurston-Attwater, *Lives of the Saints*, III, 398-399, reject it, while summarizing the story well. The explicit reference in the account of Genesius' martyrdom to Diocletian's vicennial visit to Rome and the entertainments connected with it, in which Genesius performed, would seem to go far toward establishing a presumption of historicity, for it fits exactly with the historical situation, without any anachronism. Also in favor of historicity is the complete absence of fabulous material from the story we have, and the fact that somewhat similar incidents have been reported in modern persecutions of Christians, as in the Soviet Union.

⁷⁹ Ricciotti, *Age of Martyrs*, pp. 50-52; *Cambridge Ancient History*, XII, 340.

⁸⁰ Ricciotti, *Age of Martyrs*, p. 51.

⁸¹ So well established historically is Constantius' policy of forbearance toward Christians during the Diocletianic persecution that many scholars use it as the primary argu-

ment for challenging the authenticity of every account of martyrdom in Gaul and Britain during this period—of which there are not many. Perhaps the most notable accounts are of the martyrdoms of Donatian and Rogatian at Nantes in Gaul (Butler-Thurston-Attwater, *Lives of the Saints*, II, 38-1382) and of Alban, the protomartyr of Britain (*ibid.*, II, 612-614) for which considerable evidence of historicity can be marshalled. While clearly Constantius did not initiate any persecution of Christians, he may not have thought himself legally entitled to block persecutions undertaken by over-zealous local governors, in view of the commitment of both Augusti to the persecution and the long-standing law that it was not licit for Christians to exist.

[82] Ricciotti, *Age of Martyrs*, pp. 93-98, 122-123; Butler-Thurston-Attwater, *Lives of the Saints*, I, 303-304; II, 19-21; IV, 175-178 Two other martyrs mentioned for many centuries in the canon of the Mass, Anastasia and Chrysogonus, are indicated by their Acts to have had some connection with the martyrdom of Agape, Irene and Chione. However, while both had an early cult and undoubtedly were real persons and true martyrs, in their cases no critical scholar can put any reliance upon their Acts. We cannot claim to know anything definite about them beyond the fact and the probable places (Sirmium in Pannonia and Aquileia in northern Italy, respectively) of their suffering and death for Christ, and that their martyrdoms probably took place during the Great Persecution. See Butler-Thurston-Attwater, *op. cit.*, IV, 418-419, 613-614.

[83] Ricciotti, *Age of Martyrs*, p. 128.

[84] *Ibid.*, p. 95.

[85] Donald Attwater, *Martyrs* (New York, 1957), pp. 61-62.

[86] Butler-Thurston-Attwater, *Lives of the Saints*, IV, 83-85.

[87] Eusebius, *Ecclesiastical History*, VIII, 9.

[88] Butler-Thurston-Attwater, *Lives of the Saints*, I, 133-137. The Acts of St. Agnes are a premier example of the kind of narrative, abounding in excessive miracles, presenting a stylized "damsel in distress" situation (a Christian virgin forced into a brothel) and very little else, that is rightly not regarded as a source of historical truth. Even the earlier traditions about St. Agnes, current in the latter half of the fourth century and reported by Ambrose, Prudentius, and Pope Damasus, are vague, confused, and in disagreement both with one another and with the Acts in essential details, such as the means by which Agnes was killed. The best the historian can say is summed up in the deeply perceptive comment of Paul Allard: "So died this girl, of whom only two things are known for certain: she lived purely, and died a martyr. She had, without doubt, entranced her contemporaries by the high spirit of her sacrifice, rich testimony for Christ and the Church, by words full of life and grace, a cry, a gesture, revealing a soul of exquisite beauty." (*"Ainsi finit cette jeune fille, dont on sait au moins deux choses certaines: elle vécut pure et mourut martyre. Elle avait sans doute ravi ses contemporains par l'élan de son sacrifice, une généreuse protestation en faveur du Christ et de l'Église, une parole pleine d'énergie et de grace, un cri, un geste, découvrant une âme exquise."*—Allard, *Persécution de Dioclétien*, I, 408) This is perhaps also the appropriate point to make the brief mention which is all the critical historian can properly give, of the martyrdom of St. Lucy, like Agnes honored for centuries in the canon of the Mass, which did take place, at Syracuse in Sicily during the Great Persecution, but of which no historically reliable memory remains; her Acts are obviously a conflation of what was known or believed about the martyrdom of Sts. Agnes and Cecilia, for there is hardly anything in them that is not taken from what is recounted in their Acts. See Butler-Thurston-Attwater, *op. cit.*, IV, 548-549.

[89] The circumstances of St. Eulalia's martyrdom were quite similar to those of the martyrdom of Justus and Pastor. Good evidence exists showing that there was an early

written account of it dating from the sixth or possibly the fifth century, though her extant Acts are later in date. (On this point see especially Garcia Villada, *Historia Eclesiástica de España*, I, 290-291). Eulalia has long been one of the most honored saints of Spain. Since about 500 her feast has been celebrated in Barcelona on a different day (February 12) than elsewhere in Spain (December 10). This led to the development of a tradition that there were two St. Eulalias, the one of Mérida and the other of Barcelona—a tradition still defended by Garcia Villada, *op. cit.*, I, 282-300. But the evidence of the separate feast days alone cannot prevail over the convincing evidence of otherwise almost identical Acts and traditions testifying to the identity of the supposed two St. Eulalias.

[90] Butler-Thurston-Attwater, *Lives of the Saints*, III, 270-271; Ricciotti, *Age of Martyrs*, pp. 98-100.

[91] Ricciotti, *Age of Martyrs*, pp. 85-87; Lebreton and Zeiller, *Primitive Church*, II, 1046-1049, 1204-1205.

[92] Ricciotti, *Age of Martyrs*, p. 88; Barnes, *Constantine and Eusebius*, p. 38; J. P. Kirsch, "Marcellinus, Saint, Pope," *The Catholic Encyclopedia* (1913). Kirsch's is the best summary of this controversial question which this writer has seen. Frend, *Martyrdom and Persecution*, pp. 375-376, presents a rather confused argument for the proposition that Marcellinus did lapse, accepting the correctness of Donatist charges that not only he, but three of the next four Popes following him—Marcellus, Miltiades, and Silvester I—all sacrificed to pagan gods during the Great Persecution. Such a quadruple Papal apostasy is absurd on the face of the matter. We are asked to believe that the electors of Rome on three separate occasions during six years (Marcellus was elected in 308, Miltiades in 311, and Silvester in 314) chose a man who had denied the Faith as head of the Church! The exaggeration and prejudice of the Donatist charge are obvious. The formal apostasy of even one Pope, to say nothing of four within a decade, could hardly have been a secret from everybody except a few Donatist propagandists a hundred years later. If it had happened, it would probably have destroyed the Papacy; most certainly it would have been widely discussed. Consider, for example, the widespread, sad Christian comment on the surrender of the famous Bishop Ossius the Confessor of Córdoba to the Arian heretics at the age of 101, in 358 (see Volume II, Chapter One, of this history). Barnes, *Constantine and Eusebius*, p. 38 says that Marcellinus delivered up copies of the Scriptures to the persecutors, and consequently was regarded as an apostate and therefore somehow automatically deposed as Pope. The only evidence for his having delivered up the Scriptures is much later Donatist calumny, and there is no contemporary evidence whatever that anyone ever considered him as having been deposed. Omission of his name in some later Papal lists may have many explanations, but cannot be held to indicate deposition or resignation in the absence of other evidence; even if such had happened (and it is maintained herein that a Pope cannot be deposed) the Pope had still been Pope before quitting the office.

[93] Barnes, *Constantine and Eusebius*, p. 38; Ricciotti, *Age of Martyrs*, pp. 88-89. Barnes dates the Papal consecration of Marcellinus' successor Marcellus to November or December 306.

[94] Other martyrs whose passions can be dated with reasonable probability to the year 304, and about whom we have some significant and historically reliable information, not elsewhere discussed in the text or notes, are: Irenaeus, Bishop of Sirmium in Illyria, on April 6 (Ricciotti, *Age of Martyrs*, pp. 133-135); Pollio, lector of the church of Cibali in Illyria, April 27 (*ibid.*, p. 140); Florinus and forty companions in Noricum, May 4 (*ibid.*, p. 141); Euplus of Catania in Sicily, August 12 (*ibid.*, pp. 146-148); Romanus, deacon of Caesarea in Palestine, at Antioch in the very presence of Galerius, November 18 (Downey, *Antioch*, p. 329); Crispina of Theveste in Numidia, December 5 (Ricciot-

ti, *op. cit.*, pp. 91-93); Timothy and Thecla at Gaza in Palestine (Butler-Thurston-Attwater, *Lives of the Saints*, III, 355); Marcellinus, a priest (not to be confused with the contemporary Pope of that name) and Peter, an exorcist, in Rome, both later mentioned in the canon of the Mass (*ibid.*, II, 452-453). See also the entries in Butler-Thurston-Attwater, *op. cit.*, for the other saints mentioned.

[95] Ricciotti, *Age of Martyrs*, p. 54.

[96] *Ibid.*, pp. 52-53; Smith, *Constantine*, p. 58. Ricciotti follows Lactantius in presenting Galerius as having forced an unwilling Diocletian to abdicate; Smith gives a contrary opinion, but without reasons. Lactantius' testimony is probably to be preferred; however, after his breakdown Diocletian must have realized at least to some extent his incapacity for continued rule, which would have substantially weakened any resistance he might have offered to Galerius' pressure.

[97] St. Ambrose (*De obitu. Theodis*, 42) is the authority for Helena's occupation before her marriage. His statement is supported by other authorities and is now generally accepted (*e.g.*, Smith, *Constantine*, pp. 15-16).

[98] Smith, *Constantine*, pp. 1-2, 26-28, 55-58.

[99] The best retelling of this tremendous story is in Baker, *Constantine*, pp. 84-86. Smith, *Constantine*, pp. 58-60 tries to complicate it with a conspiratorial theory based on the assumption that Galerius was a man with a cool head, sound judgment, and strong Machiavellian tendencies, and that Constantine's escape could have been foiled by signal stations on the Bosporus. These assumptions about Galerius are dubious to say the least, and the signal stations on the Bosporus would have done him no good if not alerted. Since, as shown in the text, Constantine crossed the Bosporus before Galerius woke up and before the alarm was raised over his departure, the point falls to the ground.

[100] Baker, *Constantine*, pp. 84-86.

[101] *Ibid.*; Smith, *Constantine*, pp. 60-61. Barnes, *Constantine and Eusebius*, p. 27, appears to doubt the truth of the account of Constantine's ride, but gives no specific reasons other than a telescoping of later events whereby some ancient authorities report Constantine as reaching his father only as he was dying (actually he lived for the better part of a year after his son joined him). But other ancient authorities report this point correctly (Barnes, *op. cit.*, p. 298); and in any case the error involved is natural, relatively minor, and surely insufficient to invalidate the entire account as mere romancing.

[102] Smith, *Constantine*, p. 62; Frend, *Martyrdom and Persecution*, p. 379; Ricciotti, *Age of Martyrs*, p. 116.

[103] Ricciotti, *Age of Martyrs*, pp. 104-108.

[104] *Ibid.*, p. 108.

[105] *Ibid.*, pp. 138-139.

[106] *Ibid.*, pp. 56-59; Barnes, *Constantine and Eusebius*, pp. 29-32.

[107] Smith, *Constantine*, pp. 75-77.

[108] Frend, *Martyrdom and Persecution*, pp. 377-380. There were, however, some notable martyrdoms in those two years of which we have authentic accounts: Theodosia of Tyre at Caesarea in Palestine in 307 (Ricciotti, *Age of Martyrs*, p. 116); Valentina and Thea and Paul at Gaza in Palestine (*ibid.*, pp. 114-115) and Quirinius, Bishop of Siscia in Illyria (Butler-Thurston-Attwater, *Lives of the Saints*, II, 472-475).

[109] Lloyd B. Holsapple, *Constantine the Great* (New York, 1942), pp. 137-140. In a thorough review of the question of who held Spain from the abdication of Diocletian and Maximian to the victory of Constantine before Rome, De Clercq (*Ossius of Cordova*, pp. 137-140) concludes that the evidence does not permit a firm historical judgment.

[110] Lebreton and Zeiller, *Primitive Church*, II, 1203-1204. Barnes, *Constantine and Eusebius*, pp. 38, 303-304, holds that Marcellus was elected in November or December

306, immediately after Maxentius was proclaimed emperor in Rome on October 28 of that year. But Barnes admits in his notes that this assumption requires changing no less than three specifically recorded dates in the ancient sources on the assumption that they were wrongly copied, accepting the later Donatist charges that Pope Marcellinus betrayed the Church, and accepting the theory that this alleged betrayal caused Marcellinus to be regarded as deposed (see Note 92, above). These are all too many assumptions with very little warrant.

[111] Barnes, *Constantine and Eusebius*, p. 38; Ricciotti, *Age of Martyrs*, p. 90.

[112] Frend, *Martyrdom and Persecution*, pp. 380-381.

[113] The often highly critical J. B. Segal states that the extant accounts of the martyrdoms of Shmona and Gurya in Edessa in 309, and of Habbib there in 310, "deserve to be accepted as historical documents" establishing that "Edessa was a Christian city" (*Edessa*, pp. 83-86). For Adrian and Eubulus, martyred at Caesarea when coming to visit Christian confessors imprisoned there, see Butler-Thurston-Attwater, *Lives of the Saints*, I, 484-485.

[114] Ricciotti, *Age of Martyrs*, pp. 109-113.

[115] Smith, *Constantine*, pp. 87-90; Barnes, *Constantine and Eusebius*, pp. 34-35, 40-41. Barnes brands the assassination story "a deliberate invention" (*op. cit.*, p. 305); it is hard to see how he can be quite so sure of that.

[116] Barnes, *Constantine and Eusebius*, pp. 35-37; Holsapple, *Constantine*, pp. 143-145; Frend, *Martyrdom and Persecution*, p. 384.

[117] Ricciotti, *Age of Martyrs*, p. 62; Smith, *Constantine*, pp. 90-91. Barnes, *Constantine and Eusebius*, p. 41, dates Diocletian's death to December 3, 311.

[118] Ricciotti, *Age of Martyrs*, pp. 150-151.

[119] *Ibid.*, pp. 151-153; Frend, *Martyrdom and Persecution*, pp. 381-383. For the text of this famous decree see Eusebius, *Ecclesiastical History*, VIII, 17.

[120] Ricciotti, *Age of Martyrs*, p. 153; Frend, *Martyrdom and Persecution*, p. 383; Holsapple, *Constantine*, p. 148. The last martyrdom in Palestine during this persecution was that of Eubulus in March 310 (Frend, *op. cit.*, p. 381).

[121] Eusebius, *Ecclesiastical History*, IX, 1.

20.
TRIUMPH OF THE CROSS (311-324)

The incomprehensible kindness of our God by no means allows the state of man to stray for too long a time in the darkness, nor does it suffer the odious wills of some so to prevail as not to grant men a new opportunity for conversion to the truth by opening up before them through its most glorious light a path to salvation. Of this indeed I am assured by many examples and I can illustrate the same truth from my own case. For at the first there were in me things which appeared far removed from the truth and I did not think that there was any heavenly power which could see into the secrets of my heart. What future ought these things which I have mentioned to have brought upon me?—surely one overflowing with every evil. But Almighty God Who sits in the watchtower of Heaven has bestowed upon me that which I did not deserve. Truly, most holy bishops of the Savior Christ, at this time I can neither describe nor number these gifts which of His heavenly benevolence He has granted to me, His servant.—Emperor Constantine to the Council of Arles, August 314.

The Great Persecution was ended—though it was to have two strong last echoes during the decade following the death of Galerius—but Christianity remained apparently no better situated than it had been at the end of the earlier persecutions: tacitly tolerated in most of the empire, but still without the legal

524

right to exist. This was the best status Christians had been able to achieve at any time since the Crucifixion, almost three hundred years before.

Was the heroic virtue required to sustain martyrdom, or at least to anticipate and accept the possibility of martyrdom at any time, always to be demanded of Christians? If so, Christianity would remain confined to a small minority of the spiritually elite. Yet Christ's whole life and teaching made it vividly clear that He had come not only for a spiritual elite but for all men, including—or especially—the poor and the weak, and that He wished to see all men regularly helped and sustained by their brothers in community. Ultimately this meant a Christian society, so structured as to encourage rather than discourage men and women in following Christ's road to salvation.

In a Christian society, Christ's reign would be explicitly acknowledged and its extension in men's minds and hearts encouraged by public law as well as by private devotion; His Church would be formally recognized as the arbiter of morality and the guarantor of truth about the ultimate questions of God, human life, and the universe; yet temporal government would remain, in its proper sphere, fully separate from the Church. Such a Christian society was to be Christendom, in its visible aspect. Even after the victory of the martyrs, Christendom still awaited its founder. He could not be a clergyman, for the clergy did not—and should not—have the temporal power to bring about even the beginnings of this enormous social-political transformation themselves. The founder of Christendom could only be a layman who honored the Church and understood her correctly, at least in essence; and, given the nature of the human condition and the magnitude of the transformation required, he must be a ruler, or at least one with great influence on the ruler. The dangers that would beset any attempt to establish Christendom, as so defined, were almost as great as its potential benefits. But it was an attempt that serious Christians, deeply conscious of the *universality* of the mission given them by the Savior of their souls and the Founder of their Church, had to make.

The man to make this attempt, for the Roman empire, was a convert, not even baptized until the end of his life. His grasp of Christian truth and his practice of Christian morality were often imperfect. His own statement which stands at the head of this chapter shows that he would not have sought to exculpate himself entirely from the reproaches which his many modern critics have so fiercely flung at his life and his faith. Constantine was an emperor of Rome, eventually sole emperor. His predecessors had been personally deified; he ruled as the servant of God.[1] He had nothing in this world to gain, and much to lose, by affiliation with the still widely despised Christians.[2] There is no indication that he was especially impressed with them in his early years, though—like his father—he had never hated or persecuted them. Constantine's emergence as the founder of Christendom cannot be convincingly accounted for on any grounds of human calculation or emotional predilection. It is fully explicable only as Constantine himself explained it: that Christ Himself chose him for the task.[3] As Christ had chosen Peter and the Twelve to build His Church; as He had chosen Paul on the road to Damascus to be His Apostle to the Gentiles, "taking him as prey";[4] so He chose Constantine to establish the first great temporal kingdom in which He would reign.

This view of Constantine has not found much favor with twentieth-century historical scholarship. Most modern writers, even when relatively favorable to Constantine, are uncomfortable with the theocentric view of his life (the recent study of Constantine by Paul Keresztes is a very welcome and much needed exception), while critics point to his unworthiness, hesitancy, mistakes, and crimes, his later partial support of the Arian heresy, and his long postponement of the essential sacramental initiation into Christianity which is baptism.[5] Many of their charges against Constantine are well founded. But all they show is the age-old truth that men are imperfect instruments for God's work—especially when they have no access to sacramental graces. Yet, as Christ told Nicodemus, the Holy Spirit, like the wind, blows where it will.[6] It would seem that Constantine was chosen not because he was, or was to become, a very holy man, but because at the hour of the martyrs' victory he was the best man available in a position to begin the great task of founding Christendom, which their sacrifices and prayers and example had at last rendered possible; and above all, as his own words quoted above show so well, because he was willing to listen to Christ the Lord, and in His sign conquer.

Let us set the stage, at the end of the Year of Our Lord 311. Galerius is dead, apparently unrepentant, the decree of toleration for the Christians wrung from him, through fear of death and Divine vengeance, in April, ignored by his old comrade-in-arms Maximin Daia who has begun a new persecution in September. Bishop Peter of Alexandria has been martyred in this persecution, in November; the monk Anthony, the hermit of the desert who has become a legend in his own life-time, has come out of the wastelands with other solitary ascetics to strengthen and sustain the Egyptian confessors and martyrs and to offer himself for martyrdom—an offer he is now making daily in Alexandria, which none of Daia's bloodthirsty officials dares accept.[7] From Syria and Palestine, Christians have fled for refuge to southern Armenia beyond the Tigris River; Daia is pursuing them with a punitive military expedition.[8] Licinius rules Eastern Europe and has been betrothed to Constantine's sister to seal an alliance with him. Maxentius, the son of Diocletian's old imperial partner Maximian, rules Italy and the province of Africa, specially favoring the people of Rome, largely neglected in recent years by other emperors. Neither Licinius nor Maxentius is or has been a systematic persecutor of the Christians like Galerius or Daia; they are strictly men of the moment, men of the sword, incapable of imagining any goal and purpose for their lives beyond power for themselves. Maxentius' rule in Rome is marked by flagrant immorality and arbitrary tyranny;

pagans as well as Christians testify that there was no respect for virtue or for law under his regime.[9] The election of Miltiades, an African, as Pope in July has finally reunited the church in Rome after its prolonged dispute over the question of penance and reconciliation for the lapsed after the persecution of Diocletian;[10] but the African church is now about to go into schism on very much the same question. In Gaul, Constantine has pacified the Rhine frontier; he has a veteran, loyal army, but it is substantially inferior both in numbers and in equipment to the massive forces Maxentius can deploy in Italy.[11]

Early in 312, as reports of threatening moves by Maxentius reached him, Constantine called his officers into a council of war at his winter quarters in Alsace, to discuss the prospects for success of a march on Italy. Their response was overwhelmingly unfavorable. First the former Caesar Severus, then Galerius himself, had marched against Maxentius in Italy with the full resources of the rich eastern half of the empire behind them, yet neither had been able to maintain himself in the Italian peninsula; the venture had cost Severus his life. Maxentius had at least double Constantine's strength. There was no immediately prospect of military help from Licinius.[12]

Constantine was above all a man of action. The division of the Roman empire had left him with the poorest portion. No one could seriously imagine, after the near-chaos of the past six years, that there remained any legal way to settle the question of the imperial succession or of the division of the empire among its claimants. The sword must decide. Those among the contenders who did not move first and effectively were likely to perish first. His instinct was to strike, to take the offensive while he could, aiming for the traditional power center of the empire: Rome. But he was shaken by the negative recommendations of his officers. He consulted the haruspices—the famous soothsayers of Roman (originally Etruscan) paganism who claimed to read the future in the livers of sacrificed animals. The haruspices, too, were unfavorable.[13]

Where had Constantine heard, and how much had he heard, of the God of the Christians by the winter of 312? We have little evidence on this vital point; what there is indicates very slight familiarity on his part with the Christian creed. But, as an intelligent and widely travelled ruler of a portion of the Roman empire, the son of a former Augustus of the west, Constantine must have gained clear impressions of the extraordinary courage and fidelity of the Christian martyrs during the recent persecutions. It is obvious from his own and his father's conduct as well as from his own later statements that, like many other non-Christians in the empire, he abhorred those persecutions.[14] Perhaps what came through to him most clearly at this time was that the Christian God was strong, a real help and support to those in trouble or facing death. He was in trouble; very possibly, he faced death. Therefore Constantine opened his heart in prayer to this strange God, so dimly understood.[15] When he had done so, he saw and heard Him calling.

Original historical sources for the reign of Constantine provide us with four separate testimonies for visions seen by Constantine during 312, the year of his campaign against Maxentius in Italy, and a contemporary confirmation of the most famous of those testimonies: (1) the account in the *Life of Constantine* by Eusebius, the first Christian historian, written about twenty years after the event, that Constantine and his army on the march in Gaul that year saw a cross in the sky in front of the sun with the words *In hoc signo vinces* ("In this sign you shall conquer"), whereupon Constantine ordered a golden and jewelled cross made, and atop it the *labarum* (bearing the Greek letters Chi and Rho, the first two letters of Christ in Greek, superimposed) as a standard for his army—an account which Eusebius emphasizes was given to him personally by Constantine on oath;[16] (2) the almost immediately contemporary account of the rhetorician Lactantius, a Christian convert, in his *On the Deaths of the Persecutors*, of a dream of Constantine on the night immediately preceding his decisive battle with Maxentius in Italy, in which he was told to place the *labarum* on the shields of his soldiers before the battle, and "in this sign you shall be the victor";[17] (3, 4) little-noticed passages in pagan panegyrics to Constantine delivered in 313 and in 322, the second being on the occasion of the tenth anniversary of the decisive battle, referring to remarkable visions seen in the sky in Gaul by Constantine just before his invasion of Italy, and widely known to his troops, showing that "there was a secret divine power working within him"—though no cross is mentioned, but rather apparitions of celestial armies.[18] The confirmation is found in the appearance of the words *in hoc vince* on the graffiti wall adjoining the original red-wall monument over the grave of St. Peter, which was marked by Christian pilgrims during the years from 312 to 330, before Eusebius' *Life of Constantine* had been published.[19]

The third and fourth sources and the graffiti are particularly important because they tend to confirm the first and most contested source; nor is the second by any means contradictory to the first, often though this has been alleged. There is no reason why a man who has been vouchsafed one great Christian vision should not later, on the eve of the most critical day of his life, receive another reinforcing it.[20] As many scholars have pointed out, the accounts of Eusebius and Lactantius cannot refer to the same event; but they do not need to do so. Both can be true; it is maintained here that both are true.

Something very powerful and dramatic in the realm of the spirit must have happened to Constantine during the year 312; on this all but the most prejudiced commentators agree. At the beginning of the year he is still a pagan consulting animal livers to learn the future; at the end of it he is proclaiming himself the protector and benefactor of the Christians, giving the Lateran palace to the Pope;[21] he has constantly at his side for advice and doctrinal teaching the renowned Ossius the Confessor, Bishop of Córdoba in Spain;[22] he attributes his triumph before Rome entirely to the Christian God.[23] Is the vision of the *labarum* on the night before his victorious battle alone enough to account for all this? This

Battle of Saxa Rubra, or the Milvian Bridge, took place on October 28, 312. By December, Constantine's benefactions to the Church and involvement in its internal affairs had already begun. Was just one month time enough for the necessary instruction and familiarization regarding Christianity for a man who knew so little of it before that year that, by his own testimony, he was not even quite sure what the cross signified?[24]

It seems far more reasonable to accept the authenticity of both visions, which would place Constantine's conversion experience and the making of the standard of the cross and the *labarum* (a considerable work, as Eusebius describes it) in Gaul during the spring of 312, with the call to put the *labarum* on the shield of each soldier the night before the decisive victory in October simply a seal upon it.[25]

Many historians, even orthodox Catholics, hesitate to trust Eusebius' *Life of Constantine* because of what they regard as its excessively laudatory character. It is indeed written much in the style of a panegyric. All the details may not be reliable; some unpleasant facts are suppressed. But on the essential point, the reliability of Constantine's own solemn testimony to Eusebius about what he saw in the sky, those endorsing the common modern rejection of this testimony must hold either that Eusebius flatly lied about what Constantine said to him, or that Constantine flatly lied to Eusebius. The argument is very similar to that on the authenticity of the authorship of the Gospel of John (see Chapter Fourteen), except that it is doubtless easier to picture Constantine as a deliberate liar, even on such a matter, than the Beloved Disciple or his pupils. But it is still far from easy. Constantine's religious experience of 312, whatever it may have been, was evidently the turning point of his whole life. Is it really likely that he would have lied about it on his solemn oath, in describing it to a fellow Christian, the first Christian historian? It is hardly more likely that Constantine would have been honestly confused in his memory of such an event, though we may doubt that all his army actually saw the cross in the sky, since such visions are rarely seen by everyone present.[26]

Assuming, then, the reality of Constantine's vision of the cross in the sky, and that he saw it while still in Gaul in the spring of 312, we are well prepared to understand his sudden transformation from doubt to absolute certainty; his fearless, lightning descent into Italy with an army less than half, perhaps no more than a quarter the size of his opponent's; his clemency to the people of the cities that resisted him—either out of a dawning Christian charity, or as a result of his complete personal assurance that he would ultimately rule these people and sought their good will (for terrorism, when not a product of malice, is usually the result of fear); and his defeat of a far more experienced general, Ruricius Pompeianus, near Verona in northern Italy.[27] However it may scandalize modern ears, the God of the Christians is still—though far more and much else—*Dominus Deus Sabaoth*, Lord God of armies.[28] War is a great evil; but when God's children must fight, He will help them fight well.

The decisive battle of the campaign—the battle of the *labarum*—was fought at Saxa Rubra, the Red Rocks, nine miles north of Rome on the banks of the Tiber, where stood a villa which had belonged to Livia, Caesar Augustus' wife of fifty-two years. The best of Maxentius' army was the Praetorian Guard, maker and unmaker of emperors for a century and a quarter at Rome, now making their last stand (for Constantine in victory was to abolish them forever). They held the critical left wing, away from the river. The center was held by prodigiously armored cavalry, the *cataphracti*, a development of Persian military technology never used in European warfare before this campaign. Maxentius' confidence in the *cataphracti*, together with doubts about the loyalty of the Roman populace to him arising from Constantine's growing popularity and impressive military achievements in northern Italy, probably suffices to account for his decision to engage Constantine in the open field rather than standing a siege behind Rome's massive walls, which Constantine with his small army would have found very difficult to master without aid from within. Constantine had trained a corps to deal with the *cataphracti* by means of heavy maces. He led it in person to the attack. The *cataphracti* were dispersed, the unbreakable Praetorian Guard outflanked, and Maxentius was driven in rout toward Rome. The city could only be reached from the battlefield by crossing the Tiber on the Milvian Bridge. The bridge collapsed under the weight and panic of the fugitives. Maxentius fell into the river; in his heavy armor he sank into the mud, and there he drowned. The gates of the city were opened, and the next day—October 29, 312—Constantine entered Rome in triumph.[29]

He proved remarkably merciful in victory. There were no proscriptions or confiscations; only a handful of those who had been closest to Maxentius were executed.[30] A statue of Constantine was erected in his honor; he put a cross in its hand.[31] A triumphal arch was voted, which still stands in Rome; in his inscription upon it, Constantine attributes his victory to the inspiration of "divinity," without specification or further explanation. (At this time he still sought accommodation with his pagan subjects—a substantial majority of the total population of the empire—where he could achieve it without violating his Christian conscience. However, he refused to perform the customary pagan sacrifices on the Capitoline Hill giving thanks to Jupiter for his victory.)[32] The memory of the imperial persecutors—Diocletian, Maximian, Galerius—was condemned in a stern edict; their monuments in Rome were destroyed. Having been proclaimed "First Augustus" by the Senate, Constantine ordered Daia to stop his persecution of the Christians. Whether or not Daia accepted Constantine's authority in theory, he judged it prudent at this time to comply with his order, pretending that he had never favored the executions of Christians that had taken place under his rule during the past year.[33] As amends for the effects of the persecutions, Constantine returned all the property which had been taken from

the 25 titular churches of Rome, and granted them substantial additional donations. A like restoration took place in Africa,[34] and very probably in the other
provinces under Constantine's immediate rule.

In Africa he went much further toward the official subsidization of the
Church. We have a letter from Constantine to Bishop Caecilian of Carthage,
probably to be dated in the winter of 312-313, ordering a payment of 3,000
folles (double denarii) for the support of "certain specified ministers of the lawful
and holy Catholic religion" as designated by Ossius, his principal Christian advisor. This grant was specifically stated to be for current expenses (rather than
as amends for the past persecution).[35] Thus, at this very early date, Constantine
was already undertaking the policy of government financial support of the
Catholic Church—a policy still followed in most Catholic countries and, for
Protestant churches, in several Protestant countries of Europe. The church
designated to receive state funds has come to be called the "established church."
The arrangement is mainly known to Americans as one which their Constitution explicitly forbids; but the case against it is by no means as strong as most
Americans assume. Historically, from the time of Constantine onward, governments have given financial support to Christian churches because their existence
and active functioning were regarded as commanded by God and essential to
the common good—as, in Christendom, indeed they must be. But the problem,
from the beginning until now, has been how to keep the church and all its operations free of government control once it is receiving aid from the public treasury.

In February 313 Constantine and Licinius met at Milan to solemnize, in splendid ceremonies, Licinius' marriage to Constantine's sister Constantia. The occasion provided an opportunity of which Constantine promptly took advantage,
to obtain the formal pledge of the indifferent Licinius to full toleration for the
Christians and restoration of their confiscated property throughout the empire.
This policy was later set forth in writing in an edict. The copy we have was
issued by Licinius from Nicomedia in June 313, applying to all the lands he
ruled. It specifically states that it reflected a joint decision with Constantine,
who in all probability wrote it himself and published in the West shortly before
Licinius published it in the East. Neither Licinius' earlier nor his later record
provides the slightest basis for assuming that he took any independent action
in this matter.[36]

In his subsidization of the church in Africa beginning in 313, as in his series
of Christian-oriented laws discussed later in this chapter, Constantine was moving
well beyond a policy of mere toleration of Christianity and restitution of its tangible losses from the persecution of Diocletian and Galerius. But Licinius could
be brought no further than this; it was to him that the Milan agreement was
really directed.

The firming up of the alliance between Constantine and Licinius meant an
overmastering threat to Daia, as he well knew. His only chance was to strike

while Constantine was preoccupied by a barbarian attack on the Rhine frontier, as happened in the spring of 313. Daia then attacked Licinius in Thrace. This conflict cast Licinius, somewhat uncomfortably, in the role of Christian champion against the persecutor Daia. He played that role (for this one year only) with some skill, even presenting his troops with a vaguely monotheistic prayer at the outset of a major battle with Daia—a prayer which Licinius said, probably in imitation of Constantine's now famous dream of the *labarum*, had been dictated to him by an angel in a dream the night before. Many of Licinius' troops, even those not Christians, had been deeply impressed by Constantine's victory over Maxentius and his view of the cause of that victory. They wanted and expected to be part of a similar victory similarly won, under Licinius.[37]

Badly defeated near Hadrianople on April 30, 313, Daia fled at top speed first to Nicomedia, then deep into Asia Minor. Finally run to earth at St. Paul's Tarsus, he died under controverted circumstances after at last decreeing full liberty for Christians and ordering the massacre of pagan priests, whom he said had deceived him about Christianity. By September Daia the persecutor was dead and Licinius completely victorious, as was Constantine on the Rhine frontier.[38]

Meanwhile a storm had been building in the church in Africa which was to lead to the first really long-lasting and large-scale schism in the Church of Christ since Marcion's two hundred years before. After each major persecution, as we have seen, two factions appeared in the church: rigorist and laxist. The rigorists demanded prolonged or permanent excommunication and deprivation of all ecclesiastical offices for all who had collaborated in any way with the persecutors, and viewed very dubiously any bishop who had avoided—by whatever means—imprisonment, torture, or martyrdom. The laxists, on the other hand, called for readmission of the lapsed into full Christian communion with the bare minimum of delay, examination, and penance. In Africa the rigorists had always been especially strong, perhaps partly due to the continuing influence of the memory of Tertullian and his often harsh, unforgiving writings. They still upheld Cyprian's position, despite its rejection by the Popes, requiring the re-baptism of heretics—and, they now added, of collaborators with the persecutors.[39] In 312 this division of the church in Africa came to a head when the moderate Caecilian was named and consecrated Bishop of Carthage, the principal see in the African church, before the rigorist bishops from Numidia, led by Secundus of Tigisi, could arrive to voice their objections. These rigorists then proceeded to declare Caecilian's election null and void on the grounds that his three episcopal consecrators (or at least one of them, Felix of Aptunga) had collaborated with the persecutors. Then they proclaimed one of their own group, Majorinus, to be bishop of Carthage. When Majorinus died the next year they replaced him with Donatus, who lived a very long time and gave his name to their faction and its ultimate schism and heresy.[40]

Donatus was a man of great ability—and of great pride. His own record, and that of some of his major suporters, was not nearly so pure as the principles their faction espoused might suggest. He himself had shown a schismatical temper in 311 even before the contested election of Caecilian, so obnoxiously that his later admirers had to pretend that the schismatic of 311 was a different person with the same name;[41] one of his principal adherents, Bishop Silvanus of Cirta, was later clearly proved to be not only himself a collaborator with the persecutors, but also guilty of theft, embezzlement, and simony (sale of church office);[42] another principal adherent, Bishop Purpurius of Limata, was by his own confession an unrepentant murderer.[43] The more one examines the background of the Donatist leaders—and through the most fortunate preservation of a single manuscript in medieval Paris, we are in possession of documentation on them unusually ample for this early period[44]—the more one is repelled by their malevolence and their hypocrisy, bearing more than a passing resemblance to the malevolence and hypocrisy of the Pharisees who condemned Christ.

In a letter to Anulinus, proconsul of Africa, directing the restoration of property taken from the Christian churches during the persecution—probably sent about the same time as his letter to Bishop Caecilian mentioned earlier—Constantine made it clear that he had heard of the disturbances in the African church and intended the restored property to go to the church headed by Caecilian, which he called "the Catholic Church of the Christians." The Donatist response was a direct appeal to Constantine on April 15, 313, asking him to designate three named bishops from Gaul to hear and decide their case against Caecilian.[45]

Since the acceptance of this appeal by Constantine is often presented as the first major intervention of state power in the internal affairs of the Church,[46] it should be carefully noted that: (1) the appeal was generated by Constantine's own directive to Anulinus to restore confiscated property only to churches in communion with Caecilian, threby giving him no just reason for refusing to respond to a petition to investigate the reasons why much of the African church was *not* in communion with Caecilian; (2) Constantine was not asked himself to give judgment in the case, but to recognize a commission of bishops for this purpose; (3) in response, Constantine simply turned the appeal over to the Pope, who proceeded to set up a council to hear the case, controlled by 15 Italian bishops appointed by him, though the council did also include the three bishops from Gaul requested by the Donatists.[47] If these three points are borne in mind, Constantine's action will be seen to have been substantially correct even by the more developed standards of the later Catholic Church in such matters.

Pope Miltiades' special council met at Rome for three days in October 313, under his own presidency (he was himself an African), with Donatus on hand to plead his cause. The evidence of Donatus' schismatical agitation in the past, even before the consecration of Caecilian, was brought forward. By his own admission, he had re baptized members of opposing factions won over to his own, and even re-consecrated lapsed bishops—wholly contrary to the law and teaching of the Church, as consistently upheld by the Popes and specifically by Pope Stephen I in his controversy with Cyprian in the preceding century, that baptism, ordination, and episcopal consecration put permanent sacramental marks upon the soul, and therefore may never be validly repeated. Of evidence against Caecilian, there was virtually none. Donatus was condemned, as the principal author of the schism. His followers were called upon to rejoin the Catholic Church; any who would do so immediately would be presumed to have been in good faith, though misled, and would not be penalized.[48]

The Council of Rome in 313 should have settled the Donatist question. But, as the whole long tumultuous history of Church councils and their after-effects was to show, while councils with Papal approval can and do resolve many theological issues definitively, they rarely settle any historical controversy within the Church which is presented in the ecumenical forum for the first time. The Council of Rome was for the Donatists as that of Nicaea for the Arians, of Ephesus for the Nestorians, and of Chalcedon for the Monophysites, a beginning rather than an end. In this case as in all the others mentioned and many more, the worst of the evil with which the council was called upon to deal came after it.

For Donatus and his followers had not the slightest intention of submitting to the authority of Pope Miltiades, his council, or anyone except themselves. Their *non serviam* rings as though from a trumpet out of the ancient parchment of their documents. Their response was fully in the spirit of the response of their Bishop Purpurius the murderer when Caecilian offered to be consecrated by any bishops the Donatists might choose: "Let him come; instead of laying our hands on him we will split his head open by way of penance."[49] They charged that the Council of Rome had been packed, renewed their demand for a judgment from Gaul, and loudly objected that the Council of Rome had not even considered their point that Bishop Felix of Aptunga, one of the consecrators of Caecilian, was a traitor to the Church[50]—despite the fact that they had presented no evidence on this point to the council and that it had established, by its ruling on re-consecration, that even if the charges against Felix were true, they would not affect his canonical sufficiency to consecrate.

The Donatist charges were made in the form of more petitions to Constantine, accompanied by reports from his governors in Africa of the large and growing popularity of the Donatist movement due to its vigorous leadership, excellent organization, and the popular impression (however contrary to fact) that these men stood for a strict and demanding moral code. Constantine was not so much angered at this time as scandalized, as his letter to the Bishop of Syracuse (probably dateable to January 314) makes clear:[51]

These very ones, who ought to be of one mind in brotherly love, are rather shamefully separated from one another, and furnish the men who have souls foreign to this most holy religion the occasion for scoffing, whereby it has become a matter of conscience with me to insist that what should have ceased by voluntary agreement after the judgment had been rendered, even now may possibly be ended in the presence of so many.[52]

Constantine was still a very new convert; it was less than two years since he had seen the cross in the sky. St. Paul, after Jesus took him on the road to Damascus and he had briefly and rather unsuccessfully attempted to preach Christianity in that city as a neophyte, had gone into retreat for at least a full year before beginning his great missionary work.[53] Christ Himself had spent forty days on Jebel Qarantal in preparation for his public life. Constantine had done nothing of the kind, but rather had been plunged into ceaseless political, military, and administrative activity from the moment of his great vision. Strange though it may sound to say it of a strong and mature emperor with wide experience of the world, in his new-found faith Constantine was naive. He expected long-time Christians, especially bishops and priests, always or at least usually to act like Christians. Those who had come through the age of persecution had to be strong personalities. Constantine was only now beginning to learn that the strong personality perverted, especially when already—or once—a Christian, is the worst enemy of the Church, more deadly than all the implements of torture wielded by Decius, Valerian, Galerius, Daia and their men.

In his naivete, in his well-justified concern with the scandal being given both to Christians and to unbelievers by this ugly quarrel, Constantine reopened the Donatist question, which should have been treated as settled once and for all by the Council of Rome. He called for an official investigation of Felix of Aptunga's alleged betrayal of the Church, and for a new and larger council to meet at Arles in Gaul to hear the Donatists.[54]

Were these acts of Constantine in any sense a defiance or supersession of Papal authority? Pope Miltiades died January 11, 314; we know nothing about how soon he became ill after the Council of Rome ended the preceding October, but he may well have been incapacitated or dying when Constantine made his decision. And Miltiades' successor in the chair of Peter, Sylvester I, elected January 31, 314, is one of the most shadowy and puzzling Popes in history. He had a very long pontificate—21 years, until 335—during which numerous exceedingly important events in the history of the Church took place. Faithful reports were regularly made to Pope Sylvester by councils and prelates; a significant number of them have survived. But we have almost nothing *from* this Pope. It seems that he did not leave the city of Rome during his entire pontificate, though most events of importance both religious and political were then occurring elsewhere. He appears to have performed his duties as head of the Church to little more than a minimal degree. So extraordinary was his passivity in times of such activity that some have supposed Pope Sylvester I to have been seriously and chronically ill during much of his pontificate. Whatever the explanation may be, the fact of this 21-year near-vacuum in the leadership of the Church at such a critical period does much to explain the extent of Constantine's involvement in Church affairs during that period, which comprised almost all the remainder of his reign as emperor. Finally it should be remembered that for much of this period Constantine was regularly advised by Bishop Ossius on all matters pertaining to Christianity; it is a reasonable presumption that many of his major decisions on such matters during these years were deeply influenced, if not entirely guided by Ossius' advice.[55]

As it turned out, the Donatists gained nothing from the reopening of their case. Constantine's official investigation quickly established the total falsity of their accusations against Felix of Aptunga; indeed, they were actually shown to have forged "evidence" against him. The Council of Arles, meeting in August 314 with 46 bishops from all over the empire in attendance (but not the Pope), confirmed in every respect the findings of the Council of Rome, and went even further by finally condemning and excommunicating all who persisted in the Donatist schism. The Donatists who appeared before the Council of Arles were described by the Council as obstinate and dangerous men. Re-baptism and re-ordination were again forbidden. Christians accused of collaborating with persecutors could be refused communion, as being publicly in mortal sin, only if the accusation of collaboration could be proved from official documents. All the canons drawn up by the Council of Arles were submitted to Pope Sylvester I with a very deferential letter from the Council. The irreconcilable Donatists appealed again to Constantine, whose response further defines his true perception of his relationship to the Church: "O insolent madness! They appeal from heaven to earth, from Jesus Christ to a man."[56]

There now arose one of the most fundamental issues deriving from the concept of Christendom itself: What is the proper role of the state when acting as the "secular arm" of the Church? When, and under whose direction, should it so act? The facile answer that the state should never act in matters involving churches simply will not bear close scrutiny. No state can, or ever has been able to remove itself entirely from questions of church jurisdiction. At the barest minimum, the state's judicial process must ultimately decide which organizations are legitimate churches, and who owns contested property claimed by one or more churches.

It was at precisely this minimum level of state involvement in church affairs that Constantine had to address the Donatist schism after the Council of Arles. Many Christian church buildings and property in Africa were now occupied by Donatists; in most cases they were also claimed by Catholics faithful to Caecilian and to Rome. The determination of the rightful owner might be delegated to the Church, but the enforcement of the ecclesiastical decision so as to secure the rightful owners in possession of their property could only be accomplished by the state. Constantine could not have withdrawn from the entire matter after the Council of Arles, since it was clear that the majority of the Donatists (a minority were reconciled as a result of its rulings) were going to defy that council as they had defied its predecessor in Rome. But he was trail-blazing in a whole new field—the relation of church and state in a Christian society—to which no one before, even among the greatest Christian thinkers, had given really serious thought. (Tertullian had stated that a Christian government of the empire was not ever likely to happen.)[57] He had the guidance of Ossius—who may at this point have been almost as bewildered by the Donatist problem as Constantine—but not of the Pope, with whom apparently he never had much personal contact.

It is therefore not surprising that during the next two years (315 and 316) Constantine hesitated, reconsidered, reviewed his decisions, and in the process gave way to occasional outbursts of irritation and overstatement which suggested that he saw himself as having a right and even a duty to exert much more authority within the Church than an unbaptized layman, even if emperor and a great benefactor, could properly claim. The important facts are not his occasional imprudent expressions but his final decisions, which were to uphold unequivocally, with his full temporal authority, the rulings of the Councils of Rome and of Arles regarding Caecilian and the Donatists (November 316) and to send imperial troops to enforce restitution to the Catholics of churches occupied by the Donatists in Carthage (March 317).[58]

The Donatists resisted furiously. Horrible scenes occurred as pitched battles were fought in and around three of the churches in Carthage which they held. At two of these the Donatist bishops were killed; at the third there was a general massacre of the defenders. Since this was a military operation enforcing public law, many pagans were involved, who tended to dislike all Christians, thus making it easier for the Donatists to depict their dead as martyrs. Since no attempt was made to regain control of Donatist-occupied churches in Numidia, the principal center of their strength, the effect of this action in Carthage was to deepen and extend the existing hostility without significantly reducing the Donatists' power in the church in Africa and over African church property. Constantine himself recognized this four years later. When even the revelation in 320 that a leading Donatist bishop, Silvanus of Cirta, had collaborated with persecutors, sold ordinations, and embezzled church funds—proved in open trial and followed by his conviction and exile—failed to weaken their cause, it was clear that the matter had gone beyond the possibility of rational resolution. Within a year Silvanus was not only back in Cirta, but had seized its basilica which Constantine had built for the Catholics. War with Licinius being imminent, Constantine could do nothing but suggest that another church be built in

Cirta for the Catholics, leaving the existing basilica to the Donatists. Thus the Donatists became firmly established in Africa—though nowhere else in the world—for more than a hundred years, teaching that theirs was the only true and faithful church. But there remained large numbers of loyal Catholics in Africa as well, and in the time of St. Augustine they finally prevailed.[59]

From all of this Constantine might have learned a fundamental principle of the history of the Church of Christ: that truth and loyalty in His Church only win their great battles *slowly*. Instant triumphs are almost always either illusory, or unimportant.

About the year 314 a man bearing the marks of years of privation came down out of the cold fierce mountains of Armenia to the city of Caesarea in Cappadocia where he had grown up, whence a veritable galaxy of saints was to emerge in this fourth Christian century. His father had been involved in the murder of the king of Armenia; but he had become a Christian, pledging his life to the service of Christ, hoping to expiate his father's crime through the conversion of Armenia. His name—very common in those parts—was Gregory. He had spent fifteen years in prison for the faith in Armenia, during the epoch of the great Roman persecution which had found its echo in this frontier region where Roman suzerainty had been established as a result of a successful campaign by the Caesar Galerius in 298 after an initial setback. There had been martyrs in Armenia, notably the virgin Rhipsime and her companions at the Armenian capital of Valarshapat, which consequently was to become, in Christian Armenia, the holy city of Etchmiadzin. But Gregory had survived—and he had just converted the king, Tiridates. Now he sought episcopal consecration from the bishop of Caesarea, head of the church where he had found the Faith, so as to become the head of the new Armenian church. His consecration was approved, and bestowed on the occasion of a synod held at Caesarea and attended by twenty of the bishops of Asia Minor.[60]

St. Gregory the Illuminator, the apostle of Armenia, is unfortunately too thickly shrouded in the mists of time and legend for us now to be able to give an historically accurate account of his great mission. The earliest account of it we have was written about 175 years after the event, and in view of the almost complete lack of literacy in Armenia in Gregory's time, it is unlikely to have been based on contemporary documents. Oral tradition there certainly was, and we can unhesitatingly affirm the historical existence of St. Gregory the Illuminator and the overall character and results of his missionary work. But most of the details given in our sources, abounding in marvels of all kinds, are too evidently fabulous to command belief; there are serious discrepancies among them; and the chronology is vague and confused, so that while the main tradition puts the conversion of King Tiridates shortly before that of Constantine, a recent review of the evidence strongly suggests a near equivalence in time between the two royal conversions.[61]

Working very closely together, King Tiridates and St. Gregory the Illuminator destroyed all the old pagan shrines in Armenia, beginning with those of the goddess Anahit and the god Tir, for whom the king had been named. Crosses were erected in their place. Very large numbers of people were baptized. The difficulties of transportation and communication in the mountainous country, and the fact that St. Gregory seems to have received little help from established Christian communities elsewhere, meant that a full understanding of Christian doctrine could not be disseminated immediately to all or most of these new converts. Nor was any priesthood available for the new Christian nation, except for its own old pagan priesthood. Consequently those pagan priests who would confess Christ were permitted by Gregory to act as Christian priests. All references to pagan gods were of course immediately eliminated from the liturgy, but some of the old pagan practices remained despite considerable incongruity with Christianity—notably animal sacrifices like those of the Jews in the Temple at Jerusalem, which continued for centuries and were actually performed as preliminary to (though never as a substitute for) the Mass, the Eucharist, and the handing down of priesthood by inheritance, in the manner of the Jewish priestly and levite families.[62]

It was a very risky procedure, never followed again to such an extent in the subsequent history of Christian missions; but Christian orthodoxy nevertheless put down ever-deepening roots in Armenian soil, triumphing there until the consolidation of the Monophysite heresy following the Council of Chalcedon. Within a single generation, as is often the way with recent converts whether individual men and women or whole nations, Armenian Christians were sending out missionaries of their own, deep into the Caucasus Mountains.[63]

In Rome, Constantine was undertaking a similar but vastly greater task: that of transforming a pagan structure of life and law nearly a thousand years old into a Christian structure which could become a framework for Christendom. Paganism, even in its religious form, was still much too strong to be abolished by law.[64] But Constantine could begin to introduce Christian laws for a people he hoped would become, in time, truly and fully Christian. Of the new laws evidently inspired by Christianity which he decreed from 315 to 321 we have, unfortunately, only the bare texts—no contemporary commentary on them, no explanation by Constantine or his advisors of how they were suggested or why they were adopted. But the magnitude of the change in the whole understanding of human government which they represent, is clear enough.

In ancient Roman legal tradition, only free citizens had rights. The master had power of life and death over his slaves. The head of the house had power of life and death over his wife and children. The landlord had virtual power of life and death over his tenants. The life of the convicted prisoner or captive in war was forfeit, even when he was allowed to keep it; his captors could do anything to him that they wished. While some modifications of these iron laws in the direction of greater human consideration had been made over the centuries, their spirit still brooded over the legal structure of the empire.

In view of how often the Church of Christ has been criticized or condemned as indifferent or even opposed to human rights, an ally of political absolutism, and of how often it is thoughtlessly assumed that the rule of the first Christian emperor began such a perversion of Christ's teachings, the legislation of Constantine on human rights deserves the strongest emphasis. During the years 315-321 he issued laws prohibiting the torture and killing of slaves by their masters; safeguarding tenants from unjust treatment by their landlords; safeguarding children from major physical abuse by their parents; and protecting convict prisoners from cruel treatment, including abolition of the practice of branding them on the face "which is formed in the image of heavenly beauty."[65]

The world now heard, from an Emperor of Rome, that man is made in the image of God, and that this, and only this, is the indestructible foundation of his just rights.

No more intractable problem faced the Christian social conscience than slavery in the ancient world. No genuine Christian could be comfortable with the existence of slavery, for he could not fail to know that every man is a child of God, redeemed by the Blood of Christ, given the ultimate in freedom—the choice of his own salvation or damnation—by God. To enslave him is a crime. No man can ever rightfully pretend to own another.

Yet the total instant abolition of slavery in the Roman world at the time of Constantine would have destroyed that world, for its whole economy—in the complete absence of machines—had become dependent on slave labor. The ancient Roman republic which had beaten Hannibal, though it had many slaves, could probably have survived without them. Half a millennium later, the evil had become so pervasive and so deeply rooted that this was no longer possible. The empire's years were numbered in any case—not least because of this vast multiplex curse of slavery—but no ruler could now abolish it, and survive. Nor did the Church advocate abolition, though from Paul's letter to Philemon down the years, she encouraged the freeing of slaves.[66] Ossius of Cordoba preached it to Constantine. In 321 Constantine, in a rare gesture, addressed a law for the whole empire under his rule to an individual—to Ossius, his Christian teacher. This law gave full legal validity (and, by implication, strong official encouragement) to the freeing of slaves *in Christian churches*, with the priest as witness:

> The Emperor Constantine Augustus to Bishop Hosius:
> Those who from the motives of religion should give deserved liberty to their slaves in the midst of the Church should be regarded as having given the same with the same legal force as that by which Roman citizenship has been customarily given with the traditional solemn rites. But this is permitted only to those who give liberty in the presence of the priest.[67]

It was one of the most important first steps in the building of Christendom. When that building was complete, centuries later, there would be hardly a slave left in Christian Europe.

Finally, in that same year 321, a law of Constantine formally designated Sunday as a day of rest for all, when no public or commercial business might be transacted.[68] The originally Jewish concept of observing every seventh day as a day of complete suspension of public and commercial business, widely followed even by non-Jews in the empire but never before made law, was now applied to the day of Christ's Resurrection, and has remained a fundamental element in Christendom ever since, even in our own largely apostate age. Attempts of the French and Communist revolutionary governments to abolish the observance of Sunday have been uniformly unsuccessful. For more than seventeen hundred years this cornerstone in the edifice of Christendom, laid by Constantine in 321, has stood firm.

To bring about the full establishment of the Christian Roman empire, there remained the disposal of Licinius. It is hard to feel much sympathy for this man, despite the ostentatious mourning for his fate characteristic of bitterly anti-Constantinian historians. He was the last surviving ruler of the age of the persecutions, the age of the dominion of the sword in the Roman empire. He neither gave nor represented anything to the world but the naked power of his office, originally granted to him by Galerius the persecutor. In 314 he had been discovered intriguing with Constantine's brother-in-law Bassianus, who had been appointed Caesar over Italy. In a brief war, Constantine had wrested from Licinius most of Eastern Europe (all but Thrace, roughly comprising modern Bulgaria, eastern Greece, and Turkey in Europe).[69] Evidently Licinius wished to regain this lost territory. But when he next struck, it was not at Constantine but at the Christians in his own eastern realm, who, because of Constantine's open championship of their faith, were suspected by Licinius of being Constantine's subversive agents.[70]

Licinius began in 319 or 320 by denying Christian bishops permission to meet in synod, as some in the east had met at Ancyra in 314 to deal with the difficult question of the lapsed wich had brought on the Donatist schism in Africa.[71] Then Christian soldiers and government officials were ordered to sacrifice to pagan gods or be dismissed from their posts. Christians were forbidden to visit prisoners, on pain of the visitors being thrown in jail with those they came to comfort. The assembling of men and women together at Christian public meetings and the private instruction of women by Christian clergymen were prohibited on the specious pretext that such meetings and instruction encouraged immorality. Finally, the bishops themselves were called upon to apostatize by offering sacrifice to idols, as in the dark days of the Diocletianic persecution. Bishop Basil of Apamea in Pontus, upon refusing to do so, was cut into small pieces by sword-strokes and the pieces were thrown into the sea to be devoured by fish.[72]

In the uplands of Asia Minor, near the frontier of now Christian Armenia at Sebaste near Melitene, about a hundred miles north of Christian Edessa, the Twelfth Legion was stationed. Its soldiers, like all Roman legionaries of that time, were closely and personally tied to the region of their service. The status of legionary had become hereditary; and though the fathers might be of old Roman ancestry, the mothers were from the immediate area. The strongly Christian character of their region meant that more of the legionaries of the Twelfth were Christian than was usual in Roman armies, where the Faith had generally progressed more slowly than among the civilian population. When Licinius' order for all soldiers to sacrifice to the pagan gods arrived in Sebaste, forty young Christians of the Twelfth Legion refused to obey. Thrown into prison, they prepared a "testament" which has been preserved, and bears the marks of authenticity. Eventually they were sentenced to die by being forced to stand in a frozen pool at night in mid-winter—in full view of a row of well-lighted hot baths.[73] This last of the great martyrdoms of this age bears the same mark of fiendish ingenuity, of Satanic laughter, as the first, when the human torches were lit in the gardens of Nero.

Through the agonizing hours the young men stood in the freezing water until they died, never moving to save themselves by denying Christ. At long last, one gave way; but as of old, one of the pagan guards thereupon proclaimed Christ and took his place. In the morning the icy corpses were gathered up; forty more had been crowned in Heaven.[74] It is against the backdrop of this act under the authority of one who had put his hand and seal to an edict of toleration for all Christians just seven years before, that the war of Constantine against Licinius—and Licinius' ultimate fate—ought to be judged.

Probably in the year 323,[75] after a campaign against Sarmatian barbarians invading across the Danube had brought him into Licinius' Thracian domains, Constantine led an army of 130,000 against a somewhat larger force under Licinius. Constantine marched under the *labarum*, with the battle-cry *Deus summus Salvator!* (God the Supreme Savior!) Licinius took his stand with the old gods, but was so terrified of the *labarum* that he ordered his soldiers not to attack it or even to look at it. Defeated before Hadrianople, Licinius was besieged in Byzantium, relying on a superior fleet in the Hellespont; but his fleet was badly handled and broken up by a storm, and he was forced to retreat into Asia.[76]

Crossing the Bosporus and marching toward Nicomedia in pursuit of Licinius, Constantine as leader of a mighty army and champion of Christianity was now retracing exactly the route he had travelled eighteen years before as a lone, hunted young man on a succession of stolen horses, riding for his life from the Emperor Galerius. It was on that very same road that he now fought and won the decisive battle against Licinius at Chrysopolis; and it was at Nicomedia that he received Licinius' surrender and, at the plea of Constantia, consented—for a time—to spare his life. Within a few months he had concluded—for reasons we do not know, but from Licinius' whole history may well guess—that the peace of the world required his execution.[77] To condemn his decision outright, or to call it non-Christian, is unreasonable. The Church has never condemned all capital punishment. In our own time we have seen the surviving leaders of Nazi Germany removed from the world by death at the hands of the leaders of government of the Christian West, with general approval, and Adolf Eichmann executed by the Jews of Israel for his crimes against their people. The infliction of death upon the martyrs of Sebaste was fully in the style of these men of our own day who were executed as enemies of mankind.

Along the road from the Bosporus to Nicomedia, before and after the Battle of Chrysopolis, Constantine must have found crowding into his mind the memories of that long-past night of his ride for life, along with the pageant of all that had happened to him since, illuminated throughout by the light from that cross in the sky. He knew Who had made him victorious; he knew very well that it was not his own prowess and worth. He had been God's instrument for the destruction of the enemies of the Faith and for the founding of Christendom. With simplicity and clarity he expressed this central experience and truth of his life in words which appear in the introduction to his final edict of protection and support for the Christians, following shortly after his victory over Licinius:

> God sought my service and judged that service fitted to achieve His purpose. Starting from Britain God had scattered the evil powers that mankind might be recalled to true religion instructed through my agency, and that the blessed faith might spread under His guiding hand. And from the West, believing that this gift had been entrusted to myself, I have come to the East which was in sorer need of my aid. At the same time I am absolutely persuaded that I owe my whole life, my every breath, and in a word my most secret thoughts to the supreme God.[78]

NOTES

[1] Constantine to the Council of Arles, August 314, quoted at the head of the chapter, as translated in Norman H. Baynes, *Constantine the Great and the Christian Church*, 2nd ed. (London, 1934), p. 13. The phrase translated "his servant" (servant of God) is *famulum suum*. For an excellent commentary on this immensely important letter, supporting the interpretation given in the text, see Hermann Dörries, *Constantine the Great* (New York, 1972), pp. 38-39; for a specific commentary on the significance of Constantine's use of the appellation "Servant," see *ibid.*, pp. 63-64.

[2] On this point see particularly A. H. M. Jones, *Constantine and the Conversion of Europe* (London, 1948), pp. 79-80, and Valerian Sesan, *Kirche und Staat in römisch-byzantinischen Reiche seit Konstantin dem Grossen* (Czernowitz, Austro-Hungarian Empire, 1911), pp. 123-126.

[3] Dörries, *Constantine*, pp. 61-67. It is very significant that A. Alföldi in *The Conversion of Constantine and Pagan Rome* (Oxford, 1948), after denigrating the accounts

of Constantine's visions by interpreting them in the light of the pagan religious atmosphere of the time, using the harshest language (*e.g.*, "abortions of excitable religious fancy . . . debased form of religion . . . spread of ideas of primitive religion and magic") (pp. 19-21), climaxed by "the Christianity of Constantine, then, was not wrapped in the glory of the true Christian spirit, but in the darkness of superstition" (p. 23), is forced to add in the very next sentence: "But to deny the sincerity and urgency of his religious convictions is to make a very grave mistake." (*ibid.*)

[4] See Chapter Seventeen, above, text and Note 24.

[5] For a comprehensive review of historical literature on Constantine, both favorable and unfavorable, in all modern Western languages up to 1931, see Baynes, *Constantine*, pp. 33-40; for subsequent bibliography and treatment, see Dörries, *Constantine* (favorable); Paul Keresztes, *Constantine, a Great Christian Monarch and Apostle* (Amsterdam, 1981), very favorable, with many conclusions closely in agreement with those of this history; and John Holland Smith, *Constantine the Great* (London, 1971), generally hostile.

[6] John 3:8.

[7] W. H. C. Frend, *Martyrdom and Persecution in the Early Church* (New York, 1967), pp. 385-386; Henri Quéffelec, *Saint Anthony of the Desert* (New York, 1954), pp. 145-162.

[8] Giuseppe Ricciotti, *The Age of Martyrs* (Milwaukee, 1959), pp. 78, 180-181.

[9] Smith, *Constantine*, p. 96; Lloyd B. Holsapple, *Constantine the Great* (New York, 1942), pp. 150-151; Timothy D. Barnes, *Constantine and Eusebius* (Cambridge MA, 1981), p. 42. A striking example of the character of Maxentius' tyranny in Rome (sometimes now judged by historians not to have been particularly harsh) is furnished by the suicide of the wife of Junius Flavianus, the prefect of Rome, when Maxentius summoned her to his presence to demand sexual favors. Flavianus consequently resigned his office in February 312, when Constantine was already on the march.

[10] Ricciotti, *Age of Martyrs*, pp. 89-90; J. P. Kirsch, "Miltiades, Saint, Pope," *The Catholic Encyclopedia* (1913).

[11] Holsapple, *Constantine*, pp. 152-154; Smith, *Constantine*, pp. 80-82.

[12] Ricciotti, *Age of Martyrs*, p. 157; Smith, *Constantine*, pp. 96-97.

[13] Ricciotti, *Age of Martyrs*, pp. 159-160.

[14] *Ibid.*, pp. 160-162; Do''rries, *Constantine*, pp. 11-12.

[15] Ricciotti, *Age of Martyrs*, p. 162; Baynes, *Constantine*, pp. 8-9.

[16] Eusebius, *De vita Constantini*, I, 28-32; Ricciotti, *Age of Martyrs*, p. 163; Jones, *Constantine*, pp. 95-97; Keresztes, *Constantine*, pp. 10-30; Henri Leclercq, "Labarum," *Dictionnaire d'Archéologie chrétienne et de Liturgie* (DACL), VIII (1), 940-943; Paul Allard, *La Persécution de Dioclétien*, 2nd ed. (Paris, 1900), II, 216-224. Eusebius describes in detail the *labarum* standard which he himself saw in its place of special honor. He makes it very clear that it was not the *labarum*, but a simple cross, which appeared in the sky; the *labarum* was first used later, atop the great cross-standard Constantine had made for his army. On the general reliability of the *De vita Constantini* as history, often controverted, see Baynes, *Constantine*, pp. 40-49; for a review of the very extensive literature on the *labarum* up to 1931, see *ibid.*, pp. 60-65. Though Eusebius does not specify where the great vision occurred, it can hardly have been anywhere else but in Gaul if we trust Eusebius' narrative at all (Leclercq, DACL, VIII [1], 943-947), and is clearly stated to have occurred there by Sozomen, *Ecclesiastical History*, I, 5 ("it was then no easy matter to dwell in Gaul, in Britain, or in the neighboring countries, in which it is universally admitted Constantine embraced the religion of the Christians, previous to his war with Maxentius, and prior to his return to Rome and Italy"—

since clearly the vision must have come either in Gaul or in Italy, and Sozomen's statement explicitly rules out Italy, only Gaul remains). The beginning of Allard's striking description of Constantine's conversion experience is as close as we are ever likely to get to the truth on where it happened: "It was on horseback, at the head of his troops, on some Gallic road or some steep pass of the Alps . . ." (*"C'est à cheval, à la tête de ses troupes, sur quelque route gauloise ou quelque col escarpé des Alpes"—La Persécution de Dioclétien*, II, 220). The fact that Eusebius does not mention the apparition of the cross in the sky in his *Ecclesiastical History*, of which much is made by critical historians attacking the historical authenticity of his vision, probably means only that at the time of its writing (about 325) Eusebius had not yet become sufficiently intimate with Constantine to have heard the story directly from his own lips (Leclercq, DACL, VIII [1], 947-948; Jones, *Constantine*, p. 96).

[17] Lactantius, *De mortibus persecutorum*, XLVIII, 5-6; Leclercq, "Labarum," DACL, VIII (1), 948-950. It must be remembered that Lactantius was a rhetorician, not a formal historian; *De mortibus persecutorum*—a very brief treatise—is his only work of history. The many scholars who have preferred his account of Constantine's dream to Eusebius' account of his vision, because it was written a little closer in time to the event, have often ignored this. Leclercq argues strongly that Lactantius' reference to the *labarum* being identified in the dream the night before the Battle of Saxa Rubra as a *caeleste signum* (celestial sign) refers at least by implication to the vision of the cross in the sky, which Lactantius does not mention; Baynes (*Constantine*, p. 63) rejects this, citing authors who say that *caeleste* in this context can simply mean "sublime" ("celestial" has the same double meaning, literal and figurative, in English), but the use of the word is still at least suggestive of a link with Eusebius' account in *De vita Constantini*, even if not conclusive.

[18] Holsapple, *Constantine*, p. 163; J. R. Palanque, *The Church in the Christian Roman Empire* (London, 1949), I, 22n; Leclercq, "Labarum," DACL, VIII (1), 949-950; Allard, *Persécution de Dioclétien*, II, 224-225.

[19] John E. Walsh, *The Bones of St. Peter* (Garden City NY, 1982), pp. 48, 91-93.

[20] This is the traditional view, most effectively defended in the twentieth century by Henri Leclercq, who sums up: "There are two clearly distinct episodes which ought not to be confused: Lactantius, speaking of the second, makes, by emphasizing the same terms, reference to the first." ("Labarum," DACL, VIII [1], 950—*"Il y a deux épisodes bien distincts, et que l'on ne doit pas confondre: Lactance, racontant le second, fait, par les termes mêmes qu'il emploie, allusion au premier."*)

[21] Ricciotti, *Age of Martyrs*, pp. 176-177.

[22] Victor De Clercq, *Ossius of Cordova* (Washington, 1954), pp. 149-158.

[23] Jones, *Constantine*, pp. 92-93.

[24] This point has been curiously taken by many historians as strong, even conclusive evidence against the historical reliability of Eusebius' account of the apparition of the cross in the sky to Constantine (*e.g.*, Palanque, *Christian Roman Empire*, I, 15; De Clercq, *Ossius*, p. 161; and especially Smith, *Constantine*, pp. 104-105, who calls it "the most damning . . . inconsistency" in Eusebius' story because Constantine had been at Nicomedia when the persecution of the Christians by Diocletian began there, and must have known that the first Christians arrested and tried there were accused, among other things, of exerting magical powers by means of the sign of the cross. Aside from the obvious hazard of assuming what a young man at the imperial court in 303, probably not then much interested in religious controversy—though later impressed, as were so many others, by the repeated examples of constancy unto death offered by the Christian martyrs— "must have known," the fact that the sign of the cross was falsely said to be a magical

device was hardly sufficient to teach Constantine or anyone else its place in Christian theology!) What Eusebius actually says is that Constantine "sent for those who were acquainted with the mysteries of His [Christ's] doctrines, and inquired who that God was, and what was intended by the sign of the cross he had seen" (Eusebius, *De vita Constantini*, I, 32). This does not say, and hardly implies, that Constantine had no idea what the cross meant; what he was asking for was systematic Christian instruction combined with an explanation by qualified Christian teachers of what his vision signified for his life and mission. This he soon obtained, it appears primarily from Ossius of Cordoba (De Clercq, *Ossius*, pp. 150-153). As Sesan points out (*Kirche und Staat ... seit Konstantin*, p. 97n), he may have known quite well what the cross signified to Christians, but not yet been sure—until he had discussed it with Christian priests—whether Christ would help one still formally a pagan, such as himself. For Constantine's rapid involvement in the internal affairs of the Christian Church, see Hubert Jedin and John Dolan, eds. *History of the Church*, Volume I: "From the Apostolic Community to Constantine" (New York, 1965), pp. 415-416 (this volume was originally published under the general title *Handbook of Church History*).

[25] See Note 19, above; Allard, *La Persécution de Dioclétien*, II, 226-229; and particularly Keresztes, *Constantine*, pp. 19-30, who upholds the view of the full authenticity of both visions stated in the text. Most scholars (*e.g.*, Alföldi, *Constantine*, pp. 17-18) either try to harmonize Eusebius' and Lactantius' accounts (a very difficult task, primarily for chronological reasons) or simply reject Eusebius outright (*e.g.*, Palanque, *Christian Roman Empire*, I, 21-22, whose flat assertion that "one must definitely set aside" Eusebius' account is a most regrettable example of unfounded scholarly dogmatism). Sesan takes the unique position of accepting both the vision of the cross in the sky and the dream of the *labarum* while attributing them both to the day before the Battle of Saxa Rubra/Milvian Bridge, one in the afternoon and the other in the evening (*Kirche und Staat ... seit Konstantin*, pp. 93-101). This would seem to compound the difficulties rather than resolving them.

[26] Even the great apparition of the dancing and falling sun at Fátima in Portugal in 1917 was seen only by a part—though apparently by the greater part—of the 70,000 people present (see Volume Six of this history).

[27] Ricciotti, *Age of Martyrs*, pp. 157-159; Smith, *Constantine*, pp. 107-109.

[28] Traditionally translated "Lord God of hosts," now ludicrously mistranslated "Lord God of power and might," this phrase in the Hebrew means precisely "Lord God of armies." The writer is indebted to his colleague William H. Marshner, Professor of Theology at Christendom College and a highly competent student of Hebrew, for this translation.

[29] Ricciotti, *Age of Martyrs*, pp. 170-174; Smith, *Constantine*, pp. 109-115.

[30] Ricciotti, *Age of Martyrs*, p. 175; Barnes, *Constantine and Eusebius*, pp. 45-46.

[31] Eusebius, *Ecclesiastical History*, IX, 9; Baynes, *Constantine*, pp. 62-64; Dörries, *Constantine*, pp. 41-42. Fragments of the statue still exist at the Conservatory Palace in Rome, as Dörries points out—a fact rarely mentioned by those who challenge its authenticity. Baynes declares that "this account of the statue given by Eusebius it is, in my judgment, difficult to question" and argues strongly that the statue bore an actual cross and not the *labarum* (*pace* Alföldi, *Constantine*, p. 17).

[32] See Baynes, *Constantine*, pp. 10, 66-68, on the much-discussed phrase in the inscription on the Arch of Constantine identifying the source and cause of his victory, *instinctu divinitatis*; see *ibid.*, pp. 95-103, for a brilliant presentation of the theory that the representations of Sol Invictus, the Unconquered Sun, which continued to appear on Constantine's official coinage down to 323, were capable of bearing a Christian as

well as a pagan interpretation in that age and were thus acceptable to both groups while offending neither. Baynes points out that "the personal pagan deities—Jupiter, Mars—disappeared" very soon from the imperial coinage in the West after Constantine's victory, while Sol Invictus remained for eleven years However, Christian symbols also appeared on coins and official medallions beginning soon after the victory (Alföldi, *Constantine*, p. 17; Dörries, *Constantine*, pp. 42-43). For his refusal to make sacrifice to Jupiter on the occasion of his victory, see Barnes, *Constantine and Eusebius*, p. 44. Sesan emphasizes the dual character of Constantine's conception of himself and of his public position after his victory before Rome, as a deeply believing Christian with the personal obligations this entailed, yet also the ruler of an empire still 90 per cent pagan with the public duties this entailed, including the maintenance for the time being of some official continuity with pagan public traditions (*Kirche und Staat ... seit Konstantin*, pp. 120-127). Nevertheless, it seems clear that Constantine refused to permit sacrifices to the pagan gods of Rome to be made on the occasion of his triumphal entry in 312 (Keresztes, *Constantine*, pp. 31-32).

[33] Alföldi, *Constantine*, p. 7; Ricciotti, *Age of Martyrs*, pp. 183-184.

[34] Eusebius, *Ecclesiastical History*, X, 5.

[35] *Ibid.*, X, 6.

[36] *Ibid.*, X, 5; Baynes, *Constantine*, pp. 11, 68-74; Palanque, *Christian Roman Empire*, I, 7-12; Keresztes, *Constantine*, pp. 40-53. The astonishing obfuscation of the overwhelming probabilities in this matter, arising from prejudice against Constantine, is well demonstrated by Keresztes. He also points out that Eusebius, *Ecclesiastical History* IX, 9, clearly suggests that the Edict of Milan was sent to Maximinus Daia as a final order to stop his persecutions.

[37] Ricciotti, *Age of Martyrs*, pp. 184-186.

[38] *Ibid.*, pp. 186-187; *The Cambridge Ancient History*, Volume XII (Cambridge, England, 1939), p. 692.

[39] Ricciotti, *Age of Martyrs*, pp. 236-239; John Chapman, "Donatists," *The Catholic Encyclopedia* (1913).

[40] Ricciotti, *Age of Martyrs*, pp. 230-233; De Clercq, *Ossius*, pp. 162-163.

[41] Palanque, *Christian Roman Empire*, I, 36-37.

[42] Ricciotti, *Age of Martyrs*, p. 245.

[43] W. H. C. Frend, *The Donatist Church* (Oxford, 1952), pp. 12-13.

[44] Baynes, *Constantine*, pp. 75-78.

[45] De Clercq, *Ossius*, pp. 163-167; Palanque, *Christian Roman Empire*, I, 38-39.

[46] *e.g.*, Ricciotti, *Age of Martyrs*, pp. 233-235, and Frend, *Donatist Church*, pp. 146-147 (from opposite points of view).

[47] Palanque, *Christian Roman Empire*, I, 39; Keresztes, *Constantine*, pp. 60-62.

[48] Ricciotti, *Age of Martyrs*, pp. 236-237; Charles J. Hefele, *A History of the Christian Councils* (Edinburgh, 1894), I, 179.

[49] Ricciotti, *Age of Martyrs*, p. 232.

[50] Palanque, *Christian Roman Empire*, I, 40.

[51] Ricciotti, *Age of Martyrs*, p. 237; Frend, *Donatist Church*, p. 150.

[52] Eusebius, *Ecclesiastical History*, X, 5.

[53] See Chapter Seventeen, Note 25, above.

[54] Palanque, *Christian Roman Empire*, I, 40-41.

[55] *Ibid.*, I, pp. 30-32; De Clercq, *Ossius*, pp. 175-183.

[56] Ricciotti, *Age of Martyrs*, pp. 238-240; Hefele, *Councils*, I, 180-197; Chapman, "Donatists," *Catholic Encyclopedia* (1913).

[57] Tertullian, *Apologeticus*, XXI, 24.

[58] Palanque, *Christian Roman Empire*, I, 45-47.

[59] Frend, *Donatist Church*, pp. 159-168; Chapman, "Donatists," *Catholic Encyclopedia* (1913).

[60] R. W. Thomson, ed., *Agathangelos' History of the Armenians* (Albany, NY, 1976), pp. x-xii, xlvii-lii, lxiv-lxvi; *Cambridge Ancient History*, XII, 336-337; Vahan M. Kurkjian, *A History of Armenia* (New York, 1958), pp. 117, 120-121; Barnes, *Constantine and Eusebius*, p. 65.

[61] Thomson, ed., *Agathangelos' History of the Armenians,* pp. xxviii-xxxvii; *Butler's Lives of the Saints*, edited, revised and supplemented by Herbert Thurston and Donald Attwater (Westminster, MD, 1956), III, 693-694; Adrian Fortescue, "Gregory the Illuminator," *The Catholic Encyclopedia* (1913). Kurkjian, *History of Armenia*, pp. 155-158, gives the traditional view of the conversion of Armenia before Rome. Thomson (*loc. cit.*) presents a well-crafted, scholarly argument for the thesis that the Roman restoration to the Armenian throne of the King Tiridates who became the convert of St. Gregory the Illuminator cannot have happened at the traditional date of 287 because neither Roman nor Persian records indicate any externally imposed political change in Armenia at that time. Thomson concludes that the royal murder in which Gregory's father was involved is what took place in that year, with another Tiridates, uncle of Gregory's convert, then taking the throne, displaced in turn in 298 by the victorious Romans in favor of Tiridates the convert-to-be. Gregory's fifteen years in prison would then cover almost exactly the span of the persecutions of Diocletian, Galerius, and Maximin Daia in the Roman empire, up to the probable date of the synod of Caesarea, known from independent sources, when he was consecrated bishop.

[62] Thomson, ed., *Agathangelos' History of the Armenians*, pp. lxvii-lxix; Kurkjian, *History of Armenia*, pp. 118-119; article "Armenian Church," *The Encyclopedia Britannica*, 11th edition (1910). The semi-legendary account of the mission of St. Gregory the Illuminator by Agathangelos speaks of four million baptisms in one week. While this is obviously fabulous, it probably reflects a strong oral tradition of the baptism of very large numbers in a comparatively short time during this period in Armenia.

[63] Leon Arpee, *History of Armenian Christianity* (New York, 1946), pp. 9-20. The full unity of the church in Armenia with the Roman Catholic Church up to the Council of Chalcedon is solidly established, not only by the fact that St. Gregory the Illuminator went publicly to the bishop of Roman Caesarea for consecration, but also by the following items of evidence presented by Arpee (who is a Protestant): (1) the very first historical reference to Armenian Christians, by Eusebius, tells of their receiving a letter of instruction and advice from Bishop Dionysius of Alexandria, about the middle of the third century; (2) a similar letter, rather pointedly admonishing the Armenians regarding some dubious liturgical practices and heretical ideas which had been reported in their land, was sent to them by Bishop Macarius of Jerusalem about 330, at the request of Vertanes, then head of the Armenian church; (3) by the time of St. Basil the Great in the late fourth century, Armenian bishops were still obtaining consecration from Catholic (or Arian) bishops in Asia Minor, while Nerses, the fourth head of the Armenian church in succession to St. Gregory the Illuminator, appealed to the bishops of *Italy* (obviously including the Pope) for aid against Arianism.

[64] See Note 31, above. Sesan, *Kirche und Staat ... seit Konstantin*, pp. 120-125, greatly overemphasizes the importance of this relatively brief period of official toleration of paganism alongside Christianity and of the maintenance of laws favoring the practice of pagan religion as well as of Christianity. While he exalts Constantine as an individual and his strong Christian faith, Sesan seems not to believe that it was Constantine's purpose from the beginning to build Christendom, and he says very little about Constan-

tine's Christian laws.

⁶⁵ De Clercq, *Ossius*, pp. 179-180.

⁶⁶ See the discussion of Christianity and slavery in the late Roman empire in Dörries, *Constantine*, pp. 92-103.

⁶⁷ De Clercq, *Ossius*, pp. 179-180.

⁶⁸ Dörries, *Constantine*, pp. 118-126.

⁶⁹ Smith, *Constantine*, pp. 129-132; Ricciotti, *Age of Martyrs*, p. 208.

⁷⁰ Smith, *Constantine*, pp. 162-165. Barnes, *Constantine and Eusebius*, pp. 66-67, suggests that Constantine was trying to remove his brother-in-law Bassianus (who was executed at this time for plotting Constantine's overthrow with Licinius) so as to secure the succession of his recently conceived, but yet unborn child by Fausta, and that Licinius was innocent of any tampering. It is a striking example of how far astray the prevailing extraordinary prejudice against Constantine (trenchantly criticized recently in Kerezstes, *Constantine*) can lead even a careful historian whose work is not otherwise marked by prejudice. If Constantine were going to murder his brother-in-law to remove a potential future rival to the succession of his son, elementary common sense would counsel (1) waiting until the child was born to see if it *was* a son (we know it was, but Constantine did not); (2) waiting to see if the child actually lived to be born and survived birth, which could never be counted on in those days of high infant mortality.

⁷¹ For the Synod of Ancyra and the text and an analysis of its 25 canons, see Hefele, *Councils*, I, 199-222.

⁷² Ricciotti, *Age of Martyrs*, pp. 209-210; Keresztes, *Constantine*, p. 103.

⁷³ Ricciotti, *Age of Martyrs*, pp. 211-212.

⁷⁴ *Ibid.*, pp. 212-213.

⁷⁵ The year of Constantine's triumph over Licinius is still not surely known. It is either 323 or 324. The text follows the carefully devised chronological reconstruction of Smith, *Constantine*, pp. 176-179, which places all the battles between Constantine and Licinius, and the surrender of Licinius to Constantine, in the summer (July to September) of 323. De Clercq, *Ossius*, pp. 186-191, argues for 324, but admits that this leaves hardly sufficient time for the development of the Arian heresy to the point where it required the calling of the ecumenical council at Nicaea in 325, rapid through we know that its development was (see Volume Two, Chapter One, of this history). Barnes, *Constantine and Eusebius*, pp. 76-77, and Keresztes, *Constantine*, p. 101, also opt for 324.

⁷⁶ Smith, *Constantine*, pp. 166, 170-174.

⁷⁷ *Ibid.*, pp. 174-180. Smith, whose account of these events is as comprehensive as the relatively meager sources permit, puts the worst possible construction on Constantine's motives and actions regarding Licinius and the best possible construction on the motives and actions of Licinius. We have no "hard" information whatever about Licinius' activities during the period, apparently several months in length, between his surrender and his execution.

⁷⁸Baynes, *Constantine*, p. 17. The authenticity of this edict of Constantine, quoted in Eusebius' much controverted Life of Constantine and doubted in the past, has been confirmed by the discovery of a papyrus containing a fragment of it (Jedin and Dolan, *History of the Church*, I, 408).

BIBLIOGRAPHY

A comprehensive bibliography of the history of Christianity and of Christendom would fill at least as many volumes as this history. Any reasonable use of space calls for simply listing the references cited in the notes, together with some other especially useful authorities, and brief annotations indicating the orientation, character, and value of the listed titles whch are particularly significant for the subject of this history.

Orientation is important. Christian history, even more than other kinds of history, is impossible to write without a point of view. The point of view shapes the historical questions which are asked; consequently, authors with a radically different viewpoint from that of a particular reader or researcher will often simply never ask the questions for which that reader or researcher is seeking answers. Therefore it is only fair to the reader and student to indicate, in a bibliography such as this, what the viewpoint of the listed author is, since his viewpoint will govern his whole approach to his subject matter.

To take the most obvious case, a life of Christ by a secular humanist will not only come to very different conclusions from a life of Christ by a believing, orthodox Christian, but often will not even take up points which especially concern the believer. A study of the Book of Exodus by a scholar who is convinced that Moses did not exist as an historical personage, or that virtually nothing can be known about him if he did, will proceed along almost totally different lines from a study of the same material by a scholar who believes not only that Moses existed historically, but also that he did most of what the Book of Exodus tells us that he did, and wrote at least a substantial part of that Book himself.

This is evident enough; but as soon as one begins to describe the orientation of a book so as to classify it along these lines, there is an immediate outcry against "labelling." Too hasty and superficial labelling is clearly a hindrance to sound thinking and thorough analysis. But to refuse to classify at all is simply to avoid fundamental issues. In many books on Christian or Old Testament

550

history, the view point of the author is as apparent to any intelligent reader as it was to the author himself (or, sometimes, more so). Why then should it be taboo to state it?

The terms of identification used—orthodox, Protestant, Roman Catholic, Eastern Orthodox, Jewish, Modernist, and secular humanist—are not really confusing to anyone, despite the often vehement rejection of their applicability to scholarly discourse. In essence they represent clear-cut, distinct and definable positions, though of course individual men and women will by no means always hold those positions with perfect consistency. Long essays could be written on the full definition of each term. Here we must make do with a sentence.

The *orthodox Christian* viewpoint affirms that Jesus of Nazareth, the Christ, is God Incarnate, fully God and fully man; that He was born of the Virgin Mary, lived and taught in first-century Palestine, performed miracles, died on a cross for the redemption of all men, physically and literally rose from the dead, and will return in glory to judge the world. The *Modernist* viewpoint, while maintaining the name of Christian, doubts or attempts to reinterpret most or all of the above affirmations; and since they are all made unequivocally in the New Testament, must and does hold that even when the New Testament writers are reporting what seem clearly to have been actual historical events, their reports are not always, or even in most cases, historically true. The same view is taken of the Old Testament. The *secular humanist* viewpoint rejects the whole body of Christian belief together with the Christian name identification, assuming either that God does not exist, or that if He does, He has no real significance and certainly no direct involvement in men's lives and history.

A *Roman Catholic* is a Christian who accepts the doctrinal infallibility and ecclesiastical authority of the Bishop of Rome as the head of the Church Christ founded; an *Eastern Orthodox* denies those two points of Roman Catholic belief but accepts all other major Catholic dogmas; a *Protestant* is any other Western Christian; a *Jew* is one who at least to some extent believes in Judaism, accepting the Old Testament as divinely inspired—it is not simply an ethnic designation.

This bibliography is primarily *historical*, containing works significant for the religious and political events and conditions relevant to a history of Christendom. Only a limited selection of social and cultural studies is included. Scholarly biographies are particularly featured, in keeping with the emphasis on human personality in this history. The line between histories of events and personalities presented in Scripture, and commentaries on the text of Scripture, is sometimes rather fine; but for the most part the commentaries have not been included. Exceptions are made only for points of Biblical criticism (such as the theory of the plurality of Isaiahs and the order in which the four Gospels were written) which are fundamental to the historical reconstruction of important phases in the history of the People of God.

Most of the works cited are in English; but some French, and a few German and Spanish works of particular importance for matters discussed in this volume, are included. French Catholic historical and Scriptural scholarship has always been outstanding.

Among its other purposes, this bibliography is intended as a short guide to orthodox Christian historical scholarship for the period covered by this volume. Many of the works listed are out of print, little known, and increasingly or already exceedingly difficult to obtain. It is hoped that as a result of their listing here, a few more of these books may be rescued from oblivion and restored to an honored place in public and private libraries where a Christian interest exists.

I. GENERAL REFERENCE AND ORIGINAL SOURCES

Scripture. The two best recent Bible translations for study and reference are *The New Oxford Annotated Bible*, ed. Herbert G. May and Bruce Metzger (New York, 1977), including the Roman Catholic as well as the Protestant books and several of the Apocrypha, and *The Jerusalem Bible*, ed. Alexander Jones (New York, 1966), including the Roman Catholic books. The Oxford Bible uses the Protestant Revised Standard Version of the Old Testament (1952) and a more recent translation of the Roman Catholic books and of the New Testament; the New Testament translation remains close to the Revised Standard Version of 1946. The Jerusalem Bible is a new English translation of a new French translation, both by Roman Catholics, in most cases very well done, but often with a considerable departure from the traditional English wording of familiar Scripture passages.

Commentaries on Scripture are legion, and deeply influenced by prevailing theological currents. The Protestant *Interpreter's Bible*, ed. George Buttrick et al, 12 vols. (New York, 1952-57) and the Roman Catholic *Jerome Biblical Commentary*, ed. Raymond E. Brown et al (Englewood Cliffs, NJ, 1968) lean heavily—though not always uniformly—toward Modernism. The older *Catholic Commentary on Holy Scripture*, ed. Bernard Orchard et al (London, 1952) still accepts some significant Modernist premises. No complete scholarly commentary on the whole Bible, based on the premise of the essential historical accuracy of the Word of God, has been produced in English in the twentieth century. Such a commentary is desperately needed.

Fathers of the Church. The *only* complete collection in English of the writings of the Ante-Nicene Fathers (before 325, the period covered in this volume) is the magnificent 10-volume set, *The Ante-Nicene Fathers*, ed. Alexander Roberts and James Donaldson, originally published in Scotland in the nineteenth century, reprinted in the 1950's by the leading orthodox Protestant publishing house in the United States: William B. Eerdmans Co., Grand Rapids, Mich. The footnotes and editing display a strong anti-Catholic bias, but the scholarship is outstanding. There is a Roman Catholic *Fathers of the Church* series, ed. Roy J. Deferrari, published in New York from 1946 to 1974, which reached 67 small volumes. It also is edited with the highest scholarly standards, but is incomplete; many vitally important early patristic works (notably Irenaeus' *Against Heresies*) have not yet appeared in this series, and since no volumes have been published since 1974, may never appear. There is also the *Ancient Christian Writers* series in 40 volumes, ed. Johannes Quasten et al (Westminster, MD, 1946-1975), which fills some, but by no means all of the gaps in the *Fathers of the Church* series; it is also Roman Catholic. In addition to Irenaeus' *Against Heresies*, patristic works of particular importance for this volume include the following writings of the "Apostolic Fathers": the letter of Pope Clement I, the letters of St. Ignatius of Antioch, and *The Shepherd of Hermas*; Tertullian's *De paenitentia, De pudicitia, Ad nationes, Apologeticus*, and *Adversus Valentinianum*; the *Philosophumena* of Hippolytus; Origen's *Contra Celsum*; and the letters of Cyprian.

Church History; Lives of the Saints and Martyrs. No history of the early Christian church could ever have been written without Eusebius' fourth-century *Ecclesiastical History* as a foundation. There are many editions of Eusebius' history; that in *The Fathers of the Church* series, with excellent annotation by Roy Deferrari, is used here. Jerome's commentary on Eusebius' *Chronicle*, and Jerome's *De Viris Illustribus*, are important supplements to Eusebius' *Ecclesiastical History*; the former, strangely, has never been translated into English and apparently not into any other modern Western language; it must therefore be consulted in the original Latin in the *Patriologia Latina*. *De Viris Illustribus* is in the later Protestant patristic series, *The Writings of the Nicene and Post-Nicene Fathers*, ed. Philip Schaff and Henry Wace (also published by Eerdmans in Grand Rapids), Volume III, pp. 359-384. Eusebius' famous and controversial *Life of Constantine*, a very important work which may be regarded as in some sense a sequel to the *Ecclesiastical History*, is in the Nicene Fathers series, ed. Schaff and Wace, Volume I, pp. 471-559, while Lactantius' *De mortibus persecutorum*, describing the last phase and the ending of the great Diocletianic persecution, is in *The Ante-Nicene Fathers*, ed. Roberts and Donaldson, Volume VII, pp. 77-81. Prudentius' poem *Peri Stephanon* (there is a volume on Prudentius in *The Fathers of the Church* series) gives further details about the martyrs of that persecution.

For the lives of the saints and martyrs, much the best source in English is *Butler's Lives of the Saints*, as edited and, indeed, almost completely rewritten by Herbert Thurston and Donald Attwater, 4 vols. (Westminster, MD, 1956). Though the entries on the early saints are sometimes very superficial (notably those on the Apostles) and sometimes excessively and destructively critical, the authors include an extraordinarily large number of saints and give sufficient information and above all such outstanding bibliographies on each, that any historical investigation of a saint by an English-speaking scholar should begin here. Most of the principal early authentic Passions of the martyrs are collected, with extensive annotation, in E. C. E. Owen, *Some Authentic Acts of the Early Martyrs* (London, 1927), and without annotation by Donald Attwater in *Martyrs* (New York, 1957). Aside from the accounts of martyrdoms taken from Eusebius, these Passions include those of the following martyrs: Agape, Chione, and Irene; Carpus; Cassian; Cyprian; Fructuosus; James and Marian; Justus; Lawrence; Marcellus; Perpetua and Felicity; Philip and Hermes; Pionius; Polycarp; Procopius; the Scillitan martyrs.

For many saints, and for specific points of early Church history, even the advanced student may profitably consult articles in the old *Catholic Encyclopedia* (1906-1912)—generally much more useful, because of the longer and more scholarly articles, than *The New Catholic Encyclopedia* (1965), except for bibliography, on which the new encyclopedia does exceedingly well. Especially to be recommended, for the student with a command of French, is the magnificent *Dictionnaire d'Archéologie chrétienne et de liturgie*, in 15 double volumes, ed. Fernand Cabrol and Henri Leclercq (Paris, 1924-1953). A substantial portion of this enormous work was written by Leclercq himself, a man whose scholarship can only be described as awesome.

Jewish History. For a modern synthesis, consult *The World History of the Jewish People*, ed. Abraham Schalt (multi-volume, in progress since 1964, published by Rutgers University). The indispensable original source, after the Old Testament (including the Roman Catholic books, notably 1 and 2 Maccabees) is Josephus. His *Antiquities of the Jews* is, astonishingly, still available in English only in the antiquated and ponderous eighteenth-century Whiston translation. Josephus' *The Jewish War* has recently been translated and very well commented upon, with the inclusion of the famous and controversial Old Slavonic additions pertaining to Christ, by G. A. Williamson (London,

1970).

Ancient World History. The history of the Middle East and of the Graeco-Roman classical world in ancient times (the span of this volume) are most thoroughly presented in English in *The Cambridge Ancient History*, the best and most recent of the collectively written Cambridge histories. Its first two volumes were completely rewritten, doubled in size, and issued as four volumes in a third edition in the 1970's, covering the first two millennia of recorded history (3000-1000 B.C.) and reflecting the vast increase in our knowledge of this very early history during the past fifty years. The remaining ten volumes, published in the 1920's and 1930's and covering the years from 1000 B.C. to 313 A.D., are close to definitive; they are the best starting point for serious study of the political history of the Middle East and the West during these centuries, though they are of comparatively little value—except occasionally for chronology—for sacred history at any stage. The volumes after 1000 B.C. are as follows:

III	*The Assyrian Empire* (1000-600 B.C.)
IV	*The Persian Empire and the West* (600-478 B.C.)
V	*Athens* (478-401 B.C.)
VI	*Macedon* (401-301 B.C.)
VII	*The Hellenistic Monarchies and the Rise of Rome* 301-218 B.C.)
VIII	*Rome and the Mediterranean* (218-133 B.C.)
IX	*The Roman Republic* (133-44 B.C.)
X	*The Augustan Empire* (44 B.C.-70 A.D.)
XI	*The Imperial Peace* (70-192 A.D.)
XII	*The Imperial Crisis and Recovery* (192-313 A.D.)

II. THE HISTORY OF ISRAEL

Abrahams, Israel. *Campaigns in Palestine from Alexander the Great* (London, 1927). Focusses on the wars of the Maccabees; Jewish viewpoint.

Ackroyd, P. A. "Samaria," *Archaeology and Old Testament Study*, ed. D. Winton Thomas (see).

Aharoni, Yohanan. "The Israelite Sanctuary at Arad," *New Directions in Biblical Archaeology*, ed. David Freedman and Noel Greenfield (see).

_____. *The Land of the Bible, a Historical Geography* (Philadelphia, 1967).

Albright, William F. *From the Stone Age to Christianity*, 2nd ed. (New York, 1957). Seminal work by a great, generally orthodox Christian scholar who revolutionized Biblical archeology, proving that modern archeology generally supports the historical accuracy of the Old Testament.

_____. *Recent Discoveries in Bible Lands* (New York, 1955).

Allis, Oswald T. *The Unity of Isaiah* (Philadelphia, 1950). Orthodox Protestant study, one of the many often overlooked but well presented arguments against the theory of a plurality of authors of Isaiah.

Beegle, Dewey M. *Moses, the Servant of Yahweh* (Grand Rapids MI, 1972). Full, orthodox Protestant life of Moses.

Belloc, Hilaire. *The Battleground: Syria and Palestine* (Philadelphia, 1936).

Bickerman, Elias. *From Ezra to the Last of the Maccabees* (New York, 1949). Necessarily brief survey by an outstanding Jewish authority of the least known period in Israel's history since the Exodus.

Birmingham, George A. *God's Iron* (London, 1956). Rather speculative and popularized, but well-knit life of the prophet Jeremiah.

Bodenheimer, F. S. "The Manna of Sinai," *The Biblical Archaeologist Reader*, ed.

G. Ernest Wright and David N. Freedman (see).

Boling, Robert G. *The Anchor Bible: Joshua* (Garden City NY, 1982).

Bright, John. *Early Israel in Recent History Writing* (London, 1956). Hard-hitting critique by a major recognized authority on the history of Israel, of the excesses of Modernist Old Testament criticism as applied to the early history of Israel.

_____. *A History of Israel*, 3rd ed. (Philadelphia, 1981). Clearly written, comprehensive survey by a generally orthodox Protestant.

Burrows, Millar. *The Dead Sea Scrolls* (New York, 1955).

_____. *More Light on the Dead Sea Scrolls* (New York, 1958). A much-needed corrective to sensational and misleading reports about these famous scrolls and their contents.

Cassuto, Umberto. *The Documentary Hypothesis and the Composition of the Pentateuch* (Jerusalem, 1961). Strong critique of reigning theories in Old Testament criticism, of which the "documentary hypothesis" remains the most widely accepted despite the extent to which it runs counter to what the Scriptural texts tell us about themselves.

Congar, Yves. *The Mystery of the Temple* (Westminster MD, 1962). Reflective and profound; orthodox Roman Catholic viewpoint.

Cross, Frank M. Jr. *The Ancient Library of Qumran and Modern Biblical Studies*, 2nd ed. (Garden City NY, 1961). Perhaps the best synthesis of our knowledge of the Dead Sea scrolls and what they revealed.

_____. "The Priestly Tabernacle," *The Biblical Archaeologist Reader*, ed. G. Ernest Wright and David N. Freedman (see).

Dahood, Mitchell. *The Anchor Bible: Psalms*, 3 vols. (Garden City NY, 1966-1970). New translation, with extensive notes including comparisons with Ugaritic texts, often sharply divergent from the traditional wording; excellent background analysis; generally orthodox Roman Catholic.

Danielou, Jean (Cardinal). *The Dead Sea Scrolls and Primitive Christianity* (Baltimore, 1958).

Daniel-Rops, Henri. *Israel and the Ancient World* (New York, 1964). The first volume in his universal sacred history from the orthodox Roman Catholic viewpoint; not up to the level of his later volumes and now quite outdated, having originally been written in the 1930's and not subsequently revised significantly.

Dothan, Moshe. "Ashdod of the Philistines," *New Directions in Biblical Archaeology*, ed. David N. Freedman and Jonas C. Greenfield (see).

Dubnov, Simon. *The History of the Jews from the Beginning to Early Christianity* (New York, 1967). Jewish viewpoint.

Ellison, H. L. *Ezekiel: the Man and His Message* (Grand Rapids MI, 1956). Orthodox Protestant viewpoint.

Fairweather, W., and J. S. Black. *The First Book of Maccabees* (Cambridge, England, 1899). Commentary.

Finegan, Jack. *Let My People Go* (New York, 1963). Well-written, semi-popular view of the Exodus as history; contains excellent historical insights.

Freedman, David N. and Jonas C. Greenfield, eds. *New Directions in Biblical Archaeology* (New York, 1969). See separate entries for especially significant articles.

Freyne, Sean. *Galilee from Alexander the Great to Hadrian* (Wilmington DE, 1980). Outstanding, comprehensive and well-balanced recent treatment of the history of Galilee during the period which includes the life of Christ. Jewish viewpoint, but firmly rejects the theory that Jesus was a political revolutionary.

Gaubert, H. *Abraham, Loved by God* (New York, 1968).

Glueck, Nelson. *Rivers in the Desert, a History of the Negev* (New York, 1959).

Focusses on Abraham's time, reporting archeological researches in the region in which Abraham wandered, tending to confirm his historicity. Jewish viewpoint.

Goldman, Solomon. *The Ten Commandments* (Chicago, 1965). Jewish viewpoint.

Gonzalez, Angel. *Abraham, Father of Believers* (New York, 1967).

Gottwald, Norman K. *All the Kingdoms of the Earth* (New York, 1964). Study of Isaiah's political views and policies; Modernist viewpoint.

Gray, John. *The Legacy of Canaan: the Ras Shamra Texts and Their Relevance to the Old Testament* (Leiden, 1965). Important, highly technical linguistic study.

Gross, W. J. *Herod the Great* (Baltimore, 1962).

Harland, J. Penrose. "Sodom and Gomorrah," *The Biblical Archaeologist Reader*, ed. G. Ernest Wright and David N. Freedman (see).

Harrison, R. K. *Introduction to the Old Testament* (London, 1970).

Hartman, Louis F. and Alexander A. Di Lella. *The Anchor Bible: Daniel* (Garden City NY, 1978).

Heinisch, Paul. *Christ in Prophecy* (Collegeville MN, 1956). The only really scholarly examination from orthodox Christian premises of the Old Testament prophecies of Christ to be published in English in relatively recent years; Roman Catholic.

_____. *History of the Old Testament* (Collegeville MN, 1952). Fully orthodox Roman Catholic review of the history of Israel.

Heschel, Abraham J. *The Prophets* (New York, 1962). Thoughtful, sensitive survey; Jewish viewpoint.

Hollis, Christopher and Ronald Brownrigg. *Holy Places* (New York, 1969). A survey of the holy places of the Old Testament in Palestine and the evidence pertaining to their historical authenticity.

Holt, John M. *The Patriarchs of Israel* (Nashville TN, 1964). Modernist viewpoint.

Hort, Greta. "The Plagues of Egypt," *Zeitschrift für die alttestamentliche Wissenschaft*, LXIX (1957), 84-103 and LXX (1958), 48-59.

Jones, A. H. M. *The Herods of Judaea* (Oxford, 1938).

Kaufman, Yehezkel. *The Religion of Israel, from its Beginnings to the Babylonian Exile* (Chicago, 1960). Jewish viewpoint; accepts some Modernist premises, but also offers needed correctives to some Modernist Old Testament criticism, especially with regard to the Book of Joshua.

Kenyon, Kathleen M. *Archaeology in the Holy Land*, 3rd ed. (New York, 1969). The best available survey.

_____. *Jerusalem; Excavating 3000 Years of History* (London, 1967).

_____. *Royal Cities of the Old Testament* (New York, 1971).

Kissane, Edward J. *The Book of Isaiah*, 2 vols. (Dublin, 1943). Orthodox Roman Catholic commentary.

_____. *The Book of Psalms*, 2 vols. (Westminster MD, 1953).

Kitchen, Kenneth A. *Ancient Orient and Old Testament* (Chicago, 1966). It is difficult to exaggerate the importance of this little book, which applies the standards and methods of current scholarship on the ancient Middle East to the history of Israel and Old Testament criticism, revealing major shortcomings in the latter. Orthodox conclusions, but the author does not state his own viewpoint.

_____. *The Bible and Its World* (Downers Grove IL, 1977). An update of *Ancient Orient and Old Testament*.

Kline, M. G. *Treaty of the Great King* (Grand Rapids MI, 1963). Revealing analysis of portions of the Book of Deuteronomy; orthodox Protestant viewpoint.

McCarthy, Dennis J. *Treaty and Covenant, a Study in Form in the Ancient Oriental Documents and in the Old Testament*, Analecta Biblica 21 (Rome, 1963).

McCullough, W. Stewart. *The History and Literature of the Palestinian Jews from Cyrus to Herod* (Toronto, 1975).

McKenzie, John L. *The Anchor Bible: Second Isaiah* (Garden City NY, 1968). Modernist viewpoint.

MacVeagh, Rogers and Thomas B. Costain. *Joshua* (New York, 1948). Striking reconstruction of Joshua's life and conquests, presented in vivid narrative; orthodox Protestant viewpoint.

Maly, Eugene H. *The World of David and Solomon* (Englewood Cliffs NJ, 1966).

Manley, G. T. *The Book of the Law; Studies in the Date of Deuteronomy* (Grand Rapids MI, 1957). Scholarly, orthodox Protestant commentary.

Margalioth, Rachel. *The Indivisible Isaiah* (New York, 1946). Penetrating study by a Jewish scholar who rejects the theory of the plurality of Isaiahs.

Mauchline, John. *Isaiah 1-39, Introduction and Commentary* (New York, 1962). Modernist viewpoint.

Mendenhall, George E. "The Census Lists of Numbers 1 and 26," *Journal of Biblical Literature* LXXVII (1958), 52-66.

_____. "Law and Covenant in Israel and the Ancient Near East," *The Biblical Archaeologist* XVII (1954), Numbers 2, pp. 26-46, and 3, pp. 49-76.

Myers, Jacob M. *The Anchor Bible: Ezra, Nehemiah* (Garden City NY, 1965).

Newman, Murray L. Jr. *The People of the Covenant* (Nashville TN, 1962). Modernist viewpoint.

Noth, Martin. *The History of Israel*, 2nd ed. (London, 1960). Modernist viewpoint; at odds with Bright's parallel history of Israel on a series of major points.

Parrot, André. *Abraham and His Time* (Philadelphia, 1968).

Pearlman, Moshe. *The Maccabees* (New York, 1963). A particularly good popularization; useful for the scholar in integrating data.

Perowne, Stewart. *The Life and Times of Herod the Great* (New York, 1957). Somewhat sympathetic to Herod.

Pfeiffer, Charles F. *The Dead Sea Scrolls and the Bible* (New York, 1969).

Purvis, James D. *The Samaritan Pentateuch and the Origin of the Samaritan Sect* (Cambridge MA, 1968).

Ricciotti, Giuseppe. *The History of Israel*, 2 vols. (Milwaukee, 1955). Probably the best history of Israel, by a great orthodox Roman Catholic scholar, brought down to the last Jewish uprising against Rome under Bar-Kokhba in 135 A.D.; unfortunately now out of print and difficult to obtain.

Rowley, H. H. "Elijah on Mount Carmel," *Bulletin of the John Rylands Library* XLIII (1960), 190-219. Vindication of the historicity and supernatural character of the Carmel miracle by a leading Old Testament scholar.

_____. *From Joseph to Joshua; Biblical Traditions in the Light of Archaeology* (London, 1950). Generally upholds the historicity of Moses and Joseph, but drastically reinterprets the narrative in Genesis and Exodus.

Schedl, Claus. *History of the Old Testament*, 5 vols. (New York, 1972). Though the volumes are small, this is a comprehensive history, almost as good as Ricciotti's, by a fine Austrian scholar who is a fully orthodox Roman Catholic.

Schürer, Emil. *A History of the Jewish People in the Time of Jesus Christ*, 2 vols. (New York, 1891). Classic work on rabbinic Judaism in the period from the Maccabees to the destruction of the Temple, by a great German Protestant scholar; still a very valuable source despite its age.

Skehan, Patrick W. "The Scrolls and the Old Testament Text," *New Directions in Biblical Archaeology*, ed. David N. Freedman and Jonas C. Greenfield (see).

Speiser, E. A. *The Anchor Bible: Genesis* (New York, 1964). Some Modernist premises, but these are not always dominant; a work of profound scholarship by a great Jewish exegete.

Tcherikover, Victor. *Hellenistic Civilization and the Jews* (Philadelphia, 1959). Jewish viewpoint.

Thomas, D. Winton, ed. *Archaeology and Old Testament Study* (Oxford, 1967). See separate entries for especially significant articles.

Thompson, John A. *The Bible and Archaeology* (Grand Rapids MI, 1962).

Van der Ploeg, J. *The Excavations at Qumran, a Survey of the Judean Brotherhood and its Ideas* (London, 1958).

Van Seters, John. *Abraham in History and Tradition* (New Haven CT, 1975). Written to refute the historicity of Abraham as defended by Albright, Bright, Kitchen, and others; secular humanist viewpoint.

Vaux, Roland de. *Ancient Israel, its Life and Institutions* (London, 1961). Profound cultural study by an orthodox Roman Catholic.

_____. *The Early History of Israel* (Philadelphia, 1978). Comprehensive and very learned.

Vawter, Bruce. *The Conscience of Israel* (New York, 1961). Survey of the prophets by a Roman Catholic, who was orthodox at the time of its writing.

_____. *A Path Through Genesis* (New York, 1956).

Whitley, C. F. *The Prophetic Achievement* (London, 1963).

Wright, G. Ernest. *Biblical Archaeology*, rev. ed. (Philadelphia, 1962). Probably the best survey of the subject for the intelligent general reader; orthodox Protestant viewpoint.

_____ and David N. Freedman, eds. *The Biblical Archaeologist Reader* (Chicago, 1961). See separate entries for especially significant articles.

Yadin, Yigael. *Hazor, the Rediscovery of a Great Citadel of the Bible* (London, 1975). Full archeological description of probably the most important excavation of a major Palestinian city destroyed at the time of the Israelite conquest; Jewish viewpoint.

Yamauchi, Edwin M. *The Stones and the Scriptures* (Philadelphia, 1972). Summary review and comparison of Biblical archeology and history; orthodox Christian viewpoint.

Young, Edward J. *The Book of Isaiah*, 3 vols. (Grand Rapids MI, 1965-1972). Monumental study by a strongly orthodox Protestant who holds there was only one Isaiah; includes a complete translation. Indispensable for the orthodox student of Isaiah.

_____. *An Introduction to the Old Testament*, 2nd ed. (Grand Rapids MI, 1960).

_____. *My Servants the Prophets* (Grand Rapids MI, 1952). Good introduction to the Prophets from the orthodox Protestant viewpoint.

_____. *The Prophecy of Daniel* (Grand Rapids MI, 1949). The only relatively recent, fully scholarly study and commentary which accepts Daniel as having lived in the time of the Babylonian empire, when his book says that he lived, rather than in the time of the Maccabees; by no means uncritical, steers a careful course among the many diverse interpretations of the prophecies of Daniel.

Zeitlin, Solomon. *The Rise and Fall of the Judaean State* (Philadelphia, 1962). History of the Maccabees, from a strongly Jewish viewpoint.

_____. *The Second Book of Maccabees, with Introduction and Commentary* (New York, 1954).

III. THE ANCIENT MIDDLE EAST AND THE ANCIENT ORIENT

Albright, William F. *From the Stone Age to Christianity*, 2nd ed. (New York, 1957).

Unique blend of Israelite and Middle Eastern history by a great Christian scholar.

Aldred, Cyril. *Akhenaten, Pharaoh of Egypt* (London, 1968). Original and thorough; critical of Akhenaten.

Anati, Emmanuel. *Palestine before the Hebrews* (New York, 1963). Archeology of early Canaan.

Basham, A. L. *The Wonder that Was India* (London, 1954). Probably the best general survey of early Indian history and culture up to the coming of the Muslims.

Belloc, Hilaire. *The Battleground: Syria and Palestine* (Philadelphia, 1936).

Bermant, Chaim and Michael Weitzman. *Ebla, a Revelation in Archaeology* (New York, 1979). First book-length published survey of the remarkable discoveries in the recent excavation of a third millennium B.C. city in Syria with some apparent links to the early Israelites.

Bille-De Mot, Eleonore. *The Age of Akhenaten* (New York, 1966).

Burn, A. R. *Persia and the Greeks; the Defence of the West* (New York, 1962). Includes an extended introduction on Persian and Assyrian history as preliminary to its outstanding narrative of the Persian Wars of Greece.

Chiera, Edward. *They Wrote on Clay* (Chicago, 1938). Thoughts on ancient Mesopotamian history, culture and mentality by an archeologist who spent much of his professional lifetime working there.

Clark, Grahame and Stuart Piggott. *Prehistoric Societies* (New York, 1965).

Conze, Edward. *Buddhism, its Essence and Development* (New York, 1959).

Cook, J. M. *The Persian Empire* (New York, 1983). This excellent presentation of the current state of knowledge on the Achaemenian Persian empire was reviewed just before going to press, and found to support or not to contradict the material on Persian history presented herein.

Creel, H. G. *The Birth of China* (New York, 1937).

————. *Confucius and the Chinese Way* (New York, 1960).

Frye, Richard N. *The Heritage of Persia* (Cleveland, 1963). Good survey of Persian history and culture up to the Muslim conquest, by a major authority.

Gardiner, Alan. *Egypt of the Pharaohs* (Oxford, 1961). The most thorough recent overall survey of our knowledge of ancient Egyptian history.

Gurney, O. R. *The Hittites*, 3rd ed. (London, 1961).

Heidel, Alexander. *The Gilgamesh Epic and Old Testament Parallels* (Chicago, 1946). Includes a very careful, annotated translation of the epic of Gilgamesh.

Hinz, Walther. *The Lost World of Elam* (New York, 1972).

Hirth, Friedrich. *The Ancient History of China* (Freeport, N. Y., 1969; originally published 1908).

Jacobsen, Thorkild. *The Treasures of Darkness; a History of Mesopotamian Religion* (New Haven CT, 1977). The best study of the subject available, but often very speculative; takes a patronizing attitude toward the epic of Gilgamesh.

Kenyon, Kathleen M. *Amorites and Canaanites* (London, 1960).

Kitchen, Kenneth A. *The Third Intermediate Period in Egypt* (Warminster, England, 1973). The most thorough scholarly coverage of the obscure but important period 1100-650 B.C. in Egyptian history, contemporaneous with almost the entire history of the independent Israelite monarchy.

Kosambi, D. D. *The Culture and Civilisation of Ancient India in Historical Outline* (London, 1965).

Kramer, Samuel N. *The Sumerians; Their History, Culture and Character* (Chicago, 1963). The best survey of Sumerian history and culture during the third millennium B.C.

Kwang-chih Chang. *Shang Civilization* (New Haven CT, 1980).

Laessöe, Jörgen. *People of Ancient Assyria* (New York, 1965).

Li, Dun J. *The Ageless Chinese* (New York, 1965).

Macqueen, James. *Babylon* (London, 1964).

Mellaart, James. *Catal Hüyük, a Neolithic Town in Anatolia* (New York, 1963).

Merton, Thomas. *The Way of Chuang Tzu* (New York, 1965).

Montet, Pierre. *Everyday Life in Ancient Egypt in the Days of Ramesses the Great* (New York, 1958).

Moscati, Sabatino. *The World of the Phoenicians* (London, 1968).

Murray, Margaret. *The Splendour That Was Egypt* (New York, 1963).

Narain, A. K. *From Alexander to Kanishka* (Varanasi, India, 1967). The outlines and chronological difficulties of early Indian history.

Olmstead, A. T. *History of Assyria* (Chicago, 1923). Now somewhat outdated, but still the most comprehensive work in its field.

_____. *A History of Palestine and Syria* (New York, 1931). Thorough, but increasingly outdated; principally valuable for Syria, since its coverage of the history of Israel is duplicated by more recent histories specifically on that subject. Modernist viewpoint.

_____. *History of the Persian Empire* (Chicago, 1948). The most comprehensive general treatment of the history of Persia during the Achaemenid period.

Oppenheim, A. Leo. *Ancient Mesopotamia, Portrait of a Dead Civilization* (Chicago, 1964). Scholarly and profound.

Piggott, Stuart. *Prehistoric India to 1000 B.C.* (London, 1950).

Roux, Georges. *Ancient Iraq* (New York, 1964).

Saggs, H. W. F. *The Greatness That Was Babylon; a Sketch of the Ancient Civilization of the Tigris-Euphrates Valley* (New York, 1962).

Schmidt, John D. *Ramses II, a Chronological Structure for His Reign* (Baltimore, 1973).

Sharma, Ram Sharam. *Sūdras in Ancient India; a Survey of the Position of the Lower Orders down to c. A.D. 500* (Delhi, 1958).

Tuker, Francis. *The Yellow Scarf* (London, 1961). History of the Thug stranglers, a cult of the early Hindu goddess of destruction, Kali.

Van Seters, John. *The Hyksos, a New Investigation* (New Haven CT, 1966).

Wellard, James. *Babylon* (New York, 1972).

Wheeler, Mortimer. *Civilizations of the Indus Valley and Beyond* (New York, 1966). Survey by the principal original excavator of the two great cities of the Harappa civilization in the Indus valley.

Wilson, John A. *The Burden of Egypt, an Interpretation of Ancient Egyptian Culture* (Chicago, 1957). Very thoughtful and penetrating analysis.

Zacharias, H. C. E. *Human Personality, Its Historical Emergence* (St. Louis, 1950). Misleading title; primarily significant for the early Orient; some good insights, but some very questionable sections; orthodox Roman Catholic viewpoint.

_____. *Protohistory* (St. Louis, 1947). Same comments as on the above title by Zacharias.

Zimmer, Heinrich. *Philosophies of India*, ed. Joseph Campbell (Cleveland, 1956). One of the best introductions to this important, yet often almost impenetrable subject; emphasizes the influence of pre-Aryan thought and culture upon Hinduism, Jainism, and Buddhism.

IV. THE GRAECO-ROMAN WORLD BEFORE CHRIST

Astin, A. E. *Scipio Aemilianus* (Oxford, 1967). Rome from the defeat of Antiochus the Great to the Gracchi, from the standpoint of the leading Roman during these years (185-129 B.C.).

Badian, E. *Roman Imperialism in the Late Republic*, 2nd ed. (Ithaca NY, 1968).

Baker, G. P. *Sulla the Fortunate* (New York, 1927, 1967). Sulla and Rome during his lifetime, 138-78 B.C.

Bevan, Edwyn R. *The House of Ptolemy*, rev. ed. (Chicago, 1968). The most complete history of Ptolemaic Egypt.

_____. *The House of Seleucus*, 2 vols. (New York, 1902). Still the most complete history of the Seleucid empire.

Buchan, John. *Augustus* (London, 1937). Comprehensive, well-written biography of the greatest of the Roman emperors.

_____. *Julius Caesar* (London, 1932).

Burn, A. R. *The Lyric Age of Greece* (New York, 1964). Brilliant, insightful survey, exceedingly well written; covers Greek history during what is probably its most difficult and confusing period, 750-500 B.C., with unsurpassed clarity.

_____. *Persia and the Greeks; the Defence of the West* (New York, 1962). Very thorough, very well written—much the best modern history of the Persian Wars available in English.

Bury, J. B. *A History of Greece* (New York, n.d.). Classic work, up to Alexander the Great.

Carter, John M. *The Battle of Actium* (New York, 1970).

Cary, M. *A History of the Greek World from 323 to 146 B.C.*, 2nd ed. (London, 1963).

Cowell, F. R. *Cicero and the Roman Republic* (London, 1948). Strongly pro-Cicero and anti-Caesar.

Debevoise, Neilson C. *A Political History of Parthia* (Chicago, 1938).

Dickinson, John. *Death of a Republic*, ed. George Haskins (New York, 1963). Very good narrative and analysis of the fall of the Roman republic, sympathetic to the republicans and hostile to Caesar; introduction gives an excellent summary of the complex governmental system of the Roman republic, essential to understanding its history in the years before Christ.

Dorey, T. A., and D. R. Dudley. *Rome Against Carthage, a History of the Punic Wars* (New York, 1972).

Downey, Glanville. *A History of Antioch in Syria* (Princeton NJ, 1961). A work of towering scholarship, definitive on the 900-year history of Hellenistic, Roman, and Christian Antioch.

Eddy, Samuel K. *The King Is Dead; Studies in Near Eastern Resistance to Hellenism* (Lincoln NE, 1961). A trail-blazing work of scholarship in a little studied but important subject, the underground resistance to Hellenism in the Middle East during the centuries following Alexander's conquests.

Errington, R. M. *The Dawn of Empire; Rome's Rise to World Power* (Ithaca NY, 1972).

Fine, John V. A. *The Ancient Greeks, a Critical History* (Cambridge MA, 1983). An excellent synthesis of modern knowledge and scholarly interpretation of the events of Greek history up to the Macedonian conquest.

Forrest, W. G. *A History of Sparta, 950-192 B.C.* (London, 1968).

Froude, James A. *Caesar* (New York, 1908). Vehemently—and excessively—pro-

Caesar, but a good corrective to the usually republican viewpoint of later historians, and very thorough.

Fuller, J. F. C. *The Generalship of Alexander the Great* (New Brunswick NJ, 1960).

_____. *Julius Caesar: Man, Soldier and Tyrant* (London, 1965).

Gelzer, Matthias. *Caesar, Politician and Statesman* (Cambridge, MA,, 1968).

Grant, Michael. *The Ancient Historians* (New York, 1970).

_____. *The Army of the Caesars* (New York, 1974).

_____. *Cleopatra* (New York, 1972). The only really scholarly biography in English of this remarkable and significant woman.

_____. *The Jews in the Roman World* (New York, 1973). Secular humanist viewpoint.

Green, Peter. *Armada from Athens* (Garden City NY, 1970). Very well researched and well written account of Athens' pivotal Sicilian expedition in the Peloponnesian War.

Greenhalgh, Peter. *Pompey, the Roman Alexander* (London, 1980). Well researched and exceptionally well-written first volume of the best modern life of Pompey, covering his conquest of Palestine. Totally indifferent toward both Judaism and Christianity.

_____. *Pompey, the Republican Prince* (London, 1981).

Hamilton, Charles D. *Sparta's Bitter Victories* (Ithaca NY, 1978). The brief Spartan ascendancy after the defeat of Athens in the Peloponnesian War, 405-386 B.C.

Hammond, N. G. L. *Alexander the Great, King, Commander and Statesman* (Park Ridge NJ, 1980). A thorough scholarly biography of Alexander, based upon all the most recent research. Excellent on most purely factual issues of his career, but lacks the perceptiveness and vividness of Lane-Fox's biography of Alexander.

Hansen, Esther V. *The Attalids of Pergamum* (Ithaca NY, 1947). The only history in English of this important Hellenistic kingdom, willed to Rome by its last king in 133 B.C.

Holmes, T. Rice. *Caesar's Conquest of Gaul* (London, 1899). Much the most thorough study of this familiar subject in English, practically definitive.

_____. *The Roman Republic and the Founder of the Empire*, 3 vols. (London, 1923). The most complete narrative history of the public life of Julius Caesar.

Huxley, G. L. *The Early Ionians* (New York, 1966). The Greek settlements and culture on the eastern shore of the Aegean.

Huzar, Eleanor G. *Mark Antony* (Minneapolis MN, 1978).

Hyde, Walter W. *Ancient Greek Mariners* (New York, 1947). Greek maritime expansion.

Jones, A. H. M. *Augustus Caesar* (London, 1971).

_____. *Sparta* (Cambridge MA, 1967).

Kagan, Donald. *The Archidamian War* (Ithaca NY, 1974). The first phase of the Peloponnesian War, 431-421 B.C.

Lane-Fox, Robin. *Alexander the Great* (New York, 1974). The best biography of Alexander the Great in English, and much the best. Secular humanist viewpoint.

Leon, H. J. *The Jews of Ancient Rome* (Philadelphia, 1960).

McDonald, William A. *Progress into the Past; the Rediscovery of Mycenaean Civilization* (New York, 1967).

Marlowe, John. *The Golden Age of Alexandria* (London, 1971).

Marsh, Frank B. *A History of the Roman World from 146 to 30 B.C.*, 3rd ed. (London, 1963).

Momigliano, Arnaldo. *Alien Wisdom; the Limits of Hellenism* (Cambridge, England, 1975). Traces the beginnings of the long delayed interaction between Greek and Jewish learning and culture.

Myres, John C. *The Political Ideas of the Greeks* (New York, 1972).

Narain, A. K. *The Indo-Greeks* (Oxford, 1959). Greek penetration into India, from Alexander to the time of Christ.

Nilsson, N. P. *History of Greek Religion*, rev. ed. (Oxford, 1949).

Owens, Joseph. *A History of Ancient Western Philosophy* (New York, 1959).

Parsons, Edward A. *The Alexandrian Library, Glory of the Hellenic World: Its Rise, Antiquities and Destruction* (New York, 1952).

Peters, F. E. *The Harvest of Hellenism* (London, 1972). General survey of the history and culture of the Hellenistic age.

Petersson, Torsten. *Cicero* (New York, 1963). Comprehensive biography.

Picard, Gilbert C. and Colette. *The Life and Death of Carthage* (New York, 1968). Presents most of what little is known about the history and culture of Carthage, outside the Punic Wars themselves.

Pratt, Fletcher. *Hail, Caesar!* (London, 1938). A particularly good popularization; useful to the scholar in integrating data.

Reinhold, Meyer. *Marcus Agrippa* (Geneva NY, 1933). Biography of Caesar Augustus' "right-hand man."

Rostovtzeff, M. I. *The Social and Economic History of the Hellenistic World*, 2 vols. (Oxford, 1941). A classic work.

Sainte-Croix, G. E. M. de. *The Origins of the Peloponnesian War* (London, 1972).

Scullard, Howard H. *From the Gracchi to Nero* (London, 1963).

_____. *A History of the Roman World from 753 to 146 B.C.*, 3rd ed. (London, 1961). Excellent, standard presentation of early Roman history by one of the major modern scholarly authorities.

_____. *Scipio Africanus, Soldier and Politician* (Ithaca NY, 1970). Presents very well virtually all that is known of the Roman victor over Hannibal, one of the most significant figures in Roman history.

Sealey, Raphael. *A History of the Greek City-States* (Berkeley CA, 1976).

Sherwin-White, A. N. *The Roman Citizenship*, 2nd ed. (Oxford, 1973). Very thorough.

Smallwood, E. Mary. *The Jews under Roman Rule, from Pompey to Diocletian* (Leiden, 1981). Very thorough. Secular viewpoint, but not anti-religious. The best study on the subject to date.

Stockton, D. C. *Cicero, a Political Biography* (Oxford, 1971).

Syme, Ronald. *The Roman Revolution* (Oxford, 1939, 1960). A classic work.

Tarn, W. W. *Alexander the Great* (Boston, 1948). Strongly pro-Alexander.

_____. *The Greeks in Bactria and India* (Cambridge, England, 1957). The most distant of Alexander's successor states and Greek penetration into India.

_____. *Hellenistic Civilisation*, 3rd ed. (Cleveland, 1961). Cultural survey.

Taylor, Lily R. *Party Politics in the Age of Caesar* (Berkeley CA, 1949).

Toynbee, Arnold J. *Hannibal's Legacy*, 2 vols. (Oxford, 1965).

Walbank, F. W. *A Historical Commentary on Polybius*, 3 vols. (Oxford, 1929). Encyclopedic.

_____. *Philip V of Macedon* (Cambridge, England, 1940). A profound and scholarly study; the only biography of this king (a contemporary of Hannibal) in English.

Ward, Allen M. *Marcus Crassus and the Late Roman Republic* (St. Louis, 1977).

Wilcken, Ulrich. *Alexander the Great* (New York, 1967).

Wilcoxon, George D. *Athens Ascendant* (Ames IA, 1971). Focusses on Athens from the Greek defeat of Persia in 440 B.C.

Woodcock, George. *The Greeks in India* (London, 1966).

Wunderlich, Hans. *The Secret of Crete* (London, 1974). New interpretation of the ruins of Knossos and what they signify for the nature of Cretan-Mycenaean civilization, the immediate predecessor and ancestor of the Graeco-Roman.

Zimmern, Alfred. *The Greek Commonwealth*, 5th ed. (Oxford, 1931). A classic work, brilliantly evoking Hellenic civilization in the Age of Pericles, profoundly—and perhaps excessively—sympathetic to that civilization.

V. THE LIFE OF CHRIST

Barbet, Pierre. *A Doctor at Calvary* (New York, 1953). The most striking and comprehensive presentation of the case for the authenticity of the Holy Shroud of Turin as the burial sheet of Christ, showing physical evidence of His Passion, to appear in English before Ian Wilson's *The Shroud of Turin*. The author, a doctor, provides expert commentary on the medical significance of the evidence.

Belser, J. E. *History of the Passion, Death and Glorification of Our Saviour Jesus Christ* (St. Louis, 1929). Minute analysis of the last month of Christ's life; immensely learned and thorough.

Brandon, S. G. F. *The Fall of Jerusalem and the Christian Church* (London, 1957). Secular humanist viewpoint; presents Jesus solely as a revolutionary political leader.

Bruce, F. E. *New Testament History* (New York, 1971). Generally orthodox Protestant viewpoint, though accepting many Modernist premises about the dating of books of the New Testament.

Bruckberger, Raymond-Leopold. *Mary Magdalene* (New York, 1953). Brilliant modern-day argument for the traditional view of Mary Magdalene as identical with Mary of Bethany and the sinful woman who anointed Christ; orthodox Roman Catholic viewpoint.

Butler, B.C. *The Originality of St. Matthew, a Critique of the Two-Document Hypothesis* (Cambridge, England, 1951). Strong and effective argument for the traditional view of the priority of Matthew among the Gospels.

Cutler, Allan. "Does the Simeon of Luke 2 Refer to Simeon the Son of Hillel?'', *Journal of the Bible and Religion* XXXIV (1966), 29-35.

Danielou, Jean (Cardinal). *The Infancy Narratives* (New York, 1968). A defense of their historicity by a world-renowned scholar.

Daniel-Rops, Henri. *The Book of Mary* (Garden City, N Y, 1963). Careful review of our limited historical knowledge of the Blessed Virgin Mary; orthodox Roman Catholic viewpoint.

_____. *Jesus and His Times* (New York, 1954).

Edersheim, Alfred. *The Life and Times of Jesus the Messiah*, 2 vols. (New York, 1886). Orthodox Protestant viewpoint; very thorough; especially notable for the author's encyclopedic knowledge and effective use of Jewish background material for the life of Christ.

Eisler, Robert. *The Messiah Jesus and John the Baptist* (London, 1931). Secular humanist viewpoint; learned but fanciful in arguing that Jesus was only a political revolutionary.

Fernandez, Andres. *The Life of Christ* (Westminster MD, 1958). Semi-popular but comprehensive and well researched; orthodox Roman Catholic viewpoint.

Filas, Francis L. "The Dating of the Shroud of Turin from Coins of Pontius Pilate" (article length, privately published, Youngtown AZ, 1980). Very recent evidence dating the Shroud by coin impressions to 28-30 A.D.

Fillion, L. C. *The Life of Christ, a Historical, Critical and Apologetic Exposition*, 3 vols, 2nd ed. (St. Louis, 1928). Voluminous, sometimes very useful, but frequently superficial; orthodox Roman Catholic viewpoint.

Fouard, Constant. *The Christ the Son of God*, 2 vols. (New York, 1890). Orthodox Roman Catholic viewpoint; somewhat outdated.

Freyne, Sean. *Galilee from Alexander the Great to Hadrian* (Wilmington DE, 1980). Comprehensive and clearly analyzed; very valuable for discerning the true situation in Galilee while Jesus lived there. Jewish viewpoint; rejects the thesis of Jesus as a political revolutionary.

Hoehner, Harold W. *Herod Antipas, a Contemporary of Jesus Christ* (Cambridge, England, 1972). Largely orthodox Protestant viewpoint, displays extensive and thorough acquaintance with sound modern research on the life of Christ and His contemporaries as history.

Jeremias, Joachim. *The Eucharistic Words of Jesus* (New York, 1966). Minute analysis of their meaning and full evidence of their historicity.

Kopp, Clemens. *The Holy Places of the Gospels* (New York, 1963).

Kraeling, Emil G. *The Disciples* (New York, 1966). The lives of the Twelve Apostles.

Lagrange, Marie-Joseph. *The Gospel of Jesus Christ*, 2 vols. (Westminster MD, 1938). Not a Gospel commentary, but an historical life of Jesus by one of the greatest of the orthodox French Catholic Biblical scholars; contributes decisively to solving several of the most difficult questions in the history of Christ's life.

Lebreton, Jules. *The Life and Teaching of Jesus Christ*, 2 vols. (New York, 1957). Orthodox Roman Catholic viewpoint.

Miguens, Manuel. *Church Ministries in New Testament Times* (Arlington VA, 1976). Scripturally based study of the apostolic succession; orthodox Roman Catholic viewpoint.

_____. *The Virgin Birth, an Evaluation of Scriptural Evidence* (Westminster MD, 1975). Indispensable and conclusive on this subject; orthodox Roman Catholic viewpoint.

Most, William G. *The Consciousness of Christ* (Front Royal VA, 1980). The proof that Christ was always fully aware of His divinity.

Prat, Ferdinand. *Jesus Christ: His Life, His Teaching, and His Work*, 2 vols. (Milwaukee, 1950). Thorough and profound; orthodox Roman Catholic viewpoint.

Ricciotti, Giuseppe. *The Life of Christ* (Milwaukee, 1947). An outstanding historical biography, available in a full scholarly edition and an abridged popular edition—only the former should be used; orthodox Roman Catholic viewpoint.

Robinson, John A. T. *Redating the New Testament* (Philadelphia, 1976). Modernist premises but orthodox conclusions.

Ruckstuhl, Eugen. *Chronology of the Last Days of Jesus* (New York, 1965). Evidence for dating the Passion and Resurrection of Christ to April of 30 A.D.

Thackeray, H. St. John. *Josephus, the Man and the Historian* (New York, 1929).

Walsh, William T. *Saint Peter the Apostle* (New York, 1948). Popularized biography; contains some remarkable reflections on the events of Christ's life as Peter would have seen them; historical rather than devotional approach; orthodox Roman Catholic viewpoint.

Willam, Franz M. *The Life of Jesus Christ in the Land of Israel and among Its People*, ed. Newton Thompson (St. Louis, 1931).

Wilson, Ian. *The Shroud of Turin* (Garden City NY, 1978). A survey of recent scientific research supporting the authenticity of the Holy Shroud as the burial sheet of Jesus Christ, and a brilliant exposition of its probable history from Christ's time to our own—the first complete narrative of the history of the Shroud; a landmark in recent Christian historical research and writing.

VI. THE EARLY CHURCH

Allard, Paul. *Histoire des Persécutions pendant les deux premiers siècles*, 2nd ed. (Paris, 1892). An outstanding, comprehensive, thoughtful, beautifully written orthodox Roman Catholic work, first in a series of three on the Roman persecutions of the Church (the others listed below). Should long since have been translated into English.

_____. *Les Persécutions du troisième siècle*, 2nd ed. (Paris, 1898).

_____. *La Persécution de Dioclétien et le Triomphe de l'Église*, 2nd ed., 2 vols. (Paris, 1900). Even better than its predecessor volumes.

_____. *Ten Lectures on the Martyrs* (London, 1907). The only historical work of Allard which has been translated into English; unfortunately not of particular importance.

Arpee, Leon. *A History of Armenian Christianity* (New York, 1946). Protestant viewpoint.

Atiya, Aziz S. *History of Eastern Christianity* (Notre Dame IN, 1968). Useful summary of the early history of the churches in Egypt, Syria, Armenia, and India which are now, to a large extent, not in communion with Rome. Eastern Orthodox viewpoint.

Aube, Benjamin. *Histoire des Persécutions de l'Église*, 4 vols., 2nd ed. (Paris, 1875-1886). Comparable in length to, but not as insightful as Allard's volumes.

Bardy, Gustave. *The Church at the End of the First Century* (London, 1938).

Barnes, Arthur S. *Christianity at Rome in the Apostolic Age* (London, 1938). Some very good insights, some far "off the mark"; no scholarly apparatus.

Barnes, Timothy D. *Constantine and Eusebius* (Cambridge MA, 1981). New and erudite study of Constantine's career and Eusebius' scholarship; tends to avoid disputed issues of high religious content, such as the historicity of Constantine's vision of the Cross in the sky.

_____. *Tertullian, a Historical and Literary Study* (Oxford, 1971). Very thorough, but tends to be hyper-critical.

Batiffol, Pierre. *Primitive Catholicism* (New York, 1911). Orthodox Roman Catholic.

Blackman, E. C. *Marcion and His Influence* (London, 1948). A thorough and well-balanced scholarly survey of the great second-century heretic, the first to construct a separate church. Orthodox Protestant (Anglican).

Brandon, S. G. F. *The Fall of Jerusalem and the Christian Church* (London, 1957). Secular humanist viewpoint; regards the early Christians as political revolutionaries, with consequent drastic rewriting of early Christian history.

Brown, L. W. *The Indian Christians of St. Thomas* (Cambridge, England, 1956). Rejects the historicity of the Apostle Thomas' mission to India.

Bruce, F. E. *New Testament History* (New York, 1971).

_____. *Paul: Apostle of the Free Spirit* (Exeter, England, 1977). Orthodox Protestant viewpoint; generally defends the historicity of the deeds and letters of St. Paul while avoiding where possible open disagreement with hyper-criticism.

Cadbury, H. J. *The Book of Acts in History* (London, 1955). Modernist viewpoint.

Cadoux, Cecil J. *Ancient Smyrna, a History of the City from the Earliest Times to 324 A.D.* (Oxford, 1938). Much the most thorough available presentation of the history of the very important Christian community in Smyrna, with special emphasis on the martyrs Polycarp and Pionios. Approaches Downey's *Antioch* in quality. A very valuable though little-known study.

Carrington, Philip. *The Early Christian Church*, 2 vols. (Cambridge, England, 1957). An attempt to write a connected narrative of early Church history according to Modernist premises regarding the dates of composition of the New Testament books. The result does not fit well together.

Chapman, John. "Callistus I, Saint, Pope," *The Catholic Encyclopedia* (1913).

_____. "Cornelius, Saint, Pope," *ibid.*

_____. "St. Cyprian," *ibid.*

_____. "Donatists," *ibid.*

_____. *John the Presbyter and the Fourth Gospel* (Oxford, 1911). The best treatment of the later life and writings of the Apostle John, the Christian communities he influenced in Asia Minor, and the theory of a dual authorship of the Gospel of John and the Apocalypse, which this writer has seen. Orthodox Roman Catholic viewpoint.

_____. *Matthew, Mark and Luke, a Study in the Order and Interpretation of the Synoptic Gospels* (London, 1937). Historically important arguments on the original language, authorship and sequence of the Synoptic Gospels; particularly significant on the Gospel of Matthew. Fragmentary because the author died before its completion, but deserves much more attention than it has received.

_____. "Novatian and Novatianism," *The Catholic Encyclopedia* (1913).

_____. "Paul of Samosata," *ibid.*

_____. *Studies in the Early Papacy* (London, 1928). Includes an outstanding article on St. Cyprian by this keen and immensely learned orthodox Roman Catholic scholar.

Clercq, Victor C. de. *Ossius of Cordova* (Washington, 1954). A definitive biography—has the last word, among other subjects, on the Council of Elvira.

Colson, Jean. *Lyon, Baptistère des Gaules* (Paris, 1975).

Corwin, Virginia. *St. Ignatius and Christianity in Antioch* (New Haven CT, 1960). Protestant viewpoint.

Cranfield, C. E. B. *I and II Peter and Jude, Introduction and Commentary* (London, 1960). Accepts the historicity and Petrine authorship of 1 Peter.

Cullmann, Oscar. *Peter: Disciple, Apostle, Martyr*, 2nd ed. (Philadelphia, 1962). Orthodox Protestant viewpoint; holds that Peter was martyred in Rome, but was never Bishop of Rome, nor head of the Church after leaving Jerusalem.

Danielou, Jean (Cardinal) and Henri Marrou. *The Christian Centuries*, Volume I: *The First Six Hundred Years* (New York, 1966). The first half of this useful book is by Cardinal Danielou and covers the history of the early church up to Constantine. A good survey with many valuable references, dealing with many important points often overlooked.

Danielou, Jean (Cardinal). *Origen* (New York, 1951).

Daniel-Rops, Henri. *The Book of Mary* (New York, 1960).

_____. *The Church of Apostles and Martyrs* (New York, 1960). The first volume in Daniel-Rops' great history of the Church from the orthodox Roman Catholic viewpoint—perceptive, well-written, but unfortunately lacking source citations and substantial bibliography.

Dauvilliers, Jean. *Les Temps apostoliques* (Paris, 1969). Very comprehensive; generally orthodox Roman Catholic viewpoint. Probably the best recent treatment of Church history in the first century; definitely deserves translation.

Delehaye, Hippolyte. *Étude sur le Légendier Romain, les Saintes de Novembre et de Decembre* (Brussels, 1936).

_____. *Les Origines du Culte des Martyrs*, 2nd ed. (Brussels, 1933). Hypercritical of the traditions of the martyrs.

Dix, Gregory. *Jew and Greek, a Study in the Primitive Church* (London, 1953). A much needed corrective to the exaggerations of scholars bemused by the controversy over the admission of Gentiles to the Church and the extent to which they were to be compelled to obey the Law of Moses. Orthodox Protestant viewpoint.

Dobschütz, Ernst von. *Christian Life in the Primitive Church* (London, 1904).

_____. *Christusbilder* (Leipzig, 1899). Reviews the circumstances of the appearance of the picture of Christ "not made by hands" in Edessa (the Holy Shroud of Turin, according to Ian Wilson's theory) on the assumption that it was not authentic. The only thorough treatment of this subject before Wilson.

Donaldson, Stuart A. *Church Life and Thought in North Africa, A.D. 200* (Cambridge, England, 1909).

Downey, Glanville. *A History of Antioch in Syria* (Princeton NJ, 1961). By far the best available treatment of the history of the early Christian community in Antioch.

Duchesne, Louis. *The Early History of the Christian Church*, 2 vols. (London, 1909).

_____. *Le Liber Pontificalis, Texte, Introduction et Commentaire*, 2 vols. (Paris, 1892). The classic edition of the indispensable Latin source on the early history of the Papacy, with a very extensive and profound French commentary.

Dvornik, Francis. *The Idea of Apostolicity in Byzantium and the Legend of the Apostle Andrew* (Cambridge MA, 1958). The only available reasonably sound scholarly study of the traditions about the Apostle Andrew (or about any of the less well known Apostles).

Edmundson, George. *The Church in Rome in the First Century* (London, 1913). A very important, badly neglected book whose significance is noted by Robinson in *Redating the New Testament*. Provides data and analysis almost indispensable for reconstructing the actual history and chronology of the Apostolic Age.

Farquhar, J. N. "The Apostle Thomas in North India," *Bulletin of the John Rylands Library* X (1926), 80-110.

_____. "The Apostle Thomas in South India," *ibid.* XI (1927), 20-51.

Fichter, Joseph. *St. Cecil Cyprian* (St. Louis, 1942).

Fortescue, Adrian. "St. Gregory the Illuminator," *The Catholic Encyclopedia* (1913).

Fouard, Constant. *St. Peter and the First Years of Christianity* (London, 1892). This old book and its companion volumes (listed below in chronological order of the history covered) stand, in this writer's considered opinion, as the best single treatment of the history of the Apostolic Age available in English. Their use of fact and argument in dealing with the often obscure and controverted events of this vitally important period is superb. Orthodox Roman Catholic viewpoint.

_____. *St. Paul and His Missions* (New York, 1899).

_____. *The Last Years of St. Paul* (New York, 1900).

_____. *St. John and the Close of the Apostolic Age* (New York, 1905).

Frend, W. H. C. *The Donatist Church* (Oxford, 1952). Thorough and scholarly; very favorable to the Donatists, hostile to the Catholics.

_____. *Martyrdom and Persecution in the Early Church* (New York, 1967). No perceptible Christian viewpoint; scholarly and comprehensive, yet often misses important points; still a valuable reference work for the Roman persecutions.

Garcia Villada, Zacarías. *Historia Eclesiástica de España*, Volume I (Madrid, 1929). Orthodox Roman Catholic viewpoint; the best source on the early history of the Spanish church.

Goppelt, Leonhard. *Apostolic and Post-Apostolic Times* (London, 1970). Very learned and very cautious—avoids most controversial issues.

Gregg, John A. F. *The Decian Persecution* (Edinburgh, 1897). The only full history of this persecution in English, and an excellent one; now a very rare book.

Griffe, Elie. *La Gaule Chrétienne à l'Époque romaine* (Paris, 1964). The most thorough recent coverage of Christianty in Roman Gaul. Contains virtually all available information pertaining to this subject down to 325.

Guarducci, Margherita. *The Tomb of Saint Peter* (New York, 1960).

Guéranger, Prosper. *Life of St. Cecilia, Virgin and Martyr* (Philadelphia, 1866). Translated from the second French edition; orthodox Roman Catholic viewpoint. The best and almost the only real source of information on St. Cecilia in English; does not reflect Guéranger's later change of view regarding her date.

_____. *Saint Cécile et la Société romaine aux deux premiers siècles*, 2 vols. (Paris, 1897). The eighth French edition of Guéranger's study of St. Cecilia, reflecting his final views on the subject.

Gunther, John J. *Paul: Messenger and Exile, a Study in the Chronology of His Life and Letters* (Valley Forge PA, 1972). Tries to balance traditional and Modernist chronologies of St. Paul, with varying success.

Gwatkin, Henry M. *Early Church History*, 2 vols. (London, 1909). Orthodox Protestant viewpoint.

Hardy, E. G. *Christianity and the Roman Government* (New York, 1894, 1971). Develops the theory that Christians were persecuted in the Roman empire only under general police regulations, not a specific persecuting law.

Harnack, Alfred von. *The Expansion of Christianity in the First Three Centuries*, 2 vols. (London, 1904-1905). Classic history; Modernist viewpoint.

Healy, Patrick J. *The Valerian Persecution* (Boston, 1905). The only full history of this persecution in English, and an excellent one. Orthodox Roman Catholic viewpoint.

Hefele, Charles J. *A History of the Christian Councils*, Volume I (Edinburgh, 1871). The first volume of the classic, definitive work on this subject, covering every council and major synod in the ancient and medieval history of the Church. Orthodox Roman Catholic viewpoint.

Hertling, Ludwig and Englebert Kirschbaum. *The Roman Catacombs and Their Martyrs*, 2nd ed. (Milwaukee, 1956). A small book whose full value is not apparent at first sight. Based on excellent scholarship; very good in re-creating major events in early Roman Christian history, in which the catacombs were central. Orthodox Roman Catholic viewpoint.

Holmes, T. Scott. *The Origin and Development of the Christian Church in Gaul during the First Six Centuries of the Christian Era* (London, 1911).

Holzner, Joseph. *Paul of Tarsus* (St. Louis, 1944).

Hosten, Henry. *Antiquities from San Thomé and Mylapore* (Mylapore, India, 1936). Reports research on the shrines of the Apostle Thomas, including his original burial place in India.

Jacquier, E. "Matthew, Saint, Apostle and Evangelist," *The Catholic Encyclopedia* (1913).

Jalland, Trevor G. *The Church and the Papacy* (London, 1944). Orthodox Protestant viewpoint.

Jedin, Hubert and John Dolan, eds., *History of the Church*, Volume I: "From the Apostolic Community to Constantine" (New York, 1965). Comprehensive, but constantly hobbled by excess of scholarly caution.

Jonas, Hans. *The Gnostic Religion; the Message of the Alien God and the Beginnings of Christianity* (Boston, 1963). Probably the best presentation of Gnosticism in English; includes data from the recently discovered Gnostic library at Nag Hammadi (Chenoboskion) in Egypt.

Kehimkar, H. S. *The History of the Bene-Israel of India* (Tel Aviv, 1937).

Kenrick, T. D. *St. James in Spain* (London, 1960). A review of the history of the Spanish legend and shrine of Santiago.

Kidd, B. J. *The Roman Primacy to A.D. 461* (London, 1936). Orthodox Protestant viewpoint, argues that Papal primacy was not generally recognized in the early Church.

Kirsch, J. P. "St. Cecilia," *The Catholic Encyclopedia* (1913).

_____. "Dionysius, Saint, Pope," *ibid.*

_____. "Marcellinus, Saint, Pope," *ibid*.

_____. "Miltiades, Saint, Pope," *ibid*.

_____. "Urban I, Saint, Pope," *ibid*.

Kirschbaum, Englebert. *The Tombs of Saints Peter and Paul* (New York, 1957). Detailed discussion of the excavations under St. Peter's Basilica by one of the excavators.

Knox, John. *Philemon among the Letters of Paul* (Chicago, 1935).

Knox, W. L. *St. Paul and the Church of the Gentiles* (Cambridge, England, 1939). Modernist viewpoint.

_____. *St. Paul and the Church of Jerusalem* (Cambridge, England, 1928).

Kraeling, Emil G. *The Disciples* (New York, 1966). Lives and legends of the Twelve Apostles.

Kurkjian, Vahan M. *A History of Armenia* (New York, 1958). Good summary of the traditional view of the relatively little that is known about the Christian conversion of Armenia.

Lagrange, Marie-Joseph. *L'Évangile selon Saint Matthieu,* 2nd ed. (Paris, 1923). Includes an extensive presentation, at the highest scholarly level, of the case for the priority of Matthew among the Gospels in time of writing, and for its original composition in Aramaic.

Lake, Kirsopp and Henry J. Cadbury, eds. *The Beginnings of Christianity,* 5 vols. (London, 1933). Modernist viewpoint.

Lawlor, Hugh J. *Eusebiana; Essays on the Ecclesiastical History of Eusebius* (Oxford, 1912).

Lebreton, Jules and Jacques Zeiller. *The History of the Primitive Church,* 2 vols. (New York, 1949). The first two volumes of the immense 21-volume Fliche-Martin history of the Church—two of the only three of those volumes which have been translated into English. Probably the best overall view of the subject, though sometimes vague or evasive on controversial subjects. Orthodox Roman Catholic viewpoint.

Leclercq, Henri. "La Légende d'Abgar," *Dictionnaire d'Archéologie chrétienne et de liturgie*.

_____. "Cécile, Crypte et Basilique de Sainte," *ibid*.

_____. "Édesse," *ibid*.

_____. "Gril," *ibid*.

_____. "Labarum," *ibid*.

_____. "Laurent, Saint," *ibid*.

Lietzmann, H. *The History of the Early Church* (Cleveland, 1937, 1961). Modernist viewpoint.

Lightfoot, J. B. *Dissertations on the Apostolic Age* (London, 1892). By a great orthodox Protestant scholar, who did more than any other man of his time to defend and establish the essential historicity of the development of the early Church, after the Resurrection of Christ, as reported in Scriptural and patristic sources.

Martin, J. P. Paulin. *Les Origines de l'Église d'Édesse et des Églises syriennes* (Paris, 1889). The last scholarly study to defend the essential historicity of the conversion of Edessa to Christianity in the first century. Very important and very rare.

Marucchi, Orazio. *Manual of Christian Archaeology* (Paterson NJ, 1935). Detailed and comprehensive, emphasizing the early church and the catacombs.

Mason, Arthur J. *The Persecution of Diocletian* (Cambridge, England, 1876).

Miguens, Manuel. *Church Ministries in New Testament Times* (Arlington VA, 1976). Brilliant scholarly analysis of apostolic succession from Scripture and the earliest Christian documents outside the New Testament; orthodox Roman Catholic viewpoint, but accepts substantially later than traditional dating for the composition of the Gospels.

Mingana, A. "The Early Spread of Christianity in India," *Bulletin of the John Rylands Library* X (1926), 44.

Moraes, George M. *A History of Christianity in India, A.D. 52-1542* (Bombay, 1964). The most thorough recent scholarly treatment of this subject; orthodox Christian viewpoint.

Mosshammer, Alden A. *The "Chronicle" of Eusebius and Greek Chronographic Tradition* (Lewisburg PA, 1979).

Mourret, Fernand. *A History of the Catholic Church*, Volume I (St. Louis, 1931). Orthodox Roman Catholic viewpoint.

Mundadan, A. Mathias. *Sixteenth Century Traditions of St. Thomas Christians* (Bangalore, India, 1970). A most important source for reconstructing the apostolic career of St. Thomas in India.

O'Connor, Daniel W. *Peter in Rome; the Literary, Liturgical and Archeological Evidence* (New York, 1969). Concludes that Peter was in Rome briefly but that almost nothing can be known about what he did there. Excessively cautious and skeptical.

Ogg, George. *The Chronology of the Life of Paul* (London, 1968). Generally defends the traditional chronology of Paul's life though placing his conversion within two years of the Crucifixion.

Ort, L. J. R. *Mani; a Religio-Historical Description of His Personality* (Leiden, 1967). Very thorough, scholarly examination of all available records concerning Mani personally.

Palanque, J. R., et al. *The Church in the Christian Roman Empire*, 2 vols. (London, 1949). The third volume in the Fliche-Martin history of the Church and the last which has been translated into English. Useful, but not quite up to the level of the first two volumes in this history, by Lebreton and Zeiller.

Perumalil, A. C. *The Apostles in India*, 2nd ed. (Bangalore, India, 1971).

Phillips, George, ed. *The Doctrine of Addai the Apostle* (London, 1876). Complete translation of the Syriac Doctrine of Addai, with commentary.

Podipara, Placid J. *The Thomas Christians* (Bombay, 1970).

Quéffelec, Henri. *Saint Anthony of the Desert* (New York, 1954). Popularized, but the only full biography of St. Anthony available in English, and based on sound scholarship.

Quentin, H. "Sainte Cécile," *Dictionnaire d'Archéologie chrétienne et de liturgie*.

Ramsay, W. M. *The Church in the Roman Empire before A.D. 170*, 3rd ed. (London, 1894). Orthodox Protestant viewpoint.

_____. *The Letters to the Seven Churches* (London, 1906). Excellent discussion of early Christianity in Asia Minor in light of the Book of the Apocalypse.

Ricciotti, Giuseppe. *The Age of Martyrs* (Milwaukee, 1959). History of the reign of Diocletian, the advent of Constantine, the Diocletianic persecution, and the passions of the martyrs, done with all the skill and accuracy characteristic of this great orthodox Roman Catholic historian.

_____. *The Book of Acts: Text and Commentary* (Milwaukee, 1958).

_____. *Paul the Apostle* (Milwaukee, 1953). Much the best historical life of Paul in English—particularly good on the difficult chronological problems of his apostolic career and epistles.

Robinson, John A. T. *Redating the New Testament* (Philadelphia, 1976). The first "break" in the solid Modernist scholarly front against an early dating of the Gospels. Adopts many of the traditional dates, though for non-traditional reasons.

Segal, J. B. *Edessa, the Blessed City* (Oxford, 1970). Very thorough modern scholarly study of Edessa; rejects the tradition of its first century conversion; secular humanist viewpoint.

Sherwin-White, A. N. "The Early Persecutions and Roman Law Again," *Journal of Theological Studies*, n.s. III (1952-3), 199-213. Summary of the recent status of the prolonged argument on the juridical basis of the Roman persecution of the Christians. Gives insufficient weight to the enduring strength of the argument for a general law making it illegal simply to be a Christian in the Roman empire.

Smallwood, E. Mary. "The Date of the Dismissal of Pontius Pilate from Judaea," *Journal of Jewish Studies* V (1954), 12-21. Very important for the chronology of the martyrdom of Stephen and therefore for the conversion of Paul and the whole early history of the Church.

Thackeray, H. St. John. *Josephus, the Man and the Historian* (New York, 1929).

Thomson, R. W., ed. *Agathangelos' History of the Armenians* (Albany NY, 1976). The lengthy introduction by Thomson is much the best presentation in English on the difficult and often obscure subject of the conversion of Armenia to Christianity. This is also the first full English translation of the oldest history of the Armenians.

Thurston, Herbert. "The Letter of Our Saviour to Abgar," *The Month* LXXVI (Sept.-Dec. 1892), pp. 39-61.

Wallace-Hadrill, David S. *Eusebius of Caesarea* (London, 1960).

Walsh, John F. *The Bones of St. Peter* (New York, 1982). Account of the discovery and authentication of St. Peter's grave and bones.

Walsh, William T. *Saint Peter the Apostle* (New York, 1948). A popularization, with some excellent and memorable insights.

Weiss, Johannes. *Earliest Christianity, A.D. 30-150*, 2 vols. (New York, 1937). Modernist viewpoint.

Weltin, E. G. *The Ancient Popes* (Westminster MD, 1964). The only connected history in a single volume of the Papacy from Peter to Leo the Great, in English. Often superficial, but in the absence of any similar work, a valuable reference. Modernist viewpoint.

Wilson, Ian. *The Shroud of Turin* (New York, 1978). Impressive presentation of the evidence that the Holy Shroud of Turin was brought to Edessa in the first century.

Wilson, R. M. *The Gnostic Problem* (London, 1958).

Winter, Michael M. *Saint Peter and the Popes* (Baltimore, 1960). Orthodox Roman Catholic viewpoint.

Woodcock, George. *Kerala, a Portrait of the Malabar Coast* (London, 1967). Reviews the question of the apostolate of Thomas in India, generally favorably to its historicity.

Workman, H. B. *Persecutions in the Early Church*, 4th ed. (London, 1926). Orthodox Protestant viewpoint.

VII. THE ROMAN EMPIRE FROM TIBERIUS TO CONSTANTINE

Alföldi, A. *The Conversion of Constantine and Pagan Rome* (Oxford, 1948). Tends to be hostile to Constantine.

Baker, G. P. *Constantine the Great and the Christian Revolution* (New York, 1967).

_____. *Tiberius Caesar* (London, 1929). Very well written and perspicacious; however, no scholarly apparatus.

Balsdon, J. P. V. D. *The Emperor Gaius* (Oxford, 1934). The only biography of Gaius "Caligula" in English, and a very good one; scholarly.

Barrow, R. H. *Slavery in the Roman Empire* (London, 1928).

Baynes, Norman H. *Constantine the Great and the Christian Church*, 2nd ed. (London, 1934). Profound scholarship and excellent analysis of some of the principal problems of Constantine's life, notably his conversion. Tends to be favorable to Constantine.

Birley, Anthony. *Marcus Aurelius* (Boston, 1966). An outstanding, well written scholarly biography, perhaps the best available narrative of second century Roman history.

_____. *Septimius Severus, the African Emperor* (New York, 1972). Another very fine scholarly imperial biography.

Bryant, E. E. *The Reign of Antoninus Pius* (Cambridge, England, 1895).

Carcopino, Jerome. *Daily Life in Ancient Rome*, ed. Henry T. Rowell (New Haven CT, 1940; New York, 1971). A classic work.

Coleman, C. E. *Constantine the Great and Christianity* (New York, 1914). Mostly devoted to criticizing later legends about Constantine. Doubts the sincerity of his conversion.

Dörries, Hermann. *Constantine the Great* (New York, 1972). Favorable to Constantine.

Downey, Glanville. *A History of Antioch in Syria* (Princeton NJ, 1961). Definitive on all matters concerning Antioch and the Roman empire.

Farquharson, A. S. L. *Marcus Aurelius, His Life and His World* (Oxford, 1951).

Gaudemet, J. "La Législation religieuse de Constantin," *Revue d'Histoire de l'Église de France* XXXIII (1947), 25-61.

Glover, T. R. *The Conflict of Religions in the Early Roman Empire* (London, 1909).

Grant, Michael. *The Climax of Rome* (Boston, 1968). Survey of the Roman empire in the third century.

_____. *The Jews in the Roman World* (New York, 1973). Secular humanist viewpoint.

Greenhalgh, P. A. L. *The Year of the Four Emperors* (New York, 1975).

Griffin, Miriam T. *Seneca, a Philosopher in Politics* (Oxford, 1976).

Gsell, Stephan. *Essai sur la Règne de l'Émpereur Domitien* (Paris, 1893).

Henderson, Bernard W. *The Life and Principate of the Emperor Hadrian* (London, 1923). Collects virtually all that is known about Hadrian. Secular humanist viewpoint.

_____. *The Life and Principate of the Emperor Nero* (London, 1903).

Holsapple, Lloyd B. *Constantine the Great* (New York, 1942). Lengthy but somewhat superficial. Favorable to Constantine. Orthodox Roman Catholic viewpoint.

Homo, Leon. *Vespasien, l'Émpereur du bon Sens* (Paris, 1949). Outstanding, thorough study; shows Vespasian's essential role in the Roman recovery after the "year of the four emperors" in 69 A.D.

Huttman, Maude A. *The Establishment of Christianity* (New York, 1914). An important study of Constantine's legislation pertaining to Christianity and paganism, or as influenced by Christian principles.

Jones, A. H. M. *Constantine and the Conversion of Europe* (London, 1948).

_____. *The Later Roman Empire, 284-602*, 2 vols. (Norman, OK, 1964). Encyclopedic study, primarily of Roman governmental administration.

Keresztes, Paul. *Constantine, a Great Christian Monarch and Apostle* (Amsterdam, 1981). Provides very important corrective analysis to counterbalance the extremely hostile view of Constantine common in modern scholarship, though sometimes Keresztes veers too far in the other direction of uncritical apology.

Lepper, F. A. *Trajan's Parthian War* (Oxford, 1948).

Levick, Barbara. *Tiberius the Politician* (London, 1976).

Magie, David. *Roman Rule in Asia Minor to the End of the Third Century after Christ*, 2 vols. (Princeton NJ, 1950). Encyclopedic and definitive on Roman administration in Asia Minor, but gives almost no information about Christianity there despite the fact that this region was one of the primary centers of Christianity in the Roman empire before Constantine.

Marsh, Frank B. *The Reign of Tiberius* (London, 1947).

Momigliano, Arnaldo. *Claudius, the Emperor and His Achievement* (Oxford, 1934).

Oliva, P. *Pannonia and the Onset of Crisis in the Roman Empire* (Prague, 1962). Focusses on conditions at the end of the second century. Very thorough.

Perowne, Stewart. *Caesars and Saints* (New York, 1963).

_____. *Hadrian* (London, 1960). A somewhat superficial, but occasionally useful semi-scholarly biography.

_____. *The Later Herods* (New York, 1959).

Platnauer, M. *Septimius Severus* (London, 1918; Westport CT, 1970).

Ricciotti, Giuseppe. *The History of Israel*, 2 vols. (Milwaukee, 1955). Brings the history of the Jews down to the Bar-Kokhba revolt. Particularly good on the Jewish War and the fall of Jerusalem.

Rostovtzeff, Michael. *The Social and Economic History of the Roman Empire*, 2 vols. (Oxford, 1926). A classic work.

Salmon, Edward T. *History of the Roman World 30 B.C.-138 A.D.* (New York, 1963).

Scramuzza, Vincent M. *The Emperor Claudius* (Cambridge MA, 1940).

Seager, Robin. *Tiberius* (London, 1972). Well-balanced and well-written biography of this troubled and very important second emperor of Rome.

Sesan, Valerian. *Kirche und Staat in römisch-byzantinischen Reichs seit Konstantin dem Grossen* (Czernowitz, Austro-Hungarian Empire, 1911). Thorough review of the events surrounding Constantine's conversion, upholding its genuineness; Eastern Orthodox viewpoint.

Seston, W. *Dioclétien et la Tétrarchie*, 2 vols. (Paris, 1946). Covers the years 284-300, before the Great Persecution.

Shinnie, P. L. *Meroë, a Civilization in the Sudan* (New York, 1967). The history and culture of the kingdom known to the ancients as Ethiopia, though located mostly in what is now the Sudan.

Smallwood, E. Mary. *The Jews under Roman Rule, from Pompey to Diocletian* (Leiden, 1981). Very thorough and very valuable. Secular viewpoint but not anti-religious.

Smith, John Holland. *Constantine the Great* (London, 1971). The most thorough and scholarly biography of Constantine in English, but decidedly anti-Constantine.

Stark, Freya. *Rome on the Euphrates* (New York, 1966).

Taylor, L. R. *The Divinity of the Roman Emperor* (Middletown CT, 1931).

Turton, Godfrey. *The Syrian Princesses* (London, 1974). Semi-scholarly account of the influence of the women of the family of Empress Julia Domna, wife of Septimius Severus, on Roman policy during the four succeeding reigns (of Caracalla, Macrinus, Elagabalus, and Alexander Severus).

Vaughan, Agnes C. *Zenobia of Palmyra* (Garden City NY, 1967).

Warmington, B. H. *Nero, Reality and Legend* (New York, 1969). Attempts to rehabilitate Nero.

Wellesley, Kenneth. *The Long Year—A.D. 69* (London, 1976). Probably the best history of the tumultuous and memorable "year of the four emperors"—detailed, scholarly, and well written.

Yadin, Yigael. *Bar-Kokhba* (New York, 1971). Major recent discoveries about the last great Jewish uprising against Rome, substantially revising previously held views about its character and duration, by a leading archeologist of the state of Israel.

Index

Apollonius (general of the Seleucid Empire 165 B.C.), 238

Apollonius the Apologist, St. (martyr of Rome, c. 182 A.D.), 464-465, 482

Apollos (Christian of Alexandria, first century A.D.), 421

Apologetics, Christian, 287-288, 294

Apophis (Hyksos king in Egypt, 17th century B.C.), 48

Apostles, dispersion of the (42 A.D.), 402-407, 410, 413, 433

apostolic succession, 387-388, 451

Aqaba, Gulf of (in Palestine), 73, 94

Aquila and Priscilla (Christians in Rome and Corinth, first century A.D.), 417

Ara Pacis (Altar of Peace, dedicated by Augustus 9 B.C.), 281

Arabia, 23, 93, 159, 169, 197, 205, 306, 314, 395, 399, 406, 411, 418, 431
  early Christianity in south Arabia, 434

Arabian Sea, 204, 417

Arad (town in Palestine), 100

Aramaeans, 108

Aramaic language, 338, 403, 407-408

Arbela (city in Mesopotamia) (SEE also Gaugamela), 200

Archelaus (Ethnarch of Judea 4 B.C.-6 A.D.), 306, 313
  deposed by Augustus (6 A.D.), 321, 358

Archidamos II (King of Sparta 476-427 B.C.), 178, 182, 186

Archilochos (early Greek poet, 7th century B.C.) 166

Ardashir I (King of Persia 226-241 A.D.), 471

Aretas (King of the Nabataean Arabs, 28 A.D.), 328

Arginusae Islands, Battle of (naval:, Athens vs. Sparta, in Aegean Sea, 406 B.C.), 187

Argos (city in Greece), 214

Arian heresy, 501, 526, 534, 548, 549

Arioch, King of Ellasar, 42, 54

Ariovistus (German king 58 B.C.), 260, 262

Aristides "the Just" (Athenian leader c. 530-c. 468 B.C.), 180

Aristides (early Christian apologist c. 145 A.D.), 480

Aristobulus I (High Priest and Ethnarch of the Jews 104-103 B.C.), 254-255, 267, 282

Aristobulus II (King of the Jews 67-63 B.C.), 258

Aristobulus III (High Priest in Jerusalem 36-35 B.C.), 278

Aristobulus (son of Herod the Great), 283

Aristophanes (Greek comic playwright c. 448-c. 380 B.C.), 188

Aristotle (Greek philosopher 384-322 B.C.), 194, 197-198

Ark of the Covenant, 60, 70, 73, 79, 92, 110-111, 129, 258
  brought to Jerusalem (10th century B.C.), 89
  destroyed by the Babylonians (587 B.C.), 129, 137, 146
  in Solomon's Temple (10th century B.C.), 93, 94
  Philistines capture but return (11th century B.C.), 85-86

Arles, Church Council of (314 A.D.), 535-537

Armenia, 40, 158, 250, 257, 274, 276, 280, 318, 406, 455, 526, 542
  animal sacrifice in, liturgy of, 539

church united with Roman Catholic Church before 451 A.D., 548
  conversion of (early fourth century A.D.), 538-539, 548
  priesthood by inheritance in the church of, 539

Arses (King of Persia 338-336 B.C.), 195

Artaxerxes I (King of Persia 464-424 B.C.), 183, 185, 190

Artaxerxes II (King of Persia 404-358 B.C.), 190, 193, 194

Artaxerxes III (King of Persia 358-338 B.C.), 195

Artemision, Battle of (naval:, Persians vs. Greeks, in Aegean Sea, 480 B.C.), 180-181

Arthur, King (of the Britons), 27

Aruni (Hindu philosopher), 161-162

Aryans of India 31-33

Asa (King of Judah 913-873 B.C.), 103

Asclepiades, St. (martyr of Smyrna, 250 A.D.), 492

Asculum, Battle of (Epirus vs. Rome, in Italy, 279 B.C.), 213-214

Ashdod (Philistine city in Palestine), 85, 97, 124

Asherah (goddess of Phoenicia and Canaan), 114, 128

Ashoka (Asoka) (King of India c. 265-238 B.C.), 172

Ashur (city in Assyria), 27, 131

Ashur-dan I (King of Assyria c. 1160 B.C.), 107-108

Ashur-etillu-ili (Crown Prince of Assyria 627 B.C.), 128

Ashur-uballit II (King of Assyria 612-609 B.C.), 131-132

Ashurbanipal (King of Assyria 668-627 B.C.), 28, 128-129, 149

Ashurnasirpal II (King of Assyria 884-860 B.C.), 108

Asia, continent of, 24, 47, 49, 65, 165, 177, 201

Asia, Roman province of (in western Asia Minor), 256, 276, 461, 463
  Christianity in, 420, 455-456

Asia Minor, 70, 108, 113, 177, 178, 181, 194, 199, 206, 212, 214, 227, 230, 232, 233, 256, 272, 274, 276, 312, 404, 405-406, 412, 415, 424, 450, 453, 455, 462, 463-464, 467, 475, 495, 532, 538, 542
  Christianity in, 495, 505, 542, 548

Askelon (city in Palestine), 70, 134, 145

Aspasia (companion of Pericles), 187

Assassins, 369

Assumption SEE Mary the Blessed Virgin

Assyria, 27, 42, 107-113, 116, 123-132, 141-142, 255
  downfall prophesied by Isaiah, 120-121, 126, 142
  Iran, rule in, 167-168
  Judah vassal to, 123-124
  sent "lost ten tribes" of Israel into captivity (721 B.C.), 113, 117, 149-151

Astarte (goddess of Phoenicia and Canaan), 103-104, 114

Astyages (King of the Medes 585-550 B.C.), 149, 152

Aten (god of Akhenaten in Egypt), 49-50

Athaliah (Queen of Judah 842-837 B.C.), 109-110

Athens, 178, 181-183, 215, 231
  citizenship limitations of, 215-216
  executed Socrates (398 B.C.), 193-194
  in the Peloponnesian War (437-404 B.C.),

CHRONOLOGICAL TABLE OF MIDDLE EASTERN KINGS 922-721 B. C.

JUDAH	ISRAEL	DAMASCUS	ASSYRIA
Rehoboam 922-915	Jeroboam I 922-901	Rezon I 950-916	Ashur-dan II 934-912
Abijah 915-913		Tabrimmon 916-900	
Asa 915-913	Nadab 901-900		Adad-nirari II 911-891
	Baasha 900-877	Ben-Hadad I 900-880	Tukulti-ninurta II 890-884
	Elah 877-876	Ben-Hadad II 880-842	Ashurnasirpal II 883-859
	Zimri 876		
Jehoshaphat 873-849	Omri 876-869		
	Ahab 869-850		Shalmaneser III 858-824
	Ahaziah 850-849		
Jehoram 849-842	Jehoram 849-842*		
Ahaziah 842			
Queen Athaliah 842-837	Jehu 842-815	Hazael 842-810	
Joash 837-800	Jehoahaz 815-801		Shamshi-Adad V 823-811
		Ben-HadadIII 810-772	Adad-nirari III 810-773
Amaziah 800-783	Jehoash 801-786		
Uzziah 783-742	Jeroboam II 786-746	Tabeel 772-740	Shalmaneser IV 782-773
			Ashur-dan III 772-755
	Zechariah 746-745		Ashur-nirari V 754-745
	Shallum 745		
	Menahem 745-738		Tiglath-pilser III 744-727
Jotham 742-735	Pakahiah 738-737	Rezon II 740-732	
	Pekah 737-732	Assyrian conquest	
Ahaz 735-715	Hoshea 732-724		Shalmaneser V 726-722
	Assyrian conquest		Sargon II 721-705

*These were two different Jehorams.

SOURCES FOR THE TABLE: John Bright, *A History of Israel* (2nd ed., Philadelphia, 1972), Chronological Charts: A. Leo Oppenheim, *Ancient Mesopotamia* (Chicago, 1964), list of Mesopotamian kings.

CHRONOLOGICAL TABLE OF MIDDLE EASTERN KINGS 721-582 B.C.

JUDAH	ASSYRIA	BABYLONIA	EGYPT
Ahaz 735-715	Sargon II 722-705		(Nubia) Pinakhi 747-716
Hezekiah 715-686	Sennacherib 705-681		Shabako 716-702
			Shebitku 702-690
Manasseh 686-642	Esarhaddon 581-669		Taharka 590-664
Amon 642-640	Ashurbanipal 669-627		
			Tantamani 664-656
	(Sin-shar-ishkun 627-612	Nabopolassar 626-605	Necho 610-595
Jehoahaz 609	Ashur-uballit II 612-609		
Jehoiakim 609-598	Babylonia conquest609	Nebuchadnezzar 605-562	
1st deportation 597			
Zedekian 597-587			Psamtik II 595-589
2nd deportation 587			Hophra (Apries) 589-570
3rd deportation 582			

SOURCES FOR THE TABLE: John Bright, *A History of Israel (Philadelphia, 2nd ed., 1972), Chronological Charts; John Bright, The Anchor bible: Jeremiah* (New York, 1965), pp. xxxvi-xliii; A. Leo Oppenheim, *Ancient Mesopotamia* (Chicago, 1964), list of Mesopotamian kings; K. A. Kitchen, *The Third Intermediate Period in Egypt* (Warminster, England, 1973), pp. 399-404, 468.

COURSE FOR DISASTER

COURSE FOR DISASTER

From Scapa Flow to the River Kwai

by

RICHARD POOL

Leo Cooper

To Those Who Did Not Come Home

First published 1987 by Leo Cooper Ltd

Leo Cooper is an independent imprint of
the Heinemann Group of Publishers,
10 Upper Grosvenor Street, London WIX 9PA.

LONDON MELBOURNE JOHANNESBURG AUCKLAND

Copyright © Richard Pool 1987

ISBN 0-85052-6000

Filmset by Deltatype, Ellesmere Port
Printed by Mackays of Chatham Ltd
Chatham, Kent

Contents

Illustrations

No. 4 is reproduced by kind permission of the Imperial War Museum.

Maps

Introduction

This book has been written in response to the urgings and with encouragement from friends and others who have at some time heard me speak of the strange and unexpected experience that befell me in 1942. It was never intended that this should be another war book, but rather an account of an unusual event resulting from the war.

Together with forty-six officers and men, among which were the Rear Admiral Malaya, Rear Admiral E. J. Spooner, and the Air Officer Commanding Far East, Air Vice Marshal L. E. Pulford, I found myself marooned on a small tropical island midway between Singapore and Java. At first sight the island appeared to be a paradise, with its lagoons, palm-fringed beaches and luxuriant vegetation covering its rocky promontories almost to the point where they entered the sea. The reality was very different as we experienced its virulent swarms of mosquitoes and sandflies.

These were as nothing compared to the blanket of deep depression that settled with devastating effects on us all. It was something quite beyond our experience and expectation. It almost immediately led to a terrible debilitating lassitude as the hopelessness of our situation became apparent. One by one many simply lost the will to survive. Those of us who managed to hold out ultimately became Prisoners of War of the Japanese.

I have been advised by those versed in authorship of this kind that people who may read this account like to know what sort of a person you are and something of the events surrounding such an experience. This has led inevitably to a brief description of my early life and motivation; it thus includes some details of my wartime experiences.

It is an eye witness account of events and impressions by a junior officer at the time. The major incidents are indelibly printed on my mind and backed up by brief notes throughout the period covered by the book. On each occasion of loss, I rewrote them at the first opportunity. The last editions were secreted in the false bottom of my old Army pack when a Prisoner of War. Earlier notes up till the outbreak of war were taken from my journal kept officially by all midshipmen in the Navy.

I should like especially to thank my wife and family for their encouragement over the many years that I struggled with the manuscript. To Dr Sydney Hamilton for his many helpful suggestions and comments. Also to Jean Hunt and Pat Lawrence for deciphering my handwriting and typing the resultant manuscript. Lastly and perhaps most importantly to Marion Crinoch for her determination that the story should not be allowed to 'grow cobwebs any longer'.

CHAPTER 1

The Early Years

As far back as I can remember I was fascinated by water and anything that floated on it; first I made boats for myself, then model yachts, gradually moving up the scale to sailing and racing dinghies. I read everything I could find about real seagoing ships, especially warships.

My home at Felixstowe faced the sea, with the estuaries of the Rivers Orwell and Deben to the west and east, each with their typical Suffolk foreshores of marsh, dykes and oyster beds, so I had plenty of scope to practise and fulfil my interest. I found history an absorbing subject and was easily able to equate the two interests. Thus it seemed natural that I decided to enter the Navy. I had always been encouraged in this aim by my father, a general practitioner who had served as a Naval Surgeon during the First World War.

At thirteen and a half years of age, after a successful interview, I sat the written entry examination for Dartmouth. It was February, 1933, the recession was at its height, the competition was great, and I was not successful. This was a disappointing setback but my resolve remained as strong as ever and so it was decided that I should try to enter via the Nautical College, Pangbourne. This time I succeeded and entered Pangbourne in the autumn of the same year.

Life at Pangbourne was a continuous rush, or so it seemed. We ran, or in naval parlance 'doubled', everywhere, we were always changing from uniform to P.T. rig or games clothes of one kind or another. I was completely unused to the stiff collars of my uniform shirts and, by the time I had forced the stud through the stud hole and tied my tie, my collar was dirty and distorted.

I was terribly homesick and, although I never disliked Pangbourne, I longed for the holidays. When we did have any spare time, I often spent long periods just sitting on the hillside, the College being situated three hundred feet up on the Berkshire Downs, just gazing over the receding folds of the countryside to the east, imagining that beyond the most distant fold lay the marshes and estuaries of Suffolk.

The long summer holidays, when at last they came, were a constant delight, sailing and exploring the still unspoilt estuaries, guarded by their sand and shingle banks which were a challenging entry to the sea beyond, about which I spent so much time dreaming. The romance that I found in such books as Erskine Childers' classic of pre-World War One, *The Riddle of the Sands*, became almost real as I gazed out into the North Sea mists. The vision of those childhood summers with their memories of hot sun, of the distant boom of the Lightship, of the 'Belle' steamers arriving at the long pier, paddle wheels thrashing, of sailing and swimming, of trailing my dinghy over the Suffolk heathlands to crowded regatta days at Waldringfield and Aldeburgh – these were all to stand me in good stead in the years to come, providing me with a will to see them all again.

These breaks apart, I lived the normal life of a boy of my age. I loved games and usually managed to struggle into the lower realms of most teams at the College. I was not academic and found studies hard, except for history and geography, which came easily.

One highlight of my time at Pangbourne came in July, 1935, when the whole College went down to Portsmouth and spent a day at sea in the Reserve Fleet ships to witness the Review of the Fleet by King George V on his Jubilee. My party was accommodated in what was then the Reserve Fleet Flagship, the cruiser *Effingham*. It was a perfect day and we were, as Cadets, enthralled by the spectacle of the assembled ships from the various Fleets then maintained by Britain at home and overseas. Each ship was 'dressed overall', with the many-coloured signal flags whipping and cracking in the stiff Spithead breeze and sunshine. It was a romantic view of the Navy but it strengthened my determination to succeed in my ambition.

At last, after three and a half years, in the summer of 1937 I once again sat an Admiralty Interview and written examination. Several weeks later, while I was on holiday, an OHMS envelope arrived to say that I had been successful. This was followed soon after by my first appointment 'By Command of the Commissioners for Executing the Office of Lord High Admiral of the United Kingdom to Mr R. A. W. Pool Cadet R.N.' directing me to repair on board His Majesty's Ship *Erebus* at Portsmouth on 1 September.

CHAPTER 2

Peace to War

My joining instructions to the *Erebus* directed me to arrive at Portsmouth and Southsea station by a certain train from Waterloo, the first of many such journeys. At Waterloo I found that I was one of about seventy other cadets. On arrival at Portsmouth and Southsea station we left the train and were collected up by a number of very vociferous Petty Officers who soon had us embarked in Naval buses for the next stage of our journey. This was to the pierhead at Whale Island, the home of the Navy's premier Gunnery School, HMS *Excellent*. A short passage by harbour launch and we boarded the *Erebus*, which turned out to be a converted First World War Monitor[1] used by the Gunnery School as a turret training ship.[2] She had also been partially converted for the accommodation of the Naval Special Entry Cadets, being Cadets other than those of the Dartmouth entry.

During the next few days we quickly became acclimatized to our surroundings and new way of life. The first thing we became aware of was the constant noises of the ship, the continuous humming of fans and thumping of pumps, also, the sense of confinement in the small living spaces, the unusual mode of sleeping in hammocks, which had to be 'lashed up and stowed' correctly in hammock nettings. The daily routine was ordered by bugles and 'pipes' – the latter being a boatswain's call – and what at first seemed almost a new language, naval terminology, or 'navalese'. We learnt that we were to undergo three months' basic training in all aspects of our career before ultimately joining the training cruiser for sea training.

[1]Monitors were shallow-draught ships equipped with heavy guns, for bombarding land positions close inshore.
[2]*Erebus* had one 15-inch gun-turret as its main armament.

Our training was the special responsibility of a Bligh-like figure, Lieutenant R. F. Jessel, a strict, but absolutely fair, disciplinarian; he was assisted by a small staff of Officers and Petty Officers. We had very little time to ourselves and life was full and very interesting. The mornings or forenoons were mostly taken up with technical subjects and drills. In the afternoons we played games, which took place on the Whale Island playing fields and were followed later, back on board *Erebus*, by a talk on some general naval subject. Saturday and Sunday afternoons, unless you were in a team, were your own.

The highlight of the week was 'Friday Divisions', held in the great drill shed in which the whole of the Gunnery School assembled. The *Erebus* Cadets took their turn in forming the 'Guard', which meant performing a set drill before the entire company present – most of the Navy it seemed to us. It was particularly awe-inspiring when it was one's duty to be the Guard Commander.

In these first months we got used to being shouted at by our Petty Officer Instructors, particularly the Gunner's Mate Drill Instructors, and many 'gems' would flow from their lips to be repeated for weeks after. One such was when a party of Cadets were being instructed in the drill for a Funeral Firing Party. At the appropriate moment in the drill the Gunner's Mate shouted hoarsely at the ranks of Cadets before him, 'And now what next? One pace forward?' 'Yes,' replied one innocent. 'No you bloody don't, as if you did you'd be down the bloody 'ole wouldn't you?'

Our basic training passed quickly and it proved to be an interesting and stimulating time. The international situation was deteriorating and the Navy was beginning to expand as Britain's long-delayed rearmament gained momentum. Every week a new cruiser or destroyer arrived in Portsmouth before departing to join the Fleet. Their capability, speed and armament were all eagerly discussed. In the dockyard itself, work on refits and modernization went on with increased urgency and I remember, as I passed the dry dock, looking down on the completely gutted hull of the battlecruiser *Renown* which was practically being rebuilt.

In January, 1938, after a short Christmas leave, we all moved on to the next stage of our training. This was to the *Vindictive*, an old cruiser[1] specially converted to accommodate Cadets for training, then in Chatham dockyard. Here we were to 'work ship' as part of the ship's company, as well as to continue our instruction in purely theoretical subjects. We joined a new term of Dartmouth Cadets as

[1] *Vindictive* was completed as a seaplane carrier in 1918, but converted to a cruiser in 1923.

4

well as a senior term of Special Entry. The *Vindictive*, in which we were to undertake two three-month cruises, would first take us to the West Indies. The Captain was E. J. Spooner, DSO. We seldom had any contact with him, except when he inspected us at Divisions or if one was appointed his 'doggie'.[1]

One of my first memories of the *Vindictive* was cleaning her up after leaving the dockyard. A number of us were washing the paintwork of the quarterdeck crane support in a bitterly cold wind in that bleakest of English anchorages, Sheerness, known to the Navy as 'Sheernasty'. Every time we reached up to wash above our heads the cold, dirty, soapy water ran down our arms and up our sleeves. The following day we sailed for the West Indies and within twenty-four hours had run into a very severe gale which persisted for several days. We were all terribly seasick and spent most of our time huddled behind what shelter we could find on the upper deck. It was during this gale that most of us had our first experience of the majesty, beauty and power of the sea. The colours of the huge waves, as the sun shone through their breaking crests, were breath-taking. Salt spray curled inboard, soaking us, while the mastheads drew great arcs across the sky as the ship rolled and pitched her way westward.

After sixteen days we anchored in the Virgin Isles. There is always a special thrill in arriving in a new anchorage and we all felt it for the first time as the steep, scrub-covered volcanic slopes came into view. In those days the islands were virtually deserted and it was an ideal place to clean up the ship and shake down. As an exercise in self-sufficiency and initiative, half the Cadets left the ship at a time in the ship's boats to live wherever and however they could for several days. The only rule was that we were not allowed back to the ship except in an emergency.

Onboard we settled down quickly to a busy routine of working ship and instruction, both practical and theoretical, in all the technical subjects of our career. Each evening we had a full programme of competition sport and games, one of the most strenuous being deck hockey. This was played with curved sticks between two teams of up to six players, the object being to hit a circular ring of rope through the opposite goal.

The standard of our calls was set by our first, to San Juan, the capital of Puerto Rico. I well remember the scene as we steamed into harbour, the whole ship's company 'fallen in', in white tropical

---

[1] The term 'doggie' was used to describe the Cadet who at all times followed the Captain or any other designated officer, both to act as a messenger and to see at first hand what the officer's duties were.

uniform, our marine band playing on the quarter deck, our saluting guns firing a national salute of twenty-one guns, the answering salute from the old Spanish fort and a squadron of United States Marine Corps aircraft flying overhead.

This was followed by the paying and returning of official calls by our Captain and the Puerto Rican authorities. There were many entertainments ashore and return parties on board. During such visits our routine went on as usual, although those of us not on duty partook to the full of the entertainment offered, as part of our education as future Naval Officers. We called at several more of the beautiful West Indian Islands. It was fascinating to visit English Harbour in Antigua, and to see the relics and remains, many still standing, of Nelson's presence there. We passed and saluted Diamond Rock, off Martinique, once commissioned as a British man-of-war during the Napoleonic wars.

Our last port of call on our homeward passage was to Funchal in Madeira. Here we bought lace tablecloths, ate delicious profiteroles at Reid's Hotel and made the journey to the tiny mountain-top chapel to see the body of the last Emperor of Austria-Hungary lying in its glass coffin. It was an eerie experience as the wind soughed amid the thin maritime pines. The return down the steep mountain track was by wooden sled, sliding at breakneck pace over the cobbled surface and only restrained by ropes in the hands of two of the locals.

Our second cruise was to the Baltic, where we should have visited Finland, Sweden, Estonia and Denmark, but sadly the ship's company was hit by an epidemic of measles and the programme had to be altered. So, after visiting ports on the south coast of England, we went north to Rosyth and Invergordon before setting out for the Baltic. Our first port of call was the Finnish capital, Helsinki. It was fascinating, steaming through the Kattegat past Hamlet's castle of Elsinore, then north through the calm but deep brown waters of the Baltic. As we steamed north, the already short summer night turned into daylight for most of the twenty-four hours. Helsinki was a delightful city in every respect and, for those of us who sailed, the Yacht Club showed us great hospitality. Then it was on to Sandhamm, in Sweden.

Regretfully, we sailed back to Chatham, where an inspection, and the awarding of prizes by the Chief of the General Staff, Field-Marshal Viscount Gort, VC, brought the cruise and our Cadet's time to a close. Within a few weeks we had all been appointed Midshipmen to various battleships and cruisers in the Fleet.

6

I joined the Home Fleet Battleship *Royal Sovereign*[1], then lying at Sheerness, with four of my contemporaries. The ship was preparing for the autumn cruise and exercise period. We 'Snotties', as we now got used to being known, though still under instruction, were allocated specific duties, such as taking charge of the ship's boats, watchkeeping at sea and in harbour, as assistants to the Officer of the Watch, as well as many other duties in the administration of the ship. The Captain was J. W. S. Dorling, whose brother was the well known author 'Taffrail'. I soon discovered that he was a very keen dinghy sailor.

A few days after storing and oiling we left Sheerness to join up with other Home Fleet ships at Invergordon. The next few weeks were busy times with a full programme of gunnery and other exercises, carried out at sea and in harbour. I was given the duty of Second Officer of Quarters of the new 4-inch twin high-angle guns. We exercised continually, in particular firing at sleeve targets towed by aircraft, and at a 'Queen Bee' wireless-controlled aircraft.

In harbour we were just as busy. I was made Midshipman of the launch, a heavy forty-five foot open boat used for carrying stores and liberty men from ship to shore. I found it quite an ordeal at first, going in late at night, in the strong tide, to jockey for position at the pier, in order to collect up to one hundred sailors, most of whom were very full of beer!

During all this time of internal preparation, the international situation had continued to deteriorate. The second of Mr Chamberlain's visits to Hitler took place at Godesberg on 22 September, 1938. It became known that the talks had broken down by the evening of the next day and the Prime Minister returned to London on the 24th. On the forenoon of that day the Fleet sailed for its war station at Scapa Flow.

It was grey and blustery with the wind whipping up white horses on the Cromarty Firth. The first to leave Invergordon were the ships of the 1st Minesweeping Flotilla, followed closely by the destroyers of 5th and 6th Flotillas, each ship as it passed, piping 'The Still', and being answered by the big ship's bugle calls, their signal flags standing out bright and clear in the fresh breeze as they swept by us. Then came the 2nd Cruiser Squadron, led by the new cruiser *Southampton*, her rakish lines seeming to be a personification of the new ships joining the Fleet every day. Now bugle answered bugle and the Royal Marine bands played on the quarterdecks. Next came the

[1]An 'R' class battleship of 29,000 tons displacement with a main armament of 15-inch guns.

aircraft carrier *Courageous*, with her band playing 'Roll Along Covered Wagon, Roll Along'. Then, last of all, the battleships led by the Fleet Flagship *Nelson*. Our sister ship, *Revenge*, steamed slowly past us with her band playing alternately 'John Brown's body lies a mould'ring in the grave', and 'If you were the only girl in the world'. It was a moving and stirring sight, and we all felt proud to be part of it.

As soon as we left harbour, all hands turned to, to bring up and fuse ready-use ammunition; this went on until all the lockers were filled and firing circuits had been tested. The Home Fleet steered north through thickening mist and rain squalls. Exciting though it was, it seemed unbelievable that we were actually heading for Scapa Flow and war with Germany, just twenty years since the last war. That evening we steamed into the Flow and anchored.

The next two weeks were spent exercising inside the Flow and at sea. Other units gradually joined us as mobilization took effect. Scapa Flow was a magnificent anchorage of 300 square miles of water surrounded by low heather-clad hills. The Munich Crisis, as it was known, finally passed, when Czechoslovakia was sacrificed. There was great dissatisfaction at this outcome of the negotiations.

At the end of the first week of October, *Royal Sovereign*, with most other ships, returned to Invergordon and continued exercises. It was during one of these, in a night attack by destroyers, that our ship was struck by a practice torpedo which damaged one of the propellers. We were ordered to go to Devonport for repairs. We remained there for the whole of November when, our damage repaired, we left for sea trials. It was while carrying out one of these that we received orders to shadow one of the German pocket battleships returning to Germany up the Channel. We swung on to a shadowing course and worked up to full speed. It was very misty, with high seas; at one time we burst out of the mist into a patch of sunshine and found ourselves very close to a small British tramp steamer, which must have received quite a shock. We continued on our course for several hours before we gave up, having seen nothing of the Germans. We then went on to Sheerness to give Christmas leave.

We sailed again in early January, 1939, for the Fleet's spring cruise to the Mediterranean. Despite very rough seas and bad weather, we exercised continually with other ships. It was a busy round of action stations, drills and strategic and tactical exercises, which continued until our arrival at Gibraltar. At the Rock we carried out a full programme of firings with every part of the armament. Life became even more hectic when Rear Admiral Holland hoisted his flag as Rear Admiral Second Battle Squadron in the ship and we painted overall in preparation for a visit to Golfe Juan in the south of France.

The international situation seemed to be getting worse, and the Spanish Civil War still raged, though it did appear that the Nationalist Forces of General Franco were at last winning. There was always something of interest with a number of foreign warships calling at Gibraltar and the Spanish Government destroyer *Jose Luis Diez* interned there. We also saw the Nationalist cruiser *Canarias* in Algeçiras Bay on several occasions and a French Cruiser Squadron paid a courtesy visit. All the British ships were ordered to be at anti-aircraft readiness when within range of the Spanish coast, and there continued to be an atmosphere of uncertainty. In early February the ship paid a call to Golfe Juan which was very much a social event, with dances and tennis and cocktail parties.

Another lesson was in store for me. One night, with several other officers, I was invited to a big charity ball at the Casino in Cannes, in aid of the Sunnybank Hospital for the Blind. My host was a retired Captain R.N. then living at Cannes. We were all slightly late, due to a delayed boat, and when we arrived my host was waiting to hurry me off to his table where about a dozen people were already seated. Just before reaching the table, he turned to me and said, 'Now, there is only one thing you must remember to do, and that is to bow to the Archduchess Sophie of Austria'. He either omitted to tell me which she was, or more likely, I did not take it in. Anyway, I rather panicked and went straight to the lady I thought looked most imposing, and made my bow. 'Good God child!' she exclaimed. 'Don't bow to me, I am Mrs Marks.[1] There's Sophie over there!'

In another incident I did rather better. An American couple had been dancing several of the popular dances of the day and were concluding with 'The Big Apple'. As they finished, my host turned to me and said, 'Go on young man, ask that pretty girl for a dance'. I was petrified, but he would not take no for an answer and told me that the Navy was not what it was in his young day! 'Come on,' he said, 'I will introduce you.' Off we went, and I duly had my dance. We all ended up in a Night Club later, where, after several more dances, I had quite lost my heart to my redheaded American!

Once back at Gibraltar, the Mediterranean Fleet joined us for the high point of the Spring Cruise, manoeuvres by the Combined Fleets. Over the next two weeks many stirring battles were fought between Red and Blue Fleets. It was a magnificent sight to look down

[1] Of Marks and Spencer

on the harbour from a vantage point on the Rock and see it filled to capacity with warships in the light grey of the Mediterranean Fleet, and the dark grey of the Home Fleet, the entire strength of Britain's two premier Fleets.

The exercises concluded, both Fleets went their separate ways at the end of March, the Mediterranean Fleet to Malta and the Home Fleet back to England for Easter leave. The Italian dictator Mussolini had invaded Albania at this time and orders were given for the anti-aircraft guns of the Fleet to be manned the whole time we remained at Sheerness.

As spring turned to summer, we found ourselves at Portland with other ships, busy working up once again with intensive weapon training and exercises. In May *Royal Sovereign* paid an official call to Brest, the base of the French Atlantic Fleet. There was a great feeling of *Entente Cordiale*. What a good thing we did not know what was going to happen almost a year to the day later![1] From Brest we went to Llandudno in North Wales, and were in the middle of what was proving to be a very happy visit, when suddenly orders were received to return to Sheerness and give early summer leave.

This unexpected news was the cause of much speculation and was ascribed to the dangerous international situation. In the Far East the Japanese were blockading our Concession in Tientsin and putting great pressure on the Government, while in Europe the question of Danzig and the Polish Corridor filled the news. Perhaps the final straw was the German announcement of an Army test mobilization in August.

Our passage back to Sheerness was fully occupied with exercises and action drills. The day we arrived back the Foreign Minister made a strong speech warning Germany that, should she try to annex Danzig, she would find herself at war with Britain. All through the leave period, while one half of the Ship's company was on leave, the drills, particularly the AA ones, were continued by the other half.

It was to prove my last peaceful leave. On my return I found myself, with my contemporaries, appointed to the battleship *Revenge*, with orders to join her at Portsmouth forthwith.

The *Revenge*, a sister ship to *Royal Sovereign*, was commanded by Captain E. R. Archer, a caricature of the bluff sea-dog, but a perfectly charming man. *Revenge* had just been re-commissioned after a refit and was in the throes of storing and ammunitioning, so,

---

[1]Immediately after the fall of France, the Royal Navy was forced to attack and immobilize ships of the French Fleet, wherever they were lying. Many French lives were lost and feelings were bitter.

10

from the moment of our arrival, there was an immense amount of work to be done. Our programme was to work up at Portland and then join the Home Fleet.

The Reserve Fleet was to be mobilized with Naval Reserves called up, as an exercise. All these ships were to assemble in Weymouth Bay for a Review by the King. For a short preliminary period during this period I was attached to one of the big ship's drifters. At that time each capital ship and cruiser had a steam drifter attached to it for general purposes. I was appointed to the *Shower*, which was attached to the *Newcastle*, one of the new Town-Class cruisers, in the Second Cruiser Squadron, and was being 'lent' to the Reserve Fleet. Our duty was to convey stores and libertymen between Weymouth and the various Reserve Fleet cruisers. We were worked very hard, at all hours of the day and night, but were well taken care of by our parent ships. A holiday spirit prevailed and all the reservists were obviously having a marvellous time back in the Navy, as they then thought for a fortnight. Returning them to their various ships, late at night, after a 'run ashore' was no picnic for us. Full of beer and good spirits, they very often did not bother with the pier, but just waded into the sea, waist-deep from the beach, and then would try to clamber aboard. A lot of the officers had left the Navy at the time of the 'Geddes Axe' of 1922, and many of their uniforms reflected the cut of nearly two decades earlier.

On 9 August, a grey, drizzly day, the King reviewed the Reserve Fleet and his passage through the lines of ships was the signal for all the Naval ceremonial that such occasions demanded. History was repeating itself, for just over twenty-five years earlier, in the troubled European situation of July, 1914, the King's father, George V, had reviewed his Fleet, which included the mobilized Reserve Fleet. It was not to be demobilized for a further four and a half years. The following day the Reserve Fleet ships, including fourteen cruisers and nearly sixty destroyers, sailed out of Weymouth Bay for exercises. *Revenge*'s work-up continued at even greater intensity and we were joined by another sister ship – the *Resolution*.

We learnt that we were now to become part of a new Channel Fleet based at Portland, and so the last two weeks of August, 1939, and peace, slipped away. On 1 September the Germans invaded Poland and the British ultimatum to Hitler was sent. The die was cast and the Prime Minister's momentous broadcast to the nation at 11 a.m. on 3 September came as no surprise. Within the hour air raid warning Red was signalled and we closed up at first degree of anti-aircraft readiness, but it proved to be a false alarm. I remember the brand-

11

new destroyer *Kelly*, commanded by Lord Louis Mountbatten, entering harbour and her company immediately setting to work to paint over her Mediterranean light grey with dark war grey.

There was much speculation among us as to what would happen and where we might go, and also a general feeling among us Midshipmen of how lucky we were to be in at the start, but, as we very soon found out, we had little idea of what war really meant.

CHAPTER 3

War – The First Year

At first it seemed that nothing had changed. We exercised daily at sea off Portland with an escort of MASBs,[1] carrying out gunnery control exercises and other drills. The weather was perfect, and it was in the evening of one such perfect day, while returning to harbour, that I saw, sailing up from the west, four or five of the Twelve-Metre racing yachts which annually raced at the big regattas round our coasts. Their programme always ended in the West Country and their last regattas had been cancelled on the declaration of war. Now they were returning to their home berths to be laid up for the duration of the war. It was the end of an era, for they were never to grace our coasts again as a class. They presented a beautiful but sad sight as they beat slowly into the light breeze past the Dorset cliffs and into the pale blue-mauve haze to eastward.

It was incidents such as this that brought home to us the fact that we were now at war. As the September days passed, there were other reminders, such as the shorter leaves ashore, but now in uniform and not plain clothes. The frequent comings and goings of the destroyers and smaller patrol craft, all of which were beginning to show the unmistakable signs of sea-time – rust streaks and funnels white with encrusted salt spray. Weymouth Bay, now a contraband control anchorage, was gradually filling up with merchant ships waiting for clearance.

Always the war news reminded us that elsewhere the war was intensifying: the early loss of the liner *Athenia* and the aircraft carrier *Courageous*, both torpedoed by U-boats, the crushing of the last resistance in Poland and the reports of British and German air raids.

One day in early October, amid great security, a special train

[1] Motor Anti- Submarine Boats.

arrived in Portland dockyard. We learned that it contained bullion which was to be trans-shipped to *Revenge* and *Resolution*. It was only later that we learned that it was to pay for the first big arms procurement programme in the United States. The immensely heavy gold ingots were rather precariously transferred, in half a gale, from the train to our rolling and pitching boats lying alongside the small stone jetty. After a short journey to our ship, they were manhandled into the bomb room, where they were to be stowed for the sea passage.

The Squadron sailed the next day with an escort of dazzle-painted destroyers down-Channel and out into the Western Approaches. We were later told that our destination was Halifax, Nova Scotia. As we cleared the coast, we strained our eyes for periscopes and other signs of the enemy, but nothing was sighted. When well out in the Atlantic we were joined by the 11th Cruiser Squadron, consisting of the elderly cruisers *Enterprise*, *Emerald* and *Caradoc*, all from the recently mobilized Reserve Fleet.

Our passage across the Atlantic proved uneventful and, as we finally approached the Nova Scotia coast in the clear cold light of an October morning, we were met by Canadian destroyers. As always, there was that exciting feeling when entering a new and, to most of us, strange harbour, with the flat pine-clothed coastline, the brilliant red lightship and, just discernible in the haze ahead, Halifax itself. At slow speed we steamed up the long approach channel to berth alongside and secure at the main pier where the bullion was quickly unloaded under the watchful eyes of the Royal Canadian Mounted Police. Rear Admiral Bonham-Carter, who had commanded the Squadron, left us to become Admiral-in-Charge, Halifax, and we were left wondering what was in store for us next.

While we waited, Halifax gave us a wonderfully hospitable welcome. There were numerous parties, dances and invitations to people's homes, and many of us were to make lasting friendships. Halifax was a convoy assembly port and merchant ships were to be seen daily passing up the harbour to their anchorage in Bedford Basin. One by one the ships of our Squadron left on various duties. Our turn was soon to come and we found ourselves once more at sea, acting as Ocean Escort to a succession of eastbound convoys. As the winter advanced, the weather conditions grew steadily worse. As a convoy's Ocean Escort our task was to escort the convoys through the area in which it was thought most likely that an attack by German surface raiders would take place. We, of course, longed for just such an encounter, but on each occasion that such an attack did take place we were many hundreds of miles away.

14

This convoy duty was very monotonous, steaming slowly eastwards, zigzagging against submarine attack and watching over the slow grey columns of heavily laden merchant ships as they ploughed towards England, pitching and rolling in the Atlantic seas. As soon as the position was reached in mid-Atlantic where an attack was considered to be unlikely, we would turn westwards and increase speed, heading back to Halifax.

Just after Christmas, while escorting a convoy, instead of turning back we were ordered to proceed to Plymouth. There the dockyard fitted us with the latest protection against magnetic mines. This took the form of an electrical circuit which was wound right round the ship, and when a current was switched on, it had the effect of reversing and neutralizing the ship's magnetic field; this was known as 'De-Gaussing'. There was just time for a few days' leave before we sailed again for Halifax, arriving there to find that the Canadian winter had taken over and everything lay under thick snow. At sea intense cold was now added to the normal hardships of an Atlantic winter. Spray froze everywhere it touched the ship, and steam had frequently to be used to clear our upperworks and particularly to free the anchors and cables before returning to harbour. Special articles of Canadian cold weather clothing were issued, among which was a pair of enormous fleece-lined combinations. Many of the sailors always wore these outside their normal clothing, a most incongruous sight with the large rear flaps inserted for bodily needs marked 'X Door, No Clips'.[1]

It was difficult to know how to dress, particularly at night. We would start off by wearing all we had, for we slept at our action stations, my own being aloft in the 6-inch Control Top. As the ship passed from the cold Labrador Current into the Gulf Stream, or if the wind came aft and brought the hot and suffocating funnel gases into our cramped positions, the increase in temperature woke us up in a bath of sweaty discomfort.

All through these first months of war instruction to fit us Midshipmen for our forthcoming examination for the rank of Lieutenant in Seamanship and Navigation had continued, in addition to our ship's duties. I well remember the practical part of our Seamanship exam. The six of us senior Midshipmen were given the task of stepping and fitting a main top and topgallant mast.[2] The old

[1] Watertight doors in British warships were labelled X, Y, or Z, according to their importance.
[2] Because of the size and height of ship's masts they were constructed in sections, in *Revenge*'s case lower top and topgallant, each some sixty-eight feet in length.

15

mast, which had been the highest in the Navy, at two hundred and five feet, had been carried away in a severe gale in January. A new, but less massive, spar of Oregon pine had been ordered as a replacement and was waiting on the jetty for us on our return from a convoy escort. Under the direction of the Warrant Boatswain, we stepped and secured the new spar as a replacement, a task that took us all day to accomplish.

In March we Senior Midshipmen left the *Revenge* and awaited the arrival of the battleship *Malaya*, where we were duly examined by a full Seamanship Board, constituted by the Captain and Officers; afterwards we sailed for England in her. Among her Midshipmen was John Groom who had been at Pangbourne with me. A short leave followed and with it promotion to Acting Sub-Lieutenant and appointment to *Excellent*, the Gunnery School on Whale Island at Portsmouth. It was fun to meet once more all my contemporaries and hear of their experiences, for all of us were to be accommodated here while doing technical courses for the rank of Lieutenant.

The 'phoney war' in Europe had at last become a hot war, though this expression had never applied to the war at sea. The German invasion of Norway had been followed on 10 May by the Blitzkrieg in the Low Countries and France. As this attack grew in scale and ferocity and the Allied Armies fell back before it, we found it increasingly frustrating to be 'out of it', as we then thought.

Our turn was soon to come and, towards the end of May, groups of us found ourselves suddenly snatched from our respective courses and detailed to report immediately to ports on the south-east coast. In my own case I had just completed the short trip by harbour launch from Whale Island pier to *Vernon*, the Torpedo School. As we climbed the steps the pier master told my group to report back to *Excellent* at once. I was ordered to report to the Commodore Sheerness and, within the hour, with no more than a tooth-brush and my railway warrant, I caught the next train to London. At London Bridge station I became aware of the large numbers of tired and begrimed soldiers sitting on their packs or asleep on the platforms, and discovered that they had just been evacuated from France.

On arrival at Chatham we were told that there was a big operation taking place in which the BEF was having to be evacuated directly from the beaches at Dunkirk. We were told that our task was to man the many small craft now collecting at Sheerness and take them over to Dunkirk to assist in the evacuation of the larger part of our Army in France.

The train from Chatham puffed and clanked its way through the

16

countryside, over the heavily guarded bridge across the River Swale, and arrived at Sheerness in the late afternoon. With another Sub-Lieutenant, J. D. F. Kealey, I reported to Commodore H. A. Taylor, OBE, a retired Rear Admiral who had been recalled to service, at his operations room in the old Admiralty House close to Garrison Point Fort, HMS *Wildfire*.[1] I could see from the windows that the dockyard basin was filled with a multitude of small craft of every description, requisitioned for this special task. The Staff Officer Operations, Lieutenant-Commander D. E. Holland-Martin, whom I had last seen when playing rugger against him as an *Erebus* Cadet, when he was a divisional Officer in *St Vincent*, the Boy Seaman's training establishment at Gosport, gave me my orders which were to take command of a group of Thames river steamers and take them to Ramsgate, leaving at dusk that evening.

I at once set off to find the Chart Depot to obtain a chart, parallel rulers and dividers. At the Chart Depot the clerk in charge refused to issue me with anything because I did not have the appropriate forms! I told him that my river steamers were not warships and I had no access to such forms. He was adamant. I could get nowhere and returned hurriedly to the operations room to report my lack of success. Commodore Taylor was absolutely furious and at once returned with me to the Chart Depot. He stormed in and told the clerk to whom I had spoken what I needed the charts for. The clerk replied that he knew his duty, or words to that effect, and that I was not entitled to them. The Commodore at once picked up a pair of heavy ebony parallel rulers and made as if to strike the unfortunate clerk, at the same time telling me to take what I wanted and set out for Ramsgate immediately. There was no further resistance!

I found my way to the basin steps alongside which the group of river steamers lay, ascertained that all was ready, took the wheel and ordered the crew to cast off, shouting to the other three steamers to follow. I carefully manoeuvred my way out of the basin into the Medway. The crew consisted of a recently mobilized Petty Officer Reservist from Lowestoft, an old pensioner Leading Stoker, in charge of the engine and boiler, and two very young 'hostilities only' Ordinary Seaman, just out of basic training.

It was a beautiful late May evening as my little flotilla made its way out past Garrison Point Fort and I felt very proud of my command straggling out astern. Suddenly, as we were passing the first of the channel buoys, the old Stoker pushed his head out of the engine-room hatch and shouted unceremoniously to me, 'We shall have to

[1] The establishment name given to Naval Command at Sheerness.

17

draw the bloody fires, Sir!' He was so obviously in great earnest that I immediately told him to do so. With our remaining steam I immediately headed for one of the buoys and secured to it. I asked the reason for having to draw fires. Of course, it was simple. The steamers, which normally plied between Maidenhead and Henley, had been designed to run on the fresh water of the Thames, whereas now the boiler tubes were furring up with salt water. In the great urgency of the crisis, no one had taken this into consideration!

A quick look round showed all the remainder in the same straits. What next? No other vessel was in sight. We had no means of signalling in the now quickly fading light. At *Wildfire* there had been reports of German E-boats marauding up the estuary during the night, a frightening prospect. However, just as darkness was closing in, a Balloon Barrage drifter hove in sight, steering up the Channel towards us. As soon as she was close enough we hailed her, with the result that she took us all in tow and we returned ignominiously to the Dockyard Basin. There was nothing more to be done and, after reporting back to the Commodore, I went off to the Wardroom for a drink and something to eat.

Early the next morning I was ordered to take a large modern motor cruiser named *Marsaryu* round to Ramsgate and set out to go, but had hardly got clear of the basin when she failed to answer the helm. With great difficulty we managed to get back into the basin to find the rudder had dropped off! An hour later I finally got away in an old water lighter, *X217*. These lighters from the Pool of London had been specially built for the Dardanelles campaign in 1915. With three similar craft following, I crept along the North Kent coast and out into the Channel. My orders this time were to go straight to Dunkirk. I soon discovered that our compass was very unreliable, but managed visually to get clear of the coast. So, on sighting a Light Vessel, I closed it and discovered that it was the North Foreland. I went close alongside and asked the skipper the way to Dunkirk. He was amused but told me to 'keep straight on and take the first on the left!' It was not long after this that a dense cloud of smoke appeared on the horizon ahead, towards which I steered, assuming that this must be Dunkirk. Soon we were being passed by destroyers returning at full speed to England, their upper decks crowded with troops. They were a brave sight as they swept past us, with enormous bow waves, sterns down and almost hidden by their wakes, guns pointing skyward, some grey, others in startling camouflage paint. The wakes as they reached us caused us to roll violently and our wheelhouse, loaded with heavy sandbags, creaked and groaned like an empty matchbox squeezed between thumb and finger!

I could now see a lot of shipping of every kind either entering the channel or leaving it, the latter crowded with troops. A large dredger that I had last seen at Portsmouth passed us, its buckets clanking metallically in the seaway. From its bridge waved Kenneth Martin, another of my contemporaries.

The scene that now unfolded as we turned into the channel left one in no doubt that we were taking part in a war. Dense clouds of thick black smoke billowed across the town and port, casting dark shadows on the pale sands that stretched away north-eastwards towards La Panne. The beaches were crowded with thousands of troops waiting in groups and columns as far as the eye could see, stretching down into the sea, some up to their armpits. There were lorries and transport vehicles of all sorts driven into the sea to form piers behind the beaches. At this distance the hotels and houses bordering the beach looked undamaged, but here and there plumes of smoke told another story. What a different scene from that of only twelve months ago! The tideline was littered with the wreckage of small boats, naval cutters and whalers, lifeboats from merchant and civilian craft. Lying off the beach, and moving up and down the roads, were ships of every description; destroyers, sloops, minesweepers, trawlers, tugs, cross-channel steamers, paddle-steamers that had been such a familiar sight around our coasts in summer, with their cargoes of day-trippers. With the larger ships, there appeared every variety of smaller craft from lifeboats to lighters. Lastly, I could see numerous open boats being towed in and out from the waiting ships to the beach and back.

Overhead at that moment I briefly noticed two of our fighters engaging a large number of Messerschmitts, which ended with one of our fighters being shot down, a single parachute descending, but not opening properly.

I had originally been told that I would receive instructions on arrival; clearly there were to be none. I wondered where I would be the most use, and decided on a part of the beach to the north of the harbour entrance which looked least congested. At slow speed I approached the shallow water and, knowing the tide to be falling, we laid out an anchor as a kedge so that we might haul ourselves off should we get stuck on the beach.

The nearest group of soldiers turned out to be French and at first I had great difficulty in persuading them to wade out to us, as we had grounded some twenty-five yards out from the water's edge. The two 'hostilities only' Ordinary Seamen were rather overcome by the situation and were not a great help. Finally my Leading Seaman jumped over the side and, taking a rope towards them, he managed to encourage the bolder spirits to wade out to the two long ladders we had lashed to either side of the bow to enable anyone to climb on board more easily.

While this was happening an air attack developed. A considerable number of Stukas dive-bombed the shipping in the roads and a large formation of Heinkel bombers flew along the line of the beach bombing it and the adjoining edge of the sea. There was a tremendous noise of explosions from the bombs and the anti-aircraft guns defending the port. In the roads destroyers and other warships twisted and turned amid the splashes with all their guns firing in their efforts to defend themselves from the dive-bombers. It was my baptism of fire and it was both very frightening and intensely exhilarating at the same time. The wash from the destroyers made it hard to maintain our position and many of the troops wading out were knocked off their feet. During the short lulls between the air attacks and the tremendous noise they brought about, I could distinctly hear the gunfire of the land battle. It was slow work getting the troops aboard, weighed down as they were with their greatcoats and packs, utterly exhausted and with many wounded. As they were Senegalese troops of the Soixante-Deuxième regiment, we had a difficult language problem.

The air attacks were frequent, with up to thirty aircraft bombing both shipping and the troops on the beach, and, if they were Stukas, machine-gunning as well.

In the midst of this embarkation I was hailed by yet another of my course mates, Walter Timbrell, a Canadian. He was skippering a motor yacht lying not far from us but had gone in too close and was hard aground. As he was almost full up we temporarily broke off our operation to tow him off, which we achieved with some difficulty, transferring those troops that had boarded us in the process. I then returned to our original patiently-waiting column for more. I realized that we could have approached much nearer if we had not been carrying hundreds of gallons of water for the troops on the beaches, unrequired as it turned out.

While loading up once again, I spoke to a British Army Officer who told me that the beaches were not a very healthy place to be during the night, as the Germans usually shelled them. It was my intention, when loaded to capacity, to get out and transfer my troops to a larger vessel in the roads. So, when I judged that I could pack no more troops on board, I gave the order to go astern into deep water. This proved more difficult than I had thought as a maze of floating ropes and warps forced me to stop the engines frequently to avoid fouling my large single propeller. It was while doing this that I had an altercation with a Commander in a naval whaler, who appeared to be drawing yet another hawser across my stern.

Once away from the beach I steamed slowly up the roads to the north, looking for a larger ship to which I could transfer my troops. Though I hailed several I could not find anyone who was prepared to stop, possibly because, as I now became aware, the light was already fading in the east. I realized that I had been at Dunkirk for some five hours. The sea was also becoming rougher with a distinctly chill wind freshening from seaward. I had no orders as to whether I should stay or return to England, and so under the circumstances, I decided to return to Ramsgate with my load, some two hundred and fifty soldiers crammed into the hold like sardines.

As I knew my compass was faulty, I turned my stern to the fires of the burning port and steered a course to keep them in that position. I knew it must be nearly high tide and decided to take the risk of passing over the sandbanks lying to seaward. Gradually, as the noise of the battle receded, the only sound was of our ancient Bolinder diesel engine thumping away above the splash of our bow wave. At a steady four to five knots, our maximum speed, we butted through the short Channel seas and on into the night. We were unlit and had no means of identifying ourselves to our own patrols, with the constant risk of being run down by other shipping or even being attacked by E-Boats. Once or twice I looked down into the hold but there was no sign of life; the troops had all fallen into an exhausted sleep.

Gradually the glare of Dunkirk dropped astern and, after fourteen hours of continuous activity and no food, I suddenly began to feel utterly weary and cold. At this stage the only other person awake besides myself was my engine-room hand. A mist had begun to form, limiting visibility still further. I was fighting sleep and straining to keep our indistinct wake in line with Dunkirk, now a faint glow astern. Our course had become a wide weave which I hoped was towards the English coast.

After an eternity of time dawn came at last and I found we were shrouded in a cold and clammy sea-mist with visibility only a few hundred yards. I had very little idea of our position. After another hour I decided to turn to the east as the mist began to clear. Not long after I saw a trawler crossing our bows from right to left. I turned to follow it, soon afterwards sighting the Gull Light Vessel, and so, joining a motley stream of craft heading for Ramsgate, which soon appeared, I steered to enter the harbour. As I did so I misjudged the

21

strong tide and *X217* hit the eastern jetty with a resounding crash, effectively waking up the last of our sleeping passengers. I was directed into the inner harbour to join many other small vessels, where my Frenchmen were disembarked and taken away in buses to a transit camp.

I then made my way to the office of the Naval Officer-in-Charge where I met Captain W. R. Phillimore R.N. and his Chief Staff Officer, Commander Duffy. Captain Phillimore was then addressing a group of similarly dishevelled officers. The gist of his remarks was that the situation at Dunkirk was rapidly worsening and that only craft with a minimum speed of fifteen knots were required and these should preferably be manned by volunteers. Returning to the *X217*, which obviously did not qualify, I found that her crew were not particularly anxious to 'volunteer', so I decided to see what I could find for myself. But before this, as I had had nothing to eat since early the previous morning, I found a hotel where I had breakfast and a bath 'on the house'. After a shave at the first barber's shop I saw, I returned to the harbour and started my search among the miscellany of craft lying there for one with the right speed requirements. My eye soon fell upon a large War Department high-speed target-towing launch named *Marlborough*, flying the Army's defaced Blue Ensign, which lay alongside the western breakwater. The crew, who appeared to be civilians, were on deck, and I called down to them, asking whether they needed a spare hand who could bring a Lewis gun. They referred me to the Officer-in-Charge, who turned out to be an R.A.S.C. Captain, who said he would be glad to take me along with my Lewis gun and that *Marlborough* was to sail that afternoon for Dunkirk.

I returned to *X217* to collect my Lewis gun and to tell the Coxswain to await further orders from the NOIC. *Marlborough* set out at 2 p.m., her upper deck loaded with cans of petrol for the refuelling of small craft at Dunkirk. My Lewis gun was mounted on the forehatch. I felt much more comfortable as we roared along at 20 knots. Not long after leaving the coast we met an armed trawler which ordered us to stop and identify ourselves, which we had some difficulty in doing as we apparently had not been allotted any identification signals. This trawler informed us that things were critical and the operation was almost over.

Marlborough resumed her course and some minutes later sighted another trawler on patrol. We made out the French ensign and, in view of the last encounter, decided to keep our distance. Suddenly, as we watched, we saw a large cloud of dirty black and brown smoke envelop her and seconds afterwards heard the rumble of an explosion. As the smoke blew away we saw that the trawler had disappeared. We turned towards the spot where she was last seen and closed it at full speed. As we got nearer we could make out floating débris, and amongst it, bobbing aimlessly in the swell, a number of bodies. They were all dead. Hanging in their heavy cork life jackets, it seemed as though their necks had been broken. The sea was covered with a black sooty deposit. There was nothing further to do and, speculating on the cause of such a sudden explosion, we resumed our course once again at full speed.

Hardly had we left the scene when I pointed out to the R.A.S.C. Captain two French Torpedo Boats closing us at high speed from an easterly direction. We watched intently as they crossed astern of us, heeling over as they turned to our course to overhaul us, their guns trained. I guessed that they hadn't recognized our miniature Blue Ensign and, as we had no recognition signals, they probably thought *Marlborough* was an E-Boat. I persuaded a rather shaken Captain to hoist the White Ensign which I had brought with me from the *X217*. This appeared to have the desired effect and they turned away to continue their patrol. Obviously everyone was very jumpy.

We were now within sight and sound of Dunkirk and could see the procession of small craft still making their way seaward. We also saw a hospital ship being attacked by dive-bombers and altered course towards her in case she should need assistance. While our attention was focused on the hospital ship, which we were approaching at full speed, *Marlborough* suddenly staggered and shuddered as an enormous column of dirty grey water erupted very close to us. We had been completely surprised and now found ourselves under attack by seven JU87 Stuka dive-bombers, the second of which was already diving on us. At full speed we swung this way and that to avoid the repeated attacks that now followed.

This was my first experience of being the sole target of an enemy attack and I was thankful that I was able to concentrate on firing my Lewis gun, which I did until it jammed. The Stukas were also using their guns as they dived and, although we were hit several times, providentially none of the cans of petrol lashed to the upper deck were struck. The Captain now ordered these cans to be cut loose. As they went overboard they formed a line of black shapes in our wake. The attack continued until the Germans ran out of bombs or ammunition. They then flew away low over the sea to the east.

The hospital ship had survived the attack unscathed and was making for England at full speed. As the *Marlborough* was by now back in mid-channel, the Captain decided he would return to Ramsgate. As we approached the coast, we sighted two trawlers, one of which had a heavy list. Closing them, we saw they were both packed with troops. When we had come within hailing distance, the trawler with the list told us that she was aground and asked us to transfer her troops to the second trawler. This we did; then, with a capacity load ourselves, we went on to Ramsgate. Once alongside, our soldiers disembarked. No sooner had this taken place than the *Marlborough's* civilian crew expressed their unwillingness to make any further trips of this nature; saying that they were not employed for this sort of duty, they packed their kit and left.

Reporting back to the office of the NOIC, I learnt that a great effort was to be made that night to lift still more troops but that interference was expected from E-Boats which had now moved to Ostend. To counter them a force was to be formed of all available high speed craft at Ramsgate to co-operate with the Dover-based Motor Torpedo Boats.

It was now too late to do anything further that night and I suddenly realized how tired I was, having had no sleep for forty-eight hours. So I set out to find a bed. I soon found a 'Board Residence' on the sea-front overlooking the harbour and rang the door bell. The landlady answered and I enquired whether she had a spare bed. She replied that she had, so long as the gentlemen to whom she had let the room didn't mind sharing it. The two gentlemen turned out to be David Pollock, a well-known International 14-foot dinghy sailor, and a friend, Bill Randall, both 'doing Dunkirk' for the weekend. I asked them if they would like to join *Marlborough* and they were delighted.

Sunday, 2 June, 1940, dawned a perfect day and I reported to the 'Office' once more. For the moment no craft were being sent out, and I was told to report back in two hours. Returning to the *Marlborough* to see that all was well, I was suddenly accosted by a young and smartly uniformed Army officer who asked me whether I would spare a few moments to come and speak to his General. Somewhat mystified, I went with him to the head of the 'inner basin' where a staff car was waiting. As we reached the car, the door opened and the General put his hand out and shook mine. He asked me my name and whether I had been over to the other side. As he grasped my hand he said that the Army would never forget what the Navy was doing for it during these desperate days. He then wished me 'Good Luck' and said 'Goodbye'. I never found out his name.

On returning to the 'Office' I learned that our problems over an engine-room crew for *Marlborough* had been solved by the arrival of two R.A.F. Engine Fitters and quite by chance, Tom Thornycroft, the manager of Napier Lions, so we were now a complete crew. We were to stand by for an operation at 6 p.m. that night.

For the remainder of the day we scrounged spare guns and ammunition, practised handling *Marlborough*, 'topped up' with fuel and collected some food and coffee for another night out. The operation that night was to be a 'last lift', in company with our sister launch, the *Haig*. Commander H. R. Troup, Chief Staff Officer to Commodore Taylor in *Haig*, was to be Senior Officer. We were both to tow a large merchant-ship-type lifeboat to increase our lift capacity.

A few minutes before six, as we lay alongside the jetty, our engines started, spluttering and roaring. We were suddenly asked if we would take a passenger, who immediately introduced himself as a retired Army officer. He could easily have been a Field-Marshal and was determined to 'have a go at the Hun', as he put it. He had brought his own Lewis gun and it was impossible to say no. Anyone who could produce any sort of weapon for use against aircraft could always get a trip. At six o'clock *Marlborough* followed *Haig* out of the harbour to rendezvous with a trawler which had our two lifeboats alongside. *Haig* took hers and went on. Ours turned out to be almost half-full of water. We started off by trying to pump it out as we towed, but in her semi-waterlogged state so much water came inboard from the choppy sea that our pumps were ineffective and, after wasting a precious half-hour, we were forced to abandon the lifeboat and to press on after *Haig*.

We caught up and, following astern, entered the 'Roads' just as dusk was falling. Picking our way through the outcoming shipping and the many submerged wrecks with just masts, funnels, or sometimes upperworks showing, we finally arrived off the harbour entrance. *Haig* now signalled us to go ahead and to make for a small jetty just outside the canal entrance which was at the head of the East Mole or *Jetée d'Est*. We hoped this would be a good and easy place to pick up troops. Heading slowly in through the thick black smoke that was drifting across the harbour, we hugged the mole, visibility being only a few yards at times. Dunkirk seemed a terrifying place, full of menace, an acrid smell of burning oil, warehouses on fire and general ruin. Eventually we discovered what we took to be the correct place and went alongside. One of the first things we noticed was that many of the iron ladder rungs cemented into the jetty had been sawn through, perhaps by fifth columnists. However, as the top of the bridge and wheelhouse were almost level with the top of the jetty, we decided it would have to do.

Two of us went along the jetty to find and direct troops to our position. I was most anxious to find an old boyhood friend from Felixstowe, Michael Turner, who I knew was with the Second Battalion of the Cameronians in the B.E.F., and at intervals I shouted 'Any Cameronians?', but there was no answer above the rumble of gunfire and the sound of burning buildings. Among several shadowy lines of troops there seemed to be no British. Time was short and it was not a place to linger, but we succeeded in directing a column of French troops to our position. When they saw the outline of *Marlborough*'s wheelhouse below, we found it very difficult to persuade them to jump the few feet to reach it. Occasionally the darkness was stabbed by a sudden flare-up of a fire, or a bursting starshell, but always the continual noise from the guns and once a number of low-flying aircraft passed close overhead, which we were not able to see. Nonetheless tracer fire followed them from all sides. Our military passenger and Geoffrey Carew-Hunt took the opportunity and opened up with our Lewis guns for good measure.

It was almost 1 a.m. and we were full to capacity, with some seventy troops crammed in like sardines, and there was nothing else to do but head for home. The passage out to sea was even more difficult than our entry, or so it seemed to us. Three hours later we were approaching Ramsgate out of a thick dawn mist. As the pier ends came into sight we were met by several bursts of fire from the machine-gun posts sited on them. These we had noticed were manned by OCTU Cadets, obviously on the lookout for possible E-Boats. Turning broadside on, we gave them a better opportunity to identify us, before finally heading into the harbour. We first disembarked our troops at the east jetty and reported to Captain Phillimore before edging carefully, as it was dead low water, alongside our berth on the west jetty.

It was another beautiful summer morning and all was still in the glass-like calm of the harbour. Having secured and shut down the engines, we all walked to the end of the jetty. Here relays of local ladies had been working indefatigably since the operation started, serving hot drinks and something to eat for all comers. In its way this small effort by those wonderful ladies made everything seem doubly worthwhile. For many it was the first food that they had eaten in days. We then went off to our respective lodgings to find a bed and get some sleep. Our landlady was not at all put out by having her door bell rung at six in the morning! I think she thoroughly enjoyed mothering us.

We were woken at midday and given a good lunch before reporting once more to the 'Office'. There were to be no daylight runs again but we were warned to stand by for another operation that night. However, as the *Haig* had been damaged, we were told that some of us would have to join other craft in order to make way for some rather more senior crew members from *Haig* to take over in *Marlborough*. This struck us as very unfair and our protest was so vehement and immediate that Commander Duffy, somewhat taken aback by this rebellion by a number of very junior officers, relented.[1] I think he was very sympathetic towards us.

Our orders were to leave Ramsgate at six-thirty that night and sail to Dunkirk by the most direct route. In mid-Channel we were to rendezvous with and embark Commodore Taylor who was crossing in the motor yacht *Mermaiden*. On arrival at Dunkirk we were to go up to the easternmost arm of the harbour, the *Jetée d'Est*, as far as we could, and then at the most suitable point establish a small craft assembly point, which we understood to be the *Quai Félix Faure*. This was definitely to be the last night of the evacuation and a maximum effort was to be made.

We left Ramsgate at six-thirty p.m. and set course for Dunkirk. Whenever we sighted anything that fitted the description of Commodore Taylor's motor yacht, we came up alongside it and asked if he was aboard. Eventually we found the right craft and, going alongside, took him on board. The now familiar pall of smoke was soon in sight as we closed the French coast. A short, steep sea made the spray fly as we made our way up the roads to the harbour entrance, making it difficult for us to see the numerous obstructions. The Commodore sat in the corner of the wheelhouse, complacently munching his sandwiches, seemingly oblivious of the scenes of war on either hand. I think he was amused at the 'Soviet' he found in command of his flagship.

On reaching the harbour entrance we reduced speed to dead slow and turned to port to run up between the long curving eastern arm of the harbour and the stone jetty inside it. Visibility was poor and once again we had to keep the wooden *Jetée d'Est* in sight as a guide. We passed several burnt-out and sunken ships, and in particular a large

---

[1] The crewing of *Marlborough* was rather a 'soviet'. There were five Acting Sub-Lieutenants with the senior, Robert Don, as nominal skipper. Having 'found' *Marlborough*, I appropriated the Coxswain's duties myself, as I so enjoyed the thrill of driving such a high-speed craft. In practice we all took a turn, though. In addition we had our three civilians and to begin with two and then one R.A.F. Engine Fitter.

tanker, stark and black against the burning buildings. Once more the strong smell of burning was all-pervading. Dunkirk looked and felt doomed. We crept up for an interminable time but at last came to some lock gates, which were shut. We stopped and, manoeuvring carefully, turned round to face seawards. We selected a suitable run of jetty for the assembly point and went alongside.

The Commodore now took Don ashore and set off to contact the troops, in this case 500 French Marines. *Marlborough* returned to the harbour entrance to collect as many small craft as possible. This proved no easy task in the almost impenetrable smoke and the ever-present danger of being hit by other ships. We managed to collect five or six and lead them back to the assembly point. A second attempt to find more small craft proved fruitless; we simply could not contact any so we went back into the harbour again.

While alongside the jetty, waiting for the Commodore and Don to reappear, some of us had a look at the many abandoned vehicles on the dockside. We found abandoned an almost brand-new Army motor-bike and went for a short ride on it, but the state of the *pavé*, as well as a strange air of foreboding, soon curbed our curiosity!

It was 1.30 a.m. before the Commodore returned. There was obvious confusion, no more small boats and no troops to be found. We knew that blockships were due in the harbour entrance at 3 a.m. and it was therefore time to leave. With our engines at slow ahead we moved slowly down the channel between the mole and jetty. As we passed the derelict tanker we noticed a trawler ahead of us listing and slewing round in such a way that she would shortly block the passage out. I was conning *Marlborough* and instinctively opened all three throttles and headed for the rapidly closing gap, which we just got through. Seconds later, with a dreadful jarring impact, *Marlborough* ran on to some underwater obstruction. I shut down the engines immediately and we tried to find out what had happened. Starting up the engines again, I gently put them into gear. Immediately the engines began to race. It was obvious that the shafts were damaged. *Marlborough* was already settling deeper into the water and it seemed that her bottom must be damaged as well.

What now? It was obvious that somehow we must get clear of the harbour. We tried to use some gratings to paddle with but, at the most, we could just move her by handing her along the side of the mole. We knew the harbour was to be abandoned within a short time and I think we all had visions of a prisoner-of-war camp. The future looked as black as the smoke engulfing us. We were just considering abandoning *Marlborough* and trying to find some other craft when we heard the noise of high-powered engines approaching from ahead. The Commodore thought it might be an E-Boat and I think he rather hoped it was! He was full of fight and we prepared to give it as hot a reception as possible with our two Lewis guns.

Then out of the smoke we saw one of our MA SBs coming up the opposite side of the canal. We hailed her, telling her that we were disabled and asked for a tow. Her Captain replied that he would do his best, but that his rudders were damaged and he could only manoeuvre with difficulty. He had also lost two of his crew.

With some difficulty MA SB *S07*, for this it proved to be, took *Marlborough* in tow. Seeing their difficulty in getting the towline secured, I jumped across to her foredeck to help. With the towline secured despite her condition, *S07* managed to get *Marlborough* down the canal and into the harbour entrance. At this point, in the thickest of the smoke, the tow parted and *Marlborough* was at once lost sight of. After making two wide circles trying to regain contact, *S07*'s Captain told me that he could not spend any more time searching as he had special orders to pick up Admiral Abrial, the French Commander of the Port. So once again that night I found myself on my way up the canal.

At the end of the jetty the MA SB's First Lieutenant was sent ashore to try and contact Admiral Abrial and he was soon making his way along the mole into the darkness. *S07*'s Captain soon became anxious as time was by now fast running out. He then sent me to find the First Lieutenant and tell him to return at once. After a few hundred yards I found him returning but without the French Admiral whom he said he had been unable to contact. As soon as we were back, *S07* set out for the harbour entrance. We kept a careful lookout for the *Marlborough* but we saw no sign of her. We then went outside the harbour to a position just off the *Jetée d'Est* and waited for the blockships to appear. They soon came into sight from the west, with their escorting MTBs. As we lay gently lifting to the swell, with our engines at low revolutions, gurgling and spluttering as the exhaust and circulating water ports alternately submerged and came clear of the water, we watched as the little party turned into the harbour entrance and was lost to sight in the swirling smoke. After a short time the MTBs reappeared and headed seawards down the Roads. At once three green rockets burst in the sky, the signal for 'Operation Completed', which had been made on Rear Admiral Wake Walker's orders from *MTB 102* in which he was embarked.

As we headed seawards, following *102*, we took our last look at Dunkirk. The whole area of the port lay under the ruddy glow of fires, which were reflected off the opaque black ceiling of the smoke clouds, and silhouetted against this were the masts, funnels and superstructures of the sunken shipping, the débris of a week's fierce fighting. Most poignant of all were the long columns of Poilus, the last shattered remnants of the French Seventh Army, ordered to hold Dunkirk to the end. They lined the *Jetée d'Est* in the vain hope of being evacuated.

Once we had cleared the roads, we increased speed and I went below to try and get some sleep. This, however, proved quite impossible as we shuddered through the seas at thirty knots. I wondered what had happened to *Marlborough* and whether she had managed to get a tow out of the harbour, and if she too was now on her way home. Dawn brought with it the usual thick sea mist, cold and damp, but we were soon back in *S07*'s berth in Dover harbour. Shortly after our arrival the old First War Coastal Motor Boat *Mosquito* entered harbour and, as she came slowly to her berth, we saw two oilskin-covered bodies lying across her foredeck, casualties from the blockship crews which *Mosquito* had been detailed to bring off.

After a rather liquid breakfast of bacon and egg in whisky, I managed to get a staff car to take me back to Ramsgate. The First Lieutenant of *S07* asked me if, on my way, I would send a telegram addressed to the Provost, Eton College, which read 'Greetings from a Tug at Dunkirk'. During the twenty-mile drive back to Ramsgate I found I was very moved by the peace and tranquillity of the countryside and felt that this was something really worth fighting for. At Ramsgate I once more reported to NOIC and learnt that *Marlborough* had managed to get back safely and that Commodore Taylor was at that very moment on his way to Ramsgate from Dover. I was told to report to him in an hour's time. This I did, and was lectured on not leaving senior officers in the lurch! Afterwards he offered me bread, butter and coffee, and told me to write a report on the past day's activities. In fact, all of us at Ramsgate were doing the same thing, and there was a great 'scrounging' of pens and paper from the one and only Wren writer.

After saying goodbye to our landlady who had looked after us so well in the past few hectic and disjointed days, we caught the train back to Sheerness. As with the morning's car journey from Dover, the quietness and peace of the countryside made an indelible impression on us. The next morning in London we reported to Rex House, where NA2SL[1] was accommodated, and were sent on four days' leave before rejoining Sub-Lieutenants' courses at Portsmouth.

[1] The abbreviation for Naval Assistant to the Second Sea Lord, responsible for officers' appointments.

We Sub-Lieutenants resumed our courses amid a new atmosphere that reflected the seriousness of the situation. Air raids were becoming more frequent and, with France defeated, England was now alone in the field and the Germans were preparing to invade.

The fact that France had been defeated gave rise to a new and potentially dangerous problem, the future of the powerful French Fleet. There were at Portsmouth a number of French warships. On Tuesday, 2 July, with afternoon instruction at the Signal School just ended, we were all enjoying a cup of tea in the Wardroom of the Royal Naval Barracks before returning to Whale Island. Suddenly above the chatter of conversation we heard the message broadcast that all officers were to report back to their establishments immediately.

On our arrival back at Whale Island we found everyone assembling on the lawns in front of the Wardroom. We fell in in our various instructional groups and waited. There seemed to be a great deal of activity by the Staff, and after a few minutes individuals were called out and told to report to one or another senior officer.

Frank Seymour, Tony Catlow and myself reported to a Lieutenant-Commander Kidd and were later joined by Nigel Johnstone and Lieutenant Dyer. We were told we now belonged to Party 'G' for George and would each be taking charge of a party of ratings of the same designation. We were told to draw pistol equipment, then to change into an old seagoing uniform, put on gym shoes with a pair of stockings over them, have supper and be ready to leave 'the island' at 8 p.m. As we carried out these instructions there was, of course, much speculation as to what was in store for us. One of the most popular rumours was that we were to raid tomato houses in the Channel Islands.

By a quarter to eight we once more assembled in the Drill shed and, party by party, loaded into buses. Promptly at 8 p.m., having been warned that we were not to let our arms be seen as we passed through the town, our buses left for the Royal Naval Barracks. We arrived and drove through the main gates which we noticed had been screened by canvas, the gates being immediately closed after us. Once inside, we left our buses and entered the gymnasium. Inside we found the entire personnel from the barracks and other establishments already fallen in by groups. The ratings of 'G' group, all Officer Candidates, known as 'Upper Yardsmen',[1] some twenty in number, were waiting

[1] In the old sailing navy, the best and most agile sailors always manned the upper and most dangerous yards, for setting and furling the sails. Hence the expression 'Upper Yardsmen'.

for us and in addition there were ten Stokers under a Warrant Engineer Officer. All were armed with entrenching tool helves or truncheons.

Apart from a slight murmuring here and there, we waited in silence for some ten minutes. Then a number of senior officers entered, one of whom addressed us. After a brief preamble about the French collapse and armistice with the Germans, he passed on to the future of the French Navy and the impossibility of allowing any of its ships to return to France where they might fall into the hands of the Germans. The reason we were here, he said, was to take part in an operation timed for the early hours of the next morning, the object of which was to seize those French warships in Portsmouth at that moment. Bloodshed was to be avoided if possible, but we were to tolerate no resistance on the part of the French.

The details of the plan were then explained. Each lettered party was to seize a ship, or group of ships. Zero hour was to be 3 a.m. Parties were to take control simultaneously of the Officers' quarters, the messdecks, machinery spaces and the upper deck close-range weapons. The latter task was to be entrusted to parties of Royal Marines, who would meet us in the dockyard.

Fifteen minutes before zero hour, an officer was to board each ship and deliver an ultimatum to the Commanding Officer, which stated that he had the option of serving on in his ship to fight the Germans or handing his ship over to the British and be repatriated. Frank Seymour and Tony Catlow were detailed for this unpleasant task because they both spoke French.

Party 'G' was given as its target two torpedo boats lying at the north-west corner jetty. These were *La Flore* and *La Melpomene*, sister ships of 850 tons, with a complement of about one hundred officers and ratings. Our orders having been given, we were told we were not to leave the building and to get some sleep on the hammocks laid out on the concrete floor.

At a quarter to two the next morning we were woken up and given breakfast. This went some way to easing the uncertainties and quelling the butterflies in our stomachs with which we had been wrestling as we tried to sleep on the hard floor. At two-thirty we moved off by groups, through the back gates of the Barracks and into the dockyard by the Marlborough Gate.

As soon as we were inside we were joined by our detachment of Royal Marines who drove in and left their transport with a loud clatter of hobnailed boots! We then moved off as directed to the north-west corner. Part of our route lay through the interior of some of the machine shops where the night shift stared in amazement as the long column of armed seamen and Marines filed through under the glare of the workshop lights.

We finally arrived at our waiting position under the half-built hull of the new light cruiser *Sirius*, surrounded by cranes, stages and all the paraphernalia of the building slip. A light drizzle had begun to fall, which we thought would be an aid to the operation as the French watchkeepers might be less vigilant. A hundred to a hundred and fifty yards away we could make out the superstructures, funnels and masts of the French ships, whilst behind us on the other side of *Sirius* loomed the large bulk of the old French battleship *Courbet*.

At quarter to three exactly, as the butterflies fluttered in our stomachs, Frank Seymour and Tony Catlow boarded their respective ships to deliver the ultimatum. At zero hour Commander Kidd blew his whistle and we all raced for the brows. We were on the upperdeck in a matter of seconds, with not a Frenchman to be seen. I quickly led my five seamen down the ladder to the Officers' quarters, whilst Nigel Johnstone did the same into the ship's company messdecks forward; the Marines occupied the close-range gun positions and the engine-room party disappeared down into the machinery spaces. I was not sure what I would find as I jumped down into the cabin flat. The lights were all on and the curtains were pulled across the doors.

Moving quickly from cabin to cabin, I woke up the officers, most of whom were already awake, ordered them to dress and surrender any arms in their possession. I then stationed guards to cover the hatches and cabin doors, ordering that no French officer was to leave his cabin without permission. As soon as I had done this, which took about two or three minutes, I made my way to the Captain's cabin from which I could hear the sound of a heated exchange.

The French Executive Officer, a large bull-like man with a bald head, and his Captain were arguing vehemently with Lieutenant Commander Kidd and Tony Catlow. They were absolutely furious and refused to accept the ultimatum. They demanded to know by whose orders they had been so treacherously attacked. The Executive Officer was livid with rage, and was shouting abuse at '*Les Anglais*' and '*L'Angleterre*'. The gist of his outburst was that they had always fought us and hated us, and this act showed that we had never changed from the 'Perfidious Albion' of history. He and his Captain refused to hand the ship over.

In fact the ship was already in our hands, the operation had gone like clockwork and all was over within ten minutes. I now went round each of the officers' cabins. I found their occupants sitting dejectedly on their bunks. Some asked on whose authority we had acted. I replied that Admiral Muselier, the senior Free French naval representative, had been informed and that he approved. They shrugged their shoulders and said that no French officer would accept his orders, that he was a traitor, as was General de Gaulle.

By daylight it was obvious to all that the operation had been completed successfully. The ships were securely in our hands; none of the French officers and ratings, apart from a few dozen sailors, wished to stay or have anything to do with the options they had been offered. They collected their kit and prepared to leave their ship. The French Captain then asked permission to address his ship's company for the last time. He made a long and impassioned speech. He obviously felt his position acutely. Apparently the ship had been decorated for its record at Dunkirk and at this point the Captain produced a box of Croix de Guerre which he distributed to each man!

As the French sailors began to file slowly ashore with their kit bags, they looked in a sullen, dejected mood and many were crying openly. At this time, and quite spontaneously, a tall thin sailor jumped on a hatch and addressed a small group which was waiting its turn to leave. He danced round and round, imitating a machine gun, shouting in a staccato way *Les Allemands, les Allemands, boom, boom, boom*', and then, very slowly *Les Anglais, boom . . . boom . . . boom*', as if to emphasize that we were all finished anyway and the Germans were so much the better. After the French sailors had been marched away to their waiting transport, their Captain, now calmer and more resigned, asked us to have a final drink with him and his officers before they too left. His toast to us was: '*A bas les Allemands, toujours à bas les Allemands!*' After they had had a meal and were allowed to burn any papers or documents they wished, they left the ship. Then the French Tricolor was lowered and the White Ensign hoisted.

We heard on the wireless that night the news from Oran. We were all agreed that there was no other course of action we could have taken in our desperate situation, but at the same time we felt very sympathetic towards the French in their humiliation and defeat. As one of them said to me, 'You must be crazy to think we will use our ships to blockade our own families, upon which in any case the Germans would take reprisals'.

Returning once more to our courses, we laboured away at Signals, Anti-Submarine Warfare and Gunnery. In the evenings we played tennis, tasted the night life of Portsmouth and had the occasional long weekend at the end of each subject. I had just returned from one such

34

a weekend in early July when the sirens sounded an Air Raid Warning.

On previous occasions to date the sirens had proclaimed only false alarms, and so we all took our time to get to our cabins for 'tin hats'. This time, however, it was different, and within a few minutes the crash of anti-aircraft guns started up, so we hurriedly made our way to our respective air-raid shelters.

It was a beautiful summer's day and, as we watched the grey-brown shell bursts in the sky, we soon picked out the German aircraft coming in from the south. They were twin-engined Junkers 88s flying in threes and heading straight for the dockyard, and of course us. The blue sky became pock-marked with bursts as more and more batteries came into action and opened fire. The battleship *Queen Elizabeth*, then completing the last stages of her modernization, appeared to be the principal target. As the aircraft neared the *Queen Elizabeth* amid increasingly heavy fire as the ships' guns and close-range weapons opened up, they dived steeply down in a succession of threes and released their bombs. The raid lasted about twenty minutes, a crescendo of diving aircraft, thundering bangs and crashes of hundreds of guns, the thudding explosions of the bombs, our own fighter aircraft now engaging the bombers, and Germans parachuting from their smoking and crashing aircraft.

I could not help feeling sorry for those Germans swinging from their parachutes to land in the creeks and mud-flats of the harbour. As soon as the 'All Clear' was sounded, armed parties were sent out in harbour launches to collect them. Looking over towards the dockyard, the *Queen Elizabeth* seemed undamaged, but from other parts spirals of smoke were rising. I spent the rest of the day guarding two young Germans until the R.A.F. came to collect them in the evening.

Air raids now became quite frequent both by day and night as the Germans launched the blitz in earnest. Our routine was amended as we now spent long hours of our nights in the shelters. We started our instruction much later and went on until later in the evening. Fears of an enemy parachute landing increased and the defence of Portsmouth became the Navy's responsibility. We were formed into local defence battalions and given sectors to defend. I became company commander of a company of pensioner stokers, all armed with old American Ross rifles permanently sighted at four hundred yards. Our task was to defend Portsmouth airfield. I shudder to think what would have happened if such an attack had ever come.

We struggled on through our instruction. Not unexpectedly, as a result of so many diversions, our course failed its parade training, known to us as Field Training. We had to retake it, and this time during an air raid in front of a dugout full of W.R.N.S. all giggling at us. The W.R.N.S. were still very much of a novelty to those of us who had been at sea since the war began, but were voted a great success and there was much competition to take them out in the evenings.

Officially our 'courses' for the rank of Lieutenant came to an end on Saturday 31 August. We were all sent on leave. John Howard, Frank Seymour and myself hired a taxi to take us to Havant Station, to catch our train to London, as the line into Portsmouth had been closed due to bomb damage. After a night spent at the Savoy Hotel, we went again to Rex House to find out what was in store for us in the way of our next appointment. We were all to be sent to 'Big Ships' to obtain the last requirement for promotion to Lieutenant, a Watch-keeping Certificate, which would certify that we were in every respect fit to take charge of a watch at sea, in one of His Majesty's ships.

I arrived home in the afternoon of 3 September, for a few days' leave. In fact it was to be for only two days. I found home much changed by the austerity of war. No housemaids or cook, petrol strictly rationed, and an air-raid shelter in the garden. We had to remove the distributor head from the car when we left it at all times, in order to immobilize it, thus safeguarding it against invading parachutists or Fifth Columnists. I just had time to make a nostalgic trip to Waldringfield where my dinghy was laid up in Nunn Bros' yard for the duration of the war. I drove across the familiar heathlands of heather, bracken and pine trees, past the pillboxes and strongpoints on the now closed Martlesham road leading through the aerodrome to the village, hazy and still in the warm September sunshine. Here the reminders of war were everywhere; the river was empty of yachts, their places taken by hundreds of spiked railway sleepers moored so as to act as anti-invasion obstacles. A changed world after one year of war, but strangely exciting and uplifting in a way that I had often thought of in my childhood fantasies, when I relived those first days of the First World War that I had heard about so often from my mother and father.

NO. THE
ROTOR ARM

36

CHAPTER 4

War – The Second Year

On 5 September, 1940 I received the familiar OHMS buff envelope. Opening it under my parents' anxious eyes, I read: 'The Lords Commissioners of the Admiralty hereby appoint you Sub-Lieutenant R.N. of His Majesty's Ship *Repulse*, and direct you to repair on board that ship at Scapa Flow on 7 September, 1940.' Attached was a first class railway warrant.

The journey north from Felixstowe to Thurso was like any other wartime journey. The train travelled through the quiet countryside of Suffolk and Cambridgeshire, arriving at Peterborough just in time for our connection with the Flying Scotsman. Servicemen, with their piles of kitbags, and weary civilians crowded the platforms of the larger junctions – Bury St Edmunds, Peterborough, York – then a short stop at Edinburgh before continuing to Perth. Here we had time for a rather meagre wartime dinner of cold meats and salad before changing trains for the last lap through the night to Thurso. The train, now carrying mostly service personnel, rattled along. At a small halt early next morning we were given buns and thick sweet tea from buckets by a number of local ladies, before continuing to Thurso. We went straight to the small hotel where we had baths and breakfast of kippers, toast and coffee.

At midday we boarded the steamer *St Ninian* at Scrabster harbour, then rolled and pitched our way across the Pentland Firth and passed through the Hoxa Gate into the calm waters of Scapa Flow. A grey mist shrouded the Fleet and we saw little until we arrived alongside the base ship *Dunluce Castle*. Here we disembarked with our baggage to wait for a passage to the Fleet anchorage. I drank a cup of tea and looked out into the grey murk, the rain swirling and spattering against the stateroom windows. History welled up again in my mind when I thought of all I had read of the Grand Fleet lying here waiting for the German High Seas Fleet to put to sea only twenty-two years ago.

Eventually everyone was called by name of ship and, after our gear was loaded, we embarked in a drifter for the Fleet anchorage. I eventually arrived alongside *Repulse*, a beautiful battlecruiser of 38,000 tons, which, with the *Hood*, formed the 1st Battlecruiser Squadron. The formalities of the quarterdeck were soon over and I went to be introduced to the Gunroom which was to be my responsibility. There I met twenty-five midshipmen and three other Sub-Lieutenants.

The invasion scare was at its height and early the next day we put to sea with two cruisers, *Norfolk* and *Suffolk*. This was one of the frequent anti-invasion sweeps[1] to cover the waters between the Orkneys and Iceland. I found myself on the bridge at once as Officer of the Watch, under the Senior Watchkeeper, Lieutenant O'Brien, who was also the Senior Pilot for the ship's two Swordfish aircraft. I had a very difficult time mastering the station-keeping problems caused by the constant anti-submarine zig-zagging. After two days, nothing having been sighted or reported, we returned to the Flow.

September passed with several more anti-invasion sweeps towards Norway in company with our own Flagship, the *Hood*. Watch-keeping was not easy; station-keeping on a dim shadow and pin-point of light was a constant strain at night. The blitz was at its height and we listened to the daily scores for and against. Invasion scares succeeded one another, but all turned out to be groundless. While returning from one such sweep, *Repulse* was ordered to Rosyth where we arrived on 2 October.

The Firth of Forth was grey and misty; the wet smells of autumn were carried to us on the moist winds that gusted across the Firth. We slowly steamed up to our berth, passing the Flagship of the Home Fleet, the battleship *Nelson* and the new light cruiser *Naiad*. *Repulse* was to enter drydock for a short refit and leave was to be given in two watches. Before going into dock the ship had to be de-ammunitioned and everyone in the ship took part in this operation.

I was to go on the first leave and, while waiting for the 'Night Scot', there was time for dinner with Dennis Aldridge, our senior Marine subaltern at the Aperitif, where I ate my first haggis! By midday the following day I was home. The few days passed all too quickly, trawling in the still unobstructed lower reaches of the River Deben

---

[1] The word 'sweep' was often used to describe a search over a given area for enemy ships.

one day and partridge shooting on another. It was glorious late autumn weather and it seemed to me that the Suffolk countryside had never looked lovelier. Even in this tranquil setting, however, the signs of war were always evident: the blackout curtains, strict petrol rationing, car lights reduced to slits of light and my father's Home Guard equipment in the hall of our house ready for instant use.

Leave was soon over and the long journey north to the ship quickly brought one face to face again with the daily routine of watchkeeping, with the odd evening in Edinburgh.

By the end of the month we were back to the austerity and bleakness of Scapa Flow. Within a few days of our arrival we were at sea again on another wide search for the German pocket battleship *Admiral Scheer* which had just sunk the armed merchant cruiser *Jervis Bay*.

Repulse was a wet and uncomfortable ship at sea in rough weather. Pitching into the long Atlantic seas, as the bow rose, the stern would sink with a kind of twisting motion, as her propellers thundered and water streamed in down the barbette walls of Y Turret.[1] As a result of this the Wardroom cabin flat, immediately below, was constantly awash with dirty water slopping from side to side almost up to the cabin door sills. Overall, a stale, damp and seasick smell pervaded the ship's after compartments.

November and December, 1940, were occupied by constant sorties and sweeps into the Atlantic, searching for raiders, or other special operations. We slogged, punched and rolled our way through the long, grey winter seas. On one such an occasion we acted as distant cover for the light cruiser *Naiad* while she intercepted a German trawler carrying a meteorological party who were attempting to establish a weather station on Jan Mayen Island, well to the north of Iceland within the Arctic Circle. The weather was foul for the majority of the time as gale succeeded gale.

Inside the Flow we exercised continually with anti-aircraft and sub-calibre firings. At regular intervals these were followed by full-calibre firings – the fifteen-inch and four-inch guns – in the Pentland Firth.

The constant round of watch-keeping was enlivened at times by such incidents as the occasion when one of the Fleet Air Arm's Blackburn Skuas flew over the Flow inside the prohibited zone and over the Fleet anchorage. A furious anti-aircraft barrage opened up

[1] *Repulse*'s main armament consisted of six fifteen-inch guns mounted in three turrets, A and B forward and Y aft.

from both ship and shore batteries,[1] the sky turning brown with the barrage of shell bursts, fortunately for the Skua to no avail, as it flew on unscathed! There were said to be a lot of red faces on all sides after this incident.

I remember, too, the pitch black nights, when, as Boat Officer with the duty part of the watch, in dripping oilskins we hoisted boats by the faint light from dimmed torches, the boats' crews trying desperately to hook on the slings as the boats plunged and lifted to the storm-lashed waters of the Flow.

Christmas Day, 1940, dawned cold and grey and proved more eventful than expected. My old Divisional Officer in the Training Cruiser, now a Commander and Captain of the destroyer *Beagle*, came alongside to share the facilities of a big ship, a common practice to ease the discomfort of the small ships. The day started off traditionally with a Church service and the Captain's rounds of the mess decks.

Later, in the middle of the champagne cocktail party given by the Gunroom, a signal was received to raise steam for full speed. At 1.30 p.m. the order to prepare for sea was given; half an hour later we left the Flow.

Once at sea, *Repulse* was despatched with the cruiser *Nigeria* to intercept the German heavy cruiser *Hipper* which had been in action with one of our cruisers, the *Cumberland*, when she tried to attack a troop convoy in the latitude of Gibraltar. After an extensive but fruitless search we returned to Scapa Flow five days later.

Not long after we were once again at sea, in company, this time, with the Home Fleet to patrol the stretch of water between Iceland and the Faeroes. One of our scouting cruisers, *Naiad*, reported sighting a darkened ship. She was ordered to search to the north at full speed and we were ordered to support her.

Repulse, screened by three of the big Tribal Class destroyers, steered north at full speed. At dawn we could see the snow-covered and mountainous coastline of Iceland on our port hand. One of our Swordfish aircraft was catapulted off to fly north as far as its endurance would allow and then to return to Iceland. It was the last we were to see of it for weeks. It was bitterly cold with continuous snow flurries, though the sea was calm. Even so, at full speed, great gushes of water spouted up through our hawsepipes where the anchors were housed. By the late evening *Naiad* reported she had

[1] It was said at the time that the Fleet anchorage at Scapa Flow was the most heavily defended point in the British Isles.

reached the ice edge and had made no further contact, so we were ordered to rejoin the Fleet. Later it was learned that the ship which *Naiad* had sighted was one or other of the two big German battlecruisers, *Scharnhorst* or *Gneisenau*, breaking out into the Atlantic.

We never knew until a few hours beforehand what was in store for us, hence the welcome news in early February that we were to go into drydock at Rosyth was a great surprise. We sailed that evening and the following day we were steaming up the Firth of Forth; suddenly out of the mist came a German Heinkel bomber, flying low over the ship and disappearing ahead. I wondered who was the most surprised!

Soon after anchoring, lighters came alongside to remove our ammunition before we moved into dock which we did in a blinding snowstorm. Four days' leave was granted to each watch and once again I was among those to have first leave.

For a short time we remained in Rosyth Dockyard in company with the new battleship *Prince of Wales*, our flagship *Hood*, a County Class cruiser and a number of destroyers and frigates. What a target! But no German aircraft challenged the defences. Finally, after fuelling, storing and ammunitioning, we sailed for the Clyde under snow-laden skies, escorted by two of the new Hunt Class destroyers.

The Clyde presented a scene of great activity. Amid the surrounding ring of snow-covered hills lay columns of assembled merchantmen, destroyers and escorts of all types, assault landing ships, balloon-barrage trawlers and all the many types of craft common to a large assembly port in wartime.

We anchored off the Tail o' the Bank and our orders and destination at once became the main topic of conversation. We did not have long to wait, for on the following day we sailed in company with the aircraft carrier *Furious* and two troopships, *Alcantara* and *Aquitania*. Our destination was Gibraltar by a route which took the convoy well out into the Atlantic to keep clear of air attack from enemy bases in north-west France. After three days *Repulse* was ordered ahead with *Furious*. Not long afterwards we were steaming past Cape Trafalgar and it was a marvellous feeling after the cold greyness of the Atlantic to see the lights of the Spanish and North African coasts.

At 3 a.m. we turned into Algeciras Bay. We secured half an hour later, just astern of the submarine depot ship *Maidstone* and her submarines at the south mole. Gibraltar showed few signs of war except for the half-submerged wreck of a trawler sunk in a retaliatory air-raid by French aircraft after the Oran operation.

As soon as *Repulse* and *Furious* had refuelled, we sailed south. Watchkeeping now became a joy, such was the contrast in conditions, zig-zagging at twenty-two knots under blue skies and hot sunshine, the sea changing from grey-green to blue and finally to the deep cobalt of the tropics. At night the sea was alive with phosphorescence, particularly bright in the wakes of our two ships. Once a dolphin or some other big fish rushed towards the ship leaving a glittering track that momentarily made those of us who saw it think we were about to be torpedoed.

Our destination proved to be Freetown, the capital of Sierra Leone, a hot and dusty but surprisingly elegant colonial town of another more gracious age. A small gathering of naval vessels was present, including the *Vindictive*, now reconverted to her original role as a seaplane carrier. Two action interludes included an air-raid which turned out to be a reconnaissance flight by the Vichy French from Dakar, and a high-speed dash out into the Atlantic in response to a report from the battleship *Malaya*, escorting a convoy, that she had sighted the German battlecruisers *Scharnhorst* and *Gneisenau*.

There was always light relief to be had from among the collection of natives who surrounded the ship in their dugout canoes, clustering round our garbage chutes. One character in particular, usually stark naked except for a top hat which was inscribed 'Mr Nobody', turned out to be a great wit, much to the detriment of the ship's routine with his repeated calls of 'Up spirits' or 'Stand Easy'!

After a few days, during which the opportunity was taken to camouflage the ship by painting her in a dark and light grey pattern, the *Repulse* sailed to rendezvous with a north-bound convoy, and was accompanied to sea by the P. & O. liner *Narkunda* which had been awaiting an escort. Each day, as a morale booster, the Captain would show the ship off to the convoy by steaming up through the columns of merchant ships with the band playing and the ship's company carrying out massed P.T. exercises on the forecastle.

Gradually, through colder and more inhospitable seas, we steamed north, until we ultimately arrived back in the Clyde. Two days later we were again heading out as ocean escort to a fast convoy of transports for North Africa. Apart from U-Boat alarms and being shadowed by a Focke-Wulf 'Kondor' reconnaissance plane the passage to Gibraltar was uneventful.

During the four days the ship spent in harbour I had the opportunity to tour the defences. I was fascinated by the galleries tunnelled out of the rock, and especially the concentration of guns of all calibres which studded the north face overlooking the border with Spain.

We now became part of the famous 'Force H' consisting of our sister ship *Renown*, now modernized and wearing the flag of Admiral Somerville, the aircraft carrier *Ark Royal*, sunk so many times by 'Lord Haw Haw', and the cruiser *Sheffield*. For the next three weeks *Repulse* carried out a distant patrol off Brest where the *Scharnhorst* and *Gneisenau* had put in after their long Atlantic raid. We returned to Gibraltar to refuel on being relieved by other ships. Our first relief proved to be the now fully modernized battleship *Queen Elizabeth* and on the next occasion the County Class cruiser *London*, also having been completely reconstructed. There was always an air of majesty and power as these big ships came into sight for the first time. They would suddenly appear out of the murk, signal lamps flickering greetings and operational messages.

It was after our relief by *London* that we were ordered back to the Clyde. We lay there for the next two days refuelling and storing, watching convoys arriving and assembling. I met a number of my old Canadian term-mates, who were serving in the Canadian destroyer flotilla based at Greenock.

Repulse had been ordered to act as Ocean Escort to another convoy, W.S.8B., sailing on 20 May, but at midday these orders were suddenly cancelled. We learned that the new German battleship *Bismarck* had been sighted off the Skaw, the northernmost tip of Denmark, steaming north. For two more days we waited in the Clyde for further news. Then the expected and hoped-for signal was received to prepare for sea; our destroyer escort arrived and as soon as they had fuelled we sailed under orders to join the Home Fleet, which itself was sailing from Scapa Flow that evening.

Steaming north at twenty-five knots through the Minches[1] under grey skies, there was an air of great expectancy in the ship. In the early evening of the following day, 23 May, we joined the Commander-in-Chief to the north-west of Cape Wrath, with the new battleship *King George V* wearing the flag of Admiral Tovey, and the even newer aircraft carrier *Victorious*. She looked formidable in her patterned dark grey, light grey and white camouflage paint. Far ahead and out of sight were the cruisers *Galatea*, *Aurora*, *Kenya* and *Hermione*, spread on a line of search.

Later that evening we heard that *Bismarck* and the new heavy cruiser *Prinz Eugen* had been sighted and were now being shadowed

[1]   The sea passage between the Western Isles and Skye.

by Admiral Wake-Walker, with his cruisers *Suffolk* and *Norfolk*. Both the German and British ships were just on the edge of the ice at the northern end of the Denmark Straits that lie between Iceland and Greenland. The signal to increase speed to twenty-seven knots was received and soon the familiar bursts of spray whipped up through the hawsepipes and blew down the forecastle, covering the forward turrets. To all of us this looked like the real thing and the excitement in the ship was intense as the action reports of the enemy's movements were received.

During my turn as Officer of the Watch on the bridge, wedged in between the gyro and standard compass pedestals[1], I huddled into my duffle coat, constantly checking engine revolutions and course, squinting through the distance metre to check that the ship remained at the correct distance from the next ahead. Just to my left the Captain sat on his seat, immobile except for an occasional sweep of the horizon through his binoculars. The Navigating Officer, Lieutenant-Commander Langworthy, stroking his red beard, popped back and forth from the charthouse just abaft the compass platform, while the Principal Control Officer gazed silently ahead from the starboard fore corner of the compass platform. The small bridge windows were up, but, despite this, a chill draught blew in and eddied round the rear of the bridge. Behind us and in the rear wings stood the Chief Yeoman of Signals and duty signalmen, messengers and voice-pipe members.

Our thoughts were with the *Suffolk* and *Norfolk*, playing cat and mouse with the enemy amid the mists and snow flurries of the ice edge far to the north. A third force consisting of the *Hood* and *Prince of Wales* were far ahead of us and now steaming at full speed to intercept the enemy force at dawn, as it passed the southern end of the Denmark Straits. Half an hour before dawn we went to Action Stations, but with daylight came the shattering news that in a brief action with the enemy the *Hood* had blown up and sunk. The *Prince of Wales* was engaging the enemy. Our speed was increased still further and great clouds of spray swept the ship, the screening destroyers frequently lost from sight amid the increasing seas. Far ahead, the cruisers, in a long line spread along a bearing at right-angles to our course, could only occasionally be glimpsed through the greyness of sky and sea. We later heard that the *Prince of Wales* was damaged and had to break off the action, though she and *Suffolk* and *Norfolk* were still shadowing the enemy.

[1] Although the gyro compass was the operational compass, the magnetic or standard compass was kept as an insurance against breakdown.

44

All that day we steered south-west to intercept. This we learned would be at dawn tomorrow at the present course and speed. At 4 p.m. the *Victorious* was detached to get as close to the enemy as possible to launch an attack to try and slow her down. The destroyers were by this time running short of fuel and were being sent back to Reykjavik in Iceland to refuel. We were also running low on fuel and the C-in-C signalled to us to return that night. The Captain was not pleased, as this would mean we should miss the expected action the next morning. He immediately asked the C-in-C if we could remain with him until dawn, and then be allowed to go into Conception Bay, Newfoundland, to refuel, as this would just be possible. The C-in-C replied that he accepted our bargain but that we were under no account to come under the guns of the *Bismarck*.

We plunged on through the night keeping station on the dim white patch of the Flagship's wake. Soon after midnight reports of the attacks on the *Bismarck* by *Victorious*' aircraft were received. They were apparently carried out in the face of very intensive anti-aircraft fire. Dawn on the 25th brought the news that contact with the *Bismarck* had been lost. The *Prinz Eugen* had also slipped away earlier. At daylight we were detached to refuel. We were all disappointed that what had promised to be such a great moment looked as though it had slipped away.

Repulse now steamed at half-speed through the huge, cold, grey-green seas and fog patches of the Labrador Current. We remained at action stations, with a brief break for quick meals. 'Where were the *Bismarck* and the *Prinz Eugen*?' was the question in everyone's thoughts, and, despite our desire to go into action, there was always the question of whether we would suffer the same fate as the *Hood*. The ship was a shambles below decks, fittings carried away, anything in our cabins not secured broken, and everywhere wet and foetid. Finally, on the afternoon of the 26th, we felt our way into Conception Bay and anchored off Belle Isle with only three per cent of useable fuel left. It had been a close call. The following day we received the news that *Bismarck* had finally been brought to battle and sunk only five hundred miles short of Brest. Many of us could not help admiring her achievement and gallant last fight, crippled as she was, against overwhelming odds.

Conception Bay, Newfoundland, was a wonderful anchorage, almost land-locked with a dense forest of pine trees sweeping away from its shores. As there was no anti-submarine protection, our Walrus aircraft flew anti-submarine patrols by day, while our fast picket boats armed with aircraft depth charges did the same by night.

Later two of the Flower Class corvettes came up from Halifax to take over. A small harbour oiler from Halifax 450 miles to the south came a number of times to fill our tanks. Meanwhile the fishermen among us were soon busy with lines catching numerous fish, their scales covered in a red deposit, presumably from the rich iron ore mines.

Once refuelled, we were soon at sea again, searching for *Bismarck*'s consort *Prinz Eugen*, and as we quartered the cold foggy seas between Labrador and Cape Farewell, at the southern tip of Greenland, we took the opportunity to carry out target practice on the many icebergs. Eventually we were ordered south into Halifax for essential repairs to the damage sustained during our high-speed steaming after the *Bismarck*. Upper deck fittings, including our breakwater, had been badly distorted or carried away. It was a delightful interlude and a most welcome respite from seagoing in the cold northern waters. I was able to renew many friendships made at the outbreak of war. The Canadians, once again, gave us all a wonderful, if hectic, round of entertainment.

The end of June found us at sea escorting the third Canadian troop convoy. Zig-zagging in a thick Banks fog, in close proximity to numbers of large liners, was always a nerve-racking experience, especially for the O.O.W. On one occasion I 'zigged' when I should have 'zagged' and found myself crossing the bows of some of these large ships!

Delivering our convoy to the Clyde, we were soon back in Scapa Flow where we were at once engaged in a full programme of gunnery exercises and firings with every portion of our armament. Our operational efficiency having been brought up to date, we steamed south to Rosyth for a short refit and seven days' leave to each watch.

Back in the ship, amid the familiar grime and metallic smells of the dockyard, life quickly took on its customary pattern and it seemed I had never been away. The main purpose of our refit was the installation of fifteen Swiss Oerlikon guns, the newest and most effective of the close-range weapons now being fitted in all ships.

While at Rosyth, the ship had been seething with rumours, the most popular being that our new destination was America where we were to undergo a full modernization. We were soon back in Scapa Flow, where the greater part of August was spent 'working up' to full efficiency again. The Flow now looked at its best, the heather just purpling the hills and islets, the evenings still, with the ships mirrored in the calm water. I well remember one evening while pacing the quarterdeck as Officer of the Watch, suddenly hearing and then seeing a solitary piper playing on the quarterdeck of the *Prince of*

Wales, lying close by. The effect was magical and was accentuated a short time later by the bugle notes of the 'Last Post' echoing across the anchorage as the ships lowered their ensigns at sunset. Each time we left the Flow for an exercise we would be preceded by a screen of three or four Tribal Class destroyers, always a stirring picture as they swept past us, each flying signal flags indicating their pendant numbers, and with long white wakes streaming astern.

Orders were received to proceed to the Clyde and on the last day of August, 1941, accompanied by the *Sheffield*, we sailed with our destroyer escort. Steaming down the Minches, the west coast of Scotland was looking its magnificent best in the late afternoon sun, a mauve haze of heather on the closer shores and headlands, fading into the distant blue of the hills. The same sun bathed the light, almost white-grey of the *Sheffield* in pale pink. I always found such interludes to be a tremendous uplift and antidote for the many unpleasant times that were inevitable under wartime operating conditions. The discomfort, cold and wet were forgotten in the beauty of such scenes. The following morning we arrived in the Clyde to find the usual great gathering of shipping at the Tail o' the Bank. We learned that a troop convoy to Africa was now ready to sail.

On a glorious September morning, the second anniversary of the outbreak of war, the *Repulse* sailed out to act as the convoy's Ocean Escort. First we steamed west into the Atlantic, before turning south to the Equator. Soon, after several uneventful days, blue uniforms were exchanged for white and canvas swimming baths were rigged as the temperatures climbed.

When well to the south we were detached to rendezvous and fuel from an oiler. Steaming at slow speed, the tanker came alongside, the hawsers were passed and fuel hoses connected. I remember the acrid smell of the oil and watching the pulsating armoured hoses as fuel was pumped through them over our hot steel decks. The tropical sun beat down on us and, at the slow refuelling speed, there was no relief to be had from the cooling breeze so welcome when steaming at normal speed.

By way of Freetown, and back with the convoy once again, we crossed the Equator on 22 September. The traditional 'Crossing the Line' ceremony was carried out and for the majority of us there was no escaping the Bears of Neptune's Court! Four days later we paid a call to St Helena, having left the convoy for this purpose.

As we approached the island out of the dawn from the East I thought how grim and austere it looked and tried to imagine

47

Napoleon's thoughts as he approached in 1816. We anchored off the little cleft in the precipitous cliffs which sheltered Jamestown, the island's capital. *Repulse* was once again topped up with fuel from an oiler which came alongside. Leave of two hours was given to each watch.

Rounding the Cape, we headed north for Durban, where we arrived a few days later. There followed a packed four days of hospitality for everyone, subject only to watchkeeping duties. When we sailed again to rejoin the convoy, it seemed that the whole of Durban had turned out to line both shores of the harbour entrance, cheering and waving us away to the blaring of hundreds of motor horns. We steamed majestically out past the Bluff, the Royal Marine band playing on the quarterdeck. At the same time firing circuits were tested with the characteristic 'cracks' followed by the hollow whine made by the tubes, especially in the 15-inch gun barrels. Our course was north up the Mozambique Channel, through the deep blue East African sea. Apart from the ever-present danger from U-Boats, there was the added possibility of attack by Vichy French submarines from Madagascar.

Repulse usually took station between the two centre columns of the convoy by day, while at night we moved out ahead. At least once a day the ship would steam up between adjacent lines of the convoy to give the troops a good look at us, and we hoped, confidence in our ability to protect them. The tropical sun beat down remorselessly and great use was made of our canvas swimming pool. Weapon drills and various evolutions such as preparing to tow or fuel were performed daily. Most of us slept on safari beds on the upper deck, for sleep below was almost impossible in the great heat and inadequate ventilation. The sea was almost always calm except at midday, by which time a fresh breeze would cool us and whip up white horses to contrast with the deep blue of the sea. Night in the tropics fell quickly and almost at once the great grey troopships, their rails lined with khaki, would be swallowed up astern as *Repulse* moved out to her warning station ahead of the convoy. Despite the fears of trouble the passage through the Mozambique Channel proved uneventful and at its northern end *Repulse* left the convoy and headed for Mombasa. On arrival we were ordered to form Force 'T' with the small aircraft carrier *Hermes* and the old light cruiser *Emerald*. The remainder of the month was spent covering large areas of the western Indian Ocean, flying constant air searches for enemy surface raiders and supply ships, requiring us to identify any ships found.

Mombasa became our base during this period and we paid two

visits to this pleasant East African port. The ships berthed at Kilindi Docks, glaring white concrete and shimmering in the heat of the tropical sun. Mombasa itself proved as hospitable as Durban, and a host of invitations arrived. This meant that the time between watchkeeping and ship's duties was quickly filled. From the docks the town of Mombasa was reached after a dusty drive of a mile or so, and consisted of a number of whitewashed square buildings reflecting the standard colonial architecture of the period. The shops seemed to be mostly owned by Indians, though inevitably there was an 'Old English Tea Room'.

Another port of call, chiefly for fuel, was Victoria, capital of the Seychelles on the island of Mahé, almost a thousand miles to the east. Here it was even hotter than Mombasa. French was the spoken language and French tastes and customs prevailed.

After another searching sweep we found ourselves back in Durban. Field-Marshal Jan Smuts came down to talk to us and in a witty and forceful speech he gave us a short history of South Africa, of Anglo-Dutch enmities and relationships, and of South Africa's part in the war. This elder statesman who had fought against the Empire in the Boer War, standing on a dais on the catapult deck in an ordinary civilian suit, addressing the ship's company of a British battlecruiser, made an indelible impression on everyone. It was while we were still in Durban that I was promoted to Lieutenant and my second stripe was well and truly wetted at a big dance at the Country Club.

All too soon we were at sea again heading north through the Mozambique Channel, escorting yet another troop convoy destined for North Africa. Another short stay in Mombasa to refuel, and then we put to sea en route for Ceylon, another step in our progress to San Francisco – or so the 'buzz' had it! As we steamed slowly out of Kilindi the Paymaster Commander was heard to remark, somewhat gloomily we all thought, 'And that's the last time we shall see Mombasa before war breaks out in the Far East'. I think it was fair to say that at that time, certainly among the junior officers, there was little idea of war with Japan.

It was at this time that some of us who had been accustomed to sleeping on camp beds under the tail of Y turret experienced a salutary warning of the dangers we ran. Normally the calm seas and gentle swell gave us a feeling of complete security, but one night a freak wave broke inboard and washed us out of our beds! I found myself, bed and all, halfway through the starboard guardrails. I never again slept on the quarterdeck at sea.

On 22 November we entered Colombo harbour to find the whole port in the grip of a dock strike. Armed parties from *Repulse* were at once organized to assist the authorities in running the port and docks. These measures proved successful and matters were restored to normal within the next forty-eight hours.

The following Sunday we listened to a brilliant and inspiring sermon preached by the Bishop of Ceylon at our morning service, held in the traditional naval fashion on our quarterdeck. The six-inch gun-cruiser *Glasgow* entered harbour the same morning and I was invited over to a more modern naval occasion, the buffet supper, by an old school friend, Colin Sandeman, and my term-mate Tom Collier.

The next day *Repulse* left harbour early and carried out an efficiency test for the Commander-in-Chief East Indies, Vice-Admiral Arbuthnot, which involved firing our main armament guns at a battle practice target. This exercise was carried out successfully, although we nearly ran down a large Arab trading dhow which strayed onto our firing course. We were so close when the third salvo was fired that some of the dhow's crew were seen to jump overboard with fright! *Repulse* then returned to Colombo where the Admiral left the ship in his barge which had come out to just outside the harbour. We then headed south to round Dondra Head before standing up the east coast to Trincomalee in thick monsoon weather.

Trincomalee, where we arrived the next day, looked a rather dismal spot under the grey watery haze of the monsoon rain. A large bay, ringed by dense mangrove swamps, was a great contrast to the other sunny harbours we had become accustomed to. In a brief visit ashore the only impression I gathered was of a number of old Portuguese forts overgrown by jungle with little or nothing in the way of base facilities.

Our stay was short and at six o'clock on the evening of 29 November we left the harbour and were soon ploughing through rough seas.

Once clear of Trincomalee the Captain broadcast to the ship's company that we were to rendezvous the next morning with the new battleship *Prince of Wales*, flagship of the newly formed Far Eastern Fleet, whose Commander-in-Chief was to be Admiral Sir Tom Phillips. By now the Far Eastern situation was deteriorating rapidly and war with Japan became a distinct possibility, although this had not really played a part in our thinking, for we were still Europe – and Germany – orientated. Now, as some of us began to look at the strength of the Japanese Navy, the feeling grew that here was a real chance to see action and with an enemy likely to be numerically superior.

CHAPTER 5

Prince of Wales and *Repulse*

As the rendezvous drew nearer and our RD/F receiver[1] picked up the *Prince of Wales* and her escort, all of us on the bridge focused our binoculars on the bearing on which we expected her to be sighted. Then, suddenly, into our vision came the distinctive and massive silhouette of the *Prince of Wales*, screened by her escort of four destroyers, throwing up a large white bow wave as she thrust into the seas.

Admiral Phillips had flown on ahead to Singapore, so Captain Tennant, being the Senior Officer, signalled the *Prince of Wales* to take station astern. We learned afterwards that this signal created no small stir in the *Prince of Wales*!

Dawn the following day brought Sabang and other islands at the northern tip of Sumatra into sight and, as soon as we had turned south into the calmer waters of the Malacca Straits, the destroyers came alongside the big ships in turn to be refuelled. *Repulse* refuelled the *Jupiter*, one of the new J Class destroyers.

The passage down the Straits was uneventful; watch followed watch and, as we approached the southern end, we saw glimpses of the cloud-shrouded mountains of Malaya; the sight of an occasional Chinese trading junk provided for most of us the first authentic taste of the East. By dawn the next day we were passing through the more confined waters of the southern end of the Straits. The low hills of Johore and jungle-covered Singapore Island came into sight towards midday. We turned eastwards and glimpsed Singapore itself and the shipping lying in the roads of Keppel Harbour, the whole shimmering under the heat haze. Captain Tennant now signalled *Prince of Wales* to take station ahead. She made an impressive sight as she passed close by us.

[1] Radar was originally known by the British as RD/F.

We were met by three of the new China gunboats, recently withdrawn from the China Station, *Scorpion*, *Dragonfly* and *Grasshopper*. They steamed past us on opposite courses at full speed and made a brave sight with their pendant numbers blowing straight out in the breeze. The sun was swelteringly hot and the atmosphere very humid and we were glad of the breeze made by our own speed.

The Fleet approached the boom to enter the Straits of Johore abreast Pulau Ubin which divides the Straits in the middle. At this point the destroyers fell astern. At slow speed we passed up the narrowing waters of the Straits. The shore on the north side was largely jungle, interspersed with small fishing villages, each with their own fish pagars.[1] On the Singapore side, in marked contrast, were the new buildings of Changi Barracks and the Royal Air Force Station, Seletar, with its hangars, slipways and Catalina flying boats moored offshore. At last came the Naval Base itself, with its impressive collection of new buildings – the Commander-in-Chief's house, Fleet Shore Accommodation (F.S.A.), the cranes, floating docks, marine shops and stores of the dockyard itself. A number of other ships could be seen, belonging to the local flotilla and others undergoing repairs. *Repulse* came to her buoy off the dockyard while *Prince of Wales* went alongside.

The next two days were spent in fuelling, storing and taking in the atmosphere of our new surroundings. It was rumoured that *Repulse* would shortly be off south to 'show the flag' in various places and in particular Port Darwin in Northern Australia. Information of Japanese movements and intentions did not seem very apparent to the majority of us.

The rumours proved correct and on 5 December we sailed for Darwin, screened by the old destroyers *Vampire* and *Tenedos*. Once clear of the Straits we headed south, the destroyers returning to Singapore early the next day. In perfect tropical weather and a calm sea we passed by the numerous islands including Banka and Billiton. This idyll was abruptly ended when we were ordered to return to Singapore in the early evening of the 6th. It was understood that there was a 'flap on'.

Our standard cruising zig-zag ceased, speed was increased to twenty-eight knots and we steered north into the rapidly falling tropical night. Early in the forenoon of the next day 7 December, 1941, our destroyers met us to screen us through the swept channel

---

[1]   A pagar is a fish trap consisting of a length of piles driven into the mud in lines to hold nets stretched between. There is usually a small hut on the piles at the seaward end.

past the Horsborough Light. We arrived back at the Naval Base at 4 p.m. and immediately an oiler secured alongside to top us up with fuel.

The ship was soon buzzing with news and rumours. We learnt that Admiral Phillips had flown to Manila for discussions with Admiral Hart, the Commander of the United States Asiatic Fleet, and had only just returned. There was also news of Japanese troop convoys being sighted in the Gulf of Siam, and there seemed to be a general air of expectancy that great events were about to take place.

That night after dinner groups of officers were standing about on the quarterdeck keeping cool in the still tropical air. The lights of the Naval Base and of various other ships shone out and were reflected in the still waters lapping gently against the ship's side. There was supposed to be a 'brown out' in force, with lighting at reduced brilliance, though this was not very evident and we compared it unfavourably with the strictness of blackout regulations at home.

I, personally, was looking forward to a 'night in' after the watchkeeping of the previous night and so turned in as soon as things quietened down. Most Officers returned to the wardroom for a nightcap before the bar closed.

Some time later I was awakened by the alarm rattlers sounding out their harsh burr-burrs. I noticed the Commander dash outside in his pyjamas. I was sleeping on my safari bed just outside his cabin, and then, over the broadcast came the strident bugle notes of 'Repel Aircraft'. Still in my pyjamas, with a reefer jacket over them and clutching my tin hat and gas mask, and struggling to put on my anti-flash gear, I raced up to my action station on M2 Pom Pom.[1]

A strange hush fell over the ship after the first hurried and noisy moments of closing up; it was broken only by the quiet whirring of the training motors at the guns, the opening and shutting of the ammunition ready-use lockers, the thump of shells and ammunition boxes as the loading numbers 'stood to' and a few subdued commands from the Captains of Guns. I looked at my watch; it was almost 4 a.m. We were not kept waiting long, for within a few minutes the long white fingers of the searchlights ashore began searching the sky.

The stark order 'alarm port' was received over the broadcast and all eyes turned to the bearing indicated. Then, quite suddenly, over the

---

[1] *Repulse* was armed, as part of her close-range air defence armament, with three eight-barrelled 2-pounder mountings, one on each side and one overlooking Y turret. Their effective range was 2500 yards and with a very high rate of fire. M2 was on the port side.

54

1. The author as Midshipman, 1938.

2. Cadets taking sights.
(Author second from right).

3. Captain E. J. Spooner, DSO, 1938.

4. HMS *Repulse* and the *Prince of Wales* under attack, 10 December 1941.

5. HMS *Repulse* under attack. (Watercolour by the author).

port quarter, from the direction of Singapore city, we saw the searchlight beams converge on a formation of nine aircraft flying straight towards us at an estimated height of ten thousand feet. Almost at once the port high-angle guns opened fire, their flashes blinding us. A series of terrific flashes and detonations from the base indicated that the 5.25-inch guns of the *Prince of Wales* were also in action. From our viewpoint no bursts appeared to be very close to the enemy formation. From the base itself and from many of the smaller ships we could see the tracer from the batteries of Bofors guns streaming skywards to curve away thousands of feet below the target.

It was not an impressive display of fire control discipline and a terrible waste of ammunition. We noticed also that in many parts of the base lights seemed not to have gone out, but to have been switched up to full brilliancy! No bombs were dropped by the aircraft as the formation passed overhead and disappeared in an easterly direction. After a short time the air-raid 'Yellow' was received, whereupon the lights all went out! At the 'White' warning they all came up again at full brilliancy. This seemed to us to be a poor augury of the general preparedness for war of the Naval Base, if not of the whole of Singapore. The 'Secure' was sounded and we fell out to return to our bunks and hammocks, full of excited questions. These were soon answered by the Commander broadcasting to the ship's company. He said that the aircraft had been Japanese, probably flying from Saigon, that the Japanese Fleet had attacked Pearl Harbor, that the Japanese Army was at this moment landing in north Malaya, and we were now, together with the U.S.A., at war with Japan. The date was 8 December, 1941.

We then settled down to get some rest during what remained of the night. For the majority of us, our reaction to this piece of news was, 'How lucky we are to be in at the outset of this new extension of the war. There is a large Fleet arrayed against us and therefore a challenge worthy of our mettle, and, most important, nobody else to steal our thunder.' Morale was very high.

The forenoon of the first day of the Far East War found me as Officer of the Watch. In between the multifarious duties of a busy forenoon watch, I joined with various others in speculating on our next moves; most of us thought we should be off to sea and not sitting in harbour. At eleven o'clock we went to stations to 'Repel Aircraft' when the alarm sounded. Nothing came of it, but it served to keep us all on our toes and brought a heightened sense of expectancy after the somewhat easy time we had had since leaving the more active war zone.

Shortly after this the Captain left the ship to go to the *Prince of Wales* for a conference of Commanding Officers. The ship was brought to two hours' notice for sea. Captain Tennant returned at 2 p.m. and the ship was given the news that we were going to sea that evening, in company with the *Prince of Wales*, on an operation. Spirits soared; at last we were going to have our chance. Two newspaper correspondents arrived on board, O. D. Gallagher of the *Daily Express*, and an American, Cecil Brown of C.B.S. They were accompanied by an official Admiralty photographer, Horace Abrahams.

At 5 p.m. all was ready and *Repulse* slipped from her buoy, 'pointed ship' and slowly gathered way, saluting the flagship as we passed her. The thunderous vibration of the ship's propellers while turning slowed to a more rhythmic beat as we steamed down the channel to the sea, following astern of the destroyers *Vampire* and *Tenedos*. The two other destroyers of our screen, *Electra* and *Express*, were already at sea, waiting for us outside the boom. The *Prince of Wales* followed astern of us.

Once through the boom *Prince of Wales* passed ahead and the destroyers took up screening stations on either bow. The force, now given the code name 'Z', headed east into the night. Captain Tennant told us, 'We are off to look for trouble. I expect we shall find it. We may run up against submarines, destroyers, aircraft and surface ships. We are going to carry out a sweep to the northward to see what we can pick up and what we can roar up. We must all be on our toes.'

The tropical night closed in quickly and the weather began to deteriorate with heavy rain squalls which made station-keeping difficult. The faint stern light of the flagship was just visible above the pale scut of her wake, and the broad zigzag which the force was carrying out did not make things easier. I think most people were thinking that this time we were going to see action and, as the Captain had warned us to be, we really were on our toes. I don't remember any sense of fear as to the possible outcome.

After dawn Action Stations on the 9th we reverted to the second degree of readiness, with half the ship's company closed up. I became 'watch on' and 'watch off' as Officer of the Watch. As soon as we cleared the Anambas Islands to the east, Force 'Z' turned north and headed up into the Gulf of Siam. Every hour steamed now brought us into greater likelihood of contact with the enemy. *Vampire* reported sighting an enemy aircraft shortly after dawn, but this sighting was unconfirmed.

The ships were zigzagging at seventeen knots, steering to the north-west, and conditions were ideal for concealing our approach, mist patches alternating with rain and a moderate wind and sea. The hot and humid conditions, however, made life below very uncomfortable, with all watertight doors and hatches closed.

Admiral Phillips sent a long informatory signal of events that had taken place during the night. This signal, together with four or five long 'operating intentions' signals, gave us all a clear idea of what we were attempting to do:

'THE ENEMY HAS MADE SEVERAL LANDINGS ON THE NORTH COAST OF MALAYA AND HAS MADE LOCAL PROGRESS. OUR ARMY IS NOT LARGE AND IS HARD PRESSED IN PLACES. OUR AIR FORCE HAS HAD TO DESTROY AND ABANDON ONE OR MORE AERODROMES. MEANWHILE FAT TRANSPORTS LIE OFF THE COAST. THIS IS OUR OPPORTUNITY BEFORE THE ENEMY CAN ESTABLISH HIMSELF. WE HAVE MADE A WIDE CIRCUIT TO AVOID AIR RECONNAISSANCE AND HOPE TO SURPRISE THE ENEMY SHORTLY AFTER SUNRISE TOMORROW WEDNESDAY. WE MAY HAVE THE LUCK TO TRY OUR METAL AGAINST THE OLD JAPANESE BATTLECRUISER *KONGO* OR AGAINST SOME JAPANESE CRUISERS AND DESTROYERS WHICH ARE REPORTED IN THE GULF OF SIAM. WE ARE SURE TO GET SOME USEFUL PRACTISE WITH THE HA ARMAMENT.[1] WHATEVER WE MEET I WANT TO FINISH QUICKLY AND SO GET WELL CLEAR TO THE EASTWARD BEFORE THE JAPANESE CAN MASS TOO FORMIDABLE A SCALE OF ATTACK AGAINST US. SO SHOOT TO SINK'.

The weather protected us until nearly 5 p.m. that day, but about then the low visibility suddenly cleared and the horizon revealed the presence of three single-engined float planes, obviously catapulted off Japanese warships! This was the worst possible luck and our hopes for a surprise attack were lost.

Darkness brought an atmosphere of uncertainty, not so much of menace, but for what now lay ahead of us. Was it to be another abortive operation? Would the enemy still be there? Whatever the outcome, we knew we had a full day and night, and possibly even another day at action stations. We all prepared for it, laying out our anti-flash protective clothing and clean underwear. Dinner was rather stark as the mess furniture had been secured and pictures and curtains taken down as the Gunroom was to be occupied by one of the Damage Control Parties.

Force 'Z' continued on to the north till darkness had fallen and then at 7 p.m. course was altered to the west towards Singora in order to confuse any shadowers that might still sight us and speed was increased at the same time. At about this time we learnt that *Tenedos*

[1] High-Angle guns for use against aircraft.

had been detached and ordered to return to Singapore as her fuel endurance was insufficient for her to remain with us any longer.

Later, at 8.55 p.m., the Admiral told the force: 'I have most regretfully cancelled the operation because, having been located by aircraft, surprise was lost and our target would be almost certain to be gone by the morning and the enemy fully prepared for us.'

Course was now altered to the south-east in order to return to Singapore via the Anambas Islands.[1] The receipt of this signal was a great anti-climax. The ship's company did not react at all well and were very cast down as the news filtered round, but the routine and duties of the night watches took over as we steamed south at twenty knots. The night now seemed especially cold and cheerless in our disappointment. I went off watch at midnight and lay unable to sleep in the damp heat of my cabin. I became aware of an increase in speed by the increased propeller noise but did not realize the reason until I came onto the bridge again for the morning watch. Apparently, just after midnight course was again altered and we swung round to the south-west and increased speed to twenty-five knots. This change of plan was the result of a signal received from Singapore that an enemy landing had been reported at Kuantan on the east coast of Malaya, about 180 miles to the north of Singapore, the intention being to arrive off the town at dawn and see what we could do to help. It was immediately noticeable how spirits were revived at this further promise of action, as I realized when I returned to the bridge for dawn Action Stations.

An hour before dawn the ship's company were sent to breakfast in two watches. I remember the frightful 'fug' in the Gunroom after its all-night occupation by Fire and Repair parties, and also the vibration of the ship's propellers at twenty-four knots. Our early breakfast at 4.30 a.m. consisted of scrambled or boiled eggs and a slice of ham. Ten minutes only were allowed and I remember that I burnt my tongue trying to swallow my coffee. As I left the Gunroom, I wished one of the midshipmen, Kit Bros, 'Good Luck' before returning to the bridge for dawn Action Stations.[2] As the Commander reported to the Captain that the ship was at First Degree of Readiness, the darkness began imperceptibly to lighten from the east. Our binoc-

[1] Unknown to either side, Force 'Z' was at this moment only twenty-two miles to the south of a Japanese force of four heavy cruisers. Also unbeknown to us, a Japanese submarine, *I-65*, had sighted and reported the force at 1.45 that afternoon.

[2] Kit Bros was stationed far below in the 15-inch transmitting station, and was reported to have calmed a panic as the ship was sinking, when men had tried to climb through the one small hatchway. He lost his life as a result. It was later understood that he was posthumously recommended for a V.C.

ulars swept the horizon and all appeared to be clear, and then at about 5 a.m. what was taken to be a small tug towing three or four barges was sighted to the north. No action was taken as it was thought that, if they were enemy, they could not affect the situation at Kuantan, as we should be there first. The next incident occurred at about 6.30 a.m., when an aircraft was seen low to the east for a short time before disappearing. The sun was now well above the horizon and provided a welcome warmth after the damp chill of the long night.

An hour later, as we neared the coast, one of *Prince of Wales'* Walrus amphibian aircraft was catapulted off to carry out a coastal and river reconnaissance. The coast was now clearly visible. The sharp outline of conical blue hills, their lower slopes enshrouded in white wreaths of mist rising from the jungle, were a beautiful sight. I, like many others, wondered what the mist could be concealing. Kuantan lay in a small gap in the hills and *Express* was ordered ahead to make a close examination of the little port itself. Some time later she signalled by light that 'All was as quiet as a wet Sunday afternoon'.

During this period we had been steaming south at reduced speed on a course parallel to the coast. *Express* rejoined at 8.45 a.m. and course was then altered to the east and then again to the north to investigate the tug and barges seen earlier. As I had the forenoon watch, I left the bridge to go below for a quick wash and shave. On returning to the bridge I found that we were steaming south again, zigzagging at twenty-one knots and I had to concentrate on station-keeping. At 1015 our RD/F detected an aircraft to the east and *Prince of Wales* reported it as a shadower. The Admiral now signalled First Degree of anti-aircraft readiness. Speed was increased to twenty-five knots. Very soon after this and just as I was once again leaving the bridge to go down to my action stations, the Chief Yeoman of Signals sighted a merchant ship which on identification proved to be the SS *Haldis* en route from Hong Kong to Singapore.

I was hardly at my station as Fire Distribution Officer at M2 when aircraft were reported to be closing from the starboard bow. I just had time to put on my anti-flash gear and tin hat.

It was now a beautiful clear sunny day and about 11.15 a.m. Suddenly I saw *Prince of Wales'* starboard 5.25-inch guns open fire, followed by our own 4-inch. Both ships were now swinging to starboard and I looked ahead to the port bow as the port side guns opened up. Looking up, I saw eight small silver aircraft flying towards us in a tight line-abreast formation. They were clearly going to fly straight over *Repulse* and there was a strange inevitability about

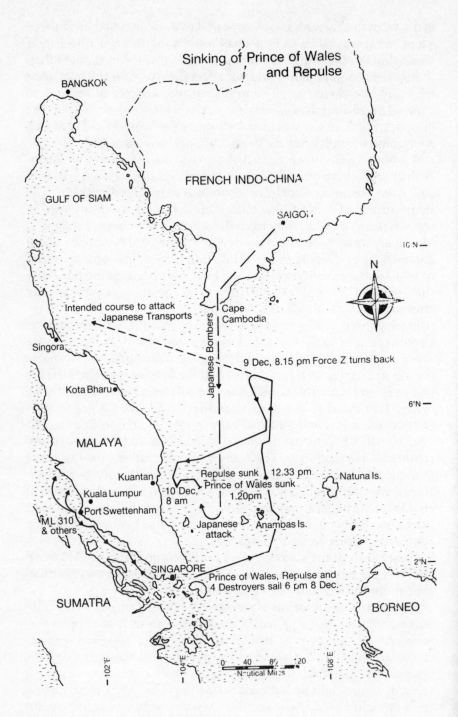

Sinking of Prince of Wales and Repulse

BANGKOK

FRENCH INDO-CHINA

GULF OF SIAM

SAIGON

10 N —

Intended course to attack
Japanese Transports

Cape
Cambodia

Singora

9 Dec, 8.15 pm Force Z turns back

Kota Bharu

6°N —

MALAYA

Repulse sunk | 12.33 pm

Kuantan

Prince of Wales sunk

Kuala Lumpur

10 Dec,
8 am

1.20pm

Natuna Is.

Port Swettenham

ML 310
& others

Japanese
attack

Anambas Is.

2°N —

SINGAPORE

Prince of Wales, Repulse and
4 Destroyers sail 6 pm 8 Dec.

SUMATRA

BORNEO

0   40   80   120
Nautical Miles

60

their intention. The HA guns were crashing out in steady salvoes and their cordite smoke blew back across the ship. As the enemy aircraft were flying at 10,000 feet, M2 and the other close-range guns were out of range. I held on to the gun platform's safety rails, saw *Prince of Wales* enveloped in yellow brown cordite smoke through which flashed the flame of each salvo. Our wakes streamed astern like great white snakes. The aircraft were passing right over us, while round about them the grey and black shell-bursts pockmarked the blue sky. We suddenly became aware of the scream of descending bombs. It was an extraordinary feeling – excited by the action and noise and at the same time knowing that within seconds you might be dead.

In a split second the ship was engulfed in water from towering bomb splashes on either side of us abreast the main hangars and catapult deck. The bombs had been dropped simultaneously and had straddled us. At once I noticed that smoke was coming from the port aircraft hangar. As there were no other aircraft immediately in sight, I made my way down the boat deck and saw a small jagged hole through the deck at the after corner of the hangar. It was no more than nine inches in diameter. A quantity of paunch mats and other boat deck gear were smouldering; the fire hoses were not fully effective, as apparently pressure was low in the fire main caused by bomb damage. The Senior Engineer[1] was soon up on the boat deck with a damage control party. He told me that the bomb had penetrated to the Marines' mess deck, where it had exploded on the armoured deck. There was also a fire on the catapult deck and one of our Walrus amphibian aircraft was so badly damaged that it had to be jettisoned.[2]

As I made my way back to M2 I thought what an accurate and determined attack it had been, as good as anything seen from the Germans. The hit by one or more bombs did not, however, appear to affect the ship's performance and a brief announcement confirmed this impression. We did not learn of the numbers of dead and injured until later. I noticed that my new khaki shirt and shorts were covered in small black spots from the bomb splashes that had engulfed the ship. There was now a lull of about twenty minutes before the next attack by enemy aircraft was detected and fire re-opened by both ships. I watched carefully as about eight or nine large twin-engined

[1] The 'Senior Engineer' was the title given to the Engine Room Department's second-in-command. He was always responsible for the ship's damage control parties.
[2] The other of the ship's Walrus had been flown off as an A/S Patrol ahead of the Force. It was unable to return to the ship when the action commenced, staying in the vicinity until forced from lack of fuel to return to Singapore.

bombers lost height in succession. At this early stage it was not clear which of us was to be the target. I remember being struck by what I chose to think was their rather sinister and oriental appearance; why I didn't know, but that is how I felt at the moment. As soon as they had reached the level at which they were going to release their torpedoes, for they were obviously going to carry out a torpedo attack, they turned towards us. It was soon apparent that they were attacking *Prince of Wales*, except for one aircraft which was headed straight for *Repulse*. Now all the close-range guns opened fire, firing barrage[1], as were both our 4-inch HA guns as well as our 4-inch Triples of the secondary armament. Our starboard side guns were also firing at a second attack developing on our starboard side. In *Repulse* the noise was stupendous. The entire AA armament was now firing, 4-inch as well as Pom-Poms, Oerlikons, Vickers .5-inch machine guns and even Lewis guns. The flash and blast of these guns pounded the senses and deafened one, even with our new ear-protectors. The resultant haze of cordite smoke enveloped the upper decks. By now both ships were manoeuvring independently at twenty-five knots, heeling over as they altered course to avoid the torpedoes that were being launched at us. *Repulse* was swinging to starboard to comb the tracks of the main starboard side attack and this enabled us to see clearly the effect of the attack on *Prince of Wales*. I saw two enormous columns of dirty sea spring up; she was clearly hit portside aft and was heeled over to starboard.[2] Whether this was due to her alteration of course to port, or was the immediate result of being hit, I could not say. She presented a vivid sight, heeled over enveloped in browny-yellow smoke from her guns and obviously badly damaged. *Repulse* had not been hit by the torpedoes launched at her and was now swinging back to port, taking *Prince of Wales* out of sight. Everything was a bedlam of noise and activity. It was during this attack that I had the impression of our Walrus, catapulted off earlier to carry out an anti-submarine patrol, diving down to sea level through the attacking planes.

Almost at once, at 11.48 a.m., we were attacked by another group of high-level bombers and our 4-inch guns were continually in action. The loading numbers on the close-range guns such as M2 were furiously clearing the spent cartridge cases and ammunition boxes out

[1] The shells were all fused to explode at a set range.
[2] *Prince of Wales* was hit almost simultaneously by two torpedoes. The port outer propeller shaft was buckled: at the time it was still revolving at the revolutions for 25 knots. This opened up watertight compartments along the port side and her speed was reduced to 15 knots and she was never under control again. She became a sitting duck.

of the way of the gun mountings. Again we heard the screaming of plunging bombs, and I was thankful, while still being conscious of the fear the noise occasioned, that I was so fully occupied with my search for new attackers on our port side. The scream and crash of the arriving bombs and high columns of water on either side indicated that we had been straddled once again, but this time there were luckily no hits.

Our ship was being brilliantly handled by the Captain. He now steadied her on a new course to close the badly damaged *Prince of Wales*, which was now listing and, we could see, had the 'Not Under Control' black balls hoisted. Captain Tennant signalled to the flagship, which was about a mile away, to know whether he could be of any assistance, but there was no reply. During the slight lull that followed the high-level attack everybody worked feverishly to resupply ammunition and be ready for the next attack.

With a new attack threatening some eight to ten minutes later, speed was once again increased as the Captain manoeuvred our ship to evade the new attack. Seven aircraft were approaching and dropped down low to deliver another torpedo attack. One aircraft flew across to the starboard side and I lost sight of it. The remaining six came in in two groups of three straight for us. Once again a cacophony of sound broke out as all the guns, now in barrage fire, opened up, the whole ship shook and shuddered with the continuous firing. I sat on the guard rails at the rear of M2 gun, hitting the Trainer's shoulder and indicating with my arm a change of target. Shouting directions was out of the question with the continuous noise of the guns.[1]

As the aircraft came in and dropped their torpedoes, they continued flying straight at us, firing machine guns right up to the moment that they swooped up over us to bank steeply away. It was possible to have a really close look at them. I noticed that they were all painted a dull green with pale lower parts and a red Japanese sun or 'poached egg' outlined in white on their wings and fuselage sides. Watching the tracks of the torpedoes approaching, one was mesmerized by their approach, knowing the destructive power which they possessed. It was only our training and the excitement of the

[1] The two key members of the close-range guns' crews were the 'Trainer' who moved the gun in the lateral plane and the 'Layer' who moved the gun in the vertical plane. It had been previous experience that in the 'heat' of an action the 'Trainer' could become 'locked on' and blind to any new and more threatening danger. Any officer not otherwise employed in our anti-aircraft action was designated as a 'Fire Distribution Officer' with the express duty of directing the Trainer on to the new target.

moment that enabled us to keep our minds on the task of continuing to fire at the attacking aircraft. The gun drill was perfect; nobody made the slightest mistake that I could see. It seemed impossible that the aircraft could fly through the barrage in front of them, they were almost lost to sight amid the bursting of hundreds of shells. The yellowy-grey smoke from the bursts floated astern of us as we continued to manoeuvre at twenty-five knots.

After a lull of about a quarter of an hour, during which time a jam was cleared in two of our eight barrels, more ammunition got ready and spent shells cleared away, another attack started to develop. So far we had had a charmed life. Our confidence in the Captain's ability to evade attacks was high, but the odds seemed to be increasing. This time the attacking aircraft split into two groups to attack *Repulse* from either side. Again all guns went into barrage firing. It seemed that the attackers were releasing their torpedoes well outside our barrage range. One could clearly see the torpedoes splashing into the sea and the start of the track towards us. This time one track was so close and still heading for the ship that, with a despairing feeling, I knew we were about to be hit. For what seemed like an eternity, though in reality was only a few seconds, I held on to the guard rails of the gun in anticipation of the explosion. It came with a great jarring shudder, as though a giant hand had shaken the ship, which brought gear crashing down. It seemed to have hit us amidships, just abaft the port hangar. However, we continued to steam at high speed and manoeuvrability was seemingly undiminished, until a second torpedo hit us further aft abreast 'Y' Turret and again the great column of spray towered up from the point of the explosion. At the same moment I realized that T2 triple 4-inch gun, trained on the beam, was masking M2's line of fire, and, as I judged M2 to be the more effective weapon, I ordered Petty Officer Kent, the Captain of T2, to train fore and aft, but we found the training rack was damaged and we had to resort to a block and tackle. It was slow and hard work, but effective.

The starboard guns were in action against the attack developing from that side. I continued to search the portside horizon to pick up at the earliest moment any further attack from that side. I could see more aircraft attacking the already crippled flagship and, as I watched, I saw three or four swing round and head for us.

Again the sky was blackened with shell-bursts from our fire, but the aircraft came on relentlessly to drop their torpedoes, the tracks of which could be seen heading straight for us. With the ship already committed to a swing to starboard to meet the attack from that side, the torpedoes were unavoidable and we were hit three times with only seconds separating the explosions. The first exploded near the Gunroom, the second abreast the mainmast, which shook and swayed, the heavy steel wire shrouds whipping violently. The ship seemed to stagger in her stride and I knew instinctively that this was the end, that *Repulse* was doomed.

It was during this attack and while watching the tracks of the approaching torpedoes that I saw one that seemed to hit the ship at a very oblique angle. I waited for the explosion, but none came. After a few seconds I saw this torpedo running slowly up the port side apparently in contact with the ship, and I distinctly noticed its yellow warhead.

It was at this point in the action that I ceased to follow the rules of a Fire Distribution Officer and allowed the guns to continue firing as the planes came on. One aircraft turned parallel with the ship only a few hundred yards away. We were firing at point-blank range; every detail was clear with flames eating their way along the fuselage from its tail to its transparent nose. The pilot and nose gunner or bomb aimer could be seen struggling to free themselves from the inferno engulfing them. Then, as we watched, quite suddenly the nose dipped and the aircraft dived into the sea, leaving a smoking patch of wreckage which passed rapidly astern.

All this time the starboard guns were going hammer and tongs at the attack on their side, but another huge shock told us that we had been hit yet again. We were firing continuously and shot another aircraft down on the port bow, and, as we passed it, with its tail sticking out of the water, a great cheer went up from all who could see it. These last attacks, and the great activity they produced, in reality occupied only a few minutes (1222–1225), though time seemed to stand still, so intense were these events.

As soon as the attacks were over, I had a moment to take stock and look around and was immediately aware of the heavy list to port that the ship was taking, and also of our failing speed. Looking aft, I could see that the quarterdeck abreast 'Y' turret was already awash. Immediately forward of us I noticed men scrambling up the steepening slope of the flagdeck. The Gunnery Officer was now leaning over the rear of the Admiral's bridge shouting to all hands to 'Abandon Ship'. At about the same time I suddenly realized that M2 gun was at maximum elevation due to the list on the ship, and would no longer bear on an approaching target, had there been any. Even so, I had the greatest difficulty in persuading the Trainer and Captain of the gun, Leading Seaman Davies, to leave; he was full of fight and wanted to stay.

The time had come when obviously no more could be done. The ship's list was increasing rapidly and we all began to scramble up the flagdeck and round the forward funnel to reach the starboard ladder down to the upper deck. There were a number of ominously slippery patches on the deck, caused by the blood of the dead and wounded, killed by enemy machine-gunning.

On reaching the ladder I saw it was crowded with men trying to descend and decided to go further forward to the starboard triple 4-inch gun, and there climbed over the guard rails in order to slide down the screen onto 'B' gun deck, which I did by climbing down over a still-secured Carley raft. I slipped back twice on this now steeply tilting deck, trying to reach the guard rails. I finally succeeded, climbed over them and, sliding down the forecastle screen over the paravane and ammunition derrick, I reached the forecastle deck itself. A number of dull booms and crashes could be heard from below as various fixtures such as lockers and other heavy gear broke away, crushing and mutilating anyone in their path.

It was obvious that there was very little time left and so once again it was over the guard rails of the upper deck and then the strange sensation of walking down the ship's side just abreast of the bridge. As I reached the bilge keel, the ship was still moving through the water, the ship's side was horizontal and I was standing upright. Glancing fore and aft down the whole length of the starboard side, I was reminded of that classic photograph of the German armoured cruiser *Blücher* sinking at the battle of the Dogger Bank in January, 1915, a picture I had carried in my mind ever since I was a young boy, fascinated and awed by the magnitude and tragedy of the scene. As with the *Blücher*, hundreds of men were now standing on the ship's side and bilge keel, some already sliding down the rounded bottom, before making a last jump. At least, I thought, this was not the bitterly cold grey North Sea in January, but a warm South China Sea with the sun shining.

I took my cap and shoes off and looked at the numerous heads of those who, forward of me, had already jumped and were floating past as the ship was still moving ahead at about five knots, even though on her beam ends. It was now or never and I took a deep breath and jumped. As soon as I surfaced I struck out to put as much distance between me and *Repulse* as I could; the danger of being caught in her still revolving propellers was uppermost in my mind during the first few seconds in the water.

Having rid myself of all encumbrances, I swam as hard as I could, remembering stories of survivors being sucked down by sinking ships. I must have swum for three or four minutes before turning on my back to see what was happening to the ship. I was just in time to see the last of her. About sixty feet of *Repulse*'s bow was sticking out of the water, the sun glittering on her light grey topside and on her red anti-fouling bottom. The ship seemed to hang poised for a few seconds and then, to the accompaniment of subterranean rumblings, *Repulse* slid under the surface.

Up until this moment I had not really felt any fear as, during the action, there had been too much to do for fear to dominate one's thoughts. Now, momentarily, it did. I realized that I had neither my inflatable waistcoat, sent to me by my parents on the outbreak of war, nor my naval inflatable life-ring on. In a moment of fear, I pulled my clothes off in order to swim more easily. It was only hours afterwards that I realized I had thrown my gold watch, cuff links and money away, having put them in my shirt pocket that morning.

The sea was a mass of bobbing heads; someone called for three cheers for the 'Old Girl', which were heartily given. I believe, but am not certain, that I then called for three cheers for the Captain – somebody did at any rate! The sea was calm and warm and I began to think of a more permanent means of supporting myself. Strangely, I did not think of sharks. It was with difficulty that the realization of what had happened began to sink in. I just could not seem to acknowledge it during those first moments.

Nearer the position where the ship had sunk, I saw a half submerged whaler[1] filled with men. I was by now several hundred yards away. In the distance I could see a heavily listing *Prince of Wales*, still under attack. The men around now started to sing 'Roll out the Barrel'; morale was still high even in such adversity and in the face of such disaster.

By now I estimated I had been in the water about half an hour, alternately treading water and swimming. I noticed the glassy slick and acrid smell of oil fuel spreading out from the position where I judged *Repulse* to have sunk. It seemed to me that some men were already suffering from the effects and called to everyone near me to keep their heads up and mouths shut. Some distance away two of our destroyer screen were stopped and seemed to be picking up survivors, so I started to swim towards them. It seemed a long time before I got near enough to feel that I was going to be picked up. As I got closer to the nearest destroyer, I had to swim into the oil fuel and

[1] A 27-foot Naval pulling boat.

smelt its overpowering stench. At last I reached her side and swam with many others to one of the scrambling nets hanging over her side, looking up at the guard rails lined with men encouraging us and helping us to clamber up the now slippery oil-covered netting and hand ropes. It was terribly difficult to get a grip, but at last I got up and, as I was helped over the guard rails, a feeling of great relief came over me.

The destroyer's upper deck was crowded with oil-covered survivors standing or lying, exhausted and wounded among air intakes, torpedo tubes and lockers.

The stench of oil fuel pervaded everything. I picked my way aft along the hot steel decks, to reach the crowded quarterdeck. My whole body was stinging and smarting from exposure to oil fuel and the tropical sun. I now realized how foolish I had been to take off my clothes.

As soon as we had recovered our breath, those of us who had climbed on board *Electra*, for she it was, turned to help her ship's company to assist the many still in the water and struggling to climb on board. It was necessary to go over the side to tie lines round those too exhausted to climb up unaided. In the middle of this the gun crews were ordered to stand by and *Electra* went ahead under the threat of attack, but the formation of enemy aircraft flew over us without dropping any bombs. *Electra* now went slowly astern again, towards the groups of survivors she had had to leave, and the rescue work restarted. One of the last to be picked up was *Repulse*'s Captain of Marines, Bob Lang. He was very weak and was desperately trying to reach a line that had been thrown in his direction.

When it appeared that everyone in her immediate vicinity had been picked up, *Electra* got under way and headed towards the position that *Prince of Wales* had been reported sunk. We all lined the guardrails looking for anyone swimming. The whole area was covered with her floating wreckage, including a number of boats which apparently had floated off the boat deck and were now crowded with survivors. Her launch was actually cruising around under power picking up survivors. I also remember the Commander-in-Chief's barge floating with its cover still on, its green enamel paint stained brown with oil sludge. In a way this symbol of what had been made the tragedy more compelling. A last look-round was being taken when the launch came alongside and asked for additional fuel to get to Singapore under her own power. Those in it were sharply ordered to come on board. Then, with no further survivors to be seen, *Electra* set course for Singapore.

Everybody now settled down as best they could; *Electra* was soon steaming at twenty-five knots with 500 survivors of both big ships on board. To preserve stability we were all ordered to lie down and as many as possible went below. It was fortunate that the sea was calm, as even the slightest use of helm for whatever reason resulted in a long and potentially dangerous roll. A tot of rum was served out to everyone, using up the entire ship's supply, and most of her food was distributed between us. I went down to the wardroom for some lime juice, having missed the rum, but it was packed tight with oily, grimy and tired men, so I returned once more to the quarterdeck.

Not long after we had set a course for Singapore a number of our Brewster Buffalo fighters appeared and circled round. A lot of men shook their fists and shouted, 'You ought to have been here two hours ago', abuse which, as we later found out, was unjustified.[1]

As well as the inevitable reaction of tiredness, I was beginning to feel distinctly chilly in the late afternoon at thirty knots, being still in my birthday suit, and set out to try and find something to put on. I was able to borrow a shirt and trousers from the Sub-Lieutenant. It was while putting them on in his cabin that I became aware that not only his face was familiar, but also that of his girlfriend, whose framed picture was on his chest. I discovered that he had been one of the 'Upper Yardsmen' in my party, 'G' for George, when we boarded the French torpedo boat *La Flore* at Portsmouth in 1940. The girlfriend had been one of Whale Island's prettiest and most popular Wrens at the same time.

Lying down on the quivering, vibrating deck, we tried to sleep, but the oil on our skins and in our eyes burnt and smarted so much that it was impossible, tired though we now were. Men were curled up and huddled everywhere. Night came and uncomfortable, hungry and cold, we longed for Singapore. There was a scare at about 9 p.m. when we passed four United States destroyers steaming north at full speed to search for survivors. They had apparently made the wrong reply to our challenge, but fortunately somehow correct identities were established in time and we continued on our course.

The remainder of our passage was uneventful and we finally berthed alongside *Vampire*, who had preceded us, at the Naval Base shortly after midnight. Elaborate arrangements had been made to receive us and we could see a line of ambulances standing by on the

---

[1] No signal reporting the attack had been sent by the flagship and Singapore did not know where we were until Captain Tennant, taking matters into his own hands, made an emergency W/T report at 1158, to 'ANY BRITISH MAN OF WAR; ENEMY AIRCRAFT BOMBING', giving his position.

dockside as we secured. Under the sickly light of the reduced power, the walking wounded were helped over the brows from ship to ship and ship to jetty by medical orderlies and volunteers from other ships at the base. Then it was the turn of those of us remaining. As we slowly moved forward to the brow, we sadly passed a row of blanket-covered bodies of those who had died on board during the brief passage to Singapore from wounds and oil fuel poisoning. As we passed across *Vampire*, each man gave his name and rank to an officer or 'writer'.

The ship's company were taken direct to the F.S.A. in buses waiting on the quayside. The officers were guided the few yards to the *Exeter*.[1] *Exeter*'s wardroom had been made ready for our reception with a wonderful and welcome buffet dinner. Captain Tennant, with a bandage round his head, was there to greet all of us individually, sure in the knowledge that he must have stood high in our esteem and respect, not only for his magnificent display of ship-handling during the action, but, at the last, his timely decision to abandon ship, which saved so many lives.

We were all able to see which of our friends had survived, and which had not come back.[2] We also learned that Admiral Sir Tom Phillips and Captain Leach had lost their lives. Two hours later, comfortably replete and with some stiff tots of whisky, we were transported to the F.S.A. After being issued with a set of shorts, shirts and toilet gear, we made our way to the Officers' Club, where we scrubbed ourselves in the showers for the next hour to get the worst of the oil and grime off. After this we were presented with yet another meal and, at last, bursting with food and utterly exhausted mentally and physically, we collapsed on to piles of mattresses which had been spread out on the floor of the Club. It was just twenty-four hours after going to dawn Action Stations off Kuantan.

[1] Victor of the *Graf Spee* action, December, 1939, and later to be sunk in her turn in the Battle of the Java Sea.
[2] 27 officers and 486 men were lost. 42 officers and 754 men survived.

CHAPTER 6

Malayan Campaign

Most of us awoke late on 11 December, having fallen deeply asleep, totally exhausted from the previous day's events. Telegrams were sent via the Admiralty to our next of kin, and read 'Safe, Well. Love'. We were then given an outline of the day's programme; collecting a minimum of kit, filling in compensation forms for lost kit, writing letters home, and, most important, preparing our reports for a Court of Inquiry to be held the next day.

During the following few days any number of invitations were received from the residents of Singapore. It was then that we learned of the enormous blow to morale that the sinking of the big ships had caused. People everywhere simply could not believe it, and I think we really felt the same, even after several days.

The greater part of 12 December was occupied by the Court of Inquiry which was held in the War Room at the Naval Base. Each officer and key rating was required to submit a brief account of the action, as well as to answer questions put to them by the Court, in order to ascertain exactly what had happened. A last parade of *Repulse*'s ship's company was held, at which Captain Tennant, after saying how well all had fulfilled their duties, said goodbye. As the senior surviving officer, he had been ordered to return to London to make a personal report to the Admiralty.

The main topic of conversation among those of us who remained was what our immediate future was to be. It appeared that the majority of the non-executive officers were either to be sent home or to a reserve manning pool, forming at Colombo, for a new Far Eastern Fleet. For the rest of us it seemed that there was more than enough to do. A party was to be sent to Surabaya, the Dutch Naval Base in Java, to man and bring back to Singapore a number of motor torpedo boats; another was to man a battery of Bofors AA guns and a naval battalion was to be formed.

It was to the latter that I was appointed, as adjutant to Commander M. Goodenough, its Commanding Officer. Bob Lang, who was the Officer in Charge of *Repulse*'s Royal Marine detachment, was to act as military adviser. The next few days were a nightmare. Not only was I very ignorant of my military duties, but there was the added frustration of the excessive bureaucracy encountered while trying to collect the equipment for the battalion. But, after four days, the order to disband the battalion was issued and our hard-won equipment was returned to store! Clearly a great deal of uncertainty and confusion reigned, but personally I was glad that this particular idea had come to nothing. The Japanese were advancing rapidly in North Malaya and several of the more senior surviving officers were now being sent home. There was nothing else to do but wait and see. These two or three days were spent swimming and relaxing at the F.S.A. My chief wish was to be sent home. I was not enamoured with the scene as I saw it and found it all very unsettling.

It was on the Monday night, 21 December, that I became aware of someone awakening me out of a deep sleep. It turned out to be Victor Clark, one of *Repulse*'s Lieutenant-Commanders. He sounded most mysterious as he whispered, 'Do you want a special job?' Of course I said yes. He then unfolded a plan to form a force of small patrol craft to carry out raids against the coastal lines of communication of the advancing Japanese Army which would operate in conjunction with a special force to be provided by the Army.

The operation was to be mounted with all possible speed, so the next two days were a non-stop rush to find certain key personnel, all the more difficult because it had to be kept secret. This involved me in innumerable journeys, sometimes four or five a day, back and forth between the Naval Base and Singapore, ten miles away. At times we became absolutely desperate, battling with the Naval Stores organization, trying to shortcircuit the system, dependent upon 'supply and demand' notes which we had not got. It may have been adequate in peacetime, but was the opposite in a wartime emergency.

I found there was a great scarcity of suitable craft for the final stages of the clandestine landings proposed. These craft had to be suitable for transporting at least twenty fully armed men from a patrol craft lying off-shore to a landing site which could be several miles away up a mangrove creek. They also had to be reliable as well as small enough to remain concealed in the mangroves until the troops could be re-embarked. The Navy just did not possess anything of this sort and the intention was to commandeer suitable craft from civilian or other sources. It was a question of surveying the myriad small craft lying in the creeks among the wharves of Keppel Harbour. Such craft were mostly owned by Chinese, but as soon as the Chinese heard of what was afoot they immediately removed some vital part of the engine. However, despite all the difficulties, we managed to obtain five or six motor boats.

The next task was to organize suitable towing craft from the resources available. The Harbour Defence Motor Launches, (HDMLs), manned by the Straits Settlement and Malayan RNVR were an obvious choice. These craft were 72 feet long with two diesel engines, giving them a speed of fourteen knots, and armed with a three-pounder gun. It was characteristic of the haphazard organization in Singapore at this time that it was left to me, a very junior Lieutenant, to approach the Captain Auxiliary Vessels (A/V), under whose command these HDMLs came, to persuade him to allocate them for this purpose.

The Captain A/V was a senior and long-retired Captain R.N. named Mulock, who had been recalled for war service and was responsible for organizing all local patrols. He was based in the Straits Settlement RNVR Drill Ship, the old First World War Flower Class sloop *Laburnum*. It was to this officer that I made my request and, by dint of a lot of persuasion, convinced him of the importance of the operation and the need for secrecy. He was very understanding, though he appeared not to have been given any information about the operation; but he allocated us two HDLMs, *1062* and *1063*.

The operation also required a base ship for the maintenance of the MLs and the motor boats, as well as accommodation for the Naval personnel. The Rear Admiral Malaya (R.A.M.Y.), Rear Admiral E. J. Spooner, now in charge of all Naval operations locally, placed the old Straits steamship *Kudat* at the force's disposal. The *Kudat* was immediately ordered round to the Naval Base to store up with the necessary food, fuel and ammunition to maintain the force up country for some weeks.

That evening Victor Clark took me out to dinner at the home of the Senior Army Officer, Major A. J. C. Rose of the Argyll and Sutherland Highlanders. Angus Rose had been second-in-command of the 2nd Battalion which was at this time the talk of Singapore, with the reputation of being the best unit in Malaya, and in no way inferior to the Japanese in the art of jungle warfare.

After dinner the operation was discussed in detail. As his wife brought us coffee, we crawled about the floor of the sitting room studying the maps of our possible operating areas. The force was to be known as 'Rose Force', as it was apparently Angus Rose who had first suggested to G.H.Q. that an attempt to interrupt the Japanese communications down the west coast of Malaya should be made. The G.O.C. Malaya, Lieut-General A. E. Perceval, had issued orders that the force was to disrupt enemy communications west of the Perak River. Fifty Australians from the Australian Imperial Force (A.I.F.) were to provide the troops.

We discussed the details of the first raid which was to be launched as soon as possible, with the landing to be made near Trong, the Force operating from Port Swettenham. Our discussion broke up at midnight and Victor Clark and I drove back to the Naval Base.

Be great exertions the *Kudat*, with the base party, sailed the next morning, 23 December, accompanied by HDML *1063* towing two of the motor boats on the 250-mile passage to Port Swettenham. By now our party consisted of Lieutenant J. Darwall R.N., Sub-Lieutenant (E) Kustner, RNVR, both from *Repulse*, Lieutenant P. O'Rourke, R.N., lent from the destroyer *Isis*, repairing after the Mediterranean bomb damage in the dockyard, Lieutenant N. Kempson and Sub-Lieutenant R. Ripley, R.N.V.R., both from *Prince of Wales*.

The following morning, Christmas Eve, HDML *1062*, Lieutenant MacMillan, in which I took passage, left the Naval Base towing two more motor boats. In the early dawn mist we were soon clear of the base and slipping down the Johore Straits. By midday we had passed Singapore and Keppel Harbour and were turning northward into the Malacca Straits. The weather then began to deteriorate and typical north-east monsoon weather set in; the sea became rough and, with the double towlines continually parting, progress was slow. A succession of fierce tropical rain storms drenched us and, to complete our discomfort, the Chinese cook became so seasick that we were reduced to tinned food.

A seemingly endless night was spent recovering parted tows and changing over exhausted and drenched crews. Christmas Day, 1941, proved no different as the weather did not moderate until the early afternoon. A lunch of condensed milk and prunes was the best we could manage, though a Christmas cake and some chocolate was produced for tea. We consoled ourselves with thoughts of a good dinner when at last we arrived alongside the *Kudat* in Port Swettenham.

By the early evening we were making our way up the winding channel to Port Swettenham. Our brown muddy wash rolled along the edges of the mangroves on either bank and the thought of nights

Malay Peninsula

N

MALAYA

PENANG

TAIPING
Trong
Dindings
Pangkor
Is.
Perak River

Sungei
Bernam

Selangor
Kuala River
Selangor
KUALA LUMPUR
Port Swettenham
Morib

MALACCA
Muar
Batu Pahat

SUMATRA

SINGAPORE
BINTANG

75

spent lying up in such places began to lose its attraction, if it ever had one! We rounded the last bend and the wharves and harbour buildings of Port Swettenham came into view, with the *Kudat* lying alongside.

As we secured we were met by Johnny Darwall. We rather wearily made our way along the jetty to board *Kudat*. Her upper deck was deserted and no one showed any interest at all. Our long-anticipated Christmas dinner had apparently long since been eaten and all that remained for us was some cold fish and chips! Johnny Darwall told us of his innumerable difficulties and frustrations, as the *Kudat*'s officers seemed quite indifferent to the needs of the force. I think they resented the upheaval and urgency of a new situation. Johnny told us that Victor Clark and Angus Rose had already gone ahead in *1063*, towing two motor boats and with twenty-five Australian troops embarked. Victor Clark had left orders for *1062* to rendezvous with him at the entrance of the Sungei Bernam the following afternoon.

So, early on Boxing Day, we set out with a further twenty-five troops on board, towing our motor boats. A rubber planter by the name of Bill Harvey joined us to act as a guide. Apart from the difficulties already experienced in towing our motor boats, the day passed uneventfully with no sign of enemy activity and by 4 p.m. we were approaching the rendezvous. It was no easy matter navigating the main channel and it was only by the most careful dead reckoning that we were able to pick our way through the maze of fishing pagars that covered the large expanse of shallow water forming the estuary. Finally we picked out *1063* ahead of us.

As soon as we reached her we went alongside for a short explanation and final orders for the raid. We were to attack the Japanese line of communication between Taiping and the pontoon bridge over the Perak River. The troops were to be landed at first light the next day. After towing the motor boats as close as possible, the two HDMLs were to return to Port Swettenham to re-fuel before returning to pick up the raiders in two days' time.

At last light we set out up the coast, following the faint white stern light of *1063*. The night was very dark, with a return of the frequent heavy showers and we all became very wet and cold, the troops huddled under their capes under whatever cover they could find on the cramped deck, the only noise being the steady roar of the ML's engines. As the course changed from north to east, we knew we were heading in towards the coast. Our eyes strained ahead as impercept-ibly the darkness lightened until we could faintly see the outline of *1063* ahead. Weaving and twisting at slow speed through the fishing

76

stakes, and shrouded in long white mist wraiths, we slowly closed the coast. Ahead of us the pale blue mountains of the Central Highlands could be seen above the rising mist. The expedition had obtained the services of a local pilot, a Eurasian named Newbrunner, who obviously knew these shallow channels like the back of his hand.

Suddenly *1063*'s signal light flashed 'Stop. Disembark Troops'. The motor launches lost way and were soon rolling gently in their own wakes, their engines spluttering and gurgling. The Australians climbed down into the motor boats alongside. There was no land in sight, all being hidden under the veil of mist. We knew we were now many miles behind the Japanese front lines and a sharp lookout was kept for Japanese aircraft.

Then the first mishap occurred – our motor boat's engine refused to start. It was soon apparent that, with daylight rapidly approaching, we should have to clear the area quickly to avoid compromising the operation, having already wasted much time; so, reluctantly, we were forced to sink her. *1063* was already retiring and was barely visible to seaward as we turned to follow her at full speed. However, the extra weight of our twenty-five Australians reduced our speed and we soon lost sight of her. We then set our own course and continued out to sea before turning south on the direct course for Port Swettenham.

About midday, when we were just abreast of the Bernam River, we sighted a small native dugout canoe, known as a *koleh*. We could see its occupants were trying to attract our attention, so we altered course towards them. As we came up to them we saw that there were three Europeans, a Chinese and a Malay. We took the former on board; the Chinese and Malay, to whom we gave some cigarettes, turned in towards the coast as they did not want to come on board. The Europeans, a man, his wife and twelve-year-old daughter, who were all suffering from severe sunburn and thirst, told us their story. He was a planter on Langkawi Island, off the Malayan-Siamese border. Aware of the imminent arrival of the Japanese, he had left with his wife and daughter in the small *koleh* from which we had rescued them. They had tried to make for Penang but found the Japanese had got there before them so they continued south, but always with the same result. By the time we picked them up they had travelled nearly three hundred miles, no mean feat in a fifteen-foot-long dugout canoe.

Back in Port Swettenham, we said goodbye to our passengers and set to work re-fuelling and taking in stores for the return trip to the Trong River. That night, in brilliant moonlight, which showed every detail of the *Kudat* and the port's quays and go-downs, there was an air-raid. Although a number of bombs fell close by, the *Kudat* and the MLs escaped damage and we finally turned in after the raid was over to get some much-needed sleep.

The peace of the next morning, Sunday, was shattered by the roar of aircraft overhead, quickly followed by the noise of a battery of Bofors AA guns opening fire. The aircraft looked like Blenheims and they certainly had British markings. Almost at once one was shot down and crashed into the mangroves to the west of the town. As soon as it was confirmed that it was indeed British the two MLs set off to search for it, but, although we searched for an hour, we could find no trace of it and returned sadly to the *Kudat*.

The following night we were again bombed and this time the *Kudat* was hit, though not seriously, and some more harbour works were damaged. The Japanese were obviously directing their attacks at the *Kudat* and it became imperative to find a shore base without delay. Welcome reinforcements now arrived from Singapore in the form of two of the much larger and faster Fairmile[1] motor launches, nos *310* and *311*, commanded by Lieutenants Maynard and Christmas; also Lieutenant-Colonel Warren of the Royal Marines, who was the Liaison Officer between G.H.Q. Far East and 1107 Special Training School. He immediately left in *311* to reconnoitre a forward base some hundred miles nearer to our operating area, while *1062* left to recover our raiding party.

At the same time an attempt to enlist the help of local Chinese pilots was made and I set out in *310* with a Customs Officer named Simms, who knew the area. Our destination was a large Chinese fishing village on Pangkor Island, a hundred miles to the north. We left in the early evening and reached the island soon after midnight where we anchored close in but out of sight of the village. Over mugs of cocoa we discussed our landing plans and then turned in for a few hours' sleep.

The village was known to have many Communist sympathizers and therefore would, we hoped, be strongly anti-Japanese. Covered by the early morning mist we crept into the village and landed Mr Simms. We were to give him an hour only, because of the danger of Japanese air attack. He returned, unaccompanied, after forty-five minutes. He told us he could not persuade anyone to come forward as they were all scared of the Japanese.

[1] Fairmile was a class of coastal patrol boat then being produced in large numbers for a wide range of inshore duties. Armed with one 3-pounder gun and a miscellany of machine guns, they were 112 ft long and had a speed of 21 knots.

78

Before leaving the area we decided to explore the channel leading to the mainland, known as the Dindings, and while doing so sighted a small tug apparently aground on a sandbank. Partly to show the flag and also to deny the tug to the enemy we shelled it to render it useless. The noise of the 3-pounder gun reverberated in the still morning air. Having put some shells through its boiler and engine room we turned out to sea at full speed.

About an hour later an aircraft was sighted right ahead flying straight towards us. It passed down our port side and we could clearly see the pilot's and observer's faces looking down at us. It was an enemy reconnaissance plane and we gave it two long bursts with our Lewis and Hotchkiss guns as it flew past us. We now expected the worst and prepared for the inevitable air attacks which we were sure would follow.

For another hour nothing happened and the Captain reduced speed, which I thought was inadvisable and said so. However, as an observer, I could only press my point so far. Shortly after this I was down in the wheelhouse helping the First Lieutenant, who was responsible for the navigation, to check our position, when we were suddenly flung off our feet by a violent crash and at the same time the alarm rattlers sounded. I dashed up to the bridge and realized we had been 'near-missed' by a bomb which had fallen just astern. Overhead were three enemy aircraft which had completely surprised us. I found the Captain leaning on the side of the bridge obviously very shaken. As soon as he saw me he said, 'You had better take over; you know more about this sort of thing than I do'. Another bomber was already diving on to us and so I immediately took command.

Steadying the helmsman on his course and going up to full speed, I ordered the signalman to report immediately he could see a bomb released, and the First Lieutenant to keep all guns firing. In fact the Japanese had little to fear from us as our machine guns were outranged for most of the time. Each time a bomber came in I kept the ML on a steady course and, as soon as the bomb was released, I altered course hard a-port or starboard. I thanked my experience in *Marlborough* at Dunkirk. This proved highly successful and for the next three-quarters of an hour we played a cat-and-mouse game and our hopes and confidence grew as attack after attack failed to hit us. But the nervous strain was considerable and I was beginning to wonder how much longer I could continue to make the right decision. They had been attacking in shallow glides individually and dropping single bombs. Fortunately at about this time they must have used up their last bombs, because they turned away and flew off to the north.

At full speed we headed for Port Swettenham and took stock of our casualties – one stoker wounded and one of the seaman gunners shot through the stomach. This was Able Seaman Carter from the *Repulse*, who was already unconscious. We signalled *Kudat* and asked for an ambulance to meet us on return. Except for the Captain of the ML, everyone had done well, especially the Malays who made up a proportion of the crew. I am sure our firing continuously with all our guns helped to keep morale high.

All was ominously quiet on arrival in harbour and we berthed just ahead of *Kudat*, which we soon discovered was deserted. The authorities were telephoned for an ambulance since our signal had not been received, and after some time had elapsed one arrived and our wounded were taken to Kuala Lumpur. Poor Carter looked very bad and we learned not long after that he had died of his wounds. The whole place was deserted. Apparently a force of twelve bombers had attacked during the morning and the *Kudat* had had to be evacuated by her crew.

Simms and I made our reports at the new Force headquarters in the Harbour Master's house where he and his wife were most helpful and hospitable. We learnt that *1062* had successfully picked up the raiding party, though the raid had not been as successful as we had hoped, due to the landing force being at half-strength. A convoy of Japanese motor transport had been ambushed, some vehicles destroyed and a Japanese Colonel killed.

However, all was not well, for Major Rose had said he would not go again with the Australians; they for their part said they would not go again with him! This was a serious setback and was brought about by a disagreement over tactics. A second raid was planned to go in at once, but was postponed because of this discord and also because we had been unable to obtain the local pilots we needed to guide us into the rivers. Johnny Darwall and I took the opportunity of this enforced lull to drive into Kuala Lumpur to arrange for additional stores, and so ended the last day of 1941.

The new year opened with another heavy air raid on the port. From then on raids intensified and there were often four or five in a day. To resolve the differences between Major Rose and the Australians, a party of forty Royal Marines, survivors from the *Repulse* and *Prince of Wales*, arrived under the command of Lieutenant Davies, *Repulse*'s junior subaltern. The Marines were to work directly with Major Rose, while the Australians would work under their own senior Officer.

Another point at issue was the question of which were the most suitable landing craft to use. The Marines wanted to continue to use the motor boats: the Australians wanted to try the small native *kolehs*. These could be carried by the MLs until much nearer to the moment of landing, thus enabling the passage to the point of attack to be made more quickly and silently. Another advantage was that they could be hidden more easily and be less suspicious if found by a Japanese patrol. This view was strengthened by the agreement of Lieutenants Pip O'Rourke and Nigel Kempson who had accompanied the motor boats on the first raid.

The next two days were spent searching the headwaters of the many creeks for seaworthy *kolehs*. Returning from one of these searches, we sighted a strange-looking craft on the beach at Morib. Thinking it might be a Japanese landing craft, we turned our lorry into a clump of palms, jumped out and, with weapons at the ready, crept to the edge of the beach. Seeing no sign of life, we went cautiously down the beach to examine it. We noticed numerous bullet holes and other signs of damage, and then noticed some instructions on its engine in English. We reported our find on the telephone before returning to Port Swettenham where we learned what it was. Apparently five fast American landing craft known as Eurekas had been sent up from Singapore to provide us with more suitable craft for raids and inshore patrols. Off Morib, some miles south of Port Swettenham, the group had been surprised by Japanese aircraft and sunk or driven ashore. This particular Eureka was repaired and put into service.

In the first week of January we were ordered to carry out patrols by night, as close inshore as possible, especially at the mouth of the Selangor River. The Japanese were trying to turn the Army's left flank by launching small bodies of troops down the coast under cover of darkness. The original aim of Rose Force, the carrying out of offensive raiding, now became overshadowed by this new development. We were all disappointed and some of us felt that this was too negative an approach.

The sailors' morale now gave cause for concern. They were all survivors of the two big ships and had been sent up country to do a special job under difficult circumstances, but a succession of operations had been cancelled and the enforced inactivity led to frustration. This was accentuated by the now frequent air-raids against which we had no response. The Japanese were flying over the port at will, bombing and machine-gunning anything that moved. There were hardly any Malays or Chinese left, they having taken refuge in the jungle.

The *Kudat* had attempted to leave in order to return to Singapore, but had been bombed and burnt out. Some of our original party were now recalled to Singapore, among whom were Pip O'Rourke to his destroyer *Isis* as her repairs neared completion, also Nigel Kempson and Ralph Ripley, a Canadian Sub-Lieutenant who had been an ordinary seaman in *Repulse* when I first joined her.

The remainder of our party had established a new headquarters in a large bungalow on the edge of the town. It had belonged to a Customs Officer named Hewitt, who was now serving with the Volunteers. His wife had only recently been evacuated with just two cases of their personal belongings, leaving the remainder of their possessions behind. We felt very sorry for them, and thousands like them, who had to abandon virtually everything they owned. We did our utmost to respect the house and its contents. I lived out of my kitbag on the floor rather than use the drawers and cupboards which were full of Mrs Hewitt's clothes. Whether or not the Japanese knew of our presence I don't know, but on several occasions it seemed that our immediate vicinity was singled out for attack.

All the available craft now patrolled nightly, leaving harbour so as to be in position by dark. At first we patrolled the coastal islands and river mouths to the north of Port Swettenham, but, as the Japanese advance continued, we drew back until we were patrolling the channels leading to Port Swettenham itself. The north channel was the easier of the two main ones, being wider and deeper than the southern one which was very shallow and tortuous.

The most exciting part of the patrol of the northern channel was the frequent investigation of the lighthouse on a small island at the entrance. We used to close in as slowly and as quietly as possible, watching intently for any sign that might indicate the presence of the enemy. When we had got as close as possible, a small dinghy was manned and, with Tommy guns at the ready, two or three of us rowed the last few yards to the jetty, climbed the steps and searched the rocky islet. In fact the lighthouse remained unoccupied, so far as we knew, right up to the time we left Port Swettenham.

The southern channel was quite different, ten to twelve miles long and at places so narrow that the mangroves almost overhung it. Our wake slapped and gurgled against the dark and evil-smelling mud-banks. We always tried to be at the seaward end by last light so as to be sure the Japanese didn't slip in before we got there. We then slowly retraced our course, using engines at irregular intervals and drifting on the tide, listening. The amazing volume of insect, bird and reptile noises never failed to astonish us. The croaking of millions of frogs, the drone and hum of mosquitoes and other insects, the slither and plop as some reptile slid over the mud into the water, combined with the various bird songs, drowned most man-made noises, so we had to rely very largely on our eyes.

The fantastic shapes the night and our imagination gave to the twisted and gnarled mangroves gave rise to many false alarms. Something black ahead would look, for a few tense seconds, as if it were a boat filled with men, and bring us instantly to a full alert. Usually it turned out to be a drifting tree trunk. The lights we saw, and even opened fire on at times, turned out to be fireflies. After very few hours on this patrol we were continually seeing things and became very jumpy.

This intensive patrolling was not done without cost to engines and machinery. Wonders were done in repairs by a small maintenance staff, headed by Sub-Lieutenant (E) Kustner, another survivor from *Repulse*, despite utterly inadequate facilities.

As the Japanese advance moved south, we were forced to give up driving into Kuala Lumpur to collect rations. One afternoon towards the middle of January Johnny Darwall and I made our last journey. Having loaded up our car with rations, we decided to have tea at the Majestic Hotel. It was deserted but for one or two old Indian waiters, who, when we asked for tea, just turned to us with the palms of their hands upturned in a gesture of hopeless resignation.

A Japanese landing at Kuala Selangor led to the Australians being moved up to counter this threat and this effectively spelt the end of any further attempts at raiding. It was this that spurred me on to have a confrontation with Victor Clark, my senior officer,[1] during which I expressed my disapproval of the way our operation was developing. I pointed out to him the very low state of morale that now existed among our sailors. I think that neither he, nor Angus Rose, nor Colonel Warren, had appreciated how low this had become. I realized afterwards that it was a most insubordinate act on my part. Victor Clark was furious and I was ordered to make my own way back to Singapore and there to await the results of my outburst.

However, before I could leave the Japanese advance came so close that it was decided to evacuate Port Swettenham. All serviceable small craft were to be taken south to Singapore, while the remaining harbour installations and the go-downs were prepared for demo-

---

[1]Lieutenant-Commander V.C.F. Clark had been Captain of a destroyer in the earlier part of the war and had been awarded a D.S.C. In *Repulse* he had been the Principal Control Officer with whom I shared many hours of watchkeeping. A fine seaman and a very spirited officer from whom I learned a great deal.

lition. Until demolition was ordered, the go-downs were to be protected against looting. The trouble lay in the bonded warehouse where there were great quantities of wines and spirits which had been stocked for Christmas. These stocks would normally have been dispersed all over Central Malaya. Word came through from the Police that troops, including some of our own sailors, were trying to get at this liquor. There and then the Chief Customs Officer decided to destroy the lot. It was an appalling sight to see cases and cases of wines and spirits being smashed. Thousands of gallons of beer, by bottle and cask, all ran to waste that night. Fortunately, from the fire risk point of view, no bombers came over. The remaining few days saw other warehouses with their assorted merchandise scattered everywhere. As with the wines and spirits, all these stores had been intended for central Malaya's Christmas supplies.

On the evening of 5 January the Harbour Master was due to leave for Singapore in the largest of the tugs and it was decided that I should accompany him in a smaller tug named the *Elizabeth*. As the latter had no compass, it was a question of 'follow my leader', but when darkness fell and the *Elizabeth* could not keep up, I found that I simply could not see; visibility in the constant rain was virtually nil. So I decided to turn in towards the coast and anchor.

When dawn broke I realized we were just to the south of the southernmost entrance to Port Swettenham. I knew that the port was not due to be evacuated until that night so I decided to return to try and obtain a compass and chart. At our best speed we steamed up the northern channel. On nearing the port a strange sense of disquiet came over me. Would I find the Japanese in possession? On turning the last bend in the channel and passing the Chinese fishing village the harbour came into view. There appeared to be no sign of life. For a moment I thought the evacuation must have taken place, and then suddenly I saw and heard the cause of the unnatural quiet. Over the roofs of the go-downs flew a Japanese reconnaissance plane. He flew over us at virtually masthead height and seemed as surprised as we were. Luckily the pilot did not attack us, as we had no means of defence.

We secured alongside the jetty and I immediately set out for the bungalow to try to find a compass. At the Police Station a sergeant told me that the Japanese had been sighted at Klang, only five miles away, during the night. Reaching the bungalow, I found the remainder of the party still in occupation, though ready to leave. After a quick discussion, it was decided that *Elizabeth* should accompany *1062* to Malacca, approximately one hundred miles to the south, that night. The plan was to establish a new base there.

At dusk, just as we were making ready to leave harbour, I remembered that I had left my binoculars at the bungalow and I at once set out on a bicycle to recover them. The deserted town had produced a strange feeling of menace in the bright sunlight of the morning, but now, in the half-light of the tropical twilight, the feeling was far more apparent. The buildings were already blurred and indistinct and shadowy figures were moving between them. At first I thought they might be Japanese, but then realized they were looters. I kept my revolver ready as I opened the door. There was no one about, although I thought I heard a faint scuffling. Recovering my binoculars, I was soon pedalling back down the main road as fast as I could.

Within a few minutes we were under way and following *1062* down the channel. Sitting in a deckchair beside the helmsman, I strained to keep *1062*'s sternlight in view. It was cold and wet and I was glad when dawn came and with it the warming sun. Some time after 9 a.m. Malacca came into view. Once more a strange feeling of disquiet manifested itself, but I soon saw the reason. A number of aircraft were circling the town and almost immediately I saw columns of black smoke rising, followed by the noise of explosions.

There were two large Straits Settlement steamships in the roads, apparently in the act of anchoring. Lieutenant Macmillan took *1062* right into the harbour, but the *Elizabeth*'s deep draught caused her to go aground and we only got off again with difficulty on the rising tide. A boat was sent out to bring me in. The only European left was the Harbour Master, who gave me a message from Victor Clark ordering us to continue south to Muar. Malacca had been evacuated, so we decided to push on at once and were soon heading south at our best speed.

The two large steamships were now steaming south ahead of us. Not long after, another formation of enemy aircraft appeared and attacked the larger of the two, which we later learned was the S.S. *Kinto* and, though she was hit on several occasions and set on fire, her Master, by skilful and violent manoeuvring, escaped being sunk. *1062* and *Elizabeth* were machine-gunned, but suffered no casualties or damage.

Our little flotilla arrived at Muar at 1 p.m. that afternoon and headed in towards the entrance. Muar appeared to be a most attractive town with its white government buildings half-hidden behind tropical pines. We found our way into the river and tied up alongside a jetty almost in the centre of the town. I went ashore at once to contact the local W.V.S. to try and organize a meal and a bath for the sailors.

The efficient and charming lady in charge, the Chinese wife of a British planter, got everything organized very quickly and the sailors were able to get away for a short time. The Captain of *1062*, his First Lieutenant Johnny Bull, and I went up to the Rest House, where we had a meal and a shower, in the middle of which an air-raid started. We dashed outside to see a group of Japanese bombers apparently dive-bombing the pontoon bridge across the river over which Army units were crossing. We made our way back to *1062*. There was considerable confusion in the town and panic-stricken Malays, Chinese and Tamils were running all over the place.

As we were sitting in *1062*'s wardroom discussing the situation and waiting for the sailors to return, somebody who said he was the District Commissioner arrived in a very agitated state and demanded that we leave Muar immediately. He told us that this was the first time that the town had been attacked and the reason was our presence! This was too much for me and I told him that we would not be leaving until we were ready and had had orders to do so. I took out my revolver and ordered him to leave *1062* immediately. He left, threatening me with all sorts of official action. Shortly after this, Victor Clark arrived and told us to move south to Batu Pahat, another three to four hours away.

Our little flotilla left just after midnight and we just scraped our way over the bar before turning south down the coast. We arrived off Batu Pahat in the early morning and, thanks to Johnny Bull's accurate pilotage, the *Elizabeth* just found enough water in the poorly marked channel to reach the town. We secured alongside some old junks where Johnny Darwall met us and took us off for a wash and breakfast. Headquarters of what remained of Rose Force was established in some bungalows just outside the town. During the day we heard that a party of Japanese troops had landed the previous night and had established themselves in the lighthouse at the entrance of the river. If this was the case, we must have passed very close to them on our way in. We resumed patrolling that night but only saw one junk which we boarded to find a very old Chinese fisherman on it. Once again the problems of night patrols were manifesting themselves, with insufficient and basically unsuitable craft, no H.E. ammunition for our 3-pounders and no ready-use stores of any kind.

It became obvious during the next day that the Japanese advance was continuing without serious check and, despite our spasmodic

6. The shore on which M.L. 310 was beached.

7. The reef on the eastern shore at low tide.

8. Headman and Mohammedan Priest on Tjebia in 1945.

9. The 'White House', Tjebia, 1945.

attempts to patrol the coast, there were continual rumours of enemy infiltration. We were ordered to sail for Singapore that same night and at 11 a.m. the next day *Elizabeth* entered the Naval Base in the middle of an air raid.

After we had secured and discharged the crew to the F.S.A., I turned *Elizabeth* over to the authorities, before reporting to the Staff Officer Local Operations, Commander P. G. Frampton, in the War Room. There I made a verbal report of my recent activities and ended by saying that I had been sent back to Singapore because of my disagreement with Victor Clark over the general conduct of our operation up country. I was told to be ready to join the old destroyer *Tenedos* when she next returned from convoy escort duties. I returned to my quarters to sort out and collect what kit I could in preparation for this appointment.

The F.S.A. presented a strange spectacle in the last days of January, 1942. It seemed to me that morale among the large numbers of personnel still there was low. A general lassitude and air of despondency prevailed. Japanese bombers were attacking targets on the island several times a day and I found it a disturbing experience, sitting inactive in an air-raid shelter listening to the scream of descending bombs.

With the Japanese advancing further south each day, I was surprised that, as far as I could see, no attempt was being made to prepare for the defence of the dockyard area. As I waited for *Tenedos* to return, I could see the situation deteriorating daily. One afternoon, while having tea in the wardroom, I rather flippantly remarked to one of the more senior officers who had been brought back from retirement, 'Well, Sir, the Japs will soon be on the other side watching us eat our tea!' He was not amused and seemed quite unable to recognize that such a state of affairs could ever happen. I was sharply reprimanded for defeatism.

On 27 January I received a message from Commander Frampton to say that he wished to see me in the War Room. He told me that the plan to hold a bridgehead in Johore had now been abandoned in view of the rapid advance of the Japanese. As a consequence the Navy would have to intensify their in-shore patrols round the island and especially in the Johore Straits. He, as Staff Officer Local Operations, was directly responsible to the Admiral for these patrols and he now wanted me to be his assistant. He said that he realized I would rather get back to sea in *Tenedos*, but that, if I would carry out this duty for a short time until things had stabilized, he would do his utmost to get me a better sea appointment than *Tenedos*. Under the circumstances I felt I had to agree, so as of that moment I became Assistant Staff Officer Local Operations on the Rear Admiral Malaya's Staff. As Commander Frampton's other duties seemed to occupy him fully, it became clear that the main responsibility for organizing the in-shore patrols would be mine.

I was given authority to requisition a car, since, as before, I would obviously have to travel between the Base and Captain A/Vs in Singapore. In addition to the off-shore patrols there was a very limited in-shore patrol in being. My idea was to build on this and gather the extra craft to meet the demands of a more permanent patrol routine.

There was no shortage of personnel to man extra craft, but finding them was a problem. If it had been difficult four weeks previously, it was doubly hard now. So, thankful to have something worthwhile to do, I went straight over to see Captain A/V in *Laburnum* at Singapore. He was the operational Commander of all the patrol vessels engaged in the present extended patrols.

Although there were plenty of ratings available at the Fleet Shore Accommodation, the arrangements with the Drafting Office were tedious; equally, the provisioning and storing of such craft as I did manage to find proved far from easy. Once more there seemed to me to be an inherent inability to cope as quickly as the emergency demanded. I never knew whether the faults rested with the individuals or the system but the following incident is typical of the general situation. While searching out suitable craft, I discovered in the dockyard boathouse the barge of the Commander-in-Chief China Station. It was a twin-engined 45-foot power-boat capable of twenty knots and very suitable for our purpose. I told the Senior Dockyard Supervisor who I was and said I wanted the boat put in the water straight away. In the event it took the better part of the afternoon. I tried to telephone the Maintenance Constructor of the Dockyard, apparently the only official who could give such authority, only to find he was playing golf, and this on 30 January, 1942! In the end it was the Rear Admiral Malaya to whom I had to appeal. He gave direct orders that the boat be put in the water and camouflaged ready for operations that night.

That evening, on my return to the F.S.A., I learned that my great friend from *Repulse*, Johnny Darwall, had died of meningitis in Johore Bahru hospital. Johnny had been my R.N. predecessor in *Repulse* as Sub-Lieutenant of the Gunroom and had been a very good friend to me during the fifteen months we had been in the ship together.

The evacuation of the Naval Base had now become imperative and every effort was being made to get the more important stores away, especially the stocks of torpedoes. All the ships being refitted were hurriedly made seaworthy, so that they could be towed if they were unable to leave under their own power. There was a growing shortage of local labour. As the enemy bombing intensified, increasing numbers of the workforce stayed away. Admiral Spooner had long wanted to take the only step possible in such circumstances, to feed the workforce in the dockyard, whereas official policy had been to provide them with bulk rations which they simply took home to their villages and then stayed there. Despite this and other difficulties, and mainly due to herculean efforts by their crews, the cruiser *Mauritius*, the destroyer *Isis*, the submarine *Rover* and the small floating dock were all got away, as well as large quantities of stores.

During my drives to and from the base I had the opportunity to think about the general situation, which was becoming critical. The Japanese were almost on our doorstep, the bombing increased each day and all of us who had pinned our faith in the Hurricane fighters were bitterly disappointed by their failure to bring any relief. Hurriedly uncrated and assembled, they were sent up piecemeal, with little or no squadron unity. They were originally destined for the Middle East and were not tropicalized, so their performance never matched that of the Japanese Zero. The Army had not been able to hold the enemy anywhere and had been on the retreat continually down the length of the peninsula. We all knew these things, but thought that at the end of the day the situation would be retrieved. No one thought of defeat, but equally no one knew how the tide could be turned.

On the last day of January, while driving back from Singapore to the Base, I was stopped at an Army roadblock within sight of the causeway which linked the island to the mainland. As I sat waiting in my car, I suddenly became aware of a column of troops, led by a solitary piper, crossing the causeway onto the island. I found out that they were the rearguard of the Argyll and Sutherland Highlanders, the last British troops to leave the mainland. They had been accorded this honour in recognition of their tremendous fighting record during the long retreat from the Siamese border. The single piper was from the Gordon Highlanders. Even though this scene was one of sadness and defeat at the abandoning of the mainland, it was also an inspiring one, giving rise to all those emotions that the sound of the pipes always evokes. I watched the two files of tired, battle-stained troops march past. Immediately a tremendous explosion signalled the demolition of the causeway, the only road and rail link with the mainland. A seventy-foot gap had been blown. Singapore Island was now under siege.

A few minutes later I drove on to the F.S.A. to collect my kit. It was virtually deserted and I paused for a few moments to reflect on the turn of events over the past weeks. I remembered our first sight of the magnificently laid-out F.S.A. and Naval Base when we arrived that day in early December. I remembered the parade ground where Captain Tennant had made his farewell speech to his ship's company; the huge swimming pool, empty and now cracked by bombs; the Officers' Club where, after it had been damaged in one of the early raids, the only stocks of wine and spirits left turned out to be champagne and creme de menthe, which we had drunk as a cocktail known as 'Arise My Love', after the current film of that name. I thought too of the Base itself with its impressive War Room, its walls covered with large charts of the adjoining sea areas. This was where the Admiral explained the operational situation to visiting Captains of ships either just in or about to leave. It seemed unbelievable that the scene of all these recollections was now to become the front line for the Army, who, only seven weeks earlier, had lain along the Siamese frontier on the Kra Isthmus, four hundred and fifty miles to the north.

With the withdrawal of the Army to Singapore and the evacuation of the base, a joint three-service headquarters was established at the Syme Road Golf Club, and it was there, on Sunday, 1 February, that the question of the patrol organization was discussed again. This meeting was attended by R.A.M.Y. Captain Mulock, the Extended Defence Officer and also still Captain A/V, Commander Frampton, and Commander Bailey, the senior Malayan RNVR Officer. Commander Bailey was now appointed Captain A/V in place of Captain Mulock. I was appointed assistant to him, as well as retaining my responsibility to Commander Frampton on R.A.M.Y.'s staff. The reorganization now gave Commander Bailey the overall responsibility for all local patrols, distant and inshore. The latter were my special responsibility. I had an excellent New Zealand Volunteer Reserve Officer to assist me.

A further meeting was held on the same date in Captain Mulock's office at Fort Canning, Fortress Command's H.Q., to discuss further details of the patrols and their limits. This was attended by all, except the Admiral, but with the addition of Lieutenant-Colonel Crawford, the Fortress Command's GSO 1. There was considerable disagreement and, mainly because of this, the original proposals that

I had put to Commander Frampton were accepted. These were the withdrawal of all patrol craft from the inner straits at night, leaving the Army defences a clean field of fire. This ruled out the need for recognition signals, an important factor in view of the 'jumpy' state of some of the troops. There were too few craft, which in any case would have been quite unable to counter any serious attempt by the enemy to cross the straits. The few which were released by this measure were turned over to the army to use as they saw fit.

The remaining regular naval craft, such as the Fairmiles, HDMLs and converted customs launches, now spared of their commitments up-country, were allocated to patrol the Western Johore Straits to the south and west of Pasir Laba and that part of the Straits extending to the south and east of Pulau Ubin, an island in the eastern Johore Straits. These patrols remained in force except for some gaps caused by the diversions for special emergencies until the last few days, when lack of fuel and maintenance for damaged craft forced their gradual abandonment.

However, the organization soon showed signs of strain for another reason. It had originally been the intention that the mainly Malayan and Straits Settlement Volunteer Reserves manning the local patrol craft would be based on their Drill Ship, the old Flower Class sloop *Laburnum*, and would use their own homes as their normal accommodation, but circumstances altered as the emergency grew more serious. To make matters worse, as the Malay ratings' places were taken by active service ratings, mostly survivors from the two big ships, as well as crews specially sent out from England to man the Fairmile Flotilla then forming, there were no base facilities for these men, except at the Union Jack Club and the Seamen's Mission where they were for the most part unreachable in the event of an emergency.

An old Straits Steamship, the *Sui Wo*, was commandeered to act as depot ship for the Malay ratings who were now almost entirely unemployed and whose discipline and morale were, not unnaturally, failing. As she had plenty of room, it was decided to allocate one deck to the European ratings and one to the Malays. The *Sui Wo* was then commanded by a long-retired Lieutenant-Commander R.N.

I paid several visits to the ship to see how the preparations to receive the men were going, but I found none. There was no organization worthy of the name and the situation became worse daily, so it was decided that there was no alternative but to use the Union Jack Club and the Seamen's Mission, despite their drawbacks.

Labour shortages were becoming more crippling every hour and damaged patrol craft were taking longer to repair. Fear of the bombing, as raids became more frequent, coupled with what many thought to be a mistaken policy of making a large rice issue to last several weeks, led to wholesale desertion by labourers and their families to the surrounding country and jungle. Ship repair and building firms such as Thornycrofts lost nearly all their labour at this critical time.

Despite these almost insuperable difficulties, a number of successful small operations were carried out, one of which involved the evacuation under the noses of the Japanese of a large body of troops from the mainland on the night of 1 February. The actual lifting was carried out by the HDMLs *1062* and *1063*, towing naval whalers and covered by the three China gunboats *Dragonfly*, *Scorpion* and *Grasshopper*, whose senior officer, Commander Hoffman, had consistently given wonderful support to the Army and to our small patrol craft.

Cracks in morale appeared not only among the Malays, but in numerous instances among the Europeans. Even a few of the officers were found wanting on occasions. Some clearly could not cope when the situation became remotely difficult. In one of the Fairmile Flotillas, for example, the Commanding Officer had to be relieved twice during the short campaign for 'inadequacy'. To be fair, the conditions were extreme, facing an enemy who completely dominated the scene, continual retreat on land and loss of command of both sea and air. For many of the local reserve officers, the shattering blows to morale caused by the sinking of *Prince of Wales* and *Repulse* within two days of the outbreak of war, and later by the failure of hurriedly assembled or flown-in Hurricanes to turn the tide in the air, were too much to bear.

Captain A/V now shifted his headquarters from the *Laburnum* to the K.P.M. Building, but communications still remained chaotic and I had to use my car as an office and as a means of passing messages direct to those patrol craft lying alongside. It was impossible to obtain a staff car for lack of drivers. The three services, even at this late date, were competing with one another over wage rates! Anything you could not do yourself never got done. Singapore still seemed to be organized on a civilian basis, which in its way was a splended example of British phlegm, but it was not the answer in the circumstances and the siege conditions prevailing. The frustrations and difficulties were beyond belief.

In the overall defence plan the island had been divided up into three different areas, each with a Naval Liaison Officer. Victor Clark was now attached to the Western Area, mainly A.I.F., while John Hayes, one of *Repulse*'s senior Lieutenants and Assistant Navigator, was with Northern Area, Third Indian Corps, of which the newly arrived 18th Division was part. If some special patrol or operation was asked for, I used to drive out and discuss it with them. My shiny blue and silver Pontiac was an unpopular visitor and was always purposely plastered with mud by the time I drove it back to town. The day's work was endless, lasting the full twenty-four hours on occasions and I kept at it until I was exhausted or in need of a meal. I often used to stop and just walk up to somebody's house and ask for a bed for the remaining part of the night.

Despite the serious situation, I found the attitudes of some senior officers quite extraordinary. A few nights after the retirement to the island I was ordered to arrange a reconnaissance by two officers of the Independent Company of the mangrove swamps along the north-western coast of Singapore Island for the purpose of recommending measures for its defence. This was carried out by *ML 310* without interference from the Japanese. On our return to Keppel Harbour I accompanied the two officers, Captain Hoffman and Lieutenant Holland, to Fort Canning to report to Fortress Command's G.S.O.1 and I accompanied them in *310*. Their recommendation was that strongpoints and machine-gun positions should be established on the edge of the mangroves with the object of attacking Japanese assault troops before they reached the cover of the mangroves. They proposed that this could easily be done by establishing these positions on floating rafts or even native boats. The Navy's part would be to put such rafts into place. The whole idea was turned down in a most disdainful manner and with such remarks as, 'You are all afraid of these little yellow bellies and you think that they can do superhuman things'.[1] There then followed a reprimand for appearing before a senior officer dirty and unshaven. All three of us had been up all night and Hoffman and Holland had been reconnoitring in the mangroves!

On 5 February the last troop convoy bringing in the remaining formations of the 18th Division arrived in Keppel Harbour. Unfortunately one ship, the *Empress of Asia*, was bombed and caught fire just off Keppel Harbour. She had to be abandoned with all the equipment for the troops of the Division already landed, as well as those embarked. All available craft left harbour to rescue survivors. One of the Fairmiles, *311*, commanded by Lieutenant Christmas, did especially well in taking off large numbers, 300 in one trip alone.

[1] The Japanese first landed through the mangroves on the north-west corner of the AIF sector on the night of 8 February.

Miraculously the remaining big liners were unloaded and escorted out to sea again undamaged, in spite of fierce bombing attacks.

On the evening of 7 February an operation was planned to take place on the following night, which would involve the majority of the Inshore Patrol Craft. This was to be a reconnaissance in force across the Johore Straits by the 55th Brigade of 18th Division. I met John Hayes at Syme Road and together we drove out to the Brigade H.Q., situated in a Chinese cemetery. First we had dinner, which, considering the circumstances, was excellent. I was fortunate to be seated next to Lieutenant-General Sir Louis Heath, who was one of the few Generals to have enhanced his reputation during the campaign, while commanding 3rd Indian Corps during the retreat.

As darkness fell we set off to get to the 'Battle Box' at Seletar aerodrome where the operation was to be discussed. However, the Japanese started to shell the area and it proved to be an eerie and frightening experience as we picked our way through the gravestones with shells exploding all around us.

We finally got into the 'Battle Box' just as a fresh Japanese barrage began to register on the immediate area. As we gathered round a large table in the dimly-lit operations room, we could hear the heavy 'crumps' of the exploding shells through the thick concrete walls. My memory went back to the last time I had been in this room, just before going up country with Rose Force, trying unsuccessfully to persuade the R.A.F. Station Commander to let me have one of his Air Sea Rescue launches.

Brigadier Massey-Beresford, the Brigade Commander, first outlined the operation's objectives and went through the proposed plan – a landing across the straits to carry out a reconnaissance, destroy a battery of Japanese guns believed to be within the area and return the following night. The Navy would supply the craft to ferry the troops over and to protect them while doing so. There was considerable discussion about our ability to do this, which I felt was very doubtful in the light of past experience. However, it was decided that it could be done. The next question was what to do with the Chinese villagers in a large fishing village in the landing area. It was finally decided that the matter had to be referred to higher authority. At the conclusion of the meeting we found that we were unable to leave the 'Battle Box' as the enemy barrage was so intense, so we had to remain where we were for another hour. The next night, 8 February, the Japanese invaded the island, so the operation was postponed indefinitely.

The Japanese made rapid progress inland and it was decided that an effort should be made on the night of 9th/10th to penetrate the

94

Western Straits as far as possible, with the twofold purpose of harassing Japanese communications across the Straits and to pinpoint as many of their batteries and embarkation points as possible for counter-battery fire. I was given orders by Admiral Spooner to plan and lead this operation.

There were still only two fully operational Fairmiles, *310* and *311*. Two others were not ready and the HDMLs were too slow. I arranged that they should proceed to the island of Pulau Bukum to embark a platoon of the Independent Company which had been assigned to the operation, and who were then guarding the oil installations. At Pulau Bukum I called a short meeting with the two Commanding Officers, Bull of *310* and Christmas of *311*, as well as Captain Hoffman and Lieutenant Holland of the Independent Company. We made a simple plan and agreed on a special code of signals, before setting out so as to be at the seaward end of the Straits at dusk. The Independent Company troops were divided between the two Fairmiles to provide additional close-range fire power. A course was set as nearly as possible in the middle of the Straits so as to remain at maximum distance from both now hostile shores. Any small craft sighted at the outset was to be treated as hostile and sunk by ramming if possible, so as to avoid giving our presence away until the last possible moment.

A small *koleh* was sighted in the gathering darkness, coming from the mainland shore. *310*, the leading boat, increased speed and headed straight for it, cutting clean through it. I did not really like having to do this, but if we were to complete the operation successfully there was no alternative.

The gun flashes of a Japanese battery firing from Johore enabled it to be pinpointed shortly after we had entered. We continued our course at slow speed so as to keep our engine noise to a minimum. As we approached the narrowest part of the Straits, we sighted a number of dim shapes ahead. Closing at full speed we saw them to be small motor boats each carrying a number of men. We opened fire as we came within range and they were quickly sunk, one blowing up. At this time a series of flickering lights were noticed; on closer inspection they appeared to be special light buoys obviously laid to guide the Japanese assault craft across the Straits.

We circled slowly once or twice but no other craft appeared, so we resumed our course towards the causeway, but now keeping to the Singapore shore where the deeper shadows gave us greater concealment, as the centre of the Straits was illuminated by the burning oil tanks at Kranje. By 10.30 p.m. we had reached the causeway and turned round for the run out. We expected that the Japanese would be ready for us this time and sure enough they were. As we turned in a wide circle, we passed close to the Johore Bahru road on which we were able to make out a number of vehicles. These we engaged with high explosive shells from our 3-pounders.

I was determined that we should destroy the light buoys before we left, and, on sighting them again, we got as close as possible before opening fire with small arms. Immediately, we were engaged by enemy fire from both sides of the Straits. We had great difficulty in extinguishing the light buoys, which appeared to be armoured, so we tried hand grenades with some success. The enemy fire was now intense from small-arms and anti-tank guns, and, to add to this, two searchlights were trying to illuminate us. As we directed our fire at the points of Japanese fire we seemed to silence them, but as soon as we ceased fire they would start again.

With our unprotected high-octane fuel tanks, I decided that discretion was the better part of valour and gave the signal to retire. Our 3-pounders were in action again within a few minutes when we engaged what was shown on the chart as a brickworks on the mainland. It appeared to us as if it was being used as an observation post as well as an embarkation point for crossing the Straits.

We were engaged twice more by enemy gunfire, positions which we duly marked on our chart. By 1.30 a.m. we cleared Pasir Laba battery and, after landing the Independent Company at Pulau Bukum, we entered Keppel Harbour and secured alongside. We had sustained no casualties and had only superficial damage, though *310* had had a lucky escape. On the wardroom table we found a solid unexploded shell. On examining it, we found 'Made in Birmingham 1927' stamped on it. It had apparently struck the steel edge of the bridge platform, ricocheted down through the deck to the engine room plating, passed through the after bulkhead, missing the fuel tank by inches, partially severed a steering cable and ended up on the wardroom table!

I went at once to Syme Road and reported the outcome of our raid to Admiral Spooner. Air Vice-Marshal Pulford, the Air Officer Commanding Far East, was also present. After a quick bath and clean-up at 69 Holland Road, where I had found temporary accommodation, I returned to the K.P.M. Building but on arrival could see no sign of Captain A/V. I was informed that he had gone down to the harbour, so I set off immediately to find him. I was just in time to see him, with his secretary, in a small dinghy leaving the *Laburnum* wharf, and was then told that he had said he was shifting his headquarters to SS *Bulang* lying off. I now had no means of getting in touch with him nor he with me and as it was impossible for him to issue further orders from *Bulang*, I decided that I must return to Syme Road at once and report Captain A/V's absence. Before doing so, I telephoned Commander Frampton to say that I was coming personally to report to the Admiral, which I duly did.

After hearing my brief verbal report, the Admiral sent a signal to the *Bulang* for 'the Captain A/V to re-establish his headquarters ashore forthwith'. No reply to this signal was received. A short time later the Admiral was informed that the *Bulang* had moved into the roads to avoid the bombing. A further signal was sent to Captain A/V 'to report in person at Syme Road'. Whether or not this signal, again sent by W/T, was ever received was not known; there was certainly no acknowledgement. Soon after it was reported that *Bulang* had sailed for Batavia. The final signal addressed to the Naval Authorities in Batavia sent out by Admiral Spooner stated that 'Captain A/V was to be held in Java pending the Admiral's arrival.'[1]

Events were now moving rapidly to a climax. It was becoming obvious that the Army was having to pull back into an ever-shrinking perimeter. Many areas of Singapore were on fire, others heavily damaged and the streets flooded with water from burst mains. The air raids were very frequent and the only resistance now was from the heavy AA batteries, which stuck to their task manfully, regardless of the fact that they had now become prime targets.

General Wavell, the newly-appointed overall American-British-Dutch-Australian (ABDA) Commander in South-East Asia, visited the island on the 10th and ordered a general counter-attack, but it never really started and by now most of us realized that Singapore was doomed. At the K.P.M. Building I was now in charge, but, as order and counterorder followed one another, it became clear that there was little that could be done. The final realization that we were running short of fuel and certainly had no more octane-90 for the Fairmiles rendered further operations impossible.

I reported this to the Admiral, who now occupied an office in Fort Canning in the centre of Singapore, the Japanese advance having forced the evacuation of Syme Road Joint H.Q. I received orders that the smaller patrol craft were only to be used on absolutely essential tasks, retaining enough fuel to leave Singapore and reach Java, should

---

[1]   To the best of my knowledge nothing further was heard of this incident after the war.

an evacuation be decided upon. All patrols were accordingly withdrawn.

The next two days were spent carrying out one or two essential tasks, one of which was to bring off the Independent Company on Pulau Bukum, which I was ordered to do on the night of 12th. On arrival, the Officer Commanding said that he had no orders to leave! He, in his turn, wanted us to tow some *tonkans*[1] full of petrol and other equipment back into Keppel Harbour. On my own initiative, I refused this request in view of the waste of critical octane-90 fuel in the Fairmiles. In the end the O.C. returned with us to go personally to Fort Canning and receive orders. Civilians continued to be evacuated and a number of Naval and R.A.F. Staff Officers left on this night in the light cruiser *Durban* and the destroyer *Jupiter*.

The evacuation of the civilians had been left much too late and there were not enough vessels to take them out, whereas empty troopships had left in the previous few weeks, any one of which could probably have embarked them all.

Despite the chaotic state of affairs, certain Singapore establishments were still trying gallantly to function as usual. During snatched moments during those last few days, I managed time off for a cold beer at the Cricket Club and, on another occasion, a ham and cheese sandwich at Arthur's Bar. Although I didn't know it then, this was to be my last bar meal until September, 1945. On the night of 11 February I thought it was more sensible to move into the city than to stay out at 69 Holland Road where I had been spending the odd night with a Major Clive, whose house it was, and Tony Sheldon, another of *Repulse*'s Sub-Lieutenants. The Japanese were now getting very close and the city was coming more and more under field artillery fire. I had been offered a suite in the Raffles Hotel by Jack Gifford, my assistant, whose partially completed HDML I had ordered to leave that night. So it was to the Raffles that I drove, having been out to Holland Road to collect my kit and say goodbye to my kind friends. I found they were leaving too. As I registered at the reception desk at the Raffles I noticed a most striking and exotic oriental female watching me and the words of a recent popular song, 'Olga Polofski, the beautiful spy', came immediately to mind. Shortly after this, while sitting on the bed in my room deciding whether or not to have a bath, the doorbell rang. I opened the door and outside were two attractive Eurasian girls who asked for Jack and a companion who had been sharing the suite with him. They seemed very disappointed when I told them that Jack and his friend had left. I suddenly became

[1] A type of Chinese barge.

98

very uneasy; snipers were said to be active and I suspected that I had been fired on that afternoon on my way up to Fort Canning. This, plus the rumours and the strange woman in the foyer, convinced me that I should leave, which I did, making my way to the harbour and *310*.

It must have been now that I decided to send a telegram to my parents saying I was still all right. The greater part of the next day, the 12th, I spent helping to collect, load and send away small craft. Many of the Naval officers left on this day. I saw Nigel Kempson of Rose Force, who left in my old tug *Elizabeth* with Dick Beckwith, who had been the second Gunnery Officer in the *Prince of Wales*.

It was on this day too that I bought a new wristwatch at Robinsons, the well-known department store, which despite the mounting chaos, was still doing business as usual. I remember saying, rather as an aside than anything else, to one of the supervisors that it hardly seemed worthwhile paying for the watch. The gentleman concerned told me that the Americans had landed large numbers of troops at Penang and that Singapore would soon be relieved!

Friday, 13 February dawned to the continual grumble of gunfire, punctuated by the deep booms of the 15-inch and 9.2-inch coastal defence guns, firing off their virtually useless armour-piercing shells into the Japanese rear areas. These shells had been supplied to contest the passage of the Straits by surface warships. The familiar, acrid smell of burning hung in the still, foetid air. The morning passed helping to supervise the many evacuees, now mostly Asiatic, trying to find a ship on which they could leave. At regular intervals the Japanese bombers and fighters launched devastating raids, against which there was little opposition other than the heavy AA batteries of 3.7-inch guns. One of these batteries was sited just inside the gates leading to *Laburnum* wharf and its guns, almost continually in action, were fought magnificently.

That afternoon the Admiral called a meeting in his office at Fort Canning. He told us that earlier that day the decision that Singapore could not hold out had been taken and orders for all remaining Naval and Air Force personnel, as well as selected Army technicians, to leave Singapore that evening had been given. The latter had been limited to three thousand, due to the shortage of remaining shipping. The final embarkation was to be made as soon after dark as possible in order to allow all craft to get clear of Singapore and its approaches before daylight the following morning. The first Japanese bombers could be expected soon after this. I was ordered by the Admiral to be ready to take him and Commander Frampton to Batavia that night.

In addition the Air Officer Commanding Far East, Air Vice-Marshal Pulford, and one other Staff Officer would be accompanying him.

I left Fort Canning for the last time and drove down to the harbour. It did not require much imagination to understand why the decision had been taken to leave. The heavy and continuous bombing had caused an immense amount of damage – ruined buildings, rubble-filled streets, fires as far as the eye could see and burst water mains gushing water. Overall hung a great pall of black smoke from the burning oil installations on Pulau Bukum and huge shadows drifted over the city to the background of almost continuous gunfire.

For the past weeks muddle and chaos seemed to have ruled supreme, but here at last was a definite order and I felt almost refreshed as I picked my way carefully back to Keppel Harbour.

As soon as I arrived at the Telok Ayer Wharf I set about passing the orders for the night's operation to all craft, all of which had already been warned to be in readiness to leave. In effect this meant a personal visit to each as no other means of communication was available. Inevitably this took time and one couldn't be sure of contacting everyone.

All day long columns of evacuees filed patiently along the approach road and on to the wharf and gradually found spaces in the miscellany of craft that now thronged the harbour and dockside. Unfortunately, despite all efforts, some military, at the point of a gun, forced their way on board.[1] Every conceivable kind of boat, including yachts, was being pressed into service and my thoughts returned to those days of Dunkirk almost two years before. I could not help wondering why such an outflow of civilians, Europeans as well as Asians, should have been allowed at this late hour. I think many of us felt at the time that it was yet another example of the lack of firm leadership. Whereas many Europeans certainly, and particularly those whose homes in up-country Malaya had been overrun, had been previously evacuated, far greater numbers should have been sent away earlier in much greater safety and comfort.[2] It was a pitiful sight to see the pathetic, bewildered groups of evacuees being separated from their belongings, and in some cases from other members of their families, to be ferried out to the many and widely assorted craft in the harbour.

The incident that stands out most in my mind of these last hours was the magnificent bravery and fortitude of a group of Australian

[1] The popular and able Captain of the dockyard, Captain Atkinson, was shot while barring the way to one such group.
[2] Of the hundreds of evacuees who left Singapore for Java on 12 and 13 February, only a handful survived, albeit to face three and half years as POWs or internees under savage and inhuman treatment.

nurses who were waiting their turn to be evacuated. The air-raids were following one another in quick succession and causing heavy casualties among the evacuees. To the noise of the guns was added the screams and cries of the dying and wounded. Smouldering and dismembered bodies lay everywhere among the pathetic remains of scattered burst-open suitcases. It was essential to calm and succour the survivors if a complete panic was not to set in. These brave nurses were always the first to answer calls for assistance and by their bearing and spirit were in stark contrast to some of the opposite sex.

As the sun set and the shadows quickly lengthened, the small patrol craft earmarked for the final lift began to come alongside. Events moved very slowly, frustratingly so at first. One reason was apparently the fact that the message ordering the special Army technicians selected for evacuation to make their way back to Keppel Harbour for evacuation had been very late in reaching the personnel concerned. In any case, the front was by now very disjointed and units were mixed up, with nobody knowing who was where.

With darkness the scene took on a more desperate aspect; the glow from the many fires seemed brighter and every thirty seconds or so the sky was illuminated by the flash of the heavy guns, followed by their deep boom. Inevitably under such conditions, collisions occurred between vessels moving alongside. Two of the hard-pressed China gunboats collided, but luckily neither suffered serious damage.

At 7.30 p.m. Admiral Spooner came down to see how things were progressing and I took him on a quick tour of inspection, telling him that I had arranged for him to take passage in *ML 310*, commanded by Lieutenant J. Bull, RNZVR. The Admiral said that he would send his and his party's kit down shortly and would follow later with the Air Marshal.

The darkness seemed to bring increasing uncertainties and a general jumpiness became apparent as the slow trickle of Army personnel made its way to the wharf to be allocated to the various vessels alongside. There were frequent rumours of Japanese break-throughs on this or that section of the front. With the unstable situation at the front line, clearly anything was possible.

At about 10.30 p.m. the Admiral, accompanied by the Air Marshal, Commander Frampton, Wing Commander Atkins and Lieutenant Ian Stonor of the Argyll and Sutherland Highlanders, who had been released from his ADC's duties by General Perceval, arrived on board. In addition a small number of Army and R.A.F. personnel had also embarked earlier.

After a quick and frugal meal in the wardroom, the Admiral, Commander Frampton and I set out for a final tour of the wharf to see progress and, above all, to urge everyone to get a move on and get clear of the harbour as soon as possible. A number of craft had already left and those remaining were taking on board the last of those waiting to leave. There being nothing further to be done, the Admiral informed Johnny Bull that he would like to leave at 11 p.m. With a few minutes left, I walked down to the wharf to where my faithful car was standing and pushed it over the edge into the water. Then, as I passed the now abandoned and sad old Straits Settlement training ship *Laburnum*, on a sudden impulse I climbed the gangway on to the deserted quarterdeck and lowered the White Ensign, returning with it to the ML.

Exactly at eleven p.m. *ML 310* slipped and went slowly astern until she was clear of the wharf. Apart from the whine of the engines, the ringing of the engine room telegraph and Johnny Bull's helm and engine orders, no one talked as the wharf slipped away into the night. On the bridge the Admiral and the Air Marshal stood silently watching the ruin of their commands. Just abaft the bridge I could see that Commander Frampton and Wing Commander Atkins were watching as well.

ML 310 threaded her way at slow speed towards the breakwater entrance. I remember looking at my watch, the one I had had to pay for in Robinsons a few days earlier, and noting that it was still Friday, 13 February. I was afterwards to consider many times whether our fate would have been different if we had waited those few minutes until another day!

Pilotage proved very difficult as thick swathes of choking smoke drifted across the harbour and the dark shapes of other vessels appeared and disappeared. Astern the few remaining craft alongside and the outlines of the Telok Ayer go-downs were silhouetted against the burning city. A signal lamp winked at us from our starboard beam announcing that this was *Trang*, a local vessel converted to mine-sweeping duties, aground with a large number of troops embarked. After a close inspection of the chart, the Admiral decided that there was nothing we could do for her and regretfully told her we were sorry but we could render no worthwhile assistance.

CHAPTER 7

Departure from Singapore

Out in the Straits navigation continued to be difficult, with marks indistinct and lights already reduced in brilliance. It was only fleetingly that they were visible in between the drifting smoke patches. Our navigation became ninety per cent 'dead reckoning'. Shortly before we were due to alter course to the south down the Phillips Channel, our steering broke down and, although the engines were immediately stopped, the ML made a wide circle off course. The hand steering was eventually connected and, making the best estimate of our position, the engines were once more put ahead and our course resumed. Some five minutes later we altered course into the Phillips Channel.

Almost immediately a series of grinding jolts checked the way of the ML and we realized we were aground. The engines had been stopped at the instant of first grounding and we hoped that the propellers, shafts and rudder were undamaged. The ML rapidly began to take up a list, which increased even though we made every effort to lighten ship. The most likely explanation was that we had 'stood on' beyond the position where we should have turned, the strong ebbing tide and our wide circle being the cause. We believed that we were now aground on a small reef to the east of St George's Island. There was little chance of refloating until the flood tide set in. On the other hand, if we had suffered underwater damage, particularly to the propellers, then there was little point in our remaining and our best course of action was to seek help from other passing vessels.

Since I felt that I was responsible for the Admiral's and Air Marshal's safety, I volunteered to go over the side and carry out an underwater inspection to the best of my ability. It was an obvious first step, so, with a rope secured to me, over I went to inspect the propellers and shaft. It was much more difficult than I had expected and I found that I could not maintain my position in the strong tide. The ML's small dinghy was then lowered to help me hold my position while I groped about between the ML's bottom and the sharp coral. So far as I could feel, everything appeared to be alright and I was returning to the upper deck when I slipped and fell between the dinghy and the ML. This elementary error of seamanlike safety, about which I had warned others on countless occasions, resulted in two crushed fingers on my left hand. It was an awful moment and I was convinced that I had lost the fingers. For a long time afterwards I heard that dreadful crunch!

Eventually the tide turned and everything was now made ready for a quick getaway as soon as it had risen sufficiently. All loose gear had been secured on the steeply sloping decks and there was nothing to do but wait as patiently as possible until the tide rose high enough for us to refloat. The list gradually decreased and we estimated that we would be afloat just after dawn. Imperceptibly the light grew and we noticed several other vessels anchored in the channel waiting for daylight. We recovered some of the items jettisoned from where they were lying on the clear coral bottom. To the north of us Singapore lay quiet under an ominous and now familiar pall of smoke.

By 6.30 a.m. *ML 310* was afloat once more and the engines were put cautiously astern to back off the reef. Hardly daring to breathe, we turned our bows south into the deeper water of the channel. Other ships which we had seen anchored were all now underway ahead of us and we too, with our stern to Singapore, increased to full speed. As if in protest at our desertion, the distant noise of gunfire was heard. Half an hour later we turned into the Durian Strait and began to overhaul the later departures. About this time we sighted an aircraft approaching from the north; it was flying low and we manned our anti-aircraft weapons. The aircraft, which the Air Marshal thought was a Messerschmitt 110, several of which, he said, the Japanese had, flew low but out of range down our starboard side. It was obviously a reconnaissance plane and therefore likely to be the forerunner of heavy air attacks on the large number of vessels crammed with evacuees, steering south for Batavia, at the western end of Java, three hundred miles to the south.

In view of the intense enemy air activity it had been our intention to proceed only at night and lie up in the day. Now that we, along with many other vessels, had been sighted and reported, it became imperative to seek cover quickly. We had of course hoped to be much

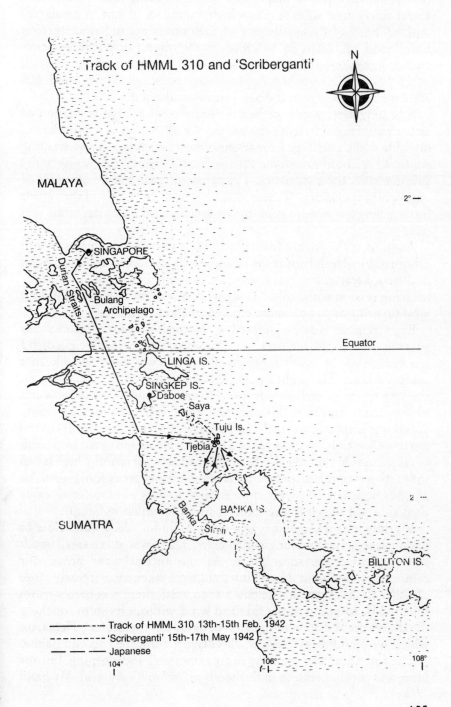

Track of HMML 310 and 'Scriberganti'

N

MALAYA

2° —

SINGAPORE

Durian Straits

Bulang
Archipelago

Equator

LINGA IS.

SINGKEP IS.
Daboe
Saya
Tuju Is.
Tjebia

BANKA IS.

SUMATRA

Banka Strait

2 ---

BILLITON IS.

————·— Track of HMML 310 13th-15th Feb. 1942
- - - - - - - 'Scriberganti' 15th-17th May 1942
— — — Japanese

104°
106°
108°

further south, but now had to turn into the Bulang Archipelago only about thirty-five miles south, which we did at 10 a.m. A small bay with a Chinese fishing village lying behind a fringe of palm trees was found and we crept in as close to the shore as possible before anchoring. Camouflage nets were quickly rigged and we took all other possible measures to conceal our presence. We noticed *ML 1062* make its way into the bay just beyond ours.

Not long afterwards we heard the noise of a large formation of aircraft approaching from the north. We all stayed as motionless as possible while two large formations of bombers flew over us, heading south. One could not shake off the fearful feeling that we were the prime target, the experience, I suppose, of two and a half years of enemy air superiority. We learned afterwards that many of the vessels leaving Singapore were sunk by air attacks in the Durian Strait that day.

As soon as the enemy formations had passed, a small party rowed ashore to buy fresh fruit at the Chinese village; others enjoyed a swim in the cool water. For me, forbidden to swim, began a painful hand-dressing session with Stoker Townsend, one of the engine room staff, who turned out to be a most efficient medical orderly.

By 5 p.m. it was considered a reasonable risk to resume our passage, so camouflage nets were lowered, the anchor weighed and our course to the south resumed. Everyone was ordered to keep a sharp lookout. The night's passage proved uneventful and dawn on the 15th found us well on our way and approaching the northern end of the Banka Straits with rather too much open sea for our liking. Speed was increased to reach the Tuju Islands lying thirty miles to the north of Banka Island, the latter's presence being indicated by a bank of large cumulus clouds. We headed for the largest island which lay to the eastward of the main group, named on the chart as Katjangan. An anxious hour later we were close enough to pick out the details of its west side and to select a suitable position in which to lie up.

We duly found a small bay and crept in, finding deep water close to under steep scrub and jungle-clad cliffs. There was also a small beach and it seemed the ideal place. As the anchor went down our camouflage nets went up and it would have taken an extremely close scrutiny to discover us. The bay was so small there was barely room for the ML to swing to the tide and wind without its stern touching the shore. Immediately to the west of us lay another island, Tjebia, on which we could make out a small village among the coconut palms.

The forenoon was spent by most swimming and sleeping, but for me it was another session in the hands of Stoker Townsend. My hand was in bad shape; it had become inflamed and I had a slight fever. The sea looked so inviting and I would have given anything to have been able to swim. On one occasion we saw a single aircraft flying south some way to the west of us, while on another we heard, but could not see, what must have been a much larger formation. It was very worrying to see the Japanese already so far to the south; we had hoped we would be beyond their range by this time.

Towards midday my whole arm had become inflamed and swollen and the fever was worse. The Admiral and Air Marshal agreed that I must see a doctor as soon as possible and it was decided that we should make for Muntok, the principal port on the north-west corner of Banka Island, approximately forty miles to the south-west. Although I was quite prepared to see a doctor I had visions of being left behind in Banka, a prospect which worried me, and I asked Admiral Spooner not to leave me there since another twenty-four hours would see us in Batavia[1] anyway. At 2.30 p.m. we weighed anchor, took down the camouflage nets and set course for Banka Island. We had not seen or heard anything in the way of enemy air activity for the past two hours and so it was felt to be a reasonable risk to make the passage in daylight.

A few minutes after starting we sighted a small *koleh* with two men in it, paddling across the channel between Katjangan and Tjebia. As they were obviously trying to attract our attention, we steered towards them. In between paddle strokes, one man appeared to be waving what looked like a letter, which it turned out to be. As the *koleh* came alongside we saw there were two natives in it, one of whom handed up the letter. The letter purported to come from the Commandant of a Dutch Military look-out and radio station on Tjebia. The Wing Commander, who spoke Malay, questioned the two men and learned that they came from the village we had seen earlier, living by collecting coconuts and fishing. The letter said that large numbers of warships were in the vicinity with many other ships. The Admiral was not inclined to attach much importance to this news. He said that, as there were no Allied warships in the area, they must therefore be Japanese and since there had been many such reports in the past few weeks, which in each case had been untrue, he proposed to ignore this one.

Course was resumed and everyone, except me, settled down to what was regarded hopefully as a pleasant interlude and a visit to a new port of call. I was made to go below and try to get some sleep, having been dosed with aspirins. Tossing and turning in my fever, I

[1] Now Djarkarta

found I just could not sleep so I decided to go up to the bridge and see how we were progressing.

It was perfect weather as I made my way along the upper deck from the wardroom hatch to the bridge, puffy cumulus clouds chasing one another across a blue sky, a deeper blue sea flecked with white horses and every now and then a burst of cooling spray whipping across the deck. On the port bow the mountains of Banka stood up clearly, while to starboard a line of cloud betrayed the low-lying coast of Sumatra. As my glance took in the horizon, I suddenly became aware of the masts and funnels of two ships ahead; a second was sufficient to identify them as the unmistakable silhouettes of two Japanese cruisers.

From the bridge they must have been in sight for fully three or four minutes and that no one had sighted them was extraordinary. I raced to the bridge, pressed the alarm rattlers and gave the order hard a' starboard and full speed. In the wheelhouse the ML's First Lieutenant who was on watch had been trying to identify the mountains ahead on the chart and was quite oblivious of the danger threatening.

As I gave the orders I had a horrid feeling in the pit of my stomach that the Japanese lookouts could not have failed to have sighted us. I handed over to Johnny Bull, who, with the Admiral, was on the bridge in seconds. The only course of action open to us was to retire at our utmost speed and try to regain the shelter of the islands with the intention of making a break for it under cover of darkness.

During the few minutes that our reversal of course had taken no less than three cruisers and two destroyers had come into sight. We watched them intently and with great anxiety. Suddenly we saw a flash from one of the forward guns of the leading cruiser. It was a ranging shot and we counted the seconds until it fell with a large splash a hundred yards astern and almost in our wake. The second cruiser, we now saw, had flown off an aircraft which immediately turned and headed in our direction.

Although we were now at full speed, it was at least four knots below our maximum due to our extra load of passengers, their gear and not least, a hundred R.A.F. Browning machine guns stowed below in the fore peak. In such circumstances it was obvious that we could not reach the shelter of the islands before the aircraft was overhead. As it came closer it was now seen to be a single-float seaplane. When it came within bombing range we started to zig-zag violently, heeling over at every alteration of helm. Fire was opened with our machine guns. We could clearly see two bombs under each wing. Suddenly the aircraft dived down to release its bombs and we watched them come slicing down to burst in the sea close astern. The shock of their explosions shook the ML severely. Bombs released, the aircraft banked steeply away and headed back to the cruisers.

We could now see that one of the two destroyers was also heading in our direction, but by now we had reached the southernmost point of Tjebia Island and lost sight of it. Our intention was to place the island between ourselves and the enemy in order to try and gain enough time to conceal ourselves if possible. Speed was reduced for better observation of possible hiding places and navigation. The whole of the eastern side of the island was now revealed to us, a jumble of rocks at the southern end giving way to a long coconut-palm-fringed beach, with, at its northern end, a steep-sided rocky promontory, behind which there seemed to be a chance of possible shelter.

Course was altered to run up towards this promontory, but shortly after steadying up on the new course, a series of violent jarring thuds, all too familiar, betokened the fact that we had run aground once again. Cutting the corner of the island too closely, as well as not appreciating the extent of the reef shown on our chart, had caused this latest mishap. The engines were immediately stopped and the dinghy lowered. Our kedge anchor with some chain was hurriedly lowered into the dinghy; the First Lieutenant and one of the seamen then rowed away, whilst a hawser attached to the chain was paid out from the ML. The idea was to lay the anchor in deeper water to seaward of the reef, and then to try and haul the ML off the reef. This operation was much harder than we anticipated; rowing the dinghy through the rough sea built up by waves breaking on the reef was hard and long.

The Admiral now decided that his and the AOC's presence should remain unknown to the Japanese, if, as seemed probable, the ML could not be refloated by the time they arrived, as also seemed likely. The ML's crew were to remain and to do all they could to refloat her. Everyone else was to get ashore and conceal themselves in the jungle, so as quickly as possible everyone lowered themselves over the side and waded ashore through the surf. If boarded, the ML's Officers and crew were to do all they could to put the Japanese off the scent of those who had gone ashore. The anchor had been laid out by now, but no movement was possible.

Because of my condition, I was rowed ashore in the dinghy. Once on the beach, I lay down in the shelter of some large rocks in a position where I could watch the ML and made no attempt to follow the others who were making their way inland. I watched as the dinghy made its way back to the ML with some difficulty. It reached

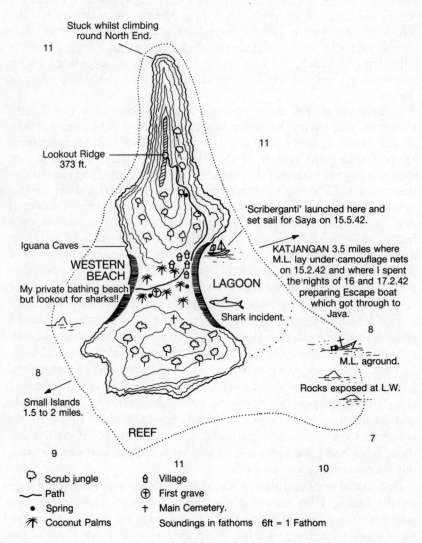

N

Rough Sketch Map of Tjebia drawn
by the author in 1942

Stuck whilst climbing
round North End.

11

11

Lookout Ridge
373 ft.

'Scriberganti' launched here and
set sail for Saya on 15.5.42.

Iguana Caves

WESTERN
BEACH

My private bathing beach
but lookout for sharks!!

LAGOON

KATJANGAN 3.5 miles where
M.L. lay under camouflage nets
on 15.2.42 and where I spent
the nights of 16 and 17.2.42
preparing Escape boat
which got through to
Java.

Shark incident.

8

M.L. aground.

8

Rocks exposed at L.W.

Small Islands
1.5 to 2 miles.

REEF

7

9

11

10

🌳 Scrub jungle   ❁ Village
— Path   ⊕ First grave
• Spring   † Main Cemetery.
🌴 Coconut Palms   Soundings in fathoms   6ft = 1 Fathom

it just as a destroyer appeared round the southernmost point of the island. She turned broadside on for a few minutes while her Captain summed up the situation. Seeing that the ML was hard aground, and that there was obviously no further danger to be expected from us, she went ahead and swung away to the south to rejoin her consorts.

As I watched her disappearing into the distance my thoughts were very mixed. On the one hand it seemed that our reprieve was too good to be true and that we now would have more time to refloat the ML, but on the other hand the obvious fact was that, in addition to the threat from the air, we now had the sure knowledge that the Japanese Navy was between us and our destination. This seemed to be a great setback to our chances of successfully reaching Batavia.

I now began to feel very unwell, the reflected heat from the rocks I was lying among seemed to have made my fever much worse. This, added to the fact that the destroyer was already hull down, decided me that my best course of action was to return to the rather cooler conditions of the ML, so I stood up and attracted their attention, indicating that I wanted to return. The dinghy was sent in for me. As I stood on the beach waiting, I was joined by Wing Commander Atkins, as he too had decided to return to the ML.

Once back on board I began to feel much better and was able to discuss the situation with Johnny Bull and the Wing Commander. I felt terribly frustrated to be in such poor shape when every action now required physical effort of one kind or another. Taking stock of the situation, it was obvious that the ML was really hard aground and suffering damage every minute as she pounded and ground on the coral; she had to be refloated quickly to save her, let alone to escape into concealment. It was decided to try and get the kedge further out; the attempt was made, but without much improvement, and, despite all our efforts, we could not move the ML. By this time the seas running over the shallows of the reef had swung the bows to the north. A thorough examination of the hull revealed extensive flooding in the engine room, the deck plates being almost covered with water entering via the propeller shafts. The propellers themselves could be heard grinding into the coral at every movement, though the remainder of the hull still seemed sound. We decided to replace the kedge, using one of the bigger bower anchors, and to try once more to regain deeper water.

It was in the middle of this operation that a Japanese aircraft suddenly appeared and there was only just time to man our guns before it had released two bombs which burst close by, severely shaking the ML and throwing up columns of water and splintered coral. Another Japanese destroyer was then sighted approaching from the south; so we had not been forgotten and were not going to be left alone. We were certainly not going to be allowed to refloat unmolested.

During the destroyer's approach, the pros and cons of resistance were quickly discussed and decided against. Our only anti-ship gun, the 3-pounder, was on the forecastle and would not bear to the south and against a destroyer our light machine guns would have had no effect. Immobile on the reef, we were a sitting target. Our instructions to divert attention from the presence of the Admiral and Air Marshal also pointed to this path. Their kit was therefore quickly thrown overboard on the side away from the Japanese and the code and signal books, together with the charts, were destroyed, and the radio rendered inoperable.

There was just enough time to do this before the destroyer hove-to about a mile away on our port quarter. She presented a picture of great menace, a long, low hull, the peculiar rake of her masts and funnels, large white name and flotilla markings in Japanese characters standing out on the dark grey background of her paintwork. As she lay to, pitching and rolling gently in the long blue seas, we saw that her upper deck and superstructure were lined with sailors. The Rising Sun ensign blew out from the peak of her short mainmast.

We could see her armament trained on us and her motor boat was lowered from her port side davits. As the boat moved away from her side, we saw a puff of yellow-grey smoke blow from the midships gun, followed a second later by the dull thud of its firing. A shell screamed overhead to explode in the coral ahead of us, to be followed by several more single shots, obviously to cover the approach of the motor boat with its boarding party. Although the shelling was accurate, we were hit only once, our klaxon horn on the mast being blown off.

During the shelling the ML's crew were sent ashore, so as not to expose them to needless casualties from gunfire that we had no way of responding to. Johnny Bull, along with his First Lieutenant, Lieutenant Henderson, the Wing Commander and I took what cover we could behind the wheelhouse. The motor boat had, by this time, reached the edge of the reef and was now, with the aid of a long sounding pole, picking its way through the breakers. We could see it carried a party of armed sailors with two officers standing in the stern sheets. I could not help feeling, once again, how 'Japanese' not only its occupants obviously looked, but also the boat itself, long and narrow-gutted. It was the same feeling that I had had on seeing the

Japanese bombers closing in on their first attack on *Repulse*. When the boat was about fifty yards off, we walked slowly and deliberately along the listing deck to the small ladder at the port quarter for which point the boat was making.

It was not a pleasant feeling, standing on the listing deck waiting for the Japanese, about to come face to face with this new enemy, quite a different sensation to the almost impersonal confrontation by gunfire at long range which is the experience of most sailors and airmen. We were not at all sure what to expect, whether they would believe our story that apart from the crew and ourselves, there was no one else on board. As the motor boat came alongside, I had a very close view of the boarding party and to me they seemed, their oriental features enhancing the impression, as hostile as any group of men I had ever seen. I was fearful of what was to come. We already knew of their reputation in this respect. We were not allowed much time for speculation, however. The Japanese literally swarmed aboard and we were at once cuffed and hit about the face and shoulders for a few unpleasant seconds until the Officer in Charge came on board and with a few short words of command put an end to this behaviour. During those few seconds I think it flashed through all our minds that we too wished we had taken to the island. Last-minute ideas of resistance also ran through our minds, but discretion quickly became the better part of valour, particularly as we remembered our aim, which was to do all we could to persuade the Japanese not to land on the island, thus inevitably leading to the discovery of the two senior officers.

This little interlude apart, the Japanese appeared well-trained and seemed to know exactly what to do. They moved purposefully about the ML on pre-arranged tasks. The second of the two officers was obviously an engineer and he took two of the party down the engine-room hatch, from which we soon heard the sounds of heavy thuds and bangs which left no doubt in our minds that, if the ML had been in a bad state before, she was in a worse one now. Another party was rummaging in the wheelhouse, while a third group, consisting of three sailors armed with light automatics, kept us covered at the stern of the ML. The Officer in Charge turned out to be a Midshipman, who, with his few words of English, asked me if I was from the 'Naval Academy'. This was followed by one or two more random questions which seemed unconnected with the occasion.

Some minutes later one of the boarding party came up to the Midshipman, spoke quickly and looked rather pointedly at us. I had a feeling that he was angry that we had immobilized the wireless set. It then seemed to me that the Midshipman was rather at a loss and I seized the opportunity to ask him, mostly by sign language, if he was going to take us on board his ship and if so could we collect some of our belongings. He nodded his head, which I took to mean yes, so I then asked him if we might go below to get them. Again he nodded his head and, with a wary eye on the automatics, we then climbed down the accommodation ladder into the wardroom where we hurriedly threw a few things into a bag.

We returned to the upper deck expecting to be told to get into the motor boat and stood waiting for some kind of indication. Suddenly there were some grunted words of command as a result of which we were hustled and pushed aft. I remember we started to protest, but to no avail and found ourselves forced right up against the guard rails at the stern. The Midshipman now announced by sound and gesture that he could not take us on board his ship as they had no space.

The full significance did not dawn on us for some moments, then, as we realized that the entire boarding party was standing in a half-circle in front of us with their weapons trained on our middles, the truth filtered through to us. I think the first to say anything was the Wing Commander, who muttered out of the corner of his mouth, 'This is it boys, I think they are going to shoot us'.

How long we actually stood there I don't know, but in reality it must have been no more than a minute. I can remember taking in the appearance of the Japanese – the Midshipman's white ducks, long trousers and button-up tunic, quite unlike our own tropical working rig of shorts and shirt. He was holding his Samurai-style sword, its hilt and scabbard covered in coarse white canvas. He was looking straight at us. The engineering officer seemed to be looking away as if he did not wish to witness what was about to happen. The members of the boarding party, whose fingers seemed to be tightening on the triggers, were dressed in white canvas suits in the same coarse material as the Midshipman's sword scabbard. They also wore little white kepis on their heads with a blue anchor on the front above the peak.

My thoughts were racing now. Was there a way out? Did one have to die? I wondered if I could sense that final pressure on the triggers. Could I fall backwards over the stern just before that final movement? Was it possible to hold my breath long enough to get away under water? These thoughts ran through my mind until they were superseded by the realization that I could not move. A mental and physical sickness stultified all thought and movement except that in the next few seconds everything would be over. The feeling of utter hopelessness was so great that there was no longer any question of fear. It seemed as though one was rooted to the spot.

Then, gradually, I sensed thought returning and with it an awareness that the Midshipman was motioning us to get into the ML's dinghy which was still secured alongside. It became clear that we still had some time left; a new situation was developing if we could take advantage of it; perhaps we only had a few minutes. We scrambled down into the dinghy and, ridiculously at such a moment, Johnny Bull handed down our bags. We set out for the shore, Johnny rowing, Henderson in the bows and the Wing Commander and myself in the stern. Wing Commander Atkins voiced our thoughts when he said, 'They will shoot us now, less messy this way!' Johnny was the only one of us who could see the Japanese and our suspense grew and remained until Johnny suddenly said very quietly, 'They are getting into their motor boat'.

For the first time since we had collected some kit to go aboard the Japanese destroyer we thought we had a chance. A new hope took hold of us; Johnny redoubled his efforts and pulled as hard as he could, trying to keep the overloaded dinghy stern on to the breaking seas as they ran over the reef. In quick glances over our shoulders we could see the Japanese heading out through the passage in the reef. We reached the beach and quickly pulled the dinghy clear of the seas before taking cover amid the rocks and scrub beyond.

We now watched the Japanese, who had reached their ship. The motor boat was quickly hoisted and the destroyer turned out to sea; her stern was soon buried below a huge white wake as she rapidly increased speed. We watched till she had disappeared from sight and it was only then that we began to find some relief from the strain and tension of the past hours. For a short period anyway we felt we would be left in peace and be able to take stock of our situation.

CHAPTER 8

Tjebia Island

The first thing to do was obviously to contact the remainder of the party, of whom there was no sign, so we set off along a path which led along just behind a fringe of tall coconut palms on the edge of the beach. After a few minutes we came to a collection of native houses clustered round a clearing about thirty to forty yards from the beach. We saw one or two inhabitants moving furtively between the houses, but as they did not seem overjoyed to see us, we were glad when we saw one of the ML's crew coming down another path from the interior of the island towards us.

He told us that the whole party had gathered further back among the palms which stretched inland for some distance. Following him, we walked along a sandy path for a short way before coming to a clearing in which the men were assembled. There was no need to tell them what had happened, as they had witnessed the proceedings from the shelter of the coconut palms fringing the beach.

Admiral Spooner now held a short conference to decide our immediate needs and the best plan to adopt. There was not a moment to lose, as the Japanese seemed to be in full command of the surrounding seas, and, if we were to succeed in breaking through to Batavia, then each hour and especially this night was of vital importance. There was also the risk that the Japanese might return and decide to take us prisoner. It was decided that the first thing to do was to carry out a thorough inspection of the ML to see if there was a last chance of getting her afloat and running again.

To make this inspection, Johnny Bull took with him his First Lieutenant, the Coxswain, the Petty Officer Motor Mechanic and the Telegraphist. He was accompanied by a second party to collect sufficient food for a meal for the whole party. Wing Commander

116

Atkins was also sent up the hill to contact the Dutch Military Observation Post situated at the north end of the island, to find out whether their wireless was working so that we could send a message for help to the Allied Headquarters in Batavia.

During the time that the Japanese had been shelling and boarding the ML, some of the party had been finding out as much as they could about the island. It was already known from the chart, now destroyed, that it was Tjebia Island, and was one of the Tuju or Seven Islands group. The inhabitants of the village, most of whom had already departed for Banka, used the island for fishing and the collection of copra, and those still remaining intended to follow them, as they had been badly frightened by the bombing and gunfire. It did not take long for Johnny Bull's inspection party to get back and report that the ML could not be made ready for some days, if at all. The Japanese had badly damaged the fuel lines, cooling and ignition systems, obviously the results of the hammering and banging we heard while they had been below. The engine room was apparently badly damaged and the site of the leak could not be found. In addition, the wireless equipment was hopelessly smashed and beyond repair. Taking all these facts into consideration, it was decided that a small party should be sent off that night in one of the several fishing boats known in Malay as *prahus* which we had seen on the beach, with the object of trying to slip past the Japanese forces clearly lying between us and Java, report the situation and then guide a rescue operation back. The remainder of the party were to make arrangements for a stay on the island for at least a week.

While the investigation of the ML's damage was being carried out the Commandant of the Dutch Army Post had appeared, accompanied by two of his men. He told the Admiral, through the Wing Commander, who spoke Malay, that he had destroyed all the wireless equipment at the post, because he thought the ML had been an enemy warship! This we did not altogether believe and told him that we should like to send our telegraphist to have a look as soon as he returned from the ML.

Johnny Bull and I then made our way down to the beach to select the most suitable of the *prahus*. When we arrived on the beach in front of the village where the *prahus* lay we realized that we were already too late, for while we had been talking and deciding what to do, the villagers had quietly faded away in the remaining seaworthy craft and had left the island. Only one or two rather dilapidated *prahus* remained. One of these, though very small, was a possible but we could see that it was obviously not seaworthy enough for a three-hundred-mile voyage starting that night. We judged that it would take at least a day's work to make it seaworthy. This was another bitter blow to our hopes. It seemed as if nothing would go right.

By this time it was dark, but enough supplies had been brought from the ML for one of the passengers, Mr Richardson, a tough old retired Warrant Boatswain, to prepare an evening meal, which he did most excellently. This and its accompanying mug of hot tea gave our flagging morale a much-needed lift. After the meal we sat around a fire of crackling coconut fronds and husks and once more discussed the situation – our immediate plans for repairing the *prahu*, who should form the party and a timetable for the passage to Batavia.

It was decided that, in case the Japanese returned or otherwise disturbed us, it would be best for the *prahu* party to leave before first light the next morning, row or paddle over to Katjangan immediately to the east, and there beach her at the little cove we could see at its southern end, very close to where the ML had anchored that morning.

There we would work on the *prahu* and hope to slip away unobserved at dusk. From then on the days would be spent lying up wherever we could and the nights on passage. We estimated it would take us ten days to reach Java. On arrival there, the position of the party would be explained and help requested by submarine or flying boat. Both Admiral Spooner and Air Marshal Pulford agreed that only this means of rescue stood any chance of success in the face of the situation that was believed to confront us. The Admiral also stressed that one of the party should return with the rescuers to show them the exact location of the island.[1] Ten days from the *prahu's* date of departure those on the island would keep a special lookout for the arrival of a rescue party, especially by night.

There was still much to do that night. A crew was selected – Johnny Bull, his Coxswain, Leading Seaman Brough, Petty Officer Motor Mechanic Johncock, Able Seaman Hill and myself. While Johnny and other members of the ML's crew collected the necessary materials and tools to effect the repairs and checked the *prahu's* sails and oars, Mr Richardson and I measured out ten day's rations from the meagre supplies brought ashore from the ML. Meanwhile, the remainder of the party who were not actively preparing for the sail to Java continued unloading essential stores from the ML and another group set about selecting and preparing the now deserted native huts for habitation. Latrines were dug and a reconnaissance along another

[1] There were numerous other small islands in the area and subsequent events were to show how important correct identification would be.

10. The Naval Store and canteen.

11. The burial area on Tjebia; photo taken after the war.

12. The Imperial War Graves Commission visits Tjebia after the war.

13. Memorial Service at the site of the eighteen graves.

pathway leading towards the foot of the hill on which the Dutch Army Post was situated, led to a spring which looked as though it had adequate fresh water. At last, very tired, at about 11 p.m., having done all that was possible, we turned in to get what rest and sleep we could.

I found myself sharing what had been the village headman's house with the Wing Commander and Ian Stonor, who had been General Perceval's A.D.C. Despite my tiredness, sleep was quite impossible. The floor boards on which we lay were verminous and the air so thick with mosquitoes that we could hardly breathe without getting them up our noses or into our mouths; their vicious whine as they hovered round us was unceasing, as were their bites. Outside the house, the chirping of millions of crickets and croaking of frogs mingled with the hum of other tropical insects. As if this was not enough, the fears of the unknown dangers of the forthcoming attempt to sail to Java for help, as well as the disasters of the day, constantly turned over and over in my mind. I was dispirited by the succession of disasters that had occurred since *Repulse* was sunk, but, despite all, and the uneasy feeling it induced in the pit of my stomach, I still longed for the dawn, when we were to cross over to Katjangan.

I suppose inevitably I must have dropped into some kind of troubled sleep. At last the dawn came and I awoke with a shake from the Wing Commander. It was still dark and he helped me find my small kitbag, which I carried down to the cookhouse and there found that always welcome mug of hot tea. While drinking this, my hand was re-dressed, a painful but still necessary operation in the light of what we anticipated lay ahead.

A number of the party turned out to help drag the *prahu* down to the edge of the lagoon and launch her. It was nearly 6 a.m. by the time we were afloat and all our gear and food had been stowed. The sky to the east was already starting to brighten as we set out to pull across the channel separating Tjebia from Katjangan. Our great fear was that we should be seen by some prying Japanese aircraft. After some time of steady pulling with a small *koleh* alongside and our extra two helpers paddling away, we noticed that we were being set down to the south-east by a strong current running in that direction. To make matters worse, the *prahu* was leaking badly despite last night's hastily caulked seams.

Our progress was much slower than we had hoped and it was fully light by the time we had got halfway across the channel. The rowers changed over at intervals in order to rest, but those resting had to bale hard to keep pace with the water coming in through the leaking seams. With my one sound hand I steered, which proved very necessary with the unbalanced oars we had constructed. I shouted the time and encouraged the rowers to make that extra effort, and became quite hoarse in the process. As well as shouting encouragement, I kept an anxious lookout at the sky. Gradually the far shore drew nearer, until, quite exhausted, we finally grounded on the sandy beach of a little cove at the island's southern end.

After a short rest, we all set to to repair the *prahu*. First our stores had to be unloaded so that the hull was accessible. All the seams needed caulking and some strengthening of the hull was also necessary. While the able-bodied members of the party undertook this work, I set to with a needle and twine to repair and strengthen the rotting stitching of the sails and rigging. Once or twice during the forenoon we heard the distant noise of aircraft, but saw nothing. The work went steadily on and every inch of the old boat was examined and repaired where necessary, to the best of our ability with our limited materials and tools. We worked on until well after midday to complete the repairs and then allowed ourselves a meagre meal of biscuits from our carefully planned daily ration.

Everyone then settled down under what shade could be found in the scrub at the back of the beach to get some rest before the first night's sail to Banka. Once more, as on the previous night, sleep evaded me, try as I would. The events of the last two days continued to course through my mind. It was a repetition of the previous night. It seemed that, almost from the first few minutes of our leaving Singapore, things had gone successively wrong. Friday the 13th had indeed lived up to its reputation! My fever and incapacity did nothing to help my frame of mind and I could not ward off the deepening sense of depression. The future had always seemed so secure and certain, but now all that had changed dramatically and the prospects of our forthcoming voyage, with all its dangers, in a leaky decrepit sailing boat through enemy-held waters, seemed daunting in the extreme.

It was our intention to set out just before sunset in order to get clear of the islands and surrounding rocks and reefs before darkness fell, so at about 5.30 p.m. we turned to again. The stores were re-stowed, the mast stepped and sails rigged. We said goodbye to Stoker Tucker and Marine Robinson who had come over with us to help with the repairs and watched them paddle off on their return journey to rejoin the main party. As soon as they had left, the *prahu* was launched and we pulled clear of the beach before hoisting sail for our journey. However, we made little progress, turning slowly round and round with our sail idly slatting about. It became obvious that there was insufficient wind and, thinking we might still be under the lee of the island, we decided to continue pulling in order to get clear. After another half hour, and with darkness falling, we still had not managed to clear some small rocks off the southern end of the island. As there seemed no prospect of more wind, we decided to return and put off the attempt for that night. In the gathering darkness we pulled back to the little cove and hauled the *prahu* up the beach clear of the sea.

It was a bitter disappointment, not least because I think we were all anxious to escape the unfortunate atmosphere of this scene of our worst misfortune. We ate another small meal and prepared to spend the night on the beach. We wondered what the others in the main party would make of our fire; we could see theirs flickering through the palms. It was surprising how secure they appeared to be, compared to the isolation of our own position.

The previous night in the village headman's house had seemed a nightmare of discomfort and we thought that at least tonight, lying on the sand of the little beach, we would be cooler and more comfortable. Somehow the sand seemed to be just as hard as the rough floor boards, the sand crabs more numerous than the bed bugs, the mosquitoes no less vicious than those of the village, and sleep only came in brief periods of dozing. In between, the realities of our lonely and exposed position were uppermost in our thoughts. The hours dragged by until dawn brought relief in the shape of a cooling swim and wash in the sea.

We made a scanty meal from some dried biscuits and watery tea, being afraid to eat more, as our rations had been strictly apportioned for a ten-day passage and we had already consumed three meals and made no progress. The biscuits tasted horrible. They had all become sodden with sea water on the way over from Tjebia Island and had been laid out on the sand to dry out, becoming a mixture of flour, salt, sugar and sand.

Johnny and I decided that there was no point in crossing the channel to the main party but that it would be better to stay where we were and do some more work on improving the sea-worthiness of the *prahu*. Twice during the morning we took cover under the scrub as Japanese seaplanes arrived to bomb the ML. This was a worrying development which showed that they had not lost interest in us and that their ships were still close. Midday came, and with it another meagre meal.

As before, we settled down to get some rest in preparation for a second attempt to get away that night. By 5 p.m. we were again loading up and preparing to launch the *prahu*, though the conditions did not look hopeful. There was an oily swell and little wind, but shortly before 6 p.m. we once more pulled out clear of the beach and hoisted our sail. After half-an-hour's battling with the current with sail and oars, we decided that we had no option but to put back to our beach and await more favourable conditions, having a faint hope that the wind might fill in sufficiently to allow us to start later. Darkness fell, but no wind came and we realized that we had another night to spend with the mosquitoes and land crabs.

It was another blow to morale and we were all very cast down. It seemed nothing could go right for us and as we tried to sleep we looked longingly across to the imagined security of the main party's fire, flickering invitingly from the village. Eventually, with that same overwhelming sense of misfortune, we fell into an uneasy, broken sleep.

Dawn on the 18th brought a momentary feeling of oblivion; however, reality soon returned as we prepared for our third morning on the little beach. Breakfast consisted of two or three biscuits and, to boost morale, we dipped into our precious ration of cocoa. As we started to eat we saw a small *koleh* approaching from Tjebia and, as it came closer, we were able to make out its occupants as Tucker and Robinson, our two helpers who had originally come over with us to help with the repairs. They brought us a message from the Admiral to say that he had some news for us and wished us to return to Tjebia that evening, instead of setting out on our journey. So, for the third consecutive day, we lay up and waited. We had no materials left with which to do more repairs, so there was nothing to do but wait. Again we watched the Japanese bomb the ML though they did not appear to hit her despite the spouts of sea and coral fragments. At 5 p.m. we set out to return to Tjebia.

We arrived back after dark and went to see the Admiral. The news he had for us was that on the previous night the Dutch native Commandant had attempted to leave the island with some of his men in another *prahu*, which must have slipped our notice in our hasty search on the evening of the 15th. However, this *prahu* had proved so unseaworthy that the attempt had been abandoned soon after starting, the party only just getting back before it actually sank under them. The Commandant had then approached the Admiral with the proposition that our party, which he had obviously been observing, would stand a much better chance of getting through if he accompanied them. This made sense to the Admiral, and so, knowing we had not managed to get away, he had sent the message for us to return.

The Commandant now announced that he wished to take two of his men with him, which of course meant that two of our party would have to drop out. The Admiral, rather surprisingly, agreed to this. The logical first choice, given my disability, was myself, the second being Petty Officer Motor Mechanic Johncock. It was decided that the re-arranged party would set sail the following evening. My feelings were mixed; a part of me really wanted to take part in this adventure which I had helped to plan, but the other part, probably due to my injury, felt a certain relief. That night we enjoyed a not unappetizing meal at a makeshift table on the veranda of the headman's house. It was a great improvement on our scanty biscuit meals on Katjangan. During our absence, Mr Richardson had turned another large hut near the beach into a cookhouse, complete with stove. With the limited stores and facilities available, he produced some quite palatable, if unusual, meals.

That night, without the dominating anxiety of the long and hazardous sail, I slept more deeply than I had been able to do on the previous four; perhaps it was sheer exhaustion.

The next day was spent checking over the *prahu*'s gear once more and doing some more work to improve her seaworthiness. We also topped up the food for the voyage which had been depleted by our continued failure to get away. As the day drew on, a good steady breeze set in and at last there was every prospect of Johnny and his party getting away, and so it proved. At 5 p.m. on 19 April I shook Johnny's hand and wished him and his crew good luck. We launched the *prahu* from the same beach we had first landed on and I sat and watched them sail away to the south.

My feelings were sad as I made my way slowly back along the path to the village. I was intensely disappointed not to be with them, but with my injured hand I realized that I would have been a liability if real trouble were met. The light was fading fast as I passed the dark shape of the ML lying out on the reef. I could hear, and just see, the men, under the direction of the ML's First Lieutenant, splashing in and out through the shallows of the lagoon bringing back stores and food.

The nights seemed to be the worst times and that night was no exception. Once more it was hours before I fell into a fitful sleep. My thoughts were with Johnny and my late companions in the *prahu*. How were they faring? How far had they got? How would they evade the enemy patrols? Were they still afloat and above all, would they succeed in reaching Java and summoning help? The wind seemed to have died away to a calm and I could hardly sense any movement in the palm fronds above us. I pictured them labouring away at the oars, something in which I could not really have helped. I did reassure myself that, however disappointed I was, it was right not to have accompanied them.[1]

[1] Long after the war I learned that Johnny Bull's party had succeeded in reaching Java and reporting the position on Tjebia. Apparently no aircraft or submarine was available in Java for a rescue mission and so the Admiral's instruction that one of the party should return with it could not be implemented. However, the American submarine *S-39*, Lieutenant James W. (Red) Coe, was returning southward in waters adjacent to the Tuju group of islands at this date. She was ordered by Commander Submarine Asiatic Fleet to rescue the British party on Tjebia island. According to *S-39*'s log, she reached Tjebia on 27 February. For two consecutive nights the *S-39* was manoeuvred close inshore and messages were flashed to the island and a radio call sent. The *S-39* withdrew and remained submerged each day. Finally, on the third night, a party was sent ashore to search the island, but after 55 minutes returned to the submarine, reporting that there was no sign of life, only some native huts, smashed to the ground, presumably by a Japanese landing force. The remainder of the night and the next day were spent observing Tjebia and Katjangan, but, as no sign of life was seen and a Japanese destroyer was sighted steering past the islands, the *S-39* withdrew.

There is a mystery about the *S-39*'s mission to rescue the party on Tjebia. The published log entries for this operation do indicate the position and details of Tjebia and Katjangan islands. However, there is a discrepancy between the log and the account on page 81 of *US Submarine Operations in World War II* by Theodore Roscoe. Roscoe states that 'the landing party was led by Coe and that they searched the island from end to end, finding only a series of footprints at the water's edge'. *S-39*'s log states that 'C.I.E.M. Peterson was sent in to search which he did for 40 minutes.' He stated on his return that he had made 'a thorough search but had found no trace of the British party, nor of life of any kind, but he had found native shacks, beaten to the ground, apparently deliberately, pots and pans scattered about, and finally, footprints in the sand, on the beach'. However, there is no doubt from the experiences narrated that no one landed on, or searched, Tjebia at this time. The only huts on the island were those occupied by our party and were in a conspicuous clearing. They were still standing when the party left and when a War Graves party visited the island at the end of the war.

An intense and keen watch was kept over this period, at all points of the island, especially the South-west point. Nobody was seen, nor were any signals by light seen or received. This watch, by day and night, never saw any sign of the Japanese destroyer reported by *S-39*. Since we were expecting a rescue attempt at this time, it seems incredible that our twenty-four-hour watch failed to sight either the rescue party or the Japanese destroyer. One must draw the firm conclusion that *S-39* never landed anybody on the island, nor did she send any continuous signals to the island. Could it have been another island? If so, why does the log record positions and details of Tjebia?

After the war Admiral Helfrich, the Dutch Naval Commander, Jarva, in his unpublished notes, commented that at the time they did not know anything about the story but 'if I had known, it would have been easy to rescue them by sending a submarine, the *K14* was near the place'.

CHAPTER 9

Marooned

The preparation of the *prahu* and the planning of the escape and rescue voyage had obviously been the priority task. However, while this had been taking place, the remainder of the party had settled down to preparing themselves for a stay of at least three weeks. Accommodation in native houses[1] had been selected and stores of all sorts were being obtained from the ML. The villagers had quietly decamped from the island on the night of our arrival, so that, as far as we knew, there was only the remainder of the Dutch Army lookout party apart from ourselves left on the island.

The senior member of our party was Rear Admiral Spooner who had, as Rear Admiral Malaya, acted as the senior Naval Officer after the demise of the Far Eastern Fleet at Singapore. He was a very active and forceful personality, who had commanded *Repulse* immediately prior to his appointment as Rear Admiral. Air Vice-Marshal L. E. Pulford, Air Officer Commanding the Far East Air Force, had been ordered to leave Singapore with the Admiral, and in character and temperament he was very much the opposite of the Admiral. He had been the Operational Commander of the Air Force during the Malayan Campaign and had witnessed the destruction of his command by an overwhelmingly superior enemy. He had suffered from malaria and was generally in very low spirits. These two senior Officers were each accompanied by a member of their staffs, the former by Commander P. G. Frampton, a rather large, florid man under whom I had served on the local operations staff. He had left the Navy as a young officer in the early twenties under the 'Geddes Axe' and, like many of his contemporaries, had been recalled in the rank of Commander at the outbreak of war. Wing Commander Atkins, like

[1] Post-war medical analysis described this as the worst thing to have done.

Commander Frampton, had been a civilian until war broke out. He was a quiet and reflective man who had spent a long time out in Malaya and spoke Malay.

Apart from myself, there were three other officers. Lieutenant Ian Stonor of the Argyll and Sutherland Highlanders, who had been General Perceval's ADC and had been told by him to join the party at the last minute; Lieutenant Henderson, the First Lieutenant of the ML, a tall red-haired Australian volunteer reserve officer, and lastly an old and immensely tough Warrant Boatswain from the naval base, Mr Richardson. Since the first meal on the island, Mr Richardson had taken over the responsibility of feeding and cooking.

The remainder of the party was made up of a mixed bag of servicemen from all three services. There were thirteen remaining crew members of *ML 310*, the senior rating of whom was now Petty Officer Motor Mechanic Johncock. Among the other naval personnel were Petty Officers Keeling, late of *Repulse*, and Firbank, of the *Prince of Wales*. Also from the two big ships were Sergeant Hornby and five marines. The Army was represented by three Royal Engineer Staff Sergeants and Sergeant Wright and five members of the Military Police. There were also two aircraftsmen.

There were still stores of food to be unloaded from the ML and Henderson, with his crew, continued this work at low tide, wading out to the ML, returning again and again splashing through the shallows with their loads. A continuous supply of water and fuel for the cookhouse also had to be collected, the former twice and sometimes three times a day, and from a considerable distance.

The best of the village huts and houses had been taken over. They were the typical native houses of that part of the world, very primitive and really no more than shelters, made of wood with one or two rooms divided by flimsy mat partitions. Some had wooden floorboards with an attap roof, raised on stilts a few feet off the sandy soil and now being shared by two or three men.

The village headman's house, which had already been named the White House because of what was left of the coat of white paint, I now shared with the Wing Commander and Ian Stonor. It was rather grander than most, having three rooms, a small veranda and, at the back, a lean-to which did duty as a store and kitchen. The rooms were full of decaying mosquito nets, hangings of various kinds and a number of framed inscriptions in Malay. We were forever uncovering strange pots and earthenware jugs, which mostly contained mildewed spices or stagnant water and to the very end of our stay we were always coming across something new. We had quickly

126

discovered that the house was alive with bedbugs and similar unpleasant creatures, but these were as nothing to the vicious clouds of mosquitoes and other insects with which we fought night and day.

The Admiral and the rest of the officers shared another large house, which appeared to have been the communal meeting hut, on the veranda of which we ate our meals.

During the next few days life settled into a well-defined pattern. Sunrise was the signal for movement and breakfast consisting of a large mug of tea with tinned milk and sugar, although these luxuries soon came to an end. This was supplemented by any fruit we could find. At about 9 a.m. the ML's bell, salvaged and now hanging outside the cookhouse, was rung and this was the signal for us to foregather. Everyone would then be detailed off for the various tasks for which they were most suited – for example, the Royal Engineer Sergeants to another old *prahu* that Commander Frampton was attempting to repair.

Stoker Robinson, having collected the small first aid kit from the ML, set up a sick bay for treatment of cuts and other minor troubles. I was a regular early morning patient for the bathing and dressing of my fingers in a basin of hot water.

The largest party worked on Commander Frampton's abandoned *prahu*, for he had little faith in the success of Johnny Bull's attempt to reach Java and was determined to set out on his own. It seemed to me that this work was somewhat misdirected, although pushed along with great urgency and vigour.

The drawers of water and hewers of wood had the hardest tasks, especially the former. They carried five-gallon cans of water between them, slung on long poles, and had to walk from the cookhouse through the village, following a twisting path up the banks of a narrow stream until they reached a small spring halfway up the main hill. All the water for drinking and cooking had to be boiled, and large quantities were needed. This task had to be repeated several times a day. It was equally hard for the wood collectors, chopping up fallen palm trees and cutting down smaller trees with inadequate tools, and then having to carry the wood back to the cookhouse. Those foraging for wild fruits and sweet potatoes had a less fatiguing and more interesting task.

Mr Richardson had a team of cooks brewing tea in discarded fuel cans and boiling up rice, a number of sacks of which had been discovered, in a large cauldron. Food was never far from our thoughts and wonders were done with the few supplies we had. Fortunately, as well as the sacks of rice, he had found some of tapioca flour and two drums of coconut oil, and these, together with a fair supply of tinned food brought from the ML, provided initially a basic but monotonous diet. We also learned how to take the heart out of the coconut palm which we called a 'coconut cabbage' and which made a passable vegetable when eaten hot. It bore some resemblance to celery when eaten fresh. At first we managed three somewhat meagre meals a day, two of which consisted of rice with the addition of perhaps a tinned sausage, or a tinned herring, or a sardine. Occasionally, as a special luxury, we had a slice of bully beef. To these basics we added various vegetable stews and wild fruits. The food was, of course, a complete change from anything we had been used to – very limited in quantity and lacking in variety – but it might have been a lot worse. Unfortunately, the general health of the company suffered from the lack of a balanced diet and very soon many men refused to eat their solitary tinned herring or sausage, and sometimes threw their rice away with it! In order to add to the diet, attempts were made to catch fish. The Air Marshal and Ian Stonor discovered an old native fishing net which they laboriously repaired. They took this out in the evenings to try their luck, but their efforts met with little success and after several expeditions they abandoned the idea.

For the first few days I climbed the narrow twisting path to the top of the hill and watched for a time the long lines of anchored Japanese transports and their escorting cruisers and destroyers, a constant reminder of the power of the enemy.

Towards the end of the second week of our stay, Commander Frampton decided that his *prahu* was ready for launching. With my experience of the work that had been necessary on the original *prahu*, I was very doubtful. However, he was absolutely determined that he was not going to remain on the island for a day longer than he had to and was certainly not going to wait for what he considered to be the unlikely success of Johnny Bull's attempt to summon help.

The *prahu* was launched early in the morning, with everyone pushing, pulling and straining, but it was so hurriedly done that proper precautions could not be taken. There were insufficient skids, made from old, dried and hardened coconut palm fronds, in place for the *prahu* to slide easily from one to another, and not enough men. The result was a disaster – the *prahu* fell over onto its side and was badly damaged, its old and rotten side cracked open. At this piece of bad fortune, albeit brought about by his own impetuous haste, Commander Frampton completely lost heart in the venture. A few days later he developed a bad chill, with violent shivering fits. With no doctor in the party, we could only suspect malaria[1]. From this moment on, he appeared to lose all interest in the life and work on the island.

During this period, before the end of February, we had three additions to our party. The first was Private Donelly of the Gordon Highlanders, who Ian Stonor and I found on the western beach. He was a survivor of another small craft which had left Singapore on the 13th. He told us that he had been drifting about for days in a small dinghy. When we found him he was suffering from exposure and was very ill with dysentery. The second arrival was a naval rating, Stoker Scammell, who had also drifted onto the western beach clinging to a piece of wreckage. We now began to look regularly on the western side of the island for other survivors, and, within a day, found our third and last, also from a ship sunk by the Japanese, a civilian dockyard employee named Dimmit, who was Australian. He had been drifting on a raft carried by the current from island to island, living off coconuts, and said he had been in the vicinity of Tjebia for almost two weeks. He was certainly in a bad way and was covered from head to foot in white sores.[2]

When Commander Frampton first became ill, as the next senior RN Officer apart from the Admiral, I took over the administrative responsibilities of our daily life. As February passed to March, it was time to look out for the hoped-for rescue. With extra lookouts posted on both the eastern and western beaches, and also at the southern-most extremity of the island, we waited expectantly.

As the first two weeks of March drew to a close with no sign of a submarine or Catalina flying boat, there was a noticeable lowering of spirits. A listlessness and sense of hopelessness visibly overcame many. We had calculated that we could expect help for a period of three weeks from the departure of Johnny Bull's party, but if by then it had not materialized, we should have to make our own way out.

Early on Sunday morning, 7 March, Commander Frampton died. For some days he had been delirious with a high fever which had gradually got worse. Despite this, because he seemed to have been ill for such a short time, it was both a surprise and a shock when he died so suddenly. The cause of death was beyond our amateur diagnosis.[3]

He was buried in a glade of coconut palms beside the path leading

[1] This was confirmed after the war.
[2] Most probably salt water ulcers.
[3] In the medical analysis that was conducted after the war the cause of death in this and subsequent similar cases was definitely malaria. It was also considered that this might have manifested itself in a cerebral form. The term 'Tjebia Fever' was in common use.

from the village to the western beach. His body, wrapped in a native mat and covered with a Union Jack, was lowered awkwardly into the shallow grave while the Admiral read the words of the burial service. Once again, as it did so often, the whole chapter of our misadventure passed through my mind, with now an extra scene to add. It seemed so unreal to be standing round this grave, a small group of men in stained and crumpled tropical uniforms, while overhead the palm fronds rustled gently in the wind with patches of blue sky showing through them. Unfortunately it was real. Leaving some men to cover the grave in, the remainder of us made our way back to the village to take up the day's duties. One could sense the blow to the already sagging morale and it was one from which the party as a whole never recovered.

By now there were six or seven others sick from various causes, the most serious of whom was the Air Marshal. He, too, had seemed to catch a chill, we thought possibly from fishing late into the evenings. As with Commander Frampton, it had developed into a fever and delirium. Apparently in Singapore he had suffered very badly from malaria and had not been properly fit at the commencement of hostilities. The subsequent strain of the hopeless campaign had further undermined his health, mentally and physically. Finally, with no aircraft left at Singapore, he had been ordered to leave by the G.O.C. when all the remainder of his command had already been evacuated.

Since his arrival on Tjebia, he had been in very low spirits. He kept his revolver loaded and was quite determined that the Japanese should never capture him alive. He felt deeply about all that had happened in Malaya. On many occasions in the evening, sitting on the veranda of the Meeting House over the last two bottles of gin salvaged from the ML, he and the Admiral would discuss the course of the recent campaign; both were bitterly critical of its handling. There was no doubt that, among other things, they considered the influence of the Governor of the Straits Settlements, Sir Shenton Thomas, to have a had a baneful effect. The Air Marshal had said during these discussions that the main reason why fighter support for Force Z had been withdrawn was the insistence of the Governor of the priority of the Air Defence of Singapore Town. This malign influence subsequently affected many defensive and other measures that needed to be taken to combat the Japanese more effectively. Examples they quoted were the refusal to allow scorched earth policies or clear fields of fire to be prepared, the unwise decision to allocate bulk supplies of food such as rice, to the population, thereby denuding the island's services and workshops, particularly the dockyard and shipyards of labour during the latter stages of the campaign. As a junior officer attempting to keep the smaller patrol craft operational I had experienced this at first hand.

The Air Marshal, in his delirium, continually saw Japanese tanks bursting through the jungle. At other times he would get up in the middle of the night and wander off through the village. The moment either Ian Stonor or myself noticed that he was gone we went in search of him. We often found him hunting through the debris of an old hut, looking, as he would tell us, for the 'Elixir of Life' and it would take all our persuasive powers to get him back to bed, clutching a half-full bottle of stagnant mosquito-infested water.

We were extremely ignorant of the Tropics and our knowledge of such common diseases as malaria and dysentery was almost non-existent. A fever followed by a chill seemed to be the main cause of our growing sick list. We thought this chill might be caused by throwing off all clothing at nights. It was next to impossible to persuade the majority of the party to obey any instructions or orders with regard to their health. Repeated warnings about eating unripe fruit made no impact; it was continually eaten by all who could find it, resulting in the most unpleasant sores in the mouth, particularly from the few pineapples.

One item of drugs, however, of which we had a good supply was quinine. Mr Richardson had discovered a large bag of the powered form. The Dutch Commandant had told us on arrival that Tjebia was known as 'Fever Island' and in view of this we had been at great pains to try to get everyone to take a daily dose, but we were only partially successful. The majority went to extraordinary lengths to avoid taking the equivalent of a teaspoonful, which was our best guess as to the correct dose to take. It was absolutely foul to take in the powder form and one had to exert the utmost willpower to swallow it. It also had the unpleasant side-effect of making one deaf.

Three days after Commander Frampton's death the Air Marshal died. I received the news in the afternoon on being relieved from lookout duty on the western beach. The news was not unexpected because he had been unconscious since the previous day. Nonetheless his death was a further great blow, for he had been respected and greatly liked by all. A pioneer of the early days of torpedo bombing, he had transferred from the Navy to the Air Force in 1918.

Early the following morning, 11 March, he was buried in a clearing near the old village burial ground, about a hundred yards to the south of the village. Once more we found ourselves standing round a

131

shallow grave, the same shapeless form wrapped in a blanket, over which the Union Jack was laid, lying beside the grave. The body had been carried on the shoulders of six volunteers. The same blue sky showed through the palm fronds high above, insects hummed and crickets chattered. As Admiral Spooner read from the prayer book, the body was lowered into the grave, and, as the vision of the Air Marshal faded, I thought again of our situation.

It now seemed certain that the original plans for our rescue had faded, yet I found it hard to accept the finality of this and all it implied. I felt that I must go on setting our extra lookouts. The more I thought and wrestled with the problems that we faced, the more reluctant I was openly to give up hope, as I would seem to be doing if I failed to set them. It was now an act of faith. What was fate doing to us? Could no single thing go right? I returned to the village with the others, turning over in my mind for the umpteenth time the events of the last disastrous month.

Once back in the village I forced myself to ring the bell and set the day's routine in motion. The ingrained habit of a daily routine became the most important means, apart from food, of keeping us all going and so, in spite of my disturbing thoughts, each morning I rang the bell for daily work.

At this time one of our main concerns was how we would remain at liberty should the Japanese arrive – essential if we were finally to get away by whatever means. The most obvious method of evading capture was, of course, to disperse and hide up in various parts of the island until any landing party had left. To this end Ian Stonor and I got into the habit of thoroughly exploring the island every afternoon. This exercise served not only to prevent us from dwelling unduly on our misfortunes, but also to keep us off our backs, an easy option which was beginning to subtly undermine many of the party's will to survive.

Tjebia Island was shaped rather like a figure of eight, being a little over a mile from north to south and perhaps half a mile wide at its widest point, which was its southernmost part. The spine of the island lay north-north-west to south-south-east, with each end dominated by a thickly wooded and scrub-covered hill, the one to the north being about three hundred feet high, while that to the south was only some hundred and fifty. These two hills' seaward sides were rocky and fell steeply to the sea, the one at the north end being impossible to negotiate as I found to my cost.

I tried to do this one afternoon and, after half an hour of climbing and traversing the tumbled rock face, I found that I could not go on nor retrace my steps. I descended to sea level, but found no way on or back there either. Climbing back up I was very near to panic; nobody knew where I was, as I had not specifically told Ian Stonor where I was going. Finding a small ledge, I sat down to think things over and to calm down before making another attempt to extricate myself. This I finally managed to do by climbing diagonally back and upwards until I reached the shoulder of the hill when it became a case of literally cutting my way through very thick scrub. After half an hour of very hard work, I eventually came to a path which I followed down to a point where I realized it joined the path that led north out of the village and here I met Ian Stonor coming out to look for me!

Lying between the two hills was a large central plantation of coconut palms which stretched right across the island. Beaches of sand and volcanic ash formed the eastern and western coasts, the beaches themselves being divided into small coves by rock outcrops. We discovered three fresh-water springs, a large one to the north of the village at the foot of the hill, which we used for drinking water, while the smaller ones, one near the main western beach and the other just to the west of the village, were used for washing.

It was a great pity that the majority of our party could not summon sufficient energy and willpower to discover the island for themselves. Unfortunately, the easiest thing to do was to throw ourselves down after the midday meal, overcome by the tropical heat and a deadly lethargy that was sapping all powers of resistance to the fate which had overcome us. We all succumbed to this from time to time, repeatedly going over all the mishaps and misfortunes that had led to our present predicament. When one finally roused oneself to face life again, an overwhelming sense of depression bore down on one.

A typical case of this debilitating state of mind was that of the ML's second-in-command, Lieutenant Henderson, who had done such excellent work retrieving everything that was useful from the ML. He had worked far into the night during the first two weeks on the island, wading out through the shallows of the lagoon at low tide with his working party, collecting stores of all kinds and carrying the loads back to the beach. With that task completed, he said he was tired and would take it easy for a few days. Nobody thought much about it; certainly he deserved a rest. However, as the days became weeks and he showed no inclination to get up and play his part in our daily life, we began to wonder why. It seemed as though he simply lacked the will to make the effort to take his place once more in the community. He remained lying down and every effort either to persuade or bully him into action failed. He took less and less care of himself until he became so unpleasantly smelly and dirty that he had to be put into a hut of his own. He was by then a pitiable figure, but at the time, beset by our many problems, we could find little sympathy. He died towards the end of March, apparently a victim of loss of will to overcome the depression and soul-destroying lassitude that became more marked each week.

The absence of any medical knowledge among us was frightening. Our troubles from disease and sickness of one sort or another grew rapidly from the time of Commander Frampton's death. At first the numbers were manageable, and with Stoker Townsend's devoted care we were able to keep abreast of things by improvising treatment on the advice of Mr Richardson and Wing Commander Atkins, both of whom had lived in the tropics for some time and had some knowledge of tropical fevers and sickness.

However, there were occasions when a man was struck down quite suddenly and in a frightening way. One such case was that of Petty Officer Keeling, a fellow survivor of *Repulse*. Keeling had been on lookout duty one morning up on the hill. During his watch he had complained to his fellow watchkeeper that his throat felt sore; this had apparently developed while he was on watch. On his return to the village he discovered, while having his midday meal, that his throat had swollen to such a degree that he was unable to swallow anything.

I was always told when anyone became ill and went along to his hut to see him at once. I immediately saw that his throat was swollen to the point where his jawbone and neck were one continuous line and he could hardly speak. We moved him over to the sick hut at once, but, of course, having no idea of the cause, little could be done for him and he died that night. P.O. Keeling was an apparently fit man who had succumbed to some ailment so lethal that he was dead in less than twenty-four hours.[1]

The next morning the now familiar and sad ritual of another burial service took place. For some days afterwards we puzzled over the cause of his death, arriving at the conclusion that it might have been caused by some kind of a bite or sting, which, if true, could have happened to any one of us.

Death took its steady toll, but at least there were other incidents to divert our minds for some of the time. One such occurred one evening when the Wing Commander, Ian Stonor and myself decided that we would bring the small dinghy in which Private Donelly had

[1] Medical comment on this case was that a tracheotomy would have been the only hope of saving his life.

arrived on the island round from the western beach to the lagoon by the village.

Our first plan had been to try to carry it the shorter distance through the coconut plantation, but we found the weight beyond our by now weakened strength. It was decided that the Wing Commander and I would paddle it round the southern tip of the island while Ian Stonor would make his way round by the shore, since it was a part of the island that we had not yet explored.

It was on such rare occasions as this that one could try, and sometimes succeed, to forget our present difficulties and future uncertainties. As we slowly paddled out towards the south-western point, the stillness and peace of the tropic evening seemed to soak into our tired and stale minds. To the west the sun was still above the horizon, while just visible to the south were the mauve outlines of the mountains of Banka Island, so near and yet so far.

We reached the south-west point just as Ian came into view, scrambling through the scrub and stumbling over the rocky shoreline. Looking down into the water, we could see that the seabed was an ever-changing pattern of colours, blues and greens of every shade tracing the contours of sand, coral and rock. Here and there vivid patches of red and brown splashed the cool depths indicating swaying patches of seaweed. Shoals of small fish darted continuously in and out of their refuges. Leaning out over the side, my head almost immersed watching all this, I felt briefly that I was in another and quite different world from our fever- and trouble-ridden island.

The sun set almost before we realized it and cut short our escape from reality. We now had to paddle briskly in order to get round the southernmost point and into the lagoon before darkness fell. The seabed, so clear and beautiful a few moments before, now became a blurred purple and our view was disturbed by the ripple and splash of our paddles. On rounding the point, *ML 310*, lying forlornly on the reef, came into view, and with it the village with the cookhouse fire glowing and flickering through the palms – a haven of a kind, but also a reminder of our situation. We paddled into the beach through the shallow channel between the reef and the rocky promontory that we had once been so anxious to place between us and the Japanese and beached the dinghy.

As soon as my hand had healed sufficiently not to be reinfected by sea water, I used to begin and end my day with a swim, either in the lagoon or from the western beach. On one occasion out of the corner of my eye I saw a swirl in the water not ten yards away. I instinctively flung myself up the beach. I was just in time. As I turned to see what had impelled my reaction, I saw the unmistakable dorsal fin of a small shark only feet from where I would have been in the water.

My luck, for once, was in. If I had been a few seconds slower in my reaction, I would have suffered a severe injury, as the shark appeared to be about four or five feet in length. For the next hour it cruised round the lagoon and we took pot shots at it, though we did not succeed in hitting it. We thought it must have come into the lagoon at high water and become trapped as the tide ebbed.

This little scare made me change my swimming habits. The possibility of danger from sharks or other fish had not occurred to me and I had often swum out some distance. Now, however, I took much greater care, never entering the water before having a good look. I never ventured far out of my depth, if at all. A swim was virtually the only pleasure available, and it always surprised me that so few took advantage of it.

Strange incidents continually occurred and I became the victim of another in about mid-April. I had just completed an early morning swim and was sitting on some rocks in the sun carrying out a careful search of the horizon with binoculars, always with the faint hope that, by some miracle, help might appear. After one or two sweeps with the glasses I paused for a few seconds to rest my eyes, when suddenly, as I put the binoculars to my eyes, my vision became completely blurred by a red haze. At first I thought the colour filter had fallen down, but as I removed the glasses I realized that it was my sight that had failed. I blinked and rubbed my eyes, to no avail; I just could not see. Sitting still for some minutes, I tried to think about what could have happened. After about ten minutes I noticed slight vision returning to my left eye.

As soon as I could make out the blurred outlines of my surroundings, I stood up and groped my way back to the village and the White House where everyone had a good look at my eyes, which, apart from being slightly bloodshot, appeared normal, and nobody could see any reason for my loss of sight. A few days passed before I could see well enough to move about and another two weeks before my sight returned properly to my left eye. My right eye had no sight and it was several months before I could see sufficiently to read and then only the tops and bottoms of any letter or object.[1]

It must have been in the third week of March when we received a visit from Tjebia's former inhabitants. One afternoon a party of ten, led by their Headman, arrived in the village. At first the atmosphere

---

[1] The Civil Consultant in Ophthalmology to the Navy gave it as his opinion that the cause was exposure to excessively bright light.

was rather tense and frigid; it was clear that the islanders did not like the way we had taken over their former houses. However, the Wing Commander and the Headman quietly talked matters over and an agreement was reached. We could not afford to be too hostile for obvious reasons. They, on their part, saw that we were able to pay them reasonably well in return for a small amount of help.

The Headman said that they had come back to the island in order to catch fish and gather copra. They could not do this at Banka where they now lived. The Japanese allowed them little freedom to pursue their own ways and they obviously did not like the turn events had taken. It also became clear from the information that the Wing Commander was able to extract that our worst fears were confirmed. It was our first definite news that the Japanese had captured Java as well as Sumatra and Borneo. Obviously any hope of escape lay with us and not from outside assistance.

They were persuaded to do a day's fishing for us each time they came to collect fish and copra. They promised also to bring us news of the Japanese movement as well as any news from the outside world. Once the ice was broken, the islanders became friendly and helpful.

We were shown how to find turtles' eggs, which, from then onwards formed an important addition to our diet. You took a long stick and walked the sandy beaches looking for turtles' nests which were betrayed by a small hole in the sand. Into this hole you then poked a stick, and if, when you pulled it out, it was covered in yolk, you knew that a few feet down there was a nest. The nest might contain fifty or more eggs, each egg being the size of a pingpong ball. The strange thing about these eggs was that no amount of boiling would produce any change; the albumen remained transparent and the shell soft. They did not taste like ordinary eggs in any way, having a strong fishy taste, which was not in any way unpleasant.

The fish that they caught for us were also excellent. On subsequent occasions when the islanders returned to us, they always caught sufficient for a good meal. The fish were of two main kinds, the large and excellently flavoured *ikan meura* and the small *ikan bilas*, rather similar to whitebait and just as good to eat. On occasions when fish was available Mr Richardson always used some of our precious frying oil, so we were able to have that old British favourite, fish and chips, the chips in this instance being cut from rather coarse, unripe bananas!

The Headman also agreed to try and buy us some bread and other small items of food on Banka Island, for which we gave him some money. He also said that he thought he might be able to get us some medicines as there was still a Dutch Controller near his present village, and that, surprisingly, civilian officials were still functioning. On hearing about the Controller, we decided to send him a letter, setting out our situation and adding a request for food and drugs. During the latter part of these talks, Wong, the very pleasant Javanese second-in-command of the lookout post, had come down the hill and joined us.

CHAPTER 10

Escape to Captivity

Spirits were low as the islanders set sail for Banka. I do not think any of us really believed we would get any help from the Dutch, even if they were still there. The Japanese tide of conquest had rushed so far south that there seemed no possible way out. By the end of March half the party was ill and the hut used for the sick was full. Men were now suffering from dysentery, malaria, beri-beri and pellagra, a skin disease caused by vitamin deficiency. Accompanying the sickness, and usually preceding it, were acute depression and despair. In most instances there seemed to be no will to fight for life. I now spent a great deal of time going round talking to everyone. I often used to ask men point-blank whether or not they wanted to see their wives and families again, and, unbelievably, the answer was often that they did not care. It was very much a case of having to drive yourself in order to occupy your mind to the full. Occasions such as the visit of the islanders were always a great help in combating this state of introspective despair.

Stoker Townsend himself was now sick and his place was taken by Mr Dimmit. The strain was so great, however, and exposure to disease such, that before the month was out they had both died, Dimmit from sheer exhaustion and Townsend from what looked like a combination of everything.

Even the Javanese were suffering. Wong told us that three had already died. When I went up the hill, at Wong's invitation, most of them were huddled under their blankets, obviously fever-ridden. Their little lookout post was dirty and uncared for. Wong himself had a fever and had lost all his old vitality and cheerfulness.

Relations between the Javanese and ourselves had gradually deteriorated, mainly as a result of their coming down the hill and catching the chickens that roamed the village. The Admiral became so angry at this that he sent for Wong to come and see him. This Wong quite naturally refused to do. It was an extraordinary situation and I was not at all sure what the outcome would be. Eventually Wong let it be known that he was prepared to come to the foot of the hill, but no further. A meeting point was arranged by the spring at the base of the hill where we drew our water.

I was worried how the situation would develop, as the Admiral was very angry, so I took the precaution of taking my revolver. The chickens, of course, originally belonged to the villagers, but had run wild since we arrived on the island and really we had no more right to them than Wong's party. However, the food situation was critical and their eggs were the only suitable food that the very sick could eat. We had no idea how many chickens there were, but collected their eggs from the various points where we knew they habitually laid. After a long discussion, with the Wing Commander interpreting, a compromise was reached and it was agreed that the Javanese would be allowed two chickens a week.

It was now obvious to most of us that if we remained on the island much longer we would all die of disease, if not starvation. We estimated that our food stocks, apart from what we could find on the island, would run out by the end of April. The food we obtained from the island was mainly fruit, the potato yam and turtles' eggs. An uncertain extra was fish caught by the villagers on their visits. Our daily ration was reduced to a cup of rice, with half a tinned sausage or sardine on it, plus what fruit or vegetables we could find. This diet was clearly not sufficient to give the resistance needed to combat the many illnesses of this unhealthy place.

The Admiral thought that, if we could obtain sufficient seeds and clear an area for a plantation, we could become self-sufficient. His idea was to obtain the seeds from the villagers. Ian Stonor, the Wing Commander and I thought our only chance was to leave the island. To this end we once again turned our attention to the ML. Was it possible at this late stage to refloat her, patch up any hull damage and try to sail her away?

It was now the first week in April and, before we had had a chance to take another look at the ML, the Japanese rather unexpectedly took a hand. Just after breakfast one morning the lookout from the western beach came running into the village to report that a ship was approaching from the direction of Banka. Running down to a point from where we could see the southern approaches, we saw the unmistakable outline of one of the older Japanese light cruisers nearing the island.

We quickly put our dispersal plans into effect. Carrying the sick, the party divided into several groups and made for previously hidden food dumps. Fires were raked out and other evidence of our presence hidden. Mr Richardson stayed to observe the movements of the cruiser as it steamed slowly past the southern end of the island and stopped abreast of the ML. A motor boat was lowered and went straight to her. Two of the boat's crew boarded her and appeared to make a general inspection of the upper deck before going below. After some minutes they reappeared and gave some instructions to the motor boat's crew. It looked as if they were trying to trace the cable laid out to the kedge anchor and shift its position. While this was happening Mr Richardson was able to observe the men on board the ML carefully. He was certain that one of them was a European, presumably German or Italian. After about half an hour they gave up whatever they were trying to do and returned to the cruiser, which then steamed off in a north-easterly direction.

As soon as we were certain that she had really left, all the parties returned to the village to resume the daily routine. In the afternoon, as soon as the tide was low enough, several of us waded out to the ML to see if we could find any sign of the reason for this sudden visit. She lay heeled over on her port side at the edge of the reef. We clambered aboard her sloping deck and were met with a stale smell of stagnant water, mixed with oil from the bilges. We opened as many hatches and scuttles as we could in order to ventilate her. We looked for some sign of the recent visit of the Japanese, but found nothing but a small scrap of paper pinned to the engine room bulkhead, on which was written in English 'How much bread?'. We took this to be a way of asking what endurance the ML had. She was a complete shambles below, every bit of moveable gear that had been left had been flung down into the filthy oily water, gurgling and sloshing about in the bilges, the result of six weeks' pounding on the reef. We also tried to trace the kedge cable which the Japanese had been seen trying to move, but this was now in deep water and impossible to see. It was obvious that things had deteriorated to such a degree that we could never make any use of the ML and all thoughts of her possible use must be abandoned.

There were on the beach in front of the village two *prahus*, one of which had been unsuccessfully fitted out by Commander Frampton. A second one was high and dry behind the seaward fringe of palms and looked in such a dilapidated state that we had, up till now, only considered it fit for firewood! However, Petty Officer Johncock and one of his engine-room crew had been looking it over again and had come to the conclusion that it had more possibilities for rebuilding than the other. In fact they had already made a start.

I now, despite the great disparity in rank, had a long argument with the Admiral over the need to put every man who could be of use to work on the *prahu*. The Admiral was reluctant to acknowledge the facts and although, from now on, a special *prahu* party was detailed each day for work, he never really agreed to it.

The *prahu* needed almost completely re-planking, as well as several new timbers to make the hull seaworthy. The rigging, mast and sails all had to be made. We were fortunate in having three Royal Engineers, Staff Sergeants Lockett, Ginn and Davies, and these three, with Stoker Tucker and Corporal Schief, started work at once.

Our problem was accentuated by the steady decline in numbers by death and sickness, as well as by the increasing apathy of all those still alive. There was so much to do and time was running out. It became necessary to work a much stricter routine in order to get the work done. It also helped to take our minds off our situation, and so afternoon work was now introduced.

As soon as everyone had started their various tasks, I visited the sick. Looking after them was the most unpopular of all duties and we had no regular sick attendant after Stoker Townsend and Mr Dimmit died. They were usually in the most wretched state in the morning, for many were too weak to get outside to the latrine.

The morning shift usually went fairly well and there was little reluctance to start work. But the afternoons were much more difficult. It was so easy to lie down during the hottest part of the day, but, having done so, it took considerable willpower to start work again. Some would always be there to do what was asked of them, while others had to be almost forced out of their huts. They refused to face the fact that, without an all-out effort, we should never survive. The afternoon work period lasted from 4 to 6 p.m.

The nights were always an eternity of waiting, thinking and fighting off the swarms of insects. Try as we would, it was impossible to ward off the great gulf of loneliness, hopelessness and frustration that slowly seemed to engulf us. This was hard enough for those of us who had sufficient resistance to fight it off by day, but for those who could not, and these were the majority, the nights were an agony of mind and spirit. Sleep was impossible until sheer fatigue took over. We dripped with sweat if we pulled any form of mosquito protection over us, but if we did not, we bled from the profusion of bites. The unfamiliar diet, based on rice, forced us to get up each hour through the night to relieve ourselves. Outside, the moonlight was so brilliant as to be almost like day, the greens and yellows of the palms and jungle now turned silver, blue and purple. The rustling of the palm fronds in the fitful night breeze could just be heard above the background noise of millions of insects and the twittering and squealing of the bats and flying foxes. Sleep, when it did come at about four in the morning, was soon disturbed by the crowing of the few remaining cockerels.

It was a sign of our general lack of energy that we were almost glad when the change in the monsoon brought heavy storms that swept across the island during April. These 'Sumatras', as they were called, formed over the central mountains of Sumatra. They provided just the excuse, that we accepted too easily, to put off facing the daily tasks. With the deluge would come the wind, roaring and tearing through the protesting palms and leaving in its wake a cold chilling damp. I, at any rate, got some enjoyment from this, as it reminded me of England, and for a short time it covered the everlasting blue skies, which I associated with our misfortunes, with thick grey cloud. This, I realized, was sheer escapism, which I strove to put aside to concentrate on the job in hand.

Escapism was always with us and we found it easy to dream of what we should do when the *prahu* was finished, where we would sail to, whether we would find another island, and above all, whether we could remain free long enough for the Japanese to be defeated in this area.

Other ways of forgetting the present were shooting expeditions to kill a cockerel for the sick. On these occasions I was accompanied by Corporal Turner, the son of an Essex farmer, and we would make believe that it was a 'walkround' after pheasants.

During April we received a number of visits from passing Javanese and Sumatran voyagers on their way to and from Banka, or to the islands of the Lingga Archipelago to the north. Wing Commander Atkins used to question them and we gathered that the Japanese had passed on to operations further south and that the seas between Singapore and Sumatra and Java were now comparatively quiet. Some were very communicative, others less so. We were told that most of the islands of the Lingga group to the north were still being administered by the Dutch and, most important, that there was a hospital functioning at Daboe, the principal town on Singkep island, and in which were a number of wounded white men being looked after by nuns. In Daboe itself, there was apparently still a Dutch

Controller. This news seemed to confirm what the former inhabitants of the village had told us. We assumed that the Japanese had just by-passed many of the smaller islands and left the local Dutch administration to carry on.

It was now decided that we should try once more to get help. A few days later a small *prahu* called in to collect coconuts before going north to Daboe and we took the opportunity. For some time the ML's Chinese cook, Charlie, had wanted to go to Daboe, where he said he had a relation who was a rich merchant and who would be sure to help us. It was agreed that he should travel north. Once there, he would contact this relation, who would then arrange for a fishing junk to come back to Tjebia and collect everyone. If this were not possible then he was to contact the Controller or the hospital and try to bring us back some medical stores and food, for which he was given three hundred Straits dollars. Charlie sailed that night on the understanding that he would be back in a week's time. The outcome was very different – he fooled us completely and we did not see him again for almost seven weeks, and then under very different circumstances.

It was shortly after Charlie had left for Daboe that we received another visit by a party from Banka. On this occasion two of the R.E. Staff Sergeants, Lockett and Ginn, left the island for Banka in an attempt to contact the Controller said to be still there. We were not very happy about this and feared for their safety since the natives looked particularly unsavoury. In addition, Lockett and Ginn were skilled craftsmen and an enormous help in the reconstruction of the old *prahu*, where they would be badly missed. Personally, I pinned much more faith in completing the *prahu* than in trusting native reports of what lay at the end of any such journey, even supposing you were allowed to reach the end of it. In the event neither Lockett or Ginn reached Banka; probably they were murdered for the money they carried. In any case, they were never heard of again.

Although I tried hard to dissuade the men from going I felt I could not actually forbid them because the Admiral was keen that they should go and had given them a letter addressed to the Controller, setting out our circumstances and asking for help. The death rate was steadily reducing our numbers and the progress with the *prahu* was only just keeping pace with our diminishing food stocks, so if somebody was prepared to take the chance, he had to be allowed to go. It also meant that there were less mouths to feed.

The money that we were able to give to such parties came from us all, paid into a common pool and kept by the Wing Commander. A small proportion of it was what we happened to have on us when we left Singapore. Most, however, came from the bundles of currency thrown into the harbour on Government orders that all currency should be destroyed prior to surrender. A number of these large packages of notes were fished out of the water by the sailors. It was no use telling anyone that the money was worthless. However, as it turned out, this money was legal tender for another six months and remained illegally in circulation for the rest of the war. This money, amounting to many hundreds of thousands of Straits dollars, was invaluable to us; without it I am sure the natives would never have fished for us, and might well have turned us straight over to the Japanese if the opportunity had occurred.

April proved to be by far the worst month for deaths. All through March, as our resistance to disease grew weaker, more and more men became unfit for work and lay about, openly saying they wished they could die. Rations were reduced twice and there was a strong inclination to favour the remaining fit rather than the weak, for obvious reasons. The desperate need was to complete the *prahu*. It was interesting to note that those who worked hardest kept fittest, though all suffered bouts of malaria and dysentery.

A death now occurred every few days and the macabre thought that each death extended the rations of the remainder could not be put out of one's mind. I personally never got used to handling and burying those who died, though it usually fell to Mr Richardson or myself to supervise the removal and burial of the dead men. Very often a death was not noticed until the morning, the man having probably died during the early part of the night. As soon as a death was reported we would go to the hut where it had occurred to take what particulars we could. Men dying in such conditions were not a pleasant sight – the deathly pallor of the emaciated face and body, lying contorted in rigor mortis, and overall the smell of vomit and excrement. Before the body could be wrapped in its blanket and rattan mat, the limbs had to be straightened, always the most distasteful part of a death. The actual burial itself was, of course, a sad and moving occasion, not least because it allowed our memories of the past and fear for the future full rein. The body, trussed up with a length of native sisal rope, was carried to the grave which had previously been dug. We only had two entrenching tools and so little more than a shallow scrape could be made. The soil was very light and sandy and there was always great difficulty in stopping the sides caving in. The Admiral usually read the burial service, but sometimes the Wing Commander or Ian Stonor did it.

Work became increasingly harder as our physical condition deteriorated. The two essentials were servicing the cookhouse and re-building and fitting out the *prahu*. There was now no sick hut, the sick remaining in their own huts, where they were looked after by their companions as best they could.

Much of the planking of the old *prahu* had been repaired with wood from huts demolished for the purpose and with planks sawn from a few felled palm trees. To help watertightness, the greater part of the hull was sheathed with beaten five-gallon fuel cans from the ML. This task was carried out with great expertise by one of the ML's engine room staff, Stoker Paddon, who had been a plumber's mate before the war. We also found a barrel of pitch under one of the huts and this was heated and poured into the bottom of the *prahu* as we were none too sure of the watertightness of the keel fastenings. The nails and fastenings we salvaged from the ML and sometimes from the village huts. The rigging, masts and spars were all fashioned by Petty Officer Firbank from the *Prince of Wales* and Able Seaman Oldnall from the ML. The sails were made up from old and rotten native sails, a new cotton yacht mainsail which I had obtained in Singapore and oddments of clothes and kitbags. These were all cut out and stitched together by Corporal Schief, who was an upholsterer in peacetime. I had previously drawn out a rough set of plans as well as a sail plan for us to work to.

In the last week of April the Admiral died. His death was very sudden and unexpected. It came as a great surprise as he had always appeared to be one of the fittest members of the party. From our first moments on the island he had seemed to be the least concerned about our troubles; his refusal, at least outwardly, to let them get him down, helped us all.

His daily routine never varied. It began at sunrise when he made his way down to the cookhouse and collected the early morning tea, always brewed by Mr Richardson. He would then bring this back to our hut and hand it round to all of us, a habit he maintained to the very end. After breakfast he would wander over to the western beach, where he wrote his diary and swam. After the midday meal he would go off to the site he had chosen for his plantation and furiously slash away with a native *parang* for at least an hour, at the hottest time of the day. Except for official occasions such as funerals or taking our Sunday service, when he invariably wore his uniform cap and shoulder straps, he dressed in a white smock which he had made himself, similar to a monk's habit, and with it he always wore a tweed check cap.

146

He had never agreed to the rebuilding of the *prahu*, believing that we should concentrate on getting seeds and becoming self-sufficient. As a junior Lieutenant I was in a quandary, not knowing what to do. In the end I fell back on the excuse that an extraordinary situation needed extraordinary measures and disregarded his feelings.

One afternoon he said to Ian and myself that he was going to give himself an enema. He had been complaining of indigestion for the past few days and had refused even our scanty food. We watched him walk off across the clearing to our latrine. We thought no more of it until we realized that some twenty minutes had elapsed and he had not reappeared. We went over to see if he was all right and found him slumped on the seat breathing heavily. He did not answer when we asked him if he was OK, so we got him to his feet and, with his arms round our shoulders, helped him, indeed dragged him, back to the hut and laid him down on his bed. He seemed to be unconscious. We had no idea what to do, so we just covered him up with his blanket and hoped he would recover. We kept watch on him at intervals through the afternoon, but his condition did not change. Just before the evening meal I went to see him, intending to try and wake him and persuade him to have a drink. However, the moment I reached him and looked more closely, I noticed his strange yellow pallor and saw a trickle of vomit or saliva from the corner of his mouth. He was quite still and did not appear to be breathing. I held his shaving mirror over his mouth and nose but could see no sign of misting. Ian and Mr Richardson came up and agreed that the Admiral was dead.[1]

That night we sat and puzzled, as we had so many times before, over the cause of death. The Wing Commander was too ill with malaria to take part. We came to the conclusion that it must have been a stroke or heart failure.

The Admiral was buried next morning. As we stood round his grave my mind went back to that first occasion when Commander Frampton was buried. At each of the fifteen deaths since, the Admiral had read the burial service, and now it was his body that lay under the Union Flag. As always on such occasions I had the same feeling of unreality. It just did not seem possible that our lives should have so utterly changed in such a short time.

If there were any among our dwindling company who doubted the need to finish work on the *prahu* and get away from this island that was so insidiously killing us, I think the Admiral's death finally made up their minds.

It was about this time that we realized that we had not seen any of

[1] Most probably an acute pulmonary embolism or cerebrovascular catastrophe.

the Javanese from the hilltop lookout post for a while. Knowing that they had been suffering like ourselves, Ian and I decided to visit them. The laborious climb up the winding path through the scrub proved hard going. Neither of us had been up for some weeks and it was an indication of how our strength was declining. On arrival at the post, we could see no signs of life or any evidence of recent occupation. This was a surprise as we had not expected them to leave such a well-placed camp site. Our immediate conclusion was that, for whatever reason, they must have moved down to another site, possibly nearer to a spring, so we set out to look for them.

Finding no sign of anyone living near the springs we knew of, we decided to search the shores of the island. After several hours we had found no trace and were forced to the conclusion that the Javanese must have left the island without our knowledge. We were sure that there were no other craft capable of taking them other than the two *prahus* at the village, so the only explanation had to be that they had been taken off by a passing fisherman. They had, however, left behind another reminder of the island's hostility. At their post we counted almost as many graves as we ourselves had.

The food situation was now a constant preoccupation and we had continually to revise our rationing scales. This was done by Mr Richardson on my estimation of a completion date for the *prahu*. Apart from a meagre supply of tinned food, the only protein foods now came from the occasional supply of fish from visiting fishermen and from our limited finds of turtles' eggs. Ian and I scoured the island for fresh fruit and vegetables, which formed the larger part of our diet, but the areas where they grew were small and were soon denuded and we had to look further afield every few days. Bananas were the most plentiful apart from coconuts. Ian discovered over forty varieties of banana, ranging from delicious orange-fleshed ones two inches long to completely tasteless three-sided ones nearly a foot in length. These we used for cooking by slicing them up and boiling or occasionally frying them as chips. There were also plenty of limes, but having no sugar prevented the best use being made of them. There were a few pineapples, breadfruit and paw paws, but insufficient for general use.

For vegetables there were a few patches of yams and a good supply of coconut palm hearts which tasted not unlike celery, although these were difficult to obtain. We thoroughly searched all the derelict huts for any food that the villagers might have left behind. In this way we found several tins of coconut oil and what we thought was a bag of tapioca flour. One of our party, Corporal Shrimpton, a baker by

148

trade, said that he would try and make biscuits from it. However, after several attempts, he was obliged to admit defeat.

From time to time Ian and I went on an iguana hunt. These reptiles lived in caves on the western side of the island. They soon discovered the presence of the newly interred bodies of our dead and tried to dig them up. We found evidence of this both at Commander Frampton's grave and in the graveyard to the south of the village. On one occasion, when we were exploring the rock outcrops on the north-western corner of the island, we saw a very large reptile. They were always very elusive and previously we had had only fleeting glimpses. It too disappeared in a few seconds among the big boulders and by the time we got to where we had first seen it, there was no trace of it.

On another occasion we thought that we had discovered the trail of one leading from the western beach towards the graveyard. We followed the trail only for it to vanish in a thick patch of scrub and rock. I think we only succeeded in firing one shot during all our hunts, so quick and elusive were they.

The *prahu* was now within measureable time of being ready and our thoughts turned to where we could go. I don't think any of us thought that total escape to Australia or India was a possibility. It was beyond our powers to sail clear of the areas of Japanese control, and the best we could hope for was to remain at large in the area in the hope that somehow we might make contact with Allied Forces. Therefore we would have to find some other island that, unlike Tjebia, would support life while we made further plans. This island had to be close enough to be able to make two trips if all of us were to leave Tjebia.

From the information we had gathered from visiting natives, it appeared that the Dutch Civil Administration still retained a measure of control in this area. We had been told that there were Controllers on Banka and to the north at Daboe, where we understood there was a hospital still functioning. The frailty of our *prahu* and the onset of the south-west monsoon made a voyage south towards Banka very hazardous. This fact, added to the temptation of the hospital at Daboe, decided us that our direction must be to the north. We planned to sail northwards to an island some thirty or forty miles from Tjebia known as Saaya. We understood from the natives that this was quite healthy and had supplies of water, also that a certain amount of food might be obtained from a small fishing village there. We should have to make two or three trips in order to take everyone off Tjebia. Once we had achieved this, we would try to make contact with the hospital at Daboe still further to the north.

It was now the first week in May, the *prahu* was almost ready and the problem of launching had to be faced. This was no easy task, as we had seen when Commander Frampton had tried in March. The *prahu* itself lay some fifty yards from the edge of the lagoon and behind the first line of palms. There were only ten men fit enough to do the heavy manual work needed. At first I thought that a system of tackles could be rigged to move the *prahu* on to the beach for launching, but we soon found that we did not have enough rope. Our next idea was to dig a channel along which we might float her into the lagoon. Again it did not take us long to realize that this was not possible either. It seemed that our only hope lay in help from the villagers on one of their periodic visits. The question was whether they would arrive before our food ran out. But, for once, fortune smiled and on 10 May the villagers returned.

We told them of our plans and they willingly agreed to help us launch the *Scriberganti*, as she was called, on the high tide the following morning. We were told that the name was Malay for 'by the grace of God'. Very early the next morning the villagers began making their preparations. First coconut fronds were cut or collected and laid out as skids under the keel. At last the great moment arrived and, with all available hands pushing and heaving, to the accompaniment of much shouting, *Scriberganti* was manoeuvred over the palm fronds. As each palm frond came clear under the stern it was carried forward and placed under the bows for the next slide. Gradually the *prahu* slid down the beach and finally into the lagoon where we secured her between two upright posts to prevent a recurrence of the disaster that had attended the first launching. The villagers seemed as pleased as we were that all had gone so well. After all, as the Headman said, *Scriberganti* had once been one of the villagers' finest *prahus*. I wondered, too, whether it might not be the thought that at long last they would get their island back which made them so cheerful. That night at low tide I surveyed a passage through the reef, rowing out with a sounding pole and probing until I found a passage through which *Scriberganti* could pass.

The next morning the villagers helped us to tow her through the reef and anchor[1] her off its seaward side abreast the village and half a mile north of the wreck of the ML.

Most of that morning I spent with Able Seaman Oldnall, hoisting the sails and checking how they fitted. I couldn't help feeling as I used

[1]   Constructed native-style of a large stone to which a wooden shank and fluke were lashed.

14. The railway bridge at Kanchanaburi today.

15. One of the few surviving sections of the railway.

16. Gravestone of Vice Admiral
E. J. Spooner, DSO, at Kranji, Singapore.

17. Gravestone of Air Vice Marshal
C. W. H. Pulford, CB, OBE, AFC.

18. The Burma-Siam railway in 1986.

to in that unbelievable world of peace when about to go for the first sail of the summer at Waldringfield or Felixstowe Ferry.

As we returned in the ML's dinghy, I felt a surge of hope such as I had not had since our arrival on the island when I looked back to seaward and saw *Scriberganti* riding to her anchor on the edge of the reef. The next thing to be decided was who should make the first journey and who would remain behind. It seemed obvious that the first party should be chosen from those who were still reasonably fit as it was essential that the voyage should succeed if help was to be obtained. There were other considerations. For instance, although he was ill, the Wing-Commander's ability to speak and understand Malay, as well as his smattering of Chinese, could prove of vital importance. Ian Stonor, at that time probably the strongest member of the party, Petty Officer Johncock and Stoker Tucker, whose original interest in *Scriberganti* gave them a claim, and finally Able Seaman Oldnall and myself, to navigate and helm, were selected.

To check on directions and navigation I climbed the hill for the last time, accompanied by the Headman. He pointed out to me the faint rounded hump of Saaya, just visible to the north. I had taken the ML's boat's compass with me to take a bearing. The Headman told me that Singkep lay an equal distance further north of Saaya and that from the highest point of Saaya you could see Singkep island.

We decided to set out on the afternoon of 15 May and made our plans accordingly. That last night on Tjebia found me assailed by the same doubts and uncertainties as I had had before making the abortive departure immediately after our arrival on the island. I prayed that this time all would go well. There is no doubt that under such conditions there is a great temptation to succumb to the belief in the saying 'Better the Devil you know than the Devil you don't' and this feeling played its part in the uncertainties, difficulties and hopes that lay before us.

My bad luck had not quite deserted me, for on the last morning, as I was slicing off the top of a coconut for a drink, I succeeded in slicing off the tip of my left thumb. I almost fainted from loss of blood and was in poor shape for several hours. This time there was no one to take my place and our last remaining field dressing was literally pressed into service!

The villagers had remained to see us on our way and were a great help in carrying our few items of kit, two cans of water and a large quantity of bananas and coconuts out to *Scriberganti*. All the remaining rations were left with Mr Richardson, except for an emergency ration for each of us sailing in the *prahu* of a tin of herrings in tomato sauce. Mr Richardson was left with the sick and two of the fitter men to fetch the water and do the heavier chores. If we did not return or send help within one week, Mr Richardson was to act as he saw fit, using the ML's dinghy or constructing a raft, for which purpose we had set aside a supply of timber and fastenings.

Our last meal on Tjebia was at midday and after a short siesta we made our way out to *Scriberganti*. Mr Richardson with his entire rear party were there to see us away. We wished each other luck.

Just before four p.m. on 15 May we hoisted sail and got under way, drifting very slowly northwards through the channel between Tjebia and Katjangan, our sails barely filled by the light southerly breeze. My thoughts were a mixture of emotions – professional interest in the set of sails and rigging, the flood of memories of all that had taken place on those seemingly green and peaceful islands, fear of the unknown hazards that lay before us, but above all the unbelievable realization that we had actually left Tjebia.

Progress was very slow; the tide seemed to be setting to the south and at first we barely held our own. Then, with the wind failing, *Scriberganti* began to be swept south and we were forced to anchor. Half an hour later the fitful catspaws became stronger, our sails filled and we weighed our anchor and started to sail. Far to the south-west over Banka, I noticed some dark clouds building up. The southerly wind gradually became stronger and *Scriberganti*, with many creaks of protest, began to make good progress and I was thrilled to feel how well she handled. Everyone settled down as well as they could among the bunches of bananas and coconuts.

The sky astern of us was now rapidly darkening and the wind increasing. It was evident that a Sumatra was developing and we made preparations to shorten sail. We needed some moments of thought because nobody was familiar with the crudities of our gear. I knew that there was a particularly nasty reef extending from the north-west corner of Katjangan which I was anxious to clear before the storm overtook us. I felt that with shortened sail we might not be able to weather it. In my anxiety to make the necessary 'offing', we held on to our sail almost too long and when the first stiff squall hit *Scriberganti*, she was almost overpowered. As it was still doubtful whether we were far enough to seaward to clear the reef we decided to hold on for a few more minutes.

As the second squall threatened to blow our flimsy sails to shreds or even dismast us, we struggled to lower them. The main strength of the Sumatra was now upon us and *Scriberganti* was tearing along at a tremendous speed, yawing from side to side as the Wing-

Commander and I strove to hold her on a course which we hoped would clear the end of the reef. The mainsail had jammed halfway down the mast and was thrashing furiously about in the hands of the other three who were trying to control it.

The next fifteen minutes or so were terrifying, *Scriberganti* creaking and straining in a manner that I knew she could not sustain for long. She had also developed a serious leak and bailing had to be carried out by every possible means and for a time it looked as though the water was gaining. The wind shrieked and icy cold rain and spray from the tops of the breaking seas reduced visibility to nil and it was impossible to hear anything unless it was shouted in one's ear. There was nothing to do but hope and hang on for as long as we could.

We now heard, above the noise of the wind, the ominous and deepening roar of the sea breaking onto the reef and realized that we were approaching the worst of our dangers. I guessed that we had not managed to gain enough offing and that our only hope was that by some miracle we might be carried through a gap in the reef, or even lifted over it on a big wave. We could now catch the occasional glimpse of white breakers as they burst on the reef, throwing spray high into the air. The noise was like thunder and it was obvious that we were almost on the reef. I just noticed a number of fierce swirls amid the waves and intermittent bursts of spray, then imperceptibly, the sea became easier, the noise faded and the wind gradually eased. The miracle I had prayed for had happened and not only had we passed safely through the reef, but the storm had moved ahead of us. For some time no one spoke; the feeling of deliverance was immense and all-embracing.

The wind gradually died away and within half an hour we lay in the wake of the storm, *Scriberganti* creaking and her sails flapping in the swell. We were soaked to the skin and dripping with salt, spray and rain. Then the sun came out and the clouds dispersed to the north. *Scriberganti* lay some four miles to the north of Tjebia. To our amazement she appeared to be none the worse for her buffeting. We soon had her baled out, the sails rehoisted and our clothes off to dry in the sun.

A cool evening breeze replaced the calm after the storm and we began to make fair progress on our course for Saaya, which we sighted at sunset. By the last light of the short tropical sunset we had a small meal of rice biscuits and sardine which Mr Richardson had prepared for us. We then arranged watches for the night and sailed on into the darkness.

The night proved surprisingly cold and when my turn for sleep came, I found it impossible because of the cold and damp. The wind was so fitful that we made little headway, but soon after dawn a light but steady breeze filled our sails and enabled us to continue our course for Saaya. We now had time to check *Scriberganti* thoroughly and found that she had stood up to last evening's ordeal very well. Nothing was damaged and we sorted out the mainsail attachment to the mast to ensure it would not jam again. We were also able to wash and use, albeit precariously, the lavatory seat extending out from *Scriberganti's* after end!

We made good progress until midday when the sun killed our wind and once again we found ourselves idly slatting about, our bows 'boxing' the compass many times over. This calm lasted the greater part of the afternoon and the heat of the sun forced everyone but the luckless helmsman to curl up and take what shelter we could, but the wide V-shape of the *prahu* made any proper shade unattainable. We tried to catch some fish over the side by lines, but, as always, we were unsuccessful.

One of the strange things about the whole of the past months was our total inability to catch fish. The sea, we knew, swarmed with fish which the locals seemed to have no trouble in catching. From the earliest days the Air Marshal, Ian and others had tried using an old native net with equal lack of success. The best we had managed to achieve was by stunning them either by firing a rifle at a visible shoal, when the impact of the rifle bullet had some effect, or by choosing a small outcrop into the sea, waiting until a shoal arrived, and then lobbing a hand grenade in. However, the fish seemed to recover before we could pick up more than one or two.

The heat was intense and we longed to go over the side for a swim, but the fear of sharks, especially after my recent experience, prevented us. We had hoped to reach Saaya that day, but, with our slow progress, we estimated there was no chance now until the next day. Towards sunset a few light airs began stealing across the water towards us, some never reaching us, while others died soon after having done so, and we resigned ourselves to another night at sea. After another hour, however, these slight airs had settled into a steady breeze.

By darkness *Scriberganti* was beating in towards Saaya at a rate which meant our arrival would, we estimated, be about midnight. We wanted to get to the fishing village that we had been told about but were not sure where it was. We decided that the best plan was to get as close into the island as possible, so that when daylight came, and with

154

it perhaps a calm, we could use our two sweeps[1] to pull in and find it. The idea of doing this in the dark, amid unknown reefs and rocks, seemed too dangerous. The dark 'loom' of the island grew closer as we continued to beat towards it. The cloudy night made it difficult to make out any details but we thought the island would have deep water close inshore, so we decided to make good use of the wind and get as close as possible.

It was a strangely exciting feeling as we beat in closer and closer to this unknown island. What should we find? We wondered if this, at last, would be our safe haven after the depression of Tjebia. It seemed to us a real achievement to have reconstructed the derelict and rotting *Scriberganti*, and to have sailed her this far. We had now got as close to the island as we judged safe and were on the point of standing off to anchor when we thought we saw lights inshore. Surely this must be the village we were looking for. The lights looked so enticing that we decided to get a little closer still to see if we could make out any details. A mixture of imagination and wishful thinking now over-ruled our common sense. We thought we could make out a lagoon, a beach and the lights which must be from the fishing village. It seemed such a short way to the beach that we decided against spending another night at sea. We would try to sail into the lagoon where we could anchor off the village in calm water.

We continued to sail steadily towards the lights, straining our eyes to make out the way ahead, at the same time conjuring up in our minds the security of a village free from all the disastrous influences of Tjebia. Suddenly, quite close ahead, we heard the surge of the sea on rocks or a reef. We immediately rounded to and dropped anchor until we could be sure of what lay ahead. As soon as we had lowered our sails, we tried to identify the features we thought we could see. Somebody said he thought the reef was getting closer and that we must be dragging our anchor. Quickly feeling our anchor rope, we found that this was so; the bottom appeared to be hard rock over which we could feel the improvised anchor dragging.

Astern of us we could now faintly make out the surge and accompanying phosphorescent effect of the sea breaking on the reef. This was coming closer all the time. There was obviously not a moment to lose. We hurriedly hoisted the mainsail, while at the same time the sweeps were got out and an effort made to pull and sail clear. By now, however, *Scriberganti* had reached the disturbed sea bordering the reef and all our efforts proved in vain. Within a few minutes, as we fell into the trough of each wave, the *prahu* crashed on

[1] Rudimentary oars.

to the bottom. Each successive wave lifted us further on and, despite the utmost we could do, *Scriberganti* soon swung broadside on to the seas and it became impossible to keep our feet. I expected the *prahu* to break up at any instant, but by some miracle she held together.

Dimly now, we could make out a dark mass of rock close by us and we decided the moment had come when we must abandon ship. We all scrambled out and found ourselves waist-deep, standing on extremely sharp rock. We then managed to secure *Scriberganti*'s bow and stern ropes to two large rocks and were thus able to prevent her from being swept away. We next set about salving what we could of our limited stores which took some time in the difficult conditions and with the *prahu* threatening all the time to break up as she pounded and crashed on the bottom. Our feet and footwear got badly cut by the rocks. At last everything possible was removed and we settled down, huddled together, as far as we could judge, on a rocky ledge just clear of the sea, but not high enough to avoid being drenched by the burst of each successive wave on the ledge below us. Sleep was out of the question because of this and the swarms of small crabs.

As the light grew with the dawn, we were able more fully to realize our predicament. It appeared that we were at the foot of a small rocky islet perhaps fifty yards square, surmounted by three or four coconut palms, the only other vegetation being some coarse grass. On the side opposite to where we had struck, separated by perhaps a hundred yards of water, lay Saaya itself, steep, rocky and tree-covered, but of the 'village' that had lured us in, there was no sign. Below us lay *Scriberganti* on her side, forlorn and waterlogged and still being battered by each wave as it broke on the reef.

The first thing to do was to have something to eat and, if possible, a hot drink. We found a shallow hollow at the top of our refuge to which we moved our stores. Searching around we collected some palm fronds and dry grass and made a fire, someone having had the foresight to keep some matches dry. As we ate our meal we tried to decide what was the best thing to do. All were agreed that we must make an attempt to get across to Saaya and see if we could make contact with any of its inhabitants.

We still had with us the little flat-bottomed dinghy that had drifted ashore on Tjebia with Mr Dimmit. It seemed sensible for the Wing-Commander with his knowledge of Malay to go over to Saaya, rowed by Stoker Tucker and Able Seaman Oldnall. They set off immediately. We had already noticed that there was a considerable current running through the narrow channel separating us from the main island and hoped they would overcome it. But it proved too strong and after some ten minutes Able Seaman Oldnall collapsed and Stoker Tucker only got the dinghy back with the greatest difficulty. There was nothing for it but to wait until the current became slacker.

While we were waiting we sighted a small fishing *prahu* coming round the point of Saaya. We had brought, as part of our equipment, a Very pistol and this we decided to use to attract the fisherman's attention. We waited to see how close he would come as we only had one cartridge. When it looked as though he had come as close as he was likely to, although still a considerable distance off, we fired our cartridge and waited on tenterhooks. Then to our great joy we saw the *prahu* turn and head towards us.

As soon as the fisherman came within earshot, the Wing-Commander hailed him in Malay, asking him to come inshore as we needed help. After some moments of obvious doubt the fisherman came close inshore. The Wing-Commander asked whether there were any inhabitants on Saaya and he said nobody lived there any more. The Wing-Commander then explained who we were and what had happened and asked him to take us to his village so that he might speak to the Headman.

The fisherman said he had come from Daboe, and we asked him whether there were any Japanese there. He replied that there were not and went on to corroborate most of our previous information about Daboe. So far as the Japanese were concerned he did not give a very clear answer, but we understood that they had been there but were not there now.

We realized that we had little option but to persuade him to take us up to Daboe, whatever the risk. Our present situation was untenable and our priority must be to get help of any kind to those remaining on Tjebia. So we asked him to take us to Daboe. After a certain amount of haggling he finally agreed to do so for three hundred Straits dollars each and what remained of *Scriberganti*.

The *prahu* was very small and could not take us all at the same time, so it was decided that we should go in two trips – the Wing-Commander, Petty Officer Johncock and myself in the first, to be followed by Ian Stonor, Stoker Tucker and Able Seaman Oldnall in the second. We set off just before noon to sail the thirty miles to Daboe.

There was a fine sailing breeze from the south-west and, although at first a little dubious of the seaworthiness of the narrow-gutted little *prahu*, we were soon reassured by the confident manner with which our fisherman handled his craft. In fact it quickly proved to be one of the more enjoyable interludes in our troubles. To his skill as a helmsman, our fisherman added extraordinary dexterity in cooking us an enamel basin full of the most beautiful flaky white rice, while scudding along in a flurry of spray, holding the tiller with his foot! The single sail was held with one hand while he cooked with the other. Into his bowl we mixed our emergency tin of 'herrings in', plus one of sardines.

The afternoon passed uneventfully, but for a few minutes hiding under a fishing net when a Japanese aircraft flew overhead. By the end of the afternoon Singkep Island was plainly in view and our thoughts turned to what lay in store for us on our arrival. The Wing-Commander tried to get some more information from the fisherman, but without success. We were now without food and in two or three days Mr Richardson's party would have none either. We came to the conclusion that if the Japanese were at Daboe we should just have to accept the fact that we had run our race as far as possible; we were neither fit enough, nor had the means, to go any further. On the other hand, if they were not there then it might still be possible to put our original plans into effect by buying a small Junk, collecting the Tjebia party and trying to exist among the islands.

At sunset we were still about two miles from Daboe, which we felt at least meant an unobserved approach in the dark. The wind dropped away to a calm and so our fisherman lowered the sail and got out two long oars, which, while standing in the raised stern, he plied with some vigour, propelling us onwards at much the same speed as under sail. As we got closer to Daboe, we could see the lights reflected in the waters of the harbour. Then we heard the noise of a motor boat's engine approaching. Our fisherman motioned to us all to lie low and keep quiet, as this would be the police launch. Within minutes the launch hailed us and was answered by the fisherman. Suddenly we were illuminated by a searchlight. We hardly dared to breathe as, for a few seconds, the launch's occupants examined us. Then, as suddenly as it had come on, it was shut off and we heard the noise of the engine receding in the distance.

The first indication we had that our journey was over was the sound of water slopping against the piles of a pier. As we passed down the side of it, a cautious glimpse showed us a number of moored junks, and, with a sinking heart, I noticed that from each drooped a white flag with the red sun of Japan. The first instinctive reaction was to conceal ourselves while there was still time, but there was nowhere to go, so we resigned ourselves to whatever reception we should

158

receive and, as the *prahu* glided alongside some steps, we prepared to clamber up on to the pier.

Within a few minutes we were stretching our cramped legs on the deserted pier while our gear was flung up to us by the fisherman. That done, he announced that he was going off 'to telephone the hospital'. We sat down on our kit to wait and see what happened. We were so weary, however, that within minutes we had fallen asleep. The next thing any of us knew was a torch shining straight into our eyes, and, in its light, the gleam of bayonets, behind which we could make out a number of armed men. With the bayonets prodding us we struggled to our feet and tried to take the situation in. They appeared to be Dutch Indonesian troops from what one could see of their uniforms. At any rate they were certainly not Japanese. The Wing-Commander elicited the information that there was a lorry at the end of the pier waiting to take us to hospital. We wearily made our way along the pier, were bundled into the waiting lorry and were soon bumping off down a road to the hospital.

About five minutes later we arrived outside a long low stone building which turned out to be the local police station. Here we were each searched and everything taken from us. We were next questioned by an officer as to who we were, where we had come from and what we were doing. Having answered these questions, the Officer told us that we were now in the custody of the Javanese gendarmerie who were in charge at Daboe. We were then taken to individual cells and locked in.

The cells were small, hot and stuffy; the only air inlet seemed to be through a small metal grille at the junction of the ceiling and wall. The only furniture in the cell was a small folding seat; there was nothing upon which one could lie except for the concrete floor. All this, in addition to a bright overhead light, made sleep difficult. I was able to talk to the Wing-Commander through the grille and we quietly discussed our situation, reaching the conclusion that we had no further options and must just sit tight and see what the morning brought.

The morning brought a small bowl of rice and another of weak vegetable stew. We were also told that we would shortly be taken to the hospital, which we didn't really believe. However, we were surprised when, a short time later, we were led out to a lorry which took us there. Again this proved to be another long single-storey building very similar to the police station. We climbed down from the lorry, watched by a curious crowd of mainly Chinese. We then carried our kit to the 'ward' that had been specially set aside for us. As

159

we passed down a long connecting corridor opening on to a number of wards, we noticed that these were mostly filled with Chinese and a few Javanese or Sumatrans. Our own ward was furnished with a number of plain wooden boards mounted on iron trestles, which we understood were to be our beds; there was no other equipment of any kind. The Chinese orderly who had shown us to the ward told us that the doctor would visit us and that when he did we were to stand at the foot of our beds and to be sure to treat him with proper respect. Two of the gendarmes remained as guards in the corridor outside.

The doctor arrived five minutes later. It was immediately evident why we had been instructed to treat him with respect. He was a very westernized and dandified Javanese, clad in a white coat. He at once, with a great flourish and some facetious remarks, took a blood slide from each of us, which he then took away for examination. He returned within a few minutes to inform us that we had not the slightest signs of fever and were perfectly healthy! And this in spite of the fact that the Wing-Commander was already having a rigor. We later heard from a Chinese dresser who had been detailed to look after us that until a short time ago the 'doctor' had been head dresser to the resident Dutch doctor and that he had assumed his title of 'doctor' the moment the Dutch had left, that he now spent the greater part of his time pursuing the Chinese nurses and that everyone hated him for the grand ways he had assumed. Nevertheless, when I showed him my hand and thumb, he dealt with the wounds very expertly, freezing them to remove the remnants of the old dirty dressings, cleaning and re-dressing them quickly and painlessly.

The old Chinese dresser proved a good friend to us during the next few days and brought us in a number of excellent Chinese meals with the money we gave him. He also brought us up to date with a lot of news. He said the hospital had become very busy after the fall of Singapore, as large numbers of wounded survivors from the fleet of small vessels that left on the last few days had been brought to or had found their way to Daboe and the hospital. The hospital had, in fact, been at full pressure until only a few days ago when the Japanese first arrived. They immediately shipped everyone, including the Dutch nursing staff and nuns, to Sumatra.

Our Javanese gendarmes, too, became quite talkative. They told us that the Japanese were not at present on the island but would be returning in a few days. They had been brought up from Java to police the largely Sumatran and Chinese population. The Japanese policy apparently was to use Sumatrans to police the Javanese and Chinese areas, and the Javanese to police the Sumatran and Chinese areas. They also told us that Australia had fallen and India was now being invaded, half of the British Fleet had been sunk and that Japan had almost won the war – news which, even if taken with a large grain of salt, was not calculated to raise our spirits. On the other side of the coin, it was evident that the Japanese were feared and hated by almost everyone.

On our second day we were much relieved to see Ian Stonor, Able Seaman Oldnall and Stoker Tucker arrive. We knew that there had always been a risk that the money we gave to the fisherman would just be taken and that he might abandon the other three on their rocky islet. However, he had kept his word and obviously gone straight back to collect Ian and the others.

We spent about five days in the hospital, during which time, apart from using some of our funds on food, we also provided money to pay for some of the braver elements in the town to throw stones at the police station and generally to stir up as much trouble as possible. How successful this little effort of resistance was we were never able to find out.

On the morning of the fifth day there seemed to be an unusual 'bustle' going on and, on asking our guards what it was all about, we learnt that the Japanese had returned and we were to be taken away. The Japanese duly arrived at about 9 a.m., entering our ward with a great show of officious arrogance and not a few shouts of displeasure at anyone who seemed out of place, or not to show proper respect. It was our first experience of the Kempeitai, the Japanese Secret Police. I remember thinking that their appearance resembled exactly the familiar cartoons of the Japanese that, over the years since the Manchurian incident, we had become so accustomed to.

Their party consisted of three sergeants who gave us a distinctly uneasy feeling as we studied them in their ill-fitting uniforms, with Kempeitai arm-bands. They were accompanied by two civilians, one of whom had an enormous black beard and the other a rather oily and sly look. We soon discovered the former to be a police officer and the latter an interpreter.

A table was brought in and placed at one end of our ward and, one at a time, we were sharply ordered to come and stand in front of it. We were told, first in Japanese, then through the interpreter, that we were now prisoners of the Imperial Japanese Army and that we must obey its orders on pain of death. The same questions that had been put to us by the gendarmerie were again put to us. In our turn, we asked that the 'stay-behind-Tjebia-party' be picked up as a matter of urgency and were told that they were being collected and that we should then all be taken to Singapore.

Two days later we were ordered to collect our scant belongings and were then escorted out of the hospital to a waiting lorry. This took us down to the harbour, under the curious gaze of the townspeople, to the pier where we had originally landed. There to my amazement lay my old tug *Elizabeth*, and on board were Mr Richardson and his party. There were also a Dutch planter and his wife, together with his assistant, who, we later learned, was a white Russian. They had been picked up from another island. Another passenger for Singapore, we discovered, was a very downcast and shamefaced Charlie, who could not meet our eyes.

As soon as we were all embarked, the *Elizabeth* cast off and headed out of Daboe. At the same time we were all forced below into the after peak which was anything but comfortable. We were very crowded and had to crouch down against the damp and sweating steel sides of the tug. There was insufficient height to stand and very little air. It was hot and foetid and through the compartment ran the unprotected propeller shaft. As the shaft revolved, half in and half out of the slimy, oily bilge water, its connecting blocks threw up a spray of odorous liquid which we could not avoid. During our two-day passage, threading our way north through the islands, we were occasionally allowed on deck a few at a time for fresh air and to attend to our bodily needs. Most of us had mild dysentery, which made conditions very unpleasant. On approaching a village, whatever we were doing, we were immediately ordered below. The Dutch planter, his wife and assistant were confined elsewhere.

Once more we were faced with the shock of conditions of which we had no experience and, in our debilitated state, it took every ounce of fortitude to hold on to our sanity and hope.

At two o'clock on the afternoon of 23 May, 1942, we arrived at Clifford Pier, Singapore, and were ordered up into the blinding sunlight from our dark and unsavoury quarters. It was a strange situation, to be back after almost thirteen weeks. Of the nine officers and thirty-five men who had originally left Singapore in *ML 310*, in addition to the three who had joined the party on Tjebia, nineteen had died on the island. One more, Lance-Corporal Shrimpton, was to die a few days later, and two were missing. We were quickly counted, a mania with the Japanese, as we were soon to know, loaded into an old British Army lorry and driven through the bomb-battered streets to what had once been the British American Tobacco building, here to be delivered into the tender mercies of the Kempeitai, the building being their headquarters in Singapore. A new adventure was about to begin.

CHAPTER 11

Prisoner of War

Our journey through the streets of Singapore awoke strange emotions. Very little of the structural damage seemed to have been repaired beyond make-shift patchwork. The streets had a dingy and forlorn look. We arrived outside the British American Tobacco building and had our first experience of the shouting and hustlings that accompanied all Japanese supervision of our movements. We were shouted at to get out of the lorry with our baggage and make our way into the building. Once inside, we climbed several flights of stairs before finding ourselves on the top floor in a room completely clear of all fittings or furniture. Lying round the floor with backs to the wall were a large number of Chinese, Indians and a few Malays. They were made to crowd closer together in order that we should take our places.

We settled ourselves down as best we could under the curious gaze of the other occupants. There was little room and the floor was hard and cold. No one spoke above a whisper and we gathered that talking was not encouraged. The only washing and sanitation facilities were in a small adjoining room and were hopelessly inadequate for the sixty or seventy of us in the room. Later two of the Chinese were ordered out of the room and returned after a short while with a table and three chairs, whereupon the Dutch planter, his wife and assistant, who had come up from the islands with us, were brought in and took their places at the table.

Every half hour a Japanese, usually dressed in a white vest, baggy khaki breeches and wooden sandals, entered the room and sauntered round, his expression a mixture of malevolence and contempt. He had a small automatic strapped to his hip. The outlook did not appear good, especially when we learnt that we were in the Kempeitai

Headquarters. The Kempeitai were rightly feared as being a cruel and sadistic offshoot of the Japanese Military Police.

Twice a day food was brought in. It consisted of a bucket of watery stew, and, to judge by the fish heads, tails and bones, the Japanese 'leavings' thrown in, a dreadful and unsavoury mixture. For several days we held out and didn't try to scrummage for a share, relying instead on the last of our iron rations, but when these ran out we were forced to join in the scramble. The only conversation we managed was a hurried word in the washroom.

We learned that all the Asiatics were here because of suspected contacts with the British, or for crimes against the Military Government. The Chinese, in particular, suffered terrible beatings and a number were killed in this way. The Dutch and their assistant, who we learned was a White Russian, were allowed to send out for food, the delicious smells from which made our lot much harder to bear and did not make them popular. However, one could not but admire the great dignity shown by the planter's wife who managed somehow to change over her two dresses each day.

After several days of lying around we officers were interrogated in turn. This interrogation was very thorough and lasted over several days. My turn duly came and I found myself seated at a small table facing a Japanese Colonel and an interpreter. To begin with the questions concerned my identification. Who was I? Where had I come from? What was I doing on Tjebia and what and where was my ship? I soon realized that name and rank were not enough for the Japanese, who in any case did not recognize the Geneva Convention.

I was repeatedly asked what I had been doing in Singapore and where I had come from. On several occasions the Colonel became very angry and drew his Samurai sword which he placed across the back of my neck. Each time I was told that unless I told the truth, my head would be cut off! I just repeated my story. I was often confronted with startling news of Japanese advances and the loss of major British or American ships. 'The Japanese armies had invaded India and Australia. Did I know about this news?' Of course I did not, and said so. On another occasion, having been told of a sweeping Japanese naval victory, I was asked if I still thought Britain and America could win the war. I answered that ultimately they would. When asked why I was so sure, I told the Colonel, rather chancing my arm, of the reply that General Ludendorff had made when asked, after the First World War, 'Why the British Army had beaten the Germans'. 'Because the British have a sense of humour, the Germans do not!' I said that the same applied today and that neither the

Japanese nor the Germans had a sense of humour. The Colonel then flew into a towering rage and left the room. I was rather afraid I had over-stepped the mark and waited anxiously. After a few minutes the Colonel returned, seemingly in quite a good humour, and asked me if I would like a drink. I said that I should very much like a glass of cold milk. This was brought to me with a plate of Huntley and Palmer's biscuits! It was explained to me by the interpreter that the Japanese were always very happy or in a rage! I was to find this very true. I also think that in a technical sense I was lucky my interrogator was an Army Officer and not a Naval Officer.

The days passed and we witnessed some bad beatings of some of the Asiatics by the Kempeitai, though, apart from the odd instance of unprovoked 'cuffing' or kicking, we were not seriously molested. A few days after our arrival Lance-Corporal Shrimpton died of severe beri beri and malaria. On 6 June, we four officers were told to collect our baggage, not very much by now, as we were leaving. We were then crammed into an old British staff car and driven to Changi, where all the British prisoners had been sent after the capitulation.

On arrival we were taken to the British hospital, then housed in Roberts Barracks. Here we were examined. Ian Stonor was detained with malaria, while the Wing-Commander and I were taken up to have supper with Major-General Keith Simmons at Southern Area Command, to whom we told our story. In our turn we learned that the Japanese had left the Prisoners of War in the Changi cantonment with its barrack blocks and bungalows to administer themselves. The various Army Commands had their own areas, but each area was guarded by Sikh troops who had been retained by the Japanese for this purpose. They were the forerunners of the Indian National Army, and went out of their way to be unpleasant and officious. They had to be saluted each time we passed them.

After our experience on Tjebia and at the Kempeitai headquarters, it was a great relief to be with our own people once again. It was not the same lonely battle against depression and isolation. Changi was well organized and, though the conditions, by the standards which we had hitherto taken for granted, were very different, life was bearable. I was accommodated in a large bungalow shared by a number of other naval officers, a handful compared to the soldiers. There was a lot to do, camp fatigues such as woodcutting, and local purchase parties, going outside the camp pulling old lorry chassis, as well as lectures and entertainments. There were many old friends to talk to, as well as new ones to be made.

Our Senior Officer was Commander H.R.D. Alexander who

organized us along naval lines. I shared a room with a New Zealander, Bruce Clarke, who I found shared my interest in sailing. In my spare time I decorated the walls of our wardroom with chalk drawings of warships, including some of the newer classes of ships, which the mainly local reserve and volunteer officers had never seen before. Occasionally we braved the Sikh guards to visit other areas and I went up to Temple Hill several times to have dinner with Ian Stonor, now back with General Perceval. The first time I sat next to the General I was patiently listened to as I got a lot off my chest! Not long afterwards the Japanese announced that 5000 officers and men were to be sent to Japan, and included in this party were all the senior officers of full Colonel's rank and above. Ian was to go with the General and came up to see me in hospital, bringing me a tin of fish and some Worcester sauce from the headquarters mess.

For several weeks at a time I was in hospital with malaria and mild beri-beri. I was there during the notorious Selerang Incident. The Japanese suddenly decided that we should sign a document to the effect that we would not attempt to escape. It was pointed out by our Command that we should be breaking our military code if we did so, but this had no effect on their demand. Nonetheless this Japanese demand was refused by our people and on 2 September all prisoners were ordered to move into Selerang Barracks. From the hospital in Roberts Barracks we watched the long columns of men streaming in via all the approach roads; they were all in by 6 p.m. Literally every square foot of space on all the floors and the parade ground was occupied. We heard that the Japanese had shot four of our people for attempting to escape that same day. Japanese and Sikh troops surrounded the area and we knew there could only be one answer in the end.

The next day was the anniversary of the outbreak of the war three years before and it brought about an intensification of pressure. Latrines which had been dug in the parade ground and barrack surrounds were having to be re-dug, and space was almost exhausted. I thought of this day in 1939, sitting in the Gunroom of *Revenge* at Weymouth listening to the Prime Minister telling us that from 11 a.m. the British Empire would be in a state of war with Germany. Not in my wildest dreams could I then have envisaged such a scene as I was now witnessing. 4 September brought heavy rain and by that evening conditions had become impossible and, with the threat that all supplies of food and water to the hospital, in which there were several thousand men, would be cut off, our Senior Officers recommended our signing the parole document. Our opposition had been taken as far as it was sensible and we signed under duress.

From the top of the hospital block it was possible to see far out into the Straits and on occasions we could see Japanese ships passing. Seeing those grey, purposeful cruisers and destroyers, and once, two cruisers of the new Mogami class, steaming into a heavy head sea, and throwing sheets of spray over their forecastles, brought back a nostalgia for my own lost way of life.

Sometimes, during the heavy rains of late August and the grey and overcast conditions that accompanied them, it reminded me of England. I think the hospital had just had its electricity supply connected and I was shaving early by a rather dim naked bulb. It was dark outside and it somehow reminded me of coming back from Pangbourne for the Christmas holidays, of Paddington Station with its Christmas decorations. I was reading A. G. Street's *A Year of my Life* at the time, so my thoughts were very much of home. I returned to my surroundings with a horrid shock.

News of the war was almost nonexistent, but occasional rumours filtered in from outside and it seemed as though the Japanese had at last been checked in the Solomons, but, encouraging though this was, the Solomons were a long way from Singapore and we knew there would be many more frustrating and boring months, if not years, before we would be free. I met numbers of people from various regiments, especially the 4th Suffolks; John Wysock-Crundall, Geoffrey Clarke, Bobby De Quincy and Sam Flick, among many others.

I celebrated my twenty-third birthday with a tin of Libby's peaches, a bad attack of quinine deafness, and forming a yacht club with Colonel Stitt of the Gordons.

All through October large parties of P.o.Ws from Java arrived. Among them were many American, Australian and Dutch survivors from the disastrous naval battles in the Java seas, including the last battle of the *Exeter* and the destroyers of our Force Z screen. The account of the epic night action of the *Perth* and the American cruiser *Houston* in the Sunda Straits only served to depress us further.

At this time we received two consignments of South African Red Cross supplies. They consisted of a tin of milk, cocoa, ¾lb biscuits, ¼lb guava jam, flour, dall and atap flour, 65 cigarettes, 4 tins of bully beef, sugar, some porridge and some vitamin caramels. Our doctors said we should eat the bulk of it at once in order to get the maximum nutritional value.

The Japanese now seemed to be clearing Java and Singapore of

P.o.W.s. There were rumours of parties going 'up country' whatever that meant. Geoffrey Hulton, *Repulse*'s senior Royal Marine Subaltern, had already left with a small party. On 26 October, having been warned two days previously, I left with a large party of officers.

After a good breakfast, thanks to our Red Cross parcels, we marched from our quarters, with all our baggage, to Changi village. Here lorries awaited us and, after being counted and re-counted, we packed ourselves in, just like sardines. Our journey now started. We had a vague idea from the Japanese that we were going to 'health camps' in the hills of Siam, now called Thailand. After several lengthy stops, including one at Changi Jail, where we had to sign pay reduction forms, we arrived at Singapore Station. Our journey of about fourteen miles had taken nearly five hours. We now settled down on a platform, surrounded by our baggage and waited another two hours for our train. The Japanese supplied no food and we had to do with the rations our cookhouse had so wisely issued to us on leaving, a meat pasty, bully beef sandwich and two boiled eggs.

At last at 3 p.m. our train arrived. It was entirely made up of closed steel wagons, into which we were told to pack ourselves, thirty men plus baggage to a wagon. We had no idea of how long our journey was to be, but it was clearly not going to be a comfortable journey. An hour later, with much jerking, crashing and banging, we started, and rumbled across the island until the causeway was reached. The train then crept very slowly across the temporary bridge. There was a short stop at Johore Bahru, but we were not allowed out and guards patrolled the length of the train. From what we could see through the half-closed doors, the countryside seemed quite normal; a few curious Malays, Chinese and Tamils watched us pass. The odd Japanese railway patrol car passed us at intervals. The night was very cold and the steel sides of our wagon sweated, and, sitting as we were, with our backs against it, it was most uncomfortable.

Tuesday morning, in pouring rain, we reached Kuala Lumpur, where we made another short stop and were able to buy some fruit. We were soon away again, clanking our way north up the peninsula. The acute discomfort of this means of travel became very evident. It was impossible to sit or lie comfortably; somebody or his baggage was always in the way. The cold and damp of the night was exchanged for oven-like temperatures by day. We took it in turns to be beside the half-open sliding doors, one on each side, which was a mixed blessing because although you got some fresh air and could see out, you also collected smuts, smoke and a drenching when it rained. We had two stops a day, usually on a siding outside the station, where a few buckets of the usual watery rice stew were provided for us. We were also allowed out, under the watchful eye of our guards, to attend to the needs of nature. As this was always where previous trains had stopped, the state of the area was indescribably foul. This was insufficient for some, who had mild dysentery or other troubles; they had to be held, with their backsides out of the doors, while the train rumbled along.

We stopped just before dark at Kuala Kubu Road, which, for those who lived in or knew Malaya must have evoked memories of Fraser's Hill and the Cameron Highlands; no air-conditioned coaches on this trip! We glimpsed the rusting remains of Bren-gun carriers at Slim River.[1] During the night it rained hard and most of us received a soaking. Though we were all very tired by now, sleep was impossible due to the discomfort and the bone-shaking jolting of the wagons.

Prai was reached early on the 28th and we were able to see Penang. I personally felt very low, aching in every joint and unwashed. However, here for the only time we managed a perfunctory wash in the waiting room and, luxury of luxuries, a hard-boiled egg and a cup of coffee. We felt almost civilised again. But we were soon herded back in our trucks again and the illusion was lost. The railway now left the lush vegetation of the hills and rubber plantations for the embankments and paddy fields of the State of Kedah. We passed the airfields of Butterworth and Sungei Pantani, Jitra and Kangar, all names that evoked bitter memories of the campaign.

We arrived at the Siam border at 4 p.m. and stopped at the first station, I think it was Ban Hat Yai, where we became the focus of attention for many curious Siamese. They seemed friendly enough and were keen to barter food for items of clothing, not that we had much to offer. The police and railway personnel were conspicuous, with high and over-large brims to their caps. We noticed that there was little love lost between them and the Japanese, and they would not accept Japanese money. The station stank of human excrement and refuse lay everywhere. It had obviously been used by many such trains before our arrival.

The train was now travelling up the Kra Isthmus, flat and rather uninteresting country with a mixture of paddy fields and low scrub, with occasional limestone conical hillocks rising above the level plain. We saw very little life; only at the small halts were the locals to be seen. Another night and whole day passed as the train rumbled north. We had almost lost any idea of where we were; the journey had

[1] The heavy fighting leading up to 12th and 28th Brigades of the 11th Indian Divisions being almost destroyed at the Slim River Bridge on 7 January, 1942.

become a nightmare of discomfort and degradation, particularly at the halts, although at least here we could stretch our legs. Another night, our fourth, during which I lost my new Red Cross boots, and then, early the next morning, 30 October, we arrived at a station where we were ordered to leave the train with our baggage.

The whole party was ordered to parade in the square in front of the station, which we learnt was Ban Pong. Then followed the interminable procedure of roll call, the counting over and over again, even dead bodies having to be paraded. I believe one man had died on the train. In this respect the Japanese made no concessions at all. Finally satisfied, they ordered us to pick up our baggage and march off to our next destination. Fortunately it was only a short distance along some rather dirty and smelly streets. On either side of us were rather dilapidated two-and three-storey houses, the lower floors of which were open-fronted shops. Our camp consisted of a series of long low huts, set close together on muddy ground, which looked very unsavoury to us. Adjacent were similar huts, housing Japanese troops; everywhere was dirt and filth, and conditions were appalling. We learned from some of our people already there that when it rained the whole camp area was under water and the contents of the latrines between the huts overflowed. There was a great shortage of water for drinking, cooking and, of course, washing. Three times a day we queued up for some slushy rice and vegetable stew, in which, if you were lucky, you might find a half-cooked piece of buffalo meat, about an inch square.

After a day and a half, during which we did our best to clean up, transport arrived to take us on the next part of our journey. As with all Japanese journeys, space was totally inadequate and we were crammed in with our baggage to drive thirty miles to Kanburi (Kanchanaburi). This proved a pleasant interlude by comparison with the past week since leaving Singapore. Although a sunny day, there was a cool breeze as we passed by well-irrigated fruit plantations, paddy fields and, here and there, clumps of scrub and bamboo. Our lorry broke down and during the two hours it took to repair it, we lay about in the shade of some roadside trees, eating bananas and pomeloes. Hordes of little Siamese boys darted round behind the guards, making faces at them and drawing fingers across their throats, which showed their feelings more eloquently than any words. The lorry was repaired by one of our people and we climbed in and continued on our way. We understood that Kanburi was near the hills and we soon saw ahead of us the pale blue hummocks of the first hills.

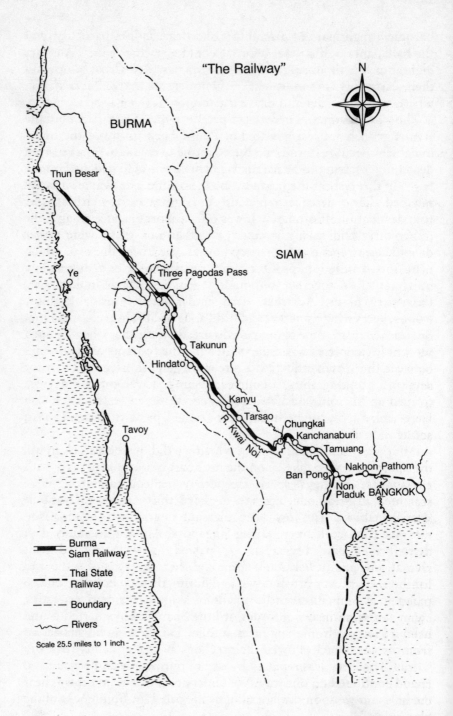

"The Railway"

N

BURMA

SIAM

Thun Besar

Ye

Three Pagodas Pass

Takunun

Hindato

Kanyu

Tarsao

R. Kwai Noi

Chungkai

Kanchanaburi

Tavoy

Tamuang

Nakhon Pathom

Ban Pong

Non
Pladuk BANGKOK

Burma –
Siam Railway

Thai State
Railway

Boundary

Rivers

Scale 25.5 miles to 1 inch

In the early evening we reached Kanburi, a small riverside town at the confluence of the Rivers Kwai Yai, coming down from the north, and the Kwai Noi, from the west. The camp itself was sited on a small common just outside the town, known as the 'aerodrome camp'. The air was much fresher and cooler than in Singapore. Each party was allocated to a hut. These huts were constructed of a bamboo framework, about two hundred feet long and twenty-five feet wide, and about ten foot high to the ridge pole. The roof was thatched with atap and a continuous raised platform of split and flattened bamboo, running down each side, served as beds, theoretically two feet to each man; an aisle of about six feet wide ran up the middle. The huts were full of mosquitoes and the bamboo slats with bed bugs. Soon after the usual meal of rice stew, the word passed round to put up our badges of rank, pips and shoulder-straps once again. This little return to normality was an immediate boost to morale. At Changi, by ordering such emblems to be removed, the Japanese had sought to humiliate the officers before their men. It had had no effect.

The next day, 2 November, we were warned that we were to move out once again. We were marched through the ramshackle little town, with its main street of packed mud, down to a wide expanse of river bank sloping down to the water's edge. Along this edge were moored several big open barges, about forty foot by twelve foot by seven foot, as well as a number of motor boats. We waited under some very large tamarind trees while the arrangements for our transport were settled. We then clambered aboard our allotted barge, which, with our baggage, left us little room. As each barge was filled it was towed out into the stream by a motor boat, 'crabbing' its way across the current, which was very strong, it being the beginning of the rainy season. We slowly made our way to the western river, the Kwai Noi, where the current seemed less strong. We tied up to a large bamboo raft moored in midstream. There were a number of these huge rafts, as well as some made of teak logs, moored along the banks of the river. Each had a little atap shelter in which the steersman lived on the long passages down from the forest. As there seemed to be no prospect of immediate further movement, most of us had a welcome swim and wash in the cool and, for once, unlimited water. We also used the last of our money to buy a little fruit and a packet of biscuits from the local traders.

In the evening the motor boat took us in tow again and headed up-river. For the next four days we puttered our way up against the current. The limestone hills gradually became higher and the bamboo clumps and scrub jungle closed in to the river's edge. At frequent intervals we pulled in to the bank at small clearings in which stood several native huts. We had had no Japanese-supplied food since our meal before leaving Kanburi and, as the days passed, so our hunger pangs grew. On the third day we stopped and were allowed to leave our barges at a P.o.W. camp called Tarsao. We understood it was a base camp for a railway being constructed from Ban Pong to Burma. Tarsao itself had been constructed by earlier parties and consisted of the now familiar bamboo and atap thatched huts and lay about forty miles up the river from Kanburi. It was pouring with rain and the camp was a sea of mud. However, we were given a meal, albeit the same old soggy rice and vegetable stew that seemed to be all that the Japanese rations allowed.

Back again in our barge, we continued up the river. The current was now very strong and progress slow; once or twice we ran aground. When this happened our Korean guards, who now seemed to have taken over from the Japanese, would order us 'to push', not from the outside, but from inside the barge itself! We were also passed by a number of bamboo rafts being piloted downstream on the current. In the late evening of 7 November we reached our destination, a small clearing in the forest called Kanyu. A number of partly-built huts awaited us. The camp was situated on the river bank at the foot of a steep jungle-clad hill, and surrounded by huge thirty- to forty-foot-high bamboo clumps. Each side was marked by two streams flowing from the hill. Our task, we were then told, was to build a road from the river to the top of the hill, really an escarpment, along the top of which a road and a railway were to be built.

Our party was known as 'W' Battalion, was commanded by Lieutenant-Colonel Moore and was entirely made up of officers. We were put to work at once – so much for the health camp in the mountains! It was by now mid-November, the height of the rainy season, and it sometimes rained for days on end. We were issued with *chunkols*, a cross between a pick and a spade, and with them gouged our way in a zigzag path up the face of the hill. Other parties were ahead, cutting down trees and clearing the scrub. While this was going on, we were still trying to complete the camp buildings – huts, cookhouse, latrines and, in defiance of the Japanese, a hut for the hospital. It was not long before we were urgently in need of the latter. By the end of the month there were many suffering from dysentery and malaria and a number of men had died.

There was very little free time, though we managed a small Remembrance Day service on 10 December to mark the sinking of *Prince of Wales* and *Repulse*. All through this month sickness

174

worsened and by the end of it only thirty officers out of one hundred and thirty were fit. It also became very cold at nights and it was impossible to keep warm. Some of the men had bartered their blankets and jerseys at Ban Pong, and suffered a great deal. Occasionally we heard news of friends and I heard that Geoffrey Hulton was at the next camp above. On Christmas Day the cook-house made a special effort, and already, in the short time that they had been cooking rice, had developed great skills with biscuits, porridge and coffee. One of the gunners, Captain Pearson, known as 'Fizzer' to us, produced virtually a one-man concert party. For a short time we forgot our plight, as we squatted round in a half-circle, faces lit by the glow of the blazing and exploding bamboo logs, behind and around us the dark outlines of bamboo thickets and overhead the dark blue sky.

Early in the new year work was intensified. We were now directly under the Japanese Engineers responsible for the construction of the railway. As soon as the road up the hill had been completed, a large part of the camp was moved up to construct a new camp by the side of the road which was also under construction along the top of the escarpment. Working parties were sent out in both directions to link up with those from other camps. The route of the railway first had to be cleared of trees and other vegetation, then the ground levelled or cut through limestone outcrops which lay in the path of the railway.

The day began at sunrise with breakfast, consisting of a mug of black tea and a tin of rice porridge. This was followed by a roll call after which we all set out on whatever task we were detailed to. Everyone had to go, including the sick carried on makeshift stretchers. Before we could start work there was a stiff march uphill. Of all the jobs at this time, the worst and the hardest was clearing the rock and other débris that had been dynamited by carrying it on a rice sack threaded on two bamboo poles. The same method was used to bring up ballast from the river bed. The heat in the narrow gullies was terrific and our bodies were white with sweat. The ferocity and intolerance of the engineers was beyond belief.

A short break, though not always, for a meal of rice and stew, carried in our mess tins, and then on through the afternoon until late in the day. We would then descend to the river, and when things were quieter, were allowed to swim. At last, the evening rissole, with the addition of a sweet rice biscuit. On the other hand, when a 'speedo' was on, it was usual to work from sunrise to sunset.

By April, 1943, the track was getting closer and a redoubled 'speedo' was ordered and my party was moved to the upper camp. An elephant party was now close to the camp, bringing down teak logs for sawing into sleepers, and I had a rather frightening experience with them. On one of the very rare rest days, 'yasmi' days in Japanese, I had left the camp to have a shower and wash under a small waterfall not far away. After this deliciously refreshing interlude, I set out to return to the camp. Somehow I lost my bearings and after some time I suddenly found myself amid a herd of elephants. In fact they were tethered, though I did not realize this at the time. I hurriedly retired into the forest. It seemed to me that the elephants were between me and the camp. An extra anxiety was that I now realized that the light was fading. Evening roll call could not be far off and I had to fight hard to control my fear that I could easily end up being lost or shot. I turned to go back in what I thought was the direction of the waterfall and, by tremendous good fortune, stumbled across the stream below the waterfall. I knew it passed close by the camp and so followed its course until, in the last light, I saw the glow of the camp's fires and crept quietly in, just minutes before the roll call. I never ventured into the forest again.

As April passed into May the pressure of work was unrelenting, the food was at its worst, and, with the continuing rains, the tolls of sickness grew heavier. Being on the road, we saw many thousands of prisoners going through in lorries or on foot, evidence of the increased tempo of work. Tamils and Chinese workers also passed by. One of the troubles, as I found from bitter experience, was that there was never time to recover from dysentery, malaria or any of the many ailments now rife. We heard horrifying accounts of cholera outbreaks in other camps up-river, particularly among the native labour who had no medical staff nor any idea of hygiene. They were just isolated and left to die. On one or two occasions, when permitted, British medical staff did what little they could.

The doctors scattered among the camps were magnificent. With the totally inadequate supplies of drugs with which they left Changi, they had to treat the full catalogue of tropical diseases under inhuman conditions and with no medical assistance from our captors. The most elementary tropical hygiene was non-existent in the camps and, in attempting to apply it, the doctors had to act, in many cases, in the face of Japanese opposition and brutality.

I was a member of a party that made several trips down to Tarsao with the engineers to load compressors into lorries, carry dynamite for blasting, and, one day, to manhandle large boulders. It was heavy and unpleasant work, for which at the end of the day we received a bucket of uncooked rice. We had then to collect firewood before we could cook and eat it. However, the worst part of such trips was our overnight accommodation. This was a so called bath-hut on the edge of the river which was black with mosquitoes.

More news filtered through of friends. Sam Flick, who was second-in-command of 4th Suffolks, told me that John Crundall was down at Chungkai with jaundice. My old room-mate from Changi, Bruce Clarke, minus beard and looking comparatively fit, passed through, as did Colonel Johnson and Bobby De Quincey of the Suffolks.

Sickness was now approaching a peak, with 560 sick out of 800 at Kanyu, myself amongst them. I had continual diarrhoea and was very weak. On a so-called fluid diet, with many others, I struggled to the latrine, black with blow-flies and below us a seething mass of maggots. With the mud and the stench, the weeks now passed in a blur of misery and degradation. A death each day was now commonplace.

With others judged seriously sick, I was now sent down to the larger hospital at Tarsao. It was another nightmare journey as we had first to get ourselves down the hill to reach the barges for the journey down-river. At Tarsao tests revealed amoebic dysentery and it was a question of holding on until some supplies of emertine could be obtained. Even then we were told there would be only enough for a 'holding dose' and not sufficient for a cure.

A month later another large party of sick, of which I was one, were evacuated by railway to Tamakan, known as the Bridge Camp because of its proximity to the bridge the Japanese had built across the Kwai Yai. We travelled slowly down the line and it was interesting to see the part of the line that had been completed at such cost. On two occasions we stopped in sidings to allow troop trains through. On one of these a train briefly stopped opposite us. One of its wagon doors was in line with ours and to our surprise it was full of Japanese girls. These girls, dressed in short white skirts and blouses, were in startling contrast to ourselves and, indeed, to their own troops. One of them told us, rather sadly, that she was a university graduate who had volunteered to serve her country overseas. She had been sent to Indo-China where she found she had to do so on her back. These girls were known as 'comfort girls' and were on their way to Burma.

Tamakan camp was sited on the east bank of the Kwai Yai River, just above its junction with the Kwai Noi, and within a hundred yards of the bridge carrying the railway across it. Almost entirely a hospital camp, the Senior British Officer was Colonel Toosey[1]. Philip Toosey, or 'Champagne Toosey' as he was known, was an inspiring leader. Always immaculately turned out, he was the epitome of the British Officer and was never overawed by our captors. We found the food much better than anything we had seen up-river, mostly because of its proximity to the food-producing areas.[2] The medical attention was not as good as at Tarsao, but this was possibly due to overcrowding. The Japanese had by now realized that, in order to finish the railway and still have enough labour to maintain it, they had to move the most seriously sick nearer to the food supplies.

Our life style changed dramatically, though living conditions were still as primitive as ever. The intense work that we had been used to changed to normal camp fatigues needed to sustain the camp itself. The whole atmosphere was more hopeful and we were encouraged by the war news obtained by the secret radio in the camp. There was also time to read and I began to paint. On leaving Changi, each of us had brought a book, and these formed the nucleus of a library, run by a camp librarian. There were regular concerts and plays, all of which were quite brilliantly produced and were watched by the Japanese. The skill and ingenuity of those who made the props and costumes out of rotten clothes, mosquito nets with dyes extracted from vegetation and soil, to say nothing of the skills of actors and players, were beyond belief. Equally great was the debt we all owed to those who, in addition to their kit, had added the weight of a musical instrument, not to mention nurturing it through the great physical difficulties encountered on the railways.

Towards the end of July enough of the drug emertine began to be available for those many like myself, suffering from amoebic dysentery, to receive a holding dose. The results were miraculous and after a few days I was out of hospital for the first time in fifteen weeks, and able to eat something like normal camp rations. With a meagre pay allowance reaching us, we had a little to spend on local purchases, mostly duck eggs in my case, with a little fruit. I was also able to take part in camp duties once more. One of the first of these was to take my turn guarding the stores in which the camp tools were kept. Some of these tools, used by the working parties, had been stolen. The Japanese were sure that it was either our people or the Thais and they

---

[1] Lieutenant-Colonel P.J.D. Toosey DSO, OBE, Commanding Officer of 135 Field Regiment Royal Artillery the Lenarkshire Yeomanry.
[2] Another reason for this was the corrupt system operated by the Japanese themselves of taking their cut of supplies passing through, to the detriment of camps further up the railway.

ordered us to guard them. We had all seen enough of their methods of punishment to make sure that it was done effectively. One night, in bright moonlight, I was doing my turn of duty, patrolling round the outside of the hut. Armed with a pick helve, I was moving cautiously through the long grass when suddenly I heard a movement in front of me. I dropped down to a crouching position, the better to see anyone coming, and not to be seen myself. As the stealthy movement drew nearer, I saw an indistinct figure almost on top of me. I sprang up and hit out, catching the figure fair and square. Something heavy dropped onto the grass, followed by a grunt of pain and surprise as the figure turned and fled. I immediately looked to see what had dropped and found a Japanese rifle! I, too, beat a hasty retreat towards our Adjutant's tent to report the incident. Colonel Toosey was called and decided that I should return to my own hut while we awaited developments. His appreciation, which turned out to be correct, was that the guard concerned would be so terrified at losing his rifle that he would not dare to report it.

We were by now hearing occasional aircraft and then suddenly Liberators from Burma or India bombed the bridges one day and, although a frightening experience for us, it also cheered us up and we all had the feeling that at last the war was moving our way.

At the end of November a large party, including myself, marched up to Chungkai, which we found had become an even larger hospital camp than Tamakan, and here I joined the 'amoebics' in a large hut known as 'amoeba hall'. The weather was now fine and dry and the nights comparatively cool. I certainly felt cold under my threadbare blanket and used to put on my only spare shirt and a rather thin jersey. All those who had shortsightedly bartered such things for cigarettes felt it very much and suffered accordingly, many of the latter either having to get up and walk about and a few even had to go to the latrines and keep warm by standing over the excrement-filled pits.

The hospital now contained many of the survivors of those first terrible months while the railway 'speedo' was on. They suffered from a full range of tropical diseases, aggravated by malnutrition, unhygienic conditions and virtual slave labour. Even though some drugs were beginning to filter through in limited supplies via the Red Cross, albeit indirectly and with the clandestine help of the Thais, they were only just sufficient to hold the various ailments at bay – dysentery, malaria, dengue fever, beri-beri and various skin diseases. Perhaps the worst of all were the tropical ulcers, some extending from the knee to the ankle, open to the bone and giving off an appalling smell. These often led to amputations, which like all other cases requiring surgery were carried out in the most primitive conditions, often with home-made instruments.

Christmas Day, 1943, passed pleasantly. The Japanese had come to recognize it as our special day. The cookhouses surpassed themselves and we even had roast beef for lunch. In any event the rations were now better and we were able to supplement them by local purchases and from the camp canteen. Our actual pay received was about eight ticals[1] a month, out of supposedly 122 ticals, the pay of a Japanese Second-Lieutenant. All but fifteen was retained by the Japanese for accommodation, lighting and food! Of our fifteen we put five into hospital funds and two into unit funds.

The railway was completed in October, 1943, though many of us did not realize it, and, although a large number of prisoners were required to maintain it, for the majority who were permanently sick in one form or another, life became somewhat easier, but only by comparison. There was time now for a more organized camp life. Letters began to arrive, but only a small fraction of what were sent from home. I received my first letter in March, 1944, and learnt that my parents had heard that I was a prisoner on Christmas Day, 1942. Two Red Cross parcels arrived, the first since Changi, and proved a great boost to morale, as well as to our health.

Many people gave talks on countless subjects of interest. We could listen to a 'test match', through the memory of Jim Swanton, the sports commentator and wartime gunner major, or pay visits to many well-known London or Parisian restaurants with Jack Bowman, Coldstream Guards and 18th Division Brigade Major. It was even possible to 'go to the races' with Willy Tosh, a well-known bookmaker and now also a gunner.

But we were never free of the periodic Japanese 'hate'. There were sudden searches, looking for secret radios of which at least one was now operating in each camp. Most were constructed as well as operated by Max and Donald Webber, in whose debt all of us who were sustained by the news they brought in will always be. It was on one of these searches that I lost the majority of the paintings that I had managed to do of this time, as well as of my previous sea experiences. The originals had been lost in *Repulse*. My scanty diaries, concealed in the false bottom of my pack, survived these searches.

From time to time and with very little warning, large parties of either 'heavy sick' or 'light sick' were moved from camp to camp. During these moves, the travelling conditions were, as always with

[1] Thai unit of currency equivalent to approximately one shilling and three pence.

180

the Japanese, intensely uncomfortable, particularly those which involved travelling by train.

I was numbered among the 'heavy sick' and was moved from Chungkai to Tamuang on 12 May. In this case we travelled by barge down-river to the camp five miles below Kanburi. The familiar railway country of jungle and steep limestone hills was left behind, and on either bank were many beautiful 'Flame of the Forest' trees, spectacular with their vivid splashes of red against the otherwise monotonous greens of scrub and bamboo. The camp was largely incomplete, organization poor and food appalling. We were glad to leave, which we did exactly a month later.

Paraded, searched and counted early in the morning, we marched, carrying our by now scanty baggage to a railway halt where we waited in the hot sun for four hours before boarding the train, thirty-two men and baggage to one enclosed steel wagon. The train headed east and joined the main line to Bangkok at Ban Pong. We stopped for the night five miles further on, in a siding beside another camp at Non Pladuk. A meal from this camp was brought to us and we learned that this was in fact another P.o.W. camp. All the discomforts of our long journey up from Singapore plagued us, heat, cold, mosquitoes and sandflies. None of this was helped by the fact that most of us had dysentery.

Nakhon Pathom was reached early the next morning. The town was situated in a large flat area of paddy fields and fruit plantations and was dominated by the largest wat, or temple, in Siam. Its golden spire-tipped conical roof glinted in the morning sunshine. The camp itself was supposed to be a base hospital camp. Its buildings were better than those up-country but the camp was liable to be flooded in heavy rains and the food was poor. On the other hand, drugs seemed to be more easily available and most of us were given sufficient to settle our dysentery down.

The fight to stay alive now gave way to seemingly endless days of captivity, cut off from all vestiges of our former life. In a way this was made worse by the exciting news of the war in Europe now reaching us via the clandestine news bulletins. The Allies had landed in Europe and we felt very out of the great events. We often heard our bombers flying over and the noise of explosions from the direction of Bangkok.

After another severe relapse, I was lucky enough to receive sufficient EBI tablets to clear this up and began to feel quite well again. I used to take a two-mile walk each day round the camp with Bryan Yonge. On my twenty-fifth birthday, encouraged by the news of the war and the frequency of the bombing raids on Bangkok, I celebrated by spending most of my month's allowance on supplementing my meals from the canteen, which cost me a whole tical.

Christmas, 1944, passed quietly – a big congregation at a Free Church service and a splendidly produced pantomime entitled 'Alf's Ring'. A few days later there were rumours of moves back up-country. A Japanese medical team arrived to classify us into sickness categories. I was now classified as 'light sick', despite having only just had another bout of amoebic dysentery, which lasted several weeks. Moves were always an occasion to take stock of one's rapidly decaying kit – blanket completely patched, shorts and a shirt which had in fact belonged to Air Vice Marshal Pulford, almost transparent, a pair of socks and boots, still reasonably sound.

We left by lorry on 10 January, passed the wat and its gardens. For me, the chief memory of Nakhon Pathom will be its wat, the last rays of the setting sun on its golden dome, and streams of flying foxes leaving its shelters to feed among the fruit plantations. The long straight road was flanked by tamarind and mango trees, behind which lay paddy fields. Everywhere there were hundreds of ducks, the source of the life-saving eggs for us.

We halted at Non Pladuk and met Colonel Toosey once again, full of confidence and encouragement. His cookhouse gave us a good meal before we were allotted a hut for the night. We marched the short distance to Ban Pong and the river where barges waited to take us up to Tamuang. On our arrival I wondered if there was any significance in numbers; number 13 party, 113 men, travelled on 13 January, allocated to hut 13!

Immediately we heard of the current rumours that very shortly the officers were to be separated from the men and sent to Kanburi. Rumour became fact and we said goodbye, paying over what little money we had to the unit funds. The men gave us a wonderful farewell party, which, considering all we had been through, was a splendid effort.[1] On 21 January we travelled up-river by barge, landing at the same point on the river bank which we had left two years and three months ago. This time we marched back up the main street to the 'aerodrome' camp.

Kanburi had changed considerably since our last visit and was now a large camp. We were at once put to work on strengthening the 'bund' and deepening the ditch surrounding the camp. This was hard

[1] From the earliest days of our captivity, the Japanese had done their utmost to split the officers and other ranks. Humiliations of every sort had been heaped on the officers, but they had signally failed.

182

work, involving the carrying of soil dug out of the ditch to the top and sides of the bund, using the 'rice-sack-on-two-poles' method. It was the kind of work which those of us with amoebic dysentery could not do without risk, but the Japanese would allow no exception.

On the credit side the food was much better. There was a great gathering of old friends, some of whom one had not seen since Changi. John Crundall and Bruce Clarke were down from Tamakan. Also there were George Allan, John Clayton, Peter Ricketts, Tony West, Tony Pender-Cudlipp and Americans from the *Houston*. The improving war news was discussed very guardedly in open places where there was no likelihood of being overheard. Security was a matter of life and death. After the bund had been strengthened to the satisfaction of the Japanese, the work eased off and there was time for reading, painting and walking round the top of the bund with Bryan Yonge, whom I had first met in the dysentery tent at Kanyu.

With, as we now knew, Germany defeated, there was much speculation as to how long Japan would last, and even more as to how we would finally be released. We surmised that the Japanese were not happy with our presence so close to the men, and so it proved for in late July and the first few days of August, 1945, parties started leaving by train eastwards. As a Section Commander of 'J' party, I left on the 5th, in the usual closed wagon.

The landmarks and stations were becoming familiar, as were the discomforts. At Ban Pong we took the Bangkok line, changed trains at Non Pladuk, where we saw signs of allied bombing. The next day, after passing Nakhon Pathom, we reached a large river, the Me Nam, on the outskirts of Bangkok. The railway bridge had been badly bombed and it was impassable by train. We had to leave our train and cross the river by a kind of bamboo swing, and it was a considerable time later that we climbed into another train on the far side. We finally stopped in what we took to be the port area of Bangkok, at 11 p.m., very tired. We were at once put to work loading up barges with various stores before finally embarking ourselves, sixty to a barge. The barges were then towed down the river to an area of large 'go-downs' where we had to unload the barges. Later, while we were waiting in the 'go-downs', we saw through the open doors some kind of exercise being carried out by the Japanese and Thai coastal motor boats.

At midday we clambered into another train and were shunted endlessly about among sidings. There had been bombing during the night and we noticed considerable damage to rolling stock, locomotive sheds and the main station. We also saw large numbers of

Japanese wounded being looked after by Japanese nurses, very pink and white amid the surrounding squalor. Finally, attached to a long train carrying wounded as well as ammunition, we set out eastwards once more. No one seemed to know where we were going, though Saigon and Japan itself were strongly tipped. The train progressed very slowly through the night, until, at nearly midnight, we stopped at a small station which may have been Prachin Buri, sixty miles east of Bangkok. It was pitch black and pouring with rain.

At 4 a.m. on 10 August, 1945, we set out on yet another march to a new camp. It was to be the hardest march yet. We understood it to be near a place called Nakhon Nayok, twenty miles away. Besides our own kit we were carrying stores for the camp. We were shouted at and bullied along by our Korean guards. The weather conditions were terrible, alternate hot sunshine and drenching monsoon rain. Our Senior Officer, Colonel Lilley of the Sherwood Foresters, was absolutely splendid. He moved back and forth along the struggling column, encouraging us all to stick it out. Even so, a number of the utterly exhausted fell by the wayside. The road was red laterite and this, combined with the heavy rain, destroyed all the best boots. I remembered John Milford, who, in peacetime worked with Yardleys, marching on two enormous balloon-like blisters. We stopped briefly at a Buddhist monastery in the village of Nakhon Myo for a meal. As the rice was ladled into our mess tins, so it was splashed out by the enormous raindrops teeming down. A few minutes only were allowed and we were soon on the march again, forcing ourselves to keep going as it grew dark. It was not until 3 a.m. the next morning that we reached the camp, to be guided to our partly-built hut. We had marched for twenty-three hours with one small stop.

We were turned out at dawn and set to work building our hut. There was to be no rest and it almost seemed as if we had returned to the conditions on the railway. The camp was made up entirely of officers and was situated in wild hilly country. Japanese front-line troops were very much in evidence and it was thought that we were in the middle of a complete Japanese Army Corps, en route from China to Singapore.

The camp was still very much under construction and there was a lot to do. I joined a transport section working with Mongolian ponies. I was the only sailor and I think I was asked because I was the odd man out. It was great fun though, and, as our task was to go out and collect supplies, it provided a chance to see the country.

The signs were that the war was obviously almost over, but what worried us was the question of whether the Japanese would accept defeat, and if not what chances did we have at this last hour?[1] News of the first atom bomb reached us, not that we knew what it was. Suddenly, on 16 August, the Japanese Camp Commandant informed the Senior British Officer that the war was over and that he was to take command. It seemed an anticlimax after the long years of waiting.

The next day a British officer, and, a little later, an American officer visited the camp to make contact and take a Liaison Officer to Bangkok. A huge supply of Red Cross stores was handed over. For the next few days, while we waited for transport, a point-to-point was held with our ponies as mounts. Food parties were sent out to requisition immense quantities of food, especially buffalo meat. Transport eventually arrived and lorry-load by lorry-load we were collected and taken direct to Bangkok airport. Here we filled in next-of-kin forms and in turn flew out in Dakota transports which had brought in airborne troops to occupy key points.

It was a tremendously exciting moment as we settled down on the floor of the Dakota for the three hundred and seventy mile flight to Mingaladon in Burma. Each was given a tin of K rations, told to hold on to the many straps hanging along the aircraft interior, and then we were away, roaring down the runway and watching Siam drop away beneath us. Our aircraft was representative of the Commonwealth. Its crew included Canadian, British and New Zealand members. The flight path lay over the line of the railway, though we did not see anything of it. Moulmein was given a wide berth as a Japanese anti-aircraft battery was still active there.

Mingaladon airfield, newly constructed, was full of aircraft – fighters, bombers and transports, all standing on the expanded metal tracks. Formalities were nil and we were soon enjoying a drink in the mess. We also had our first experience of the WASBs[2], dressed in their jungle green uniforms identical to those of the army and a new idea to us. We understood they had been serving right up to the front lines. We were given temporary transit accommodation in tents, each tent having a WASB attached to look after our welfare.

In the next two or three days everyone was given a thorough medical check-up in the military hospital at Rangoon, kitted up in jungle green before returning to our tents to await evacuation.

[1] Later we learned that the Japanese had segregated the officers from the men because they feared that the officers would lead their men against the Japanese in the event of our unexpected airborne invasion of Siam, which was actually contemplated.
[2] Women's Auxiliary Service, Burma.

I received an invitation from Captain T. Kerr, R.N., the Senior Naval Officer Rangoon, to come and have drinks in his office. As I came through the door he greeted me with, 'When your sister heard that I was coming to the Far East, she said to me "Find my brother". Now that I have done so I shall send her a telegram.' He explained that my sister had been a boat's crew Wren and had been the Coxswain of his motor boat at the Coastal Forces base at Felixstowe, he being the Captain Coastal Forces there.

Eventually we embarked in the troopship *Worcestershire* and sailed down the Irrawaddy to the sea. During the long voyage home, each table in the dining room included one lady taken from the many Women's services. This was to help us back to normality after years away from any feminine influence! These delightful ladies must have had a lot to contend with. Finally, on a beautiful late October evening, we steamed into Liverpool Bay, the kind of day as well as 'the day' we had all dreamed about for so long. There was a tremendous turnout to welcome us and it was an emotional moment, as *Worcestershire* edged slowly alongside the dock in the gathering gloom, to realize that at last we had come home. A special train took the majority of us down to London. It was late when we arrived, and with my table's feminine influence I set out in a Royal Marine R.T.O.'s jeep to find accommodation, but could find nothing at that late hour. Armed with an introduction from John Crundall to his wife's mother, wife of the Governor of Chelsea Hospital, I called at the Porter's Lodge at the main entrance in the small hours. We were offered the use of an enormous pile of mattresses in one end of the main block, and here we slept, perched precariously on top of about thirty of them! The next morning we called at the Governor's house and were made very welcome with a bath and breakfast. General Liddel asked me where we had spent the night and when I told him, he said, 'Well, young man, you have made history. You must be the first man to have slept with a woman in the pensioners' quarters!'

Later that morning, having collected and changed into my uniform, ordered in July, 1941, at Messrs Gieves, I was making my way to the Berkeley Buttery, when I heard my name shouted across Piccadilly from the Ritz Arcade. It was my sister, whom I had arranged to meet for lunch.

CHAPTER 12

Reflections

As a Prisoner of War and often during the years that have passed since the events narrated in this book, I have thought of why things happened as they did and what their course would have been 'if only' this or that action had or had not been taken. I have considered their effect on my life at the time and subsequently. I have also compared one event with another.

Discounting my pre-war service, the war lasted for me, twenty-nine months. There then followed three further months 'lost' on Tjebia Island before, having fallen into enemy hands and becoming a prisoner, the final thirty-eight months till the end of the war.

Like many others, being on the receiving end during those early years there was a sense of bitterness towards the politicians, who between the wars had allowed such a state of unpreparedness to develop. They were continually warned and it was in the face of all the lessons of history. Also, the gullibility of the public who as a whole accepted this reading of events, must accept their share of criticism.

In all the early operations of the war, during which we suffered so grievously, there was always a feeling of anger at our inadequate equipment and material. However, such was our faith in our country that we never for one moment doubted the belief that we would win the war. This sureness of ultimate victory gave us enormous inner strength and without it many would not have survived.

For most of us, especially those under thirty years of age, the war was an exciting and stimulating time, there were bad moments as well as frightening ones, but there was a lot of fun too. New places to see, we never, certainly in the Navy, knew where we would end up once having left harbour. Most of us had no doubt that we were carrying

187

out an essential task, it was what we had trained for and we believed in. Back in England one felt we were part of a great national crusade, everyone pulled together and it was a wonderful feeling. Similarly overseas all doors were open to us and people's kindness was unstinting.

However remotely it might have been, when the ship was part of a big operation there was a feeling of intense excitement and at the end one felt that you had played a part in a great event.

There was always a great difference between those operations where you were part of an organised unit: *Repulse*, for instance, and having to act more or less on your own initiative such as Dunkirk and Singapore. Both large evacuations in the face of a dominant enemy, but otherwise very different.

At Dunkirk, however extempore the operation may have been with a large margin for personal initiative, one always had the feeling that there was an efficient organisation backing you up. The object always remained clear. Time was short and urgent.

Singapore was on a different time scale, much longer with the first civilian evacuees leaving in Ocean Liners on scheduled sailings, then on the same ships as they brought in reinforcements and finally and too late in a last desperate attempt on any available vessel. Where Dunkirk had almost seemed a gay adventure, Singapore was the sad culmination of unrelieved defeat and battered morale. Those of us who played a part found it a frustrating and dispiriting experience.

The question that I pondered perhaps longer than any other was what would have been the outcome if all those ships and small craft that left Singapore on 13th February had not been ordered south to Batavia. Part of the answer was a grave lack of information on Japanese movements caused by the premature destruction of codes and cyphers, a question in itself. Even so the question remains. A secret supply route into Singapore had been designated. This lay through the west Sumatran port of Padang thence by road to the Inderagiri river and the east coast and then up to Singapore through the Lingga and Riouw islands. This route was successfully used 'force majeur' by many survivors of the small ships sunk en route to Batavia. However much one thinks about it, it remains one of the 'if onlys'.

For those such as ML 310 and others who managed to get as far south as the Banka Straits, there was little hope as they ran straight into the main Japanese invasion force moving on Java.

I often thought about our grounding on leaving Singapore and speculating on the delay caused to progress to the south. If it had not occurred we should have been seventy five miles further on. Would we then have managed to pass ahead of the Japanese? Also I should not have injured my hand to the extent that decided the Admiral to leave the shelter of Katjangan in broad daylight. Even if we had not got any further south at that point of time, we would have waited, as was our plan, for darkness and perhaps passed clear to the eastward of the Japanese.

The 'ifs' are raised endlessly and it seems that chance and luck play a great part in events. A further example was the chance hit by a Japanese torpedo on one of the propeller shafts of the *Prince of Wales*. Had this not happened the course of the Far East conflict might well have been changed and with it the events described above. Of course with the evidence collected since, the whole operation of Force Z was studded with 'if only' at every stage.

So far as these reflections of the events I have described go, I have no doubt of the dreadful reality of Tjebia island. The three months spent there were worse than the whole time as a Prisoner of War.

I have often, since I first heard of it in the late sixties, thought about an explanation of the report by the Commander of the United States Submarine S-39. My conclusion about this mysterious episode is that, right or wrong island notwithstanding, S-39's Commander was not prepared to take too much trouble and more important risk. One has to remember the extreme dangers under which he was operating. It was his first war patrol with the odds impossibly loaded against him. The seas alive with Japanese ships, the air with their aircraft. He had expended his torpedoes, his patrol was over. The safety of his submarine was paramount. He probably decided he was not going to risk his crew further; after all what was an unknown British Admiral to him? The reported search of Tjebia island simply did not take place.

However we do know that Johnny Bull did get through and make his report. One of the suggested means of rescue had been sent, but for whatever reason had failed.

It is difficult to weigh up the effect that my Prisoner of War experience had. Of course I was completely divorced from my professional career and the accumulation of experience that I would have gained had I remained free. On the other hand I was brought into contact with men of virtually every other walk of life. People whom probably never have met in a lifetime and learned about ways of life far removed from that of a professional sailor. The conditions under which we lived were like nothing any of us had experienced or even imagined. We were simply expendable until the moment the

Japanese realised that the death toll was becoming such that they might be unable to complete or maintain the railway.

Those of us who survived all had one thing in common 'a will to survive'. If that 'will' was lost for more than a few days you died. Tjebia island made this very evident to me. We all had different components leading to this 'will', but common to most was a certain vitality and enjoyment of life, the ability to transport your thoughts away from the squalid hardships of the present to the almost fantasy world of England, its life, customs and culture. I constantly saw my own Suffolk coast and the many faces of the weather, contrasting it to the monotony of our tropical climate. Reading whenever possible would often bring this home forcibly. Such quotations as 'a golden September in an English Park' from Andre Maurois' Chauteaubriand would evoke the strongest memories and for a short time at least shut out our surroundings.

The versatility of talent displayed amongst such a gathering was another stimulating and life-saving force.

Perhaps in conclusion my final reflection on this whole story is that given the circumstances, the course events took were inevitable. The human participants mostly good, but some weak, displayed a fortitude and a sense of humour which our enemy would not understand, particularly as we had, in their eyes, forfeited all honour. These views formed at the time have not changed in the light of hindsight and all that has been published.

Epilogue

On my arrival at Liverpool I was greeted by Admiral Dorling, my old Captain in *Royal Sovereign*. He told me that the First Sea Lord, Admiral of the Fleet Sir Andrew Cunningham, would very much like me to call and see him when I got down to London. In London the next morning I telephoned his secretary and a meeting was arranged for that afternoon. At the Admiralty I was taken up to the First Sea Lord's room, overlooking the Horse Guards. As I entered, A.B.C. (as Admiral Cunningham was known throughout the Navy) got up from his desk and came to meet me. He immediately asked me if I would like some tea. He always had doughnuts with his tea and would I like some too? He then asked me many questions about events in Singapore and he particularly wished to know about Admiral Spooner. At the end of my account, he gave me Mrs Spooner's address and asked me if I would write to her.

As a result of my letter Mrs Spooner asked if I would meet her and Mrs Pulford to tell them about events on Tjebia. Some days later I met Mrs Spooner at the Ladies' Carlton. Sadly Mrs Pulford felt she could not face the story. For a few minutes our conversation turned to the previous occasions on which we had met – at Seaford, when she had had lunch in *Vindictive* when I was a cadet, and later at Admiralty House in Singapore when she and the Admiral had given a cocktail party the day after *Repulse* arrived at the Naval Base.

Mrs Spooner then said to me, 'Before you tell me what happened, I should like to tell you what I know.' She said that she had always known what was happening to Jack. He was in the room now. She went on to describe very vividly several incidents and occurrences on Tjebia; the scene after our first landing, our strained relationships with the Javanese, the house where the Admiral had lived and the white habit that he used to wear, and most strangely, she had sensed our great depression of spirit. There was much more to this than a vivid imagination; her story was much too detailed. She told me that she was not psychic and did not have such knowledge about anything else. So far as Tjebia was concerned, she could not have got the information from anyone else, I believe I was the first survivor home.

In my turn, I told her the whole story from the time she left Singapore until the time we left the island. I then gave her one of her husband's shoulder straps, which I had kept since his death for this moment, should it ever come.

APPENDIX I

A NOMINAL ROLL OF COMPLEMENT AND PASSENGERS IN H.M.M.L. 310 WITH SUBSEQUENT ADDITIONS ON TJEBIA.

Complement of H.M.M.L. 310

Lieut. J. Bull, R.N.Z.V.R. Commanding Officer.	(Reached Java)
Lieut. Henderson, R.A.N.V.R. Executive Officer.	(Died on Tjebia)
Lieut. Sea. Brough. Coxswain.	(Reached Java)
A. B. Hill	(Reached Java)
A. B. Oldnall	(P.O.W.)
A. B. Johnstone	(P.O.W.)
A. B. Gibson	(Died on Tjebia)
A. B. Flower	(Died on Tjebia)
A. B. Haward	(Died on Tjebia)
A. B. Russell	(Died on Tjebia)
Tel. Tweedale	(P.O.W.)
P.O. Motor Mech. Johncock	(P.O.W.)
Sto. Tucker	(P.O.W.)
Sto. Paddon	(P.O.W.)
Sto. Townsend	(Died on Tjebia)
St. Little	(Died on Tjebia)
Cook 'Charlie'	(Survived)

Taking Passage

Rear Admiral E. J. Spooner R.A.M.Y.	(Died on Tjebia)
Air Vice Marshal C. W. Pulford A.C.C. Far East	(Died on Tjebia)

Cdr. P. L. Frampton, R.N., S.O.L.O.	(Died on Tjebia)
W/Cdr. P. A. Atkins. R.A.F.V.R.	(P.O.W.)
Lieut. R.A.W. Pool R.N.	(P.O.W.)
Lieut. I.W. Stonor Argyll and Sutherland Highlanders	(P.O.W.)
Mr. Richardson Warrant Boatswain R.N.	(P.O.W.)
P.O. Keeling	(Died on Tjebia)
P.O. Firbank	(P.O.W.)
Sto. P.O. Bale	(Died on Tjebia)
Tel. Smithwick R.N.	(P.O.W.)
Serg. Hornby	(Died on Tjebia)
Mne. Sully	(Died on Tjebia)
Mne. Robinson	(P.O.W.)
Mne. Smith	(P.O.W.)
Mne. Sneddon	(P.O.W.)
Mne. Day	(P.O.W.)
Staff Serg. Lockett R.E.	(Missing)
Staff Serg. Ginn R.E.	(Missing)
Staff Serg. Davis R.E.	(Died on Tjebia)
Serg, Wright M.P.	(P.O.W.)
L/Corp. Shrimpton M.P.	(Died Singapore)
L/Corp. Turner M.P.	(P.O.W.)
L/Corp. Schief M.P.	(P.O.W.)
L/Corp. Stride M.P.	(P.O.W.)
A/C Smith	(P.O.W.)
A/C Bettany	(P.O.W.)

Joined the party on Tjebia

Sto. Scammell	(Died on Tjebia)
Pte. Docherty Gordon Highlander	(Died on Tjebia)
Mr. Dimmett R.N. Dockyard Singapore	(Died on Tjebia)

Total Died and Missing whilst at Tjebia Island	18.
Died at Singapore within a week of leaving Tjebia	1.
Reached Java by boat	3.
Survived to become Prisoners of War	22.
Returned to Singapore but later arrested	1.
Missing	2.
TOTAL	44.

APPENDIX II

Copy of letter written by Rear Admiral E. J. Spooner to Captain Cazalet, dated 10/2 on Naval Message Pad. In Imperial War Museum among Cazalet's papers. Handwritten by Spooner.

S. 1320c *NAVAL MESSAGE.* (Revised October 1935)
For use with S. 1320b

My Dear Cazalet,

Singapore will probably be captured tonight or tomorrow. The story of ineptitude, bad generalship etc. is drawing to a close. I am sending with this 3 trunks, (tin) and one short(?) box of mine and my wife's. Please take to Batavia and turn over to Collins or to my wife who is staying with Lady Sanson at Bandoeng. My wife left here in *Scout* last night. I am getting away all the Sailors & Officers I can in the various patrol boats, and intend to follow myself in an M.L. at the last, and not be captured if I can avoid it.

The present state of affairs was started by the A.I.F. who just turned tail, became a rabble and let the Japs walk in unopposed.

My marines have been cut up. The young N. Officers in M.L.s & Fairmiles have been splendid.

A certain number of officers and sailors may come with you. As they come in from various boats & jobs all over Island am sorting them out as boats crews & getting surplus away – I do not intend that any be taken prisoner if I can help it.

You must go by midnight – all good luck & tell my wife I'll follow soon.

Yours,

195

APPENDIX III

The 'Vision' of Mrs Fitzwilliam

In the Spring of 1985 I received a letter from the mother of a brother officer who was lost in *Repulse*. She was then a very old lady of ninety and had heard me talking of the action whilst taking part in Granada's Television series on the 'End of Empire'. She told me that she had heard very few details of his death and as I must have known her son could I help her.

I wrote to her telling her all the details of her son's time in *Repulse* that I could remember, including a fall from the foremast control position the day before the action. As a result of this fall he was in the sick bay on the morning of 10th December. He was seen on the upper deck shortly before the ship sank, but was not seen thereafter.

Mrs Fitzwilliam's reply thanking me contained this strange premonition of her son's death. I quote her exact words. 'You may think I am mad when I tell you on the Monday December 8th I saw what was happening to the ship, the bombers which to me were black, the torpedoes falling and then all I could see was the stern of the ship sticking out of the water – I told my husband but to me the ship was sunk, the only difference being I was two days early.'

She apparently could not get this out of her mind. I understand this first became manifest early in the morning. Bearing in mind that Singapore time was 7 hours ahead, this must have been nearly the exact time the ships sank, although two days early.